The New Antoinette Pope School **COOKBOOK**

The New
Antoinette Pope School

COOK

BOOK REVISED EDITION

by Antoinette and Francois Pope

MACMILLAN PUBLISHING CO., INC.
New York

COLLIER MACMILLAN PUBLISHERS
London

IN APPRECIATION OF THEIR ENDLESS COOPERATION AND
ASSISTANCE IN THE PRODUCTION OF OUR COOKBOOKS, WE
DEDICATE THIS REVISED AND UPDATED EDITION TO OUR
LOYAL AND DEVOTED SONS, BOB AND FRANK, AND TO
OUR ADOPTED SISTER, ALICE POPE GIERUM.

Macmillan Publishing Co., Inc.
866 Third Avenue, New York, N.Y. 10022
Collier-Macmillan Canada Ltd., Toronto, Ontario

LIBRARY OF CONGRESS CATALOG CARD NUMBER: 72-12448

Printed in the United States of America

▶ *Contents*

Introduction	vii
Important Facts Regarding Measurements	xi
Glossary of Cookery	xiii
Appetizers: Hors d'Oeuvres, Canapés, Open-Face Sandwiches, Dips, Fillings, Spreads	1
Fondues, Quiches, Hot Dips, Rarebits	88
Soups and Chowders	101
Meats	114
Poultry and Dressings	196
Seafood and Fish Dishes	236
Eggs, Omelets, Soufflés, and French Toast	256
Vegetables: Vegetable Molds and Vegetable Casseroles	270
Sauces and Gravies for Meats, Fish, Poultry, and Vegetables	321
Salads: Salad Bowls and Salad Dressings	343
Chafing Dishes and Casseroles: Luncheon, Supper, and Dinner Dishes	375
Party-Style Molds	418
Quick Breads: Waffles, Biscuits, Pancakes, Popovers, Doughnuts, Specialty Breads, and Non-Yeast Coffee Cakes	475
Yeast Breads: Rolls, Breads, Coffee Cakes, Doughnuts, and Pastries	492
Cakes and Tortes: Special Occasion Cakes	531
Icings and Frostings: Professional Cake Decorating	609
Desserts: Cheese Cakes, Strudels, Puff Pastry, and Tarts	630
Cookies: Bars and Slices, Plain and Fancy	682
Pies	731
Italian Dishes	758
Oriental Cookery	822
Smörgåsbord, or American-Style Buffet	856
Teas and Coffee-Making	858
Party-Style Punches	862
An Introduction to Wines	866
Vegetable Carving and Butter Molding	870
Pickling and Preserving	875
Home Freezing	880
Menus	901
Index	916

▶ *Introduction*

EVER SINCE THE ANTOINETTE POPE SCHOOL OF FANCY COOKERY IN CHICAGO has been in existence, requests for recipes have come from people who had heard of the school but were unable to attend. Now anyone who wishes to serve delicious food such as the Antoinette Pope School is noted for can do so by using this book. It can be easily understood, and excellent results will be obtained if directions are followed as closely as possible. The authors also recommend that you read the preface in each category several times for more detailed informative material regarding the various recipes.

Beginners, as well as the more experienced cooks who wish to add to their repertoire of fine dishes, can try these carefully tested recipes with assurance. Over 40 years of experience in creating new recipes and improvising on old, and many thousands of hours of research, testing and re-testing, and teaching cookery have gone into the preparation of this book. Its purpose is to help not only the average homemaker, but anyone interested in food preparation to increase her knowledge and skill in cooking.

In addition to many thousands of women and men beginners in cooking, personalities in every field have attended the Pope Cooking School, including prominent physicians; attorneys; leading home economists; food editors; caterers, restaurant owners, and others.

One of the amusing questions frequently asked the Popes is just how did you get this way about cooking? They claim that it all stems from their childhood days. On both sides of the families there were professional cooks (French and Italian). One relative in particular conducted a Parisian café and had many continental chefs as friends. Through this association and the Popes' inborn love of good food, their many friends among American and European chefs, leading home economists, and many other food experts, have made it possible to keep their recipes and other valuable information regarding food updated.

This does not necessarily mean that all the Pope preparations are Latin or Gallic in style and taste. American cookery predominates. The Popes have also combined different forms of foreign and oriental cookery with our native style and the result is a never-ending array of eye and taste appealing dishes for everyone and every occasion. Plain (fundamental) cookery gets attention it deserves in the Pope book. It is the foundation which must be laid before it is advisable to learn about advanced or fancy cookery. The Popes realize this fact fully and hundreds of recipes are the day-to-day kind of cookery done in most homes. These include the proper roasting, broiling, braising, and frying of meats; proper cookery of vegetables so that taste appeal and nutrition values are retained; simple desserts, and numerous other plain foods that can be perfectly cooked and made very attractive. They know that it is their responsibility to help their students get a thorough knowledge of these fundamentals.

The Pope School was the outgrowth of suggestions from a few friends who liked the food the Popes served them in their home and who continually asked to know more about their method of cooking. They prevailed upon the Popes to give them a few lessons in cookery, and that was the beginning of the Antoinette Pope School of Fancy Cookery forty years ago, when Mrs. Pope taught a class of ten in her dining room. Within a short time, a kitchen-school room had to be built in the basement of their home, and Mr. Pope opened classrooms in still another address. In 1942 the co-directors decided to take a central location with room for expansion, and today the school occupies almost three thousand square feet in a prominent building on the world famous Michigan Boulevard in Chicago with a large auditorium that accommodates 150 students, in addition to laboratories, experimental kitchens, reception rooms, offices, etc.

No other private cooking school, to our knowledge, has had the success, attendance, and recognition in this field as the Popes. In 1951 until 1963, for almost thirteen years, they conducted a daily television cooking show, "Creative Cookery," on three major television stations—local and network—and were given academy awards for the best educational program on television during those years.

Previous editions of the Pope Cookbook have been best sellers since 1948, including the new Antoinette Pope School Candy Book, that was acclaimed by many authorities as the best candy book ever published for the professional candy maker as well as for the homemaker who wishes to prepare fine candies in her home kitchen.

Mrs. Pope has been listed in *Who's Who of American Women* since its inception and was recently nominated for the coveted Achievement Award, which is presented to the foremost Italian-American women in America for their meritorious accomplishments, at the auspicious AMITA banquet, at the Biltmore Hotel in New York City.

It is the hope of the authors that the use of this book will stimulate the desire of many more thousands for further knowledge in the fine art of cookery.

Introductory Note by August F. Daro, M.D.

Mrs. Antoinette Pope requested that I write a few words about nutrition in her updated cookbook. I feel honored to do so, since she is famous not only for conducting a very successful cooking school for over 40 years, but also for earlier editions of her cookbook which have been best sellers for almost twenty-five years. The art of cooking and the young science of nutrition are changing so rapidly in trying to keep pace with the progress in medical and other sciences that Mrs. Pope was inspired to revise the fourth edition of her famous best seller cookbook. Her new cookbook is up-to-date not only in the cooking art, but also in nutrition, as she covers the value of vitamins, minerals, and proteins and emphasizes proper cooking methods to preserve the nutritive value of foods.

The science of nutrition is a young one and dates back to the beginning of this century. At the present time and especially in the past year, there has been a tremendous surge of interest in nutrition in medical and lay journals. Articles emphasize the effect of poor nutrition on the unborn child, the older individual, and the general public. Poor nutrition affects the rich and the middle class, as well as the poor.

As Mrs. Pope points out, if you cook vegetables immediately upon obtaining them from the garden, they are more tender, tastier, and have their full mineral and vitamin content in comparison with vegetables that have been transported long distances or that have been stored in freezers for a long period of time. In addition, food processing methods tend to diminish the vitamin and mineral content of foods. It seems important, therefore, to provide a supplement to the daily diet with chelated mineral and vitamin tablets to insure that the billions of body cells are properly nourished.

Physicians are dedicated to the elimination of disease and the prolongation of life. The study of individuals living a long, relatively disease-free life illustrates the validity of the therapeutic tools which physicians have available from the growing discoveries in nutrition involving cell membranes, enzymes, chelated minerals, vitamins, proteins, carbohydrates, and fatty acids.

Malnutrition continues to be a serious and mounting problem, even though many nations are veritable cornucopias of food stuffs. Unfortunately, the mass producing of foods, paradoxically, has increased quantity

* *Doctor Daro is Professor of Obstetrics and Gynecology at the Loyola Stritch School of Medicine, in Chicago, and has written many medical and nutritional papers.*

but not, in all cases, the retention of the factors necessary for health maintenance and disease prevention. In addition, the abundance of food stuffs has created a superfluity of high calorie, low-nutrient foods.

Dr. C. Edith Weir, Assistant Director of the Human Nutrition Research Division of the U.S. Department of Agriculture, states that most of the health problems underlying leading causes of death in the United States could be altered by an upgrading of the diet.

In the future, physicians, as they become acquainted with the new discoveries in nutritional therapeutics, will influence the public consumption of food. Ultimately, this will lead to food companies formulating increasing varieties of foods for specific therapeutic purposes. Hopefully, this will replace the present hit-and-miss system where physicians hope that their patients will include the correct combination of foods in their diets to meet prescribed nutritional intakes.

▶ IMPORTANT FACTS
REGARDING
Measurements

THERE ARE TWO WAYS TO MEASURE FOR ACCURACY: ONE, BY WEIGHING; THE other, by using standard measuring cups and spoons. All recipes in this book have been developed with standard measuring cups and spoons because this method is more practical and time-saving for household use.

We must emphasize that in order to have excellent results with our recipes, standard level measurements must be used, and the method of procedure must be the same as ours in every detail.

Liquids: Liquids are the easiest to measure, but we have found that many good cooks have a tendency to avoid filling the cups or spoons full of liquid; furthermore, they fail to empty them completely. This, of course, will cause cakes and other baked goods to be dry.

Fats: Fats are more difficult to measure because there is a tendency for large air spaces to form, especially when fats are cold. It is therefore safer to allow fats to stand in room temperature for a short time until somewhat plastic, then pack solid into measuring cups or spoons and level off the top. If a recipe calls for cold, firm fat, store it in refrigerator until ready after it is measured.

Flour: More trouble is encountered in measuring flour than any other ingredient. After many years of experimental work, we have concluded that the most reliable way to measure flour is to sift it directly into the measuring cup, having it slightly overfull, then to level off the surface with the edge of a knife or spatula. All our recipes were developed with this method, which is the equivalent of a tablespoon less per cup than if the flour is first sifted into a bowl and then put into the measuring cup with a spoon. Flours are divided into two categories. By this we do not mean brands of flour, but kinds. Bread and other yeast doughs require all-purpose flour milled from hard wheat, which contains a tenacious, elastic gluten. This strong gluten is necessary for the slow rising action of yeast. Cakes and pastries, however, require a flour of fine gluten quality, which yields easily to the action of baking powder, and such a flour is milled from soft winter wheat. It contains a very small amount of delicate gluten. Cake flour gives cakes a finer, lighter, and more tender texture than ordinary bread or all-purpose flour. Cake flour, used in our recipes, must not be confused with the so-called prepared "pastry flours" or cake mixes, under various brand names, that contain baking powder, sugar, and other ingredients. All flours should be kept in a cool, dry, well-ventilated place. If flour appears damp at any time, sift it several times before the open door of a heated oven. Let cool a few minutes before using.

Granulated Sugar: Granulated sugar packs very slightly. Sift same as flour to remove lumps, etc.

Confectioners' Sugar: If this sugar is lumpy, it must be rolled and sifted before it is measured if using our recipes. Proceed as with flour.

Brown Sugar: We prefer light brown sugar; should be rolled to remove lumps, then packed solidly into the cup—unless otherwise specified in recipe.

Baking Powders, Baking Soda, Cream of Tartar: It would not be practical to sift these ingredients because of the small amount used. We suggest, however, loosening powder with a spoon, then picking up and leveling with edge of spatula. Most of our recipes have been developed with double-acting baking powder unless otherwise stated in specific recipe. If a double-acting baking powder is substituted for single-acting, use ¼ teaspoon less for each teaspoon called for in recipe. If single-acting powder is substituted for double, use ¼ teaspoon more. If possible use type of baking powder specified in recipes.

Subdivided Glass or Metal Cups: This style of cup is not dependable because it is difficult to pack a piece of slippery fat into the bottom of cup and also to level off the top. It is safer to use a set of individual measuring cups and spoons that may be purchased in hardware and department stores.

Size of Bowls: You will observe that we often mention the number of the bowl used for the various recipes. When we state the number, we mean the width of the bowl across the top. For example, a No. 8 bowl would mean a bowl that measures 8 inches across the top.

Size of Pastry Tubes: See Professional Cake Decorating (page 623).

A GLOSSARY OF
Cookery

After-Dinner Coffee: Strong black coffee usually served after dinner without sugar or cream.

À la King: Meats, poultry, or vegetables in a rich cream sauce made with milk, cream, and stock.

Al Dente: An Italian term meaning slightly firm and not soft used to describe texture of food, especially spaghetti and similar items.

Amandine: Any dish or sauce prepared with sautéed almonds. *Amandine* is the French word for almonds.

Appetizers: Attractive, small open-faced sandwiches or other small portions of foods or beverages served before the meal or as a first course of a dinner or luncheon. Also served at cocktail parties.

Au Gratin: Meats, poultry, or vegetables in cream sauce, covered with fresh pulled or dry bread crumbs and sprinkled with parmesan or American cheese, then baked or broiled until top is brown and crisp.

Au Jus: Natural juices obtained from cooking meats, combined with small amount of stock or water, and seasoned.

Bake: To cook (meats, cakes, yeast doughs, etc.) by dry heat, especially in oven.

Baked Alaska: Usually sponge cake, topped with very firm ice cream, then completely covered with a meringue and baked in a very hot oven until meringue has a golden color. Follow our directions for best results.

Bananas: Bananas should not be refrigerated until they are ripe. Refrigeration stops further ripening. It is best to buy them *slightly* green, then allow to ripen at room temperature, about 70° to 75° F. When ripe the skin is yellow and at this point banana should be eaten or refrigerated. Best to use within 2 or 3 days—before the skin turns black. Very dark skin does not affect the taste appreciably, but overripe bananas are not as desirable.

Barbeque: To cook (meats, fish, or poultry) on a spit and baste with piquant sauce. Excellent results are obtained in an oven if you follow our recipes and directions.

Bar-le-Duc: A French fruit preserve made of white currants, and often with berries.

Baste: To moisten (meats or poultry) with melted fat or liquid or drippings in pan while baking.

Batter: A semiliquid mixture of flour, liquid, etc.

Bearnaise Sauce: Basically a Hollandaise sauce with added tarragon, parsley, and other ingredients.

Beat: To blend thoroughly, using a rotary motion.

Beef Tartar: Fresh, lean ground beef, highly seasoned, and served raw as a spread on crackers, melba toast rounds and squares, pumpernickel, etc. Often served at cocktail parties. Only the leanest and best quality beef should be used for this purpose and must be strictly fresh, not more than a day old after it is ground.

Blanc Mange: A white sweet pudding made with milk and cornstarch, and flavored with vanilla, rum or brandy, etc.

Blanch: To cover with boiling water for time suggested in recipe. Also to loosen skins from almonds.

Blend: To mix several ingredients until well united.

Boil: To cook in water or other liquids kept in continuous motion. Temperature of boiling point at or near sea level is 212° F.

Bouillabaisse: A thick French soup or stew, made with several kinds of fish and shellfish.

Bouillon: A clear broth made from lean meat.

Bouquet Garni: A combination of herbs tied with a string, or if dry herbs are used, they are wrapped in a piece of cheesecloth and tied. Used to flavor stews, sauces, etc.

Braise: To brown in small amount of fat, then *simmer* over very, very low heat until tender in a covered saucepan or skillet in small amount of liquid.

Brioche: Very light, rich yeast-raised French rolls.

Broil: To cook by direct exposure to heat.

Brush: To dip brush into butter, beaten egg, etc., and spread on various foods.

Canapé: Small piece of fancy-cut toasted or sautéed bread, covered with highly seasoned food and garnished. Served before luncheons or dinners, or at cocktail parties.

Capers: A flower bud which is pickled and used to garnish and season salads, sauces, and other foods. It is a shrub of the Mediterranean regions and used in many gourmet dishes.

Capon: A rooster which has been castrated to improve its flesh. Usually weighs more than 5 pounds and is very desirable for roasting for special occasions.

Caramelize: To melt granulated sugar over low heat until it changes color to golden brown without scorching or burning, which would impart a bitter taste. Used for coloring and flavoring foods and candies.

Cassoulet: A popular French dish, made with white beans and a combination of pork, poultry, sausage, and mutton, cooked in a large pot of water, well seasoned. There are many versions of this famous dish, depending on local traditions.

Castor Sugar: A fine granulated sugar, similar to our superfine. This term is used in England.

Chapon: A medium piece of crust of Italian or French bread, well rubbed with fresh garlic and blended with salad greens to add garlic flavor. It is usually discarded, but can be eaten.

Chaud-Froid Mold: Chicken, lobster, crab meat, etc., covered with a French chaud-froid (hot and cold) sauce, then garnished and glazed with a clear aspic. See our recipes.

Cheese, Cheddar and American: These terms are used interchangeably. Are the same but come under different brand names and quality.

Cheese, Processed: A pasteurized cheese made with a combination of several kinds of natural cheese and emulsifying agents into a homogenous plastic mass. It is more bland than natural, aged cheeses, but is preferred by many, and has many uses.

Cheese, Parmesan and Romano: Parmesan cheese is milder and not as salty as the Romano. Grated Parmesan is used more frequently in this country to season soups, casseroles, sauces, and pastas. The Italian people usually prefer the Romano cheese, freshly grated, then stored in the refrigerator for a short time. Romano is more commonly used in the southern part of Italy and by a majority of the Italians in America. The grated Italian cheeses are not as desirable as when you buy it by the wedge or piece and grate as needed, then refrigerate for a short time.

Chop: To cut into small, medium, or large pieces.

Citron: A fruit grown for the peel only, it is like the lemon in appearance and structure. After some preparation, it is then candied, and sold principally as an ingredient in fruit cakes and other desserts. It is usually available halved, but also comes by the piece, diced, in strips, in bulk, or in jars.

Combine: To blend ingredients.

Confectioners' Sugar–Powdered Sugar: Basically the same. It is also sometimes called icing sugar. For best results, sift before measuring and combining with liquid, unless otherwise suggested.

Consommé: A light-colored clear soup, usually made from several meats and vegetables, well seasoned.

Coq au Vin: This is a classic French chicken dish, cooked in wine, onions, herbs, garlic, mushrooms, etc. Lastly the sauce is thickened with small amount of flour, and simmered for several minutes.

Court Bouillon: A highly seasoned stock made from fish and sometimes used as a liquid in which to cook fish.

Cream: To beat shortening, sugar, and eggs until fluffy, about 5 minutes.

Crêpe: A thin French pancake.

Croquettes: A mixture of minced, ground, or chopped meat, fowl, vegetables, rice, etc. Combined with a thick sauce, coated with crumbs, eggs, and crumbs again, then ordinarily fried in deep fat.

Croutons: Small cubes of bread, fried or toasted until crisp, and served with soups or as a garnish for various dishes.

Cube: To cut into small or medium-sized square pieces.

Curry: An East-Indian dish similar to a stew but characterized by the pungent flavor of curry powder, which contains numerous spices.

Cut: To divide with a knife or scissors. To combine solid fat with dry ingredients with the least amount of mixing, allowing fat to remain in small pieces.

Degrease: To remove surplus fats from surface of boiling or cold liquids. An easy way to do this is to pour hot liquid into transparent glass cup or bowl and let stand a few minutes so that fat rises to the surface. Then with a large spoon remove fat from surface, and also tilt utensil so that a thicker amount of fat will accumulate on one side, making it easier to remove. If you have time to chill the liquid, the fat congeals on the surface and can be removed easily.

Deglaze: To blend in required amount of liquid with meat drippings in pan after most of fat has been removed. Rich drippings and juices are dissolved in the liquid. This operation is the usual basic step in preparing a sauce or gravy for fried, sautéed, or roasted meats and poultry.

Deviled: Seasoned with hot condiments.

Dice: To cut meats, vegetables, cheeses, etc., into small cubes.

Dissolve: To melt or liquify.

Dot: To cover the surface of food with small pieces of butter, cheese, etc.

Dredge: To sprinkle thickly with flour or other ingredients.

Drippings: Fat and juice dripped from meat or poultry while roasting.

Eviscerated, or Drawn, Poultry: Completely cleaned poultry. Generally the gizzard, neck, heart, and liver, which can be used to make stock for the gravy, are wrapped in paper and placed in the cavity of the bird.

Fat: Butter, lard, margarine, vegetable shortenings, suet that has been rendered, and oils.

Fillet: Boned cut of meat, poultry, or fish.

Flake: To separate into small pieces or flakes, removing any bones.

Fold In: To add (whipped cream or beaten egg whites) to another ingredient without loss of air.

Fouet: The French name for a wire whisk or whip, that comes in various sizes, and can be used to whip egg whites, sauces, etc.

Fricassee: A dish made of poultry or meat cut in pieces and stewed in a gravy, sauce, or stock.

Fry: A small amount of fat is used to pan-fry; a large amount to deep-fry.

Garnish: Decoration of parsley and other vegetables, used to add color and eye appeal to another food.

Giblets: The edible viscera of poultry, such as the heart, liver, and gizzard.

Glaze: To brush with a prepared or cooked syrup, or with aspic, meat gravies, etc.

Gluten: The rubbery substance in all-purpose flour that forms an elastic framework capable of surrounding and holding the carbon dioxide gas bubbles formed by yeast. There is also a small amount of gluten in cake flour.

Grate: To pulverize by rubbing on a grater.

Grill: To broil on a grill.

Grind: To put (meats, fish, poultry, nuts, etc.) through a food chopper.

Hollandaise: A French sauce made with a large amount of butter and egg yolks, and served with fish and vegetables and some meats.

Hors d'Oeuvres: Relishes or small appetizers served before the main dishes. The terms "hors d'oeuvres" "canapés," and "appetizers" are used interchangeably.

Infusion: To steep tea, coffee, leaves, etc., in a liquid so as to extract the soluble properties of the ingredients.

Instant Flour: A granular flour, the consistency of fine granulated sugar or salt. The only advantage we see in using it is that it dissolves more easily than regular flour in sauces and gravies.

Julienne: To cut into very narrow long strips, as for meats, vegetables, cheeses, etc.

Knead: To work and press (bread or other doughs) with the hands until smooth.

Lardoon: Long strips of fat used in larding lean meats.

Lukewarm: Tepid or moderately warm; temperature 98° to about 110° F.

Marinate: To soak in an acid mixture (marinade) for some time before actual preparation.

Marinade: A seasoned liquid in which meats, fish, poultry, vegetables, etc., are steeped or soaked before cooking.

Mask: To coat food with a sauce or a glaze.

Melt: To dissolve by heat.

Meringue: A combination of beaten egg whites and sugar used as a topping for pies then baked until golden color, or formed into various shapes and baked.

Mince: To cut or chop as fine as possible.

Mix: To unite or blend by beating or in any manner to effect distribution.

Mocha: A flavor used in cakes and icings obtained from a coffee infusion or a combined infusion of chocolate and coffee.

Monosodium Glutamate: A white powder, water soluble, used to intensify the flavor of meats, vegetables, and other foods. Commonly refered to as M.S.G. under different brand names, its use is now frowned on by nutritionists. However, most Chinese home cooks and restaurant chefs do use M.S.G. and many use it in great quantities. An optional teaspoon of M.S.G. can be added to any of the Oriental recipes with excellent results. Use your own judgment and the tastes of your family as your guide.

Mornay Sauce: A white sauce seasoned with Parmesan cheese and wine.

Nutmeats: Shelled nutmeats must be refrigerated as soon as possible after you purchase them to prevent rancidity. It you purchase them in quantities, freeze. Remove from freezer only amount you will use within a day or two. To freeze, place in plastic bags or freeze containers, and squeeze out air. Tie tightly. They may be kept frozen for many months without becoming rancid.

Pan-Broil: To cook in a very hot skillet rubbed with a piece of suet, pouring off fat as it accumulates in skillet.

Par Boil: To drop into rapidly boiling water and cook gently only until partially done.

Pare: To cut off the outside skin of apples, potatoes, etc.

Peel: To strip off the skin or rind of fruits or vegetables.

Peppercorn: The whole pepper berry, before it is ground.

Petits Fours: Very small rich butter cakes, cut into various shapes, then covered with a glossy fondant, and decorated.

Planked Foods: To serve meat and fish, also very tender small broilers, on a heavy wooden plank, which is then garnished with border of Duchesse potatoes and assorted colorful cooked vegetables.

Poach: To cook, submerged in simmering liquid about 185° to 200° F.

Purée: Food cooked until very soft, then pressed through a sieve or ricer. Also a soup prepared with food put through a sieve and made thinner with the addition of milk, cream, or stock.

Quiche Lorraine: An open-face pie, with a tender crust. Filling is made with or without cheese (usually Swiss), cream, eggs, bacon, seasonings. Crab meat and other seafood can also be used. See our recipes for more details. Very delicious served as an appetizer.

Ravigote: A cold sauce made of tarragon vinegar, seasoned with chopped capers, finely chopped green onions, parsley, etc., served on fish, seafood, and salad ingredients.

Risotto: An Italian dish of rice cooked with broth and flavored with grated Italian cheese, a bit of saffron, and other seasonings.

Roast: To cook (meats and poultry) by dry heat, ordinarily in an oven.

Rock Cornish Hens: Small birds, weighing anywhere from 1 to 1½ pounds, that are a cross between a Rock Cornish and a White Rock. Available only frozen.

Roll: To roll dough on a pastry cloth or on a floured board with a rolling pin.

Saffron: A spice made from the dried orange-colored stigmas of the Autumn Crocus. It is used to color rice, rolls, and other dishes. Must be used sparingly as indicated in recipes to add color and a very distinctive taste.

Sauerbraten: Usually pot roast of beef soaked in a marinade made with seasoned vinegar, wine, and spices for many hours to help make it more tender.

Sauté: To cook lightly in a small amount of fat in a hot skillet.

Scald: To heat (milk or other liquid) below the boiling point—about 200° F. Milk is scalded when a thin skin forms over surface. The term is also applied to food immersed in boiling liquid for a short time.

Scallop: To combine with sauce or other ingredients, usually in layers, and bake.

Sear: To expose the surface to a very high temperature for a short time, either in a hot oven or skillet.

Shortening: Various kinds of fat used in baking and cooking.

Shred: To cut with a very sharp knife or special shredder into thin narrow slices.

Sift: To put (flour, sugar, or other fine dry ingredients) through a sifter.

Simmer: To cook in liquid kept just below the boiling point—about 185° to 200° F.

Skewer: A long metal or wooden pin for holding meat or vegetables together while being cooked, or any similar pin used to fasten or hold an item in position.

Soufflé: A light baked dish made fluffy with beaten egg whites combined with egg yolks, white sauce, and cheese, seafood, or other ingredients. Similar dishes are prepared with fruit juices, chocolate, vanilla, etc., and served as a dessert.

Squabs: Young domestic pigeons raised especially for gourmet consumption. They can be prepared same as cornish hens, and served in the same way. Not easily available unless you go to a specialty shop.

Stock: The liquor or broth prepared by boiling meat, fish, vegetables, etc.

Sweetbreads: The thymus glands of a calf. Treated very much like brains. They must be soaked for at least 2 hours in cold water before they are cooked. A whole sweetbread usually weighs about 1 pound. They are a delicacy, and may be prepared in many ways. Follow directions in recipes, and use them within a day or two.

Truffles: Called the diamonds of cookery by Brillat Savarin. They are a fungus growth that are found underground around the bases of oak trees, and are a kin to the more popular sponge mushroom. They are extremely expensive, even in the regious of France and Italy where they are found, because no method of cultivating them has been discovered. They are used in gourmet cooking for their pungency and flavor. There are several varieties and can be purchased in many of the finer food stores in cans. Occasionally fresh truffles are imported by a few specialty shops, but their price is prohibitive.

Hen Turkeys–Tom Turkeys: There is no appreciable difference in the tenderness of hen and tom turkeys today. Practically all turkeys, whether hens or toms, in the market are from 3 to 6 months old, and are equally tender when properly prepared.

Welsh Rabbit, or Rarebit: A dish consisting of melted cheese, cream or milk, seasoned with spices and a little wine, served in a chafing dish on toast. May also be served as a fondue in a fondue pot.

Table d'Hôte: A meal of several courses planned by the restaurant and served at a set price.

Wild Rice: A long, aquatic grass, and not a true rice at all. It has an interesting texture and flavor when properly cooked and seasoned.

Wok: A Chinese cooking pan that resembles a salad bowl with handles. Use it as directed in recipes. Comes in various sizes and metals.

Zuppa Inglese: Literally translated it means English soup, but is a delicate Italian cake flavored with liquors, whipped cream, and sometimes candied fruits.

► *Appetizers*

HORS D'OEUVRES, CANAPÉS,
OPEN-FACE SANDWICHES,
DIPS, FILLINGS, SPREADS

FOR AN ELABORATE MEAL IT IS NOT NECESSARY TO INCLUDE A LARGE VARIETY of heavy foods in the menu. A simple, well-prepared dinner or luncheon can be enhanced with tasty and attractive hors d'oeuvres or canapés—hot or cold—served in the living room with a cocktail. The object of these appetizers is to stimulate the appetite rather than to dull it. Therefore, they should be well seasoned and small in size.

The cocktail party has grown tremendously in popularity and has become a definite part of the entertainment schedule for every household. However, now foods for these parties are no longer limited to a few open-face sandwiches. Besides a selection of delectable hot and cold individual hors d'oeuvres, limited to cocktail parties, we are including more substantial preparations that are molded beautifully, and others that are served hot in chafing dishes for cocktail and snack luncheon or supper parties.

How to Store Hors d'Oeuvres

Most hors d'oeuvres may be made hours or a day in advance if stored in wax-paper-lined boxes, holding paper in place with Scotch tape, or place boxes in large plastic bags, to prevent drying out. Keep in refrigerator or cold place, not warmer than 40°-50° F.

Freezing Hors d'Oeuvres

The majority of these foods may be prepared two weeks in advance and frozen, with the exception of hard-cooked eggs, fresh tomatoes, fresh celery, and hors d'oeuvres containing large amounts of mayonnaise or glaze. Glaze for hors d'oeuvres and canapés may be found on page 3. Do not garnish until shortly before serving. If a freezer is not available, many of these appetizers may be prepared a day or two in advance and stored in covered containers—preferably in boxes, then in plastic bags, to prevent

1

dehydration. All *frozen* hors d'oeuvres should stand in room temperature for about 2 hours to defrost in covered containers, or may be defrosted in refrigerator for about 5 or 6 hours. Cold refrigerator hors d'oeuvres may be served at once.

Seafood and Poultry Casseroles—Frozen

May be put together and frozen, but do not bake before freezing. Frozen casserole dishes must stand in room temperature for about 6 hours before baking or in refrigerator for 12 hours or longer for better results. Baking time must be almost doubled and temperature reduced about 25 degrees. It is best to test before removing from oven by inserting a meat thermometer in center of food. It should register about 150° F., never higher than 180° F., but do not overbake. If a freezer is not available, these dishes may be prepared a day or two in advance and stored, covered, in coldest part of refrigerator. Let stand in room temperature about an hour before baking, increasing baking time about 15 minutes.

Cream Cheese

This is one of the most versatile foods used. During warm weather or at any time if cream cheese appears too moist or soft for decorating and molding of cold preparations, we recommend adding 1 teaspoon of plain gelatin combined with 2 tablespoons of cold water. Stir gelatin and water gently and let stand about 5 minutes, then dissolve it over simmering water. Add dissolved gelatin to *1 pound of cream cheese*, stirring quickly until well blended. Add coloring at this point if desired. Cover cheese tightly and refrigerate for at least 2 hours before using. It is not always necessary to stabilize cream cheese with gelatin for these purposes. Test it first by making several rosettes or other designs. If they do not retain their shapes, add gelatin. Other soft cheeses may be stabilized with gelatin if necessary. For cheese decorations on hors d'oeuvres that are to be baked, it is best to add 2 tablespoons of sifted all-purpose flour and the coloring to *each pound* of cheese just before cheese is to be used for making decorations. Cheese must be of medium consistency for this purpose.

Toasted Bread Foundations for Hors d'Oeuvres

Cut sliced white or dark bread that is 2 or 3 days old into desired sizes and shapes. Place on baking sheet and cover with another baking sheet of same size—to prevent breads from curling. Bake at 300° F. about 15 minutes on first side, then turn over, cover, and bake another 15 minutes, or until golden brown but not too dark. If breads are not completely dry and crisp when brown, remove upper baking sheet, *shut off heat*, and allow breads to dry about 10 more minutes, watching closely.

To make bread foundations for hors d'oeuvres and canapés less resistant to moisture when they are to stand for more than an hour or two after they are prepared, brush the toasted and crisp breads (after they have baked about 30 minutes) with egg white (that has been beaten until slightly foamy with Dover beater) on one side. Continue to bake at 300° F. or lower temperature 7 or 8 minutes, until absolutely dry. May be prepared several days in advance if kept in covered container.

Sautéed Bread Foundations for Hors d'Oeuvres

Cut bread that is 2 or 3 days old into desired shapes and sizes. Cover with wax paper and let remain in room temperature until dry. This will prevent grease-soaked foundations and will produce crisp tender beads.

To sauté, melt 1 tablespoon butter in a 9- or 10-inch skillet. Place cut dry breads in hot butter and sauté about 1 minute over moderate heat, watching closely that they do not become too dark. Remove breads, add another tablespoon of butter, and when hot, sauté second side, pressing down gently with fork to help retain shape. Remove from skillet and let cool on wax paper before spreading with various fillings. May be prepared several days in advance if kept in covered container in cool place.

Glaze for Hors d'Oeuvres, Canapés, Centerpieces, and Fruits

Glaze is used not only to glorify these foods, but also to preserve their freshness. To make glaze, combine 1 tablespoon of plain gelatin with ¼ cup cold water. Stir gently and let stand about 5 minutes in a small saucepan, then pour 1 cup of boiling water or clear light veal or chicken stock over thick gelatin. Stir gently until completely melted. Keep in a cold place or refrigerator until *slightly congealed*, about the consistency of unbeaten egg white. Place hors d'oeuvres on cake cooler with drip pan underneath, and with a spoon or small saucepan pour thickened gelatin. With a rubber scraper pick up glaze that falls through and remelt if necessary over warm water, and stir gently until of right consistency. If it becomes too thin, place saucepan in ice water for a few minutes but watch closely that it does not become too quick. Refrigerate glazed hors d'oeuvres until set, then with a spatula release them from cake cooler and transfer to wax-paper-lined boxes. Cover tightly and refrigerate until serving time if made day in advance.

Daisy Centerpiece for Hors d'Oeuvres Platter

Select firm white round turnips or potatoes that are at least 3 inches in diameter for large flowers. With sharp knife slice about ⅛ inch in thickness. Cut through with daisy cutter. For center use a thick round slice of carrot. Hold together with heavy toothpicks. Place on half of an orange, apple, grapefruit, or potato, or on styrofoam around base. Fill in open spaces with parsley or green leaves. These flowers may also be used to garnish cold meat platters, finger sandwiches, and tea sandwiches. *If using potatoes dip flowers into lemon juice to prevent darkening.* Use smaller vegetable for small cutter.

Basic Pastry Dough for Hot Hors d'Oeuvres

Makes about 24 medium size

1½ cups sifted all-purpose flour
¼ teaspoon salt (increase to ½ teaspoon if using unsalted shortening)
½ teaspoon baking powder

½ cup butter or margarine, cold and firm
2 tablespoons beaten whole egg, combined with about ¼ cup very cold water, or just enough to form a medium soft dough

Sift dry ingredients together 2 or 3 times. Cut butter into dry ingredients until it looks like a coarse meal. Add beaten egg combined with the cold water, adding only enough liquid to form a medium dough. Work ingredients with a knife or fork until it leaves sides of bowl. Turn out onto floured pastry cloth and knead gently for about ½ minute until smooth. Shape into a square piece and cut in halves. Wrap in wax paper and store in refrigerator for at least ½ hour, but do not permit it to become too firm. Use according to specific recipes.

Hors d'Oeuvres Patty Shells

Makes about 20 patty shells

To form patty shells, roll ½ recipe Basic Pastry Dough to measure about 8 x 8 inches. With a 2-inch cutter, cut out as many rounds as possible. Press scraps of dough together very gently and roll again to same thickness. Cut more rounds. From half of rounds cut through with a 1¼-inch cutter forming rings. Scraps and small cut-out rounds may be rolled again until dough is completely used up; chill scraps before rolling if too soft to handle. Brush solid rounds with beaten egg combined with 2 teaspoons milk and ¼ teaspoon salt, place rings over solid rounds, brush rings with beaten egg. Puncture center of shells with a toothpick. With spatula transfer onto very lightly greased baking sheet or silicone paper. Place in refrigerator for about 15 minutes, then bake in a 400° F. oven 10 minutes; lower heat to 325° F. and bake about 10 more minutes or until delicately brown, but not too dark. Watch closely toward end to prevent burning. If shells are not sufficiently brown after 20 minutes, shut off heat and allow to finish browning and drying for another few minutes with oven door partly open. They may be prepared several weeks in advance if stored in a covered container in refrigerator. May be frozen for several months. If frozen, let stand in room temperature 4 or 5 hours to defrost in covered container.

These patty shells may be filled with creamed preparations such as crab meat, lobster, shrimp, chicken, ham, etc., for hot hors d'oeuvres, having them slightly round at top. Place caps on and heat in a 350° F. oven for about 10 minutes, watching closely toward end to prevent overbrowning. Sprinkle with paprika. Serve as soon as possible. For cold hors d'oeuvres, fill with finely cut cold seafood or chicken salad, garnish tops with parsley, sliced stuffed olives, or cheese rosettes and leaves. They may be filled several hours in advance if fillings are not too soft, and refrigerated.

Bread Cases for Hot Hors d'Oeuvres

With a 2-inch round or oval cutter, cut out twice as many breads as hors d'oeuvres to be prepared. With open end of No. 7 large star cookie tube, or small 1¼-inch round cutter, remove center from half of breads. Brush solid rounds with little soft butter or margarine and cover with cut-out rounds. Fill, brush top with melted butter, and broil or bake as suggested in recipe.

▶ HOT APPETIZERS ◀

Mushroom Pastry Crescents or Diamonds

Makes about 24 medium-size crescents

2 tablespoons finely chopped onion
2 tablespoons hot butter or margarine
½ pound fresh mushrooms (or 3-ounce can) chopped very fine
(Instead of using mushrooms, you may use ¾ cup finely chopped ham, seafood, or chicken)

About 1 teaspoon salt (omit if ham used)
⅛ teaspoon pepper
2 tablespoons Italian cheese
1 tablespoon cornstarch, combined with ½ cup cool milk

Sauté onion in butter for several minutes. Add very finely chopped mushrooms and cook 2 or 3 minutes. Season with salt, pepper, and Italian cheese, mixing well. Last, add cornstarch combined with milk and continue to cook over *low heat* about 3 minutes after it thickens. Remove from heat and let stand until cool before spreading on dough.

How to Form Crescents. Roll ½ recipe Basic Pastry Dough (page 4) to measure about 10 x 10 inches. Spread half of cool filling on upper half of dough. Flatten with spatula or dinner knife, fold uncovered half of dough onto filling. Pat dough gently with rolling pin to uniform thickness if necessary, and cut through filled dough with a medium-size crescent cutter, dipping cutter into flour occasionally to prevent sticking. Brush crescents with well-beaten egg combined with 2 teaspoons milk and ¼ teaspoon salt. Pick up with a spatula and place onto very lightly greased baking sheet. Small, leftover pieces of dough may be formed into various designs for tops of crescents. Brush again with beaten egg. Bake at 400° F. about 15 to 20 minutes, or until golden brown. Watch closely last few minutes to prevent burning and drying out. Serve hot. May be baked several days in advance, wrapped well, and stored in refrigerator in covered container. Reheat at 350° F. for about 7 or 8 minutes just before serving. May be frozen.

Mushroom Surprises

Makes about 24

Use 1 pound strictly fresh, firm, *medium-size* mushrooms, as uniform in size as possible. Wash thoroughly in lukewarm water, drain and dry on towel. Slice off stems. Stems may be used for Mushroom Pastry Crescents. Sauté whole buttons, rounded side down first, in small amount hot butter. Turn over and brown second side. Takes about 3 minutes on each side. Do not overcook. Season well with salt, pepper, and a little garlic or onion salt. Let stand until cool before shaping.

How to Form Mushroom Surprises. Roll ½ recipe Basic Pastry Dough (page 4) to measure about 9 x 12 inches, and then cut into 3-inch squares with a pastry wheel or knife. Place a whole mushroom on each piece of dough and enclose, pinching ends and rolling very gently in hand to form smooth balls. Surplus dough may be pinched off from bottom when necessary if mushrooms are small. Place balls on lightly greased baking sheet or silicone paper, having smooth side up. Brush with well-beaten egg. Form small strands of dough from leftover scraps and place on each ball to simulate a swirl. Brush again with beaten egg. Bake about 20 minutes at 425° F., watching closely toward end to prevent burning. One pound fresh mushrooms will make 24 Mushroom Surprises and about 24 Mushroom Crescents. If mushrooms are small, place two together and enclose in dough. Small well-seasoned meat balls or sautéed shrimp and a little sautéed onion are delicious prepared this way.

Hot Ham Bouches

Fills about 30 bread cases

In 2 tablespoons of butter or margarine, sauté for 5 minutes 1 medium peeled tomato cut very fine, or ½ cup drained canned tomatoes. Add 2 tablespoons finely chopped green onions and tops, and ½ cup finely chopped ham. Add 2 large whole eggs, slightly beaten, and cook over low heat until thick, adding ¼ teaspoon salt and a little pepper. Let cool. Fill 2-inch round or oval bread cases with this preparation and sprinkle with parmesan or American cheese. May be prepared hours in advance, kept covered with wax paper in refrigerator. Bake on heatproof platter or flat baking sheet at 400° F. for about 10 to 12 minutes, or until brown and crisp.

Hot Mushroom Meringues

Makes about 8 appetizers

Wash 1 cup fresh mushrooms and dry well, or use ½ cup best quality canned mushrooms. Chop fine and sauté in 2 tablespoons butter. Season with about ⅛ teaspoon salt, ⅛ teaspoon garlic salt, and a pinch of pepper. Combine 2 slightly beaten egg yolks with 2 tablespoons coffee cream or milk and add to hot cooked mushrooms. Continue to cook over *very low heat* until thickened—about 5 minutes. Spread on 2-inch rounds of *untoasted* bread (in baking, bread will toast on bottom), sprinkle with a little parmesan cheese. Beat the 2 leftover egg whites until they just cling to bowl. With a teaspoon, place on entire surface of mushroom mixture, and bake at 400° F. on a lightly greased baking sheet, 10 to 15 minutes, or until whites are delicately brown. Do not broil as meringue will toughen. First part of these appetizers may be prepared in advance, but egg whites must not be beaten and spread until ready to be baked and served. Very unusual and delicious.

Hot Mushrooms in Chafing Dish

Prepare first part of Hot Mushroom Meringues recipe (omitting the egg whites for top) and increase cream or milk to 4 tablespoons for each recipe. Simmer mixture only until thick and creamy, 5 minutes, but not too heavy. This is a very convenient way to serve large groups and when there is a shortage of help. If chafing dish is equipped with a tray underneath, arrange several kinds of crackers, wafers, or melba toast as attractively as possible around chafing dish, with a large serving spoon on one side. Guests will help themselves. One cup finely cut crab meat, lobster, or shrimp may be added to basic mushroom preparation for a special gourmet dish.

Hot Mushroom Bouches

In ¼ cup butter or other shortening sauté 2 tablespoons fine-chopped onion and 1 cup fresh mushrooms (or ½ cup good quality canned). Cook about 5 minutes, then add 4 hard-cooked eggs chopped fine, 1 tablespoon parsley, 1 teaspoon salt, and a little pepper. Add 1 slightly beaten egg and cook only until thick. Spread or fill bread cases (page 5), sprinkle with cheese, and bake at 400° F. about 12 minutes.

Stuffed French-Fried Shrimp Gourmet

Cook 2 pounds shelled raw medium or large shrimp in simmering water about 5 minutes. With small sharp knife make a very deep slit through rounded part of shrimp, but do not cut through. Marinate shrimp in special marinade (page 9) for several hours, then drain well.

Special Filling for 2 Pounds Shrimp or Lobster Tails

½ cup cooked ham, pork, or any other meat (or seafood) finely chopped

¼ cup onion (or ½ cup fresh green onion and tops) finely chopped

About ½ cup finely chopped Chinese water chestnuts (one 5-ounce can)

½ teaspoon salt if using unsalted meat; ¼ teaspoon if using ham

¼ teaspoon pepper

¼ teaspoon garlic salt

½ cup dry bread crumbs, to be used in filling

2 whole eggs, well beaten with a fork for a few seconds

About 2 tablespoons more or less of warm water or stock (if needed)

Additional bread crumbs and egg for coating

Combine all ingredients in a bowl, except the warm water and the additional crumbs and eggs to be used for coating. Stir well for about a minute until smooth. If preparation appears dry, add the 2 tablespoons of water or stock, and allow filling to stand for at least 15 minutes or longer. Now test preparation in hand to see if it holds its shape; if not, add a little more liquid. Fill open end of shrimp with this filling, rounding it smoothly and firmly. Now cover shrimp carefully with dry fine light bread crumbs, dip into well-beaten egg combined with a tablespoon water, ¼ teaspoon salt, ⅛ teaspoon pepper, then into crumbs again, pressing crumbs onto surface until smooth. Let stand on wax paper in room temperature about 10 minutes, turning them over after 5 minutes, then fry as per directions given below.

To Fry French-Fried Shrimp Gourmet. Lower crumbed shrimp carefully into deep hot fat—350° F. (see page 123 for Deep-Fat Frying directions)—and cook them about 5 or 6 minutes, or until brown and crisp if they are to be served at once. They may be fried for only 2 or 3 minutes, hours (or a day) in advance, and refried at 350° F. for several minutes until brown and crisp just before serving. If partially cooked shrimp are to stand for more than an hour, they must be refrigerated in covered container. Can be frozen and refried before serving.

Stuffed Lobster Tails Gourmet

Cook 2 pounds lobster tails (5 or 6 ounces each, not larger) gently in boiling water 5 minutes after boiling begins. Drain well, and when cool remove shells. Cut crosswise in about 1-inch pieces. Marinate in special marinade for several hours. Drain well, and make a slit about ⅔ way down, stuff opening with filling smoothly and firmly. Cover with crumbs, egg and crumbs and fry at 350° F. about 5 or 6 minutes. Serve on frilled toothpicks.

Special Marinade for 2 Pounds Shrimp or Lobster Tails

⅓ cup salad oil
⅓ cup lemon juice or wine vinegar
1½ teaspoons salt
About ¼ teaspoon pepper

About ½ teaspoon garlic salt
About ¼ teaspoon dry tarragon or other herb

Combine all ingredients in medium-size bowl, and with egg beater beat for about 1 minute.

Please Note: Instead of crumbing these appetizers, they may be carefully dipped into standard batter (page 244) and French-fried at 350° F. for about 5 or 6 minutes.

To Serve: Arrange around a bowl of Hostess Dipping Sauce (page 334).

Pancho Almond-Shrimp Appetizers

1 pound uncooked large shrimp, peeled and deveined
Flour
Batter (below)

About 2 cups blanched almonds, put through nut chopper
½ cup dry bread crumbs
Cooking oil
Pancho Dipping Sauce (below)

If shrimp are small, split them butterfly fashion, if large cut in halves. With a heavy knife or cleaver flatten them slightly. Roll in flour, then dip into batter; let drip well, holding in fingers, then cover completely with chopped untoasted almonds, combined with bread crumbs. Deep fry at 350° F. for about 5 or 6 minutes. Serve around a bowl of Pancho Dipping Sauce.

To prepare almonds, drop them into hot water and let simmer several minutes; *remove skins*, then put them while quite moist through nut chopper, or use commercial blanched sliced almonds, crushed with rolling pin.

Batter for Pancho Almond-Shrimp Appetizers

2 eggs well beaten for a few seconds   About 1½ teaspoons salt
¾ cup milk   ¼ teaspoon pepper
1 tablespoon oil   ½ teaspoon baking powder
1 cup sifted all-purpose flour

Combine all ingredients in a bowl, and with egg beater beat until smooth. May be used within a few minutes, or cover and put aside for several hours in a cool place.

Pancho Dipping Sauce

3 small cans tomato sauce   ⅛ teaspoon onion salt
¼ cup cider vinegar   1 teaspoon chili powder
1 teaspoon paprika   1 tablespoon cornstarch, combined
1 tablespoon brown sugar   with 1 tablespoon water (op-
⅛ teaspoon celery salt   tional)
⅛ teaspoon hot pepper

Combine all ingredients except cornstarch and water. Stir well, and cook uncovered about 10 minutes. Now add the cornstarch and water only if a thick sauce is preferred and simmer for several minutes. Serve in bowl in center of platter; surround with cooked shrimp. Sprinkle top of sauce with very finely chopped green onion or parsley for additional color.

Pancho Shrimp Luncheon Style

Use very large shrimp for luncheon or supper main dish. Shrimp can be fried in advance for hors d'oeuvres or main dish, then reheated in a 400° F. oven on cake racks with drip pan underneath for about 5 minutes after they are removed from refrigerator. Do not refry. For main dish serve with plain rice or Turkish Pilaf (page 312) and Pancho Sauce.

Shrimp Louisiana (in Chafing Dish)

1 pound cooked shrimp, left whole if   ½ teaspoon garlic salt
small or medium; split lengthwise   1 tablespoon brown sugar
if large   ¼ teaspoon celery salt
½ cup chili sauce   2 tablespoons cornstarch combined
¾ cup catsup   with 1 cup water or tomato juice
1 tablespoon prepared horseradish   ½ cup fresh green onions and ½ cup
(optional)   green onion tops, cut in ½-inch
About 1 teaspoon salt   pieces

Combine all ingredients except starch mixture and green onions. Mix well, cover bowl, and let marinate for at least an hour. About 10 minutes before serving, add dissolved cornstarch to ingredients, mix well and cook over moderate heat for about 5 minutes after simmering begins if shrimp are large; cook about 3 minutes after simmering begins if shrimp are small or medium. If sauce is too thick add a little water. Last, fold in the fresh green onions and tops. Pour into chafing dish and serve with crackers, wafers, or melba toast. This also makes an excellent buffet or luncheon dish served with plain hot rice.

Cantonese Egg Rolls

Purchase noodle-dough squares that measure about 7 inches if making large rolls, or 4-inch squares for individual size, available in Chinese noodle factories or Chinese stores. They are more economical and satisfactory than homemade noodle dough. These factories supply the leading Chinese restaurants. There are about eighteen 7-inch squares to the pound. Keep them in their original wrapper, covered with a very damp towel, until ready to be used (to prevent drying out), and store in refrigerator. It is best to use them within 3 days after they are purchased. You may use Noodle Dough for Egg Rolls (page 823).

Cut off about 1½ inches from two corners and 1 inch from other two corners of each square. Measure ¼ cup filling (see below) solidly packed, and form a 5-inch roll (about 1 tablespoon for individual). Place filling on wide end of dough nearest you. Brush edges of dough with well-beaten egg combined with ¼ teaspoon salt, and roll up, turning edges in while rolling. Keep rolls on wax paper until all have been completed.

As soon as rolls are completed, heat oil to 360° to 375° F. Dip rolls into Cantonese Fritter Batter, then lower into hot fat carefully and fry until *very lightly colored* and set for about 2 minutes. Lift out and drain on cake coolers. If to be kept more than an hour before serving, cover and store in refrigerator. About 30 minutes before serving, remove from refrigerator, let stand in room temperature. When ready to be served, lower gently into hot oil 360° to 375° F. and fry until *golden brown* and crisp—about 5 minutes. Remove from fat, cut each roll crosswise into 3 or 4 pieces and serve at once. Serve individual rolls whole.

Cantonese Fritter Batter

1 medium egg	¼ cup sifted all-purpose flour
2 tablespoons chicken stock or milk	½ teaspoon salt

Combine all ingredients in a small bowl and, with egg beater, beat until smooth. Cover and let stand about 10 minutes, or longer. If batter is too thin, add a little more flour; if too thick add more liquid. It is best to have a thin batter.

Filling for 8 Large Egg Rolls

1 cup cooked shrimp (canned may be used; reduce salt)

1 cup cooked pork, veal, or ham finely chopped with knife

1 cup celery, chopped very fine

½ cup canned Chinese water chestnuts, chopped (not too fine)

½ cup fresh green onion and stems, chopped very fine, or 2 tablespoons chopped dry onion

1 teaspoon salt (less if using ham or seasoned meat)

1 teaspoon sugar

⅛ teaspoon black pepper

3 tablespoons melted butter, or more

2 tablespoons peanut butter, or more

Chop all ingredients with heavy knife or cleaver. Do not grind. Add seasonings. Combine all ingredients in a bowl, and with hands work well until thoroughly blended. If mixture appears too dry, add a little more peanut butter. Mixture should appear moist and hold its shape when pressed in hand but not wet nor too dry. Cover and store in refrigerator until ready to be used. May be prepared a day in advance but *must be refrigerated*.

Cantonese Fried Shrimp

Serves 6

1 pound raw shrimp weighed with shells

1 very large egg (⅓ cup)

½ cup chicken stock, milk or water (more or less, depending on flour)

2 teaspoons salt

1 tablespoon cornstarch

About ¾ cup sifted flour

¾ teaspoon baking powder

¼ teaspoon garlic salt

Shell shrimp and remove vein if necessary. Split lengthwise. If shrimp are very large, flatten with cleaver and cut in 2 pieces to insure thorough cooking. If small or medium, they may be left whole. Wash under cold running water and drain very thoroughly for about 15 minutes, then on paper towel.

Combine all ingredients (except shrimp) in a bowl, and with egg beater beat until smooth. Cover and let stand at least 15 minutes. Drop well-drained *raw, split* shrimp into batter. Pick up one piece at a time, drain a little, and drop into deep hot oil—about 350° F. Do not fry too many in first frying at one time to prevent clinging together. Fry until *very light brown* if to be prepared in advance and refried. If to be served at once, fry until *golden* brown and crisp—about 5 minutes. Best to fry second time. Drain on cake cooler and serve as soon as possible. If after frying 1 or 2 shrimp, the coating appears too thin, add a little more flour. If it appears too thick, add a little more liquid.

These shrimp may be fried first time several hours or a day in advance, stored in refrigerator after they are cool, then refried for several minutes before serving, or until crisp, and golden brown. *Watch second frying as they darken quickly*. Keep temperature about 350° F.

Serve with Sweet-Sour Sauce (page 17) or Hot Sauce (page 18).

Cantonese Barbecue Ribs and Pork

2 pounds ribs, pork tenderloin, or pork loin
¼ cup granulated sugar
2 tablespoons catsup
2 tablespoons soy sauce
½ teaspoon Chinese molasses
2 teaspoons salt
¼ teaspoon black pepper
¼ cup chicken stock

For marinade, combine all ingredients (except meat) and mix well. Pour over meat on both sides. Cover with wax paper, and let stand in refrigerator 7 or 8 hours or longer, turning occasionally and brushing several times with sauce that settles in dish while standing.

About 2 hours before serving, remove meat from refrigerator, place it on a rack with drip pan underneath, adding about 1 cup cold water in drip pan to prevent smoking.

Ribs. Roast ribs at 350° F. about 1½ hours, turning them over after 45 minutes, and baste them occasionally with leftover marinade. After 1½ hours, test ribs, and if not done, roast a little longer. Very thick back ribs may take 25 or 30 minutes longer. It is better to have them a little overcooked than undercooked. Before serving, cut with a very sharp knife into single ribs and serve with sauce. If meat is browning too rapidly, cover loosely with aluminum foil or lower temperature to 325° F. Ribs are done when you can pull them apart easily.

Pork Tenderloin. Follow above directions. Roast about 2 hours if tenderloins are large and thick, turning over after 1 hour. Chinese cooks use the center and leanest part of a pork loin for this purpose.

Pork Loin. Prepare same as pork tenderloin, but cook for longer time, allowing about 40 minutes per pound for 3- or 4-pound pieces. Use meat thermometer and cook to 170° F. Oriental cooks trim the pork loin, removing most of visible fat. It is more moist and tender than the pork tenderloin.

Won Tons

Makes about 40

1 whole egg
¼ teaspoon salt
1 recipe of Chinese Noodle Dough (page 823) or
½ pound of commercial Chinese noodle dough
Peanut oil

Beat egg and salt 15 minutes in advance.

Cut moist noodle dough in about 2½-inch squares. Place 1 slightly rounded teaspoon of meat filling on each, spreading it flat. Brush edges of squares with beaten egg, fold over, forming triangles. Press edges well together. Puncture top 2 times with toothpick. Deep-fry Won Tons as soon as possible after they are filled, at 350° F., until golden brown and crisp on one side, then with fork turn over and fry second side. Lift out with perforated spoon, and drain on cake racks. May be kept hot in a low oven (about 250° F.) for about 15 minutes, or they may be deep-fried hours in advance, refrigerated then reheated on cake racks with drip pan underneath in a 350° F. oven for about 8 to 10 minutes. Do not refry.

Won Ton Meat Filling

½ pound (1 cup packed) very finely ground lean raw pork, chicken, or beef (cooked meat may be used)
⅛ teaspoon pepper
2 tablespoons finely chopped water chestnuts

1 teaspoon cornstarch
1 tablespoon finely chopped fresh green onion and stems
About 1 teaspoon salt
2 teaspoons soy sauce

Combine all ingredients and blend well. Use 1 slightly rounded teaspoon for each Won Ton.

Oriental Appetizers on Bamboo Sticks

Makes about 15 to 20

1 pound of beef or pork tenderloin, sliced about ¼ inch thick, 1¼ inch squares, *not larger* (top-quality aged sirloin tip or top of round may be used, if sprinkled with meat tenderizer about 20 minutes after they are removed from marinade and before they are sautéed)

or 2 pounds medium-size raw shrimp
6-inch very thin bamboo sticks
Small canned mushroom caps
Cocktail onions
Pineapple cubes, or cubed water chestnuts

Insert pointed end of bamboo sticks through one piece of meat, then through a mushroom cap, small cocktail onion, cube of pineapple or water chestnut, then another piece of meat. (If shrimp is used instead of meat, first cook shrimp in simmering water about 3 to 5 minutes. When cool, drain well and place on bamboo sticks.) Place appetizers in a medium-size flat container, and cover with marinade. Refrigerate for at least 8 hours, turning them over several times.

To Cook Appetizers. Drain well, and sauté over *medium* heat on well-oiled flat side of griddle pan, or heavy large skillet, about 1 minute on each side. It may be necessary to lower or increase heat from time to time, also to add little more oil, or a little water on griddle during cooking process. Do not overcook. May be kept hot on heatproof dish or other flat pan in very slow oven (250° F.) for about ½ hour. Or appetizers may be grilled hours or a day in advance, cooled, then refrigerated. Shortly before serving remove from refrigerator and brush them with leftover marinade, reheat on griddle or in skillet about ½ minute on each side, or large amount may be reheated in a 350° F. oven for about 10 minutes just before serving.

To Serve. Arrange on a 12- or 14-inch round platter, with bowl of Hot Sauce (page 18) in center, or serve without sauce.

Marinade

2 tablespoons granulated sugar
2 tablespoons catsup
¼ cup soy sauce
½ teaspoon Chinese molasses

¼ teaspoon pepper
¼ teaspoon garlic or onion salt
1 cup chicken or meat stock (add bouillon cube to 1 cup hot water)

Combine all ingredients and blend thoroughly. Pour over appetizers.

Oriental Shrimp

1 pound raw whole large shrimp (25 to 30)
3 tablespoons soy sauce
1 teaspoon Chinese molasses
¼ teaspoon salt

½ cup chicken or meat stock
¼ teaspoon garlic or onion salt
¼ teaspoon black pepper
1 pound thinly sliced bacon
1 large can water chestnuts (halved)

To cook shrimp, drop them into boiling unsalted water and let simmer about 5 minutes as soon as they come to boiling point. Remove shells and vein, if necessary. If using top-quality cooked canned shrimp, omit salt in recipe. If shrimp are very large and thick, split in halves lengthwise.

Stir ingredients except bacon, shrimp, and chestnuts well for about ½ minute and pour over the cooked whole shrimp and sliced water chestnuts. Mix well and let marinate for at least 2 hours, turning them over occasionally. When ready to be prepared, drain well. Wrap a thin whole or half slice of bacon around a whole shrimp and slice of water chestnut firmly, and secure with plain heavy toothpicks. This may be done hours or a day in advance if refrigerated in a covered container.

To Serve. Place appetizers on cake racks with drip pan underneath (pour 1 cup hot water in pan to prevent smoking) and bake at 425° F. about 8 minutes on first side, then turn over and bake about 7 more minutes on second side. Remove from oven, and replace plain toothpicks with frilled ones if desired. Serve hot. These appetizers may be *completely cooked* hours in advance and stored in refrigerator, covered, as soon as they are cold, then reheated in oven at 400° F. on racks for about 7 or 8 minutes. May be frozen for 1 week. (Reheat for about 10 minutes if frozen.)

Oriental Chicken Liver Appetizer

Makes about 20

2 tablespoons soy sauce
¼ cup water or stock
¼ teaspoon salt
¼ teaspoon garlic salt
¼ teaspoon black pepper
½ pound chicken livers, each cut in two or three pieces, depending on size

5-ounce can Chinese water chestnuts, each sliced lengthwise in two pieces
½ pound bacon, each slice cut in two pieces crosswise (not lengthwise)

Combine all ingredients except chicken livers, water chestnuts, and bacon, and stir until well blended. Place a piece of chicken liver and a thick slice of chestnut on one end of bacon, roll tightly, and insert a heavy toothpick through bacon, chestnut, and liver to hold together as securely as possible. Place appetizers into bowl of marinade, cover and refrigerate for several hours or longer. Omit salt if marinated for longer than 2 hours.

To Bake and Serve. Place 1 cup hot water in a drip pan. Arrange marinated appetizers on a cake rack, leaving about an inch space between each one, and bake in a preheated 450° F. oven 10 minutes. Now turn over and bake another 8 to 10 minutes. Plain toothpicks may be removed and replaced with frilled picks. Serve appetizers on a heated platter. Will remain hot for about 15 minutes. They may remain in oven with heat shut off and door slightly open for a short time if necessary before serving. These appetizers may be completely prepared and baked for a little shorter time, several hours or a day in advance, if refrigerated, then reheated on cake racks in a 400° F. oven for about 6 or 7 minutes just before serving.

Hot Oriental Delight Appetizers

Makes about 45

1 can Chinese water chestnuts (6½- or 8-ounce size) chopped medium, not too fine
3-ounce can chopped mushrooms, chopped fine
4½-ounce can shrimp or 1 cup freshly cooked, chopped medium, not too fine
½ teaspoon salt if using freshly cooked shrimp and unsalted

cooked pork (omit salt if using canned shrimp and ham)
2 teaspoons soy sauce
¼ teaspoon pepper
¼ cup fresh green onion and stems mixed, chopped fine
¾ pound of ham or cooked pork (1½ cups packed), chopped fine
5 whole eggs
4 cupfuls light bread crumbs

Add ingredients (except eggs and bread crumbs) to White Sauce and stir well until evenly blended. Cover, and refrigerate for 2 hours or longer, or until firm enough to handle and shape. Can be prepared day in advance.

To shape, pick up 1 level tablespoon of preparation, and with hands shape into very smooth balls, dampening hands *slightly* if sticky. Cover balls with light bread crumbs, then dip into well beaten whole eggs, let drain (add no water to eggs). Roll again in crumbs, then in egg, and the third time in crumbs. This is important to prevent bursting and to produce a crisp crust. Place on wax paper and let stand about 20 minutes, turning balls over several times. Lower gently into deep hot fat, about 375° F., until lightly colored, for about 2 minutes, then refry a second time just before serving at 375° F. for about 2 minutes. It is best to fry these appetizers a second time for crisp crust even if they are to be served within a short time. They may be fried once a day in advance, and then refried shortly before serving. Store them in covered container in refrigerator. Or they may be frozen for several weeks. Let stand covered in room temperature for about 2 hours after removing from freezer, but do not allow to become warm; or defrost for longer time in refrigerator.

Note. If using French-fry basket, place 8 to 10 appetizers in basket at one time, and lower into fat. They will brown evenly if placed in fat at one time. In reheating the second time twice as many may be placed in basket at one time, at 375° F. Do not allow fat to cool, but increase heat as necessary.

To Serve. Arrange balls in chafing dish, or on a large platter around a bowl of Hot Sauce (page 18). Frilled toothpick on top center of each adds color, and makes them easy to pick up.

White Sauce

Prepare with 3 tablespoons melted butter or margarine, add ¼ cup sifted all-purpose flour, stir until smooth, than add ½ cup lukewarm milk. Cook, stirring continuously until thick and smooth. Simmer 2 or 3 minutes. Add little more milk if sauce is too stiff to cook.

Sweet-Sour Sauce—No. 1

¼ pound dry apricots
1 cup water
¼ teaspoon salt

½ cup granulated sugar, more or less
About ½ cup cider or white vinegar, more or less

Cook apricots in water in covered saucepan very slowly about 30 minutes, or until very soft and most of water has been absorbed by apricots. (You can substitute canned apricots.) When soft, put apricots through food mill.

Combine all ingredients, and with egg beater beat until smooth and thoroughly blended. Taste and season further if necessary. Serve with Cantonese appetizers. May be made days in advance and stored in covered jar in refrigerator.

Sweet-Sour Sauce—No. 2

¼ cup vinegar
½ cup pineapple juice
⅓ cup brown sugar, solidly packed

1½ tablespoons cornstarch
2 tablespoons water
About 1 teaspoon salt

Combine all ingredients in saucepan and bring to boiling point, stirring constantly. Let simmer about 5 minutes. Let cool and serve with appetizers. May be made in advance. If sauce is too thick, thin out with pineapple juice or vinegar.

Hot Sauce

½ cup cool water
About 1½ tablespoons dry mustard, more or less, to suit taste

About ¾ cup catsup
About 1 teaspoon salt

Combine all ingredients and, with egg beater or large spoon, beat until smooth and thoroughly blended. Serve with appetizers. May be made days in advance and stored in covered jar in refrigerator.

Mustard Sauce

To each cup mayonnaise, add about 1 teaspoon dry mustard, 1 teaspoon sugar, 3 tablespoons prepared mustard, or enough to suit taste. Add a little lemon juice if too thick.

Seafood Gourmet Appetizers in Patty Shells

Will make about 36

Rich Flaky Dough for Patty Shells

1 cup (½ pound) salted butter, cold and firm (half margarine may be used)
2 cups sifted all-purpose flour

1 egg yolk, slightly beaten
¾ cup commercial sour cream
1 egg white
½ teaspoon lemon juice

With pie blender, cut cold firm butter into flour until it looks like coarse meal (same as for pie dough). Now add yolk combined with sour cream, and with a dinner knife or fork stir until dough leaves sides of bowl. Turn out onto lightly floured pastry cloth and knead very gently for a few seconds. Divide dough into 4 equal parts, and shape each into uniform square pieces. Wrap well and refrigerate for about 8 hours or longer. Dough may be frozen for several weeks. To prepare patty shells, roll each piece of dough with covered rolling pin on lightly floured pastry cloth to measure 7 x 8 inches.

With 2-inch-round cutter, cut out as many rounds as possible. Remove center from half of rounds with open end of large No. 3 cookie tube, or a very small 1⅛-inch cutter. Place scraps together gently, roll dough and form more patty shells. Full recipe will make about 36. Puncture solid rounds and rings with a fork, brush them gently with egg white combined with lemon juice, beaten for ½ minute. Place rings on solid rounds, picking them up carefully with spatula and transfer to very lightly greased baking sheet. Refrigerate for at least 15 minutes. Bake in 400° F. oven about 15 to 20 minutes, and watch closely toward end to prevent overbrowning. Shut off heat, leave oven door partly open for about 20 more minutes.

Special Seafood Gourmet Filling

2 tablespoons melted butter or margarine
3 tablespoons sifted all-purpose flour
1 cup warm milk
¾ teaspoon salt
⅛ teaspoon cayenne pepper, or ½ teaspoon hot sauce
¼ cup chopped toasted almonds

¼ cup finely chopped green onion and stems
2 tablespoons pimiento cut into ¼ inch pieces
1 tablespoon dry sherry wine (optional)
6- or 7-ounce package or can cooked crab meat, cooked lobster meat, or shrimp, chopped fine

Combine flour with melted butter and stir until smooth. Add the warm milk slowly. Cook until thick, now add dry seasonings and simmer several minutes. Last, add all other ingredients, and do not cook further. Simply mix well. Taste and season further if necessary. Let cool, refrigerate in covered bowl until needed if not to be used within an hour. May be prepared day in advance if refrigerated.

To Serve. Fill patty shells with a scant tablespoon of filling, having top nicely rounded and smooth. Place cap on, and bake about 10 to 12 minutes in a preheated 350° F. oven just before serving. May be sprinkled lightly with paprika.

Quick Flaky Cheese Sticks

Makes about 60 sticks

Prepare Flaky Dough same as for Patty Shells (page 18). Divide dough into 4 pieces, wrap and chill for 8 hours or longer. Roll each piece on lightly floured cloth to measure 5 inches wide and 16 inches long. Brush entire surface with egg white combined with ½ teaspoon lemon juice, beaten ½ minute. Puncture well with a fork, sprinkle with 1 tablespoon grated Italian cheese and a little paprika. Trim off uneven ends, and cut dough into about fourteen 5-inch strips, about ¾ inch wide. Form coiled sticks, place them on well-greased baking sheet (or better, on silicone paper) about 1 inch apart. Chill for at least 15 minutes, or until firm to the touch, then bake in 400° F. oven about 12 to 15 minutes or until golden brown, but not dark. Remove sticks that are done if center ones are not brown. This is important to prevent overbrowning. Let cool on cake racks. Store in covered container if not to be served within a few hours. Cheese sticks make a nice accompaniment for seafood, molds, soups, etc. Baked Patty Shells and Sticks may be kept for several weeks if well wrapped and refrigerated, or may be frozen for several months. Pastry dough also freezes well.

Hot Cheese Soufflé Hors d'Oeuvres

½ pound (2½ cups without packing) freshly shredded (on small shredder) *firm* processed American or cheddar cheese (do not use cheese *spread*, but you can use ½ pound cream cheese instead of American; in this case use only yolk of egg, and spread 1 level tablespoon cream cheese filling on each round of bread)

1 large egg (measure scant ¼ cup)
⅛ teaspoon salt
⅛ teaspoon garlic or onion salt
About twenty 2-inch rounds of thick sliced bread, or about forty 1½-inch rounds (at least 2 days old)
Soft butter

Shred firm cheese just before combining it with other ingredients. Beat egg slightly, add salt and cheese little at a time to egg, mixing well with a fork or spoon for about 1 minute, then with hand, until well blended and firm. This preparation must be very firm for best results and must not stick to hands when shaping rounds. Small or medium eggs may require a little less cheese, but it's better to add a little extra cheese if egg appears thin.

For the large 2-inch rounds of bread, pick up 1 rounded standard measuring teaspoonful of cheese preparation (that is, 2 level teaspoons) and in palms of hands shape into very smooth balls. Flatten balls and place them on lightly buttered bread rounds, leaving ¼ inch of bread free of cheese all around. If using smaller cutter—1½-inch size—form small balls with 1 level measuring teaspoon cheese preparation. About 5 or 6 minutes before serving, place them on center of a small baking sheet in a preheated 425° F. *broiler*, 2 inches from heat until brown and puffed. Takes about 5 minutes. These soufflés may be broiled hours or even a day in advance, then kept in a covered container until shortly before ready to serve. To reheat place them on a heatproof platter (or baking sheet) *in oven* (not broiler this time) preheated to 425° F. for about 5 or 6 minutes. This is an excellent way to serve large groups. An entire large platter or baking sheet may be *reheated* at one time and served immediately.

Ham and Cheese Soufflé Hors d'Oeuvres

1 recipe Cheese Soufflé (page 20)
Some cooked very *thinly* sliced ham
   (or other cooked meat) cut in
   small squares

Large stuffed green olives, each cut in
   6 very thin slices
Bread rounds and soft butter

Place very *thinly* sliced meat squares on lightly buttered bread rounds, then thin slice of olive. Form balls with 1 rounded measuring teaspoon cheese preparation for the 2-inch breads and 1 level teaspoon for the 1½ inch. Flatten cheese and place it over olive and ham as smoothly and uniformly as possible. Broil, etc., according to directions page 20.

Seafood Cheese Soufflé Hors d'Oeuvres

Spread buttered bread rounds with a thin layer of finely chopped crab meat, lobster, shrimp, or salmon and a drop of hot sauce. Cover with cheese rounds, etc., and broil according to directions page 20.

   Note. If preferred, these hors d'oeuvres may be put together completely without broiling in advance. Keep them well covered, in a cold place (must be refrigerated if using meat or seafood), then broil as needed. It is important to cut bread rounds into uniform thickness, also to flatten cheese to uniform thickness to prevent uneven topping and dripping.

Mushroom Soufflé Appetizers

Prepare 1 pound large, firm fresh mushrooms (strictly fresh—about 20 to 24 to the pound). Wash mushrooms in lukewarm water several times, then dry them well in a towel. Sauté caps of fresh mushrooms in several tablespoons hot butter or margarine about 2 minutes on each side, but do not overcook. Should remain firm. Place them upside down on wax paper to drain well, then sprinkle inside very lightly with salt before stuffing them with cheese preparation (page 22).

   Chop mushroom stems very fine. Combine them with about 2 tablespoons fresh green onion and 2 tablespoons onion stems, very finely chopped. Sauté chopped mushrooms and onions in about 1½ tablespoons butter. Now season with about ½ teaspoon salt, ⅛ teaspoon *crushed* rosemary, ¼ teaspoon pepper, ⅛ teaspoon hot sauce. Combine 1 egg yolk with ¼ cup milk, stir well, and add to mushroom preparation. Continue to cook over *very, very low heat* only until thick for several minutes. Let cool before spreading this preparation on bread rounds.

   With a 1½-inch-round cutter (use little larger cutter, about 2-inch size, for large mushrooms) cut out as many rounds of thickly sliced bread as mushrooms to be prepared. Spread top of bread thickly with 1 slightly rounded measuring teaspoon mushroom preparation, and with tip of finger make slight depression in center. Place whole mushroom cap with open end up on top of filling, fitting it in firmly. Now form uniform smooth balls with 1 level teaspoon cheese preparation and insert one in opening of each mushroom.

Flatten balls very slightly with tip of finger. If mushrooms are very large, make balls a bit larger. Arrange appetizers on center part only of small baking sheet, and broil them at 425° F. about 2 inches from heat source for about 7 minutes or until puffed and brown. Watch closely the last minute or two to prevent burning. Transfer them at once to a heated serving platter, insert a frilled toothpick through top center of each, and serve at once, or may be baked in oven on upper rack at 450° F. for about 12 to 15 minutes.

Note. It is best to use thickly sliced bread that is at least 2 days old for these appetizers. Filling, mushrooms, and cheese balls must be placed together as symmetrically as possible to prevent tilting of mushrooms after they are broiled. Also be sure to use a baking sheet that is not warped or out of shape in any way for this purpose.

Cheese Preparation

1 large egg (to measure not more than ¼ cupful) beaten with a fork

½ pound (about 2½ cups) finely shredded processed firm American cheese (Soft cheese foods and spreads do not give as good results. They flatten out more but can be used, if preferred); ½ pound cream cheese may be used instead of American, in which case use as for Hot Cheese Soufflé, page 20

¼ teaspoon salt

Combine ingredients and mix well with a heavy spoon until smooth for at least 1 minute, forming a *very stiff preparation that does not stick to hands when forming balls.*

Hot Crab Meat Soufflé

Makes 18

½ cup mayonnaise
1 teaspoon lemon juice
¼ teaspoon garlic or onion salt
¼ teaspoon hot sauce or dash of hot pepper
About ⅓ teaspoon salt

1 can or package frozen crab meat (about 6 to 7 ounces), well drained, flaked, and chopped medium
1 medium egg white
About eighteen 2-inch-thick bread rounds

Combine all ingredients except white of egg and bread rounds in a medium-size bowl and blend thoroughly. Now beat white of egg in small 5-inch bowl until it clings to bowl and fold it into preparation until evenly blended. Pick up 1 scant tablespoon and pile on rounds of bread, keeping it higher in center and as smooth as possible, with a small spatula or dinner knife.

Preheat broiler at 400° F., place appetizers on a small baking sheet, about 3 inches from heat, for about 5 minutes or until tops are golden brown and puffed. Serve hot, *or* they may be placed on large double baking sheets and baked on center rack of oven at 425° F. for about 10 to 12 minutes or until golden brown and puffed. Bread cases may be used instead of single rounds. In this case use a slightly round tablespoon of filling, spreading it on upper bread ring and keeping it high in center. These cases must be baked and not broiled.

Note. This preparation is best made a day in advance and stored in refrigerator, or may be placed on bread rounds or in bread cases several hours in advance, refrigerated. Then broil or bake as per general directions.

Hot Seafood Melty Appetizers

Makes 20

½ pound cream cheese, medium consistency (room temperature about 1 hour)
Yolk of 1 large egg
About 1¼ teaspoons hot sauce, more or less (optional)
¼ teaspoon onion or garlic salt
About ¼ teaspoon salt

About twenty 2-inch rounds of thickly sliced white or dark bread
Paprika
1 cup packed cooked canned or frozen crab meat (6- or 7-ounce can or frozen), cooked shrimp, or lobster meat (flake crab meat, cut other seafood into small pieces)

With electric mixer or heavy spoon, beat cream cheese for about 1 minute. Add yolk, and beat until well blended. Now add the hot sauce, onion or garlic salt, plain salt, and mix well. Last, add seafood and stir until thoroughly blended. Place 1 level standard measuring tablespoonful of preparation on each bread round, having it rounded and higher in center. Spread surface smoothly with small spatula or dinner knife. Sprinkle lightly with paprika. This may be done long in advance if refrigerated, covered well with wax paper or plastic bag.

To Serve. Preheat oven about 15 minutes in advance at 450° F. Arrange appetizers on small baking sheets (not large), and place under broiler about 2 inches from heat, for about 5 to 6 minutes, or until they are golden brown and puffy. Watch closely the last minute or two. A frilled toothpick may be placed in center top of each, and serve at once.

Note. These appetizers may be completely broiled in advance, and refrigerated or frozen if well wrapped, then reheated on baking sheet in oven, center rack, *not broiler*, at 400° F. for about 7 to 10 minutes. A large baking sheet can be reheated at one time in this way, and avoids last-minute preparation.

Crab Meat au Diable

2 tablespoons butter or margarine
2 tablespoons flour
¾ cup milk
½ teaspoon salt
¼ teaspoon chili powder
⅛ teaspoon hot sauce
1 slightly beaten egg yolk

½ cup finely chopped canned mushrooms (3-ounce can)
1 tablespoon butter
2 tablespoons finely cut green onion
6- or 7-ounce canned or packaged frozen crab meat, chopped in small pieces

Melt butter, add flour, mixing until smooth. Add milk little at a time, and cook until thick. Sauté mushrooms in 1 tablespoon butter for 2 or 3 minutes. Combine all ingredients except crab meat, and simmer about 5 minutes. Last, fold in crab meat. Mix gently and serve hot in chafing dish or let cool and refrigerate if not to be used at once.

To Serve. Serve in chafing dish or in Patty Shells (page 4). Fill tiny Patty Shells, having filling slightly rounded, and bake at 350° F. about 10 minutes just before serving. Fills about 24 shells. May be filled in advance and refrigerated in covered container. Sprinkle tops with paprika.

Oysters Rockefeller Appetizers

Makes about 24

1 can frozen oysters (12-ounce size) drained and dried well on towels. Must not retain too much moisture.

About twenty 2-inch oval *thick* commercially sliced bread
1 recipe Topping Rockefeller

To Prepare Appetizers. Place raw oysters on ovals of breads, leaving about ⅛ inch of bread uncovered all around. (Cut through bread with a large oval cutter made by shaping a 2-inch round cutter into an oval. It is best to have bread that is several days old, or dry out ovals of bread on baking sheets in a 300° F. oven for about 10 minutes.) If oysters are large cut them about 1¼ inches long and ½ inch wide. Two or 3 small pieces may be put together. Spread 1 heaping (measuring) teaspoon Topping Rockefeller on top and sides of oysters smoothly with small spatula, keeping it rounded in center.

Place appetizers on greased baking sheet, and bake in preheated 425° F. oven about 5 or 6 minutes, or until underside of breads is golden brown and crisp. If appetizers have been put together in advance and refrigerated, increase baking time to about 8 minutes, and test, then place them under broiler for about 3 minutes, 2 inches from heat. Will remain hot for about

10 minutes, but best to serve as soon as done. Pick up with a small spatula or dinner knife and arrange on a warm platter. Top of each may be garnished with a thin slice green stuffed olive.

Topping Rockefeller

¼ cup fresh parsley, cut with scissors fine as possible

½ cup uncooked defrosted, frozen spinach, chopped fine as possible, well drained, then very gently press out surplus moisture in a strainer

¼ cup finely chopped green onions and stems, chopped fine as possible

½ cup (1 stick) butter or margarine, first measured then melted (use warm)

About 1 teaspoon hot sauce

Scant ½ teaspoon salt

⅛ teaspoon black or white pepper

½ teaspoon garlic salt

2 tablespoons grated Italian cheese

¼ cup unseasoned dry bread crumbs, or little more if preparation is too soft

Combine all finely chopped ingredients in medium-size bowl, mixing thoroughly to form a pasty, moist preparation, of spreading consistency. If made in advance and stored in refrigerator, it must stand at room temperature or in bowl of warm water for at least an hour to soften, or will be difficult to spread.

Sombreros

1 jar or can tamales

1 recipe Crisp Tortilla Bases or large sesame crackers

Sauce from tamales

¾ tablespoon cooked bacon

1 rounded teaspoon American cheese

Remove tamales from container carefully to prevent breakage. Release them from wrapper, and cut tamales crosswise in 1-inch pieces. Place each piece in center of a Tortilla Base (or sesame cracker) with cut side down. Pick up a little of the sauce and pour it over top, then sprinkle top and base with very finely chopped cooked bacon (cut raw bacon into very small pieces, then pan-fry until done, but not too dry). Over bacon sprinkle finely shredded American cheese. Arrange on flat baking sheet and bake in center of oven at 400° F. about 6 or 7 minutes just before serving. Serve at once. If preparing only a few, bake about 5 minutes.

Crisp Tortilla Bases

1½ cups yellow corn meal

1 cup sifted all-purpose flour

2 teaspoons salt

¼ teaspoon black pepper

¼ teaspoon oregano

¼ teaspoon garlic salt

2 tablespoons shortening

About ¾ to 1 cup lukewarm water

Mix dry ingredients together. Cut in shortening with pie blender until mixture is finely divided. Add ¾ cup water and mix well. If it appears too heavy or dry, add more water, a little at a time. Dough should be medium consistency. Knead for about 1 minute. Wrap and let it stand for about 15 minutes or longer. If dough seems too soft add a little flour, if too stiff wet hands and knead gently.

Break off piece of dough at a time and roll *very very thin* on floured pastry cloth. With 2¾-to-3-inch-round cutter, cut out dough. Puncture each round with a fork. Place rounds on wax paper, and when all are cut out (may be piled on top of each other) deep-fry at 375° to 400° F. until golden brown on one side and turn over to brown other side. Will float to top. Use tongs to turn and to remove from fat. Do not fry more than 4 or 5 at a time to prevent crowding. Let cool. May be prepared several days in advance. Fill top as suggested above or with any desired filling.

Crab Meat, Lobster, Shrimp, or Chicken Blintzes

Prepare batter for Russian Blintzes (page 652). Then make any of the creamed seafood or chicken fillings, increasing flour slightly to make a stiffer sauce. Let fillings cool, fill blintzes, and roll. Sauté, and arrange in flat attractive baking dish. Refrigerate if not to be served at once. Reheat in a 350° F. oven for about 15 to 20 minutes before serving. Top of Blintzes may be spread with a mushroom sauce before reheating.

Cocktail Flaky Horns

Prepare Rich Flaky Horn Pastry (page 729). Use a stiff seafood, chicken, meat, or mushroom preparation to fill. If made in advance, they must be refrigerated, then reheated at 350° F. for about 10 minutes just before serving.

Cocktail Chili Tacos

Makes about 30 tacos

½ cup finely chopped onion (1 medium)
2 tablespoons hot melted fat
1 pound ground round steak or other lean beef
About 2 tablespoons chili powder (or less) or taco seasoning mix
About ½ teaspoon salt, depending on seasoning in tomato sauce
1 clove garlic finely chopped (or put through garlic press) or ½ teaspoon garlic salt

¼ teaspoon black pepper
⅛ teaspoon, more or less, hot cayenne pepper (optional)
1 tablespoon flour (increase to 1½ tablespoons flour for each recipe if preparing large amounts)
8-ounce can tomato sauce
¼ cup water (little more if needed)
Crisp Tortilla Bases (page 25) or large seasame crackers, about 2 inches in diameter
American cheese

Cook chopped onion in the hot fat for about 5 minutes in an 8-inch skillet. Add the ground beef, and continue to cook, separating meat with a fork, for about 10 minutes, until brown. Add seasonings and blend thoroughly. Sprinkle the tablespoon flour over entire surface, and stir well. Last add the can of tomato sauce and ¼ cup of water, mix, and cook until thick, stirring constantly, over medium heat. Let simmer about 5 minutes. If preparation appears very heavy, add a little more water to loosen it a bit, but must be thick and not spread. If preparation is too soft, add 1 teaspoon cornstarch diluted in 1 teaspoon water, and simmer for 3 minutes.

To Serve: Place 1 level standard measuring tablespoon of hot filling on center of each Tortilla Base or sesame cracker. Keep higher in center and rounded. Sprinkle top of meat with 1 teaspoon finely shredded American cheese.

Serve hot. May be reheated in a 350° F. oven about 5 minutes after they are on a baking sheet. If preparation is made in advance, it is better to reheat it in skillet or saucepan on top of stove, adding a little water if necessary.

Turkish Dolmas

Makes about 50

1 jar grapevine leaves (may be purchased in Greek grocery stores and some supermarts), pickled in salt brine, 10 ounces net weight

1½ pounds of ground lamb from shoulder (or leg), or beef with some suet, or part ground pork shoulder

1 medium very finely chopped onion (½ cup)

3 tablespoons finely chopped fresh parsley (or ½ tablespoon dry)

About 1½ teaspoons salt
¼ teaspoon black pepper
About ½ teaspoon cinnamon, more or less
⅓ cup uncooked rice
½ cup cool water
2 cups tomatoes
About 2 cups hot water or stock
1½ teaspoons salt
¼ teaspoon pepper
¼ teaspoon baking soda

Simmer leaves in a large pot of water for about ½ hour. Drain thoroughly and let cool. Put aside.

Combine next 8 ingredients in the order given, in a large bowl, and with hands blend thoroughly. If preparation appears dry, pour about ½ cup of warm water over surface and mix well. Now form oval 2-inch rolls with 1 level tablespoon of meat, and place them on one end of large leaves (use 2 leaves if small). Roll firmly, turning in ends as you roll. Place in a 3- or 4-quart saucepan or Dutch oven, with open ends down, ⅛ inch apart. Several layers may be prepared at one time, but do not overfill pot.

Now add the tomatoes crushed with hands into medium-size pieces, combined with the hot water, salt and pepper, and baking soda. Rolls must be completely covered with liquid. If short, add little more water or tomatoes. Place a heavy heatproof dish on top of meat. This will prevent Dolmas from floating and opening. Plate is not necessary if Dolmas are simmered gently. Simmer, covered, about 1 hour or until meat and rice are tender. Test 1 by cutting through with a fork. Sometimes takes about 15 minutes longer. When done, shut off heat, and if too much liquid remains, carefully pour it into a smaller pot, and let it simmer for about 20 minutes uncovered until it is reduced to about half. These Dolmas are often served cold, but are more delicious served quite warm in a chafing dish topped with remaining liquid and tomatoes in pot for cocktail and buffet parties, with Lemon Sauce on the side. Be sure to have some plates and forks on table and a large serving spoon.

Note. Instead of grapevine leaves, the outer leaves of green cabbage, cut in proper size, may be used instead. The grapevine leaves are more unusual for cocktail parties and lend a diffrent taste to this dish. A very thin lemon sauce is usually served with Dolmas, but we are giving our own excellent basic recipe of Lemon Sauce that has more body and taste appeal.

Lemon Sauce

2 tablespoons melted butter or margarine
2 tablespoons all-purpose flour
1 cup warm milk (less for thicker sauce)

About ½ teaspoon salt
⅛ teaspoon white pepper
About ¼ cup lemon juice (more or less to suit taste)

In a 1-quart saucepan melt butter, add flour and stir until smooth. Add warm milk slowly. Simmer about 5 minutes. Add salt, pepper, and lemon juice slowly, and let simmer about 1 more minute. Serve warm or cool. May be refrigerated and reheated in top part of double boiler or over direct low heat, until warm. Best to serve it warm, not too hot, and not cold. May be used on asparagus, broccoli, and fish instead of Hollandaise.

Flaky Crab Meat Appetizer

⅓ recipe New Quick Puff Paste dough (page 136)

Egg white glaze
¼ teaspoon salt or lemon juice

Roll ⅓ recipe of New Puff Paste to measure about 16 x 16 inch square on well-floured pastry cloth. Cut into 4 uniform strips (each measuring about 4 x 16).

Spread a scant ½ cup of Crab Meat Filling down center of each strip of pastry. Bring sides up to enclose filling, overlapping a little if possible. Press down small ends. Pick up with both hands and carefully place on

12 x 18 baking sheet covered with silicone or parchment paper, evenly spaced. A 12 x 18 sheet will hold 4 strips. Bake at 400° F. in a preheated oven, center rack, about 20 or 25 minutes, or until top and sides of pastry is lightly colored.

Have egg whites at room temperature or lukewarm. For each egg white, beat with *fluffy beater* a few seconds until foamy, then add ¼ teaspoon of salt or lemon juice, and beat again a few seconds until well blended and foamy. Let stand at least 15 minutes before using. Now brush entire top and sides with egg white glaze. Lower temperature to 300° F. and bake about 15 to 20 more minutes, or until underside is golden brown and crisp. Remove from oven, let stand about 10 minutes, then with small light-weight serrated-edge knife cut each strip crosswise in about 1¼-inch pieces. (⅓ recipe of pastry and 1 recipe filling will make 4 strips, each cut into about 12 pieces crosswise, or about 48; full recipe of pastry and 3 recipes of filling would make approximately 150 appetizers). Serve quite warm but not too hot, nor cold. May be baked in advance and refrigerated well wrapped for 2 days.

To reheat, place on baking sheet, and reheat at 350° F. for about 7 to 10 minutes, depending on amount. May also be frozen several weeks if properly wrapped. Best to defrost slowly in refrigerator then reheat for about 7 to 10 minutes.

Crab Meat Filling

1 cup cream cheese (½ pound), room temperature until soft
Yolk of 1 egg
1 cup, little more or less crab meat, flaked, or chopped medium (other seafood may be used)

About 1¼ teaspoons hot sauce or ⅛ teaspoon cayenne pepper
¼ teaspoon onion or garlic salt
About ¼ teaspoon salt

With heavy spoon or mixer cream cheese until soft. Add the yolk, chopped crab meat or other seafood, and blend thoroughly. Add rest of ingredients, and beat until well blended. Makes scant 2 cupfuls.

Baked Hot Molded Glazed Ham

1½ pounds (3½ cups solidly packed) cooked ham, ground or chopped fine
1½ cups dry light bread crumbs
2 very large eggs (½ cup) or 3 small, slightly beaten with fork
1½ cups of milk, little more or less, room temperature

½ cup finely chopped green onion and stems, mixed
A little salt, if necessary
¼ teaspoon black pepper
¼ teaspoon hot sauce or ⅛ teaspoon cayenne pepper
1 teaspoon Worcestershire sauce
Pancake syrup

Combine all ingredients, and beat well for about 2 minutes. Let stand about 15 minutes. May be mixed with hands. If preparation appears very heavy, a bit more milk may be added, but must hold shape. Place preparation on a piece of heavy well-greased foil or piece of silicone paper and with hands mold it to shape of ham, keeping it high and smooth in center. Make an opening on small end, about 1-inch deep, for decoration. Score top (but not necessary) and place whole clove in each section. Drizzle warm dark commercial syrup (or any pancake syrup) over entire top. Carefully cut away surplus foil from base of ham, and with pancake turner pick up ham and place it on a cake rack, with drip pan underneath. Pour cup hot water into pan, and bake ham at 350° F. for about 1½ hours or until crusty, glossy, and firm to the touch. When ham has baked about ¾ of an hour, brush or drizzle again with warm syrup and pour more water into pan. When done remove from oven, and brush once more with warm syrup; let drain well. With dinner knife loosen around base of ham, and with pancake turner pick up and transfer to center of a 16- or 14-inch round (or oval) platter. Surround base of ham with crackers for cocktail parties or Petit Sweet Potato Delights for buffets. Serve hot or warm. Very delicious for snacks, buffet suppers, or luncheons.

How to Garnish. Insert a small well-trimmed fresh pineapple (or artificial pineapple) top into opening of small end of ham, supporting it underneath, if necessary, with piece of foil. Place whole or half well drained (and dried on paper towel) red maraschino cherries on half toothpicks, close together around base of pineapple top, or, if preferred, a good size wax-paper frill (like used on ends of chicken legs) may be made and held in small end of ham with a long wooden skewer.

Petit Sweet Potato Delights

About 4 pounds sweet potatoes, more or less	1 egg
Granulated or brown sugar	1 teaspoon water
Flour	Corn flakes

Scrub unpeeled fresh sweet potatoes, and cook in small amount of boiling water, in covered saucepan, until tender, but not too soft. Drain well, and dry out over low heat. Peel, mash, and to each cup mashed sweet potato add 1 teaspoon granulated (or brown sugar). Some brand canned potatoes are excellent for this purpose. Form balls with 1 slightly rounded tablespoon of potatoes. Roll well in flour, then dip into beaten egg combined with 1 tablespoon water, then in medium crumbled corn flakes, being sure that surface is completely covered. Place balls on greased wire cake rack, with drip pan underneath, and bake in a 400° F. oven about 12 to 15 minutes, leaving at least ½-inch space between each Delight. Potatoes may be stuffed with a very small cube (not more than ½-inch square), well drained, and dried on paper towel, of canned pineapples, or with a miniature marshmallow. These Delights may be prepared long in advance, if well covered, and baked about 15 minutes before serving. Arrange them around base of ham.

Cantonese and Meat Cocktail Strudels

Prepare 1 recipe Strudel Dough (page 655). Spread filling over ½ of cut dough (about 14 inches wide) and sprinkle top with ½ cup finely shredded American cheese. Roll, brush top with melted butter and bake at 400° F. about 30 to 40 minutes, or until brown. May stand in oven with heat shut off for at least ½ hour before serving. Best served quite warm.

This is an excellent light luncheon or supper dish, served with cheese sauce, tomato sauce, or mushroom sauce and a vegetable; or serve plain as a snack and at cocktail parties. May be baked a day in advance and refrigerated and reheated for about 20 minutes at 325° F. just before serving.

To Make Smaller Strudels. Follow directions for American Cheese smaller strudels (page 32), using 1¼ or 1½ cups Cantonese or Meat Filling for each strudel.

Cantonese Strudel Filling

1 pound cooked pork, veal, ham or chicken
½ pound cooked shrimp (1 pound before cooking), crab meat, or lobster meat
1 small or large can Chinese water chestnuts
1 cupful celery
1 cupful fresh green onions and stems (or ½ cup plain onion)
About 1 teaspoon salt (use less salt for ham)
½ teaspoon black pepper
¼ cup soy sauce

Place first 5 ingredients on chopping board, and with a cleaver or large heavy knife chop into medium pieces. Place in a bowl. Season with salt, pepper, and soy sauce, and blend well. Taste and season further if necessary.

Meat Strudel Filling

1½ pounds freshly ground veal, pork, lamb or beef (with some suet) or cooked chicken, ham, or corned beef
¼ cup hot butter or margarine
About 1½ cups very thinly sliced onions
About 2 teaspoons salt
¼ teaspoon pepper
1½ tablespoons pimiento, cut ¼ inch wide and 1 inch long (optional)
⅓ cup parsley, finely chopped or
⅓ cup green onion tops, cut about ½ inch long

Sauté meat for about 5 minutes, separating it with a fork during cooking process. Add the thinly sliced onions and continue to cook about 5 more minutes. Add seasoning and all other ingredients. Let cool for about 15 minutes.

American Cheese Cocktail Strudels

Prepare 1 recipe Strudel Dough (page 655). Cut stretched dough into several long narrow pieces (about 14 inches wide). Drizzle each piece of dough with melted butter and sprinkle with crumbs. Cover ½ of surface with about 6 cups coarsely shredded (not grated) American or cheddar cheese and sprinkle lightly with salt. Roll, etc., following directions for Cantonese and Meat Cocktail Strudels. Bake at 375° F. about 30 to 35 minutes.

Serve warm as a light luncheon or supper dish, or as a snack. Very delicious with soups or salads.

To Make Smaller Strudels. For each strudel, use 2 pieces of stretched dough that measure about 10 x 18 inches. Brush each with warm melted butter, sprinkle with crumbs. Cover ½ of top layer with 1¼ cupfuls coarsely shredded American cheese and sprinkle lightly with salt. Roll from large end, forming a narow 18-inch strudel. Place 3 strudels on greased 12 x 18-inch baking sheet. Bake at 375° F. about 15 to 20 minutes or until golden brown, but not dark.

This recipe will make 3 narrow cocktail strudels. *These strudels must be served quite warm.* Before serving, cut them into about 2-inch serving pieces, keeping them close to each other in pan. Place in a preheated 325° F. oven for about 15 minutes. Serve as soon as possible. They may be prepared a day or two in advance and stored in a cool place, well wrapped for a day or two, or they may be properly wrapped for freezing and frozen for several weeks. Let defrost completely before reheating.

Pastry Squares

1 recipe of Pastry Dough for Calzoni (page 35)	1 recipe of American Cheese or Meat Filling (page 33)
	Milk

Cut dough in 2 pieces, using about ⅔ for bottom crust, ⅓ for top. Roll dough for bottom to measure about 11 x 16 inches. Pour filling in 9 x 13 x 1-inch baking sheet on top of pastry dough, and spread evenly. Roll dough for top crust to measure about 10 x 15 inches, puncture it well with a fork, fold in half, pick up carefully with both hands and place it on top of filling. Go around edges with a fork to seal well, cutting off any surplus dough. Brush entire top with milk. Bake in preheated 350° F. oven about 35 minutes or until top is dark golden color. Remove from oven, and let stand until quite warm but not too hot or cool. Best served warm. Cut in squares and oblongs.

May be baked in advance and reheated for about 15 minutes at 350° F., or until quite warm. Meat pastries must be stored in refrigerator if not to be served within 2 hours.

These pastries are very delicious served as snacks or for brunches. Cheese pastries cut into strips are very attractive served with salads or soups.

Note. Please use dark burned-out tinware baking sheets for tender brown undercrust. If tinware pan is new, place it (empty) in center of 375° F. oven for at least 4 hours. (New shiny tinware does not absorb heat as easily.) Or use aluminum pan.

American Cheese Filling for Pastry Squares

1 pound of firm American or cheddar cheese, coarsely shredded

5 large whole eggs, well beaten with a fork
¼ teaspoon or more salt (optional)

Combine ingredients in a medium-size bowl and stir until very well blended, for at least 1 minute. In addition to the pound American cheese, ½ pound of creamed small or large curd cottage cheese (do not drain) may be used. Blend thoroughly.

Meat Filling for Pastry Squares

1 pound finely ground beef, veal, pork, lamb or ham
1 small onion cut into fine strips
2 tablespoons butter or margarine
1¼ teaspoons salt (omit if using ham)

⅛ teaspoon garlic salt (optional)
⅛ teaspoon cinnamon
⅛ teaspoon pepper
1½ tablespoons cornstarch combined with ½ cup cool water

Sauté the ground meat and onion in hot butter for about 10 minutes, turning several times, separating meat. Before it is done, add all other ingredients and cook until thick, then simmer about 5 minutes. Let cool before spreading on pastry dough.

Cocktail Croquettes

Prepare Chicken Croquette Mixture (page 223) or use finely chopped shrimp, lobster, crab meat, tuna fish, or well-drained salmon. When cold and firm, form small balls or ovals with 1 level tablespoon or tiny chickens with 2 level tablespoons. Coat with crumbs and beaten egg and then crumbs. Let stand about 15 minutes. Deep-fry until brown and crisp. Serve on toothpicks with Special Hostess Sauce (page 334) or Tartar Sauce (page 334).

In Chafing Dish. Prepare basic chicken or seafood croquette mixture. When cold and firm shape in medium-size balls. Follow general directions.

Serve in a chafing dish with hot Medium White Sauce (page 224) on the side.

Note. Croquettes may be reheated on cake racks in a 350° F. oven for 12 to 15 minutes for large; 7 or 8 minutes for small, but are less crisp, or may be fried to lighter color, then refried for about 2 minutes before serving.

Shrimp de Jonghe

2 pounds fresh raw shrimp, or 1 pound cooked and peeled
¼ cup butter or margarine
½ to ¾ cup cold firm butter or margarine
1 clove garlic chopped as fine as possible or put through garlic press
1 teaspoon salt

1 cup, or little more, lukewarm dry sherry or sauterne wine (half water may be used)
½ cup very finely chopped parsley
1¼ cups dry bread crumbs
About ¼ cup grated Italian cheese
About ¼ cup melted butter or margarine

Cook raw shrimp gently in salted boiling water 3 to 5 minutes depending on size. Remove shells and intestinal vein, if necessary, Split lengthwise and sauté shrimp in the ¼ cup butter for a few seconds. Beat ½ cup or more cold, firm butter until very light—about 3 minutes. Add the garlic, salt, wine (a little at a time), parsley and the bread crumbs alternately. Pour sautéed shrimp into a greased shallow round baking dish that measures about 10½ × 1⅓ inches or preferably in 17-inch stainless steel oval dish. Spread crumb preparation over shrimp with a fork as uniformly as possible. Sprinkle with grated Italian cheese and drizzle with melted butter. Bake at 350° F. about 40 minutes (10 minutes longer if casserole is put together long in advance and ingredients are cold), then broil until brown and crisp for 2 or 3 minutes.

Calzoni Squares

Roll ⅔ recipe of Pastry Dough (page 35) to measure 11 × 16 inches for bottom crust. Place it in dark well-greased 9 × 13 × 1-inch baking sheet (1 teaspoon shortening to grease pan), bringing it up on all sides of pan. Pour filling into pan, and spread as evenly as possible. On floured pastry cloth roll other piece of dough to measure about 10 × 15 inches, puncture it well with a fork, fold in half, pick up carefully with both hands, and place it on top of filling. Go around edges with a fork to seal well, cutting off any surplus dough. Brush entire top with milk. Bake in preheated 375° F. oven about 30 minutes, or until dark golden color. Remove from oven, place on cake rack and let become lukewarm before cutting. This pastry is best served lukewarm or cold, but not hot. It may be prepared in advance, and stored in refrigerator until shortly before serving, then reheat at 350° F. for about 10 minutes until lukewarm.

Pastry Dough for Calzoni

2¼ cups sifted all-purpose flour
1½ teaspoons double-acting baking powder
¾ teaspoon salt

¾ cup butter or margarine, firm
1 very large egg, well beaten with fork, combined with
¼ cup milk

Sift dry ingredients together in 8-inch bowl. Add butter or margarine, and with pie blender cut through until it looks like fine meal. Add beaten egg and milk all at once, and with large spoon blend thoroughly until leaves sides of bowl. If appears dry, add little more milk. If too soft, add very little more flour. Turn out onto floured pastry cloth and knead gently about 1 minute, or until smooth, adding more flour if sticky. Cut dough in two pieces, using about ⅔ for bottom crust, ⅓ for top. If dough feels soft, best to wrap it in wax paper and chill for about ½ hour or longer.

Ricotta-Sausage Filling for Calzoni

2 large whole eggs, well beaten with fork
1 pound fresh ricotta cheese (do not drain)
¼ to ½ cup milk, depending on moisture in ricotta
1 pound fresh Italian sausage, cut in 3-inch pieces

¼ cup grated Italian cheese
⅛ teaspoon black pepper
About ¾ teaspoon salt (½ teaspoon if using commercial peperoni sausage)
2 tablespoons fresh chopped parsley, or ½ teaspoon crushed leaf oregano

In a 10-inch bowl add the beaten eggs to the ricotta, and stir until well blended. Add milk, and beat well. Sauté sausage in small amount fat until well browned, turning several times. Then add ¼ cup water, cover skillet and steam for about 10 minutes. Let cool, then slice ¼-inch thick, and cut in 2 or 3 pieces to facilitate cutting squares. (Instead of fresh Italian sausage, ½ pound of top-quality dry commercial peperoni sausage may be used. Simply slice peperoni same as for fresh, and combine with other ingredients.) Add all other ingredients in the order given.

Mozzarella Hors d'Oeuvres (Italian-Style Quiche Lorraine)

1 cup and 2 tablespoons sifted all-purpose flour
½ teaspoon salt
¾ teaspoon baking powder

⅓ cup butter or margarine
1 small egg beaten with fluffy beater a few seconds
Milk

Sift dry ingredients together. Add butter and with pie blender cut through until like a fine meal. Add beaten egg, little at a time, and stir well with a heavy fork or dinner knife until dough leaves sides of bowl. If too dry, add little milk or water. It is not always necessary to use the entire egg. Keep dough medium, not too soft, and not firm. Turn out onto lightly floured pastry cloth and knead gently for a few seconds. Cut it in 2 parts, having 1 piece a little larger for bottom crust. Form in square pieces, wrap well and refrigerate if not to be used within a few minutes. If it is refrigerated for some time, it is best to let stand in room temperature for a few minutes before rolling.

Roll larger piece to measure 9-inch uniform square, trim uneven edges if necessary, and place on bottom of lightly greased 7-inch square pan, having it come up on sides about 1 inch. Pour in filling. Roll dough for upper crust to measure 8 inches; puncture well with a fork, fold over and place it on top of filling carefully. With fingers seal edges by pressing down. Brush top with milk and bake on bottom rack of 400° F. oven for about 25 to 30 minutes, or until brown. Remove from oven, and let cool for about 20 minutes before serving. Or it is better if allowed to cool completely and reheat at 400° F. about 10 to 12 minutes. Use a serrated-edge knife to cut panful in 6 strips, then crosswise in 6 uniform squares. This is a nice tiny cocktail size, but may be cut little larger for general snacks.

Filling for Mozzarella Hors d'Oeuvres

¼ pound (1 cup packed) mozzarella cheese (scamorza cheese or Swiss cheese may be used instead) very coarsely shredded or cut in very small pieces

2 large eggs, beaten with a fork for a few seconds

⅓ cup warm whipping cream
¼ teaspoon salt
⅛ teaspoon pepper
⅛ teaspoon oregano or thyme
¼ teaspoon garlic or onion salt

Combine all ingredients in a medium bowl and stir until well blended.

Sautéed Shrimp, Italian Style

Serves 6

2 pounds uncooked shrimp
½ pound fresh mushrooms
4 large green peppers
⅓ cup butter or oil

2 teaspoons salt
½ teaspoon pepper
1 teaspoon oregano
2 tablespoons sauterne

Wash, shell, and devein shrimp; dry. Wash mushrooms in salted water, dry and slice. Slice green peppers into strips 3 inches long and 1½ inches wide.

Melt butter, or heat oil until hot, add green peppers, sauté about 3 minutes, add shrimp and sliced mushrooms and sauté about 5 minutes. Season with salt, pepper, and oregano. Add sauterne.

Sauté about 3 more minutes or until shrimp are done. Serve at once in chafing dish.

Italian Salami Hors d'Oeuvres Puffs

2 cups sifted all-purpose flour combined with
4 teaspoons double-acting baking powder
2 whole eggs
1 cup milk
About 1 teaspoon salt
½ teaspoon garlic salt

¼ teaspoon basil or oregano
¼ teaspoon black pepper
½ teaspoon celery salt
1½ teaspoons fennel seed
2 teaspoons oil or melted fat
1 tablespoon grated Italian cheese
½ cup fine-chopped Italian salami

Combine all ingredients except chopped salami, and with egg beater or electric mixer, beat until smooth. Fold in chopped salami. Pick up with a teaspoon and with another spoon or finger push into deep hot fat, 350° F. Fry until golden brown, turning over when necessary. It is best to fry enough at one time to cover entire surface. This will prevent puffs from rolling over. Serve hot in a chafing dish or on a hot platter with Sauce Gourmet (page 342) in center.

Italian Cheese Appetizers

½ pound scamorza or mozzarella cheese, cut in ¼-inch cubes
2 whole eggs
About ½ cup sifted all-purpose flour, or enough to make right consistency
About 1 teaspoon salt
¼ teaspoon pepper
⅛ teaspoon dry basil
⅛ teaspoon garlic salt

⅛ teaspoon oregano
2 tablespoons grated parmesan cheese
1 tablespoon dry light wine (optional)
Light dry bread crumbs (almost white)
2 eggs beaten well with a fork and combined with
2 teaspoons water
Fat

Combine all ingredients except crumbs, the last 2 eggs, and fat. Mix thoroughly. Cover and let stand at least 30 minutes. Pick up 1 level tablespoonful at a time. Drop into crumbs, form balls or ovals, dip into egg mixture, then into crumbs. Dip again into egg mixture and into crumbs. Shape smoothly in palms of hands. Let stand on wax paper about 15 minutes or longer, turning them over once or twice. The balls may be shaped several hours in advance. In this case keep them well covered with wax paper in refrigerator. To serve, deep-fry at 350° F. about 3 or 4 minutes. Insert a plain or frilled toothpick in top of each and serve at once. These appetizers may be served in a chafing dish for buffet parties. Serve plain or with a dipping sauce.

Italian Meat Ball Appetizers

Prepare Italian Meat Balls (page 795), making them size of a very large marble. Sauté according to general directions until brown. Serve them hot on toothpicks, or in a chafing dish with Basic Italian Tomato Sauce for dipping (page 766).

Miniature Pancake-Sausage Hors d'Oeuvres

Prepare Pancake Mixture (page 480). Pour 1 level teaspoon batter for each appetizer on hot ungreased griddle pan, leaving space between pancakes. Turn over when tops are bubbly, and cook second side until brown. This can be done several hours in advance.

Now sauté Premium Brown 'N Serve pork sausages several minutes, then cut them crosswise into halves or smaller pieces. Spread center of pancakes with a little catsup, prepared mustard, or plain butter. Place a piece of sausage on each pancake and hold together with heavy toothpicks. Reheat in a 400° F. oven about 5 or 6 minutes, or until hot. Plain picks may be removed and replaced with frilled ones just before serving.

Tamale-Bacon Appetizers

Cut canned tamales into about 1-inch pieces crosswise, thin bacon slices in halves crosswise, and sliced American cheese in ¾-inch squares. Place cheese on corn meal part of tamale, and wrap bacon around tamale firmly. Hold in place with heavy toothpicks.

About 10 minutes before serving, place appetizers on cake rack with drip pan underneath. Pour 1 cup hot water into pan to prevent smoking. Bake 5 minutes in a preheated 550° F. oven, then turn over and bake bottom side about 3 minutes. The plain picks may be replaced with frilled picks as soon as appetizers are removed from oven. Serve at once. These appetizers may be put together a day in advance if stored in covered container in refrigerator.

Frankfurter-Bacon Appetizer

Proceed as for Tamale-Bacon Appetizers, using skinless frankfurters instead of tamales.

Bacon-Sausage Appetizer

Cook Premium Brown 'N Serve pork sausages until brown. Cut them into 1-inch pieces. Slice Chinese water chestnuts in halves lengthwise. Cut thin bacon slices in halves croswise. Cut sliced Swiss cheese in ¾-inch squares. Wrap bacon *firmly* around a piece of sausage, a slice of chestnut, and a square of cheese. Hold together with heavy toothpicks.

About 15 minutes before serving, arrange them on a cake rack with drip pan underneath. Pour a cup of hot water into pan to prevent smoking. Bake appetizers 10 minutes in a preheated 425° F. oven, then turn them over and bake about 5 more minutes. Serve hot. May be baked in advance and reheated at 425° F. about 5 minutes just before serving.

Rouquefort Puffs

Makes about 20

1 cup cream cheese, medium consistency

2 ounces roquefort cheese, mashed until very fine

2 tablspoons slightly beaten egg

2-inch rounds of bread

Anchovy butter, garlic butter, or plain butter

Beat cream cheese about ½ minute. Add the roquefort cheese, and blend well. Last, add 2 tablespoons slightly beaten egg, a little at a time, and mix well. If mixture appears very soft, chill for about half an hour.

Spread rounds of bread that have been toasted on one side only (or use untoasted) lightly with anchovy butter, garlic butter, or plain butter. With large plain tube or plain opening of coupling, pipe a mound of cheese mixture on each bread round, leaving about ¼-inch space uncovered to prevent dripping on sides. Broil at 350° F., about 3 inches from heat, until brown and puffed, for about 4 or 5 minutes, watching closely toward end. Serve as soon as possible as hot hors d'oeuvres, or with soups and salads. May be prepared a day in advance if stored in covered container in refrigerator, and broiled before serving. May be frozen.

Toasted Ham Rolls

1 cup ham chopped very fine or minced

4 hard-cooked eggs chopped very fine

¼ cup mayonnaise

1 teaspoon prepared mustard

¼ cup fine-chopped fresh green onion

About 1 teaspoon salt

About ⅛ teaspoon hot sauce

White bread

Cream cheese (optional)

Combine all ingredients and beat well. If too thick, add small amount of milk or cream to make of spreading consistency.

Cut white bread very thin. (Thin-bread slicer is excellent for this purpose.) Remove crusts. Spread slices thinly with filling. Roll. Place on a baking sheet with open end down. Pipe a scroll or rosette and leaves of flour-stabilized cream cheese (page 2) on each, or leave plain. Bake in a 450° F. oven about 7 or 8 minutes, or until bread is golden brown and crisp. Serve hot. Rolls may be prepared in advance, refrigerated, and baked just before serving.

Brown 'N Serve Roll-up Appetizers

With sharp knife or scissors remove crust from fresh commercially sliced bread (preferably standard size slices, not small). Cut bread into strips about 1-inch wide and about 3½-inches long and flatten slightly with rolling pin if necessary.

Place dab of mustard, chili sauce, or catsup in center of strips, and 1-inch pieces of Premium Brown 'N Serve sausage in center. Roll up, overlapping bread to prevent opening. Fasten with toothpick.

Brush entire surface of bread lightly with warm melted butter or margarine, and sprinkle exposed part lightly with paprika. Place appetizers on a baking sheet, and bake at 450° F. about 6 to 8 minutes, or until crisply golden brown. Replace plain picks with frilled ones, if desired, and serve hot.

These appetizers may be put together hours or a day in advance, if refrigerated. Bake a minute or two longer if very cold, and serve at once.

Grilled Sardine and Swiss Cheese Appetizer

Spread round crackers or round melba toast lightly with anchovy butter. Place 2 or 3 very small sardines, a little prepared mustard, a little chopped onion, and a small square of Swiss cheese on each cracker. Brush cheese with French dressing. Bake at 400° F. about 5 or 6 minutes, only until cheese has melted. Sprinkle each with paprika and serve hot. *Do not freeze.*

Toasted Cheese Roll Ups

Spread thin-sliced day-old white bread (use thin-bread slicer) lightly with anchovy paste. Cut cheddar or Swiss cheese in strips about ¼ inch shorter than bread and about ⅓ inch thick. Wrap bread around cheese. Tie up each roll with a narrow strip of lean bacon that is about 6 inches long. Place on rack with drip pan underneath. Pour 1 cup hot water into pan. Bake at 400° F. about 10 minutes, or until golden brown and crisp. They may be frozen, or prepared a day in advance if kept in covered container in refrigerator.

These are equally suitable served with soups or salads.

Rolled Cream Cheese Toasted

Remove all crusts from unsliced loaf of bread. With sharp knife slice as thin as possible. If too thick, flatten with rolling pin. Spread with creamed butter and cream cheese and a bit of anchovy paste, or any desired filling. Roll gently and arrange on cookie sheet, open ends down. Shortly before serving, place under broiler at 400° F. until golden brown. Serve hot.

Oriental Pagoda Appetizer

About ¾ pound cooked pork loin or ham, cut ½ inch thick, into 1-inch-square pieces (beef tenderloin slices, sautéed 3 or 4 minutes on each side, then cut into square pieces, may be used instead of pork loin or ham)

5-ounce can Chinese water chestnuts, each cut lengthwise in 3 slices
6-ounce can large button mushrooms, left whole
1 recipe Marinade Oriental

Place the cooked cut meat, sliced chestnuts, and whole mushroom caps in bowl with marinade. Let stand in refrigerator several hours or longer.

Pick up meat and arrange on cake rack about 1 inch apart (have drip pan underneath with 1 cup water). Place slice of chestnut on meat, and whole mushroom cap on chestnut with rounded side up. Insert heavy plain toothpick through each appetizer, and dip into lukewarm Glaze Oriental. Bake at 400° F. about 8 to 10 minutes. Place on hot serving platter, and replace plain toothpicks with frilled picks to make appetizers more attractive. Serve hot.

Note. These appetizers may be put together hours in advance (without glazing), and kept covered in refrigerator. Just before serving, dip into glaze and bake.

Marinade Oriental

2 tablespoons soy sauce
1 teaspoon Chinese molasses
¼ teaspoon garlic salt
¾ cup water or liquid from mushrooms

Combine all ingredients in a 7-inch bowl. Mix well.

Glaze Oriental

To strained marinade above, add 1 tablespoon cornstarch diluted in 2 tablespoons water. Mix well and cook over medium heat until thick, then simmer about 3 or 4 minutes. Let stand until lukewarm.

Lobster à la Newburg

2 cups cooked lobster meat chopped medium-fine (lobster tails may be used)
2 tablespoons butter
½ cup dry sherry

4 egg yolks slightly beaten
1 cup cream
About 1 teaspoon salt
A little pepper

Sauté lobster meat in butter 2 or 3 minutes; add wine, egg yolks, and cream. Cook gently over *very low heat* until thickened (about 5 minutes). Add salt and pepper toward end. Ingredients may be put together in advance, but do not cook until just before serving. Serve in a chafing dish or heated bowl with crackers, melba toast, or as desired.

Crab Meat, Lobster, or Shrimp Filling

Prepare sauce with 1 tablespoon melted butter, 1 tablespoon flour, and ½ cup warm milk. Cook until thick, then add 1 tablespoon dry sauterne wine, ½ teaspoon salt, 1 cup flaked crab meat, lobster, or shrimp, and 1 tablespoon very fine-chopped or minced fresh green onions. Spread on toasted or sautéed breads, or fill Bread Cases (page 5). Sprinkle with parmesan cheese and broil just before serving for about 5 minutes at 400° F.

Creamed Ham Filling

Prepare sauce as for Crab Meat Filling (above). Add 1 tablespoon dry sherry, 1 cup fine-chopped or minced ham, ¼ cup fine-chopped and sautéed mushrooms, 1 tablespoon chopped green stuffed olives. Spread on toasted or sautéed breads, or fill Bread Cases (page 5). Sprinkle with American cheese and broil just before serving for about 5 minutes at 400° F.

Creamed Chicken Filling

Prepare sauce as for Crab Meat Filling (above). Add 1 tablespoon dry sauterne wine, ½ teaspoon salt, 1 cup chicken cut in very small pieces, 1 teaspoon capers, and 2 tablespoons medium-chopped toasted almonds. Spread on toasted or sautéed breads, or fill Bread Cases (page 5). Sprinkle with parmesan cheese and broil just before serving for about 5 minutes at 400° F.

Crab Meat Thermidor in Pastry Shells

Serves 4 to 6

1 cup (6 or 7 ounces) crab meat	2 tablespoons butter or margarine
2 tablespoons butter or margarine	½ teaspoon salt
3 tablespoons flour	2 tablespoons parmesan cheese
1 cup warm half & half cream	Hors d'oeuvres Patty Shells (page 4)
1 tablespoon dry sauterne wine	
Pinch cayenne pepper	1 tablespoon parmesan cheese
⅛ teaspoon dry mustard	Little warm melted butter
1 cup fresh mushrooms	

Flake crab meat. In a saucepan, melt butter, add flour and then the half &

half a little at a time, stirring constantly. Allow mixture to simmer about 2 or 3 minutes after it thickens. Then add wine, cayenne pepper, mustard, mushrooms (which have been sautéed in butter or margarine), crab meat, salt, and 2 tablespoons parmesan cheese. Mix well and pour into Hors d'Oeuvres Patty Shells. Sprinkle other tablespoon of parmesan cheese on top of shells. Drizzle with melted butter.

Bake in 350° F. oven for 10 minutes.

Hot Frankfurter Filling

Cook 4 medium-size frankfurters in simmering water about 5 minutes. Drain, and chop fine. Combine with 1 teaspoon prepared mustard, 2 tablespoons piccalilli, and enough mayonnaise to moisten. Spread on toasted breads, or fill Bread Cases (page 5). Sprinkle with shredded American cheese and broil at 400° F. just before serving for about 5 minutes. May be served cold.

Chicken Liver Filling

Sauté 1 tablespoon fine-chopped onion in 2 tablespoons butter about 2 minutes. Add ½ cup fine-chopped, uncooked chicken livers (calf liver may be used) and continue to cook about 7 or 8 minutes over medium heat, turning often. Then add ¼ cup minced or fine-chopped ham, ¼ cup minced or fine-chopped mushrooms, and about ⅛ teaspoon salt. Cook together about 5 minutes. Last, bind with 1 whole egg slightly beaten, and cook only until thickened but not dry. If dry, add a little coffee cream or milk. Spread on toasted or sautéed breads, or fill Bread Cases (page 5). Sprinkle with cheese and broil just before serving at 400° F. about 5 minutes.

Scrambled Egg and Salami, Ham, or Cervelat Filling

To 2 slightly beaten eggs add 3 tablespoons very fine-chopped or minced salami, ham, or cervelat, 1 teaspoon minced parsley, ⅛ teaspoon salt, a pinch of pepper. Sauté over medium heat in 2 tablespoons hot butter until medium thick, but not dry. Mix and cut through with a fork during cooking process. Spread on toasted or sautéed breads, or fill Bread Cases (page 5). Sprinkle with cheese and broil just before serving at 400° F. about 5 minutes.

A Man's Favorite Appetizer

Cut sliced bread into ovals or rounds. Spread with butter or margarine and a little mustard. Cover thickly with mashed Braunschweiger liver sausage or Chicken Liver Filling (page 43), that has been seasoned with a little grated onion or onion salt, keeping it high in center, and as smooth as possible. Place under broiler set at 400° F. about 1 inch from heat and broil 7 to 10 minutes or until hot and puffy. May be garnished with a slice of stuffed green olive just before serving. Serve hot.

Petit Hamburger Hors d'Oeuvres

Makes 35 to 40

1 pound beef ground fine	About 1 teaspoon salt
2 tablespoons dry bread crumbs	2 large eggs
2 tablespoons fine-chopped parsley	2 tablespoons milk or water
2 tablespoons grated onion	Butter
¼ teaspoon black pepper	2-inch rounds of bread

Combine first 8 ingredients in a bowl and beat until thoroughly blended. Measure with level tablespoon and shape into small thick patties. Sauté in hot butter until brown on one side over moderate heat about 2 minutes. Turn over and fry second side. Serve on sautéed rounds of breads. Surround hamburgers with fine-chopped sautéed onion, or spread center top of hamburger with Sautéed Onion.

Sautéed Onion for Petit Hamburger

2 medium onions chopped fine	About ¼ to ½ teaspoon paprika, de-
¼ cup butter	pending on color
½ teaspoon salt	

Sauté onion in hot butter for several minutes. Season with salt and paprika. Cover and steam until tender, but not too soft, about 5 minutes.

Swedish Meat Balls

1 pound finely ground beef	About 2 teaspoons sugar
¼ pound finely ground pork shoulder	¼ teaspoon pepper
1 medium-sized red potato, boiled un-	¼ teaspoon cinnamon
til tender, then peeled and	¼ teaspoon nutmeg
mashed	1 large egg, beaten with fork
¼ cup dry bread crumbs	¼ cup coffee cream or rich milk
1 medium-size onion chopped very	About 2 teaspoons, or less, salt
fine	

Combine all of the ingredients in the order given, and beat after each addition until well blended. In palms of hands form smooth balls with 1 level tablespoon of preparation, dampening hands occasionally if necessary. Pan-fry in about ¼ inch of hot salad oil or other fat, over medium heat, until brown on all sides, about 5 or 6 minutes. Do not overcrowd skillet, being sure to leave space between each meat ball as you sauté them, and do not turn them until very brown on underside. These meat balls may be cooked in advance and refrigerated in a covered container for a day or two.

Before serving, prepare glaze with drippings in pan. Add 1 cup water or stock to drippings, and to each cup of liquid, add 1 tablespoon cornstarch first diluted in 1 tablespoon cool water. Cook until thick and glazy, about 5 minutes after simmering begins. Add little gravy coloring and season to taste. Pour only enough of this glaze over meat balls to moisten them, and simmer gently in a skillet for several minutes. Pour into chafing dish. Sprinkle top with finely chopped green onion or parsley. Frilled picks may be inserted on top of meat balls for cocktail parties, or place a large serving spoon on chafing dish tray.

Cocktail Stuffed Hamburgers

Prepare meat and onions as for Petit Hamburgers (page 44). Wrap 1 level tablespoon meat around ½ teaspoon sautéed onion. Flatten to thick patty. Sauté, etc. These hamburgers may be prepared and placed on breads several hours or a day in advance and kept in covered container in refrigerator. About 10 minutes before serving, place in 350° F. oven. If possible reheat in heatproof platter and serve from same platter to keep hot.

French-Fried Shrimp Remoulade

Serves 4

1 pound fresh raw shrimp
About 1 cup light dry bread crumbs
  (seasoned with ¼ teaspoon marjoram, ¼ teaspoon salt, ¼ teaspoon pepper)

1 egg slightly beaten (combined with 1 tablespoon water; seasoned with ½ teaspoon salt)

Shell shrimp, remove vein, if necessary, and split lengthwise. If shrimp are large and thick, flatten them with a cleaver and cut in 2 pieces to insure thorough cooking. If small, they may be left in 1 piece. Wash under cold running water, drain thoroughly, and dry in a towel. Roll shrimp in seasoned bread crumbs, dip into egg mixture, then into crumbs again. Press crumbs well onto shrimp. Let stand on wax paper about 20 minutes, turning over several times while standing. Deep-fry at 375° F. about 5 minutes or until brown and crisp. Arrange in center of oval platter and cover with Sauce Remoulade (page 46). Garnish platter with lemon wedges and parsley, or serve sauce separately.

Sautéed Shrimp Remoulade. If preferred, shrimp may be sautéed in a small amount of butter or other fat until golden brown on both sides, instead of deep frying, for about 5 minutes.

Note. This dish is also recommended as a first course at dinner.

French-Fried Oysters Remoulade

Serves 4

1 pound large oysters (frozen breaded oysters may be used)
About 1 cup light dry bread crumbs (seasoned with ¼ teaspoon thyme, ¼ teaspoon salt)

1 egg slightly beaten (combined with 1 tablespoon water; seasoned with ½ teaspoon salt)

First, roll oysters in seasoned crumbs, then dip into egg mixture, then into crumbs again. Press crumbs well onto oysters. Let stand on wax paper about 20 minutes, turning them several times while standing. After 20 minutes drop oysters into deep hot fat, 375° F., and fry until golden brown and crisp, about 5 minutes. Drain well, arrange on platter, and pour Sauce Remoulade over them. Garnish platter with parsley and lemon wedges, and serve at once. Or serve sauce in a small attractive bowl in center of a large round platter and surround bowl with fried oysters.

Sautéed Oysters Remoulade. If preferred, oysters may be sautéed in a small amount of butter or other fat about 5 minutes until golden brown on both sides instead of deep frying.

Note. This dish is also recommended as a first course at dinner.

Sauce Remoulade

½ cup mayonnaise
1 tablespoon chili sauce
¼ teaspoon dry mustard
⅛ teaspoon garlic salt
1 tablespoon lemon juice

2 tablespoons fine-chopped green stuffed olives
1 hard-cooked egg chopped fine
1 tablespoon piccalilli or India relish
¼ teaspoon hot sauce

Mix all ingredients and blend thoroughly. Refrigerate for at least 8 hours before serving.

▶ COLD APPETIZERS ◀

Hard-Cooked Eggs

Cover eggs with warm water; bring to boiling point over medium heat, stirring gently 7 or 8 minutes, or until they come to the boiling point. Remove from heat, *cover tightly,* and let remain in very hot water about 15 minutes for small eggs, 20 minutes for medium, and 25 minutes for very large. (Stirring eggs the first 7 or 8 minutes will help to centralize yolks. This is not necessary if fresh eggs, that are properly stored in refrigerator and not more than one week old, are used.) When eggs are done, pour cold water over them at once; crack the shell on entire surface and roll the eggs between the palms of hands gently to free the thin tough skin from the egg, and facilitate shelling. Holding eggs under cool running water helps to release shell. Cut or slice eggs at once to prevent the yolks from discoloring.

Tulip Eggs

Best to use eggs not more than one week old. Hard-cook eggs. Shell them carefully, and place 1 at a time into ½ cup hot water, combined with ½ teaspoon food coloring. Pick up with perforated spoon, drain well, and place on a cake rack or paper toweling. As soon as eggs are cool enough to handle, with paring knife cut 3 rounded petals on small end of egg, leaving about ½-inch space at top. Do not cut below top of yolk. Insert stiff green onion stems in large end, whole clove in center of yolk. Arrange egg tulips attractively on hors d'oeuvres or meat or sandwich platters, around salad molds, or as desired.

Deviled Egg Birds

Best to use eggs not more than one week old. Hard-cook 8 eggs. Shell them, and at once cut them crosswise in 2 parts. Remove thin slice from bottom of each. Release yolks gently from white shells, and put aside the 12 most attractive white shells. Put all of yolks and remaining whites through a food mill, grater, or strainer. Combine them with ¼ cup soft cream cheese, 2 tablespoons mayonnaise, 1 teaspoon vinegar, ½ teaspoon salt, ⅛ teaspoon garlic powder, 1 teaspoon prepared mustard, and ⅛ teaspoon dry mustard. Blend all ingredients thoroughly, and if very stiff add a little more vinegar, lemon juice, or mayonnaise. Taste and season further if necessary. Partially fill the 12 white shells with a seafood, ham, or chicken paste or ¼ teaspoon anchovy paste, or leave plain.

To Form Birds. With plain opening of coupling and bag (or large plain tube), pipe egg mixture to simulate chest and head of bird. Cut narrow strips crisp carrots, about ½ inch long and very narrow, and insert several on each side to simulate feathers, and several on back end for tails. Cut very small flat wedges of carrot for beak. Use 2 tiny whole black pepper for eyes. Or make eyes with bits of dry currants or raisins, rolled into balls between fingers. Or eyes may be made with skewer dipped into red coloring.

To Serve. Arrange eggs on an attractive platter covered with fresh parsley, shredded endive, or green lettuce, and serve as an hors d'oeuvre. Or may be arranged grouped in center of platter, and surrounded with other hors d'oeuvres. These birds may be prepared a day in advance if stored in a covered container in refrigerator. It is better, however, to cut carrot strips and garnish eggs not more than an hour or two before serving to prevent carrots from wilting slightly.

Fancy Stuffed Deviled Eggs

Hard-cook 4 eggs. Cut in 2 parts crosswise and remove thin slice from bottom lengthwise. Remove yolks carefully, and put them through food mill. For 8 halves, combine yolks with about ½ cup cream cheese (or additional eggs). Add 1 tablespoon mayonnaise, 1 teaspoon prepared mustard, ¼ teaspoon salt, 1 teaspoon vinegar, bit dry mustard, ⅛ teaspoon garlic salt, or season as desired. Keep preparation medium consistency. With No. 7 large star cookie tube and bag, pipe a large straight rosette in each shell. Decorate top with pink cream cheese rosette and tiny green cheese leaves, using No. 24 tube for rosettes, No. 65 for leaves. Arrange attractively.

Colored Easter Eggs

Hard-cook eggs, and while still hot, place them one at a time into ½ cup hot water, combined with ½ teaspoon or little more food coloring, for about 1 minute, or until desired color is obtained. Pour the ½ cup hot water into a standard tall measuring cup and add coloring. Eggs must be submerged in colored hot water, and it may be necessary to add more hot water and coloring if a large number of the same color eggs are prepared.

Pick up eggs with a large spoon and transfer them to paper toweling. Let stand a few minutes until dry, then store them in refrigerator if not to be used within several hours.

To glaze eggs, with fingers rub them with a little salad oil shortly before serving.

Crab Apple Egg Appetizers

Hard-cook small or medium eggs, not more than 15 minutes. They should not be cooked too firm. Remove at once from heat and cover with cold water. Shell carefully while eggs are quite warm, and as soon as possible press both ends gently with thumb and forefinger for about ½ minute to form permanent impression. Impression should be deep on large end. To color eggs, place them in warm water combined with a few drops of food coloring, and let remain in colored water for several minutes. Drain well on towels or cake rack in upright position. With skewer, gently make an opening in center of large end, and insert a sprig of parsley. Serve as centerpiece in a bed of leaf lettuce, shredded lettuce, or endive, or use several to garnish center of an hors d'oeuvres tray, or as desired.

Egg Roses

Use small or medium-size eggs. Cook and shape as for Crab Apple Eggs (page 48). Tint pink or leave white. When cold, pipe two rows of yellow cream cheese with ½ teaspoon measurement, to simulate petals, starting on large end of egg, holding egg with thumb and forefinger.

Have ready 2-inch rounds of bread that have been spread with savory butter or cheese. Place decorated egg in center of bread. Center top of egg may be filled with black caviar. With No. 67 tube and green cheese, pipe leaves around base of egg. Cheese for this purpose must not be too stiff. Let stand in room temperature until medium consistency, and if necessary soften with not more than 1 tablespoon cream to each ½-pound cheese. Any type of cheese spread may be used instead of plain cream cheese.

These eggs make attractive centerpieces for hors d'oeuvres, meat, and salad platters, and are excellent served as a first course for luncheons and dinners. May be prepared a day in advance if stored in closed container in refrigerator. Lift up with pancake turner when transferring to serving dish.

Tomato Tulip Hors d'Oeuvres

Select 8 to 10 attractive small plum tomatoes. Wash them and dry well. Cut 3 scalloped petals on each tomato to simulate a tulip. Scoop out about ⅔ of pulp (pulp can be used for cooking purposes). Sprinkle inside lightly with salt. Drain upside down on a rack about 15 minutes.

With tip of spoon or a bag and plain opening of coupling, place small amount of cheese filling into opening of tomato, having it come up almost to tip of petals. Cut small rounds of black ripe olive, brush with oil, and place on filling. Rub tomatoes with a little plain Italian or French dressing (or salad oil) to impart gloss.

Serve these tulips on a bed of watercress, lettuce, endive, or lemon leaves. May be used as a centerpiece on an hors d'oeuvres platter, sandwich platter, meat platter, etc.

Filling for Tomatoes

Combine ¼ cup roquefort cheese with ¼ cup cream cheese and work it with a fork or spoon until smooth. Slowly add about 1 tablespoon French dressing and blend well.

Plum Tomato Tulip Hors d'Oeuvres Spray

Wash and dry plum tomatoes; cut petals as above. With a wooden skewer or pointed knife make a deep opening in stem end, and insert a crisp onion stem in each. Arrange spray on a flat platter, using 8 to 10 tulips (more or less, depending on size of platter). Cut long pointed leaves from fresh green onion stems and insert between tulips. Arrange individual hors d'oeuvres around tulips. These tomato tulips are very unusual and decorative.

Note. Any minced filling, such as ham, chicken, etc., may be used to fill these tulips.

Pineapple Hors d'Oeuvres Centerpiece

For a large centerpiece use about 2 pounds of minced cooked chopped chicken livers or Braunschweiger liver sausage, combined with chopped green olives, green chopped onion, etc. Minced chicken, ham, or cheeses may be used instead. If mixture appears too dry to mold, add some soft butter or cream cheese to bind. Chill mixture for at least an hour, then on a small plate shape it to simulate a fresh pineapple. Make an opening on center top and insert a fresh pineapple top (or imitation top may be used). Spread entire surface of mold with very little soft butter, and cover with large stuffed green olives (sliced thin in advance and kept on wax paper, covered). Surround base with crackers, wafers, or melba toast.

This pineapple centerpiece is more attractive glazed. To glaze, remove pineapple top, lift mold off plate with pancake turner and place it on a small round cardboard covered with foil, on a cake cooler. Follow general directions for glazing (page 3). Let stand in refrigerator until glaze is set for at least an hour, then with pancake turner, transfer mold onto serving platter. Place pineapple top just before serving. Instead of using sliced olives, soft cheddar cheese may be piped on pineapple with No. 3 cookie star tube.

Cheese Apple Hors d'Oeuvres Centerpiece

1 teaspoon plain gelatin	⅓ pound roquefort or bleu cheese, well
2 tablespoons cold water	mashed with a fork or pie blen-
⅔ pound cream cheese (1⅓ cups packed)	der (⅔ cup packed)

Combine gelatin with cold water. Let stand until thick, then dissolve over simmering water, *and at once* add to the cream cheese. Blend well, and combine it with roquefort or bleu cheese. Mix well until evenly blended, adding a little green coloring if desired. Pack it into a small deep bowl and refrigerate for 2 hours or longer.

To Shape. Go around bowl with a dinner knife and release cheese. With hands shape preparation to simulate an apple. Go over entire surface with a spatula, to make it smooth. Sprinkle paprika on surface if to be served alone as a centerpiece. If to be served with another centerpiece sprinkled with paprika, it is better to sprinkle only half of apple with paprika. Use artificial apple leaf or one made with fresh green pepper. Cut oval of green pepper, mark top to simulate veins in leaf. Cut strip of green pepper for stem and place on top of apple.

Note. If using meat or seafood preparation, shape into apple, let become cold and firm, then spread smoothly with green cream cheese. Do likewise with other fruits.

Large Strawberry Hors d'Oeuvres Centerpiece

Follow general directions as for Cheese Apple Centerpiece (above). Pack into a small bowl and refrigerate until firm. Release from bowl and shape mixture to simulate a large strawberry. Sprinkle entire surface with bright paprika, or cover with red bread crumbs. Place it on a small round cardboard covered with foil or wax paper.

With small daisy cutter, cut through a wide strip of fresh green pepper or cucumber peel. Make a small opening in center of hull with point of a skewer. Use a strip of pepper for stem. Place hull and stem on large end of strawberry, or pipe green cheese hull with No. 3 cookie star tube.

Pear Hors d'Oeuvres Centerpiece

Follow general drections as for Strawberry Centerpiece. A sharp cheddar cheese spread combined with at least half white cream cheese would be attractive for pear. Shape to simulate pear and go over entire surface with a spatula to make it smooth. Place a whole clove or raisin on large end and a green pepper leaf and stem on small end. Cut an oval of green pepper, mark top to simulate veins. Use green pepper strip for stem. Sprinkle upper round part of pear with bright paprika.

Note. A combination of the large green apple, strawberry, and pear appetizer molds are very unusual and attractive served on a large platter or tray. In this case use contrasting sharp cheeses and other preparations. Place apple in center, and strawberry and pear on sides, making the strawberry and pear half the size of apple. Use small round cardboard bases covered with wax paper or foil underneath each fruit to help support them when transferring from one platter to the other. For very large groups, the pineapple mold can be included in this arrangement. Serve assorted wafers, crackers, and melba toast on same platter, or separately.

Lobster Centerpiece

Cook a small (1-to-2-pound size) live lobster about 20 minutes in simmering water, or purchase already boiled. When cold, brush with salad oil and place in center of a large round or oval platter. Surround with hors d'oeuvres.

Sandwich Loaf

Remove top and side crust from day-old unsliced sandwich style loaf of bread. Cut lengthwise into about ½-inch slices. Dark and white bread may be used in same loaf, using 2 slices of white and 2 of dark. Cut a cardboard about same size as bread and cover it with first slice of bread. Spread bread with Whipped Butter or Margarine, then with ham (or other meat) that has been cut fine or put through a food chopper. Season with a little mayonnaise, grated onion, finely cut green onion tops or green pepper, and pimiento. Place second slice over filling and spread with butter, then with a fine egg salad or filling used in Coronation Appetizer (page 67), or filling used in Deviled Eggs (page 48). Place third slice over filling and spread with butter and chicken liver paté, or other meat paste that has been seasoned with stuffed green olives, etc. Cover with fourth slice of bread.

After sandwich loaf is completely filled, with a very sharp knife trim uneven sides and ends if necessary. Spread entire loaf smoothly with soft, pale pink cream cheese. With No. 27 or 30 star tube pipe straight lines on sides and ends of loaf. This will make it appear larger. Have ready about 10 roses and 6 rosebuds made of cream cheese of a deeper shade of pink. These roses should be made at least an hour in advance and kept in refrigerator until absolutely cold and firm enough to facilitate removal with a dinner knife or pair of scissors. Pipe a mound of pink cheese in center of loaf and place roses over it. With No. 67 leaf tube and green cream cheese, pipe leaves in open spaces. Pipe long green leaves and fine long stems on top and sides of loaf. Use No. 4 plain writing tube for the stems, and with the same tube and white cream cheese, pipe liles of the valley. Serve this sandwich loaf on an attractive oval or oblong platter or tray. Garnish ends with 3 yellow vegetable jonquils and parsley, or as desired.

This loaf may be prepared a day in advance. In this case, spread entire surface wth cream cheese and cover it with wax paper and a damp towel. Keep in refrigerator. Several hours before serving, remove towel and wax paper. Spread entire surface again with cream cheese and decorate. Keep in cold place until ready to be served. *It must be kept cold, but allow it to stand in room temperature about 30 minutes before slicing to prevent from cracking.* Loaf may be completely decorated day in advance if stored in a closed container.

Note. Numerous other fillings from the hors d'oeuvres section may be used in these sandwich loaves. For tea parties, fill loaf with various jams, preserves, or jellies. For cocktail parties a seafood loaf would be very interesting.

Whipped Butter or Margarine

Beat very cold, firm butter or margarine with high-speed electric mixer for about 5 minutes, or until it looks like whipped cream. Excellent for spreading on fancy sandwiches, hors d'oeuvres bases, vegetables, and hot rolls. Do *not* use in baking cakes.

Seafood Cocktail Horn of Plenty

2 pounds net drained weight cooked crab meat, lobster meat, shrimp, or salmon (remove any bones)

1 cup celery, cut into narrow crosswise pieces

1 dozen hard-cooked eggs, chopped medium

¼ cup each fresh green onion and tops, chopped medium

¼ cup (very small jar or can) pimiento, cut into ½-inch squares

2 tablespoons plain gelatin, combined with ¾ cup cold water (mix well, let stand until thick, then dissolve over simmering water, and add it to 1½ cups mayonnaise)

Combine all ingredients in the order given and mix well. Taste and add little salt if needed and ¼ teaspoon cayenne pepper or hot sauce. Pack down in bowl, cover, and refrigerate for at least 4 hours or until firm to the touch.

Meanwhile cut out a cardboard Horn of Plenty to measure about 10 to 12 inches long and make opening about 7 inches wide. Cover cardboard (so that wide open end is on right-hand side) with light-weight foil, holding in place underneath with Scotch tape if necessary.

When salad is firm, turn it out onto pattern of horn on a 12 × 18 baking sheet, covered with wax paper. Shape horn attractively and smoothly. Refrigerate for a few minutes (longer if it feels soft), or can be shaped day in advance and kept well covered in refrigerator.

To coat and glaze horn, prepare Chaud-Froid Mayonnaise (page 54); let stand a few minutes. Slide hands underneath cardboard and horn, and transfer it carefully onto a long cake rack with drip pan underneath. Spread entire surface with about 1 cup Chaud-Froid Mayonnaise. Refrigerate for a few minutes, then go over surface again with about ½ cup Chaud-Froid

Mayonnaise making sure to cover any open spots. Refrigerate again for a few minutes.

Now stir rest of Chaud-Froid Mayonnaise, having it tepid and of pouring consistency, but not too thin and not thick. May be necessary to place pan in warm water for a few seconds if it appears thick. From saucepan pour rest of sauce quickly and smoothly over entire surface of mold. If coating is too thin, pick it up with rubber scraper, place into pan, stir until smooth over cool water a few minutes, and pour again. It will be necessary to spread open end with a spoon. Now refrigerate for about ½ hour. Meanwhile, or in advance, prepare Clear Glaze (page 55).

After ½ hour, pour Clear Glaze that is about the consistency of unbeaten egg white over entire surface, and if too thin, cover again. May be necessary to do this several times. Rerigerate for at least ½ hour.

To transfer horn to serving 16-inch round platter (be sure refrigerator is large enough to hold platter unless you have another cold place to store it, about 40° F. or colder) with a dinner knife release bottom edges of mold from rack, slip both hands underneath cardboard and carefully lift up and place horn on platter, having open end of horn on right-hand side.

Place a few toothpicks in open end of horn to hold the first layer of Glazed Shrimp in place, as close together as possible. After supporting first layer of shrimp with picks, rest of shrimp will cling together very nicely. Arrange them as attractively as possible in open end and some on platter.

This is a very beautiful and delectable mold for cocktail parties, buffet suppers, or as a first course. Serve Quick Flaky Cheese Sticks (page 19) separately. Instead of shrimp this horn may be filled with assorted olives and other relishes; with small hors d'oeuvres, etc.

To Decorate Open End and Tail End of Horn. Beat 1 pound (or less) cream cheese until smooth and of medium consistency; add few drops of green coloring and very little yellow, matching color as close as possible to coating on horn. With bag and No. 7 large star cookie tube pipe large E border on rim of open end. Do likewise on tail end.

Chaud-Froid Mayonnaise

2½ tablespoons plain gelatin, combined with 1 cup cold water (stir and let stand until thick for several minutes, then dissolve over simmering water)

3 level cups commercial mayonnaise (room temperature at least 1 hour)

A few drops of green coloring and a little yellow coloring, diluted in ½ teaspoon water

Add the dissolved warm gelatin slowly to the mayonnaise, then the diluted food coloring. Stir well until evenly blended. For coating molds of this type, it should be cool, but not cold or warm, better on the tepid side.

If too thick, place pan in another pan of warm water and stir until smooth. If too thin, place it in a pan of cold water. Use as directed.

Clear Glaze

In a 1-quart saucepan combine 2 tablespoons plain gelatin with ¾ cup cold water. Stir until thick and let stand several minutes. Now pour 2 cups of boiling water slowly over thick preparation and stir gently until dissolved. Remove any foam from top of gelatin to keep it clear as possible. Let cool to unbeaten egg white consistency and use as directed. If too thick, place in pan of warm water, if too thin place it in pan of cold water.

Glazed Shrimp for Open End of Horn

¼ cup cider vinegar
1¾ cups water
About 1 teaspoon salt
1 or 2 teaspoons sugar
1 small clove garlic sliced, or ½ teaspoon garlic or onion salt
2 pounds raw shrimp cooked about 5 minutes, then peeled if necessary (any size can be used)

Red and yellow coloring diluted in 2 teaspoons warm water
2 tablespoons plain gelatin, combined with ¾ cup cold water (let stand until thick, then dissolve over simmering water)

Combine all ingredients except dissolved gelatin and food coloring. Blend well and pour over the cooked cleaned and peeled shrimp. Stir well, cover and refrigerate for at least 1 hour to marinate.

To glaze shrimp, drop them into a fine strainer. Warm up strained marinade, add the dissolved gelatin and diluted red coloring with very little yellow to produce an attractive coral shade. Place well-drained shrimp on cake rack with drip pan underneath. Now cool marinade combined with gelatin until it is the consistency of unbeaten egg white. Can be forced over cold water. Pour thickened glaze over entire surface of shrimp. Pick up glaze with rubber scraper, and pour again if necessary until a nice uniform coating is obtained; may be necessary to do this several times. This not only adds color to the shrimp, but adds flavor and preserves them. Let shrimp remain on rack in refrigerator or cold place for at least 15 minutes, then release them from rack with a dinner knife or small spatula.

Epicurean Pumpkin Cheese Hors d'Oeuvres Centerpiece

1 pound cream cheese
¼ pound roquefort or bleu cheese
1 teaspoon Worcestershire sauce
1 tablespoon dry wine (optional)

1 pound yellow cheese spread (soft cheese in 2-pound package excellent)

Let cream cheese and roquefort stand room temperature for a *short* time until medium consistency, not too soft. Mash and combine; add Worcestershire sauce and wine, and blend thoroughly. Form ball and wrap firmly in wax paper. Refrigerate for a short time, and shape again to make as uniform as possible; return to refrigerator until very firm for several hours.

Meanwhile let yellow cheese stand in room temperature for several hours until it can be rolled easily. If too firm, place it in a bowl, then in a pan of hot water (about 150° F.) for a short time, turning it over to keep uniform in temperature. Mix with a spoon or hand, and when of proper consistency, not too soft, place it on sheet of wax paper and roll round to measure about 10 inches in diameter. Place firm cheese ball in center, and wrap yellow cheese around ball as evenly and smoothly as possible. Form pumpkin, making it as smooth as possible by dampening hands, or dipping small spatula into hot water from time to time. Chill if necessary.

With flat handle of a dinner knife or a long skewer make 8 lengthwise impressions on surface of pumpkin. Make a thick-pointed stem with piece of citron, or thick green gum drop, or green pepper, or a piece of green celery. If using citron, place stem in colored water for a short time, and dry it well. Make a slight depression on top of pumpkin, and insert stem, having pointed end up. With tiny brush and green coloring, tint around stem end, also very lightly on body, and tint body also with a little orange coloring if cheese is very light.

Place pumpkin on a small round cardboard covered smoothly with foil, and arrange it in center of round platter. Surround it with assorted hors d'oeuvres crackers and breads.

Chicken Liver Paté Hors d'Oeuvres Centerpiece

1 pound chicken livers, well drained
½ cup butter
½ cup finely chopped fresh green onion and stems
½ cup finely chopped celery
1½ teaspoons salt
¼ teaspoon pepper
1 teaspoon Worcestershire sauce
4 slices of thin bacon, cut into very small pieces (pan fry slowly until crisp, drain)
4 hard-cooked eggs
¼ cup mayonnaise

Cook livers in butter for 7 or 8 minutes. Let cool. With heavy knife chop until fine. To the remaining fat in skillet, add chopped livers and all ingredients except eggs and mayonnaise and cook together about 5 minutes over low heat.

Now add the 4 hard-cooked eggs, mashed fine with pie blender, and the ¼ cup of mayonnaise (or cooked salad dressing), and stir until evenly blended. Taste and season further if necessary. Cover and refrigerate for about 2 hours, or until firm enough to mold, but not too stiff. If too firm, let stand in room temperature for a short time.

With hands form chicken, dipping hands into warm water as necessary to keep it smooth as possible. Make eyes with tiny round pieces of maraschino cherry, and comb for top of head with half of cherry, and half cherry on tail end.

Place chicken-shaped paté in center of nest (see below). Spread exposed rim and sides of nest *very* lightly with mayonnaise, and cover thickly with about ¾ cup of very finely chopped green onion stems, or parsley. Refrigerate until serving time. Carefully pick up with a broad pancake turner and place in center of a 16-inch (or smaller) platter. Surround with assorted cocktail crackers, melba toast, etc.

Nest for Chicken Liver Paté Centerpiece

An extra half recipe of Chicken Liver Paté preparation may be made for nest (or use about 2 cups of any other hors d'oeuvres paste or soft cheese). Cut out an oval cardboard to measure about 6 inches wide and 7 inches long, and cover it with light-weight foil, sealing bottom with Scotch tape, keeping flat as possible, or cover with silicone paper. Place preparation on cardboard and shape it into a smooth uniform oval, making a slight depression in center. Chill until firm.

Bleu Cheese Hors d'Oeuvres Mold Centerpiece

1 pound bleu cheese (roquefort or gorgonzola may be used)
1 pound creamed cottage cheese, large curd (do not drain)
¼ cup fine-chopped chives or fresh green onions and tops
½ teaspoon salt
⅛ teaspoon cayenne pepper

2 teaspoons plain gelatin, combined with ¼ cup cold water (stir gently and allow to stand until thick, then dissolve over simmering water)
½ cup whipping cream, beaten until medium thick but still slides out of bowl

Crumble bleu cheese into small pieces. Combine it with cottage cheese, chives, salt, and cayenne pepper. Add dissolved gelatin to whipped cream, and fold it into other ingredients as uniformly as posible. Pour into an oiled 1-quart plain mold or bowl. Cover with wax paper and refrigerate 7 or 8 hours, or until firm to the touch.

To Serve. Loosen around edges and invert onto platter. Sprinkle top with paprika. Place leaf lettuce or other greens attractively around mold (using leafy part only). Garnish base of mold with thin-sliced small tomatoes, overlapping slightly. Or omit lettuce and tomatoes and arrange round crisp crackers or other hors d'oeuvres bases around mold. In this case platter can be garnished with carved vegetable flowers and parsley bouquets.

Glazed Shrimp Centerpiece

Prepare French Dressing Glaze as follows: In the small bowl of electric mixer combine ½ cup vinegar, ½ tablespoon paprika, 1½ teaspoons salt, a dash of red pepper, 1 small clove garlic, 1 or 2 tablespoons granulated sugar, 1 whole egg, a few drops red coloring. Mix well, then slowly (about 1 tablespoon at a time) add 1 cup salad oil and beat until thick. Combine 2 teaspoons plain gelatin with 3 tablespoons cold water. Let stand until thick; then dissolve over boiling water. While *hot*, add slowly to French Dressing and mix very thoroughly until smooth. Place in refrigerator or force over ice water until very cold and thick, about 1 hour or longer. Stir every 5 or 6 minutes, until thick, during cooling process to keep in uniform consistency.

Dip cold whole freshly cooked shrimp, that have been placed securely on heavy toothpicks with rounded side up, into this dressing. Let drain for a moment or so, and stick into a grapefruit, an eggplant, an orange, or an apple. Let drain in refrigerator or cold place about 30 minutes. Then remove shrimp and stick them into a clean vegetable or fruit. Pipe top of each shrimp (scraping surface with point of tube) with a rosette, using No. 24 or No. 27 tube and pale-pink cream cheese, and with No. 65 or No. 67 leaf tube, pipe green leaf on each side or leave plain. Glaze may be poured over shrimp and served in a compartment dish.

Note. It is best to use French Dressing Glaze as soon as it is thick enough to cover shrimp, in about 1 hour. It should have the consistency of a medium custard. If glaze must stand longer, stir it gently before dipping shrimp, and if it appears too solid, place it in a pan of warm water for several minutes, then stir until of proper consistency, but not thin. If it becomes too thin, chill again and watch closely, stirring often. One recipe of glaze will cover about 30 shrimp, depending on size.

Shrimp Salad Louisiana

1 pound cooked shrimp (2 pounds raw shrimp)	2 cups celery, cut ⅓ inch wide crosswise

Cook raw shrimp in simmering water about 5 minutes if large, 3 or 4 minutes if medium. Shell and remove vein. Leave shrimp whole for this salad if small or medium; split in halves lengthwise if large. Pour ½, more or less, Sauce Louisiana over shrimp and celery, and blend well. Arrange dome-fashion in medium-size serving platter and cover entire surface with rest of Sauce Louisiana.

Garnish base of salad with cold cooked asparagus tips that have been marinated in Italian Dressing (page 368) for about 20 minutes. Top may be garnished with about 8 thick half slices of lemon, overlapping each other.

Sauce Louisiana

½ cup catsup
1 cup chili sauce
½ teaspoon hot sauce or ⅛ teaspoon hot pepper
½ teaspoon salt
1 small clove garlic, minced fine or put through garlic press
2 tablespoons fresh green pepper minced fine (optional)

¼ cup fresh green onion and tops, cut fine
2 tablespoons prepared horseradish
2 teaspoons plain gelatin, combined with ¼ cup cold water (stir and let stand until thick, then dissolve over simmering water)

Combine all ingredients except gelatin and mix well. Now add warm dissolved gelatin and stir quickly and thoroughly. Refrigerate sauce for about ½ hour, stirring it gently several times. This sauce may be prepared several days in advance or longer if kept in covered container in refrigerator. In this case, remove sauce from refrigerator about 15 to 30 minutes before combining it with seafood. Makes a delicious cocktail and dipping sauce for hors d'oeuvres.

Lobster Salad Imperial

4 pounds frozen lobster tails (will give about 2 pounds net after cooking)
About 2½ cups Seafood Tartar Sauce (page 60)

2 medium-ripe Calavo pears, lemon juice
1 can artichoke hearts
1 recipe Tomato Aspic (page 60)
Paprika

Defrost lobster tails. Cover with hot water and bring to boiling point. Lower heat and simmer 5 to 12 minutes for small and medium and 18 minutes for large tails. Let cool in water slightly, shell and cut into about 1-inch pieces, or larger. Moisten lobster meat with about ½ cup of the Seafood Tartar Sauce and put aside. Cut pears in halves lengthwise. Remove seeds, brush cut sides of pears at once with lemon juice to prevent discoloration. Place with cut side down on wax paper and *cut tip* into about 1-inch pieces with small serrated-edge knife.

Cut center part of pear in ⅓ inch horseshoe slices. Dip or brush each one with lemon juice. Reserve 8 most attractive slices to garnish top of salad. With small sharp paring knife pare slices. Moisten the 1-inch pieces with a little Seafood Tartar Sauce. Open can artichoke hearts and reserve 6 most uniform and attractive ones to garnish base of mold. Pour a little Italian Dressing (page 368) on artichokes, cover and let stand in refrigerator for about ½ hour. Drain thoroughly. Cut irregular artichoke hearts into about 1-inch pieces and combine with the lobster meat, cut-up pears, and more Seafood Tartar Sauce to moisten. Mix *very* gently and pour onto an oval 17-inch platter, forming a mound (20-inch oval platter may be used). Spread rest of Seafood Tartar Sauce as smoothly as possible over entire surface of salad.

With a 2-inch round or medium crescent cutter, cut Tomato Aspic into 18 crescents. Leave rest of aspic uncut until needed for top of mold. Place 3 aspic crescents on each end of salad to simulate a flower. Form 2 flowers on each side. Drain artichokes thoroughly, open slightly in center and sprinkle with paprika. Place 1 on each small end of aspic flowers, or use colossal green or black ripe olives, fresh or preserved kumquats, etc. With a small 1¼-inch round cutter, cut out 6 tiny crescents from rest of Tomato Aspic. Garnish top of salad with the horseshoe slices of pears and small aspic crescents. Fill in open spaces around base of salad with ripe or green olives dried in a towel, then rubbed with a bit of salad oil. Sprinkle outside edge of mold with paprika.

Seafood Tartar Sauce

2 cups commercial mayonnaise
1 small clove garlic, chopped very fine or put through garlic press
⅓ cup fresh green onions, chopped very fine
½ cup fresh green onion stems, chopped very fine
¼ cup chopped pickles
¼ cup chopped green stuffed olives
¼ cup lemon juice
About 1 tablespoon granulated sugar
2 teaspoons plain gelatin, combined with ¼ cup cold water (stir gently and let stand until thick about 5 minutes; dissolve over simmering water)

Combine all ingredients except gelatin mixture. Dissolve gelatin and while warm stir into sauce and mix well. Chill in refrigerator for about 30 minutes, not longer, stirring every 5 minutes to keep at uniform consistency. Best not to prepare this sauce until needed. It will set if kept in refrigerator if not stirred often. If it must be refrigerated, remove and let stand room temperature until soft before stirring to prevent curdling. This is a delicious sauce and may be used with any seafood salad or cooked fish.

Tomato Aspic

4 cups tomato juice
1 bay leaf
⅛ teaspoon whole pepper, crushed
1 small onion sliced
1 tablespoon celery leaves
1 tablespoon parsley
1 sliver garlic
1 teaspoon salt
1 teaspoon sugar
2 tablespoons lemon juice or vinegar
3 tablespoons plain gelatin, combined with ½ cup cold water or white wine
Red food coloring

Simmer all ingredients except lemon juice and gelatin mixture for 15 minutes. Strain, and while very hot, add the lemon juice and thick gelatin mixture. Stir until completely dissolved. Add little red coloring. Let stand until cool, then pour into a lightly oiled baking sheet that measures about 10 x 14 inches. Keep in refrigerator until firm to touch for 8 hours or longer. This aspic may be poured into fancy small or large oiled molds. Use as directed in Lobster Salad Imperial, or as desired.

Crab Meat Salad Ravigote

5 (6-ounce) packages frozen crab meat, or 5 small cans top quality (about 7 ounces)

¼ cup tarragon vinegar

3 cups pascal celery, peeled lightly and cut crosswise about ⅓ inch thick, then washed, drained and dried thoroughly in a towel

About 1 teaspoon salt

About 1 teaspoon capers, well drained (optional)

1 tablespoon fresh green onion, cut fine

¼ cup fresh green onion tops, cut about ½ inch

1 cup *stabilized* mayonnaise

About ¾ cup or more *unstabilized* mayonnaise to spread over entire surface of salad

4 hard-cooked egg yolks, put through a fine grater or sieve

Paprika

Defrost crab meat if frozen. Leave in large pieces, removing any bones. Pour the tarragon vinegar over crab meat and mix well with two forks. Cover and keep in refrigerator for about ½ hour or longer. Drain very thoroughly, pressing out excess moisture. Combine the crab meat, celery, salt, capers, fresh green onion and tops, and the cup of *stabilized* mayonnaise. Blend well, press down into 8-inch bowl, cover and place in refrigerator for about 30 minutes. Be sure to chill salad right in bowl for about 30 minutes or longer, before turning it out onto platter. Mound salad on a 17-inch oval platter, pressing it into shape with hands. At this point do not stir. Spread entire surface with about ¾ cup plain mayonnaise and cover with the grated egg yolks. Sprinkle paprika lengthwise of mold, to cover about 1 inch of center of surface.

Garnish base of salad alternately with thinly sliced tomatoes and cucumber or groups of kumquats, cocktail mix, large black or green olives, pickled rinds, etc. Place bouquet of parsley on each end. This salad may be prepared hours or a day in advance. In this case, do not garnish with grated yolks, tomatoes and cucumber slices until about an hour before serving.

Stabilized Mayonnaise

Combine 1 teaspoon plain gelatin with 2 tablespoons cold water. Mix gently, and let stand until thick, about 5 minutes, then dissolve over simmering water. Pour warm gelatin at once slowly into 1 cup of commercial mayonnaise and mix well. Stabilized mayonnaise can stand in refrigerator for ½ hour (not longer), if stirred several times to keep it at uniform consistency. If it remains in refrigerator until extremely cold and set it will curdle when combining with other ingredients. The small amount of gelatin added to mayonnaise absorbs excess moisture in seafood and other ingredients that usually settles in platter.

Colonial Doll Centerpiece

1 large grapefruit
China doll head
Heavy rounded toothpicks

Very firm medium-size stuffed green olives (dried in a towel)
Cream cheese, or cheese spreads
Very fresh parsley

Remove 1 slice from bottom of grapefruit, and place it on a small round plate. Cut out an opening at top of grapefruit, insert 5 or 6 heavy toothpicks and then China doll head. With a skewer make shallow holes on grapefruit, leaving about 2-inch spaces between them. Insert sprigs of parsley in some of the openings. Place firm green olives on heavy toothpicks, and with No. 101 or No. 104 tube, pipe a rose on each with white or colored cheese. Place in openings of grapefruit until grapefruit is attractively covered with roses. Rows of white, pink, and light-yellow or green roses are very attractive on this centerpiece.

Keep in refrigerator until serving time. May be made several hours in advance, or a day in advance if kept tightly covered in a deep container to prevent cheese from discoloring or drying out. This makes a very colorful and beautiful centerpiece for a large hors d'oeuvres platter.

Seafood Hors d'Oeuvres Platter

To serve 12

1 pound cooked lobster meat or top-quality salmon or tuna
1 pound cooked shrimp, jumbo size preferable (2 pounds before cooking) split lengthwise if large and thick
1 pound cooked crab meat (canned or frozen may be used)
Colossal green ripe olives (8-ounce can contains about 20 olives)

8-ounce jar colossal black stuffed olives
2 packages frozen (or canned) asparagus tips, cooked until just tender, not too soft (serve 3-inch part of tips only)
2 bunches carrots cut in 3-inch thick wedges, cooked until just tender, about 15 minutes

Heap the lobster meat, salmon, or tuna in center of 16-inch round platter, having it about 2 inches high, forming a slight dome. Surround the lobster meat with the cooked shrimp, overlapping one another. Leave little space between each row of seafood for the olives. Separate the lobster and shrimp with a ring of colossal green stuffed olives. Surround shrimp with a ring of crab meat. Separate the shrimp and crab meat with a ring of colossal black ripe olives dried on towel then rubbed lightly with a little salad oil. Complete the platter with a ring of 3-inch long asparagus tips and a ring of carrot wedges.

This Seafood Hors d'Oeuvres Platter may be put together several hours in advance. In this case, cover it well with wax paper and refrigerate. Just before serving drizzle and brush top of foods with a little of the Vinaigrette Tarragon Dressing to add moisture and gloss. Spread some Tarragon Mayonnaise Dressing over lobster meat in center only, and sprinkle with paprika. Serve with salad sticks, crackers, melba toast, etc.

May be served as first course for special dinner parties, hors d' oeuvres suppers, buffet parties, or for snack parties.

Vinaigrette Tarragon Dressing

2 cups salad oil
½ cup cider vinegar
¼ cup tarragon vinegar
2 teaspoons salt

¼ teaspoon pepper
1 small clove garlic sliced thin or put through garlic press

Combine all ingredients in a jar. Cover and shake well until thoroughly blended. Let stand in refrigerator for several hours before using. After several hours shake again and pour part of dressing on the various foods listed above to moisten. Blend well, cover and refrigerate for several hours. To serve, drain each food thoroughly.

Tarragon Mayonnaise Dressing

2 cups mayonnaise
2 tablespoons tarragon vinegar, more or less
¼ cup finely chopped stuffed green olives
¼ cup chopped fresh green onion
¼ cup chopped fresh green onion stems
1 tablespoon sugar (optional)

½ cup finely chopped pickles
About 1 tablespoon lemon juice, more or less
1 small clove garlic very finely chopped or put through garlic press
Salt to taste if necessary

Combine all ingredients and blend thoroughly. Serve this sauce separately in an attractive bowl with the Seafood Hors d'Oeuvres Platter.

Salmon for Hors d'Oeuvres

Use fine-quality salmon; break into medium-size pieces. Add only enough Tartar Sauce (page 336) or other dressing to make it appear moist. Arrange in one of the sections of a compartment dish, and sprinkle top generously with finely chopped fresh green onions, chives, or green stuffed olives.

Crab Meat in Tomato Cups

Use best quality frozen, canned, or fresh crab meat. Flake, and combine with a little mayonnaise to which a little prepared horseradish has been added. (Use 3 parts mayonnaise and 1 part horseradish.) Stuff very small scooped-out whole or half fresh tomatoes with this preparation. Plum tomatoes are excellent. Place a thick slice of stuffed black olive and green pepper leaves on each, or rosettes and leaves. Arrange in longest section of compartment dish and surround them with tiny pickled cocktail onions, or as desired.

These foods are very attractive in oblong or round hors d'oeuvres trays. Decorate center of trays with vegetable flowers and parsley, or as desired. May be served as a first course on a cocktail table in living room, or for a light supper or luncheon.

Kippered Herring Snack Mold

14-ounce can plain kippered herring, very finely chopped
¼ cup minced fresh green onion
¼ cup minced fresh green onion stems
About ½ cup sour cream

¼ cup finely chopped green stuffed olives
¼ cup sour cream
Several black pitted olives or green olives
Green onion stems

Combine the chopped kippered herring, minced onion, onion greens, the ½ cup sour cream, ¼ cup finely chopped green stuffed olives. Blend thoroughly. Mound on an oval dish, keeping it higher in center. With a spatula smooth surface and spread with the ¼ cup, or more, sour cream. Pit and cut black ripe olives or green olives to simulate petals. Form several flowers on top of mound, and insert green onion stems. Place a round piece of red pimiento in center of flowers. Make green onion leaves. Surround mound with round or oval crackers, melba toast, or potato chips.

Dainty Finger Sandwiches

Remove crusts from bread and slice with thin bread slicer. Spread gently with Whipped Butter (page 79) and a soft meat paste, cheese, or sweet filling. Place on flat dish or pan. Cover with wax paper and place in plastic bag. Keep in refrigerator or cold place until shortly before serving. Cut into fingers, or as desired. Decorate tops with cream cheese rosettes and green leaves, using No. 24 or No. 27 tube for rosettes, and No. 65 or 67 tube for leaves.

Serve in alternate rows with Dainty Triangle Sandwiches.

Dainty Triangle Sandwiches

Prepare bread as for Dainty Finger Sandwiches; cut into triangles. Decorate with rosettes or tiny sprays of flowers. Use No. 2 tube for stems, No. 24 or 101 tube for flowers, and No. 2 tube for bulbs and imitation leaves.

Arrange above sandwiches in alternate rows on an oblong or rectangular tray, with doily underneath. Center of tray may be garnished with vegetable carved flowers and parsley.

Basket Tea Sandwiches

With medium-sized (2 inch) plain round cutter, cut out as many rounds of bread as needed. Spread each one with soft or Whipped Butter (page 79), and then with finely minced chicken or other meat paste. Put 2 rounds together and place in a medium-size petit fours cup, shaping cup to simulate base of a basket. Place a dab of cream cheese on each side of cup so that it will adhere to bread. Pipe a handle and a bow with No. 4 plain tube and green cheese. Then, with No. 24 or 27 tube, pipe pink cheese rosettes, front and back. With No. 65 or 67 tube, pipe green leaves.

Peanut Butter Party Sandwiches

Use sliced bread; cut out as many stars as desired. Spread entire surface with smooth peanut butter. With No. 24 tube, pipe edge with peanut butter. Place a plain whole salted peanut on each point, and with No. 24 tube, pipe a pink cream cheese rosette in center, and with No. 65 tube, pipe green leaves around rosette.

Clover Leaf Party Sandwiches

With medium-sized clover leaf cutter, cut out as many bread clovers as desired. Spread entire surface with creamed butter or margarine and then place over each bread a clover leaf of commercially sliced American cheese, ham, or other meat, cut the same size, or spread with meat paste. With No. 4 plain decorating tube, pipe edge with a plain white line (or leave plain), and with No. 24 star tube, pipe a rosette of yellow or pink cream cheese in center and green leaves with No. 65 tube.

Tulip Party Sandwich

With tulip cutter, cut out as many bread tulips as desired. Spread entire surface with Whipped (or soft) Butter or Margarine (page 79) and then with No. 24 star tube, fill in flower part with *old cheddar cheese* (or other cheese) that has been thoroughly creamed and all lumps removed. With No. 24 star tube or No. 70 leaf tube, pipe leaves and stem with green cream cheese. These tulips may also be covered with a thin slice of ham or cheese cut same size and decorated as desired.

Crescent Party Sandwiches

Cut out as many bread crescents as needed. Do likewise with sliced cheese or sliced cold meats. Spread breads with Whipped Butter or Margarine (page 79) and place meat or cheese over butter. Pipe a yellow rosette on top center with green leaves on each end, using No. 24 tube for rosettes, and No. 65 tube for leaves.

Bacon-Egg Canapé

Makes about 20 to 24 appetizers

6 hard-cooked eggs, chopped fine
About ¼ cup, or more, mayonnaise
3 medium green stuffed olives, chopped fine
¼ cup finely chopped green onion and stems

About ¾ teaspoon salt
½ teaspoon hot sauce
5 slices bacon, pan-fried until crisp, pouring off fat as it accumulates in skillet (when cool, chop or crumble fine)

Combine all ingredients except bacon and blend well. Spread 1 level table-spoon on 2-inch rounds of sautéed or toasted breads. With finger make a depression in center of each. Fill center with the finely chopped cooked bacon. Garnish with sprig of parsley. May be served cold.

Very delicious if made in advance and reheated for about 7 or 8 minutes in a 350° F. oven just before serving. Do not freeze. May be made a day in advance if stored in covered container in refrigerator.

Gruyère Caviar Hors d'Oeuvres

If using gruyère Swiss cheese in wedge shape cut each wedge crosswise in 2 or 3 uniform slices. Cut rye bread same shape and size. Spread breads with savory butter. With very small round cutter ¾ inch wide (large end of a decorating tube may be used as cutter) cut out round section of cheese from wide end. Place cheese on buttered bread. Fill opening with well-drained black caviar, having it come up to level of cheese, flattening caviar with a spatula, or dinner knife. With No. 24 or 27 star tube pipe pink cheese rosette near pointed end, and green leaves with No. 65 tube.

May be frozen, or made a day in advance and kept in covered container in refrigerator.

Shrimp in Cocktail Sauce Hors d'Oeuvres

With a 2-inch cutter, cut out twice as many rounds of rye or white bread as hors d'oeuvres to be made. Spread half of rounds with Anchovy Butter (page 79). Cover with rest of bread rounds. Pour about ½ teaspoon cocktail sauce or catsup, to which a little horseradish has been added, in center of bread, and spread it to about ¼ inch from edge of bread. Split medium-size cooked shrimp in halves lengthwise, or leave whole; brush with a little Italian Dressing (page 368), or leave plain and lay them on top of sauce. Sauce should show around shrimp for contrast and appearance. With No. 24 tube, pipe white or colored cheese border around edge of bread. With No. 24 tube pipe white, pink, or yellow rosette and green leaves with No. 65 tube on top center of shrimp.

These hors d'oeuvres may be made smaller with a 1½-inch cutter if to be served before luncheon or dinner. In this case only 1 round of bread may be used.

May be frozen, or refrigerated for a day if kept covered in refrigerator. May be glazed if not frozen.

Caviar-Egg Appetizer

Small or medium eggs are best for this appetizer. Hard-cook as per general directions (page 46). Shell, and with egg slicer, cut them crosswise into rings. Remove yolks carefully so as not to break white rings. Put yolks through a food mill or mouli grater. Cut rounds of dark or white bread with a cutter that is a little larger than diameter of egg white rings, about 1¾ inches wide. Sauté bread rounds in small amount butter until crisp and lightly browned on both sides, or leave plain. Let cool, spread ends with Whipped Butter (page 79) and dip ends into grated yolk. Place white egg rings on each. Fill center with black or red caviar that was removed from container several hours in advance, seasoned with a little lemon juice, and stored covered in refrigerator. Pipe 2 tiny pale pink cheese rosettes with No. 24 tube and green leaves with No. 65 tube.

Coronation Appetizer

Spread small 1½-inch (or larger) rounds of bread with butter, then sprinkle with a little garlic salt. With egg or cheese slicer or very sharp knife slice 6 hard-cooked eggs crosswise into about 4 slices each. Remove yolks carefully. Place white rings over the bread. Put yolks and ends of whites through a food grater or sieve. Combine them with 1 tablespoon soft butter, 1 tablespoon mayonnaise, ¼ cup cream cheese, 1 teaspoon vinegar, ½ teaspoon salt, ⅛ teaspoon dry mustard, ⅛ teaspoon garlic salt.

Blend thoroughly. Taste and season more if necessary. If mixture is too heavy, add a little lemon juice or mayonnaise; if it is too soft, add a little more cheese or additional sieved hard-cooked egg. With No. 7 star cookie tube and bag, press this mixture into the egg rings, about 1 inch high. Decorate tops with pink cheese rosettes and green leaves. Glaze if desired.

Surprise Olive Hors d'Oeuvres

Cover small or medium-size stuffed olives with soft chicken-liver paste, ham paste, Braunschweiger sausage, or spreading cheese; work it gently in palms of hands. Roll into very fine-chopped or grated pecan or walnut meats, and place each on small round buttered crackers or breads. Decorate top with soft cream rosette with No. 24 or No. 27 star tube, and green leaves with No. 65 or No. 67 tube.

Italian Cornucopias

Slice Italian-style capocollo or prosciutto in thin slices. Cut each slice in half. Form cornucopias, pressing open ends well. Pipe a small bulb of cheese on toasted rounds, squares, or ovals of bread. Place cornucopias on bread. Insert a strip of gruyère cheese in each to represent pistil. Pipe one or more green cheese leaves at base with No. 65 or No. 67 leaf tube. Serve cold. May be frozen or prepared a day in advance if stored in refrigerator.

Caviar Grape Hors d'Oeuvres

Cut out ovals of breads; toast, sauté, or leave plain. Spread lightly with savory butter, then with white cheese spread. Place 3 small mounds of well-drained black caviar on bread to stimulate clusters of grapes. With No. 4 plain tube and green cheese, pipe stems and imitation leaves. Serve cold. May be frozen, or stored in refrigerator in covered container if made a day in advance.

Stuffed Olive Pinwheels

Remove all crust from day-old unsliced sandwich-style loaf of bread; slice it lengthwise, about ⅓ inch in thickness as uniformly as possible. Flatten slices with rolling pin. Spread some of slices with a sharp yellow cheese, beaten until smooth, or with a white cheese to which a few drops of green coloring have been added. Pit medium-size, or preferably large, black or green olives; stuff them solidly with pimiento, meat paste, fine-chopped chicken, ham, tongue, or other stuffing. Place 3 or 4 olives on small end of each slice, depending on size of olives and width of bread. Roll tightly to form a pinwheel. If a very wide pinwheel is preferred, use 2 slices of bread. Wrap tightly in wax paper, slip into a plastic bag, and refrigerate several hours or longer. May be prepared a day in advance. Instead of olives, these slices can be spread with various fillings and rolled the same way. Jellies or jams are especially nice for children's parties and teas. When ready to be served, with a very sharp knife slice crosswise in about ½-inch slices. Arrange them attractively on a platter, overlapping slightly. They may be cut in advance if well covered with wax paper or plastic bag and kept in a cool place.

Gherkin Fan Appetizers

Cut ovals of bread. Spread with savory butter or any meat or seafood paste. Sprinkle *lightly* with paprika. Cut tiny uniform firm gherkins in 4 or 5 sections, leaving ¼ inch uncut on bottom, to simulate a fan, and place on bread. Pipe white cheese rosette at base of pickle with No. 24 tube, and green leaves with No. 65 tube. Serve cold. Do not freeze.

Sunbonnet Canapés

With a 2-inch cutter, cut out as many rounds of dark or white bread as canapés desired. With a 1¼-inch round cutter, cut same amount. Do likewise with sliced cold cuts or sliced cheese. Spread large rounds with Anchovy Butter (page 79). Place cut meat or cheese rounds on each. Spread bottom of small rounds of breads with butter and place them on larger ones, having smaller ones close to edge. With No. 24 tube and pink or yellow cheese, pipe tiny rosettes around sides of small rounds, then with No. 65 tube pipe tiny green leaves between rosettes. Pipe green cheese bow on back of small rounds. Meat Sunbonnets are attractive decorated with pale pink cheese. Cheese Sunbonnets are attractive with pale yellow decorations, or they may be decorated in contrasting color.

Serve as cold appetizers or tea sandwiches. May be made with larger cutters for party sandwiches.

Cheese-Meat Swirls

Spread commercially thin-sliced pressed ham (or other fine grained square cold cuts) with heavy cream cheese (or spread that comes in glasses or tubes). Meat must be purchased already sliced by packer, or have marketman slice with slicing machine, not by hand. Roll firmly. For wide rolls, use 2 slices of meat. Wrap in wax paper and chill for several hours or longer. Cut in about ¾-inch slices, insert toothpick near open end and place on grapefruit, apple, or orange. Decorate top with rosettes and leaves. Or place each slice on lightly buttered rye or white breads. Pipe colored cheese rosette and green leaves on top of each. Serve cold.

Sail Boat Appetizers

Cut small pickles in halves lengthwise; if very small leave whole. With small paring knife remove part of center. With bag and No. 24 or 27 star tube, pipe an oval of pink or yellow colored cheese in opening of pickles. Insert a wedge of thinly sliced *hard* salami or firm cheese in center of each to simulate sail. Place pickles on ovals of buttered well-seasoned bread, and with No. 24 or 27 tube and blue colored cheese, pipe around base of pickle to simulate water. A small artificial flag may be placed on one end if desired.

Hotel Rainbow Canapés

Remove all crusts from day-old unsliced sandwich style loaf of bread. With long sharp knife slice lengthwise about ½ inch thick. Spread slices with soft butter and a little anchovy paste or any smooth meat or seafood paste preferred, for hors d'oeuvres; spread with jam or jelly for tea sandwiches. With No. 27 star tube and bag, pipe crosswise pink and green colored cream cheese (or other soft sharp cheeses) alternately on entire slice, starting from small end. Refrigerate slices on a flat pan or platter until firm to the touch, then cover with glaze according to directions (page 3), and refrigerate again until shortly before ready to be served.

To serve, cut each slice into long narrow strips, about 1½ inches wide, then into diamond shapes. Arrange 6 or 7 together to simulate a flower. Garnish center of each flower with a large black olive that has been rubbed lightly with salad oil to impart glaze. A platter filled entirely with these canapés is very attractive.

Bon Bon Elites

With a 1½-inch cutter, cut out as many rounds of bread as hors d'oeuvres to be prepared. Spread with green cheese and dab of anchovy paste, then press a small bulb of cheese onto center. Place a large stuffed black olive (well dried and rubbed very lightly with oil) on each round of bread. Starting at top of olive, pipe a swirl of white cream cheese with No. 4 plain tube. Then with No. 24 star tube pipe a colored cheese rosette on top of olive and two green leaves with No. 65 leaf tube. With No. 24 tube, pipe a flat green border of cheese on edge of breads, or leave plain. Chill, and glaze if desired (see directions, page 3).

Swan Shrimp Appetizer

Cut ovals of rye or white bread and sauté them on both sides in a small amount of butter until golden brown. When cold, pipe an oval of green cheese in center of each with No. 27 tube, then a dab of anchovy paste. Sauté freshly cooked firm shrimp in small amount of butter and season well with a little garlic or onion salt. When cold, place a shrimp, with rounded side down, on each bread oval to simulate a swan. With sharp scissors cut off small pieces from pointed end to make it flat. With No. 4 plain tube and pink cheese pipe head of bird, and eyes with No. 2 plain tube and green cheese. With No. 24 or 27 star tube pipe green tail and feathers on each side of body. If preferred, white cheese may be used for tail and feathers.

Italian Salami-Anchovy Appetizer

Have Genoa salami or other style cold cuts sliced thin. With a 2-inch cutter, cut as many rounds as appetizers to be prepared. Cut out same number of bread rounds. With a very small round cutter (about ¾ inch) cut out small round centers from salami. Place salami rings on buttered breads. Insert a whole rolled anchovy (or tiny heart of artichoke) in opening. Pipe several green leaves around base of anchovy. May be frozen or prepared a day in advance if stored in covered container in refrigerator.

Sesame Breast of Chicken Cold Hors d'Oeuvres

Makes about 24

½ pound cooked chicken breast (1 pound raw breast simmered about 30 minutes will give about ½ pound or 1¼ cups packed; when cold, with a heavy knife or cleaver chop medium; do not grind)

½ cup celery, chopped fine

1 tablespoon fresh green onion and 1 tablespoon onion stems, chopped fine

¼ cup coarsely chopped toasted almonds

½ teaspoon sesame seed (optional)

⅔ cup mayonnaise

About ½ teaspoon salt, a little more if needed

½ teaspoon hot sauce (or Worcestershire)

1 teaspoon plain gelatin, combined with 2 tablespoons cold water (stir and let stand several minutes until thick, then dissolve over simmering water)

In a medium-size bowl, combine all ingredients in the order given, adding dissolved gelatin last, and stir for about 1 minute, or until thoroughly blended. Cover and refrigerate for at least 2 hours. May be prepared a day in advance.

Place a level tablespoon of preparation in center of large round 2⅛-inch sesame crackers, forming a smooth mound, leaving ½ inch space all around uncovered. Sprinkle lightly with paprika. Break off part of bottom of a frilled pick, and insert through center top of each. An attractive alternative is to pipe tiny rosettes of pink cheese on entire surface with No. 24 star tube, leaving a little space for leaves. With No. 65 tube and green cheese, pipe tiny leaves. Or may be simply garnished with a cheese rosette with No. 27 star tube and green leaves with No. 65 leaf tube.

May be put together many hours in advance if thick crackers are used and stored in refrigerator, covered.

Sesame Breast of Chicken Hearts. Spread a scant tablespoon of preparation on thick 2-inch bread hearts, having it high and rounded in center, smooth as possible. Sprinkle top lightly with paprika, or leave plain. Insert several pieces of slivered toasted almonds center top, or garnish with cream cheese rosette and leaves, or a frilled pick.

Strawberry Appetizer

These appetizers may be made with minced cooked chicken liver preparation, ham, Braunschweiger liver sausage, or other meat pastes, or cheese spreads of medium consistency. A combination of ⅔ cup cream cheese and ⅓ cup roquefort or bleu cheese is delicious for this appetizer. If meat paste is too dry to mold, add some soft butter or soft cheese to make proper consistency. First form uniform-size balls with 1 rounded teaspoon meat or cheese in palms of hands, then roll into finely grated Red-Colored Bread Crumbs. Shape to simulate strawberries, and place a sprig of parsley, or an imitation strawberry leaf on large end. May be glazed if desired (see directions, page 3). Place on small rounds or ovals of bread, crackers, or melba toast, holding them down with a dab of soft cheese if necessary.

Red-Colored Bread Crumbs

Combine ¼ teaspoon red food coloring with 1 teaspoon or little more cool water, mix well, and pour it over ¼ cup of *light golden* (not too dark) dry fine bread crumbs. Blend well with a fork, then thoroughly in palms of hands. If crumbs are not red enough, add another drop or two of coloring and water and rub crumbs in hands. Spread them out on wax paper and let dry in room temperature for a few minutes, or longer, before using. This amount will cover 12 to 14 strawberry appetizers, depending on size.

To dry out white bread, remove crust from sliced bread, and place it in a very slow oven, about 250° F. for 15 to 20 minutes, then shut off heat and let remain in oven until absolutely dry (or use light commercial crumbs). Grate, or put through food mill, sift if necessary, then add coloring. Colored crumbs may be kept for several weeks after they are dry in a closed container if stored in refrigerator or a cold place.

Honolulu Pineapple-Strawberry Bird Appetizer

Fresh pineapple
Strawberries; gently wash, drain well, and dry them in towel, then remove hulls (medium-size berries best, leave them whole; if extremely large, cut in halves)
Frilled toothpicks
Fruit Salad Dressing (page 371)

In making pineapple bird, do not peel, simply slice off about ⅓ from large end. Now carefully release center of pineapple in chunks as large as possible, leaving a thick wall. Cut removed pineapple in about 1-inch squares and ½ inch thick.

Insert pineapple pieces through frilled toothpick first, then insert a whole strawberry with wide end in first, having tip out. Melon balls may be used instead of strawberries.

Make bird's neck and head (page 343), tint yellow, then stripe it with red and green coloring. Use clove for eye. Fill with one recipe Fruit Salad Dressing without adding whipped cream. Arrange appetizers around base on platter attractively.

Keep in refrigerator until ready to be served. Can be put together several hours in advance and kept well covered in refrigerator or very cold place.

Seafood Basket Hors d'Oeuvres

Makes about 24

6- or 7-ounce package of frozen or canned crab meat (cooked lobster, shrimp, drained salmon or tuna fish may be used, chopped medium)
2 hard-cooked eggs, chopped very fine
½ cup celery, chopped very fine
2 teaspoons finely chopped green onion (reserve green stems for topping)

1 tablespoon red pimiento, cut into small pieces (optional)
About ½ teaspoon salt, more or less
½ teaspoon or less hot sauce, or 1/16 teaspoon cayenne pepper
1 teaspoon plain gelatin, combined with 2 tablespoons cold water (stir and let stand until thick, then dissolve over simmering water, and add it to ¼ cup mayonnaise; blend well)

Flake crab meat. If using salmon or tuna fish, drain well, and chop medium. If using lobster tails or shrimp, cook until tender, then chop medium. Combine seafood with all other listed ingredients and stir until well blended. Cover and refrigerate for several hours or longer.

Seafood Basket

To prepare baskets, cut out 24 rounds of rye, white, or whole wheat bread with a 1½-inch round cutter. Cut out narrow crescents for handles with small round cutters. Spread top of each bread round with 1 rounded teaspoon of seafood preparation, keeping it higher in the center, and as smooth as possible.

Add 2 teaspoons lemon juice to 3 tablespoons of mayonnaise and blend well. Pour it into a small flat dish. Dip narrow crescents lightly in the mayonnaise and cover with very, very finely chopped green onion stems. To prepare onion stems, wash them well and dry thoroughly in a towel. With scissors slit them down, then cut crosswise as fine as possible, or may be chopped on a cutting board with a large knife. Measure ½ cupful for entire recipe. Wrap it in paper toweling for a few minutes to remove surplus moisture. Place crescents on rounded part of appetizer, pressing down gently to make them cling. With fingers sprinkle little more chopped onion stems on handles if not well covered.

Last, with pink, yellow, or white cream cheese and No. 24 tube pipe rosette on top center of handle, and with green cheese and No. 65 tube pipe leaves.

These hors d'oeuvres may be made several hours or a day in advance if stored in covered container and refrigerated. May be made large with 2-inch cutter.

Cold Meat Sweet Pea Appetizers

Use firm salami or other fine-grained sausage that is about 2 to 3 inches wide (or you can use the commercially sliced thin salami in packages). Have marketman slice meat with No. 1 or No. 2 machine slicer. Remove casings. Fold slices in halves, keeping back part a little higher. Fold slices in quarters, pressing together firmly to prevent opening. Spread 2-inch rounds of rye (or other bread) with plain or Anchovy Butter (page 79). Pipe a bulb of cream cheese with No. 27 star tube on top, front part. Place folded meat over cheese on breads, pressing down well to keep it in place and prevent opening. At once pipe a cheese rosette bottom center of sweet pea with No. 27 tube, and a leaf on each side with No. 65 or 67 leaf tube. Refrigerate at once, preferably in a covered container if made in advance. May be made many hours in advance if properly stored.

Sardines on Toast

Use edges of bread left after cutting out centers for hors d'oeuvres. Cut uniform long strips, leaving crusts on. Toast in oven until well dried out and golden brown. Place a small sardine on each strip, decorate with a dab of mayonnaise, a strip of pimiento, and parsley.

Italian Tomato-Tuna Fish Appetizers

Attractive firm plum tomatoes, or regular small firm tomatoes
Salt
Black pepper
6½-ounce can tuna fish (mashed with fork if in large pieces)

2 tablespoons fine-chopped fresh green onion and tops
¼ cup fine-chopped Italian finochio (Pascal celery may be used)
¼ cup Italian Dressing (page 368), more or less

Slice plum tomatoes in halves lengthwise. Remove seeds and part of pulp, leaving a thick wall. If using regular tomatoes, cut each into 4 or 6 wedges, depending on size of tomato. Remove seeds and part of pulp. Drain well. Sprinkle inside of tomatoes with little salt and black pepper. Combine all other ingredients and blend well. Fill tomatoes, having them slightly rounded and smooth. Sprinkle tops lightly with paprika and garnish one end with sprig of parsley.

Shrimp-Pineapple Appetizers

Cut a fresh pineapple in halves lengthwise. With a small sharp knife cut out meat of pineapple in chunks as large as possible. Then scoop out rest of pineapple, leaving a medium-thick wall. Place the 2 pineapple halves in center of a large platter. Fill them with Special Dressing for Seafood Fruit Appetizers. Surround pineapple shells with chunks of pineapple and shrimp held together with a frilled or plain toothpick. Cut pineapple in pieces about ½ inch thick and 1 inch square. Use medium-size shrimp, having shrimp at bottom. Canned pineapple may be used when fresh is not available.

Shrimp- or Lobster-Melon Appetizers

Cut a fresh melon in halves and proceed same as for Shrimp-Pineapple Appetizer.

Special Dressing for Seafood Fruit Appetizers

To each cup of mayonnaise, add about ½ cup commercial sour cream, and a little juice of red maraschino cherries, or liquid from beets. Serve very cold.

Glazed Shrimp Farci

1 pound raw shrimp, large size is best (cook gently about 5 minutes, peel and devein if necessary; refrigerate until ready to be stuffed)
1 recipe Tart Dressing (below)
1 tablespoon plain gelatin, combined with ⅓ cup cold water (stir and let stand several minutes until thick, then dissolve over simmering water)
½ pound soft cream cheese, most of it colored green and a little of it colored pink
About 20 bread rounds cut with 2-inch cutter (or smaller if using small shrimp)

Pour Tart Dressing over cooked shrimp and let stand several hours in refrigerator.

With No. 27 star tube and green cheese, pipe rosette border in open end of shrimp, holding tube as close to shrimp as possible. Place shrimp on cake rack and refrigerate about 30 minutes or until cheese feels firm. When dressing is consistency of a thin egg white, place shrimp on rack and pour glaze. It may be necessary to cover them a second time if glaze is too thin. Keep shrimp on cake rack and refrigerate a few minutes. Pick up shrimp carefully with a small spatula and place them on rounds of bread, or round crackers, or melba toast, that have been spread lightly with anchovy paste. Last, with No. 24 star tube and pink cheese, pipe a rosette on large end or in opening of shrimp, and with No. 65 leaf tube, pipe leaves on each side with green cheese. Keep cold until ready to serve. Very attractive and delicious.

To Make Glaze. Drain shrimp, reserving dressing. To dressing add dissolved gelatin. Add a *tiny* drop of red and yellow coloring and put aside to thicken.

Tart Dressing

1 cup water combined with 2 tablespoons cider vinegar
1 teaspoon sugar
¾ teaspoon salt
1 small clove garlic, cut into small pieces, or ¼ teaspoon garlic salt

Combine all ingredients.

Stuffed Dill Pickle Appetizers

Cut 2 large dill pickles into several sections crosswise and scoop out centers very carefully with slender paring knife. Melt 1 tablespoon butter, add about 1 teaspoon minced onion and minced parsley, and about ¼ pound of smoked liver sausage that has been mashed with a fork. Cook together several minutes and then add center of the pickle that was scooped out. When cool, pack mixture firmly into pickles, wrap in wax paper, and allow to stand in refrigerator several hours. Cut crosswise into about ⅓-inch slices, place over small rounds of buttered rye bread. Garnish with parsley.

Sardine Crescents

Remove bones from sardines, or use boneless sardines. Mash with fork until pasty. Add a little lemon or onion juice. Cut unsliced white or dark bread lengthwise and then into crescent shapes with cutter. Toast bread, if desired, until thoroughly dry. Spread sardine paste rather thick over the center of the crescent, bringing it down thinner at the edges. Select very small leaves from a bunch of watercress or parsley and press the tiny short stems into sardine paste near both ends. Sprinkle tops with sieved hard-cooked egg whites, then egg yolks and a dash of paprika.

Switzerland Anchovy Appetizers

3 level tablespoons all-purpose flour
2 tablespoons melted butter
1 cup milk
About 1 teaspoon salt
¼ teaspoon pepper
¼ pound Swiss cheese, coarse-shredded

4 anchovies, cut into very small pieces
Very light dry bread crumbs (almost white)
2 eggs beaten well with a fork and combined with 2 teaspoons water
Fat for frying pan

Add flour to melted butter, then the milk slowly. Add salt and pepper. Cook until thick, and simmer about 5 minutes. Let sauce stand until luke-warm, stirring occasionally. Add cheese and anchovies. Blend thoroughly. Refrigerate until firm, at least 1 hour. May be prepared and refrigerated a day in advance.

Pick up 1 level tablespoonful at a time, drop into light dry bread crumbs and shape into balls. Dip into egg and then into crumbs. Dip into egg a second time and into crumbs again, rolling in palms of hands. Let stand at least 15 minutes before deep-frying at 350° F. about 2 minutes, or until golden brown and crisp. These appetizers may be egged and crumbed several hours in advance. In this case, keep them covered with wax paper in refrigerator. To serve, insert a plain or frilled toothpick in top of each and serve as soon as possible, or serve in a chafing dish for buffet parties. Serve plain or with a dipping sauce.

Italian Prosciutto and Melon Appetizers

Use thin-sliced Italian prosciutto (other ham can be used). Wrap it around strips of melon (any kind of melon may be used) cut about 1½ inches long and ¾ inch wide. Insert frilled toothpicks through each to hold together, and serve cold. May be prepared hours in advance if refrigerated in a covered container.

▶ CANAPÉ BUTTERS, FILLINGS, SPREADS, AND DIPS ◀

For open-face sandwiches use small round, oval, crescent, diamond, or heart cutters. Dark and white breads or crackers are used. Sandwiches are more palatable if breads are toasted or sautéed in butter or margarine. If sandwiches with very moist fillings are to be made hours in advance, it is better not to toast breads, as they will soften. Simply spread with about ¼ teaspoon canapé butter and then with respective fillings. These untoasted sandwiches may be made a day in advance and kept in refrigerator in boxes lined with wax paper.

It takes about 1 tablespoon of filling for each sandwich. Keep filling slightly rounded in center and spread as smoothly as possible. Shortly before serving, pipe white rosettes and green leaves on colored sandwiches. Make pink, yellow, or orange rosettes on the lighter-colored ones. Pipe some with a simple scroll for variety. Use No. 24 or No. 27 tube for rosettes and scroll, and No. 65 or No. 67 tube for leaves. When ready to serve, arrange attractively on a platter, grouping those of one kind together and placing the groups in alternate rows—or each kind can be served on a separate platter.

Canapé butters are used instead of plain butter to add tanginess to hors d'oeuvres, canapés, and finger sandwiches.

Cheddar Cheese Butter

With electric mixer, beat ½ cup soft cheddar cheese until creamy—about 3 minutes. Add 2 tablespoons soft butter and 2 slices crumbled, crisp-fried bacon. Beat only until thoroughly blended. Add a little salt if necessary.

Garlic and Parsley Butter

With electric beater beat ½ cup firm butter until it has the consistency of whipped cream. Add 2 tablespoons coffee cream, about ¼ teaspoon garlic powder, ¼ teaspoon table salt, and ¼ cup minced parsley.

Pimiento Butter

With electric mixer, beat ½ cup firm butter until it has the consistency of whipped cream. Slowly add ¼ cup canned pimiento that has been put through a sieve or food mill. Add ¼ teaspoon celery salt, ¼ teaspoon onion salt, and ¼ teaspoon table salt. Beat until thoroughly blended.

Anchovy Butter

Beat ½ cup cold, firm butter with electric mixer for several minutes, then add 1 teaspoon anchovy paste, and continue to beat until well blended, but not runny. Chill.

Anchovy Cream Cheese Spread

Beat ½ cup cold, firm cream cheese for several minutes, then add 1 teaspoon anchovy paste. Beat until well blended, but not too soft. Chill.

Whipped Butter or Margarine

Beat very cold, firm butter or margarine with high-speed electric mixer for about 5 minutes, or until it looks like whipped cream. Excellent for spreading on fancy sandwiches, hors d'oeuvres bases, vegetables, and on hot rolls, but do not use in baking cakes.

Anchovy or Sardine Butter

With electric mixer, beat ½ cup firm butter about 3 minutes, or until it has the consistency of whipped cream. Slowly add to butter 2 tablespoons cold coffee cream and 1 tablespoon anchovy or sardine paste. Beat until well blended.

Roquefort or Bleu Cheese Butter

With electric mixer, beat ½ cup firm butter about 3 minutes, or until it has the consistency of whipped cream. Slowly add to butter 2 tablespoons cold coffee cream and ½ cup mashed roquefort or bleu cheese. Beat until well blended.

Horseradish Butter

With electric mixer, beat ½ cup firm butter about 3 minutes, or until it has the consistency of whipped cream. Slowly add to butter about 2 tablespoons cold coffee cream, 3 tablespoons prepared horseradish, and ¼ teaspoon salt. Beat until well blended.

Shrimp, Lobster, or Crab Meat Butter

With electric mixer, beat ½ cup firm butter about 3 minutes, or until it has the consistency of whipped cream. Slowly add to butter 2 tablespoons cold coffee cream and ¼ cup fine-chopped or minced shrimp, lobster, or crab meat. Beat until thoroughly blended.

Pecan Butter

With electric mixer, beat ½ cup firm butter about 3 minutes, or until it has the consistency of whipped cream. Then slowly add ½ cup cream cheese that has been mashed with a fork, 1 cup fine-chopped pecans (may be put through food mill), and ½ teaspoon salt. Beat until thoroughly blended.

Olive Butter

With electric mixer, beat ½ cup firm butter about 3 minutes, or until it has the consistency of whipped cream. Slowly add 2 tablespoons cold coffee cream and 3 tablespoons fine-chopped or minced green pimiento-stuffed olives. Beat until well blended.

Ham or Tongue Butter

With electric mixer, beat ½ cup firm butter about 3 minutes, or until it has the consistency of whipped cream. Slowly add 2 tablespoons cold coffee cream, ¼ cup fine-chopped or minced ham or tongue, and 1 tablespoon prepared horseradish.

Coronation Egg Spread

Hard-cook 4 eggs. When cool, shell and put through a mill or sieve. Bind with a little soft butter, soft cream cheese, or mayonnaise. Season with about ¼ teaspoon prepared mustard, ½ teaspoon vinegar, ¼ teaspoon salt, ⅛ teaspoon garlic salt, a pinch of cayenne pepper. Mix with a fork until blended. Use as desired.

Egg Salad Spread

Hard-cook 4 eggs. Cut up and put through a food mill. Combine with ½ cup minced or fine-chopped celery, 1 tablespoon fine-chopped green onion, 2 strips bacon fried until crisp and cut into small pieces, about ¼ teaspoon salt, and only enough mayonnaise to bind mixture.

Watercress Filling

With electric mixer, beat ½ cup cold cream cheese until light—about 3 minutes. Add ¼ cup fine-chopped, blanched toasted almonds, 2 tablespoons fine-chopped watercress, and ¼ teaspoon salt. Blend well and use as desired.

Anchovy-Walnut Spread

To 1 cup soft cream cheese, add ½ tablespoon anchovy paste, ¼ cup walnuts chopped fine, 1 cup celery cut very fine or minced, 8 small green stuffed olives chopped very fine, and about 1 tablespoon coffee cream, or enough to make of consistency to spread.

Caviar Spread

Add about 1 tablespoon caviar to 4 eggs that have been hard-cooked and put through a food mill or sieve. Season with 1 tablespoon lemon juice, ¼ teaspoon garlic salt, and ⅛ teaspoon table salt. Add about 2 tablespoons coffee cream to make of proper consistency to spread.

Cucumber, Bacon, and Celery Filling

Peel cucumber and chop fine to make 1 cup. Drain. Add ½ cup celery chopped fine, 4 strips bacon fried crisp and cut into small pieces, about ¾ teaspoon salt, a pinch of cayenne pepper, and enough mayonnaise to bind. It is better to use Gelatin Mayonnaise (page 82) to absorb surplus moisture.

Salmon Spread

To 1 cup drained flaked salmon, add 1 tablespoon minced green onion, 2 tablespoons fine-chopped black olives, ⅛ teaspoon garlic salt, and about ¼ cup French dressing to bind. Add a little salt if necessary.

Tuna Fish Spread

To 1 cup mashed tuna fish, add about ¼ cup mayonnaise, 2 tablespoons piccalilli, and 1 tablespoon fine-cut fresh green onion.

Chicken Salad Spread

Combine 1 cup fine-chopped or minced chicken with ½ cup minced celery, 1 tablespoon minced pimiento, 1 tablespoon minced green pepper, and about ⅓ cup mayonnaise to bind.

Ham Salad Spread

To 1 cup cooked minced ham, add ½ cup fine-cut celery, 1 tablespoon minced pimiento, 1 tablespoon minced fresh green onion, and about ⅓ cup mayonnaise to bind.

Crab Meat Spread

Flake 1 cup crab meat, being sure to remove all bones. Add 2 teaspoons capers, 2 tablespoons minced green pepper, a few drops Worcestershire sauce, and only enough French dressing or mayonnaise to make proper consistency for spreading.

Lobster Spread

Chop 1 cup cooked lobster meat (lobster tails may be used for this purpose) as fine as possible. Add 1 tablespoon prepared horseradish, 2 tablespoons black olives cut fine, ½ teaspoon salt, and enough mayonnaise or boiled dressing to bind. One tablespoon chopped chives and ¼ cup fine-chopped celery may be added.

Tongue Spread

To 1 cup minced cooked tongue, add 2 teaspoons prepared mustard, 1 tablespoon capers, and enough mayonnaise to bind (about ¼ cup).

Gelatin Mayonnaise

Combine 1 teaspoon plain gelatin with 2 tablespoons cold water. Stir gently and let stand until thick. When thick, dissolve over simmering water. Add warm gelatin mixture to 1 cup mayonnaise and blend thoroughly. Add required amount to various recipes.

Note. Used in salads and fillings containing celery or when necessary to avoid watery condition.

Green Olive and Sardine Spread

To 1 cup mashed sardines (boneless), add about ¼ cup mayonnaise, ½ tablespoon lemon juice, 2 tablespoons chopped stuffed green olives, and 1 teaspoon grated onion. Mix well.

Sardine and Egg Filling

Combine ½ cup mashed boneless sardines with 2 hard-cooked eggs that have been put through a food mill or sieve. Season with a little salt, a pinch of cayenne, 1 teaspoon lemon juice, and enough French dressing to make proper consistency for spreading. Spread on toasted or sautéed breads, and garnish.

Salmon and Cucumber Filling

Combine ½ cup flaked, cooked salmon with ¼ cup peeled, fine-chopped drained cucumber. Season with 1 tablespoon chopped, fresh green onion, a little salt if necessary, and a pinch of cayenne. Add only enough mayonnaise to make of spreading consistency. Use as desired.

Cheddar Cheese and Ham Spread

Combine ½ cup soft cheddar cheese with ¼ cup minced or fine-chopped ham, ⅛ teaspoon Worcestershire sauce, and about ¼ cup coffee cream, or enough to make proper consistency for spreading.

Cream Cheese and Roquefort Cheese Spread

Mash cheese with fork. To ½ cup of each, add ¼ cup coffee cream, a little at a time, and 2 tablespoons fine-chopped green stuffed olives.

Pimento Cheese Spread

Combine 1 cup soft pimento cheese with 1 tablespoon fine-chopped green onion tops, and 2 strips bacon that have fried until crisp and cut into very small pieces. Add a little coffee cream to make of spreading consistency. A little salt may be added if needed.

Savory Anchovy Filling or Topping

Makes about 18

Beat ½ cup cream cheese until of medium consistency. Add 2 teaspoons cream and 1 teaspoon (or less) anchovy paste, a little at a time, then ¼ cup pecans, chopped coarse or broken with fingers, and about 2 tablespoons chopped green stuffed olives. Fill tiny patty shells and garnish tops with rosette and leaves, or spread about ¼ inch thick on cool toasted split beaten hors d'oeuvres biscuits and garnish top as desired. This is a very delicious, rich concoction, and is especially good served on small bases of melba toast or toasted biscuit before luncheons or dinners. Serve cold.

Paprika Sour Cream Dip

Makes approximately 1 cup

1 cup sour cream
⅛ teaspoon garlic powder
Pinch of ground ginger
½ teaspoon onion powder
Pinch of cayenne pepper

¾ teaspoon salt
2 tablespoons crumbled bleu cheese
¾ teaspoon paprika
Paprika for garnish

Combine first 8 ingredients and beat with a rotary beater. Place in small serving bowl. Garnish top with paprika. Surround with raw vegetable relishes, such as slices of cucumber, radish roses, potato chips, and crackers.

Parmesan Garlic Dip

Serves 4

Two 3-ounce packages white cream cheese (softened)
½ cup cream
¼ cup grated parmesan cheese

2 teaspoons grated onion or ½ teaspoon onion powder
¼ teaspoon garlic powder
1 teaspoon Worcestershire sauce

Gradually add cream to softened cream cheese. Add remaining ingredients and mix well.

Note. If dip is too thick, add more cream until of desired consistency.

Tropical Dip

Serves 4

Blend together until creamy two 3-ounce packages cream cheese and 5 tablespoons mayonnaise. Stir in ½ cup fine-chopped nuts, 1 teaspoon chopped ginger, and ⅓ cup well-drained canned crushed pineapple. Sprinkle surface with chopped mint or paprika.

Roquefort Cream Cheese and Wine Dip

1 pound cream cheese
¼ pound roquefort cheese
¼ cup fine-chopped blanched almonds

About ¼ cup dry sauterne wine
Salt to taste, if needed
Paprika

Blend cream cheese, roquefort, almonds, and wine until smooth. Season with salt to taste. Place cheese dip in round bowl and sprinkle top with paprika.

May be prepared hours in advance and kept in refrigerator. Serve at room temperature.

Sardine Dip

1 can sardines, boned and mashed until pasty
⅓ cup cream cheese
¼ teaspoon hot sauce
¼ cup minced green onion

2 tablespoons cream
About ¼ teaspoon garlic salt
¼ teaspoon celery salt
About ⅓ cup French dressing to make proper consistency

Combine all ingredients, adding French dressing a little at a time, and blend thoroughly. Chill at least 1 hour. Serve in a bowl surrounded with crackers, bread sticks, or potato chips.

Tuna and Egg Dip

1 small can tuna fish, mashed
2 hard-cooked eggs, chopped fine
⅛ teaspoon garlic salt
⅛ teaspoon cayenne pepper

⅛ teaspoon celery salt
¼ cup fine-chopped onion
⅓ cup soft strong cheese
About ½ cup French dressing

Combine all ingredients, adding French dressing slowly to make mixture of proper consistency, and blend thoroughly. Chill at least 1 hour. Serve in a bowl surrounded with crackers, bread sticks, or potato chips.

Crab Meat Dip

1 small package frozen crab meat (or 1 small can)
¼ cup minced green onion
2 hard-cooked eggs, chopped fine

¼ teaspoon cayenne pepper
About ½ teaspoon salt
About ½ cup thick French dressing
1 tablespoon horseradish

Combine all ingredients and blend thoroughly. Chill at least 1 hour. Serve in a bowl surrounded with crackers, bread sticks, or potato chips.

Pimento Cheese Dip

½ cup cream pimento cheese
½ cup ripe olives chopped fine
¼ cup fine-chopped fresh green onion
1 tablespoon lemon juice
¼ teaspoon Worcestershire sauce

About ¼ cup cream, or enough to make dipping consistency
1 tablespoon dry light wine (optional)
About ½ teaspoon salt

Combine all ingredients and blend thoroughly. Chill at least 1 hour. Serve in a bowl surrounded with crackers, bread sticks, or potato chips.

Anchovy Dip

1 small can anchovies, chopped fine
¼ cup stuffed green olives, chopped fine

1 pound, or more, cream cheese
¼ teaspoon hot sauce
About ⅓ cup cream, or enough to form proper consistency

Combine all ingredients and blend thoroughly. Chill at least 1 hour. Serve in a bowl surrounded with crackers, bread sticks, or potato chips.

Liver Paté Dip

4½-ounce can liver pâté
2 tablespoons mayonnaise
2 tablespoons chopped stuffed green olives

1 tablespoon strong prepared mustard
2 tablespoons chopped onion (fresh green preferred)
2 tablespoons cream

Combine all ingredients and blend thoroughly. Chill at least 1 hour. Serve in a bowl surrounded with crackers, bread sticks, or potato chips.

Braunschweiger Dip

1 cup mashed Braunschweiger
2 tablespoons very fine-chopped green stuffed olives
⅛ teaspoon hot sauce
½ cup soft sharp cheese spread

2 tablespoons fine-chopped fresh green onion and stems
1 teaspoon prepared mustard
Enough cream to make proper consistency

Combine all ingredients and beat well until thoroughly blended. Serve in an attractive bowl surrounded with crackers, wafers, melba toast, or potato chips.

Fluffy Cheese Dip

½ pound cream cheese, cold and firm
1-ounce package roquefort or bleu cheese, crumbled into small pieces
Few drops hot sauce
⅛ teaspoon Worcestershire sauce (optional)

About ⅛ teaspoon garlic or onion salt
About ¼ cup coffee cream, more or less, to suit taste
2 tablespoons, more or less, fine-cut chives or green onion stems

With electric mixer, beat cream cheese until of medium consistency, add roquefort cheese and continue to beat about 1 minute. Start adding cream, a tablespoon at a time, and beat after each addition about 1 minute. Mixture should look like heavy whipped cream. Do not overbeat. *It must not be runny.* Season with hot sauce and other ingredients. Fold in chives. Sprinkle top with paprika.

Serve in an attractive bowl, in center of a large round platter, and surround with crisp potato chips or small crackers.

Cucumber and Bacon Dip

1 large cucumber, peeled and chopped very fine (2 cups drained)
8 slices bacon cut in small pieces and fried until crisp, drained
About ¼ cup sour cream
About ¼ cup mayonnaise
About 1½ teaspoons salt
4 hard-cooked eggs, put through a sieve or food mill
1 tablespoon lemon juice
¼ cup minced green onion

Combine all ingredients and blend thoroughly. Serve in an attractive bowl surrounded with crackers, melba toast, or potato chips.

Fondues, Quiches, Hot Dips, Rarebits

▶ FONDUES ◀

Swiss fondue cookery has become very popular in this country and many versions of the classic fondue have been developed in the last few years. While the classic Swiss recipe made with Swiss cheese and wine is undoubtedly the most popular, a beef bourguignon created recently by the French, while not in the strictest sense of the word a fondue, is now sweeping the country, and is served by the most discriminating hostesses everywhere. A third type of fondue that we are including in this section is the chocolate version, served as a dessert. We are also including a delectable American or cheddar cheese fondue for cocktail parties, snacks, etc.

Fondue pots come in a variety of shapes, sizes, and materials. Please follow directions from the manufacturer. Whereas pottery pots can be used for cheese fondue, they should not be used for beef fondue and other foods that are cooked in very hot oil. The constant high heat required for oil cooking would cause pottery pots to crack and break. A metal pot or the newer heavy gauge aluminum alloy with baked enamel finish (that comes in colors) is the most attractive and practical for all fondues, including the cheese. Besides fondue forks, one for each guest, be sure to provide extra regular dinner forks for eating; also small plates, dishes for sauces, and cocktail napkins.

To Serve Fondue

When the fondue is ready, it is placed in the center of the table (a round table is preferable). Then, taking regular turns, each guest spears a cube of bread, meat, or cake on a fondue fork and swirls it into the hot preparation or oil, keeping it in continual motion until the next guest dunks his food. The swirling motion is important, as it keeps the fondue at a good dipping consistency. The food is then transferred to a dinner fork (fondue fork would be too hot to eat from), then the luscious morsels are popped into the mouth, sometimes dipped into a zesty sauce, sometimes not. The fondue must remain hot all the time. If it becomes too thick a small amount of heated wine must be stirred into the mixture to keep it at the right temperature. Never allow wine to boil, never hotter than simmer. Adjust heat accordingly.

A hot beverage may be served with any of the fondues, or the same wine used in preparing the dish may be served. Let your own tastes be your guide.

Choose guests who are likely to enjoy this kind of a party. About 6 are all that can comfortably cook and eat out of one fondue pot.

Cheese for Fondues

Cheeses used in fondues must be well aged or the fondue will be stringy. In Switzerland the minimum aging period is about 4 months, and is often extended to almost a year. Fondues of mildest flavor are made with *emmenthaler* cheese alone, known as Swiss cheese. It has large eyes and is one of the finest used in other cooked dishes. *Gruyère* is also a Swiss cheese (manufactured also in France) but has smaller and sometimes nonexistent eyes. Gruyère is richer in flavor and melts more easily than the emmenthaler. Either may be used alone in fondues, or may be combined. About ¼ cup of grated Italian cheese (parmesan or romano) may be added to the shredded Swiss cheese for additional flavor, but this is not necessary. It is best to cut cheese into small pieces or to shred as it melts more easily and smoothly than when it is grated. Remember to use only natural Swiss and gruyère cheeses, that are properly aged, for best results, and not the pasteurized kind.

Liqueur and Wine for Fondues

Kirsch (cherry brandy) is the liqueur commonly used by the Swiss in making fondue, but any kind of liqueur may be used, or it may be omitted entirely. The wine adds sufficient flavor to any fondue. *Use only dry white wines, preferably of the rhine or chablis type.*

Bread for Fondues

Have ready cut in advance 1-inch square cubes of Italian or French bread, with some crust left on one side. This is very important. Keep cubes wrapped until needed. Each guest spears a piece of bread on a fondue fork through soft part of the bread first, then through the crust so that he does not lose his bread in the preparation. Cubes of bread must be swirled in the fondue to keep it at the right texture.

Meat for Fondues

Have all ingredients measured in advance and stored on a tray. Meat cubes must be dry and in room temperature at least ½ hour in advance. Dry the pieces of meat on paper toweling. Wet or very cold meat will cause spattering and cooling of the fat. For meat and similar fondues, have pot about ⅔ filled with oil. Heat it in a 2-quart saucepan directly on top of range to about 400° F., then carefully transfer to fondue pot and place it on stand in center of table. Adjust flame on fuel container to maintain oil temperature. Spear beef cubes with long-handled fondue forks. Immerse in hot oil long enough to cook to degree of doneness desired, about 20 to 30 seconds for rare, 40 to 60 seconds for well done. Cool slightly before transferring with a second cold fork to small plate. Serve with sauce, etc. See individual recipe.

Classic Swiss Cheese Fondue

Makes about 3 cups

2 cups of any dry white wine (preferably of the rhine or chablis type)

1 pound aged natural Swiss cheese, coarsely shredded or diced into small pieces (you can use half gruyère cheese)

2 tablespoons all-purpose flour

2 tablespoons cornstarch, combined with ¼ cup cool dry white wine until smooth

About ½ teaspoon salt

⅛ teaspoon nutmeg

⅛ teaspoon pepper

⅛ teaspoon garlic or onion salt

Italian or French bread cubes, cut into about 1-inch squares, leaving some crust on one side (important)

2 tablespoons any dry brandy added to the 2 cups dry white wine, but not necessary

Most recipes suggest that you pour wine into fondue pot and set it over low heat on top of range, but we find it is easier and safer (and prevents scorching) if you prepare it in a 2-quart saucepan, directly over low heat of range, then pour it into fondue pot. When wine begins to simmer (never boil), temperature about 185° to 200° F., add cheese tossed with flour, handful at a time, stirring constantly with a long heavy spoon, in one direction only (which helps to prevent curdling) until cheese begins to melt. As soon as cheese appears soft and melted, add the cornstarch combined with the ¼ cup cool wine, and continue to cook and stir briskly until smooth and thickened. Then simmer about 3 minutes; do not boil. Add seasonings and blend well. Taste, and season further if needed.

Remove pot from range, and pour preparation into fondue pot on stand, over low flame to prevent cheese from becoming stringy and scorching. Adjust heat as necessary.

This will serve 6 as an appetizer, or 3 as an entrée.

To Serve. Each guest impales a cube of bread (follow general directions, page 88) on fondue fork thrust through soft part, then through crust, and swirls it in the fondue until the next guest is ready to dunk his food. The hot food must be released from fondue fork with a cold dinner fork and cooled slightly before eating, or it may be transferred to small plates.

If fondue becomes too thick toward end, add a little heated wine and stir well, or increase heat slightly. Toward the very end some of the melted cheese will form a brown crust at the bottom of the utensil. When that happens, keep heat as low as possible to prevent utensil from cracking. The cheese crust can easily be lifted out with a fork. It is considered a delicacy, and can be eaten.

American or Cheddar Cheese Fondue

1 pound of soft American cheese food or spread (or cheddar cheese), cut in small pieces	⅛ teaspoon nutmeg
	⅛ teaspoon white pepper
	⅛ teaspoon onion salt
2 tablespoons butter	About 2 tablespoons or more any kind
½ cup hot half and half cream	dry light wine

In a 2-quart saucepan combine the cut-up cheese, butter, and cream and set over low heat on top of range, stirring continuously until completely melted and quite warm. Now stir in seasonings and the wine, blend well. Remove from heat and pour into fondue pot. Place on stand, over low heat, adjusting flame to prevent scorching. Test consistency of preparation with a cube of French or Italian bread on long fondue fork, swirling it in for a few seconds. Lift out and observe consistency. If too thick, add a little more warm wine or warm cream. Serve as suggested in general directions (page 88).

Beef Fondue Bourguignon

As an entrée allow at least ⅓ pound of well-trimmed beef tenderloin for each person, cut into about 1-inch squares. Refrigerate meat, loosely covered with wax paper (do not wrap tightly) until about ½ hour before preparing. Meat may be marinated in a wine marinade, then drained well, and dried with paper toweling to prevent spattering. Please read general directions (page 90).

In a 1- or 2-quart heavy saucepan heat about 2 cups of oil directly on top of range to about 400° F. Test temperature with a thermometer for best results. Now pour hot oil into fondue pot and carefully place it on its stand in center of table. Adjust heat to keep oil hot, but do not allow fat to smoke at any time. For additional flavor (but not necessary) a small amount of clarified butter (page 328) may be added to the hot oil.

To Serve. Spear beef cubes with long-handled fondue fork. Immerse into hot oil long enough to cook to degree of doneness desired, about ½ to 1 minute. This beef is best served rare or medium. Release hot meat from fondue fork with a cold dinner fork onto a dish. Serve with Sauce Bearnaise (page 341), Sauce Tartar (page 334), chili sauce, Special Hostess Sauce (page 334), or as desired. As a main dish, you can serve crusty French or Italian garlic bread, a tossed salad, and French fried potatoes, if desired.

Be sure to have medium-size plates, cocktail napkins, and sauces on the table for each guest in advance. Any hot beverage may be served with fondue, or you can serve dry wine.

Swiss Milk Chocolate Fondue

1 pound Swiss-type milk chocolate, cut into small pieces (dark sweet chocolate may be used)
⅔ cup whipping cream (combine with ¼ cup milk, then heat until quite warm, but not too hot)

1 teaspoon vanilla
2 tablespoons or more brandy or rum (optional)

Combine cut-up chocolate, warm cream and milk, and vanilla in a 2-quart saucepan, and place it over very, very low heat of range. Stir preparation continuously and quickly until chocolate is melted and quite hot. Now let simmer about 5 minutes until it thickens slightly. Do not let mixture boil at any time as it will change texture of chocolate. Best keep temperature of melted chocolate below 210° F. Add the brandy or rum, if desired. Stir well, pour into fondue pot, and place it on stand over very, very low flame. Heat must be adjusted often to prevent scorching.

To Serve. Each guest impales a 1-inch cube of Angel Food (page 570) or Sponge Cake (page 572) (do not use butter cakes) on fondue fork, and swirls it in the Chocolate Fondue until the next guest is ready to dunk his cake. Release the chocolate-dipped cake with a cool fork, etc. Whole large marshmallows, pineapple chunks, banana chunks, and other foods may be dipped in Chocolate Fondue.

Additional Fondue Recipes

Any of the hot dips and rarebits given in this section can be served as fondues by making a slight adjustment. They are all very delectable preparations for snack and cocktail parties. Increase liquid in these dip recipes if using as fondues, to make proper consistency. A little wine may be added to the basic preparation. Test consistency with a cube of bread, etc.

▶ QUICHES ◀

Basic Quiche Lorraine

1 partially baked 9-inch pie shell (see directions below)

¼ pound Swiss cheese (1¼ cups), coarsely shredded and combined with 1 tablespoon flour

½ pound thinly sliced bacon, cooked until medium crisp (not too dry) drained, leaving 2 tablespoons of drippings, and cut into ½-inch pieces

3 large whole eggs (to measure ¾ cupful) beaten with fluffy beater ½ minute

2 cups rich milk or half cream (do not use skim milk), warm

⅛ teaspoon nutmeg

¾ teaspoon salt

¼ teaspoon pepper

¼ teaspoon garlic or onion powder

Pie Shell

Prepare pie shell with 1¼ cups sifted all-purpose flour, ½ cup shortening, ½ teaspoon baking powder, ¾ teaspoon salt, and about ¼ cup cold milk or water. Mix as per general directions for Basic Pie Dough (page 732), and roll into 13½-inch circle. Place into 9-inch pie plate, and crimp edges. Grease the outside of an 8-inch glass pie plate with ½ teaspoon shortening, and place it inside of larger plate lined with pastry. This inner plate will keep crust smooth and prevent pastry from buckling. Prebake crust for about 15 minutes at 400° F. Remove from oven, and carefully lift out inner plate. Now place a strip of foil that measures 34 inches long and 2½ inches wide around edge of plate to prevent crust from overbrowning, holding it in place with a pin.

Combine shredded cheese and cut up-cooked bacon, and place on bottom of partially baked crust. Combine all other ingredients in the order given, blending them well until evenly mixed. Pour most of this preparation over bacon and cheese. Place plate into preheated 425° F. oven center rack. With a cup or small saucepan pour in rest of preparation. This is done to prevent spillage onto crust.

Bake quiche at 425° F. for about 20 to 30 minutes, or until filling puffs and is lightly browned, testing it in center with tip of paring knife after 20 minutes. If knife comes out clean, remove quiche from oven. If top is not brown, place it under broiler for a minute or two, but watch very closely to prevent burning.

Let quiche cool on a cake rack for at least ½ hour. Should be served warm, but not too hot, and can be served cool. Cut into wedges, and serve with coffee or cocktails, etc.

Quiches may be baked in advance and refrigerated. To serve, cut into serving portions right in plate, then reheat in preheated 400° F. oven for about 15 minutes. Let cool for about 5 minutes before serving. May be frozen for about two weeks if properly wrapped. Defrost before reheating same way.

Mushroom Quiche Lorraine

1 partially baked 9-inch pie shell (prepared as per general directions above)

3- or 4-ounce can chopped mushrooms, drained well, save liquid (*or better, use* ½ pound fresh sliced mushrooms), sautéed about 5 minutes in 2 tablespoons butter

¼ pound (1¼ cups) coarsely shredded Swiss or gruyère cheese

1 cup warm whipping cream, combined with ¼ cup mushroom liquid or water

2 large or 3 medium eggs to measure ½ cupful, beaten with fluffy beater ½ minute

4 slices thin bacon, pan-fried until medium crisp, drained, cut into ½-inch pieces

¼ cup finely chopped green onion and ¼ cup chopped onion stems, sautéed in 2 tablespoons butter for about 2 minutes

½ teaspoon salt

⅛ teaspoon pepper

⅛ teaspoon garlic or onion powder

About 1 teaspoon hot sauce (optional)

Prepare same as Basic Quiche Lorraine (page 93). Bake 25 to 30 minutes, test.

Ham and Gruyère Cheese Quiche Lorraine

1 partially baked 9-inch pie shell (prepared as per general directions, page 93)

1 cup cooked ham, cut in ¼-inch cubes, lightly packed (⅓ pound)

1¼ cups coarsely shredded gruyère cheese, lightly measured (¼ pound)

1 tablespoon instant onion, minced or flaked (or 2 tablespoons finely chopped sautéed onion)

About ¼ to ½ teaspoon salt

⅛ teaspoon pepper

¼ cup or less grated Italian cheese

½ teaspoon hot sauce (optional)

3 large whole eggs, well beaten with wire whisk about ½ minute (¾ cup)

1½ cups rich milk (not skim), or half cream, warm

Prepare partially baked 9-inch crust. Remove from oven, let cool slightly, remove inner plate. Place strip of foil around rim, as suggested in general directions to prevent overbrowning. Combine cut-up ham, shredded cheese, and all of seasonings in a bowl, and pour them into bottom of shell. Now combine well-beaten eggs and milk, blend well, and pour into crust over other ingredients. Bake in a preheated 425° F. oven about 25 to 30 minutes, or until filling puffs and is lightly browned. May be tested by inserting blade of paring knife in center of filling. If comes out clean, quiche is done. Remove from oven, let stand on cake rack, for about ½ hour, or until cooler if desired. Cut and serve.

Crab Meat Quiche Lorraine

1 partially baked 9-inch pie shell (prepared as per general directions, page 93)

1 cup cooked crab meat (frozen or canned, or fresh, about 6 to 7 ounces), cut in about ½-inch pieces, then sautéed in 2 tablespoons butter for ½ minute only

1¼ cups coarsely shredded Swiss cheese (¼ pound)

1 cup cool dairy sour cream, combined with 1 cup warm rich milk (do not use skim milk)

3 large whole eggs (¾ cupful)

2 tablespoons dry sherry or other dry wine (optional)

⅛ teaspoon nutmeg

1 teaspoon salt

¼ teaspoon pepper

¼ teaspoon onion salt

1 teaspoon hot sauce

Prepare and bake like Basic Quiche Lorraine (page 93). Bake about 25 to 30 minutes and test.

Shrimp or Lobster Quiche

Prepare same as Crab Meat Quiche, using 1 cup chopped cooked shrimp or cooked lobster meat. Bake about 25 to 30 minutes and test.

▶ HOT DIPS ◀

Hot Chicken Dip or Puffs

¼ cup minced onion

½ cup minced fresh mushrooms

¼ cup butter

⅓ cup flour, unsifted

2 cups chicken stock or milk

About 1 teaspoon, or more, salt

¼ teaspoon pepper

½ cup medium chopped toasted almonds

2 cups cooked chicken, finely chopped

½ cup finely chopped green onion

Sauté the onion and mushrooms in the hot butter for 5 or 6 minutes. Add the flour and blend well. Add chicken stock or milk slowly. Add seasonings. Cook until thick, then simmer about 5 minutes. Fold in the chopped toasted almonds and cooked chicken just before serving. Serve in a chafing dish (sprinkle top with ½ cup finely chopped green onion) with crackers, melba toast, etc. If too thick, add a little stock or milk. Or allow mixture to become cold, then spread 1 level measuring tablespoonful on 2-inch rounds of bread, leaving about ¼ inch around bread uncovered with filling. Bake in a 450° F. oven about 5 or 6 minutes, then broil at same temperature for 2 or 3 minutes.

Hot Shrimp Dip or Snack

2 tablespoons minced onion
2 tablespoons butter
2 tablespoons flour
1 cup warm milk
1 cup cooked shrimp, finely chopped

¼ cup sharp soft cheese
About ⅛ teaspoon hot sauce
¼ cup finely chopped fresh green onion stems
Salt (optional)

Cook the minced onion and the butter for several minutes. Add flour and blend well. Add milk slowly. Cook until thick, then add the shrimp, cheese, hot sauce, and fresh green onion stems and a little salt if needed. Simmer about 5 minutes just before serving in a chafing dish, surrounded with crackers, melba toast, potato chips, etc.

Hot Mushroom Dip

1 pound fresh mushrooms, washed, drained, chopped very fine
⅓ cup butter
2 tablespoons butter
¼ cup finely minced onion

¼ cup flour
2 cups warm milk
About 1 teaspoon, or less, salt
⅛ teaspoon cayenne pepper
2 tablespoons parmesan cheese

Sauté the chopped mushrooms in ⅓ cup hot butter for about 5 or 6 minutes and put aside. In a separate saucepan melt 2 tablespoons butter and add onion. Cook for several minutes, add the flour and blend well. Add milk slowly, and then the seasonings and cheese. Cook until thick. Add sautéed mushrooms and simmer altogether about 5 minutes just before serving Serve in a chafing dish or attractive heated bowl, surrounded with crackers, melba toast, or as desired.

Lobster or Crab Meat Thermidor Dip

¼ cup finely chopped onion
¼ cup butter
¼ cup flour
2½ cups warm milk
⅛ teaspoon cayenne pepper
⅛ teaspoon dry mustard
About 1¼ teaspoons salt
¼ pound fresh mushrooms, chopped fine and sautéed in 1 tablespoon butter

2 cups cooked lobster or crab meat, chopped medium (lobster tails may be used)
¼ cup grated parmesan cheese
2 tablespoons light dry wine (optional)
½ cup finely chopped onion (optional)

Sauté the onion in hot butter for about 5 minutes, add flour and blend well. Add the warm milk and seasonings and simmer about 5 minutes. Add mushrooms, lobster or crab meat, grated cheese, and wine and cook another 5 minutes just before serving. Serve in chafing dish with crackers, melba toast, etc. Sprinkle top with ½ cup finely chopped onion, if desired.

Italian Tomato Dip

2 tablespoons chopped onion
2 tablespoons butter
½ cup ham or salami, finely chopped
1 cup chopped fresh or drained canned tomato
Pinch of baking soda

⅛ teaspoon oregano
⅛ teaspoon black pepper
¼ teaspoon salt
2 tablespoons Italian grated cheese
1 egg, slightly beaten

Sauté onion in the butter for several minutes, add the ham or salami and all other ingredients except the slightly beaten egg. Cook about 5 minutes, then add the egg and continue to cook and stir for another minute or two until thick. Serve hot in a chafing dish surrounded with toasted garlic French bread, cut thin.

▶ RAREBITS ◀

Sardine Rarebit

Serves 4

2 tablespoons butter
½ pound cut-up American cheese food
6 to 8 tablespoons hot cream
⅛ teaspoon salt
½ teaspoon Worcestershire sauce
¼ teaspoon dry mustard

1 tablespoon madeira or sauterne
1 egg yolk
4 slices toast
2 cans sardines (3-ounce size)
Paprika

Melt butter in a chafing dish or saucepan, using low heat. Add cheese, stirring until melted; then slowly add cream, salt, Worcestershire sauce, mustard, and wine. Continue to stir until cheese is completely melted and cream is blended with cheese. Last, add egg yolk and blend well.

Serve hot on slices of toast that are topped with about 6 to 8 sardines. Sprinkle paprika on top of rarebit sauce.

Tomato Rarebit on Toast with Anchovies

Serves 6

3 large fresh tomatoes
2 tablespoons oil
2 tablespoons fresh lemon juice
1 teaspoon salt
⅛ teaspoon ground black pepper

½ cup shredded cheddar cheese
2 tablespoons fine dry bread crumbs
¼ cup butter or margarine
6 rounds hot buttered toast
Anchovies for garnish

Wash tomatoes, cut into halves, and place on a baking sheet, cut side up. Sprinkle with oil, lemon juice, salt, and black pepper. Place under broiler 5 minutes. Sprinkle with cheese and bread crumbs. Dot with butter or margarine. Place under broiler to brown, 2 to 3 minutes.

Serve on rounds of hot buttered toast. Garnish as desired with anchovies.

Spanish Welsh Rarebit

Serves 6

¼ cup fine-chopped green pepper
¼ cup green onions chopped fine
¼ cup hot butter
2 tablespoons flour
1 cup warm milk
½ pound American cheese food, cut into small pieces

1½ cups tomatoes (fresh or canned), crushed into small pieces
¼ teaspoon baking soda
2 eggs slightly beaten with a fork
About 1½ teaspoons salt
½ teaspoon dry mustard
⅛ teaspoon cayenne pepper

In a 2- or 3-quart saucepan, sauté green pepper and onion in butter for about 5 minutes. Add flour and blend until smooth. Slowly add milk. Cook, stirring constantly, until smooth and thick. Add cheese and keep over low flame, stirring constantly, until melted.

Heat tomatoes in a small saucepan, add soda, and simmer about 5 minutes. Add tomatoes to cheese mixture, a little a time, stirring constantly. Add ½ cup of this hot mixture to eggs and blend well, then return egg mixture to complete preparation. Add seasonings, and simmer about 5 minutes, stirring continuously.

Serve at once in a chafing dish, on toast, with crackers, or as desired.

Shrimp and Cheese Rarebit

Serves 4

2 tablespoons butter or margarine
3 tablespoons flour
¼ cup cream
½ cup liquid drained from canned mushrooms
½ cup water
¼ cup shredded American cheese

¼ cup chili sauce
¼ teaspoon Worcestershire sauce
3- or 4-ounce can drained mushroom stems and pieces
5-ounce can drained shrimp
3 cups cooked rice (optional)
Parsley (optional)

Melt butter in a 2-quart saucepan. Gradually stir in flour; then add cream, mushroom liquid, and water, and cook and stir over medium heat until thickened. Add cheese, chili sauce, Worcestershire sauce, mushrooms, and shrimp, and cook over low heat until cheese is melted.

If you prefer, serve shrimp mixture over warm rice and garnish with sprigs of parsley or parsley flakes.

Frankfurter Rarebit

Serves 4

6 slices bacon, cut into small pieces
¼ cup bacon drippings
1 pound frankfurters, cut into ¼-inch pieces
½ cup chopped onion
¼ cup chopped celery
2¼ cups warm milk

⅓ cup all-purpose flour
½ cup shredded American cheese
½ teaspoon salt
½ teaspoon garlic salt
1 tablespoon prepared mustard
Toast (optional)
Tomatoes, sliced (optional)

Sautè bacon until crisp. Remove from pan and drain, being sure to save ¼ cup bacon drippings. Pour drippings into a large skillet and sauté frankfurters, onion, and celery for 5 minutes. Combine milk with flour and add to frankfurters in skillet. Cook until thick, about 5 minutes after simmering begins, stirring constantly. Add cheese, seasonings, and mustard, and continue to cook 5 more minutes. Last, add reserved bacon and mix well.

Serve from a chafing dish or on toast with sliced tomatoes.

Ham Rarebit

Serves 4 to 6

¼ cup butter
2 tablespoons flour
1 teaspoon dry mustard
1 cup coffee cream
2 teaspoons Worcestershire sauce

1 cup shredded cheddar cheese
2 tablespoons madeira or sauterne
1 cup diced cooked ham
Buttered toast
Paprika

Melt butter; add flour and dry mustard. Stir to make smooth paste. Add cream a small amount at a time, then Worcestershire sauce, cheese, and wine. Continue to stir until cheese is completely melted and cream is blended with cheese. Last, add ham and heat a few minutes.

Ham Rarebit may be prepared in a saucepan or skillet and then transferred to a chafing dish. Serve on buttered toast and sprinkle with paprika.

Welsh Rarebit

½ pound soft American cheese, coarse-shredded or cut into small pieces
1 tablespoon butter
About 2 to 4 tablespoons hot cream
¼ teaspoon salt

1 tablespoon madeira or sauterne
½ teaspoon Worcestershire sauce
¼ teaspoon dry mustard
1 egg yolk

Combine cheese and butter in top of double boiler, but directly over flame. Stir vigorously until cheese is completely melted. Now place over hot water and add cream, about 1 tablespoon at a time, stirring vigorously, seasonings, and wine. Last, add egg yolk, and blend well.

Serve over freshly toasted bread or crackers as a snack or for brunch.

Welsh Rarebit Open-Face Sandwiches

Welsh Rarebit is delectable when poured onto sliced chicken, ham, or seafood open-face toasted sandwiches. Sprinkle top with a little paprika, and place under broiler a few minutes to brown lightly.

▶ *Soups and Chowders*

MEATS OF ALL KINDS (EXCEPT PORK) AND FOWL ARE USED IN THE PREPARATION of soup stock. A thin or clear soup, such as a consommé or bouillon, is ordinarily served with a heavy meal, but if the meal is light, it is better to supplement it with one of the cream soups. Hot soups, to be palatable, must be served piping hot in heated soup dishes or bouillon cups.

▶ STOCKS ◀

Stocks are the basis of many soups and sauces, and are also used to enrich many other foods. We are including in this chapter easily prepared, flavorful Brown Meat Stock, White Meat Stock, White Poultry Stock, and Fish Stock, or Fumet. They may be prepared in advance and refrigerated for several days, or frozen for several months.

If you prefer, you can substitute canned beef bouillon, canned chicken consommé, or bottled clam juice for the homemade stocks. Today these convenient products are used by most homemakers and even by some of the leading chefs. However, while these substitutes are satisfactory, they do not equal the perfection of a well-prepared homemade stock.

Instant bouillon cubes and dehydrated stocks can also be used, according to directions in recipes or on labels of the products.

Brown Meat Stock

2 pounds shin of beef or boneless beef
Butter or margarine
Unsalted shortening
About 8 cups cold water
3 cloves
1 small bay leaf
¼ teaspoon thyme

¼ teaspoon marjoram
¼ teaspoon whole or crushed black pepper
About 1 tablespoon salt
¼ cup chopped parsley
1 medium chopped onion
¼ cup chopped celery

Cut meat in about 2-inch pieces, dry it well, and brown it thoroughly in a small amount of butter or margarine combined with a small amount of unsalted shortening, to prevent scorching. Cover meat with the 8 cups of cold water, and heat slowly to the boiling point. Tie seasonings in a

cheesecloth bag and add to the meat and water with the chopped vegetables. Partially cover pot leaving an open space for the steam to escape.
Simmer (do not boil) slowly for about 3 hours. Skim from time to time
if it is to be used as a clear stock. Do not skim if to be used for the family-
style plain thick soups, as the scum contains valuable nutrients.

Note. In preparing meat stock, much of the flavor of the meat is retained
in the cooking liquor. The meat still has some flavor and food value and
is delicious when served with horseradish, or any other highly seasoned
sauce.

White Meat Stock

Use about 2 or 3 pounds of lean, raw veal shank meat, or boneless veal.
Some cracked veal bones may be included. Do not brown meat for a white
stock. Follow directions given on page 101 for Brown Meat Stock, using the
same seasonings and vegetables.

White Poultry Stock

You can use about 5 pounds of chicken wings, necks, bones, and giblets
of raw chicken, in addition to a pound of veal shank. Or you may use
a whole or parts of a stewing hen, along with the seasonings and the
vegetables. The chicken may be removed when tender, and the stock
simmered for a longer time. Follow cooking directions given for Brown
Meat Stock (page 101).

Fish Stock (or Fumet)

Fish stock does not keep as well as other stocks in the refrigerator for
more than a day or two. It is best to prepare it as needed unless it is frozen.
The less expensive lean fish is best for this purpose. Do not use oily fish.
Instead of raw fish you can use bottled clam juice.

About 2 pounds of lean raw fish (or use 2 cups of bottled clam juice)	¼ cup chopped parsley stems (not the leaves)
6 cups water if using raw fish (4 cups if using bottled clam juice)	⅓ cup fresh mushroom stems
1 cup dry wine	1 bay leaf
1 medium sliced onion	2 teaspoons lemon juice
	1 sliced carrot

Combine all ingredients in a large stainless steel saucepan. Bring slowly
to the boiling point. Simmer about 2 hours if using raw fish; cook only
30 minutes if using bottled clam juice. Strain and clarify according to general directions. Clam juice is very salty, and may not require additional

salt. Taste and season as needed. Fish stock is excellent for fish veloute sauce, and is excellent for poaching fish, etc. Use as indicated in recipes.

Clarified (Clear) Stock

As soon as stock is done, strain it, and let cool. Taste for seasoning before it is clarified. Refrigerate cool stock until very cold and all of fat rises to top. Remove all fat from surface, and pour stock to be clarified into stew-pan. Allow the whites and shell of 1 egg for each quart of stock. Beat whites a few sconds and combine them with the crumbled shell and 2 tea-spoons of water, and add to the cold stock to be clarified. Place over moderate heat and stir constantly only until boiling begins. Shut off heat and let stand about 20 minutes *without stirring*. The egg whites will now have risen to the surface.

Line a colander with a double-thickness cheese cloth wrung out in hot water, and place colander over a deep bowl so that bottom will remain above surface of the clarified liquid. Very gently ladle the stock and egg whites into colander so that it drains through the cloth. Let cool uncovered, then store in a covered container in refrigerator, or may be frozen. Use as indicated in recipes for consommés, aspics, etc.

Meat Essence or Meat Glaze

This is a very useful preparation to have on hand, and can be made by reducing to a syrup-like consistency any of the stocks listed above. Keep stock over medium heat in the beginning and as the essence becomes thicker, gradually reduce the heat. When it coats a wooden spoon and has a syrupy consistency, it is done. Pour it into small sterilized jar and refrigerate. One quart of stock will reduce to about ½ cupful, but a tea-spoon or less of this highly concentrated glaze stirred into a sauce or soup will enhance the flavor greatly. Homemade essence has a much better flavor than the commercial meat extracts. (A good brand of meat or beef extract may be used as a substitute. Instant bouillon and bouillon cubes are often used also.)

▶ HEARTY SOUPS ◀

French Onion Soup

For each cup of clear stock, use about ½ cup onion, sliced thin in rings or lengthwise, sautéed in ½ tablespoon butter. Allow to cook until delicately brown. Add stock to onion. Cover, and simmer about 15 minutes or until onions are tender. Butter both sides of 2-inch rounds of white bread (very attractive if cut with daisy cutter), and dip into grated parmesan cheese. Place under broiler until golden brown on both sides. Place 1 round in each soup plate, and pour boiling onion soup over bread. Sprinkle top with very fine-chopped parsley, and serve at once. Add pinch of nutmeg to each cupful of onion soup just before serving. It is not necessary to clear stock for onion soup.

Quick Onion Soup

To ¾ cup boiling water, add 1 teaspoon instant bouillon or 1 bouillon cube, a pinch of nutmeg, and 1 small sliced onion sautéed a few minutes. Cook gently about 15 minutes. Place cheese crouton in each plate, sprinkle with parsley, etc.

Gumbo Chicken Soup

Serves 6 to 8

½ cup chopped fresh green onions
½ cup fine-chopped green pepper
1 cup tomatoes, fresh or canned
⅛ teaspoon baking soda

1 can okra or fresh okra cooked until tender (20 minutes) and cut up
1 full recipe White Poultry Stock (page 102)
½ cup, or more, cooked rice

Sauté onions until delicately brown. Then add green pepper, tomatoes, baking soda, and okra. Cook all together 5 minutes and then add it to poultry stock. Simmer together about 20 minutes, adding rice 5 minutes before end of cooking time.

Quick Vegetable Meat Ball Soup (Italian Style)

1 recipe Meat Balls for Soup (page 105)
8 cups cold water
½ cup chopped celery and leaves
½ cup thinly sliced carrots
¼ cup chopped fresh parsley
1 medium onion, sliced thin
1 bay leaf

½ cup canned or fresh peeled tomatoes, broken into small pieces (optional)
About 1 tablespoon salt
¼ teaspoon black pepper
About 1 cup fresh green beans or peas
½ cup or less of washed uncooked rice, or 1 cup uncooked broken macaroni or other pasta

Pour meat balls and drippings into a large stewpan; add the 8 cups of cold water, and *slowly* bring to the boiling point over medium heat. Cover pot, and simmer about 1 hour. If you prefer a thick soup, cook uncovered. After 1 hour, add the rest of the ingredients, and continue to simmer about

20 more minutes, covered, or uncovered. (Instead of using the various vegetables listed above, you can use a 10- or 12-ounce package of frozen mixed vegetables.) This soup freezes well.

This is a very hardy delicious soup and can be served as a light family meal with Italian or French garlic bread and a salad. Serve grated Italian cheese separately.

Note. Please refer to chapter in Italian cookery for two more very special Italian soups.

Meat Balls for Soup

1 pound ground beef
1 large whole egg
¼ cup sifted all-purpose flour
1½ teaspoons salt
1 clove garlic, put through garlic press, or ½ teaspoon garlic salt

2 tablespoons finely chopped parsley, or ½ teaspoon dry oregano leaves, crushed in fingers
¼ cup grated Italian cheese
¼ cup butter, combined with shortening or oil

Combine all ingredients, except butter and shortening or oil, in the order given in a medium-size bowl, and mix very thoroughly with a large spoon or with hands. Shape about 1 teaspoon (little more or less) of meat into smooth balls, dampening hands when necessary to prevent sticking. Do not have hands wet, just damp. Sauté balls in butter and shortening or oil until very brown, but do not scorch.

Oyster Stew

Serves 6

¼ cup butter
1 pint oysters with liquor
2 cups milk
2 cups coffee cream

1½ teaspoons salt
⅛ teaspoon pepper
1 tablespoon sauterne

Melt butter; when hot, add oysters and liquor. Cook slowly until oyster edges curl. While oysters are cooking slowly, bring milk and cream to scalding point.

When oysters are cooked, add them to scalded milk and cream. Add salt, pepper, and wine, and serve hot immediately.

Vichyssoise

2 tablespoons butter
1 cup chopped white part of leeks or green onions
2 tablespoons flour
4 cups White Poultry Stock (page 102)

3 cups finely shredded raw potatoes
About 2 teaspoons salt
¼ teaspoon garlic salt
2 cups cold coffee cream
Extra fine-chopped chives or green onion tops

In a 3-quart saucepan melt butter, add chopped leeks or onions, and sauté until lightly brown. Add flour, and blend well. Add warm stock slowly, stirring all the time, then the raw shredded potatoes. Add all of seasonings, and cook covered for about 30 minutes. Now pureé the soup through a fine sieve. This soup should be of a heavy consistency. Stir in the cream and blend well. Taste and season further if necessary. Refrigerate, and serve in chilled soup cups or plates. Sprinkle tops with the extra fine-chopped chives or onion tops.

Clear Bouillon with Petits Quenelles

1 recipe Clear Stock (page 103)
1 cup finely chopped and solidly packed meat left over after making soup stock
¾ teaspoon salt
1 teaspoon finely chopped parsley
⅛ teaspoon onion salt
2 tablespoons flour
⅛ teaspoon black pepper
1 teaspoon parmesan cheese
1 large egg, slightly beaten

Combine all ingredients except stock and blend thoroughly, using egg to bind preparation. Form into tiny balls (quenelles) with about 1 teaspoon of mixture, and brown nicely in hot butter. Add 8 to 10 quenelles to each serving of clear hot stock. Sprinkle top with a bit of chopped parsley and parmesan cheese.

Beef Barley Vegetable Soup (Scotch Broth)

1 recipe Brown Meat Stock (page 101)
½ cup sliced carrots
½ cup sliced turnips
1 large onion, sliced
½ cup sliced celery
1 cup fresh or canned tomatoes, broken into small pieces
½ cup or more uncooked green beans or peas
½ cup quick all-purpose pearled barley, or ½ cup uncooked rice

Strain stock and add all ingredients except green vegetable, barley or uncooked rice; simmer about 30 minutes. Now add the quick barley or rice, and green vegetable, and simmer for about 20 more minutes.

Lentil Wiener Soup

4 strips bacon
½ cup fine-chopped celery
½ cup fine-chopped onion
2 tablespoons flour (combine with ¼ cup cool water, to make a paste)
About 1 tablespoon salt
¼ teaspoon pepper
½ pound lentils cooked in 8 cups water for about 2 hours
½ cup sieved tomatoes, with pinch soda, or ½ cup tomato paste
½ pound or more frankfurters, sliced crosswise ¼ inch thick
Butter or margarine

Chop bacon fine and sauté for several minutes. Add chopped celery, onion, and flour mixture. Cook together in a small skillet until thickened, and add to the cooked lentils. Season with salt and pepper. Add tomatoes or paste and cook together about 30 more minutes. Sauté the sliced frankfurters in a small amount of butter or margarine and add to soup the last 10 minutes. If you prefer a thick soup do not cover pot during the cooking process.

Hearty Ham and Bean Soup

½ pound navy beans
Ham bone and any small bits of left-over ham
1 medium onion, chopped and sautéed in 2 tablespoons ham drippings or other fat
¾ cup shredded raw potatoes
¾ cup chopped celery and ¼ cup chopped celery leaves

About 1 teaspoon salt, depending on amount of ham used
¼ teaspoon pepper
½ cup drained tomatoes (fresh or canned), cut into medium-size pieces
½ cup fresh green onion tops

Wash beans well, then cover with 6 cups warm water. Let stand overnight. Next day pour beans and water in which they were soaked into a large saucepan.

Combine all ingredients except tomatoes and green onion tops. These two ingredients may be omitted, but they add much color to the dish. Add them last 10 minutes to retain color. Cook soup in a covered saucepan slowly about 3 hours or until beans are very soft. When done, taste, and season further if necessary. If soup appears too thick toward end, add a little water or stock. If it appears too thin, cook uncovered a few minutes. Add tomatoes and onions last 10 minutes, and cook slowly uncovered.

▶ CREAM SOUPS ◀

Cream soups should never be allowed to boil after they have simmered for the time suggested in recipes. If you are not ready to serve them at once, they may be kept hot by placing a sheet of heavy wax paper over opening of pot, then cover tightly. Place pot in a pan of simmering water until you are ready to serve the soup. Never keep pot over direct heat after soup has thickened, as it will thin out soup and also may cause curdling. The wax paper and tight cover prevent crust on soup.

Cream soups may be prepared in advance, stirred several times until cool, then stored in a covered container in refrigerator, or they may be frozen. To reheat refrigerated cream soup, place it over very low heat, and as soon as it starts to melt at the bottom, stir gently with a spoon. Let simmer for several minutes (not boil) and serve at once.

If cream soups have been frozen, it is better to place container holding soup into a pan of very hot water, and allow soup to soften before placing it over low heat. Stir gently and frequently until soup begins to simmer; simmer for several minutes, and serve at once.

If cream soups are too thick to serve, add a little milk or cream. If they are too thin, add 1 or 2 tablespoons of Kneaded Butter (page 108), or a little cornstarch dissolved in a little water. Pour into thin soup, stir until simmering begins; then simmer about 1 or 2 minutes, not longer.

Cream of Tomato Soup

Serves 4 to 6

To one No. 2½ can of tomatoes, add ¼ cup parsley, 1 small bay leaf, ½ small onion stuck with 3 cloves. Simmer all together about 10 minutes in a covered saucepan. Then put through a food mill or ricer, or press out through a strainer. Add to strained tomatoes ¼ teaspoon baking soda and can Italian-style tomato paste. Mix until smooth. In a medium-size saucepan melt ¼ cup sifted flour, and gradually add 2 cups rich milk or cream. Cook until thick and smooth, stirring constantly. Add 1 teaspoon salt. Simmer about 5 minutes after it thickens. Then add tomato mixture, a very little at a time, to the white sauce, and blend well. Add 1 tablespoon sugar. Bring to simmering point and serve at once.

If it is necessary to reheat tomato soup, do not allow it to boil, as it is likely to curdle, depending on the acidity of the tomatoes. It is better to bring it to the simmering point *and serve at once.*

Cream of Mushroom Soup

Serves 4 to 6

Chop ½ pound fresh mushrooms very fine, and cook gently in an uncovered saucepan with 3 cups milk about 15 minutes. After 15 minutes measure, and add enough more cream or milk to make 4 cups. In a medium-size saucepan melt ¼ cup butter, add ¼ cup sifted flour, and mix well to form a smooth paste. Then very slowly add mushroom mixture and 1 teaspoon salt to flour paste. Cook over low heat until it comes to the simmering point; then allow to simmer about 5 minutes longer.

Cream of Fresh Pea Soup

Cook 12-ounce package of frozen peas gently with 1 small fine-chopped onion and 2 cups water in covered saucepan about 15 minutes. When very soft, put through a food mill or strainer. Measure pulp and liquid, and add enough rich milk or cream to make 4 cups. In a medium-size saucepan melt ¼ cup butter; add ¼ cup sifted flour. When smooth, add pea mixture, a little at a time. Cook slowly to simmering point, add about 1 teaspoon salt, and cook about 5 more minutes.

Cream of Spinach Soup

Serves 4 to 6

In an uncovered saucepan cook 1½ pounds fresh spinach or 1 package frozen spinach in 1 cup water until tender. When done, cut up in small pieces and put through a food mill or press. Melt ¼ cup butter; add 2 tablespoons grated onion and ¼ cup sifted flour. Gradually add 3½ cups milk or coffee cream, stirring constantly, and let simmer until thick and smooth; then slowly add spinach and spinach water, a small amount at a time. Let cook until thoroughly combined, and simmer 5 minutes, stirring continuously. If too thick, it may be thinned out with more milk or cream. Add about 1 teaspoon salt toward end of cooking.

Cream of Celery Soup

Serves 4 to 6

Cut celery and leaves into small pieces to make 4 cups solidly packed. Cover with 4 cups water and 1 teaspoon salt. Cook *gently* in an uncovered saucepan about 1 hour or until very tender. Put through a food mill or ricer, and press out as much of the pulp as possible. Add enough milk or cream to celery mixture to make 4 cups. In a medium-size saucepan melt ½ cup butter; add ¼ cup sifted flour, blend well. Then slowly add above mixture, a little at a time, stirring constantly. Cook slowly to simmering point, season further if necessary, and cook several more minutes.

Cream of Cauliflower Soup

Serves 4 to 6

Pour 4 cups water over 1 pound fresh cauliflower or 1 package frozen cauliflower. Cook gently in an uncovered saucepan until very tender (about 45 minutes for fresh cauliflower, 15 minutes for frozen). Put through a food mill or strainer. Measure liquid and pulp. Add enough milk or cream to make 4 cups. In a medium-size saucepan, melt ¼ cup butter, add ¼ cup sifted flour, then add above mixture very slowly. Bring slowly to simmering point, season with about 1 teaspoon salt, and continue to cook about 5 more minutes.

Cream of Asparagus Soup

Serves 4 to 6

Use 1 pound fresh asparagus or 1 package frozen asparagus. Remove about 1 inch of tender tips from asparagus and put aside. Cut rest into small pieces. Cover with 4 cups cold water and cook in an uncovered saucepan until tender, about 45 minutes. Then drain liquid (there should be about 2 cups). Put asparagus through a food mill. Cook tips in above asparagus liquid until tender (about 10 minutes). Strain and put aside. Combine asparagus liquid with pulp and enough rich milk or cream to make 4 cups. Melt ¼ cup butter, add ¼ cup sifted flour, and mix until smooth. Then slowly add asparagus mixture. Let come to simmering point, stirring constantly. Then cook about 5 minutes, adding about 1 teaspoon salt last few minutes. Add asparagus tips.

Cream of Potato and Green Onion Soup

Serves 4 to 6

Use 1 pound peeled Idaho potatoes and 1 large bunch fresh green onions. Reserve about ½ cup green onion tops, cut crosswise into fine rings, to be added to soup just before serving. Cut up rest of onion into small pieces and combine with potatoes cut into small pieces and 3 cups water. Cook gently in a covered saucepan until very tender—about 1 hour. Then put through a food mill or ricer. Add to potato mixture enough milk or cream to make 4 cups. In a medium-size saucepan melt ¼ cup butter, add ¼ cup sifted flour, and slowly add potato and milk mixture, a small amount at a time. Let cook slowly to simmering point, season with about 1 teaspoon salt, and continue to cook several minutes. Just before serving, fold green onion tops into soup.

Cream of Chicken Soup

Serves 6 to 8

Pour about 10 cups water over 5-pound stewing chicken that has been cut up in about 12 pieces. Season with ¼ cup celery, ¼ cup onion, ¼ cup parsley, 1 very small bay leaf, and ½ tablespoon salt. Cook gently until chicken is tender—about 3 hours—in a covered saucepan. Then measure stock. If too rich, remove some of fat. In a saucepan melt 1 tablespoon butter (chicken fat may be used) and 1 tablespoon flour for each cup of stock. Add lukewarm stock slowly. Cook about 5 minutes after it comes to simmering point.

Cream of Corn Soup

Serves 4 to 6

Combine 1 can cream-style corn with 4 cups milk. Cook gently in an uncovered saucepan about 20 minutes. Melt ¼ cup butter, add ¼ cup sifted
flour, then slowly add corn mixture to sauce, a little at a time. Cook until
thick, season with 3 tablespoons sugar and 1 teaspoon salt, and continue to
cook several more minutes.

Soup of Two Colors

Place any style of cutter with open top in center of a flat soup dish. Pour
a very thick cream soup in cutter. Around cutter pour a cream soup of
contrasting color. Lift out cutter very gently and serve at once. For a
thicker soup, increase flour by 1 tablespoon.

▶ CHOWDERS ◀

Corn Tomato Chowder

Serves 4

2 ounces (¼ cup) salt pork or bacon, diced
¼ cup diced onions
1 small bay leaf
16-ounce can tomatoes
17-ounce can cream-style corn
1 cup diced raw potatoes
1½ cups boiling water
1 cup hot milk
Salt and pepper to taste

Fry salt pork or bacon until brown, add diced onions, and cook until
tender. Add bay leaf, tomatoes, corn, diced potatoes, and water. Cook
slowly uncovered until potatoes are tender. Remove bay leaf. Slowly stir
in hot milk, and season with salt and pepper to taste.

Clam Chowder

Serves 6

2 slices bacon, cut fine
½ cup dry onions, minced
2 tablespoons fine-chopped celery
Liquid from 2 (8-to-10-ounce) cans minced clams
2½ cups diced raw potatoes (½-inch cubes)
½ cup hot water
¼ cup domestic sauterne
Minced clams from 2 (8-to-10-ounce) cans
1½ cups milk
2 tablespoons butter
1 teaspoon salt
⅛ teaspoon cayenne pepper
¼ teaspoon white pepper

Sauté bacon, onions, and celery together until golden brown. Add clam liquid, diced potatoes, water, and wine, and cook in a covered saucepan until potatoes are tender (about 10 minutes) but still firm.

Add clams, milk, butter, salt, cayenne pepper, and white pepper. Bring to boiling point, stirring occasionally. Serve hot.

Note. For Manhattan Clam Chowder, omit milk and add 1½ cups canned tomatoes.

Vegetable Clam Chowder

Serves 6 generously

4 cups water	6 medium-size potatoes, cut into 1-inch cubes
4 slices bacon, cut into small pieces	
3 carrots, chopped fine	1 quart milk
1 small green pepper, chopped fine	7-ounce can minced clams
1 cup onions, chopped fine	½ tablespoon salt, more or less
	¼ teaspoon pepper

Heat water to boiling point. While water is heating, partially sauté diced bacon until light brown; then add bacon and drippings to boiling water along with carrots, green pepper, onions, and potatoes. Cover saucepan and simmer 45 minutes. Stir in milk, clams with clam liquid, and seasonings. Serve piping hot.

Corn Chowder

Serves 6 to 8

½ cup cubed bacon	2 cups milk
1 small onion, cut fine	3 tablespoons flour
1 cup raw potatoes, cubed	1½ teaspoons salt
1 cup water	¼ teaspoon pepper
1½ cups cooked corn	½ teaspoon garlic salt

Sauté bacon in a frying pan a few minutes; then add onion, and continue to cook until onion is soft. Parboil potatoes in water about 5 minutes, or until tender. In a saucepan combine bacon, onions, potatoes with water, and corn. Combine milk and flour, and add to other ingredients. Stir over heat until mixture comes to a boil. Add seasonings, simmer several minutes, and serve hot. If too thick, add additional milk.

Scallop Chowder

Serves 6

¼ cup butter or margarine	2 cups rich milk
½ cup diced onions	¾ pound scallops, diced
1 cup or more diced potatoes	1 teaspoon salt
1 small bay leaf	¼ teaspoon white pepper
3 cups water	Paprika

Melt shortening, add onions and sauté until golden. Add diced potatoes, bay leaf, and water. Cover saucepan, and simmer vegetables 15 minutes or until potatoes are tender. Add milk, scallops, salt, and pepper, and simmer about 5 minutes. Sprinkle with paprika just before serving.

▸ *Meats*

It is generally conceded by the best scientists that a liberal protein allowance is required for optimum health and that the foods of animal origin, such as meat, are of high nutritive value. In addition to this, meat has an important place in meal planning because of its appetite appeal and satiety value. The council on foods of the American Medical Association made the following statement: "Meat is especially noted for its protein, needed for body building and repair, but it makes other valuable contributions to the balanced diet. It is rich in iron, phosphorus and Vitamin G."

Fundamentally, there are only three principles involved in cooking meat: (1) dry heat, (2) moist heat, and (3) frying.

The tender cuts are cooked by dry heat because they contain little connective tissue, but moist heat is required to make tender those cuts which contain much connective tissue. There are exceptions to this general rule, as will be seen on cooking the specific kinds of meat in this section. Certain inherent characteristics of beef, veal, pork, and lamb make it necessary to modify these methods of cooking in order to get the best results.

It has been found that the temperature of the oven is an important factor in getting the best results. A moderately low temperature (300° to 350° F.) for the greater part of the cooking period should be used. Higher oven temperature increases cooking losses, by evaporation and by dripping.

Before you start the actual cooking of meats, we think it is essential for you to have some definite facts regarding quality and how to identify it. Variation in price depends first on the grade of the animal from which it comes, and second on the cut, and because fresh meats are sold at all prices, the consumer is often confused.

In order to help and protect the consumer, in 1927 the meat packers and the government developed a systematic method of grading beef, and later lamb, mutton, and veal. Although there are federal grades of pork, they have not been widely used because pork, especially those which have been cured and smoked, carry identifiable packer brands. The stamp or

We wish to express our thanks to Swift & Company and to the National Life Stock and Meat Board for their cooperation in compiling many of the facts and other information regarding meat cookery.

For many specialized dishes in meat cookery, please refer to chapters in Italian Cookery, Oriental Cookery, and Casseroles.

brand is put on in such a way that all retail cuts are marked, and you do not have to depend entirely on the retailer's word. Many packers establish their own grade names, usually referred to as *brand* names. Some of the brand names may parallel the government grades. There is often a great difference in the quality (or tenderness) of the same cut of meat, depending on brand or grade. The government grades of fresh meat recommended for home cooking are listed below.

Government Grades of Fresh Meats

U.S. PRIME. The finest grade, but it is not available in the majority of retail stores. It is sold primarily to the very best hotels, high-class restaurants, and deluxe railroad cars.

U.S. CHOICE. A high grade of beef available in almost any retail market. U.S. Choice mature beef has a thick covering of white firm fat, and the lean is bright red and well marbled. Marbling—flecks of fat within the lean—is an important factor affecting the quality in meat. Marbling enhances palatability by increasing juiciness, flavor, and tenderness.

U.S. GOOD. A good grade of beef for those who want economy. It has good flavor, is reasonably tender, and not wasteful, but is not as fine as U.S. Choice. It has less fat, which is yellowish, and the lean meat is darker.

How Much Meat to Buy

Several factors affect the meat-buying decision, relating to cuts and quantity. These points should be considered:

The individual appetite of family members. Men, especially those who are active, and teen-agers usually have hearty appetites. Therefore, more generous servings of meat should be allowed than for preschoolers or other members of the family whose capacities are smaller.

Because of varied appetites, it is difficult to define an "average" serving. Too, the kind and amount of foods accompanying meat to the table affect the amount of meat eaten at a meal. Sometimes a 12-to-16-ounce steak may be enjoyed by 1 person, and on another occasion a pound of ground beef might serve 3 or 4 people well.

How much meat is in the cut? With steaks and chops, this is easy to see. For bone-in roasts, the proportion of meat to bone may not be so readily apparent. A general guide to follow is to plan on a 6-pound bone-in roast to yield approximately 2½ to 3 pounds of boneless cooked meat. This would provide about 5 to 8 servings, depending on the portion size.

Allow ½ pound of boneless uncooked meat for each serving. This includes boned roasts and steaks, hamburger, boneless stew, boneless lamb and veal.

For meat with some bone allow at least ¾ pound for each serving.

For very bony cuts, such as spareribs, short ribs, shoulder, 1 pound for each serving.

Storing Meat

Store prepackaged fresh meats from a refrigerated self-service case in original wrap without breaking the seal if to be used within 1 or 2 days. If to be kept longer, the wrapper should be loosened at the ends, to allow meat to breathe, or it is likely to spoil.

Fresh meat not prepackaged should be removed from the market wrapping paper and stored unwrapped or loosely wrapped in waxed paper.

Variety meats and ground or chopped meats are more perishable than other meats and should be cooked in 1 or 2 days if not to be frozen.

Cured and smoked meats, sausages, and ready-to-serve meats also should be stored in the refrigerator, and left in their original wrappings. Follow directions on label.

Canned hams, picnic hams, and other perishable canned meats should be stored in the refrigerator unless storage recommendations on the can read to the contrary. These meats should not be frozen.

Cooked meats which are left over should be cooled quickly, covered or wrapped promptly to prevent drying and spoilage, and stored in the refrigerator. Bones may be removed to conserve storage space, but meat should be left in as large a piece as posible.

Meats cooked in liquid for future serving should be cooled quickly, uncovered, then covered and stored in its own liquid in the refrigerator. To speed cooling, when meat is cooled in liquid, the pan containing the cooked meat may be set where there is good circulation of cool air, or it may be cooled by setting the pan in cold or running water.

Note. For information on handling frozen meats, see freezing section, page 880.

Aging of Meats

In the normal process of moving fresh meat from packer to retailer to consumer to kitchen range, there is a time lapse of from 6 to 10 days. This is usually long enough for some tenderizing to take place. For customers who prefer "aged" meat, however, some retailers will hold ribs and loins of beef from 2 to 4 weeks. This will increase the tenderness and flavor and the price of meat considerably, as there is waste to the retailer in trimming the meat for the consumer. Only ribs and loins of high quality beef, lamb, and mutton usually are aged. These cuts are naturally tender so the major purpose of aging is to develop additional tenderness and characteristic flavor. To be suitable for aging, meat must have a fairly thick covering of fat to prevent discoloration of the lean and to keep dehydration at a minimum.

Premium Meats

Beef. In recent years scientific research has developed a tenderizing process that provides dependable tenderness with retention of the basic quality and flavor of steaks and roasts. The process consists of tenderizing from within by the use of natural protein food enzymes that are distributed uniformly through all the cuts of meat through the capillary system. The enzyme is inactive in all stages of raw meat. The tenderizing action starts when meat temperature reaches about 120° F. and then passes the inactive stage at about 180° F. The advantages to homemakers are dependable tenderness, reduced cooking time, and additional variety of cuts of beef that can be cooked by dry heat methods. This beef is fully identified at the wholesale and retail levels as it is marked "Pro'Ten—Tendered with Papain."

Normally, cuts of beef suitable for roasting or broiling are from the rib and loin. As these represent only about 25 percent of the beef, they command higher prices than other cuts that cannot be cooked satisfactorily by dry heat. On the other hand, the tenderizing process, identified with the Pro'Ten label, is now available from the forequarters and rounds of Premium beef. As these tendered cuts cook in shorter time periods, care must be given to cooking suggestions so as to avoid overcooking.

We recommend Pro'Ten roasts, but of family size, in the neighborhood of 6 to 8 pounds. For occasions requiring large roasts, we recommend reducing the size by cutting in half, which will avoid overcooking and will again appreciably reduce the cooking time to produce tender palatable roasts.

Pork. Through careful selection for leanness, and expert grading and trimming, a new pork is available wearing the name, Premium Tend'r Lean Pork. This new Tend'r Lean Pork is delightfully tender, has consistent leanness—and superb flavor.

Pork chops of this new pork can now be broiled, and should be at least 1 inch thick. Pork loins are best roasted to an internal temperature of 170° F. instead of 185° F. Cook all other large cuts of pork also to 170° F.

This new Tend'r Lean Pork is also marketed in 2-pound boneless consumer-style roasts called Tend'r Lean Pork Roast and Tend'r Lean Pork Loin Roast. They come frozen, ready to cook in their own foil pans, and with a garnish. They roast in about 2 hours without thawing.

Pork is good for you, as it is the richest source of thiamine and contains high quality complete proteins. Best of all an average serving of this new pork contains just 240 calories compared with 377 calories for the pork of yesterday.

Lamb. All lamb cuts of Premium quality lamb are tender. In addition to the leg and crown roast for roasting, there are now several new netted rolled lamb roasts available to the homemaker, such as boneless rolled shoulder, rolled Scotch roast, etc. Leg of lamb is the traditional feast at Easter, and the racks and regal crown roasts are holiday favorites, known as gourmet cuts. Roast these meats right in the net slowly, at 325° F., for about ½ hour per pound. They can be basted with a favorite sauce, or seasoned simply with salt and pepper.

These cuts can be served medium rare, delicately pink in the middle, and rich golden brown on the outside. These boneless netted rolled lamb roasts should stand about 20 minutes before serving. Remove net before carving at the table. The meat will easily cut into firm, rounded slices, as thick as you desire. They can also be sliced before cooking into choice steaks for broiling or pan-frying.

Veal. Veal is young beef, and is almost as delicately flavored as chicken. In Europe it is prepared in many delicious ways, and is served in the finest restaurants.

The most desirable cuts of top-quality Premium veal for roasting are the leg and boned and rolled shoulder.

Premium quality veal steaks and chops can even be broiled, but at a lower temperature, until well done. Because veal comes from a young animal and is deficient in fat it is advisable to brush it well with melted butter or margarine several times during the broiling process.

For roasting, it may be covered with several strips of salt pork or bacon, and cooked with the fat side up, uncovered, or it may be basted with a special sauce continental, as suggested in our Italian meat section, in addition to numerous other delectable veal preparations.

Premium veal cutlets and chops, not more than ½ inch thick, plain or breaded, can be sautéed or fried in unsalted shortening or oil about 5 to 7 minutes on each side, over low heat, *without braising*. Test piece by cutting through with side of fork, and if not tender enough, cover skillet tightly, add no liquid, and cook for about 5 minutes longer over low heat.

Corned Beef. For your convenience and the eating pleasure of your family, enjoy a revolutionary new kind of corned beef brisket, Premium Corned Beef Brisket.

No longer is it necessary to simmer corned beef in water in a covered kettle for hours. Now you can place a Premium Corned Beef Brisket on a rack in an open pan in a slow oven and never look again until the roast is tender when tested with a sharp-tined fork.

This new corned beef brisket is a joy to slice and is tender enough to cut with a fork. Best of all, no flavor is lost in the cooking water. Directions come with each piece. Request it at your markets, and be sure to specify Premium Corned Beef for *Oven Roasting*. The regular corned beef that is cooked in water is not the same.

Special Beef Cuts

Fillet or Tenderloin of Beef. The fillet, or tenderloin of beef, is the most expensive, most tender, and most elegant cut of beef, provided you purchase branded Premium Pro'Ten beef, or Prime aged U.S. beef. It can be roasted whole—as beef tenderloin in Puff Paste, called Beef Wellington; Chateaubriand, etc.—or it may be cut into individual thick steaks to make filets mignons, tournedos, etc. It is also the most desirable cut to use for beef Stroganoff, peppered steaks, and any oriental or other special fancy dishes that call for quickly cooked thinly sliced beef that cooks in 2 or 3 minutes.

The fillet, or tenderloin of beef, must be completely trimmed and oven prepared by your butcher (not by an inexperienced person), making sure that all the surplus fat and sinew is trimmed off, and the thin tough skin is removed from the entire tenderloin. Also request him to remove about 1 or more inches from the large round sinewy end. This part of the tenderloin is very tough and cannot be eaten unless it is chopped fine for some other dish. The long flat, pointed, narrow end may be tucked under with heavy wood pins, removing them before serving the meat, or it may be removed entirely and used for some other dish. Always purchase this cut of beef from a reliable, high-class butcher shop, and make sure also that the round sinewy end is not included in an order of individual fillets mignons or tournedos that are ordered and cut in advance. Best to investigate this very closely as many butchers include it in their orders. It would be very embarassing to serve this undesirable end of tough meat to one of your guests.

Eye of the Round of Beef. Very few homemakers are familiar with this cut of beef and few butchers carry it at all times, but it can be ordered several days or longer in advance. It is a long thick boneless piece of beef that looks like a very large beef fillet, or tenderloin, but is less expensive and excellent in quality and tenderness *if you purchase* Premium Pro'Ten or U.S. Prime aged beef. This cut must be trimmed by your butcher, removing any undesirable fat, sinews, and skin, and about 1 inch, more or less, from each end.

We have done some very interesting research and experiments with the eye of the round of beef, with great success. This cut is especially desirable for Beef Wellington, and for all other recipes that call for whole beef tenderloin. Follow general directions given for the tenderloin of beef, but cook meat for Beef Wellington to about 140° to 150° F. interior temperature the second cooking, and the same for other whole roasts, when using the eye of the round of beef. This cut can also be used for Chateaubriand, and for other dishes that call for thinly sliced quickly sautéed beef. This cut is just as desirable and in some dishes we prefer it to the much more expensive tenderloin of beef. The retail price in the Chicago area at the present time is more than 50 percent less for the eye of round than for the tenderloin, which is a tremendous saving. It makes more attractive slices when roasted whole and there is less waste. Do try it, but remember to buy top-quality branded meat.

Rib Eye or Beef. This cut has become very popular in recent years and can be used in recipes that call for tenderloin of beef with the exception of the Beef Wellington. Be sure to purchase only Premium Pro'Ten or U.S. Prime beef for excellent results and tenderness. Best to order it several days in advance—and from a reliable butcher shop.

▶ HOW TO COOK MEAT ◀

Meat Marinade for Beef, Veal, or Lamb

1 cup dry white or red wine
¼ cup cider vinegar
1 cup salad oil
2 teaspoons salt
¼ teaspoon black pepper
⅛ teaspoon dry tarragon

1 bay leaf, crushed into small pieces
½ teaspoon thyme or marjoram leaves,
   crushed
1 large clove garlic, chopped fine, or
   better put through garlic press

Combine all ingredients in a medium bowl, and with egg or wire beater beat for about 2 or 3 minutes. Soak meat in this marinade and turn it over often, and baste it from time to time with marinade that settles at the bottom of the dish. Four hours in marinade will add a subtle delectable flavor to the meat. Keep meat in refrigerator, but let stand in room temperature for 1 hour before cooking, either in or out of marinade.

Note. Place meat to be marinated into an enamel, glass, or stainless steel utensil, *and not in other utensils made of metal*, as very often the acid in the marinade will act upon the metal chemically and develop an unpleasant taste in the food.

Salt in Meat Cookery

Salt is used to enhance the flavor of almost all cooked foods; without it food would be tasteless. But it must be used with discretion. The amounts suggested in our individual recipes may be used as a guide, and may be increased or decreased to suit individual taste.

In meat cookery, a good rule to follow is ¾ level measuring teaspoon salt for each pound of ground meat; ¾ teaspoon salt for 1 pound boneless meat cutlets, sliced ½ inch thick or less; ½ teaspoon salt for chops, cut about ½ inch thick; ⅓ teaspoon salt for each pound of steaks with bone, and other meats with much bone.

The same rule can be used for poultry and fish.

Cooking Methods

The most important guide to follow in all meat cookery (except oven broiling) is to use a low cooking temperature. This keeps the juice and flavor in the meat, cuts down shrinkage, keeps the meat more tender and palatable, and prevents burnt fat drippings. There are three methods used for cooking meat: *dry heat*, which consists of oven roasting, oven broiling, and pan-broiling; *moist heat*, which consists of braising and water cooking; and *frying*, which consists of pan-frying and deep-fat frying.

Time schedules for cooking various cuts of meat are given with each recipe. These schedules are a guide to the approximate cooking time required to make the meat tasty and tender.

To *test for doneness of meat*, always use a meat thermometer when roasting meats. More details are given with roasting instructions (page 127). To test broiled meats, cut a small slit in the meat near the bone and note the color and degree of doneness inside. To test braised and water-cooked meats, pierce the meat with the point of a paring knife or sharp-tined meat fork for tenderness, or cut through a piece with a dinner fork, after meat is sliced. It must cut through without much pressure to be tender.

Important. If you are able to procure the fine-quality meats discussed earlier—Fresh Pro'ten Beef, Fresh Tend'r Lean Pork, Fresh Premium Quality Veal and Lamb, Fresh Premium Quality Processed Meats—you will notice that they require less time to cook because of their high quality and tenderness. While our time tables are excellent guides, we suggest that you test the meat for doneness a ½ hour before cooking time is up, and to use a meat thermometer whenever possible. Other details are given in each recipe.

To Sauté or Pan-Fry Uncoated Meats, Poultry, and Fish

Use an open skillet. Melt amount of fat suggested in individual recipes until it is quite hot. We like to use half butter and half unsalted shortening or oil.

Meat must be dry on the surface, and in room temperature at least ½ hour. (If meat is too cold or if it is wet, steam will form, preventing it from browning.) Do not season meat until it is brown on one side. Salt tends to draw out the juice and retard browning.

Do not crowd meat in pan. It is important to leave empty spaces between pieces.

Do not turn meat until it is well browned on first side, or until the blood begins to form on upper part. If the meat seems to be steaming, *increase heat at once,* but watch closely to prevent scorching.

When meat is done, remove to hot platter, and at once add small amount of water, stock, or light dry wine to drippings. With wooden spoon release the brown drippings and residue in the pan, lower heat and simmer about 2 minutes. Pour over meat, or serve separately.

Important. If fat scorches or burns during the cooking process (at any time) it must be discarded, and fresh fat added.

To Brown Meat for Braising, Pot Roasting, and Stewing

Braising, pot roasting, and cooking in water are methods for cooking less tender cuts of meats. Some tender cuts also are best if braised. It is important to follow cooking directions given in each recipe.

Use a heavy skillet and a small amount of fat (half butter or margarine and half unsalted shortening or oil give excellent results). Do not have more than ⅛ inch of very hot fat in pan. Meat must be dry. If it is not to be coated with flour or crumbs, wipe meat well with paper toweling. Do not crowd the pan, as this would cause steaming and prevent browning. Meat must be browned slowly for at least 7 or 8 minutes on each side to give a more lasting brown which will not wash off when the liquid is added. *If the fat appears scorched, discard it,* as it would impart a bitter taste to the meat. If necessary you can add a little fresh fat to skillet after the burnt fat has been discarded. If meat is browned too rapidly, it will not have an attractive appearance when done.

After meat or poultry has been well browned, it is very important to remove surplus fat from drippings in skillet before you pour suggested amount of liquid over meat in skillet. A very small amount of fat may be left in but too much fat prevents formation of steam that is absolutely *essential* in tenderizing the meat or poultry during the braising process. Fat simply sizzles and does not produce moisture.

Add the liquid and seasonings as suggested in the individual recipes, and cook as directed. If a rack is not used after meat has browned, meat should be turned occasionally during the cooking process to prevent it from getting too brown on the underside. Add more liquid as needed.

To Cook Meat and Poultry in Water

Cover meat with water or liquid suggested in individual recipes, and simmer. Do not boil. Cook meat until you can penetrate it easily with sharp point of a paring knife or a two-tined fork. Tests prove that meats are more tender if cooked at a simmering rather than a boiling temperature, and there is less shrinkage.

Braised meats cooked with the addition of liquid, in a tightly covered pan, must be cooked over *very, very low heat* (simmer burner) after liquid comes to a boil. If heat is even a bit too high, moisture evaporates quickly, which causes drying and scorching, and steam is not created. Add a small amount of liquid as needed until meat is tender.

Braising and pot roasting may be done on top of the stove, covered tightly, or in covered pot in oven set at 325° to 350° F. until tender. Add more liquid from time to time to prevent scorching, and also to create steam. We prefer oven-braising.

To Deep-Fat Fry Meat, Poultry, and Fish

Deep-fat frying isn't new. It was used by the ancient Romans and the Orientals for centuries. Today inexpensive cooking utensils and thermometers makes it easier. Even a beginner can turn out delicious foods using this very popular method of cooking if our simple directions are followed and you use a good deep-fat thermometer, available in the houseware sections of department and hardware stores.

The old test for temperature of hot fat was done with 1-inch cubes of bread. If the bread browns within 60 seconds the temperature is desirable for the majority of foods, about 375° F. However, this is not a reliable test. Unless you are equipped with a good deep-fat thermometer we do not recommend deep-frying because many foods require higher or lower temperatures. Too-high temperature will form a crust too rapidly before the food is cooked through. On the other hand, if temperature is too low the food will be grease-soaked and heavy.

Do's and Don'ts. You don't need a special pot for deep-fat frying. Any deep heavy pot will do. A frying basket, easily available in houseware departments, is a practical necessity for best results in frying any amount of small items such as potatoes, fritters, shrimp, etc. Pot should be deep enough so that it is never more than half-full of fat. There must also be room in the kettle for the bubbling up of the fat which occurs in frying potatoes and other wet items. Surplus moisture must be removed from wet foods with toweling before you lower them into the fat. Always lower the basket gradually so that you can observe the amount of bubbling and be ready to lift it up if it looks as though the fat might be going over the top.

The fat you use is one of the most important aspects of deep-fat frying. It is closely related to temperature. Lard, solid shortenings, and liquid oils, such as corn, peanut, and cotton-seed, are the most commonly used and available for household use. Never wait for the fat to smoke before adding the food, as this would decompose the fat, making it useless for further frying. Fat may be used several times if the temperature is kept below the smoking point, but it is best to add some fresh fat to the used for the next frying. After used fat becomes thick and dark, it is best to discard it. Never use margarine, butter, or drippings for deep-fat frying as they smoke at very low temperatures. When you have finished frying, cool the fat slightly; line a strainer with several thicknesses of cheese-cloth or ordinary facial tissues and strain. Store the leftover fat in a cool place or refrigerator.

Whenever possible, foods to be deep-fried should be at room temperature at least ½ hour when they are lowered gently into the hot fat, using a long slotted spoon or pair of tongs. Always dip spoon or tongs into the hot fat *first* so that the food will not cling to them when they are released.

Do not increase the amount of fat and sugar in each recipe, nor in the batter, because if the food is too rich it will absorb more fat during the frying process, and some items like fritters may actually disintegrate in the hot fat, or the batter may slide off some foods. If you are using frozen foods to be deep-fried be sure to follow directions given on label.

Put only moderate amounts of foods into the hot fat at one time to prevent boiling over of fat, which might catch on fire. If this occurs, have a *heavy metal lid* at hand to place over the kettle at once. The flame may also be smothered with salt. Never use water. *Skim any small particles of food or foam from the fat as they accumulate during the frying process, and discard.* After frying 1 batch, allow temperature of fat to rise again to required heat. Don't poke the foods with a fork. Remove them with a slotted spoon or tongs, and place them onto a tray covered with several thicknesses of absorbent paper. Deep-fat fried foods should be served immediately. If not, leave them on the paper toweling and place in 250° to 300° F. oven to keep warm for a short time.

Follow directions given in each recipe for special handling or reheating foods cooked in advance.

To Prepare Breaded Meats, Poultry, Fish

Dampen very lightly and season food to be breaded with salt, pepper, etc. Dip into flour or fine dry bread crumbs, shaking off loose crumbs. Dip into beaten egg diluted in a little milk or water, as suggested in individual recipes. Some items require a heavier coating than others. Do not overbeat eggs for this purpose. Use a small wire whisk or egg beater for a few seconds until yolk and whites are well blended but not too foamy. Drain food well, and cover completely with sifted dry crumbs, being sure that there are no vacant spots. Press crumbs onto food gently, and allow loose crumbs to fall off.

Place breaded food on a flat pan covered with wax paper, and let stand about 20 minutes in room temperature, turning it over several times. We do not recommend placing breaded foods in the refrigerator unless indicated in recipe.

To brown breaded foods, heat about ¼ inch of unsalted shortening or oil (do not use butter or margarine) in a heavy skillet, and when it is quite hot (about 350° F.; tilt skillet and check temperature with a deep-fat thermometer) lower food gently into hot fat, reduce heat slightly, and cook until golden brown and crisp on underside. With tongs carefully turn food over to brown second time. Keep heat medium, and leave spaces between each piece to prevent steaming.

Some thin cuts of food may be done after they have been nicely browned on each side. For thick cuts, *place browned food on a trivet,* add about ½ cup (more or less) of water, stock, or wine in a 10-inch skillet and ¼ cup of water in an 8-inch skillet. Cover tightly and braise until meat is tender, when you can insert point of paring knife easily into thickest part. Check moisture in pan, *and add more liquid as necessary* to produce steam at all times until meat is tender. Adjust heat from time to time. Keep liquid below trivet. May be braised in a 350° F. oven.

Breaded meats may be braised without placing them on a trivet directly in skillet, but they will be soggier and the crust is likely to peel off and cling to bottom of pan. The advantage of the trivet is that you can add a much larger amount of water or stock to produce steam for meats that require longer cooking without the meat actually resting in the liquid.

Instead of pan-frying breaded foods, many can be deep-fat fried as suggested in individual recipes.

Note. If you are preparing a large amount of breaded pan-fried foods, we suggest that you clean skillet with paper toweling after each panful is completed. Use fresh fat each time, to keep crust on meat attractive and prevent sticking to pan.

For extra flavor, a little clarified butter (page 328) may be added to the shortening or oil for breaded meats, but watch closely to prevent scorching.

Bread Crumbs and Other Coatings for Meat, Poultry, Fish, Croquettes, etc.

It is important to use the kind of crumbs called for in recipes. In many cases they cannot be used interchangeably with good results.

Commercial Bread Crumbs (dry). Can be used in any of our recipes calling for dry bread crumbs provided they are not flavored. If you do use the commercial flavored crumbs *omit* some of seasoning in recipe.

Leftover white bread that is several days old is especially desirable for this purpose. The crust may be left on or may be removed. Place the sliced bread on center rack of oven set at 250° F. for about 15 more minutes, or until it is very, very lightly colored (pale golden color). If bread feels slightly soft when time is up, shut off heat and leave it in oven with door open for 15 or 20 minutes longer, or until firm. When bread is cool, crush it with rolling pin, or put through food chopper or grater. Sift before measuring and using.

Homemade crumbs do not keep as well as the commercial. They can be stored in the freezer, however, for several months, using only the amount needed for each recipe. Commercial crumbs contain a preservative and can be kept for several weeks or longer in a cool dry place.

Cracker Crumbs. The commercial crumbs are excellent and can be used in majority of recipes that call for dry bread crumbs.

Browned Bread Crumbs. Add 1 cup of dry toasted crumbs to ¼ cup warm melted butter or margarine, and blend well with a fork. If they appear too dry, add a bit more melted fat; if too moist, add little more crumbs, and blend well.

Moist or Soft Bread Crumbs. Best to have white bread several days old, or older. Remove crust. For large pulled fresh crumbs called for in our recipes, simply pull bread apart with fingers into about ½-inch pieces, using very little pressure to keep the texture light. For finer moist crumbs, support sliced white bread gently on a solid surface with fingers of left hand, and with fork in right hand pull the bread apart in size desired. Best to store soft moist bread crumbs in refrigerator or in freezer to prevent molding.

Other Commercial Coatings Sold Under Various Brands. We have not had good results with some of the high-priced meat coatings. We find that coatings do not cling well to the product unless it is first dipped into diluted egg, as suggested in our recipes.

Finely Crushed Corn Flake Coating. This coating cannot be used on foods that require more than several minutes' cooking without overbrowning and burning. You might use it on foods that are precooked, then covered with this coating and sautéed only a minute or two until brown and crisp. They can be used on foods that are baked in oven after they are coated. Read directions on labels.

Seasoned Flour for Coating Meat, Poultry, Fish, etc.

¾ cup sifted all-purpose flour	½ teaspoon garlic, or ⅛ teaspoon
1 teaspoon salt	garlic powder
⅛ teaspoon pepper	1½ teaspoons paprika
	⅛ teaspoon poultry seasoning

Combine all ingredients in a small paper or plastic bag, and shake until well blended. Dampen meat or chicken slightly, place 2 or 3 pieces in bag, hold tightly and shake well to cover completely. Pick up and let loose flour drop off.

For more fragile foods, it is best to pour some coating onto a square piece of wax paper. Flatten it out, place food on top, and lift up corners of paper and shake gently to prevent breakage of food. Sprinkle any uncoated parts with fingers. Press down gently to make coating cling well.

This gives a very thin, simple coating, but for a thicker and more adhesive crust, dip the food into beaten diluted egg after it is floured, then into bread or other crumbs, and cook as per directions on each recipe. Best to have the beaten diluted egg in a flat wide soup plate or Pyrex pie plate, not a narrow bowl. Two or 3 teaspoons water are usually added to 1 whole egg, then beaten a few seconds until well mixed, but not foamy.

To Roast Meats

Allow meats to stand in room temperature for a least 1 hour before roasting.

Wipe meat with clean damp cloth. Place on a rack in a roaster or in a baking sheet. Always put the meat in the pan with the fat side up. This makes basting unnecessary. As the fat melts, it will baste the roast.

Salt and pepper may be added to the meat either before or after roasting.

Do not add any water first half of roasting time and do not cover. A cover on the pan means the condensation of steam and the result is a pot roast rather than a roast.

Searing does not keep in juices, nor keep a roast from drying out. A roast which is seared shows greater shrinkage than one which is not seared. Meat cooked at a constant low temperature will have an attractive browned appearance even if it is not seared. A roast cooked at high temperature will lose more weight than one cooked at a constant low temperature.

An accurate roast meat thermometer tells exactly when a roast has reached the desired degree of doneness, by registering the internal temperature. Rare, medium, and well done are marked at the proper temperatures on the thermometer. The thermometer is inserted in the meat so the center of the bulb reaches the center of the largest muscle. It remains in the roast throughout the cooking period. (To make sure that the bulb of thermometer is in the center of the meat, we recommend moving thermometer up and down slowly during the latter part of roasting period. If temperature drops at any point, leave thermometer at this particular point until meat is done to desired degree. Do not take into consideration about ¼ inch of tip of thermometer when measuring.) For flat or small roasts, it is better to insert thermometer into thick end of meat if it is less than 3 inches thick.

For veal, cover meat with strips of salt pork, bacon, or suet. Then as the fat melts the roast actually bastes itself. However, no fat is necessary for veal that is roasted in a covered pan.

A boneless rolled roast or boned leg should be turned over several times during the roasting process. This will insure more uniform cooking and browning. In this case the meat thermometer may be inserted the latter part of roasting period.

Important. After meat has been roasting for a while, watch drippings closely and if they appear *scant or to scorch,* pour a cup of hot water or stock into pan and loosen drippings with a spoon. If drippings are not sufficiently brown for gravy when meat is almost done, add commercial gravy coloring.

After Removal from Oven. Cooking action will continue in oven roasts for a few minutes after removal from ovens because the surface temperatures tend to equalize with the center temperatures of the roast. Therefore, in following thermometer calculations, it is well to remove the roasts from the oven, particularly Pro'Ten roasts, when they reach a temperature of about 5° F. for small roasts, 10° F. for very large roasts, less than the recommended temperature for the doneness you prefer. Roasts permitted to stand for 20 to 30 minutes after removing from the oven lend themselves to easier carving.

Timetable for Roasting Meats

Rib Roast of Beef

Rare	325° F. About 25 minutes per pound
Medium	325° F. About 30 minutes per pound
Well Done	325° F. About 35 minutes per pound

Pork Loin and
all large pieces of pork — 325° F. About 35 minutes per pound

Lamb—leg, breast,
shoulder, loin crown roast — 325° F. About 30 to 35 minutes per pound

Veal—leg (covered with several strips of salt
pork, or use covered roaster) — 325° F. About 30 minutes per pound

For small roasts weighing less than 5 pounds, increase roasting time about 10 minutes per pound, and roast at 350° F. for beef, lamb, and veal; 350° F. for pork. If not brown at end of cooking period, raise temperature to 400° F. and brown well, adding a little water to drippings to prevent smoking.

About 10 minutes per pound should be added to above timetable for boneless rolled roasts.

Note. The timetables for roasting are only a guide and not specific, therefore, we recommend increasing the temperature to 400° F. toward end of roasting period and to add 1 cup of stock or water to drippings if meat is roasting too slowly. If, however, it is roasting too rapidly, reduce temperature to lowest point.

Thickened Gravy for Roasted Meats

When meat is done, remove most of fat from drippings in roasting pan, leaving about ½ tablespoon of fat for each cup of gravy to be made. Add stock, milk, or water to drippings, and with a wooden spoon carefully loosen any brown residue on rack and in pan. Stir the gravy over low heat until the particles of the residue are dissolved. To thicken, measure, and to each cup of drippings and liquid add slowly about 3 tablespoons flour diluted in ¼ cup water and stir until smooth. Cook until thick, stirring continuously, then simmer about 5 minutes. Taste and add salt, pepper, and a little commercial gravy coloring if needed. Sautéed mushrooms and other seasonings may be added. Use less flour for a thinner gravy; more for a very thick gravy.

Note. See pages 321-327 for Gravy Au Jus and other gravies.

To Broil Steaks and Chops

The two most popular and healthful methods used in cooking tender steaks and chops are oven-broiling and pan-broiling. To broil means to cook by direct heat or to grill. Broiling may be done over hot coals or under a gas flame or an electric unit.

Studies on broiling, together with other meat cookery investigations, have established certain fundamentals which have made it possible to standardize broiling methods within limits. The type of equipment used may necessitate some modifaction of the method.

The timetables for broiling are only a guide and not specific. Variables influencing the cooking time include thickness of cut and surface area (the steak with the larger surface takes somewhat longer), the type of broiler used, the temperature of the meat before it is placed in the broiler, and the degree of doneness desired. Experience is the best judge as to how to modify the general methods given to obtain the results desired. In oven-broiling the best results are obtained if broiler pan is almost filled. In broiling only a single small steak, 1 or 2 lamb chops, or beef tenderloins, the best results are obtained if they are pan-broiled; if oven-broiled, time must be reduced.

Extra-thick steaks or chops should be broiled with reduced heat, or the broiler pan should be lowered so that the meat cooks through without burning. Broilers differ in size, type of broiler rack, heat equipment, and depth of broiler oven, and therefore the distance the meat can be from the heat source differs. For these reasons learn to adjust the broiling time to your broiling oven. Our time schedule is only a guide and we suggest that you make notes of variations so you have a time schedule to suit your own broiling oven.

Gas Ranges Equipped With Smokeless Broiler. With this type of range the broiler may be preheated or not. Some manufacturers do not recommend preheating. With some broilers thick steaks and chops may be cooked without preheating. It is best to follow directions given by manufacturer of your particular type of stove and to ascertain whether the broiler is of the smokeless type. If your stove is equipped with a smokeless broiler, *set regulator to "broil"* and follow our general directions for broiling.

Gas Ranges Not Equipped With Smokeless Broiler. This type of range has an ordinary wire rack or single broiling pan which causes smoking. *We recommend that the regulator be set to 450° F. and to leave oven door (not broiler door) partially open.* This will cause better circulation of heat, thereby prevents smoking. In leaving oven door open with regulator set at 450° F., temperature is equivalent to 550° F.

Electric Ranges or Other Broiling Equipment. It is best to follow directions given by the manufacturer and to make notes for future reference.

Allow steaks and chops that are to be broiled to stand in room temperature for about 1 hour loosely covered with wax paper. When ready to broil the steak, rub with a clove of garlic, if desired, and brush with melted butter or margarine. This helps to brown the meat. Slash the fat edge in several places to prevent curling. Cut a piece of fat from the meat, pull the broiler part out of oven and grease the surface, then lay the meat on the central portion of the rack, and have the top of the meat about 2½ inches from flame or heating element. Allow meat to cook for time specified on 1 side. Sprinkle with salt and pepper, turn and cook on second side. Large steaks, such as sirloin, will take 2 or 3 minutes longer to cook. The same is true if broiling more than 1 steak at a time. *It is therefore well to test steaks for doneness several minutes before the end of the second half of the cooking time specified. To do this, simply cut a small gash along the edge of the bone, bend the meat back and note its color.*

When the meat is done, salt the second side and quickly remove to a hot platter. Place about 1 tablespoon softened butter on top of meat, if desired, and serve it as quickly as possible.

It is best *not* to add the salt before browning because steaks and chops have relatively large exposed surfaces and the fact that salt draws out juices must be considered.

Because beef tenderloin patties and lamb chops have a small surface area, *the broiling times must be modified.* Brush beef tenderloin patties with melted butter or margarine before broiling, or wrap strips of salt pork or bacon around each patty and hold in place with a wood pin.

Timetable for Broiling Meats

Steaks 1 Inch Thick
Rare
> About 6 minutes first side; and little less time on second side

Medium
> About 8 minutes first side; and little less time on second side

Well Done
> About 12 minutes first side; and little less time on second side

Steaks 1½ Inches Thick
Rare
> About 10 minutes first side; and little less time on second side

Medium
> About 12 minutes first side; and little less time on second side

Well Done
> About 15 minutes first side; and little less time on second side

Beef Tenderloin Patties (Filet Mignon) or Lamb Chops 1 Inch Thick
Rare (for tenderloin only)
> About 5 minutes first side; and little less time on second side

Medium (for lamb or tenderloin)
> About 6 minutes first side; and little less time on second side

Well done (for lamb or tenderloin)
> About 8 minutes first side; and little less time on second side

Beef Tenderloin Patties (Filet Mignon) or Lamb Chops 1½ Inches Thick
Rare (for tenderloin only)
> About 6 minutes first side; and little less time on second side

Medium (for lamb or tenderloin)
> About 8 minutes first side; and little less time on second side

Well done (for lamb or tenderloin)
> About 10 minutes first side; and little less time on second side

For thicker steaks and chops, increase broiling time several minutes on each side. If meat is not sufficiently brown at the end of each broiling period, remove broiler and brush meat again with melted butter, and place it closer to heating element or flame for a minute or two, then lower broiler when meat is turned over.

If broiler rack is of the semisolid type, heat transfer through the rack may cook the meat from the bottom, shortening the cooking time. Therefore decrease time as necessary *on second side*.

▶ BEEF ◀

Planked Steaks

The board for planked meats or fish should be of oak or hickory at least 1 inch thick. The more a plank is used, the better the flavor of the food cooked on it. The plank must be thoroughly heated in the oven for about 10 minutes before the meat or fish is placed on it, and the first few times it should be brushed over with oil, butter, or other shortening, but after it is thoroughly seasoned this becomes unnecessary. Never scrub a plank, but after use, wipe it with a clean damp cloth and rinse surface only with boiling water *and dry it thoroughly before storing*. Keep it wrapped in a cool, airy place until ready to be used.

Planked foods are always served on the plank with their accompanying vegetables and garnishes. Trays of silver or other metals are sold in which the plank may rest for table service, or it may be laid on a stainless steel, silver, or aluminum platter.

Oven-broil or pan-broil a tender steak or individual beef tenderloins on 1 side for half of the time suggested, depending on thickness. Remove steak from broiler to buttered heated plank with unbroiled side up. Pipe close to edge a thick border of seasoned mashed or Duchesse Potatoes (page 301), using pastry bag and No. 7 star cookie tin tube for large planks and No. 3 star tin tube for small planks. Place under broiler about 2½ inches from heating element or flame, and cook until steak is done and potatoes are brown (about 10 to 15 minutes, depending on thickness of meat). Remove plank from broiler and fill in exposed parts of plank with hot cooked and buttered seasoned vegetables, such as green beans, whole or sliced carrots, corn, asparagus tips, brussels sprouts, peas, sautéed mushrooms, etc. If using tomatoes, place on plank at same time as potatoes and broil; then add other vegetables.

Just before serving, spread or brush steak with melted or very soft butter, and serve at once. Top of steak may be garnished with sliced or whole sautéed mushrooms.

If plank must stand after it is completed, it may be kept hot in a 300° F. oven for a few minutes (not longer).

Pan-Broiled Steaks

Place the steak over medium heat in a hot skillet or on a grill that has been lightly rubbed with a little steak suet. Brown first on 1 side, then on the other. Pour off the fat as it accumulates. Do not cover pan and do not add water. Season last few minutes. (Steaks that are cut ¾ inch thick or less are better prepared in this way.) Definite times for pan-broiling cannot be given. When almost done, test by cutting a small gash close to bone and note the color of the meat. For medium done, it takes about 7 minutes each side for ¾ inch steaks. Decrease or increase cooking time, according to thickness. Keep heat medium.

Whole Roasted Beef Tenderloin

See page 127 before preparing meat. Have a large fillet of beef (about 3 to 4 pounds) well trimmed, ready for roasting. Rub with a cut clove garlic. Place it on a rack with drip pan underneath. Brush well with soft or melted butter. Sprinkle with salt and pepper. Roast fillet at 425° F. for 30 minutes, then turn meat over, reduce *heat* and continue to cook at 300° F. about

> 15 more minutes per pound for rare
> 20 more minutes per pound for medium
> 25 more minutes per pound for well done

or tenderloin may be roasted at 400° F. for about 1 hour total time, turning over after 30 minutes.

It is better to use meat thermometer to determine doneness of meat, which may be inserted on thickest end of meat. Baste meat every 15 minutes with melted butter or drippings in pan, or even better with 1 recipe French Dressing (page 333) for Cornish Hens. Watch closely and as soon as drippings appear in pan, add 1 cup of hot stock or water to prevent scorching. Add more liquid if and as needed. Any leftover liquid with drippings in pan can be used for gravy.

When meat is done, remove to a hot platter with attractive side up. Let stand about 15 minutes before slicing and serving.

Meanwhile prepare gravy with drippings in pan. Add more liquid to make required amount of gravy. For each cup of liquid add 1½ tablespoons, more or less, cornstarch diluted in 2 tablespoons cool water (or 3 tablespoons flour diluted in ¼ cup water). Cook until thick, then let simmer about 5 minutes, adding salt and other seasonings to taste if necessary.

To Serve. Pour a recipe (more or less) of Risotto Milanese (page 805) or mixed vegetables into a large oval platter. Pack down smoothly, making a slight depression in center to place the sliced tenderloin, overlapping slices. Pour some of the gravy over meat. Cornstarch will give a more attractive and glazy gravy than flour. Garnish top of meat with large Sautéed Carved Mushrooms (page 134), preferably with stems sliced off, and brush them with a little gravy. Two packages cooked buttered asparagus spears, broccoli, or peas may be served around base of platter. Garnish ends of platter with parsley bouquets and vegetable roses or other flowers.

Special Mushroom Gravy

Makes 2 cups

In 2 tablespoons (or more) hot butter sauté 1 cup sliced or chopped fresh mushrooms for several minutes, turning to brown evenly. Add 3 table-spoons cornstarch diluted with ¼ cup water or stock (or ⅓ cup water or stock). Add 2 cups of cool vegetable or meat stock slowly and ¼ cup finely cut fresh green onion and stems. Let simmer about 3 minutes. Last, add a little salt if needed, a few pieces of pimiento cut in ½-inch pieces, a little gravy coloring if necessary, and 1 or 2 tablespoons dry wine if desired. Simmer several minutes longer.

Sautéed Carved Mushrooms for Beef Tenderloin

Purchase large firm stuffing mushrooms. (This size mushroom must be ordered several days in advance as they are not always available.) May be brushed with lemon juice to keep light. Wash them well, dry on towels. Slice off stems (do not pull off). Flute to simulate a flower or leave plain. Sauté mushrooms in ¼ cup butter or margarine with rounded side down first over moderate heat. Turn and brown second side. Cover skillet if mushrooms are very large and thick, and steam about 3 or 4 minutes, but do not overcook. They should retain their shape. This can be done an hour or longer in advance and kept covered. Reheat very gently for 2 or 3 minutes just before serving.

Fillet of Beef Wellington

1 whole well-trimmed oven-ready fillet of beef (remove tail end, and cut off about 1 inch from large end, to make uniform as possible in thickness), weighing about 3½ to 4½ pounds

¾ recipe New Quick Puff Paste (page 136), or ¾ recipe Classic Puff Paste (page 645), made with butter

Your favorite French dressing, or ours (page 368), or instead beef may be brushed with melted butter several times, and seasoned to suit taste

Cornstarch

Dry wine (optional)

Sliced sautéed mushrooms

Please read page 127 before preparing meat. Brush fillet of beef well on entire surface, top and bottom, with French Dressing or melted butter, cover and refrigerate for several hours, brushing it with more French Dressing several times, until ready to be roasted.

Several hours before serving, place meat on long rack in a shallow baking sheet, and roast in a 400° F. preheated oven 30 minutes on first side, then turn over carefully and roast underside about 35 more minutes, or until meat thermometer (placed into thickest end of meat) registers about 130° F. for rare, 140° F. for medium rare. Beef Wellington should not be served well done. Temperature of meat will rise a few degrees while cooling. Brush meat several times during roasting time with French Dressing or melted butter. As soon as drippings appear in pan, add about 2 cups hot stock or water, very little at a time, to prevent scorching and to be used for gravy.

When meat reaches desired temperature, remove from oven at once. Let meat cool, room temperature, but not too cold if to be served within a short time. However, if preferred, meat may be roasted long in advance, but must be refrigerated if to stand for more than about an hour. If cooked meat has been refrigerated, remove about an hour in advance. *Reserve drippings for gravy to be made later.*

To prepare Wellington, roll ¾ recipe Puff Paste (you can use a rich pie pastry instead) to measure about 18 inches square for a fillet weighing about 3½ to 4½ pounds after it is completely trimmed and oven-ready. For more servings 2 fillets may be put together, to make 1 long fillet. In this case roll full recipe of Puff Pastry to measure about 20 inches square.

Prepare Chicken Liver Paté (page 137) and let cool to lukewarm and of spreading consistency. If made long in advance and refrigerated, reheat it gently for a few seconds until tepid, but not too warm. Spread top and upper part only of sides of cool tenderloin with paté, smooth as possible. Roll pastry to recommended size, 18 × 18 inches. Carefully pick up meat with both hands *and place it with paté side down onto center of rolled pastry.* Brush 1 end of pastry with Egg White Glaze (page 137). Trim off opposite side, leaving enough dough to overlap, about 1½ inches. Reserve trimmings for top decorations. Enclose fillet in pastry dough, sealing all open ends. Now lift up carefully and place on large flat baking sheet covered with greased silicone paper, placing seam side down. Brush entire surface and sides of exposed pastry with Egg White Glaze.

Now roll scraps of pastry about thickness of pie crust, and cut out 5 daisies with large daisy cutter. With 1 teaspoon pastry dough form flat balls and place 3 on top, evenly spaced, and 1 on center of each end. Brush again with Egg White Glaze. Place a daisy on top of each flat ball, and 1 on each end. Brush daisies with Egg White Glaze. With about ½ teaspoon dough form pencil-like strips about 3 inches long, and form coils. Place 1 on center top of each daisy. Roll rest of leftover scraps, thicker than for daisies, and with pizza wheel cut out wide 3-inch-long leaves, about 8 in all; place on top and ends of pastry. Brush leaves with Egg White Glaze. Other pastry decorations may be cut out with various cutters. Bake as soon as possible.

Bake Wellington in preheated 425° F. oven 20 minutes, or until golden brown. Lower heat to 300° F. *and brush light top part of pastry with Egg*

White Glaze. Continue to bake at 300° F. about 30 more minutes, but watch closely toward end to prevent overbrowning or burning. May be kept hot for a short time in oven with heat shut off, door partially open.

About 15 minutes before Wellington is done, prepare gravy with reserved drippings from first cooking of fillet. Keep meat in oven with heat shut off until gravy is made. Remove surplus fat from drippings, adding more stock or water to make required amount. Add about 1½ tablespoons cornstarch with little water for each cup of liquid. Combine and cook until thick, then simmer about 5 minutes. Add a little dry wine if desired, and some sliced sautéed mushrooms. A little gravy coloring may be added if necessary.

To Serve. When done place a pancake turner on each end of meat, and transfer carefully to a heated oval or oblong platter. Arrange grilled Parmesan Tomatoes au Gratin (page 318) around base, and short broccoli or asparagus spears brushed with melted butter and seasoned. Serve Sauce Bearnaise (page 341) separately for vegetable. Serve meat gravy separately. Slice meat crosswise with a very sharp knife, at least 1 inch thick, or better 1½ inches.

Note. Allow about ⅓ pound or little more of uncooked trimmed fillet of beef for each serving.

New Quick Puff Paste

4 cups sifted unbleached all-purpose flour (or more if needed)	half cups (must be spreading consistency)
3 teaspoons, or less, salt	1⅛ cups warm water, combined with
2 cups *soft* swiftning, divided in 4	2 slightly beaten egg yolks

Sift flour and salt together in an 8-inch bowl. Add ½ cup of the very soft shortening, and with pie blender cut through until it looks like a very fine meal. Add the warm water and yolks, all at once, and with a large wooden spoon blend well, until difficult to mix further. Turn dough out onto floured pastry cloth and knead gently several minutes until smooth. If dough is sticky and clings to hands during kneading process, *add little more flour*, keeping it medium consistency. Now place smooth dough into well-greased 8-inch bowl, cover tightly in plastic bag, and place in *freezer* about 15 minutes, or in coldest part of refrigerator for 30 minutes.

After 15 minutes in freezer (or 30 if in refrigerator), roll dough to measure about 12 × 24 inches, and with rubber scraper spread ½ cup of the soft shortening over entire surface. Fold in thirds, place on flat baking sheet covered with wax paper, wrap well, and place in freezer 15 minutes (or coldest part of refrigerator 30 minutes). Repeat rollings and spreading of shortening in 15- (or 30-) minute intervals until all shortening has been used. *After last* rolling, pastry must be kept in freezer at least 30 minutes, not more than 40 minutes, if to be used at once, or in refrigerator 1½ hours, or as long as 2 days (not longer), well wrapped. May be frozen for 2 weeks. If pastry feels very stiff when ready to use, let stand room temperature, covered, a few minutes, but not soft. Cut off rolled ends from dough.

Egg White Glaze for Top of Puff Paste

Have egg whites room temperature or lukewarm. For each egg white, beat with *fluffy beater* a few seconds until foamy, then add ¼ teaspoon of salt or lemon juice, and beat again a few seconds, until well blended and foamy. Let stand 15 minutes or longer. Use as indicated in each recipe.

Chicken Liver Mushroom Paté

¼ pound chicken livers, well drained and dried on towel, sautéed gently in 2 tablespoons butter about 10 minutes, then well drained

¼ pound fresh mushrooms, washed, dried thoroughly, and sautéed in 2 tablespoons butter about 5 minutes, or 1 medium-size can chopped mushrooms, well drained

½ cup cooked ham

¼ teaspoon pepper

¼ teaspoon oregano leaves

Salt

¾ cup chicken or beef stock (can use bouillon cube), combined with ¼ cup sifted flour, forming smooth mixture

About 2 or more tablespoons dry wine

1 clove garlic, put through garlic press, or chopped very fine

Place cooked livers, mushrooms, and ham on cutting board, and with large heavy knife chop until medium consistency, not too fine, and not too coarse.

In a large skillet combine leftover drippings from livers and mushrooms; add 1 more tablespoon butter, and when hot, add chopped ingredients. Add pepper, oregano leaves, and a little salt if needed. Cook together about 5 minutes over medium heat. Now add the flour combined with stock, stir well and cook until thick, then simmer about 5 minutes, adding wine and garlic the last 2 minutes. Let cool to tepid before spreading onto meat. If made in advance, must be refrigerated. Taste and season further if necessary.

Chauteaubriand

Please read page 119 before preparing this recipe. Chateaubriand is prepared from the choicest and most tender center cut of a prime beef tenderloin, and is a favorite of French chefs and epicureans. It is usually served whole, roasted or broiled, and is sliced at the table. In recent years many of the fine continental restaurants serve individual Chateaubriands, cut about 1½ inches thick, weighing anywhere from 6 to 8 ounces; or they will serve a larger size for two, as requested. For individual servings, if the whole tenderloin is not thick, have it cut or cut it yourself in 2-inch pieces, then flatten with a cleaver, or strike top cut part of meat with bottom of a small skillet or saucepan to desired thickness. Then meat may be dipped into melted butter and broiled according to general directions for Filet Mignon (page 129). We have a very special way to prepare and serve the whole Chateaubriand for formal occasions.

Whole Chateaubriand for Special Occasions. Purchase a large thick prime tenderloin, well trimmed, peeled, and all sinew removed by the butcher. Cut away about 6 or 7 inches of the narrow end and a 1½-inch piece from thick end. Only the thickest and most attractive part of the meat is used for this dish. If the meat is not neat and firm, tie it with string in several places until it is done, then remove string.

Place the uncooked meat into an enamel, glass, or stainless steel dish and cover it with Meat Marinade (page 120). Do not use other metal utensils for soaking meat (except stainless steel) as often the acid in the marinades will act upon the metal chemically and develop an unpleasant taste in the meat. Let meat soak for about 4 hours, turning it over, and basting it often. Keep it in refrigerator, but let stand in room temperature in marinade at least an hour or longer before cooking.

When ready to cook, drain meat well, *dry surface with paper towel.* Place it on a rack in a flat pan, in 400° F. oven for about 1 to 1½ hours, depending on size and thickness, or until thermometer reads 130° F. for rare; 140° F. for medium-rare. It is important to brush meat with soft or melted butter from the very start and several times during the roasting period, to brown it attractively. Marinades do not brown well because of the moisture content but do add flavor. Pour a cup or more of stock or water into roasting pan to prevent scorching, as this will be used later for glaze. Allow about 1½ hours for a large thick tenderloin that weighs about 4 pounds, less time for smaller sizes. Watch closely and add more liquid to drippings as needed. When meat is done, remove from oven, and serve it hot with Sauce Bearnaise (page 341), Vegetables Vinaigrette (page 318), Glazed Stuffed Artichoke Bottoms (page 273), and Marinated Mushrooms (page 293).

For An Elaborate Cold Buffet Dinner. Prepare and roast meat as directed above about 2 *hours before you are to serve it, or even a day in advance.* If to stand for more than 2 hours in room temperature, please refrigerate. About an hour before serving, brush entire surface of meat with lukewarm Glaze given below. Let stand a few minutes and glaze it a second time. Let drain well, then lift meat up carefully and place it in center of a large oval platter. Garnish top of meat with a row of glazed Marinated Mushrooms (page 293) or with Stuffed Artichoke Bottoms (page 273), also brushed with Glaze. Surround base of meat first with a thick border of cold Carrot Wedges Vinaigrette, then with a thick border of Broccoli or Asparagus Tips Vinaigrette (see Vegetables Vinaigrette, page 318). This is one of the most unusual and delectable dinners for special occasions. Meat may be sliced in ½-inch slices before it is garnished, or sliced at the table.

Individual Oven-Broiled Chateaubriands

Tie individual 1½-to-2-inch-thick tenderloins top and bottom if meat is not neat and firm. Marinate them for about 4 hours as directed for whole Chateaubriand. Drain well. Brown in very hot butter in a skillet on top of stove for about 2 or 3 minutes on each side. Place on a rack in shallow pan, and in a 450° F. preheated oven, *not broiler*, pour cup hot water or stock into pan. Brush meat well with melted butter several times (not marinade) and allow about 15 minutes for 1½-inch-thick pieces, turning them over when top is brown. *It is important to remove meat from refrigerator about 1 hour or longer before cooking.*

Individual oven-broiled Chateaubriands may vary in cooking time from 2 to 3 minutes depending on temperature and thickness of meat. Best to allow an extra 5 minutes. Test 1 by making an incision down center of bottom side, and observe color. They are always best cooked rare or medium-rare, but not well-done. This is an excellent way to prepare individual tenderloins as it is easier, meat is more delectable, requires less watching, and more meat may be prepared at one time than when using broiling section.

Unmarinated Chateaubriands may be *oven-broiled* for the same length of time, first dipping them into melted butter.

Individual tenderloins are attractive served on rounds of sautéed breads cut same width as meat, and top of meat garnished with a glazed Marinated Mushroom (page 293) or Stuffed Artichoke Bottoms (page 273) or Sauce Bearnaise (page 341).

Glaze and Gravy for Chateaubriands

Use the drippings and liquid remaining in roasting pan after meat is done. Add more stock or water to make required amount. Strain, and to each cup use 4 level teaspoons cornstarch diluted in 2 tablespoons water. Cook until thick, then simmer at least 5 minutes, stirring all the time. Add a little commercial gravy coloring. Let stand until lukewarm, and if too thick add a bit of water.

Corned Beef

Purchase only top-quality branded corned beef for good results. Wash corned beef thoroughly under cool running water. Place it on a rack in a large pot, cover with cool water and bring slowly to the boiling point. Now lower heat and simmer until fork-tender. For pieces weighing 5 to 7 pounds, cook 45 to 60 minutes per pound, depending on quality. For pieces over 7 pounds, cook 30 to 45 minutes per pound. Keep pot covered and add more hot water during the cooking process to keep meat always submerged in liquid. Turn meat over every hour and continue to cook until it does not cling to dinner fork when tested in leanest part, and meat remains in pot when fork is removed. Allow meat to remain in its own liquid for at least ½ hour after it is done. If it is to be served cold, plunge it into ice water as soon as removed from hot liquid, and keep it in ice water for several hours. Then drain well, wrap in wax paper and refrigerate until ready to serve. This will firm up meat, making it easy to slice thin. Or let it cool in liquid, then refrigerate.

Carving. Always slice corned beef against the grain when possible. If meat is to be served hot, sprinkle it with paprika after it is removed from liquid, place on a rack with drip pan underneath, and bake for about 10 minutes at 450° F., basting meat with some corned beef liquid several times, and sprinkle with more paprika.

To Serve. Surround corned beef slices with boiled cabbage or Brussels sprouts, potatoes and carrots, or as desired.

Beef Stew Gourmet

2½ pounds of beef chuck, heel of round, top of round, sirloin tip, or neck, cut into 1¼-inch pieces
Flour
¼ cup butter or margarine (best to use part oil or unsalted shortening)
About 3 teaspoons salt
½ teaspoon pepper
½ teaspoon marjoram
½ teaspoon celery salt
½ teaspoon thyme
½ cup, more or less, of dry red or white wine

About 2½ cups of meat or vegetable stock (or add 2 teaspoons instant boullion to 2½ cups water)
1 cup or more very small whole carrots, or cut into 3-inch thick wedges
1 cup whole very small onions (if medium cut in quarters); canned whole onions can be used
1 cup whole new very small potatoes (optional), or can use whole canned potatoes
1 small package frozen peas, or cut green beans, defrosted
Cornstarch

Dry meat well on paper toweling, or roll lightly into flour; brown it thoroughly in the hot butter, or preferably half shortening or oil, over medium heat. Do not rush it. Add seasonings, the wine, about 2½ cups of stock, or enough to submerge meat. Cover stew pan, and *simmer* meat gently until it is almost tender, about 1 hour if you are using Premium Pro'Ten beef (cook longer for other grades). May take anywhere from

1½ to 2½ hours, depending on quality. When meat is almost done, add the carrots, onions, and potatoes. Cover and continue to simmer for about 20 more minutes, or only until meat and vegetables are tender, not too soft. Now add the green peas or string beans, and simmer about 7 or 8 more minutes.

Last, drain all of liquid from stew, measure, and if less than 2 cups, add water or stock. To each cup of liquid, add 1½ tablespoons cornstarch dissolved in 2 tablespoons water. Stir well, and cook gravy until thick, then simmer about 5 minutes. Add a little gravy coloring if needed. Taste and season further if necessary.

Arrange stew attractively in a chafing dish or deep serving platter. Pour part of glossy gravy over stew, reserving some to serve separately with buttered, seasoned noodles or rice.

Corned Beef for Oven Roasting

Purchase Premium Corned Beef *For Oven Roasting.* Cut end of wrapper and remove roast. Place roast, fat side up on a rack in a shallow open pan. Do not cover or add water. Roast in a slow oven (325° F.) about 3 hours, or until fork tender. If a sharp-tined meat fork can be inserted and removed easily the meat is tender. Let the cooked roast stand 15 minutes before slicing.

This roast may also be used for rotisserie cooking. Rotisserie cooking time is about the same as oven roasting time. Or if desired, this corned beef may be braised in a small amount of water in a tightly covered kettle until fork-tender.

Do not use meat thermometer in this roast.

Pot Roast of Beef

A top-quality pot roast has as much nourishment and flavor as a rib roast if it is properly cooked. Pot roast is not the name of a cut of meat. It's a way of cooking. There are several good cuts of beef for pot roasting, such as Boston cut, round bone or arm cut, flat bone, heel of round, or boneless rump.

Top of Stove Pot Roasting. Select a piece 4 to 5 pounds in weight. Wipe it with a damp cloth. Rub well with flour. Brown the meat on all sides in a heavy kettle in about 3 tablespoons of butter and shortening. Slip a rack under the meat and add ¼ cup or more hot water. Cover tightly and cook slowly (simmer) until tender about 45 minutes per pound, or until fork-tender and meat separates from bones, depending on quality of meat. Turn occasionally and add about 4 tablespoons of hot water from time to time as needed to prevent scorching during cooking process. When meat is half done, season it with salt, pepper, sliced onion, and a little celery, a small bay leaf, and continue to cook until done.

Oven Pot Roasting. Pot roasting can be done in the oven instead of on top of stove. First brown meat on all sides, according to our general directions; place it on a trivet, add about ½ cup hot water, cover pan and roast at 325° F. about 45 minutes per pound, or until meat is fork-tender and separates from bones, depending on quality of meat and size of roast. When meat is almost done, about last half hour, *remove cover*, and continue to cook until attractively brown.

Carving. With some pot roasts it is easier to remove a section of the meat from the bone, turn it on its side, then cut across the grain. Always carve it thin if using the *round or a lean* piece of beef. There is about twice as much beef available for pot roasting as the choicer cuts, and because it is a very nutritious and economical piece of meat it should be used often in the diet.

Gravy for Pot Roast of Beef

Remove meat and most of fat from drippings; add water or stock to drippings in pan. Season further if necessary. If a thicker gravy is desired, add about 2 tablespoons of flour combined with a little cold water to form paste for each cup of liquid. Cook until thick, about 5 minutes after simmering begins. A little commercial gravy coloring may be added if necessary.

Uniform size whole potatoes and carrots may also be added the last hour around pot roast, or they may be cooked separately and then added the last few minutes to take on flavor.

Meat Loaf De Luxe

2 pounds lean ground beef and ¼ pound ground beef suet, or 1½ pounds beef and 1 pound ground pork or lamb shoulder, lean	½ teaspoon any kind meat seasoning
	1 very small clove garlic, chopped fine or put through garlic press (optional)
1 cup dry bread crumbs, or less	
1 cup milk (part catsup or chili sauce may be used)	1 small onion, chopped fine (may be sautéed in 1 tablespoon fat)
About 2 teaspoons salt	2 large whole eggs, beaten slightly
½ teaspoon thyme	2 or 3 slices bacon (optional)

In a large bowl mix above ingredients, except bacon, in the order given. Place meat on an oval 17-inch heatproof serving platter, and with hands shape it into a loaf that measures about 12 inches long and 2½ inches thick, tapering ends slightly. Bake in preheated 400° F. oven 30 minutes, then lower heat to 325° F. Add about ¼ cup water or stock to drippings in pan, and more as needed to prevent drippings from scorching during baking process. Continue to bake meat about 45 minutes more to 170° F. Reduce time by 15 minutes for half recipe of meat. Baste meat with drippings in platter from time to time.

For additional flavor, 2 or 3 slices of bacon may be placed crosswise on meat after it has baked the first 30 minutes. If bacon slices are long, cut them in halves crosswise.

When meat is done, remove from oven; let it stand about 15 minutes before it is cut and served. Meanwhile, drippings in baking dish may be removed and served separately, or they may be combined with a little water or stock and thickened with cornstarch or flour, using 1 tablespoon cornstarch or 2 tablespoons flour diluted in 2 tablespoons water for each cup of gravy to be made. Taste and season further if necessary with a bouillon cube and commercial gravy coloring. Let simmer about 5 minutes. Arrange cooked vegetables and potatoes, or well seasoned, buttered noodles around base of meat loaf, and serve hot.

Note. Meat loaves may be served hot or cold. To reheat leftover meat loaf, slice and sauté in small amount hot butter or margarine about 2 minutes on each side.

Meat loaf may be baked in a loaf pan, but baking on a flat pan produces a more delectable and brown crusty surface. If it is baked in a loaf pan, let it stand in room temperature in pan about 20 minutes to absorb the meat juices *before turning* it out onto serving platter. Meat loaves may be shaped and baked on cake racks with drip pan underneath, following our general directions. Let cool 15 minutes, then release meat from rack with a large spatula or knife, and carefully slide it onto a serving platter.

Stuffed Cabbage Leaves

Makes about 12 medium-sized rolls

1 pound ground beef, veal, pork or lamb (add ½ cup warm water to raw beef and ¼ cup to other meats)
¼ cup, or more, uncooked rice
¼ teaspoon pepper
1 medium onion chopped fine
1½ teaspoons salt

2 pounds loose cabbage
2 cups fresh or canned cut-up tomatoes, to which add ¼ teaspoon soda, 2 teaspoons salt, and ¼ teaspoon pepper
About 3 cups or more water, tomato juice, or extra tomatoes

Combine meat, rice, chopped onion, salt and pepper. Mix well. Cut cabbage in halves. Discard outer tough leaves. Remove core and separate leaves. Cook them in boiling water for several minutes until soft enough to roll. Drain well, and when cool place a roll of the meat mixture on each leaf and roll to enclose meat. In 3-quart pan, place rolls carefully in layers, ¼ inch apart, with open ends down. Cover with tomatoes and liquid to cover rolls, and place a heavy heatproof plate over rolls to prevent floating. Plate is not necessary if heat is kept at simmer. Cook slowly in a covered saucepan about 1¼ hours if using veal, pork, or lamb; 1½ hours if using beef. Test a roll for doneness before serving. Cook longer if necessary.

Beef Bordelaise

1 hard-cooked egg, chopped fine
1 small onion, sliced thin
About 1 teaspoon salt and ¼ teaspoon pepper
Pinch nutmeg on each piece of meat
About 2 tablespoons fresh chopped parsley
1 anchovy cut into small pieces, or a little anchovy paste (optional)

2 tablespoons finely chopped suet or bacon (or small pieces of firm butter or margarine)
1 pound round steak (or flank steak) sliced thin and pounded, or cubed
Flour
¼ cup butter and shortening
1 cup water or stock
About 1 tablespoon cornstarch
1 tablespoon dry red wine
About ¼ cup sautéed mushrooms

Sprinkle egg, onion, salt, pepper, nutmeg, parsley, anchovy and suet over pounded meat slices. Roll carefully and tightly. Hold rolls together with wood pins wherever necessary. Roll them in flour, and shake off loose flour. Brown well on both sides in combined hot butter and shortening over medium heat. Season with a little more salt and pepper. Place in a small heavy saucepan or skillet if preparing only 1 pound of meat. Add 1 cup water or stock, cover tightly and cook slowly at simmering point, turning rolls over several times, for about 1½ to 2 hours or until meat is fork tender. When meat is done, pour off liquid, measure, and to each cup add about 1 or more tablespoons cornstarch combined with 2 tablespoons water. Cook until thick and smooth, and simmer about 5 minutes. Now add dry wine and sliced sautéed mushrooms. Taste and season further if necessary.

How to Serve Beef Bordelaise. Brush meat with hot gravy; arrange it in center of large round platter. Place individual fruit or vegetable salad around meat, alternately with Italian Potato Croquettes, page 813.

Hamburgers with Smothered Onions

Have good quality round steak or boiling beef freshly ground. If beef is very lean, have butcher grind with it 2 ounces of beef suet. *Omit suet if beef has some fat.* The extra suet will add flavor, moisture, and tenderness to the hamburgers. Season each pound of meat with about 1 teaspoon salt, ¼ teaspoon garlic salt or ⅛ teaspoon garlic powder, ⅛ teaspoon celery salt, ⅛ teaspoon paprika, ⅛ teaspoon black pepper. Combine these seasonings with 2 tablespoons hot water and mix well. Pour mixture over the chopped meat and blend well with a fork. For large hamburgers, measure ½ standard measuring cup of meat; shape it into balls, then flatten into 5-inch round patties, or use hamburger former. Sauté on a hot griddle or in a heavy hot skillet, over medium heat, in a small amount of butter or margarine. Cook 2 minutes on each side for medium, or about 3 minutes on each side for well done. Do not turn until meat is brown on first side, *and do not overcook.*

A large amount of hamburger seasoning can be prepared at one time, stored in covered container and used as needed. Shake well. Use 2½ teaspoons seasoning combined with 2 tablespoons hot water for each pound of meat.

Note. If using heavy griddle pan or heavy nonstick skillet, it is not necessary to use butter or other fat. Simply rub hot griddle lightly with piece of beef suet or shortening. Place seasoned meat on hot grill and cook over moderate heat until brown on one side, about 2 or 3 minutes. Turn over and brown second side about 2 or 3 minutes.

Smothered Onions

Slice onions and sauté them in a small amount of butter or margarine in an uncovered skillet until lightly brown. Sprinkle with salt and paprika. Cover and allow to steam about 5 minutes, or until crisply tender.

Broiled or Sautéed Salisbury Steaks

1 pound ground beef, with some ground suet	⅓ cup commercial dry crumbs (½ cup home-type)
1 recipe Thick White or Mushroom Sauce (page 146)	About 1½ teaspoons salt
	¼ teaspoon pepper
	1 large egg

In a medium-size bowl combine all ingredients, and beat until well blended. Let preparation stand at least ½ hour before shaping steaks into 4 large oval patties, about 1 inch thick. Place them on well-greased pan (not broiling rack) to keep them moist. Brush top and bottom of meat with warm melted butter or margarine. Broil at 500° F. about 3 inches from heat about 7 minutes on each side for well done; only about 5 minutes each side for medium. Serve plain, or garnish top with sautéed sliced mushrooms.

Note. Instead of broiling, these patties may be sautéed for about 5 minutes on each side in a small amount of hot butter combined with a little oil or unsalted shortening.

Thick White Sauce

2 tablespoons butter or margarine   ¾ cup very hot milk
3 tablespoons sifted flour

In a 1-quart saucepan, melt butter, add flour, and stir until smooth. Add very hot milk all at once, and quickly stir continuously over low heat until smooth and thick. Let simmer several minutes. Do not season if using in Salisbury Steaks, as seasonings were included in the meat preparation.

Thick Mushroom Sauce

¼ cup very finely chopped canned mushrooms, or ½ cup fresh
2 tablespoons butter or margarine
3 tablespoons sifted flour
¾ cup very hot milk

In a 1-quart saucepan sauté mushrooms in the 2 tablespoons hot butter for several minutes over low heat. Add flour, and blend well. Last, add very hot milk *all at once*, and quickly stir continuously over low heat until smooth and thick. Let simmer several minutes. Do not season if using in Salisbury Steaks, as seasonings were included in the meat preparation.

Jumbo Stuffed Baked and Broiled Green Pepper Beefburger

Serves 4

1 pound of fine-ground beef with some extra suet
1 teaspoon salt
¼ teaspoon black pepper
1 medium-size onion, minced
1 egg
¼ cup milk
⅓ cup dry bread crumbs
¼ cup chili sauce

Combine all ingredients except chili sauce, and blend thoroughly. Let stand ½ hour. Divide into 2 portions. Shape each piece into a 6 × 8-inch oval. Place Green Pepper Filling on one, spreading it to about 1 inch from edges. Place rest of meat over top and pinch ends to enclose filling. Shape as uniformly as possible on an oval 17-inch baking platter (or round glass baking dish). Brush top with ¼ cup chili sauce. Bake on bottom rack of oven at 450° F. about 15 minutes then place under broiler at 450° F. about 3 inches from heat about 7 or 8 minutes, but watch closely that it does not scorch.

To Serve. Place whole cooked vegetables and potatoes around meat and serve with chili sauce or catsup in an attractive bowl.

Green Pepper Filling

Sauté 2 cups fresh green pepper, cut about 2 inches long and 1 inch wide, in ¼ cup shortening about 5 minutes. Add 2 slivers of garlic, ½ teaspoon salt, and cook about 2 more minutes.

Jumbo Stuffed Mushroom and Green Pepper Beefburger

Serves 4

1 pound fine-ground beef with some extra suet	1 egg
1 teaspoon salt	¼ cup milk
¼ teaspoon black pepper	⅓ cup dry bread crumbs
1 medium-size onion, minced	¼ cup chili sauce

Combine all ingredients except chili sauce, and blend thoroughly. Let stand ½ hour. Divide into 2 portions. Shape each piece into a 6 × 8-inch oval. Place Mushroom and Green Pepper Filling on one, spreading it to about 1 inch from edges. Place other meat over it, and pinch end to enclose filling. Shape as uniformly as possible on an oval 17-inch baking platter (or round glass baking dish). Brush top with ¼ cup chili sauce. Bake on bottom rack of oven at 450° F. about 15 minutes; then place under broiler at 450° F. about 3 inches from heat for about 7 or 8 minutes, but watch closely that it does not scorch.

To Serve. Place cooked vegetable, potatoes, noodles, or rice around meat, and serve extra chili sauce or catsup separately.

Mushroom and Green Pepper Filling

Sauté 1 cup fresh green pepper, cut 2 inches long and 1 inch wide, in 2 tablespoons shortening with 2 slivers of garlic until lightly browned, about 5 minutes. Sauté 1 cup fresh mushrooms, sliced medium-thin, in 2 tablespoons shortening about 3 minutes. Combine peppers and mushrooms, and season with about ½ teaspoon salt, ¼ teaspoon pepper. Cook about 2 or 3 minutes.

Jumbo Baked and Broiled Cheeseburger

Serves 4

1 pound fine-ground beef	¼ cup milk
1 teaspoon, or less, salt	⅓ cup dry bread crumbs
¼ teaspoon black pepper	¼ pound coarse-shredded American
1 medium-size onion, minced	cheese
1 egg	

Combine all ingredients except cheese, and blend thoroughly. Let stand ½ hour. Place ½ of meat about ½ inch thick on an oval greased heatproof serving platter. Cover center of meat with shredded cheese, leaving about 1 inch all around uncovered with cheese. Place rest of meat carefully on top; pat and pinch edges of meat to enclose cheese. Brush with melted butter and bake at 450° F. on lowest rack of oven 15 minutes; then place under broiler about 2 inches from heat at 450° F. until top is brown, about 6 or 7 minutes. Arrange Pan-fried Potatoes (page 300) and another cooked buttered vegetable around meat, and serve with a salad and Special Hostess Sauce (page 334).

Mushroom Beefburgers

1 pound beef ground with ¼ cup beef suet	⅛ teaspoon celery salt
1 teaspoon, or less, salt	⅛ teaspoon paprika
¼ teaspoon garlic salt	⅛ teaspoon black pepper

Combine all ingredients and blend well. Divide into 8 uniform portions. Shape into balls, then into 4-inch patties on wax paper. Place ¼ of Mushroom Filling on each of 4 patties. Place plain patties over filling. Pinch ends well. Pick up and with hands shape into uniform round patties to measure about 3½ inches in diameter. Keep them on individual pieces of wax paper until ready to be cooked.

Turn meat patties onto a well-greased hot grill or heavy skillet, and cook about 5 minutes on each side over moderate heat.

Serve on large round buns or sliced bread, or as a meat course with vegetables, potatoes, rice, or noodles.

Mushroom Filling

Sauté one 3- or 4-ounce can sliced or chopped mushrooms (or ¼ pound fresh mushrooms, chopped) in 2 tablespoons butter or other shortening with ¼ cup fine-chopped fresh green onion about 5 minutes over moderate heat. Divide into 4 equal portions.

Green Pepper and Mushroom Beefburgers

1 pound beef ground with ¼ cup beef suet	⅛ teaspoon celery salt
1 teaspoon, or less, salt	⅛ teaspoon paprika
¼ teaspoon garlic salt	⅛ teaspoon black pepper

Combine all ingredients and blend well. Divide into 8 uniform portions. Shape into balls, then into 4-inch patties on wax paper. Place ¼ of Green Pepper and Mushroom Filling on each of 4 patties. Place plain patties over filling. Pinch ends well. Pick up and with hands shape into uniform round patties to measure about 3½ inches in diameter. Keep them on individual pieces of wax paper until ready to be cooked.

Turn meat patties onto a well-greased hot grill or heavy skillet, and cook about 5 minutes on each side over moderate heat.

Serve on large round buns or sliced bread, or as a meat course with vegetables, potatoes, rice, or noodles.

Green Pepper and Mushroom Filling

In 2 tablespoons oil sauté ¾ cup fresh green pepper, cut into pieces 1 inch long by ½ inch wide, about 3 minutes until lightly browned. Cover and steam about 3 minutes; add a little minced garlic and ½ cup fresh mushrooms cut into small pieces, and sauté about 3 minutes longer. Season with ¼ teaspoon salt and ⅛ teaspoon black pepper. Divide into 4 equal parts.

Onion Beefburgers

1 pound beef ground with ¼ cup beef
    suet
1 teaspoon, or less, salt
¼ teaspoon garlic salt

⅛ teaspoon celery salt
⅛ teaspoon paprika
⅛ teaspoon black pepper

Combine all ingredients and blend well. Divide into 8 uniform portions. Shape into balls, then into 4-inch patties on wax paper. Place ¼ of Onion Filling on each of 4 patties. Place plain patties over onions. Pinch ends well. Pick up and with hands shape into uniform round patties to measure about 3½ inches in diameter. Keep them on individual pieces of wax paper until ready to be cooked.

Turn meat patties onto a well-greased hot grill or heavy skillet. Cook about 5 minutes on each side over moderate heat.

Serve on large round buns or sliced bread, or as a meat course with vegetables, potatoes, rice, or noodles.

Onion Filling

Sauté 1½ cups sliced onion in 2 tablespoons oil or shortening about 5 minutes until lightly browned and crisply tender, not too soft. If too firm, cover and steam about 5 minutes. Season with about ¼ teaspoon salt, ⅛ teaspoon pepper, and ⅛ teaspoon paprika.

Green Pepper Beefburgers

1 pound beef ground with ¼ cup beef
    suet
1 teaspoon, or less, salt
¼ teaspoon garlic salt

⅛ teaspoon celery salt
⅛ teaspoon paprika
⅛ teaspoon black pepper

Combine all ingredients and blend well. Divide into 8 uniform portions. Shape into balls, then into 4-inch patties on wax paper. Place ¼ of Green Pepper Beefburger Filling on each patty. Place plain patties over filling.

Pinch ends well. Pick up and with hands shape into uniform round patties to measure about 3½ inches in diameter. Keep them on individual pieces of wax paper until ready to be cooked.

Turn meat patties onto a well-greased hot grill or heavy skillet, and cook about 5 minutes on each side over moderate heat.

Serve on large round buns or sliced bread, or as a meat course with vegetables, potatoes, rice, or noodles.

Green Pepper Beefburger Filling

Sauté 1½ cups fresh green peppers, cut about 1 inch long and ½ inch wide, in 2 tablespoons oil or shortening about 3 or 4 minutes or until lightly browned. Then cover saucepan, and steam about 3 or 4 minutes. Peppers should be crisply tender, not too soft. Season with about ⅓ teaspoon salt and ⅛ teaspoon pepper during cooking process. When done, divide into 4 equal portions.

Broiled Cheeseburger Dinner or Luncheon

Serves 3 to 4

1 pound fine-ground beef with some suet	1 egg
	¼ cup milk
1 teaspoon, or less, salt	⅓ cup dry bread crumbs
¼ teaspoon black pepper	¼ cup coarse-shredded or chopped
1 medium-size onion, minced	American cheese

Combine all ingredients except cheese, and mix well. Let stand ½ hour. Divide into 8 uniform portions. Form round patties ½ inch thick. Place 4 of the patties on a greased heatproof serving platter. Cover center of meat (leaving about 1 inch uncovered) with cheese. Place rest of meat patties over cheese, pinching ends of meat well to enclose cheese. Shape smoothly. Brush tops with melted butter. Bake on lowest rack of oven set at 450° F. about 10 minutes. Then remove from oven and place under *broiler* about 2 inches from heat until top is brown, about 6 or 7 minutes. Do not turn over, as underside will be done.

Duchesse Potatoes (page 301) are very attractive and delicious around these cheeseburgers. Use bag and No. 7 cookie star tube, and pipe potatoes before cheeseburgers are placed in oven. Open spaces may be filled with buttered carrots, corn, or green vegetables just before serving. Serve Special Hostess Sauce separately.

Special Hostess Sauce

1 cup chili sauce	¼ cup prepared horseradish
½ cup catsup	2 teaspoons Worcestershire sauce

Combine all ingredients and blend well.

Deviled Hamburgers

1 pound ground round steak	1 teaspoon Worcestershire sauce
¼ cup chili sauce	1 teaspoon, or less, salt
2 teaspoons prepared mustard	¼ teaspoon pepper
1 teaspoon horseradish	2 teaspoons grated onion
1 very small clove garlic, minced	4 hamburger buns

Combine all above ingredients except hamburger buns, and blend well. Divide meat mixture into 4; flatten to 5-inch-round patties.

Sauté on a hot griddle or in a heavy hot frying pan, over medium heat, in a small amount of butter. Cook 2 minutes on each side for medium or about 3 minutes on each side for well done. Do not turn meat patties over to other side until brown on one side.

Split hamburger rolls in halves, brush with melted butter, and toast in broiler until golden brown. Serve at once.

Cornish Pasties

½ pound ground beef with some suet	¼ teaspoon pepper
¼ cup (or more) raw fine-chopped onion	About ½ cup vegetable or meat stock (if bouillon cube is added to
1 cup raw fine-chopped potatoes	water, reduce salt to about ¾ tea-
About 1 teaspoon salt	spoon)

Mix all ingredients and blend well. Do not add all of stock if mixture appears too soft. Divide into 4 equal parts.

Roll dough to measure about 16 × 16 inches square. Cut into 4 uniform squares. Place ¼ of the filling on each. Brush edges with beaten egg. Turn ½ of dough over filling. Turn edges, forming a seam. Go around with a fork to seal securely. Make several small gashes on top of each pasty. Brush with milk and bake at 400° F. about 40 to 45 minutes, or until golden brown.

Serve with a green vegetable and mushroom sauce for a light luncheon or supper, or serve hot as a snack.

Dough for 4 Large Pasties

1½ cups sifted all-purpose flour	1 medium-size egg beaten with fork,
½ teaspoon baking powder	combined with about ¼ cup milk
½ teaspoon salt	⅓ cup shortening

Sift dry ingredients. Cut shortening into dough until it looks like a fine meal. Add egg and milk to make medium dough, not too soft. Knead gently a few seconds until smooth. Wrap in wax paper and chill in refrigerator while preparing filling.

Cheeseburger Pie

1 pound fine-ground beef	1 medium-size onion chopped very
1 egg	fine
1 teaspoon, or less, salt	⅓ cup dry bread crumbs
¼ teaspoon black pepper	⅓ cup milk
	3 slices American (or other) cheese

Combine all ingredients except cheese, and blend thoroughly. Let stand ½ hour. Pat ½ of meat smoothly over bottom of 7-inch skillet that has been well greased on bottom and sides with 2 teaspoons shortening. Place cheese slices evenly over meat; then cover with rest of meat, patting smoothly. Cut (right in skillet) into 4 pie-shaped wedges. (If preparing 1½ recipes in an 8¼-inch skillet, cut into 6 wedges.) This dish may be prepared hours in advance and stored in refrigerator until about 20 minutes before serving. Cook on top of stove over moderately high heat about 10 minutes, or until browned on bottom and sides. Wrap handle of skillet with aluminum foil, brush top of meat well with melted butter, and broil at high temperature, about 2 inches from heat, 6 or 7 minutes, or until brown. Let stand in room temperature a few minutes, then lift out with pie or cake server, and serve with a vegetable, potatoes, and a salad.

Creole Round Steak Roll

Serves 4 to 6

1 cup moist bread crumbs	¼ cup melted butter or shortening
½ cup minced celery	1 large slice round steak (1½
¾ cup minced onion	pounds), cut about ⅓ inch thick
1 tablespoon chopped parsley	3 tablespoons shortening
1 teaspoon salt	2 cups canned tomatoes
⅛ teaspoon pepper	½ cup chopped green pepper
1 teaspoon sage	

Combine bread crumbs, celery, onion, parsley, salt, pepper, sage, and melted butter. Blend well.

Spread mixture over entire surface of round steak, and roll like jelly roll. Tie roll or hold together with wooden toothpicks. Brown meat roll in shortening. Place browned meat roll in a casserole to fit. Pour tomatoes and green pepper over meat. Cover casserole and bake in preheated 350° F. oven about 2 hours, or until tender when tested with fork.

About 45 minutes before meat is done, arrange small potatoes around meat. If drippings in casserole are too watery, thicken with 1 tablespoon cornstarch combined with 2 tablespoons water, and add to drippings about 15 minutes before meat is done.

Puffy Meat Patties

Serves 4

3 egg yolks
½ pound ground beef
¾ teaspoon salt
¼ teaspoon baking powder
¼ teaspoon black pepper

1 tablespoon, more or less, minced parsley, or 1 teaspoon dry
1 small grated or fine-chopped onion
3 egg whites beaten until they cling to bowl
Shortening

With egg beater, beat egg yolks about 1 minute. Add ground beef, salt, baking powder, pepper, parsley, and grated onion. Mix thoroughly. Last, fold in stiffly beaten egg whites and blend gently. Pick up with a large spoon and lower gently into about ⅛ inch of very hot shortening. Fry about 2 minutes on each side over moderate heat for medium-rare, or 3 minutes on each side for well done. Do not turn meat until well browned on first side.

Serve as soon as done, with potatoes, vegetables, or as desired.

Meat Balls Gourmet

Serves 4

½ pound ground lamb
½ pound ground veal
⅓ cup dry bread crumbs
⅓ cup milk
1 whole egg

1 teaspoon, or less, salt
¼ teaspoon pepper
¼ teaspoon dried mint, crushed
1 small clove garlic chopped fine or put through garlic press

Combine all ingredients, and beat with spoon until well blended. Let stand ½ hour. Form medium-size balls, and sauté in ¼ cup shortening until brown on all sides. Do not sauté too many at one time, and do not turn until underside is brown. When all meat balls are done, cover them with Sauce Gourmet, cover saucepan and simmer about 20 minutes.

To Serve. Pour meat balls and sauce in center of a bed of mixed well seasoned vegetables, rice, or noodles. Delicious and economical.

Sauce Gourmet

2 tablespoons butter or other fat
¼ cup minced onion
¼ cup fine-chopped celery
1 cup chili sauce (or catsup)

¼ cup stock or water
2 tablespoons dry wine
1 tablespoon brown sugar

Sauté onion in butter several minutes. Add all other ingredients, and blend well.

Swiss Steak

Serves 6

2-to-2½-pound piece of round steak,
   sliced 1½ to 2 inches thick
Flour
¼ cup butter
½ cup chopped onions
1 small clove garlic

2 cups canned tomatoes
¼ cup dry red wine
¼ cup celery leaves
2 teaspoons, or less, salt
¼ teaspoon pepper

Wipe meat with a damp cloth. Dredge well with flour. Melt butter and brown meat on all sides. In last minute or two sauté onions and garlic with meat.

Add tomatoes, wine, celery leaves, salt, and pepper. Cover saucepan, and simmer very gently about 2½ hours, or until tender when tested with a fork.

Swiss Steak can be placed in a 325° F. oven in a covered casserole and cooked about 2 hours, or until tender.

If gravy is too thin, thicken with flour or cornstarch.

Chicken-Fried Sirloin Steak, Top of the Round, or Cubed Steaks

Have top-quality meat sliced *as thin as possible*. Cut into individual servings. Pound sirloin or round steaks. Sprinkle with salt and pepper, dredge with flour, then dip into well-beaten egg to which 1 tablespoon water has been added. Melt a small amount of butter or margarine in a skillet, and when very hot, add meat and cook over moderately high heat about 1½ minutes on each side, or until brown, for very thin steaks. Do not overcook.

Sautéed Roast Beef Hash

Serves 2

1 cup leftover roast beef, boiled beef,
   or pot roast, cut into small cubes
1 cup boiled peeled potatoes, cut into
   small cubes
⅓ cup fresh green onion or dry onion,
   chopped fine

2 tablespoons fresh green pepper, cut
   into small pieces
About 1 teaspoon salt
¼ teaspoon pepper
2 tablespoons shortening

Combine all ingredients except shortening in a bowl. Blend well. In an 8-inch skillet heat fat until very hot. Add hash ingredients and cook over medium heat about 5 minutes. Turn over with a large spoon and cook another 5 minutes. Turn over again, and with a large spoon pat it down firmly. Continue to cook over medium heat about 5 more minutes. It will take about 15 minutes in all.

Pick up hash with a large spoon or pancake turner and mound it on an oval serving platter, keeping it as smooth and compact as possible. Surround it with buttered asparagus tips, arranged in small bunches with a strip of pimiento to add color. Green beans or peas may be used instead of asparagus. In this case fold ¼ cup small pimiento strips into the vegetable.

Serve with a tomato sauce or mushroom gravy.

Note. For a 10-inch skillet, double the recipe.

Chili Con Carne

Serves 6 to 8

4 tablespoons shortening or oil	6-ounce can tomato paste
½ cup onions, chopped medium	2 teaspoons sugar
1 clove garlic, chopped fine	2 teaspoons salt
1 tablespoon fine-chopped beef suet or 1 slice bacon, chopped fine	2 tablespoons chili powder, or less, diluted in 2 tablespoons warm water
½ cup green peppers, diced medium	
1 pound ground beef	2 cups red kidney beans (No. 2 can), drained
2 cups canned tomatoes (No. 2 can)	

Heat shortening or oil, add onions, garlic, suet or bacon, and green peppers, and sauté until golden brown. Then add ground beef, and stir until meat is lightly browned. Add tomatoes, paste, sugar, salt, and chili powder diluted with water. Cover saucepan and bring to a quick boil. Lower heat and simmer slowly 30 minutes. Then add drained red kidney beans and simmer an additional 15 minutes. Serve piping hot.

Note. Reserve red kidney bean liquid, and if Chili Con Carne needs additional liquid, add bean liquid.

Sauerbraten (American style)

Serves 8

5-pound piece rump or top of round, or round-bone pot roast	¼ teaspoon ground sage
1 tablespoon, or less, salt	¾ cup tarragon vinegar
½ teaspoon pepper	2 (6-ounce) cans tomato paste
1 tablespoon dry mustard	2 cups Brown Meat Stock (page 101)
6 tablespoons butter or shortening	3 carrots, chopped fine
1 cup onions, minced	½ cup celery leaves, chopped fine
½ teaspoon oregano leaves, crushed	¼ cup dry red wine
1 bay leaf, crushed	1 tablespoon cornstarch, diluted in 2 tablespoons cold water

Wipe meat with a damp cloth. Rub entire surface with salt, pepper, and dry mustard. Melt butter in a 5-quart Dutch oven, and sauté onions until delicately golden brown. Add meat, and brown on all sides. Remove meat from Dutch oven. Add oregano, bay leaf, sage, tarragon vinegar, tomato paste, meat stock, carrots, and celery leaves. Bring to a good boil. Place meat back in Dutch oven on a rack. Cover tightly, and simmer gently over very low heat until meat is tender when tested with a fork, about 3½ hours. Turn meat over 2 or 3 times during simmering period. Last 30 minutes add wine. When meat is done, remove to a warm oven while thickening sauce with 1 tablespoon cornstarch diluted with 2 tablespoons cold water. Cook sauce uncovered about 5 minutes.

To Serve. Cook 1 pound noodles and place on large oval platter. Slice meat and arrange attractively in center of platter. Pour sauce over noodles and meat. Serve rest of sauce separately in a gravy boat.

Potted Oxtails

Serves 6

3 pounds oxtails	½ teaspoon black pepper
Flour	½ teaspoon garlic salt
¼ cup shortening	1 tablespoon, or less salt
2 medium-size onions (1 cup), chopped	⅛ teaspoon nutmeg
¼ cup fresh celery leaves	⅛ teaspoon mace
1 cup canned tomatoes	⅛ teaspoon thyme
½ cup water	6 carrots, cut into 1-inch pieces
½ cup rhine wine or dry sauterne	1 package frozen peas

Have oxtails cut into about 2-inch pieces, dredge in flour, and brown on all sides over moderate heat in ¼ cup hot melted shortening. Add chopped onions, celery leaves, tomatoes, water, wine, and seasonings, and simmer slowly in a covered saucepan about 3 hours, or until meat almost falls off bones. Add carrots and peas and cook another 20 minutes, or until vegetables are tender. If gravy is too thin, thicken with 1 tablespoon cornstarch, combined with 2 tablespoons water, and cook about 5 minutes.

This recipe can be prepared a day in advance, adding carrots and peas 15 minutes before serving.

▶ LAMB ◀

Oven-Broiled Lamb Chops

Have lamb chops cut 1 inch thick. Allow to stand in room temperature about 1 hour before broiling. Set oven temperature to broil. Rub broiling rack with a little lamb chop suet and place lamb chops on it close together.

Top of lamb chops should be about 2½ inches from flame or heating element. For medium well done, broil about 7 minutes on each side. If using a nonsmokeless broiler, leave oven door partly open, and broil at 450° F.

Pan-Broiled Lamb Chops

Place a heavy skillet over moderate heat and allow it to become quite hot. Rub entire surface with a little lamb chop suet; lower heat to medium and place chops on it. For chops 1 inch thick, pan-broil 6 or 7 minutes on each side for medium well done, pouring off fat as it accumulates in skillet, *and press meat down often to brown well.*

Grilled Lamb Chops

Have grill very hot; lower heat to medium and rub with a little lamb suet or shortening. Place chops on grill and cook on one side about 6 or 7 minutes for 1 inch chops, medium well done, *pressing meat down with fork to brown well.* Season just before serving.

Spring Lamb Stew

½ cup onions, sliced	¼ cup fresh celery leaves
¼ cup butter or margarine	2 teaspoons salt
2 pounds lamb shoulder	⅛ teaspoon marjoram
2 tablespoons, or more, tomato sauce	1 whole clove
¾ cup water	3 medium potatoes, quartered, or 1
2 tablespoons dry red wine	cup, small
1 teaspoon paprika	1 bunch carrots
¼ teaspoon pepper	¼ pound fresh mushrooms, sautéed 5
⅛ teaspoon thyme	minutes
1 very small bay leaf	1 package frozen peas, defrosted

Sauté onions several minutes in the ¼ cup butter. Cut lamb into 2-inch pieces and add to onions and sauté until meat is lightly browned. Place meat in a 4-quart saucepan. To rich drippings and onions in skillet add all the above ingredients except carrots, potatoes, mushrooms, and peas. Blend well and pour over meat. Cover saucepan and bring to a quick boil. Reduce heat, and simmer for 60 minutes. Then add potatoes and carrots and simmer an additional 25 minutes, or until meat is fork tender. Last 5 minutes add sautéed mushrooms and peas. Taste and season further if necessary. Thicken gravy if desired with 1½ tablespoons of cornstarch diluted in 2 tablespoons of water and add to gravy. Cook for 5 minutes, stirring occasionally. Add a little liquid if too thick.

Braised Shoulder Lamb Chops or Lamb Shanks

If using chops, have them cut about 1½ inches thick. Dredge meat with flour and brown thoroughly in a very small amount of butter or margarine. Place on a trivet, add ¼ cup or more hot water, cover pan and cook slowly 1½ to 2 hours, or until tender, depending on quality and thickness of meat and utensil used. Turn meat occasionally. Add about 2 tablespoons of water from time to time as necessary during cooking process. When meat is about half done, add some thinly sliced onion, ½ teaspoon salt for each pound of meat, a little pepper, celery leaves, and 1 small bay leaf. When meat is tender, remove to a hot platter. Pour off most of fat from skillet, add desired amount of water or stock to drippings, scraping them well with a wooden spoon. Measure, and to each cup of liquid, add 1 or 1½ tablespoons cornstarch, combined with 1 tablespoon cold water. Cook until thick and clear, about 5 minutes after simmering begins. Add some cooked diced carrots and green peas to this gravy and pour over meat just before serving. If drippings are not dark brown when meat is removed, add a little commercial gravy coloring.

Arrange meat over seasoned buttered noodles, or diced carrots and green peas, in an oblong or oval platter; pour gravy over meat, and garnish ends of platter with vegetable flowers and parsley bouquets.

Savory Lamb Chops and Fresh Green Peppers

Serves 4

1 pound loin or rib lamb chops, cut about 1 inch thick	1 teaspoon salt
	1 sliver garlic
¼ teaspoon oregano	2 tablespoons cider or wine vinegar
¼ teaspoon black pepper	

Rub hot skillet with lamb chop suet. Add chops, and brown them well over moderate heat. Season with all other ingredients. Cover, and cook about 7 minutes for medium rare, or 10 minutes for well done. Turn chops over while cooking. Cook uncovered 2 or 3 minutes. Serve chops attractively with Green Peppers. If any drippings remain in pan, add 1 or 2 tablespoons hot water and place over heat until very hot. Pour over meat and peppers.

Green Peppers

1 pound fresh green peppers, cut into 1½-inch strips	¼ teaspoon black pepper
	⅛ teaspoon cayenne pepper
1 sliver garlic	2 tablespoons cider or wine vinegar
½ teaspoon salt	2 tablespoons cooking oil
¼ teaspoon oregano	

Sauté green pepper strips in hot fat until delicately brown. Add garlic and all other seasonings. Cover, and steam about 5 or 6 minutes, or until peppers are crisply tender. Let cook uncovered 2 or 3 minutes.

Balkan Lamb with Eggplant

Serves 6

2 pounds leg of lamb or lamb shoulder, cut into 2-inch pieces
Flour
¼ cup hot butter or margarine
1 small clove garlic, chopped fine
½ cup onions, sliced
2 teaspoons salt
½ teaspoon black pepper

½ teaspoon marjoram
1 large unpeeled eggplant, cut into 2-inch squares
¼ cup celery leaves
2 cups canned or fresh tomatoes
2 tablespoons cornstarch, combined with ¼ cup water

Dredge meat with flour. Melt butter, add chopped garlic, and brown meat. Place meat and rich drippings in a 2- or 3-quart saucepan; add all other ingredients except cornstarch and water. Cover saucepan, and simmer slowly 50 to 60 minutes, or until meat is tender. Then add cornstarch combined with water, and cook 5 minutes uncovered, stirring occasionally.

Lamb Curry Stew

Serves 4 to 6

1½ pounds shoulder or leg of lamb, cut into 2-inch pieces
¼ cup butter
2 large onions, sliced
1 small clove garlic, cut fine
2 teaspoons, or less, salt
¼ teaspoon pepper
1 teaspoon curry powder
1 small bay leaf

2 tablespoons cornstarch, combined with 1½ cups cool water or stock
1 very small eggplant, peeled and cut into 2-inch pieces (optional)
1 pound red boiling potatoes, whole if small, cut into large pieces if large
8 medium-sized peeled carrots
Salt and pepper
2 tablespoons sauterne (optional)

Brown lamb in butter. Add sliced onion and garlic, and continue to cook over moderate heat about 5 more minutes, turning several times. Season with salt, pepper, curry powder, and bay leaf. Combine cornstarch with water or stock and add to meat (tomato juice may be used instead of water). Cover and simmer about 1½ hours, or until meat is almost tender. Sprinkle eggplant, potatoes, and carrots with a little salt and pepper, and add to meat; stir well. Cover, and continue to cook until vegetables and meat are tender, about 30 minutes, testing with fork last 15 minutes. Add wine last few minutes.

Serve stew around a mold of plain rice. Sprinkle top of mold with paprika.

Braised Barbecued Lamb Riblets

Serves 4

1 breast of lamb, cut into riblets
¼ cup hot shortening, or more if needed
About 1½ teaspoons salt
¼ teaspoon pepper
1 clove fresh garlic, cut into small pieces or put through garlic press
1 small onion, sliced thin

1 cup chili sauce, combined with 2 tablespoons dry wine (wine may be omitted)
1 cup stock (or add bouillon cube to water)
½ teaspoon dried mint, crushed
8 small carrots, or 4 large cut in thick long pieces

Have butcher cut lamb breast into small riblets. Roll them in flour, and brown them in hot shortening. When brown, add salt, pepper, garlic, onion, chili sauce, stock, and mint. Cover, and simmer gently about 45 minutes. Now add raw carrots and continue to cook until meat and carrots are tender, about 25 to 30 more minutes. Taste sauce, and season further if necessary. A package of frozen peas may be added the last 7 or 8 minutes.

To Serve. Pack cooked plain rice or Rice Pilaf (page 312) into a greased bowl. Turn it out onto a large round serving platter. Sprinkle top of rice with paprika. Pick up lamb riblets and carrots with a perforated ladle, and arrange them around base of rice. Serve sauce separately.

Lamb Chops Maintenon

Serves 4

4 thick rib or loin lamb chops, cut about ¾ inch thick
1 tablespoon butter
½ cup fine-chopped fresh green onions
6 medium-size fresh mushrooms, chopped fine

About ½ teaspoon salt
⅛ teaspoon pepper
⅛ teaspoon thyme
⅔ cup dry bread crumbs
1 cup hot stock or milk

If using rib chops, scrape bone clean. Cook them in hot butter over moderate heat until brown on both sides. Remove, and sprinkle lightly with salt and pepper. Place on a dish until needed. In drippings sauté onion and mushrooms about 7 or 8 minutes. Season with salt, pepper, and thyme. Pour hot stock or milk over bread crumbs; mix well with a spoon until it looks like a thick custard. Add sautéed onion and mushrooms to bread mixture, and beat well until smooth. If it appears thin, add a little more crumbs; if too thick, add a little more stock or milk. Spread about 1 tablespoon of this mixture over 1 side of each lamb chop, forming a smooth dome, with a wet spatula or dinner knife. Drizzle lightly with melted butter.

Place in a 400° F. oven on a baking sheet (uncovered) about 15 minutes, then under broiler, 2 or 3 minutes.

To Serve. Place chop frills if using rib chops. Arrange attractively around a mound of cooked peas and julienne glacèed carrots. A quick tomato sauce or mushroom sauce may be served separately with these chops.

Barbecued Breast of Lamb

Serves 3

About 3 pounds breast of lamb, cut into serving pieces, well seasoned with salt and pepper
2 tablespoons hot shortening
½ cup chopped onion
¼ cup chopped celery
¼ cup chopped green pepper
2 tablespoons chopped mint leaves (optional)

1 small can tomato paste or sauce, combined with ¾ cup stock or water
2 tablespoons vinegar or lemon juice
About 2 teaspoons, or less, salt
¼ teaspoon black pepper
⅛ teaspoon cayenne pepper

Brown meat in hot shortening. Add chopped onions, celery, green pepper, and mint leaves, and continue to sauté another 5 minutes. Then add all other ingredients. Cover, and cook gently on top of stove or in a 350° F. oven about 1½ to 2 hours, or until meat is tender when tested with a fork. Uncover last 15 minutes and baste with sauce in dish until done. Serve in a bed of plain seasoned rice or Rice Pilaf (page 312).

Lamb Shish Kebab

Serves 4

1 pound, net weight, lamb from leg or shoulder, cut into pieces about 1½ inch square
1 large fresh green pepper, cut into 1½-inch squares

1 large firm red tomato, cut into 1½-inch squares
6 large firm fresh mushrooms, or 3 very small onions, cut into thick slices

Drop pieces of meat into marinade (page 162), mix well, cover, and let stand in refrigerator about 12 hours or longer, turning occasionally. This will tenderize meat.

To Broil Shish Kebab. On long metal skewers alternate meat with green pepper, tomato, mushrooms, or slices of onion. Brush meat and vegetables well with marinade, and sprinkle a little salt and pepper on vegetables only. One pound of meat will make 3 medium Shish Kebab. Place under broiler, set at 500° F., about 2 inches from heat. Broil about 12 minutes on each side for medium rare, a little longer for well done.

To Roast Shish Kebab. Place on rack in a shallow roasting pan, and roast in a 400° F. oven about 50 minutes, turning several times. Then place under broiler several minutes if necessary to brown.

Baked Shish Kebab. Place in roasting pan without rack. Over meat pour over ½ cup tomato purée or paste combined with 1 cup stock or water seasoned with ½ teaspoon salt and a little pepper. Cook about 1 hour in a 400° F. oven, turning several times and basting with sauce.

To Serve Shish Kebab. Pack Turkish Rice Pilaf (page 312) in a mold. Turn out onto a large dish and surround with Shish Kebab. Or serve on dinner plates with individual molds of rice and broiled eggplant.

Gravy for Broiled or Roasted Shish Kebab

Pour 1 cup stock or hot water into drippings; scrape gently, and thicken with 1 tablespoon cornstarch combined with 2 tablespoons cold water. Pour into a small saucepan and cook until thick; then simmer about 5 minutes. Taste and season further if necessary. This gravy is very delicious served on rice or potatoes.

Marinade for 1 Pound Meat

2 tablespoons cider vinegar	¼ teaspoon oregano or marjoram
1 tablespoon wine (optional)	⅛ teaspoon dry basil
¼ cup salad oil if meat is lean (use a	⅛ teaspoon ground black pepper
little less if meat is very fat)	2 small slivers garlic
About 1½ teaspoons salt	1 small thin slice lemon with skin

Beat these ingredients with egg beater about 1 minute.

Lamb Shashlik

Serves 4

Prepare lamb as for Shish Kebab (page 161). Remove lamb from marinade; dip into white bread crumbs. Stick through metal skewers. Brush with oil or butter, and bake in a 350° F. oven about 50 minutes or until golden brown on all sides. Turn skewers around once or twice during cooking.

Serve Shashlik with Hot Sauce, Turkish Pilaf (page 312), saffron rice, or baked tomato stuffed with rice.

Hot Sauce Served with Shashlik

2 cups chili sauce	1 cup catsup
1 tablespoon piccalilli	1 tablespoon honey
1 tablespoon prepared horseradish	1 tablespoon vinegar
1 tablespoon chopped chutney	½ teaspoon salt
¼ teaspoon pepper	

Blend ingredients well, and chill for several hours.

Lamb Shashlik en Brochette

2 pounds leg of lamb cut into 1½-inch squares

Marinate lamb 24 to 48 hours in Burgundy Marinade. Prepare as above.

Burgundy Marinade

2 cups burgundy wine
1 bay leaf
2 teaspoons salt
1 teaspoon mixed whole spices

1 medium-size onion, minced
1 teaspoon black pepper
1 tablespoon Worcestershire sauce

Blend all ingredients together.

▶ VEAL ◀

Hungarian Veal Paprika

2½ pounds veal steak, sliced in 2-inch squares, ⅓ inch thick
¼ cup butter or margarine
4 slices of bacon, cut into ½-inch pieces
1 small onion, cut into small pieces
1 clove garlic, chopped fine
¼ cup chopped celery leaves
1½ teaspoons salt
¼ teaspoon black pepper

1 tablespoon paprika
1 small bay leaf
¼ cup light dry wine
1 tablespoon tomato sauce
1 cup stock or water, combined with 1 teaspoon instant bouillon
¼ cup sifted flour, combined with ⅓ cup cool water until smooth
1 cup commercial sour cream

Sauté sliced veal in the butter for several minutes on each side until lightly brown. Pour meat and drippings into a saucepan. Cook bacon several minutes, add the onion, garlic, and celery leaves and cook about 5 more minutes. Add cooked vegetables to the veal, and all other ingredients except flour and sour cream. Cover saucepan and cook meat gently, simmering point, about 30 minutes if using top-quality veal, or a few minutes longer if necessary. Test meat by cutting through 1 piece with a fork. Do not overcook.

When meat is tender, pour off gravy into another saucepan or skillet. Now add the diluted flour and sour cream, a little at a time stirring continuously until evenly blended. Cook over low heat until thick or simmering begins, then simmer for several more minutes. Do not boil. Add meat to sauce the last minute or two, and serve at once in a bed of seasoned broad buttered noodles, rice, or vegetables. Part of sauce may be served separately in a gravy dish.

Veal Cutlets à la Creole

Serves 6

2 pounds veal steak, sliced ½ inch thick
¼ cup butter or other shortening
¾ cup celery, cut up
½ cup green peppers, cut into 1-inch squares
¼ cup chopped onions
2 teaspoons, or less, salt
¼ teaspoon pepper
6-ounce can Italian tomato paste
6 ounces water
1 bouillon cube
¼ teaspoon baking soda
3- or 4-ounce can mushrooms or ¼ pound fresh mushrooms, sautéed

Cut veal steak into serving portions and sauté in butter or shortening until brown. Add celery, green peppers, and onions; sauté 2 or 3 minutes. Add salt and pepper. Add tomato paste, diluted with water, and bouillon cube. Cover saucepan, and simmer gently about 20 minutes, adding baking soda and mushrooms last few minutes.

Serve in a bed of cooked rice, noodles, or fancy macaroni.

Veal Maréchal

Serves 4

Very thin slice veal (about 1 pound) cut into pieces about 4 × 6 inches (put smaller pieces together, and treat as 1 piece)
Salt and pepper
Thyme
4 tablespoons firm cold butter, cut into uniform pieces
¼ cup fine-chopped fresh green onions, sautéed in 1 tablespoon butter 5 minutes
½ cup fine-chopped fresh mushrooms, sautéed in 1 tablespoon butter 5 minutes and seasoned with ¼ teaspoon salt and a pinch of pepper
Dry light bread crumbs
2 eggs, diluted with 1 tablespoon water and beaten a few seconds
Fat for deep-frying
Frilled toothpicks

With a rolling pin, pound and roll veal until flat. Sprinkle very lightly with salt and pepper, and put a pinch of thyme on each piece. Place piece of butter in center of each, and cover butter with part of sautéed onions and mushrooms (divide mushrooms and butter into 6 portions). Roll meat around butter, shaping it to simulate a drumstick. Press well with both hands. Dip in bread crumbs, then into diluted egg, into crumbs again, then into diluted egg, and into crumbs a third time, pressing crumbs well onto surface of meat. Place on wax paper and let stand about 20 to 30 minutes, turning meat over several times while standing, to permit surface to dry slightly. Deep-fry at 300° F. about 10 or 11 minutes, keeping temperature of fat between 275° and 300° F. If higher, meat will be slightly uncooked in center.

Place a frilled toothpick on one end of each piece just before serving.

Important. After veal steaks are stuffed and covered with crumbs, let stand in cool room not more than ½ hour, or else butter is likely to soften. To insure meat's cooking all the way to center, it is advisable not to refrigerate veal before cooking. Serve this delicious Veal Maréchal as soon as done, or keep hot in a slow oven for a few minutes if necessary. Very delicious with asparagus with Hollandaise Sauce (page 340) and Duchesse Potatoes (page 301).

Veal Cutlets Romano (Saltimbocca)

Serves 4

1 pound veal from leg, sliced thin, then cut into rectangular (or square) pieces about 2 × 3 inches, and pounded
½ pound sliced Swiss, provolone, or scamorza cheese
½ pound thinly sliced Italian prosciutto or ham

2 eggs well beaten with a fork, combined with 1 tablespoon milk, seasoned with ½ teaspoon salt, ¼ teaspoon crushed oregano or thyme, ¼ teaspoon pepper
Flour
Very light dry bread crumbs
¼ cup butter and ¼ cup unsalted shortening

Put 2 slices of veal together, sandwich fashion, with 1 slice cheese and 1 slice ham between, having cheese and ham a little smaller than veal. Hold firmly, and cover completely with light dry crumbs, then dip into beaten egg preparation, then into crumbs again. Press crumbs down onto meat to seal it well. Let stand on wax paper about 20 minutes, turning cutlets over several times. About 15 minutes before serving, heat butter and shortening in a large skillet. When very hot, place cutlets in skillet, leaving at least 1-inch spaces between them, and sauté over *low* heat 7 or 8 minutes on first side, then with a pancake turner turn them over carefully and sauté second side 7 or 8 minutes. To insure thorough cooking of veal, it must be sliced thin; crumbs must be very light in color, and meat cooked over low heat.

Serve cutlets on a bed of well-seasoned buttered noodles, Risotto Milanese (page 805), or vegetables, with a quick gravy made from drippings in skillet.

Note. If you use Premium quality veal cutlets or chops, sliced not more than ½ inch in thickness, it is seldom necessary to braise meat in covered pan after it has cooked about 5 to 7 minutes on each side. Before braising veal in any of our recipes, test meat by cutting through 1 piece with side of fork after you have sautéed it on each side as per directions. Then if not tender enough, cover and braise for a few minutes as indicated in recipe.

Gravy for Veal Cutlets Romano

To prepare gravy, add to drippings 2 more tablespoons butter, ½ cup fresh mushrooms, sliced or chopped, and ¼ cup fresh green onion and stems chopped fine. Sauté about 5 minutes. Now add ¼ cup flour, blend well, and last, add 1½ cups stock or milk, a little at a time, and cook until thick and smooth, stirring continuously. Let simmer about 5 minutes; then add 2 tablespoons dry sherry or sauterne, a little salt and pepper as needed, and cook 2 or 3 more minutes. Serve separately.

Mock Chicken Legs—No. 1

Makes 6 medium or 4 large

½ pound pork shoulder, pork tenderloin, or lamb steak, sliced about 2 inches thick
Salt
Pepper
1½ pounds veal steak, sliced thin
Very light dry bread crumbs (not white)

2 beaten eggs, combined with 2 tablespoons water, in small deep bowl
¼ inch shortening or oil
½ cup water

Place wooden skewer through a piece of pork or lamb. Sprinkle well with salt and pepper and roll a long strip of veal steak over pork, shaping to simulate a drumstick, mold with hands, and hold in place wherever necessary with heavy toothpicks. Sprinkle with salt and pepper. Roll in bread crumbs, then dip in egg and then in crumbs again. Let stand on wax paper about 20 minutes, turning occasionally; after this, brown meat on all sides over medium heat in about ¼ inch hot shortening or oil (about 350° F.). Do not turn meat until brown underneath. After meat is thoroughly brown, place it on a trivet.

Add water to drippings in pan, cover and let braise slowly on top of stove about 1½ to 2 hours, or until tender, depending on quality of meat and size of legs.

May be baked in a *covered* pan at 350° F. for about 1½ hours after legs are first browned in skillet on top of stove. Chicken legs may also be baked at 350° F. *uncovered* about 1½ to 2 hours for dry crust, after they are first browned in fat on top of range. If necessary, add about 2 tablespoons of water to the drippings from time to time to prevent drying out and burning.

Mock Chicken Legs—No. 2

An easier way to prepare this meat is to have butcher cut veal steak and pork shoulder steak in 1½-inch square cubes. Arrange 1 of each alternately on long wooden skewers. With hands, mold meat close together to simulate drumstick. Now proceed to coat with crumbs, egg, etc. Cook same as Mock Chicken Legs—No. 1.

Note. All veal or all pork shoulder may be used. For extra large legs, use 3 pieces of meat instead of 2.

Gravy for Mock Chicken Legs

Remove meat from drippings in pan and place it in a very slow oven or skillet over very low heat to keep hot until gravy is made. Remove most of fat from drippings. Add the desired amount of stock or water to drippings and blend well. To each cup of liquid add 3 tablespoons, or more, of flour combined with ⅓ cup cool water until smooth. Cook until thick, then simmer about 5 minutes.

For a glazy gravy, use 1½ tablespoons of cornstarch combined with 2 tablespoons water for each cup of liquid. More or less flour or cornstarch may be used, depending on thickness of gravy desired. Add a little commercial gravy coloring and seasoning to gravy during simmering process, if required. Two tablespoons dry wine and about ¼ cup of sautéed mushrooms may be added for additional flavor.

Veal Birds Bordelaise

Serves 4

1 pound veal steak, sliced thin and cut into 3 or 4 serving portions
1 teaspoon salt
¼ teaspoon pepper
¼ teaspoon rosemary
2 tablespoons grated parmesan cheese
2 slices very dry toast covered with cool water until it swells, then squeezed dry
¼ pound pork sausage, sautéed 5 or 6 minutes and loosened with fork
½ cup fresh green onion and ¼ cup onion stems

¼ cup flour, combined with ½ teaspoon paprika, ¼ teaspoon salt, ⅛ teaspoon pepper
¼ cup shortening
1 cup meat or vegetable stock
1 tablespoon cornstarch or 2 tablespoons flour
2 tablespoons tomato paste
½ teaspoon salt and ¼ teaspoon pepper (in addition to other salt and pepper)
2 tablespoons light dry wine (optional)

First, pound veal steak. Sprinkle it with salt, pepper, rosemary, and cheese.

Combine toast, sausage meat, onion, and a little more salt and pepper if necessary. Blend ingredients well. Place some of this dressing in center of each slice of pounded veal, and roll to enclose filling. Hold together with heavy toothpicks. Roll meat in seasoned flour, and brown it in hot shortening over moderate heat.

Combine stock with cornstarch or flour, tomato paste, ½ teaspoon salt, ¼ teaspoon pepper, and wine. Pour over meat and simmer (over low heat) about 40 minutes if veal is sliced thin and of top quality, a little longer if sliced thick. Meat should be tender when tested with a fork, but do not overcook, or it may become fibrous and dry.

To Serve. Arrange veal birds in center of a large platter (heatproof if available), and surround meat with Duchesse Potato nests filled with peas and carrots. This makes a very colorful arrangement. Prepare 1 recipe Duchesse Potatoes (page 301). Cook 1 package frozen peas and carrots a few minutes in advance. Arrange about 15 minutes before serving time, and keep it in a moderate oven 350° F. about 15 minutes. If preferred, peas and carrots may be omitted. In this case simply pipe Duchesse Potatoes around meat, using No. 7 cookie star tube. Pour remaining sauce over meat, or add a little more stock, and serve separately.

Veal Birds Smetana

Serves 3 to 4

1 pound veal steak, sliced thin and cut into 3 or 4 serving pieces
1 teaspoon salt
¼ teaspoon pepper
¼ teaspoon rosemary
¼ teaspoon dried parsley

¼ cup flour, seasoned with ¼ teaspoon salt, ⅛ teaspoon pepper, ¼ teaspoon paprika
¼ cup shortening
½ cup water or stock (may use bouillon cube)
½ cup sour cream

First, pound veal and sprinkle it with salt, pepper, rosemary, and parsley. Place some of Dressing on each piece of veal. Roll and hold together with wood pins. Roll meat into seasoned flour, and brown it well in ¼ cup hot shortening. Add ½ cup water or stock. Cover saucepan, and simmer about 45 minutes, or until tender when tested with a fork.

Remove meat when tender, add ½ cup sour cream, a little at a time, to the drippings, mixing well until smooth. Place meat back into sauce and simmer (as gently as possible), do not boil, about 10 minutes. Serve in a bed of buttered noodles or as desired.

For Special Occasions. Surround veal birds with grilled thick tomato slices, each topped with a sautéed mushroom, and small bundles of buttered asparagus tips between tomatoes. To grill tomatoes, remove both ends and cut each tomato crosswise into 2 thick slices. Brush with melted butter, salt, pepper, and parmesan cheese, and broil about 5 minutes. It is best to arrange entire meal on a heatproof platter and keep in slow oven a few minutes before serving.

1 medium-size chopped onion, sautéed in 3 tablespoons hot shortening
½ teaspoon salt
⅛ teaspoon pepper
½ teaspoon dry parsley
⅓ cup dry bread crumbs
⅓ cup cool water

Combine all dressing ingredients. Mix well. Let preparation stand ½ hour.

Veal Collops Braunschweiger

Serves 3 to 4

1 pound leg of veal, sliced about ¼ inch thick and cut into serving pieces
1 teaspoon salt
¼ teaspoon pepper
¼ teaspoon marjoram
Very light dry bread crumbs
1 egg slightly beaten and combined with 1 tablespoon water
About ¼ cup shortening or oil
½ cup stock or hot water
Thin-sliced American cheese

First, pound veal steaks; season them with salt, pepper, and marjoram. Cover meat well with very light bread crumbs, then dip into beaten egg combined with water, then into crumbs again. Press crumbs onto meat. Let stand on wax paper about 20 minutes, turning over once or twice while standing. Brown meat in hot shortening on both sides. Place it on a trivet; add ½ cup hot water or stock to drippings; cover skillet and steam about 25 minutes.

Remove meat from skillet, place it on a baking sheet, spread some Braunschweiger Topping on each, forming a slight mound in center. Place a small thin slice American cheese on each. Bake at 400° F. about 10 or 12 minutes, or until cheese is fully melted.

Sprinkle top lightly with paprika, and serve attractively with potatoes, rice, vegetables, or buttered noodles.

Note. These Collops are attractive if baked in a heatproof platter, surrounded with Duchesse Potatoes (page 301), or small precooked browned potatoes.

¼ pound Braunschweiger sausage
¼ cup minced fresh green onion and stems
½ tablespoon prepared mustard

Combine all ingredients.

Veal Balls Smetana

Serves 6

1¼ pounds ground veal and ¼ pound
  ground suet
1 large clove garlic, put through
  press
¼ cup fine chopped parsley
2 teaspoons salt
¼ teaspoon pepper

2 slightly beaten eggs
½ cup dry bread crumbs, combined
  with ½ cup meat or vegetable
  stock or milk
¼ cup butter
2 tablespoons oil

Combine all ingredients except butter and oil in the order given. Blend
well. Let stand ½ hour. Shape into medium-size balls, using ¼ cup for
each. Dip hands in water and have them slightly damp if meat clings to
hands when shaping balls. Brown meat on all sides in very hot butter
and oil. Pour Smetana Sauce over balls. Cover, and simmer gently (do not
boil) about 20 minutes. Serve in center of buttered noodles. Sprinkle top
of meat balls with fine-chopped fresh green onion tops or parsley.

Smetana Sauce for Veal Balls

½ pound fresh sliced mushrooms
2 tablespoons butter
¼ teaspoon salt
⅛ teaspoon pepper
1 tablespoon cornstarch (or 2 tablespoons flour), combined with ½
  cup milk

1 cup sour cream
1 teaspoon salt
¼ teaspoon pepper
About 1 teaspoon gravy coloring

Sauté mushrooms in butter about 3 minutes. Season with salt and pepper.
Add cornstarch or flour combined with milk; then add sour cream. Simmer
about 3 or 4 minutes. Season sauce with 1 teaspoon salt, ¼ teaspoon
pepper, and gravy coloring.

Veal Chops Maintenon

Serves 6

6 veal chops, cut about ¾ inch thick
3 tablespoons butter or margarine
About 1½ teaspoons salt
¼ teaspoon pepper

1 very small clove garlic, slivered
3 tablespoons water or stock
Paprika

Brown chops in very hot butter on both sides; season with salt, pepper,
water, and garlic. Cover skillet, and gently steam chops about 15 minutes,
turning over twice while steaming. If drippings appear scorched, add 1
or 2 tablespoons stock or water. Place chops on a heatproof platter, cover

with Sauce Maintenon, sprinkle with paprika, and bake in a 400° F. oven about 10 minutes; then place under broiler until top is brown.

Serve with small browned potato balls or cubes. Add ¼ cup stock or water to drippings left over from sautéing veal; cook gently, season to taste, and serve with potatoes.

Sauce Maintenon

2 slices bacon, chopped fine	½ teaspoon salt
2 tablespoons chopped onion	⅛ teaspoon black pepper
¼ pound fine-chopped fresh mushrooms, or 1 small can	½ cup stock or milk
2 tablespoons flour	Paprika

Sauté bacon until medium-crisp; then add onion and mushrooms. Sauté all together 7 or 8 minutes; then sprinkle with flour, salt, and pepper, and stir in stock or milk. Cook until thick; then let simmer about 5 minutes. Let sauce cool before spreading neatly on partially cooked veal chops.

Veal Chops Madrid

Serves 4 to 6

Use 6 rib veal chops cut ½ inch thick. Scrape rib bones clean, forming French chops. Sauté chops in hot butter or other fat over moderate heat until brown on both sides. Add 2 tablespoons hot stock or water, cover, and steam about 25 minutes. Sprinkle lightly with salt and pepper. Remove from skillet and let cool. Then spread on each side about 1 tablespoon dressing (below) having dressing slightly rounded, using a wet knife or spatula. Cover each chop well with very light dry bread crumbs; then dip into 1 beaten egg combined with 1 tablespoon water, then into crumbs again, pressing crumbs well onto surface. Let stand on wax paper about 20 minutes, turning over several times. When ready to serve, deep-fry at 350° F. until brown and crisp or bake at 400° F. about 30 minutes. Keep in warm oven until ready to be served. Put a frill on each bone and serve around a mound of vegetables or as desired. Serve with Sauce Madrid.

Dressing for Veal Chops Madrid

½ cup fine-chopped fresh mushrooms	⅛ teaspoon thyme
¼ cup fine-chopped fresh green onions	½ pound (1 cup solid-packed) cooked ground ham
2 tablespoons hot butter	
About ¼ teaspoon salt	¼ cup sifted all-purpose flour, combined with 1 cup stock or milk
⅛ teaspoon pepper	

Sauté mushrooms and green onion in hot butter about 5 minutes. Add all other ingredients and cook until thick; then simmer about 5 more minutes. Let stand until cold before using.

Sauce Madrid for Veal Chops

½ cup sliced fresh mushrooms
1 tablespoon hot butter
¼ cup thin-sliced green pepper strips
2 tablespoons dry sherry or sauterne
   (optional)

2 tablespoons cornstarch, combined
   with 2 cups stock or tomato juice
About 1 teaspoon salt
¼ teaspoon pepper
¼ teaspoon thyme
Veal chop drippings

Sauté sliced mushrooms and green pepper strips in hot butter about 5 minutes. Add wine, cornstarch mixed with stock or tomato juice, salt, pepper, and thyme. Pour these ingredients into veal-chop drippings, scraping pan well, and cook until thick; then simmer about 5 minutes. If using stock instead of tomato juice, add 1 or 2 tablespoons tomato paste to sauce. Taste and season further if necessary.

Veal Patties Farci (Stuffed Veal Hamburgers)

Serves 4 to 6

1 pound ground veal
¼ pound suet or bacon ground with
   veal
⅓ cup dry bread crumbs
⅓ cup milk

1 egg
1 teaspoon salt
¼ teaspoon pepper
¼ teaspoon garlic salt

Combine all above ingredients and mix thoroughly. Pick up ¼ cup meat and stuff with about 1 tablespoon Stuffing for Veal Patties Farci. Mold with hands to enclose stuffing and form thick patties. Fry patties in hot butter or shortening over moderate heat until brown on both sides. Place them in a baking dish. Pour over them Tomato Sauce for Veal Patties Farci, and bake covered about 30 minutes at 400° F.

   Serve with rice, noodles, or potatoes, and a green vegetable.

Stuffing for Veal Patties Farci

¼ pound cooked ham or bacon chopped
   fine. (If using ham, sauté in 1
   tablespoon butter. If using bacon,
   fry it slowly about 5 minutes,
   pouring off part of fat.)
¼ pound fresh mushrooms chopped
   fine, or 1 small can chopped
   mushrooms

½ cup fine-chopped fresh green onion
   and stems
2 tablespoons pimiento cut into small
   pieces (optional)
⅓ cup dry bread crumbs
About ½ teaspoon salt
⅛ teaspoon pepper
¼ teaspoon marjoram

Add chopped mushrooms and onion to sautéed ham or bacon, and cook about 5 minutes. Then add all other ingredients and blend well. If mixture appears dry, add a little stock or water—only enough to bind. Let cool.

Tomato Sauce for Veal Patties Farci

⅓ cup thick tomato paste, combined with 1 cup meat or vegetable stock (bouillon cube may be combined with water)

¼ cup fine-chopped onion

½ cup chopped mushrooms (optional)

2 tablespoons shortening

About ½ teaspoon salt

⅛ teaspoon pepper

⅛ teaspoon marjoram

Sauté onion and mushrooms in shortening about 5 minutes. Add tomato paste, stock, and seasonings. Simmer about 5 minutes.

Veal Stew Tarragon

Serves 4 to 6

2 pounds boneless veal, cut into thick 2-inch pieces

½ cup flour, combined with 1 teaspoon salt, 1 teaspoon paprika, ½ teaspoon tarragon, ¼ teaspoon pepper; sift together

About ⅓ cup hot shortening

1½ cups vegetable or meat stock (bouillon cube may be added to water), combined with 1½ tablespoons cornstarch

2 tablespoons tarragon vinegar

1 teaspoon salt

¼ teaspon dried parsley

¼ teaspoon dried celery

¼ teaspoon pepper

2 tablespoons tomato paste (or omit tomato paste and add about ½ teaspoon commercial gravy coloring)

8 small peeled potatoes and 4 large carrots, cut into thick long wedges

Roll meat in seasoned flour. Brown it well in hot shortening. Add all other ingredients, cover saucepan, and simmer until meat is tender when tested with a fork, about 45 minutes, depending on quality of veal.

Veal Chops Provincial

Serves 2 to 3

1 pound loin or rib veal chops, sliced 1 inch thick

2 tablespoons butter

2 tablespoons oil

1 teaspoon salt

⅛ teaspoon black pepper

⅛ teaspoon each thyme, rosemary

2 tablespoons lemon juice or dry wine, combined with 1 tablespoon tomato paste

¼ cup stock or water

Brown chops on both sides in butter and oil. Season, and add all other ingredients, cover and cook gently about 25 minutes. Add Green Peppers. Continue to cook covered about 7 or 8 minutes more.

These veal chops and green peppers are delicious served in a bed of fancy noodles or rice.

Green Peppers for Veal Chops Provincial

Cut 1 pound fresh green peppers into 1½-inch strips and sauté in 2 tablespoons cooking oil until delicately brown. Season with about 1 teaspoon salt, ⅛ teaspoon black pepper, and 1 sliver of garlic. Cover, and steam about 3 or 4 minutes before adding to meat.

Baked Veal in Casserole

Serves 4

1 pound boneless veal, cut into 2-inch pieces
About ¼ cup butter
2 tablespoons oil
1 pound potatoes, peeled and cut into 2-inch pieces
1 pound onions, peeled and cut into 2-inch pieces
1 small clove garlic, slivered

2 teaspoons salt
½ teaspoon each pepper, oregano
2 tablespoons parsley, chopped fine
2 cups fresh-peeled tomatoes, or one No. 2 can tomatoes
2 tablespoons cornstarch, combined with 2 tablespoons tomato juice or water

Brown meat well on all sides in hot butter and oil; then add potatoes, onions, and garlic, and continue to cook over moderate heat until vegetables are delicately brown. Add seasonings, then tomato and cornstarch mixture. Blend well, and simmer about five minutes. Pour into a small oblong 10 × 6½ × 2-inch casserole (or other baking dish). Cover with foil (unless dish comes with cover) and bake at 325° F. about 45 minutes, or until meat and vegetables are tender.

Serve with a green vegetable.

Curry of Veal with Rice

Serves 4 to 6

2 pounds boneless veal, cut into 2-inch pieces
¼ cup butter
2 tablespoons oil
1 medium-size onion, sliced thin
About 2 teaspoons salt and 1 teaspoon curry powder, more or less to suit taste

2 tablespoons cornstarch diluted in 1 cup meat stock (or use water and a bouillon cube)
1 tablespoon tomato paste added to stock
2 tablespoons light dry wine (sauterne preferable)

Brown veal in very hot butter and oil. Add all other ingredients in the order given. Cover, simmer about 40 minutes, or until meat is tender. If sauce appears too thick, add a little more liquid.

Serve in a rice ring or around any style molded rce.

Rice for Curry of Veal

Sauté 2 tablespoons fresh green onions, 1 small clove garlic, ¼ cup fresh green pepper, and 2 tablespoons fine-cut mushrooms in ¼ cup hot fat about 5 minutes. Then add 1 pound rice and about 3 cups hot stock (or water with bouillon cube) and 1 teaspoon curry powder. Cover, and cook gently about 30 minutes, or until tender. Stir gently 2 or 3 times toward end.

Braised Veal Chops à la Sauterne

6 veal chops
4 tablespoons butter
2 tablespoons oil
¼ cup fine-chopped onions
1 small clove garlic, chopped fine
¼ cup sauterne

1 teaspoon salt
¼ teaspoon white pepper
½ cup sliced stuffed green olives
2 tablespoons pimiento, cut into 1-inch squares

Sauté veal chops in hot melted butter and oil until they are brown on both sides. Add onions, garlic, wine, salt, and pepper. Cover saucepan, and simmer over low heat until chops are tender when tested with a fork, about 40 minutes, turning them over several times. After chops are cooked, add olives and pimiento, and blend well.

Arrange veal chops on serving platter, and pour sauce over meat.

Plain Breaded Veal Cutlets

Proceed same as for Parmesan Veal Cutlets (page 786), but omit sauce and cheese on top of cutlets. Plain breaded veal cutlets may be served with any type of gravy or tomato sauce.

Note. If a crisp crust is preferred on veal cutlets, cover them with egg and crumbs, as per general directions. Let stand, etc. Do not have them sliced more than ½ inch in thickness, better ¼ inch, to insure thorough cooking. Deep-fry cutlets at 325° F. in oil or shortening for about 7 or 8 mintues, until golden brown and crisp without further cooking. Or they may be baked on a rack with drip pan underneath at 350° F. uncovered for about 20 to 30 minutes after they have been browned in hot fat in a skillet on top of stove. Pour about 1 cup of hot water in drip pan to prevent smoking. When meat is tender, pour sauce on top and place sliced cheese over sauce, and continue to bake until cheese is fully melted for about 7 or 8 minutes.

If Premium quality veal is used and it is sliced less than ½ inch thick, it may be covered with egg and crumbs, etc., then fried slowly in ¼ inch of oil or shortening about 7 or 8 minutes on each side *without braising.*

Green Pepper Veal Stew

Serves 6

1 pound boneless veal, cut into 2-inch pieces
About 2 tablespoons hot butter
2 tablespoons oil
1 teaspoon salt
¼ teaspoon pepper

¼ teaspoon rosemary or thyme
1 tablespoon flour
¾ cup fresh or canned tomatoes, cut into small pieces and combined with ⅛ teaspoon baking soda

Sauté veal in hot butter and oil until brown on all sides. Add all other ingredients, mix well, and simmer covered over low heat about 40 minutes. When meat is tender, add Sautéed Green Peppers, and serve with Macaroni for Green Pepper Veal Stew or cooked rice.

Sautéed Green Peppers for Veal Stew

1 pound fresh green peppers, cored and cut into 1-inch wide strips
3 tablespoons oil or other fat
½ teaspoon salt

¼ teaspoon rosemary or thyme
1 small clove fresh garlic, slivered fine

Sauté peppers in hot fat until delicately brown on both sides. Add seasonings, and continue to cook over low heat about 7 or 8 minutes.

Marcaroni for Green Pepper Veal Stew

Cook 1 pound fancy macaroni (plain may be used) in about 4 quarts salted boiling water until tender. Drain well; season with ¼ cup melted butter (or remove excess fat from top of veal stew and use instead) and ¼ cup grated parmesan cheese. Blend well with two forks.

Continental Meat Patties

Serves 3

½ pound ground veal
½ pound ground pork
¼ cup dry bread crumbs
¼ cup milk
¾ teaspoon salt

¼ teaspoon dried marjoram
¼ teapsoon garlice salt
1 tablespoon grated Italian cheese
1 whole egg

Combine ingredients and blend well. Let stand ½ hour.
  Continental Stuffed Meat Patties—Broiled. Use ¼ cup meat for each

patty, 3 inches round. Spread half of these with 1 tablespoon, or a little more, Roquefort Filling. Place another 3-inch round patty over each cheese-covered patty. Pinch ends. Place meat on well-greased flat pan. Brush top of meat with melted butter, and broil 3 inches from heat at 500° F. about 6 minutes or until top is brown. Turn over and cook second side about 6 minutes.

Continental Meat Patties with Roquefort Topping—Broiled. Use ½ cup meat for each patty, 3 inches round. Place meat on greased flat pan. Brush top of meat with melted butter, and broil at 500° F. about 6 minutes; then turn over and broil other side about minutes. Now spread top of each with 1 tablespoon or more Roquefort Topping, sprinkle with paprika, and place under broiler about 2 minutes, or only until cheese has melted.

Continental Stuffed Meat Patties—Sautéed. Follow directions for shaping Continental Stuffed Meat Patties (above), and sauté in a small amount of butter about 5 or 6 minutes on each side.

Continental Meat Patties with Roquefort Topping—Sautéed. Use ½ cup meat for each patty, 3 inches round. Sauté on first side about 5 or 6 minutes. Turn over and sauté second side 5 or 6 minutes. Now spread top of each with 1 tablespoon or more Roquefort Topping, sprinkle with paprika, *cover skillet*, and continue to cook about ½ minute more or until cheese has melted.

Roquefort Filling or Topping

½ cup (¼ pound) roquefort or bleu cheese

1 tablespoon salad oil
1 tablespoon wine vinegar

Mash cheese with fork until it is of medium consistency. Add oil and vinegar 1 teaspoon at a time, and blend thoroughly. This recipe will yield enough filling or topping for 2 pounds meat patties. It may be kept several weeks in a covered container if refrigerated.

Gravy for Continental Meat Patties

¼ cup fine-chopped onion (or ½ tea-spoon onion salt)
½ cup fine-chopped fresh mushrooms
¼ cup butter or margarine (or meat drippings)
¼ cup sifted all-purpose flour

2 cups stock (or add 2 bouillon cubes to 2 cups water)
About ½ teaspoon salt if using un-salted stock (no salt if using bouillon cubes)
¼ teaspoon pepper
¼ teaspoon crushed dried marjoram

Sauté fine-chopped onion and mushrooms in butter about 5 minutes. Add flour and blend well. Add stock, a little at a time, and all seasonings. Cook until thick; then simmer about 5 minutes. Taste, and season further if necessary. Add a little commercial gravy coloring if desired.

▶ HAM ◀

Fully Cooked Ham

The following directions are for Premium fully cooked hams. The trend today is toward this type of ham. They can be purchased with the shank, shankless, and boneless. They are fully cooked and delightfully mild-flavored and tender. For cold service, just slice and serve. If to be served hot, let stand room temperature about 1 hour, then place ham in a 325° F. oven on rack with fat side up, and cook according to schedule given on wrapper, or when internal temperature reaches 130° F. on meat thermometer. Takes about 10 minutes per pound to heat.

How to Score and Glaze Ham. The majority of hams today are sold skinned. About 30 minutes before ham is heated through and ready to serve, remove it from oven, and with a long sharp knife cut fat into diamond shapes, if desired, or leave plain. Spread surface of ham weighing 10 to 12 pounds with very thick glaze. Increase temperature of oven to 425° F. Pour about 4 cups hot water into roasting pan to prevent smoking when part of glaze drips into pan. Bake about 20 to 30 minutes or until ham is glazy and brown.

Glaze for Ham

1 cup brown sugar, solidly packed
2 tablespoons all-purpose flour
¼ cup corn syrup or honey

About 1 or 2 tablespoons pineapple or other juice

Combine all ingredients except juice. Mix well, then add about 1 tablespoon juice at a time, forming a very, very thick paste.

Uncooked Ham

In some localities the ham that must be cooked before eating is available. This ham is tenderized when you purchase it, but it is not fully cooked. It must, therefore be cooked according to directions given on wrapper before eating, or cook in a slow oven 325° F. according to schedule below, or until internal temperature reaches 160° F. on meat thermometer.

Cooking Schedule for Uncooked Ham

8 to 10 pounds—about 3½ hours
10 to 12 pounds—about 3½ to 4 hours
12 to 15 pounds—about 4 to 4½ hours
15 to 18 pounds—about 4½ to 5 hours

18 to 22 pounds—about 5 to 6 hours
22 to 24 pounds—about 6 to 6½ hours

Glazed Orange Daisies for Decorating of Hams

With paring knife, mark 8 sections on skin of 3 large or 4 medium California oranges, being careful not to cut too deeply. Remove skins carefully, cover with cold water and bring to a boil; then lower heat and simmer about 15 minutes, having skins always submerged in water. Drain and trim to simulate large or small petals. In 2-quart saucepan prepare a syrup with ¾ cup granulated sugar and ¾ cup hot water. When clear, add the orange petals and cook them in this syrup for about 15 minutes or until they look glazy and somewhat transparent. When done, drain well, and when cool arrange 7 or 8 large petals on upper largest part of ham, holding them down with long stemmed cloves if necessary. Place rest on shank end, holding them in place with toothpicks. Place whole red maraschino or candied cherry on each pick. Use red cherries for center of flower, holding it down with toothpick if necessary. The leftover oranges may be cut crosswise into very thick slices brushed with French Dressing (page 368) and served around ham topped with individual Strawberry-Rhubarb Molds (page 440). Fill open spaces with parsley bouquets. (Or use pineapple rings.)

During the Easter season it is traditional to garnish ham with Colored Eggs (page 48), vegetable flowers, endive, etc.

Ham Cutlets Madrid

Serves 6

1 cup fine-chopped fresh mushrooms
½ cup fine-chopped fresh green onions
¼ cup butter
1 pound (about 2 cups solidly packed) cooked ground ham
½ cup sifted all-purpose flour, combined with 2 cups stock or milk

About ½ teaspoon salt
¼ teaspoon pepper
⅛ teaspoon thyme
Dry bread crumbs
1 beaten egg, combined with 1 tablespoon water

Sauté fine-chopped mushrooms and green onions in hot butter about 5 minutes. Add next 5 ingredients and cook until thick, then simmer about 5 minutes. Let stand until cold, preferably in refrigerator. When mixture is cold, shape into cutlets about ½ inch thick. Cover with dry bread crumbs; then dip into beaten egg combined with water, then into crumbs again, pressing crumbs well onto surface. Let stand on wax paper about 20 minutes, turning over 2 times. When ready to serve, deep-fry at 350° F. until brown and crisp. Cutlets may be kept hot in a 250° F. oven about 20 minutes.

Serve around a mound of vegetables, potatoes, or Rice Pilaf (page 312), with Sauce Madrid. This is an excellent way to use leftover ham.

Sauce Madrid for Ham Cutlets

½ cup sliced fresh mushrooms
¼ cup thin-sliced green pepper strips
2 tablespoons hot butter
2 tablespoons dry sherry or sauterne (optional)

2 tablespoons cornstarch, combined with 2 cups stock or tomato juice
About 1 teaspoon salt
¼ teaspoon pepper
¼ teaspoon thyme

Sauté sliced mushrooms and green pepper strips in hot butter about 5 minutes. Add wine, cornstarch mixed with stock or tomato juice, salt, pepper, and thyme. Cook these ingredients until thick; then simmer about 5 minutes. If using stock instead of tomato juice, add 1 or 2 tablespoons tomato paste to sauce. A little gravy coloring may be added. Season further if necessary, and serve separately with Ham Cutlets Madrid.

Spinach Timbales and Ham Casserole

Serves 4

Prepare Spinach Timbales and Cheese Sauce (below). When sauce is done, pour it into an oval flat 17-inch stainless steel casserole (or glass casserole). Place 4 thick slices of ham over sauce. If commercially thin-sliced ham is used, fold each slice in half. With a paring knife loosen timbales from custard cups and invert 1 on each slice of ham. Slice hard-cooked eggs with commercial cutter; dip part of one end in paprika. Garnish top of each timbale with slice of egg. Instead of sliced ham, 1 cup or more of leftover small pieces of ham may be folded into sauce, and timbales may be placed on top of sauce. Bake casserole at 350° F. about 20 minutes before serving if ingredients are warm, 30 minutes if cool.

This makes an attractive and delicious luncheon or supper dish. Duchesse Potatoes (page 301) or mashed potatoes may be served separately.

Spinach Timbales

¼ cup fine-chopped onion
2 tablespoons butter or shortening
2 tablespoons all-purpose flour
1 cup cool milk
¼ cup shredded or grated American cheese
About 1 teaspoon salt
⅛ teaspoon pepper

1 package or more frozen chopped spinach, cooked in ½ inch of water about 5 minutes (drain spinach well; it should measure 1½ cups)
½ cup dry bread crumbs
3 large eggs, beaten about ½ minute

Sauté onion in butter or shortening about 5 minutes. Add flour, mix until smooth. Add milk slowly, stirring all the time. Cook until thick; then add cheese, salt, and pepper. Continue to cook about 5 more minutes. Pour this sauce over the cooked spinach, bread crumbs, and beaten eggs. Beat until thoroughly blended about ½ minute. Pour into 4 custard cups that measure 3¼ inches wide and 2¼ inches deep and have been well greased with ⅓ teaspoon shortening for each cup. Place in a pan of hot water and bake at 350° F. about 50 minutes or until firm to the touch in center.

Cheese Sauce for Spinach Timbales and Ham Casserole

¼ cup butter
¼ cup flour
2 cups cool milk
½ teaspoon salt

⅛ teaspoon pepper
½ cup freshly shredded American or cheddar cheese
4 slices ham

Melt butter, add flour, and stir until smooth. Add milk slowly. Cook until thick; then add seasonings and cheese. Continue to cook about 5 more minutes.

Glazed Ham Loaf

Serves 8

3½ cups ground cooked leftover ham, packed
1½ cups dry bread crumbs
2 large or 3 medium-size eggs, beaten a few seconds

About 1 to 1½ cups milk
½ cup fine-chopped green onion and stems
¼ teaspoon dry mustard
A little salt if necessary

Combine all ingredients. Beat well until smooth, or mix with hands. It is best to add only 1 cup milk at first. After ingredients are well blended, add more milk only if mixture appears very heavy. It must, however, hold its shape. Place mixture on a piece of aluminum foil and mold it to simulate a whole ham. Score top; place whole cloves in each section. Drizzle dark commercial syrup over entire surface. Carefully cut away surplus aluminum foil around base. With a pancake turner pick up ham and foil base and transfer to a cake rack with baking sheet underneath. Bake at 350° F. about 1½ hours, or until crusty, glossy, and firm to the touch.

Remove from oven and drizzle again with dark commercial syrup.

Lift up with pancake turner and place on an oval platter. Arrange canned spiced crab apples around ham, with whole glazed carrots between apples. Or apples and carrots may be arranged in groups. A sprig of parsley may be inserted in large end of carrots for additional color. The small end of ham may be studded with 5 or 6 maraschino cherries on toothpicks, or with a wax-paper frill held in meat with a small skewer. Serve Special Gingersnap Raisin Sauce (page 182) separately.

Special Gingersnap Raisin Sauce

6 small gingersnaps (⅓ cup crumbled)
½ cup brown sugar, packed
¼ cup white vinegar
1 cup hot water

¼ teaspoon salt
1 very small lemon, cut into small thin slices
¼ cup seedless raisins

Combine all ingredients in a saucepan and bring to boiling point. Lower heat and let simmer about 10 minutes, or until sauce is thick and transparent.

Ham and Spinach Roll Ups in Casserole

Serves 4

About ½ cup fine-chopped onion
⅓ cup bacon drippings or other fat
2 packages frozen spinach, cooked until just tender, drained very thoroughly (press out excess moisture, then chop medium-fine)
About 1 teaspoon salt

¼ teaspoon black pepper
¼ teaspoon dried marjoram, crumbled
1 pound commercial sliced cooked ham (10 or 12 slices)
1 recipe Thick Cheese Sauce for Ham and Spinach Roll Ups
1 recipe Duchesse Potatoes (page 301)

Sauté chopped onion in fat about 5 minutes. Add spinach, salt, pepper, and marjoram, and cook together 2 or 3 minutes. Let cool about 15 minutes. Place ¼ cup spinach mixture lengthwise on each slice of ham and roll to enclose spinach. Place roll ups on greased baking dish, with open end of ham down. Carefully pour Thick Cheese Sauce over top. With bag and No. 7 large star cookie tube, pipe Duchesse Potatoes around end of platter. Bake at 400° F. about 20 minutes if ingredients are warm; about 25 minutes if casserole was prepared in advance. Place under broiler to brown top if necessary when time is up.

Remove from broiler, and garnish top of casserole with hard-cooked egg cut into 8 uniform lengthwise sections to simulate a flower, placing a curled strip of pimiento or red maraschino cherry in center. Instead of Duchesse Potatoes, small whole cooked carrots, brushed with melted butter, may be arranged around these roll ups.

Thick Cheese Sauce for Ham and Spinach Roll Ups

½ cup bacon drippings (or butter or other fat)
½ cup sifted all-purpose flour
2 cups warm milk
About 1 teaspoon salt

¼ teaspoon pepper
¼ teaspoon marjoram, crumbled
2 cups or less freshly shredded American cheese (½ pound)

Melt fat, add flour, and blend until smooth. Add milk slowly. Cook until thick. Add seasonings and shredded cheese, and continue to cook about 5 more minutes, or until cheese is fully melted. Let stand about 15 minutes; then stir it vigorously and pour over roll ups. Sprinkle lightly with paprika.

▶ PORK ◀

Plain Broiled Pork or Veal Chops

This recipe is for young tender pork and veal loins weighing 8 to 10 pounds and of top quality; otherwise it is better to braise meat, covered, with some moisture added.

Have marketman cut about 6 chops 1 inch thick. Let chops stand at room temperature covered with wax paper about 1 hour. Set regulator at 550° F. if using a smokeless broiler (set it at 450° F. if using a nonsmokeless broiler, but leave door of oven, not broiler, partially open to prevent smoking). Brush chops lightly with melted butter or margarine on both sides (this browns meat attractively and adds more flavor), sprinkle lightly with salt and pepper, then cover both sides of meat with a thin coating of light dry crumbs. This protects the meat from drying out. Place under broiler, about 2½ inches from heat, and broil for about 12 to 15 minutes on each side.

Stuffed Broiled Pork or Veal Chops

Have marketman cut chops 1 inch thick, and make pocket for dressing on outside. Stuff pockets lightly with Dressing. Prepare and broil same as plain broiled chops above.

Dressing for 6 Chops

¼ cup finely chopped celery	¾ teaspoon salt
¼ cup finely chopped onion	⅛ teaspoon pepper
2 tablespoons hot shortening	¼ teaspoon poultry seasoning
¼ cup, or more, hot water or stock	A little chopped green onion and
3 small slices very dry toasted bread broken into very small pieces	pimiento (optional)

Sauté the chopped celery and onion in the shortening for about 5 minutes. Add the hot water or stock, blend well and pour over the broken dry toast. Add seasoning as listed, and mix well. Let stand at least 10 minutes before using.

Pan-Braised Breaded Pork or Veal Chops

Have chops sliced about 1 inch thick or less (may be stuffed as in preceding recipe if desired). Sprinkle with salt and pepper and light bread crumbs. Press crumbs onto chops. Dip into beaten egg to which 1 tablespoon water has been added, then into crumbs again. Let stand about 20 minutes, turning several times. Fry slowly in ¼ inch unsalted fat or oil until golden brown on each side. Place on a trivet, add about ¼ cup of hot water, cover tightly and let simmer (adding a small amount of water from time to time if necessary) about 30 to 45 minutes, or until tender when tested.

Pork tenderloin patties may also be prepared this way. Have pork tenderloin patties flattened to about 1 inch in thickness. Prepare according to general directions. Cook 20 to 30 minutes, or until fork tender.

Plain Fried Pork or Veal Chops

Pork chops and veal chops of top quality, without breading, cut not more than ½ inch thick, and from young tender loins, can be pan-fried in unsalted shortening or oil over medium heat without braising. Use medium heat, and keep turning meat several times during the cooking process until brown and tender. Do not cover. Total cooking time is 10 to 12 minutes. Season when almost done. Acceptable but drier than if they are covered after browning and braised in about ½ cup or more water for about 15 minutes.

Plain Braised Pork or Veal Chops

If these chops are sliced thicker than ½ inch they cannot be cooked successfully by pan-frying unless they are first browned well on both sides in small amount of butter and oil combined (about 2 tablespoons for each pound of meat). Then they may be placed on a trivet, or left right in pan.

Add about ½ cup hot water or stock, cover skillet and cook meat over very, very low heat (simmer burner), until tender, about 30 to 60 minutes, depending on quality of meat. Turn meat over from time to time and if moisture has evaporated, add 2 tablespoons more at a time, but keep heat low (high heat will cause evaporation quickly, low heat will produce steam to cook meat). Stay with it and check moisture in skillet toward end. Season meat after it has been browned well, or the last few minutes of cooking. Shoulder lamb chops may also be prepared this way.

Deep-Fat-Fried Pork Chops, Pork Tenderloin Patties, and Veal

Pork chops, pork tenderloin patties, and veal sliced not more than ½ inch thick, coated with flour, then dipped into beaten egg, then into dry light crumbs, may be deep-fat-fried at 325° F. for about 7 to 10 minutes, total time, or until golden brown. They are more quickly cooked in deep fat and are nice and crisp on the outside.

Baked Crisp Crust Pork Chops, Pork Tenderloin Patties, and Veal

Coat meat with flour, dip in egg, then into crumbs as per general directions preceding recipe. Brown them in ¼ inch unsalted shortening or oil on each side until light golden color, not too dark, as they will darken further in oven. Place chops on cake rack or trivet with pan underneath, pour ½ cup hot water into pan, and bake in a preheated 350° F. oven, *uncovered,* about 40 minutes for chops and patties sliced ¾ inch thick; bake 1 hour for 1 inch thickness. Turn meat over after first half of cooking time. Good prepared this way, but not as moist and flavorful as when braised. Crust is dry but not as dry as when fried in deep hot fat.

Pork tenderloin patties are always more tender and moist when breaded or dipped into a batter and French-fried. If a recipe calls for sliced pork tenderloin without breading, it will be more tender if a little dry meat tenderizer is sprinkled over moist meat, punctured with fork. Let stand a few minutes and sauté on each side about 3 to 5 minutes, depending on thickness.

Roasted Stuffed Pork Tenderloin

Serves 6 to 8

2 large pork tenderloins weighing about 1 pound each
Salt and pepper
Melted butter
1 large thin-sliced onion
1 cup celery, sliced thin crosswise
⅓ cup hot butter or shortening
5 slices of very dry toasted white bread, soaked in cool water until it swells, then squeezed dry.

(Place bread in a 300° F. oven about 30 minutes, turning it over several times. Be sure it is a deep golden color and thoroughly dry before soaking.)
About 1 teaspoon salt, ¼ teaspoon black pepper, ½ teaspoon meat seasoning, 2 tablespoons fresh parsley or 1 teaspoon dry parsley
1 whole egg, slightly beaten

Split pork tenderloins lengthwise, but do not cut through. Season both sides well with salt and pepper, and brush with melted butter.

Prepare dressing. Sauté onion and celery uncovered in hot butter or shortening about 5 minutes. Cover and steam about 5 minutes. Pour cooked vegetables over dry fluffy bread. Add seasonings and slightly beaten egg. Blend well with 2 forks.

Spread dressing over one of the tenderloins, keeping it away from edge of meat. Place other tenderloin over dressing, forming an attractive roll. Tie with a string or use heavy round toothpicks to hold together. Place in an oblong glass baking dish that measures about 12 × 8 × 2 inches. Brush well with melted butter or margarine. Cover dish with greased aluminum foil and bake at 350° F. about 1 hour. Remove foil, and place meat under broiler (raising temperature to *broil*) until top is brown on both sides. Place back into oven and continue to bake at 350° F. uncovered about 1 hour, or until meat is tender. A little commercial gravy coloring and stock may be added to drippings in baking dish for additional color.

To Serve. Arrange meat in center of an oval platter. Surround with vegetables or browned potatoes.

Vegetable Daisy Meat Dinner

Cover a Premium Daisy (uncooked smoked shoulder butt) with warm water and bring to the boiling point. Now lower heat and simmer meat about 1 hour per pound for pieces weighing less than 2½ pounds. For larger pieces cook about 50 minutes per pound, or until fork-tender. After meat is done, allow it to remain in liquid for about ½ hour.

To Serve. Remove meat and slice crosswise. Arrange in center of large oval platter, and around it place buttered Brussels sprouts, whole small cooked buttered carrots, and buttered whole potatoes. Cook Brussels sprouts only until crisply tender, about 10 to 15 minutes; cook small whole carrots about 20 to 25 minutes; medium-size potatoes until tender, but not too soft, about 25 to 30 minutes. Please see pages 281, 283, 299 for more details. The vegetables are more delicious if cooked in Daisy meat liquid when meat is almost done, or when it has been removed from liquid.

Note. The Daisy meat is a delicious and economical piece of meat as there is no bone or any waste. Instead of cooking it in water, it may be baked at 325° F. on rack with drip pan underneath about 1 hour per pound. We prefer cooking it in water as it is less salty and more moist.

Continental-Style Baked Pork Tenderloin

Serves 6

2 whole pork tenderloins (leave whole if small; cut in halves crosswise if large)

About 1 teaspoon salt and ⅛ teaspoon each pepper, oregano, and celery salt

4 large potatoes peeled and quartered, then browned in hot fat and seasoned

¼ cup oil or shortening

2 cups tomatoes crushed in small pieces

Another 1 teaspoon salt and ½ teaspoon black pepper

¼ cup grated parmesan cheese

1 small clove garlic chopped fine

⅛ teaspoon baking soda

2 tablespoons dry light wine (optional)

¼ teaspoon oregano or marjoram

¼ teaspoon dried parsley or 1 tablespoon of fresh parsley

¼ teaspoon dried celery

Over medium heat brown meat in oil or shortening. Season with the 1 teaspoon salt, ⅛ teaspoon pepper, oregano, and celery salt. Place meat in a large 12-inch casserole (or large round glass pie plate). Arrange browned potatoes around meat. Combine all other ingredients, mix well, and pour over meat and potatoes. Cover with another dish of the same size (or with heavy aluminum foil) and bake at 325° F. about 1½ to 2 hours, or until meat is tender. Test with a fork before removing from oven.

Serve with a vegetable and salad.

Continental-Style Baked Pork Loin

Serves 8

4-pound piece pork loin (backbone removed)	1 small clove garlic, chopped fine
2 tablespoons hot shortening	⅛ teaspoon baking soda
About 1½ teaspoons salt	2 tablespoons dry light wine (optional)
¼ teaspoon pepper	
¼ teaspoon oregano	¼ teaspoon oregano or marjoram (in addition to oregano above)
2 cups tomatoes, crushed into small pieces	
1 teaspoon salt and ½ teaspoon pepper (in addition to salt and pepper above)	¼ teaspoon dried parsley or 1 tablespoon fresh parsley
	¼ teaspoon dried celery or 1 tablespoon minced fresh celery
¼ cup grated parmesan cheese	1 pound macaroni, cooked until tender in salted boiling water

Over medium heat brown meat well in hot shortening. Season it with salt, pepper, and oregano. Place meat in a deep baking dish or casserole. Combine all other ingredients except macaroni, and pour over the meat. Cover dish (aluminum foil may be used) and bake at 350° F. about 2½ to 3 hours, or until tender. When meat is done, remove from sauce. Pour part of sauce over cooked macaroni, and blend well. Pour macaroni into a large serving platter. Slice meat and arrange it in center of macaroni. Pour rest of sauce over meat, and serve with a vegetable and a salad.

Sweet-Sour Spareribs with Sautéed Cabbage

Serves 4 to 6

3 pounds spareribs cut into serving pieces, well seasoned with salt and pepper, celery salt, and garlic salt	½ cup chopped green pepper
	½ cup chili sauce, combined with ½ cup pineapple juice
2 tablespoons hot fat	¼ cup brown sugar solidly packed
½ cup chopped green onion and stems	2 tablespoons cornstarch, combined with ¼ cup lemon juice
¼ cup chopped celery	

Brown spareribs in hot fat. Add chopped onion, celery, and green pepper, and continue to cook about 5 more minutes. Add all other ingredients and pour over meat. Cover, and back at 350° F. about 2 hours, or until meat is fork tender.

Serve in a bed of Sautéed Cabbage and Onion.

Sautéed Cabbage and Onion for Sweet-Sour Spareribs

1 large loose cabbage	1 large onion, sliced thin
Salad oil or other shortening	Salt and pepper

Wash cabbage. Cut in halves, place with flat side down on cutting board, and cut in ¼-inch slices. Loosen cut cabbage. Measure, and for each cup cabbage heat 1 tablespoon salad oil or shortening. Add onion slices and cook gently about 5 minutes. Now add cabbage, and blend thoroughly a minute or two over medium heat. Cover and steam (without adding water) about 10 to 15 minutes or until cabbage is tender enough to suit taste. Turn several times during cooking process, and add a little more oil or shortening if it appears dry. Season with salt and pepper when almost done, and continue to cook.

Pork Tenderloin Slices Gourmet

Serves 3

1 pound pork tenderloin, sliced ⅓ inch thick	¼ cup stock or water
¼ cup hot butter or shortening	1 tablespoon lemon juice
1 teaspoon salt	1 tablespoon brown sugar
¼ teaspoon black pepper	½ teaspoon onion salt
1 cup chili sauce or catsup	¼ teaspoon dried rosemary, crushed

Sauté sliced tenderloin in hot butter or shortening over moderate heat until brown on 1 side. Season with salt and pepper, and brown other side.

When meat is browned on both sides, add all other ingredients. Cover saucepan, and simmer about 20 minutes, or until tender. Do not overcook. When done, serve it in center of a bed of well-buttered seasoned green noodles or rice.

Pork Hocks with Boiled Vegetables or Sauerkraut

Serves 4 to 6

4 pork hocks	4 small potatoes
½ tablespoon salt	4 small white onions
1 teaspoon caraway seeds	(Or No. 2½ can sauerkraut instead
1 small clove garlic	of vegetables)
4 small carrots	

Wash hocks and place in large saucepan. Cover with hot water, add salt, caraway seeds, and garlic. Cover saucepan and bring to a quick boil. Reduce heat and simmer approximately 3 hours, or until meat is tender and almost falls from bones.

For boiled vegetable dinner, about 30 minutes before meat is done, add vegetables and cook slowly about 30 minutes, or until tender.

If serving sauerkraut with pork hocks, add sauerkraut 20 to 30 minutes before meat is done, and simmer slowly.

To Serve. Place pork hocks in center of platter and arrange cooked vegetables around them. Sprinkle vegetables with paprika and serve hot. In serving pork hocks and sauerkraut, remove pork hocks and place on platter. With a ladle pick up sauerkraut, allow surplus liquid to drain, and place sauerkraut in center of platter. Serve at once.

Barbecued Baked Pork Tenderloin

Serves 6

2 whole pork tenderloins (leave whole if small; cut into halves crosswise if large)
¼ cup shortening
About 1 teaspoon salt and ⅛ teaspoon pepper for each pound of meat
1 medium-size onion, chopped fine
1 cup chili sauce

1 cup stock or water with bouillon cube
2 tablespoons vinegar
2 tablespoons brown sugar
¼ teaspoon salt
⅛ teaspoon cayenne pepper or little hot sauce
¼ teaspoon dry mustard

Over medium heat brown meat well in ¼ cup shortening. Place meat in a 10½-inch glass pie plate. Sprinkle it well on both sides with salt and pepper. Prepare a barbecue sauce by adding chopped onion to leftover meat drippings (add little more fat if necessary). Sauté onions about 5 minutes; then add all other ingredients. Continue to cook slowly uncovered 7 or 8 minutes. Pour this sauce over meat. Cover plate with greased foil and bake in a 325° F. oven about 1½ to 2 hours, or until meat is tender when tested with a fork.

Creole-Style Pork Tenderloin Patties

1 pound serves 3 or 4

Have 1 pound pork tenderloin patties sliced and flattened to about 1 inch in thickness. Season with salt and pepper. Roll in flour or bread crumbs, dip into beaten egg combined with 1 tablespoon milk, then into very light bread crumbs again. Let stand on wax paper about 20 minutes, turning them over twice while standing. Brown meat in about ¼ inch hot fat on both sides over moderate heat. Pour 1 cup crushed tomatoes over meat (crush with hand), ½ teaspoon salt, ¼ teaspoon pepper, 1 small thin-sliced onion, and 1 small thin-sliced green pepper that has been sautéed in a little shortening about 5 minutes. Add ¼ teaspoon baking soda. Cover and *simmer* about 20 to 30 minutes, or until meat is tender when tested with a fork. Do not overcook, and keep heat low.

Baked Pork Chops and Potatoes in Casserole

Serves 4

¼ cup butter or shortening	2 tablespoons flour
4 pork chops, sliced about 1 inch thick	1½ cups crushed tomatoes and juice
Salt and pepper	½ teaspoon salt
½ pound onions sliced thin (1 cup)	¼ teaspoon pepper
1 pound raw potatoes sliced very thin (3 cups)	½ teaspoon marjoram or other herb

In hot butter or shortening brown chops on both sides. Season with salt and pepper. In a round glass pie plate, 10½ × 1⅓ inches, place half of sliced potatoes, sprinkle with salt and pepper, then place onions over potatoes, season same way, and cover onions with rest of sliced potatoes. Place browned chops over potatoes. Add flour to drippings in pan and mix until smooth. Then slowly add crushed tomatoes and juice. Season with salt, pepper, and marjoran or other herb. Cook until thick; then simmer several minutes. Pour sauce over meat and vegetables. Cover with greased foil, and bake at 350° F. about 1 hour if chops are thick, less time for thinner chops. Test meat and potatoes after 50 minutes. Overcooking will make meat stringy and dry.

Serve from baking dish with a green vegetable.

Veal chops or shoulder lamb chops may be prepared in same way.

Pork Roast and Sauerkraut

Serves 6 generously

1 large can sauerkraut	1 clove garlic
3-pound piece boned pork roast	¼ cup shortening
Salt	1 pound potatoes
Pepper	

Empty sauerkraut into a colander and run cold water through it. Do not drain too thoroughly. Place sauerkraut in a roasting pan. Season pork roast with salt, pepper, and garlic, and brown on all sides in hot shortening. Place browned pork roast on top of sauerkraut, pour drippings over meat, cover, and roast in preheated 325° F. oven about 2½ hours or until pork roast has reached 170° F., the well-done stage. One pound potatoes that have been peeled, quartered, and browned in shortening on top of stove may be added to roast the last hour.

▶ INDOOR BARBECUED MEATS ◀

Barbecued Spareribs—No. 1

Cut ribs into serving-size portions. Steam them in a covered saucepan with meaty side up in 1 cup of hot water for about 30 to 45 minutes, depending on thickness and amount of ribs. Turn them occasionally during steaming process. When meat is tender, season it with salt, pepper, a little garlic, and celery salt. Pour Barbecue Sauce (page 193) over each rib and let marinate for at least 1 hour. About 30 minutes before serving, place marinated ribs on racks in a shallow roasting pan, with meat side up, and roast for about 30 to 30 minutes at 350° F., turning over after 10 or 15 minutes. *Pour 2 cups water into roasting pan below rack to prevent smoking.* Do not overbake ribs to prevent drying out. Brush them several times with additional Barbecue Sauce.

These ribs may be stuffed with Bread Dressing before they are baked. Place dressing on skin side and cover with another rib. Tie if necessary.

Ribs may be steamed and marinated a day in advance and refrigerated. Then they require only a very short roasting time before serving. Or ribs may be completely cooked in advance, then drizzled with a little Barbecue Sauce, covered with aluminum foil, and reheated in a 350° F. oven for about 20 minutes for single recipe. Cook about 10 minutes longer for larger recipes.

Bread Dressing for 3 Pounds Barbecued Ribs

½ cup warm water or stock	1 teaspoon salt
6 slices white very dry toasted bread, broken or cut into about ½-inch pieces	¼ teaspoon pepper
	¼ cup pimiento, cut into ½-inch pieces (optional)
2 tablespoons or more shortening	¼ cup fresh green onion tops, cut into ½-inch pieces (optional)
1 large onion (½ cupful), sliced thin	
½ cup celery, cut into narrow short strips	1 large whole egg, beaten few seconds

Pour the ½ cup of warm water or stock over the broken pieces of toast and let stand about 10 minutes. Melt shortening, add sliced onion and celery and sauté for about 5 minutes. If vegetables appear dry add 2 tablespoons water, cover and steam over medium heat for 7 or 8 minutes. Pour cooked vegetables over bread, and season dressing with salt, pepper, pimiento and green onions. Last, add beaten egg and blend well with 2 forks.

Barbecued Spareribs—No. 2

Cut raw ribs into serving-size portions. Sprinkle them on both sides with salt, pepper, garlic salt, and celery salt. Place them on racks in a shallow roasting pan meat side up, *pouring 2 cups hot water into roasting pan.* Roast at 450° F. 20 to 25 minutes, then turn them over, lower heat to 300° F. and continue to cook about 30 minutes. Now brush them with Barbecue Sauce (page 193), turn them over, having meat side up; brush well with Barbecue Sauce and continue to cook for about 20 more minutes; 15 minutes longer for very thick back ribs.

Ribs are done when you can pull them apart with fingers, but do not dry them out by overcooking. It may be necessary to add more water to roasting pan to prevent smoking.

Ribs may be completely cooked in advance, then drizzled with a little Barbecue Sauce, covered with aluminum foil and reheated in a 350° F. oven for about 20 minutes for single recipe. Cook about 10 minutes longer for larger recipes.

Barbecued Spareribs—No. 3

Steam and marinate ribs in Barbecue Sauce (page 193) same as for method No. 1. Place them on broiler rack and broil on each side about 10 to 15 minutes, at 325° F., about 3 inches from heat. Watch closely that they do not burn. Brush them with Barbecue Sauce when turning over.

Barbecued Short Ribs of Beef

Short ribs of beef are delectable prepared according to general directions for Barbecued Spareribs, method No. 2.

Barbecued Boneless Rolled Beef, Pork Loins, Veal, or Lamb

Follow our general cooking directions for Roasting of Meats, page 127–129. When meat is about ¾ done, baste it every 15 minutes with Barbecue Sauce. Turn meat over several times to brown underside during latter part of roasting process, and add water or stock *as needed to drippings* in roasting pan to prevent scorching and smoking. Serve additional sauce separately.

Barbecued Steaks and Chops

Follow our general directions for the Broiling of Steaks and Chops, page 129. Brush both sides of meat lightly with Barbecue Sauce the last minute or two, and serve more sauce separately.

Barbecued Hamburgers

Prepare and grill hamburgers according to general directions, page 129. Brush meat lightly on both sides with Barbecue Sauce the last minute. Serve more sauce separately.

Barbecue Sauce

1 medium size onion, chopped fine	1 tablespoon brown sugar
2 tablespoons shortening	1 tablespoon Worcestershire sauce
1 cup tomato catsup	¼ teaspoon dry mustard
1 cup water or stock from steamed ribs	1¼ teaspoons salt
2 tablespoons vinegar or ¼ cup lemon juice	¼ teaspoon (or more) red hot pepper
	¼ teaspoon black pepper
	¼ teaspoon celery seed

Sauté onion in the shortening for about 5 minutes. Add remaining ingredients except seasonings and cook in covered saucepan for about 20 minutes. Add seasonings and continue to simmer about 10 more minutes. If sauce is too thick, add little more stock, water or vinegar.

This is sufficient sauce for about 3 pounds of ribs or 2 small chickens. It is a delectable basic all-around barbecue sauce. More or less seasonings may be added to suit taste. May be prepared days in advance and kept covered in refrigerator, or may be frozen.

▶ FRANKFURTERS ◀

Frankfurter Quails

Split Premium frankfurters lengthwise but do not cut through bottom. Rub inner surface lightly with mustard. Place a ½-inch-wide strip of commercially sliced American cheese in center of each frankfurter; then wrap with a whole or ½ slice thin bacon cut crosswise. Arrange on rack in dripping pan and bake about 12 to 15 minutes in 425° F. oven, or until bacon is done enough to suit taste. Pour 1 cup hot water in pan. Last, place under broiler for several minutes.

Frankfurters à la Duchesse

Serves 4

1 pound large thick dinner-style frankfurters
Prepared mustard
1 recipe Duchesse Potatoes (page 301)

Shredded American cheese
1 package frozen peas and carrots,
  cooked until tender and seasoned

Split frankfurters lengthwise, but do not cut through lower skin. Open them and spread cut side of each with ½ teaspoon prepared mustard. With bag and No. 7 large star cookie tube, pipe Duchesse Potatoes in each frankfurter. Sprinkle top of potatoes with freshly shredded American cheese. Pipe rest of potatoes in center of a heatproof serving platter, forming a nest. Fill center of nest with cooked peas and carrots. Sprinkle top of vegetables and potato nest with cheese. Arrange frankfurters on platter attractively, and just before serving bake at 450° F. about 12 to 15 minutes, or until cheese is melted and browned.

This makes a delicious luncheon, supper, or dinner, served with a salad and hot rolls.

▶ LIVER ◀

Baked Whole Calf's Liver

A 2-pound baked calf's liver will serve 6

1 whole calf's liver (about 2 pounds)
1 teaspoon salt
¼ teaspoon pepper
1 cup thin-sliced onions
2 slices salt pork or 6 slices of bacon

½ cup hot water
½ cup dry red wine
¼ cup fresh celery leaves
¼ pound fresh mushrooms

Remove the thin skin and membrane from whole calf's liver. Place in a casserole or small roasting pan. Season with salt and pepper. Place ½ of onion slices on top of liver, then slices of salt pork or bacon on top of onion, holding them in place with toothpicks. Add water, wine, and celery leaves.

Cover casserole or roasting pan and place in a preheated 350° F. oven. Bake 1 hour and 15 minutes for 2-pound liver or 1 hour and 30 minutes for 2½- to 3-pound liver.

When done, transfer baked liver to a hot platter. Pour drippings into a saucepan, add sautéed mushrooms, and if drippings are too thin, thicken with 1 tablespoon cornstarch combined with 2 tablespoons cold water, and cook until thick (about 5 minutes).

Serve with mashed potatoes and a vegetable.

Chicken-Fried Liver

Have calf or beef liver sliced thin. Proceed as with Chicken-Fried Sirloin Steak (page 154), but do not pound liver. Fry on each side about 5 minutes, or until brown. Serve with Smothered Onions (page 145).

▶ BACON ◀

How to Fry Bacon. A simple way to fry bacon without separating the slices is to remove the required number of slices in 1 piece and put the remaining section back in the refrigerator. Place bacon in a cold skillet and heat *slowly*. Turn and separate the slices when they begin to loosen. This method will prevent tearing slices when trying to separate them when they are chilled. Continue to fry and turn, keeping heat low. Do not pour off the drippings during cooking, since fat helps float the slices and brown the slices more uniformly without raw or burned spots. More bacon can be fried at one time with this method because the cooking depends on the heat of the melted fat rather than on the heat of the bottom of the pan. Drain on absorbent paper, and serve at once.

How to Broil Bacon. Allow bacon to stand in room temperature about 15 minutes to facilitate separation of the slices, thereby preventing tearing of slices. Lay them on a broiling rack about 3 inches from heat source, watching closely to see that they do not burn. Turn slices over in about 3 minutes to brown evenly.

Our Preferred Way to Cook Bacon. Allow bacon to stand in room temperature 15 or 20 minutes to facilitate separation of slices. Place slices crosswise on ribbed side of top-of-the-stove grill, over low heat. Cook and turn often until bacon is done to suit taste. Melted fat from bacon will drip into groove of grill, thereby keeping bacon slices dry and crisp.

How to Bake Bacon. This is an excellent way to prepare larger amounts of bacon at one time. It is not necessary to turn the bacon. Let bacon stand in room temperature about 15 minutes, then carefully release slices; place them on a rack set in a baking pan. Bake in an oven at 400° F. for about 10 to 12 minutes, or until brown and crisp to suit taste.

Bacon Drippings. Strain drippings and store them in a covered jar in refrigerator or a cool place. They are excellent for pan-frying eggs, meats, and vegetables.

▶ *Poultry*
AND DRESSINGS

POULTRY PROVIDES A GOOD VALUE FOR WISE MEAL PLANNERS. IT IS GENERALLY liked, is available and a good buy the year round, and is a fine source of body-building nutrients. Poultry contributes protein, niacin, riboflavin, vitamin A, phosphorus and other minerals to maintain good health.

Modern-day poultry is beautifully cleaned and requires little kitchen preparation to make it pan ready. Conveniently packaged, poultry is easy to buy and store in the home freezer or refrigerator. Use frozen poultry within 2 to 3 months for maximum flavor quality, and use fresh whole or cut-up poultry stored in the refrigerator within 2 days.

Poultry lends variety to meals and is so versatile. Oven- or rotisserie-roasted, pan-, deep-fat-, or oven-fried, fricasseed, or stewed poultry is delicious for hot service. What is left is tasty served cold or combined in favorite casseroles, creamed dishes, and salads.

Cooked poultry meat properly wrapped freezes well for impromptu as well as planned meals. Best to use the frozen cooked poultry within 2 weeks. Use cooked poultry stored in the refrigerator within 2 days.

Poultry Definitions

Rock Cornish Hen. The smallest, youngest member of the chicken family, suitable for roasting, especially with a stuffing. May also be baked, broiled, or fried. It usually weights 1½ pounds or less; many people serve an individual bird to each diner.

Broiler-Fryer. The all-purpose chicken, a young meaty bird about 9 weeks old that weighs 1½ to 3½ pounds. Don't be deceived by its name; a broiler-fryer may be roasted, simmered, or sautéed as successfully as broiled or fried, for chicken dishes with moist, succulent meat.

Roaster. A little older and larger than the broiler-fryer, the roaster weighs 3½ to 5 pounds, is about 12 weeks old, and has tender meat.

Bro-Hen. A plump, meaty laying hen, about 1½ years old, 4½ to 6

We wish to express our thanks to the Swift Dairy & Poultry Company, a division of Swift & Company, for their cooperation in compiling many of the facts and other information regarding poultry cookery.

pounds in weight, that is excellent for simmered chicken dishes and for baking as well. Provides ample tender meat for dishes made with "cooked chicken."

Capon. This is the desexed male chicken, 4 to 7 pounds, with plenty of white meat for roasting or simmering. Capons are large, plump, and tender chickens excellent for company dinners. Follow directions on the package for roasting. Or, thaw, stuff, and prepare according to directions, page 207.

Duckling. Duckling is a richer, bolder-flavored bird in the poultry family and is favored by many gourmets. Ducklings are available in the markets frozen and vacuum packaged in weights from 3½ to 5½ pounds. In buying allow about 1½ pounds per person. Follow the directions on the package for roasting, or directions, page 231.

Turkeys. Turkeys specially bred and fed to yield a greater proportion of delicately flavored white meat to the richer flavored dark meat are available frozen and vacuum packaged. Weights range from 4 to 24 pounds. Turkeys are also available already stuffed in weights of 6 to 16 pounds. Buy 1½ pounds per person of the regular turkeys and 1½ to 2 pounds per person of the stuffed turkeys. Some markets feature cut-up turkeys. Halves, quarters, or pieces are packaged and are available for smaller families or those who prefer just light or dark meat.

Toughness in Poultry

Occasionally chicken, and especially the breast meat, because it is so sensitive, is slightly tough after it has been cooked properly, even by experts. There are several reasons for this condition.

First. All freshly slaughtered poultry must be aged in the refrigerator or in slushed ice for at least 24 hours, loosely wrapped or covered with wax paper.

Second. Poultry must not be cut into individual pieces until rigidity (stiffness of the muscles) disappears, which takes about 24 hours after it has been slaughtered. It has been observed by experts in the poultry field that this stiffness occurs at the surface first, and in a few minutes spreads to the entire muscle when it is cut too soon after it has been slaughtered. If you purchase fresh poultry (that is not frozen) ask your marketman if it has been on ice at least 24 hours. If he is unsure, it is best that you refrigerate fresh poultry, loosely wrapped in wax paper, for at least 12 more hours after you purchase it, before it is cooked, or frozen. If poultry is bought direct from a farmer, it is best to refrigerate for 24 hours.

It is also important not to freeze poultry for long periods. The quality is always more desirable and more tender after short freezer storage. Most supermarts have poultry sales every week or two. We seldom purchase more than 2 weeks' supply, and in addition we double wrap poultry—as it has more tendency to toughen in the freezer than other meats. Some experts say that freezing some meats makes them more tender, but this does not apply to poultry.

In addition, the breed and the feed the bird has received may have some effect on the tenderness, but if you purchase a top well-known brand, you will be assured of quality.

Braising

Braising is one of the most practical methods to tenderize poultry, and even the breast meat is often prepared with this method. To cook gently over low heat means to place cooking utensil on *simmer burner* after the liquid in the pot starts to boil. Cover tightly when braising. You will observe that this very low simmer will create more steam (that is important to tenderize the meat) than if you use higher heat. You must use a small pot for small amounts, to avoid too much evaporation and scorching of drippings. This evaporation and scorching is also caused if the heat under pot is a little too high—and you will notice that no steam is created. There must be steam emanating from the pot and its cover when you lift off cover. If not, add a little hot water or stock, cover and cook over *simmer burner*, until tender.

Before you remove meat from the heat, test it with a two-tined fork or paring knife in the thickest piece. *If breasts are included, they should be removed about 10 minutes before the less tender pieces are done.* Follow each recipe in detail. If you can penetrate the meat and release the fork or knife easily without effort, and if the juices run clear yellow without any trace of pink, the meat is done. Our timing is only a guide, and it is better to test tenderness a few minutes before the time is up. Poultry is always more palatable cooked to the well-done stage, but overcooking it until it falls apart will make it tough and fibrous. Because of the difference in individual birds even of the same brand, you may often have to cook poultry a few minutes longer or less.

Braising is especially excellent for cooking less tender birds and other meats. Braising in most cases means cooking in a small amount of liquid. This method tenderizes the meat and also brings out its flavor. Braising meats in the oven instead of top of the stove requires less attention and results are more delectable. First brown chicken on top of stove as indicated in each recipe; add small amount of liquid, bring to the boiling point on top of stove, then place meat on a trivet (or not as you prefer). Cover tightly and at once place skillet into a preheated 350° F. oven for

Please refer to Italian Cookery chapter and Casseroles chapter for more interesting chicken dishes.

40 to 50 minutes, more or less, depending on quality, size, etc. Remove breasts about 10 minutes before the less tender pieces are done.

It is not always necessary to add liquid in the beginning in braising meats if you are using a very heavy skillet with a tight cover and you are preparing small young chickens, not more than about 2½ pounds drawn weight, and of top quality. Young chickens and other tender meats will cook in their own juices provided they do not require long cooking and the heat is kept very low. If you do not use a trivet in braising meat, meat must be turned over during the cooking process several times to prevent its sticking to bottom of pan. If you use a trivet, at least ¼ cup hot water must be added to produce steam, from time to time, as needed.

Top of Stove vs. Oven Braising. If you are preparing only several pieces, please use a small skillet, about 8-inch size, and cook on top of stove or in oven. In a 10- or 12-inch skillet, many more pieces of chicken can be prepared at one time, and better results are obtained if braised in oven, as it requires less attention. Follow general braising directions.

After meat or poultry has been well browned (always over medium heat, not high—to prevent toughness on outside layer of chicken or other meat) it is very important to remove surplus fat from drippings in skillet before you pour suggested amount of liquid over meat in skillet. A very small amount may be left in, but too much fat prevents formation of steam that is absolutely essential in tenderizing the meat or poultry. Too much fat simply sizzles and does not produce moisture.

Nonstick Skillet. This is an excellent utensil to use for cooking meats, fish, chicken, omelets, etc., but it must be used carefully. Never use it over extremely high heat, as the surface is likely to corrode when the temperature reaches about 450° F. The manufacturers are constantly improving these utensils, and it is therefore always best to purchase a top brand and to read label for directions. While it is true that some meats can be cooked in these utensils without addition of fat, most foods require some fat, and it is important to use the amount of fat suggested in our recipes for breaded meats and other breaded foods in order for a crisp crust to form. For omelets and egg cookery, you can cut amount of fat suggested in half.

Trivets and Racks for Braising and Steaming. It is better but not absolutely essential to use a trivet for braising breaded meats. We recommend using a trivet because it prevents crust of meat from sticking to bottom of pan and prevents a soggy coating. More water or other liquid can be added to skillet when you use a trivet provided meat does not rest in the liquid. Meat must be turned over several times if a trivet is not used in braising.

Trivest and racks are available in hardware and department stores, in various sizes and styles, to fit the smallest and the largest skillet or saucepan. They are recommended in the text books published by Iowa State College and the University of Chicago, department of Home Economics, and are used as suggested in our recipes.

Deep-Fat Frying Poultry

See pages 123–127 meat cookery.

To Cook Chicken and Turkey Breasts

As far back as 1920 (almost fifty years ago) Charles Ranhofer, former chef of the famous Delmonico Restaurant in New York City, and author of the outstanding cookbook of the century, *The Epicurean,* devoted many pages to the preparation of chicken fillet and breasts, and in all his recipes this delicate morsel was cooked quickly in clarified butter (page 328) *without addition of water or other liquid.*

The breast of chicken and turkey is very delicate and delicious when properly cooked. To keep it moist and tender it should be sautéed or fried quickly over low or medium heat in clarified butter (or plain butter combined with small amount oil or unsalted shortening) for the time suggested in recipes. For *best results,* whenever possible, do not cook chicken or turkey breasts in liquid unless suggested.

A quick way to prepare breasts of chicken or turkey for recipes calling for cooked meat is to remove skin and bones from breasts. Flatten them to about ⅓ inch in thickness on large end. Wash and dry meat thoroughly. Use about 1 tablespoon of *clarified* butter for each ½ breast of chicken in a skillet over low heat. When butter is quite warm, but not too hot, add breasts, and turn them over and around for a few seconds until they are well coated with the butter. Do not allow butter to burn. Now cover skillet and poach breasts over medium heat (do not allow them to brown) *about 3 minutes on each side.* Remove from heat, season and use as desired. To test breast for doneness, press it with forefinger when time is up; if it feels springy, it is done. If it feels soft, cook it another minute.

An excellent way to prepare chicken meat for various recipes, creamed chicken, à la king, casseroles, etc., is to prepare a *whole simmered chicken* (page 211). Today's broiler-fryers are so moist and tender that the legs and thighs can also be used in many dishes that call for chicken breast.

In many recipes where all parts of cut-up chicken are included, it is best to remove breasts about 10 minutes before the less tender pieces are done. Whenever possible it is best to cook the breasts separately. If this tender meat (breast) is cooked in water or other liquid, it is acceptable, but not as moist and tender as when cooked over low or medium heat (not over high heat), in butter or other fat suggested in recipes. Boned chicken breasts and sliced turkey breasts, not more than ½ inch in thickness, coated with flour, then egg, then crumbs, sautéed 6 to 8 minutes on each side will be tender and moist without further cooking. If breast is less than ½ inch thick, sauté it only about 4 or 5 minutes on each side.

If bone is left on ½ breasts of chicken, it is best to flatten them slightly on bony side with a cleaver or large heavy knife; cover with crumbs, etc., brown them in ¼ inch hot unsalted fat, then place breasts with meat side up in a skillet. Cover tightly and braise for about 25 minutes for small; about 30 to 40 minutes for medium and large size. If heat is kept very low, it may not be necessary to add any water or stock, but it is usually safer to add about ¼ cup of liquid to produce steam. The breast meat is tender and done when you can separate it easily from the rib bones without effort, using 2 forks to make test with 1 piece.

Another excellent and quick way to prepare sliced boned turkey and boned chicken breasts, flattened to not more than ⅓ inch in thickness, is to coat meat lightly with seasoned flour, then sauté quickly over *medium* heat about 3 or 4 minutes on each side, uncovered or until delicately colored, not too brown. Overcooking will toughen meat. Use about 1 tablespoon clarified butter or margarine (half oil may be used) for each medium breast. Serve it at once. Very delectable if handled properly.

Whenever possible it is better to leave the rib bone on the split breasts. Remove the heavy breast-bone and cut away any small pieces that are uneven from edges of meat. Now with a cleaver or heavy butcher knife (or bottom of small saucepan) strike bony side of breasts to flatten to uniform thickness, about ½ inch thick. You may remove the skin, or leave on until it has cooked. The bones and skin will keep meat more moist and tender, and it will shrink less. It is best to prepare chicken breasts used as a main dish using this method without removing bone before or afterward. Skin may be removed at any time. For competely boneless breasts see directions page 200.

Important. If breasts (or any other parts of poultry) are extremely cold when you are ready to cook them (especially deep-fat frying) it is important to dip each piece into a pot of hot water for about ½ minute, then dry them well on paper toweling if suggested in recipe, or have pieces moist if to be rolled into flour or crumbs.

Note. It is not necessary to presteam chicken breasts regardless of size for sautéing or any type of plain or deep-fat frying *provided* large half breasts are cut crosswise in 2 pieces, with or without breast bone removed. Then flatten them slightly with a cleaver or large heavy knife. Dip first into hot water for about ½ minute, then prepare according to directions in each recipe. We do not recommend deep-frying or sautéing raw breasts and other parts covered with corn flake crumbs as they brown too quickly and center of meat is not done. If you prefer to use corn flake crumbs, please prepare chicken (presteamed) as suggested on page 215 for Crunchy-Crust Deep-Fat Fried Chicken.

If using plain (not clarified) butter, melt it over low heat and do not add food until butter foams up and the foam starts to subside. At this point butter should be *hot and very lightly colored,* but not brown. Add the food to be sautéed, 1 piece at a time, and cook as directed in recipe, leaving a space between each piece. Plain butter combined with unsalted shortening or oil is heated the same way, and is preferable to plain butter alone. Please be sure that food to be sautéed is dry on the surface. Remove any noticeable moisture with paper toweling, unless the food is coated with flour or crumbs.

Marinades for Poultry and Meats

Place poultry or meats to be marinated into an enamel, glass, or stainless steel utensil, and not in other utensils made of metal (except stainless steel), as very often the acid in the marinade will act upon the metal chemically and develop an unpleasant taste in the food. Let food soak in the marinade for the time suggested in recipe, turning it over, and basting it often with marinade in pan. Keep refrigerated, but let stand in room temperature about 1 hour before cooking, either in or out of marinade, as suggested in recipes.

▶ TURKEY ◀

Fresh or Frozen Turkey

Fresh turkeys are advertised frequently at a premium and priced over frozen. Fresh (unfrozen) turkeys deteriorate, so their freshness depends on how many days old they are. If you purchase a fresh turkey cover it loosely in wrapper and store in the refrigerator for 2 or 3 days.

Flavor and tenderness tests show no distinguishable difference in turkeys due to freezing. The most reliable turkey, from a quality standpoint, is the frozen turkey with a well-known brand name. Another advantage is that the label or tag on these birds is your buying guide. You can check it for weight, price, cooking directions, and the U.S. inspection stamp, which denotes a quality, wholesome bird. We use and recommend the Deep-basted Butterball turkeys. They are deeper in the breast with more white meat and are always tender and juicy. Most leg tendons are removed for easier carving. "Deep-basted" means a special basting mixture is added deep inside where hand-basting cannot reach. The result is a perfection of tenderness and juiciness every time.

Methods of Thawing Turkey. Frozen turkeys should be thawed slowly, never at room temperature or in warm water. Thaw the frozen turkey in the original bag on a tray in the refrigerator. Allow 2 to 3 days, depending on the size of the bird. When sufficiently pliable, remove giblets to speed thawing. If you buy a turkey at the last minute and must thaw it rapidly, place turkey in unopened bag in pan. Cover with cold water. Change water frequently for 2 to 6 hours. If you have a freezer, you can buy a turkey a week or two in advance and keep it in the freezer until 2 to 3 days before cooking. It is best to use a thawed turkey as soon as possible or within a day after it is completely thawed.

Neck and Giblets

Simmer in salted water, about ½ hour for the liver and 2 to 2½ hours for neck, heart, and gizzard.

To Prepare Turkey for Roasting

Free legs and tail from tucked position. Remove neck and giblets from body and neck cavities. Rinse turkey and drain. Stuff neck and body cavities lightly (about ¾ cup stuffing per pound purchased weight). Fasten neck skin to back with skewer. Fold wings back so that wing tips will hold neck skin in place. Fasten body cavity with steel skewers by placing them across the opening at regular intervals. With heavy twine bring the skin edges together by "lacing" the twine around the pins, thus closing the opening. (Deep-basted Butterball turkeys require no lacing. Simply return drumsticks and tail to tucked position. Push drumsticks under band of skin.) Tie a cord around lower end of each drumstick. This prevents the muscle and skin from drawing away from the leg bone during roasting. Push drumstick close to body, but not too tightly, tying leg ends to the tail piece. Pull the string firmly so that the bird will retain its shape. Cut string after 3 hours.

Bread Stuffing for Turkey

For 15-to-18-pound turkey

1-pound loaf white sliced bread (about 16 slices)

1 cup butter or margarine, or ½ pound bacon cut into small pieces

Turkey liver and heart, cut into small pieces

2 cups onions, sliced about ⅓ inch thick

2 cups celery, cut crosswise, about ⅓ inch thick

1¼ cup or more hot water or stock

2 teaspoons, more or less, thyme

½ cup fresh parsley, finely chopped

About 2 teaspoons salt

½ teaspoon pepper

2 large eggs, beaten with a fork

With fingers break bread (including crust) into about 1-inch pieces. Spread on large baking sheet. Toast in 325° F. oven about 20 to 30 minutes, or until light golden color and crisp. Turn over several times with a long spoon after the first 10 minutes to keep bread uniform in color. Melt butter or margarine, or sauté bacon until medium done, about 5 minutes. Add liver and heart. Cook 5 minutes. Add onions and celery. Stir well and add ¼ cup water. Cover and steam about 10 minutes, or until vegetables are tender. Add 1 cup of hot water or stock to vegetables. More liquid may be added for a moist dressing. Pour vegetables over toasted bread. Season with thyme, parsley, salt, and pepper. Add eggs. With 2 forks mix ingredients until well blended. If any dressing remains after bird is stuffed, it may be baked separately in a well-greased baking dish on upper rack the last 40 minutes, covered with greased foil. Extra dressing may be prepared.

Note. Place the stuffing in the turkey just before roasting. The dry ingredients may be measured in advance and the other ingredients may be cut up in advance and refrigerated. The ingredients are safer combined just before stuffing. There are now turkeys on the market that are already stuffed for convenience and are becoming increasingly popular. These turkeys are prepared under government inspection and controlled and sterile conditions in a manner not generally possible in the home. These stuffed birds are flash frozen and should be kept frozen according to the directions on the wrapper.

Important. For best results it is better to roast turkeys weighing more than 18 pounds without stuffing. Stuffing can be baked separately in a heatproof baking dish. Place in oven when removing turkey from oven. Let turkey stand 30 minutes to allow juices to set for easier carving. Drizzle top of dressing with melted butter or margarine and a little more water. Cover with greased foil. Bake in a 400° F. oven about 45 minutes, or until top is brown and crusty. Roasting turkey without stuffing shortens roasting time.

To Roast Turkey

Use uncovered pan for attractive turkey to carve at the table. Use a covered pan to shorten roasting time though bird will be less attractive. If a portable electric roaster is used, follow manufacturer's directions and time schedule. It is not recommended that you wrap the entire bird in foil if using these methods and roasting temperatures.

Roasting in Uncovered Pan

Weigh stuffed and trussed bird to estimate total cooking time. A bathroom scale is excellent for this purpose, or use weight of bird purchased as a guide. Place turkey, breast side up, on a rack in a shallow open pan. Use no water or cover. Insert meat thermomenter into center of the largest part of the thigh meat next to the body cavity, not touching bone. Rub skin with shortening for a golden color. Shield skin of neck cavity with small square of aluminum foil. Roast in a 325° F. oven. When skin is light golden brown, place a sheet of lightweight aluminum foil loosely over turkey breast and thighs to prevent overbrowning.

Roasting in Covered Pan

Place turkey, breast side up, on rack in deep roaster pan. Use no water. Cover with lid, vent open. Roast in 350° F. oven. Remove lid toward end of roasting if further browning is necessary.

Roasting times were determined using dark enamel roasters. If shiny, light colored roaster is used, it may be necessary to increase time up to 1 hour.

Timetable for Roasting (approximate)

Weight as Purchased	Uncovered Pan 325° F. Oven	Covered Pan 350° F. Oven
4 to 8 pounds	3½ to 4½ hours	2½ to 3 hours
8 to 11 pounds	4½ to 4¾ hours	3 to 3½ hours
11 to 14 pounds	4¾ to 5½ hours	3½ to 4 hours
14 to 20 pounds	5½ to 6 hours	4 to 4½ hours
20 to 24 pounds	6 to 7 hours	4½ to 5 hours

Important. After turkey has roasted 2 or 3 hours it may be necessary to add about ½ cup of stock or water from time to time to drippings in pan if they appear scant or scorched. This is very important to preserve flavor and color of drippings to be used for gravy.

Test for Doneness. Our timetable is only a guide to determine when to put the turkey in the oven. Roasting times vary depending on the temperature of turkey when placed in the oven as well as oven temperature, pan, and shape of turkey. It is always desirable to plan the roasting schedule so that the turkey is out of the oven at least 30 minutes for easier carving. This period given the meat a chance to absorb the juices. To tell whether turkey is done, move the drumstick up and down. If the leg joint gives readily or breaks, the turkey is done. Or, press the thickest part of the drumstick, protecting fingers with cloth or paper. It is done if the meat feels soft. When a meat thermometer is used, it should register 180° to 185° F.

To Serve. Carve with a very sharp, thin-bladed knife and fork with guard. Don't, under any circumstances, allow the turkey, stuffing, or gravy to stand outside of the refrigerator after the meal is over. Before refrigerating, remove all stuffing from the bird and put it in a covered bowl. Wrap the entire bird if only 1 side has been carved. Otherwise, remove the remaining meat from the bones. Cover well. If you plan to make turkey soup, crack the bones, wrap well and refrigerate.

Glazy Gravy for Roasted Turkey

Combine neck, gizzard, cut-up stalk of celery and carrot, ¼ cup parsley, 1 small cut-up onion, and 1 bay leaf in a medium-size sauce pan. Add 6 cups cold water and 1 tablespoon salt. Cover and cook slowly for several hours or until gizzard is tender. Strain. Remove most of fat from drippings in roasting pan, leaving about 1 tablespoon for each cup of gravy to be made. Add strained stock to drippings, measure, and for each cup add about 1½ tablespoons of cornstarch dissolved in 2 tablespoons of cool water. Cook until thick. Simmer until clear, about 5 minutes if using cornstarch. If gravy appears too thick, thin out with a little more liquid. Taste gravy and season further if necessary. Brush turkey with this gravy just before serving to impart an attractive glaze, if desired. A little commercial gravy coloring may be added if a darker gravy is preferred.

Deep-Basted Breast of Young Turkey

To suit those who prefer white meat of turkey, Deep-basted Premium Breast of Young Turkey is available in the majority of markets. They are "deep-basted" to assure tenderness and juiciness, and are frozen while fresher than "fresh-sold" birds, and are vacuum sealed. Weights range from 2½ to 7 pounds. Cook them according to directions on label or in recipes calling for breast of turkey or breast of chicken.

Butter-Basted Turkey Roasts (White and Dark Meat or All-White Breast Meat)

These are interesting items and come packaged as 2-pound boneless roasts. They have generous patties of butter nestling between the skin and the roast. This handy frozen turkey roast is oven-ready in its own foil pan when purchased. Cooking directions appear on each package.

▶ CHICKEN AND OTHER POULTRY ◀

For best results purchase only top-quality poultry. It is available fresh or quick-frozen. Do not freeze for long periods.

Removing Skin and Bones from Uncooked Poultry

Skin and bones may be removed before cooking, unless otherwise indicated in recipe. However, the skin and bone help to keep the meat more moist, more tender, and more flavorful. Chicken breasts are often skinned and boned for some dishes, but generally it is better not to remove them until cooked. Follow directions in each recipe. A chicken stock can be made with bones and skin and used as a base for chicken gravy.

Whole Roasted Chicken

Wash drawn chicken under cold running water and dry it well. Do not stuff chicken ahead of time, but just before roasting. Stuff body and neck cavities lightly with Bread Dressing (page 208), and truss.

To Truss. This assures more even cooking and browning and the chicken will be more attractive and easier to carve. Draw neck over onto the back and fasten with a skewer. Fasten wings onto back by twisting the tip ends. To close the main cavity insert skewers and lace together with string, or simply close opening with 1 or 2 metal skewers. Tie drumsticks together loosely to tail end.

To Roast. Brush skin thoroughly with melted fat, and place trussed bird, breast side up, on a rack or trivet in a shallow open roasting pan (broiler pan may be used).

For large birds, weighing more than 4 pounds, a loose sheet of aluminum foil or a thin cloth moistened with fat may be placed loosely on top of bird from the beginning, *or* after it has partly cooked, to prevent over-browning and to keep it moist. Cover breast with cloth moistened with unsalted shortening or foil as soon as it is brown.

Roast bird at a constant temperature according to chart (page 208). The chart is only a guide and cannot be depended upon entirely. *Premium poultry may take less time to roast.* Brush bird with additional fat or drippings in roasting pan from time to time. If the drippings in pan appear scant or to scorch at any time, *add about ¼ cup of stock or water, as needed.* A low roasting temperature assures excellent drippings, rich in color and flavor for the gravy. *If chicken is cooking too rapidly lower temperature toward end. If too slowly raise temperature and add a little water to drippings.*

To Test for Doneness. Compute cooking time, allowing an extra 15 or 20 minutes. It is always better to allow bird to stand in room temperature away from drafts a short time after it is done. This facilitates handling and carving. Chicken is done when you can penetrate the thickest pieces easily with a two-tined carving fork or the blade of a slender paring knife, and the juices run clear yellow without any trace of pink. To test for doneness, press the thickest part of the drumstick between the fingers—meat should feel soft, and not rigid. Protect the fingers with wax paper or cloth.

Roasted, or whole simmered, chicken is done when the drumstick thigh joint and the shoulder joint move easily and leave body without effort. If you are roasting more than one chicken at the same time, at least 3 inch space must be left between each bird, and the roasting time will have to be increased about 15 minutes. Best to make suggested tests before removing chicken from oven.

Timetable for Roasting

Ready to Cook or Stuffed Weight	Oven Temperature	Approximate Roasting Time
2 to 3 pounds	350° F.	1½ to 2 hours
3¼ to 3¾ pounds	325° F.	2¼ to 2½ hours
4 to 5 pounds	325° F.	2¾ to 3 hours
Capons 5½ to 7 pounds	325° F.	3¼ to 4 hours

Bread Dressing for Chicken

½ pound white bread (about 8 slices)
½ cup butter, or ½ pound bacon cut into small pieces
Liver and heart, cut into small pieces
1 cup onions, sliced about ⅓ inch thick
1 cup celery, cut crosswise about ⅓ inch thick

2 tablespoons water
½ cup hot water or stock
1 teaspoon, more or less, thyme
¼ cup fresh parsley, chopped fine
About 1 teaspoon salt
¼ teaspoon pepper
1 large egg, beaten with fork

With fingers break bread (including crust) into about 1-inch pieces. Spread on a large baking sheet and toast in a 325° F. oven for about 20 to 30 minutes, or until golden brown and crisp, turning it over several times with a long spoon after the first 10 minutes, to keep bread uniform in color. Melt butter, or sauté bacon until medium done, for about 5 minutes. Add the chicken liver and heart and cook 5 more minutes. Now add the sliced onions and celery, stir well. Add the 2 tablespoons water. Cover pan and steam gently about 10 minutes, or until vegetables are tender. Add the ½ cup of hot water or stock to vegetables. More water may be added for a moister dressing. Pour vegetables over toasted bread, season with thyme, parsley, and salt. Last, add beaten egg, and with 2 forks mix ingredients until well blended. If any dressing remains after chicken is stuffed, it may be baked separately in a well-greased baking dish on upper rack the last 40 minutes, covered with greased foil. This is enough stuffing for 3 to 4 pound fully drawn chicken.

Gravy for Roasted Chicken

Cover gizzard and neck with 2 or more cups cold water. Add 1 teaspoon salt, 1 small bay leaf, 1 small sliced onion, and ¼ cup celery. Cook in covered saucepan about 1 to 1½ hours, or until gizzard is tender. When done, strain. Remove surplus fat from drippings in roasting pan, if necessary. Add 1½ tablespoons (more or less) cornstarch, combined with 2 table-spoons water (2 tablespoons flour may be used instead) to drippings for each cup of gravy to be made. Now add the lukewarm strained stock and with a fluffy beater or spoon blend well. Cook until thick and simmer about 5 minutes. Taste and season further, if necessary. Giblets may be cut up and added to gravy. A little commercial gravy coloring may be added for additional color.

Quick Chicken Gravy

½ cup fresh mushrooms, chopped fine; or ¼ cup canned
¼ cup finely chopped onion
Use leftover drippings from any cooked chicken, or use about ¼ cup butter or margarine
¼ cup sifted all-purpose flour
2 cups chicken stock (made from bones, skin, neck gizzard, etc.), or 2 teaspoons instant chicken bouillon dissolved in 2 cups hot water
About ½ teaspoon salt
Bit pepper
2 tablespoons light dry wine (optional)

Sauté the chopped mushrooms and onion in the drippings or ¼ cup of hot butter or margarine for about 5 minutes. Add flour and continue to cook and stir for about 3 minutes. Now bring the 2 cups of stock to a boiling point and add it immediately all at one time to the flour preparation. *At once* stir continuously over medium heat until smooth and thick, then simmer about 5 minutes. Taste and season further, if necessary. Add gravy coloring and wine if desired and cook about 2 more minutes.

This delicious gravy can be prepared for any type of chicken dish.

Quick Chicken Pan Gravy

This can be made by removing any surplus fat from drippings in pan. Add about ½ cup of stock (or part wine) to the drippings, and scrape gently over low heat. Strain if necessary. Taste and season.

Chicken Breasts for Fancy Dishes

Split whole breasts in 2 pieces. Skin and bones may be removed after cooking. Place breasts in a deep skillet or saucepan, with bone side down; add about ½ inch hot water or stock. Cover pot tightly, bring to the boiling point. Lower heat to simmer burner (do not boil), and cook small

(4 to 5 ounces) breasts about 20 to 30 minutes; 6-ounce size about 35 minutes; up to 8 ounces about 40 to 45 minutes, or until breast bone can be easily loosened from meat, but do not overcook—to prevent toughness. This is the best way to judge doneness. Add more hot liquid to pot as required and watch closely that steam is created when you lift off cover. *Keep heat low as possible,* and test to see if done a few minutes before time is up.

When meat is tender, you can release it easily in 1 piece after it has cooled to lukewarm. Now remove skin, and use whole half breasts for special gourmet dishes, such as Chaud-froid Breast of Chicken, and other fancy glazed dishes. This is the most practical way to cook breasts for this purpose.

Many continental chefs braise the whole chicken, then carefully release the breast meat in 1 piece from each side. The breast meat is usually more moist and more tender when chicken is cooked whole, but is not too practical and economical for this purpose. Do not remove bone and skin from breasts until after they are cooked—to prevent more shrinkage, and to retain a better shape and tenderness.

Sautéed Breasts of Chicken (Braised)

½ cup sifted all-purpose flour
1½ teaspoons paprika
1 teaspoon salt
⅛ teaspoon pepper
⅛ teaspoon thyme
⅛ teaspoon garlic salt

1 pound breasts of chicken, split in halves
About 2 tablespoons butter and 2 tablespoons oil or shortening, heated

Sift dry ingredients together. Place them into a paper or plastic bag. Shake 1 or 2 damp breasts at a time in the bag to coat thoroughly. Sauté breasts over moderate (*not high*) heat in the hot combined butter and oil, with flesh side down first until golden brown, then turn over and brown bony side. Place browned breasts with bone side down into a small skillet or saucepan to prevent drying out if preparing only small amount. Add ¼ to ½ cup hot water. Cover tightly and steam (or braise) gently over very low heat (see general directions for braising, page 198). Cook about 25 minutes for very small breasts weighing 4 to 5 ounces, 35 to 40 minutes for those about 6 to 7 ounces, and 45 to 50 minutes for large breasts weighing 8 ounces or larger. Add more water to produce steam if necessary. Heat must be kept low (simmer burner excellent). Remove cover last 5 minutes and continue to cook gently, turning breasts over, until they appear nice and brown. A trivet may be used in the skillet or saucepan, but it will be necessary to add more water from time to time.

Sautéed Chicken Legs (Braised)

Prepare same as Sautéed Breasts (page 210) but increase cooking time to about 40 to 60 minutes.

To Serve. Sautéed breasts or legs are very delicious and attractive served in the center of a bed of well-seasoned, buttered green or yellow noodles with a vegetable and a salad. The top of each breast or leg may be garnished with a large carved whole sautéed (or plain) mushroom and parsley bouquets on each end for special occasions.

Pan-Fried Chicken in the Rough

Broilers, frying chickens, roasting chickens, and small young broiler-type turkeys may be prepared in the rough. Split small broilers in halves, cut larger chickens in quarters, or serving-size pieces. Do likewise with small young turkeys. No coating of flour or crumbs is generally used on this type of fried chicken, but we prefer coating it with seasoned flour same as Sautéed Breasts of Chicken (page 210). The skin may be pulled off or left on, as you prefer. If chicken is not floured, it must be thoroughly dried on a towel.

Sauté pieces same as for Sautéed Breasts of Chicken, then place in a deep skillet with fleshy side up after it has browned on all sides. Now add ¼ to ½ cup hot water, cover tightly and cook over low heat 40 to 45 minutes for broilers; 50 to 55 minutes for frying chickens; 60 to 70 minutes for roasting chickens; and about 1½ to 2 hours for young turkeys. Turn pieces over 2 or 3 times during cooking process, keeping bony side down for greater part of time. Add more hot water to drippings as needed to produce steam. Follow detailed directions for Sautéed Breasts of Chicken. If breasts have been separated from leg, remove them about 10 minutes before the less tender pieces are done. When meat is tender, remove cover and continue to sauté a few minutes on each side until attractively brown.

Simmered Whole Chicken

1 whole broiler-fryer (or larger) chicken	½ cup celery tops
2 cups hot water	1 teaspoon salt
1 small onion, sliced	½ teaspoon pepper
	1 small bay leaf

Place whole chicken on a trivet (if you have one, but not essential) in deep pot with breast side up; add remaining ingredients. (If preferred seasonings may be omitted in simmered chicken.) Bring to a boil; now lower heat at once, cover tightly, and simmer 40 to 60 minutes, or until leg and wing joints move easily, and can be removed from body without effort. When done, let cool, and use as indicated in recipe. The skin is usually discarded or can be left on for family meals. If not to be used at once, refrigerate chicken and broth together to keep it moist. A 3-pound broiler-fryer chicken yields about 2½ cups cooked meat, packed, and approximately 2½ cups of broth.

To Simmer a Bro-Hen or Other Larger Chickens. Increase water to 3 cups, salt to 2 teaspoons, and all other seasoning slightly. Cook these larger chickens for 2 to 3 hours, depending on tenderness of bird and size. Make test for doneness as suggested for smaller birds.

Note. This is the best method to prepare chicken for recipes that call for cooked chicken meat (chicken à la king, creamed chicken, casseroles, etc.). It is best to cook chicken whole for this purpose for more moist and tender meat, and for less shrinkage.

Basic Fried Chicken (in Shallow Fat)

1 broiler-fryer chicken about 2½ pounds, cut into serving pieces	1 teaspoon salt
	1 teaspoon paprika
½ cup sifted all-purpose flour	⅛ teaspoon pepper or desired herb

Separate leg from thigh (or leave whole if small). Remove large breast bone from breast halves, and flatten each with cleaver to ½-inch thick. Sift dry ingredients together. Dampen chicken pieces lightly and roll in flour to cover completely. Shake off loose flour. Or you can dip floured chicken into well-beaten egg combined with 1 tablespoon water, then cover well with *light* dry bread crumbs. Let breaded chicken stand about 20 minutes on wax paper, turning it over several times.

To Fry. Bring temperature of shallow ½ inch unsalted shortening or oil to 300° F. Place legs and thighs in first, then backs, wings, and breasts. If pieces are cooked all at one time in a large uncovered skillet, remove breasts after they have cooked about 7 or 8 minutes *on each side* if bones were left on. Cook flattened *boned breasts* only 3 or 4 minutes on each side. Turn only once. Cook wings about 10 minutes on each side; backs about 12 minutes on each side; thighs and legs about 15 to 20 minutes on each side, depending on size of chicken. It is best to check temperature of fat with a deep-fat thermometer. If temperature is too high chicken will not be cooked in center; if temperature is too low, it will take longer to cook and surface of chicken will be greasy. Do not overbrown.

Note. Any unsalted shortening or cooking oil may be used for deep-fat and for shallow-fat frying. Test temperature of fat with thermometer for best results and to prevent tough upper layer of chicken. Do not use butter, margarine, or drippings for this purpose. See page 123 for details about deep-fat frying.

Crispy-Crust French-Fried Chicken (in Deep Fat)

1 cut-up broiler-fryer, weighing 2 to 2¾ pounds (not larger), washed and dried in paper towels, then each piece seasoned lightly with salt and pepper

1 recipe Crispy-Crust Batter (page 214)
Oil or unsalted shortening for deep-fat frying

Chicken must stand in room temperature, covered with wax paper, for at least an hour. If it feels very cold, best to dip each piece into hot water for a few seconds, then dry meat well on paper towel, to prevent thinning of batter.

To Deep-fry Raw Chicken. Dip raw pieces into batter, hold in fingers and let surplus batter drip off for a few seconds. Lower gently into deep hot fat heated to 325° F. Cook legs and thighs about 15 to 18 minutes, until golden brown and crisp. Keep temperature of fat around 300° F. (not over 325° F.) after frying begins to insure thorough cooking in thick parts of chicken. Do not overcrowd frying basket, and wait a few seconds before you add each piece. This will prevent chicken pieces from clinging together.

Breasts with bones left on are dipped into hot water, and dried well, then dipped into batter, and French-fried for only 8 or 9 minutes at 325° F. without turning, if they are completely submerged in the hot fat. Boned breasts are cooked only about 4 to 5 minutes at 375° F. Wings will be done in about 10 minutes, backs about 12 minutes.

Keep cooked chicken in prewarmed oven on rack if necessary. Prewarm oven at 300° F. for 15 minutes, *then shut off heat.* Place fried chicken on rack on baking sheet, and it will remain crisp and hot for at least ½ hour.

Or this chicken can be fried to a slightly lighter brown in first frying, then refried at the original temperature about 300° to 325° F. for several minutes until brown and crisp. You can do first frying day in advance if cooked chicken is refrigerated and well wrapped. Let stand room temperature about an hour before refrying.

To Deep-fry Presteamed Chicken. For chickens that weigh more than 2¾ pounds drawn weight, it is safer to presteam the chicken pieces (except breasts) in covered pot in about 1 inch of simmering water, for about 35 minutes for small, 40 to 50 minutes for medium or large broiler-fryers that weigh up to 3½ pounds, or until just tender, but do not overcook.

Dip the pieces of chicken into the batter, then deep-fry at 375° F. (higher temperature than raw chicken) for only about 6 or 7 minutes, or until brown and crisp. It is best to cut leg away from thigh if chickens weigh more than 2 pounds to insure thorough cooking close to bone.

It is not necessary to presteam breasts regardless of size for this method of frying provided large breasts (split in halves) are cut crosswise in two pieces, then flattened slightly with a cleaver or large heavy knife on boney side. Simply dip them into hot water for a few seconds, drain well on paper towels, then dip pieces into batter and deep-fry about 8 or 9 minutes at 325° F., completely submerged in fat. If bones have been removed from breasts, flatten them slightly on thick end, dip into batter, but reduce cooking time to 3 or 4 minutes at a higher temperature of 375° F. Overcooking this tender part of the chicken will make it tough and stringy.

Never allow coating on the chicken to become overbrown at any time. This would cause outside layer to be less tender.

Crispy-Crust Batter

½ cup sifted all-purpose flour	½ teaspoon garlic salt
¼ cup unsifted white corn meal or flour	¼ teaspoon pepper
½ teaspoon baking powder	1 large egg, beaten about ½ minute with wire beater
1 teaspoon salt	½ cup cool water or chicken stock
⅛ teaspoon any kind herb	1 teaspoon salad oil or melted fat

Sift dry ingredients together. Combine beaten egg with water or stock and oil or fat. If chicken stock appears oily, omit the teaspoon of fat in batter. Add dry ingredients to the beaten egg, water, and teaspoon of fat in a small bowl. With a fork or spoon, stir only until smooth. If batter appears very thick, it is important to add a little more water or stock. Heat does not penetrate a very thick batter (unless chicken has been presteamed), but a thinner crust on chicken is more desirable. Test it by frying 1 piece of chicken after it is dipped in batter. If batter appears too thin, a bit more flour can be stirred in. If you are using part corn meal in this batter, it is important to use batter within a few minutes, to keep it crisp.

Breaded Deep-Fat Fried Chicken

If you prefer a breaded, very crisp crust on deep-fat fried chicken prepare chicken as for Crispy-Crust French-Fried Chicken (page 213). Instead of dipping pieces into batter, roll them in flour, then dip into beaten egg combined with 1 tablespoon water, drain in fingers, and cover completely with light dry bread crumbs (or cracker meal). Breaded chicken should stand on wax paper about 20 minutes, turning it over several times. Now follow cooking and timing directions for Crispy-Crust French-Fried Chicken.

Braised Pan-Fried Breaded Chicken

Coat damp uncooked chicken with seasoned flour, then dip into well-beaten egg combined with 1 tablespoon water, drain in fingers; now cover well with light dry bread crumbs. Let stand on wax paper about 20 minutes, turning pieces over several times.

Brown chicken well on each side over medium heat in about ¼ inch of unsalted hot shortening or oil. Place pieces with fleshy side up on a trivet (if you have one) for best results. Add ¼ to ½ cup hot water or stock to drippings in pan, depending on size of skillet and amount of chicken you are preparing. Cover skillet tightly and braise (cook gently) about 40 minutes for small broilers, 45 minutes for fryers, and about 1 hour or longer for roasting chickens. Always test thick part of thigh with a two-tined fork or pointed paring knife for doneness. Chicken must be well done to be palatable. When done, remove cover and lift out trivet, and allow chicken to sauté uncovered for a few minutes, turning pieces over once or twice. This will impart an attractive, sautéed appearance to the crust. Remove breasts 7 to 10 minutes before *less* tender pieces are done. Breasts are done when rib bone can be released easily from meat with a fork.

Important. More water or stock must be added to drippings in pan if they appear scant at any time to prevent scorching. Braising must be done over very, very low heat after liquid begins to boil. High heat will cause evaporation of moisture within a few minutes and cause drippings to scorch. Steam is easily produced over a *simmer burner* and much less liquid will be required.

Braised Oven-Fried Breaded Chicken

Prepare as above, and bake covered in a 350° F. oven for about same time, or may be baked uncovered, increasing cooking time a few minutes longer if you prefer a drier crust.

Crunchy-Crust Deep-Fat Fried Chicken

For this method all parts of chicken can be used *except the breast*. Chicken pieces must be presteamed in covered saucepan as per general directions until tender. Now season pieces with salt and pepper. Roll damp chicken into flour, then dip into beaten egg combined with 1 tablespoon buttermilk or coffee cream, drain in fingers, and cover completely with regular corn flakes that have been crushed medium, and part crushed fine, and blended together. Do not use the commercial type fine corn flake crumbs, as the results are not as satisfactory. Press corn flakes well onto surface of chicken, keep on wax paper for about 20 minutes, turning over several times. Now lower into 325° F. hot fat or oil, having pieces completely submerged in the fat. Cook only 3 or 4 minutes, as this coating burns fast.

This type of chicken can be completely cooked and fried in advance, then reheated in a 350° F. oven for about 20 minutes if chicken is cold, 15 minutes if it is room temperature. Do not refry as coating will burn instantly.

Butter-Crisp Baked Chicken

Wash chicken in cold water, *drain thoroughly*, but do not dry. (If chicken pieces are fried in any style *without a coating* of any kind, they must be thoroughly dry on the surface or they will not brown properly.) Coating will cling better if chicken pieces are moist but not too wet. Shake several pieces of chicken in the bag of Seasoned Flour at a time, being sure that each piece is thoroughly coated. Shake off loose flour. Sauté pieces in about ¼ inch half butter and half oil or shortening until golden color on each side, not too brown, as they will darken more in oven. Arrange chicken 1 layer deep in a well-greased shallow uncovered baking pan (broiler pan excellent). Brush chicken well with additional melted fat, and pour remaining drippings in skillet over top.

Bake chicken at 350° F. about 35 minutes for small breasts and wings; 45 minutes for legs, thighs, and backs. Bake about 15 minutes longer for chickens weighing more than 2 pounds drawn weight. Test with point of paring knife or two-tined fork. If you are preparing 2 layers at one time, increase baking time to about 1¼ hours, or longer, depending on size and quality, but remember to remove breasts and wings about 10 minutes before less tender pieces are done. Keep them warm in a covered skillet until rest of pieces are ready. Brush chicken with melted butter or drippings in pan several times during the baking process to keep it moist and tender.

If this chicken is prepared in an attractive heatproof serving platter, fill in open spaces with well-buttered and seasoned vegetables or sautéed potatoes just before serving.

Seasoned Flour for Coating Chicken

¾ cup sifted all-purpose flour	⅛ teaspoon garlic powder or salt
1 teaspoon salt	1½ teaspoons paprika
⅛ teaspoon pepper	⅛ teaspoon poultry seasoning

Combine all ingredients in a small paper or plastic bag and shake well to blend thoroughly.

Broiled Chicken

Purchase tender, small chickens, preferably about 2½ pounds or smaller, drawn weight. Have them split in halves lengthwise, with neck and back bone removed. It is best to break the drumstick, hip, and wing joints to keep the bird flat during broiling. Bring wing tip onto back under the shoulder joint. Brush well with melted butter. Season each half on both sides with about ½ teaspoon salt, ⅛ teaspoon white pepper, and a pinch of thyme or rosemary. Place chicken, with cut side up, in bottom of broiling pan—not on rack—so that chicken is kept moist, about 3 inches from heat, with temperature set at 425° F. to 450° F.

Broil slowly, 15 to 25 minutes on each side, depending on size and quality. Premium chickens may take less time. Baste with additional butter several times during broiling process. Turn over when chicken is done on first side and continue to broil until brown and crisp on the outside. Chicken is done when the thickest part of the drumstick and wing joints is easily penetrated with a two-tined fork, and there is no pink color visible, or when thigh separates easily from body. Turn chicken around whenever necessary so that it browns evenly. To broil larger chickens up to 3 pounds, broil at about 400° F. to 425° F. about 30 minutes on each side.

Breast of Chicken (or Turkey) Romanoff

1 pound boneless chicken or turkey breasts (½ inch thick), sliced	2 tablespoons salad oil
1 egg, combined with 1 tablespoon water and beaten well with fluffy beater or fork	2 tablespoons butter

To Marinate Breasts. Pour Marinade (page 218) over sliced boneless breasts. Mix well, cover and refrigerate for at least 2 hours, turning them over and around several times during this period. May stand in refrigerator all night.

To Fry Breasts. Pick up marinated breasts, hold in fingers and let drain a few seconds. Dip into beaten egg, then cover completely with Crumb Coating (page 218). Place on wax paper, and let stand about 20 minutes, turning over twice. In a 10-inch skillet heat salad oil and butter. When hot, place coated breasts into skillet gently, leaving about an inch space between each piece, and sauté over medium heat until golden brown, about 8 minutes. With pancake turner, turn over and brown second side. It is important to clean skillet with paper toweling after sautéeing each panful in order to prevent sticking and to keep breasts attractive in color. Pour any remaining drippings over cooked breasts. Add more fresh oil and butter to skillet for next frying.

If breasts are not to be baked in oven, it is important to cook them at least 8 minutes on each side on top of stove if cut ½ inch thick. We prefer to place them on oven rack with drip pan underneath, at 350° F. about 20 minutes if meat is warm; 30 minutes if breasts were sautéed in advance and refrigerated. For 2 layers, increase baking time to about 40 minutes. It is not necessary to bake sautéed top-quality breasts if sliced not more than ½ inch thick. Simply sauté 7 or 8 minutes on each side. If sliced thinner, sauté only about 4 minutes on each side but increase heat slightly to brown crust.

Note. It is very convenient to bake the breasts in a 17-inch steel platter (or any other attractive heatproof platter), instead of on a rack, to eliminate transferring them to another dish.

To Serve. Garnish top of cooked breasts with slivered sautéed almonds, or serve plain. May be surrounded with seasoned mixed vegetables, or asparagus. Garnish ends of platter with parsley bouquets and vegetable flowers.

Marinade for Breast of Chicken (or Turkey) Romanoff

⅓ cup dairy sour cream
1 tablespoon lemon juice
1 sliver garlic, chopped fine
1 tablespoon grated Italian cheese

¼ teaspoon oregano or other herb
¾ teaspoon salt
¼ teaspoon pepper

Combine all above ingredients in a small bowl, and with fluffy beater or heavy spoon beat until smooth.

Crumb Coating for Breast of Chicken (or Turkey) Romanoff

1 cup dry light golden bread crumbs
¾ teaspoon paprika
¾ teaspoon salt

⅛ teaspoon pepper
⅓ teaspoon crushed thyme or other herb

Combine all dry ingredients and mix well.

Chicken Kiev

6 medium-size half chicken breasts about 6 ounces, each to measure about 4 × 5 inches when flattened out (do not use any larger breasts)
6 tablespoons firm butter (a little more may be used)
Salt
Pepper

Pinch rosemary
Garlic salt
Light dry bread crumbs
2 large whole eggs, beaten well with a fork and combined with 1 tablespoon water
Fat for deep-frying
Toothpick frills

With medium-sharp knife and fingers release meat from chicken breasts. With rolling pin, pound and flatten meat. Sprinkle each breast lightly with salt, pepper, garlic salt, and a pinch of rosemary, or use other seasonings. Place 1 tablespoon or little more of cold, firm butter in center of each, and roll meat firmly around butter, shaping it to simulate a drumstick. Press well with damp hands and cover with dry bread crumbs. Dip into diluted egg, then into crumbs, into diluted egg again, and then a third time into crumbs. Press crumbs well onto surface of meat. Let stand at room temperature on wax paper about 20 to 30 minutes, turning them over every 7 or 8 minutes, to permit entire surface to dry slightly.

Shortly before breasts are ready to be served, lower them gently into deep hot fat at 300° F. and cook for about 10 minutes, keeping temperature of fat between 275° F. and 300° F. If stuffed breasts are cooked at a higher temperature, center of meat is likely to be slightly underdone.

Place a frilled toothpick on one end just before serving, and serve as soon as removed from hot fat if possible. May be kept hot in a warm 300° F. oven for a few minutes if necessary.

Note. Breasts may be stuffed, shaped and rolled in crumbs twice, then refrigerated covered for many hours in advance. However, it will be necessary to remove them from refrigerator at least ½ hour in advance, and to dip them into beaten egg and crumbs a *third* time and let them stand on wax paper, turning them over several times, in room temperature about 30 minutes before deep-frying.

To Serve. Arrange Chicken Kiev on a bed of well-seasoned, buttered peas or other vegetables, noodles, or rice. Garnish top of each breast with a large sautéed mushroom, and place parsley bouquet on each end of platter. Pipe Duchesse Potatoes (page 301) around Kiev breasts. Sprinkle with paprika.

Spanish-Style Chicken with Rice

2 broiler-fryers, about 2½ pounds each
Seasoned Flour for Coating Chicken (page 216)
¼ cup butter and ¼ cup oil, heated
1 cup chopped onion
1 clove garlic, put through garlic press
1 cup fresh green pepper, cut into 1-inch squares
1 pound uncooked rice
½ cup pimiento, cut in 1-inch squares
¼ teaspoon or more chili powder
2 tablespoons or more tomato paste
2 teaspoons salt
½ teaspoon black pepper
3 cups chicken stock (or add instant bouillon to water)

Cut chicken into serving pieces, roll damp chicken well in Seasoned Flour, and over medium heat brown it in the hot butter and oil. After chicken is browned, remove from skillet. In the same skillet sauté the onion, garlic, and green pepper for about 5 minutes. Now add rice, pimiento squares, seasonings, tomato paste, and the 3 cups chicken stock. Bring to boiling point. Pour into a 3-quart casserole, arrange chicken over top attractively. Cover casserole, and bake in a 350° F. oven for about 1¼ hours, or until chicken is tender. Test after 1 hour, and if chicken and rice are tender, do not cook further.

This recipe may be cut in half, and prepared in a 2-quart casserole, for little less time.

Chicken in the Pot With Vegetables

2 broiler-fryers, about 2 pounds each
8 cups cold water (2 quarts)
1 small bay leaf
¼ cup celery leaves
2 tablespoons minced onion
2 tablespoons or less salt
¼ teaspoon pepper
1 bunch fresh carrots, cut into 2-inch wedges
8-ounce package fine noodles
1 small package frozen peas

Cut chicken into serving pieces and wash under cold running water. Place it in a 5-quart saucepan with the 2 quarts cold water, the bay leaf, celery leaves, and minced onions. Cover saucepan and bring to quick boil. Reduce heat, and simmer gently about 30 minutes. Now add salt, pepper, and carrots. Cover saucepan and simmer about 15 minutes longer. Last, add the uncooked noodles and the package green peas, and cook uncovered about 10 minutes longer.

How to Serve. First, serve chicken soup with a few noodles and peas. Then pour off most of remaining soup from chicken, carrots, peas, and noodles, and serve chicken with other ingredients separately in an attractive tureen or any other attractive deep casserole. Garlic French or Italian bread is delicious served with this family-style meal.

Chicken Breasts Imperial

From the famous Imperial House Restaurant in Chicago

4 split chicken breasts (trimmed as per general directions page 200), about 6 or 7 ounces each
Salt
Pepper
Thyme
Garlic salt
About ½ cup sifted flour
2 medium eggs, well beaten with a fork and combined with ¼ cup milk, ½ teaspoon salt, ¼ teaspoon pepper
1 cup dry bread crumbs, combined with ¼ cup grated parmesan cheese (mix well)
¼ cup butter and ¼ cup oil, heated
4 slices ham
4 slices pineapple
4 half slices tomatoes (remove thin slice from tops and bottoms; slice 2 tomatoes crosswise, each in 2 pieces), seasoned
1 package frozen asparagus, cooked until just tender and still green, rolled in melted butter and parmesan cheese
4 very large thick plain or fluted mushrooms, sautéed until lightly colored

Sprinkle half breast (with bones left on) with salt and pepper, pinch thyme on each, and a bit of garlic salt. Roll in flour, then dip into egg mixture, then in crumbs well mixed with parmesan cheese. Press crumbs well on entire surface of breasts. Let stand on wax paper about 15 minutes, turning them over 2 or 3 times. Melt butter and oil, and when lightly colored (but not brown) add breasts with meaty side down first, and sauté gently over medium heat. When light brown on one side, turn over and brown second side. Do not overbrown as they will darken further in the oven during baking process.

On a heatproof good-size shallow platter (or a baking sheet) arrange slices of ham. Fold ham if it is thin and large. Place a slice of pineapple on each piece of ham, and a sautéed breast on each slice of pineapple. Pour drippings (if they are not too dark; if so discard them) over breasts. Arrange thick slices of tomatoes on platter. Bake in a preheated 350° F. oven about 35 minutes for small, 4-ounce, breast; 40 to 45 minutes for 6-ounce breast; 50 minutes for 8-ounce breast. Brush breasts with melted butter the last few minutes.

When done, remove from oven and garnish edge of platter with cooked buttered asparagus spears. Place a sautéed mushroom on top of each breast, and serve at once.

Barbecued Chicken

Have broiler or frying chicken weighing 1½ to 2 pounds split in halves; larger chicken cut in quarters. Wash chicken under cool running water and dry it on paper towel. Brush both sides well with soft butter or margarine, sprinkle with salt, pepper, celery salt, and paprika. Place chicken on rack in a shallow pan, pouring 2 cups hot water into pan. Roast chicken with skin side up, first at 400° F., about 20 minutes. Brush again with butter, turn over, brush with butter, and roast about 15 minutes on second side. After 35 minutes at high temperature, reduce heat to 300° F. Now brush both sides well with Barbecue Sauce (page 222), and continue to roast about 10 more minutes for small birds up to 2 pounds; about ¼ hour for larger chickens weighing 2½ to 3 pounds. If you can loosen leg easily from body, meat is done. If you are barbecuing quartered chickens, cook breasts 10 to 15 minutes less time. Add more water to drippings in pan from time to time as needed to prevent scorching especially after birds are brushed with Barbecue Sauce. Any remaining liquid and drippings may be added to leftover Barbecue Sauce and served separately with chicken.

Note. If you are preparing 2 layers of chicken at one time, increase baking time by 10 to 15 minutes.

Barbecue Sauce

1 medium-size onion, chopped fine	1 tablespoon Worcestershire sauce
2 tablespoons shortening	¼ teaspoon dry mustard
1 cup tomato catsup	1¼ teaspoons salt
1 cup water or stock	¼ teaspoon or more red hot pepper
2 tablespoons vinegar or ¼ cup lemon juice	¼ teaspoon black pepper
1 tablespoon brown sugar	¼ teaspoon celery seed

Sauté onion in the shortening for about 5 minutes. Add remaining ingredients except seasonings and cook in covered saucepan for about 20 minutes. Now add seasoning to taste and continue to simmer about 10 minutes. If sauce is too thick, add little more stock, water, or vinegar.

This is sufficient sauce for about 3 pounds of ribs or 2 small chickens. It is a delectable basic all-around Barbecue Sauce. May be prepared days in advance and kept covered in refrigerator.

Chicken à la King

About 4 pounds roasting or frying chicken	1 cup sifted all-purpose flour
4 cups hot water	2 tablespoons sherry or sauterne wine (optional)
1 tablespoon salt	½ pound fresh mushrooms, sliced and sautéed about 5 minutes, or 3-ounce can, sliced
1 small bay leaf	
1 small carrot, cut up	
½ cup celery and leaves	1 package frozen peas, cooked about 5 minutes
1 small onion, cut up	
¼ teaspoon pepper	4-ounce, or smaller, can pimiento, cut into 1-inch pieces (optional)
½ cup butter or margarine	

Wash whole chicken under cool running water, place it on a trivet in a deep saucepan; add the 4 cups hot water, tablespoon salt, bay leaf, cut-up carrot, onion, and pepper. Cover tightly and steam chicken until tender, about 1 hour, or until leg and wing joints move easily, depending on size. Other qualities and large roasting chickens will take longer. Stewing chickens require much longer cooking, anywhere from 2½ to 4 hours. When done, drain well, and when chicken is cool, remove meat from bones, remove skin, and cut meat up in large 1½-inch pieces. Strain stock from the cooked chicken, and if it measures less than 3½ cups, add a little water to make up difference. If it measures more, cook it uncovered for a few minutes.

In a 3-quart saucepan melt the butter or margarine, add the cup of flour, a little at a time, forming a smooth mixture. Slowly add the lukewarm strained chicken stock, and cook over moderate heat until thick, stirring continuously, then lower heat, and let simmer about 5 minutes.

Now add the cut-up chicken, sautéed mushrooms, peas, the wine and pimiento. Simmer together about 7 or 8 minutes, stirring gently and often. Taste and season further if necessary. If sauce is too thick, add a little stock or water.

If Chicken à la King is to stand for more than a few minutes after it is cooked, keep it in a cold place or it is likely to sour. When leftover Chicken à la King is cool, store it at once well covered in refrigerator. It may be reheated in top part of double boiler or over direct *low heat,* adding a little milk or water, and stir gently until smooth and hot.

Note. Chicken à la King is an excellent dish for buffet parties, served in a chafing dish, or serve it in Classic Puff Paste patty shells (page 645), or on large split tea biscuits.

Chicken Croquettes

Makes about 10 croquettes

2½ cups of roasted or braised chicken (or veal, beef, or pork), put through a food chopper (measured and *packed solidly* after it is ground)
1 cup Thick White Sauce
Salt, if needed
⅛ teaspoon pepper
A little grated onion or ½ teaspoon onion salt
Dry sifted bread crumbs
Beaten egg, combined with 1 tablespoon water
Oil or shortening
Whole cloves for eyes

Mix meat with Thick White Sauce. Season with about ¾ teaspoon salt, a little pepper, and grated onion or onion salt. Other seasonings or herbs may be added. Cover and place preparation in refrigerator until thoroughly cold and solid, for several hours or longer.

Measure ¼ cup and shape with hands to simulate chickens or pyramids. Sprinkle well with crumbs, dip into diluted egg and then into crumbs again. Let stand about 20 minutes before deep-frying until golden brown, at 375° F. in oil or shortening.

May be kept warm in 275° F. oven on a cake rack for about 15 minutes. Use whole cloves for eyes. Serve with Medium White Sauce (page 224).

Note. Before cooking, a 3-pound chicken will give about 3 cups of meat; a 3-pound piece of veal with bone will give about 3 cups of meat; a 2-pound piece of boneless veal or pork will give about 3 cups of meat.

Thick White Sauce

3 tablespoons butter or margarine
3 tablespoons sifted all-purpose flour
1 cup warm milk
About ½ teaspoon salt

Melt butter or margarine, add flour, and when well blended, add warm milk very slowly. Cook over low heat until thick and smooth, stirring constantly. Add salt and simmer 5 minutes.

Medium White Sauce

2 tablespoons butter or margarine
2 tablespoons sifted all-purpose flour
   (3 may be used)

1 cup warm milk
About ½ teaspoon salt

Same method as for Thick White Sauce.

Chicken and Rice Curry, Company-Style

Serves 8

4- to 5-pound roasting chicken
1 tablespoon salt
3½ cups boiling water
1 small bay leaf
¼ cup celery leaves
¼ cup sliced onion
1 pound whole medium-size mushrooms
About ¼ cup butter
½ teaspoon salt
White pepper
1 medium-size fresh green pepper
1 tablespoon butter
½ cup butter

1 small clove garlic, chopped fine
1 cup fresh mushrooms, chopped fine
2 tablespoons green onion, chopped fine
1 pound long-grained rice, top quality
3 cups chicken stock
1 teaspoon, more or less, curry powder
1 teaspoon salt
1 small can pimientoes, cut into ½-inch squares
Salt and pepper

Place chicken on a trivet; add salt, boiling water, bay leaf, celery leaves, and sliced onion. Cover and cook chicken gently until tender, about 1½ hours, or until leg and wing joints move easily. When cool enough to handle, remove skin, release meat from bones, and cut chicken into about 2-inch pieces.

Wash mushrooms in lukewarm water, drain well, and dry in a towel. Sauté whole mushrooms in ¼ cup hot butter until brown. Season mushrooms with ½ teaspoon salt and a little white pepper. Cook about 3 minutes, not too soft.

Cut green pepper into slivers about 2 inches long and very narrow. Sauté gently 2 or 3 minutes in 1 tablespoon butter.

In ½ cup hot butter, sauté garlic, the chopped mushrooms, and green onion about 5 minutes, but do not allow to become brown. Then add rice, chicken stock, curry powder, and 1 teaspoon salt. Cook gently until tender, about 30 minutes, depending on quality of rice. If rice appears too dry toward end, add about ¼ to ½ cup more hot chicken stock, and continue to cook covered until tender.

Keep chicken and rice quite hot over very low heat or simmering water while preparing Special Curry Sauce.

Add chicken, whole sautéed mushrooms, pimiento squares, and sautéed green pepper strips to rice, and mix gently. Pour Curry Sauce over combined ingredients and blend well. Mound on a large oval hot platter, and serve at once.

Special Curry Sauce for Chicken and Rice Curry

1 cup (more if desired) chicken stock	½ teaspoon salt
1 tablespoon cornstarch diluted in 2 tablespoons water or stock	2 tablespoons sauterne
⅛ teaspoon powdered saffron	2 egg yolks

Combine all ingredients except egg yolks, and cook until thick and glazy, about 5 minutes after it starts to simmer. Combine about ½ cup of this mixture with slightly beaten egg yolks, a little at a time; then add to rest of sauce slowly.

Arroz con Pollo—No. 1 (Chicken with Rice, Cuban-Style)

¼ teaspoon, or a little more, saffron combined with ½ cup hot water	1 pound best-quality rice
1 large roasting chicken, about 5 pounds, or 2 frying chickens, about 2½ pounds each, cut into serving pieces	1 tablespoon salt
	¼ cup butter and oil to sauté mushrooms
Flour	½ pound, or more, fresh mushrooms (if small, leave whole; if large, cut into very thick slices)
¼ cup butter and ¼ cup oil to brown chicken	¼ teaspoon salt
1½ teaspoons salt	Pepper
Pepper	1 teaspoon oil to sauté green pepper
¼ cup butter and oil to sauté onion and garlic for rice	1 small green pepper, cut into narrow 2-inch strips
1 small onion, cut into fine pieces	Cornstarch
1 small clove garlic, minced	¼ cup pimiento, cut into narrow 2-inch strips

Let saffron and water stand about 1 hour. Then simmer about 10 minutes. Strain.

Roll cut-up chicken in flour, and sauté in about ¼ cup or more hot butter and ¼ cup oil until golden brown on all sides. Then add ½ cup Chicken Stock; cover pan, and steam chicken until almost tender (about 35 to 45 minutes if using frying chickens, 60 to 70 minutes if using roasting chickens). Turn chicken occasionally, and toward end of cooking, season with about 1½ teaspoons salt and a little pepper.

In ¼ cup hot butter and oil sauté onion and garlic 2 or 3 minutes, being careful not to let it turn brown. If butter or oil discolors, rice will not have an attractive appearance. Add rice, 3 cups hot Chicken Stock that has been combined with strained saffron water, and 1 tablespoon salt. Cover, and bring to boiling point, then lower heat and cook *very gently* about 15 to 20 minutes, depending on quality of rice. Some brands cook in less time. When rice is half done, place pieces of cooked chicken over it; add a little more stock if rice appears dry, cover pan, and continue to cook about 20 to 30 minutes more, or until rice and chicken are tender.

In about ¼ cup of hot butter and oil, sauté fresh mushrooms. Cook only about 3 or 4 minutes. Season with about ¼ teaspoon salt and a little pepper. Let stand until needed.

In about 1 teaspoon hot oil sauté green pepper until slightly soft but still green. Do not overcook.

While rice and chicken are cooking, prepare gravy with drippings left over from sautéing chicken and mushrooms. Add enough Chicken Stock to make required amount of gravy, and for each cup add 1 tablespoon corn-starch diluted in 2 tablespoons cold water. Cook together about 5 minutes after it simmers. Season with a little salt and pepper. A few pieces of sautéed mushrooms may be added to gravy.

To serve, remove chicken from rice and keep hot in a warm oven or in a skillet over very low heat. Fold pimiento strips, sautéed green-pepper strips, and about ½ cup sautéed mushrooms gently into rice, being careful not to mash vegetables. Pack rice into a buttered No. 7 bowl, using slight pressure. Turn out onto a large round platter, preferably colored, and surround with chicken and rest of sautéed mushrooms. Serve gravy separately.

Note. About ¼ cup sauterne may be poured over chicken and rice a few minutes before it is done. Part of Chicken Stock may be replaced with tomatoes. In this case rice will not have attractive yellow color.

Chicken Stock

Gizzard and bony parts of chicken	¼ cup parsley
1 small stalk celery and leaves, cut into large pieces	1 very small bay leaf
	About 7 cups water
1 small onion, cut into medium-size pieces	

Prepare chicken stock with ingredients specified. Cook covered, about 1½ hours. When done, strain.

Arroz con Pollo—No. 2

Use same ingredients as for Arroz con Pollo—No. 1 (page 225). Sauté floured pieces of chicken in hot butter and oil until golden brown. Add 3½ cups Chicken Stock combined with the strained liquid from saffron, ½ teaspoon black pepper, about 1½ tablespoons salt. Cover, and simmer chicken about 30 minutes for roasting chickens and 20 minutes for fryers. Sauté green-pepper strips, onion, garlic, pimiento and mushrooms in ¼ cup butter and oil several minutes. Add rice, and sauté about 5 minutes. After chicken has cooked 20 to 30 minutes, add rice mixture, and cook together about 30 to 45 minutes, depending on quality of rice and tenderness of chicken. Add more stock toward end if rice appears too firm or dry. Chicken prepared this way cannot be served as attractively as in the first method.

Fricassee of Chicken

5 cups boiling water	½ cup celery leaves and celery
4- or 5-pound chicken, cut into pieces for serving	¼ cup parsley
	About 1 tablespoon salt
1 sliced onion	

Pour boiling water over chicken; add sliced onion, celery and leaves, and parsley. Cover pan, and cook gently until tender—about 1½ hours for roasting chicken, and several hours for stewing chicken, depending on quality and size. Add salt a few minutes before chicken is tender. When done, remove chicken from stock, and keep in warm place until Sauce and Dumplings are prepared.

After chicken has been cooked and is tender, it is more attractive and delicious if it is sautéed in butter or margarine before serving. After it is sautéed, brush each piece with drippings in pan or melted butter, and arrange in center of platter with Dumplings around it. Serve rest of Sauce separately.

Sauce for Fricassee of Chicken

Strain chicken stock, measure, and for each cup of stock use about 3 tablespoons sifted all-purpose flour. Add *lukewarm* stock, a small amount at a time, to flour, forming a smooth mixture. Cook about 5 minutes after it starts to simmer. Season further if necessary.

Fluffy Baking Powder Dumplings

½ tablespoon shortening	½ teaspoon salt
1 cup sifted all-purpose flour	Scant ½ cup cool milk, or enough to form medium dough (not too soft)
1 teaspoon double-acting baking powder	

Cut shortening into dry ingredients until fine. Add liquid all at once. Mix well with a fork, turn out onto a floured canvas cloth, and knead gently about ½ minute. Form in a smooth long roll and cut on bias into 8 pieces. Or pat and roll dough ½ inch thick and cut into small rounds. Place on top of Sauce. Cover, and allow to cook gently about 10 to 15 minutes, depending on size of dumplings. Do not uncover pan while dumplings are cooking, and *keep heat low* to prevent scorching and excess evaporation. When done, pick up with a perforated ladle or large spoon, and serve.

Note. To be cooked only on thick stews or very heavy sauces.

Chicken Pie

Serves 8

6 tablespoons butter or shortening	1½ teaspoons salt
3½ cups sifted all-purpose flour	4 egg yolks or 2 whole eggs, well beaten with fork
2¼ teaspoons double-acting baking powder	¾ cup cold milk

Cut shortening into dry ingredients until it looks like fine meal. Add eggs combined with milk, forming a soft dough that is not sticky. Turn out onto a covered floured pastry cloth and knead gently a few seconds. Remove about ⅓ cup dough for flowers and leaves. Then cut balance of dough into 2 parts, having one part a little larger for bottom crust. Pat and roll dough to fit a 10½-inch baking dish. Pour in filling; brush bottom rim with milk, and place on upper crust, turning crust under. Press around edge with fork. Make openings in the upper crust with a fork to allow steam to escape.

How to make roses and leaves out of dough for top of meat pies. Before using dough for lower and upper crusts, remove ⅓ cup and add about ⅓ cup more flour. Knead well until smooth. Let stand covered a few minutes; then roll very thin. With small round cutter cut out about 20 rounds of dough, using 10 for each rose. Place rounds together to simulate a rose and pinch ends well. Arrange 2 roses in center of pie. Then with scissors or knife cut out about 8 leaves from rest of dough. Make impressions on leaves to simulate veins, using a dinner knife. Arrange leaves around roses or use daisy cutter. Brush entire top with milk. Bake in a 400° F. oven about 45 minutes, or until golden brown. Extra sauce may be served separately.

Filling for Chicken Pies

2½-pound drawn frying chicken	3 cups strained chicken stock
3½ cups boiling water (4½ cups if extra sauce is desired)	Salt
	Pepper
1 small bay leaf	¾ cup firm boiled potato balls or cubes
1 slice onion	
1 sprig parsley	1 cup cooked green peas
1 piece celery	¾ cup small cooked carrot balls or slices
½ cup butter	
About ½ cup sifted all-purpose flour	¼ cup chopped fresh green onions

Wash chicken well; cook in covered pan, on a trivet in simmering water with bay leaf, onion, parsley, and celery, until tender, about 1 hour. Add 1 tablespoon salt last 10 minutes. When chicken is cool, remove meat from bones, and cut into 1½-inch pieces (about 2½ cups). Discard skin.

In a saucepan melt butter, add flour, then 3 cups chicken stock gradually, stirring constantly. Cook and stir until it comes to boiling point. Then lower heat and allow to simmer several minutes. Pour it over the meat and other vegetables, mixing gently. Taste, and season more if necessary. Let stand until lukewarm before pouring into crust.

Rock Cornish Hens Gourmet-Style

To prepare 6 Rock Cornish Hens, defrost completely, sprinkle inside with a little salt and pepper, and drizzle with melted butter or Special French Dressing below. Stuff with about ½ cup of preferred dressing, or cook without stuffing. Close opening after stuffing with a small metal poultry skewer or heavy wood pins. Brush entire surface of birds with melted butter or Special French Dressing, sprinkle with paprika, place them on a rack in an uncovered shallow pan with breast side up, about 2 inches apart, and roast at 400° F. for 20 minutes, then reduce temperature to 350° F., and roast about 25 to 30 more minutes, or until top of birds is golden brown. Now turn birds over having breast side down and continue to roast about 15 or 20 more minutes or leg can be released from body easily. This will insure uniform cooking and browning.

Baste birds several times during cooking process with melted butter, Special French Dressing, or drippings in pan. It is very important to add several tablespoons of stock or water to drippings in pan from time to time as soon as they appear to dry out to prevent smoking and scorching. Leftover drippings in roasting pan may be used for gravy.

How to Serve. For individual service, place on each plate 1 bird sprinkled on top with paprika (cover leg ends with paper frill if desired), an individual fruit or vegetable salad, and asparagus or buttered peas. If birds are prepared without stuffing, they are very attractive around a mound of wild rice (Turkish Pilaf, page 312, or Risotto Milanese, page 805). Place them alternately with individual salads, or servings of buttered asparagus tips. Hollandaise Sauce (page 340) may be served.

Special French Dressing for Rock Cornish Hens

¼ cup wine vinegar
2 teaspoons paprika
1 teaspoon savory, rosemary, or oregano leaves
2 teaspoons salt

½ teaspoon white pepper
2 teaspoons sugar
1 clove garlic, cut into small pieces or put through garlic press
1 cup salad oil

Combine all ingredients in a jar, cover and shake for 1 minute until well blended. Keep in a jar with tight cover. Shake well each time before using.

Wild Rice Stuffing for Rock Cornish Hens

¾ cup uncooked wild rice, washed according to directions on package

2¼ cups stock or water

1 teaspoon salt

½ cup butter

Finely chopped giblets of birds

½ cup finely chopped fresh green onions

¼ cup chopped green onion tops

¾ cup finely chopped celery

1 cup finely chopped fresh mushrooms (or ½ cup canned)

½ teaspoon poultry seasoning or sage

1 tablespoon finely chopped fresh parsley, or 1 teaspoon dry parsley

About 1 teaspoon salt

¼ teaspoon black or white pepper

Cook rice for about 45 minutes in boiling stock or water, seasoned with 1 teaspoon salt, in tightly covered saucepan. This will give 3 cups cooked rice; or follow directions on package. In medium-size saucepan or skillet melt butter, add chopped giblets and sauté for about 5 minutes. Add all other ingredients except rice and continue to cook uncovered for about 5 more minutes, mixing ingredients as they cook. Now cover and steam for 5 minutes. Pour these ingredients over the cooked rice and blend well. If stuffing appears dry, add a little more melted butter or cream. Use about ½ cup of stuffing for each bird, and close opening with small metal poultry skewers or heavy wood pins. White rice may be used instead of wild rice.

Bread Stuffing for Rock Cornish Hens

½ cup melted butter

Finely chopped giblets

½ cup finely chopped celery

½ cup finely chopped fresh green onion

¼ cup onion stems

¼ cup water or stock

4 cups tiny toasted white bread cubes (about ¼ inch size)

About 1 teaspoon salt

¼ teaspoon pepper

1 teaspoon poultry seasoning or sage

¼ cup fresh chopped parsley, or 1 teaspoon dry parsley

2 eggs well beaten with a fork

Sauté the chopped giblets for 5 minutes in the butter, then add celery and onion, and continue to cook 5 more minutes uncovered. Now add ¼ cup water or stock, cover pan and steam about 5 minutes. Pour these ingredients over the toasted bread cubes, mix well with 2 forks. Add seasonings, parsley, and beaten eggs. Blend well. Stuff birds according to directions given for Wild Rice Stuffing.

Special Tettrazini Gravy for Cornish Hens

½ pound fresh mushrooms, washed and sliced

¼ cup finely chopped green onion

¼ cup butter

3 tablespoons cornstarch, combined with ¼ cup cold water

About 2 cups stock or water added to drippings in roasting pan; strain if necessary

About 1½ teaspoons salt

¼ teaspoon pepper

¼ cup green onion tops, cut into about 1-inch pieces

¼ cup pimento, cut into ½-inch squares

2 tablespoons dry sherry or other dry wine

Sauté the mushrooms and onion in the ¼ cup butter for about 5 minutes. Add diluted cornstarch, and then slowly add the 2 cups of warm stock or water, the salt and pepper. Cook until thick, stirring constantly, then let simmer about 5 minutes. Last, add green onion tops, pimiento, and wine and cook for about 1 more minute. Birds may be brushed with this gravy just before serving to impart glaze. Serve rest separately.

Roast Ducklings Gourmet Style

Have ducklings weighing 4 or 5 pounds each drawn by butcher, or preferably use Premium Quick Frosted Long Island Drawn Ducklings. Wash inside and outside of bird and dry with a towel. Sprinkle inside of duckling with salt before roasting. Stuff if desired, with Bread Dressing (page 232), or cut 2 medium-sized oranges, leaving skins on, into large pieces and stuff bird. Apple or onion cut up the same way may be used instead. The orange, apple, or onion add flavor and should be discarded when duckling is ready to be served.

Weigh and truss duckling, put on a rack in an open pan, breast side up, and roast at 350° F. ⅔ of roasting time, allowing about 30 minutes per pound for birds weighing over 4½ pounds, and 35 minutes per pound for smaller ones. Last ⅓ of roasting period, turn bird, having breast side down, so that it may brown uniformly. Watch closely toward end of roasting period, and if necessary increase or decrease time a little, but do not overcook. Birds are done when leg joints move easily.

When bird begins to brown, baste every 15 or 20 minutes with ½ cup orange juice to which a little shredded or grated rind has been added. When done, drain off most of fat in pan, leaving about 1 tablespoon. To the drippings, add 1 cup hot water or stock and scrape well. Strain and add 1 cup of orange juice, ¼ cup currant jelly, ¼ cup brown sugar. Thicken with about 3 tablespoons cornstarch combined with ¼ cup cold water, and cook until thick and clear, about 5 minutes. Serve separately. *Makes enough gravy for 1 or 2 ducklings.*

To Serve. Place 1 or 2 ducklings on a large round platter. Arrange Sweet Potato Delights (page 309) around birds, alternate with parsley bouquets or colorful individual fruit salad, salad molds, etc. Ducklings may be left whole to show platter or they may be carved and arranged attractively on top of dressing, and brushed with gravy just before serving. Serve rest of gravy separately.

Note. If preferred, duckling may be roasted as above, omitting orange juice for the basting. Brush bird with fat in pan occasionally. When done, pour off most of fat, leaving about 1 tablespoon. Add 1 cup hot stock or water, scrape well and strain. Add about 1⅓ tablespoons (more or less) cornstarch combined with ¼ cup cold water for each cup of gravy. Cook until thick and smooth, about 5 minutes.

Bread Dressing for Duckling

½ pound white bread (about 8 slices)
½ cup butter, or ½ pound bacon cut into small pieces
Liver and heart, cut into small pieces
1 cup onions, sliced about ⅓ inch thick
1 cup celery, cut crosswise about ⅓ inch thick

½ cup hot water or stock
1 teaspoon thyme, more or less, poultry seasoning, or sage
¼ cup fresh parsley, chopped fine
About 1 teaspoon salt
¼ teaspoon pepper
1 large egg, beaten with fork

With fingers break bread (including crust) into about 1-inch pieces. Spread on a large baking sheet and toast in a 325° F. oven for about 20 to 30 minutes, or until golden brown and crisp, turning it over several times with a long spoon after the first 10 minutes to keep bread uniform in color. Melt butter or sauté bacon until medium done for about 5 minutes. Add the liver and heart and cook 5 more minutes. Now add the sliced onions and celery, stir well. Cover pan and steam gently about 10 minutes, or until vegetables are tender. Add the ½ cup of hot water or stock to vegetables. More water may be added for a more moist dressing. Pour vegetables over toasted bread, season with thyme, parsley, and salt and pepper. Last add beaten egg and with 2 forks mix ingredients until well blended. If any dressing remains after duckling is stuffed, it may be baked separately in a well-greased baking dish on upper rack the last 40 minutes, covered with greased foil.

Broiled Cornish Hens

Split birds, sprinkle with salt and white pepper, and brush well with melted butter or Special French Dressing (page 229). Place with flesh side down on greased pan, about 3 inches from heat, and broil at 425° F. about 15 to 20 minutes, or until attractively brown and tender. Baste with melted butter or Special French Dressing several times during broiling process.

To Serve. Arrange birds with flesh side up around a rice mold, alternate with individual fruit or vegetable salads. Cover leg ends with paper frill if desired.

Cornish Hens Oriental

3 tablespoons wine vinegar
1½ teaspoons paprika
¾ teaspoon savory or rosemary herb
2 teaspoons salt
½ teaspoon black pepper, 1 teaspoon sugar

1 small clove garlic, sliced or chopped
⅓ cup soy sauce
1 teaspoon Chinese molasses
½ cup salad oil
3 Cornish hens, split in half

Mix all ingredients until well blended, and at once pour over split hens, in a deep utensil. Let marinate for at least 8 hours, turning them over and around a few times.

About 1½ hours before serving, arrange hens on rack with flesh side down first, in a large shallow roasting pan, or broiler pan. Pour about 2 cups hot water in bottom of pan to prevent smoking, and roast at 375° F. 30 minutes, then turn over and continue to roast about 30 to 40 minutes, depending on size of birds. It is important to brush birds often with left-over marinade after the first 15 minutes. Test 1 of hens for doneness, by loosening leg from body. If it is resistant, continue to cook longer. When done, brush with glossy gravy made with drippings in pan and any remaining marinade.

To Prepare Gravy. Add water or chicken stock to drippings in pan (or use water and instant bouillon). For each cup of gravy add 1½ table-spoons starch diluted in 2 tablespoons water. Taste and season further with little salt, pepper, and soy sauce, if desired. Cook until thick and glazy about 5 minutes after simmering begins. Sliced sautéed mushrooms may be added to sauce. Brush birds with glaze before serving. Serve on a bed of fried rice, or vegetables, or both. Garnish ends of platter with vegetable flowers and parsley bouquet. Sprinkle top with finely chopped green onion and stems if desired.

Crispy-Crust French-Fried Cornish Hens

Serves 4 to 6

Use 3 Cornish hens weighing about 1 pound each. Wash and dry thoroughly in a towel; then cut each into 4 pieces. Sprinkle lightly with salt and pepper and let stand in room temperature, loosely covered with wax paper, about 30 minutes before frying.

Prepare Crispy-Crust Batter (page 234). As soon as possible after batter is prepared, dip seasoned pieces of Cornish hens into batter, let surplus batter drain off, and deep-fry at 325° F. about 10 minutes, or until crust is golden brown and crisp. Do not fry more than a few pieces at a time to prevent clinging together and lowering temperature of fat appreciably. Try to keep temperature of fat between 300° to 325° F. If batter on birds appears too thin after frying 1 piece, add 1 or 2 more tablespoons of flour; if too thick, add 2 or 3 teaspoons water.

Fried pieces may be kept hot and crisp at least 30 minutes in a pre-warmed oven. To prewarm oven, light it at 400° F., and after about 15 minutes, *shut off heat* before storing cooked birds.

To Serve. Mold Curried Rice in a 7-inch bowl, and turn over onto platter. Sprinkle top with paprika. Arrange Cornish hens around rice alternately with groups of asparagus, or other vegetable. Serve Mushroom Gravy separately.

Crispy-Crust Batter for French-fried Cornish Hens

1 cup sifted all-purpose flour
½ cup white corn meal
1 teaspoon baking powder
2 teaspoons salt
½ teaspoon garlic salt

½ teaspoon white pepper
2 medium-size eggs, well beaten with a fork, and combined with 1 cup cool water and 2 teaspoons salad oil or melted fat

Sift dry ingredients together several times; then combine them with egg mixture. With a fork or spoon stir only until smooth.

Curried Rice for French-fried Cornish Hens

Giblets from Cornish hens, cut into small pieces
¼ cup fresh green onion and ¼ cup green onion tops, cut into ½-inch pieces
¼ cup butter
¼ cup tomatoes, cut into small pieces

1½ cups stock (a bouillon cube may be added to water)
1½ teaspoons salt
⅛ teaspoon white pepper
1 teaspoon, more or less, curry powder
1 cup uncooked rice

Sauté cut-up giblets and onion in butter about 5 minutes. Add tomatoes and all other ingredients, and stir well. Cover, and cook slowly about 30 minutes, or until rice is tender. If it appears dry, sprinkle about ¼ cup more stock or water over top, and cook a few minutes longer.

Mushroom Gravy for French-fried Cornish Hens

¼ cup butter
1 cup fresh mushrooms, sliced thin
½ cup fresh green onion and tops, cut into small pieces
2 tablespoons or more cornstarch, diluted in 2 tablespoons water

2 cups chicken stock (or add bouillon cube to water)
About 1 teaspoon salt
½ teaspoon curry powder
¼ teaspoon pepper

In butter sauté mushrooms and green onions about 5 minutes. Add diluted cornstarch and all other ingredients, a little at a time. Cook until thick, stirring constantly; then let simmer several minutes. Add about 1 teaspoon (more or less) commercial gravy coloring. Taste, and season further if necessary.

▶ *Seafood*
AND FISH DISHES

UNTIL THE LAST FEW YEARS FISH BOUGHT AT OUR MARKETS WERE NOT CLEANED, which discouraged the homemaker because it entailed too much preparation on her part. Today, however, fish can be purchased ready to cook.

Fish should be included as often as possible in our diet not only because it adds variety to our meals but because it is rich in mineral salts and vitamins A and D.

No matter what method is used in cooking fish, it is done when the flesh flakes when you cut it through with a fork, and the flesh is no longer translucent.

It is best to bake or broil fish on an attractive heatproof serving platter so that it is not necessary to transfer it to another platter. To prevent breakage lift fish off baking platter with 1 or 2 pancake turners (1 on each end for large fish).

Marinade for Seafood and Fish Fillets

Enough for 1 pound

2 tablespoons salad oil
2 tablespoons lemon juice or wine vinegar
½ teaspoon salt
⅛ teaspoon black pepper
⅛ teaspoon garlic salt
⅛ teaspoon dry tarragon (other herbs may be used)

Combine all ingredients and beat well with egg or fluffy beater for about 1 minute. Pour marinade over 1 pound of seafood or fillets and let stand for about 1 hour, covered, in a cool place. When ready to cook, pick up, drain and dip into batter or cover with crumb and egg, and deep-fry, according to directions given in recipes. Broiled fish is also delectable if marinated in this dressing for about 1 hour before broiling.

Shrimp may be deep-fried without precooking. In this case, remove shell, split shrimp lengthwise, flatten them slightly with a cleaver or heavy knife to insure thorough cooking. Dip in batter or cover with crumbs, and deep-fry at 350° F. until golden color and crisp, about 5 minutes.

Note. Place seafood or fish to be marinated into an enamel, glass, or stainless-steel utensil, and not in other utensils made of metal, as very often the acid in the marinade will act upon the metal chemically and develop an unpleasant taste in the food. Let food soak in the marinade for time suggested in recipe, turning it over, and basting it often with a large spoon with marinade in pan. Keep in refrigerator, but let stand in room temperature for about 1 hour before cooking, either in or out of marinade.

▶ FISH DISHES ◀

Whole Baked Stuffed Whitefish à la Creole

Start with a whitefish (other fish may be used), weighing about 2½ to 3 pounds net weight after it is scaled and boned, leaving it whole. Wash it thoroughly in lukewarm salted water just before stuffing, and dry it well with paper towels. Head and tail may be removed or left on fish. Sprinkle inside with about 1 tablespoon salt, and brush well with melted butter or margarine. Place Bread Dressing carefully into body of fish, without packing, and do not overfill, so that fish can be closed by bringing ends together.

Place fish on a piece of well-greased silicone or parchment paper (or smooth aluminum foil) cut same size and shape as fish. Brush entire fish well with melted butter or margarine, and bake it in a preheated 400° F. oven about 15 minutes, then lower heat to 300° F. and continue to bake about 1 more hour, depending on thickness of fish. About 10 minutes before it is ready, pour part of Sauce Creole (page 238) over fish, and baste it 2 or 3 times with more sauce before removing from oven. Serve rest of sauce separately. Stuffed fish, like stuffed poultry or other meat, takes longer to cook per pound. A whole unstuffed fish weighing same weight will be done in less time.

A large baked or poached fish may be tested for doneness by inserting a meat thermometer into the thickest part of fish (not in dressing). It is done when temperature reaches about 140° F., not lower, and never over 150° F. No matter what method is used in cooking fish, it is done when the flesh flakes when you cut through it with a fork, and the flesh is no longer translucent.

Bread Dressing for Baked Stuffed Whitefish

½ cup warm stock or water

6 slices of very dry toasted bread, broken or cut in ½-inch pieces

½ cup hot butter or margarine

1 small green pepper, cut into 1-inch strips

1 large onion, sliced thin (1 cupful)

½ cup celery, cut crosswise ½ inch wide

2 more tablespoons stock or water

1 teaspoon salt

¼ teaspoon pepper

½ teaspoon sage or thyme

1 large whole egg, beaten

Drizzle the ½ cup stock or water over the broken toasted bread, and let stand while preparing rest of dressing. In the ½ cup of hot butter sauté the pepper, sliced onion, and celery for about 5 minutes. Now add the 2 tablespoons water or stock, cover pot and cook gently about 10 minutes. Pour this preparation over the toasted bread, and blend well. Season with salt, pepper, and sage. Blend well with 2 forks. Add beaten egg, and mix well. If dressing appears dry, a little more liquid can be added. Taste dressing, and season further if necessary. Dressing not used in stuffing fish may be baked separately in greased heatproof baking dish, covered with greased foil, on upper rack the last 30 minutes.

Creole Sauce for Baked Stuffed Whitefish

2 tablespoons chopped onion
2 tablespoons chopped green pepper
2 tablespoons parsley, chopped medium
2 tablespoons finely chopped celery
¼ cup butter

6-ounce can Italian-style tomato paste
¾ cup of water
1 bouillon cube (optional)
About ½ teaspoon salt
¼ teaspoon pepper
⅛ teaspoon baking soda

Sauté the onion, green pepper, parsley, and celery in the ¼ cup butter for about 5 minutes. Add the tomato paste, water, and seasonings. Cover and cook slowly about 20 minutes. Pour over fish as suggested. Extra sauce may be prepared and served separately.

Whole Poached Salmon Gourmet-Style

Serves 12

Whole fresh or frozen salmon, 4 to 6 pounds (best to remove head and tail)
3 eggs
Fresh green onion stems

Several whole cloves
1 recipe Clear Glaze (page 239)
1 recipe Chipped Lemon Gelatin Ice (page 240)
2 fresh lemons

Wrap salmon in a large sheet of wet silicone paper or cheese cloth, and tie it in center; place it carefully into Court Bouillon (page 239) with open end of silicone up. Leave ends of paper untied. Pour enough hot water into pot to submerge salmon completely. Cover pan, and simmer fish about 10 minutes per pound. Do not overcook. When done, remove pan from heat and let fish cool in liquid until it is lukewarm. Now very carefully, with both hands, lift out fish with the paper or cheese cloth, and slip it onto a stiff cardboard cut a little smaller than fish, smoothly covered with lightweight foil, or silicone paper. At once with fingers and a dinner knife, carefully remove all dark skin from top part and sides of fish. Hold it under gently running cool water to wash away any small bits of skin, etc. Drain well on cake rack; place rack with fish on it in a long flat pan, and re-frigerate until very cold.

Hard-cook 2 or 3 eggs: Cover eggs with cool water. Bring to a boil. Re-move from heat, and keep tightly covered 15 minutes for medium eggs, 20 minutes for large. At once pour cold water over eggs, and immediately peel from large end. Use special wedger to section each egg in 6 wedges. Keep on wax paper on plate, covered with wax paper until needed.

Wash fresh green onion stems and dry them well. Do not cut until needed.

When fish is cold and Clear Glaze is the consistency of unbeaten egg white, begin to pour it over fish. Do this several times. Refrigerate fish between pourings for a few minutes. Cut 3 thin onion stems, making 1 longer than the other 2. Dip stems in a little cool Glaze and arrange them on fish, with longest in center. Form tulips with 2 wedges of egg for each, dipping lower part of egg into a little Glaze. Place a whole clove in center of each. Cut diamond leaves, dip them into Glaze and arrange on stems attractively. If egg wedges slide off, place 1 or 2 toothpicks below lower petals (picks are removed when fish is completed). *Refrigerate fish until decorations cling well, for at least 15 minutes.* Then pour Clear Glaze over entire surface several times, chilling fish between pourings.

To Serve Salmon. With a dinner knife release bottom edge of salmon from rack, and with 2 pancake turners, 1 on each end (or slide hands underneath), pick it up and transfer to a large oval or round platter. Sur-round fish with Chipped Lemon Gelatin Ice. Place thin ½ slices of fresh lemon attractively in ice, or omit lemon slices, and surround fish with Stuffed Glazed Tomato Slices (page 318) (or rounds of canned tomato aspic) on top of lemon ice, making slight depression.

Court Bouillon

3 cups cold water
½ cup lemon juice
1½ cups celery and leaves, mixed
1 teaspoon whole peppercorns
1 teaspoon allspice
1 large bay leaf

1 tablespoon fresh parsley, or 1 tea-spoon dry
¾ cup salt
½ cup cider vinegar
(For smaller fish, use less salt and other ingredients)

Simmer all ingredients for about ½ hour in a large deep oval roasting pan or large Dutch oven.

Clear Glaze

⅓ cup plain gelatin, combined with 1 cup cold water (stir and let stand until thick, about 5 minutes, dis-solve over simmering water)

3 cups strained fish stock
3 cups cold water

Combine all ingredients, and let stand until consistency of unbeaten egg white.

Chipped Lemon Gelatin Ice

¼ cup plain gelatin, combined with 1 cup cold water (stir and let stand until thick, about 5 minutes; dissolve over simmering water)

⅔ cup strained lemon juice
⅔ cup granulated sugar
½ teaspoon salt

Pour 2 cups boiling water over above ingredients. *Then add 2 cups cold water.* Stir gently. Pour into 9 × 9 × 2-inch pan, and refrigerate for at least 8 hours. Can be prepared a day or two in advance. When ready to serve, cut through with a dinner knife or with a round cutter to simulate fine chipped ice.

Halibut Steaks with Tomato-Cheese Sauce

Serves 4 to 6

Combine 2 cups moist bread crumbs, ½ teaspoon salt, ¼ teaspoon pepper, ¼ teaspoon thyme, ⅓ cup melted butter, and 1½ tablespoons chopped parsley for stuffing.

Place a halibut steak weighing 1 pound in a well-greased baking pan. Cover with stuffing, and place another 1-pound steak on top. Fasten together with toothpicks or skewers. Pour 1 can tomato sauce over steaks, and bake in a 350° F. oven 40 to 45 minutes. Sprinkle with ¼ pound shredded American cheese, and continue baking until cheese melts. Garnish.

Baked Lake Trout with Shrimp Sauce

Serves 6 generously

3 pounds lake trout (or whitefish)
¼ cup diced onions
1 cup chopped celery
2 tablespoons butter
2 teaspoons salt
¼ teaspoon pepper
¼ cup chopped parsley

3 cups moist bread crumbs
2 eggs, beaten
About 2 tablespoons sauterne
½ pound small cooked shrimp
2 additional tablespoons butter
2 additional tablespoons sauterne

Have marketman bone lake trout, leaving head and tail on. Rinse fish in lukewarm water, and dry well with towel. Sprinkle inside with a little salt. Prepare stuffing by sautéing onions and celery in 2 tablespoons butter. Add to sautéed vegetables, salt, pepper, chopped parsley, bread crumbs, beaten eggs, and enough sauterne to moisten stuffing. Do not have stuffing soggy, just fluffy.

Stuff trout, and close openings. Brush fish with melted butter, and place in a greased baking dish or pan, on greased parchment or silicone paper or aluminum foil. Bake in a preheated 400° F. oven for 15 minutes. Then lower heat to 300° F. and continue to bake about 1 more hour.

Just before removing from oven, sauté shrimp in butter, add a little sauterne, and cook several minutes. Pour shrimp and wine sauce over fish after it has been arranged on serving platter. Garnish with bouquets of parsley and lemon slices.

Whitefish Fillets Hollandaise

Serves 4

Wash whitefish fillets in lukewarm salted water. Dry on a towel. Brush with melted butter; sprinkle with salt and paprika. Broil on a flat greased pan about 12 to 15 minutes with flesh side up, about 2 inches from heat, at 450° F. Do not turn, as fish will be done. Remove from broiler and spread with Hollandaise Sauce (page 340). Place back in broiler and broil several minutes until top is brown. Serve at once.

One recipe of Hollandaise Sauce will be sufficient for about 2 pounds of fillets. It is better to prepare Hollandaise Sauce several hours in advance, allowing it to become cool and thick before spreading on fillets.

Pompano en Papillote

Serves 4

1 cup hot water	2 tablespoons dry white wine
1 teaspoon salt	Lemon juice
¼ teaspoon pepper	Butter
1 tablespoon lemon juice	½ cup cooked lobster meat, cut into
1 tablespoon parsley	medium-size pieces, or 8 medium-
1 tablespoon sliced onion	size cooked shrimp
1 tablespoon chopped celery	
2 pompanos weighing 1½ pounds (or smaller) each, boned and split, making 4 fillets	

Combine water with salt, pepper, lemon juice, parsley, onion, and celery. Cook gently in a covered saucepan about 15 minutes. Add fillets of pompano and wine. Cover, and simmer about 15 minutes, turning it over during cooking process. Let cool in stock while preparing Dressing (below). Then lift out carefully with pancake turner, and let drain on cake rack.

To Cook. Cut parchment paper, silicone, or foil into 4 very large hearts, about 4 inches larger all around than the pompano fillets. Brush papers with hot melted butter or oil. Brush pompano fillets on both sides with lemon juice and butter; place on 1 side of paper, having skin side down. Arrange cooked lobster meat or shrimp on each fillet. Spread Dressing over lobster or shrimp, forming a slight dome. Fold paper over, and roll and pinch edges together securely, using several paper clips *only* if necessary. Place on a greased baking sheet and bake in a 400° F. oven about 20 minutes, or until paper is light brown.

Pompano en Papillote may be prepared in advance and refrigerated until serving time. In this case increase baking time to 30 minutes, and reduce temperature to 375° F.

To Serve. Lay baked papillotes on hot individual serving plates. Cut around sides of the papillotes with the point of a paring knife or scissors, and turn up flap to expose pompano. This should be done in the dining room just before fish is served to guests. The fish is eaten directly from the paper. Serve with a green vegetable and a salad bowl.

Dressing for Pompano en Papillote

¼ cup hot butter	1 teaspoon salt
¼ cup fine-chopped green onion and stems	¼ teaspoon pepper
	⅛ teaspoon mace
¼ pound fresh mushrooms, sliced thin	2 egg yolks, beaten with a fork
1 tablespoon flour, combined with ½ cup stock from pompano, blended until smooth	

In hot butter sauté chopped onions 2 or 3 minutes. Add sliced mushrooms and continue to cook about 3 more minutes, turning often. Add flour combined with pompano stock, salt, pepper, mace, and egg yolks. Simmer all together about 3 minutes. If Dressing appears unusually thick, add a little more pompano stock. It should have the consistency of a soft custard when hot. Allow Dressing to stand until cool and thick, as it will be easier to work with.

Whitefish Fillets en Papillote

Serves 2 to 3

Prepare dressing with ½ pound fresh mushrooms chopped fine (or 4-ounce can mushrooms) and sautéed in about 2 tablespoons butter. Add 2 tablespoons chopped green onion, ½ teaspoon salt, ⅛ teaspoon black pepper, ⅛ teaspoon cayenne pepper, ½ cup dry bread crumbs, and ⅓ cup stock or rich milk, to form a medium consistency. This is enough dressing for 1 pound of fillets.

Wash fillets in lukewarm salted water. Dry on a towel. Brush with melted butter; sprinkle with salt and paprika. Broil about 12 to 15 minutes on greased flat pan with flesh side up, about 2 inches from heat, at 450° F. Do not turn, as fish will be done. Remove from broiler, and spread 1 tablespoon dressing on each side of fillets. Cut parchment or silicone (or foil) into very large hearts, about 4 inches larger all around than fillets. Brush papers well with melted hot fat or oil; place a fillet on each. Roll and pinch edges of paper together securely, using several paper clips if necessary. Arrange on greased baking sheet and bake at 400° F. about 10 minutes if fillets are warm and if dressing is warm. If ingredients are cool, or if prepared in advance, bake at 350° F. about 30 minutes. This method keeps all juices and flavor in food.

To Serve. Cut around sides of the papillote with a small sharp knife or scissors, and turn up the flap to expose fish. The fillets are eaten from the paper cases. Serve with a green vegetable and a salad.

Baked Stuffed Fillet of Perch

Serves 2 to 3

Use 1 pound fillet of perch. Flatten between wax paper with a cleaver, or pound with rolling pin to uniform thickness; then cut into serving portions. Brush each fillet with melted butter, and sprinkle lightly with salt and pepper. Place half of fillets on well buttered baking dish. Cover top of fillets with Cheese Dressing, then place rest of fillets over dressing with flesh side up. Brush well with melted butter and sprinkle with paprika. Cover dish, and bake at 350° F. about 40 minutes; then place under broiler for a minute or two just before serving. During baking process, drizzle about 1 more tablespoon hot melted butter over top.

Cheese Dressing for Fillet of Perch

In 2 tablespoons hot butter or margarine sauté ½ cup thinly sliced onion and ½ cup thinly sliced celery for about 5 minutes. Cover and steam about 5 more minutes. Add ¼ cup stock or water to vegetables, and pour vegetables over 2 cups of toasted bread cubes. Blend well. Season with about ½ teaspoon salt, ¼ teaspoon pepper, ¼ teaspoon thyme. Last, fold in 1 cup coarse-shredded American cheese and ¼ cup finely chopped parsley.

Broiled Whitefish, Halibut, Haddock

Have halibut sliced about ¾ inch thick. Have other fish scaled, boned and cut. Wash fish in lukewarm salted water just before cooking. Dry it well on paper towels. Rub with cut clove or garlic or sprinkle lightly with garlic or onion salt, and brush with melted butter on both sides or use Marinade (page 236). Arrange fish in a well-greased flat baking sheet (or 17-inch stainless steel heatproof serving platter). Pipe a border of Duchesse Potatoes (page 301) with No. 7 tube. Sprinkle fish with salt and paprika. The paprika will produce a very beautiful golden brown surface after fish is done. Broil it at 450° F. about 2 inches from heat, about 12 to 15 minutes, *with flesh side up* and skin side down, without turning. Raise heat to highest point the last minute or two if necessary. Do not overcook. Fish is done when it flakes. Remove from broiler, pick up carefully with a pancake turner and arrange on serving platter (or leave on 17-inch steel platter), filling in empty spaces with colorful cooked mixed vegetables. Serve with desired sauce or topping.

Breaded Deep-Fried Fish, Shrimp, Scallops

Cut flat fillets of fish (not more than ½ inch in thickness) into desired size pieces, or if small, leave whole. Wash them in lukewarm salted water just before cooking and dry well on paper towels. Marinate if desired (page 236). Roll into very light dry bread crumbs, dip into beaten egg combined with 1 tablespoon water and 1½ teaspoons salt, then cover with crumbs again, pressing crumbs well onto surface. Let stand on waxed paper for about 20 minutes, in room temperature, turning over several times. Then lower into deep hot fat (350° F.) and cook for about 5 minutes, or until brown and crisp. Raw scallops, shrimp, raw fillet of perch, sole, haddock, pike, white fish, halibut, etc., may be prepared in this way. Serve with Tartar Sauce (page 336), Hollandaise Sauce (page 340), Creole Sauce (page 335), Sauce Amandine (page 329), etc. Scallops are best breaded.

Standard Batter for French-Fried Fish, Shrimp, and Onion Rings

For 2 pounds

1 cup sifted all-purpose flour	1 tablespoon oil (optional)
1 egg	About 1½ teaspoons salt
About ¾ cup milk	About ¼ teaspoon pepper
1 teaspoon double-acting baking powder	About ½ teaspoon hot sauce
der	About ¼ teaspoon garlic salt

In a No. 6 or 7 bowl combine all above ingredients and with egg beater beat until smooth. Cover and let stand at least 15 minutes before using. This is a general batter and may be used for: Raw flat fish fillets, not more than ½-inch thick, dipped into warm salted water. Cooked shrimp (simmer about 3 minutes with shells on, then peel), or use raw shrimp, flattened. Raw onion rings, cut about ⅓ inch wide.

Dip fish, shrimp, or onion rings into batter. Allow surplus batter to drain, lower into hot fat (350° F.) and cook until golden brown and crisp, for about 5 or 6 minutes. If coating is too thick, add little milk; if too thin add little flour after frying first piece.

Note. Onion rings, fish, and shrimp in a batter may be fried hours in advance (to a light color) then refried at the same temperature for several minutes just before serving. Much more fish or shrimp can be refried at one time and the crust is more crisp and delectable. Or fish and onions may be fried the first time a few minutes before serving and fried a second time for extra crispness. (See page 123 for deep-fat frying information.)

Crispy-Crust Batter for Shrimp and Fish

For 1 pound

½ cup sifted all-purpose flour, combined with ¼ cup yellow or white corn meal
½ teaspoon baking powder
1 teaspoon salt
½ teaspoon garlic or onion salt
¼ teaspoon white pepper
1 medium well-beaten egg, combined with ½ cup cool water and ½ tablespoon oil

Sift all dry ingredients together. Combine them with beaten egg, cool water, and ½ tablespoon salad oil. With a *fork* stir only until smooth. Do not overmix. It is best to use this batter as soon as possible after it is made. If coating on fish is too thick after frying 1 or 2 pieces, add about 2 teaspoons more water, and if too thin, add another tablespoon or 2 of flour and blend well.

To Fry. Split raw shrimp and flatten them with a cleaver or heavy knife. Dip into batter; let surplus drain off, and deep-fry at 375° F. for about 5 minutes, or until golden brown and crisp. Do not fry too many at one time to prevent them from clinging together. When done, drain well and serve as an appetizer, or as desired. Fish fillets may be fried in same way, but dip into warm salted water first and dry on towel.

Shrimp and other fish may be fried in this special batter a day or several hours in advance *for a little less time, or until light golden color,* then refried for about 2 or 3 minutes at 375° F. just before serving.

Pan-Fried Fish

Any fish fillet, sliced fish not more than ½ inch thick, or small whole fish may be pan-fried. For each pound of fish sift together ½ cup all-purpose flour, 2 or 3 teaspoons paprika, about ⅓ teaspoon salt, ⅛ teaspoon pepper, ¼ teaspoon garlic or onion salt, and about ¼ teaspoon crushed herbs. Fish must be room temperature for at least 30 minutes, and it is best to dip it first into warm salted water. (Add 2 teaspoons salt to 1 quart water.) Drain and dry it on paper towels, then dip into beaten whole egg combined with 1 tablespoon water and then into seasoned flour, fine dry bread crumbs, or cracker meal, covering it well. Pan-fry in about ¼ inch very hot cooking oil or shortening, and cook over moderate heat about 5 minutes on each side, depending on thickness of fish, or until brown and crisp and fish flakes easily.

Broiled Fillets of Haddock

Serves 2

1 pound fillets of haddock (completely defrosted if purchased frozen)	½ teaspoon salt
	⅛ teaspoon pepper
2 tablespoons melted butter	¼ teaspoon garlic salt

Brush fillets with melted butter; sprinkle with salt, pepper, and garlic salt. Place fillets on greased flat baking pan. Broil at 500° F. 3 inches from heat, 10 minutes if fillets are about ½ inch thick, 12 minutes if thicker. Remove from broiler (do not turn over) and spread fillets with Special Topping for Broiled Fish (below), sprinkle with paprika, and place under broiler several more minutes, or until attractively brown. Pick up with pancake turner to prevent breaking, and serve hot with lemon wedges, etc.

Special Topping for Broiled Fish

3 tablespoons thick mayonnaise	¼ teaspoon dried basil or oregano, crumbled in fingers
2 teaspoons lemon juice	
¼ teaspoon hot sauce	½ teaspoon salt

Combine all ingredients, and spread over fish.

Broiled Halibut Steaks With Soufflé Topping

Serves 6

About 3 pounds halibut steak, cut into 6 serving portions, ¾ inches thick	2 egg whites
	Pinch of salt
2 tablespoons salad oil	1 teaspoon lemon juice
1 teaspoon salt	¼ cup Thousand Island dressing
Pepper	Sliced stuffed olives
Rosemary	Lemon wedges

Brush halibut steaks with oil. Broil at 450° F. until fish is almost done, about 12 minutes. Sprinkle top of steaks with 1 teaspoon salt, a little pepper, and pinch rosemary.

While halibut steaks are broiling, beat egg whites with salt and lemon juice until stiff; fold in Thousand Island dressing. Spoon or spread egg dressing on top of each halibut steak; return to broiler; broil until topping is lightly browned.

With pancake turner carefully transfer soufflé-topped halibut to a warm serving platter. Garnish fish with sliced stuffed olives and lemon wedges, and serve immediately.

Halibut Steak à la Creole

Serves 4

¼ cup butter
2 pounds halibut steak, cut ½ inch thick
1½ teaspoons salt

¼ teaspoon pepper
½ cup onion, sliced thin
1 cup canned tomatoes, drained

Brush baking dish with melted butter. Arrange halibut steak in dish. Season with salt and pepper. Brush with melted butter. Cover fish with sliced onions and tomatoes, and bake in a preheated oven at 400° F. about 30 minutes.

Baked Fish Steaks with Bread Stuffing

Serves 3 to 4

1½ pounds fish steaks (halibut, haddock, salmon, etc.), about ¾ inch thick, dipped into warm water
1 teaspoon salt
½ teaspoon ground black pepper
2 cups soft bread cubes or crumbs
1 tablespoon dried onion flakes

1 tablespoon dried parsley flakes
1 teaspoon poultry seasoning
3 tablespoons butter or margarine, melted
½ cup beef broth or water
1½ tablespoons butter or margarine
⅓ cup boiling water

Purchase 2 fish steaks the same size and shape, which can be placed 1 on top of the other. Place 1 steak in an oiled baking dish. Mix ½ teaspoon salt and ¼ teaspoon black pepper, and sprinkle over fish slices. Combine remaining salt and black pepper with bread cubes or crumbs, onion and parsley flakes, poultry seasoning, melted butter or margarine, and beef broth or water. Spread over fish. Cover with second fish steak. Dot with 1½ tablespoons butter or margarine. Pour boiling water in pan around fish. Bake in a preheated moderate oven (350° F.) 30 to 40 minutes, or until fish flakes when tested with a fork.

If desired, garnish with lemon slices and paprika. Serve with hot Lemon-Mayonnaise Sauce.

Lemon-Mayonnaise Sauce

Heat ½ cup mayonnaise, 2 tablespoons fresh lemon juice, and a pinch of white pepper together in the top part of a double boiler, stirring constantly, only until warm.

Sautéed Frogs' Legs Provincial

2 pairs of frogs' legs will make 1 generous serving portion

1 dozen pairs large frozen frogs' legs (about 2½ pounds)	4 eggs, well beaten
	¼ cup butter
Salt and pepper	1 tablespoon minced onion or 1 small
About 2 cups dry bread crumbs	clove garlic, minced

Thaw frozen frogs' legs. Rinse in cold water and dry them well on paper towel.

Sprinkle each pair of frogs' legs with salt and pepper and dip in dry bread crumbs, then in beaten eggs, and again in bread crumbs. Allow to stand in room temperature on a sheet of wax paper about 15 minutes, turning them over twice.

Melt butter, and when it is hot, add minced onion or garlic, and sauté frogs' legs over medium heat until golden brown on 1 side; then turn to other side. Cooking takes about 15 minutes, depending on size of frogs' legs.

Serve frogs' legs with Tartar Sauce (page 336) and lemon wedges.

Note. Frogs' legs can be purchased in three sizes: small, large, and jumbo.

Poached Fish

To retain its delicate texture and fine flavor, fish should never be boiled, but poached (simmered) in a highly seasoned water, known among chefs as Court Bouillon (page 239).

Instead of Court Bouillon, fish may be poached in white dry wine, milk, cream, tomato juice, or thin tomato sauce, seasoned to suit taste.

Whole or Thick Pieces. To prevent breaking when fish is removed from hot liquid, tie it in cheesecloth (or in wet parchment or silicone paper if it is available). Place wrapped fish on a rack in a saucepan with about 2 inches of Court Bouillon. Cover pot tightly, and simmer until fish is flaky, about 8 minutes for fish 1 inch thick, about 12 minutes for fish 2 inches thick. When done, lift carefully out of saucepan with pancake turner, let drain. Place fish in a skillet, keeping it covered while preparing Fish Sauce (page 249) with which it is to be served.

Arrange fish on serving platter, pour sauce over top, and sprinkle with sautéed slivered almonds, fine-cut green onion, or parsley.

Fillets. Pour about 1 inch of Court Bouillon into a deep skillet, and bring to the boiling point. Place fillets carefully in skillet, lower heat, and simmer gently about 8 to 10 minutes, or until fish flakes when tested with a fork. With a perforated pancake turner, lift fish out of liquid, let drain, and serve on a hot platter with leftover juices in pan, or a sauce.

Court Bouillon for Poached Fish

An excellent court bouillon may be prepared with 2 quarts water, about 1 cup light dry wine or vinegar, 1 large carrot cut into 1-inch pieces, 1 large onion cut into 1-inch pieces, 1 small bay leaf, 1 sprig parsley (or 1 teaspoon dried parsley), ¼ teaspoon peppercorns slightly crushed, 2 teaspoons salt, 2 whole cloves, and ¼ teaspoon celery seed or salt. Bring these ingredients slowly to a boil; then simmer about 15 minutes.

Fish Sauce

Strain leftover Court Bouillon, and for each cup of liquid melt 2 tablespoons butter or margarine, add 2 tablespoons flour, and blend well. Now add liquid slowly, and cook until thick; then simmer about 5 minutes. taste, and season further if necessary. For additional flavor, add 1 tablespoon soft butter, 1 teaspoon lemon juice and dry white wine to thickened sauce.

Scallops Louisiana

¼ cup shortening
½ cup chopped fresh green onion
1 small green pepper, cut into 1-inch strips
1 small clove garlic, cut fine (or ¼ teaspoon garlic salt)
About 1½ teaspoons salt
¼ teaspoon black pepper
6-ounce can Italian-style tomato paste, combined with 1½ cups stock or water added slowly to 2 tablespoons flour
2 tablespoons dry wine (optional)
1 pound scallops uniform in size (cut large ones into halves)
½ pound fresh mushrooms sautéed in 2 tablespoons shortening (leave small mushrooms whole; cut large ones into thin slices)
¼ teaspoon baking soda (optional)

Melt shortening, and when hot add onion, green pepper and garlic. Cook about 5 minutes over moderate heat. Add salt and pepper, then tomato paste combined with stock and flour. Cook until thick; then simmer in a covered saucepan about 5 minutes. Add wine, scallops, and mushrooms, and continue to cook about 10 minutes over low heat at simmering point. Add baking soda last 2 or 3 minutes if desired. If mixture appears too thick, add a little water or stock.

Serve around rice that has been molded in a bowl. Sprinkle top of ice with a little paprika. Garnish edge with buttered asparagus tips or serve in a bed of buttered noodles.

Oysters à la Rockefeller

About 15 minutes before they are to be served, place oysters on half-shells in a baking sheet that is filled to top with rock salt (ice-cream salt).

Bake in a 450° F. oven about 5 minutes, or until edges of oysters begin to curl. Remove from oven, and quickly spread about 1 tablespoon Green Butter Dressing over entire surface of each oyster. Return to oven and bake about 5 minutes longer. For genuine Oysters Rockefeller, the oysters should not be allowed to brown; they should be served rare. However, they are more palatable to many persons if placed under the broiler for a few minutes to become crisp.

Green Butter Dressing for 16 to 18 Oysters

½ cup fine-chopped parsley
½ cup fine-chopped green onion tops
½ cut fine-chopped fresh uncooked spinach
⅓ cup dry bread crumbs
½ teaspoon hot sauce

½ cup melted butter or margarine
½ teaspoon salt
¼ teaspoon black pepper
⅛ teaspoon garlic salt
2 tablespoons parmesan cheese

Put parsley, green onion tops, and spinach through a fine food chopper, or chop fine with a heavy knife or cleaver. Sprinkle hot sauce over chopped vegetables, then bread crumbs, melted butter, salt, and other seasonings. Mix well.

This dressing may be prepared several days in advance and kept in refrigerator until ready to be used; then let it stand in room temperature until soft enough to spread, or beat until of spreading consistency.

Shrimp Pilaf

Serves 6

½ cup chopped onion
½ cup chopped celery
¼ cup chopped green peppers
¼ cup butter
3 cups cooked rice
1½ cups cooked shrimp, split into halves

1 teaspoon salt
⅛ teaspoon pepper
½ teaspoon paprika
3 cups canned tomatoes
2 tablespoons parmesan cheese
¼ cup pimiento, cut into ½-inch squares

Sauté onions, celery, and green peppers in butter until onions and celery are golden brown. Add cooked rice, shrimp, and all other ingredients. Pour into a buttered 2-quart casserole and bake covered at 325° F. about 30 minutes.

Note. Instead of shrimp, crab meat may be used.

Broiled Lobster

Put in a deep kettle enough boiling water to cover lobster; add about 2 teaspoons salt for each quart of water. Take lobster by the back and drop it head first into boiling water. Cover and let *boil* about 5 minutes. Remove cover, and allow to simmer gently about 15 minutes for small lobsters weighing 1 to 1½ pounds or about 20 minutes for lobsters weighing about 1½ to 2 pounds. Rapid cooking makes the meat tough. (A lobster that was in good condition when it was boiled has its tail curled, and when the tail is straightened out it will snap back into place.) Allow lobster to remain in water in which it was cooked about 1 hour; then remove, and when cool, split, and remove intestinal tract and stomach. Brush with melted butter, sprinkle with a little salt, and broil at 550° F. 3 inches from heat about 5 minutes, or until brown, or prepare as desired.

How to Split a Live Lobster. Live lobsters should be pegged or have rubber bands on claws when delivered. (After arrival of lobsters in the market, they usually stay alive about 24 hours.) Wash under cool running water. Drain well. Grasp the lobster firmly by its back. With both hands, overlap the claws; this enables one to hold the lobster securely and easily with one hand. With a sharp, heavy knife make a deep incision through the body and the entire length of tail. Pull the 2 halves apart without breaking them, and remove the "body" or stomach, which is high in the body shell or back of eye. Remove the intestinal vein, which runs from the stomach to the tip of the tail.

Fish dealers will kill and split lobsters or boil them for you, if requested to do so.

Broiled Live Lobster

Prepare lobster as above. Crack, and remove edge and tip of claws. Break shell and forearm to facilitate eating. Heat broiler thoroughly, setting it at 450° F. Place lobster flesh side up, brush with melted butter, and sprinkle with a little salt. Broil 15 minutes for lobsters weighing about 1 to 1¼ pounds each, 20 minutes for lobsters weighing about 1½ to 2 pounds each. Have top of lobster 3 inches from heat. If not brown at end of broiling time, raise heat to 550° F. Brush with melted butter several times during the broiling period. Do not turn lobster, as juices will be lost, but place in the upper part of oven for about 5 minutes before serving. Pour more hot melted butter over it before serving.

Arrange attractively on individual plates, and garnish with parsley and lemon slices. Serve hot melted butter separately.

Note. Better results will be obtained if lobsters are baked at 450° F. in upper part of oven about 20 minutes, and then broiled at 550° F. several minutes until golden brown. This method is simpler, and more lobsters can be prepared at one time.

Lobster Tails

Lobster tails are not to be confused with the true Atlantic lobster of the large meaty claws. They come from rock lobster, which are really large crayfish, but are very meaty and delectable if properly prepared. They come in various sizes, but commonly weigh 4 to 12 ounces, frozen in attractive packages. At least 8 ounces should be prepared for each serving. It is best to thaw the lobster tails before cooking.

How to Thaw Lobster Tails. The best way to thaw lobster tails is to remove them from the freezer, and to store them in a normal refrigerator temperature overnight. They may be thawed out more quickly in room temperature for several hours, or if in a great hurry, cover them with cool water and let stand 30 to 60 minutes. Prepare as soon as defrosted, or refrigerate.

Boiled Lobster Tails

To prevent them from curling, insert long metal skewers lengthwise in each tail before dropping them into the boiling salted water to cover. Simmer tails weighing 4 to 12 ounces, about 5 to 13 minutes, depending on size, then let remain in hot water for about 15 minutes to absorb moisture.

To Remove Meat. First remove metal skewers, and with heavy kitchen scissors cut down the middle of the upper or underpart of tail. We prefer to cut upper part. With fingers loosen and pull out meat. Cut and use for Lobster Thermidor (below), salads, or as desired.

Lobster Tails Thermidor

Boil lobster tails (preferably those weighing at least 8 ounces each) as per general directions. With large kitchen scissors, cut through center top hard shell as suggested above. Remove meat from tails, cut up and prepare thermidor same as for casserole (page 253). Allow preparation to cool at least 30 minutes before placing it smoothly and high in center of tails. Sprinkle top with paprika, and bake in oven on aluminum foil on baking sheet, at 500° F. about 10 minutes for small, 15 minutes for those weighing more than 10 ounces each. Then place them under broiler, 3 inches from heat for several minutes, or until top is brown.

To Serve. Arrange tails attractively on a large round platter, alternately with individual fruit or vegetable salads, around a heap of French-fried potatoes, or well-seasoned buttered vegetables. This makes a very colorful and delectable party-style luncheon, dinner, or supper meal.

Broiled Precooked Lobster Tails

Follow general boiling directions given above, *but reduce* simmering time to half, being sure to insert long metal skewers in each one to prevent curling. When cool enough to handle, remove skewer, and with heavy kitchen scissors, cut down the middle of the back (top hard shell). Open out the tail and bend it backward as far as possible to crack the shell side so that the meat is exposed. With fingers, loosen meat from sides and bottom of shell leaving meat in shell. Brush top well with melted butter or Seafood Marinade (page 236), sprinkle with salt and paprika, and broil 3 inches from heat, about 7 to 12 minutes, or until golden brown. If you prefer, tails may be split through the center in 2 pieces (loosen meat) then placed with meat side up, seasoned and broiled in the same way. Or you may cut away the undershell (soft part) completely and neatly; loosen meat from sides and bottom (but leave in shell), and broil at 500° F.

Lobster Tails Broiled Without Precooking

Defrost tails completely; wash and dry them in a towel. Cut or split them in any of the 3 ways suggested for the Broiled Precooked Lobster Tails above and loosen meat. We prefer cutting hard upper shell. Insert metal skewers lengthwise in each tail, or each half of split tails, to prevent curling. Place them with meat side down on well-buttered aluminum foil, on a flat baking pan, and broil at 500° F. about 3 inches from heat about 5 minutes for very small tails, 7 or 8 minutes for those up to 12 ounces. Now turn them over, having meat side up. Brush them well with melted butter, or Seafood Marinade (page 236). Sprinkle with salt and paprika, and broil about 6 or 7 minutes for very small tails, and 10 to 12 minutes for up to 12 ounces. For tails weighing more than 12 ounces each, increase cooking time several minutes on each side. Serve hot with melted butter and wedge of lemon. Lobster tails are more moist broiled without precooking in water.

Lobster Thermidor in Casserole or Chafing Dish

Serves 6 to 8

¼ teaspoon dry mustard
¼ teaspoon garlic salt
2 teaspoons salt
¼ teaspoon pepper
½ cup butter or margarine
⅔ cup sifted all-purpose flour
3 cups warm half & half cream, or rich milk
2 tablespoons light wine
¼ cup grated Italian cheese
⅛ teaspoon cayenne pepper

4 cups cooked lobster meat, cut in 1-inch pieces (3 pounds uncooked lobster tails will give about 4 cups cooked)
½ pound fresh mushrooms, sliced and sautéed in 2 tablespoons butter several minutes and seasoned with ½ teaspoon salt and a little pepper; or use medium can sliced mushrooms

Cook lobster tails according to general boiling directions (page 252).

Melt butter, add flour and blend until smooth. Add warm cream slowly, stirring continuously, and cook until thick, and then simmer about 5 minutes. Add the wine and all other ingredients and cook together several minutes, stirring continuously. If too thick, add a little more cream or milk. Best to have sauce thick as it will soften when thermidor is baked. Pour into 17-inch stainless steel casserole, spread smoothly, forming a slight mound in center, and sprinkle with paprika. Bake in a 300° F. oven about 30 minutes if ingredients are warm, or 40 minutes if casserole has been refrigerated. If top is not brown when time is up, place it under broiler for several minutes and watch closely.

To serve, arrange well-seasoned and buttered asparagus or peas around base. Garnish with a vegetable flower and parsley. This is a delectable preparation for buffets, cocktail parties, supper parties, luncheons, and dinner parties.

It may be prepared a day in advance and refrigerated, well covered, as soon as it is cool.

Other style heatproof casseroles may be used, *or increase cream* and serve in chafing dish. Sprinkle center of chafing dish with paprika and a ring of finely chopped green onion or parsley on ends.

Shrimp de Jonghe

Serves 4 to 6

2 pounds fresh raw shrimp, or 1 pound cooked and peeled	1 cup or little more lukewarm dry sherry or sauterne (half water may be used)
¼ cup butter or margarine	
½ to ¾ cup cold firm butter or margarine	½ cup very finely chopped parsley
1 clove garlic, chopped as fine as possible or put through garlic press	1¼ cups dry bread crumbs
	About ¼ cup grated Italian cheese
	About ¼ cup melted butter or margarine
1 teaspoon salt	

Cook raw shrimp gently in salted boiling water 3 to 5 minutes depending on size. Drain. Remove shells and intestinal vein, if necessary. Split lengthwise and sauté shrimp in the ¼ cup butter for a few seconds. Beat ½ cup or more cold, firm butter until very light, about 3 minutes. Add the garlic, salt, wine (a little at a time), parsley, and the bread crumbs alternately. Pour sautéed shrimp into a greased shallow round baking dish that measures about 10½ × 1⅓-inches, or preferably in stainless steel oval dish. Spread crumb preparation over shrimp with a fork as uniformly as possible. Sprinkle with grated Italian cheese and drizzle with melted butter (about ¼ cup). Bake at 350° F. about 30 minutes (longer if casserole is put together long in advance and ingredients are cold), then broil until brown and crisp for 2 or 3 minutes.

Shrimp Arnaud

Serves 4 to 6

Drop 2 pounds of uncooked shrimp (will give about 1 pound cooked) into rapidly boiling salted water, and cook gently about 5 minutes for large shrimp, 3 minutes for medium. When done, remove shells and intestinal vein, if necessary, and split shrimp in halves lengthwise. Pour about ⅓ of Sauce Arnaud over shrimp, mix well, cover and refrigerate for at least 4 hours before serving.

To Serve. Form a mound on an oval 12-inch dish, pour and spread rest of Sauce Arnaud over top. Place relishes or hors d'ouvres crackers around base, and garnish end or top with small vegetable flowers and parsley. This is an excellent dish for cocktail and buffet parties, or may be served as a first course before dinner.

Sauce Arnuad

2 tablespoons wine vinegar, or other vinegar
⅓ cup salad oil
1 tablespoon paprika
¼ cup prepared strong mustard
About 1 teaspoon salt, more or less
1 cupful celery chopped as fine as possible

½ cupful fresh green onion and tops, chopped as fine as possible
¼ cup parsley, chopped as fine as possible
1 clove garlic, chopped very fine or put through garlic press
More vinegar or lemon juice, as needed

Combine all ingredients in a bowl and blend thoroughly. Now, it is important to add more vinegar or lemon juice to make spreading consistency; do not have too oily. Use on cooked shrimp, crab meat or lobster.

► *Eggs*

OMELETS, SOUFFLÉS, AND FRENCH TOAST

THE EGG IS ONE OF OUR MOST VALUABLE FOODS. HIGH NUTRITIONAL VALUE, versatility in cooking, mild, delicate flavor, and ready availability characterize the egg as unique among foods.

It deserves the attention of the homemaker who plans and prepares family meals as well as the individual who dines out.

Eggs may be served in hundreds of ways. They are easily and quickly prepared by cooking in the shell, frying, broiling, baking, poaching, scrambling, and by using them in simple omelets.

Eggs combine well with other foods. They are useful in the preparation of beverages, breads, cakes, desserts, salads, salad dressings, sandwiches, sauces, and soups, as well as in cereal, cheese, fish, meat, and vegetable dishes. In cookery, eggs *thicken* as in custards and puddings; *leaven* when they are beaten to incorporate air as in cakes; *add color, richness, and flavor* to individual dishes; *coat* as in breaded meats; *garnish* as in canapés, salads, and soups; *bind* as in meat loaves and croquettes; *emulsify* as in salad dressings and cream puffs; *clarify* as in preparation of consommé or in "boiled" coffee.

Cooking Hints for Good Results

Take from refrigerator only the number of eggs needed.

Remove eggs from refrigerator about 15 minutes before using, since the separation of yolks from whites is quicker and better if eggs are quite cool, but not extremely cold. Eggs beat up faster and to larger volume when brought to room temperature.

Store leftover whites in a tightly covered jar in the refrigerator. They may be held a week to 10 days.

Store leftover yolks in a tightly covered jar in the refrigerator. They may be held 2 or 3 days. Or hard-cook the yolks. Use in salads, scalloped dishes, sandwiches, etc.

Four to 6 whole eggs, 8 to 10 egg whites, or 12 to 14 egg yolks are the equivalent of 1 standard measuring cup.

256

Always serve hot egg dishes on *warm* plates.

Nonstick skillets are excellent utensils for sautéing, frying, and scrambling of eggs, and are especially recommended for all omelets, provided you do not keep them over very high heat, which would corrode the lining of the pan. Fat can be reduced or eliminated with this type of cookware. Otherwise follow general directions in recipes.

Egg Quality Is Easily Determined

The position of the yolk, the condition of the thick and thin white, and the size of the air cell determine interior quality. A high-quality egg, when broken out on a plate, has a high-standing yolk, well centered and banked in thick white. There is a little thin white. As the egg loses quality, the air cell becomes larger due to moisture loss. Thick white becomes thin. The yolk floats to the side or top of the egg. When broken out on a plate, the lower-quality egg has a flattened yolk and the white is watery and thin.

People sometimes ask about a little dark speck that, very infrequently, may appear in eggs. These are blood spots, formed when the egg is produced. They may be lifted out of the egg before cooking. They do not alter the nutritive value or the cooking performance.

Grades. Eggs are graded on the basis of outside appearance, weight, and interior quality. Interior quality is judged by candling. Candling consists of holding and turning the egg before a beam of light strong enough to reveal the interior. Eggs may be graded according to federal, state, or private standards. The federal standards use the letters, A, B, C, for designation. Many fine-graded eggs are sold under a brand name or trademark without a letter grade.

Graded eggs carry their grade and size—and in some cases the date of candling—on the carton in which they are packed. Graded eggs are usually available in all markets.

Eggs Come in Several Sizes

Eggs are grouped according to size. Most eggs are classified.

	One dozen weighs at least:
Extra Large	27 oz., or 1 lb. 11 oz.
Large	24 oz., or 1 lb. 8 oz.
Medium	21 oz., or 1 lb. 5 oz.
Small	18 oz., or 1 lb. 2 oz.

Small eggs are usually more plentiful in the later summer and fall. The size does not affect the quality but does affect price. The various qualities of eggs may be found in all sizes. Weight for weight, the nutritive value and cooking performance of small eggs are equal to those of large eggs of the same quality.

Large eggs are used in our recipes unless otherwise specified.

Eggs Vary in Color

Shell color may vary from white to deep brown. Color is a breed characteristic. Shell color does not affect the flavor the nutritive value, or the cooking performance. Neither is it a guide to yolk color. There is no advantage to the consumer in paying more for brown or white eggs of equal quality and size.

The yolk color may vary from light to deep yellow. Yolk color is influenced by heredity and diet. It does not necessarily affect flavor or nutritive value.

Egg Care Is Easy

Proper refrigeration helps to maintain the original quality of eggs. Eggs may be stored commercially for several months at temperatures as low as 32° F. In the home, egg quality is maintained by storage in the refrigerator. Always buy eggs that have been kept under refrigeration.

▶ BASIC EGG DISHES ◀

Poached Eggs

Fill a deep skillet about ⅔ full of water. Bring to a boil, then reduce heat to hold temperature at simmering point. At once, break eggs, 1 at a time, into a saucer and slip into simmering water. Cover pan and cook 4 to 6 minutes, depending on firmness desired and number of eggs cooked at one time. The steam from the cover of skillet will form a nice uniform film over the yolks, making it unnecessary to pour hot water over top of eggs as they cook. When done, remove eggs with a large perforated spoon or pancake turner, drain well, and serve on buttered toast, or as desired.

Adding salt and vinegar to water does not appreciably prevent whites from spreading. Either may be omitted and excellent results are obtained. For more uniform round poached eggs, use a buttered poacher, which can be purchased in hardware stores or housewares departments of large stores. Bring water in poacher to a boil, break each egg directly into buttered inset cup of poacher, cover tightly, and steam eggs 4 to 5 minutes.

Fried (or Sautéed) Eggs—No. 1

Use a small smooth heavy skillet and ½ tablespoon warm butter, margarine, lard, or strained bacon fat *for each egg*, to prevent sticking. Break eggs carefully, 1 at a time, into a saucer, and slip them into warm fat, 1 at a time. Cook over *very, very low heat* about 4 or 5 minutes, depending on degree of doneness desired and number of eggs you can cook at one time. (It is better not to cook more than 4 eggs at once and to have fat warm and not too hot.) Spoon the fat over top of eggs during cooking process to help set yolks and to keep them hot. Season with a little salt and pepper when almost done. To serve, pick up eggs with pancake server, cutting through whites if necessary, and transfer to warm plates. Pour leftover fat over eggs if desired.

Fried (or Sautéed) Eggs—No. 2

Proceed same as for Method 1. As soon as eggs are partially cooked, after 1 or 2 minutes, pour 1 teaspoon hot water over each egg. Season, and cover skillet tightly. Continue to cook gently over very low heat about 3 more minutes. This method forms an attractive film on yolks and does not require basting.

Note. As little as ½ teaspoon fat can be used for each egg, provided a nonstick skillet is used; otherwise eggs will stick.

Fried Eggs and Bacon

To prevent eggs from sticking to skillet (unless you use nonstick skillet) when preparing this combination, cook bacon first over very low heat, then pour off bacon fat into another clean smooth skillet. Now cook eggs in the bacon fat, following general directions, and serve together.

The sugar used in curing many brands of bacon causes a sticky residue when bacon is cooked. If this is not objectionable, cook bacon until almost done, then add eggs 1 at a time. When done, loosen eggs and bacon from skillet with a pancake turner.

Scrambled Eggs—No. 1

Add 1½ tablespoons milk or cream, ⅛ teaspoon salt, a little pepper or any other seasoning to each egg. Beat eggs slightly with a fork if streaks of white and yellow are prefered; beat longer if a uniform color is preferred. Use a small 6-inch skillet if preparing only 2 or 3 eggs; a 7- or 8-inch skillet if preparing 4 or 5 eggs. For each egg heat 1 teaspoon or 1½ teaspoons fat until it begins to sizzle but not brown. Pour in egg mixture and cook over low heat until it begins to set. With a fork or spoon stir and scrape from the bottom and sides of pan until eggs are done to suit individual taste.

Scrambled eggs are always more delicious served soft, creamy, and piping hot, with buttered toast, a slice of ham, or crisp bacon.

Scrambled Eggs—No. 2

A simple but slower way is to scramble eggs in a double boiler, stirring them occasionally. This method prevents eggs from overcooking.

▶ OMELETS ◀

Basic French Omelet

For 6- or 7-inch skillet (best to use nonstick skillet), use 1 tablespoon butter (or margarine, lard, or bacon drippings), 2 large (or 3 very small) eggs, about ¼ teaspoon salt, pinch of pepper, and 1 tablespoon milk. Other seasonings may be used.

For 8- or 8½-inch skillet, use 1½ tablespoons butter (or margarine, lard, or bacon drippings), 3 large (or 4 very small) eggs, about ⅓ teaspoon salt, pinch of pepper, and 1½ tablespoons milk. Other seasonings may be used.

In skillet melt butter or other fat over moderate heat until it sizzles, but do not allow to brown. At once combine eggs and other ingredients, and heat with egg beater about ½ minute. Pour eggs into hot skillet, and cook over *moderate* heat (not low and not high) until the underside is set, about 2 minutes. With a spatula or dinner knife, lift up edges of omelet *all around* to permit uncooked egg to run to bottom. Continue to cook for 2 or 3 more minutes, or until omelet is done. A good omelet should be moist on top and brown underneath. Increase or decrease heat slightly if necessary. With 1 or 2 spatulas or dinner knives fold omelet over and turn out onto a hot platter. This is a basic French omelet and may be served plain.

Important. If omelet appears too moist at the top when almost done, cover skillet the last minute, but watch colsely not to overcook. A good omelet should be creamy and not dry.

Luncheon or Supper Omelet

For a more substantial omelet, ½ cup or more of sautéed seasoned mushrooms, sliced onions, vegetables, seafood, meat, or cheese may be poured over ½ of cooked omelet before folding it over. In this case, lift omelet out of skillet with 1 or 2 pancake turners to prevent breaking. Mushroom sauce or tomato sauce may be served separately with omelet.

Swiss Mushroom Asparagus Omelet

Serves 2

¼ pound fresh sliced mushrooms, sautéed in 2 tablespoons butter for several minutes and seasoned with ¼ teaspoon salt, a little pepper and thyme

8 cooked asparagus spears, seasoned and buttered
3 thin slices Swiss cheese
Paprika

Follow general directions for Basic French Omelet (page 260) using 4-egg recipe and an 8- or 8½-inch skillet. When omelet is done, pour sautéed mushrooms over ½ of omelet. With the aid of 1 or 2 dinner knives or spatulas turn plain side over onto filling. Place cooked, seasoned asparagus spears on top of folded omelet, then slices of cheese on top of asparagus. Sprinkle cheese lightly with paprika. Wrap foil around handle of skillet, and place skillet under broiler, set at 450° F., for several minutes, or until cheese has melted.

When done, remove omelet from skillet with 1 or 2 pancake turners, and serve at once with mushroom sauce, tomato sauce, or any other sauce desired.

Asparagus Omelet in Casserole

Serves 4 to 6

4 slices bacon, cut in small pieces and pan-fried until crisp (pour off some of fat, leaving about ¼ cup in skillet)
1½ to 2 cups cooked (1 package frozen) asparagus, cut into 1-inch pieces
¼ teaspoon each oregano, dry parsley, dry basil, crushed in fingers
¾ teaspoon salt

¼ teaspoon garlic salt
6 large whole eggs, beaten with a fork and combined with ¼ cup milk
¼ cup grated Italian cheese
2 cups pulled white bread crumbs (preferably from bread several days old)
Paprika

In a bowl combine all ingredients except crumbs and paprika. Blend gently, and pour into a well-buttered 9-inch pie plate, or oblong glass casserole that measures about 8 × 6 × 2 inches. Cover top with the bread crumbs. Sprinkle lightly with paprika, and bake at 375° F. about 25 minutes, or until center of omelet feels firm to touch.

To serve, cut in wedges if baked in round pie plate, or in squares if baked in oblong plate. Serve with meat, poultry, or fish, or as a light luncheon or supper dish with Cheese Sauce (page 315) or tomato sauce and hot rolls.

Italian Potato Omelet

Serves 4

3 medium-size potatoes, boiled with skins on, then peeled, and sliced medium-thick
1 small onion, chopped
About ½ teaspoon salt
⅛ teaspoon black pepper

¼ teaspoon oregano leaves, crumbled
About ¼ cup hot butter or margarine
3 large eggs
½ teaspoon salt
⅛ teaspoon pepper

Combine cut potatoes, onion, and seasonings, and drop into hot fat in an 8-inch skillet. Sauté potatoes about 5 minutes, turn over and sauté another 5 minutes. Now beat eggs with a fork, add salt and pepper, and pour over entire surface of potatoes. Continue to cook until eggs are set on underside. Then with a pancake turner, turn potatoes over and cook a few minutes longer, but not until too dry.

This is very delicious as a main family luncheon or supper dish, or it may be served with meat, fish, or poultry.

Fluffy Omelet

Serves 2

4 teaspoons butter or margarine
4 large (or 5 small) eggs, separated
½ teaspoon salt

¼ teaspoon cream of tarter
¼ teaspoon pepper (optional)
¼ cup milk

Preheat oven at 350° F. Melt 2 teaspoons butter in each side of 9½-inch special 2-section omelet pan, and brush sides and edges of pan with part of butter. Keep pan over *very, very* low heat.

Separate eggs, place whites in an 8- or 9-inch bowl, yolks in a 7-inch bowl. Add salt to whites and beat until foamy, then add cream of tartar and continue to beat until whites form very stiff peaks but are not dry. (This takes about 1 minute with a powerful beater, a little longer with others.) Now add pepper and milk to yolks and beat them about ½ minute without washing beater. At once fold yolk mixture, a little at a time, lightly into beaten whites, and blend well until no streaks appear, but do not over-mix.

Pour ½ of preparation into each side of heated, buttered omelet pan. With a spatula, level surface of egg, and cook over *very, very* low heat for about 5 minutes, or until underside is *lightly* browned. Lift omelet at edge to see color. After 5 minutes, place omelet in preheated oven and bake about 7 or 8 minutes, or until knife inserted into center comes out clean. If top of omelet appears too moist when done, place it under broiler for about 1 minute. When done, go around edge of pan with a dinner knife to loosen omelet. (At this point you may cover 1 side with sautéed mushrooms or other vegetables if you wish). Fold pan over, and carefully turn omelet out onto hot serving platter, releasing omelet with a dinner knife or spatula if necessary.

Serve with mushrooms and tomatoes sautéed or any other sauce.

Note. All omelets of this type shrink slightly and should be served as soon as they are done.

▶ FANCY EGG DISHES ◀

Eggs Supreme

1 tablespoon or more soft butter	Salt
5 slices white bread, toasted	Pepper
5 slices American cheese	⅛ teaspoon nutmeg
5 whole eggs	1 tablespoon parmesan cheese

Spread butter on bottom and sides of 8 × 12 × 1½-inch casserole. Trim toast so that it will fit nicely on bottom of casserole. Trim American cheese to fit toast, and with a 1-inch (or little larger) round cutter, cut out center of cheese. Place cheese over toast. Break eggs carefully, so that yolks drop onto cut-out sections of cheese. Season with a little salt, pepper, and nutmeg, and sprinkle with parmesan cheese. Bake at 350° F. about 15 minutes, or until yolks are set.

Fluffy Egg Nests à la Rosinia

Spread soft butter on sliced white bread. Place under broiler until delicately brown and crisp. Arrange on baking sheet with toasted side down. Spread upper side with soft butter; cover with thin slices of cooked ham, bacon, or cheese. Pile on white of 1 stiffly beaten egg (beaten only until it clings to bowl), to which a small pinch of salt has been added. If ham, bacon, or cheese is very salty, omit salt. Form a depression in egg white with a spoon; slip in whole egg yolk very carefully. Bake at 375° F. about 15 minutes, or until delicately brown. Serve at once.

Note. In preparing a number of these nests at one time, separate eggs carefully. Pour whites into a large bowl. Keep yolks in shells and place each on a crumpled towel to prevent breaking. Have crumpled towel in a shallow pan. Pour each yolk into white carefully.

Arrange nests attractively on a large platter and garnish with parsley bouquets or vegetable flowers.

Eggs and Spinach Florentine Baked in Casserole

Serves 6 to 8

3 (10-ounce) packages frozen cooked (or 3 pounds of fresh) spinach
Salt
Pepper
4 whole eggs
¼ pound American cheese, freshly shredded

1 small can evaporated milk, with ½ teaspoon salt
3 tablespoons melted butter, poured over
2 cups large, fresh-pulled bread crumbs

If using fresh spinach, wash thoroughly several times in lukewarm salted water. Drain and cook without additional water (use only what clings to spinach) in covered saucepan until tender—about 10 minutes. When done, *drain very thoroughly,* and chop fine; season with about 1 teaspoon salt and a little pepper.

Place spinach in a well-greased, shallow round glass pie plate that measures about 10 × 1¼ inches. Make 4 depressions with a spoon, pressing spinach well up on the sides so that a raw egg may be dropped into each. Sprinkle eggs lightly with salt and pepper.

Add cheese to the milk and cook only until cheese is fully melted. Add ½ teaspoon salt. With a spoon pour cheese sauce over eggs and spinach very carefully. Cover with buttered crumbs and bake in a 375° F. oven about 3 minutes. Place in broiler to brown, if necessary.

Eggs Benedict

Split English muffins, toast them on cut side, and spread with soft butter or margarine. Place a slice of ham that has been sautéed lightly on each muffin half. Place a Poached Egg (page 258) on top of ham, and pour some Hollandaise Sauce (page 340) over egg.

For a special brunch a slice of cooked breast of chicken or turkey may be placed over ham, then Poached Egg, and Hollandaise Sauce.

Scrambled Corn and Eggs

Serves 2

2 slices bacon
½ cup milk
1 cup canned whole-kernel corn, drained

½ teaspoon salt
Dash of pepper
4 eggs, beaten

Cook bacon until crisp and remove from skillet. Combine milk, corn, salt, pepper, and beaten eggs.

Pour into hot bacon fat and scramble. Serve topped with crumbled bacon.

Asparagus and Scrambled Eggs

Serves 4 to 6

6 eggs	1 teaspoon any salt seasoning
6 tablespoons cream	¼ cup asparagus liquid from jar (or
2 tablespoons butter or oil	from pan in which frozen or fresh
½ cup asparagus, cut in small pieces	asparagus has been cooked)
1 teaspoon minced onion	

Beat eggs and cream until frothy. Heat butter or oil in heavy 9-inch skillet; add asparagus, onion, and salt seasoning. Simmer a few minutes. Add asparagus liquid and simmer another minute. Pour in egg and cream mixture. Continue cooking at very low heat, scraping constantly from the bottom of the pan until done. Serve on buttered toast or as desired.

▶ FRENCH TOAST ◀

Grilled French Toast

Serves 2

2 eggs	About ½ teaspoon salt
2 tablespoons cream or milk	Sliced bread
2 tablespoons melted butter	

Beat all ingredients except bread together for about ½ minute. Dip sliced bread into batter, letting it soak a few seconds. Place it on a lightly greased griddle pan. When brown on one side, turn over and cook second side. Brush griddle each time with melted butter or other fat.

French Toast prepared in this way is light and greaseless. Serve at once with jellies, jam, syrup, or as desired.

Ham, Cheese, and Mushroom French Toast Sandwiches

Remove crusts from slices of white bread if desired, or leave them on for a more substantial sandwich. Brush lightly with butter. Place thinly sliced cheese on 1 slice. Place thinly sliced ham on other slice. Cover ham with a thin layer of sautéed mushrooms, well seasoned to suit taste. Make sandwich, cut in 2 rectangular pieces. Dip each piece into well-beaten egg combined with 2 tablespoons milk, about ½ teaspoon salt, and a little pepper. Pick up with tongs or fingers and pan-fry in about ¼ inch very hot butter or other fat until brown on each side.

Serve at once as a light luncheon or snack with sliced tomatoes.

These sandwiches are very attractive if arranged on an oblong or oval platter, overlapping each other slightly. Surround with sliced tomatoes and serve a quick mushroom sauce separately.

Swiss Cheese French Toast Sandwiches

Remove crusts from slices of white bread if desired, or leave them on for a more substantial sandwich. Brush lightly with butter. Fill with thinly sliced Swiss cheese. Make sandwich, cut in 2 rectangular pieces. Dip each piece into well-beaten egg combined with 2 tablespoons milk, about ½ teaspoon salt, and a little pepper. Pick up with tongs or fingers and pan-fry in about ¼ inch very hot butter or other fat until brown on each side.

Serve at once as a light luncheon or snack with sliced tomatoes.

These sandwiches are very attractive if arranged on an oblong or oval platter, overlapping each other slightly. Surround with sliced tomatoes and serve a quick mushroom sauce separately.

California Toast

Serves 6

6 egg yolks	Juice of ½ orange
½ cup cream	⅛ teaspoon nutmeg
⅛ teaspoon salt	¼ cup butter
Rind of 1 orange	12 slices 1-day-old bread

Beat egg yolks with hand beater, gradually adding cream. Add salt, orange peel, orange juice, and nutmeg.

Melt butter in large skillet or grill. Remove crusts from slices of bread. Dip slices into batter and fry until golden on both sides.

Serve with syrup made as follows: Combine 1 cup granulated sugar with 3 tablespoons water. Heat until sugar is completely dissolved, then add 1 tablespoon honey and ½ teaspoon vanilla.

▶ SOUFFLÉ DISHES ◀

The word *soufflé* in French means "puffed up." Soufflé dishes are those that are puffed up, usually by the addition of eggs. Meat and fish soufflés are very attractive and delicious served for party luncheons or suppers, and as main dishes with a sauce, a salad, and a dessert. The vegetable soufflés may be served as accompaniments to meat, poultry, or fish courses.

Cheese Soufflé

5 very large eggs
¼ cup butter or margarine
¼ cup sifted all-purpose flour
1⅓ cups warm milk

¼ pound (1¼ cups lightly measured)
American or cheddar cheese,
finely shredded or grated
½ teaspoon salt

Separate eggs very carefully, pour whites into an 8- or 9-inch bowl and let stand in room temperature at least 1 hour (or place bowl with whites into a pan of warm water). Temperature of eggs must be 75° F. to 80° F., not cold or too warm. Pour egg yolks into a small bowl. Beat yolks at once with egg beater or small wire beater for about 1 minute. Cover with a small plate, and let stand in room temperature until needed.

Set oven temperature to 350° F. Pour very hot water (about 150° F.) into a deep roasting pan or any other utensil that is about 2 or 3 inches deep. Place roasting pan with the very hot water into oven, center rack.

In a 2-quart saucepan melt butter or margarine, add flour, and stir until smooth. Take off heat, and slowly add the warm milk, stirring all the time to keep smooth. Put back over medium heat and cook and stir until smooth. Let simmer about 2 minutes. Add the finely shredded or grated cheese, and continue to cook and stir until cheese is fully melted and smooth. At this point remove from heat, add the beaten yolks, about 1 tablespoon at a time to the hot sauce, and continue to stir until all yolks have been added. Add ¼ teaspoon salt; blend well. Cover saucepan, and let stand while you beat egg whites.

In an 8- or 9-inch bowl, add ¼ teaspoon salt to egg whites and beat at high speed until they cling well to bowl, testing by tilting bowl. Beat a few seconds (not minutes) longer after they cling to bowl. Do not overheat. *At once* add the warm cheese sauce, about ¼ cupful at a time right from saucepan, and with a large wooden spoon or rubber scraper, fold and stir gently until evenly blended, and no streaks appear. Pour preparation in 1½-quart soufflé dish that has been well greased on bottom and lightly on sides, filling it to about 1 inch from top for best results.

The same amount of eggs will not always give the same amount of soufflé preparation; it depends on freshness of eggs, time of year, and other factors. If any preparation is left over after you fill soufflé dish, pour it into a small greased custard cup and bake it at the same time, removing it before the larger soufflé is done. Any heatproof 1½-quart deep bowl or casserole can be used.

Place dish carefully into deep roasting pan half filled with very hot water (at least 150° F.). Pour more very hot water around dish, having it come up on sides at about 2 inches deep. Bake in a 350° F. preheated oven anywhere from 45 to 60 minutes, depending on temperature of water, etc. Test with long blade of paring knife after 40 minutes through top center of soufflé. If blade comes out clean, soufflé is done. If unsure, it is best to bake it another few minutes. Soufflés must be served at once for best results. However, if soufflé is done before you are ready to serve it, shut off heat, and let soufflé remain in hot water for about 10 minutes, not longer if possible, *with oven door closed*. A strong draft may cause it to settle.

To Serve. Cut soufflé into serving portions with a serrated-edge cake server or knife, pick up each portion with a very large oval serving spoon (or wooden spoon) and transfer to individual plates. Serve mushrooms and tomatoes sautéed or mushroom sauce or any preferred sauce, separately. A green cooked buttered vegetable and fruit salad are excellent served with this soufflé.

Note. Some recipes suggest baking soufflés in oven without using pan of hot water. Through many tests we find that the hot water gives the soufflé better texture, and enables it to hold up better.

Corn Soufflé

Follow general directions given for Cheese Soufflé (page 267). Use only 4 large eggs, separated, ¼ cup butter, ¼ cup sifted all-purpose flour, 1 cup and 2 tablespoons milk, 1 teaspoon salt added to sauce, ¼ cup shredded American cheese or 2 tablespoons Italian cheese added to sauce, and 1 cup well-drained whole kernel corn. Add corn to the hot sauce; add ¼ teaspoon salt to egg whites and proceed same as for Cheese Soufflé (¼ cup sugar may be added to beaten whites for Corn Soufflé, not to others).

Spinach, Broccoli, Asparagus, or Pea Soufflé

Follow general directions given for Corn Soufflé, adding about ¼ teaspoon garlic salt and ¼ teaspoon pepper if desired. Use 1 cup well-drained, chopped cooked vegetable.

Frozen or Canned Mixed Vegetable Soufflé

Follow general directions given for Corn Soufflé, using ¼ teaspoon garlic salt and ¼ teaspoon pepper if desired. Use 1 cup well-drained cooked mixed vegetables.

Cooked Meat or Chicken Soufflé

Follow general directions given for Corn Soufflé. Season as desired. Omit cheese. One cup cooked chopped ham, corn beef, tongue, leftover poultry, or any other cooked meat may be used.

Fish or Shellfish Soufflé

Cooked crab meat, lobster, shrimp, tuna, or salmon may be used. Flake cooked fish, or chop medium. Season as desired. Two tablespoons grated Italian cheese may be added. Follow general mixing and cooking directions given for Corn Soufflé.

▸ *Vegetables*

VEGETABLE MOLDS AND
VEGETABLE CASSEROLES

ALL VEGETABLES ARE RICH IN VITAMINS. VITAMINS ARE NECESSARY FOR HEALTH, and if they are lacking in the diet, illness will develop.

The most natural and economical way to get vitamins is to eat proper foods. Vitamins are a group of constituents of most foods in their natural state and are often destroyed by improper cooking. Therefore, good cooking is an integral part of the balanced diet. If you want to get all the vitamin and nutritive value for fruits and vegetables, eat them as nearly raw as possible, or steam them in a small amount of liquid and eat the pot liquors (the liquids left after vegetables are cooked) with them. They contain vitamins B_1, C, and G, and should be served with the vegetables if possible, or used as a base for soups, gravies, sauces, etc. When cool, they may be stored in a tight-covered jar in the refrigerator for several days.

Because we all need a small amount of fat in our diets, use butter or enriched margarine on vegetables. Vegetables are always more satisfying and palatable when buttered.

The seven basic foods to be eaten each day should be selected from each of the following groups:
1. Green and yellow vegetables.
2. Oranges, tomatoes, grapefruits, or uncooked cabbage or salad greens.
3. Potatoes and other vegetables or fruits.
4. Milk, or milk products such as cheese, etc.
5. Meat, poultry, fish, or eggs, or legumes such as peas and beans, or nuts.
6. Bread and cereals.
7. Butter or enriched margarine.

▸ IMPORTANT FACTS REGARDING
VEGETABLE COOKERY ◂

Baking soda added to vegetables destroys vitamins B_1, C, and G.

Unless it is absolutely necessary, do not cut vegetables until they are ready to be cooked. Exposure to air means some loss of vitamin C.

If possible, avoid washing vegetables after they are cut, for washing causes loss of vitamins.

Do not peel root vegetables if it can be avoided, for the minerals and other vital qualities lie close beneath the peels. The peels are palatable after they are cooked, especially in young vegetables.

Vegetables such as carrots and parsnips should be cut lengthwise instead of crosswise whenever possible, since this prevents damage to longitudinal cells and minimizes "bleeding" of minerals and vitamins during cooking.

Cabbage, Brussels sprouts, cauliflower, and broccoli often cause digestive upsets if they are overcooked because the sulphur compounds they contain are liberated. Be sure to cook only until crisply tender.

The juice of oranges, lemons, and other citrus fruits should not be expressed until immediately before it is to be served. If it is to stand, cover tightly and keep in refrigerator, and use as soon as possible.

Add salt in beginning, but sometimes it is not added until vegetables are almost done. Note instructions in recipe.

If adding cream to vegetables, add after the heat has been turned off. This gives vegetables a more delicious and delicate flavor.

A little vinegar or lemon juice added to beets and red cabbage will help to retain the color.

A small amount of granulated sugar added to the so-called sweet vegetables—carrots, peas, corn, beets—while standing improves their flavor.

Almonds contain eight vitamins—A, B_1, B_6, G, E, niacin, choline, and biotin. They are delicious when dropped into boiling water for about 3 minutes; remove skins, split, and cut lengthwise into 4 pieces. Sauté almonds in a small amount of butter or margarine and pour them over steamed buttered green or wax beans, asparagus, etc. Almonds are an outstanding source of vegetable protein.

Steaming is the most helpful way to prepare most vegetables because it preserves important elements that are sometimes destroyed by other methods of cooking.

The steaming method requires very little water, and in many cases vegetables may be cooked in their own juices with a small amount of butter added to them, provided utensils with tight-fitting covers are used and utensils are not too large for small amounts of vegetables. When necessary to add water, use about ⅛ inch of boiling water, which is often enough, until steaming starts; then the juices begin to be drawn from the vegetables by the heat. It is best to follow specific instructions given with each recipe. Regardless of utensil used, the most essential points to remember in steaming vegetables are to use low heat after steaming has started and to stir vegetables several times to prevent scorching and insure even heat distribution.

Use as little salt as possible in steamed vegetables. Too much destroys the delicate flavor. Vegetables prepared by steaming require very little seasoning, for they retain the natural mineral salts.

To retain the greatest amount of minerals in green vegetables, and for stronger flavor, steam in a very small amount of water only until tender. In order to retain color and at the same time prevent loss of vitamins in a large amount of liquid, steam vegetables, removing cover during the last few minutes or when almost tender; continue to cook uncovered, turning often. If vegetables are to be served for a special occasion and color is an important factor, cook uncovered in enough boiling water to submerge vegetables, until crisply tender. In this case a pinch of soda may be added to green vegetables.

▶ VEGETABLE DISHES ◀

Artichokes

Purchase small or medium-size artichokes for best flavor. Wash artichokes several times in lukewarm water and drain, bottoms up. Remove loose discolored leaves around base, and clip tip of each leaf. Drop into enough boiling unsalted water to cover artichokes (to retain color); cover saucepan and let boil about 20 minutes for small, 25 minutes for medium, and 30 minutes for large, until outer leaves may easily be pulled from stem. Instead of cooking in a large amount of water, artichokes may be steamed in a small amount of boiling water, adding more water during the cooking process, if necessary, to prevent drying out. Turn artichokes several times during cooking period. When almost done, add salt and continue to cook several minutes longer. Remove from liquid and drain well, bottoms up, on rack.

Buttered Artichokes

Prepare artichokes and drain (as above). When cool enough to handle, remove chokes with a teaspoon and discard. The choke is the hairy, spiny part above the heart. Place artichokes in individual saucedishes, and pour hot melted butter or margarine (a small clove of minced garlic may be added and greatly improves flavor) into center and between leaves. To eat, pull off a leaf, hold by tip, and dip into butter in saucedish. Remove the fleshy part of the base of the leaf with the teeth, and discard remainder of the leaf. When all leaves are removed, eat the heart with a fork.

Artichokes with Cheese Sauce

Prepare artichokes (as above). Remove chokes and discard. Reheat artichokes in covered saucepan in a small amount of artichoke liquid. Place artichokes in individual saucedishes, then pour over them heavy cheese sauce made as follows: Melt 2 tablespoons butter or margarine in saucepan, blend in 2 tablespoons sifted flour. Add 1 cup artichoke liquid or milk, little at a time, stirring constantly. When sauce thickens, season with ½ teaspoon salt, and add 1 cup freshly shedded American cheese that has been measured lightly. After cheese is added, cook sauce only until cheese is fully melted.

Stuffed Artichoke Bottoms

Artichoke bottoms
2 tablespoons finely chopped onion
2 tablespoons butter or margarine
½ pound fresh mushrooms, washed, and dried thoroughly in a towel, chopped fine

About ½ teaspoon salt
⅛ teaspoon pepper
2 level teaspoons cornstarch, dissolved in ¼ cup cool stock or water

To prepare artichoke bottoms, drain them, dry thoroughly on towel, and sauté them *(rounded side down first) about 1 minute on each side.* Let cool.

Sauté chopped onion in the 2 tablespoons hot butter or margarine over medium heat, for about 2 minutes. Add chopped mushrooms, stir well, and cook for about 2 or 3 minutes. Add seasonings and cornstarch mixture and cook over low heat until thick, then simmer about 2 more minutes, stirring continuously to prevent sticking to pan. Let cool, then use 1 level tablespoon to stuff hollow part of sautéed artichoke bottoms keeping mushroom purée rounded and smooth in center.

To reheat Stuffed Artichoke Bottoms, place them on a rack in a 300° F. oven for about 10 minutes, or place on top of Individual Oven-broiled Chateaubriands (page 139) the last 5 minutes.

Stuffed Artichokes de Luxe

4 artichokes
1 large clove garlic minced or 1 small onion, minced
¼ cup butter, margarine, or oil
1 cup dry bread crumbs
¼ cup parsley, minced

1 teaspoon salt
¼ teaspoon black pepper
2 tablespoons grated parmesan cheese
1 cup hot artichoke liquid or meat stock or water
Melted butter

Prepare artichokes (as above). Remove chokes and discard. Sauté garlic or onion in shortening until delicately brown, pour over dry bread crumbs, and mix well. To crumb mixture add parsley, salt, pepper, and cheese, and mix thoroughly. Last, drizzle over ingredients the artichoke liquid or meat stock or water, mixing all gently with a fork, keeping ingredients moist without allowing them to become compact. Pour a little melted butter into each artichoke and sprinkle lightly with salt. Then pour dressing into centers and between leaves. Place artichokes close enough together to prevent spreading, and bake in a covered pan at 350° F. about 30 minutes. Pour hot melted butter over dressing just before serving.

Asparagus

Purchase fresh brittle stalks of uniform size. Keep in hydrator until ready to be cooked. Wash thoroughly several times in lukewarm water, and when stalks are clean, hold each stalk between the thumb and forefinger of each hand and exert a gentle pressure downward on each end of the stalk. It will break at the point where the stalk is still tender. If asparagus appears very sandy, it may be necessary to remove each scale with a sharp knife or vegetable peeler and then rinse in clear water; otherwise they will be gritty. Tie in 1 bundle, or in several bundles; place bundles with stem ends down in about 2 inches of boiling unsalted water. Cover (double boiler is excellent for this purpose, using either top or bottom as a cover). (Or cook asparagus in small flat skillet in ¼ cup water, covered.) Cook 10 to 20 minutes, depending on number, tenderness, and thickness of stalks. When almost done, sprinkle with salt and cook several minutes longer. Remove carefully, and serve with melted butter, Hollandaise Sauce (page 340), or as desired.

Creamed Asparagus on Toast

Cook asparagus 10 to 20 minutes. Place on buttered toast. Pour cream sauce over asparagus and serve at once. Sauce may be prepared as in Asparagus in Casserole (page 409), omitting crumbs. Excellent luncheon or supper dish.

Fresh Lima Beans

Lima beans may be purchased fresh or frozen. The fresh beans usually are already shelled, but if purchased with pods do not accept unless crisp and brittle. Wash thoroughly and keep in hydrator until ready to be cooked. Shell just before cooking. Steam in a small amount of boiling water in tight-covered utensil about 20 to 30 minutes, or until tender. Season and serve as desired. Frozen lima beans are preferred, as they are always more uniform in quality and tenderness. Cook as fresh lima beans are cooked—only until tender (about 10 minutes).

Fresh Lima Beans and Corn Baked in Casserole

Serves 6

¼ cup butter or margarine
¼ cup sifted all-purpose flour
1½ cups milk
¼ cup American or parmesan cheese
About 1 teaspoon salt
¼ teaspoon white pepper
¼ cup pimiento cut into 1-inch squares
2 cups freshly cooked lima beans or

1 package cooked frozen lima beans
2 cups kernel corn or 1 package frozen corn
½ cup green onion tops cut into 1-inch pieces
2 cups pulled fresh bread crumbs
3 or 4 tablespoons melted butter or margarine

Melt butter or margarine, blend in flour, and add milk gradually, stirring constantly. Cook until thick and then simmer 2 or 3 minutes. Add cheese, salt, pepper, and pimiento. Combine this sauce with beans and corn and onion tops. Pour all into a well-greased pie dish (about 10 × 1⅓ inches). Sprinkle top with crumbs. Drizzle with melted butter or margarine and bake about 30 minutes at 350° F. If crumbs are not brown after 30 minutes, place under broiler for several minutes and watch closely.

This is a very substantial dish and may be served as a main luncheon or supper dish with hot rolls and a salad.

Home-Style Baked Beans

Serves 6 to 8

1 pound navy beans
1¼ cups, or less, tomato catsup
4 slices bacon or salt pork, cut into small pieces
1 tablespoon salt
About ½ teaspoon black pepper

3 tablespoons cornstarch
1 tablespoon molasses
1 tablespoon light corn syrup
2 strips bacon or salt pork, cut in halves crosswise

Place navy beans in a large bowl; wash thoroughly, then cover well with warm water. Let stand overnight. Next day, pour beans *and* water in which they were soaked into a covered pan. Cook gently until very tender—about 2 hours or longer, depending on quality of beans. When done, drain, leaving about 1½ cups of liquid (best to measure liquid). Add 1 cup catsup to the beans. Add bacon or salt pork, salt, and pepper. Make a paste with the cornstarch, syrup, ¼ cup catsup, and molasses. Add all to beans. Pour into a well-greased baking dish. Arrange slices of bacon or pork over top. Bake, covered, at 275° F. about 3 hours, or until tender, removing cover toward end. If beans boil over while baking, keep cover slightly ajar. Keep dish on an old small baking sheet for entire time that beans are baking.

Dilled Beans Louisiana

Serves 6

2 packages frozen green beans	1 teaspoon dillseed
4 slices bacon, cut into small pieces	½ teaspoon black pepper
1 small onion, chopped into small pieces	

Cook defrosted beans in 1½ cups salted water until crisply tender but not soft. Drain well, saving liquid.

Fry bacon until medium crisp but not dry. Add onion, and cook several minutes. Add green beans and seasonings, and cook 2 or 3 minutes. It is best to let this cool and refrigerate several hours or longer, to develop flavor. Shortly before serving, prepare following sauce and pour over beans.

Sauce for Dilled Beans Louisiana

¼ cup butter or margarine	1 teaspoon salt
¼ cup sifted all-purpose flour	¼ teaspoon hot sauce or ⅛ teaspoon
1½ cups bean liquid (if short, add milk)	cayenne pepper
	2 tablespoons vinegar (optional)

Melt butter, add flour, and form smooth paste. Add bean liquid, and cook until thick. Then add seasonings, and simmer several minutes. Pour over beans and serve hot.

Dilled Beans Louisiana in Casserole

Serves 6

Follow directions (as above). Pour beans with sauce into a very small casserole or flat baking dish. Just before serving, sprinkle top with fresh pulled white bread crumbs, and bake in a 400° F. oven about 15 to 20 minutes, or until crumbs are brown. Casserole may be prepared hours or a day in advance and baked about 25 to 30 minutes before serving.

Marinated String Beans

Serves 2 or 3

1 package frozen string beans, cooked until just tender and still green	⅛ teaspoon marjoram
2 tablespoons salad oil	⅛ teaspoon black pepper
1 teaspoon vinegar	⅛ teaspoon dried basil or parsley
¾ teaspoon salt	1 silver garlic

Combine all ingredients except cooked green beans. With a spoon or beater, beat until thick. Pour over string beans. Blend well. Cover and refrigerate several hours or longer. Cook about 5 minutes just before serving.

Fresh Green String Beans

Wash beans under cool water. Remove ends. French cut or cut as desired. Cook in about 2 tablespoons unsalted water. Cover tightly and let cook about 10 to 15 minutes. Add salt to taste last 2 or 3 minutes. Drain and serve as desired. Frozen beans may be prepared in same way, reducing cooking time to about 5 to 6 minutes.

Fresh Green Beans
Fresh Wax Beans

Purchase fresh crisp beans, and wash thoroughly in cool water. Remove ends. Cut into diamond shapes, French cut, or leave whole. Drop into 2 tablespoons (for each package) water, cover utensil, and steam about 10 to 15 minutes, or until tender, turning several times during cooking process. Add salt to taste when almost done. Butter, or serve as desired.

Frozen beans may be prepared in same way, reducing cooking time to about 5 minutes.

Leftover beans may be served as a salad with thin-sliced onion, marinated in French or Italian Dressing (page 368) for about 15 minutes or longer. When ready to be served, add a few pieces of canned pimiento and arrange on lettuce leaf.

Beans With Sautéed Toasted Almonds

Cook beans as in preceding recipe. Drain very thoroughly. Brush cooked beans with melted butter. Drop almonds into boiling water about 3 minutes; drain well, and remove skins. Slice lengthwise into fourths, sauté in a small amount of melted butter or margarine; or sprinkle butter over almonds and place on a baking sheet in 350° F. oven until lightly browned and crisp, for about 10 minutes. Arrange beans on a large serving plate or individual serving plates. Pour almonds and butter over them, sprinkle with salt, and serve hot.

Green or Wax Beans With New Boiled Potatoes and Onions

Cook beans as above. Do not drain. In a small amount of oil or other shortening sauté some thin-sliced onion about 5 minutes; add to beans. Steam uniform whole small potatoes with skins on until tender but not too soft. When done, remove skins. Add potatoes to beans and onions; season with salt and pepper to taste. Cover and cook gently about 5 minutes, or until heated through. Serve hot. This is an unusually delicious combination.

Lima Beans and Spinach Continental

Serves 4 to 6

¼ cup salad oil
1 very small clove garlic, chopped fine
1 package frozen spinach, cooked until just tender, drained well
1 package frozen lima beans, cooked until tender, drained well or use canned lima beans)
1½ teaspoons salt
¼ teaspoon black pepper
⅛ teaspoon, or less, cayenne pepper
¼ teaspoon oregano or marjoram

In a medium-size saucepan or skillet, heat oil. Add garlic, and cook several minutes over medium heat. Add spinach and lima beans, and all other ingredients. Cover saucepan and simmer about 7 or 8 minutes.

Bean, Mushroom, and Carrot Medley Glacé

Serves 8

2 medium-size (2 cups) onions, sliced thin lengthwise
¼ cup butter or margarine
2 cups carrots, peeled if necessary, cut about ¼ inch wide and 3 inches long
1 package frozen green beans, defrosted
1 package frozen wax beans, defrosted
½ pound fresh mushrooms, sliced medium-thick and sautéed in ¼ cup butter 3 minutes
About 2 teaspoons, more or less to suit taste, salt
¼ teaspoon, or more, white pepper
½ teaspoon garlic salt
½ teaspoon savory or rosemary crushed in fingers
¼ cup, or more, melted butter

Sauté onions in ¼ cup butter about 5 minutes. Cover and steam several more minutes until crisply tender, not soft. Put aside.

Combine carrot strips, defrosted green and wax beans, and steam in ¼ cup hot water, in a covered saucepan, until crisply tender, but still colorful, about 5 or 6 minutes.

In a large skillet or saucepan, combine cooked onions, vegetables, and sautéed mushrooms. Add all seasonings and ¼ cup melted butter. Just before serving, cook over medium heat about 5 minutes. Pour Glaze (page 279) over vegetables and blend gently.

Serve on an oval platter, forming a smooth mound. Garnish ends with vegetable flowers and parsley bouquets.

Note. These vegetables may be cooked in advance, then seasoned and heated about 5 minutes. Add Glaze just before serving.

Glaze for Vegetables

Combine 1 tablespoon cornstarch with 2 tablespoons cool water, and add to 1 cup clear chicken stock (instant bouillon may be added to 1 cup hot water). Cook these ingredients, stirring constantly until thick; then simmer about 5 minutes.

String Beans Medley

Serves 4 to 6

1 package frozen green string beans	¼ cup melted butter
1 package frozen yellow string beans	About 1¼ teaspoons salt
¼ pound fresh mushrooms, sliced thin and sautéed in 2 tablespoons butter several minutes	¼ teaspoon white pepper
	1 cup cracker crumbs, blended with 3 tablespoons melted butter

Combine both packages of string beans and steam in ¼ cup of water in a covered saucepan 5 or 6 minutes, until tender. Drain well, and combine beans with all ingredients except cracker crumbs blended with melted butter. Taste, and season further if necessary. Pour mixture into a flat heatproof 10-inch pie plate or oval heatproof 12-inch plate.

Sprinkle top with cracker crumbs combined with melted butter, and bake at 350° F. about 15 minutes. Baking will require about 25 minutes if medley has been prepared in advance and stored in refrigerator.

Caramelized Glazed Beets

1 pound small uniform-size beets	2 tablespoons soft butter
¼ cup granulated sugar	

Cook beets with skins on until just tender. Rub skins off under cold running water. If beets are large, cut into thick slices or wedges; if small, leave whole. In a heavy skillet melt sugar and keep over moderate heat until it is lightly caramelized. Add butter, and stir until blended. Add warm cooked beets and stir over moderate heat until glazy, for about 5 or 6 minutes. Serve at once.

Beets

Purchase fresh young beets, wash thoroughly, dry, and keep in hydrator until ready to be cooked. Pare skin as thin as possible; cut lengthwise into uniform slices. Add a very small amount of lemon juice, a little salt, and 1 tablespoon butter or margarine for each cup of cut beets. If desired, 1 teaspoon of sugar for each cup of beets, which enhances flavor, may be added in the beginning. Cover tightly and place over high heat. As soon as they start steaming, lower heat and continue to cook about 20 to 30 minutes, depending on thickness of slices, quantity, and age. Turn several times while cooking, and watch to see that they do not scorch. If necessary, add a few drops of water. If you do not have a heavy saucepan with a tight cover, it will be necessary to add a small amount of water. If any liquid remains in pan when beets are tender, cook uncovered over high heat several minutes, or until liquid boils away.

Quick Beets Supreme

Serves 4

No. 2 can sliced beets
¼ cup sliced onions
2 tablespoons butter
¼ cup sugar
½ teaspoon salt

⅛ teaspoon pepper
1 tablespoon lemon juice
⅓ cup beet liquid or water, combined
    with 1 teaspoon cornstarch

Pour off liquid from beets and reserve. Sauté onions in butter until tender. Stir in sugar, salt, pepper, lemon juice, beet liquid or water, and starch. Add beets and cook until thoroughly heated, and simmer about 5 minutes, stirring occasionally.

Beet Greens

Fresh beet tops should not be discarded, as they are more nutritious than the roots. Remove coarse stems. Wash in several waters. When they are clean, place in a saucepan with about ½ inch of boiling water. Cover and steam about 10 minutes, or until tender, turning several times. Drain; season with salt, pepper, and butter.

To Serve. Make a large nest (or individual nests) of cooked buttered beet tops, and fill center with cooked beets. Very attractive and delicious.

Broccoli

Purchase strictly fresh broccoli with closed deep green buds. If fresh and young, it is not necessary to peel, but remove the heavy leaves and about ¼ inch from stem end. Wash several times in lukewarm water. Place with stem end in about 3 inches of boiling water, cover, and cook about 15 to 20 minutes, or until tender. When almost done, sprinkle with salt. If stems are very thick and not uniform, cut into uniform thickness before cooking. When done, drain well, and serve with melted butter, Hollandaise Sause (page 340), or as desired. Soak frozen broccoli about 10 to 12 minutes in only ¼ cup water.

Broiled Broccoli or Asparagus Mornay

Serves 4

Cook 1 package frozen broccoli or asparagus spears in ¼ cup hot water, to which 1 teaspoon salt has been added. Steam gently in covered saucepan until tender. Pick up vegetable and carefully transfer to heatproof dish. A small glass pie plate, measuring about 8 inches, is the right size for 1 package of vegetable. Increase baking time for larger recipes. Reserve liquid for sauce. Brush vegetable with melted butter. With a spoon carefully pour cool sauce over vegetable, leaving about ½ inch of vegetable uncovered. Sprinkle top with paprika. Bake at 400° F. about 10 minutes; then broil at same temperature until top of sauce is brown.

Sauce Mornay for Broccoli or Asparagus

1 tablespoon melted butter	⅛ teaspoon celery salt
2 tablespoons all-purpose flour	2 tablespoons minced onion, sautéed
Vegetable stock with enough rich milk	in ½ tablespoon butter
or cream added to make ½ cup	1 tablespoon sauterne (optional)
¼ teaspoon salt	½ cup shredded American cheese, or
⅛ teaspoon white pepper	¼ cup grated parmesan cheese

Melt butter, add flour, and blend well. Add vegetable stock and milk, seasonings, and sautéed onion. Cook until thick. Then add wine and cheese, and continue to simmer 3 or 4 minutes, being sure that cheese is completely melted. Let sauce stand until cool before spreading on vegetable.

Brussels Sprouts

Brussels sprouts may be purchased fresh or frozen. If necessary, remove outer wilted leaves from fresh sprouts, and trim stems. If not to be prepared at once, store, without washing, in coldest part of refrigerator. May be cooked whole, but to shorten cooking time cut x-mark in ends of stems or remove corelike part extending from stem into sprouts. This core requires much longer cooking than the leaves to become tender. May be quartered if desired. Wash thoroughly until water is clear, but do not soak for more than a few minutes, as soaking destroys vitamins. Cook in rapidly boiling unsalted water to cover, in an uncovered saucepan, 10 to 15 minutes, or until crisply tender. To preserve color, flavor, and texture, and to be digestible, Brussels sprouts should not be overcooked. When done, drain, season, and serve as desired.

Brussels Sprouts Breaded and Deep-Fried

Serves 4

2 cups Brussels sprouts, cooked until crisply tender

Light dry bread crumbs

1 well beaten egg, combined with 1 tablespoon water and ½ teaspoon salt

Cover cooked wet sprouts with crumbs, dip into beaten egg, and then into crumbs again. Let stand on wax paper about 15 to 20 minutes, turning over occasionally. Deep-fry at 375° F., until brown and crisp. Sprinkle with cheese and serve at once.

Brussels Sprouts Sautéed

Serves 4

1 medium-size onion, sliced thin, or 1 small clove garlic, sliced thin

2 tablespoons, or more, butter, margarine, or oil

2 cups Brussels sprouts, cooked until crisply tender

Add onion or garlic to hot shortening, cook several minutes, add sprouts, and toss gently until thoroughly heated—about 5 minutes. Season with salt and pepper and serve at once.

Green Cabbage

Cabbage is one of the most inexpensive and nutritious foods. To be perfect, it should be cooked until just tender, and if served raw as cole slaw it should be cut as fine as possible. Wash and store in refrigerator until ready to be cooked.

To cook, remove wilted outer leaves, and wash well. Cut into fourths or eighths, leaving part of core on each section to hold leaves together. It may be tied. Drop into rapidly boiling unsalted water to cover, and cook uncovered until crisply tender, from 8 to 12 minutes, depending on quality and amount prepared. Add salt last few minutes. When done, drain and season. Serve as desired.

Cabbage and Onion Sautéed

Wash cabbage (see above). Cut away core. Place on a board, and with a very sharp or saw-edged knife cut in slices about ¼ inch wide. For each cup of cut cabbage, heat 1 tablespoon salad oil or other shortening. Add thin-sliced onion or garlic (enough to suit taste) and cook gently about 2 or 3 minutes. Add cabbage (no water), mix well, cover pan tightly, and bring to steaming point over high heat. *Lower heat to medium* and continue cooking about 10 to 15 minutes, or until just tender. Turn several times. Just before it is done, season with salt and pepper. Serve hot.

Red Cabbage

Prepare same as green cabbage (page 282). It is especially delicious raw, cut fine or shredded, and used with other salad vegetables.

Carrots

Carrots are one of the most inexpensive and protective foods available. They add color to any cooked vegetable dish or salad. They are best eaten raw combined with other salad vegetables. Peel carrots *only* if necessary. If small, leave whole; if large, cut lengthwise whenever possible to prevent loss of vitamins. Place in a saucepan with only enough boiling water to produce steam (about 4 tablespoons), and cook covered about 10 to 25 minutes, depending on size, turning several times during cooking process. May be cooked uncovered the last few minutes to allow evaporation of liquid if any remains when pot liquor is not to be used. Season and serve as desired.

Baked Carrot Mold

Serves 8 to 10

1 cup butter or margarine
1 cup brown sugar
2 whole eggs
2½ cups sifted all-purpose flour
¾ teaspoon baking powder
1 teaspoon baking soda

1 teaspoon salt
2 tablespoons water
2 tablespoons lemon juice
3 cups grated carrots, lightly packed
   into measuring cup

Cream butter or margarine well, add brown sugar, and beat 1 minute. Add 2 whole eggs and beat 3 minutes until batter is light. Sift dry ingredients together and add alternately with combined water and lemon juice, beating well until smooth. Last, mix in grated carrots.

This is a heavy batter. Spoon into a well-greased (use 1 tablespoon shortening) and floured 6-cup-capacity rind mold (1½ quarts), and spread evenly. Bake at 350° F. about 45 minutes, or until firm to the touch.

Unmold while still hot. Surround mold with cooked peas, corn, beets, etc. Makes an excellent substitute for potatoes, rice, or macaroni product.

Carrots Toasted Whole

Select uniform small or medium-size carrots. Wash thoroughly—do not peel for this purpose even if slightly discolored. Steam in a small amount of water in a tightly covered saucepan 20 to 30 minutes, or until crisply tender when tested with metal skewer in thickest part. Drain thoroughly. Brush with light or dark corn syrup, or honey; roll into crumbled corn flakes. Place on greased flat baking sheet, and bake at 350° F. about 20 minutes. When done, serve attractively.

For special occasions, tiny sprigs of parsley may be inserted in large end of carrots to simulate carrot greens. First, make an opening with a metal skewer, then insert stems of parsley. This adds much color to the dish. If adding carrots to soups or stews, do not overcook. Add them 15 to 30 minutes before soup or stew is done.

Cooked carrots combine well with other foods, such as peas, green lima beans, etc. When added to other salad vegetables, shred carrots fine just before serving, or they may be cut into julienne strips for a salad bowl.

Carmelized Glazed Carrots

Serves 6

1 pound fresh carrots, peeled and cut into large thick 3-inch wedges
¼ cup granulated sugar

2 tablespoons very soft or melted butter

Cook carrots in small amount of water in covered pan until crisply tender, about 15 minutes. Drain well and keep hot. In a large 9- or 10-inch heavy skillet melt the ¼ cup granulated sugar and keep over moderate heat until it is very lightly carmelized. Add soft or melted butter and stir until blended. At once add the *hot* carrots, and with a long spoon stir over moderate heat for about 5 minutes, or until they are nicely glazed. If carrots have been steamed in advance, they must be reheated before adding them to glaze. Serve at once with meat or poultry.

Whole Glazed Carrots

8 small carrots
2 tablespoons butter

¼ cup brown sugar

Peel carrots if necessary. Leave whole. Steam them in ¼ inch of boiling water in a covered saucepan, about 20 to 25 minutes, depending on size, until crisply tender. Drain well. Melt butter and sugar in a skillet, add carrots, and continue to cook several minutes until nicely glazed. Arrange around pork roast.

Julienne Glazed Carrots

Peel carrots if necessary, or simply wash them well. Cut into uniform long narrow strips about 2½ inches and ⅛ inch thick. Cook in covered pan in *very small* amount of water about 6 or 7 minutes after they come to the steaming point, depending on thickness and amount of carrots, but do not cook too soft. Drain very thoroughly for several minutes and dry on a towel. Measure carrots after they are cooked, and for each cup, add 1 tablespoon granulated sugar and cook over moderate heat for several minutes only until carrots absorb sugar. Then brush with top part of melted butter and serve at once.

Cauliflower

Select white, compact cauliflower with no discoloration. Remove outer leaves, wash in cool water until clean, drain thoroughly, and keep in hydrator until ready to be cooked. When ready to be prepared, remove all leaves, stalks, and stems. Separate flowerettes, and wash under cool running water to make sure that all dirt is removed, but do not soak. Drop into enough boiling unsalted water to cover, and cook uncovered about 15 to 20 minutes, until crisply tender. Add salt last few minutes.

Cauliflower may also be steamed in 1 inch of boiling water.

Cauliflower Scalloped

Serves 6

2 cups Thick White Sauce (page 328), using 2 teaspoons salt in sauce	1 teaspoon salt after it is cooked and drained)
1 medium-size cauliflower, prepared as above, or 2 packages frozen (add	1 cup shredded American cheese
	6 hard-cooked eggs, sliced

In a greased pie plate (about 10 × 1⅓ inches), pour part of Thick White Sauce. Place cooked and well-drained cauliflower over sauce; then cover with a little more sauce, sprinkle with half of cheese, and arrange sliced hard-cooked eggs over cheese, pour rest of sauce, and sprinkle again with cheese. Bake at 350° F. about 30 minutes. If not brown after 30 minutes, place under broiler for several minutes and watch closely.

Cauliflower Centerpiece on Vegetable Platter

Serves 8

1 medium-size cauliflower	1 package frozen wax beans
4 slices American cheese	1 package frozen corn
Paprika	1 bunch carrots
1 bunch fresh asparagus, or 1 package frozen asparagus	Melted butter
	Salt, pepper

Wash whole cauliflower, remove green stalks, and cook covered in about 1 inch of boiling salted water about 20 minutes, or until tender.

Remove from saucepan, place on baking sheet, cover head of cauliflower with cheese, and place in a 400° F. oven about 5 minutes or until cheese is melted.

Place cauliflower in center of a serving platter; sprinkle top of cauliflower with paprika. Around base of cauliflower arrange attractively cooked asparagus, wax beans, corn, and carrots. Pour melted butter on top of vegetables, season to taste, and serve hot.

Cauliflower Sautéed

Cook cauliflower (page 285); drain thoroughly. Melt some butter or margarine; add small clove of sliced garlic or 1 small onion. Cook 2 or 3 minutes. Add cooked cauliflower and sauté 7 or 8 minutes, turning over several times. Season with salt and pepper when almost done. Use about 1 tablespoon shortening for each cup cauliflower.

Celery

Purchase crisp attractive stalks. Wash thoroughly and store in hydrator. Celery is commonly eaten raw in salads or as an appetizer with olives, etc. Tender stalks may be stuffed with cream cheese and nuts and served as an appetizer.

Celery is used in soups, stews, chop suey, etc.

Creamed Celery

Cut celery crosswise into ½-inch pieces. Cover with boiling water, and cook in covered saucepan until tender, about 20 minutes. Add salt last few minutes. When done, drain, measure liquid, and to each cup add 2 tablespoons flour combined with 2 tablespoons water to make a smooth paste. Cook until thick; pour over celery, and simmer several mintes. A little butter or margarine may be added for flavor. Cooked fresh lima beans are delicious combined with creamed celery. In this case increase water when cooking celery. Add a few pieces of canned pimiento and some fresh onion tops for color the last minute.

Chives

Chives are used as seasoning in salads, stews, soups, cottage cheese, and other dishes. Cut fine or into short strips. They have a strong flavor and should be used with discretion. Purchase only fresh grasslike shoots, and keep in hydrator until ready to be used. Leeks may be used in the same way.

Corn on Cob

Purchase corn that has fresh green husks. To judge freshness, examine kernels, which should exude a milky substance when punctured. If not to be prepared soon after purchased, remove outer husks, leaving inner layer to preserve corn. Place in hydrator or store upright in about 1 inch cold water to keep fresh. It is better to cook corn as quickly as possible after it is picked to insure tenderness and flavor. When ready to cook, remove all husks and silk, etc.; trim tips and ends. Drop into enough boiling unsalted water to cover; cover utensils and boil gently about 7 to 10 minutes, depending on quality. Corn is done when milk in kernels is set. Add salt last minute or two. Drain and serve hot with butter or margarine. Corn may be kept hot in a strainer or colander over simmering water for a few minutes.

Steamed Corn

Corn may be placed on a rack or directly in a small amount of boiling water (about ¼ inch) and steamed in a covered saucepan until just tender, 10 minutes, turning it over 2 or 3 times.

Creamed Fresh Corn off the Cob

Husk and clean corn thoroughly, removing all silk. Hold firm with stem end up, and cut downward with a sharp knife, being careful not to cut too close to cob. Combine about 3 tablespoons rich milk or cream and 2 teaspoons sugar with 1 cup corn that has been cut off cob. Simmer in a covered saucepan about 10 minutes, or until tender. Season with 1 teaspoon (or more) butter, a little salt, and pepper.

Corn Fritters

Serves 4

2 eggs	1 tablespoon sugar
⅓ cup milk	1 teaspoon salt
1¼ cups sifted all-purpose flour, combined with 2 teaspoons double-acting baking powder	¼ teaspoon pepper
	1 cup cream-style golden sweet canned corn

Separate eggs. Combine egg yolk with all other ingredients except egg whites and stir until smooth. Beat egg whites until they cling to bowl. Pour them into corn mixture and fold over and over until well blended and no streaks appear. With a teaspoon or tablespoon drop preparation into hot fat between 360° and 375° F., and cook until brown. Turn them over and brown second side.

These corn fritters are very delicious with fried chicken or other meat dishes.

Steamed Frozen Corn

Serves 4

Place 1 package frozen corn in a small saucepan with a tight cover. Add 1 or 2 tablespoons butter and 1 tablespoon sugar. Do not add any water. Place over moderate heat, and when corn is entirely defrosted, let cook about 5 minutes, turning several times. Serve hot.

Corn and Ham Fritters

Serves 4

2 eggs
⅓ cup milk
1¼ cups sifted all-purpose flour, combined with 2 teaspoons double-acting baking powder
About ½ teaspoon salt, depending on saltiness of ham

1 tablespoon sugar
¼ teaspoon black pepper
1 cup cream-style golden sweet canned corn
1 cup ham, cut into very small cubes, or chopped coarse with a knife

Separate eggs. Combine egg yolks with all other ingredients except egg whites, and beat until smooth. Beat egg whites until they cling to bowl. Pour them into corn mixture and fold over and over until well blended and no streaks appear. With a teaspoon or tablespoon drop preparation into deep hot fat between 360° and 375° F., and cook until brown. Turn them over and brown second side.

These corn fritters are very delicious with a mushroom or tomato sauce for a light family luncheon or supper dish.

Cucumbers

Cucumbers are used principally in salads. Purchase solid, green cucumbers. Wash well and keep in refrigerator. When ready to be served, slice and combine with other salad ingredients. Very fresh young cucumbers may be served with skin on if sliced very thin. If cucumbers are soft, slice and keep in *unsalted* ice water about 7 or 8 minutes before serving. Do not soak longer.

Cucumbers in Sour Cream

Serves 2 to 3

1 medium-size cucumber, sliced thin crosswise
1 small onion, sliced very thin lengthwise
½ teaspoon salt
Pinch of pepper
A little paprika

1½ teaspoons granulated sugar
1 tablespoon vinegar
½ cup, or more, commercial sour cream
1 tablespoon green onion tops, cut in ½-inch pieces

Slice cucumber and onion. Combine all other ingredients and pour over cucumber and onion. Cover and chill about 15 minutes before serving. This dressing may be used on cole slaw or other salad vegetables.

Stuffed Eggplant Halves

Serves 4

1 large eggplant
¼ cup butter
¼ cup chopped celery
½ cup green peppers, cut into ½-inch squares
¼ cup fine-chopped onion
½ pound ground beef
1 teaspoon salt

¼ teaspoon pepper
1 cup fresh tomatoes, chopped medium-fine
2 tablespoons chopped parsley
¼ cup pimiento, cut into ½-inch squares
1 cup fresh pulled bread crumbs, or corn flakes

Wash eggplant; cut into halves lengthwise and remove pulp to within ½ inch of skin. Cut up pulp into ¼-inch cubes.

Sauté, in hot melted butter, celery, green peppers, onions, and ground meat about 5 minutes. Add all other ingredients, including scooped out cut-up eggplant, except bread crumbs, and blend well. Fill eggplant halves with mixture.

Place in a greased baking dish. Bake uncovered in preheated oven at 350° F. 30 minutes. After 30 minutes sprinkle top with pulled bread crumbs or corn flakes and drizzle about 2 tablespoons melted butter on top. Continue to bake about 15 more minutes.

Arrange on attractive platter, and garnish with quartered tomatoes and parsley or watercress.

Pan-Fried Eggplant Slices

Serves 4

1 eggplant
1 teaspoon salt
⅛ teaspoon pepper

1 egg, well beaten
¼ cup butter and ¼ cup oil

Slice eggplant in ½-inch slices. Add salt and pepper to well-beaten egg. Dip eggplant slices in seasoned egg, and sauté in hot melted butter combined with oil over medium heat about 5 minutes on each side. Serve at once.

Very delicious served with any meat course.

Eggplant, Vegetable, and Meat Stew

Serves 4 to 6

1 pound lamb (preferable), beef, or veal cut into 2-inch pieces
Flour
¼ cup hot shortening
2 cups fresh tomatoes, or 1 can tomatoes (1-pound, 1-ounce size)
1 medium-size eggplant
About 4 medium-size carrots, cut into long thick wedges
1 large onion, cut lengthwise into 1-inch pieces

¼ cup parsley
¼ cup celery leaves
1 small clove garlic
1 cup frozen or fresh peas, or fresh string beans
½ tablespoon cornstarch, combined with ⅓ cup tomato juice or water
1 tablespoon salt
½ teaspoon black pepper

Roll meat in flour and brown in shortening. When thoroughly brown on all sides, add tomatoes; cover saucepan and cook slowly about 1 hour, or until meat is almost tender. Beef will require longer cooking. Peel eggplant and cut into 2-inch pieces; add to meat; then add carrots, onions, parsley, celery leaves, and garlic. Cover, and cook very gently about 20 minutes; then add peas and cornstarch combined with liquid. Continue to cook about 10 more minutes, adding salt and pepper a few minutes before it is done. This is a delicious and economical main dish.

Endive

Purchase fresh crisp endive with well-blanched centers and green outer leaves. To clean, remove stem, discard any wilted leaves, separate, and wash thoroughly in several cool waters. Drain well and keep in hydrator until ready to be used. The inner part may be cut up and used as a salad with any desired dressing. The outer green leaves are usually cooked or added to soups.

Boiled Endive, Italian-Style

Clean as above. Because of its acridity, it is better to cook endive in a large amount of rapidly boiling unsalted water until tender. Oftentimes, first water is poured off about 15 minutes after endive has cooked, and clear hot water is added to it and cooking process completed. Endive takes about 20 to 30 minutes to become tender, depending on texture of leaves. Add salt last few minutes. Drain.

For each cup of cooked drained endive, sauté 1 very small piece garlic in 1 teaspoon oil (onion may be used instead). Pour over endive; season with salt and a little cayenne or black pepper. Cook all together until heated through, about 7 or 8 minutes. Steamed peeled potatoes, cooked navy beans, or lima beans may be combined with cooked and seasoned endive; in this case, use more seasoning and oil.

Endive With Spareribs, Italian-Style

Sauté spareribs in a very small amount of shortening until brown on both sides. Add enough boiling water to produce steam, and cook about 40 to 45 minutes, or until tender. Combine with cooked endive (not too well done) seasoned with oil and garlic. Cover and steam about 15 minutes.

Escarole

Escarole has wider, thicker leaves than endive, and has same uses as endive, but is more commonly used in Italian cookery.

Garlic

This seasoning may be purchased fresh or as garlic salt or powder. Bulbs should be firm and skins brittle. It should not be stored in refrigerator, but in a cool, dry place, in a Mason jar with several openings in cover. Remove only cloves to be used. Peel the thin paperlike skin, slice, chop, or put through a garlic press. It is used for flavoring meats, poultry, vegetables, and salads.

Lettuce

Green lettuce is a much higher source of vitamin A than white blanched lettuce. It is also richer in vitamin G than white lettuce. Lettuce is used principally raw, alone or combined with other salad ingredients; also as a basis for fruit salads, and for decorative purposes. Purchase attractive fresh lettuce without discoloration. Remove any wilted or discolored leaves. Core, and allow cold water to run through head. Shake well to remove surplus water; keep in hydrator until ready to be used. Shred, cut or break with hands just before using, and pour just enough salad dressing over lettuce to moisten each leaf or piece. Mix well with 2 forks or hands. Serve as soon as possible.

Mushrooms

Purchase only firm white mushrooms; those of button variety that are tightly closed at point where top joins stem are choicer than open caps. Do not wash until ready to be used. Keep in refrigerator in tight-covered container or original package with cellophane cover. Do not keep longer than a day or two, as they become dry and moldy. When ready to be prepared, cut off thin slice from end, wash in lukewarm water several times until clean, drain thoroughly, and dry on a towel. *Do not peel.*

Broiled Mushrooms

Wash and dry (see above). With a sharp knife cut away stems—do not pull out. Dip each mushroom into melted butter or margarine to which a little minced garlic has been added. Place with round side up about 2 inches from heat, 400° F., and broil about 3 or 4 minutes until brown; turn over and broil about 3 or more minutes, depending on size and thickness of mushrooms. Season with salt and pepper, and serve. Stems may be pan-fried and used for many purposes.

Fresh Mushrooms Sautéed

Wash 1 pound strickly fresh mushrooms in lukewarm water, leaving stems on, but cut off thin slice from bottom. Dry carefully on towel. If mushrooms are strictly fresh, it is not necessary to peel them. Sauté in about 2 tablespoons of butter combined with 2 tablespoons shortening or oil with rounded side down first, turning several times. For medium-size mushrooms cook about 3 minutes total time, for large cook about 5 minutes. Do not overcook. Season with salt and a little pepper toward end. Stems may be *sliced off* if desired. Do not pull out stems.

Mushrooms and Spinach Baked in Casserole

Serves 6 to 8

1 pound fresh mushrooms	2 tablespoons melted butter or margarine
3 cups cooked chopped spinach, or 3 (10-ounce) packages frozen cooked spinach, well drained	1 cup cream or rich milk
	1 cup freshly shredded cheddar cheese
1 teaspoon salt	Garlic salt
A little chopped onion	

Wash and dry mushrooms. Slice off stems. Sauté both caps and stems several minutes, with round side down first, until brown. Line a flat pie plate that measures about 10 × 1⅓ inches with spinach that has been seasoned with salt, onion, and melted butter or margarine. Arrange sautéed mushrooms and stems over spinach.

Prepare sauce with cream and cheese. Bring to simmering point and allow to cook 2 or 3 minutes. Let sauce stand about 5 minutes. Sprinkle mushrooms with a little garlic salt. With a spoon, pour sauce over them carefully. Bake about 20 minutes at 350° F.; then broil several minutes until top is brown.

May be used as a main luncheon or supper dish, or as an accompaniment.

Marinated Mushrooms

Wash, dry, and sauté mushrooms on round side first about 1 minute in part butter and part oil; turn over and sauté second side. Mushrooms may then be marinated, for many hours in advance, in Vinaigrette Tarragon Dressing (page 336).

Stuffed Mushrooms Baked in Cream

Serves 6

1 pound very large uniform-size fresh thick mushrooms	1 teaspoon salt
⅓ cup butter	¼ teaspoon black pepper
1 medium-size onion, chopped fine	1 tablespoon tomato catsup
2¼ cups soft pulled bread crumbs (bread should be several days old)	1 tablespoon lemon juice
	Strips of bacon
	½ cup cream

Wash mushrooms. Dry well and remove stems carefully. Melt butter and cook onion and mushroom stems that have been chopped fine. Stir in bread crumbs and cook about 2 minutes. Stir in seasonings. Stuff mushroom caps with mixture; garnish tops with narrow strips of bacon to form a cross, and arrange in a glass heatproof platter. Pour cream around them and bake in a hot oven, 400° F., about 20 minutes.

Serve in platter in which mushroom are baked. Garnish platter with parsley bouquets.

Okra

Okra may be purchased fresh, canned, or frozen. Because of its bland flavor, okra is usually combined with tomatoes, green peppers, and other vegetables. Fresh okra should be washed well in several waters. Remove stems if it is to be cut before cooking. Do not remove stems if it is to be cooked whole. Drop into enough unsalted water to cover pods; cover utensil, and cook about 20 to 30 minutes, depending on freshness. Drain, and combine with other vegetables, such as stewed tomatoes, corn, sautéed green peppers, and onions. Season with butter, salt, and pepper, and serve with Hollandaise Sauce (page 340), if desired. Okra may be added to vegetable soup.

Okra Stew, Creole-Style

Serves 4

1 medium-size onion, sliced thin	½ cup cooked corn kernels
3 tablespoons shortening	1 cup cut cooked okra, or canned
1 green pepper, cut into short narrow strips	okra
	About 1 teaspoon salt
1 cup fresh (or thick, canned) tomatoes	¼ teaspoon pepper

Sauté onion in shortening. Add green pepper and cook several minutes longer. Add tomatoes and corn and cook 7 or 8 minutes. Then add okra and simmer all together about 5 minutes longer. Season with salt and pepper.

The mucilaginous liquid that comes with canned okra should not be discarded. Add with okra to stew, or use in soup.

Onions

It is better to use onions cooked whenever possible, for cooking softens fibers and releases vitamin C. Purchase onions with thin brittle skins free from sprouts. Peel under cool running water to prevent tears. Slice, grate, mince, or leave whole, and prepare as desired.

Sautéed Onions

Peel onions as above. Slice in lengthwise pieces about ½ inch wide. Drop into a small amount of hot butter or margarine. Brown lightly on all sides over moderate heat. Cover, and steam about 10 minutes, or until tender, depending on quantity and quality of onions. When almost done, season with salt, and sprinkle with a little paprika to impart attractive color.

Serve with hamburgers, steaks, etc.

French-Fried Onion Rings

1 cup sifted all-purpose flour	About 1 teaspoon salt
1 egg	About ¼ teaspoon pepper
About ¾ cup milk	About ½ teaspoon hot sauce
1 teaspoon double-acting baking powder	About ¼ teaspoon garlic salt
	Medium-size onions
1 tablespoon oil (optional)	

In a No. 6 or No. 7 bowl, combine above ingredients (except onions) to make batter. With egg beater, beat until smooth. Cover, and let stand at least 15 minutes before using. Slice onions crosswise in about ⅓-inch slices. Separate rings; dip in batter and allow surplus batter to drain. Drop into hot fat, 350° F., and cook until golden brown and crisp, about 5 or 6 minutes. If coating is too thick, add a little milk; if too thin, add a little flour after frying first piece.

Note. Onion rings in a batter may be fried in advance (to a light color), then refried at the same temperature several minutes just before serving. Onions may be fried the first time a few minutes before serving and fried a second time for extra crispness. They may be kept warm on a cake rack in a 300° F. oven until ready to be served (about 15 or 20 minutes).

Glazed Onions

Serves 4

2 tablespoons melted butter
6 tablespoons sugar
½ teaspoon salt
½ teaspoon paprika

2 teaspoons water
1 pound small onions, simmered about 15 minutes

Blend first 5 ingredients in a large skillet over low heat. Add onions. Cook, turning often, until onions are golden and glazed.

Parsley

Purchase fresh bright-green parsley. Wash thoroughly in cool water until absolutely clean. Drain well and keep in refrigerator in a plastic bag or in hydrator. If to be kept more than a few days, refreshen in cold water, and put back in hydrator. Parsley may be kept at least a week. It is best eaten raw, but should be added to stews, soups, meat loaves, meat patties or balls, and to whatever else possible. It adds color and flavor when chopped fine and sprinkled over salads, buttered potatoes, fish, meat, eggs, etc. Parsley is one of the richest vegetables in vitamin A, and it builds up resistance to infection and maintains health of the eyes. Use it freely and as often as possible.

Parsnips

Purchase smooth, firm parsnips, well shaped and of medium size (not too large). Do not accept soft or shriveled ones, for they are pithy and fibrous.

Wash, and cut a thin slice off top and bottom. Keep in hydrator until ready to be used, or they will dry out. If large, remove skin with vegetable peeler; if small or medium-size, peeling is unnecessary, as skin may be easily removed after parsnips are cooked by holding under cool running water and rubbing with fingers. To cook, leave whole if small; for larger ones, slice lengthwise into desired thickness. Cook, covered, in a large amount of water if a delicate flavor is desired, or they may be steamed in about ½ inch of boiling water in a covered saucepan. To cook parsnips requires 20 to 45 minutes, depending on thickness of slices and whether they are cooked whole.

If they are to be served buttered or pan-fried in strips, cook them only until crisply tender, testing with a metal skewer or a fork. If they are to be mashed, cook until very soft.

Pan-Fried Parsnips

Cook as above. When tender, drain well. Let cool slightly and remove woody core from center. Core is not commonly removed by cooks, but it improves flavor and palatability of parsnips if this is done. Core is tasteless, fibrous, and of no food value. Sprinkle with salt and pepper, roll in flour, then dip into well-beaten egg. Drain, and pan-fry in a small amount of hot butter or other shortening until brown on all sides, over moderate heat. Serve at once.

Parsnips Baked

Cook as above. Brush each piece with melted butter; arrange in a flat baking dish; sprinkle each layer with a small amount of brown sugar and a little salt. Sprinkle additional sugar over the top. Bake at 350° F. about 20 minutes. Serve hot.

Peas

Purchase crisp pods with bright-green color. They should be kept in hydrator until ready to be used, without shelling. Shell (never soak in water after shelling), drop larger ones into enough boiling water to produce steam, cook about 7 or 8 minutes, then add smaller ones. Peas require 10 to 20 minutes to become tender, depending on age and size. Season when almost done. The addition of several empty pods cut into small pieces while peas are cooking imparts additional flavor and sweetness. Discard pods before serving peas.

To Cook Frozen Peas. Place 1 package of frozen peas in *small* saucepan; add 1 tablespoon of butter and 1 tablespoon sugar to peas and no water.

Cover pan tightly; place it over medium heat, and when peas are entirely defrosted allow them to steam about 3 minutes. Serve at once. Frozen corn may be cooked in same way.

Peas Sautéed in Onion Butter

For each cup of unseasoned and unbuttered cooked peas, melt 1 tablespoon butter or margarine and add 1 very small fine-sliced onion. Sauté onion about 7 or 8 minutes; add peas and continue to cook over moderate heat until peas are heated through. Season with salt and pepper, and serve at once.

Green Peas Paprika

Serves 4

2 cups cooked green peas, or 1 package frozen
¼ cup butter
¼ cup finely chopped onion
¼ cup sifted all-purpose flour
½ teaspoon salt
¼ teaspoon black pepper
½ teaspoon paprika
½ cup rich milk or cream, combined with ½ cup pea stock
½ cup shredded American cheese

Cook peas in ¼ cup boiling water seasoned with ½ teaspoon salt only until tender and still green, about 3 minutes. Drain well. Melt butter, add onion, and cook until delicately brown. Add flour, salt, pepper, and paprika. Blend well. Slowly add cool rich milk or preferably cream, and cook until thick. Let simmer about 5 minutes; add cheese and keep over very low heat until cheese is fully melted. Pour green peas into a baking dish, cover with sauce and broil about 2 inches from moderate heat until top is brown. Green beans may be used instead of peas in this dish. Use a very small baking dish (about 8-inch size).

Peppers (Green and Red)

Purchase only smooth crisp peppers. Wash well, and keep in hydrator until ready to be prepared. Use in salads and for flavoring.

Pan-Fried Peppers

Wash and dry peppers. Cut in halves lengthwise; remove core seeds and inner white membranes. Cut into strips about 1 inch wide. Fry in a small amount of very hot oil, with smooth side down first. Do not turn until light brown; then fry second side. When brown, add clove of sliced garlic; cover pan, and steam over moderate heat about 5 minutes, or until crisply tender, depending on thickness and quantity of peppers. When done, remove cover, season with salt and a little cayenne or black pepper and bit of oregano; cook uncovered 2 or 3 minutes.

Serve as a vegetable with meat or fish. This also makes an excellent sandwich filling.

Peppers Pan-Fried With Tomatoes and Eggs

Serves 4

Pan-fry as above. After peppers are light brown on both sides, add 1 medium-size tomato (for 4 peppers) peeled and cut into about 1-inch pieces. Cook uncovered about 2 or 3 minutes. Cover and continue to cook until peppers are tender, about 5 minutes. Remove cover; season with salt, pepper, and oregano; add 2 slightly beaten eggs and continue to cook several more minutes.

Serve as a light luncheon, brunch, or supper dish. It is also an excellent sandwich filling.

Green Peppers and Eggs

Serves 4

1 large clove garlic	1 teaspoon salt
¼ cup oil	¼ teaspoon pepper
4 large green peppers	4 eggs
½ teaspoon oregano	

Sauté chopped garlic in oil about 2 minutes. Add green peppers that have been cut into long strips about ¾ inch wide, and cook as above with cover on pan about 5 minutes, or until peppers are tender when tested with a fork. Add seasonings, and continue to cook 2 minutes uncovered. Break eggs with a fork and add to peppers. Stir until eggs are set.

Succotash-Stuffed Baked Green Peppers

Serves 6

6 medium-size fresh green peppers	2 tablespoons sifted all-purpose flour
1 package frozen corn	1 cup warm milk
1 package frozen lima beans or green peas	1¼ teaspoons salt
3 tablespoons butter or margarine	½ cup pimiento, cut into ½-inch squares

Cut fresh green peppers lengthwise into 2 parts. Remove seeds and core carefully. Cook peppers gently about 5 minutes in simmering water to cover.

Drain thoroughly. Cook corn until tender; cook lima beans or peas until tender.

In a saucepan melt butter or margarine, blend in flour, and mix until smooth. Then add milk, a little at a time, stirring constantly. Cook until thick, adding salt toward end.

Combine corn, beans or peas, pimiento squares, and white sauce, mixing gently. Fill peppers, sprinkle with a little grated parmesan or American cheese. Arrange attractively in a baking dish, in which they are to be served, and bake about 15 minutes at 400° F. Serve hot. Fresh mushrooms that have been sautéed about 6 or 7 minutes may be served in same casserole.

This mixture may be prepared without the green peppers. Pour into buttered baking dish, and proceed as above.

Note. Please see Italian Dishes (pages 804–805) for additional fresh green pepper recipes.

Potatoes

Purchase smooth, firm potatoes of uniform size, not too large, and without sprouts. Keep in a cool dark place with ventilation until ready to be prepared. To retain vitamin C content, do not peel potatoes before cooking, unless peeling is suggested for some special dish.

Boiled Potatoes

Purchase boiling potatoes of uniform size. If irregular in size, always place larger ones on bottom. Drop into about 1 inch of unsalted boiling water; cover pan, and let steam over moderate heat until tender, about 25 to 40 minutes, depending on size and purpose for which they are intended. For mashing purposes, cook until *very* soft. For potato salads and pan-fried potatoes, cook until just tender, or slices will fall apart when cut. Do not add salt to water when boiling potatoes with skins on because skins are more likely to break and potatoes will be water-soaked. When done, drain well and dry out over very low heat for about 1 minute. Season later.

Baked Potatoes

Wash uniform-size Idaho baking potatoes and dry them well. Rub entire surface with salad oil or shortening. Bake in a 400° to 425° F. oven about 1 to 1½ hours, or until done, depending on size. Remove from oven and immediately puncture with a fork to allow steam to escape, cut a 2-inch cross on the center top of each potato, and while holding with a towel press each potato from bottom until it bursts through the cross. Top with sour cream or butter, salt and paprika.

To speed the cooking, baking potatoes may be cut in half lengthwise. Brush cut sides well with soft butter or margarine, and place them with cut sides down on a well-greased baking sheet or heatproof platter. Brush outside of potatoes also with melted fat. Bake half potatoes at 400° to 425° F. about 35 to 45 minutes, or until done. Then turn them with cut side up, drizzle well with melted butter, salt, and a little paprika; place under broiler to brown lightly.

Serve at once. If you have other foods in the oven that require lower temperatures, potatoes can be baked at the same time but will require more time to cook.

Pan-Fried Potatoes

Peel and cut 4 large potatoes into quarters, or 8 medium size in halves. Leave very small potatoes whole. Wash them well and dry in a towel to prevent splattering of fat. Brown them well on all sides in about ¼ inch very hot unsalted shortening or oil *over high heat*. When brown, reduce heat to medium, cover pan and cook about 10 to 20 minutes longer, or until potatoes are tender when crushed with a fork. Pour off all of fat and continue to cook slowly uncovered for several minutes. Season and serve around meat loaf, or as desired.

An excellent way to prepare potatoes is to place them around a roast the last ½ hour. In this case, remove most of clear fat from drippings in roasting pan and add a small amount of hot water or stock, scraping drippings. Turn potatoes around several times during the roasting process.

Pan-Fried Brown Potato Slices in Omelet Pan

Peel potatoes and slice them crosswise about $\frac{1}{16}$ inch thick to measure 3 cups. Wash potatoes under cold running water and keep in cold water until ready to prepare them. Drain well, and dry between towels. Heat 3 tablespoons unsalted shortening in one side of a standard-size omelet pan. When fat is very hot, carefully add about ⅓ of potatoes, flatten them out well, and sprinkle lightly with salt, pepper or paprika, a little onion or garlic powder, or a few thin slices of onion; add second layer of potatoes, and season; last, add rest of potatoes and season lightly. Cover potatoes with opposite side of omelet pan, and cook over medium-high heat (not too high) about 12 minutes. Then with a dinner knife lift up a small section from bottom to observe if they are brown; if not, continue to cook several more minutes, or until underside is brown and crisp. Now melt 1 tablespoon shortening in empty section of pan. Heat well. Carefully turn side of pan with potatoes over onto opposite side; flatten top of potatoes with back of a large spoon, and continue to cook potatoes, *uncovered* this time, about 10 minutes, or until underside is brown and crisp. When done, loosen around upper edges, and turn over onto hot serving platter. This is a very unusual and attractive way to prepare sliced brown potatoes.

Pan-Fried Brown Potato Slices in Skillet

Peel, slice and dry potatoes as in above recipe. To cook, heat 1 tablespoon or more unsalted shortening for each cup potatoes. Use 2 cups for a 6- or 7-inch skillet, 3 cups for an 8- or 9-inch size. It is better not to have too many layers if using this method. When fat is very hot, add ½ of potatoes and sprinkle with salt, pepper or paprika, a little garlic or onion powder, or a few slices of onion. Add rest of potatoes. Cook over medium-high heat (not too high) about 15 minutes *uncovered,* shaking pan from time to time to prevent sticking. When potatoes are brown underneath, with a pancake turner, turn them over, and continue to cook until underside is brown, about 10 more minutes. It may be necessary to turn potatoes over more than once and to cook them a little more or less time. It depends on type of potatoes and kind of skillet used. These potato slices are very attractive; they hold their shape well and at the same time are tender.

Duchesse Potatoes

Peel and cut about 2 pounds of Idaho potatoes in uniform large pieces. Cook in about 1 inch of hot unsalted water in covered pan until just tender. Do not overcook. Drain well, dry out over low heat. *Mash at once.* Measure, and to every 3 cups of mashed potatoes, add 2 tablespoons of butter or margarine, 1 small whole egg, 1 teaspoon salt, and *a little hot milk if potatoes appear very heavy.* Beat with electric mixer, or spoon *only* until smooth. With bag and No. 7 star cookie tube, squeeze rosettes or baskets onto a well-greased baking sheet; or use for border of planked steaks and casseroles. Bake about 30 minutes in 375° to 400° F. oven, or until slightly brown, and serve at once.

French-Fried Potatoes

Cut large uniform-size boiling potatoes into long strips about ½ inch wide. Allow them to remain in very cold water for about 1 hour, changing water several times to remove loose starch. Dry thoroughly on towel and deep-fry at 375° to 400° F. in desired shortening or oil about 5 minutes, depending on thickness and quality of potatoes, or until golden brown but not too dark. In lowering the cold potatoes into the hot fat, the temperature will drop considerably. Therefore, raise heat and try to keep temperature close to 375° F. It is better not to allow temperature to go any higher, as potatoes will not be cooked throughout. Drain on cake cooler. When ready to be served, refry potatoes at 375° F. and cook until crisp and brown, about 2 or 3 minutes. Sprinkle with salt and pepper and serve at once.

Do not add too many potatoes in first frying as the moisture will cause fat to bubble over. However, in reheating, a large number may be fried at one time. These potatoes may be fried the first time several hours or a day in advance. Refry several minutes before serving. May be frozen.

Note. Sweet potatoes may be fried the same way.

Lyonnaise Potatoes

Serves 2 to 3

1½ cups boiled potatoes, cut into small cubes and sprinkled lightly with paprika
About ¾ teaspoon salt
⅛ teaspoon pepper

2 tablespoons fine-chopped green onion
1 tablespoon cream or milk
2 tablespoons fat

Mix potatoes well with salt, pepper, onion, and cream or milk, using 2 forks. Drop into very hot fat in a 6-inch skillet. Flatten potatoes with a spoon or pancake turner. Have heat medium, and cook until brown and crisp on underside, about 10 or 12 minutes. When brown, fold over like an omelet and slide onto a serving platter, or pick up with a serving spoon in individual portions.

For an 8-inch skillet, double amount of potatoes and other ingredients.

Baked Potato-Cheese Mold

Serves 4 to 6

2 pounds red boiling potatoes, uniform in size, cooked until just tender, not too soft, cooled, then peeled and cut into ½-inch cubes
1 teaspoon salt
½ teaspoon celery seed
½ cup coarse-shredded American cheese

¼ cup fresh parsley chopped fine, or 2 teaspoons dried parsley
1 large egg, slightly beaten with a fork
1 recipe Sauce (page 303)
¼ cup shredded American cheese to sprinkle on top

In a large bowl combine all ingredients except ¼ cup cheese (include 1 recipe Sauce). Blend thoroughly. Pour ingredients into a 7-inch bowl (5-cup capacity) that has been greased with 1 teaspoon salad oil. Pack down gently. Cover with wax paper and store in refrigerator several hours or longer. Mixture may be prepared a day in advance. About 40 minutes before serving, with a dinner knife loosen around top edge of mold and turn it out onto center of a lightly greased heatproof serving platter. Sprinkle top part only (do not place cheese on sides, to prevent sticking to platter) with the ¼ cup cheese. Bake at 400° F. about 30 to 40 minutes, or until attractively brown.

This is especially good when served surrounded with meat balls and sauce.

Sauce for Potato-Cheese Mold

¼ cup melted butter or shortening (bacon fat or meat drippings excellent)

¼ cup fine-chopped fresh green onion and stems

¼ cup sifted all-purpose flour

1 cup milk

½ teaspoon salt

¼ teaspoon pepper

Melt shortening, add onion, and sauté 5 minutes. Stir in flour and mix until smooth. Add milk, a little at a time, and the seasonings. Cook until thick, stirring constantly; then simmer several minutes.

Baked Potato Ring Mold

Serves 6 to 8

3 pounds red boiling potatoes, uniform in size, cooked until just tender, not too soft, cooled, then peeled and cut into ½-inch cubes

1½ teaspoons salt

¾ teaspoon celery seed

¾ cup coarse-shredded American cheese

⅓ cup fresh chopped parsley, or 1 tablespoon dried parsley

2 small eggs, slightly beaten with a fork

1 recipe Sauce (page 304)

⅓ cup shredded American cheese to sprinkle on top

In a large bowl combine all ingredients (including 1 recipe Sauce) except ⅓ cup cheese. Blend thoroughly. Pour ingredients into a 9½ × 2½-inch ring mold that has been oiled with 1½ teaspoons salad oil. Pack down gently. Cover with wax paper and store in refrigerator several hours or longer. Mixture may be prepared a day in advance.

About 40 minutes before serving, with a dinner knife loosen around top of potato mold and turn it out onto center of a lightly greased heatproof serving platter. Sprinkle top part only (do not place cheese on sides, to prevent sticking to platter) with the ⅓ cup cheese. Bake at 400° F. about 35 to 40 minutes, or until attractively brown.

To Serve. Fill center of ring with buttered peas or another green vegetable, and surround it with whole glazed carrots, beets, mushrooms, or

other contrasting vegetables, or center may be filled with creamed
.am, poultry, or seafood.

Sauce for Potato Ring Mold

⅓ cup melted butter or shortening
(bacon fat or meat drippings
excellent)
½ cup fine-chopped fresh green onion
and stems, or ¼ cup dry onions

⅓ cup sifted all-purpose flour
1½ cups milk
¾ teaspoon salt
¼ teaspoon pepper

Melt shortening, add onion, and sauté 5 minutes. Stir in flour, and mix
until smooth. Add milk, a little at a time, and the seasonings. Cook until
thick, stirring constantly, then simmer several minutes.

Potatoes Vesuvio in Casserole

Serves 8

Cook 4 pounds potatoes with skins on until soft. At once peel and mash
slightly with electric mixer.

To hot potatoes add ⅓ cup soft butter, 3 teaspoons salt, and 2 whole eggs
slightly beaten. Beat only until blended. Last, add *only* enough hot milk to
form medium consistency. Usually about ¼ cup milk is needed, but more
or less may be required, depending on potatoes. Beat until smooth.

Reserve 2 cups for border, and pour rest of potatoes into baking dish
that measures about 10½ × 1⅓ inches, or an oval or rectangle baking
casserole. Form a slight mound in center; then make depression. Pipe
around base of potatoes, using No. 3 or No. 7 large tin cookie tube.
Pipe around depression and on sides if any potatoes remain. Pour Filling
into opening of potatoes. Sprinkle top of Filling only with paprika. Bake
casserole in a 400° F. oven about 30 minutes, or until delicately brown.

This can be prepared several hours in advance, and baked about 45
minutes, instead of 30 minutes, before serving. Serve part of sauce with
each serving of potatoes.

This is a very unusual and delectable dish, and especially nice for
buffets and company dinners.

Filling for Potatoes Vesuvio

1 cup coarse-shredder cheddar cheese
(¼ pound)
3 egg yolks, slightly beaten with a
fork
¼ cup melted butter

1 tablespoon coffee cream or milk
⅛ teaspoon cayenne pepper
¼ teaspoon dry mustard
¼ teaspoon salt

Beat all ingredients together until well blended.

Sautéed Whole New Potatoes

Peel small new potatoes. Melt ¼ cup oil or shortening, and when it is hot, brown potatoes on all sides. Season with salt and pepper.

Cover saucepan, adding about 2 tablespoons water, and steam over low heat until tender, about 20 to 30 minutes, shaking pan from time to time.

Potatoes Delmonico in Casserole

Serves 6 to 8

¼ cup butter	½ cup grated cheese (any kind)
3 tablespoons flour	4 hard-cooked eggs, sliced with egg
1½ teaspoons salt	slicer or cut into large pieces
¼ teaspoon pepper	4 cups cold cooked potatoes, sliced
½ teaspoon garlic salt	about ¼ inch thick
1½ cups hot milk	

Melt butter, add flour, and mix until smooth. Add seasonings and hot milk, a little at a time. Cook until smooth and thick; then simmer about 5 minutes. Blend cheese into sauce; then add eggs and potatoes. Pour into a medium-size well-greased baking dish, oblong or round; spread evenly. Sprinkle top lightly with additional cheese and a little paprika. Bake at 400° F. about 20 minutes then place under broiler until top is brown.

Serve with meat, fowl, or seafood.

Very delicious and substantial for a light luncheon or supper dish with a salad.

Swiss-Style Potato Pancake in Skillet

Serves 2 to 3

1 tablespoon fine-chopped onion, or 2 tablespoons chopped green onion	⅛ teaspoon pepper
	2 tablespoons lard or other shortening (butter may be used)
¼ cup shredded Swiss cheese	2 medium-size Idaho potatoes peeled and coarse-shredded
About ¾ teaspoon salt	

Prepare all ingredients except potatoes. Coarse-shred potatoes last to prevent darkening. Do not wash after shredding or shreds will not hold together in cooking. As soon as shredded, mix well with seasonings, using 2 forks to blend well. Pour into 1 tablespoon very hot fat in 6½-inch skillet. Pack potatoes down with back of a large spoon or pancake turner. Keep heat medium and cook on 1 side about 7 minutes, or until golden brown and crisp. *Then* place other tablespoon fat on top of potatoes, lift up with 2 forks, and turn over. Cook on second side about 7 minutes, or

.own and crisp. Lift out of skillet with 2 forks, or simply slide .co serving platter.

Larger amounts may be prepared in larger skillet, increasing all ingredients accordingly, and cooking 2 to 3 minutes longer on each side.

Fresh Potato Pancakes

Will make about 12 medium size

2 large whole eggs, beaten with fluffy beater for a few seconds
2 or little more tablespoons milk
2 tablespoons all-purpose flour
¼ teaspoon baking powder
1¼ teaspoons salt

About ⅛ teaspoon pepper
⅛ teaspoon onion salt
1 pound (2 large) raw potatoes, peeled
Strips of bacon, cut into square pieces (optional)

In a medium bowl combine beaten eggs, milk, flour, baking powder, salt, pepper and onion salt. With fluffy or hand beater beat for about 1 minute until smooth. Now shred fine raw potatoes into liquid preparation. This will prevent potatoes from turning dark.

To fry pancakes, stir well each time, pick up with a large spoon and pour into about ¹⁄₁₆ inch very hot unsalted shortening or cooking oil. With back of spoon flatten each one, and fry over medium heat until golden brown and crisp on 1 side, for about 5 minutes. Now with pancake turner, turn over and fry second side for several minutes. Square pieces of bacon may be placed on each pancake before turning over.

Scalloped Creamed Potatoes

2 pounds red boiling potatoes, peeled and sliced thin into cold water, then drained well
About 1½ teaspoons salt
¼ teaspoon pepper

1 medium or large onion, sliced very thin
About 1 cup shredded American cheese
1 recipe Cream Sauce for Scalloped Potatoes (page 307)

In a well-greased 1½-quart deep casserole place about ⅓ of the thin sliced drained potatoes. Sprinkle with teaspoon salt, little pepper, ⅓ of the thinly sliced onion, ⅓ cup of the shredded American cheese, and ⅓ of the Cream Sauce. Repeat 2 more layers, using same amounts of seasoning and sauce. Bake in a preheated 400° F. oven for 30 minutes, covered well with a greased piece of foil, unless you have a cover for the casserole. After 30 minutes, remove cover, lower heat to 300° F. and continue to bake for about 45 more minutes, or until potatoes are tender. Test with point of paring knife or fork. Best to allow a few minutes extra. If sauce begins to boil over before 30 minutes, remove cover and lower the heat. If top of potatoes is not brown when tender, place it under the broiler for a few minutes, but watch closely to prevent burning.

These potatoes will remain very hot for at least 20 minutes. Increase baking time for a larger recipe by about 15 minutes, but make test.

Cream Sauce for Scalloped Potatoes

¼ cup butter or margarine
¼ cup sifted all-purpose flour

2¼ cups milk, very hot
About 1 teaspoon salt

In a small saucepan melt butter, add flour, and stir until smooth. Add the hot milk all at once, *and immediately* stir over *low heat* with wire beater or heavy wooden spoon until thick and smooth. Takes only a minute or two to thicken, then continue to stir until very smooth, and let simmer about 5 minutes. Add salt the last minute or two. This is a medium sauce, and if it appears too thick, add a bit more milk, or a little water.

Fancy-Cut Buttered Baked Potatoes

Select uniform-size Idaho baking potatoes. Peel as smooth as possible. Slice crosswise, not quite through, so that potatoes are held together by a base of uncut potato. Wash thoroughly under cold running water and dry well in a towel. Brush with melted shortening and arrange in a well-greased baking pan. Bake at 400° F. about 1 to 1½ hours, depending on size and quality of potatoes. Brush with melted fat occasionally while baking; sprinkle with salt toward end. When tender, brush with melted fat again and place under broiler several minutes until attractively brown. Brush with melted butter and serve.

Fluffy Mashed Potatoes

Serves 6

Peel and wash thoroughly 2 pounds uniform-size Idaho potatoes cut in 2-inch pieces. Steam in about 1 inch unsalted boiling water in covered saucepan about 20 to 25 minutes, or until very soft, depending on size and quality. When done, drain thoroughly; place back over very low heat to dry out. Place in heatproof bowl, and *at once* with electric mixer beat several minutes. Add about ½ cup or more very hot milk, a small amount at a time. Beat, then add 1 teaspoon baking powder and about 1 teaspoon salt. Continue to beat only until light. Pour into a serving bowl; add about 2 tablespoons butter just before serving, and mix gently. These potatoes may be poured into a medium-size greased deep baking dish, reserving about ⅓ for top. With No. 7 tin tube and bag, pipe fancy scrolls on top. Place in a 350° F. oven about 15 minutes and serve hot. Place under broiler to brown if you wish.

New Potato Casserole

Serves 6

⅓ cup butter or margarine
2 tablespoons finely chopped onion
3 tablespoons all-purpose flour
1 teaspoon salt
¼ teaspoon paprika
1½ cups milk

1 cup (¼ pound) shredded processed cheddar cheese
2 pounds small new potatoes, cooked and peeled
½ cup pimiento, cut into ½-inch squares
1 cup pulled fresh bread crumbs

Melt 3 tablespoons of the butter; add onion, and sauté until golden. Stir in flour, salt, and paprika to make a smooth paste. Add milk slowly, and cook over medium heat until sauce is smooth and thickened. Remove from heat; add cheese, and blend until cheese is completely dissolved.

Place cooked potatoes in a buttered casserole; sprinkle cut-up pimiento over potatoes. Pour cheese sauce over potatoes. Top with pulled bread crumbs, and drizzle remaining 2 tablespoons butter over bread crumbs. Bake in a 350° F. preheated oven 20 to 25 minutes, or until crumbs are golden brown.

Note. Two No. 2 cans whole cooked potatoes may be used when new potatoes are not in season.

Pan-Glazed Sweet Potatoes

Serves 6

Steam 6 uniform-size small or 3 large unpeeled sweet potatoes until *just tender, not too soft.* When cool enough to handle, remove skins. Leave whole if small, or cut into halves.

For Glaze. In a large skillet bring to boiling point ⅓ cup brown sugar solidly packed, ⅓ cup hot water, and 3 tablespoon butter or margarine. Place potatoes in this syrup, and cook uncovered gently a few minutes until they absorb glaze, turning several times during cooking process. Pick up with pancake turner and serve hot. Pour or brush any leftover glaze over potatoes.

Oven-Glazed Sweet Potatoes

Serves 8

Cook 8 (4 pounds) medium-size sweet potatoes (yams are preferable) in a small amount of boiling water, in a covered saucepan, about 30 to 45 minutes, or until just tender, not too soft. When cool, peel and cut into halves, or if small, leave whole. Place on a greased baking sheet.

For Glaze. Combine 1 cup brown sugar solidly packed, ⅓ cup strained orange juice, and 1 tablespoon butter, and cook about 5 minutes, or until clear. Pour this glaze over potatoes, and bake about 30 minutes at 350° F., or until potatoes are soft. Baste several times with glaze in pan. When done, brush potatoes with glaze that is left in pan.

Arrange attractively on serving platter and garnish with parsley and vegetable flowers, or serve around ham.

Sweet Potato Delights

Use Jersey sweet potatoes as they are drier and easier to work with. Steam unpeeled potatoes in small quantity of boiling water in covered saucepan until *just* tender, but not too soft, about 25 to 35 minutes. Let cool, remove skins, and mash; add 1 tablespoon brown sugar to each cup. Pick up ¼ cup (or a little more) of mashed potato, make depression, and place a half large *soft* or miniature marshmallow and a small piece of pineapple in each. Shape into balls, enclosing marshmallow and pineapple. Roll in flour, then dip into well-eaten egg to which 1 tablespoon water has been added, then into crumbled corn flakes, making a slight depression on each. Let stand on wax paper about 20 minutes. Deep-fry at 350° F. Watch carefully and fry only 2 or 3 minutes, until brown. Keep in covered skillet over very low heat or in a warm oven (300° F.) for a few minutes, until ready to be served. Serve as soon as possible. Garnish top with red maraschino cherry and citron or green pepper leaves.

Instead of deep frying, these delights may be baked on a greased rack on baking sheet at 400° F. for about 15 to 18 minutes. Or they can be deep-fried to a lighter color in advance, then reheated in a 350° F. oven on greased rack for 12 to 15 minutes.

Sweet Potatoes Meringue in Casserole

4 pounds unpeeled sweet potatoes, steamed in a small smount of boiling water, covered, until just tender, not too soft (2 or 3 No. 2½ cans of sweet potatoes may be used)

½ cup brown sugar, packed
¼ cup melted butter
1 cup crushed pineapple and part of juice

Cook potatoes in covered saucepan in a small amount boiling water until just tender, not too soft (or use canned sweet potatoes). When cool enough to handle, peel and slice about 1 inch thick lengthwise. Arrange in layers in well-buttered 17-inch oval heatproof baking dish (round baking dish may be used); sprinkle part of sugar, melted butter, and crushed pineapple on each layer. Spread about ⅓ of Special Brown

Sugar Meringue over top part only of potatoes, leaving about 1 inch uncovered with meringue around base. With No. 7 large star cookie tube and bag, pipe rest of meringue around base, forming a rosette border, and pipe some rosettes at each small end and on top or sides. Work as quickly as possible and bake on bottom rack at 400° F. for about 30 minutes, or until meringue is brown.

This is a beautiful and delectable dish served with ham or poultry for special occasions.

Special Brown Sugar Meringue

1 cup egg whites	1 teaspoon cream of tartar
¼ teaspoon salt	1 cup soft light brown sugar, packed

Beat egg whites and salt until foamy. Add cream of tartar and beat until very stiff, about 1 minute after mixture clings to bowl. Add brown sugar, a little at a time, and continue to beat until well blended and very stiff.

Caramelized Glazed Sweet Potatoes

Serves 4

1 pound small-size (uniform as possible) sweet potatoes, cooked with skins on until just tender, and peeled	¼ cup granulated sugar 2 tablespoons soft butter

If potatoes are large, cut them into 2 or 4 lengthwise pieces. They must not be overcooked for this purpose. In a heavy skillet melt sugar, and keep over moderate heat until it is lightly caramelized. Add butter, and stir until blended. Add hot cooked potatoes, and stir over moderate heat until glazy, about 5 or 6 minutes. Serve at once.

Sweet Potatoes in Orange Cups

Serves 6

Wash thoroughly 6 medium-size unpeeled sweet potatoes and cook them in covered saucepan in a small amount of water until *very* tender when tested with metal skewer. Remove skins and mash well. Add 2 tablespoons butter and enough orange juice to make proper consistency to go through No. 3 or No. 7 star tin tube. About ¼ cup brown sugar may be added to mashed sweet potatoes while they are hot. Put hot potatoes into a bag with No. 3 or No. 7 tube and press into orange cups. Decorate each top with a whole glazed or maraschino red cherry and green citron or pepper leaves. Mashed sweet potatoes may be kept hot over simmering water and piped into orange cups just before serving. After they are filled, they may be kept in a 300° F. oven until ready to be served (but not more than 30 minutes).

Pumpkin

For cooking purposes, it is better to purchase small pumpkins, weighing about 6 or 7 pounds, for large ones are coarse in texture. Wash and dry well.

Cut into uniform-size pieces; remove seeds and stringy parts. Pare, and drop into enough boiling unsalted water to cover. Cook in covered saucepan until tender (about 25 minutes). They may be steamed in a small amount of water in a tightly covered saucepan. When done, drain well, mash, or put through a food mill. Season to taste and serve. If using for pumpkin pies, *drain again* after it is mashed and omit seasoning.

Baked Pumpkin

Cut into desired-size pieces, removing seeds and stringy parts, leaving rind on. Arrange on baking sheet; brush with soft butter or margarine, and sprinkle with salt. Cover, and bake at 350° F. about 1 hour, or until tender when tested with a metal skewer or fork. Pour melted butter over it and serve.

Alice Pope Gierum's Wild Rice Gourmet

1 cup wild rice	¼ cup pimiento, cut into strips (optional)
2 cups hot stock or water	
½ pound sausage meat	¼ cup green onions, chopped fine (optional)
½ pound fresh mushrooms	

Wash wild rice according to directions on package, then cook in hot stock or water in covered saucepan about 1 hour, or until tender. Meanwhile sauté sausage meat until brown, loosening it from pan with a fork. Wash and dry mushrooms and cut in about ½-inch pieces. Sauté mushrooms in 2 tablespoons of sausage drippings or butter for several minutes. When rice is done, combine all 3 ingredients and blend with 2 forks. Pimiento strips and green onions may be added for additional color and flavor. Taste, and season with a little salt or pepper if required.

Serve with any poultry, meat, or seafood dish. May be packed in a buttered bowl and turned over onto center of serving platter.

Wild Rice Mold

Wash wild rice according to directions on package. In a 3-quart saucepan melt ½ cup butter or margarine, add ¼ cup finely chopped onion,

½ cup sautéed sliced mushrooms, 1 pound wild rice, and about 1 table-spoon salt. Last, add 4 cups of boiling stock or water. Cover saucepan and simmer over low heat for about 1 hour, or until tender. When done, let remain covered about 15 minutes, then fold into the rice ¾ cup of pimiento (cut in ½-inch squares), ½ cup medium chopped parsley.

Turkish Pilaf (Rice with Mushrooms)

¼ cup butter or margarine
1 small green pepper, cut into ½-inch pieces
1 clove garlic, cut very fine or put through garlic press
1 cup fresh chopped mushrooms, or 1 small can (optional)
1 cup canned or fresh tomatoes

About 2 teaspoons salt, if using water, less if using stock
About ⅛ teaspoon black pepper
1 pound long grain white rice
About 2¼ cups vegetable or meat stock, or hot water with 1 bouillon cube if desired

In a heavy 2- or 3-quart saucepan melt the fat. Add green pepper, garlic, and mushrooms and sauté 5 minutes. Add tomatoes and seasonings, the rice, and 2¼ cups of hot water or stock. Stir only until mixed. Cover tightly; let come to a quick boil; then let it cook *slowly* over low heat about 25 to 30 minutes (depending on type of rice) or until tender, but not too soft. Do not uncover rice during cooking process, but stir it gently with a fork several times the last few minutes.

This rice is delicious served with chicken or any meat dish in place of potatoes.

Double Boiler Method. May be cooked in upper part of double boiler for about 1¼ hours, or until tender. If using double boiler, allow rice to come to a boil over direct heat, then place it over boiling water and cover. If it appears dry or firm when cooking time is up, pour a little more hot water (about ¼ cup) over rice and continue to cook a few minutes longer. When rice is done, shut off heat, and allow it to remain covered for about 20 minutes. This will fluff rice and loosen it from sides and bottom of pan.

Note. Majority of the rice growers today recommend cooking rice without washing and for a shorter time. If preferred, follow directions on package. Converted rice requires more liquid and longer cooking.

Chinese Rice—No. 1

1 pound of best-quality rice
About 3 ¼ cups hot water

1 teaspoon salt (optional)

Combine rice with hot water. Add salt. Cover saucepan tightly and bring to a quick boil. Lower heat and simmer slowly about 25 to 30 minutes, or until well puffed and dry. Keep heat very low and stir gently 2 or 3 times. If rice appears too firm toward end of cooking, sprinkle it with a little more hot water and continue to cook a few minutes longer. When rice is done, shut off heat and allow it to remain covered about 20 minutes. This will fluff up and loosen rice from bottom and sides of pan.

May also be cooked in double boiler about 1 hour or until tender (see directions page 312).

Chinese Rice—No. 2

In a 2-quart saucepan combine 1 cup rice with 2 cups cold water and about 1 teaspoon salt. Cover and bring to a good boil for about 1 minute. Lower heat and simmer about 14 minutes, or until rice is done.

For more details follow directions given on package. If using precooked or other types of rice, follow directions on package.

We prefer Method No. 1.

Fried Almonds and Rice

Serves 8 to 12

⅓ cup butter ·
¾ cup medium-size onion, chopped
½ cup medium-size green pepper, chopped
¼ cup medium-size pimiento, chopped
½ teaspoon garlic salt
½ teaspoon pepper
1 teaspoon salt
⅓ cup soy sauce
1 cup toasted slivered almonds
6 cups cooked rice

In a large skillet or saucepan heat butter; when hot add onion and green pepper and sauté about 3 or 4 minutes, or until tender. Add all other ingredients, mix well, and heat slowly about 10 minutes.

This may be served with any kind of meat, seafood, or poultry dish. It is an excellent side dish with a Chinese meal.

Salad Greens

Iceberg and other lettuces are the most frequently used salad greens. But when the following greens are plentiful, include them in your salads as often as possible, not only to improve your salads but because of their rich vitamin and mineral content. Never discard the outer green leaves of lettuce, romaine, curly endive, or other greens, as they are more nutritious than the inner ones. If they are not bruised or discolored, shred or cut fine and use them in salads, sandwiches, etc. Also include green celery tops in the salad bowl for extra flavor and vitamins. Salad greens, like other leafy and green vegetables, contain more vitamin C when fresh. Therefore, buy them as fresh as possible and keep in hydrator until ready to be used.

Vegetables Used as Salad Greens

Young raw spinach	Chinese or celery cabbage	Endive
Cabbage	Dandelion greens	Escarole
Watercress	Romaine	Radish tops

Spinach

Purchase only strictly fresh and crisp dark-green spinach. One pound fresh will give 1 cup cooked spinach. Remove roots and coarse stems and any wilted or discolored leaves. To draw out sand and dirt, wash several times in lukewarm water or until water appears free of grit. Place in a large saucepan without adding any water, as enough clings to spinach to produce steam. Cook in tightly covered saucepan over moderate heat until tender, about 5 or 6 minutes after steaming starts. Turn spinach several times while cooking. Serve as desired.

Spinach Pie

Prepare 4 pounds fresh spinach as above, or 4 packages frozen spinach according to directions on package. Drain very thoroughly, chop medium-fine, season with about 1 teaspoon salt, a little pepper, 2 tablespoons or more melted butter or margarine, a little grated or fine-chopped onion, onion salt, or garlic salt. Pour into 10-inch pie plate. Break 4 or 5 whole eggs, 1 at a time, directly on spinach, and cut through each egg with a fork. Bake at 350° F. about 30 minutes, or until eggs are set. Sprinkle with salt and a little pepper. Cut into wedges while in dish, and serve hot with meat or poultry.

Spinach, Broccoli, or Asparagus Mold

1 pound fresh pork sausage patties or ½ pound Brown 'N Serve Cooked Sausages (½ pound fresh mushrooms or 1 small can may be used instead of the sausage)	6 large whole eggs, slightly beaten
	½ cup homogenized milk
	3 cups cooked finely chopped spinach, broccoli, or asparagus, well drained, packed
½ cup finely chopped onion	4 (10 ounce) packages frozen vegetables (3 cups cooked)
¼ teaspoon nutmeg	
About 2 teaspoons salt	½ cup dry bread crumbs

We prefer the Brown 'N Serve Sausages. Simply cook them according to directions on package until brown, breaking them into small pieces. If using uncooked pork sausages cover them with warm water, bring gently to the simmering point. Allow to simmer about 5 minutes, breaking them into small pieces. Drain well, and then brown them on all sides over medium heat in a greased skillet, shaking pan, or turning sausages often to prevent bursting and sticking. Pour off fat as it accumulates in skillet. If using fresh mushrooms, wash, drain and dry them on a towel. Chop fine and sauté them in about 2 tablespoons butter or margarine. If using canned mushrooms, drain, chop and sauté them in 2 tablespoons butter or margarine. In 2 tablespoons sausage drippings or butter sauté the chopped onion for about 5 minutes.

In a large bowl, combine the cooked sausage *or* mushrooms and all other ingredients and with a spoon beat for a few seconds until thoroughly blended. Taste and season further if necessary. Grease bottom and sides of No. 11 (9 × 5 × 2¾ inches) bread pan thickly with 1 tablespoon of shortening, and line bottom and small ends of pan with a triple thickness of heavy wax paper, having paper come up about 1 inch higher than top of pan. Cut a sheet of wax paper about 14 inches long, then fold it into thirds. Grease paper with shortening. Pour mixture into pan and press down well as you pour. Place pan in a larger container of hot water and bake at 350° F. about 1¼ to 1½ hours, or until firm to the touch in center of mold. It sometimes takes a few minutes longer, depending on temperature of ingredients and water. When done, remove and let stand about 5 minutes, or if necessary it may remain in the hot water in oven with heat shut off and door partly open for about 15 minutes. To serve, loosen around sides and ends with a dinner knife all the way down to bottom of pan. Turn over onto platter carefully to prevent breaking. Peel off paper, garnish, etc.

To Serve. Unmold onto flat serving platter (oblong flat platter is preferable). Arrange additional cooked pork sausages around mold. Brush top and sides of mold with hot melted butter or sausage drippings. Cut 1 or 2 hard-cooked eggs lengthwise into 6 uniform sections and arrange on top of mold to simulate a flower. Form center of flower with a curled strip of red pimiento or a red maraschino cherry.

Serve as a main light luncheon, supper, or dinner dish, with a salad, French-fried Potatoes (page 301), and Cheese Sauce (below). Very attractive for a buffet party.

Cheese Sauce for Baked Vegetable Mold

¼ cup butter or margarine
¼ cup sifted all-purpose flour
2 cups warm milk

About 1 cup, more or less, freshly shredded cheddar or American cheese
About 1¼ teaspoons salt

Melt butter, add flour and mix until smooth. Add warm milk slowly. Cook over low heat until thick and smooth, stirring constantly. Add the cheese and salt, and continue to cook for several more minutes, or until cheese is fully melted and sauce is smooth. If sauce is too thick, add little more milk. Serve separately.

Spinach Supreme

Serves 4

2 packages frozen spinach	2 teaspoons lemon juice
2 tablespoons sauterne	½ teaspoon salt
1 teaspoon Worcestershire sauce	About ½ teaspoon pepper
2 tablespoons melted butter or margarine	

Cook spinach in a covered saucepan about 5 minutes or until done. Drain thoroughly. Combine other ingredients and pour over cooked spinach, tossing until thoroughly coated. Reheat and serve at once.

Hubbard Squash

Place cut squash, from which seeds have been removed, with skin side down in a saucepan, adding about 1 inch hot water. Cover, and let steam about 1 hour, or until tender when tested with a metal skewer or fork. Use moderate heat, and add more water whenever necessary to prevent scorching. Watch closely, and when tender remove carefully. Place on a baking sheet, brush well with soft butter, sprinkle with salt and brown sugar, and bake at 400° F. about 25 to 30 minutes, or until sugar has melted.

Baked Stuffed Summer Squash

Serves 4 to 6

2-pound squash	or leftover meat or poultry
Butter or margarine	¼ cup pimiento, cut into ½-inch squares
Salt	
Garlic salt or onion salt	⅓ cup pulled fresh crumbs
¼ cup shortening	About 1 teaspoon salt
1 small green pepper, cut into 2-inch strips	¼ teaspoon black pepper
	¼ teaspoon black pepper
1 small onion, cut lengthwise into ½-inch slices	¼ cup shredded American or parmesan cheese
½ pound (1 cup) freshly ground meat	

Wash squash well; do not peel. Place in a saucepan with about 1 inch of boiling water. Cover pan, and steam gently on 1 side about 10 to 15 minutes; turn over carefully and steam about 10 to 15 minutes more. Squash should be crisply tender, or it will break in baking. When done, let stand until cool enough to handle. Remove a slice from top; scoop out pulp. Discard seeds. Cut pulp into small pieces. Place squash in a baking dish, brush entire surface well with melted butter or margarine, and sprinkle with a little salt and a little garlic or onion salt.

To Make Stuffing. Sauté green pepper and onion in ¼ cup, or less, shortening. Cook about 5 minutes. Then add meat. Cook until meat is nicely brown, about 7 or 8 minutes. Add squash pulp that has been cut into small pieces; mix well. Last, add pimiento and pulled crumbs. Season with salt and black pepper. Stuff squash with this mixture. Sprinkle top with cheese, and bake about 30 minutes at 350° F. Place under broiler several minutes and serve hot.

This makes an excellent main luncheon or supper dish.

Baked Acorn Squash

Cut squash in halves lengthwise. Remove seeds, and brush with melted butter; place on well greased baking sheet with cut side down. Bake at 400° F. about 45 minutes to 1 hour, or until tender when tested with metal skewer. When tender, turn right side up; brush again with melted butter, and sprinkle thickly with brown sugar and a little salt. Continue to bake with right side up about 15 minutes longer, or until sugar is fully melted. Acorn squash may first be steamed about 30 minutes, then baked like Hubbard squash. Serve additional melted butter separately. May be placed under broiler for a few minutes at 450° F.

Tomatoes

Select tomatoes of bright-red color, firm, smooth, and of medium size. Wash well, dry, and keep in hydrator until ready to be used. They are best eaten raw, in salads or with center scooped out with a spoon and filled with fine-cut vegetables, fish, or meat salads.

To Peel Tomatoes. Submerge into boiling water about ½ minute. Pour cold water over them at once, and remove skins.

Stewed Tomatoes

Peel tomatoes as above; cut into quarters or eighths; place in a saucepan. For each pound tomatoes add 1 tablespoon fine-chopped onion and 1 tablespoon sugar, or less. Cover, and cook about 10 minutes, stirring occasionally. Toward end, season with salt and a little butter, and serve hot as a vegetable.

Fresh Grilled Parmesan Tomatoes au Gratin

8 servings

4 medium-size firm tomatoes (about 2½ to 2¾ inches wide)	¾ cup dry bread crumbs (not too dark)
¼ cup very warm melted butter or margarine	2 tablespoons grated Italian cheese
Salt and pepper	½ teaspoon crushed oregano leaves, or ¼ teaspoon powder

Remove thin slice from top and bottom of each tomato, then cut each into 2 uniform slices. Place cut tomatoes on greased flat baking sheet. Drizzle top of each with about 1 teaspoon warm melted butter or margarine. Sprinkle lightly with little salt and pepper. Now add the crumbs, grated cheese and oregano (mixed together) a little at a time to the very warm melted butter, and with a fork blend thoroughly. Cover top of each tomato slice with 1½ tablespoons crumb preparation, having it slightly rounded in center. Bake in a 400° F. oven about 5 minutes, then place under broiler at 400° F. about 2 inches from heat, for about 5 minutes, or until crumbs are well browned. Remove from heat, and sprinkle top center of each with pinch chopped parsley or green onion stems. Serve around Beef Wellington (page 134), with short thick spears of seasoned broccoli in between tomatoes (or as desired). Serve Sauce Bearnaise (page 341) separately for vegetables.

Stuffed Glazed Tomato Slices

Serves 8

Cut in halves crosswise 4 medium-size tomatoes (or use thick slices of canned aspic). Cook 1 package of mixed frozen vegetables until just tender, blanch at once with cold water, to retain color, drain well. Marinate in ¼ cup clear French Dressing (page 368). Add ½ cup of leftover glaze (page 239) and a few pieces of pimiento for additional color to vegetables. Refrigerate vegetables for several hours, then pick up with a spoon and mound on each slice of tomato. Place them on a rack with drip pan underneath. Pour some of remaining glaze (consistency of unbeaten egg white) over top more than once if necessary. Refrigerate for at least several hours. May be prepared day in advance.

Vegetables Vinaigrette

Peel and cut fresh carrots into about 3-inch-thick wedges. Cook them in small amount of water in tightly covered pan for about 10 minutes, after simmering begins, or until crisply tender. Cook broccoli or asparagus in about 1 inch of water, covered, for 7 or 8 minutes, but watch not to overcook. Pinch of soda may be added to green vegetable to intensify color. As soon as done, place them into a large pot of ice water to keep green color. Drain well. When carrots and green vegetables are well drained, cover with Vinaigrette Tarragon Dressing (page 336), turning them several times. Carrots may remain in dressing for many hours. Prepare green vegetable in dressing not more than ½ hour before serving, or they are likely to lose color.

White Turnips

Purchase smooth, firm, medium-size turnips with fresh green tops. Wash and keep in hydrator until ready to be used. Pare, slice, or cut into thick pieces. Place in enough boiling unsalted water to cover, and cook in an open kettle about 30 to 50 minutes, or until tender. Drain well; mash. Season with salt, pepper, and butter. Or sauté slices or pieces in melted butter or margarine and season to taste.

Rutabagas may be prepared like white turnips.

Zucchini Stew

Purchase medium-size zucchini that weigh about ½ pound each. Wash well under cool water, dry, and cut off about ½ inch from both ends. *Do not peel.* When zucchini are fresh their skins are tender and palatable. Peeling spoils their attractiveness and flavor. They may be sliced crosswise in ½ inch thickness, or we prefer to cut the whole zucchini lengthwise in 2 pieces (4 if they are very large), then crosswise into 2-inch chunks.

For each zucchini weighing ½ pound, melt 2 tablespoons butter or other fat until very hot, and sauté vegetable pieces until brown on white sides; then add 1 medium onion, sliced thin lengthwise, and 1 medium fresh green pepper cut in 1-inch narrow strips (pepper may be omitted), and cook about 3 minutes tightly covered over very low heat, or until zucchini is crisply tender. Now add ½ cup *well*-drained canned or fresh tomatoes, cut in about ½-inch pieces, ½ teaspoon salt, ⅛ teaspoon thyme or oregano leaves crushed, and ⅛ teaspoon pepper, and continue to cook uncovered only until they begin to simmer, for 2 or 3 minutes. Taste and season further before serving in a vegetable dish, with meat, poultry, or fish.

Company-Style Zucchini Stew in Casserole

Serves 4

Prepare double recipe of basic Zucchini Stew (above) for an 8-inch flat baking dish; 3 recipes for a 9 or 10 inch size. After stew has been seasoned and has started to simmer, pour into buttered baking dish. Sprinkle top with fresh pulled white bread crumbs (dry may be used) and about 2 or 3 tablespoons grated Italian cheese. Drizzle entire surface with 3 or 4 tablespoons warm melted butter or margarine, place it under broiler set at 450° F. until crumbs are brown and crisp, about 3 inches from heat, if ingredients are hot, but watch closely as it may take only 3 or 4 minutes.

If casserole was prepared in advance and is cold, best to bake it first at 450° F. for about 10 minutes. If necessary place under broiler for several minutes to brown crumbs.

Broiled Zucchini Halves

For two ½-pound zucchini, remove ½ inch from both ends, cut each with a long knife into halves. *Do not peel.* Add 1 teaspoon salt to 1 cup of hot water in a deep skillet or saucepan. Bring to a boil, then lower zucchini halves gently into water, cover pan and simmer vegetable slowly about 7 to 10 minutes, depending on the freshness. Best to test with point of a paring knife through the green skin after 7 minutes. If you can penetrate this thick area easily, remove from heat, and pour cold water into pot. Drain zucchini carefully to prevent breakage. Brush entire surface top and bottom with melted butter or margarine.

To Bake or Broil. Place zucchini on a heatproof serving dish or other utensil. Pour about ¼ inch water into dish. Now pour about 1 teaspoon or a bit more of melted butter or margarine on top surface. Sprinkle lightly with salt, pepper, crushed oregano leaves, and grated Italian cheese. Last, place a scant tablespoon of crushed drained tomatoes (canned or fresh, cut in half pieces) on each, and sprinkle again lightly with grated Italian cheese.

About 30 minutes before serving (or sooner) bake casserole in a preheated 450° F. oven for about 10 minutes if ingredients are warm; 15 minutes if have been refrigerated. Last, place under broiler set at 450° F. for several minutes, but watch closely not to scorch topping. Serve right from casserole, or each zucchini may be picked up with a spatula or pancake turner and arranged around meat or poultry. Allow 1 whole zucchini cut in halves lengthwise for 2 servings.

Note. For more delicious zucchini recipes see Italian Dishes (page 758).

▶ Sauces and Gravies

FOR MEATS, FISH, POULTRY, AND VEGETABLES

A WELL-PREPARED SAUCE OR GRAVY ADDS RICHNESS AND THE FINISHING TOUCH to meats, fish, poultry, and vegetables. To be perfect, it must be smooth, glossy, and distinctive in flavor. Good gravy is not only delicious in itself, but enhances the flavor of the meat or the starchy food with which it is served.

Gravy usually accompanies roast and braised meats, or poultry, some pan-broiled meats, fried chicken. A considerable amount of the vitamins and minerals of the meat may be leached out into the gravy, and unless all meat juices are used, even those from broiled meats, much of the nutritive value is wasted.

To Deglaze—means to blend in required amount of liquid with the meat drippings in pan after most of fat has been removed. Rich drippings and juices are dissolved in the liquid. This operation is the usual basic step in preparing a sauce or gravy for fried, sautéed, or roasted meats and poultry.

To Degrease—means to remove surplus fats from surface of boiling or cold liquids. An easy way to do this is to pour the hot liquid into a transparent glass cup or bowl and let it stand a few minutes so that the fat rises to the surface. Then with a large spoon remove fat from surface, and also tilt utensil so that a thicker amount of fat will accumulate on one side, making it easier to remove. If you have time to chill the liquid, the fat congeals on the surface, and can be removed easily.

Thickened Gravies and Sauces

There are two ways of preparing a thickened gravy or sauce. One is the conventional method where the lukewarm or cool stock or other liquid called for is added *slowly* to the cooked flour and butter (called a Roux). The second method is to bring the liquid to a boil or simmering point and *immediately* add it *all at once* (not little at a time) to the Roux. In either method the preparation must be stirred at once and constantly over medium heat until thick and smooth, preferably with a wire whisk. Then let simmer about 3 to 5 minutes. A large wooden spoon may be used to stir sauces, but a wire whisk is indispensable in producing smooth gravies in a quick time. The small household-style wire whisk is available in all hardware stores and houseware departments of large stores.

Note. The second, quicker method may be used in the preparation of all gravies, sauces, glazes, and similar preparations throughout our book that do not contain eggs or yolks. Follow direction in recipes where eggs or yolks are indicated.

In home cooking there are 2 ingredients to thicken gravies—with all-purpose flour or with cornstarch. Cornstarch has twice the thickening power of flour, and it also produces a more translucent gravy. In oriental cooking cornstarch is used to thicken the various sauces and gravies. We also prefer to use it in some of our recipes instead of flour to produce a gloss. Please use amount of thickening agent recommended in each recipe, then if you prefer a thicker gravy or sauce increase amount of flour or starch; if a thinner consistency is preferred, reduce amount.

An easy way to combine flour or cornstarch with water or stock for some gravies and sauces is to pour required amount of cool liquid in a small or medium jar first, then add the flour or starch. Cover tightly and shake vigorously for about ½ minute, or until smooth. Now add to other ingredients as indicated in recipe. Cook until thick, then simmer about 5 minutes.

Browned Flour for Sauces and Gravies

Browned flour adds flavor and color to gravies. A large amount can be browned on a baking sheet in a 400° F. oven in about 15 minutes. Stir it after the first 7 or 8 minutes, releasing it from the edges where it browns more quickly to keep it uniform in color. When it reaches a golden color (not too dark) remove it from oven, let cool, and store in a closed container. Note that browned flour has less thickening power than white, therefore use double amount, or less, called for in gravies made with white flour. Taste browned flour after it has cooled. Do not use if it has a bitter taste. Watch it closely the last few minutes to prevent overbrowning.

To Avoid Formation of "Skin"

Sauces and gravies which are not served immediately after they are prepared form a skin.

To avoid this some cookbooks suggest floating melted butter on the surface; some suggest water; others suggest floating milk or stock. We have not found these suggestions very successful. We have had excellent results, however, by *immediately* placing a sheet of heavy wax paper over open pot and *at once* covering it tightly. The paper will form a tight seal and exclude any air from entering. The pot cover alone will not do it. This is a very simple procedure if you have the paper and cover ready. The sauce or gravy will remain quite hot for at least 15 minutes.

If you wish to prepare sauce or gravy long in advance, proceed with the wax paper and cover, then place gravy pot into another utensil with simmering water. Never keep it over direct heat. Gravies and sauces are safe stored this way provided internal temperature is 150° F. or over. If you do not wish to use this simple method, be sure to stir gravy from the very beginning several times and keep it over simmering water. Gravies made with cornstarch must *not* be stirred too often and too briskly, as they are likely to become thin.

Leftover gravies and sauces can be refrigerated or frozen. They will appear very thick after they are cold. Before adding extra liquid, place pot over *very* low heat (or simmering water), and as soon as bottom of gravy begins to soften, stir it gently, and increase heat slightly, but stay with it, stirring it often. After it is heated, do not let simmer for more than 1 minute, or it is likely to break down and become thin. If it is too thick, add a little liquid; if too thin, add some Kneaded Butter (page 324), and simmer for another 2 minutes, not longer.

Butter or Margarine for Browning

If using plain (unclarified) butter or margarine, melt it over low heat and do not add food *until butter foams up and the foam starts* to subside. At this point watch it closely and as soon as butter *begins to color lightly* (but is not brown) add the food to be sautéed 1 piece at a time, leaving a space between each piece, and cook as directed in recipe. Keep heat low to prevent burning.

Butter combined with part salad oil or shortening is heated the same way, and is preferable to butter alone, unless the butter has been clarified. Clarified butter alone or combined with oil can withstand more heat and is recommended in sautéing and frying foods that require more than several minutes of cooking. (See page 328.)

The foods to be sautéed must be dry on the surface. Remove any noticeable moisture with paper toweling—unless the article is coated with flour or crumbs. Moisture will prevent the food from browning.

Important. For all sauces and gravies, use a heavy-bottomed pan to prevent scorching on the bottom. Where we do not suggest sifting required amount of all-purpose flour, loosen floor with a spoon, then measure. During the cold months when heat is used in the homes and the humidity is low, you will find that it requires a little less flour or cornstarch in preparing gravies. A thick gravy or sauce is easily corrected by adding a little more liquid after sauce has thickened. If gravies and sauces are too thin, at any time, please follow directions for Kneaded Butter or Margarine.

Kneaded Butter or Margarine

This is an excellent simple mixture of flour and slightly softened butter or margarine to have on hand, refrigerated (or may be frozen), to thicken thin sauces, gravies, and some cream soups, at the end of the cooking process, or at any time a thin precooked preparation requires thickening after it has been reheated.

To Prepare. Combine slightly softened butter or margarine with an equal amount or a bit more of all-purpose flour, and with a heavy spoon cream it together until smooth and well blended. Large amounts may be prepared with an electric mixer. Either form balls with a tablespoon of the preparation, or measure by tablespoon on a flat pan covered with wax paper. Refrigerate, and when firm, keep it covered in a plastic bag. May be kept for at least 2 weeks, or frozen for a longer time.

How to Use. Simply drop 1 or 2 balls or spoonfuls into each cup of unthickened hot liquid, and at once stir constantly until preparation is smooth and thick, then simmer about 3 to 5 minutes. Do not add kneaded butter or margarine to preparations that require long simmering. To a thin sauce always add it the last few minutes. Do not continue to cook for more than 2 minutes if the sauce was previously cooked.

The conventional method of thickening hot thin sauces and gravies with flour mixed with water causes lumping, and straining is usually required. Kneaded butter and margarine with flour, however, will blend smoothly in the hot preparation immediately as the fat melts, but it must be stirred continuously from the beginning until thickened.

▶ BROWN SAUCES ◀

Brown Roux (for Brown Gravies and Sauces)

A roux is a very convenient preparation to have on hand and can be prepared weeks in advance if you do a great deal of cooking. To prepare a roux, combine an equal amount of butter or margarine with an equal amount of all-purpose flour (standard measurements), and cook over very low heat in a saucepan until brown, but not scorched. This will take about 3 minutes. Stir preparation often to keep it smooth and prevent burning on the bottom. Let cool, and store in a covered container in the refrigerator, or use at once.

To make gravy with a roux, add 1 cup of stock, water, or milk to 2 or

3 tablespoons of roux. Blend until smooth and cook until thick, then simmer for about 3 to 5 minutes. Add seasonings.

Brown Gravies (for General Purposes)

Good gravy is not difficult to make if directions are followed. For a delicious quick gravy, prepare as follows: For each cup of gravy, brown lightly 2 or 3 tablespoons of butter or margarine over very low heat in a small heavy-bottom saucepan. Now add 2 or 3 tablespoons of all-purpose flour, stir and cook over low or medium heat for 2 or 3 minutes, or until roux is brown, but not scorched. *Slowly* add 1 cup lukewarm stock (or water combined with instant bouillon) or brown drippings and liquid from a roast or braised meat. Or for a quicker method, bring liquid to boiling or simmering point, and add it *all at one time* to the roux. For either method, *immediately* stir and cook over medium heat until thick and smooth, then simmer about 5 minutes. Add about ¼ teaspoon salt, if needed, a little pepper, or any other seasonings called for in recipe.

Note. Drippings from roasted or braised meats are oftentimes scant and not very dark for good gravy. In this case, a little commercial gravy coloring may be added. Browned flour loses part of its thickening power, therefore increase amount if a thick gravy is preferred.

If too much fat is used, gravy or sauce will curdle or separate, making it very undesirable. Most of fat must be removed from drippings in roasting pan, leaving about 1 tablespoon for each cup of gravy to be made. If curdling should occur, it may be corrected by adding about ¼ cup of water combined with a teaspoon of cornstarch slowly to the curdled gravy, stirring continuously until gravy is smooth, then simmer for about 1 more minute. Do not cook further, or it is likely to become thin. Always taste gravies before serving, and if too bland, a little instant bouillon and dry wine always add flavor and color, especially if water is used instead of stock or drippings.

Gravy au Jus

This type of gravy is never thickened. It is made from the drippings and residue left on the rack and drip pan in the broiler, or from drippings left from roasted, fried, or pan-broiled meat and poultry. All surplus grease should be skimmed off with a tablespoon, then a *small* amount of water or preferably stock is poured over the racks or into the pan with any browned residue, and the pan or rack is carefully scraped with a wooden spoon to loosen the particles. When all this residue is released, the rack may be taken off the roasting or broiling pan. Now you stir the gravy over low heat until all particles are dissolved. Taste to decide if gravy must be concentrated for better flavor, or if more hot liquid is needed. Season if necessary; heat to boiling point, strain it, and serve at once in a gravy dish.

Thickened Brown Gravy

When roasted meat is done, remove it from pan, and keep it out of draft. Prepare gravy by adding hot water or stock to drippings, stir well to release as much of the color as possible, as suggested for Gravy Au Jus. Now pour the unthickened gravy into a large glass Pyrex cup. Let stand a minute or two until fat settles on top. Remove most of fat, leaving about 1 tablespoon or less for each cup of gravy to be thickened. For a medium thickened gravy, in a small saucepan mix 3 tablespoons of all-purpose flour combined with ¼ cup cool water, until smooth, for each cup of gravy to be made. Bring liquid to the boiling point, and add it *all at one time* to the flour preparation, stirring continuously over medium heat until thick and smooth, then simmer about 5 minutes. Taste and add salt, pepper, and a little gravy coloring if needed. Sautéed mushrooms and a little dry wine may be added, then simmer 2 or 3 minutes longer. Increase flour for a very thick gravy; use less for a thinner gravy.

Mushroom Gravy

Pour about 2 tablespoons of drippings from meat (or you can use 2 tablespoons butter) into a small or medium size saucepan. Sauté 1 cup sliced or chopped fresh mushrooms and 1 tablespoon finely cut onion in the hot fat for several minutes, turning to brown evenly. Add 3 tablespoons cornstarch diluted in ¼ cup cool water to the sautéed vegetables. Now add 2 cups of very hot (simmering point) vegetable or meat stock *all at one time*, and immediately cook over medium heat until thick and smooth, stirring all the time. Simmer about 5 minutes. A little gravy coloring may be added, if needed, and about ¼ cup of dry wine. Simmer again for about 2 minutes. For additional color, you can add 2 tablespoons canned pimiento, cut into ½-inch squares, and ¼ cup fresh green onion and stems, cut ½ long, without cooking further. This will make about 2 cups of delicious gravy that can be served with any meat or poultry.

Gravy for Pot Roast of Beef

Remove meat and most of fat from drippings in pan. Floured meats usually thicken gravy sufficiently. Add stock or other liquid if necessary, taste and season further. If a thicker gravy is desired, simply add 1 or 2 tablespoons of the Kneaded Butter (page 324) and stir immediately until smooth and thick, then simmer about 5 minutes. A little dry wine and gravy coloring may be added before simmering begins, if needed. This gravy can be used with any floured braised meat dish.

▶ WHITE SAUCES ◀

In every-day cookery the white sauces occupy a more important place than the brown. They are made quickly with a white roux (butter and flour cooked together) and the addition of milk, cream, or white stock. They are used for creaming fish, eggs, chicken, veal, and vegetables. They are also the base of soufflés, cream soups, and au gratin preparations.

Two sauces form the basis of all white sauces—Veloute Sauce and Bechamel Sauce. They are both made from a flour and butter roux as thickening agent. Bechamel is made with milk or part cream, with the addition of herbs and other flavorings. Sauce Veloute is made the same way, using chicken, veal, or fish stock, often combined with some cream or milk, and seasoned with herbs, and sometimes a little wine.

There are many versions of these two basic white sauces, and any changes in ingredients gives the sauce a different name. They are also often enriched with additional butter, cream, and egg yolks. Detailed directions are given with each recipe.

How to Enrich Sauces With Egg Yolks. To prevent the yolks from curdling the sauce, we suggest that you beat the yolk or yolks first with a fork, then add a little cool milk, cream, or water, about a tablespoon for each yolk, and blend well. Stir a little of the hot sauce into the yolks, and pour the yolk mixture slowly into the hot sauce, stirring as you pour. Simmer, and use as suggested in recipe.

White Roux

Combine an equal amount of melted butter with an equal amount of all-purpose flour, and cook over low heat for about 2 or 3 minutes, *without browning*, stirring all the time. Now add the warm milk slowly, and continue to stir. Cook until thick and smooth, then simmer for several minutes.

Or you can scald the milk and add it all at one time to the cooked warm Roux, and immediately beat with a wire whisk until thick and smooth, then simmer several minutes. This second method is quick and works easily.

Thin White Sauce

1 tablespoon butter or margarine
1 tablespoon flour

1 cup warm milk
About ¼ teaspoon salt

Melt butter over low heat. Add the flour, stir and cook together for about 2 minutes, but do not allow it to brown. Now add the warm milk slowly, stirring all the time, and cook until thick, then simmer several minutes.

Or you can scald milk and add it all at one time to the cooked roux, and immediately beat with a wire whisk until smooth, then simmer for several minutes.

Medium White Sauce

Use 2 tablespoons butter or margarine, 2 tablespoons flour, 1 cup warm milk, ¼ teaspoon salt. Follow directions given for Thin White Sauce.

Thick White Sauce

Use 3 tablespoons butter or margarine, 3 tablespoons flour, 1 cup warm milk, ¼ teaspoon salt. Follow directions given for Thin White Sauce.

▶ HOT BUTTER SAUCES ◀

Many delectable foods are served with plain or seasoned hot butter instead of gravies and sauces. To prevent heated butter from burning, it is always best to clarify it, which is a very simple operation (see below). If you use the clarified butter often, a large amount can be prepared at one time and refrigerated for at least 2 weeks in a closed container, or it may be frozen for several months.

Clarified butter is always preferable for sautéing breast of chicken or turkey and many other delicate foods where the milky residue from plain butter would cause sticking and scorching, imparting a very undesirable taste to the cooked food. If you prefer to use butter without clarifying it for these purposes, it is safer to combine the butter with part salad oil or shortening. The butter will add flavor, and the shortening or oil will help to prevent scorching. The finest chefs use part oil in sautéing most foods.

In most cases it is better to combine plain butter or even the clarified butter with unsalted shortening or oil for foods that require more than a few minutes to cook.

Clarified Butter

Cut butter up into pieces and place it in a heavy-bottomed saucepan over very low heat, and do not stir. Let stand a few minutes, or until foam rises to top and butter is completely melted, being careful not to allow butter to color. Skim off the foam with a tablespoon, but leave pot over *very low heat* until no more foam rises, and all residue sinks to bottom of pan. With a tablespoon remove clear yellow fat, without picking up any of the residue at the bottom, pour into a container, and store in refrigerator, covered, if not to be used within a few minutes.

Most chefs do not discard the foam and residue removed from the clarified butter. They use it to enrich sauces and soups, and it can be kept refrigerated for at least 2 weeks or it may be frozen for several months. Hot clarified butter is often used plain on cooked lobster and other seafood without combining it with other ingredients.

Brown or Black Butter Sauce

¾ cup clarified butter
1 tablespoon or more white wine vinegar, or lemon juice

2 tablespoons chopped parsley, chives, or green onion stems
1 or more tablespoons capers (optional)

For best results, use clarified butter for this butter sauce. The sediment in unclarified butter will burn easily and make sauce speckled and bitter.

Heat clarified butter very slowly over low to medium heat until dark brown, but do not burn. Taste it. At once stir in the vinegar or lemon juice, parsley, chives, or green onion stems, and the capers if desired. Stir well and serve hot. Best not to combine ingredients until you are ready to serve sauce, but can be reheated carefully if necessary.

This sauce can be used on eggs, fish, seafood, asparagus, broccoli, etc.

▶ SPECIAL SAUCES AND GRAVIES ◀

Sauce Amandine

Drop ½ cup of shelled almonds into boiling water, and simmer several minutes, drain well, and let cool a few minutes. Remove skins, and slice almonds lengthwise. Sauté in ½ cup hot butter *over very low heat* for about 5 minutes, stirring continuously until golden brown. Season with about ½ teaspoon salt and mix well. Serve hot over fish or vegetables. May be prepared in advance and reheated over very low heat for a few seconds.

Maitre d'Hôtel Butter

Allow ½ cup butter to stand in room temperature about 30 minutes. With a heavy spoon or electric mixer, beat butter until creamy for about 1 minute. Add 2 tablespoons lemon juice, a little at a time, 1 tablespoon very finely chopped parsley, ⅛ teaspoon white pepper, ¼ teaspoon salt, and ½ teaspoon prepared mustard. Blend well. Very delicious on broiled, baked, or fried fish or vegetables.

Sauce for Chicken Tetrazzini

⅔ cup sifted all-purpose flour
½ cup melted butter
1 cup warm milk or cream
2 cups warm chicken stock

1½ teaspoons salt
2 tablespoons dry sauterne or sherry wine

Blend flour into melted butter, gradually add milk or cream and chicken stock, stirring constantly. Cook until thick and smooth, then simmer 5 minutes, adding salt and wine toward end. Let cool about 15 minutes before pouring over top of Chicken Tetrazzini (page 782). If too thick, add 1 or 2 tablespoons of milk.

Sauce Parisienne

Melt ⅓ cup butter or margarine; add ⅔ cup sifted all-purpose flour, then gradually add 2¾ cups of chicken stock or cream. (Measure chicken stock, add enough cream to make 2¾ cupfuls.) Mix well; place over moderate heat and let come to simmering point. Then add 1 teaspoon salt and let cook gently 5 minutes. Let sauce cool about 20 minutes, stirring it several times, before pouring over food such as broccoli and chicken. If too thick add little liquid.

Cheese Sauce for Baked Vegetable Mold

¼ cup butter or margarine
¼ cup sifted all-purpose flour
2 cups warm milk

About 1 cup, more or less, of freshly shredded cheddar or American cheese
About 1¼ teaspoons salt

Melt butter, add flour and mix until smooth. Add warm milk slowly. Cook over low heat until thick and smooth, stirring constantly. Add the cheese and salt, and continue to cook for several more minutes or until cheese is fully melted and sauce is smooth. If sauce is too thick, add little more milk. Serve separately with Baked Vegetable Mold (page 314).

Glazy Gravy for Roasted Turkey

Combine neck, gizzard, cut-up stalk of celery and carrot, ¼ cup parsley, 1 small cup-up onion, and 1 bay leaf in a medium-sized saucepan. Add 6 cups of cold water and 1 tablespoon salt. Cover and cook slowly for several hours, or until gizzard is tender. When done, strain. Remove most of fat from drippings in roasting pan, leaving about 1 tablespoon for each cup of gravy to be made. Add the strained stock to drippings, measure, and for each cup add about 1½ tablespoons of cornstarch dissolved in 2 tablespoons of cool water. Cook until thick and simmer until clear, about 5 minutes if using cornstarch. If gravy appears too thick, thin out with a little more liquid. Taste gravy and season further if necessary. Brush turkey with this gravy just before serving to impart an attractive glaze. A little commercial gravy coloring may be added if a darker gravy is preferred.

Chicken Pan Gravy

½ cup fresh mushrooms, chopped fine (or ¼ cup canned)
¼ cup finely chopped onion
Left-over drippings from prepared chicken, or about ¼ cup additional butter or margarine
¼ cup sifted all-purpose flour
2 cups chicken stock (made from neck, gizzard, etc.), or add 2

chicken bouillon cubes to 2 cups boiling water (milk may be used instead of water to make gravy)
Salt, and pepper to taste, if needed
A little commercial gravy coloring, if desired
1 or 2 tablespoons light dry wine (optional)

Sauté the chopped mushrooms and onion in leftover drippings or additional butter for several minutes. Add flour and continue to cook for 2 or 3 minutes. Add stock slowly and blend well. Cook until thick, sitrring continuously, and simmer about 5 minutes. Taste and season further if necessary. Add gravy coloring and wine if desired, and cook about 2 more minutes. This very delicious pan gravy can be prepared for any of our chicken dishes.

Gravy from Chicken Stock

Cover gizzard and neck with 2 or more cups cold water. Add 1 teaspoon salt, 1 small bay leaf, one small sliced onion, and ¼ cup celery. Cook in covered saucepan about 1 to 1½ hours, or until gizzard is tender. When done, strain. Remove surplus fat from drippings in roasting pan if necessary. Add 1½ tablespoons or less cornstarch, combined with 2 tablespoons water (2 tablespoons flour may be used instead) to drippings for each cup of gravy to be made. Now add the lukewarm strained stock, and with a fluffy beater or spoon blend well. Cook until thick and simmer about 5 minutes. Taste and season further, if necessary. Giblets may be cut up and added to gravy. A little commercial gravy coloring may be added for additional color.

Sauce Poulet for Chicken Alfredo

1¼ cups rich chicken stock (bouillon
   cubes may be used)
2 tablespoons light wine
1 small bay leaf

1 tablespoon celery or celery leaves,
   chopped fine
1 small piece onion
½ teaspoon salt

Combine all ingredients and simmer in a covered saucepan about 15 minutes. Strain, measure, and for *each cup stock,* melt 2 tablespoons butter, add ¼ cup fine-chopped mushrooms and 2 tablespoons fine-chopped fresh green onions, and sauté about 5 minutes. Add 2 tablespoons flour (or 1 tablespoon cornstarch) and blend well. Add stock slowly and cook until thick; then simmer about 5 minutes. Season further if necessary. Serve separately with Chicken Alfredo (page 779).

Gravy for Chicken Legs

Remove meat from drippings in pan and place it in a very slow oven or skillet over very low heat to keep hot until gravy is made. Remove most of fat from drippings. Add the desired amount of stock or water to drippings and blend well. To each cup of liquid add about 3 tablespoons of flour combined with ⅓ cup cool water until smooth. Cook until thick, then simmer about 5 minutes.

For a Glazy Gravy. Use 1½ tablespoons of cornstarch combined with 2 tablespoons water for each cup of liquid. More or less flour or cornstarch may be used, depending on thickness of gravy desired. Add a little commercial gravy coloring and seasoning to gravy during simmering process, if required. Two tablespoons dry wine and about ¼ cup of sautéed mushrooms may be add the last 2 minutes for additional flavor.

Special Orange Glaze for Sweet Potato Fluff

¾ cup brown sugar, solidly packed
1 cup orange juice, combined with 1
   tablespoon cornstarch

Rind of a small orange, and 2 tablespoons of butter

Combine all ingredients in a small saucepan. Blend well and bring to boiling point. Let simmer 5 minutes, or until clear. Pour this glaze into heatproof glass bowl in center of Sweet Potato Fluff (page 414) casserole before baking.

Old-Fashioned Whole Cranberry Sauce

1 cup water
1 cup granulated sugar

2 cups whole washed cranberries

Combine water with sugar. Mix well and boil gently 5 minutes. Add the 2 cups of whole washed cranberries and cook without stirring until the skins pop, about 5 minutes. Let cool before serving. May be prepared a day or two in advance and refrigerated as soon as cool.

Special French Dressing for Rock Cornish Hens Gourmet-Style

¼ cup wine vinegar
2 teaspoons paprika
½ teaspoon savory, rosemary, or oregano
1 teaspoon salt

½ teaspoon pepper
2 teaspoons sugar
1 clove garlic, cut in small pieces or put through garlic press
1 cup salad oil

Combine all ingredients except oil in a small bowl. With egg beater, beat for ½ minute until well blended. Add oil about 1 tablespoon at a time and continue to beat until emulsified. Keep in a jar with tight cover. Serve with Rock Cornish Hens Gourmet-Style (page 229). Shake well each time before using.

Gourmet Dressing for Salmon and Seafood Dishes

1 cup dairy sour cream
1 cup mayonnaise
¼ cup finely chopped green onion and stems
¼ cup lemon juice

1 teaspoon capers (optional)
½ cup finely chopped stuffed green olives
¼ teaspoon salt
2 teaspoons granulated sugar

Combine all ingredients in order given and blend well. Keep refrigerated until ready to serve.

Barbecue Sauce

1 medium-size onion, chopped fine
2 tablespoons shortening
1 cup catsup
1 cup water or stock from steamed ribs
2 tablespoons vinegar or ¼ cup lemon juice

1 tablespoon brown sugar
1 tablespoon Worcestershire sauce
¼ teaspoon dry mustard
1¼ teaspoons salt
¼ teaspoon or more red hot pepper
¼ teaspoon black pepper
¼ teaspoon celery seed

Sauté onion in the shortening for about 5 minutes. Add remaining ingredients except seasonings and cook in covered saucepan for about 20 minutes. Now add seasonings and continue to simmer about 10 more minutes. If sauce is too thick, add a little more stock, water, or vinegar. More or less seasonings may be added to suit taste. May be prepared days in advance and kept in refrigerator, or frozen. This is sufficient sauce for about 3 pounds of ribs or 2 small chickens.

Sauce Tartar

1 cup mayonnaise
1 small clove garlic, chopped very fine or put through garlic press
2 tablespoons fresh onion, chopped
¼ cup fresh green onion stems, chopped
2 tablespoons chopped pickle or pickle relish
2 tablespoons finely chopped stuffed green olives
1 or 2 tablespoons lemon juice or little less vinegar
1 tablespoon granulated sugar (optional)

Combine all ingredients, blend well. Keep in cool place (do not allow to freeze) until needed. Serve with any type of seafood.

Marinade for Seafood and Fish Fillets

2 tablespoons salad oil
2 tablespoons lemon juice or wine vinegar
½ teaspoon salt
⅛ teaspoon black pepper
⅛ teaspoon garlic salt
⅛ teaspoon dry tarragon (other herbs may be used)

Combine all ingredients and beat well with dover or fluffy beater for about 1 minute. Pour marinade over 1 pound of seafood or fillets and let stand for about 1 hour, covered, in a cool place. When ready to cook, pick up, drain and dip into batter or cover with crumb and egg, and deep-fry, according to directions given in recipes. Broiled fish is also delectable if marinated in this dressing for about 1 hour before broiling.

Special Hostess Sauce

1 cup chili sauce
½ cup catsup
¼ cup commercial horseradish
2 teaspoons Worcestershire sauce
1 small clove garlic, put through garlic press, or chopped fine

Mix all ingredients well and keep in covered jar in refrigerator at least 2 hours. Very delicious for shrimp and other seafood dishes.

Quick Tomato Sauce for Parmesan Veal Cutlets

In 2 tablespoons shortening sauté 1 tablespoon of finely chopped onion or 1 small clove of garlic. Add 6-ounce can of Italian-style tomato paste and 1 can of water. A teaspoon of instant bouillon or cube may be added. Season with about ¼ teaspoon salt, 2 tablespoons of grated Italian cheese, pinch of baking soda, a little nutmeg, all-spice, and pepper. Cook slowly in covered saucepan about 15 minutes. Add a little more water toward end of cooking if it becomes too thick. Should be the consistency of a medium custard. This amount of sauce will be sufficient for about 12 Parmesan Veal Cutlets (page 786). Extra sauce may be prepared and served separately. Simmer 15 minutes.

Note. See chapter in Italian Dishes for special sauces for spaghetti, ravioli, lasagna, etc.

Creole Sauce

2 tablespoons chopped onion
2 tablespoons chopped green pepper
2 tablespoons parsley, chopped medium
2 tablespoons finely chopped celery
¼ cup butter

6-ounce can Italian-style tomato paste
¾ cup water
1 bouillon cube (optional)
About ½ teaspoon salt
¼ teaspoon pepper
⅛ teaspoon baking soda

Sauté the onion, green pepper, parsley, and celery in the ¼ cup butter for about 5 minutes. Add the tomato paste, water, and seasonings. Cover and cook slowly about 20 minutes. Pour over Stuffed Whitefish (page 237) as suggested. Extra sauce may be prepared and served separately.

Tarragon Mayonnaise Dressing

2 cups mayonnaise
2 tablespoons, more or less, tarragon vinegar
¼ cup finely chopped stuffed green olives
¼ cup chopped fresh green onion
¼ cup chopped fresh green onion stems

1 tablespoon sugar (optional)
½ cup India relish, or chopped pickles
About 1 tablespoon, more or less, lemon juice
1 small clove garlic very finely chopped or put through garlic press
Salt to taste if necessary

Combine all ingredients and blend thoroughly. Serve this sauce on seafood, or separately.

Sauce Arnaud

2 tablespoons wine vinegar, or other vinegar
⅓ cup salad oil
1 tablespoon paprika
¼ cup prepared strong mustard
About 1 teaspoon, more or less, salt
1 cupful celery, chopped as fine as possible

½ cupful fresh green onion and tops, chopped as fine as possible
¼ cup parsley, chopped as fine as possible
1 clove garlic, chopped very fine or put through garlic press
More vinegar or lemon juice, as needed

Combine all ingredients in a bowl and blend thoroughly. It is important to add more vinegar or lemon juice to make spreading consistency, and not too oily. Use on shrimp, crab meat, or lobster.

Vinaigrette Tarragon Dressing

2 cups salad oil
½ cup cider vinegar
¼ cup tarragon vinegar
2 teaspoons salt

¼ teaspoon pepper
1 small clove garlic, sliced thin or put through garlic press

Combine all ingredients in a jar. Cover and shake well until thoroughly blended. Let stand in refrigerator for several hours and shake before using. Serve with Vegetables Vinaigrette (page 318).

Seafood Tartar Sauce

2 cups commercial mayonnaise
1 small clove garlic, chopped very fine or put through garlic press
⅓ cup fresh green onions, chopped very fine
½ cup fresh green onion stems, chopped very fine
¼ cup chopped pickles

¼ cup chopped green stuffed olives
¼ cup lemon juice
About 1 tablespoon granulated sugar
2 teaspoons plain gelatin, combined with ¼ cup cold water (stir gently and let stand until thick about 5 minutes; dissolve over simmering water)

Combine all ingredients except gelatin mixture. Dissolve gelatin and while warm stir into sauce and mix well. Chill in refrigerator for about 30 minutes, not longer, stirring every 5 minutes to keep at uniform consistency. Best not to prepare this sauce until needed. It will set if kept in refrigerator without stirring often. If it must be refrigerated, remove and let stand room temperature until soft before stirring to prevent curdling. This is a delicious sauce and may be used with any seafood salad or cooked fish.

Tartar Sauce

To 1 cup of mayonnaise, add 1 small clove of garlic chopped very fine (or put through garlic press), 2 tablespoons chopped fresh green onions, ¼ cup chopped green onion tops or chives, 2 tablespoons piccalilli, 2 tablespoons short pimiento strips, 1 tablespoon lemon juice, and 1 tablespoons granulated sugar. Stir until well mixed.

     Pour over 1 pound cooked lobster meat or shrimp. Serve in compartment dish; or very attractive if mounded in center of a serving platter. Spread top with a little extra mayonnaise or Tartar Sauce. Sprinkle with paprika, or garnish as desired. Arrange relishes, or slices of tomatoes, cucumber, etc., or crisp crackers around base.

Special Gingersnap-Raisin Sauce

6 small gingersnaps (⅓ cup crumbled)
½ cup brown sugar, solidly packed
¼ cup white vinegar
1 cup hot water
¼ teaspoon salt

1 very small lemon, or ½ large lemon, or 1 very small orange, cut into lengthwise pieces, then sliced crosswise into very thin slices
¼ cup seedless raisins

Combine all ingredients in a saucepan and bring to boiling point. Lower heat, and let simmer about 10 minutes, or until thick and transparent. For additional flavor 1 or 2 tablespoons curaçao may be added to this sauce. Serve with baked ham, smoked tongue, corned beef, etc.

Sweet-Sour Sauce—No. 1

¼ pound dry apricots, combined with 1 cup water and cooked until very soft (or use canned apricots)
¼ teaspoon salt

½ cup, more or less, granulated sugar
About ½ cup, more or less, cider or white vinegar

Cook apricots in water in covered saucepan very slowly about 30 minutes, or until very soft and most of water has been absorbed by apricots. When soft, put apricots through food mill.

Combine all ingredients and with egg beater, beat until smooth and thoroughly blended. Taste and season further if necessary. Serve with Cantonese Appetizers (pages 11–17). May be made days in advance and stored in covered jar in refrigerator.

Sweet-Sour Sauce—No. 2

¼ cup vinegar
½ cup pineapple juice
⅓ cup brown sugar, solidly packed

1½ tablespoons cornstarch, combined with 2 tablespoons water
About 1 teaspoon salt

Combine all ingredients in saucepan and bring to boiling point, stirring constantly. Let simmer about 5 minutes. Let cool and serve with Cantonese Appetizers (pages 11–17). May be made in advance. If sauce is too thick, thin out with pineapple juice or vinegar.

Hot Sauce

½ cup cool water
About 1½ tablespoons dry mustard, more or less, to suit taste

About ¾ cup catsup
About 1 teaspoon salt

Combine all ingredients and, with egg beater or large spoon, beat until smooth and thoroughly blended. Serve with Cantonese Appetizers (pages 11–17). May be made days in advance and stored in covered jar in refrigerator.

Mustard Sauce

To each cup mayonnaise, add 1 teaspoon dry mustard, 1 teaspoon sugar, 3 tablespoons prepared mustard, or enough to suit taste. Add a little lemon juice if too thick. Serve with Cantonese Appetizers (pages 11–17).

Lemon Sauce for Turkish Dolmas

2 tablespoons melted butter or margarine	About ½ teaspoon salt
	⅛ teaspoon white pepper
2 tablespoons all-purpose flour	About ¼ cup lemon juice, more or less
1 cup warm milk (less for thicker sauce)	to suit taste

In a 1-quart saucepan melt butter, add flour and stir until smooth. Add warm milk slowly. Simmer about 5 minutes. Add salt, pepper, and lemon juice slowly, and let simmer about 1 more minute. Serve warm or cool. May be refrigerated and reheated in top part of double boiler or over direct low heat, until warm. Serve with Turkish Dolmas (page 27), broccoli, fish, etc.

Special Thick Mushroom Sauce for Salisbury Steaks

2 tablespoons butter or margarine	3 tablespoons flour
¼ cup finely chopped canned mushrooms, or ½ cup fresh mushrooms	¾ cup milk

Sauté chopped mushrooms in the 2 tablespoons butter for several minutes. Add flour, mixing until smooth. Last add milk, and let simmer 3 or 4 minutes. Do not season. Use as directed in Salisbury Steaks recipe (page 145).

Pancho Dipping Sauce

3 (6 ounce) cans tomato sauce	⅛ teaspoon onion salt
¼ cup cider vinegar	1 teaspoon chili powder
1 teaspoon paprika	1 tablespoon cornstarch, combined
1 tablespoon brown sugar	with 1 tablespoon water (optional)
⅛ teaspoon celery salt	
⅛ teaspoon hot pepper	

Combine all ingredients except cornstarch and 1 tablespoon water. Stir well, and cook uncovered about 10 minutes. Add the cornstarch and water only if a thick sauce is preferred and simmer for several minutes. Serve in bowl in center of platter, surrounded with cooked shrimp. Sprinkle top of sauce with very finely chopped green onion or parsley for additional color.

Whipped Cream Brandy or Rum Sauce

¼ cup fresh egg whites
1 cup granulated sugar
¼ teaspoon cream of tartar
3 tablespoons cool water
⅛ teaspoon salt
½ teaspoon vanilla

½ teaspoon plain gelatin, combined with 2 tablespoons cold water
2 tablespoons brandy or rum
1 cup whipping cream, beaten just until it clings to bowl (not too stiff)

Combine egg whites, sugar, cream of tartar, the 3 tablespoons cool water, salt, and vanilla in upper part of small double boiler. Mix well with wooden spoon. Bring water in lower part to a boil, place upper part of boiler in position and at once beat (if using electric beater, remove double boiler from stove) until mixture is thick and clings to pan for 6 or 7 minutes. Remove top of boiler from water. Combine gelatin with 2 tablespoons cold water, let stand until thick, then dissolve over simmering water. Add brandy or rum to dissolved gelatin. At once add the gelatin and brandy mixture, a little at a time, to the sauce and beat by hand or with electric mixer *only* until well blended. Keep in refrigerator or cold place until cool —about 1 hour—but let stand only until cool or else it will become too thick, in which case stir well with a spoon over hot water. Then fold it, little at a time, into the whipped cream.

Keep sauce in refrigerator until ready to be served. May be prepared hours in advance. *Do not omit* gelatin or liquor will separate from other ingredients. This sauce should always be stirred gently for a few seconds before serving to insure smoothness.

Meat Marinade for Beef, Veal, or Lamb

1 cup dry white or red wine
¼ cup cider vinegar
1 cup salad oil
2 teaspoons salt
½ teaspoon black pepper
⅛ teaspoon dry tarragon

1 bay leaf, crushed in small pieces
½ teaspoon thyme or marjoram
1 large clove garlic, chopped fine or preferably put through garlic press

Combine all ingredients in a medium bowl and with egg or wire beater, beat for about 2 or 3 minutes. Soak meat in this marinade, turn it over often and baste it from time to time with marinade that settles at the bottom of the dish. Four hours in marinade will add a subtle delectable flavor to the meat.

Note. Place meat to be marinated into an enamel, glass, or stainless steel utensil, and not in other utensils made of metal (except stainless steel) as very often the acid in the marinade will act upon the metal chemically and develop an unpleasant taste in the meat or poultry, and other foods. Let food soak in the marinade for time suggested in recipe, turning it over, and basting it often with a large spoon with marinade in pan. Keep in refrigerator, but let stand in room temperature for about 1 hour before cooking, either in or out of marinade.

Glaze and Gravy for Chateaubriand

Use the drippings and liquid remaining in roasting pan after meat is done. Add more stock or water to make required amount. Strain, and to each cup, use 4 teaspoons cornstarch diluted in 2 tablespoons water. Cook until thick, then simmer at least 5 minutes, stirring all the time; add a little commercial gravy coloring. Let stand until lukewarm, and if too thick add a bit of water. Brush meat, mushrooms, or tops of artichoke bottoms with glaze. (See page 137 for Chateaubriand recipe.)

Hollandaise Sauce

Makes about 1¼ cups

¾ cup soft butter
4 large egg yolks (⅓ cup) slightly beaten
About 2 tablespoons lemon juice

¼ teaspoon or more salt
Dash red pepper
2 to 4 tablespoons very hot water (optional)

Divide butter into 3 parts. In upper part of a very small enamel or stainless steel double boiler, place egg yolks and 1 part of the butter. Bring water in lower part of double boiler to a boil, remove from heat, and place upper part over water. At once with wire whisk, sometimes called fluffy beater, sold in most department and hardware stores (or you can use egg beater), beat first piece of butter and yolks until butter is completely melted. Then add second piece of butter and beat until melted. Do likewise with third piece of butter, and continue to beat for *about 5 minutes until sauce thickens like a very soft custard.* For a thicker sauce, reheat water, but keep it below boiling point (about 200° F.). Continue to cook the sauce over hot water, stirring it continuously and vigorously with wire whisk during the cooking process. Lift upper part of double boiler from hot water occasionally if sauce appears to lump, and continue to beat off heat, then place back over very hot water (about 150° F.). Add lemon juice, salt, and red pepper and blend well.

Very hot water may be added to sauce, a tablespoonful at a time, while beating. This is an excellent way to extend sauce, is less rich, and also protects sauce from curdling.

Hollandaise sauce may be kept warm over hot water between 125° to 150° F. until ready to be served for about ½ hour, or it may be prepared hours or several days in advance. In this case, let sauce cool, then store it in a covered jar and refrigerate. To serve, place over hot water about 150° F. Cover and do not stir for 7 or 8 minutes; then stir very gently until sauce is lukewarm, not hot, or it is likely to separate.

Should Hollandise or Sauce Bearnaise (below) curdle or separate at any time, add about 1 tablespoon very hot water, a teaspoon at a time, and beat well.

Note. It is better to have upper part of double boiler rest in hot water *provided* sauce is beaten *at once and continuously*. Also, check temperature of water in lower part of boiler once or twice during the beating process and keep it as close to 200° F. as possible, but below the boiling point, 212° F. If not to be served at once, it can be kept warm over hot water, about 125° to 150° F., stirring it occasionally to prevent lumping and separating.

Sauce Bearnaise

Makes about 1¼ cups

⅓ cup egg yolks (about 4 or 5 large)
1 tablespoon or more lemon juice
¾ cup *warm* melted salted butter
2 teaspoons dry or frozen chives, or dry parsley
1 teaspoon or bit more tarragon vinegar (cider vinegar may be used)
½ teaspoon dry tarragon leaves, crushed in fingers, if using tarragon vinegar; if using cider vinegar increase leaves to 1 teaspoon
⅛ teaspoon pepper
About ⅛ teaspoon, or bit more, salt (increase if using unsalted butter)
¾ teaspoon well-drained firm capers (optional)

Bring water in lower part of a 1-quart stainless steel or enamel double boiler to a boil, *and shut off heat.* Place yolks and lemon juice in upper part of boiler, and at once with wire whisk beat about 1 minute. Now add the warm melted butter, about 1 tablespoon at a time, and beat after each addition a few seconds. After all of the butter has been added, continue to beat sauce for about 5 minutes, or until it looks like a soft custard. If sauce does not thicken after this time, reheat water to boil, shut off heat. Place top of boiler on and *at once* continue to beat until Bearnaise is thick. If sauce appears to be cooking too rapidly, lift it off water to prevent overcooking. Beat well for a few seconds, or longer if necessary. Add all other ingredients listed, and blend well with wire whisk. If sauce appears oily or too heavy, or to separate, at any time, *at once* add about 2 tablespoons very hot water, teaspoonful at a time and stir until smooth. May be kept warm over water that is 125° to 150° F. for about ½ hour. Stir occasionally until ready to be served. For a thinner Bearnaise Sauce, as much as 2 more tablespoons hot water may be added slowly and stirred gently until well blended.

Note. Follow other detailed directions given for Hollandaise Sauce (page 340). Never use an aluminum double boiler for these sauces to prevent discoloration of sauce. A small heatproof Pyrex bowl or stainless steel bowl may be placed over very hot water (about 200° F.) inside of a small saucepan to fit.

Sauce Gourmet

1 cup chili sauce or catsup	¼ cup fine-chopped fresh green onions
1 teaspoon prepared mustard	and stems
2 tablespoons lemon juice or vinegar	¼ teaspoon celery salt
½ teaspoon hot sauce (optional)	¼ teaspoon black pepper

Combine all ingredients and blend well. Serve with hors d'oeuvres puffs, etc.

▸ *Salads, Salad Bowls*

AND SALAD DRESSINGS

IT IS AN ESTABLISHED FACT THAT FRUITS AND VEGETABLES ARE THE RICHEST sources of vitamins, which are essential in maintaining good health. It is, therefore, important to serve a fruit or vegetable salad with each meal. A simple salad is ordinarily served with a hearty meal, and a more elaborate salad is served with a light dinner or luncheon.

All ingredients used in salad dressings should be fresh and strong. Various types of vinegar may be used for variety. A top-grade vegetable oil may be used instead of olive oil unless the distinctive flavor of olive oil is preferred. Shake or mix dressings thoroughly before using.

Note. Also see Party-Style Molds (page 418).

▸ SALADS AND SALAD BOWLS ◂

Pineapple Bird of Paradise Centerpiece

Place an attractive fresh pineapple on cutting board and slice off about ⅓ from one side. With sharp knife remove center of pineapple, leaving ½-inch wall. Use special cutter, or sketch and cut out pattern of bird's head and neck on stiff cardboard. Place it over slice of Idaho potato cut about ¼ inch thick, and with a small sharp knife cut around carefully. Place head in cold water with little lemon juice and yellow food coloring in a flat pan and hold down with another pan to prevent it from curling. Keep in refrigerator for at least an hour (or may be made day in advance). Shortly before using, remove from water and brush with lemon juice, then place into small amount of yellow colored water. Dry on a towel.

With tiny brush tint nose and top of head with undiluted red coloring, then dilute red and green or blue coloring with drop of water and paint a few feathers on sides of neck. Cut opening on front part of pineapple, and insert neck. If necessary trim lower part of neck very slightly to fit into opening, and hold in place with wood pin.

Bird may be filled with cut-out pineapple and other fruits or with a dressing, and used as centerpiece of a salad or hors d'oeuvres platter.

Note. If preferred, pineapple may be cut in halves, making 2 birds. Proceed same as above.

Individual Pineapple Birds of Paradise Salad Tahiti

Cut pineapple into 2 or 4 equal parts, depending on size. With sharp medium knife remove center in 1 piece, leaving ½-inch wall. Insert heads. Cut removed pineapple in about 1-inch pieces. Combine it with cut-up cooked breast of chicken, a few slices maraschino cherries, cut in rings, *or* fresh strawberries, and enough Whipped Cream Mayonnaise to moisten. Place a spoonful dressing on top just before serving, or garnish with a scroll of stiff whipped cream with No. 3 star cookie tube.

This makes an attractive light luncheon or supper dish for ladies parties. Serve finger sandwiches or small hot rolls separately.

Whipped Cream Mayonnaise

For whipped cream mayonnaise, add ½ cup whipped cream to 1 cup mayonnaise and blend well.

Individual Pineapple Birds of Paradise Cocktail

Cut pineapple into 2 or 4 equal parts, depending on size, leaving ½-inch wall. Combine cut-up pineapple with sliced fresh strawberries. Fill birds attractively. Insert heads. Just before serving, cover top with fruit salad dressing. Makes a delicious and attractive first course for special dinner or luncheon parties, or may be served as a fruit dessert.

Watermelon Salad Basket

Purchase small watermelon, weighing not more than 20 pounds unless a very large platter is used. Cut melon to simulate a basket with handle. Trim edges of basket as uniformly as possible. With knife remove center of melon in large pieces, leaving a thin red wall. Dry outside of melon thoroughly, and rub with salad oil to impart gloss. Scallop edges or leave plain.

With large end of French baller, cut out as many melon balls as possible. Remove seeds. Cut up irregular pieces of melon in about 1-inch pieces and place them in basket, forming a mound. Cover mound thickly with melon balls, starting on outer edge. Other cut-up melons and fruits or berries may be used.

Garnish handle with small clusters of black, green, or red grapes, strawberries, fresh sweet cherries, or any small fruits in season, holding them in place with small pieces of wood pins.

Place basket in center of a large platter, and on each end of platter arrange a Bird of Paradise (page 343) filled with fruit salad dressing or whipped cream. Surround basket with fresh or artificial green leaves, and if desired fresh or canned peach halves filled with fresh blueberries or blackberries, or pipe a large thick white cream cheese rosette with No. 3 star cookie tube in each cavity. Pipe leaves with No. 67 tube and green cheese. Place well-drained (dried on towel) red maraschino cherry or uniform fresh strawberry on each rosette. If using fresh peaches, plunge them into boiling water for about 1 minute, then blanch with cold water. Peel, cut and at once brush with lemon or pineapple juice to prevent discoloration.

Watermelon basket may be used as a punch bowl, floating melon balls on top.

Honey Dew or Cantaloupe Salad Basket

Select large melons if to be used as centerpiece for platter. Cut and prepare like watermelon basket. For main luncheon or supper dishes, purchase small melons. Cut like watermelon, then with very sharp knife and vegetable peeler remove skin completely. Continue to trim more layers until edible part of melon is reached. Fill inside of basket with fresh-cut fruits or berries, forming a mound, then cover completely with small melon balls. Garnish base of melons with contrasting fresh fruit in season or simply with green leaves. Canned fruits may be used.

Caesar Salad Bowl

Makes 4 to 6 portions

Caesar Salad should be made at the table where everyone can see its preparation just before serving.

2 medium-size more or less cloves of garlic	1 teaspoon coarse black pepper
1 teaspoon salt	4 fillets of anchovies, cut up in small pieces, or 2 teaspoons anchovy paste
6 tablespoons oil	
2 tablespoons wine vinegar	
1 tablespoon fresh lemon juice	1 tablespoon parmesan cheese
½ teaspoon Worcestershire sauce	1 pound cold crisp romaine lettuce
1 teaspoon dry mustard	1 coddled egg
½ teaspoon salt	24 or more small croutons

Into a large wooden salad bowl place 2 medium cloves of garlic cut in small pieces and 1 teaspoon salt; crush with fork and rub in bowl until bowl is well flavored with garlic. This takes about 2 minutes. Garlic and salt may be discarded but we prefer to leave them in bowl. (In this case omit the ½ teaspoon salt called for in recipe.)

Add oil and beat rapidly with fork until thick, about 1 minute; then add wine vinegar and lemon juice slowly and beat until thoroughly blended with oil. Add Worcestershire sauce, dry mustard, salt, pepper, anchovies, and parmesan cheese. Beat until well blended. Add chilled romaine lettuce which has been broken in medium-size pieces. Toss well with salad fork and spoon until well marinated, but not so vigorously as to bruise the lettuce. Add coddled egg and mix well. Last add sautéed croutons, mixing and tossing salad gently to prevent croutons from becoming soggy.

Serve at once in individual salad bowls.

Croutons

Cut French or Italian bread in ½-inch cubes. Sauté in oil or butter with 2 or 3 slivers of garlic in an open skillet until crisp and golden brown on each side. Croutons may be sautéed hours in advance.

Coddled Egg

Place 1 egg in very hot water, covered, for 5 minutes.

Big Apple Fruit Cocktail

Use Roman Beauty or other large attractive apples. Cut off about ¼ inch from stem end. Scoop out apples, leaving a ¼-inch wall. (Apples may be scooped out a day in advance.) Brush inside with lemon juice to prevent discoloration, and keep covered in refrigerator. Make small slit on 1 side of top of apple. Fill apples with cold diced fruits combined with a little liqueur or fruit juices. Place green straws in slit and cover with top of apple. Serve in sherbet glasses. Garnish with mint or other fresh leaves.

Fresh Vegetable Salad Bowl

Serves 6

1 large head of iceberg lettuce, cut or broken into medium-size pieces (other lettuce may be used instead)

Tomatoes cut into 1-inch pieces

Cucumber, peeled and sliced thin (optional)

About ½ cup radishes, sliced thin cross-wise

About ½ cup fresh green onions, cut into 1-inch pieces

About ½ cup watercress, or red cabbage (optional)

Have these ingredients cold, crisp, and thoroughly drained. Pour salad dressing over them. Mix well and serve. This salad is very attractive if served in a salad bowl that has been lined with fresh romaine lettuce or other greens. On top of vegetables arrange 6 or 7 slices of tomatoes that have been cut crosswise; over tomatoes arrange 6 or 7 thin rings of green pepper cut crosswise. Pour more dressing over tomatoes and peppers. Sprinkle top with medium chopped green onion or parsley.

Any fresh salad vegetable may be used in this salad bowl.

Saratoga Salad Bowl

Serves 6

1 medium-size head lettuce	⅓ cup salad oil
2 cups fresh orange sections	2 teaspoons salt
2½ cups cooked diced chicken	½ teaspoon paprika
6 tablespoons roquefort or bleu cheese, crumbled	¼ teaspoon ground black pepper
⅓ cup fresh lemon juice	⅛ teaspoon garlic powder

Wash lettuce, pat dry, and tear leaves into small pieces. Place in a salad bowl with next 3 ingredients. Combine remaining ingredients and add. Toss lightly. Serve as a main-dish luncheon or supper salad.

Anchovy Salad Bowl

Serves 4

½ cup salad oil	1 teaspoon salt
¼ cup tarragon vinegar	¼ teaspoon pepper
1 teaspoon anchovy paste	1 pound escarole
1 small clove garlic, put through garlic press	2 or 3 fresh tomatoes

In a wooden salad bowl, blend oil, vinegar, and anchovy paste until dressing emulsifies. Add garlic, salt, and pepper, and blend well. Add chilled lettuce, and blend with dressing. Cut tomatoes in wedges and arrange attractively on top of lettuce.

Bahama Salad Bowl

Serves 4

1 medium head iceberg lettuce, or 1 pound romaine lettuce, washed and dried in a towel, then broken into medium pieces	3 artichoke hearts, quartered
	1 small avocado, cut in 1-inch pieces
	1 hard-cooked egg, cut in about 8 pieces
1 small tomato, cut in 6 pieces	

Have all ingredients well chilled at least 2 hours in advance and combine with Bahama Salad Dressing (page 373). Toss well for 2 or 3 minutes and serve very cold.

Cole Slaw Salad Bowl

Wash cabbage under cold running water; drain well. Shortly before serving, shred it as fine as possible. Add desired amount of shredded raw carrots, thinly sliced onion, a few strips pimiento, and finely chopped green onion tops or green pepper. Keep in a covered bowl or in plastic bag in refrigerator until ready to be served. Just before serving, pour Cooked Salad Dressing (page 371) over vegetables, mixing thoroughly.

Cole Slaw or Lettuce Salad, Molded

Shred cabbage or lettuce as fine as possible. Combine with a little pimiento, green pepper, and shredded onion. Add only enough salad dressing to moisten. Pack into a mold. Turn onto a platter and decorate top with little mayonnaise and strips of pimiento and green pepper. Arrange ½ slices of tomatoes around base of mold.

Summer Salad Bowl

Serves 6

1 head iceberg lettuce	2 medium tomatoes
2 heads bibb, or 1 Boston lettuce	1 green pepper
1 small head curly endive	⅓ cup sliced green onions

Tear or break all lettuce into a large salad bowl and mix well. Quarter tomatoes and place on top of mixed lettuce. Core and slice green pepper and place pepper rings between tomatoes. Sprinkle entire top with sliced green onions. This basic salad is delicious served with Cream Roquefort (page 372) or garlic dressing.

Serve dressing separately after salad is served.

Piquant Salad Bowl

Serves 4 to 6

1 head iceberg lettuce, broken into medium-size pieces	1 small cucumber, peeled and cut into medium-size chunks (about 1 inch)
½ head endive, broken into medium-size pieces	½ cup fresh green onions and stems, cut into 1-inch pieces
3 tomatoes cut into medium-size chunks (about 1 inch)	4 hard-cooked eggs, cut into wedges
2 large carrots very coarse-shredded	

Combine all ingredients and moisten them well with Piquant French Dressing (page 373). Toss greens, vegetables and eggs together several minutes.

Kentucky Limestone Salad Bowl

Serves 4

1 pound of bibb lettuce

1 recipe Kentucky Limestone Salad Dressing (page 374)

Pour dressing over lettuce and blend well. Serve at once.

Shrimp Salad, Molded

Serves 8

3 pounds uncooked shrimp, or 1½ pounds cooked cleaned shrimp
2 tablespoons salt
3 quarts boiling water
1 teaspoon caraway seed
2 tablespoons lemon juice
⅓ cup French or Italian dressing (optional)
4 cups celery, cut crosswise, ¼ inch wide

2 tablespoons pimiento, cut in ½-inch squares
½ cup, or less, chopped fresh green onion and tops combined (or a little grated onion)
About 2 teaspoons salt
6 hard-cooked eggs, sliced crosswise
1½ cups thick mayonnaise-gelatin as suggested

If using uncooked shrimp, wash them thoroughly under cold running water; cook *gently* in about 3 quarts boiling water, seasoned with 2 tablespoons salt, 2 tablespoons lemon juice, and 1 teaspoon caraway seed. If shrimp are large cook them gently about 5 minutes; if medium cook them about 3 minutes, after they start to boil. Drain well, peel and devein. Split cooked shrimp in halves lengthwise if large; if small or medium, they may be left whole.

Combine cooked shrimp with all other ingredients except mayonnaise and gelatin. To prevent salad from becoming watery, even if it is to stand for only a few minutes, it is better to add 1 teaspoon unflavored gelatin combined with 2 tablespoons cold water, stir gently, and let stand until thick, then dissolve over simmering water. Add this dissolved warm gelatin slowly to the 1½ cups mayonnaise, mixing it well. At once pour mayonnaise over salad ingredients, and blend thoroughly. Pour into oiled 7- or 8-inch bowl, or, better, aluminum tower mold, pressing salad down well into bowl. Cover with wax paper and refrigerate for at least 8 hours.

To Serve. Loosen around edges with dinner knife, dip mold into warm water for a few seconds, wipe outside well, place a sheet of heavy wax paper and serving platter on top of mold, and turn over carefully. If mold is not in center of platter, it may be moved by pulling wax paper. Cut away surplus paper. Garnish and serve salad with additional mayonnaise or Whipped Cream Mayonnaise Horseradish Sauce (page 374).

This is a basic mold, and instead of shrimp you can use about 1½ pounds of cooked lobster meat, crab meat, salmon, tuna fish, chicken, or ham. Larger amounts of seafood or meat may be used in this salad. In this case, decrease amount of celery accordingly.

Colonial Doll Mold

Proceed same as for Shrimp Salad, Molded, but increase gelatin to 1 tablespoon and water to ¼ cup. Turn out onto platter. *Leave wax paper on platter* until mold is decorated. Spread entire surface of mold lightly with mayonnaise and sprinkle with 4 hard-cooked egg yolks that have been put through a sieve or mill. Insert several heavy toothpicks on top of mold, and place doll head over picks. Garnish waistline with fresh parsley sprigs. Now cut away wax paper. Arrange additional whole (takes about 1 pound) cooked shrimp brushed with French dressing around base of mold, or garnish base with sliced tomatoes. This salad can be prepared in 8 or 10 individual molds. Serve Horseradish Whipped Cream Sauce (page 372) separately.

Shrimp Salad Louisiana, Molded

1 pound cooked shrimp (takes 2   2 cups celery cut ⅓ inch wide cross-
    pounds raw shrimp)   wise

Cook raw shrimp in simmering water about 5 minutes if large, 3 or 4 minutes if medium. Shell and remove vein. Leave shrimp whole for this salad if small or medium; split in halves if large. Pour ½ (more or less) Sauce Louisiana (page 374) over shrimp and celery, and blend well. Mold with hands in dome-fashion on medium-size serving platter, and cover entire surface with rest of Sauce Louisiana.

Garnish base of salad with cold cooked asparagus tips that have been marinated in Italian dressing for about 20 minutes and then drained thoroughly. Top may be garnished with about 8 thick half slices of lemon, overlapping each other, or 4 half slices lemon and 4 half slices small tomatoes, alternately.

How to Prepare Asparagus Tips. Use only tender part of tips. Drop into rapidly boiling salted water and cook until crisply tender, about 3 minutes for medium-thick stalks if using frozen asparagus *that have been completely thawed before cooking.* Cook fresh asparagus tips about 7 or 8 minutes. Test 1 for doneness before removing from water. As soon as they are crisply tender, drain and plunge them into ice water until asparagus are very cold.

This will preserve their attractive green color and prevent loss of vitamins.

Shrimp Salad in Tomato Poinsettia

Serves 4 generously

Select uniform, red, solid tomatoes. Cut through skins into 8 sections, starting from top and leaving about 1 inch uncut. Loosen petals carefully and remove pulp and seeds. Drain well, and sprinkle with salt. Mold Basic Shrimp Salad (page 349) into tomato, using oiled custard cups or small molds. Loosen mold before turning over. Decorate top with a little mayonnaise and fine-chopped parsley or fresh green onions. On sides arrange bread-and-butter finger sandwiches.

Avocado and Shrimp Salad with Russian Dressing

Serves 2

Prepare Russian Dressing with 1 cup mayonnaise, 3 tablespoons chili sauce, 1 teaspoon fine-chopped onion, and 1 teaspoon lemon juice. Add 1 pound cooked shrimp, and blend well. Chill in refrigerator 1 hour.

Halve 2 chilled avocados. Brush with lemon juice, remove stones, and peel. Heap with the shrimp mixture; sprinkle top with paprika. Place each avocado half in a lettuce cup and serve at once. Large tomatoes can also be used instead of avocados.

Crab Meat Salad Ravigote, Molded

Serves 8

5 (6 ounce) packages frozen crab meat, or 5 small cans (about 7 ounces) top quality crab meat
¼ cup tarragon vinegar
3 cups pascal celery, peeled lightly and cut crosswise about ⅓ inch thick, then washed, drained and dried thoroughly in a towel
About 1 teaspoon salt
About 1 teaspoon capers, well drained (optional)

1 tablespoon fresh green onion, cut fine
¼ cup fresh green onion tops, cut about ½ inch
1 cup *stabilized* mayonnaise
About ¾ cup or more *unstabilized* (plain) mayonnaise to spread over entire surface of salad
4 hard-cooked egg yolks, put through a fine grater or sieve
Paprika

Defrost crab meat if frozen. Leave in large pieces. Pour the tarragon vinegar over crab meat and mix well with 2 forks. Cover and keep in refrigerator for about ½ hour or longer. Drain very thoroughly, pressing out excess moisture. Combine the crab meat, celery, salt, capers, fresh green onion and tops, and the cup of *stabilized* mayonnaise. Blend well, press down into 8-inch bowl, cover and place in refrigerator for about 30 minutes. Be sure to chill salad right in bowl for about 30 minutes or longer, before turning it out onto platter. Mound salad on a 17-inch oval platter, pressing it into shape with hands. At this point do not disturb. Spread entire surface with about ¾ cup plain mayonnaise and cover with the grated egg yolks. Sprinkle paprika lengthwise on mold, to cover about 1 inch of center of surface.

Garnish base of salad alternately with thinly sliced tomatoes and cucumber or groups of kumquats, cocktail mix, large black or green olives, pickled rinds, etc. Place bouquet of parsley on each end.

This salad may be prepared hours or a day in advance. In this case, do not garnish with grated yolks, tomatoes, and cucumber slices until about an hour before serving.

Stabilized Mayonnaise for Crab Meat Ravigote

Combine 1 teaspoon plain gelatin with 2 tablespoons cold water. Mix gently, and let stand until thick, about 5 minutes, then dissolve over simmering water. Pour warm gelatin at once slowly into 1 cup of commercial mayonnaise and mix well. Stalibilized mayonnaise can stand in refrigerator for ½ hour (not longer), if stirred several times to keep it at uniform consistency. If it remains in refrigerator until extremely cold and set it will curdle when combining with other ingredients. The small amount of gelatin added to mayonnaise absorbs excess moisture in seafood and other ingredients that usually settle in platter.

Crab Meat Salad à la Reefer, Molded

Serves 6

3 (6 ounce) packages frozen crab meat completely defrosted, or 1 pound fresh crab meat

1 cup, or more, celery, cut crosswise about ⅓-inch wide

2 medium-size avocados, cut in halves lengthwise. Brush at once with lemon juice to prevent discoloration. Place on cutting board covered with wax paper, with cut side down. With serrated knife cut carefully into slices about ⅓-inch thick. Brush slices at once with lemon juice. With sharp knife

remove skin from slices carefully to prevent breaking. Add irregular pieces of avocado to basic part of salad. Place slices on wax paper on flat surface, brush with lemon juice, cover, and refrigerate until needed.

1 recipe Reefer French Dressing (page 353)

1 recipe Reefer Tartar Sauce (page 353)

3 medium-size tomatoes cut in wedges

Paprika

Drain defrosted crab meat well, pressing out surplus moisture. Leave it in large pieces, removing bones. Combine crab meat with celery, and irregular pieces of avocados cut into large pieces. Pour Reefer French Dressing over these ingredients, mix gently with 2 forks, cover bowl, and refrigerate about 1 hour. Then pour into a colander and drain well.

To serve, combine these ingredients with ½ of Reefer Tartar Sauce and blend gently. Pour onto center of a large round platter, forming a dome. Spread rest of Tartar Sauce over entire surface with a spatula dipped into hot water, making it as smooth as possible. Refrigerate at least 1 hour. Shortly before serving, garnish top with slices of avocado to simulate a flower; sprinkle entire salad with paprika. Arrange rest of avocado slices around base of salad, overlapping one another. On outside of avocado slices place tomato wedges.

This salad may be served as an appetizer course, as a main luncheon or supper dish, as an entree for special dinners, for buffets or cocktail parties. Serve salad sticks, melba toast, or crackers separately.

Reefer French Dressing

¼ cup salad oil
1½ tablespoons cider vinegar
1 sliver of fresh garlic

½ teaspoon salt
⅛ teaspoon cayenne pepper

Combine all ingredients in a jar. Cover, and shake well about 1 minute. Pour at once over Crab Meat Salad ingredients.

Reefer Tartar Sauce

1 pint (2 cups) commercial mayonnaise
1 small clove garlic, put through garlic press
¼ cup fresh green onions chopped fine
⅓ cup fresh green onion stems chopped fine
¼ cup chopped sweet pickles

¼ cup chopped stuffed green olives
About 2 tablespoons lemon juice
About 1 tablespoon granulated sugar
1 teaspoon gelatin, combined with 2 tablespoons cold water (stir gently about 5 minutes until thick, then dissolve in a pan of simmering water)

Combine all ingredients except gelatin mixture. Dissolve gelatin, and while still hot, add it slowly to the sauce, and beat until smooth. Chill in refrigerator about 30 minutes, *stirring every 5 minutes to prevent setting*. It is best not to prepare this sauce until about 30 minutes before it is to be used. If it must be refrigerated for a longer time, be sure to stir it occasionally, and if it should set in refrigerator, remove and let stand in room temperature until creamy before stirring, or bowl may be placed in a pan of warm water a few minutes and stirred gently to prevent curdling. This is a delicious sauce and may be used with any seafood salad or fish.

Turkey or Chicken Salad Superb, Molded

Serves 6 to 8

1 small head lettuce, washed and dried thoroughly in a towel, then shred fine

1 cup Pascal celery, peeled lightly and cut ⅓ inch wide, crosswise, washed and dried thoroughly in a towel (a tomato cut in 1-inch pieces may be added)

About 1½ pounds cooked cold turkey or chicken, sliced thin (takes about 3 pounds uncooked chicken breasts)

About 3 tablespoons Italian or French dressing

2 recipes, more or less, of Salad Dressing Superb (page 368)

Combine lettuce, celery, and tomato. Moisten with as little Italian or French dressing as possible, tossing well with 2 forks. Mound vegetables on 16-inch round or oval serving platter. Cover with slices of cold turkey or chicken. Spread entire surface with most of the Salad Dressing Superb, serving any leftover dressing separately. Sprinkle with paprika. Garnish base alternately with sliced tomatoes and cucumbers that have been brushed with French dressing, or as desired. This salad may be put together and refrigerated several hours in advance.

Lobster Salad Imperial, Molded

Serves 8

4 pounds frozen lobster tails (about 2 pounds after cooking)

About 2½ cups Seafood Tartar Sauce (page 336)

2 medium ripe calavo pears

Lemon juice

1 can artichoke hearts

1 recipe Tomato Aspic (page 471)

Defrost lobster tails. Cover with hot water and bring to boiling point. Lower heat and simmer 5 to 12 minutes for small and medium, and 18 minutes for large tails. Let cool in water slightly, shell and cut into about 1-inch pieces, or larger. Moisten lobster meat with about ½ cup of Tartar Sauce and put aside. Cut calavos in halves lengthwise. Remove seed, brush cut side of calavo at once with lemon juice, to prevent discoloration. Place with cut side down on wax paper and *cut tip* into about 1-inch pieces with small serrated-edge knife.

Cut center part of calavo in ⅓ inch horseshoe slices. Dip or brush each one with lemon juice. Reserve 8 most attractive slices to garnish top of salad. With small sharp paring knife pare calavo slices. Moisten the 1-inch pieces with a little Tartar Sauce. Open 1 can artichoke hearts and reserve 6 most uniform and attractive ones to garnish base of mold. Pour a little Italian dressing on artichokes, cover and let stand in refrigerator for about ½ hour. Drain thoroughly. Cut irregular artichoke hearts into about 1-inch pieces and combine with the lobster meat, cut-up calavo, and more Tartar Sauce to moisten. Mix very gently and pour onto an oval 17-inch platter, forming a mound; a 20-inch oval platter may be used. Spread rest of Tartar Sauce as smoothly as possible over entire surface of salad.

With a 2-inch round or medium crescent cutter, cut Tomato Aspic into 18 crescents. Leave rest of aspic uncut until needed for top of mold. Place 3 aspic crescents on each end of salad to simulate a flower. Form 2 flowers on each side. Drain artichokes thoroughly, open slightly in center and sprinkle with paprika. Place 1 on each small end aspic flowers or use colossal green or black ripe olives, fresh or preserved kumquats, etc. With a small 1¼-inch round cutter, cut out 6 tiny crescents from rest of Tomato Aspic. Garnish top of salad with the horseshoe slices of calavo and aspic crescents. Fill in open spaces around base of salad with ripe or green olives dried in a towel, then rubbed with a bit of salad oil. Sprinkle outside edge of mold with paprika.

Potato Salad, Molded

Makes 6 cups

3 pounds red boiling potatoes (new red potatoes best)
¼ cup French or Italian dressing (optional)
4 hard-cooked eggs, sliced
Small amount grated onion or fresh green onion
¼ cup green pepper or fresh green onion tops, cut into ½-inch strips
¼ cup pimiento, cut into ½-inch squares
½ cup or more celery, cut crosswise, ¼-inch wide
About 1 tablespoon, or less, salt
About ¾ to 1 cup mayonnaise

Wash boiling potatoes thoroughly and cook gently, with skins on, in covered saucepan in unsalted *boiling water* until tender but not too soft, about 25 to 35 minutes. When cold, peel and slice. Add remaining ingredients, except mayonnaise, and mix well. Last, add only enough mayonnaise (beaten with a spoon) to hold ingredients together. (It is better not to have salad too soft if to be molded.) Serve more plain or Whipped Cream Mayonnaise–Horseradish Sauce (page 374) separately if desired.

To Mold. Pack potato salad firmly into well-oiled 7-inch bowl. With a dinner knife or spatula loosen salad on sides, place sheet of heavy wax paper and then a large flat platter over top of bowl and invert carefully. Shake slightly if necessary. Spread a little mayonnaise on mold and sprinkle with paprika. Top of mold may be garnished with vegetable or radish rose. Now cut away wax paper. Around base of mold place sliced cold meats and cheeses cut into triangles and garnish with several vegetable flowers or large radish roses.

Asparagus-Olive Salad Mold

Serves 6 to 8

2 cups boiling water
1 package lemon dessert gelatin
2 teaspoons plain gelatin, combined
    with ⅓ cup cold water (stir and
    allow to stand about 5 minutes
    until thick)
2 teaspoons salt, more or less to suit
    taste
⅛ teaspoon cayenne pepper
1 tablespoon vinegar

¾ cup stuffed olives, sliced crosswise
½ cup India relish, or fine-chopped
    pickles
1 package (12-ounce size) frozen cut
    asparagus, cooked until just ten-
    der
1 cup uncooked celery, cut crosswise
    about ¼ inch wide (not too
    thick)
¼ cup mayonnaise

Add boiling water to lemon gelatin, and at once add the thick plain gelatin mixture, stirring continuously until gelatin is dissolved. Add salt, cayenne pepper, and vinegar. Let stand in a cold place or refrigerator until slightly congealed, but not thick; it should have the consistency of unbeaten egg white. Combine all other ingredients, mix well, and add them to congealed gelatin mixture all at once. Blend quickly and evenly. Pour at once into an oiled 6-cup mold or bowl. Refrigerate at least 8 hours.

To Serve. Loosen around edge of mold and turn out onto a serving platter. Sprinkle top of mold with paprika. Arrange slices of tomatoes around base of mold, alternately with slices of cucumber. Slices of cold meats and cheese may also be served around this mold. Serve Whipped Cream-Mayonnaise Horseradish Sauce (page 374) separately.

Potato Salad With Bleu Cheese and Sour Cream

Serves 6 to 8

8 large red boiling potatoes
½ cup chopped celery
2 tablespoons minced parsley
½ cup toasted almonds, sliced
3 green onions and tops, chopped
About 2 teaspoons salt

¼ teaspoon ground pepper
1 pint commercial sour cream
4 ounces bleu cheese, crumbled
¼ cup wine vinegar
Radish roses
3 hard-cooked eggs

Cook potatoes gently with skins on in covered saucepan until just tender, not too soft. Peel and cut into medium cubes or slices. Add celery, parsley, almonds, chopped onion, about 2 teaspoons salt, pepper.

In a medium bowl combine the sour cream, little at a time, with the crumbled bleu cheese. Add wine vinegar, a little at a time, and blend well. Pour over potatoes and other ingredients and mix thoroughly. Cover and let marinate for several hours in refrigerator before serving. Arrange attractively on a platter, and garnish with radish roses, and slices of hard-cooked eggs.

German Hot Potato Salad

Serves 6

6 strips bacon, cut into small pieces
1 medium onion, sliced thin
2 teaspoons flour
1 tablespoon sugar
1½ teaspoons salt
¼ teaspoon pepper

½ cup water
½ cup parsley, chopped medium
⅓ cup cider vinegar
1½ pounds red boiling potatoes cooked until just tender (do not over-cook), peeled and sliced

Sauté cut bacon until medium-crisp, but not too dry. Drain off most of fat. Add sliced onion and cook about 3 minutes. Add all other ingredients except vinegar and potatoes. Cook preparation, stirring all the time, until it thickens slightly, then let simmer about 3 minutes. Now add vinegar, and simmer about 2 more minutes. Last, add sliced potatoes, and blend gently. Remove from heat and serve warm.

Petit Gourmet Relish Molds

Makes about 16 molds

1 tablespoon plain gelatin, combined with ¼ cup cold water (stir gently and allow to stand several minutes until thick, then dissolve over simmering water)
2 cups cool gingerale to which ⅛ teaspoon green coloring has been added
½ cup piccalilli, or fine-chopped sweet pickles
½ cup fine-chopped celery

¼ cup fine-chopped green stuffed olives
¼ cup fine-chopped green onion and ¼ cup fine-chopped stems
1 tablespoon, or less, prepared horse-radish
1 tablespoon, or less, prepared salad mustard (use less of strong mustard)
Tomato Aspic (page 471) or other red gelatin

Add dissolved gelatin to gingerale with green coloring. Stir well, and let stand until it begins to congeal: about the consistency of a heavy unbeaten egg white. Gingerale is likely to foam up when adding dissolved gelatin, but it will settle. When gelatin preparation is ready, remove any foam from top, and fold in all other ingredients, blending well. Pour into tiny molds that measure 1¾ × ¾ inches (molds may be larger). Place them on a baking sheet, and refrigerate at least 8 hours until firm to the touch.

To Serve. Dip molds into warm water a few seconds, wipe them well, and shake out onto palm of hand. Place each with large end up on a small 1¼-inch round (about ½ inch thick) of Tomato Aspic. Arrange attractively around ham mold. This is very delectable with seafood molds, corned beef, or any other meat course.

Individual Marinated Vegetable Molds

Makes about 16 molds, 2¾-inch size

3 cups boiling water
2 packages lemon gelatin dessert
1 package frozen mixed vegetables, or 2 cups any combination cooked vegetables

½ cup Modified Italian Salad Dressing (page 369) or your favorite French dressing
Tomato Aspic (page 471), or other red gelatin

Add boiling water to lemon gelatin and let stand until it has consistency of a heavy unbeaten egg white. Meanwhile cook vegetables until just tender, not too soft. Drain well, and combine with salad dressing. Let stand in refrigerator until gelatin preparation is ready. Now drain vegetables thoroughly, and fold them into thickened gelatin until evenly blended. Pour into lightly oiled molds that measure about 2¾ inches wide and 1 inch deep. Place them on a baking sheet and refrigerate at least 8 hours.

To Serve. Dip molds into warm water a few seconds, wipe them well, and shake out onto palm of hand. Place each on a thick slice of Tomato Aspic. Arrange 12 of these molds around salmon or other salad with very small parsley bouquets between them.

Tuna or Salmon Salad in Avocado Cup

Serves 4

6-ounce can tuna, or salmon
¼ cup celery, cut fine
1 tablespoon green stuffed olives, sliced
¼ cup fresh green onions, sliced
1 tablespoon pimiento, cut into 1-inch squares

2 tablespoons mayonnaise
1 tablespoon lemon juice
1 avocado
Leaf lettuce or lettuce cup
1 fresh tomato, cut into 8 sections

Flake tuna or salmon. Add celery, olives, onions, and pimiento; blend. Then add mayonnaise and lemon juice, and blend well.

Split ripe avocado lengthwise, remove stone, peel off skin. Brush with lemon juice.

Place leaf lettuce or lettuce cup on salad platter. On top of lettuce, place avocado half.

Pack salad into ½ cup custard or measuring cup, and unmold in center of avocado half. Place 1 teaspoon mayonnaise on top of salad. Garnish top of salad with pimiento and a sprig of parsley. Arrange tomato sections around base of avocado.

Crab Meat Salad in Avocado Cup

Serves 2

6-ounce can crab meat	Freshly ground pepper
¼ cup fine-cut celery	1 hard-cooked egg
2 tablespoons fine-cut green peppers	3 tablespoons mayonnaise
1 tablespoon pimiento, cut into 1-inch squares	1 avocado
¼ teaspoon salt	Lettuce cup or leaf lettuce

Flake crab meat; add celery, green pepper, pimiento, salt, pepper, and sliced hard-cooked egg. Last, add mayonnaise, and blend well.

Split ripe avocado lengthwise, remove stone, peel off skin. Brush with lemon juice.

Place lettuce cup or leaf lettuce on salad plate. On top of lettuce, place avocado pear half. Pack crab meat salad into ½ cup custard or measuring cup, and unmold in center of avocado half. Decorate top of crab meat salad with strips of green pepper and pimiento. Lobster or shrimp may be substituted for crab meat, if desired. Serve Thousand Island or French dressing separately.

Gourmet Seafood Cocktail or Salad

On 1 side of cocktail glass, arrange attractive leaf lettuce. Half fill it with lobster and crab meat cut into medium-size pieces, or use top-quality white tuna. Cover thickly with cocktail sauce, to which ½ tablespoon grated horseradish has been added for each cup of cocktail sauce. Garnish top with sprig parsley and 2 or 3 slices stuffed green olives. Place 3 large firm-cooked shrimp (leaving tails on if desired) on opposite edge of glass. Serve this as a main luncheon or supper dish with hot cheese puffs, cheese sticks, rolls, etc. Or dish may be made smaller and served as first course for special dinner parties. To eat shrimp, pick up in fingers and dunk into sauce.

Red Kidney Bean Salad

Serves 6 to 8

4 cups canned red kidney beans (2 No. 2 can)	3 tablespoons oil
	3 tablespoons vinegar, or lemon juice
1 large onion, chopped	1 teaspoon salt
¼ cup chopped parsley	½ teaspoon pepper
¼ cup chopped celery	

Blend above ingredients and keep in refrigerator several hours. When they are well chilled, serve on crisp lettuce leaves or in a salad bowl, and garnish with slices of tomato and cucumber.

Green Bean Salad

Serves 4

12-ounce package frozen cut green beans (or canned)
½ cup French dressing
2 tablespoons chopped onions
1 cup chopped celery

¼ cup cut green peppers
About ¼ cup mayonnaise
Salt and pepper to taste
2 tomatoes
1 cucumber

Cook green beans until just tender. Drain well. Allow to become cold. Marinate beans in ½ cup French dressing. Refrigerate about 1 hour. When ready to serve salad, add onions, celery, green pepper, and enough mayonnaise to bind ingredients together. Season with salt and pepper to taste.

Serve in a wooden salad bowl lined with leaf lettuce or in individual salad bowls. Garnish top with quartered tomatoes and sliced cucumbers.

Athenian Salad

Over thick-shredded lettuce, place several small pieces of tomato, several pieces of cucumber cut into ½-inch chunks, and a little fresh green onion and stems cut in about ½-inch pieces. Sprinkle top with fedda cheese cut into narrow strips, several anchovy strips, and a little oregano. Season with salt, cider, or wine vinegar, and olive oil. Do not mix salad ingredients, but arrange in order given.

Romaine Lettuce with Russian Salad Dressing

Serves 4 to 6

1 cup mayonnaise
1 hard-cooked egg, chopped fine
2 tablespoons chili sauce
1 tablespoon fine-chopped green pepper

1 tablespoon pimiento, cut into ½-inch squares
1 tablespoon black caviar
2 teaspoons fine-chopped chives or green onion tops

Blend well, and chill several hours. Shake and pour over 1 pound cut or broken crisp romaine lettuce.

Avocado Bird Salad

For main luncheon or supper dishes, purchase large avocados. With a very sharp knife, cut them lengthwise into halves. Remove pits very carefully. Peel if desired. Brush entire surface of avocado with lemon or other citrus juice. Make a gash in front of large end. On a heavy piece of paper or cardboard, sketch the head and neck of bird, place it on slices (cut about ¼ inch thick) of large fresh pears or apples that have been brushed with citrus juice. If avocados have been peeled, simply fill them with any desired cut-up fruits, such as strawberries, raspberries, pineapple, etc., and serve with Fruit Salad Dressing (page 371). Or they may be filled with shrimp, lobster, crab meat, chicken, etc., moistened with French or other tart dressing. Arrange bird on shredded lettuce, formed to simulate a small round nest.

Place heads of birds in cold water to which a little orange coloring has been added. Remove, and dry on towel. Paint bird's beak and neck with a little red coloring, and insert in gash, holding in place with cream cheese. With No. 27 or No. 30 star tube, pipe scrolls of white or green cream cheese on sides of birds to simulate feathers. Pipe tail same way. Use cloves for eyes. Fresh or canned pears may be prepared in this way. Small avocados may be used as a first course or as an accompaniment.

Do not cut birds' heads more than 2 or 3 hours in advance. Store in refrigerator until ready to be used. Rest of salad may be prepared in advance, covered, and stored in refrigerator.

Salmon-Pea Salad

Serves 4

¼ cup garlic French dressing
¼ cup commercial sour cream
1 tablespoon prepared mustard
1 can (16 to 17 ounces) peas
1 can (1 pound) salmon

1 cup thin-sliced celery
⅓ cup chopped ripe olives
¼ cup diced sweet pickles
½ teaspoon seasoned salt

Combine French dressing, sour cream, and mustard. Add drained peas, salmon broken into chunks, and remaining ingredients. Toss lightly, and chill. Serve in mounds on crisp salad greens.

Crunchy Salmon Salad

Serves 4 to 6

½ cup mayonnaise
¼ teaspoon salt
⅛ teaspoon pepper
2 tablespoons lemon juice
1 tablespoon grated onion
½ cup cream

1-pound can red salmon, drained and flaked
¼ cup diced sweet pickles
½ cup cut-up celery
2 cups crushed potato chips
Lettuce

Blend together mayonnaise, salt, pepper, lemon juice, and grated onion. Stir in cream. Fold in drained flaked salmon, pickles, and celery. Chill several hours.

Just before serving, mix in potato chips. With a cup, shape into mounds onto lettuce cups. Serve at once.

Party-Style Ham Salad Platter

Serves 6 to 8

¼ cup French dressing
3 cups celery, cut into ½-inch slices
1½ cups cooked green peas, or string beans
½ cup fresh green onions and tops

3 cups cooked ham, cut into ½-inch cubes
About ¾ to 1 cup mayonnaise, or enough to moisten ingredients
Large black ripe olives
6 hard-cooked eggs

Pour French dressing over celery, green peas, and green onions. Mix well and let stand, covered, in refrigerator about 1 hour. Then add ham, and moisten all ingredients with about ¾ to 1 cup mayonnaise.

Mound salad on a 16-inch oval or round platter. Smooth and flatten top with a spatula. Form a large opening in center. Fill center with large black ripe olives that have been rubbed lightly with oil. Opening may be filled with any relishes desired or with salad greens. Sprinkle salad lightly with paprika.

Garnish outside of salad with 12 halves of hard-cooked deviled, stuffed eggs. For additional color, place small sprig of parsley or large fresh pepper leaves between egg halves.

German Hot Sweet-Sour Green Bean Salad

Serves 4

12-ounce package frozen cut green beans (or canned)
2 slices bacon, diced
½ cup chopped onions
2 teaspoons granulated sugar

1 tablespoon vinegar
½ teaspoon salt
⅛ teaspoon pepper
¼ cup green-bean liquid

Cook green beans until just tender, drain, and measure ¼ cup of liquid. Cook diced bacon over moderate heat until light golden brown. Add chopped onions, and sauté several minutes. Add sugar, vinegar, salt, pepper, beans, and bean liquid, and cook about 5 minutes.

Serve hot with any meat course.

Asparagus Salad

Cook asparagus according to directions on page 274. When cool, cover, and keep in refrigerator. When ready to be served, arrange over a large thick slice of tomato and shredded lettuce; pour French dressing, or any desired dressing, over salad, and serve.

Tomato Basket Salad

Select tomatoes of uniform size. If large, cut in halves lengthwise. Scoop out center very carefully and let drain upside down. Sprinkle inside of tomato with salt. Cut up pulp, a little green pepper, onion, lettuce, celery, etc. Add desired dressing. Fill tomato, and spread top with a little creamed mayonnaise. Sprinkle with paprika. Cut narrow rings of fresh green pepper and insert into sides of tomatoes to simulate a basket. Serve on lettuce.

Tomato Rose Salad

Select medium-size well shaped *firm* tomatoes. Add a little coloring to cream cheese, or leave white. With fork, beat only until of medium consistency. If cheese is too soft after adding coloring, chill it in refrigerator until sufficiently firm. Fill smallest spoon with cheese (iced-tea spoon or baby spoon may be used), scrape it against edge of bowl, and pipe first row around upper part of tomato. Pipe another row on lower part of tomato. Arrange on bed of endive, watercress, or lettuce. Place small rosettes of parsley around lower part of tomato, holding in place close to cheese, and serve with French or other dressing. Tomatoes may be filled with salad before they are piped with cheese. Sprinkle top with grated egg yolk or fine-chopped or shredded carrot.

Banana-Pineapple Salad

1 ripe banana, brushed with pineapple juice
2 slices canned pineapple

Crisp salad greens, such as curly endive or watercress
Strawberries, blackberries, cherries

Peel banana and place a ring of pineapple around each end. Garnish with crisp salad greens, berries, cherries, and so forth. Serve with French dressing or Fruit Salad Dressing (page 371).

Waldorf Salad

2 cups diced unpeeled red apples
1 cup diced celery
½ cup chopped pecans or walnuts

1 cup mayonnaise, combined with 1 tablespoon pineapple juice
2 bananas sliced, dipped into pineapple or lemon juice

Mix together apples, celery, and pecans or walnuts. Add mayonnaise combined with pineapple juice, and banana slices. Arrange on lettuce leaf or in lettuce cup. Garnish with watercress and sprinkle lightly with paprika.

Fresh Fruit Salad Plate

1 lettuce cup	Grapefruit sections
Cottage cheese	French pineapple spears
Cantaloupe balls	Slices of oranges
Honeydew balls	Finger sandwiches with desired fillings
Watermelon balls	Walnut or pecan halves

Place on center of plate lettuce cup filled with cottage cheese. Around lettuce cup arrange attractively cantaloupe, honeydew, watermelon balls, grapefuit sections, pineapple spears, orange slices, finger sandwiches, a few whole walnuts or pecan halves. Serve with French dressing or your own favorite dressing separately.

Fresh Fruit Salad Plate with finger sandwiches is ideal to serve for luncheon, especially during the hot summer months.

Cantaloupe or Honeydew Melon Birds

Cut each melon lengthwise into 4 or 6 sections with knife. Loosen meat of melon and cut it into small sections, but do not remove. Fill with fresh-cut fruits, such as watermelon, strawberries, raspberries, pineapple, and so forth. Proceed as in Avocado Bird Salad (page 360) for head, etc.

Pineapple-Apricot Salad

Over thick slice of lettuce place a slice of pineapple that has been tinted pink. Fill cavities of 2 apricot halves or whole apricot with cream cheese and nuts and put halves together. Spread apricot with cream cheese and cover with fine-chopped nuts. Place in center of pineapple. Over apricot place ½ slice of green pineapple to simulate handle. Pipe tiny rosettes of cream cheese on top of green pineapple and around apricot, using small star tube.

Standing Pear Salad

Fill cavities of 2 halves of pears with cream cheese and chopped nuts. Press carefully together, and place, small end up, on crisp cup-shaped lettuce leaves. To cream cheese add a little orange coloring and enough fruit syrup or cream to make right consistency to pour. With a teaspoon, pour over top of pear and sprinkle with fine-chopped nuts. Pears may be tinted pale pink or yellow if desired. Tiny strips of citron or green pepper may be used as stems.

Grape-Pear Salad

Fill 2 or 3 small pears, or 1 large pear, with cream cheese and chopped nuts, and arrange on thick slice of lettuce. Spread rounded side of pear with cream cheese, and cover with seedless grapes that have been cut into halves, or use red grapes. Place green-pepper strips to simulate stems, and make tiny leaves with red and green pepper. Cheese must not be too soft when spread over pears, and grapes must be dry, or they will slip off.

Florida Salad

Over thick slice of lettuce place slice of pineapple. Fill cavity of pineapple with jam or jelly. Pipe 6 rosettes of cream cheese on pineapple. Top each rosette with whole maraschino cherry, small fresh strawberry, raspberry, or fresh black cherry. Place tiny green citron or pepper leaves on each side of rosettes. Serve with Fruit Salad Dressing (page 371).

Tropical Raspberry Salad

Place a large fresh or canned pineapple ring on slice of iceberg lettuce. Fill center of pineapple with drained creamed cottage cheese or fresh raspberries, forming a slight mound. Place grapefruit and orange segments alternately over mound. Decorate top by pipping a large rosette of cream cheese or whipped cream and adding 2 long green-pepper leaves.

Combine ½ tablespoon plain gelatin with ¼ cup cold water. Let stand until thick. Pour 1 cup boiling water over 1 package lemon- or raspberry-flavored gelatin dessert and plain gelatin. When completely dissolved, let stand until slightly congealed. Add a 12-ounce package defrosted frozen raspberries. Stir gently. Then pour into an oiled 7 × 7-inch square pan. Refrigerate 6 or 7 hours or longer, until very firm. Cut into 1¼-inch strips, then into diamonds. Garnish each plate with several raspberry diamonds to simulate flowers.

Hollywood Salad

Over a thick slice of lettuce, sliced crosswise, place 6 sections of grapefruit to simulate a flower. Between sections, place narrow strips of green pepper or citron and pimiento. Down center, pipe 3 rosettes of cream cheese with No. 27 or No. 30 star tube. Top each rosette with smallest black ripe olives brushed with oil, small blackberries, sweet cherries *or* small black grapes.

Place small green pepper or citron leaves on each side of rosettes and larger leaves in front and back. Serve French Dressing (page 368) or Fruit Salad Dressing (page 371) separately.

Happy Jack Salad

Select attractive medium or large firm tomatoes. Cut off thin slice from stem end, to be used for hat. Scoop out pulp, drain well, and sprinkle inside with salt. Drain. Fill with any desired salad, such as chicken, crab meat, lobster, ham, tuna fish, eggs, etc. Add small amount of gelatin to salad to absorb surplus moisture. On top of tomato place a hard-cooked egg, prepared as follows:

Insert several toothpicks on narrow bottom of egg so that it will stand in salad. Place 2 cloves on egg for eyes; with red coloring on end of wooden skewer paint face, and make a gash for mouth, in which place a tiny green candle to represent cigarette. Trim round slice of tomato that was removed from stem end, place it on top of egg to represent hat, holding down with a frilled toothpick. Place stuffed tomato on leaf or romaine lettuce, in bed of shredded lettuce or cup shape lettuce. Pit a large black olive and cut in halves; place one half below tip of candle to simulate ash tray. In darkened room, light candles just before guests are seated. Keep candles in refrigerator until ready to be used to prevent excessive dripping.

Turkey Fruit Salad

On lettuce leaves (preferably leaf lettuce or romaine or thick slice of lettuce) arrange ½ of firm well drained pear, or 2 halves held together with cream cheese, rounded side up. The pear may be tinted pink, or left plain. Cut pineapple slices in halves, tint green, drain well on a towel and arrange on high part of pear and ½ slice on back part, holding in place with flat toothpicks.

Sketch and cut out pattern of bird's head and neck on stiff cardboard. Place it over a slice of Idaho potato or apple cut about ¼ inch thick, and with a small sharp knife cut around carefully. Place them in cold water in a flat pan and hold down with another pan to prevent them from curling. Keep in refrigerator at least 1 hour (or may be made day in advance). Shortly before using, remove from water and brush with lemon juice, then place in a small amount of yellow-colored water. Dry slightly on a towel. Tint nose and top of head with undiluted red coloring, using a tiny brush; then dilute red coloring with a drop of water and paint a few feathers on sides of neck. Insert small whole cloves for eyes. Make slit in front of pear and insert head, trimming bottom if too thick. Press tiny white rosettes of cream cheese on pineapple, and pipe base of pear with cream cheese.

May be served as main luncheon dish, using 2 pear halves. May be used as a first course or as an accompaniment, using 1 small pear half. Serve Fruit Salad Dressing (page 371) separately.

Calavo-Cranberry Salad with Turkey Slices

Cut large calavo pears in halves lengthwise. Remove seed, and peel carefully. Brush entire surface with lemon juice at once to prevent discoloration. Fill with cranberry relish or sauce (canned cranberry sauce may be used). Serve on bed of endive or leaf lettuce. Arrange cold sliced turkey on each side. (Leftover chicken or turkey may be used in this way.) Serve French dressing separately. Pipe large rosette with No. 27 tube on small and large end of calavo, and green leaves with No. 67 tube. Excellent luncheon or supper dish, with hot rolls.

Calavo-Strawberry Salad with Cold Sliced Baked Ham

Prepare calavo as for Calavo-Cranberry Salad with Turkey Slices. Fill center with Strawberry Rhubarb Mold (page 440). Arrange cold sliced ham on each side. Garnish tip and rounded part of calavo with large cheese rosettes and green leaves. Serve Horseradish Whipped Cream Sauce (page 372) or French Dressing (page 368) separately.

Pear Mint Salad with Cold Sliced Lamb

Select large firm fresh or canned pear halves. For canned pears, marinate in own syrup, to which add a little green coloring and mint flavoring. If using fresh pears, peel, core, and cut into halves lengthwise. Brush with lemon juice. Prepare syrup with 2 parts water and 1 part sugar. Cook pears in syrup about 5 minutes if soft; 7 or 8 minutes if very firm. Lift out pears; add green coloring and mint flavoring. Place pears back into syrup and let remain until cold. Drain well. Fill openings with cream cheese and chopped nuts. Put 2 together, and serve on lettuce leaves. Place mint leaf on small end. Arrange cold sliced lamb on each side. Serve some French dressing separately. Other cold sliced roasted meats may be served instead. This is an excellent luncheon or supper dish, served with hot rolls.

Melon Boats

Cut medium-size honeydew melons and cantaloupes into 4, 6, or 8 lengthwise sections, depending on size of fruit. Remove seeds. With French baller, cut out balls from each section, leaving a small space between each ball. Place honeydew balls in cantaloupe, and vice versa. Balls may be marinated in a light wine about 1 hour before serving. Garnish ends of boats with sprigs of mint leaves. Any small leaves may be used instead. Serve as a first course if small, or use large melons for main light luncheon or supper dishes, with open-face and finger sandwiches. A fruit salad dressing may be served separately.

▶ SALAD DRESSINGS ◀

Italian or French Dressing Continental-Style

1 cup salad oil
¼ to ⅓ cup wine vinegar (other vinegars may be used)
1 clove garlic, cut in 2 or 3 pieces

About 1¼ teaspoons salt
⅛ teaspoon black pepper
⅛ teaspoon oregano

Combine all ingredients in a jar. Cover tightly and shake vigorously until thoroughly blended. Keep in cool place (best temperature about 60° F.). Shake dressing well each time before pouring over salad ingredients.

Note. If French dressing or any of the stabilized dressings given in this section become too thick at any time, do not stir nor beat, but place in a pan of warm water and stir gently until smooth and of proper consistency. If curdling should occur at any time, place bowl with dressing in a pan of hot water and stir until completely melted, then reset in refrigerator or ice water and watch closely, stirring occasionally to keep uniform in consistency.

Salad Dressing Superb

2 teaspoons unflavored gelatin, combined with ¼ cup cold water (mix and let stand until thick, about 5 minutes, then dissolve over simmering water)
1 cup commercial mayonnaise (room temperature)
1 teaspoon lemon juice
¼ cup half & half cream
¼ cup, or less, mild salad mustard or 2 tablespoons strong type

1 uncooked egg yolk
2 tablespoons granulated sugar
1 small clove garlic, chopped fine or put through garlic press
2 tablespoons finely chopped green onion
¼ cup chopped onion stems
2 tablespoons finely chopped green pepper (optional)
½ teaspoon capers, well drained (optional)

Add dissolved *warm* gelatin to the mayonnaise slowly and blend well. Now add all other ingredients and mix thoroughly. Refrigerate dressing for at least 30 minutes (not more than an hour) *and stir it occasionally* to keep it uniform and of medium consistency.

Modified Italian Dressing

1 cup salad oil
⅓ cup cider vinegar
1 clove garlic, cut into several pieces
1¼ teaspoons, or less, salt

⅛ teaspoon coarse black pepper (optional)
¼ cup, or less, granulated sugar

Combine all ingredients in a medium jar with tight cover. Shake vigorously until thoroughly blended, for at least 1 minute. Keep in cool place or refrigerator for at least 1 hour. Shake well each time before pouring onto salad ingredients. This is a very delicious, popular dressing for salad bowls and other greens. Ingredients may be increased or decreased to suit taste.

Modified French Dressing

⅓ cup cider vinegar
1 tablespoon, or less, paprika
1¼ teaspoons salt
Dash red pepper
1 clove garlic, cut into 2 or 3 pieces

¼ cup, or less, granulated sugar
1 whole egg
1 cup salad oil
Little red food coloring (optional)

Combine all ingredients except oil in a No. 7 bowl. With electric mixer or egg beater, beat about 1 minute, then add the cup of oil, about 1 tablespoonful at a time, and continue to beat until thick for about 1 more minute. Shake well each time before using. Keep in a cool place.

Zesty Sour Cream Dressing

1 cup commercial sour cream
1 teaspoon salt
⅛ teaspoon coarsely ground pepper
2 tablespoons finely minced green onion and stems

2 tablespoons prepared horseradish, or 1 tablespoon freshly grated horseradish

Combine all ingredients and stir well. May be prepared several days in advance if stored in covered jar in refrigerator. Use with vegetable and seafood molds.

Roman Dressing

Makes about 1⅔ cups

2 cloves garlic
1½ teaspoons salt
1 cup salad oil
1 egg, well beaten
Juice of 1 lemon

⅓ cup grated parmesan cheese
½ teaspoon whole pepper, ground coarse
2 teaspoons Worcestershire sauce

Mash garlic with salt. Add part of oil slowly to well-beaten egg, beating constantly with rotary or electric beater. When mixture starts to thicken, add rest of oil and lemon juice alternately, in small amounts, beating constantly.

Stir in cheese, ground pepper, Worcestershire sauce, and mashed garlic with salt. Pour over salad greens.

Gourmet Goddess Salad Dressing

1 clove garlic, crushed in press or cut very fine
2-ounce can anchovies, drained and cut into ½-inch pieces
¼ cup or more chives (frozen chives are excellent), or fine-cut green onion tops
1 tablespoon lemon juice
2 tablespoons wine or tarragon vinegar
1 cup mayonnaise
½ cup commercial sour cream
2 tablespoons minced parsley
About ¼ teaspoon coarse black pepper

Combine all ingredients, and blend well. Cover tightly, and let ripen at least 1 day in a cool place. Do not freeze. Stir well, and pour over salad greens, or use on seafood salads.

Roquefort Dressing

In a bowl or mixer combine ⅓ cup cider or other vinegar, 1 tablespoon paprika, 1½ teaspoons salt, dash of red pepper, small clove of garlic cut in 2 pieces (or ½ teaspoon garlic salt), ¼ cup granulated sugar (or less), and 1 whole egg. Mix well, and slowly add 1 cup oil, and beat until emulsified. Then add ¼ cup or less roquefort cheese broken up into medium-size pieces, and blend well. An electric mixer or egg beater may be used in preparing this dressing. Do not add too much oil at one time, especially in beginning.

Roquefort cheese is added last and blended into dressing with a wooden spoon. Keep dressing tightly covered in cold place. Shake thoroughly before using.

Mayonnaise Dressing

1 whole egg, or yolks of 2 eggs (yolks will give a richer and heavier dressing)
½ teaspoon dry mustard
1 tablespoon granulated sugar
1 teaspoon salt
Dash of red pepper (more spices may be used)
3 tablespoons vinegar or lemon juice (an extra tablespoon may be used)
2 cups salad oil

Combine all above ingredients except oil in mayonnaise mixer or in bowl, Add oil, a very little at a time (about 1 teaspoon), and beat until thick and creamy. If mayonnaise appears too oily or curdles after it is completed, add slowly about 2 tablespoons boiling water, vinegar, or lemon juice, and beat well with a wooden spoon. If using 2 yolks instead of a whole egg, it is advisable to add boiling water or extra vinegar, etc. When done, keep tightly covered in a cool place. Best temperature is between 60° and 70° F. If mayonnaise appears oily after standing, stir it with spoon or add a little boiling water and beat vigorously.

Cooked Salad Dressing for Cole Slaw

2 tablespoons cornstarch, or ¼ cup
    sifted flour
1½ teaspoons, more or less, dry mus-
    tard
1½ teaspoons salt
⅛ teaspoon paprika (optional)

¼ cup granulated sugar
1 egg yolk, beaten with a fork and
    combined with ⅓ cup milk
1½ cups warm milk
½ cup, more or less, cider vinegar

Combine cornstarch, seasonings, and sugar. Add yolk combined with the ⅓ cup cool milk, and blend until smooth. Add the 1½ cups warm milk slowly, and cook until thick and smooth, and let simmer about 3 minutes. Now, last add the vinegar slowly, blend well and continue to simmer about 3 more minutes. Let stand until cool, or use warm if desired. May be kept in tightly covered jar for several days if refrigerated. Stir or beat a few seconds before using, and if too thick, add a little milk, or vinegar.

Fruit Salad Dressing

2 tablespoons melted butter
2 tablespoons all-purpose flour
½ cup granulated sugar
2 egg yolks
½ cup strained pineapple juice
⅛ teaspoon salt

2 egg whites beaten to medium con-
    sistency
2 tablespoons granulated sugar
1¼ cups lukewarm strained pineapple
    juice
1 cup whipping cream (optional)

In a 2-quart saucepan, combine melted butter and flour; mix until smooth. Then add the ½ cup granulated sugar and the egg yolks combined with ½ cup pineapple juice, and the salt. Mix thoroughly.

To the beaten egg whites add the 2 tablespoons granulated sugar and beat until well blended. Blend egg whites gently into first mixture. Last slowly add the lukewarm strained pineapple juice. Cook slowly in heavy saucepan until thick and smooth, stirring constantly. Let simmer several minutes. Watch carefully that it does not curdle, keeping heat low. If it curdles, beat a few seconds with egg beater. Allow mixture to become cold; then, if desired, fold in whipping cream that has been beaten to medium consistency. Serve very cold.

Whipped Cream Brandy or Rum Sauce

¼ cup fresh egg whites
1 cup granulated sugar
¼ teaspoon cream of tartar
3 tablespoons cool water
⅛ teaspoon salt
½ teaspoon vanilla

½ teaspoon plain gelatin, combined with 2 tablespoons cold water
2 tablespoons brandy or rum
1 cup whipping cream, beaten just until it clings to bowl (not too stiff)

Combine egg whites, sugar, cream of tartar, the 3 tablespoons cool water, salt, and vanilla in upper part of small double boiler. Mix well with wooden spoon. Bring water in lower part to a boil, place upper part of boiler in position (if using electric beater, remove double boiler from stove) and at once beat until mixture is thick and clings to pan for 6 to 7 minutes. Remove top of boiler from water. Combine gelatin wth 2 tablespoons cold water, let stand until thick, then dissolve over simmering water. Add brandy or rum to gelatin.

At once add the gelatin and brandy mixture, little at a time, to the sauce and beat by hand or with electric mixer *only* until well blended. Keep in refrigerator or cold place until cool, about 1 hour, but let stand only until cool or else it will become too thick, in which case stir well with a spoon over hot water. Then fold it, little at a time, into the whipped cream.

Keep sauce in refrigerator until ready to be served. May be prepared hours in advance. *Do not omit* gelatin or liquor will separate from other ingredients. This sauce should always be stirred for a few seconds gently before serving to insure smoothness.

Horseradish Whipped Cream Sauce

½ cup prepared commercial horseradish, lightly drained
1 cup thick mayonnaise
2 tablespoons granulated sugar

½ teaspoon salt
1 cup whipping cream, beaten until it just clings to bowl (not too stiff)

Combine all ingredients except cream in a bowl. Blend well, then pour in the whipped cream, and stir gently until evenly mixed. Serve separately with chaud-froid and other molds.

Pope's Cream Roquefort Salad Dressing

½ cup cream cheese
1 cup sour cream
2 tablespoons mayonnaise or salad dressing

½ teaspoon salt
½ teaspoon Worcestershire sauce
¼ pound roquefort cheese, crumbled

Put cream cheese in 6- or 7-inch bowl and cream well with mixer, about 2 minutes. Add sour cream, mayonnaise, salt and Worcestershire sauce and mix only until blended. Then add crumbled roquefort and blend in gently with wooden spoon. This salad dressing can be made in advance if kept refrigerated. Before serving stir gently as it will thicken when refrigerated.

Bahama Salad Dressing

1 small clove garlic, crushed in garlic press
½ teaspoon celery salt
½ to ¾ teaspoon salt
⅛ teaspoon freshly ground black pepper

About 1½ teaspoons strong mustard (more or less to suit taste)
¼ cup red wine vinegar
½ cup salad oil

Combine all ingredients in a mason jar and shake well for 2 or 3 minutes. Refrigerate for at least 2 hours before using. Shake well before pouring over salad and toss well until completely blended. Serve at once.

Piquant French Dressing

1 large clove garlic, mashed or put through garlic press
⅛ teaspoon dry mustard
⅛ teaspoon cayenne pepper
¼ teaspoon black pepper
⅛ teaspoon celery seed
About ½ teaspoon salt
2 teaspoons granulated sugar

1 cup salad oil
⅓ cup wine or cider vinegar (tarragon-flavored vinegar may be used)
2 tablespoons anchovies, cut into small pieces
¼ cup crumbled roquefort or bleu cheese

Combine all ingredients in a jar. Cover, and shake well about 1 minute. Refrigerate, and shake again about 1 minute before pouring onto salad ingredients.

Gourmet Dressing for Salmon and Seafood Dishes

1 cup sour cream
1 cup mayonnaise
¼ cup finely chopped green onion and stems
¼ cup lemon juice

1 teaspoon capers (optional)
½ cup finely chopped stuffed green olives
¼ teaspoon salt
2 teaspoons granulated sugar

Combine all ingredients in order given and blend well. Keep refrigerated until ready to serve.

Kentucky Limestone Salad Dressing

1 clove garlic, put through garlic press
¼ teaspoon celery salt
About 1 teaspoon salt

1 teaspoon salad mustard
¼ cup pear vinegar (other vinegars may be used)
½ cup salad oil

Combine all ingredients and shake well. Refrigerate at least 2 hours. Shake again just before pouring over lettuce.

Sauce Louisiana

½ cup catsup
1 cup chili sauce
½ teaspoon hot sauce, or ⅛ teaspoon hot pepper
½ teaspoon salt
1 small clove garlic, minced fine or put through garlic press
2 tablespoons fresh green pepper, minced fine (optional)

¼ cup fresh green onion and tops, cut fine
2 tablespoons prepared horseradish
2 teaspoons plain gelatin, combined with ¼ cup cold water (stir and let stand until thick, then dissolve over simmering water)

Combine all ingredients except gelatin and mix well. Now add warm dissolved gelatin and stir quickly and thoroughly. Refrigerate sauce for about ⅓ cup of alcohol. Wipe outside of the lamp with a dry cloth. Light several days in advance or longer if kept in covered container in refrigerator. In this case, remove sauce from refrigerator about 30 minutes before combining it with seafood. Makes a delicious cocktail and dipping sauce for hors d'oeuvres foods.

Whipped Cream Mayonnaise-Horseradish Sauce

To each cup mayonnaise, add 1 or 2 tablespoons prepared horseradish and ½ cup whipping cream beaten until medium. Keep in refrigerator until ready to serve. Serve separately instead of plain mayonnaise with salad molds.

▶ Chafing Dishes and Casseroles

LUNCHEON, SUPPER, AND DINNER DISHES

WITH TODAY'S TREND TOWARD BUFFET ENTERTAINING, THE CHAFING DISH HAS made a comeback. A chafing dish, however, can be used around the clock, from breakfast to a late snack, for appetizers, main dishes, and desserts, indoors or out. With the chafing dish pan directly over the heat, it acts as a skillet for quick sautéing. With the water pan underneath, you have a perfect double boiler for delicate sauces. To save time, always fill the water pan with boiling instead of cold water.

Today, chafing dishes can be purchased at moderate prices. They come in copper, chrome, stainless steel, and aluminum. We recommend one that is equipped with a water jacket and a tray for easy and satisfactory use. The stirring spoon or fork, seasonings, and other ingredients that go into the recipe are grouped around the chafing dish on the tray.

For an alcohol chafing dish, denatured or wood alcohol may be purchased in hardware and drug stores. Fill the lamp with cotton and saturate it with about ⅓ cup of alcohol. Wipe outside of the lamp with a dry cloth. Light and regulate flame. Sterno heat may be used in these lamps instead of alcohol. If you use an electric chafing dish, follow directions given by the manufacturer.

Most of us enjoy food more if we watch it being prepared. Numerous dishes can be prepared directly in the chafing dish while guests are seated around the table, and to save time many of the ingredients can be prepared ahead of the party. For our hot preparations it is best to cook the sauce shortly in advance, and then add other ingredients at the table. This will shorten cooking time about 10 or 12 minutes.

When entertaining large groups, it is best to prepare entire recipe in advance in the kitchen and then serve it from chafing dish to keep hot. Beef Stroganoff, special stews, creamed seafood and poultry preparations, French-fried shrimp, Cantonese dishes, and many others can be served in chafing dishes. Chafing-dish preparations can be supplemented with side dishes prepared in the kitchen, especially when more than 4 people are to be served. Hors d'oeuvres dips or other similar concoctions served before a special luncheon or dinner can be prepared in the living room on a tea wagon or butler's cart in full view of guests. Be sure to have all necessary ingredients ready to be used, and also see that the cocktail plates, forks, and napkins are at hand.

All delicate sauces containing large amounts of butter and eggs, such as Hollandaise, and those made with sour cream must be cooked and kept over hot water jacket (about 125° to 150° F., never direct heat) to prevent curdling or separation.

Also please note that basic cheese dishes must be kept over water jacket after the cheese is fully melted to prevent toughening and scorching of cheese.

▶ SEAFOOD AND POULTRY CASSEROLES ◀

Casserole dishes are legion, and they are a boon to the hostess because they can be prepared weeks in advance and frozen, or they can be refrigerated for many hours or a day in advance, then baked and served piping hot to large or small groups.

The casseroles to be frozen may be prepared completely, but do not bake them before freezing. Frozen casserole dishes must stand in room temperature at least 4 hours, *or better in refrigerator to defrost about 8 hours,* before baking. Never allow them to become warm while defrosting before baking. Baking time must be increased and temperature of oven reduced about 25 degrees. It is best to test internal temperature by inserting meat thermometer into center of food before removing casserole from oven. Most desirable temperature is about 150° F. Overcooking frozen precooked foods will make them soft and less palatable. Please see section on Freezing (page 880).

If a freezer is not available, these dishes may be prepared hours or a day in advance, then covered well and stored in coldest part of refrigerator. About an hour before baking, remove them from refrigerator and let stand in room temperature, then bake, increasing time about 15 minutes to 150° F. Casserole dishes that require a cover may be covered with heavy greased aluminum foil.

Note. Today authorities warn that food must not be allowed to cool at room temperature and suggest that if it is not to be served within a few minutes to cool it rapidly in a pan of ice water; or food may be placed in the refrigerator even if it is warm. An easy rule to remember is to keep hot foods hot (at least at 140° F.) and cold foods cold (below 45° F.) at any time. Food kept for more than 3 hours between 60° and 120° F. may not be safe to eat. Salmonella, a tiny, infectious bacteria that contaminates food, thrives at room temperature. It is destroyed at a temperature of 40° F. or below, and 140° F. or above.

Salmonella is a year-round danger, and it becomes more common during the summer months when picnickers eat foods that have been improperly stored. It thrives in usual picnic foods such as potato salad, milk products, poultry, and fish. If you can't maintain these foods at the proper temperatures, don't take them along unless they are going to be cooked at the picnic site.

Convenience foods sold in stores can also become contaminated if not prepared according to directions and stored properly, and if right temperatures as suggested above are not maintained. It is always safer to insert a meat thermometer into a preparation that is reheated to make sure that temperature reaches at least 150° F. and not more than 180° F.

Lobster Oriental in Chafing Dish (or in Casserole)

Serves 8

2 pounds small lobster tails
¼ pound fresh mushrooms
2 tablespoons butter
¼ teaspoon salt
⅛ teaspoon pepper
⅛ teaspoon garlic salt
½ cup butter or margarine
½ cup sifted all-purpose flour
2 cups milk or thin cream, warm
About 1½ teaspoons salt
¼ teaspoon pepper
1 tablespoon soy sauce

1 can Chinese chestnuts, sliced medium (about 4 ounces)
¼ cup sherry wine
¼ cup blanched whole or split toasted salted almonds
2 tablespoons pimiento, cut into 1-inch pieces
About ½ cup shredded toasted almonds
Another ½ cup finely chopped green onion stems

Cover lobster tails with hot water and simmer about 7 to 10 minutes. If using very large tails increase cooking time to about 15 minutes. Let cool in own liquid for ½ hour, then remove shells and cut lobster in about 1½-inch pieces (or smaller). (One pound of cooked crab meat may be used instead of lobster tails.)

Leave mushrooms whole if very small. If large cut into thick slices. Sauté in 2 tablespoons of hot butter for about 5 minutes, turning several times. A small can of mushrooms may be used instead. Season with the ¼ teaspoon salt, ⅛ teaspoon pepper, and ⅛ teaspoon garlic salt.

Prepare sauce by melting butter or margarine, add flour and blend to a smooth paste. Add warm milk or thin cream, little at a time, and the seasonings. Cook until thick and smooth, stirring continuously, then add the cooked lobster meat, mushrooms, soy sauce, Chinese chestnuts and wine. *If preparation is too thick add more milk or wine and continue to cook about 5 more minutes.* Last, fold in the blanched toasted almonds, pimiento and green cut onion.

Pour into chafing dish or casserole, sprinkle top with ½ cup of shredded toasted almonds and garnish about 1 inch on sides with ½ cup green onion, and serve hot with crisp crackers, toast, etc.

Crab Meat au Diable (in Chafing Dish or in Patty Shells)

Serves 2 to 3

2 tablespoons butter or margarine
2 tablespoons flour
¾ cup milk
½ teaspoon salt
¼ teaspoon chili power
⅛ teaspoon hot sauce
1 slightly beaten egg yolk

½ cup finely chopped canned mushrooms (3-ounce can), sautéed in 1 tablespoon butter for 2 or 3 minutes
2 tablespoons finely cut green onion
6- or 7-ounce can or package frozen crab meat, chopped in small pieces

Melt butter, or margarine, add flour, mixing until smooth. Add milk a little at a time, and cook until thick. Add all other ingredients except crab meat, and simmer about 5 minutes. Last, fold in crab meat. Mix gently and serve hot in chafing dish or let cool and refrigerate if not to be used at once.

To Serve. Serve in chafing dish or in Patty Shells. Fill tiny Patty Shells (page 4), having filling slightly rounded, and bake at 350° F. about 10 minutes just before serving. Fills about 24 shells. May be filled in advance and refrigerated, in covered container. Sprinkle top with paprika.

Crab Meat Creole (in Chafing Dish)

Serves 6

½ cup green onion and stems, cut into ½-inch pieces
½ cup fresh green pepper, cut into ½-inch pieces
¼ cup butter or shortening
2 cups fresh tomatoes, peeled and cut into 1-inch chunks (drained canned tomatoes may be used instead)
2 cups kernel corn (fresh, or 1 package frozen, or 1 can drained)

About 1 teaspoon salt
¼ teaspoon coarse-ground black pepper
¼ teaspoon celery salt
1 pound fresh or frozen crab meat (remove bones but leave crab meat in large pieces)
2 tablespoons cornstarch combined with 1 cup stock (or a bouillon cube added to water)

Sauté green onion and pepper in butter 3 or 4 minutes. Add tomatoes, corn, and seasoning, and cook about 5 more minutes. Add crab meat and, last, cornstarch combined with stock. Mix well, bring to the boiling point, lower heat, and simmer 3 or 4 minutes. Do not cook further, to prevent toughening of crab meat. Taste, and season further if necessary. Sprinkle top with fine-cut fresh green onion stems just before serving.

This is an excellent dish for buffets or cocktail parties. This is also delicious served in Patty Shells (page 4) or on toast as a light luncheon or supper dish.

Creamed Crab Meat and Rice (in Chafing Dish)

Serves 4

2 cups Medium White Sauce (page 328)	¼ cup dry sherry wine
½ teaspoon pepper	1½ cups cooked crab meat
½ teaspoon Worcestershire sauce	2 tablespoons pimiento strips
	½ cup sautéed sliced mushrooms

Prepare Medium White Sauce, and add pepper, Worcestershire sauce, sherry, pimiento, and mushrooms. Cook about 3 minutes, add crab meat that has been broken into small pieces, and cook another 2 minutes. Serve in chafing dish on white rice.

Shrimp Louisiana in Chafing Dish

Serves 4

1 pound cooked shrimp, left whole if small or medium; split lengthwise if large	½ teaspoon garlic salt
	1 tablespoon brown sugar
	¼ teaspoon celery salt
½ cup chili sauce	2 tablespoons cornstarch, combined with 1 cup water or tomato juice
¾ cup catsup	
1 tablespoon prepared horseradish (optional)	½ cup fresh green onions and ½ cup green onion tops, cut in ½-inch pieces
About 1 teaspoon salt	

Combine all ingredients except starch mixture and green onions. Mix well, cover bowl and let marinate for at least an hour. About 10 minutes before serving, add dissolved cornstarch to ingredients, mix well and cook over moderate heat for about 5 minutes after simmering begins if shrimp are large; cook about 3 minutes after simmering begins if shrimp are small or medium. If sauce is too thick add a little water. Last, fold in the fresh green onions and tops.

Pour into chafing dish and serve with crackers, wafers, or melba toast. This makes an excellent buffet or luncheon dish served with plain hot rice.

Shrimp Creole in Chafing Dish

Serves 6

⅓ cup butter or margarine
1 small onion, chopped medium
1 cup celery, chopped medium
3 cups tomato juice
About 2 teaspoons salt
½ teaspoon celery salt
½ teaspoon garlic salt
¼ cup cornstarch, combined with ½ cup tomato juice

About 1½ pounds of uncooked shelled shrimp
¼ pound sliced fresh mushrooms, sautéed 3 minutes
1 small fresh green pepper, cut in 1-inch narrow strips, sautéed several minutes
½ teaspoon baking soda (optional)

Heat butter or margarine in a 3-quart saucepan, and sauté chopped onions and celery about 5 minutes. Add the 3 cups tomato juice, all of seasonings (except soda) and the cornstarch combined with the ½ cup tomato juice. Mix well, and cook until thick, then simmer about 3 minutes. Now add the shelled raw and deveined shrimp, and simmer 7 or 8 minutes if small, or about 12 minutes if shrimp are large. Shrimp take longer to cook in a thick sauce. Last, add the sautéed mushrooms, sautéed green pepper, and baking soda, and continue to cook about 5 more minutes. Pour into chafing dish.

To Serve. Mold rice in a bowl and surround with Shrimp Creole, or rice may be placed in a chafing dish, covered with shrimp and sauce, for buffet and cocktail parties. Garnish edge with ½ cup finely chopped green pepper or parsley.

Shrimp and Deviled Eggs Mornay in Casserole

Serves 4 to 6

⅓ cup butter or margarine
⅓ cup sifted all-purpose flour
2 cups warm milk
½ cup grated parmesan cheese, or 1 cup freshly shredded American
2 teaspoons salt
2 tablespoons light dry wine (optional)
¼ teaspoon pepper
¼ teaspoon celery salt
¼ teaspoon dried parsley
8 hard-cooked eggs, cut into halves

½ pound fresh mushrooms, sliced thick (or 3-ounce can)
½ cup fresh green onion and onion tops, cut into ½-inch pieces
2 more tablespoons butter or margarine
½ teaspoon salt
Pepper
1½ pounds fresh shrimp, cooked in gently boiling salted water about 5 minutes if large, 3 minutes if medium-size

To prepare sauce, melt butter, add flour, and blend until smooth. Add milk slowly. Cook until thick, stirring constantly. Let simmer about 3 minutes. Now add cheese and all other seasonings, and continue to simmer about 2 or 3 minutes.

Sauté mushrooms and onions in 2 tablespoons butter about 5 minutes, turning often. Season with about ½ teaspoon salt and a little pepper.

Arrange egg halves, with cut sides up on bottom of a baking dish that measures about 10 × 6 × 2 inches. Sprinkle eggs very lightly with a little salt and pepper. Combine cooked shrimp with sautéed mushrooms and onion, and place gently over eggs. Pour sauce over entire top.

Bake at 350° F. about 20 minutes if ingredients are warm or about 30 minutes if casserole was prepared in advance and ingredients are cold. Place under broiler to brown top a minute or two, if necessary.

Top of casserole may be garnished with a hard-cooked egg first cut into halves lengthwise, then each half cut into 4 sections. Arrange egg on top center of casserole to simulate a flower. Place a curled strip of red pimiento or whole red maraschino cherry in center of petals.

A tasty and satisfying luncheon or supper dish. Serve with a vegetable and salad.

Crab Meat or Lobster Creole

Follow directions for Shrimp Creole (page 380). Add about 1 pound cooked crab meat or lobster instead of shrimp the last 5 minutes, *and simmer gently.*

Haddock Creole

Follow directions for Shrimp Creole (page 380). About 1½ pounds of uncooked haddock, cut into 1½-inch pieces may be used instead of shrimp. Add haddock the last 12 minutes, and simmer gently.

Shrimp Supreme in Casserole

Serves 4

6 hard-cooked eggs, sliced into halves lengthwise	2 tablespoons butter
½ pound bacon, cut into small pieces and fried	2 tablespoons flour
1 cup cooked rice	1 cup warm milk
½ pound cooked shrimp, split into halves lengthwise	½ teaspoon salt
	¼ teaspoon white pepper
	½ cup shredded cheddar cheese
	2 tablespoons bread crumbs

Place egg halves with cut sides down in a buttered 1½-quart casserole. Over eggs place fried bacon. Cover bacon with cooked rice. Next place shrimp halves attractively over rice.

In a 1-quart saucepan melt butter, add flour, forming a smooth paste; then slowly add milk. Cook about 5 minutes until it thickens. Then add salt, pepper, and cheese, and cook over low heat until cheese has melted.

Pour this sauce over shrimp and spread uniformly. Over sauce sprinkle bread crumbs. Place in a 350° F. oven about 30 minutes. If not brown, place under broiler a few minutes.

Shrimp Jambalaya

Serves 6

1 pound raw shrimp, shelled and de-veined
¼ cup hot butter
½ cup fresh green onion and stems, chopped into ½-inch pieces
1 small clove garlic, minced
½ pound cooked ham (1 cup cut into cubes)
About 1½ teaspoons salt
¼ teaspoon black pepper

⅛ teaspoon cayenne pepper
About 2½ cups cooked rice (1 cup uncooked rice cooked in 2 cups water and 1 teaspoon salt)
2 cups thick fresh or canned tomatoes, cut into large pieces
1 can okra well drained (okra may be omitted, but does add much color and taste)

Sauté shrimp in hot butter about 5 minutes, turning them often. Add green onion and garlic, and cook several more minutes. Add ham, and all other ingredients. Blend thoroughly. Pour into a casserole that measures about 10 × 6 × 2 inches. Bake at 350° F. about 30 minutes. Sprinkle top with fine-chopped green onion or parsley, and serve hot with a salad and dessert. This is an excellent buffet supper and luncheon dish.

Creole Shrimp and Rice in Individual Casseroles

Serves 4

3 cups cooked rice
1 pound cooked shrimp, split in halves

1½ cups green peppers, cut into 1-inch squares and sautéed 2 or 3 minutes
¾ cup shredded cheddar cheese
Paprika

In each of 4 individual-size casseroles place ¾ cup cooked rice. Cover top of rice with split cooked shrimp. Cover top of shrimp with sautéed green peppers. Pour Tomato Juice Sauce (page 383) over green peppers. Sprinkle with cheese and paprika. Bake in a preheated 350° F. oven about 15 minutes. Remove from oven and place under broiler 2 or 3 minutes, or until cheese is golden brown. Serve at once.

Tomato Juice Sauce for Creole Shrimp and Rice

6 tablespoons butter or margarine	3 cups lukewarm tomato juice
⅔ cup all-purpose flour	2 teaspoons salt

Melt butter or margarine, add flour slowly; mix into smooth paste. Add tomato juice, a small amount at a time, stirring constantly to remove lumps. Add salt. Cook until thick; then cook several minutes longer, stirring constantly.

Salmon-Macaroni Casserole

Serves 6 to 8

½ pound elbow macaroni	¼ cup pimiento, cut into 1-inch squares
¼ cup butter or margarine	1 teaspoon salt
¼ cup sifted all-purpose flour	¼ teaspoon pepper
About 1¼ cups warm milk	1-pound can red salmon, well drained
¼ pound shredded American cheese	

Cook macaroni until tender. Drain very thoroughly, and pour a small amount of cold water over it.

In a separate saucepan melt butter, blend in flour, and then add milk gradually, stirring constantly; cook until thick and smooth. Add cheese, reserving ¼ cup, and add pimiento squares, salt, and pepper. Continue to cook until cheese is melted. If sauce is too thick, *add more milk.*

Flake salmon, add to cooked macaroni, blend, add ⅔ of cream sauce to macaroni and salmon mixture, and blend well. Pour in a 1½-quart casserole. Pour rest of sauce over top and sprinkle with ¼ cup cheese. Bake about 30 minutes in a 425° F. oven, or until top is brown.

Salmon Casserole

Serves 6 to 8

½ pound bacon, cubed	½ cup minced parsley
1½ cups chopped onions	½ teaspoon salt
2 cans salmon (8-ounce size), drained and flaked	¼ teaspoon garlic powder
	⅛ teaspoon pepper
3 cups cooked rice	1 cup fresh pulled bread crumbs

Fry cubed bacon and chopped onion together in a skillet over medium heat about 5 minutes. In a large bowl mix salmon with rice and parsley. Next, add bacon and onion, mixing very well with 2 forks. Last, blend in seasonings. Place mixture in a well-buttered 1½-quart casserole. Cover top of casserole with pulled or dry bread crumbs; then drizzle with a little butter. Cover with greased foil to prevent drying out. Bake at 375° F. about 45 minutes.

Tuna-Mushroom Casserole

Serves 4

¼ cup butter or margarine
¼ cup flour
2 cups scalded milk
½ cup shredded American cheese, solidly packed, or ¼ cup parmesan cheese
⅛ teaspoon garlic salt
⅛ teaspoon pepper
¾ teaspoon salt

Pinch of oregano or thyme
¼ cup pimiento, cut ⅛ inch wide and 1 inch long
2 (7 ounce) cans tuna, drained and flaked
1 medium-size can sliced mushrooms, or ½ pound fresh mushrooms
1 cup pulled fresh bread crumbs

In a 2-quart saucepan melt butter or margarine and blend in flour, making a smooth paste. Add scalded milk slowly. Cook about 5 minutes after sauce comes to simmering point, stirring constantly. Add cheese, seasonings, pimiento, and cook until cheese is melted. Add tuna and mushrooms to sauce. If using fresh mushrooms, sauté first 2 or 3 minutes. Place in a casserole, and cover top with bread crumbs.

Bake 25 minutes at 350° F. If crumbs are not brown, place under broiler a few minutes.

Fillet of Haddock or Perch Mornay in Casserole

Sauté 1 large onion sliced thin in 2 tablespoons butter or margarine for about 10 minutes until lightly browned. Add 2 packages of defrosted frozen whole spinach; season with about ½ teaspoon salt, ⅛ teaspoon pepper, and ⅛ teaspoon thyme. Cook together in covered saucepan about 7 or 8 minutes. *Drain well,* then pour spinach into a well-buttered medium-sized flat baking dish or 17-inch steel platter.

Wash 1 pound fillet of haddock or perch cut into serving portions in lukewarm salted water. Dry well in a towel. Combine ⅓ cup sifted all-purpose flour with 1 teaspoon paprika and 1 teaspoon salt. Mix well in a paper bag. Place fillets in bag and shake well, covering completely with flour mixture. Sauté fillets in ¼ cup hot oil or shortening about 6 or 7 minutes on each side until golden brown. Lift up carefully and place on top of spinach.

Prepare sauce with ¼ cup hot butter, 1 tablespoon finely minced onion, ⅓ cup sifted all-purpose flour, and mix until smooth. Add slowly 1½ cups warm milk. Cook until thick, then add ¼ cup grated parmesan (or ½ cup American) cheese. Season with about ¾ teaspoon salt, ¼ teaspoon pepper, ¼ teaspoon thyme, and 2 tablespoons light dry wine. Cook again about 5 minutes after it starts to simmer. Cool sauce ½ hour, beating it several times, then pour sauce over entire surface of fish and spinach, and spread until smooth. Sprinkle top lightly with paprika. Pipe Duchesse Potatoes (page 301) around edge of platter, and several potato rosettes on each end. Bake at 450° F. 15 minutes (20 minutes if ingredients are cold) then broil for several minutes until top is attractively brown. Very delicious and economical dish. Increase baking time by 10 minutes for double recipe.

Asparagus and Tuna Casserole

Serves 4

1 package frozen asparagus
4 hard-cooked eggs, sliced
10-ounce can cream of mushroom soup
2 cans tuna

2 tablespoons pimiento, cut into ½-inch pieces
1 cup crushed potato chips

Cook asparagus until tender and arrange on bottom of buttered 10½-inch pie plate. Cover with slices of hard-cooked eggs. Heat mushroom soup until thin, and add to tuna and pimiento, mixing until well blended. Spread this mixture over layer of sliced eggs, and then cover with crushed potato chips.

Cover with greased foil and bake in a 350° F. oven 20 minutes. Then remove cover and bake 10 more minutes.

Note. This recipe may be doubled for a 10× 6 × 2-inch casserole. In this case make 2 layers of all ingredients and bake 30 minutes covered and 10 minutes uncovered.

Tuna-Green Noodle Casserole

Serves 3 to 4

½ pound greeen noodles
7-ounce can tuna
½ pound sautéed sliced mushrooms or
    3-ounce can
½ cup pimiento strips
2 whole eggs

½ cup milk
1 teaspoon salt
¼ teaspoon pepper
½ teaspoon garlic salt
¼ cup parmesan cheese
¼ cup melted butter

Cook noodles in rapidly boiling water until tender, about 12 minutes. Drain. Place noodles in a large bowl. Flake tuna and add to noodles, mixing thoroughly. Add sautéed mushrooms and pimiento strips, and mix well. Beat eggs about ½ minute, combine with milk, and add to noodles and tuna. Last, add seasonings. Pour into a well-buttered 1½-quart casserole, and sprinkle top with cheese. Drizzle melted butter over cheese. Bake at 350° F. about 30 minutes.

Broiled Fillets of Haddock or Perch Piquant

Serves 3

Prepare Sauce Piquant (below). When ready to broil fillets (1 pound of haddock or perch), melt Sauce Piquant over very low heat until it looks like heavy cream. Pour ½ of it into a medium-flat heatproof baking dish (large-size glass pie dish may be used), and place fillets over it with flesh side up. Sprinkle fillets lightly with salt. Brush them with rest of Sauce Piquant; sprinkle lightly and evenly with paprika. Broil at 450° F., about 2 inches from heat, 10 to 15 minutes, or until top is golden brown, depending upon thickness of fillets. If fillets are not uniform in thickness, it is better to place them between sheets of wax paper and pound with rolling pin. When done, remove from broiler and with No. 7 or No. 3 star cookie tube and bag, fill in open spaces with large scrolls of Duchesse Potatoes (page 301). If preferred, potatoes may be piped into plate before broiling to take on a nice brown crusty appearance. Extra Sauce Piquant may be prepared and served hot separately.

Sauce Piquant for Broiled Fillets of Haddock or Perch

¼ cup butter, or margarine, creamed	⅛ teaspoon cayenne pepper
1 tablespoon fine-chopped fresh green onion and stem	1 tablespoon lemon juice
	½ teaspoon salt
1 tablespoon minced parsley	¼ teaspoon marjoram

Beat all ingredients together until thoroughly blended. Cover tightly and store in refrigerator for several hours before using, or longer. When stored flavor becomes more pronounced.

Baked Halibut and Cheese Casserole

Serves 4 to 6

2 pounds halibut	1 teaspoon salt
4 tablespoons butter	¼ teaspoon pepper
¼ cup all-purpose flour	2 tablespoons lemon juice
2 cups warm milk	¾ cup shredded American cheese

Wash fish in warm salted water and dry thoroughly. Cut into good-sized serving portions that can be arranged in a casserole attractively. Place on a well-greased flat pan, flesh side up. Sprinkle with salt, and broil at 350° F., 2 inches from heat, about 12 to 15 minutes. Do not turn.

While fish is broiling, prepare a cream sauce by melting butter, blending in flour until smooth, and slowly adding milk. Simmer 5 minutes, stirring constantly. Add salt and pepper.

Place broiled fish in a well-buttered 2-quart flat casserole, and brush with lemon juice. Pour cream sauce over fish. Last, sprinkle cheese over top. Bake in oven at 350° F. 20 to 25 minutes. If top is not brown, casserole can be placed under broiler a few minutes.

Baked Chicken Monte Carlo in Casserole

Serves 6

2 packages frozen broccoli or 1 bunch fresh (spinach or asparagus may be used instead of broccoli)
2 or 3 pound fully drawn chicken
2 teaspoons salt
Additional 1 teaspoon salt
¼ teaspoon pepper
⅓ cup grated parmesan cheese

½ pound or more sliced fresh mushrooms, sautéed in 2 tablespoons butter for several minutes, seasoned with ½ teaspoon salt and ⅛ teaspoon pepper (or 1 medium can, sliced)
3 tablespoons melted butter

Drop broccoli into rapidly boiling unsalted water and cook gently until just tender, but not too soft. (For stronger flavor, broccoli may be steamed in small amount of water.) Drain thoroughly and when cold cut lengthwise into uniform *thin* slices.

Wash chicken under cold running water; place on a trivet; add 1 cup boiling water; cover pan tightly and steam about 1 hour or until leg leaves body easily, adding 2 teaspoons salt last few minutes. When done, remove and let stand until cool enough to handle. Discard skin, and slice meat.

Arrange sliced broccoli on bottom of well-buttered flat baking dish. Sprinkle with 1 teaspoon salt and ¼ teaspoon pepper, and pour about ⅓ recipe Sauce Parisienne over broccoli. Sprinkle with 2 tablespoons parmesan cheese. Then cover top of sauce with sliced sautéed mushrooms. Arrange sliced chicken over mushrooms, and cover chicken with rest of Sauce Parisienne. Sprinkle thickly with rest of the grated parmesan cheese, drizzle the 3 tablespoons melted butter over cheese and bake at 350° F. about 30 minutes; then place under broiler until golden brown and crisp.

If desired, garnish top of casserole with 7 short stalks of cooked buttered broccoli and a strip of pimiento that has been rolled to simulate center of flower or red maraschino cherry. Serve hot.

Sauce Parisienne

Melt ⅓ cup butter or margarine; add ⅔ cup sifted all-purpose flour, then gradually add 2¾ cups of chicken stock and cream. (Measure chicken stock, add enough cream to make 2¾ cupfuls.) Mix well; place over moderate heat and let come to simmering point. Then add 1¼ teaspoons salt and let cook gently 5 minutes. Let sauce cool about 20 minutes, stirring it several times, before pouring over broccoli and chicken. If too thick add a little liquid.

Chicken Custard Casserole

Serves 6 to 8

2 cups cooked chicken, cut into medium-size pieces
2 cups rich milk
1 cup chicken stock (instant bouillon may be used with water)
¼ pound fine noodles, cooked until crisply tender, drained well, then seasoned with ½ teaspoon salt and 2 tablespoons butter
1 cup cooked carrots, sliced crosswise ½ inch thick
10-ounce package frozen green beans or peas, cooked until crisply tender
4 large whole eggs, slightly beaten
½ teaspoon dried basil, crushed in fingers
½ teaspoon dried parsley, crushed in fingers
2 teaspoons salt
¼ teaspoon pepper
2 tablespoons grated Italian cheese
Another ¼ cup grated Italian cheese to sprinkle on top

Combine all ingredients except the ¼ cup grated Italian cheese. Mix well, and pour into a well-buttered casserole that measures about 12 × 8 × 2 inches. Sprinkle top with cheese. Bake in a shallow pan of very hot water, 1 hour or until set, in a 350° F. oven.

This makes a very delicious meal served with a salad and desert.

Chicken-Mushroom Mornay in Casserole or Chafing Dish

Serve 8 to 12

¾ cup butter
1 cup sifted all-purpose flour
4 cups lukewarm chicken stock (if short, add rest in cream)
3 teaspoons salt
¼ teaspoon white pepper
¼ cup grated parmesan cheese (more may be used)
¼ cup dry sauterne wine (optional)
1 pound fresh firm mushrooms (large or medium-size), sliced thick and sautéed in ⅓ cup hot butter about 5 minutes (not too soft), turning several times. Season with 1 teaspoon salt, ¼ teaspoon white pepper, 1 very small clove garlic, minced as fine as possible
¼ cup pimiento cut into 1-inch squares, added to mushrooms
About 4 pounds fully drawn chicken, cooked in 4 cups hot water until tender (about 1 hour if using frying chickens, several hours if using stewing chickens); 3 pounds breasts of chicken may be used instead
About 3 cups pulled fresh white bread crumbs, from bread several days old (optional)
¼ cup melted butter

Prepare Mornay Sauce as follows: Melt butter, add flour, and blend until smooth. Add lukewarm stock, a little at a time, salt, pepper, and cheese. Cook about 5 minutes after it thickens. Add wine and let sauce cool about 20 minutes to lukewarm before using in casserole.

Pour sautéed mushrooms combined with pimiento squares into a greased baking casserole that measures about 12 × 8 × 2 inches or a 17-inch stainless-steel platter. Pour about ⅓ of Mornay Sauce over mushrooms.

Place cut chicken over mushrooms. Pour rest of Mornay Sauce over chicken, and cover surface thickly with bread crumbs. Drizzle crumbs with about ¼ cup melted butter. Bake at 350° F. about 45 minutes; then place under broiler if crumbs are not brown after 45 minutes. If casserole is prepared long in advance and ingredients are cold, increase baking time to 1 hour or a little longer. It may be prepared a day in advance, but do not bake. Store in refrigerator when casserole is cool. Remove from refrigerator about ½ hour in advance and bake.

Savory Pinwheel Chicken Casserole

Serves 6 to 8

⅓ cup butter or shortening
⅓ cup sifted all-purpose flour
2½ cups warm chicken stock or milk
2 cups, more or less, cooked chicken
10-ounce package frozen peas, defrosted

1 cup cooked carrots, cut crosswise about ½ inch thick
About 1 teaspoon salt
¼ teaspoon pepper

Melt butter, add flour, and stir until smooth. Add warm stock or milk slowly, and blend until smooth. Cook until thick. Now add all other ingredients, and simmer about 7 or 8 minutes. Taste, and season further if necessary. Pour into an oblong casserole that measures about 10½ × 6½ × 2 inches. Let the casserole stand a few minutes while preparing Savory Pinwheel Biscuits.

Place biscuits on top of casserole, spacing them evenly, and bake in a 400° F. oven 20 to 25 minutes, or until biscuits are brown. Serve hot with a salad and dessert.

Savory Pinwheel Biscuits

1 recipe Baking Powder Biscuit Dough (page 393)
½ teaspoon dried crushed basil
½ teaspoon dried crushed parsley

¼ teaspoon pepper
¼ teaspoon garlic salt
¼ teaspoon celery salt

Roll dough to measure 12 × 12 inches. Sprinkle surface with seasonings. Roll like a jelly roll and cut into 12 uniform slices.

Turkey or Chicken Timbales in Green Pea Casserole

Serves 4

⅓ cup fine-chopped fresh green onion and stems
2 tablespoons butter or margarine
2 tablespoons all-purpose flour
1 cup cool stock or milk
About 1½ teaspoons salt
⅛ teaspoon pepper
½ teaspoon poultry seasoning

1½ cups leftover turkey (or chicken), chopped with a cleaver or heavy knife
¼ cup dry bread crumbs
3 large whole eggs, beaten about ½ minute
4 large whole mushrooms
Pimiento strips

Sauté onion in butter or margarine about 5 minutes. Add flour and blend well. Add cool stock or milk, and cook until thick; then add salt, pepper, and poultry seasoning. Continue to cook gently about 5 minutes. Pour this sauce over chopped turkey, bread crumbs, and beaten eggs, and blend thoroughly. Pour into 4 custard cups that measure 3¼ inches wide and 2¼ inches deep and have been well greased with ½ teaspoon shortening for each cup. Place filled cups in a pan of hot water, and bake at 350° F. about 1 hour or until centers of timbales are firm to the touch. Prepare Creamed Peas.

With a dinner knife loosen around timbales, and turn out onto wax paper. Pick timbales up with a pancake turner and transfer to top of Creamed Peas in a straight line in center of baking dish. Garnish top of each timbale with a whole fluted sautéed mushroom and strips of pimiento around base of mushroom. Bake at 350° F. about 20 minutes before serving if ingredients are warm, about 30 minutes if casserole was put together long in advance and ingredients are cold.

Creamed Peas for Turkey Timbales

¼ cup butter
¼ cup flour
2 cups cool milk or stock
About 1½ teaspoons salt
⅛ teaspoon pepper
¼ teaspoon poultry seasoning

1 package frozen peas, completely defrosted
⅓ cup canned pimiento, cut ½ inch wide and 1 inch long
About ½ cup sliced sautéed fresh mushrooms (optional)

Melt butter, add flour, and stir until smooth. Add milk or stock slowly, stirring constantly. Cook until thick; then add seasonings and peas. Continue to simmer about 6 or 7 minutes. Add pimiento and sautéed mushrooms, and mix very gently. Pour into a 17-inch oval stainless-steel flat baking dish (oblong glass baking casserole may be used).

Chicken Creole in Casserole

Serves 6 to 8

2 broilers (about 2 pounds each)
Seasoned flour
⅓ cup butter
½ cup sauterne wine
1 cup canned or fresh peeled tomatoes
¼ cup fresh celery leaves
1 cup sliced carrots

3 teaspoons salt
½ teaspoon pepper
½ teaspoon oregano
1 large clove garlic, chopped fine
½ pound fresh mushrooms
No. 2 can okra (including liquid)

Cut each broiler into 6 pieces. Dredge in seasoned flour. Melt butter, and when it is hot sauté chicken until golden brown on both sides.

Place chicken and drippings in a heatproof casserole. Add wine, tomatoes, celery leaves, carrots, salt, pepper, oregano, and garlic. Cover casserole tightly, and bake at 350° F. 1 hour.

Sauté mushrooms and add to Chicken Creole; also add okra. Cover casserole, and cook about 15 minutes more, or until chicken is tender.

Chicken Regal Casserole

Serves 4

3½ cups cooked chicken, cut into ½-inch pieces
1 cup fresh mushrooms, sliced
¼ cup butter
½ pound cooked medium-sized egg noodles
⅓ cup milk
2 large whole eggs, well beaten

⅓ cup minced onion
⅓ cup minced celery
½ cup pimiento strips
2½ teaspoons salt
½ teaspoon garlic salt
¼ teaspoon pepper
⅓ cup of stock from chicken

Steam chicken in a skillet or large pan in a small amount of water until tender. (Reserve ⅓ cup stock for recipe.) Sauté mushrooms in butter until golden brown. Cook noodles in rapidly boiling water until tender—8 to 10 minutes.

Now combine all ingredients in a large bowl and mix thoroughly. Pour mixture into a buttered 1½-quart casserole. Cover with greased foil and bake at 350° F. 30 to 40 minutes. Garnish top of casserole with hard-cooked egg flower. Serve with Regal Sauce.

Regal Sauce

¼ cup melted butter
¼ cup sifted all-purpose flour
2 cups warm milk or chicken stock

1 teaspoon salt
1 teaspoon Worcestershire sauce
1 cup shredded American cheese

Melt butter, add flour, and mix until smooth. Add warm milk slowly, and blend well. Simmer 5 minutes, stirring constantly. Last, add cheese, salt, and Worcestershire sauce, and continue to cook until cheese is melted.

Turkey and Dressing in Casserole

Serves 4

¼ cup butter	About 4 cups leftover bread dressing
¼ cup flour	½ pound fresh mushrooms, sliced and
1¼ cups stock or milk or leftover gravy	sautéed in 2 tablespoons butter
About 1 teaspoon salt	Salt and pepper
¼ teaspoon pepper	About 2 cups leftover sliced turkey
¼ cup grated parmesan cheese	

Melt butter, add flour, and mix until smooth. Add stock and next 3 ingredients. Cook until thick; then simmer about 5 minutes. This sauce should be very stiff to prevent it from soaking into dressing.

Arrange leftover bread dressing in a medium-size casserole. Spread mushrooms over dressing. Season lightly with salt and pepper. Arrange sliced turkey over mushrooms; then pour sauce over entire top. Bake at 350° F. uncovered about 35 minutes if ingredients are warm. Bake about 45 minutes if casserole was prepared in advance. Place under broiler to brown top just before serving. This is an excellent and tasty way to reheat and serve leftover dressing and turkey.

Epicurean Breast of Chicken or Turkey in Individual Casseroles

Serves 2

2 slices of white toasted bread, each cut in 2 triangles	¼ butter or margarine
2 slices of cooked ham	⅓ cup sifted all-purpose flour
About ½ pound of cooked breast of turkey or chicken	1½ cups chicken stock (or use instant bouillon in water)
¼ pound fresh mushrooms, sliced, and sautéed about 5 minutes and seasoned with ¼ teaspoon salt	2 tablespoons dry sherry
	⅛ teaspoon white pepper
	¼ cup shredded American cheese, or 2 tablespoons Italian cheese
	Paprika

Place 2 triangles of toast in each of 2 individual casseroles. (These casseroles are available in the better department and hardware stores.) Arrange slice of ham on top of bread, and half of turkey or chicken on top of ham, then sautéed mushrooms, on each.

Melt the ¼ cup butter or margarine, add flour and blend well. Add warm chicken stock and wine slowly. Add the pepper. Cook until thick, stirring constantly, then let simmer about 5 minutes. Taste and add salt if needed. Let sauce cool for about ½ hour, stirring it several times, then pour in over top of other ingredients in each casserole. Sprinkle top of each with cheese and a little paprika. Bake at 450° F. about 10 minutes, then place under broiler for several minutes, just before serving. If casseroles have been prepared in advance and ingredients are cold, bake them 15 minutes, then broil until top is brown. Several sandwiches may be prepared and baked on a larger oval baking platter, increasing baking time by 10 minutes. Fill ends of casseroles with well-seasoned buttered peas, or short asparagus tips. Garnish with a small daisy vegetable flower and spray of parsley, if desired.

▶ MEAT CASSEROLES ◀

Beef Stew and Biscuits in Casserole

Serves 4

3 cups cooked meat, cut into 1-inch cubes

1 cup cooked potatoes, cut into 1-inch cubes

1 cup cooked green beans or green peas

1 cup cooked carrots, cut into 1-inch pieces

1 large onion, sliced thin and sautéed in 2 tablespoons shortening

2 cups thick brown gravy, combined with ¼ cup tomato paste, cooled 30 minutes (page 394)

About 1½ teaspoons salt

¼ teaspoon salt

½ teaspoon dried herbs

Combine all ingredients in order given and pour into a well-greased casserole. Prepare 1 recipe Baking Powder Biscuit Dough (below); roll to about ½-inch thickness. Cut into 1¼-inch strips, then into diamonds. Arrange diamonds over stew in center to simulate a large flower. Place a round piece of dough in center of flower. Arrange more diamonds on stew as attractively as possible. Brush biscuits with milk. Bake at 425° F. about 20 to 25 minutes, or until biscuits are brown. Serve with a salad.

Note. This is an excellent way to use up leftover beef or other meat.

Baking Powder Biscuit Dough

1¼ cups sifted all-purpose flour

2¼ teaspoons double-acting baking powder

½ teaspoon salt

¼ cup shortening

About ½ cup cool milk

Combine dry ingredients and sift together several times. Cut shortening into dry ingredients until mixture looks like fine meal. Add enough milk to form a medium consistency, not too heavy and not sticky. Knead dough about ½ minute; roll and cut as described above.

Thick Brown Gravy for Beef Stew in Casserole

¼ cup butter or margarine
¼ cup minced onion
⅓ cup sifted all-purpose flour

2 cups milk, stock, or water (if using water or milk, add 2 bouillon cubes)
A little commercial gravy coloring

Sauté onion in hot butter about 5 minutes. Add flour, and blend until smooth. Slowly add stock and gravy coloring. Cook until thick; then simmer about 5 minutes. If using unsalted stock or no bouillon, add 1 teaspoon salt. No salt is required if using instant bouillon. May add ½ teaspoon dried herbs for extra flavor. Let cool 30 minutes before using.

Beef Casserole à la Duchess

Serves 4 to 6

2 packages cooked frozen lima beans (other green vegetables may be used, such as peas, green beans, etc.), seasoned with 1½ teaspoons salt, ¼ teaspoon pepper, and 1 large onion sliced thin, sautéed for about 5 minutes in ¼ cup shortening
2 cups sliced beef
Salt and pepper

2 cups Thick Brown Gravy (let gravy cool for ½ hour, beating it several times)
2½ pounds boiled, peeled, and mashed potatoes, seasoned with 3 tablespoons butter, 1½ teaspoons salt, 1 egg, and 2 or 3 tablespoons hot milk if potatoes appear very stiff

Pour lima beans and onions into a well-greased casserole that measures about 10½ × 6¼ × 2 inches, or preferably a 17-inch steel oval platter. Arrange sliced beef over vegetable. Sprinkle lightly with a little salt and pepper. Pour lukewarm brown gravy over entire surface. Place mashed potatoes in a bag with a No. 7 star cookie tube and pipe a double rosette border around edge of casserole. Pipe large rosettes on each end. Bake at 400° F. about 20 minutes, or until potatoes are brown.

This is a complete meal and may be served with a salad and dessert.

Thick Brown Gravy à la Duchess

¼ cup very finely minced onion
¼ cup butter or margarine
½ cup sifted all-purpose flour

2 cups warm milk, stock, or water (if using water or milk best to add 2 teaspoons instant bouillon)
A little commercial gravy coloring

Sauté the finely chopped onion in the ¼ cup hot butter or margarine for about 5 minutes. Add flour and blend until smooth. Slowly add the stock and gravy coloring. Cook until thick, then simmer about 5 minutes. If using unsalted stock, add 1 teaspoon salt. No salt is required if using instant bouillon. May add ½ teaspoon dry herbs for extra flavor. Let cool (and stir several times) ½ hour before pouring over meat. If too thick add a little milk or water.

Beef Stroganoff in Chafing Dish

Serves 4

1 pound beef or pork tenderloin, sliced about ¼ inch thick and in 2-inch squares, rolled into ⅓ cup of flour combined with 1 teaspoon salt and ¼ teaspoon pepper
¼ cup butter or margarine
½ cup onions, chopped fine
1 small clove garlic, chopped fine
½ pound fresh sliced mushrooms
Another ¼ cup of butter

2 tablespoons flour
About ¾ cup beef bouillon (instant bouillon may be added to water)
2 tablespoons dry sherry wine
2 teaspoons Worcestershire sauce
About 1 teaspoon salt
1 tablespoon tomato sauce
¼ cup sliced stuffed green olives (optional)
1 cup commercial sour cream

Sauté the floured meat slices in ¼ cup of butter or margarine, about 2 minutes on each side. In another ¼ cup of butter sauté the chopped onions, garlic, and sliced mushrooms about 5 minutes.

Drain drippings from the cooked beef and vegetables, and into drippings stir flour, bouillon, sherry wine, Worcestershire sauce, about 1 teaspoon salt, 1 tablespoon tomato sauce, and the ¼ cup sliced olives. Let simmer several minutes. Now add the cup of sour cream slowly, stirring continuously, and simmer about 2 minutes, but do not boil. A little commercial coloring may be added for additional color. Last, add the cooked meat and vegetables to the sauce, and simmer about 2 or 3 minutes. Do not boil. Serve at once in chafing dish or casserole.

Baked Roast Beef Hash in Casserole

Serves 4

3 cups leftover roast beef, boiled beef, or pot roast, cut into ½-inch cubes
2 cups boiled potatoes, cut into ½-inch cubes
½ cup fresh green onions or regular onions, cut into ½-inch pieces and sautéed in 1 tablespoon butter
1 large green pepper, cut into ½-inch pieces, sautéed in 2 tablespoons butter

¼ cup pimiento, cut into ½-inch squares (optional, used principally for color)
About 1 teaspoon salt
¼ teaspoon pepper
½ teaspoon dried herbs
2 cups Thick Brown Gravy (page 394)

Combine above ingredients; mix with 2 forks, taste, and season further if necessary. Pour into a well-greased casserole that measures about 10½ × 6¼ × 2 inches. Sprinkle top thickly with pulled fresh white bread crumbs, and drizzle with a little butter (about 2 tablespoons melted). Bake at 400° F. about 20 to 25 minutes, or until crumbs are brown. Serve with a green vegetable and a salad.

Porcupine Beef Balls in Casserole

Serves 6

1½ pounds ground beef	¼ cup green peppers, diced
½ cup uncooked rice	¼ cup onions, chopped
1½ teaspoons salt	3 tablespoons all-purpose flour
¼ teaspoon pepper	1 teaspoon salt
¼ teaspoon garlic salt	⅛ teaspoon pepper
3 cups canned tomatoes, crushed	½ teaspoon baking soda
⅓ cup butter or margarine	

In a large bowl combine beef, rice, 1½ teaspoons salt, ¼ teaspoon pepper, garlic salt, and ⅓ cup crushed tomatoes. Mix well, and form 16 smooth meat balls. Place meat balls in a well-greased 3-quart casserole.

In a 2-quart saucepan heat butter or margarine, and sauté green pepper and onions about 3 minutes. Blend in flour and add remaining tomatoes. Cook until thick; then add 1 teaspoon salt, ⅛ teaspoon pepper, and ½ teaspoon baking soda. Cook a few more minutes. Pour this sauce over meat balls in casserole, cover casserole, and bake at 375° F. for 1½ hours.

This casserole may be served as is, with a vegetable, or with macaroni.

Casserole Savoy

Serves 6 generously

1½ pounds pork shoulder, cut into 1-inch pieces	½ pound green noodles
¼ cup butter	1 teaspoon salt
½ cup onions, chopped medium-fine	¼ cup butter
1 cup celery, cut into ¼-inch slices	1 small can mushroom soup, undiluted
2 teaspoons salt	1 package frozen peas, cooked
¼ teaspoon pepper	½ cup grated American, or ¼ cup parmesan cheese
½ teaspoon thyme	
1 cup water, combined with 6-ounce can tomato paste	

Sauté pieces of pork in ¼ cup butter; then add onions and fry 2 or 3 minutes until onions are light brown.

Add celery, 2 teaspoons salt, pepper, thyme, and water combined with tomato paste. Simmer all ingredients in a covered saucepan about 45 minutes, or until meat is tender. Every 10 minutes lift cover and mix all ingredients well. Keep over very low heat so that meat will be tender and juicy. About 10 minutes before meat is done, cook green noodles in 3 quarts boiling water about 12 minutes.

When noodles are tender, drain well and add 1 teaspoon salt and ¼ cup butter and blend well.

Combine noodles with meat mixture and add mushroom soup and peas. Blend all ingredients well, and pour into a 2-quart greased casserole. Sprinkle cheese on top and bake in 375° F. oven 20 minutes if mixture is hot, or 30 minutes if it was prepared in advance.

Pastitso (Greece's National Dish) in Casserole

Serves 8

½ pound macaroni, boiled gently in unsalted water until tender but not soft, about 25 minutes
¼ cup butter, melted
1½ teaspoons salt
⅛ teaspoon black pepper
2 tablespoons grated Italian cheese
1 teaspoon salt
¼ teaspoon black pepper
1 pound ground lamb, beef, pork, or veal

2 tablespoons butter
⅛ teaspoon nutmeg
⅛ teaspoon cinnamon
2 tablespoons light dry wine (optional)
¼ cup tomato paste or purée (optional)
2 large eggs
¼ cup grated Italian cheese

Add to well-drained macaroni, ¼ cup melted butter, 1½ teaspoons salt, ⅛ teaspoon black pepper, 2 tablespoons cheese.

Sauté ground meat in 2 tablespoons butter over moderate heat, about 7 or 8 minutes, until brown but not dry. Season with 1 teaspoon salt, ¼ teaspoon black pepper, ⅛ teaspoon nutmeg, ⅛ teaspoon cinnamon, and cook together about 2 more minutes. Then add wine and tomato paste or purée to meat.

Pour cooked seasoned meat over macaroni. Then add beaten eggs, and blend well. Pour into a well-buttered oblong dish that measures about 12 × 8 × 2 inches. Sprinkle top with ¼ cup grated Italian cheese, and bake in a preheated oven at 350° F. 15 minutes if ingredients are warm, about 10 minutes longer if ingredients have been standing and are cool. While macaroni is in oven baking, prepare Custard Topping for Pastitso (page 398).

Pour custard over partially baked macaroni, and sprinkle top thickly with grated Italian cheese. Bake again about 30 minutes. If top is not brown after 30 minutes, place casserole under broiler and watch closely. When top is brown, remove and let stand in room temperature 30 to 45 minutes before cutting into squares and serving. This dish will remain quite hot about 45 minutes and will spread if cut and served sooner.

This casserole may be baked several hours in advance if refrigerated and reheated at 300° F. about an hour before serving. It cuts more attractively after it is reheated, but is less creamy. Restaurants prepare this dish in advance and reheat it as ordered.

Leftover Pastitso may be cut into serving portions and steamed in a deep skillet or saucepan in a very small amount of water. Cover pan, and steam about 10 minutes, or until heated through, over moderate heat.

Custard Topping for Pastitso

½ cup butter or margarine, melted
½ cup sifted all-purpose flour
3 cups warm milk

1½ teaspoons salt
3 large eggs, beaten with Dover beater a few seconds

Place butter over moderate heat until hot, but do not burn. Add flour to butter, and stir until smooth; then add milk, little at a time. Cook until thick, and simmer several minutes. Add salt. Let stand about 10 minutes; then add sauce to beaten eggs, *very slowly*, to prevent curdling. Stir continuously while blending sauce with eggs.

Curried Pork Casserole

Serves 3 to 4

About 1½ cups leftover cooked pork, cut into 1-inch cubes, seasoned with 1 teaspoon salt, ½ teaspoon pepper (any other meat may be used)

About 3 cups, or less, cooked rice (1 cup raw rice cooked in 2 cups water) and ½ teaspoon salt

1 package frozen peas, cooked about 5 minutes after defrosted, or 1 can peas drained

1 cup carrots, cut crosswise into ½-inch slices, and steamed until tender

Combine all ingredients in casserole 10½ × 6½ × 2 inches. Spread with Curry Sauce. Bake at 350° F. about 30 minutes if ingredients are warm, about 40 minutes if casserole was prepared long in advance. Place under broiler to brown if necessary before serving.

Curry Sauce for Pork Casserole

2½ tablespoons melted butter
2½ tablespoons all-purpose flour
1½ cups milk

½ teaspoon curry powder
1 teaspoon salt
¼ teaspoon pepper

Combine melted butter with flour until smooth. Add milk slowly, and seasonings. Cook until thick; then simmer about 5 minutes.

Pork and Macaroni Casserole Louisiana

Serves 3 to 4

½ pound, or more, ground pork shoulder, sautéed in 1 tablespoon shortening about 7 or 8 minutes (drain off fat from meat)

2 medium-size onions, sliced thin and sautéed in pork drippings about 7 or 8 minutes

1¼ cups elbow macaroni, first measured and then cooked in salted boiling water until tender, and drained well

2 cups crushed canned or fresh tomatoes, combined with ¼ teaspoon baking soda

½ cup shredded Swiss cheese (other cheeses may be used)

About 2 teaspoons salt

½ teaspoon black pepper

¼ teaspoon rosemary

¼ teaspoon celery salt

¼ teaspoon cayenne pepper

1 cup fresh-pulled bread crumbs

2 tablespoons melted butter or margarine

Combine all ingredients except bread crumbs and butter. Mix well and pour into a 10½ × 6½ × 2-inch casserole. Sprinkle top with crumbs and drizzle with melted butter. Bake at 350° F. about 30 minutes if ingredients are warm, about 40 minutes if casserole was prepared long in advance. Place under broiler to brown top if necessary.

Pork Shoulder (or Tenderloin) and Mushroom Casserole

Serves 4

1 pound lean pork shoulder (or pork tenderloin), sliced about ⅓ inch thick

Bread crumbs

1 or 2 eggs, beaten slightly and combined with 2 tablespoons water

About ¼ cup hot shortening

4 slices bacon, cut into small pieces

2 cups thin-sliced onion

½ pound fresh mushrooms, sliced medium-thin and sautéed in 2 tablespons butter

1 teaspoon salt

¼ teaspoon pepper

¼ teaspoon oregano

½ cup meat or vegetable stock (bouillon cube may be added to water)

Season sliced meat (cut about ⅓ inch thick and 3 inches in diameter) and cover with bread crumbs; dip into beaten egg, then cover with crumbs again. Let stand about 20 minutes, turning twice. Brown slices in about ¼ cup (more or less as required) hot shortening. Place in a baking dish that measures 10½ × 6½ × 2 inches. Fry bacon until crisp. Drain well. Add onions to bacon drippings, and sauté 7 or 8 minutes. Combine onions, bacon drippings, and sautéed mushrooms. Season with salt, pepper, and oregano. Spread over meat. Pour stock over vegetable. Cover casserole, and bake at 325° F. about 40 minutes, or until meat is tender when tested with a fork. Bake a little longer if casserole was prepared long in advance. Serve with potatoes and another vegetable, or as desired.

Casserole of Baked Elbow Macaroni and Pork Sausages

Serves 6

½ pound elbow macaroni	About 1¼ cups warm milk
½ pound Brown 'N Serve pork sausages	¼ cup grated American cheese
¼ cup cutter or shortening	1 teaspoon salt
¼ cup sifted all-purpose flour	

Cook macaroni in boiling salted water 20 to 30 minutes, or until tender. Drain very thoroughly and pour a small amount of cold water over it.

Sauté pork sausages about 3 minutes. Cut up ½ the cooked sausages into ½-inch pieces. Leave other sausages whole.

In a separate saucepan melt butter (or use sausage drippings), blend in flour, and then add milk gradually, stirring constantly. Cook until thick and smooth. Add cheese and salt and continue to cook over low heat until cheese is melted. If sauce is too thick, add more milk. Combine ⅔ of this sauce with cooked macaroni, add cut-up sausages, and blend well. Pour into a 1-quart casserole. Pour rest of sauce over top, and arrange whole sausages attractively on top of cream sauce.

Bake about 30 minutes at 425° F. or until top is brown. This can be served as a main luncheon or supper dish.

Party-Style Ham Luncheonettes

Serves 5

5 slices boiled ham (more ham may be used)

3 large California oranges, peeled and sliced about 1 inch thick, brushed with melted butter, and sprinkled very lightly with brown sugar

3 pounds sweet potatoes (yams preferable), cooked until tender, peeled, mashed, and seasoned with about 2 tablespoons butter, 2 tablespoons brown sugar

Glaze made with 1 cup brown sugar solidly packed, ½ cup orange juice solidly packed, ½ cup orange juice, and 1 teaspoon butter, cooked about 5 minutes or until clear

5 whole maraschino cherries

1 fresh green pepper, cut to simulate leaves

1 package frozen green peas, cooked covered in 2 tablespoons butter with 1 tablespoon sugar until just tender but still green

If using commercial thin-sliced ham, fold slices and place them in a well-buttered flat 16-inch heatproof platter. Cover ham with slices of orange. (Pineapple slices and juice may be used instead of orange slices and juice.) With a No. 7 star cookie tube and bag, pipe a very large mound of sweet potato on each slice of orange. Pour glaze over potatoes and ham. Bake at 400° F. about 20 minutes. Remove from oven, and garnish top of each mound with a whole red maraschino cherry and pepper leaves. Pour peas on each side of platter and serve at once.

Served with hot rolls and a dessert, this makes a good light luncheon or supper.

Ham and Green Noodle Casserole

Serves 6

½ pound green noodles
1 package frozen green peas
2 tablespoons butter or shortening
2 tablespoons chopped onions
2 tablespoons flour
1 teaspoon salt
¼ teaspoon black pepper

2 cups warm milk
1½ cups (¾ pound) diced cooked ham
1 cup grated American or cheddar cheese
1 cup pulled fresh bread crumbs
¼ cup melted butter

Cook noodles and green peas. Preheat oven at 400° F. Melt 2 tablespoons butter, sauté onions a few minutes, add flour, salt, and pepper. Then slowly add warm milk, and cook over medium heat, stirring constantly until smooth and thickened.

Pour half of noodles into a well-buttered 10 × 6 × 2-inch casserole. Over noodles arrange ham, and over ham cooked peas. Sprinkle top of peas with grated cheese. Pour sauce over all; then place rest of noodles on top of sauce. Sprinkle with pulled bread crumbs. Drizzle butter over bread crumbs, and bake in preheated 400° F. oven about 25 to 30 minutes.

Ham and Broccoli Roll Ups in Casserole

Serves 6 to 8

1 pound fine spaghetti or green noodles
2 tablespoons salt
¼ cup melted butter
½ cup freshly shredded American cheese

¼ teaspoon white pepper
2 packages frozen broccoli spears
Melted butter
1 pound commercial sliced boiled ham
3 cups Thick Cheese Sauce (page 402)
Paprika

Cook spaghetti or noodles until tender, but not too soft, in 4 quarts boiling water containing 2 tablespoons salt. Drain well and add melted butter, cheese, and pepper.

Cook broccoli, in covered pan, in ½ inch salted boiling water about 7 or 8 minutes or until just tender, but not too soft. Drain well. Brush with melted butter. Divide broccoli into as many portions as there are ham slices, and wrap a slice of ham over each portion of broccoli. (Asparagus may be used instead of broccoli.)

Pour cooked seasoned spaghetti or noodles in a well-greased 16-inch casserole. Form a ring, with a large open space in center. Place ham roll ups in center with open ends down. Pour Thick Cheese Sauce over roll ups only. Sprinkle top of sauce with paprika and bake at 350° F. about 30 minutes; then broil 1 or 2 minutes until top is brown.

Thick Cheese Sauce for Ham and Broccoli Roll Ups

½ cup butter or margarine
½ cup sifted all-purpose flour
3 cups warm milk

1½ teaspoons salt
About 1 cup coarsely shredded American cheese

Melt butter, add flour, and blend well until smooth. Add milk slowly, stirring constantly. Bring to a boil, lower heat, add shredded cheese and seasonings, and simmer about 5 minutes being sure that all cheese is melted. Let stand about 10 mintues before pouring over roll ups.

Ham and Duchesse Sweet Potatoes in Casserole

Serves 8

⅓ cup hot butter or margarine
½ cup fine-chopped green onion, or ¼ cup chopped onion
3 cups fresh tomatoes, peeled, cut into small pieces, and drained (drained canned tomatoes may be used)
½ cup green onion tops, cut about ½ inch long

3 cups chopped cooked ham (may be put through food chopper)
About 1 teapsoon salt
½ teaspoon pepper
¼ teaspoon marjoram
6 whole eggs, slightly beaten
1 recipe Sweet Potato Delight (page 403)

In hot butter or margarine sauté onions several minutes. Add tomatoes, and cook about 5 minutes. Add green onion tops, ham, salt, pepper, marjoram, and eggs. Cook over medium heat until thick, about 5 minutes. (If it appears too moist or runny 1 tablespoon cornstarch diluted in 2 tablespoons milk may be added. Let simmer several minutes after starch is added. If cooked properly and tomatoes have been drained, it will not be necessary to add starch in most cases.) Mound mixture in center of platter, leaving about 2 inches of space all around. Pipe Sweet Potato Delight around edge with pastry bag and No. 7 large star cookie tube. If any potato remains, pipe several rosettes on each end. Bake about 20 minutes at 400° F. if ingredients are warm. If cold, bake a few minutes longer. Sprinkle center of ham with very fine-chopped green onion tops or parsley just before serving.

This is a delicious luncheon or supper dish. Excellent for buffets. Serve with a salad and dessert.

Sweet Potato Delight for Casserole

Cook 2 pounds sweet potatoes with skins on until tender, or use 2 cans sweet potatoes (some brands of canned sweet potatoes are excellent for this purpose). Mash potatoes until smooth. Add 2 tablespoons butter, ¼ cup brown sugar, ¼ teaspoon salt. Mix well.

Baked Macaroni Sizzling Squares

Serves 4 to 6

½ pound elbow or other macaroni, broken into about 1-inch pieces	1 teaspoon salt
1 teaspoon salt	½ pound sliced frankfurters, sautéed in butter for several minutes
¼ cup butter or margarine	¼ pound American cheese, cut in ¼-inch cubes
¼ cup sifted all-purpose flour	
1½ cups warm milk	Medium-size fresh tomatoes

Cook macaroni in boiling water about 25 or 30 minutes, until tender. Drain well. Pour into a large bowl and add 1 teaspoon salt to the cooked macaroni, mixing thoroughly.

Melt shortening; add sifted flour, then the warm milk a little at a time. Cook over low heat until thick, about 5 minutes, stirring constantly. Add 1 teaspoon salt toward end.

Pour the hot sauce over macaroni; mix well. Last, fold in sliced sautéed frankfurters and American cheese cubes. Pour into wax-paper-lined square pan that measures about 8 × 8 × 2 inches. Let stand in room temperature until cool; then place in refrigerator for 6 or 7 hours, or until absolutely cold and firm to the touch.

About 30 minutes before serving time, remove from pan, cut into 4 (or more) square portions, place on *well*-greased baking sheet. Pour 1 tablespoon Cheese Sauce over macaroni and place a thick slice of tomato over sauce; pour more sauce over tomato. Bake in a 400° F. oven for about 25 to 30 minutes. If not brown after 30 minutes, place under broiler a few minutes.

Serve these squares with a green vegetable and salad. May be served for supper or luncheon.

Cheese Sauce for Macaroni Squares

Melt 2 tablespoons butter or margarine; add 2 tablespoons flour, then 1 cup warm milk a little at a time. Cook over moderate heat until thick and smooth, stirring constantly. Then add ½ teaspoon salt and 1 cup freshly shredded American cheese. Continue to simmer until cheese is fully melted. This is enough sauce for tops of squares from 1 recipe, and there will be some left over, which may be served separately. If sauce is too thick to be served separately, thin down with more hot milk.

Creamed Ham and Asparagus Noodle Casserole

Serves 6

1 pound, or less, noodles
¼ cup melted butter
A little salt, if necessary
¼ cup grated parmesan cheese
½ teaspoon marjoram
2 cups Medium White Sauce (page 328)
1 package frozen cut asparagus, defrosted

About 2 cups cooked ham (leftover ham excellent), cut into ¾-inch pieces
About 1 teaspoon salt
¼ teaspoon pepper
¼ teaspoon marjoram
2 tablespoons cheese

Cook noodles in salted boiling water until tender. Drain well, and add butter, salt, cheese, and marjoram. Blend well, and pour into a large casserole that measures about 16 or 17 inches.

Make Medium White Sauce. When it is thick and smooth, add asparagus and cook about 10 minutes after simmering starts, or until tender. Add ham and seasonings to sauce. With a large spoon form a nest in noodles. Pour ham filling into center. Bake at 400° F. about 20 minutes just before serving, a little longer if casserole was prepared in advance.

Mexican Tamales

Makes 12 tamales

1¼ cups yellow corn meal
¼ cup sifted white flour or corn flour
1½ teaspoons salt
2 tablespoons shortening added to 1 cup boiling water or meat stock

12 parchment or silicone papers, 7 x 9 inches
Parmesan cheese

Sift dry ingredients together several times. Slowly add boiling water or meat stock to form a smooth thick paste of spreading consistency. If paste appears too thick, more liquid may be added. Liquid must be added to dry ingredients as soon as it comes to boiling point. Allow mixture to cool a few minutes after boiling liquid has been added. Then spread 2 level tablespoonfuls on wet pieces of parchment or silicone papers. Dip spatula in water and spread mixture into 4-inch squares. Place 2 level tablespoonfuls Meat Filling (below) on each. Roll and enclose in parchment paper. Twist ends. Place tamales about ½ inch apart in a saucepan or deep skillet.

They may be piled on top of one another. Pour Tomato Gravy (below) over tamales, being sure that they are submerged in liquid. Add water, tomato juice, or meat stock to sauce if there is not sufficient liquid. Bring slowly to the boiling point, then lower heat and simmer about 30 minutes in covered pan. Be sure tamales are always submerged in liquid while simmering. When done, let them remain in sauce until ready to be served. They should stand in sauce at least 10 or 15 minutes. They may be made several hours in advance, kept in sauce, and reheated gently about 15 minutes just before serving.

To serve, lift out of saucepan carefully, remove paper, arrange attractively on serving dishes. Pour sauce over tamales and sprinkle with grated parmesan cheese for additional flavor.

Meat Filling for Tamales

Braise or roast meat in regular way until tender. Put through food chopper or cut as fine as possible with knife. Leftover boiled, roasted, or other cooked meats or poultry are excellent for this purpose. Measure meat after it is chopped, and to 1½ cupfuls, solidly packed, add about ½ cup of Tomato Gravy (below) or enough to bind mixture. Season with about ¾ teaspoon salt, 1 teaspoon chili powder, ¼ teaspoon hot pepper. Mix well and use as directed.

Tomato Gravy for Tamales

In ¼ cup shortening sauté one medium-size clove garlic and 1 medium-size onion that have been chopped fine. Add 2 cans Italian tomato paste and about 4 cups hot water, meat stock, or tomato juice. Season with about 1 tablespoon salt, ½ teaspoon hot pepper, 1 tablespoon chili powder. Cook gently in a covered saucepan about 30 minutes. This sauce should not be too thick. Add a little water if necessary. Seasonings may be increased or decreased to suit taste.

▶ VEGETABLE CASSEROLES ◀

Creamed Peas and Carrots à la Duchesse

Serves 6 to 8

2 pounds carrots	1 cup Thick White Sauce (page 328)
¼ cup butter	2 packages frozen peas (12-ounce
¼ cup granulated sugar	size), completely defrosted

If carrots are very small, leave whole. Rub off skin after they are steamed in a small amount of water. If carrots are large, cut them into thick 3-inch wedges. Steam in a small amount of water until crisply tender. Drain well. Melt butter and granulated sugar. Add carrots, and cook gently several minutes. Prepare Thick White Sauce. When thick and smooth, add defrosted peas and continue to cook about 7 or 8 minutes, or until peas are tender.

Place carrots in a baking dish, forming a nest. Pour creamed peas in center, forming a slight mound. Cover with foil. Just before serving, bake about 20 minutes at 350° F. if ingredients are hot. If prepared in advance and ingredients are cold, bake about 30 minutes.

This is a very attractive and delicious way to serve peas and carrots. Sprinkle center of peas with paprika if desired.

Mushroom and Vegetable Medley in Casserole

Serves 8

3 packages frozen mixed vegetables, steamed covered in ¼ cup water until tender
About 1½ teaspoons salt
1 sliver fresh garlic
¼ cup butter or margarine
About ¼ teaspoon pepper
¼ teaspoon celery salt
1 pound fresh mushrooms, washed and sautéed about 5 minutes in

¼ cup hot butter seasoned with a little salt and pepper (leave mushrooms whole if they are small; if large, cut into thick slices, leaving stems on; reserving about 6 of the largest whole mushrooms to garnish top of casserole)
Grated parmesan cheese

Combine all above ingredients except cheese, and mix gently with a large spoon. Pour into a well-buttered 16-inch heatproof oval dish or large glass casserole. Pour Sauce Medley over entire top, sprinkle with cheese, and bake at 350° F. about 30 minutes if ingredients are hot. Bake a little longer if casserole was prepared in advance. Place under broiler several minutes to brown top if necessary. Garnish top with very large sautéed fluted mushrooms, or as desired.

This is an excellent vegetable dish to serve with special company dinners and buffets.

Sauce Medley

⅓ cup butter or margarine
½ cup all-purpose flour
3 cups chicken stock (or canned chicken stock or bouillon)
About 1½ teaspoons salt

¼ teaspoon marjoram
¼ teaspoon thyme
1 sliver garlic
2 tablespoons light dry wine (optional)

Melt butter, add flour, and blend until smooth. Add lukewarm chicken stock a little at a time, stirring constantly; add all other ingredients, and simmer about 5 minutes after sauce thickens. Taste, and season further if desired. More or less flour may be used to thicken sauce.

Curried Spinach and Egg Casserole

Serves 4

½ cup thin-sliced onion	About 1¼ teaspoons salt
¼ cup melted butter or bacon drippings	About ½ teaspoon curry powder
	¼ teaspoon black pepper
2 packages frozen spinach, cooked until just tender, and drained well	3 cups Curry Sauce (below)
	6 hard-cooked eggs
	Paprika

Sauté onion in butter about 5 minutes. Add spinach, salt, curry powder, and pepper. Continue to cook about 5 more minutes. Pour spinach into greased casserole that measures about 10 × 2 × 6 inches. Cover top of spinach with 3 cups Curry Sauce. Spread evenly. Over sauce place hard-cooked eggs that have been sliced with egg slicer. Separate slices slightly to show yolks. Sprinkle top of eggs well with paprika. Cover loosely with greased aluminum foil and bake at 350° F. about 25 or 30 minutes.

Serve as a light luncheon or supper dish with toast or hot rolls. It may be served as an accompaniment to meat dishes.

Curry Sauce for Spinach and Egg Casserole

½ cup butter or margarine	1½ teaspoons salt
½ cup sifted all-purpose flour	About ¾ teaspoon curry powder
3 cups warm milk	

Melt butter or margarine, add flour, and blend well until smooth; add milk slowly, stirring constantly. Bring to a boil, lower heat, add seasonings, and simmer about 5 minutes. Let stand about 10 minutes before pouring over spinach.

Casserole of Spinach

Serves 6

2 pounds fresh spinach, or 2 packages (12 ounces each) frozen chopped spinach	3 tablespoons flour
	1½ cups warm milk
	1 teaspoon grated onion
½ teaspoon salt	2 hard-cooked eggs, sliced
⅛ teaspoon pepper	1 cup pulled fresh bread crumbs
½ teaspoon lemon juice	2 tablespoons melted butter or margarine
3 tablespoons butter or margarine	

Cook spinach in a small amount of boiling water just until tender, about 5 minutes. Drain well. Chop fine if using fresh spinach. Season with salt, pepper, and lemon juice.

In a saucepan melt butter or margarine and blend in flour; gradually pour in milk, stirring constantly to prevent lumping. Cook until thickened; add grated onion and sliced eggs.

In the bottom of a lightly greased 1½-quart casserole, arrange a layer of ½ the cooked spinach; pour over ½ the egg sauce. Cover sauce with remainder of spinach and then cover with remaining egg sauce. Sprinkle with pulled bread crumbs. Drizzle bread crumbs with 2 tablespoons butter or margarine. Bake in a 375° F. oven 30 minutes.

Casserole of Mixed Vegetables Mornay

3 (10 or 12 ounce) packages frozen
   mixed vegetables
¼ cup water
1 teaspoon salt
¼ teaspoon pepper

¼ teaspoon garlic salt
3 tablespoons butter
2 cups fresh pulled crumbs (optional)
3 tablespoons melted butter or margarine

Cook vegetables in the ¼ cup water in covered saucepan until tender about 5 minutes after they are defrosted. When done, drain, saving liquid for Mornay Sauce, and season vegetables with the salt, pepper, and garlic salt. Taste and season further if necessary. Spread vegetables in a greased baking dish that measures about 10 × 1⅓ inches or medium oval platter, cover with Mornay Sauce and about 2 cups pulled white bread crumbs. Drizzle entire surface of crumbs with about 3 tablespoons hot melted butter or margarine. Bake about 30 minutes at 350° F., then broil until crumbs are brown and crisp.

Crumbs may be omitted and casserole may be sprinkled with paprika and garnished with sautéed whole or sliced mushrooms and ends of platter with parsley bouquets and vegetable roses, *or as desired.* To prepare mushrooms, purchase 1 pound or more of large thick mushrooms. Wash well in lukewarm water, dry them on a towel, cut off stems (do not pull out). Sauté mushrooms in about ¼ cup hot butter with rounded side down first until golden brown, then brown other side. Cook about 3 or 4 minutes on each side. Season with little salt and pepper. Buttered asparagus may be placed around base of platter.

Note. For a 17-inch oval steel platter, use 1½ recipes.

Mornay Sauce for Mixed Vegetables

¼ cup butter or margarine
⅓ cup sifted all-purpose flour
2 cups liquid (use liquid from vegetables and add enough rich milk or cream to make 2 cups)
¼ cup grated Italian cheese

Pinch of nutmeg or thyme
1 teaspoon salt
¼ teaspoon garlic salt
2 tablespoons light dry wine (optional)

Melt butter or margarine, add flour and stir until smooth. Add liquid gradually, stirring constantly, and cook until thick. Add remaining ingredients and simmer about 5 minutes. Taste and season further if desired. Let this sauce stand about 20 minutes then pour it over seasoned mixed vegetables.

Puffy Asparagus and Cheese Casserole

Serves 6

10- or 12-ounce package frozen asparagus, cut into about 1-inch pieces and cooked in ¼ cup hot water with ½ teaspoon salt until crisply tender (about 7 or 8 minutes)

2 cups pulled soft white bread crumbs

¼ pound (1 cup packed) coarse-shredded American or cheddar cheese

2 tablespoons pimiento, cut into ½-inch squares (optional, but adds color)

About 1 teaspoon salt

½ teaspoon dried basil crushed in fingers

¼ teaspoon onion salt

¼ teaspoon pepper

1¼ cups very hot milk, combined with 2 tablespoons butter or margarine

3 egg yolks, beaten well with a fork or fluffy beater

3 egg whites, beaten until they barely cling to bowl

In a large bowl combine well-drained asparagus, bread crumbs, shredded cheese, pimiento, and all seasonings. Blend gently with 2 forks.

Heat milk and butter, and add slowly to beaten yolks. Pour over vegetable mixture and blend well. Last, fold beaten egg whites gently into other ingredients. Pour into a well-buttered oblong casserole that measures about 10½ × 6 × 2 inches. Set in a pan of hot water and bake at 375° F. about 50 minutes, or until blade of knife comes out clean.

Note. Extra cooked asparagus tips (about 6) may be used to garnish top of casserole, to simulate a flower. Place a curled piece of pimiento or a red maraschino cherry in center of flower.

This casserole makes a delectable accompaniment to any meat, poultry, or fish dinner.

Asparagus in Casserole

Serves 6 to 8

3 cups fresh asparagus, or 2 packages frozen asparagus

¼ teaspoon salt

3 tablespoons butter or margarine

3 tablespoons flour

1 cup asparagus liquid or milk

1 teaspoon salt

½ cup freshly shredded American cheese

2 cups large fresh-pulled bread crumbs

Cook asparagus until just tender, adding ½ teaspoon salt toward end, and drain well. Cut into about 1-inch pieces, and place in a greased pie dish that measures about 10 × 1½ inches. Prepare sauce: melt butter or margarine, add flour, then the liquid a little at a time, stirring constantly. Cook until thick; add 1 teaspoon salt and cheese. Continue to cook several more minutes, or until cheese is fully melted. If sauce is too thick, add a little more liquid. Pour sauce over asparagus; cover top with bread crumbs, and drizzle with melted butter or margarine. Bake at 325° F. about 30 minutes; then place in broiler several minutes, until crumbs are brown and crisp.

Asparagus Majestic in Casserole

Serves 6

2 packages frozen asparagus
3 whole eggs
2 cups scalded milk
1 teaspoon salt
⅛ teaspoon cayenne pepper

⅛ teaspoon black pepper
⅛ teaspoon garlic salt
Pinch of oregano
2 tablespoons melted butter

Cook asparagus and cut each spear into halves. Beat eggs slightly, add scalded milk, slowly and then all seasonings. Last, add melted butter.

Arrange asparagus uniformly in a buttered casserole that measures 10 × 7 × 2 inches. Pour custard over asparagus. Place casserole in a larger pan of hot water and bake at 350° F. about 40 minutes, until blade of knife come out clean. It may be placed under broiler to brown top, but watch closely. Shredded cheese may be sprinkled on top just before broiling.

This is a most unusual way of preparing asparagus, and it will go well with any type of dinner.

Lima Bean and Sausage Casserole

Serves 4 to 6

2 packages frozen lima beans
About 1 teaspoon salt
1 pound Brown 'N Serve cooked sausage
1 large onion, sliced thin
¼ pound fresh sliced mushrooms (optional)
¼ cup butter or other shortening
⅓ cup flour

2 cups warm milk
About 1½ teaspoons salt
¼ teaspoon pepper
½ teaspoon dried savory
¼ cup or more pimiento, cut into 1½-inch squares
⅓ cup American cheese, fine-shredded
Paprika

Cook lima beans until tender, about 10 to 12 minutes, in ½ inch of water with 1 teaspoon salt. Brown cooked sausages in a greased skillet, and put aside 6 links to garnish top of casserole.

Sauté onion and mushrooms in butter about 5 minutes, turning them several times. Add flour, and blend well until smooth. Add warm milk slowly. Add all seasonings except cheese and paprika, and cook sauce until thick; then simmer about 5 minutes. Combine sauce with cooked lima beans, whole sausages (except 6), and pimiento. Pour into an oblong casserole that measures about 10 × 6 × 2 inches; sprinkle top with about ⅓ cup fine-shredded American cheese and lightly with paprika. Bake in a 400° F. oven about 20 minutes; then broil to brown top if necessary for 1 or 2 minutes. Remove from heat, and garnish top of casserole with 6 sausage links to simulate a flower, and a curled piece of pimiento or red maraschino cherry in center.

Asparagus Luncheon Rolls in Casserole

16 to 24 large cooked asparagus stalks
4 to 6 large slices boiled ham
Salt

Pepper
Melted butter

Arrange 4 to 6 stalks of asparagus on each slice of ham. Sprinkle lightly with salt and pepper, and brush with butter. Roll over to enclose asparagus. Arrange in a shallow oblong casserole or baking pan. Cover with Cheese-Olive Sauce (below) and bake in a preheated 350° F. oven about 25 minutes.

Cheese-Olive Sauce

¼ cup butter or margarine
2 tablespoons fine-chopped onions
1 teaspoon salt
⅓ cup sifted all-purpose flour
2 cups rich milk

½ cup shredded American cheese
½ cup ripe olives, cut into medium-size pieces (green stuffed olives may be used)

Melt butter or margarine, sauté onions, add salt and flour, and blend well. Add milk slowly and cook over moderate heat, stirring until thickened and smooth, about 5 minutes. Stir in cheese and olives, keep over heat only until cheese melts.

Egg and Potato Scallop in Casserole

Serves 6

¼ cup butter or margarine
2 tablespoons flour
2 cups warm milk
1 tablespoon minced fresh parsley
1½ teaspoons salt
⅛ teaspoon white pepper

6 medium-size cooked potatoes, sliced
6 hard-cooked eggs, sliced
1 cup fresh pulled bread crumbs
2 tablespoons melted butter

Melt 2 tablespoons butter or margarine, add flour, and blend well. Add warm milk. Cook over low heat, stirring constantly, until thickened. Simmer 5 minutes. Add parsley, salt, and pepper. Place alternate layers of potatoes and eggs in a greased baking dish (10 × 6 × 2 inches), and pour sauce over top. Sprinkle with pulled bread crumbs. Drizzle bread crumbs with 2 tablespoons melted butter or margarine.

Bake in a moderately hot oven (375° F.) 20 minutes, or until crumbs are browned.

For variety, use cooked peas, peas and carrots, or sliced green beans in place of potatoes.

Eggplant Grand'Mère

Serves 4 to 6

2 small eggplants, or 1 large	About 2 teaspoons salt
¼ cup hot butter or other fat	¼ teaspoon pepper
Salt and pepper to taste	¼ teaspoon rosemary
1 large onion, sliced thin	¼ teaspoon mint
Additional butter for sautéeing	About ¼ cup grated parmesan cheese
6-ounce can Italian-style tomato paste, combined with ¾ cup water or stock	

Wash eggplants. Dry well, and remove both ends. Cut small eggplants crosswise into 2 thick slices. Cut large eggplant into 4 thick slices. Do not peel. With a sharp paring knife remove part of center from each slice, leaving a thick 1½-inch rim. Reserve center. Brush eggplant slices well with melted fat, and sprinkle with salt and pepper. Place in a greased baking dish, cover bake at 350° F. about 20 to 30 minutes. Meanwhile prepare Filling (page 413).

Sauté sliced onion and centers of eggplant, chopped fine, in butter about 5 minutes. Add tomato paste combined with water or stock, salt, and next 4 ingredients. Cover, and simmer 15 minutes.

Place Filling in eggplant rims that have been partially baked, spreading Filling well over top, forming a slight mound. Pour 2 tablespoons tomato mixture on each slice; sprinkle with grated parmesan cheese. Pour rest of tomato mixture into casserole around eggplant. Cover casserole with greased foil, and continue to bake at 350° F. about 1 more hour, or until eggplant is tender when tested with a fork. When done, sprinkle center of each slice with fine-chopped green onion or parsley.

Serve with plain rice, noodles, or potatoes.

Filling for Eggplant Grand'mère

1 pound coarse-ground lean lamb
    shoulder
Hot fat

½ teaspoon salt
⅛ teaspoon pepper
½ pound fresh mushrooms, sliced

In a separate skillet or saucepan sauté ground lamb in about 1 or 2 table-spoons hot fat about 10 minutes. Season with salt and pepper. Add sliced mushrooms and cook several minutes. Add *only* enough tomato mixture (above) to meat and mushrooms to form a thick consistency.

Deviled Eggs in Casserole

⅓ cup butter or shortening
⅓ cup sifted all-purpose flour
2¼ cups warm milk
    About 1½ teaspoons salt
6 small whole cooked carrots (if
    large, cut into long thick slices)

1 package frozen asparagus, cooked
    until just tender and still green
8 Deviled Eggs (prepare recipe as
    for Deviled Egg Birds, page
    47, without making birds)
1 cup freshly shredded American
    cheese

Melt butter, add flour, and blend until smooth. Add milk slowly, then salt. Cook until thick; then simmer about 5 minutes. Pour this sauce into pie plate. Place cooked carrots and asparagus in sauce as attractively as possible. Arrange Deviled Eggs around edge and center of platter. Sprinkle shredded cheese between eggs on sauce only (not on eggs). Bake at 350° F. about 30 minutes just before serving.

Corn and Bacon Casserole

Serves 4

2 tablespoons butter or bacon drip-
    pings
3 tablespoons all-purpose flour
1 cup liquor from corn, or milk
1 teaspoon salt
⅛ teaspoon pepper
1 tablespoon parmesan cheese
2 cups whole-kernel corn (1-pound
    can, or 1 package frozen); if us-

ing canned corn, drain it well and
    reserve liquid for sauce
2 medium-size tomatoes, sliced about
    ¼ inch thick
A little thyme, salt, pepper, and par-
    mesan cheese (for tomatoes)
About 6 slices lean bacon, cut in halves
    crosswise

Melt butter, add flour, and blend well. Add corn liquor or milk. Cook until thick; then add salt, pepper, and parmesan cheese. Simmer several minutes. Combine this sauce with drained corn, and pour into a 9-inch glass pie plate. Arrange sliced tomatoes over entire surface as attractively as possible. Sprinkle tomatoes with a little salt, pepper, a pinch of thyme, and a little grated parmesan cheese. Arrange bacon strips over tomatoes to form a pinwheel, and place a curled strip of bacon in center of pinwheel. Bake at 350° F. about 25 minutes, or until bacon is cooked. It may be placed under broiler 2 or 3 minutes if desired.

This is a delicious accompaniment to any meat, poultry, or fish dish.

Sweet Potato Fluff in Casserole

Serves 8 to 12

About 5 pounds unpeeled sweet potatoes, cooked, tightly covered, in small amount water until just tender, not soft	⅓ cup soft brown sugar 2 tablespoons butter Rind of 1 orange, grated

Peel cooked sweet potatoes; mash well while hot and combine them with the brown sugar, butter, and grated rind of orange. Reserve about 3 cups for fancy border, and pour rest of potatoes into a well-buttered 8 × 14 (or 10-inch) glass pie plate. Spread potatoes smoothly with a spatula, having them higher in center. With a large spoon make opening in center of potatoes, large enough to hold a small *heatproof* glass or metal bowl that measures 4¾ inches wide by 2¼ inches deep. Place bowl in center and fill it with Special Orange Glaze (below).

With pastry bag and No. 3 large cookie star tube, pipe a fancy border around base of potatoes and around opening in center. If potatoes to be used for border appear lumpy, it is better to put them through a food mill. About 30 minutes before serving time, bake potatoes in a 400° F. oven. Casserole may be put together hours in advance and baked as soon as turkey or other roast has been removed from oven to cool before serving. This will give ample time to serve potatoes and meat hot. Garnish ends of platter with vegetable flowers and parsley just before serving.

Note. Prepare double recipe for 17-inch oval steel platter and decorate with No. 7 star cookie tube.

Special Orange Glaze for Sweet Potato Fluff

¾ cup brown sugar, solidly packed 1 cup orange juice, combined with 1 tablespoon cornstarch	Rind of a small orange 2 tablespoons of butter

Combine all ingredients in a small saucepan. Blend well and bring to boiling point. Let simmer 5 minutes, or until clear. Pour this glaze into heatproof glass or metal bowl in center of potato casserole before baking.

Potatoes Delmonico in Casserole

Serves 6

¼ cup butter
3 tablespoons flour
2 teaspoons salt
¼ teaspoon pepper
½ teaspoon garlic salt
1½ cups hot milk
½ cup shredded American or cheddar cheese

4 hard-cooked eggs, sliced with egg slicer or cut into large pieces
4 cups cold cooked potatoes, sliced about ¼ inch thick
¼ cup more cheese for top
Paprika

Melt butter, add flour, and mix until smooth. Add seasonings and the hot milk, a little at a time. Cook until smooth and thick; then simmer about 5 minutes. Blend cheese into sauce; then add egg slices and potatoes. Pour into a medium-size well-greased baking dish, oblong or round, and spread evenly. Sprinkle top lightly with additional cheese and a little paprika. Bake at 400° F. about 20 minutes; then place under broiler until top is brown.

Serve with meat, fowl, or seafood. This is very delicious and substantial for a light luncheon or supper dish with a salad.

Green Noodle Soufflé Casserole

Serves 4

8 ounces green noodles
2 tablespoons melted butter or margarine
2 egg yolks slightly beaten with a fork
½ cup hot milk
½ teaspoon garlic salt
¼ teaspoon pepper

¼ teaspoon thyme
1 cup coarsely shredded cheddar cheese
2 egg whites, beaten until they just cling to bowl
Another ½ cup shredded cheese for top of casserole

Cook 8 ounces green noodles gently in boiling salted water (use 2½ quarts water and 1 tablespoon salt) until crisply tender (about 10 minutes). Drain well and at once add 2 tablespoons melted butter or margarine and mix with 2 forks. Combine cooked noodles with egg yolks, milk, seasonings, and cheese, and blend well. Beat egg whites until they just cling to bowl. Fold them into noodle mixture and mix with a spoon until no streaks appear. Pour into a casserole 10½ × 6¼ × 2 inches that has been well greased. Sprinkle ½ cup shredded cheese over top. Bake at 375° F. about 30 minutes, or until noodles puff. Place under broiler to brown if necessary.

Serve as soon as possible. May be kept in a warm oven with heat shut off for a few minutes if necessary.

Serve with any kind of meat, poultry, or fish dinner.

Noodles Romanoff in Casserole

1 pound wide yellow noodles
¼ cup melted butter or margarine
Another ¼ cup melted butter
¼ cup sifted all-purpose flour
1½ cups warm milk
½ pound (2 cups) shredded American or cheddar cheese
About 3 teaspoons, or less, salt

⅛ teaspoon pepper
½ teaspoon thyme
1 cup sour cream
2 cups large curd cream cottage cheese
1 more cup shredded American or cheddar cheese

Cook noodles in plenty of unsalted boiling water gently, about 10 minutes, not too soft. *Drain well,* and at once pour them back into pot. Add the ¼ cup melted butter or margarine and blend well with 2 forks to prevent noodles from clinging together.

Prepare sauce with ¼ cup melted butter; add flour and stir until smooth. Now add the warm milk slowly, and cook until thick, stirring continuously. Add the 2 cups shredded cheese, salt, pepper, and thyme, and continue to cook until cheese is fully melted, about 3 more minutes after simmering begins. Now lower heat, and add the cup of sour cream, a heaping spoonful at a time, and stir well after each addition. Remove from heat, add the 2 cups creamed cottage cheese (without draining) and blend thoroughly and gently. Combine about ⅔ of this preparation with the cooked noodles; mix well.

Pour noodles into well-buttered flat baking dish (17-inch steel platter excellent). Spread rest of sauce over top and sprinkle with the other cup of shredded cheese. Bake in a preheated 350° F. oven for about 30 minutes if ingredients are warm; 45 minutes if casserole was prepared in advance. Increase heat to 500° F. and place under broiler for several minutes until top is brown.

Seasoned buttered peas may be served around base of casserole. Garnish ends with parsley and vegetable flowers. Serve with Breast of Turkey or Chicken Romanoff (page 217) or any other main dish.

Baked Macaroni in Casserole

½ pound macaroni
⅓ cup butter or margarine
⅓ cup sifted all-purpose flour
About 2¼ cups warm milk

¼ pound shredded American or cheddar cheese
1 teaspoon salt

Cook macaroni in gently boiling salted water about 25 to 30 minutes, or until tender. Drain very thoroughly. About 10 minutes before macaroni is done, in a separate saucepan, melt butter or margarine, blend in flour and then add milk gradually, stirring constantly. Cook until thick and smooth and simmer 5 minutes. Add the ¼ pound American or cheddar cheese and salt. Continue to cook until cheese is melted. If sauce is too thick, add little more milk. Combine ⅔ of this sauce with the cooked macaroni in 1-quart casserole dish or small oval steel platter. Pour rest of sauce over top. Bake about 30 minutes at 425° F., or until top is brown. Place under broiler for several minutes if necessary to brown top.

Quick Casserole

Cook ¾ pound of noodles or spaghetti (or any other macaroni product) in 3 quarts of boiling water seasoned with 1 tablespoon salt until tender, but not too soft. Takes anywhere from 10 to 20 minutes depending on thickness and quality of product. Drain well, and at once add ¼ cup soft or melted butter or margarine, ¼ cup grated Italian cheese or ½ cup shredded American cheese, ½ teaspoon marjoram or thyme, crushed in fingers, and ¼ teaspoon of garlic or onion salt. Mix well with 2 forks, taste, and season further if necessary with a little salt and pepper. Pour into a well-greased large (about 17 inch) oval (or round) baking dish, and with a large spoon form a slight depression in center.

Prepare sauce with ⅓ cup melted butter or margarine. Add ½ cup sifted all-purpose flour and stir until smooth. Add 2½ cups warm milk, a little at a time, 1½ teaspoon salt, ¼ teaspoon pepper, ¼ teaspoon marjoram or thyme, 2 tablespoons Italian or ¼ cup shredded American cheese. Cook until thick, then simmer about 5 minutes. Add 1 package of cooked asparagus cuts, peas, green beans, or lima beans (canned vegetables may be used), and 2 cups (more or less) of cooked meat, ham, or poultry, cut in flat 1-inch pieces. (Instead of meat, 2 cups, more or less, of cooked shrimp, lobster, crab meat, or any kind of cooked fish, cut in about 1-inch pieces may be used.) Taste, and season further if necessary. Pour this preparation into center of casserole, leaving a 2-inch rim all around without filling. Sprinkle center top only with paprika. Cover casserole loosely with well-greased aluminum foil and bake at 400° F. about 20 minutes if ingredients are warm, about 30 minutes if casserole was put together in advance.

Note. These casseroles are delicious and economical one-dish meals and are especially nice for buffet luncheons and suppers. They can be prepared hours or a day in advance if refrigerated, covered. Then bake for about 30 minutes at 400° F. just before serving. Instead of macaroni products, Rice Pilaf (page 312), plain rice, or Duchesse Potatoes (page 301) may be used in these casseroles.

▶ *Party-Style Molds*

THE VERSATILE MOLD CAN BE SERVED AS A FIRST COURSE, A MAIN DISH, OR as an accompaniment. It glorifies any simple luncheon or buffet table. We are including in this section many specialized, fancy layered molds not found in other cookbooks, and directions must be followed closely to insure success.

The 3-ounce packages of flavored gelatin dessert (instead of 6 ounce size) are used in our recipes. We also use the plain unflavored gelatin that comes in bulk (1 pound or smaller sizes), and which is available in most supermarts. If kept tightly covered in a cool dry place plain gelatin will last for several years without decomposing. Plain gelatin adds body to the molds and prevents them from liquifying in a warm room. The plain unflavored gelatin that comes in envelopes must be measured with standard measuring spoons.

Adding Food Coloring

If a recipe calls for food coloring to be added, it must be added while the preparation is very warm and in a liquid stage. We found it is safer to always dilute the food coloring in about 1 teaspoon of warm water before adding it to any gelatin preparation. If it has begun to congeal slightly and is lukewarm, preparation will not absorb coloring uniformly and will have a streaked appearance, depending also on the quality of the coloring. If this should occur at any time, pour preparation into a saucepan and keep *over very low heat,* stirring gently, until it is evenly colored. Do not let boil at any time. This would weaken gelatin. Simply let it stand heated until ready, then proceed with recipe directions.

Chilling Mold

Chilling can be speeded up by setting gelatin preparations into a pan or large bowl of ice and water, but never force them in a freezer. Freezing will weaken gelatin and the finished mold will break down and become watery when brought to room temperature for serving. Gelatin molds with a large amount of whipped cream can be frozen for a short time when indicated in recipe. Commercially prepared molds, sold in many stores, are made with special thickening agents that are not available in retail stores for the home-maker at the present time. However, the majority of our molds may be prepared a day or even two in advance and are nice and tender.

To Unmold

To facilitate removal of gelatin from molds, we like to oil them very lightly with a little bland oil. Too much oil would blur the surface. Before un-molding gelatin from molds, remove them from refrigerator about 15 minutes in advance, then dip them into a pan of warm (not hot) water to the depth of gelatin for about 1 minute. Remove from water and wipe metal part of mold with a towel to prevent dripping onto serving platter. Now loosen around top edge of mold with a small pointed knife, or wet fingers and gently pull gelatin away from top edge. Brush top of gelatin *and* a cool platter with water lightly. The moist surfaces make it easier to slide the gelatin into the center of the platter after it is unmolded. Place moistened platter on mold, and invert mold and platter together, holding them firmly and close to table top. Lift off mold carefully. If gelatin does not release easily, cover top and sides of mold with a thick hot wet towel for about 1 minute.

Large Molds

For large molds liquids should be reduced by ¼ cup each 3-ounce package of gelatin dessert. (This has already been done where necessary in all recipes in this section.) A firmer consistency makes molds less fragile and are less likely to crack when unmolding.

Layered Molds

Chill each layer until set, but not *too firm* before adding the next layer. If the first layer is too firm, the layers may slip apart when unmolded. Many layers may be built up in this way. The other mixtures should be cool and only slightly thickened, like an unbeaten egg white or a very soft custard, before pouring onto set gelatin in mold. If pouring mixture is too warm, it will soften the lower layer and mixtures will run together. If pouring preparation is too set, it will not cling to lower layer.

Fruits and vegetables, etc., may be added when gelatin is like a very soft custard. If it is too thin they will sink or float. If this should occur, place bowl into a pan of ice water for a short time, stirring gently until it begins to congeal and fruits or vegetables are well interspersed in gelatin. Do not let become too thick or it will not cling to layer in mold.

Fresh or frozen pineapple and pineapple juice should not be added to gelatin molds unless they are first cooked about 5 minutes. The enzyme in this fruit prevents gelatin from setting. Figs, mangoes, or papayas should not be used. Do not substitute canned-fruit syrups for plain liquids specified in recipes, since syrup may be too heavy and sweet for mixtures to gel properly.

To Whip Gelatin Desserts

Prepare as directed in recipe and chill until like a medium custard, not too thick, and not thin. Then with electric mixer beat mixture until fluffy and thick, for about 2 minutes. During warm weather, place bowl into another utensil with ice and water before you start to beat.

Clear Top Molds with Special Designs

Dissolve gelatin completely in water or other liquid suggested brought to the boiling point. Stir very, very gently to prevent bubbles on surface, then add cool liquid as suggested, and stir gently. If necessary remove bubbles from surface with a large spoon before pouring the next preparation very gently into mold. Let set as suggested in each recipe.

Decorations for Clear Gelatin Molds

Citron Peel Green Stems and Leaves

In many of our recipes for fancy top layered gelatin molds, fancy cookies, petit fours, etc., we suggest citron leaves, stems, etc. The most useful item for this work is candied citron peel, an ingredient used in holiday fruit cakes. It is available in many fancy grocery stores, sold by the piece or halved. Citron is a fruit peel (from the orange family) that is grown for the peel alone, and after some special treatment, is candied. It is light to dark green with some yellow tint.

Stems. With a very sharp knife slice citron lengthwise about ⅛ inch thick, then into about 1-inch narrow strips, about ⅛ inch wide.

Leaves. With a very sharp knife slice same thickness, then trim to uniform width about ¼ to ⅓ inch wide. Now cut strips into diamond shapes. This is a quick and excellent way to make leaves.

For other decorations, scraps and trimmings may be cut into small pieces. For additional color, it is important to soak these decorations in some green colored water (add few drops green coloring to warm water) for about 10 minutes, not longer. Then drain them well, rinse under clear cool water, and dry them thoroughly on paper towels. May be used at once, or let dry completely, and store in a cool dry place for several weeks or longer, in a covered container. Use as indicated in recipe.

Green candied pineapple may also be cut up and used in same way. Green maraschino or candied cherries are sometimes used.

Gelatin Leaves, Stems, and Other Decorations

Combine 4 level teaspoons plain gelatin with ⅓ cup cold water. Stir gently and let soak for about 5 minutes. Now add ⅔ cup boiling water over the thick gelatin preparation; stir gently until completely melted. Add 1 teaspoon sugar, a drop or 2 of green food coloring, first diluted in about 1 teaspoon warm water. Stir gently until evenly blended. Let preparation stand in room temperature until it is just warm (about 125° F.)

Add this green preparation about a teaspoon at a time to ¼ cup well-beaten cream cheese (in a 5-inch bowl), stirring well with rubber scraper after each addition. If preparation appears lumpy, strain. Pour into an 8-inch square pan lightly oiled with ⅛ teaspoon salad oil. Refrigerate for at least 8 hours.

To make leaves and other decorations, loosen around sides of pan with a small pointed knife, and turn set gelatin out onto heavy paper (or silicone paper) on a very flat surface, keeping bottom side up when cutting into various shapes. Small particles of the cheese are likely to float to top after you pour preparation into pan, but do not show after gelatin is turned over onto opposite side when making decorations.

Follow same directions for cutting of stems and leaves as suggested for citron peel. Use as suggested in recipes. This preparation may be made in various colors, and cut in many shapes and designs for top of molds. Very unique and simple to prepare.

Green Nuts for Decorative Purposes

When a recipe calls for pistachio nuts, you can use pecan meats, prepared as follows: Put pecan halves through a medium nut chopper, or crush with rolling pin. Add a few drops of green food coloring, working coloring into nutmeats with a fork, then blend them further in palms of hands. Spread nuts on a cookie sheet and allow to dry in room temperature for an hour or longer. When dry, it is important to put the colored nutmeats through a food mill or grater. Use as indicated in recipes.

How to Work With Fresh Pineapple, Pears, and Peaches

Cut pineapple from stem and into medium-thick slices. With small round cutter, remove core. Cut through or trim each slice into uniform rounds. Prepare enough syrup to cover pineapple slices, using 2 parts water and 1 part sugar (sugar may be increased). Add a drop or two diluted yellow coloring to syrup and simmer pineapple, about 5 or 6 minutes. Shut off heat and allow to remain in syrup until cold. Drain thoroughly.

For fresh pears, cut in halves lengthwise, remove core, etc. Peel, brush at once with citrus juice. Cook in syrup same as for pineapple about 5 minutes if pears are soft, 7 or 8 minutes if they are firm. Let remain in syrup until cool. A drop or two of any desired diluted coloring may be added to syrup while pears are cooling.

For fresh peaches, place in a colander, lower into rapidly boiling water for about 1 minute, remove and peel. Brush *at once* with citrus juice. It is not necessary to cook peaches in syrup. Fresh pineapple juice and pineapple (this includes the quick frosted) *must first be cooked for about 5 minutes* before using in a gelatin or jelly mold.

Shamrock Party-Style Mold

Serves 12 to 18

½ pound (1 cup) cream cheese
2 tablespoons plain gelatin, combined with ⅔ cup cold water (stir gently and let stand until thick)

⅓ cup granulated sugar
2 tablespoons strained lemon juice
2½ cups boiling water

With electric mixer beat cheese until medium, then make 3 large white, pink, or yellow carnations with No. 104 tube directly on pan covered with wax paper. Make 8 carnation buds with same tube. To remaining cheese add green coloring, and with No. 8 plain tube pipe bulb and short stem of carnations. Freeze carnations *only* until very firm to the touch, then cover.

In an 8-inch bowl combine gelatin preparation, sugar, and lemon juice. Add the 2½ cups boiling water (or use 1½ cups boiling and 1 cup cold water). For clear topping it is best to use water.

Pour ⅓ cup of this clear topping into very lightly oiled shamrock mold, and ¾ cup into large round mold (upside down cake pan that measures 9 × 2 inches). Refrigerate until firm to touch. Release carnations from wax paper with a small spatula or dinner knife and place the 3 large ones upside down in each shamrock leaf. Place buds on bottom of round pan, spacing them evenly. Pour about ⅓ cup cold clear topping around carnations in shamrock part, and ¾ cup over small carnations in large round pan. Refrigerate until set to touch, then pour ½ cup more topping into large pan and ⅓ cup into shamrock part. Refrigerate until set, then pour any remaining topping into each pan. Refrigerate until set. If carnations move around as you pour clear topping at any time, stop, and refrigerate for a short time, then continue to pour rest of topping.

With a large spoon pour Filling (page 423) into molds gently and slowly, filling them to top. Refrigerate for at least 8 hours.

To Serve. Loosen around edges with dinner knife. Dip larger mold into warm water, dry outside of mold with towel. Brush top of mold and 16-inch serving platter *lightly* with cold water. Place platter over mold, hold firmly and turn over, tipping platter slightly to centralize mold if necessary. With a towel remove surplus moisture from top center of mold. Release shamrock mold in same way, but do not brush top with cold water. This would cause mold to slide off bottom mold. Simply release top edge, and support bottom of mold with fingers, close to lower mold, and carefully turn over onto center of bottom mold.

Platter may be garnished on each side of mold with a spray of large white cream cheese or quick buttercream carnations with No. 124 or 104 tube and long thick stems and leaves with No. 8 or 10 plain tube. Will take about ¾ pound cream cheese or icing. Fresh or canned fruits and green leaves may be used instead.

Filling for Shamrock Mold

4 cups boiling water

4 packages lime gelatin dessert (3 ounce size)

2 cups ice water

2 cups fruit syrup (if short add a little water)

About ½ teaspoon green coloring, diluted in ½ teaspoon water

½ pound (1 cup) cream cheese, cold and firm

2 No. 303 cans pear halves, mashed, or crushed pineapple, drained

Pour boiling water over the 4 packages lime gelatin. Stir well until dissolved. Add the ice water and fruit syrup. Add about ½ teaspoon diluted green coloring and blend well. Let stand until cool and consistency of a very soft custard.

In a 10-inch bowl, beat the cold, firm cream cheese until creamy for several minutes. Add the green preparation, not more than 2 tablespoons at a time, and beat after each addition until smooth, scraping sides of bowl from time to time. If preparation appears thin, place it in a pan of ice water and stir gently and continuously until like a very soft custard, but not heavy. At this point, add the mashed drained pears, folding until evenly blended.

Colonial Fruit Salad Doll

Serves 12 to 18

3-ounce package lemon gelatin (first dissolve in ¾ cup boiling water, then add ¾ cup ice water; let stand until cold but not set)

2 No. 303 cans pear halves, well drained

4 (3-ounce) packages cherry or any other red gelatin (first dissolve in 3 cups boiling water, then add 1 cup ice water and 2 cups of cold

syrup left over from the canned fruits)

1 pound cream cheese (keep in refrigerator or cold place until needed)

No. 303 can fruit cocktail, well drained (will give about 1½ cups fruit)

Another ½ pound cream cheese for decorations (room temperature for at least 1 hour)

Brush both pans lightly with salad oil just before using. Turn them upside down to drain off surplus oil. This will facilitate removal of molds.

Pour ¼ cup of the cool lemon gelatin in lightly oiled 1-quart fluted mold. Refrigerate for about 20 minutes, or until like a soft custard. Cut 2 nice firm pear halves, each in 3 uniform lengthwise pieces, trimming ends if necessary to fit grooves of mold. Fill every other groove, using 6 sections of pears in all. Pour about 1 teaspoon of the lemon gelatin at a time around base of pears, using not more than 2 tablespoons in all. Refrigerate again until pears are firmly anchored to the gelatin, for about ½ hour, or longer if necessary. Now pour another ½ cup of cold (but not congealed) lemon gelatin, a little at a time, over the pears. Refrigerate again until set.

Measure and put aside 2 cups of the plain red gelatin preparation, to be used later. Add leftover lemon gelatin to the larger amount of red and refrigerate or keep in a cold place (or pan of ice water if necessary) until it is the consistency of unbeaten egg white, but not too thick. Meanwhile, with electric mixer, beat the 1 pound of cold cream cheese until it is very creamy and of medium consistency. At this point, add the slightly thickened larger amount of red gelatin, about a tablespoon at a time, beating after each addition with electric mixer. If preparation appears thin, chill it for a few minutes until the consistency of unbeaten egg white, but not thick, or else it will not cling to rest of mold. With pie blender mash rest of pears which will give about 2 cups and fold them gently into the pink cream cheese preparation. Pour 1 cup of this pink preparation over the lemon gelatin in fluted mold a little at a time and refrigerate again until set to the touch. At once pour rest of pink preparation into an oiled 9 × 2-inch upside down cake pan (or a deep layer cake pan about same size). Refrigerate until set to touch.

Chill the 2 reserved cups of plain red gelatin until it is the consistency of unbeaten egg white, and fold in the well-drained 1½ cups of fruit cocktail. Pour it over the pink preparation in the fluted mold gently, a little at a time, filling mold to the very top. Refrigerate for at least 8 hours. Best to prepare day in advance.

To Assemble Doll. With a dinner knife loosen around upper edge of-9-inch part of doll. Dip it into warm water (not hot) for a few seconds. Lift out of water, and shake mold gently to see if salad is loosened. If not, place it back into the warm water for a few more seconds, and test. Wipe outside of mold, and brush top and serving platter lightly with cold water. Place platter over mold, and invert carefully, tilting platter slightly if necessary to centralize mold. Now with a clean cloth wipe top of inverted mold to remove any excess moisture or oil. Release salad from fluted mold in same way, but do not brush with water. This would cause it to slide off lower part. Simply loosen and turn over, supporting with both hands, placing it on center top of lower mold.

Cut off an inch of tip from a long meat wooden skewer (should measure 4 inches), and insert it through top center of fluted mold as far down as possible. Place china doll head over skewer. Divide the ½ pound soft cream cheese in 2 parts, using a little more for the pink rosettes. Add a few drops of red coloring to the larger amount, and green to the other. Beat until well blended, but not too soft, and not too firm. Chill a few minutes if too soft. With No. 27 star tube pipe cluster of pink rosettes around waistline of doll, then with No. 65 leaf tube fill in with green leaves. Pipe more rosettes and leaves on entire mold, as attractively as possible. A rosette and green leaf may be piped on doll's hair unless she is wearing a hat. Small dainty cookies or cakes are very attractive arranged around this mold.

Note. This mold may be made up in the different shades of green, or any color combination preferred. Fresh cut-up fruits (except fresh pineapple) may be used instead of the canned fruit cocktail. Fresh or frozen pineapple must be cooked for 5 minutes before adding to a gelatin preparation.

Party-Style Apricot-Pear Gelatin Mold

Serves 12

3-ounce package lemon gelatin dessert, combined with 1½ cups boiling water and ½ cup cold water

1 largest can of whole or halves apricots, or 2 medium-size cans, well drained

1 largest can pear halves, or 2 medium-size cans, well drained

2 (3 ounce) packages lime gelatin dessert, combined with 2 cups boiling water and 1 cup cold fruit syrup from canned fruits

½ pound cold firm cream cheese, or 1 cup commercial sour cream

3 (3 ounce) packages raspberry (strawberry or cherry may be used) gelatin dessert, combined with 3 cups boiling water and 2 cups of cold fruit syrup (if short of syrup use water to make up difference)

Combine the 1 package of lemon gelatin dessert with the water; stir gently until thoroughly dissolved. Pour 1 cup of this preparation into lightly oiled 11¼ × 2½-inch round mold. Refrigerate until set, but not too firm. Place an apricot half with rounded side down into each cavity, and one in center cavity.

Cut most of pear halves (each into about 4 to 6 lengthwise sections), making a total of about 20. Tint half of them in green and half in pink. This is done by adding food coloring to about 1 cup of cool water in a small narrow bowl. Place cut pears into colored liquid and let remain until a good color is obtained, not too light, as they appear much lighter after mold is completed. Drain colored sections thoroughly on paper toweling, then arrange them on top of mold alternately. Now pour rest of lemon gelatin preparation, a little at a time, around fruit, and if any of the pieces appear to move around, stop adding the lemon gelatin, and place mold in refrigerator until fruit is set in place, then add remaining lemon gelatin. Refrigerate until set.

Combine the 2 packages of lime gelatin with the 2 cups water brought to a boil, then add 1 cup cold syrup. Stir until dissolved. Add a drop or 2 of diluted green coloring. Let stand until the consistency of unbeaten egg white. A few minutes before topping in mold is firm, with electric mixer beat the ½ pound of cheese until creamy, smooth, and of medium consistency, not too soft. Now add the slightly congealed lime gelatin, a little at a time, to the beaten cheese, beating after each addition with electric mixer until well blended. Pour this green preparation over the topping in mold, and refrigerate until green is set.

Meanwhile, combine the 3 packages of raspberry (or other red) gelatin dessert with the 3 cups of boiling water, then add the 2 cups of cold fruit syrup; blend well, and let stand in a cold place or in a pan of ice water (do not use too many ice cubes in water; best to let set slowly) until consistency of unbeaten egg white. This should be done when the green in mold is firm to the touch. Mash up any leftover apricots and pears, and fold them into the red gelatin preparation. If preparation appears too thin, place it into pan of cold water or refrigerator for a few minutes, but do not allow it to become too thick, or else it will not cling to the green section. Pour this over the green, and refrigerate mold for at least 8 hours.

To Serve. Loosen mold around upper edge with dinner knife; dip mold into warm water (not hot) for a few seconds; wipe pan, rub top of mold and 16-inch serving platter lightly with cold water. Place platter on top of mold and turn over. Garnish base of mold with any kind of fresh green leaves, or as desired.

Note. Instead of apricots *very small* peach halves, or large fresh or canned sweet cherries may be used. Canned colored pineapple spears may be used instead of the pear sections.

Standard-Size Della Robbia Gelatin Ring Fruit Mold

Serves 12

1½ (3-ounce) packages gelatin, combined with 1 cup boiling water and 1½ cups cold water
1 small can pear halves, color 3 pink (leave rest white)
1 small can pineapple rings, color 3 green (leave rest natural)
1 or 2 bananas, cut to fit impressions

About 8 fresh strawberries, or maraschino cherries
1½ (3-ounce) packages lime gelatin and ½ tablespoon plain gelatin
1 cup boiling water and 1½ cups fruit syrup
¼ pound (½ cup) cream cheese, or ½ cup dairy sour cream

Follow directions as for Large Party-Size Gelatin Ring Fruit Mold (below) using 10 x 2¼-inch mold.

Della Robbia Large Party-Size Gelatin Ring Fruit Mold

Serves 18

3 (3-ounce) packages lemon gelatin, combined with 2 cups boiling water, until dissolved, then add 3 cups cold water

1 large can pear halves, 4 colored pink (not too light and not too dark)

1 medium-size can pineapple rings, 4 colored green (not too light and not too dark)

2 bananas (not too ripe), cut lengthwise, then trim ends round to fit impressions

About 1 dozen fresh strawberries, or maraschino cherries, well drained

3 (3-ounce) packages lime gelatin, combined with 1 tablespoon plain gelatin (mix well; pour 2 cups boiling water over the lime gelatin and the plain gelatin; stir until dissolved, then add 3 cups cold fruit syrup from the canned fruits. Water may be used to make up the 3 cups if necessary. Add a few drops of diluted green coloring.)

½ pound (1 cup) cream cheese, cold and firm, or 1 cup cold dairy sour cream

Pour 2 cups of the lemon gelatin into 13 x 2¾-inch lightly oiled mold. Refrigerate until set, but not too stiff. Place the well-drained (and dried on paper towels) pears and pineapple rings in proper impressions, then bananas, cut and ends rounded. Place whole fresh strawberry or cherry in round opening of pineapple, and rest of berries in open spaces to add color. Now pour 1 cup of the cool thin lemon preparation around fruits, little at a time. Refrigerate until set. Pour rest of lemon preparation into mold, and if fruits appear to move around, do not add all of it. Refrigerate until fruits are well anchored to gelatin. Add rest of lemon. Refrigerate until set.

Meanwhile, let green gelatin preparation stand until the consistency of unbeaten egg white. When lemon in mold is set, beat the cup of cream cheese with electric mixer for several minutes (or use sour cream without beating). Add green gelatin, not more than ¼ cup at a time in the beginning, and beat after each addition medium speed, until smooth. If preparation appears thin after you have completed operation, place bowl in refrigerator for several minutes until *slightly congealed,* but not heavy. Cut up any leftover fruits in small pieces and fold it into green gelatin. At once pour into mold, and refrigerate for at least 12 hours, or better prepare day in advance.

To Serve. Loosen around upper edge of mold and tube with a dinner knife. Place mold in lukewarm water for a few seconds. Wipe mold. Brush large platter (about 16-inch size) *and* top of mold lightly with cold water. Place platter over mold, hold it *firmly* with both hands (it is very heavy and awkward) supporting edge on table, and turn over. A low Pyrex custard cup filled with whipped cream or Fruit Salad Dressing (page 371) may be placed in opening of mold.

Pineapple-Shaped Fruit Mold

Serves 6 to 8

Topping for Pineapple Mold

½ cup boiling water
2 teaspoons plain gelatin, combined with ¼ cup cold water in a 7-inch bowl (stir and allow to stand until thick)

2 tablespoons granulated sugar
2 tablespoons lemon juice
No. 2½ can pineapple spears

Pour boiling water over gelatin preparation. Sir until dissolved. Add granulated sugar and lemon juice. To ⅓ cup gelatin mixture add a little green coloring and a drop of yellow. Pour 2½ tablespoons of this green into leaf part of oiled pineapple mold and reserve rest of green for later. Lift body part, supporting with a towel on baking sheet. *Refrigerate until slightly congealed, but not too firm.* To rest of plain topping add 1 or 2 drops of diluted yellow and a tiny drop of red, forming a *very* light orange color. Put this aside in a cool place until needed.

When green leaf part is slightly congealed, cut up enough pineapple spears to fill in design. Now pour rest of green preparation, a teaspoon at a time, around pineapple and on top. Refrigerate again until firm to touch.

When leaf part is set to touch, remove any particles of green that might have spilled into body part, and pour about ½ of the light-orange gelatin into mold. Refrigerate until slightly congealed. Meanwhile, trim off a narrow strip from flat side of pineapple spears, so that spears measure ½ inch wide. Cut each spear into about 4 diamonds. About 8 spears will be required.

When clear orange gelatin is partially set in mold, arrange pineapple diamonds attractively. Now pour 2 tablespoons of leftover light-orange gelatin, a teaspoon at a time, around pineapple. Refrigerate until set. Then pour in rest of cold light-orange gelatin (that is not congealed), a little at a time, and refrigerate until set. Meanwhile prepare filling for mold.

Filling for Pineapple Mold

¾ cup boiling water
3-ounce package pineapple gelatin dessert
¾ cup pineapple juice
3-ounce package cream cheese, cold

and firm, or ⅓ cup commercial sour cream
Leftover pineapple spears, cut into small pieces
¼ cup broken pecan meats

Pour boiling water over pineapple gelatin. Stir well until dissolved; then add cold pineapple juice. Add some diluted yellow coloring and a little red coloring, to give gelatin a deep orange color. Let preparation congeal slightly. Meanwhile, in a 7-inch bowl beat cold firm cream cheese until creamy with electric mixer. Add congealed gelatin, about 1 tablespoon at a time, to cheese, beating well after each addition until smooth. If preparation appears thin, place bowl in a pan of ice water and stir gently until it is like a very, very soft custard. At this point, fold in cut-up pineapple and broken pecan meats. At once pour this into mold. If preparation is too thick, it will not cling to topping. If it is too thin, pineapple and nutmeats will not be evenly distributed. Refrigerate at least 8 hours.

To Serve. Dip mold into warm water a few seconds. Wipe it well. Loosen around edges; brush top of mold *and* serving platter lightly with cold water. Place platter over mold, and invert. Use 12- or 14-inch platter. Garnish with lemon or other green leaves and Frosted Grapes (page 435), other canned fruits, or fresh fruits in season.

Fresh Blueberry Party-Style Mold

Serves 12

1 tablespoon plain gelatin, combined with ¼ cup cold water (stir gently and let stand until thick)
2 tablespoons granulated sugar
2 tablespoons strained lemon juice
1½ cups boiling water
1 pint fresh blueberries, washed, and dried in a towel

12 green 1¼-inch citron leaves (let soak in water with a little green coloring for a few minutes, then drain well and dry them in a towel); or use other green leaves
3 red maraschino cherries, dried in a towel, and cut into rings

In a 7-inch bowl combine gelatin preparation, sugar, lemon juice, and boiling water. Stir gently, and let stand until cool. Pour ½ cup into lightly oiled 1½-quart ring mold. Refrigerate until set, but not too firm. At same time combine ½ cup of the fresh blueberries with 3 tablespoons clear gelatin topping in a narrow cup. Refrigerate until quite firm. Place rest of clear topping in a cool place or refrigerate until needed, but do not permit to set. Should be consistency of a thin unbeaten egg white, or simply use it cold.

When clear topping in mold is partially set, with tip of spoon pick up congealed blueberries, and place them in 6 small heaps, evenly spaced. Arrange green citron leaves and cherry rings attractively around berries. With a spoon carefully pour about ¼ cup of the clear topping around decorations and refrigerate until set. Then pour rest of clear topping into mold and refrigerate until firm. If decorations appear to float at any time as you pour in topping, stop pouring and place pan in refrigerator until decorations are firmly set, then pour rest of topping.

Prepare Second Layer of Mold. Combine 2-to-3-ounce packages of black raspberry or any other dark gelatin dessert with 1½ cups of boiling water and 2 cups iced water or pineapple juice. Stir well and let stand until consistency of unbeaten egg white. Beat ½ pound (1 cup) of cold, firm cream cheese (or use 1 cup sour cream) at high speed for several minutes until creamy. Add 1 cup of the slightly congealed dark gelatin preparation, not more than ¼ cup at a time, and beat after each addition until very smooth, scraping sides of bowl from time to time with rubber scraper. At once pour this orchid preparation slowly into mold over the set clear topping, and refrigerate again until firm to touch.

Prepare Third Layer of Mold. Put aside ½ cup of the remaining blueberries if platter is to be garnished with stuffed peaches or pears. Allow rest of dark gelatin to stand until consistency of unbeaten egg white. Now fold in rest of blueberries, and pour over the set orchid cream cheese preparation in mold. Refrigerate for at least 8 hours.

Decorations for Platter Around Mold

½ cup of the fresh blueberries

2 teaspoons plain gelatin, combined with ¼ cup cold water (stir and let stand until thick, then dissolve over simmering water; add the 2 teaspoons dissolved gelatin to 1 cup of the strained fruit syrup)

1 large can pear or peach halves (nice and firm), well drained on cake racks

About sixteen 1-inch green citron leaves

8 maraschino cherry rings

In a cup combine the ½ cup berries with ¼ cup of gelatin preparation. Refrigerate until set. Let rest of gelatin preparation stand until consistency of unbeaten egg white. Place fruit halves on cake rack with drip pan underneath. Fill cavities with spoonful congealed berries. Place citron leaves on each side and a cherry ring on top. Now pour slightly thickened glaze over entire surface of stuffed fruits. May be necessary to do this several times until well coated. Pick up glaze that falls into drip pan, stir well, and if thick, place pan in warm water for a few seconds. If too thin, place in cold water, until right consistency, and pour over fruit.

To Serve Mold. Dip mold in warm water for a few seconds, and dry it well on outside. Brush top of mold and 16- or 14-inch round platter lightly with cold water, loosen around top edges and tube; place platter over mold, hold firmly, and invert. Garnish platter with lemon leaves (or other green leaves). With pancake turner, pick up stuffed glazed fruits, and arrange on leaves, evenly spaced. Place 4½ × 2-inch Pyrex bowl in center of mold, and fill it with Fruit Salad Dressing (page 371) or with whipped cream.

Individual Cranberry Molds

Pour cranberry preparation (below) into individual lightly oiled molds and let stand in refrigerator for several hours or longer to become firm. To serve, loosen around upper edge with paring knife, dip into warm water, and turn out onto pineapple rings or thick slices of oranges. Very attractive arranged around base of roasted turkey alternately with parsley bouquets. Or serve individual molds in lettuce cup.

Cranberry Gelatin Mold

Serves 12

4 cups (1 pound) fresh cranberries	¼ cup cold water
1 large California orange	3 cups boiling water
2 cups granulated sugar	2 (3 ounce) packages lemon gelatin
1 tablespoon plain gelatin	dessert

Wash cranberries well, drain thoroughly. Cut a peeled or unpeeled orange into small pieces, and put both cranberries and orange into food chopper, and grind together, being careful not to lose any of the juices. Place small bowl under chopper to catch juices. Add 2 cups or less of granulated sugar to the chopped cranberries and orange, and allow to stand about 15 minutes until sugar has dissolved.

Let the plain gelatin stand in the ¼ cup cold water 5 minutes until thick, then dissolve it over simmering water. Pour the 3 cups of boiling water (or half boiling water and half cold) over the 2 packages of lemon gelatin. Add the dissolved plain gelatin at once, mix well, and let stand until slightly congealed; then combine thoroughly with cranberry mixture.

Brush a 7-cup ring mold (any style mold may be used) with salad oil. Pour in preparation and allow to jell for 10 to 12 hours. Keep in refrigerator until thoroughly set. When ready to be served, loosen mold around edges and tube with slender knife, brush top of mold and serving platter with cold water, dip into warm water a few seconds, and turn out onto platter.

Arrange half slices of glazed pineapple around base of mold, and in between slices place pale green glazed pear halves. Insert a half or whole maraschino cherry on large open end of each pear.

Glazed Fruit for Mold

Prepare glaze with 1½ tablespoons plain gelatin combined with ⅓ cup *cold* water. Let stand until thick, then pour 1½ cups boiling water over thickened gelatin. Add a drop of yellow coloring. Let cool until slightly congealed. Add a little diluted green coloring to liquid of pears and allow them to stand in this liquid until delicately colored. Pick up and place on cake coolers. Do not color pineapple. Simply place it on cake cooler. When glaze is slightly congealed, pour it at once onto cold fruit. Pick up glaze that falls through, stir and use again. If it becomes too thick, place over warm water and stir until smooth, then chill over ice water to make proper consistency. Glazing may be done a day in advance. Store fruit in refrigerator until ready to be used. Release from cake coolers with a spatula to prevent marking or breaking.

Party-Style Citrus Fruit Salad Mold

Serves 8 to 12

1¼ cups boiling water
1 tablespoon plain gelatin, combined with ⅓ cup cold water (stir gently and let stand until thick)
¼ cup granulated sugar
2 tablespoons strained lemon juice

1 can mandarin segments (or small orange segments), 2 red maraschino cherries, and 8 citron or green pepper leaves, cut about 1¼ inches long and ½ inch wide

In medium-size bowl pour boiling water over the thick gelatin preparation, granulated sugar, and lemon juice. Stir gently and let stand until cool and clear.

Pour ¾ cup of this clear preparation into standard 1½-quart ring mold; refrigerate until partially set, not too firm. Now form 4 flowers with mandarin or orange segments, using 3 segments for each flower, and place ½ red maraschino cherry, well drained and dried on towel, upside down on small end of flower. Place green citron or other leaf on each side of cherry. Now pour about 2 teaspoons of clear, cold topping, very little at a time, around each flower and leaves, and put back into refrigerator until flowers cling to base and do not move around. Pour rest of clear topping, a little at a time into mold, and if decorations appear to move around at any time, stop adding topping and refrigerate mold for a short time. Then add rest of topping (liquid stage). Refrigerate until set to touch.

Citrus Fruit Salad

2½ cups syrup from grapefruit and mandarin segments (if short, add a little water)
2 (3 ounce) packages lime gelatin
A drop or two diluted green coloring, if desired
2 No. 303 cans of grapefruit segments, or combined grapefruit

and orange segments, well drained
½ cup fresh strawberries, or ¼ cup sliced maraschino cherries
¾ cup granulated sugar
½ cup cold commercial sour cream or cream cheese

Bring to boil 1½ cups of the syrup and *at once* pour it over the granulated sugar and 2 packages lime gelatin. Stir well, and let stand until dissolved.

Now add rest of syrup (1 cup). Add a drop or two of diluted green coloring if desired, but not necessary. Let preparation become cold. When cold, add 1 cup of this green preparation to the ½ cup commercial sour cream (or beaten cream cheese) *a tablespoonful* at a time and blend well. Allow this to stand in a cool place until it is the consistency of a thin unbeaten egg white, then pour it into mold. Refrigerate until very set to touch.

Meanwhile allow rest of green preparation to stand until the consistency of a thin unbeaten egg white, and at this point fold in the well-drained fruits and leftover mandarin segments. Pour at once, before it thickens, very gently into mold. Refrigerate for at least 8 hours.

To Serve. Loosen around upper edge of mold and around tube; dip mold into warm water for a few seconds; wipe mold. Brush flat platter *and* open part of mold lightly with cold water. Place platter over mold and invert. If it does not come out easily, dip again into warm (not hot) water, and turn over. Garnish platter with fresh lemon leaves or other leaves, fresh strawberries, or other fruits in season, such as melon rings, cut in halves, calavos, fresh pineapple, or with canned fruits. If using fresh strawberries, insert several toothpicks on bottom sides of mold, then place a berry on each pick.

Cranberry Fluff Mold

Serves 8 to 12

2 tablespoons plain gelatin, combined with ½ cup cold water (allow to stand until thick, then dissolve over simmering water)
1-pound can whole-cranberry sauce, beaten well with a spoon
½ cup granulated sugar
½ teaspoon salt
¼ cup lemon juice
1 cup canned cranberry-juice cocktail
About ¼ teaspoon red food coloring
1 pint (2 cups) whipping cream, beaten until it clings to bowl (do not beat further) and refrigerated

Add dissolved gelatin to cranberry sauce. Then add sugar, salt, lemon juice, and cranberry-juice cocktail, a little at a time, to form a smooth mixture. Add red coloring. Beat well about 1 minute. Place bowl in refrigerator or a pan of ice water until mixture is of medium consistency, like a soft custard, not too firm.

When cranberry mixture looks like a soft custard, beat it with electric mixer about 2 minutes. Now add whipped cream, and fold over and over until no streaks appear. Pour into a well-oiled 1½-quart mold and spread evenly. Refrigerate at least 8 hours.

To Serve. Loosen around edges and brush top with cold water. Brush a platter with cold water, and invert mold on platter. Garnish base of mold with lemon or galax leaves and with fresh or canned fruits, relishes, or as desired. This mold is delicious with poultry, ham, and other meat dishes.

Yuletide Star Cranberry-Raspberry Mold (or Christmas Tree Mold)

Serves 12

1 pound fresh cranberries, picked over and washed
1½ cups hot water
2 cups granulated sugar
2 (3 ounce) packages raspberry gelatin dessert

1 tablespoon plain gelatin, combined with ½ cup cold water (stir gently and let stand at least 5 minutes until thick)
2 tablespoons lemon juice
1½ cups cold water

Combine cranberries and the 1½ cups hot water. Cover saucepan and boil about 5 minutes after boiling starts, or until skins pop open. Press through a fine sieve or food mill to remove skins and seeds. Add 2 cups granulated sugar and boil again about 1 minute, skimming top if necessary. Remove from heat and at once (while cranberry jelly is very hot) add 2 packages of raspberry gelatin dessert and the thick plain gelatin mixture. Stir for about 1 minute, or until competely dissolved. Now add the 2 tablespoons of lemon juice and the 1½ cups of cold water and stir until well blended for about 1 minute. Pour into oiled star mold (6-cup capacity). (Other style molds may be used.) Refrigerate for at least 8 hours. May be prepared 1 or 2 days in advance.

Garnish for Special Occasion

1 large can large pear halves, tinted green (or leave white)
2 cans apricot halves or small peach halves, well drained, and rounded

part tinted red with diluted coloring
3 dozen artificial marzipan leaves

Cut pears in 4 lengthwise slices. Arrange 4 sections between each point with cut sides down and round part on outside. Place 3 tinted apricot or peach halves in center and 2 between pears on each side. (Preserved kumquats may be used instead of apricots.) Place stem and leaf on top of each apricot. (Imitation marzipan leaves may be used.)

Purple Grape Mold

Serves 6 to 8

Leaf Part of Mold

1 teaspoon plain gelatin, combined with 2 tablespoons cold water (stir well, and let stand until thick, for several minutes, then dissolve over simmering water until clear)
2 more tablespoons cold water

2 teaspoons lemon juice
1 tablespoon granulated sugar
About ⅛ teaspoon diluted green food coloring
2 tablespoons commercial sour cream, or cream cheese, beaten until creamy

Combine all ingredients *except* sour cream (or cream cheese). Blend well. Pour this preparation, about *a teaspoonful* at a time, into sour cream and stir well with rubber scraper after each addition. If it appears the least bit lumpy put through tea strainer. Brush grape mold with ½ teaspoon salad oil, place it on a small flat baking sheet, raising mold so that stem end is down, supporting pointed end with a crushed wet towel. Pour preparation carefully into stem end. Refrigerate until set to touch.

Body Part of Mold

2 (3 ounce) packages dark gelatin desert

2 cups boiling water

1½ cups very cold pineapple juice (or other fruit juice or fruit syrup or water)

¾ pound of fresh dark grapes, or 1 can fruit cocktail (if fresh grapes are large, best to cut them in halves and remove seed)

Pour boiling water over dark gelatin dessert. Stir until completely dissolved, then add the 1½ cups cold pineapple juice. Pour 3 tablespoons of this preparation into body part of oiled mold. Refrigerate until partially congealed, but not too firm. At this point, place grapes in each indentation. Refrigerate for about 15 minutes. Now pour 3 more tablespoons of cold purple preparation teaspoonful at a time, over and around grapes, and refrigerate until firm to touch. If using canned fruit cocktail, use grapes for indentations, rest for body.

Let rest of purple preparation stand until it is the consistency of unbeaten egg white (not thick). At this point, fold in rest of grapes or fruit salad, and with a large spoon carefully pour into mold, filling it to top. Refrigerate for at least 8 hours.

To Serve. With a dinner knife loosen around upper edge of mold. Dip into warm water a few seconds, wipe mold, and brush top with cold water. Brush a medium-size (12 to 14 inch) platter with cold water. Place platter over mold and invert. Garnish platter with sprays of lemon or other green leaves and with bunches of Frosted Grapes, or as desired.

Frosted Grapes

Add ½ teaspoon of lemon juice (or ¼ teaspoon salt) to each egg white. Beat until very slightly foamy (not too long). Let stand at least ½ hour. Wash clusters of grapes and dry them well. Hold them in fingers and dip into egg white preparation, covering thoroughly. Let drip a few seconds, then place into a bowl of granulated sugar (or commercially colored sugar). Cover all surfaces well with sugar, shake slightly and place on cake rack to dry. May be dipped again into sugar after 15 minutes if necessary. This may be done several hours or day in advance, and kept in a cool place. Very attractive on large green leaves to garnish fruit salad molds, meat platters, etc.

Butterfly Party-Style Fruit Salad Mold

Serves 6 to 8

2 (3 ounce) packages lemon gelatin dessert
2 cups boiling water
1 cup cold pear syrup
1 large can (No. 2½) pear halves, well drained
2 (3 ounce) packages lime gelatin dessert

2 cups boiling water
1 cup cold pear syrup (if short, add water)
3-ounce package cream cheese, or ⅓ cup sour cream
Red and green food coloring

Combine the 2 packages lemon gelatin dessert with 2 cups boiling water; stir gently until completely dissolved, then add 1 cup cold pear syrup. Pour 1½ cups of this light preparation into bottom of lightly oiled butterfly mold. Refrigerate until congealed, but not too firm. Meanwhile cut up 4 pear halves, each into 4 lengthwise slices. Add about ⅛ teaspoon diluted green coloring to ⅔ cup cool water and submerge ½ of pear slices. Add ⅛ teaspoon diluted red coloring to another ⅔ cup cool water and submerge rest of slices. When pears have taken on an attractive color, *drain them well,* and store on paper towels in refrigerator until needed.

When gelatin in mold is congealed, place a thick oval white pear in center with *rounded* part down. Arrange colored pear slices alternately on each side, keeping them very close together. Cut up several red maraschino cherries into crosswise slices, and place them in open spaces to add color. At this point, carefully pour ⅓ cup of the lemon preparation with a spoon around fruit. Refrigerate until set to touch.

To remaining lemon gelatin preparation that is still in liquid stage and warm, add a few drops of diluted red coloring, stir well and refrigerate until very slightly congealed. At this point, with rubber scraper, beat the small package of cream cheese, or ⅓ cup sour cream, until creamy; add the congealed gelatin, about a teaspoon at a time in the beginning, and beat well after each addition with scraper until smooth. At once pour this pink preparation into mold and refrigerate until set to touch.

Combine the 2 packages lime gelatin dessert with 2 cups boiling water and 1 cup pear syrup. Add a little diluted green coloring and blend well. When this is partially congealed, *but not too thick,* fold in leftover pears that have been cut in small pieces or mashed with pie blender. Pour at once into mold and refrigerate for *at least 8 hours.* If this green preparation is too thick it will not cling to rest of mold. Should be the consistency of a thin custard.

To Serve. With a dinner knife loosen around upper edge of mold. Dip into warm water a few seconds. Wipe mold, and brush top with cold water. Brush a medium-size (12 to 14 inch) round platter also with water. Place platter over mold and invert. Garnish platter with sprays of lemon or other green leaves, or as desired.

Raspberry-Pineapple Mold

Serves 8 to 12

Topping for Raspberry-Pineapple Mold

2 teaspoons plain gelatin, combined with 3 tablespoons cold water (allow to stand until thick, then dissolve over simmering water)
2 tablespoons sugar
2 tablespoons lemon juice

½ cup water
Green food coloring (optional)
1 slice pineapple from No. 2 can pineapple slices (1¼-pound size), drained
1 drained maraschino cherry

Pour very hot dissolved gelatin over sugar and lemon juice. Stir. Now slowly add water. Pour ⅓ cup of this preparation into an oiled 7-cup mold (tower aluminum mold or plain bowl may be used). Refrigerate until gelatin is partially set, but not too stiff. Tint 1 slice of pineapple green (or leave yellow), drain it well on a towel, and arrange it in center of mold. Place drained red maraschino cherry in opening of pineapple ring. Refrigerate again until set to the touch. Pour rest of cold clear topping (that is not set) over pineapple, and refrigerate again until set to the touch.

Filling for Raspberry-Pineapple Mold

Drained juices from fruit
2 (3 ounce) packages raspberry gelatin dessert
½ tablespoon plain gelatin, combined with ¼ cup cold water

1 small can sweet Bing cherries, drained
Remaining pineapple slices from No. 2 can
2 tablespoons lemon juice

Measure drained pineapple and cherry juice. If there is less than 3½ cups, make up difference with additional fruit juices, gingerale, or water. Bring juices *only* to the boiling point, and pour them over raspberry gelatin and plain gelatin combined with water. Stir until completely dissolved, and add balance of liquid to make up 3½ cups. Refrigerate until partially set, but not too thick; then gently fold in drained cherries, pineapple cut into 1-inch pieces, and lemon juice. With a cup gently pour this preparation over first part of mold. Refrigerate at least 8 hours. Mold may be prepared a day or 2 in advance.

To Serve Mold. With a paring knife loosen around top edge of mold.

Dip it into warm water a few seconds. Wipe outside of mold thoroughly. Brush top of mold and platter with cold water and invert onto platter.

Garnish for Special Occasions

1 No. 2 can pineapple slices
1 jar kumquats, or 1 large can peeled
    apricots

A few sprigs fresh lemon leaves

Arrange pineapple rings, overlapping each other slightly, around base of mold. Place whole kumquat or peeled apricot in opening of pineapple. Group leftover kumquats or apricots on lemon leaves on each side of mold.

Melon Medley Salad Mold

Serves 12

4 cups hot water, combined with 1 tablespoon dried mint (or 2 tablespoons chopped fresh mint), simmered several minutes, then strained through fine cloth
3 tablespoons plain gelatin, combined with ¾ cup lemon juice, stirred and allowed to stand until thick,

then dissolved thoroughly over simmering water
1 cup granulated sugar
¼ teaspoon salt
1 cup watermelon balls
1 cup cantaloupe balls
1 cup honeydew balls

Combine all ingredients except melon balls, and stir well. Pour ½ cup into lightly oiled 6-cup mold or plain bowl. Refrigerate until it is like a soft custard, but not too firm. Now place about 14 assorted melon balls on gelatin. With a spoon gently pour ¼ cup gelatin preparation (still in liquid stage) over fruit. Refrigerate again until set to the touch. Arrange more assorted melon balls over surface of firm gelatin, and with spoon gently pour another ¼ cup, or a little more, gelatin preparation (still in liquid stage) over fruit. Refrigerate again until set to the touch. Meanwhile, chill rest of gelatin preparation until it has the consistency of unbeaten egg white (it must not be too heavy, nor too thin). At this point, fold rest of melon balls into preparation, and at once *gently* pour into mold. Refrigerate at least 8 hours.

To Serve. Dip mold into warm water a few seconds. Wipe outside well, and turn out onto a platter. Garnish base of mold with fresh mint leaves (or small lemon or other leaves) and bouquets of assorted melon balls. Insert toothpicks in melon balls to prevent them from rolling out of position. If preferred, base of mold may be garnished with half slices of cantaloupe and honeydew alternately with green leaves, or as desired. Serve whipped cream or Fruit Salad Dressing (page 371) separately.

Note. Any 1 of the 3 melons may be used alone in this mold. If using cantaloupe or honeydew melons alone, color may be added with a few well-drained red and green maraschino cherries. Scraps of melon cut into ½-inch pieces may also be used in base of mold, but not for top decorations.

Multifruit Salad Mold

Serves 8

4 egg yolks
1 teaspoon sugar
¼ teaspoon salt
2 tablespoons lemon juice
1 cup whipping cream
2 teaspoons gelatin combined with ¼
  * cup cold water
½ pound miniature marshmallows

1 pound red grapes, each cut into 3
  or 4 pieces and seeded
⅓ cup green cherries, each cut into 2
  or 3 pieces
8 slices pineapple, each cut into 10 or
  12 pieces
1 cup pecans, coarse-chopped

Beat egg yolks till lemon color (about 2 minutes), and add sugar, salt, lemon juice, and ½ cup whipping cream, beating only until blended. Cook this mixture in a 1-quart saucepan over very low heat until thick, and allow to simmer 2 minutes. Add gelatin mixture that has thickened, and stir until gelatin has melted. Pour into a large bowl and allow to cool but not to set. While this mixture is cooling, combine marshmallows, grapes, cherries, pineapple, and nuts. When custard is cool, beat the other ½ cup whipping cream until it just clings to bowl, and add to custard. Mix only until blended. Add cut fruit, marshmallows, and pecans, and blend well. Pour into an oiled 6-cup bowl or mold. This salad must stand at least 8 hours before unmolding. It is not advisable to make this salad more than a day in advance.

When ready to serve, loosen around sides and bottom of mold, and turn out onto a large round wet platter. Arrange sliced pineapple, peach, and pear halves around mold, and serve with Fruit Salad Dressing (page 371).

Strawberry-Rhubarb Mold

Serves 12 to 16

2 cups boiling water
2 tablespoons plain gelatin, thoroughly
  mixed with the gelatin dessert
  and sugar
2 (3 ounce) packages lemon or strawberry gelatin dessert
½ cup granulated sugar
A little red coloring, diluted in ½ teaspoon warm water

2 (16 ounce) packages frozen rhubarb, cooked about 5 to 10 minutes after it is completely defrosted, *and then cooled*
3 (10 or 12 ounce) packages frozen
  sweetened strawberries, defrost
  but do not cook (raspberries may
  be used)

Pour the boiling water over the 2 packages of gelatin dessert, mixed with plain gelatin, the ½ cup granulated sugar, and red coloring. Let stand in refrigerator until *slightly congealed*, then add the cooked *cool* rhubarb and the defrosted berries. Pour into a 9-cup mold that has been brushed with salad oil. Let stand in refrigerator until firm to the touch, about 8 hours or longer. Shortly before serving, unmold onto flat round platter, arrange glazed pineapple slices cut in halves around base alternately with pale green pears. Place half red cherry in open end of pears. Serve Fruit Salad Dressing (page 371) with this mold. Or omit fruit around mold and simply garnish with vegetable flowers and parsley or relishes.

Note. This recipe may be cut in half and poured into a 4- or 5-cup Easter egg mold, or it may be poured into individual molds and served in lettuce cups or on pineapple slices. The whole recipe will make about 14 to 18 individual molds depending on size. If *fancy* large or small molds are used, it is better to dip the outside of the molds in warm water for a few seconds in order to release salad without damage.

Strawberry-Rhubarb Egg Mold

Prepare half recipe of basic Strawberry-Rhubarb Mold (above). Pour it into oiled egg mold that measures 7½ inches long × 2¾ inches deep. Refrigerate for at least 8 hours. To serve, loosen around edges with a spatula or dinner knife. Brush top of mold with cold water. Place a wet 14-inch round platter over mold and invert. Around base, arrange large firm pear halves (No 2½ can) that have been cut lengthwise into 3 or 4 sections and tinted green. This is done by placing the cut pears into water to which a little green coloring has been added. Drain colored pears well. In between slices of pears, place small canned red crab apples, kumquats, or apricots. Garnish small ends of egg with several of these small fruits. Thick peach slices may be used instead of pears. Serve whipped cream or Fruit Salad Dressing (page 371) with this salad mold, or as desired.

Confetti Party Mousse

Serves 12 to 16

3-ounce package strawberry or raspberry gelatin dessert, combined with 1¼ cups biling water
3-ounce package lime gelatin dessert, combined with 1¼ cups boiling water
1½ tablespoons plain gelatin, combined with ½ cup cold water

(stir gently and let stand until thick)
1½ cups unsweetened pineapple juice (small can), combined with ⅔ cup granulated sugar
2 cups whipping cream, beaten only until clings to bowl, but not dry

Pour 1¼ cups boiling water over the package of raspberry gelatin, and 1¼ cups over the lime gelatin. Stir well and let stand in room temperature in bowl until lukewarm, then pour each into separate 7 × 7 foil pans, brushed with ¼ teaspoon salad oil. Refrigerate *for at least 12 hours* (better to prepare day or two in advance). Must be very firm. A few minutes before they are to be folded into rest of preparation, with a dinner knife cut them as uniformly as possible in ⅓-inch cubes (not more than ½ inch) right in pan. With a spatula loosen them from bottom and sides and let remain in refrigerator in pans *until needed*.

Soak the 1½ tablespoons plain gelatin in the ½ cup cold water. Stir and let stand until thick. Combine pineapple juice and granulated sugar, and bring to a boil. Remove from heat and at once add the thick gelatin preparation. Stir well until completely dissolved. Pour into 9- or 10-inch bowl and let stand in a cool place or refrigerator until slightly congealed (but not too thick).

A few minutes before pineapple preparation has thickened, in a 7-inch bowl beat the 2 cups of cream until it barely clings to bowl. Add whipped cream all at once to the slightly thickened pineapple juice and quickly stir and fold until no streaks appear. *At once* fold in the *cut-up* red and green gelatin cubes, a few of each at a time, and blend very gently. Pour into a bread pan that measures 9½ × 5½ × 2¾ (No. 22) or any 2-quart ring or other mold that has been brushed with ½ teaspoon salad oil. Keep in coldest part of refrigerator for at least 8 hours, and not more than 2 days. *Do not freeze.*

To Serve. Loosen around edges of mold, dip it into warm water a few seconds and wipe mold well. In advance cut a stiff cardboard about ½ inch smaller all around than pan, cover it neatly with foil, holding bottom part in place with Scotch tape. Place cardboard over mold, then 16-inch (or smaller) serving platter over cardboard, and invert carefully. Decorate top with large whipped cream or cream cheese roses and leaves using No. 124 large rose tube and No. 70 leaf tube, or as desired.

Stuffed Glazed Cheese Fruits

Cold firm cream cheese, or any other cheese that can be shaped easily
Whole roasted almonds, filberts, or pecan meats *or* curled anchovies *or* small stuffed green or black olives *or* small balls of minced ham, chicken, or seafood
1 recipe Clear Glaze (page 464)
Red, green, and yellow food coloring
Imitation leaves

Pick up 1 slightly rounded tablespoon cheese, and flatten it slightly in palm of hand. Place nutmeats or other filling in center, and enclose, rolling gently to form strawberries, apples, and pears. Place on wax paper, and refrigerate until cold and very firm.

Prepare glaze and separate it into 3 parts in coffee cups or small custard cups. Add a few drops of diluted yellow coloring to 1 part, red to 1, and green to the other. Let stand until glaze has consistency of unbeaten egg white. Coloring must be added before glaze begins to thicken. When colored glaze is of proper consistency, insert heavy toothpicks in stem end of fruit and dip into glaze. It may be necessary to dip several times until the proper coating is obtained. If made a day in advance, cover thickly with glaze. Place cheese fruits on cake racks as they are dipped, and let stand in refrigerator or cold place at least 30 minutes. Sprinkle pears lightly with paprika and insert a small whole black pepper or small black currant on large end of each pear; then gently remove toothpick and insert imitation green leaf, or a short strip of green pepper or citron in each. Place in small paper cups, and arrange around Confetti Party Mousse (page 440) or any salad or hors d'oeuvres platter.

Tulip Party-Style Mold

Serves 8

1 tablespoon plain gelatin, combined with ⅓ cup cold water (stir gently and let stand until thick for about 5 minutes)
¼ cup granulated sugar
2 tablespoons lemon juice, strained
1¼ cups boiling water
1 large can (No. 2½ size) pears
Several red maraschino cherries, well drained, and dried on towel

8 citron leaves, cut 1 inch long and about ⅓ inch wide
4 narrow citron stems, cut about 2½ inches long
3-ounce package raspberry gelatin dessert
⅓ cup sour cream, or cream cheese
½ cup whipping cream
1½ cups pear syrup
3-ounce package lime gelatin dessert

In medium-size bowl, combine the thick gelatin preparation, granulated sugar, lemon juice, and last the boiling water. *Stir gently,* and let stand until cool.

When cool, pour ¾ cup of clear preparation into a 1½-quart ring mold that has been very lightly rubbed with salad oil. Refrigerate until partially set, but not too firm. Now cut up 2 pear halves, each into 6 lengthwise slices. Form 4 tulips with 2 slices for each flower, having pointed ends slightly open. Space tulips evenly on top of gelatin. Place a whole *small* red maraschino cherry (or ½ if large) into open rounded end of each flower. Place stems on bases and 1 leaf on each side of stem. Pour about 1 tablespoon of clear, cool gelatin around each flower and over stems and leaves. Refrigerate until flowers cling to base. Pour rest of clear topping over flowers, a little at a time, and if decorations move around at any time, stop adding gelatin and refrigerate mold for about 15 minutes, then pour in rest of topping. Refrigerate until set to touch.

Add 1 cup boiling water (or fruit syrup) to 3-ounce package raspberry gelatin. Mix well, and chill until the consistency of unbeaten egg white. Now add this preparation to ⅓ cup commercial sour cream (or beaten cream cheese) very little at a time, and stir until smooth. Last add ½ cup whipping cream that was beaten until clung to bowl, but not too stiff. Cream can be beaten in advance and refrigerated until needed. Pour this pink preparation over clear topping that is set to touch. Refrigerate until the pink is set.

Meanwhile, add 1½ cups boiling pear syrup over 3-ounce package lime gelatin. Stir gently and let cool to consistency of unbeaten egg white. Mash remaining pears (left over from the can) and fold them into lime preparation until evenly blended. Pour this over the set pink preparation in mold. Refrigerate for at least 8 hours.

To Serve. Loosen around upper edge of mold with a dinner knife; dip mold into warm water for a few seconds. Wipe outside. Brush top of mold and serving platter lightly (14- or 16-inch size) with cold water. Place platter over top of mold and invert, shaking slightly.

Platter may be garnished by cutting pears from another can, each half in 4 lengthwise slices. Form tulips with 2 slices; arrange them around base of mold, spacing them evenly. Place ¼ of maraschino cherry in open rounded end, then place a green citron leaf (cut 1¼ inches long and ¼ inch wide) fornt and back of each cherry. Between tulips place small peach or apricot halves (well drained) and rounded side lightly tinted with red food coloring. Insert tiny marzipan leaf on each or omit and garnish with group fresh or artificial strawberries.

Center of mold may be filled with Fruit Salad Dressing (page 371), or whipped cream, piping part of cream at the top with No. 7 or 3 cookie star tube.

Cartwheel Grape-Juice Salad Mousse

Serves 12

2 tablespoons plain gelatin	1½ cups whipping cream
1 cup cold water	¾ cup sifted confectioners' sugar
½ cup boiling water	1 pound cream cheese for decorat-
2 cups grape juice	ing: ¾ pound for grapes and ¼
2 tablespoons lemon juice	pound for green stems and leaves
½ cup granulated sugar	(less may be used)
½ teaspoon salt	20 pineapple fingers
Red food coloring	2 cans tangerine segments

Combine gelatin with cold water. Stir gently, and let stand until thick —about 5 minutes. Then place over simmering water, and dissolve. In a 10-inch bowl combine dissolved gelatin with boiling water, grape juice, lemon juice, granulated sugar, and salt; add a little red coloring. Let stand in a cold place or force over ice water until slightly congealed—about the consistency of a soft custard.

While gelatin is setting, whip cream until it just clings to bowl; add confectioners' sugar, and beat only until blended. Keep cream in refrigerator until needed.

When gelatin is of the consistency of very soft custard, beat it until fluffy, about 7 or 8 minutes or longer at high speed with electric mixer. At this stage, fold whipped cream into fluffy gelatin and blend thoroughly until no streaks appear. Pour into an oiled 8- or 9-cup mold. Let stand in refrigerator until set, about 10 or 12 hours. When ready to unmold, loosen around edges with paring knife, dip into warm water, wipe mold, place a wet large flat platter over mold, and invert. Shake mold slightly, and if it does not come out easily, cover with a hot wet towel.

Decorate upper part of mold with clusters of white cream-cheese grapes, using No. 8 or No. 10 plain tube, first scraping surface with a paring knife. Pipe stems with same tube. With No. 67 or No. 70 leaf tube, pipe in empty spaces with green leaves.

Arrange about 20 pineapple fingers around base of mold, and 2 tangerine segments across each finger (2 cans). On outer edge of platter place about 12 halves or quarters of well drained colored pears. Other canned or fresh fruits in season may be used. Serve Fruit Salad Dressing (page 371) separately.

Ice Cream Fruit Salad Mold

¼ cup sifted all-purpose flour
1 cup granulated sugar
2 egg yolks, combined with 1¼ cups milk
½ teaspoon salt
1 tablespoon butter
2 tablespoons lemon juice
¼ cup pineapple juice
1 cup whipping cream
1 tablespoon plain gelatin, combined with ½ cup cold water (stir and let thicken)

4 cups diced canned or fresh fruit
2 tablespoons sliced red and 2 tablespoons green maraschino cherries (or all red)
Cream cheese or whipped cream for decorating
Green melon rings or calavo pears
Small peach halves
Chopped nuts

In a 2-quart saucepan, combine flour, granulated sugar, and yolks mixed with the milk, a little at a time. Stir well until smooth. Add salt. Cook in a heavy saucepan over direct *low heat* until thick and smooth, stirring constantly. Let simmer several minutes, then add butter, lemon and pineapple juice, and cook about 2 more minutes after simmering begins. At once add the thick gelatin preparation, and stir until melted. Remove from heat. Let stand until cool, but not cold, stirring it occasionally. Now whip the cup of cream until medium thick, and barely slides out of bowl. Fold cream into cool custard, and last add the cut-up fruits, and mix until evenly blended.

Have prepared a bread pan that measures about 10½ × 2¾ × 4½ inches (No. 22), with double thickness of wax paper cut to fit pan smoothly, having paper extend to cover top of mold. Pour salad into pan, and cover well with wax paper. Place in freezer (or freezer compartment of refrigerator turned to coldest point) for about 24 hours, or longer. If to be kept more than 24 hours, overwrap in freezer paper or foil. Shortly before serving, loosen wax paper from top, and turn mold over onto large flat platter. Remove paper.

Garnish top with pale pink cream cheese or whipped cream roses (or buttercream roses), made with No. 104 or larger 124 rose tube, and green leaves with No. 67 or 70 tube. Around base of mold, arrange ½ slices of green melon rings or calavos, first sliced, then skins removed. Brush calavo slices with lemon juice to prevent discoloration. On outside of slices, place small peach halves stuffed with cream cheese and chopped nuts, forming whole fruit, then spread with cream cheese and roll into finely chopped nuts. Clusters of black grapes are very attractive around edge of platter, or garnish as desired.

This mold may be served as a main light luncheon or supper dish with finger or open face dainty sandwiches, as a separate course for special dinner party, or as a dessert at end of meal. Serve Fruit Salad Dressing (page 371) separately.

Note. One large can pineapple chunks and 1 medium can fruit cocktail or salad, well drained, will give about 4 cups fruit. This is a delicious combination. Other canned or fresh fruits may be used instead. Fresh pineapple and fresh pineapple juice must be cooked about 5 minutes before using in this recipe or other gelatin recipes. Frozen pineapple must also be cooked 5 minutes.

Sabayon Salad Mold Mousse

Serves 8 to 12

Whites of 4 large eggs	2 tablespoons rum or brandy
¼ cup sifted confectioners' sugar	1 teaspoon vanilla
2 cups whipping cream	1½ tablespoons plain gelatin
Yolks of 4 large eggs	½ cup cold water
1 cup sifted confectioners' sugar	1½ cups coarsely crushed plain cookies

Beat the egg whites until they cling to bowl, then add the ¼ cup sifted confectioners' sugar, and beat until well blended. In another bowl, beat the whipping cream, until it just clings to bowl. Place both in refrigerator until needed. Beat yolks with electric mixer for several minutes, and add 1 cup sifted confectioners' sugar, the rum or brandy, and vanilla. Beat until smooth.

Combine gelatin with cold water, stir and let stand about 5 minutes until thick. Dissolve over simmering water. Add the dissolved gelatin to the beaten egg yolk mixture at once. Immediately add the beaten egg whites, the whipped cream, and the coarsely crushed cookies to the egg yolk mixture, and blend each one in thoroughly. Pour into oiled tower mold (8-inch bowl can be used). Let stand in refrigerator for 10 or 12 hours until set.

Before unmolding, loosen around sides. Dip into warm water. Wipe outside of mold. Brush top of mold and a flat platter lightly with cool water and invert. Shake a little if necessary. If mold does not come out, cover with hot wet towel.

Decorate top of mold with whipped cream relief roses with No. 104 tube, and leaves with No. 67 or 70 tube, *or as desired.* Sides of mold may be decorated with whipped cream, using No. 3 star cookie tube. Pipe border around base of mold with same tube. It will take at least 2 cups of whipping cream to decorate a very fancy mold (4 cups after it is whipped).

Arrange fancy small cookies or cakes on platter. Fruits may be used instead. Serve Whipped Cream Brandy or Rum Sauce separately.

Whipped Cream Brandy or Rum Sauce

¼ cup fresh egg whites	½ teaspoon plain gelatin
1 cup granulated sugar	2 tablespoons cold water
¼ teaspoon cream of tartar	2 tablespoons brandy or rum
3 tablespoons cool water	1 cup whipping cream, beaten just
⅛ teaspoon salt	until it clings to bowl (not too
½ teaspoon vanilla	stiff)

Combine egg whites, sugar, cream of tartar, the 3 tablespoons cool water, salt, and vanilla in upper part of small double boiler. Mix well with wooden spoon. Bring water in lower part to a boil, place upper part of boiler in position (if using electric beater, remove double boiler from stove) and at once beat until mixture is thick and clings to pan for 6 or 7 minutes. Remove top of boiler from water. Combine gelatin with 2 tablespoons cold water, let stand until thick, then dissolve over simmering water. Add brandy or rum to gelatin.

At once add the gelatin and brandy mixture, a little at a time, to the sauce and beat by hand or with electric mixer *only* until well blended. Keep in refrigerator or cold place until cool, about 1 hour, but let stand only until cool or else it will become too thick, in which case stir well with a spoon over hot water. Then fold it, little at a time, into the whipped cream.

Keep sauce in refrigerator until ready to be served after whipped cream has been added. May be prepared hours in advance. *Do not omit* gelatin or liquor will separate from other ingredients. This sauce should always be stirred for a few seconds gently before serving to insure smoothness.

Yuletide Eggnog Mold

Serves 8 to 12

⅓ cup granulated sugar
⅛ teaspoon salt
4 egg yolks, slightly beaten
3 cups warm commercial eggnog
1½ tablespoons plain gelatin, combined with ½ cup cold water (mix thoroughly and let stand until thick
4 egg whites (½ cupful), beaten until they just cling to bowl, then add ¼ cup granulated sugar and beat only until blended (overbeating will give a dry texture); refrigerate

1 teaspoon vanilla or brandy flavoring
1½ cups whipping cream, beaten until it just clings to bowl (do not overbeat); refrigerate
⅓ cup red maraschino cherries, well drained and dried on a towel, sliced in rings
⅓ cup green maraschino cherries, well drained and dried on a towel, sliced in rings
¼ cup coarsely broken pecan meats
2 cups whipping cream

In a 2-quart saucepan, combine the granulated sugar, salt, and slightly beaten yolks. Add warm eggnog slowly. Cook over low heat (or simmering water) until it coats spoon. Simmer about 2 minutes, stirring constantly, but do not permit to boil at any time. Remove from heat and *at once add the thick gelatin mixture.* Stir until dissolved and let stand in room temperature until cool. Then place custard in refrigerator or in bowl of ice water, until it is medium thick, stirring it often to prevent setting. This is very important. While custard is cooling beat cream and egg whites and refrigerate. When custard is of medium consistency and smooth, add the vanilla or brandy flavoring, sliced cherries and nuts, a few pieces at a time for even distribution. Fold in whipped cream. *At once* fold in egg whites and blend well until no streaks appear. Pour into well-oiled tower mold (or any mold 6-cup capacity). Refrigerate for at least 12 hours. To serve, loosen around edges of mold, brush top of mold and platter with cold water and turn out.

To Decorate. For a very fancy decoration during the holidays, whip 2 cups of whipping cream until it clings to bowl. Remove ⅓ cup to which add a drop or 2 of green coloring for leaves. With a No. 3 large star cookie tube and bag pipe rest of cream vertically around mold, leaving enough for border at base and rosettes on top. With same No. 3 tube, pipe border and several rosettes on top of mold. With No. 67 or 70 leaf tube, pipe leaves in between rosettes with the green whipped cream. Surround mold with small fancy cakes or cookies, or Fruit Cake Petit Fours (page 557).

Pineapple Cream Cheese Mold

Serves 8 to 12

2 cups boiling water
2 (3 ounce) packages lemon or lime gelatin dessert
2 teaspoons plain gelatin, combined with ¼ cup cold water
2 cupfuls of pineapple juice
½ teaspoon orange or ⅛ teaspoon green coloring, diluted in 1 teaspoon water
1 pound cream cheese (keep in refrigerator until needed)

No. 2½ can of crushed pineapple, thoroughly drained
Fresh strawberries, or raspberries, or cherries, or green or pink melon balls
Cream cheese
Sections of grapefruit, oranges, or slices of avocados, or pink melon
Pale green pears
Small peaches
Maraschino cherries

Pour the boiling water over lemon or lime gelatin dessert. Then at once add the combined plain gelatin and water which has stood until thick. Stir well. Next, add pineapple juice and coloring. Mix thoroughly and let stand in a cold place until slightly congealed. Beat cold cream cheese with electric mixer until of medium consistency. *Do not permit it to become warm.* Add gelatin mixture to the creamed cheese, very *slowly* (tablespoon at a time), using electric mixer, and continue to beat only until throughly blended. Let this mixture stand in ice water until of medium consistency. Last, fold in pineapple. Pour into an oiled ring mold that measures about 10 × 2½ inches (other style molds may be used), and allow it to stand in refrigerator for 7 or 8 hours, or longer, until firm.

When ready to be served, loosen around edge and tube. Brush top lightly with cold water. Also brush 16-inch platter with cold water. Turn out onto platter.

To Decorate. Fill center of the mold with fresh strawberries, raspberries, or cherries, or fresh green or pink melon balls that have been thoroughly washed, drained, and dried on a towel, leaving hulls on strawberries. Pipe top of mold with white cream cheese rosettes and green leaves, *scraping surface of mold with tip of tube to prevent rosettes from sliding off.* Use No. 30 tube for rosettes and No. 67 for leaves. Around lower outside edge of mold, arrange sections of grapefruit, oranges, or slices of avocados, or preferably pink melons.

Next arrange, alternately, halves of small *pale green* pears and small peaches. Inside of peach pipe a white rosette of cream cheese and place a red maraschino cherry on rosettes. Pipe center top of pear with a pink cheese rosette and green leaves.

If cream cheese does not spread easily, add a little lemon or pineapple juice and mix thoroughly. Then spread, etc.

Avocados may be sliced about ⅓ inch thick (not too thin) several hours in advance. Keep on wax paper on flat surface, brush with lemon juice, cover with wax paper, and store in refrigerator. If necessary pick up with spatula to prevent breaking.

This fruit salad platter may be used as a main course for a light luncheon or supper dish. It is also delicious as an accompaniment, or as a separate course.

Baba Crown Ice-Cream Mold

Serves 12

Prepare individual Babas (page 528), and decorate as suggested.

Prepare an ice-cream mold as follows: Line an 8-inch bowl with wax paper, making small creases where necessary to keep paper as flat and smooth as possible. Allow about 6 or 7 pints commercial ice cream to stand in room temperature about 15 minutes, until slightly soft. Pack ice cream as solidly as possible into paper-lined bowl. Cover top with wax paper and wrap for freezing. Keep in freezer until needed. When ready to serve, lift ice cream out of bowl, remove wax paper, and place mold on a thin layer of any kind of cake. (Cake may be brushed with a little brandy or other liqueur if desired.) Cake will keep mold in position, preventing it from sliding on platter. Go over entire surface of ice cream with a spatula to make it as smooth as possible. Garnish top of mold with about 30 well-drained (and thoroughly dried in a towel) red maraschino cherries, holding them close together on ice cream with toothpicks, forming a thick rounded cluster. Place 1½-inch-long citron leaves (about 30 in all) between cherries. Or cherries may be omitted and a spray of whipped-cream roses or other designs may be piped onto mold. Pipe a thick scroll of whipped cream with No. 3 cookie tube around base of mold, to cover edge of cake. Place about 12 (more or less) individual Babas around mold, and serve with brandy-flavored whipped cream or Whipped Cream Brandy or Rum Sauce (page 372).

Note. Ice-cream mold may be decorated several hours in advance and kept in freezer. If you do not have a freezer, or a sufficiently large freezing compartment in your refrigerator, ice cream should be packed in mold and served at once. Have all other items ready so that mold may be decorated as speedily as possible. Instead of ice cream, our Sabayon Mold (page 445) may be served with Babas.

Bar-Le-Duc French Cream Cheese Mold

Serves 12

1½ pounds cream cheese, room temperature about ½ hour

2 (3 ounce) jars French Bar-Le-Duc jelly, or ¾ cup raspberry jam

1 tablespoon plain gelatin, combined with ½ cup cold water (mix gently and let stand until thick, about 5 minutes, then dissolve over simmering water)

1 cup whipping cream, beaten until it clings to bowl, then add to cream ½ cup sifted confectioners' sugar and beat only until blended

Red food coloring

About ½ pound additional soft cream cheese to decorate mold (less cheese may be used for decoration)

No. 2½ can pear halves

Pale green food coloring

Pale pink food coloring

White bread

Stir jelly or jam into cream cheese until smooth. Add warm dissolved gelatin slowly and mix well. Then fold in the whipped cream and blend until no streaks appear. Pour into a heart shape 6-cup mold (other style molds may be used) that has been oiled with 1 teaspoon salad oil. Refrigerate for at least 6 hours, or until firm to the touch, but do not freeze. For best results do not prepare more than 2 days in advance.

To Serve. Loosen around edges of mold with a dinner knife or spatula. Dip in warm water a few seconds. Wipe mold. Place a wet flat 14- or 16-inch platter over top of mold and turn over carefully, shaking slightly if necessary to release mold.

To Decorate. Add a little red coloring to the half pound soft cream cheese and beat only until smooth and evenly colored, or leave white. With No. 24 or 27 star tube, pipe border around edges of both hearts in center of mold, being sure to scrape salad slightly with tip of tube as you go around to prevent jelly or jam from running out after hearts are filled. Go over top of rim a second time with cheese, to raise it enough to prevent jelly or jam from overflowing. Pipe and fill in arrow with cream cheese, also form a border around top rim of mold with same tube, and make cheese outlines around side designs of mold. Now carefully, a little at a time, with tip of teaspoon pour smooth red jelly or jam into open space of hearts and spread carefully, or decorate as desired.

Cut pears from large No. 2½ can of pear halves into 3 lengthwise sections. Tint half of slices pale green and half pale pink. This is done by adding a little food coloring to syrup or water and submerging cut pears for a few minutes in liquid. Drain pears thoroughly on paper towels, and arrange them alternately around base of mold.

With a medium heart cutter, cut out white bread hearts. Decorate center top of hearts with tiny relief rose (or rosette) with pink cheese using No. 101 tube or No. 27 star tube, and 1 green cheese leaf with No. 67 tube. Arrange bread hearts in groups of 3, leaving about 3-inch space between each group. Have 4 groups all together (12 sandwich hearts).

Dessert Rice Mold Imperial

Serves 12

1 cup granulated sugar
¼ cup sifted all-purpose flour
2 tablespoons cornstarch
⅛ teaspoon salt
2 egg yolks, combined with ¼ cup cool milk
2 cups warm milk
1 teaspoon vanilla
1½ tablespoons plain gelatin, combined with ½ cup cold water (stir and let stand until thick)
1 cup standard-type rice, cooked in 3 cups simmering water and ½

teaspoon salt, in tightly covered saucepan, until very soft, about 25 to 30 minutes, over very low heat; drain well, and measure 3½ cups cooked
1 cup whipping cream
½ cup candied fruits, marinated in 2 tablespoons brandy (optional)
1 teaspoon vanilla
Cream cheese or buttercream or whipped cream or fresh strawberries

In a 2-quart saucepan combine sugar, flour, cornstarch, and salt. Add yolks combined with cool milk, little at a time, and stir until smooth. Add warm milk slowly, and cook until thick and smooth, stirring continuously. Let simmer about 5 minutes. Now at once shut off heat, and immediately add the thickened gelatin preparation. Stir until dissolved.

In a large bowl (about 10 inch size) combine cooked rice and hot gelatin mixture. Blend thoroughly. Let stand until lukewarm. May be forced over cold water. Meanwhile, beat 1 cup of whipping cream until barely clings to bowl. Fold it into the lukewarm rice preparation, mixing gently and well blended. Add ½ cup of candied fruit (cut into ¼-inch pieces) that has been marinated in 2 tablespoons of brandy or pineapple juice, without draining. Fruit may be omitted. Add 1 teaspoon vanilla or other flavoring. Pour into a 7-cup very lightly oiled tower mold. Refrigerate for at least 24 hours.

To Serve. Loosen around upper edge of mold with dinner knife, rub top of mold *and* a platter with cold water. Place 12- or 14-inch platter over top of mold and invert. Top of mold may be decorated with a large cream cheese or buttercream or whipped cream rose or rosettes, and green leaves. Or garnish with a group of fresh strawberries held in place with toothpicks, and green citron leaves. Surround base with fresh strawberries, kumquats, or clusters of Frosted Grapes (page 435), and green leaves, or as desired.

Serve plain whipped cream, or our Whipped Cream Brandy and Rum Sauce (page 372) or crushed sweetened strawberries separately; or *serve plain.*

Note. For large party-size mold, double above recipe and pour into tyrolean mold that measures 7¼ inches tall and 9 inches wide at open end.

Cheese and Crab Meat Ring Mold

Serves 8 to 10

2 tablespoons unflavored gelatin
¼ cup cold water
1 cup chili sauce
12-ounce package cottage cheese
1 cup mayonnaise
2 cups crab or lobster meat (two 6-ounce cans)
1½ cups thin-sliced celery
2 tablespoons lemon juice
1½ teaspoons salt
1 cup (½ pint) whipping cream
Endive or romaine for garnish
Large black olives for garnish

Soak gelatin in cold water. In a 3-quart saucepan heat chili sauce until it simmers; then add congealed gelatin and stir till dissolved. Add cottage cheese, mayonnaise, crab or lobster, celery, lemon juice, and salt. Mix well until blended. Allow to stand about 1 hour until slightly congealed, or force over cold water. When slightly congealed, beat cream till almost stiff and blend with crab or lobster mixture. Pour into a well-oiled 9½ × 2-inch ring mold, and allow to stand in refrigerator at least 8 hours, or until completely set. Unmold on endive or romaine, and garnish center with large black olives.

This is excellent for buffet suppers or afternoon lunches. Surround with sliced cold cuts or cheeses.

Bavarian Almond Cream Mold

Serves 8

2 egg yolks
¼ cup sifted granulated sugar
¼ teaspoon salt
1 cup scalded milk
1 tablespoon unflavored gelatin, combined with ¼ cup cold water
2 egg whites
1 cup whipping cream
2 teaspoons vanilla
¼ cup slivered blanched almonds

In a 2-quart saucepan combine egg yolks, sugar, and salt, and blend well. Add scalded milk very slowly, stirring constantly. Then add congealed gelatin all at one time, and continue to mix until gelatin is completely melted. Cook over medium-low heat, being careful not to allow mixture to boil, until it coats spoon. Allow to cool until the consistency of unbeaten egg whites. Beat egg whites until they are stiff; then set aside. Beat whipping cream the same way. Add vanilla to cool custard, then almonds; then fold in stiffly beaten egg whites and whipped cream until well blended.

Pour into a lightly oiled No. 7 bowl and let stand in refrigerator 8 hours, or until firm enough to unmold. Can be prepared 48 hours in advance. Serve with fresh fruits and desired salad dressing or Custard Sauce.

Custard Sauce

2 cups milk
3 egg yolks
3 tablespoons sifted granulated sugar

¼ teaspoon salt
2 teaspoons vanilla

Heat milk to scalding point. In a 1-quart saucepan beat egg yolks slightly, add sugar and salt, and then *very slowly* add scalded milk, a small amount at a time, stirring constantly until all milk has been added. Cook over very low heat until custard thickens only sufficiently to coat wooden spoon. Allow to cool about 15 minutes. Add vanilla. After Custard Sauce is cold, cover and place in refrigerator until well chilled.

Hyacinth Party-Style Mold

Serves 8 to 12

4 cups crab meat, tuna fish or other seafood (four 7-ounce cans), or cooked chicken, cut into 1-inch pieces
2 cups celery, cut crosswise, ⅛ inch wide
⅓ cup fresh green onion, cut fine (or 2 tablespoons regular onion)
⅓ cup fresh green onion stems, cut ½ inch long
¼ cup, or less, pimiento, cut into ½-inch squares

About ½ teaspoon hot sauce, or ⅛ teaspoon hot pepper
About 1 teaspoon of salt
1 tablespoon plain gelatin, combined with ⅓ cup cold water (stir gently and let stand until thick, then dissolve over simmering water; now slowly add warm gelatin to 1½ cups mayonnaise and blend well)
Green food coloring
Cream cheese
Red food coloring

Combine all ingredients in order given, and pour into a 9 × 3 round loose bottom cake pan that has been oiled lightly with ½ teaspoon salad oil on sides only, and bottom covered smoothly with silicone or heavy wax paper cut same size. Refrigerate for at least 3 hours. Meanwhile prepare Topping:

Topping

½ pound cream cheese (room temperature at least 1 hour)

1 tablespoon plain gelatin, combined with ⅓ cup cold water (stir gently, and when thick dissolve over simmering water)

½ teaspoon garlic salt

½ teaspoon salt

1½ cups sour cream or buttermilk or homogenized milk (cream or milk must be lukewarm or at least room temperature; if too cold does not combine well)

Yellow food coloring

With spoon or electric mixer, beat cream cheese for about 1 minute. Add all other ingredients in order given, a little at a time, and beat after each addition only until smooth. Remove ¾ cup of this preparation to which add a little diluted yellow coloring, blend well, and pour into lightly oiled custard cup, 3¼ inches across the top. Refrigerate until needed. *At once* pour and spread rest of preparation smoothly on top of salad that is firm to the touch. Refrigerate for at least 8 hours.

To Decorate Mold. Loosen around sides of pan with a dinner knife, and lift out mold, being sure to leave salad on bottom of round pan. Place it on a 16-inch round serving platter. Now dip custard cup into warm water for a few seconds, wipe cup well, loosen around upper edges and turn out onto wax paper. Cut it lengthwise in 2 halves. Place one of halves with flat side down on lower top part of mold to simulate a flower pot.

Add green coloring to ¾ cup of white cream cheese, and blend well. With a No. 10 plain decorating tube, pipe a 4-inch-thick straight stem in center of pot. With part of green cheese and same tube pipe a thick base (about 2 inches wide and 3 inches long) on upper part of thick stem, having it slightly pointed on top, and straight at bottom. Add a little red coloring to ¾ cup of cream cheese, forming a bright pink, and with No. 24 or 27 star tube, pipe tiny rosettes on entire surface of foundation to simulate hyacinth. With green cheese and plain No. 8 tube pipe 3 curved imitation leaves on each side of flower. Place leftover green and pink cheese (1 color on each side of bag) into bag with No. 10 plain tube, and pipe a small rosette border on edge of mold.

Chipped Green Gelatin Ice to Go Around Base of Mold

2 cups boiling water

3 (3 ounce) packages lime gelatin dessert (or use lemon and green coloring)

1 tablespoon gelatin, combined with

½ cup cold water (stir gently until thick)

2 cups cold water

Green food coloring

In 8-inch bowl, pour the 2 cups of boiling water over the gelatin dessert and the thick plain gelatin. Stir until completely dissolved. Now add the 2 cups cold water and blend well. Add a little diluted green coloring. Pour into a 9-inch square or round pan, and let stand *at least* 8 hours until very firm. To use, cut through with dinner knife to simulate finely chipped ice, and arrange it around base of mold.

Cut 1 or 2 lemons in halves lengthwise, then into medium thick slices. Place 6 half slices on each side of mold upright into chipped ice leaving about an inch space between each slice.

Serve our Horseradish Whipped Cream Sauce separately with this mold (page 372). Very beautiful and delectable for cocktail and buffet suppers.

Holly Wreath Seafood Buffet Mold

2 pounds soft cheddar cheese, medium consistency (other cheese spreads may be used)
1 pound crab meat or lobster meat (cut up cooked shrimp, tuna fish, or salmon may be used)
¼ teaspoon celery salt
¼ teaspoon garlic salt

¼ cup fresh green onions and ¼ cup fresh green onion stems, cut into ½-inch pieces
½ teaspoon Worcestershire sauce
½ pound cream cheese, to which add a little green coloring and a little milk for spreading

Keep cheese in room temperature for several hours until soft. With a heavy spoon or electric mixer beat it only until creamy. Add seafood and blend well. Now add all other ingredients except the ½ pound cream cheese, 1 at a time, and mix until evenly blended. If mixture is too soft to mold, cover and place it in refrigerator for about 1 hour, or until firm. Turn it out onto a 14- or 16-inch round flat serving platter, and with hands form a wreath that measures about 9 inches wide. Keep surface as smooth as possible. Add a little green coloring and a *very* small amount of milk at a time to ½ pound of cream cheese, and blend it until evenly colored. Spread this cheese over the entire surface of mold. Decorate as desired.

Special Decoration for Holly Wreath Seafood Buffet Mold

A little lukewarm corn syrup
2 jars tiniest gherkins, split in halves lengthwise, or if large cut pickles into several thick pointed strips, then marinate in their own liquid to which a small amount of green food coloring has been added; drain and dry on towel

1 jar small pickled onions, marinated in their own liquid to which a small amount of red food coloring has been added (or use fresh uncooked cranberries); drain well and dry thoroughly on a towel

With finger tip rub *very* little lukewarm corn syrup on cut drained pickles and onions, or use cranberries. Insert pickles into top of mold to simulate holly, and at about 1 inch intervals place the red onions or fresh cranberries brushed lightly with syrup. Place thinly sliced medium tomatoes and cucumber alternately around base of mold. Add thin bread and butter fancy sandwiches, wafers, melba toast, or crackers.

Note. Basic part of mold may be made a day in advance, omitting the pickle and other decorations. In this case shape it on a piece of foil on a stiff cardboard or flat dish and refrigerate for several hours before serving. Then transfer to serving platter, insert pickles and onions and garnish as desired.

Valentine Salad Mold

Serves 8 to 12

Topping for Valentine Salad Mold

½ pound cream cheese, at room temperature

About 2 tablespoons prepared horseradish

1 tablespoon plain gelatin, combined with ¼ cup water (allow to stand until thick, and dissolve over simmering water)

About ½ teaspoon garlic or onion salt

1 teaspoon salt

1 cup commercial sour cream or buttermilk (homogenized milk may be used) *at room temperature* (must *not be cold* or will not unite well)

With electric mixer or spoon beat cream cheese. Add horseradish and all other ingredients in the order given, a little at a time, beating after each addition.

Pour this preparation into a lightly oiled 8-cup heart mold and refrigerate until firm to the touch. Then pour Filling over top, a cupful at a time, and spread gently and smoothly. Refrigerate mold at least 8 hours.

To Serve. Dip mold into warm water a few seconds; wipe it well on outside. Place a small cardboard cut about same size and shape of heart (covered with wax paper or foil) under mold to support it. Loosen around edges of mold first. Turn over. Place mold in center of a 16-inch round platter, and garnish it with Decorations for Valentine Salad Mold (page 457). Serve Horseradish Whipped Cream Sauce (page 372) separately.

Filling for Valentine Salad Mold

4 cups salmon, tuna, or any other seafood, or cooked chicken cut into 1-inch pieces

2 cups celery, cut about ⅛ inch wide crosswise

⅓ cup fresh green onion, cut fine, or 2 tablespoons chopped onions

⅓ cup fresh green onion stems, cut about ½ inch long

¼ cup or less pimiento, well drained and cut into ½-inch squares

½ teaspoon hot sauce, or ⅛ teaspoon hot pepper

About 1 teaspoon salt

4 teaspoons plain gelatin, combined with ½ cup cold water (stir gently and allow to stand until thick, then dissolve over simmering water and, while still warm, add slowly to 1½ cups mayonnaise)

Combine all ingredients in the order given, adding mayonnaise and gelatin last. Mix with a spoon until well blended, and at once pour over topping in mold.

Decorations for Valentine Salad Mold

3½ cups water (half boiling, half cold)
3 (3 ounce) packages raspberry gelatin dessert (strawberry may be used)

1 tablespoon plain gelatin, combined with ½ cup cold water (stir gently until thick)
¼ cup lemon juice (optional)
½ cup green cream cheese

Pour 3½ cups water over red gelatin and *at once* add plain gelatin combined with cold water. Stir until completely dissolved; then add lemon juice. Pour into three 9-inch round or square pans that have been lightly oiled or one 12 × 18-inch oiled baking sheet. Refrigerate at least 8 hours.

With a very small daisy cutter, cut out about 5 or 6 daisies from gelatin in pan. Lift them out gently with fingers or a small spatula, and place them on a pan covered with wax paper. With knife *cut through rest of gelatin to simulate chipped ice.* Form a spray of daisies (using 5 flowers) on top of mold, first piping bulb of green cream cheese underneath each to raise them. Then with No. 8 plain decorating tube, pipe stems, and with No. 70 tube, pipe 5 or 6 leaves toward bottom of stems. With a large spoon pick up chipped gelatin ice and arrange it thickly around base of mold.

At least ½ cup cream cheese (colored green) will be required for stems, leaves, and bulbs.

Poinsettia Buffet Log, Molded

1½ pounds cooked ham, poultry, or seafood, cut into small pieces
⅓ cup finely chopped stuffed green olives
¾ cup fresh green onion and stems, cut fine
About ¾ teaspoon hot sauce

1½ teaspoons prepared mustard
¾ cup of soft cream cheese
2 cups, or less (1 pound), soft cheddar cheese
Another 1 cup cream cheese, to which add a little green coloring

In a large bowl combine the cut-up ham, poultry, or seafood, green olives, onions and stems, hot sauce, prepared mustard, and the ¾ cup soft cream cheese. Mix well, and on a sheet of wax paper form a roll that measures about 12 inches long. Wrap firmly in wax paper and store in refrigerator on a flat pan or dish, for an hour or longer. When log is firm enough to handle, place it on a stiff cardboard covered with foil or wax paper that has been cut a little smaller than log. Now spread entire surface with the 2 cups soft cheddar cheese.

Chill log again until yellow cheese is firm, then spread entire top and sides with the cup of green cream cheese. If green cheese appears too stiff, add a very little milk or cream. With a fork mark surface of green cheese to simulate a log. Place in refrigerator until firm, for at least 2 hours. Then, slice off piece from each end to expose filling, and decorate top with Poinsettia Cream Cheese Decorations or Fresh Tomato Poinsettias. Surround log with various canned or fresh fruits, crackers, melba toast, wafers, etc.

Poinsettia Cream Cheese Decorations

½ pound cream cheese (1 cup)
Red food coloring

Green food coloring
Yellow food coloring

To ½ cup cream cheese, add red coloring. Mix well with a spoon. Add *little milk* only if necessary, but do not have cheese too soft. Add green coloring to ⅓ cup cheese and blend well. Add yellow coloring to 2 tablespoons white cheese for centers. With decorating bag and No. 67 leaf tube, pipe poinsettia in center of log. Place small amount of yellow cheese right in tube (without using bag because of the very small amount) and pipe tiny dots in center of poinsettia. Pipe stems with No. 4 tube and leaves with No. 67 tube.

Fresh Tomato Poinsettia

Cut tomato to simulate poinsettias. Use yellow cheese dots for center. Place on top center of mold with smooth side up. Pipe yellow cheese dots in center.

Chaud-Froid Fish or Seafood Mold

Serves 8

2 pounds frozen, canned, or fresh crab meat (4 cups solidly packed), or other seafood or fish such as tuna, salmon, shrimp, or lobster
3 cups celery, cut crosswise about ¼ inch wide
¼ cup green onion stems, cut 1 inch long
¼ cup fresh onion tops, cut fine
½ cup green stuffed olives, sliced crosswise

2 tablespoons pimiento, cut into ½-inch squares
About 1 teaspoon salt
⅛ teaspoon red pepper
2 cups mayonnaise
2 cups mayonnaise
1½ tablespoons plain gelatin, combined with ½ cup cold water (stir gently and let stand until thick, then dissolve over simmering water); if using salmon, increase gelatin to 2 tablespoons combined with ¾ cup cold water

In a large bowl combine all ingredients except mayonnaise and gelatin.

Blend well. Now, add the *warm* dissolved gelatin to the mayonnaise and stir until smooth. At once pour stabilized mayonnaise over other ingredients, and with a large spoon mix thoroughly. Pour into a well oiled curved fish mold (about 6-cup capacity), pressing salad down into mold. Cover with wax paper and refrigerate for at least 8 hours, and not more than 2 days. Can be molded with hands.

Note. Before pouring salad into mold, place on a cardboard with open end down and make an outline of opening with a pencil, then cut cardboard about ½ inch smaller all around. Cover cardboard with dull side of lightweight aluminum foil, holding ends of foil on underside down as flat as possible with Scotch tape. When ready to decorate mold, loosen around upper edges with a dinner knife, place cardboard over mold, then a cake rack, and turn over shaking slightly. If salad does not come out easily, lift up mold, and insert a dinner knife between mold and salad. If necessary, dip mold in warm water for a few seconds, dry it well, and turn over.

To Cover Mold with Chaud-Froid Sauce. Place mold on rack with drip pan underneath. Pour cool, slightly thickened Chaud-Froid Sauce (page 460) over mold. Pick up sauce that falls into drip pan, and strain if necessary. Pour again until mold is properly covered. It may be necessary to pour sauce over mold several times, depending on consistency. If the sauce sets before it is fully applied, simply stir it constantly over warm or hot water, and when again smooth, chill it over ice water if necessary until of proper consistency, and pour.

To Decorate Mold. Cut pimiento to simulate a flower pot. Dip it into a little slightly thickened Clear Aspic Glaze (page 460), drain well and place on top of fish.

Cut 3 green onion stems into narrow pointed strips, and some diamond shape leaves from wider stems. Dip lightly into Clear Aspic, and arrange attractively on top of fish. With very small round cutter or open end of cake decorating tube (olive pitter excellent), cut out several rounds of pimiento for center of flower. Pit black ripe olives (1 can jumbo), and cut them lengthwise into halves, then into thin slices for petals of flowers. Form flowers on fish. Place some of these thin slices of olives on tail end, close together. Pit an olive and cut it crosswise in narrow rings for eyes. Cut out 2 rounds of pimiento to fit center of olives. Place eyes on fish scraping surface slightly. Dip decorations into a very little slightly thickened Clear Aspic and pick up with a toothpick whenever necessary. Now place mold in refrigerator for at least 20 minutes.

To Glaze Mold. Remove mold from refrigerator, place it on a drip pan. Pour cool slightly thickened Clear Aspic Glaze over fish carefully and slowly several times if necessary, or until a nice even glaze is obtained. Pick up glaze that drops into drip pan, strain if necessary.

If it is too thick, place over warm water for a minute or so and stir gently until of right consistency; if too thin, place it in a pan of ice water. Glaze must be the consistency of an unbeaten egg white, but not too thick. After mold has been glazed it must stand in refrigerator at least 30 minutes before transferring it to serving platter. Then loosen around edges of base of mold with a dinner knife, and slide a wide pancake turner on each end as far to center as possible; life up and carefully transfer to 16-inch (or larger) serving platter. It is important to use a platter that fits your refrigerator unless fish is kept in a cold room that is below 40° F. for not more than a day in advance.

To Serve. Place ½ slices of lemons around base of rounded part of mold, then small pimiento rounds dipped into aspic on top center of each slice, and a tiny rosette of parsley between slices. Fill center opening of mold with chipped Lemon Ice (page 461). Place several half slices of lemon in ice, about 1 inch apart. Garnish front part of ice with a medium-size parsley bouquet.

This mold may be served as a first course and for cocktail and buffet parties. It will glorify an otherwise simple table arrangement.

Note. Cold hams, other meats, hors d'oeuvres, and numerous other molds may be covered with Chaud-Froid Sauce and Clear Aspic Glaze for special occasions.

Chaud-Froid Sauce

⅓ cup butter or margarine
⅓ cup sifted all-purpose flour
3 cups warm milk
2 tablespoons plain gelatin, combined

with ¾ cup cold water (stir gently, and let stand until thick)
½ teaspoon salt
¼ cup mayonnaise

Melt butter or margarine (but do not allow to brown), add flour and blend until smooth. Add warm milk, little at a time, and cook until thick and smooth, stirring continuously. Let simmer several minutes. Remove from heat, and *at once* add thick gelatin and salt, and stir well until thoroughly blended. Pour this hot sauce very slowly over the ¼ cup mayonnaise, stirring quickly. For yellow Chaud-Froid, add a few drops *diluted* yellow food coloring; for pink, add a few drops diluted red, and a drop or 2 of diluted yellow. Blend well. Strain sauce into another saucepan, and let it stand until cool, or about the consistency of an unbeaten egg white.

Clear Aspic Glaze

In a 2-quart saucepan combine 3 tablespoons plain gelatin with ¾ cup cold water. Stir gently and let stand until thick. Then pour 3 cups boiling water over thick gelatin and stir gently until completely melted and clear. If it appears cloudy after a minute or two place over very low heat and stir gently only to dissolve completely. Remove any foam that settles at top.

Allow this preparation to stand in room temperature at least 2 hours (best not to force it in refrigerator until it is at least lukewarm). When it is lukewarm or just cool, and you are ready to pour, place it in a pan of ice water and stir gently and continuously until it is the consistency of an unbeaten egg white. Pour at once over mold, and proceed as per directions above.

Lemon Ice

To basic Clear Aspic Glaze given above, add ¼ cup strained lemon juice, ½ teaspoon salt, and ⅓ cup sugar *while it is very hot*, and stir gently. Pour it into a 9 × 9-inch square pan or large baking sheet. Let stand in room temperature until lukewarm, then refrigerate for at least 8 hours until firm to the touch. With a dinner knife or round cutter, cut through until it looks like chipped ice.

Chaud-Froid Chicken or Meat Mold

Serves 8

4 cups of cooked chicken, ham, or other meat (4-pound roasting chicken or 3 pounds of breasts will give about right amount after they are cooked)	¼ teaspoon red pepper
	¼ cup fresh green onion tops, cut ½ inch long
6 hard-cooked eggs, sliced crosswise	About 2 tablespoons chopped fresh onion (optional)
2 cups celery, cut crosswise ¼ inch wide	1½ tablespoons plain gelatin combined with ½ cup cold water until thick, then dissolved over simmering water
¼ cup pimiento cut in ½ inch squares	
½ cup toasted almonds	2 cups mayonnaise
About 1 teaspoon salt	

In a large bowl, combine all ingredients except mayonnaise and gelatin. Now add dissolved warm gelatin to mayonnaise and stir well. At once pour stabilized mayonnaise over other ingredients and blend thoroughly. Pour into oiled mold, pressing down with spoon as you pour. Refrigerate, etc., like fish mold (page 458).

To Cover Mold With Chaud-Froid Sauce. Prepare 1 recipe of basic Chaud-Froid Sauce (page 460), and in addition to a drop or 2 of diluted yellow food coloring, add a few drops of diluted red coloring to make a nice soft pink or peach shade. Let sauce stand until proper consistency, as per general directions. Pour onto mold, decorate and cover with Clear Aspic Glaze (page 460). Refrigerate, etc.

To Decorate Mold. Cut 3 different-size long narrow pointed green onion stems, and dip them into slightly congealed Clear Aspic. Place attractively on top of mold. Form clusters of grapes with rounded slices ripe black olives, dipping them into a little Clear Aspic. Cut green leaves from wide onion stems and arrange attractively. Place thinly sliced green stuffed olives around edge of mold, pick them up with paring knife or toothpick. If olives are large, cut slices in halves. *This part of decoration may be omitted.* Place decorated mold in refrigerator for at least 20 minutes, then gently pour Clear Aspic over top and sides. Refrigerate again for about 20 to 30 minutes. Loosen around bottom of mold with a dinner knife, then slide a wide pancake turner on each end and transfer to serving platter. Garnish base of mold with overlapping half slices (or if small use whole slices) tomatoes, and place parsley rosettes between slices. Garnish small ends of mold with large parsley bouquet.

Quick Chaud-Froid Salmon or Seafood Salad Mold

Serves 12 to 16

2 16-ounce cans salmon, well drained, or 4 cans (7 ounce size) tuna fish, crab meat, lobster, or any other kind of cooked fish (about 4 cups)

½ cup green onion chopped fine, *and* ½ cup green onion stems, cut ½ inch long

8 hard-cooked eggs, chopped medium

½ cup stuffed green olives, chopped medium

1 tablespoon plain gelatin, soaked in ½ cup cold water (stir and let stand several minutes until thick, then dissolve over simmering water

1¼ cups of commercial mayonnaise (combine with warm gelatin, stirred well, just before adding to other ingredients)

Break drained fish in small pieces (discard bones) and combine it with all other ingredients in the order give above. Mix very well. Taste and add little salt if needed, about ½ teaspoon. Pack salad down in bowl with a heavy spoon, cover, and refrigerate for several hours. Meanwhile, cut a cardboard to fit bottom of fish, to measure about 3 inches wide and 14 inches long. Cover cardboard fish with lightweight foil smoothly, sealing it with Scotch tape underneath.

To shape fish, remove salad from refrigerator and turn it out onto foil-covered cardboard, supporting it on a large board or baking sheet. With hands, mold salad to simulate fish, dampening hands if necessary, forming smooth surface. Spread entire surface of fish with about ½ cup of Chaud-Froid Mayonnaise (page 463) prepared a few minutes before you are ready to use it. Refrigerate fish for about 15 minutes, then spread it again with about ¼ cup more Chaud-Froid Mayonnaise, and refrigerate again for about 15 minutes, or little longer.

Remove fish from refrigerator, and with pancake turner on each end (or slip hands underneath) lift up fish and transfer to a long cake rack that measures about 10 × 16 inches, in a large baking sheet. Pour rest of cool (not too cold) Chaud-Froid Mayonnaise slowly over entire surface of fish to cover completely and evenly. Sauce for this coating should be of a pouring consistency, not too thin and not too cool. It may be necessary to pick up sauce that drops into pan with rubber scraper (strain if lumpy) and pour over fish a second time. If sauce appears too thick, a teaspoon or 2 of hot water may be added, or place it into another pan of warm water for a few seconds and stir gently until smooth. If too thin, place it in a pan of cold water, stirring continuously until ready. Refrigerate fish for about 15 minutes.

About an hour in advance, insert a curled anchovy into center of 8 uniform large cooked shrimp and place them on a rack all in one direction, with drip pan underneath. Pour Clear Glaze (page 464) over shrimp and refrigerate for about 15 minutes, then cover them a second time with Clear Glaze, and refrigerate until needed.

Remove fish from refrigerator. Arrange 7 or 8 glazed shrimp close together, down center of fish, scraping a small area underneath shrimp with point of knife, to prevent them from sliding off. On each side of shrimp, place green onion diamond leaves (or use flat fresh green pepper leaves). Make eyes with thin slices of pimiento-stuffed black olive, and garnish tail end with thin wedges of black pitted olives. Refrigerate fish for about 15 minutes, or longer. Moisten all decorations of fish with a *little* Clear Glaze as you use them, to prevent sliding off.

Remove from refrigerator, and pour slightly congealed Clear Glaze (about consistency of thin unbeaten egg whites) over entire surface of fish. Chill fish again. May be necessary to pick up glaze with rubber scraper, strain, and pour again over fish.

To Serve. With a dinner knife loosen around bottom edge of fish; place a pancake turner on each end, or slip hands underneath, and carefully transfer to a very flat oval or rectangle platter (at least 18 inches long). A large 18-inch round platter may be used. Place 12 Individual Marinated Vegetable Molds (page 465) on slices of fresh tomato, or Tomato Aspic (page 471) around base of fish, with tiny bouquets of parsley between molds, or garnish with Lemon Ice (page 461) or as desired.

Chaud-Froid Mayonnaise

1½ tablespoons plain gelatin, combined with ¾ cup cold water (stir well and let stand until thick for several minutes, then dissolve over simmering water)

2½ cups commercial mayonnaise (room temperature for at least an hour)
A few drops of yellow coloring diluted in a teaspoon of warm water

Add dissolved warm gelatin slowly to the mayonnaise, stirring gently and continuously, then add diluted yellow coloring, and mix well until no streaks appear. For coating molds, this preparation must be cool, not too cold, and not warm. It is best not to prepare it too far in advance, but shortly before you are to use it. If it appears too thin, it can be placed in another pan of cold water, and stirred gently until of right consistency. If too thick, place it into a pan of warm water, and stir until smooth. For the last pouring a tablespoon of warm water may be added if necessary.

Clear Glaze for Molds and Other Foods

In a 2-quart saucepan combine 2½ tablespoons plain gelatin with 1 cup cold water. Stir until thick and let stand several minutes. Now pour 2½ cups of boiling water slowly over gelatin and stir gently until dissolved. Remove any foam from top. Let cool on a rack in room temperature for about an hour, then refrigerate until consistency of an unbeaten egg white. If too thick, place saucepan in another pan of lukewarm water and stir until smooth, then let stand until thick enough to pour. If too thin, place it in a pan of cold water and stir until ready to pour. Any leftover glaze may be refrigerated and used within a week or 10 days.

Chaud-Froid Lobster Salad Mold

Serves 6 to 8

1 pound cooked lobster meat (2 cups solidly packed), or cooked lobster tails (canned lobster may be used)	2 tablespoons fresh green onion tops, chopped fine
	¼ cup pimiento, cut into ¼-inch squares
1½ cups celery, cut crosswise about ¼ inch wide	About ½ teaspoon salt
	About ⅛ teaspoon red pepper
¼ cup green stuffed olives, sliced crosswise	1 tablespoon plain gelatin, combined with ¼ cup cold water until thick, then dissolved over simmering water
¼ cup fresh green onion stems, cut 1 inch long	
	1 cup mayonnaise

In a large bowl, combine all ingredients for Lobster Mold and proceed same as for curved fish mold (page 458). Cover with Tomato Glaze (page 465).

To Decorate Mold. After mold has been covered with Tomato Glaze, place 2 small black olive rings for eyes and use 2 rounds of pimiento for center of eyes. Garnish tail end with black olives that have been cut lengthwise in halves and then in thin slices. Now chill mold about 20 minutes, then cover with Clear Aspic Glaze (page 460).

To Serve Mold. Loosen bottom with a dinner knife, lift up with 2 spatulas (or hands) and transfer to serving platter. Twin lobster molds are very attractive on a large round platter. Place chipped Green Gelatin Ice (below) around base and center, and half slices of lemon in ice about 1 inch apart.

Tomato Glaze for Lobster Mold

¼ cup butter or margarine
¼ cup flour
2 cups strained warm tomato juice
1 teaspoon salt
Some diluted red food coloring and a
    little diluted yellow coloring

1½ tablespoons plain gelatin, combined
    with ¾ cup cold water until
    thick
¼ cup mayonnaise

Melt butter or margarine, add flour, then the warm tomato juice, and salt. Cook over low heat, stirring continuously until thick, then simmer several minutes. Remove from heat, and at once add thick gelatin preparation, and stir well. Now add this slowly to ¼ cup mayonnaise (that is in a two-quart saucepan) and stir continuously until well blended. Strain, and add diluted red coloring, and a few drops of diluted yellow until proper color is obtained. Let stand in room temperature about 2 hours or until lukewarm, then it may be forced over ice water. Proceed same as for basic Chaud-Froid Sauce (page 460).

Green Gelatin Ice

Prepare 3 packages of lime gelatin dessert, reducing water in each package to 1½ cups. Pour into two 9 × 9-inch square pans, or 1 large baking sheet. Let stand in refrigerator for at least 8 hours until firm to the touch. Then with dinner knife or round cutter, cut through to simulate chipped ice.

This is enough for 1 mold; use double or less recipe for 2 molds.

Individual Marinated Vegetable Molds

Makes about sixteen 2¾-inch molds

2 packages lemon gelatin dessert and
    3 cups boiling water
1 package frozen mixed vegetables, or
    2 cups any combination cooked
    vegetables

½ cup Modified Italian Salad Dressing
    (page 369) (or your favorite
    French dressing)

Add the 3 cups boiling water to the lemon gelatin and let stand until consistency of a heavy unbeaten egg white. Meanwhile, cook the vegetables until just tender, not too soft, drain well, and combine with the salad dressing. Let stand in refrigerator until gelatin preparation is ready. Now drain vegetables thoroughly, and fold them into the thickened gelatin until evenly blended. Pour into lightly oiled molds that measure about

2¾ inches wide and 1 inch deep. Place them on a cookie sheet and refrigerate for at least 8 hours.

To Serve. Dip molds into warm water for a few seconds, wipe them well, and shake out onto palm of hand. Place each on a thick slice of Tomato Aspic (page 471), or fresh tomato or other red gelatin preparation.

Chaud-Froid Ham Salad Mold

Serves 12 to 16

2¼ pounds cooked ham, cut in ½-inch pieces

6 hard-cooked eggs, cut in small pieces

½ cup fresh green onion, chopped fine

½ cup fresh green onion stems, cut in ½-inch pieces

½ cup pimiento, cut in ½-inch pieces

½ teaspoon coarse black pepper (optional)

1 tablespoon plain gelatin, combined with ½ cup cold water until thick, then dissolve over simmering water, and add to 1¼ cups commercial mayonnaise slowly just before it is to be combined with other ingredients

Combine all ingredients in the order given. Mix well and pack firmly into bowl. Refrigerate for about 2 hours. Meanwhile cut a cardboard to fit bottom of ham and cover with foil, sealing bottom with Scotch tape.

To mold, turn salad out onto cardboard onto a baking sheet. With hands shape salad to simulate ham. Spread entire surface with ½ cup Chaud-Froid Mayonnaise (page 463). Refrigerate for about 15 minutes and spread again with about ¼ cup or more Chaud-Froid Mayonnaise. Refrigerate another 15 minutes.

Remove ham from refrigerator, and with a pancake turner on each end, or slip hands underneath, lift up mold and transfer to a large cake rack (at least same size as ham) with baking sheet underneath. Pour rest of Chaud-Froid Mayonnaise that is of proper consistency over entire surface of ham. It may be necessary to pick up mayonnaise that drops into pan and pour again, but best to cover with one pouring if possible. Refrigerate again for about 15 minutes or longer.

For decorations on ham, cut long thin slices of crisply cooked carrots to measure ⅔ inch wide, then into 1½ wide diamond shape. Use 6 diamonds for each flower (scraping surface of mold slightly) and ½ red maraschino cherry for center. Make stems and green leaves with onion stems or green pepper. Three flowers are sufficient for decoration, 1 in center and 1 on each side. Moisten decorations with Clear Glaze (page 464) as you use them.

After decorations have been placed on mold, chill for 15 minutes, then pour slightly thickened Clear Glaze over entire top carefully Some of decorations which are likely to slip off may be picked up with a toothpick and placed back. Pick up glaze that drops into pan, strain if necessary, and pour again until a nice uniform thick coating is obtained. Refrigerate for about an hour or longer.

To Serve. With a dinner knife, loosen around base of mold, then with hands or pancake turner on each end lift up carefully and transfer to a 16-inch round glass platter.

Make a paper frill for shank end of ham using full width of wax paper, to measure about 11 or 12 inches long. Fold paper twice so that it is about 2½ inches wide. Now cut narrow sections halfway, turn inside out, and form frill. Hold together with a pin or paper clip; insert skewer into shank end of ham, then insert paper frill into skewer.

For decorations around base of ham, hard-cook 8 or more eggs for about 20 minutes. Shell, and remove a thin slice from bottom. Color half of eggs red and half yellow, and place them on paper towel with cut side down for a few minutes. Cut each to simulate a tulip on pointed end, forming 3 scallops to show yolk. Insert a whole clove in center of yolk. With a wooden skewer make an opening on rounded end an insert a long stiff onion stem (or long strip of green pepper). Arrange 2 red and 2 yellow tulips on each side of ham attractively, with cut side down to prevent rolling. Instead of these tulips, pineapple slices topped with whole apricots or tiny spiced apples may be used, or simply garnish with green leaves.

Chicken Salad Mold

10 hard-cooked eggs
4 cups cooked chicken, cut in small ½-inch pieces (a 3½-pound fully drawn chicken)
½ cup finely cut fresh green onion tops
½ cup pimiento, cut in about ¼-inch squares
1 cup finely chopped celery
½ cup cream cheese (room temperature)

1 cup mayonnaise
4 teaspoons plain gelatin, combined with ⅓ cup cold water (stir well and let stand until thick, then dissolve over simmering water)
About 2¼ teaspoons salt
About ¼ teaspoon white pepper
½ pound bacon, cut in small pieces and pan-fried until just crisp, pouring off fat

In a large bowl, with a pie blender chop hard-cooked eggs fine. To the eggs, add the cooked cut-up chicken, the green onion tops, pimiento, and chopped celery. In a medium-size bowl beat cream cheese until smooth. Add the mayonnaise a little at a time, and blend well. Now add dissolved warm gelatin slowly and mix thoroughly. Pour mayonnaise mixture over chicken ingredients and blend well. Add the salt, pepper, and crisp bacon. Cover and allow salad to stand in refrigerator for 4 or 5 hours, or until firm to the touch.

When cold and firm, turn salad out onto center of a serving platter, and mold it with hands to simulate a chicken. If it does not hold together, dip hands into hot water and use pressure in shaping chicken. If it appears soft after it is shaped, chill it again for a short time. Then spread entire surface lightly with mayonnaise and sprinkle with 4 egg yolks put through a food mill or grater.

Use cloves for eyes and make comb with piece of turnip or potato tinted red, or with a red maraschino cherry. Paint tip of nose with red food coloring.

Around base of mold, arrange groups of 3 or 4 green cocktail bread and butter or cream cheese sandwiches, about 24 altogether. Between sandwiches, place small, pale pink vegetable carved roses or other flowers and parsley bouquets, or garnish as desired. Serve Horseradish Whipped Cream Sauce (page 372) separately with this salad.

Egg Salad Mold

Serves 12

24 hard-cooked eggs	4 teaspoons gelatin, combined with
½ cup finely chopped fresh green onion and tops	⅓ cup cold water (let stand until thick, then dissolve over simmering water)
½ cup pimiento, cut into ¼-inch pieces	
½ cup finely chopped celery	2 teaspoons salt
½ cup cream cheese (room temperature)	¼ teaspoon white pepper
	½ pound bacon, cut in small pieces and pan-fried until just crisp
1 cup mayonnaise	

In a large bowl with pie blender chop hard-cooked eggs until fine. Add the chopped green onions, pimiento, and celery. In a medium bowl beat the cheese, add the mayonnaise and then the dissolved gelatin, beating well. Pour mayonnaise mixture over chopped egg ingredients. Last, season with the salt, pepper, and crisp bacon. Blend well, cover and refrigerate for 4 or 5 hours, or until firm.

Turn out onto platter and shape to stimulate a large egg. If it does not hold together, dip hands into hot water as necessary and mold, using pressure. Chill again if it appears soft, then spread entire surface with soft cream cheese. Add a little milk or cream to cheese if necessary to make it of spreading consistency.

Decorate top of egg with a spray of colored cheese flowers and green stems, or as desired. Do not add any milk or cream to cheese for top decorations. Simply beat it with a spoon until of proper consistency. Add coloring. It will take about 1 pound of cheese for very fancy decorations. Arrange dainty sandwiches around egg, or garnish as desired.

Lime Horseradish Mold

Serves 12

2½ cups boiling water
2 (3 ounce) packages of lime- or lemon-flavored gelatin
¼ cup granulated sugar
2½ cups cold water
½ teaspoon salt
1 tablespoon unflavored gelatin, combined with ¼ cup cold water,

until thick, then dissolved over boiling water
About ⅛ teaspoon green coloring
About ⅓ cup prepared horseradish (less may be used)
1 pound well drained creamed cottage cheese
1 very small grated onion

Pour boiling water over flavored gelatin and sugar; when dissolved, add cold water, salt, dissolved gelatin (remelt over boiling water first), and green coloring. Place in refrigerator or a pan of ice water, and let stand until *slightly* congealed (about the consistency of unbeaten egg white). Fold in horseradish, cottage cheese, and grated onion. Pour into oiled ring mold that measures 9½ × 2 inches (other style molds may be used). Allow to stand in refrigerator until firm and set.

When ready to unmold, loosen around sides of mold with paring knife. Place platter over top, and invert onto platter. If using ring mold, fill center with large black ripe olives. On outside of mold place carved vegetable flowers and parsley or endive, or slices of cold tongue, ham, corned beef, etc. Serve with Horseradish Whipped Cream Sauce (page 372).

Garden Vegetable Salad Mold

Serves 8 to 12

2 (3 ounce) packages lemon gelatin dessert
2 cups boiling water
2 cups cold water
1 tablespoon plain gelatin, combined with ¼ cup cold water (stir until smooth, allow to stand 5 minutes, then dissolve over simmering water)
1 cup firm tomatoes, cut into 1-inch pieces, well drained

½ cup fresh green pepper or onion strips, cut about 1 inch long
½ cup thin-sliced cucumber, first peeled and scored with a fork
¼ cup thin radish slices
¼ cup fresh green onion, or tablespoons chopped onion
½ cup coarse-shredded raw carrots
1 cup shredded green cabbage
About 1½ teaspoons salt
¼ cup cider vinegar

Dissolve lemon gelatin in boiling water. At once add cold water and dissolved plain gelatin. Refrigerate or force over ice water until it has the consistency of an unbeaten egg white or very soft custard.

Combine all vegetables, salt and vinegar, and let stand while gelatin is congealing. When gelatin mixture is of proper consistency, add mixed marinated vegetables and fold over and over until evenly distributed. Pour into a 7-cup oiled mold or bowl. Let stand in refrigerator at least 7 or 8 hours until firm. To serve, unmold onto wet platter and garnish edges with assorted relishes, or sliced meats.

Chicken-Tongue Mold

Serves 12

5-pound roasting chicken	3½ cups warm strained chicken stock
4 cups hot water	(remove fat if stock appears too
¼ cup celery	rich)
¼ cup parsley	1 tablespoon unflavored gelatin
1 onion, sliced	¼ cup cold water
1 very small bay leaf	8 to 10 slices cooked tongue, ⅛ inch
About 1 tablespoon salt	thick, or other cold meat

Wash chicken thoroughly; cover with hot water, add celery, parsley, onion, bay leaf, and cook slowly in covered heavy utensil until tender, about 1½ hours. It is better to cook chicken whole on a trivet, as there is less shrinkage. Add salt toward end of cooking. When cool, remove meat from bones and cut into medium-size pieces, about 1 inch. Remove fat from chicken stock.

Dissolve gelatin in cold water, let stand until thick, then dissolve over boiling water. Add gelatin to warm chicken stock; then add cut chicken. One-inch pieces of tongue may be combined with chicken. Brush a ring mold with salad oil. Arrange *around it* uniform slices of tongue (see cooking directions below) or other sliced cold meats. Pour chicken and warm stock into mold, being sure that chicken and stock come to very top of mold, or it will break when unmolding. Allow to stand in refrigerator 10 or 12 hours, until thoroughly set.

When ready to unmold, loosen top sides with a paring knife, place damp 16-inch platter over mold, and turn over. Fill center with endive, or a small bowl with sauce, and garnish outside with vegetable flowers, Lime Horseradish Mold cubes (page 469), or fancy bread-and-butter sandwiches. Serve French dressing with endive.

How to Cook Tongue. Cover a Premium smoked beef tongue with warm water, and cook until tender—about 3 or 4 hours, depending on size. Keep water at simmering point. Keep tongue always submerged in water and keep pan *covered*. Allow it to remain in the water in which it was cooked for ½ hour. Remove skin from tongue while warm. When cold, trim and slice. One large tongue weighing about 4 pounds is sufficient for 2 molds. Use most attractive slices for mold.

Tomato Aspic Mold

Serves 12

4 cups tomatoes or tomato juice	1 teaspoon salt
1 bay leaf	1 teaspoon sugar
⅛ teaspoon whole pepper, crushed	2 tablespoons lemon juice or vinegar
1 small onion, sliced	3 tablespoons plain gelatin, combined
1 tablespoon parsley	with ⅔ cup cold water or dry
1 tablespoon celery leaves	white wine and allowed to stand
1 sliver garlic	until thick

Simmer all ingredients in covered saucepan except lemon juice and gelatin mixture, for 15 minutes. Strain, and while very hot, add lemon juice and thick gelatin mixture. Stir until completely dissolved. Add a little red coloring. Let stand until cool; then pour into a lightly oiled baking sheet that measures 10 × 14 inches. Keep in refrigerator 8 hours or longer, until firm to the touch. This aspic may be poured into fancy small or large oiled molds.

Cucumber Salad Mold

Serves 8

3½ cups boiling water	3 large unpeeled cucumbers, grated
3 (3 ounce) packages lemon gelatin	or shredded very fine (add a
dessert	little water if necessary to make
Green coloring, diluted	3 cups)
2 teaspoons plain gelatin, combined	3 tablespoons grated onion, or ⅓ cup
with ¼ cup cold water (stir and	fine-chopped green onion and
allow to thicken)	stems
⅓ cup prepared horseradish	1½ teaspoons salt
⅓ cup vinegar or lemon juice	

Pour boiling water over lemon gelatin dessert. Add a little diluted green coloring and *at once* add thickened plain gelatin. Stir well until completely dissolved. Now place bowl in pan of ice water (or in refrigerator) until preparation is slightly congealed, about the consistency of unbeaten egg white. At this point fold in all other ingredients and blend well. Pour into an oiled tower mold (or any 7-cup mold). Refrigerate at least 8 hours.

To serve, dip mold into warm water a few seconds; brush top of mold and center of a 14-inch platter with cold water, and invert. Place sliced tomatoes around base, and sprinkle top of mold with paprika.

This mold is very refreshing and delicious with any cold or hot meat dish or seafood. It is especially attractive for buffet service.

Party-Style Potato Salad Mold

Serves 8 to 12

Add a little red food coloring to ⅔ cup cream cheese and blend well. Chill for a few minutes if too soft. With No. 104 tube, pipe 4 roses on nails and keep them in freezer compartment until firm to the touch, or longer. Add a little green coloring to ⅓ cup cream cheese, and pipe 12 leaves with No. 67 or 70 leaf tube on pan covered with wax paper. Store in freezer compartment until needed. (This may be done several hours in advance and frozen.) When ready to make mold, prepare Topping and Potato Salad (page 473).

Pour 1 cup of clear Topping into 1½-quart ring mold (or 7-cup bread pan). Refrigerate until almost set, but not too firm. Now with a small spatula or dinner knife release roses from nails and place them upside down onto Topping, evenly spaced. Lift off leaves from wax paper in same way and arrange them upside down around roses. Now pour about 2 teaspoons of Topping (still in liquid stage) around each rose and a very little over leaves (about a teaspoon at a time) to anchor decorations onto gelatin. Refrigerate until set to touch. Now carefully pour rest of clear cold liquid gelatin Topping, teaspoon at a time, over decorations, and if they appear to move around at any time, stop adding preparation and refrigerate for a short time. Then add rest of liquid Topping. Refrigerate until set to touch.

Remove mold from refrigerator, rub sides with a little salad oil, and pour Potato Salad into mold *carefully with a small cup*, pressing down *very gently.* Cover with wax paper and refrigerate for at least 7 or 8 hours. (May be prepared a day in advance.)

To Serve. With a small spatula or dinner knife go around top sides of mold. Dip mold into warm (not hot) water for a few seconds. Wipe outside of mold with a cloth to prevent dripping. Brush top of mold and serving platter lightly with cold water, and invert. If mold does not come out easily, cover top and sides with hot wet towels.

Garnish base of mold with tomatoes sliced crosswise, alternately with cucumber, or with cold sliced meats and cheeses or as desired.

Note. For a large 3-quart ring mold prepare 1½ recipes and make 6 roses and about 20 leaves. For bread pan that holds about 10½ cups (No. 33) prepare 1½ recipes, and make 4 or 5 roses and about 15 leaves.

Instead of cream cheese rose decorations, mold may be decorated with wedges of hard-cooked eggs, put together to simulate a daisy, with ½ red cherry in center. Make green pepper or green citron leaves. Canned tangerine segments may be arranged in same way. Follow general directions for setting.

Topping for Party-Style Potato Salad Mold

2 cups boiling water

1½ tablespoons plain gelatin, combined with ½ cup cold water (stir gently and let stand about 5 minutes until thick)

3 tablespoons lemon juice, strained

3 tablespoons granulated sugar

In medium-size bowl, at once pour boiling water over gelatin preparation, lemon juice, and granulated sugar. Stir *very* gently until dissolved.

Potato Salad for Party-Style Salad Mold

2 pounds of new red boiling potatoes, cooked with skins on until just tender, not too soft, peeled and cut in medium size slices ⅓ inch thick

1 cup celery, cut about ¼ inch wide crosswise

½ cup fresh green onion stems, cut about ½ inch

¼ cup fresh green onion, chopped fine

¼ cup pimiento, cut into ½ inch squares (optional)

4 hard-cooked eggs, cut medium

1 teaspoon dill seed (optional)

About 3 teaspoons salt

¼ teaspoon white pepper

1 tablespoon plain gelatin, combined with ½ cup cold water (stir until well blended; let stand until thick, then dissolve over simmering water)

1½ cups commercial sour cream or mayonnaise (or half of each)

Combine all these ingredients in the order given and blend thoroughly.

Buffet Party Vegetable Salad Mold

For tower mold

Marinade for Vegetables

2 tablespoons salad oil

⅓ cup cider vinegar

½ teaspoon coarsely ground black pepper

1½ teaspoons salt

1 teaspoon dry rosemary, crushed

Combine all ingredients in a small bowl. With wire whisk or dover beater, beat about 1 minute just before pouring over vegetables.

Cooked Vegetables for Salad Mold

10-ounce package frozen asparagus or green beans, cooked until crisply tender in small amount water and ½ teaspoon salt; drain well

10-ounce package frozen lima beans or peas, cooked same way, seasoned with ½ teaspoon salt

2½ cups fresh carrots, peeled and cut into long thick pointed wedges,

about 2½ inches long and ⅔ inch wide, cooked about 10 minutes, covered, in small amount of water and ½ teaspoon salt; drain well

⅓ cup pimiento, cut into ¾-inch squares (4 ounce can)

½ cup fresh green onions and stems, cut into about ½-inch pieces

Combine all ingredients in medium-size bowl, and at once pour the Marinade over vegetables. Blend thoroughly, cover, and refrigerate for at least 1 hour, turning them over and over several times.

Gelatin Preparation for Vegetable Mold

1 (3 ounce) package lemon gelatin dessert
¼ cup granulated sugar
1 tablespoon plain gelatin, combined with ¼ cup cold water; let stand until thick
¼ cup lemon juice
2 cups boiling water

In a medium-size bowl combine the lemon gelatin dessert, granulated sugar, thick gelatin mixture, and lemon juice. Add the 2 cups of boiling water at once and stir until completely dissolved.

Pour ⅓ cup of this preparation into a slightly oiled mold that measures about 5½ inches deep and 7 inches wide at open end (tower mold). Refrigerate until partially congealed, but not too firm. Place a small carved carrot or turnip rose, upside down, into center of gelatin, and arrange 6 to 8 green pepper or citron leaves, that measure 1 inch long and ½ inch wide, around rose. Instead of rose, a large maraschino cherry may be placed in center, with green pepper or carrot leaves around it. Now pour about 2 tablespoons of the cool Gelatin Preparation around decorations, a tablespoonful at a time. Stop adding gelatin if decorations move around, and refrigerate for a short time. Then add little more liquid Gelatin Preparation, using in all ½ cup. Refrigerate again until *set to the touch*.

Place rest of plain Gelatin Preparation in refrigerator or force over cold water until it is the consistency of thin unbeaten egg white. At this point fold in the marinated vegetables, without draining, until evenly blended. With a cup carefully pour vegetables over firmly set decorations in mold. Refrigerate mold for at least 8 hours, or better prepare day in advance.

To Serve. With a dinner knife loosen upper edge of mold, brush top lightly with cold water. Brush platter also with water. Dip mold into warm water for a few seconds, and wipe outside well. Place wet platter over mold and turn over, shaking slightly. Garnish base of mold with sliced tomatoes and cucumbers brushed with French dressing, assorted relishes, cold sliced meats and cheeses, or as desired. Serve Zesty Sour Cream Dressing separately.

Zesty Sour Cream Dressing

1 cup commercial sour cream
1 teaspoon salt
⅛ teaspoon coarsely ground pepper
2 tablespoons finely minced green onion and stems
2 tablespoons prepared horseradish, or
1 tablespoon freshly grated horseradish

Combine all ingredients and stir well. May be prepared several days in advance if stored in covered jar in refrigerator.

▶ *Quick Breads*

WAFFLES, BISCUITS, PANCAKES, POPOVERS, DOUGHNUTS, SPECIALTY BREADS, AND NON-YEAST COFFEE CAKES

THE BREADS IN THIS SECTION ARE VERY POPULAR BECAUSE THEY ARE MADE quickly and may be made into a large variety of foods. The leavening agents used act fast and make the mixture light in a short time. Quick breads are more palatable when served hot.

▶ WAFFLES ◀

Waffles

Makes about 5 waffles

1½ cups sifted all-purpose flour	2 egg yolks, well beaten for ½ minute
½ teaspoon salt	
1½ teaspoons double-acting baking powder	1¼ cups milk
1 tablespoon granulated sugar	¼ cup melted butter or margarine
	2 egg whites, beaten until they cling to bowl

Sift dry ingredients together several times. Beat egg yolks with egg beater and combine them with milk. Gradually stir liquid into dry ingredients and beat only until smooth. Add melted butter. Last, fold in beaten egg whites.

Pour heaping ½ cup batter in center of hot waffle iron. Cover, and allow to bake until brown and crisp, about 3 or 4 minutes.

Serve with syrup, sausages, bacon, or as desired. Delicious as a base for creamed foods, or as a dessert with sugared berries and fruits.

475

Pecan Waffles

Makes about 5 waffles

1½ cups sifted all-purpose flour
½ teaspoon salt
1½ teaspoons double-acting baking powder
1 tablespoon granulated sugar
2 egg yolks, well beaten for ½ minute

1⅓ cups milk
¼ cup melted butter or margarine
¼ cup chopped pecans
2 egg whites, beaten until they cling to bowl

Sift dry ingredients (except chopped pecans) together several times. Beat egg yolks with egg beater and combine them with milk. Gradually stir liquid into dry ingredients and beat only until smooth. Add melted butter and chopped pecans. Last, fold in beaten egg whites.

Pour heaping ½ cup batter in center of hot waffle iron. Cover, and allow to bake until golden brown and crisp, about 3 or 4 minutes.

Serve with syrup, sausages, bacon, or as desired. Delicious as a dessert with sugared berries and fruits.

▶ BISCUITS ◀

Baking Powder Biscuits

Will make about 12 (2-inch) biscuits

2 cups sifted all-purpose flour
4 teaspoons double-acting baking powder
1 tablespoon granulated sugar

1 teaspoon salt (1½ teaspoon if using salted shortening)
⅓ cup unsalted shortening
1 cup less 2 tablespoons milk

Sift dry ingredients together several times. Add shortening and cut through until it looks like a fine meal. Make a well in center; add milk all at once, and with a fork or long spoon stir vigorously for about ½ minute, or until dough is thoroughly blended. Now turn dough out onto a well-floured pastry cloth, and knead it gently for ½ minute, adding a little more flour if dough feels unusually sticky and if it is difficult to handle. Keep dough very soft. If dough feels heavy, add a little more milk. Too much liquid will produce a soggy biscuit; too little will produce a dry biscuit.

To shape biscuits, pat or roll dough to ⅔ inch in thickness. Let dough stand about 1 minute, then cut through with a 2-inch cutter, dipping cutter into flour each time to prevent sticking. With a spatula or hand carefully lift up biscuits and place them on an ungreased baking sheet about ¼ inch apart. Knead scraps of dough gently a few seconds, pat or roll to ⅔ inch thick, let stand about 1 minute, and form more biscuits. Brush tops with milk or melted fat.

Bake in a 450° F. oven about 15 minutes, or until delicately brown. (Decrease time for flatter biscuits.) Smaller or larger cutters may be used. It is best to bake these biscuits just before serving. However, leftover biscuits may be well wrapped and stored in a cool place. Sprinkle them with a little water and reheat in a 400° F. oven for about 7 or 8 minutes just before serving.

Biscuits may be mixed, shaped and stored in refrigerator, covered well with wax paper, or in a plastic bag until ready to be baked. Remove from refrigerator and let stand in room temperature while preheating oven. Bake and serve.

Note. A convenient biscuit mix can be prepared days in advance with our basic recipe, omitting the milk. Store in a covered container in a cool place. When ready to be baked, add the required amount of milk, knead, shape and bake according to our general directions.

Savory Tea Biscuits, Continental-Style

Makes about 15 (2-inch) biscuits

Prepare basic Baking Powder Biscuit dough (page 476). Roll dough ½ inch thick. Bake according to directions, and let cool. Split in halves and cover lower half with 1 teaspoon Continental Filling. Place top on, and spread top with about ¼ teaspoon filling. Reheat at 400° F. about 7 or 8 minutes just before serving. These biscuits may be filled hours in advance and stored in a covered container in refrigerator or a cool place until ready to be reheated.

These biscuits are delectable served with seafood or poultry salads, soups, chafing dish preparations, or as snacks. They may also be made smaller for delicious hot hors d'oeuvres.

Continental Filling for Savory Tea Biscuits

½ cup soft butter or margarine	¾ teaspoon coarse oregano, crushed
¼ cup or less, grated Italian cheese	between fingers, or ¼ teaspoon
1 medium or large clove of garlic, put	powdered
through garlic press, or chopped	⅛ teaspoon black pepper
very fine	

Combine all ingredients and beat until well blended. May be made several days in advance if stored in a covered container in refrigerator. Let stand in room temperature until soft before using.

Shortcake Biscuits for Berries and Other Fruits

Increase sugar in recipe for Baking Powder Biscuits (page 476) to 2 tablespoons. Use 1 whole well-beaten egg and make up difference with milk to make the required amount. Use a 3-inch cutter for large shortcakes, or bake in a layer cake pan.

▶ PANCAKES ◀

Crêpes Suzette

Serves 4 to 6

½ cupful whole eggs, beaten with egg beater about ½ minute
1 cup sifted all-purpose flour
2 tablespoons melted butter or margarine
1 cup milk (room temperature)

1 teaspoon brandy or triple sec or other liqueur (optional)
A little lemon rind, or ¼ teaspoon lemon extract
½ teaspoon salt

Beat eggs, add flour, a little at a time, alternately with the milk and melted butter or margarine, the triple sec or brandy, the rind of lemon, and salt. Beat with egg beater only until smooth. Cover, and let stand about 15 minutes or longer.

For a 7-inch skillet, pour about ⅔ of a *quarter cup measurement*. Brush skillet well with a little melted shortening for first pancake only, then occasionally if they stick. The butter added to the batter makes it unnecessary to grease skillet. After pouring batter into skillet, let cook for a *few seconds*, lift from heat and tilt pan back and forth while batter is still thin so that pancakes will be uniform in thickness. Cook until brown on first side over moderate heat; turn and cook second side until golden color. Roll each one, or pile flat on platter. After preparing first pancake, more milk or flour may be added to regulate thickness. It is better to cool skillet slightly before pouring batter for each crêpe but do not have skillet cold. This gives a thinner pancake. Pancakes may be prepared several hours in advance. Makes about 18 very thin pancakes if using 7-inch skillet. Smaller skillets may be used. In this case, use less batter (about 2 level tablespoonfuls).

Melt part of L'Aiglon Butter in a chafing dish. A skillet may be used instead. In this case, keep skillet over very low heat. Add *rolled* or *flat* crêpes to the melted L'Aiglon Butter, 1 at a time, turning often, then roll each if necessary. In preparing a large number of these crêpes at one time, they may be piled on top of one another. Drain off all excess butter that remains in chafing dish after crêpes are heated through. Now pour at least ¼ cup or more warm liqueur over crêpes; cover dish for several minutes, then remove cover, light, and bring flaming to table. Or prepare before guests in dining room. Be sure to continue turning crêpes in liqueur until flame burns out, and serve as soon as possible as a dessert or light luncheon dish. Melt any leftover L'Aiglon Butter and serve it hot in a separate dish. If flame continues to burn too long, it may be extinguished by covering chafing dish for a few seconds.

For breakfast or luncheon dishes, these pancakes may be spread with jellies, jams, softened cream cheese, commercial sour cream, cottage cheese, etc., then rolled, sprinkled with sifted confectioners' sugar, or syrup.

L'Aiglon Butter for Crêpes Suzette

½ cup cold, firm butter
1 cup sifted confectioners' sugar
Rind of 1 small orange and 1 very small lemon

½ cup warm orange juice
⅓ cup warm triple sec or any other liqueur or combination of liquors at least 80 proof

With electric beater, beat the butter until light and creamy. Add sugar, rinds, and warm juice, *a little at a time*, and continue to beat until thoroughly blended. If butter separates, place bowl in a pan of hot water for a few minutes and beat well until smooth.

German Pancakes

Serves 4

3 large eggs (¾ cup)
¾ cup cool milk
¾ cup sifted all-purpose flour
½ teaspoon salt
1 tablespoon unsalted shortening for

10-inch skillet or 1½ tablespoons unsalted shortening for 12-inch skillet
Melted butter
Granulated sugar

Combine all ingredients except shortening in a medium-size bowl. With egg or electric beater beat about 2 or 3 minutes. Melt the shortening in a 10- or better 12-inch heavy skillet. When very hot, pour in batter and bake in a 450° F. oven 15 minutes. Lower temperature to 350° F. and bake about 10 more minutes, or until golden brown and crisp. When pancake puffs up in center during first part of baking, puncture it well with a skewer or fork. When done, remove from oven and turn out onto long platter. Drizzle about 1 tablespoon hot melted butter and 1 tablespoon granulated sugar over entire surface; then spread half with warm Apple Filling or other filling. (About ½ cup very thinly sliced uncooked apples may be added to batter before baking pancakes.) Fold over to enclose apples. Drizzle top with about 1 more tablespoon hot melted butter and 1 tablespoon sugar. Cut crosswise and serve at once.

Apple Filling for German Pancakes

Sauté 1 pound peeled and thinly sliced apples in ¼ cup hot melted butter or margarine for several minutes. Add ¼ cup granulated sugar and continue to cook about 5 to 6 minutes longer, turning often. If apples appear too firm, cover pan and steam about 5 minutes. Apples should be crisply tender, not too soft. Season with ⅛ teaspoon nutmeg and ⅛ teaspoon cinnamon. Mix well. Let stand until lukewarm before using. This filling may be made several hours in advance and reheated just before pouring onto pancake.

Fresh Peach Filling for German Pancakes

Prepare same as for Apple Filling, substituting peaches.

Uncooked Strawberry, Raspberry, or Blueberry Fillings for German Pancakes

Wash 2 cupfuls fresh berries. (Do not cook.) Remove hulls from strawberries. Pour onto a towel and remove surplus moisture. Combine berries with ½ cup granulated sugar just before pouring onto pancake.

Pancakes (Griddle Cakes)

Makes about 12 depending on size

1 cup sifted all-purpose flour
2 teaspoons double-acting baking powder
1 tablespoon granulated sugar
¾ teaspoon salt

1 large egg, beaten about ½ minute
About ¾ cup milk (room temperature)
2 tablespoons butter or other melted fat

Sift dry ingredients together and pour into a medium-size bowl. Combine beaten egg, milk, and melted fat. Pour liquids all at once into dry ingredients and with a large wooden spoon stir *only* until ingredients are moist, but still slightly lumpy. This will give a more tender and puffier pancake. Place griddle over moderate heat and test by sprinkling a few drops of water over the hot surface. If water bounces around, forms tiny bubbles, it is ready. *From the tip of a large spoon* pour batter to obtain uniform round cakes. The batter should begin to bubble within a few seconds. When top of cakes are full of bubbles and a few begin to break, turn cakes over and bake on second side until golden brown.

Serve them as soon as possible with butter, syrup, jam, marmalade, jelly, cream cheese, sour cream, or as desired. (Leftover pancake batter may be used the next day if covered tightly and refrigerated.)

Note. It is not necessary to grease griddle if some fat is used in batter. Bake cakes over moderate heat, not high or low. Serve cakes as soon as possible, or keep them hot over very low heat in covered skillet, or in a very slow oven on a baking sheet for a short time. For thicker pancakes, use less milk. For thinner pancakes, increase milk.

Many variations can be made from our basic recipe by adding about ½ cupful cooked, well-drained vegetables, seafood, poultry or meat to batter just before you start to bake cakes.

For luncheon or supper plate, place 3 (4-inch) pancakes together sandwich fashion with creamed chicken, seafood, or ham, in center of dinner plate. Pour a little filling over top and sprinkle with paprika, or finely chopped green onion. Serve at once with a salad and dessert.

Southern Rice Pancakes

Makes about 12 pancakes

¾ cup all-purpose flour
¼ cup sugar
½ teaspoon, or more, salt
¼ teaspoon nutmeg
¼ teaspoon cinnamon
1½ teaspoons double-acting baking powder

¾ cup milk
1 whole egg, well beaten
2 tablespoons melted butter or margarine
1 cup cooked cool rice

Sift all dry ingredients together and place in a bowl. Add milk, egg, and butter all at one time and mix until well blended. Last, mix in cooked rice. Pour ¼ cup batter onto a hot lightly greased griddle pan and allow to bake until brown underneath. With a pancake turner, turn over and bake top side until golden brown. Serve with syrup or honey.

Blueberry Griddle Cakes

Makes about 20 cakes, depending on size

2 cups sifted all-purpose flour
3 teaspoons double-acting baking powder
1 teaspoon salt
2 tablespoons granulated sugar
2 eggs, well beaten until light

About 1½ cups milk (room temperature)
3 tablespoons melted butter or margarine
¾ cup fresh or well-drained canned blueberries

Sift dry ingredients together several times. Combine beaten eggs, milk, and melted butter. Add liquids all at once to dry ingredients and mix only until *moist but still slightly lumpy*. Then fold in blueberries.

With a large wooden spoon pour batter onto a hot ungreased griddle pan and allow to bake over moderate heat until tops of cakes are full of bubbles and brown underneath. With a pancake turner, turn over and bake top side until golden brown.

Pancakes may be kept warm in a covered skillet over very low heat until ready to be served.

Milk may be decreased for a thicker pancake. For a thinner pancake, increase milk.

Pancakes Made with Buttermilk (or Home-Type Soured Milk)

Serves 3 to 4

1 cup sifted all-purpose flour
1½ teaspoons   double-acting   baking powder
½ teaspoon baking soda
¾ teaspoon salt
1 tablespoon granulated sugar

1 large egg, beaten about ½ minute
2 tablespoons of butter or other fat, melted
About 1 cup, more or less, buttermilk or sour cream (room temperature)

Combine and prepare same as for pancakes made with regular milk (page 480).

Syrup (for Pancakes, Waffles, Etc.)

½ cup hot water
½ cup granulated sugar
1 cup brown sugar, solidly packed

2 tablespoons white corn syrup
½ teaspoon vanilla

Combine all ingredients except vanilla in a 1-quart saucepan, stir well until sugar is dissolved over low heat. Wash sides of pan with brush dipped into hot water. Place thermometer in syrup and cook to 226° F. for medium consistency. (Takes about 15 minutes over medium heat.) Do not stir after syrup begins to boil to prevent graining. When done, remove from heat and gently stir in ½ teaspoon vanilla. Serve hot, or let cool, pour into jar, cover tightly and keep in a cool place.

Corn Griddle Cakes

Makes about 12 to 16 cakes

1 cup sifted all-purpose flour
2 teaspoons double-acting baking powder
1 teaspoon sugar
½ teaspoon salt

1 small egg, beaten with hand beater a few seconds
½ cup milk
2 tablespoons butter or margarine, melted
½ cup cream-style corn

Sift dry ingredients together several times. Combine beaten egg with milk and melted butter. Add egg mixture to dry ingredients and mix only until moist but still slightly lumpy. Add corn and fold over gently. With a large spoon pour batter onto an ungreased griddle pan (if using a skillet, it is best to grease it lightly). Bake over moderate heat until tops of cakes are full of bubbles and brown underneath. With a pancake turner, turn over and bake top side until golden brown. Milk may be decreased for a thicker pancake. For a thinner pancake, increase milk. Serve with sausages, bacon, syrup, or as desired.

Corn Oysters

Makes about 12 to 16

1 cup cream-style corn
2 medium-size eggs
About 1½ teaspoons salt
¾ cup sifted all-purpose flour

1½ teaspoons double-acting baking powder
¼ teaspoon pepper

Combine all ingredients and mix until smooth. With a teaspoon (or tablespoon) drop into about ⅛ inch of very hot cooking oil, and fry over moderate heat until brown on one side. Turn them over and fry second side.

Potato Croquettes (Italian-Style)

Peel and wash 1 pound Idaho potatoes and cut in uniform large pieces (about 2 inches). Cook 20 to 30 minutes or until soft in about 1 inch boiling unsalted water, in covered saucepan. Drain well, dry out over low heat. *Mash at once while very hot* and to 2 cups (little more or less) add 1 *very small* beaten egg (only enough to hold ingredients together), 1 teaspoon salt, ⅛ teaspoon pepper, 1 tablespoon (more or less) fresh parsley chopped fine, 1 tablespoon Italian grated cheese, ¼ teaspoon onion or garlic salt. Mix well, and let cool. Then divide into 8 uniform portions (about ¼ cupful each) and form oval croquettes. Roll in fine light bread crumbs, then into beaten egg combined with 1 tablespoon water, then into crumbs again. Let stand on wax paper, room temperature about 20 minutes, turning over several times. Shake off loose crumbs and deep fry at 375° F. for several minutes until golden brown and crisp. May be kept warm in a very, very low oven on cake rack for about 15 minutes, or croquettes may be fried to a lighter color in advance and refried at 350° F. for several minutes just before serving; or may be completely fried and reheated on cake rack with drip pan underneath in 350° F. oven for about 12 to 15 minutes, not longer or they are likely to crack. May be pan-fried in about ¼ inch of hot unsalted shortening or cooking oil several minutes on each side, instead of frying in deep fat.

Fresh Potato Pancakes

Will make 12 medium-size pancakes

2 large whole eggs, beaten with fluffy beater for a few seconds
2 tablespoons, or little more, milk
2 tablespoons all-purpose flour
¼ teaspoon baking powder
1½ teaspoons salt

About ⅛ teaspoon pepper
⅛ teaspoon onion salt
1 pound (2 large) raw potatoes, peeled
Strips of bacon, cut into square pieces (optional)

Combine beaten eggs, milk, flour, baking powder, salt, pepper and onion salt. With wire whisk or hand beater beat for about 1 minute until smooth. Now grate or slice fine raw potatoes into liquid preparation. (This will prevent potatoes from turning dark.)

To fry pancakes, stir well each time, pick up with a large spoon and pour into about $\frac{1}{16}$ inch very hot unsalted shortening or cooking oil. With back of spoon flatten each one, and fry over medium heat until golden brown and crisp on one side, for about 5 minutes. Now with pancake turner, turn over and fry second side for several minutes. Square pieces of bacon may be placed on each pancake before turning over.

Hush Puppies

Serves 4

1 cup yellow or white corn meal
½ cup sifted all-purpose flour
1 teaspoon salt
¼ teaspoon black pepper
2 strips bacon, cut into small pieces and fried until crisp, then drained (optional)

⅓ cup onion, chopped fine and sautéed in 1 tablespoon bacon drippings or other fat, drained
¾ cup very hot milk
1 whole large egg
3 teaspoons double-acting baking powder

Combine corn meal, flour, salt, and pepper, and mix well. Add cooked bacon and onion. Very slowly add hot milk. Beat well about ½ minute; then add egg and beat until thoroughly blended. Cover, and let stand at least 30 minutes until cold. Just before deep-frying add baking powder and beat well. If batter appears too heavy, add a little milk or water. If too thin, add a little more corn meal. It should be of medium consistency. Pick up with a teaspoon and push into deep hot fat (about 350° F.) with finger or another teaspoon. Do not permit fat to go over 350° F. if possible, to insure thorough cooking in center of puppies. Fry until deep golden-brown color on both sides, turning over as necessary. Serve hot with fried fish, shrimp, or chicken. Leftover puppies may be reheated in a 300° F.

oven on a baking sheet 7 or 8 minutes, or they may be kept warm in a *very* slow oven for a short time.

▶ POPOVERS ◀

Popovers

Makes 6 large popovers

2 large or 3 small eggs (½ cup), beaten about ½ minute
1 cup sifted all-purpose flour

½ teaspoon salt
1 cup cool milk

In a medium-size bowl combine all ingredients and beat about 1 minute with a hand beater or ½ minute with electric beater. Pour into six 3¼-inch custard cups (each greased with ¼ teaspoon unsalted shortening) having them about half filled. Place them on an old baking sheet to facilitate handling, leaving spaces between them. Bake in a preheated hot oven, 400° F., about 30 minutes; then lower heat to lowest point and continue to bake about 20 to 30 more minutes, or until crisp and brown. About 15 minutes before removing from oven, cut a slit on side of each popover to let out steam. When done, remove at once from custard cups to prevent softening, and serve immediately.

Popovers are best served as soon as done. However, leftover popovers may be reheated in a 350° F. oven about 15 minutes until crisp.

They are delicious served with butter, jams, jellies, stewed fruits, or creamed dishes.

▶ DOUGHNUTS ◀

French Doughnuts

Makes 6 to 8 large thick doughnuts

1 cup hot water, combined with 3 tablespoons butter or margarine
¼ teaspoon salt

1 cup sifted all-purpose flour
3 very large eggs (¾ cup)
Confectioners' sugar or icing

In a 2-quart saucepan bring water, butter or margarine, and salt to a full boil. Add sifted flour all at once, lower heat and stir vigorously for several minutes, or until paste is smooth and leaves sides of pan. Transfer paste to a medium-size bowl, let cool for about 3 minutes. Now add eggs, 1 or 2 at a time, and with electric mixer beat after each addition until smooth. Beat about 3 more minutes after all eggs have been added. In doubling recipe, beat paste about 4 or 5 minutes after all eggs have added. If paste is warm, chill it for a short time until it feels cool. Best to use it within an hour.

To Form Doughnuts. Place paste into bag with No. 7 large star cookie tube, and squeeze it onto rounds of heavy wax paper, cut 3 inches in diameter, overlapping ends of dough about 1 inch to prevent doughnuts from opening. Lower them gently into deep hot fat at 375° F., keeping paper side up, and fry until golden brown on 1 side. When doughnuts come to top, lift off paper, turn doughnuts over and fry for 2 or 3 minutes until golden color but not dark. (French doughnuts must be turned over several times after they are golden color to prevent sogginess.) Remove from fat, let cool on cake racks. Before serving sprinkle thickly with confectioners' sugar or better drizzle with Coffee Cake Icing (page 510), or Icing for Cream Puffs (page 668).

Buttermilk Fried Doughnuts

Makes about 8 to 12 medium doughnuts

2¼ cups sifted all-purpose flour	2 tablespoons melted butter or shortening
1¼ teaspoons double-acting baking powder	½ teaspoon vanilla
½ teaspoon baking soda	1 very large whole egg, beaten ½ minute
½ teaspoon salt	½ cup granulated sugar
½ teaspoon nutmeg	
½ cup buttermilk (room temperature)	

Combine flour, baking powder, soda, salt, and nutmeg, and sift together several times. In an 8-inch bowl combine the buttermilk, melted butter, vanilla, beaten egg, and granulated sugar, and beat until smooth.

Add flour combined with other ingredients, a little at a time, to the buttermilk mixture, and beat with a long heavy wooden spoon until dough is smooth. When it is too stiff to beat with spoon, turn it out onto floured pastry cloth, and knead gently about ½ minute, adding only enough more flour to prevent stickiness. Pat and roll dough to ⅓ inch in thickness (not thicker) if using a 2¾-inch round cutter. (Do not use larger cutter than 3 inches round for this type of doughnut.) Roll dough only ¼ inch thick if you are using cutter smaller than 2¾ inches. Let dough stand on cloth after it has been rolled for about 1 or 2 minutes, then cut through with doughnut cutter, dipping it into flour when necessary.

To fry doughnuts, place them carefully on pancake turner and gently lower them into hot fat heated to 365° F. and fry on first side until golden brown, then turn over and fry second side. Best not to turn more than once to prevent greasy surface on doughnuts. When done, remove carefully with a longer skewer, fork, or pair of tongs, or a perforated spoon. Place on cake cooler. When cool, ice or sprinkle thickly with sifted confectioners' sugar and serve. Do not sugar doughnuts until you are ready to serve them. Store in a covered container.

Smetana Doughnut Puffs

Serves 6

1 cup commercial sour cream, combined with 1¼ teaspoons baking soda
1 teaspoon vanilla
¼ teaspoon salt
⅛ teaspoon cinnamon
⅛ teaspoon nutmeg
½ cup granulated sugar
1 large egg, well beaten with a fork
About 2 cups sifted all-purpose flour
Confectioners' sugar

Combine all ingredients except flour and with heavy spoon beat well until thoroughly blended. Then add flour, about ½ cup at a time, and beat until smooth, adding only enough flour to form a very stiff batter. Pick up with a greased teaspoon and push into deep hot fat, between 360° F. and 375° F., with finger or another teaspoon. (Do not use more than 1 slightly rounded teaspoon batter for each puff, to insure complete cooking in center. Dip teaspoon into hot fat each time before picking up batter.) Fry until golden brown, turning them over as necessary. It is best to fry enough puffs at a time to fill entire surface of the frying utensil. This will keep them in position and they will fry more uniformly. When done, remove puffs from fat and drain on cake cooler or paper. Roll in sifted confectioners' sugar before serving. Puffs may be served warm, and are very delicious and tender the following day if stored in a tight closed container. Do not sugar them until ready to serve.

Buttermilk Doughnut Balls or Puffs

Follow directions as for Buttermilk Fried Doughnuts (page 486), but reduce flour to about 2 cups, or enough to form a very stiff batter that drops from spoon in thick lumps or gobs. Pick up a slightly rounded teaspoon of stiff batter, and with another spoon or your forefinger push batter into hot deep fat heated to 365° F. Dip spoon into the fat occasionally to help release batter easily, and beat batter occasionally to keep it uniform in consistency. After balls have puffed out, keep stirring them with a long spoon, and submerge below surface of oil from time to time to brown evenly. (They have a tendency to turn over, unless you have the entire surface filled with these puffs.) Another way to keep them down below top of oil is to place the empty basket that comes with your French fryer on top of balls, using a slight pressure. This will keep them in position to brown evenly. When done, lift out with a perforated spoon, drain well, and place them on cake rack. When cool, roll well into sifted confectioners' sugar. They are delicious served warm, or may be prepared a day in advance if stored in an airtight closed container. Do not sugar doughnuts until ready to serve.

▶ SPECIALTY BREADS ◀

Banana Nut Bread

Serves 8

⅔ cup butter or margarine
1⅓ cups sifted granulated sugar
2 very large eggs (½ cup)
3 cups sifted all-purpose flour, combined with 4 teaspoons double-acting baking powder

⅓ cup milk
¾ cup finely chopped pecans
1½ cups just ripe bananas, mashed fine with pie blender (will take 3 or 4 bananas, depending on size)

Have all ingredients room temperature at least an hour. In 8- or 9-inch bowl beat butter or margarine about 1 minute. Add sugar a little at a time, and beat another minute. Add eggs, 1 at a time, beating each in about 1 minute, or until preparation looks like whipped cream. Add about 1 cupful of flour combined with the baking powder, beating after each addition until smooth. Pour into 13 x 4½ x 2½-inch pan that has been well greased with 2 teaspoons unsalted shortening, and bottom covered with silicone or heavy wax paper. Bake at 350° F. about 1 hour and 10 minutes, or until top is brown and firm to touch, in center, or when cake tester comes out dry. Remove from oven, let remain in pan on a cake rack for about 15 minutes. Then loosen around sides, and carefully turn out onto cake rack. Let cool, then wrap well, or keep in plastic bag to retain moisture. Cut and serve as desired.

Date and Nut Bread

Serves 8

⅔ cup boiling water
1 package moist pitted dates (7¼ ounce size), cut in fine pieces
¼ cup soft butter or margarine
⅔ cup granulated sugar
¼ teaspoon salt

1¾ cups sifted all-purpose flour, combined with ½ teaspoon baking soda
1 cup medium-chopped walnuts or pecans

Pour boiling water over dates, butter or margarine, sugar, and salt which have been combined in an 8- or 9-inch bowl. At once, add combined flour and baking soda a little at a time. Beat until well blended, and last add the chopped nuts, and mix well.

Pour into 2 tall, round cans (No. 2 size) that measure about 4¼ inches high and 3⅓ inches wide. Grease cans well with shortening, and line bottom and sides with heavy wax paper cut to fit smoothly. Press batter down with spoon. Cover with greased foil and bake in a 350° F. oven about 1 hour, or until firm to the touch when tested in center.

When done, turn over carefully onto cake racks and let cool. Store in a tightly covered box or keep in cans in which they were baked. Wax paper may be removed from sides, but if bread is to be kept for some time, it is better to leave paper on until ready to serve.

Slice and serve with tea or salads. Slices may be cut crosswise and decorated with cream cheese or buttercream rosettes and green leaves. Use No. 27 tube for rosettes and No. 67 for leaves.

Corn Bread

Serves 8

¾ cup unsifted yellow corn meal
1 cup and 2 tablespoons sifted all-purpose flour
¼ cup granulated sugar
1 tablespoon and 2 teaspoons double-acting baking powder

1 teaspoon salt
2 large eggs
1 cup milk
¼ cup shortening, melted

Preheat oven at 475° F. Grease 1 square pan 9 × 9 × 2 inches with 2 teaspoons shortening, greasing sides very lightly, and sprinkle with flour. Sift together corn meal, flour, sugar, baking powder, and salt. Place in a No. 8 or No. 9 bowl. In a separate bowl beat eggs with wire whisk or dover beater about ½ minute, add milk, and beat another ½ minute. Add combined milk and eggs to dry ingredients all at one time, and blend. Last, add melted shortening. Mix until blended but *do not overmix*. Pour into greased pan and bake in a preheated oven at 475° F. about 15 minutes, or until golden brown on top. When it is done, remove from oven, place on rack, and let stand 10 minutes; then loosen around sides and turn out on cake rack.

Corn-Bread Sticks

Makes about 20 sticks

Use recipe for Corn Bread (above). Preheat oven at 475° F. After oven has been preheated to proper temperature, heat special corn mold that has been well brushed with melted shortening in oven 5 minutes. After 5 minutes remove from oven and with a tablespoon pour batter into each section almost to top of pan. Bake in 475° F. oven about 10 minutes, or until golden brown. When done, remove at once from mold.

Pineapple Date and Nut Bread

Serves 6 to 8

1 egg, beaten
⅓ cup milk
⅓ cup butter or shortening
1 cup crushed pineapple
1 cup chopped pecans or walnuts
1 cup chopped dates

2¾ cups sifted all-purpose flour
¾ teaspoon salt
¾ cup granulated sugar
1 tablespoon baking powder
¼ teaspoon baking soda

Combine beaten egg, milk, melted shortening, pineapple, nuts, and dates. Sift together dry ingredients; add to batter, and stir until blended.

Pour into a greased and floured pan that measures 9 × 5 × 3 inches. Bake in a preheated 350° F. oven about 1 hour and 15 minutes, or until done when tested with a skewer.

Gingerbread

Serves 8

½ cup butter
½ cup sugar
2 beaten eggs
1 cup molasses
2¾ cups sifted all-purpose flour
1 teaspoon baking soda

2 teaspoons baking powder
¼ teaspoon salt
½ teaspoon cloves
2 teaspoons ginger
1 cup warm water

Cream butter, add sugar, and beat about 2 minutes until light. Add beaten eggs slowly and beat mixture 2 minutes longer. Add molasses and blend well. Add all dry ingredients alternately with warm water, and blend until smooth. Pour into an 8 × 8 × 2-inch square pan that has been greased with 2 teaspoons shortening and floured. Bake in a 350° F. oven about 1 hour and 5 minutes. Decorate with whipped cream.

▶ NON-YEAST COFFEE CAKES ◀

Madelaine's Coffee Cake

Serves 8

2 whole eggs
1 cup granulated sugar
¼ cup butter or margarine, melted
2 cups sifted all-purpose flour
½ teaspoon salt

1½ teaspoons single-acting baking powder
½ cup milk
½ cup brown sugar
1 teaspoon cinnamon

Combine eggs, granulated sugar, and melted butter or margarine in a medium-size bowl. Beat 2 minutes until light and fluffy. Then add sifted dry ingredients alternately with milk, and mix only until batter is smooth. Pour into a greased and floured 8 × 8 × 2-inch or 9 × 9 × 2-inch square pan. Sprinkle brown sugar and cinnamon over top, and bake about 25 minutes at 375°. This is best served the day it is made.

Danish Cinnamon Coffee Cake

1 cup butter or margarine	¼ teaspoon salt
2 cups sifted granulated sugar	3 teaspoons double-acting baking powder
3 large whole eggs	3½ cups sifted cake flour
1 teaspoon vanilla	1½ cups cool milk
½ teaspoon almond extract	

Cream butter or margarine well with electric mixer for about 1 minute. Add sugar, a small amount at a time, and continue to beat until well blended. Now add eggs, 1 at a time, and beat each about 1 minute. Beat about 2 more minutes after all eggs have been added, until batter is fluffy, but not runny. Add flavorings. Now combine salt, baking powder, and flour, and sift together 2 or 3 times. Add dry ingredients, about ½ cup at a time, alternately with milk, about ¼ cup at a time, and beat until smooth. Pour batter into 9 × 13 × 2-inch pan greased with 1 tablespoon unsalted shortening and floured. Spread evenly, and sprinkle top of batter with Topping, a small amount at a time, starting from the outside to center. Bake cake in preheated 350° F. oven about 55 minutes, and test. If necessary bake a few minutes longer. Let cool, and cut right in pan into square or oblong pieces.

Topping for Danish Cinnamon Coffee Cake

½ cup sifted all-purpose flour	1 tablespoon cocoa
½ cup sifted granulated sugar	¼ cup cold, firm butter or margarine
1 tablespoon cinnamon	

Sift dry ingredients together 2 or 3 times. With pie blender cut in the ¼ cup of firm butter until it looks like very coarse meal.

▸ *Yeast Breads*

ROLLS, BREADS, COFFEE CAKES, DOUGHNUTS, AND PASTRIES

Yeast. Active yeast in compressed or dry form is a living plant especially suited to breadmaking. It is responsible for the fermentation action that produces the light porous grain and unusual texture of baked yeast products. One of the most important functions of yeast is that carbon dioxide gas is formed during the fermentation process, which causes yeast doughs and yeast batters to rise. This process results in light porous baked products and is partly responsible for their delicious flavor and aroma.

For those who bake at home, active dry yeast is fast replacing the old-style perishable compressed yeast, long sold in foil-wrapped cakes. Active dry yeast in airtight, moistureproof packages stays fresh for several months on any cool shelf and gives uniformly fine results until the expiration date on the package.

Active dry yeast can be used in place of compressed yeast in any recipe, when dissolving directions on the package are followed. The content of each package is measured to give baking action equal to a ⅔-ounce compressed yeastcake. Packaged dry yeast remains alive, actually respiring, all the time. This keeping quality is maintained by packaging the yeast in a nitrogen atmosphere in a moistureproof container. In this almost oxygen-free package the yeast remains in a resting stage until dissolved in warm water. Then the rehydrated dry yeast works the same as compressed yeast.

Perishable compressed yeast-cakes must be kept in the refrigerator, and for no longer than a week or two. Compressed yeast can be frozen but must be defrosted at room temperature and used immediately. To determine whether compressed yeast is usable, crumble it between the fingers. If it crumbles easily, even though there is slight browning at the edges due to drying, it is still good.

Research shows that in dissolving yeast, the best results are obtained when the water temperature is 95° F. to 110° F., with the ideal temperature near

95° F. for compressed yeast and near 110° F. for active dry yeast. In using active dry or compressed yeast, too much heat can kill the action of the yeast. Not enough heat, however, can retard its action. For best results dissolve active dry yeast in warm, not hot, water and compressed yeast in lukewarm water.

The manufacturers recommend two ways to use new improved dry yeast. We prefer the Traditional Method because of its simplicity and use it in our recipes throughout this book. Just dissolve by stirring yeast into the warm water (105°-115° F.) specified in recipe and combine with other ingredients. Or if you prefer, you can use the Rapidmix No Dissolve Method printed on their label.

Flour. Wheat flour is used for breadmaking because it contains a particular protein called gluten, which has unique physical properties. The gluten stretches to form an elastic framework capable of holding the bubbles of gas produced by the yeast. Without gluten you cannot make satisfactory yeast-raised breads. The amount and quality of gluten vary with different flours. The variety of wheat, where grown, and the milling process all influence the character of the flour and the amount and kind of gluten, which in turn influence the volume and texture of the yeast-raised products. Recipes using yeast usually specify approximate instead of exact amounts of flour and do not indicate an exact number of minutes for kneading the dough or beating the batter. The amount of flour required and the time and manipulation necessary are determined by the character of the flour, particularly its absorptive property and the amount and quality of gluten. For best results, follow recipe directions. But also learn to recognize good consistency in a mixture and proper kneading in a dough.

The flour used for breadmaking in the home is enriched all-purpose flour, sometimes called family flour. Other types of flour, such as cake flour and self-rising flour, are sometimes used but do not produce the same results. Rolled oats, bran, corn meal, and rye flour are sometimes used in combination with all-purpose wheat flour to make special breads and rolls.

Liquid. Milk and water are the liquids ordinarily used in making yeast breads. Occasionally other liquids such as fruit juices are added for special flavor. The milk may be whole, evaporated, or dry. When using whole milk to make yeast breads and rolls, it should be scalded to obtain best grain and texture. Whatever the liquid, it should be lukewarm when mixed with the dissolved yeast, because too much heat can make the yeast inactive.

Water is the best and fastest liquid medium for yeast rehydration. So for best results, use only water when dissolving active dry yeast. In a recipe using liquid other than water for dissolving the yeast, substitute ¼ cup warm, not hot, water for ¼ cup of the liquid in the recipe. Dissolve dry yeast in the water and then proceed with the recipe.

Bread and rolls made with water have a wheaty flavor and crisp crust, while those made with milk have a more velvety grain and a creamy-white crumb. Milk breads also keep better and make better toast.

Sugar and Salt. Yeast and sugar work together to form the carbon dioxide that causes the dough—or batter—to rise. Salt helps control this rate of rise. The right proportion of sugar and salt contributes to the flavor of the product, and, in addition, sugar helps give a golden-brown color to the crust.

The usual sugar is white granulated, but brown sugar, molasses, honey, and corn syrup are sometimes used, depending upon the type of product being made. Salt may be plain or iodized.

Shortening. Some type of fat or oil is included in nearly all yeast-raised products. It conditions the gluten, making a dough or batter that stretches easily as the bubbles of gas expand. Shortening also adds flavor and contributes to a tender crust and an attractive sheen.

Eggs. Eggs give extra flavor and richness and make the product more nutritious. They also help produce a fine and delicate texture and, like sugar, encourage a golden brown crust. Sometimes, before baking, a beaten-egg mixture is brushed on the surface of the rolls or bread to give them a golden sheen.

Other Ingredients. Spices and herbs, fruits, nuts, and other tasty ingredients are added for flavor, variety, and extra food value.

Utensils. Standard household measuring cups and measuring spoons are essential. Select a bowl big enough to allow room for easy mixing and fermentation, and a wooden mixing spoon that is comfortable to handle.

Ordinarily, a clean towel is used to cover the dough or batter—or the shaped bread or rolls—when they are set to rise. But you can cover them just as efficiently with wax paper, paper toweling, or even a plate for the bowl rise.

Method. The Straight Dough Method is the one commonly used and with which you may be most familiar. The mixing is done in continuous operation as outlined in our recipes. The time it takes a dough to rise by the Straight Dough Method is affected by the amount of yeast. More yeast (as specified in recipes) produces an Action-Quick Dough and speeds up the rising time.

Freezing. Unbaked doughs in this section cannot be held in the freezer, unless indicated, as in our Danish Pastry Coffee Cakes which can be frozen 1 week only.

You may obtain especially developed recipes for freezing from The Standard Brands, Inc. (manufacturers of Fleischmans Yeast) New York, N.Y. 10022.

▶ ROLLS ◀

Basic Recipe for Yeast Raised Rolls

¾ cup scalded milk or hot water
2 tablespoons granulated sugar
⅓ cup soft butter or margarine
About 2 teaspoons salt
2 large whole eggs, beaten about ½
    minute

1 package dry yeast combined with ¼
    cup warm water, not hot (about
    110°-115° F.). For a faster rising
    dough use 2 packages yeast com-
    bined with ½ cup warm water
    and *reduce milk to ½ cup.*
About 4½ cups sifted all-purpose flour

In a small saucepan scald milk or use hot water. Add sugar, shortening, and salt. Let stand until completely melted over low heat. Add well-beaten eggs slowly, and when liquid is lukewarm add the dissolved yeast. Stir in the sifted flour, about a cupful at a time. When dough is of medium consistency, beat it until smooth, then add rest of flour, and beat well after each addition. When dough is too stiff to beat, turn it out onto a floured pastry cloth and knead it for about 5 or 6 minutes, or until smooth, adding only enough more flour to prevent dough from adhering to hands. Keep dough as soft as possible. Place it into a greased 7-inch bowl. Brush top with melted fat, cover with wax paper and a towel. Set in a warm place away from drafts. Most desirable temperature is 80° to 85° F. Allow dough to double in size. When you think the dough looks twice as large as it was at first, press the tip of one finger lightly and quickly about ½ inch into top of the dough. If the dent stays, the dough is light enough to be called double in bulk. If the dough springs back let it stand another 15 minutes and test it again. This will take anywhere from 40 to 60 minutes, *depending on temperature of room, temperature of ingredients, and amount of yeast used.* During cold, damp days or if your kitchen is cooler than 80° F., place the bowl with dough in a pan of lukewarm water, about 100° F., not hot, and replace water if it cools.

When dough has doubled in size, turn it out onto a lightly floured pastry cloth, roll, cut, or shape as desired. Allow shaped rolls to stand in a warm room from 15 to 60 minutes, before baking. Parker House Rolls are sometimes ready to be baked within 15 minutes after they are shaped, if the kitchen is warmer than 80° F. and if you use extra yeast, and seldom more than 40 minutes. During cool weather other rolls may take as long as 60 minutes to become light.

In preparing more than 1 recipe at a time, it is better not to use more than 1½ packages of yeast for each recipe and in this case it is important to work as quickly as possible when rolling and shaping rolls, and to store in refrigerator the portion of dough that is not being shaped. This will prevent overfermentation. Many failures are caused by overlight yeast dough.

Refrigerated Yeast Roll Dough. Double the amount of sugar and increase salt by ½ teaspoon in basic dough recipe. After scalding the milk, combine it with the sugar, shortening, and salt. Allow this to stand until absolutely cold before adding the beaten eggs, yeast, and flour. As soon as dough is kneaded, place it in a cold greased 8-inch bowl, cover tightly and store in coldest part of refrigerator to retard fermentation. (This is necessary to preserve life of yeast and flavor of dough.) The next day, remove all or part of dough from refrigerator and shape as desired. Let rise in warm place, about 85° F., until light, about 1½ to 2 hours, depending on temperature of room. It is better to use dough after 24 hours. If it must stand longer, punch it down each day but do not keep for more than 3 days. Do not freeze dough.

How to Reheat Rolls. As soon as rolls are cool, they should be stored in a tight container to prevent drying out. If more than a day old, sprinkle or brush them with a little warm water, place on baking sheet, and reheat at 425° F. for about 7 to 15 minutes, depending on size of rolls and quantity. Test one after 7 minutes and if not soft and hot, let remain in oven until ready.

Parker House Rolls

After basic dough has doubled in size turn it out onto a lightly floured pastry cloth. With covered rolling pin, pat and roll dough to ½ inch in thickness if using a 2-inch cutter, a little thicker if using a larger cutter. Let rolled dough stand about 3 minutes, then cut through with a 2-inch round cutter. With back of dinner knife, crease through center of each, pick up, turning floured side up. Brush ½ of floured side very lightly with melted butter or margarine; pull roll to elongate it slightly and fold over, pinching center of edges well together. Place rolls about ¼ inch apart on a lightly greased baking sheet. Brush tops with melted butter or margarine and allow to stand in a warm place, away from drafts, about 15 minutes during *very* warm weather, or about 30 to 40 minutes if temperature in kitchen is cooler than 80° F. Bake in a 400°-425° F. preheated oven for about 10 to 15 minutes, or until lightly browned, but not too dark and dry. Knead scraps of leftover Parker House dough together gently for a few seconds, cover and let ripen about 15 minutes, then shape into old-fashioned rolls, or other rolls listed below.

Cloverleaf or Twin Rolls

After basic dough has doubled in size, with both hands, starting in center, form a uniform long roll. Quickly cut the roll into uniform pieces. Dip fingers in flour and form rounds. Place 2 or 3 balls together into greased sections of muffin pans, having them ¾ filled. Brush tops lightly with melted butter or margarine, and let stand until very light, about 40 to 60 minutes. Then bake in preheated 400° F. oven about 12 to 15 minutes.

Old-Fashioned Rolls

Cut dough into uniform pieces, same as for Cloverleaf and Twin Rolls. Form balls and place them in a greased shallow pan, about ¼ to ½ inch apart. Brush tops with melted butter or margarine, let rise in warm place until very light, about 30 to 60 minutes, then bake in preheated 400° F. oven about 20 to 25 minutes, or until brown. These Old-Fashioned Rolls are very moist and delicious.

Braided Rolls

Follow rolling and cutting directions as for Cloverleaf Rolls; form 3 strands for each braid. Pinch ends well and form braids. Pinch opposite ends when braid is completed. Let stand about 3 minutes, then brush them with egg yolk combined with 2 teaspoons milk or water and sprinkle with poppy or other seed and a little coarse salt if desired. Let stand about 15 more minutes or longer, if necessary. Bake at 400° F. for about 12 to 15 minutes. For crusty rolls, place them at least 2 inches apart, reduce heat to 300° F. and bake about 10 minutes longer.

Knotted Rolls

Follow general rolling and baking directions as for Braided Rolls. Form single strands, and tie into loose knots. Place about 1 or 2 inches apart on lightly greased baking sheet. Bake 12 to 15 minutes. For sweet rolls, drizzle with Coffee Cake Icing (page 510), and chopped pecans.

Butterhorn Dinner or Luncheon Rolls

Makes about 16 rolls

Use Basic Yeast Dough for Pecan Rolls (page 521). For medium-size rolls, cut 1 recipe of dough into 2 pieces. Form each in round patty. Roll pieces into 10-inch circles and let stand several minutes before cutting. Brush with melted butter and cut into 8 sections as you do a pie. Roll carefully from large end to opposite point. Curve each roll into a crescent shape. Place on lightly greased pan or silicone paper with open end down. Let rise about 30 minutes, then brush with beaten yolk combined with 2 teaspoons milk, and sprinkle with poppyseed or caraway seed if desired. Let rise about 10 more minutes, then bake in 425° F. oven about 12 to 15 minutes.

Corn-Meal Yeast Pan Rolls

Serves 8

¾ cup scalded milk	age compressed yeast and 1
¼ cup shortening	tablespoons granulated sugar,
2 tablespoons granulated sugar	combined with ¼ cup warm
2 teaspoons salt	water (about 110° F.)
1 well-beaten egg	¾ cup yellow or white corn meal
1 package dry yeast, or 1 small pack-	2½ cups sifted all-purpose flour

Pour scalded milk over shortening. Add sugar, salt, and beaten egg. When lukewarm, add dissolved yeast. Combine corn meal with flour and sift together several times. Add it to liquid, about 1 cup at a time, and beat after each addition until smooth. When dough is stiff, turn it out onto a well-floured pastry cloth and knead gently several minutes, adding additional flour if dough is sticky. Keep dough as soft as possible. Place in a greased bowl, brush top with melted shortening, cover, and let double in size. Punch down, and shape into a uniform long roll. Cut into 16 uniform pieces. Shape in balls, and place them in a well-greased 10-inch layer-cake pan, leaving about ½ inch spaces between them. Brush tops well with melted butter. Let stand about 30 to 40 minutes, or until very light. Bake in a preheated 400° F. oven about 25 to 30 minutes, or until golden brown but not too dark.

These rolls are more delicious if served warm. They may be baked a day or two in advance and reheated in a 400° F. oven about 7 or 8 minutes.

French Brioches

4 cups sifted all-purpose flour	¼ teaspoon salt
½ cup granulated sugar	2 packages dry yeast, combined with
5 large or 6 medium-size eggs	½ cup warm water (110° F. to
⅔ cup soft butter	115° F.)

Make a well in center of flour and add other ingredients, 1 at a time, mixing dough with hands. If dough appears too heavy, add more egg. It should be of medium consistency. Knead dough several minutes. Place it in a bowl, cover well, and refrigerate at least 10 hours. When ready to bake, remove from refrigerator, shape ⅔ of dough into medium-size balls and ⅓ into very small balls. Place large balls in well-greased brioche molds (muffin pans may be used). Make a deep gash in center of each ball, and place small ball partly in opening. Let rise until medium-light. Brush with beaten whole egg that has been combined with ¼ teaspoon salt. Salt will liquefy egg, making it easy to spread. Let balls stand longer, or until little more than double in size. Then bake them at 375° F. until brown, about 12 minutes for small, and 15 to 18 minutes for large, depending on size.

It is better not to have brioche molds more than ⅓ filled before dough begins to rise. When dough rises almost to top of molds, bake as suggested.

Quick French Brioche Rolls

Makes about 12 large or 20 medium rolls

½ cup butter or margarine
½ cup scalded milk
2 medium whole eggs and 2 egg yolks
¼ cup granulated sugar
½ teaspoon salt

1 package dry yeast, combined with ¼ cup warm water (110° F. to 115° F.)
About 1⅓ cups sifted all-purpose flour and 1⅓ cups sifted cake flour (sifted together)

Add butter to scalded milk and let stand over low heat until completely melted. Pour all of eggs into an 8-inch bowl and with electric or egg beater beat them for about ½ minute. Add the sugar and salt and beat until well blended. Now pour the melted butter and milk *slowly* over the egg mixture. Let stand until lukewarm, and add dissolved yeast. Last add the flour, about ½ cupful at a time, and beat batter for at least 1 minute after all the flour has been added, forming a smooth loose batter, not too thin and not too thick (should fall in *soft* gobs from spoon). Cover bowl and place it into a pan of warm water (about 110° F.) for 30 to 40 minutes, or until batter appears puffy. Now beat batter for a minute, and with large pointed spoon pour it into well-greased (use unsalted shortening) medium or large muffin pans, having them ½ filled. Let stand in a warm place for about 1 hour, or until they are slightly above top.

Bake in preheated (preheat oven about 15 minutes in advance) 375° F. oven about 12 minutes for medium and 15 minutes for large, or until brown. When done, remove from oven, loosen around edges, and turn out onto cake cooler.

These rolls may be served plain, or they may be iced with Coffee Cake Icing (page 510) and sprinkled with chopped pecans. They are always more delectable reheated in a 350° F. oven for about 7 or 8 minutes before serving.

Use little extra flour for double recipe.

Kneaded Brioche Luncheon or Dinner Rolls

Increase salt in Quick French Brioche Rolls recipe (above) to about 1½ teaspoons and flour to about 3½ cups total. Add enough flour to form a very stiff dough in bowl, and turn it out onto floured pastry cloth and knead until smooth for several minutes, adding flour to prevent stickiness. Place in greased bowl, brush top with melted butter and let stand until doubled in size. Turn out onto floured pastry cloth and shape into parkerhouse, knotted, or cloverleaf rolls. Brush with melted butter or egg glaze and let stand until light, for about 30 to 45 minutes, then bake at 375° F. for about 12 to 15 minutes. Reheat at 350° F. about 7 or 8 minutes before serving.

Flaky Croissant Luncheon or Dinner Rolls

Makes about 24 medium-size rolls

Dough No. 1

1 cup butter (half margarine may be used), cold and firm, but not hard   1 cup sifted all-purpose flour

With pastry blender cut shortening into flour until it looks pasty. Turn it out onto a floured pastry cloth and knead gently for a few seconds. Shape it into a square about 5 × 5 inches. Wrap well in wax paper and refrigerate until ready to be used. It is better not to keep it in coldest part of refrigerator. Should not be too stiff when combining it with Dough No. 2.

Dough No. 2

1 package dry yeast, combined with ¼ cup warm water (about 110° F.)

½ cup scalded milk, then let it stand until lukewarm

1 whole egg and 2 yolks, beaten for about ½ minute with hand beater

2 tablespoons granulated sugar (can increase sugar to ⅓ cup for Coffee Cakes, page 515)

1 teaspoon salt

About 2½ cups sifted all-purpose flour, or enough to form a soft dough that does not stick to hand when kneading

Combine dissolved yeast, lukewarm milk, beaten eggs, sugar, salt and last add flour a little at a time. Beat until smooth when dough is of medium consistency. When too stiff to beat with spoon, turn dough out onto a floured pastry cloth and knead gently for several minutes, adding little more flour as necessary. Place dough in buttered 5-inch bowl, brush top with melted butter, cover with wax paper and let rise in room temperature until double.

When double in size, turn it out onto pastry cloth and knead it again for about ½ minute. Place again in greased bowl, brush top with melted butter, cover and let double in size second time.

After second rising, turn dough out onto floured pastry cloth and roll it to measure about 6 × 18 inches. Place Dough No. 1 in center, and turn ends of Dough No. 2 over to enclose No. 1. Roll dough to about 12 × 18 inches, fold again, and roll once more to measure about 12 × 18 inches. Fold over, wrap it in wax paper and keep in refrigerator for about 30 minutes. After 30 minutes give dough 1 more rolling to about 12 × 18 inches, fold over, wrap and refrigerate for about 1 hour. If dough must be kept longer, place it under freezing compartment to prevent over-fermentation. Best to use it within 1 hour especially during warm weather.

To Bake. After 1 hour, or when ready to be baked, remove dough from refrigerator, cut it into 4 uniform pieces. Roll each piece to measure about 6 × 18 inches, and cut it into about 6 (or more) wedges. Roll each from large end, and form croissants. Place them on ungreased baking sheet with open end down. Brush with melted butter, let rise in room temperature (do not force near heat) about 1 to 1½ hours, depending on temperature of room, and on size and thickness of rolls, but watch closely. When light, bake at 375° F. for about 20 minutes, or until delicately brown and crisp. These rolls require very close watching toward end to prevent burning.

To Reheat. These rolls are flakier reheated, and may be prepared several days in advance. Store them covered in refrigerator or a cool room. May be frozen. To reheat place them in a 350° F. oven on baking sheet for about 7 or 8 minutes or longer, depending on size. Serve at once.

English Muffins

Makes about 12 very large muffins

1 package dry yeast, combined with ¼ cup warm water (about 110° F.)
½ cup lukewarm milk and ½ cup lukewarm water (scald milk and let cool to warm)
3 tablespoons melted shortening

1½ teaspoons salt
1 tablespoon sugar
1 large whole egg, beaten about ½ minute
About 3½ cups white corn meal or more, sifted all-purpose flour to form soft dough

Dissolve yeast. Add it to lukewarm milk and water, then add all other ingredients, forming a medium dough. Turn out onto a well-floured pastry cloth and knead several minutes until smooth, adding little more flour if necessary. Place in greased bowl, brush top with melted fat, cover and let stand until doubled in size. When doubled, roll to ¼ inch in thickness, not thicker. Let stand about 5 minutes, then with a 3½- or 4-inch cutter, cut through dough. Reknead scraps of dough gently, let rest about 20 minutes, then roll and cut.

Place cut muffins on a baking sheet that has been well covered with white corn meal. Sprinkle more corn meal lightly on top. Let rise for about 30 minutes. Pick up carefully with a pancake turner and bake on an ungreased griddle pan or in heavy skillet over low heat about 7 or 8 minutes on each side. These muffins are very delicious and may be served in many ways.

Bagels

Makes 12 very large

1 package dry yeast, combined with ¼ cup warm water (stir and let stand until dissolved)
1 cup lukewarm water or milk
1 large whole egg, or 2 yolks
¼ cup, or little less, granulated sugar

3 teaspoons salt
¼ cup melted butter or margarine
About 5½ cups sifted all-purpose flour, or enough to form a medium dough that does not stick to hands during kneading process

In a 9- or 10-inch bowl combine all ingredients except flour. Stir, and add flour, about 1 cupful at a time, and beat well. When dough becomes too heavy to mix with spoon, turn it out onto floured pastry cloth and knead well for several minutes, adding more flour if dough sticks to hands. Place smooth kneaded dough in a 7-inch greased bowl, brush top with melted fat, cover and let rise until double in bulk.

When dough has doubled in size, scrape off flour from pastry cloth, turn out onto cloth and knead it for about 1 minute. Now let it rise again for about 20 minutes. After second rising, cut dough into 12 uniform pieces, and roll each piece on *unfloured* pastry cloth into pencil-like strips that measure about 10 inches long, having ends *very* slightly tapered. Dip finger in water and wet 1 inch of one end and form rings, overlapping ends 1 inch. Press ends together *very* well to prevent opening.

Now place bagels on a dry unfloured dish towel, and let rise in room temperature 10 minutes during warm weather, and 15 minutes during cold weather. Meanwhile, bring water to boiling point in a large 10- or 12-inch skillet. After bagels have risen for 10 or 15 minutes, pick each up carefully with fingers of both hands and lower gently into boiling water. A large skillet will hold 6 bagels at one time. Let simmer (not boil) 1 minute, then with a fork carefully turn them over and simmer second side 1 minute. With a flat perforated pancake turner or flat ladle, lift bagels out of water, let drain well, and turn them over (having wetter side up) onto a double-thick dish towel to absorb surplus moisture. (This will prevent them from sticking to pan during baking process.) They can remain on towels until all are cooked in water, but must be baked as soon as possible. Preheat oven right after bagels are shaped.

To Bake. Pick bagels up carefully with fingers of both hands, and place them on a 12 × 18 baking sheet that has been well greased with 1 tablespoon or more unsalted shortening. Bake at 375° F. about 30 minutes, or until brown and crisp. Brush them with warm water every 10 minutes to impart glaze.

For a very crusty bagel, allow them to remain in oven with heat shut off and oven door partially open for about 20 more minutes.

To Reheat Bagels. If more than 2 days old, it is better to dip bagels into warm water. Place on cake rack with baking sheet underneath, and re-heat at 350° F. about 10 minutes, or 15 minutes for a crispier crust.

Toasted Bagels. Split bagels in halves. Place in toaster until brown and crisp. Spread with butter. Very delicious.

Poppy Seed or Caraway Bagels

Prepare bagels as in basic recipe. Brush bagels with egg yolk diluted with 1 tablespoon water, sprinkle with seed before placing them into oven.

Hot Cross Buns

Makes 20 buns

Kuchen Dough for Hot Cross Buns

¾ cup scalded milk
⅓ cup very soft butter or shortening
¼ cup granulated sugar, sifted
1 teaspoon salt
2 whole eggs, well beaten
½ teaspoon vanilla
1 package dry yeast, dissolved in ¼

cup *warm* water (110° to 115° F.)
¾ teaspoon cinnamon
⅛ teaspoon allspice
About 3½ cups sifted all-purpose flour
¾ cup currants, simmered and drained

Pour scalded milk over butter, sugar, and salt. When completely melted, add well-beaten eggs slowly and vanilla. When liquid is lukewarm, add dissolved yeast. Blend well. Add cinnamon and allspice to flour. Add about ½ of flour to liquid slowly, beating dough until smooth. Now add currants gradually and blend well. Add rest of flour, and beat until dough is smooth and too stiff to mix with spoon.

Turn dough out onto a floured cloth and knead gently 2 or 3 minutes, adding only enough more flour to manipulate dough, using very little pressure. Place kneaded dough in well-greased No. 7 bowl, cover, and let stand in a warm room until dough has doubled in size. When dough has doubled in size, turn out onto floured cloth and knead again about ½ minute. Place again into greased bowl, cover, and let double in size a second time. After second rising, turn dough out onto a floured cloth and cut dough into halves, each half into quarters, and each quarter into 5 pieces, which will yield 20 Hot Cross Buns. Shape into round buns with hands.

Use a 10 × 14 greased baking sheet. Place 5 rows of 4 buns on greased baking sheet, and with scissors cut a small cross on the top of each bun. Let rise until double in size (about 45 minutes). Bake in a preheated 350° F. oven about 20 to 25 minutes. After buns are at room temperature, make crosses with Coffee Cake Icing (page 510), using a pastry bag and No. 6 or No. 8 tube, or pour from teaspoon.

▶ BREADS ◀

Plain White Bread

1 package active dry yeast, combined with ¼ cup warm water (110° F. to 115° F.) not hot; for faster rising dough, use 2 packages dry yeast and ½ cup warm water and reduce milk to 1 cup
1¼ cups scalded milk, or hot water (half milk and half water may be used)

2 tablespoons shortening
1 tablespoon granulated sugar
About 2½ teaspoons salt
4¼ cups, more or less, sifted all-purpose flour
Melted shortening, or beaten egg combined with 1 tablespoon milk

Combine dry yeast with the warm water, stir and let stand at least 5 minutes, or until completely dissolved. Pour scalded milk or hot water over the shortening, granulated sugar, and salt. When liquid is lukewarm (between 85° and 98° F.) add dissolved yeast, then the flour, about 1 cupful at a time beating well after 3 cups of flour have been added, until batter is smooth. Continue to add and beat rest of flour. When dough begins to leave sides of bowl and is too stiff to mix with spoon, turn it out onto a floured pastry cloth and knead it well for 5 or 6 minutes, adding more flour as needed to prevent dough from sticking to hands and pastry cloth. Place dough in a 6- or 7-inch greased bowl, brush top with melted shortening, cover and let stand in a warm place until it doubles in size— 40 to 60 minutes or longer, depending on temperature of room.

When doubled in size, turn it out onto *very* lightly floured pastry cloth and knead again about 2 minutes. It may *now* be shaped to fit greased bread pan that measures about 9 × 4¾ × 2¾, *or better it may be allowed to double again a second time, then kneaded for about 1 minute,* and shaped to fit bread pan. Brush top of loaf with melted shortening, or beaten egg combined with 1 tablespoon milk. Let rise until a little more than double, or until sides of dough reach top of pan and center is well rounded. Bake in preheated 400° F. oven 30 minutes, then reduce heat to 350° F. and bake about 30 more minutes, or until bread is brown. Cover loosely with foil toward end if it is browning too rapidly. Reduce time by 15 minutes for 2 smaller loaves.

Bohemian Rye Bread

1 package active dry yeast, combined with ¼ cup warm water (110° F.), not hot, or 2 packages yeast combined with ½ cup warm water; only ½ cup buttermilk
¾ cup boiling water
2 tablespoons shortening
1 tablespoon salt, or less

1 tablespoon caraway seed
1 tablespoon sugar
¾ cup cool buttermilk or scalded homogenized milk
About 5 cups sifted Bohemian rye and wheat flour, or 2 cups unsifted whole rye flour, combined with 3 cups sifted all-purpose flour

Combine dry yeast with warm water, stir and let stand about 5 minutes, until completely dissolved. Pour boiling water over shortening, salt, caraway seed and sugar. Very slowly add the milk. When liquid is *lukewarm*, add the dissolved yeast. Add the sifted Bohemian rye and wheat flour, or if preferred add 2 cups of unsifted whole rye flour combined well with about 3 cups of sifted all-purpose flour. Beat batter well after each addition of flour until dough is smooth. When dough is too heavy to mix with spoon, turn it out onto well-floured pastry cloth and knead about 5 or 6 minutes, adding rest of flour as needed.

Doughs prepared with rye flour are sticky. Do not add any more flour than necessary. Place kneaded dough in greased 7-inch bowl, brush top with melted shortening, cover and let double in size. Turn out onto lightly floured pastry colth and knead again about 2 minutes. It may now be shaped to fit greased bread pan that measures about 9 × 4¾ × 2¾ inches or little larger, or better it may be allowed *to double a second time*, then kneaded about 1 minute and shaped to fit bread pan. Brush top of loaf with melted shortening, cover and let rise until a little more than double, or until sides of dough reach top of pan and center is well rounded. Bake in preheated 400° F. oven 30 minutes, then reduce heat to 350° F. and bake about 30 more minutes, or until bread is brown. Cover with foil toward end. Reduce baking time by 15 minutes for 2 smaller loaves.

When breads are done, immediately remove from pans, and place on cake cooling racks.

French Bread (Home-Style)

1 package dry yeast, combined with ¼ cup warm water (110° F. to 115° F.)
About 3 teaspoons salt, or less
2 tablespoons granulated sugar
1½ tablespoons melted shortening
¾ cup scalded milk

¾ cup water
About 5 cups sifted all-purpose flour
⅓ cup egg whites, beaten until they just cling to bowl
Melted shortening
White corn meal

Combine dissolved yeast, salt, sugar, melted shortening, milk, and water in a medium-size bowl. Add 3 cups of flour, a little at a time, and beat until smooth. Now add beaten egg whites and blend well. Add rest of flour, a little at a time, and beat until smooth. When dough is too stiff to beat, turn it out onto a floured pastry cloth and knead gently about 2 minutes, adding only enough more flour to prevent excessive sticking, *keeping dough as soft as possible*. Place in a greased bowl, brush top with melted shortening, cover, and let rise until doubled. This will take about 45 minutes to 1 hour. After it rises the first time, knead it again for about ½ minute. Place it again in greased bowl and let double—about 30 minutes. After second rising, turn dough out onto a floured pastry cloth and divide it into 3 uniform pieces. Roll each piece into a rectangle that measures about 8 × 16 inches, and shape it like a jelly roll, pinch ends well. Place it with open end down on a 12 × 18-inch baking sheet that has been thickly sprinkled with white corn meal from a shaker. Place all 3 loaves on 1 baking sheet, leaving equal spaces between them.

With a sharp knife make diagonal cuts on tops of loaves, about ⅛ inch deep, spacing them 2 inches apart. Let loaves stand in room temperature about 1 to 1½ hours. Do not force near heat. (When cuts in bread are almost flat, bread is ready to be baked.) Bake at 325° F. about 1 hour and 15 minutes. After 1 hour, look at bread, and if it is brown, shut off heat and allow it to remain in oven a few minutes longer to make crust more crisp.

After 30 minutes, loaves may be brushed several times during baking time with slightly beaten egg white combined with 1 teaspoon water. This will impart an attractive glaze to loaves, but is not necessary.

To recrisp French Bread after it has been stored in a covered container, reheat it about 10 minutes in a 400° F. oven.

Raisin Cinnamon Bread

1 package active dry yeast, combined with ¼ cup warm water (110° F.), not hot, or 2 packages yeast and ½ cup warm water; only ½ cup milk

¾ cup scalded milk

3 tablespoons shortening

⅓ cup granulated sugar

1 teaspoon salt

1 large whole egg or 2 yolks, beaten a few seconds with egg beater

About 3¾ cups sifted all-purpose flour

1 cup raisins, simmered several minutes, drained, and sprinkled with flour

Melted shortening

1 egg, well beaten

1 tablespoon cocoa

1 teaspoon cinnamon

2 tablespoons granulated sugar

Combine dry yeast with the warm water, stir and let stand at least 5 minutes or until completely dissolved. Pour scalded milk over the shortening, sugar, and salt. When melted, add the beaten egg and when lukewarm add the dissolved yeast. Then gradually add about ¾ of the flour and beat batter until it is smooth. Add the raisins, a few at a time, mixing well. Add rest of flour and beat until well blended. Turn out onto very lightly floured pastry cloth and knead 5 or 6 minutes, adding more flour as needed to prevent dough from sticking to pastry cloth and hands. Place in greased 7-inch bowl, brush top with melted shortening, cover and let rise until double. (It will take longer for this rich dough to rise than the plain bread.)

When doubled in size, turn out onto pastry cloth and knead again about 2 minutes. *Place in bowl and let rise second time.* After second rising, roll dough to measure about 8 × 18 inches. Brush entire surface with part of well-beaten whole egg and sprinkle with about 1 tablespoon cocoa, 1 teaspoon cinnamon, combined with 2 tablespoons granulated sugar. Roll like jelly roll, and place it in greased pan that measures about 9 × 4¾ × 2¾ (No. 11) inches, open end down. Cover and let stand in warm place until slightly more than double, or until sides of dough reach top of pan and center is well rounded. (Will take about 1 hour, more or less.)

Bake in a preheated 400° F. oven 30 minutes, then reduce heat to 350° F. and bake about 30 more minutes, or until brown. Cover loosely with foil toward end if it is browning too rapidly.

Whole Wheat Bread

1½ cups scalded milk, or half milk and
    half water
1 tablespoon salt, or less
2 tablespoons brown sugar or honey
¼ cup, or less, shortening

1 package dry yeast, combined with
    ¼ cup warm water (110° F. to
    115° F.)
2 cups unsifted whole-wheat flour
2 cups sifted white all-purpose flour

Pour hot liquid over salt, brown sugar or honey, and shortening. When it is lukewarm, add yeast combined with water. Combine dark and white flours and mix well. Add gradually to liquid, beating after each addition. When it is too stiff to beat with a wooden spoon, turn out onto a covered board and knead about 5 minutes, adding enough flour to form medium dough. Place in a well-greased bowl. Brush top with melted fat and allow to rise until double. Turn out onto board and knead again about 3 minutes. Place in a greased bowl, brush top with melted fat, and allow to rise again until double. Shape dough to fit a medium-size well-greased pan. Brush top of loaf with melted butter or shortening, and allow to rise until about double. Bake at 400° F. 50 to 60 minutes. Lower heat during last part of baking time if bread is becoming too brown.

Whole-wheat flour may be increased in this recipe. In this case reduce white flour.

▶ COFFEE CAKES ◀

Kuchen Dough

Foundation dough for yeast-raised coffee cakes

⅓ cup scalded milk

¼ cup very soft butter or margarine

¼ cup granulated sugar (a little more sugar may be used)

½ teaspoon salt (if using unsalted shortening increase salt to 1 teaspoon)

2 large whole eggs, well beaten with egg beater about ½ minute

½ teaspoon vanilla

Several drops yellow food coloring if eggs are light in color

1 package dry yeast, combined with ¼ cup warm water (about 110° F.), not hot (stir well, and let stand about 5 minutes)

About 2½ cups sifted all-purpose flour, or enough to prevent dough from adhering to hands

Pour scalded milk over butter or margarine, sugar, and salt. When melted, add well-beaten eggs slowly, then vanilla. When liquid is lukewarm add dissolved yeast. Mix well, and add flour gradually, beating until dough is smooth and too stiff to mix with spoon. After beating in flour, turn dough out onto a floured pastry cloth and knead several minutes, adding only enough more flour to manipulate dough. Place kneaded dough in well-greased 7-inch bowl, brush with melted fat, cover with wax paper and towel and let stand in a warm place (best temperature is about 85° F.), *or place bowl in pan of lukewarm water*, about 100° F. if your kitchen is cooler than 80° F. When dough has doubled in size, turn it out onto very *lightly floured* pastry cloth and knead again about 1 minute. Place into greased bowl, cover, and let again double in size. *After second rising*, turn dough out onto lightly floured pastry cloth and shape as desired.

Very Important. Do not permit dough to become overlight after the second kneading. As soon as dough has doubled in bulk the second time, roll, fill, and shape as desired. Allow shaped coffee cake to stand in warm room, about 80° to 85° F., for 40 to 60 minutes, or until light, depending on temperature of room.

Note. During extremely cold weather 2 packages of yeast combined with ½ cup warm water may be used in each recipe, and milk reduced to 2 tablespoons. It is seldom necessary, however, to use more than 1 package yeast if your kitchen is warm.

In preparing more than 1 recipe at a time, it is important to work as quickly as possible when rolling and shaping coffee cakes, and to store in refrigerator the portion of dough that is not being shaped. This will prevent overfermentation. Many failures are caused by overlight doughs.

Refrigerated Coffee Cake Doughs

Prepare Kuchen Dough (page 508). After combining scalded milk, butter or margarine, and beaten eggs, allow liquids to stand in refrigerator until cold, about 70° F. Then add dissolved yeast and flour. Knead until smooth for several minutes. Place at once in a chilled greased bowl, cover and store in coldest part of refrigerator. Next day, turn dough out onto a lightly floured pastry cloth, and knead about 2 or 3 minutes. Place in a warm greased bowl and let stand until it doubles in size, about 1½ hours. Roll and shape as desired. Let stand until light before baking.

Coffee Cake Braid

For 2 braids, divide full recipe Kuchen Dough (page 508) into 6 uniform pieces. On very lightly floured pastry cloth, roll each piece into a 16-inch strand, giving a slight twist. Place 3 strands together and form a braid. Pinch ends well so that they do not open in baking, and place on greased sheet or silicone paper. Brush cakes with melted butter or margarine, and let stand about 1 hour; then bake about 25 minutes in a 350° F. oven. If using Pineapple Filling, with teaspoon fill open space after baking 25 minutes, and finish baking for about 5 more mintues. Glaze and ice with Coffee Cake Icing (page 510).

Pineapple Filling

Cook together until thick ½ cup crushed pineapple and juice, 2 teaspoons cornstarch dissolved in 1 tablespoon cold water, 2 tablespoons granulated sugar, pinch of salt. This filling is sufficient for 2 medium Coffee Cake Braids, or use prepared pineapple filling in cans.

Filled Walnut or Pecan Coffee Cake

1 recipe Kuchen Dough (page 508)
1 large whole egg, well beaten with fork
1½ cups walnuts or pecans, chopped medium or fine
About 3 tablespoons cream or milk
½ teaspoon vanilla
1 cup sifted confectioners' sugar
About ¼ cup cake or cookie crumbs or extra nuts (if filling is too soft)
Melted butter or margarine

Pat and roll full recipe Kuchen Dough into a rectangle about 8 × 20 inches. (If using ½ recipe roll 6 × 12 inches, and use 9-inch round pan.) Brush entire surface with part of a well-beaten egg.

In a small bowl combine walnuts or pecans, rest of egg, cream or milk, vanilla, and confectioners' sugar to form proper consistency. If preparation appears too soft, add cake or cookie crumbs or extra nuts. If too thick, add little extra milk. (If using ½ recipe of Kuchen Dough, use only ½ recipe of filling.)

With a fork spread this preparation on dough. To prevent leakage while baking, leave about 1 inch of dough on all sides free of filling. Roll, not too tightly and not too loosely, from wide end like a jelly roll. Press ends well and place cake on greased baking sheet or better silicone paper, with open end down. Brush top with melted butter or margarine and allow to stand in warm room until light, about 1 hour. Bake at 350° F. about 30 minutes, or until brown. When done, remove from baking sheet and when cool brush with lukewarm white corn syrup, if desired, then cover with Coffee Cake Icing and sprinkle with nutmeats.

Coffee Cake Icing

Combine 1 tablespoon hot milk or water, ¼ teaspoon vanilla, and about 1 cup sifted confectioners' sugar. If it is too thin, add more sugar. If too thick, add more liquid.

Swedish Tea Ring

1 recipe Kuchen Dough (page 508)
1 large whole egg, well beaten with fork
1 tablespoon milk
½ cup brown sugar, solidly packed
1 cup pecans, chopped medium or fine

1 cup raisins, simmered several minutes, drained and dried on towel (or you can use cut-up dates or Holiday Fruit Mix)
¼ cup cake or cookie crumbs or extra nuts (if filling is too soft)
Melted butter or margarine

Pat and roll full recipe Kuchen Dough into a rectangle about 8 × 20 inches if using a 12-inch pan; roll 6 × 16 inches for 9-inch pan, keeping corners square and use ½ recipe of filling. Brush with part of beaten egg. In bowl combine rest of egg, milk, brown sugar, nuts and raisins. If filling appears too soft, add cake or cookie crumbs or extra nuts. Other fillings may be used instead. With fork, spread filling to cover small ends but leave 1 inch uncovered on wide ends.

Roll like jelly roll. Bring ends together, forming a ring, and lift gently onto 12-inch round pan that has been thickly greased with 1 tablespoon soft unsalted shortening, keeping open end down, or better on silicone paper. With sharp knife or scissors cut through, spacing cuts about 1½ inches apart and turn each division upward to show filling. Press each point down. Brush with melted butter or margarine and allow to rise until light, about 1 hour. Bake in a 350° F. oven 30 minutes. When done, loosen sides *at once*. Place wax paper and rack over cake and invert, shaking pan slightly. Glaze and ice with Coffee Cake Icing (above).

Buttercream Filled Coffee Cake Loaf

1 full recipe Kuchen Dough (page 508)
½ cup cold firm butter or margarine
1 cup sifted confectioners' sugar

1 teaspoon vanilla
½ cup, or less, pecans, finely chopped
A little cinnamon (optional)
Melted butter or margarine

Prepare full recipe Kuchen Dough. In a 7-inch bowl, with electric mixer, beat the ½ cup of cold firm butter or margarine for several minutes. Add sifted confectioners' sugar and continue to beat for several more minutes, or until it looks like a heavy whipped cream. Add vanilla and blend well. Spread ¼ cup of this buttercream inside 9¾ × 5¾ × 2¾-inch pan, and put rest aside to spread on dough. (Half recipe dough can be baked in 7½ × 3¾ × 2¼-inch pan, 35 minutes. Use ½ recipe filling.)

Roll Kuchen Dough to measure about 8 inches wide and 24 inches long. Spread rest of buttercream over entire surface of dough and sprinkle with the finely chopped pecans and a little cinnamon. Cut dough crosswise into 3 pieces. Roll each from wider side to form long rolls. Twist each roll slightly, and with the 3 rolls form a tight braid. Pinch ends well together. With both hands pick up braid and transfer to bread pan that was thickly spread with buttercream. Brush top of braid with melted butter or margarine, cover and let stand in a warm place until dough comes to about 1¼ inches from top of pan. It will take about 1 hour, depending on temperature of room. Bake in a 350° F. oven about 50 minutes.

Note. This coffee cake should not be served very warm and must be baked in a loaf pan. The buttercream adds unusual moisture and cake is more delicious if served a few hours after it is baked, or the following day. After cake is cold, store it in a plastic bag or container, or wrap well in several thicknesses of wax paper. Shortly before serving, glaze and drizzle cake with Coffee Cake Icing (page 510). May be reheated if more than 2 days old.

How to Reheat. Light oven and preheat to 350° F. Sprinkle coffee cake lightly with water and place it in oven on baking sheet. Test after 15 minutes. If not sufficiently soft, bake a little longer, ice, etc.

Cinnamon Ball Coffee Cake

1 recipe Kuchen Dough (page 508)
¾ cup melted butter (half shortening may be used)

¾ cup granulated sugar, combined and mixed well with 1½ teaspoons cinnamon

After Kuchen Dough rises the second time, turn out onto pastry cloth and cut into uniform pieces about 1½ inches in diameter. Shape each piece into a ball. Dip balls into warm melted butter, then into cinnamon-sugar mixture, and place balls in a well-greased tube pan or coffee cake ring pan about 9 or 10 inches in diameter and at least 2½ inches deep. Leave about ½-inch space between balls. Form a second layer of balls, if necessary, in a zigzag formation. Drizzle top with remaining butter, sugar, and cinnamon. Let rise until about double; then bake at 400° F. about 30 minutes, or until brown and firm to the touch. Let stand in pan greased with 1 tablespoon unsalted shortening about 5 minutes, and turn out onto cake cooler. Drizzle with Coffee Cake Icing (page 510).

Individual Buttercream Coffee Cake Yeast Rolls

Makes 12 large or 16 medium-size rolls

Prepare 1 recipe Kuchen Dough (page 508). After dough has doubled in size the second time, cut it into halves. Roll each half into a 10-inch square. Spread each piece of dough with ⅓ cup Buttercream Filling (below). Roll like jelly roll, and cut into 6 uniform pieces. Place with cut side down in individual large muffin pans that have been greased with teaspoon Buttercream Filling. Spread top of each with ½ teaspoon Buttercream Filling, and sprinkle with slivered blanched almonds. Let rise until light or double in size. Bake at 350° F. about 35 to 40 minutes, or until brown. Remove from oven, and when cool, drizzle top with Coffee-Cake Icing (page 510) if desired, or brush with warm light corn syrup.

Buttercream Filling for Yeast Rolls

Beat ½ cup firm butter until light (about 5 minutes). Add 1 cup sifted confectioners' sugar, a little at a time, and ½ teaspoon vanilla. Beat with electric mixer. Cover, and keep in a cool place until needed.

Yuletide Coffee Cake Wreath

Use 1 full recipe basic dough for Glacéed Pineapple-Orange Yeast Rolls (page 519). After second rising, turn dough out onto a lightly floured pastry cloth, cut it into 2 pieces, and roll each piece into an 18-inch rope. Cut each rope into 18 (1-inch) pieces, making 36 pieces in all. Now shape pieces into balls. Dip balls into warm melted butter or margarine (using ½ cup in all), then into brown sugar combined with cinnamon (using ¾ cup soft brown sugar combined with 1½ teaspoons cinnamon in all). Place 12 balls, leaving small spaces between them, on bottom of a well greased ring mold that measures about 9½ × 2 inches. Sprinkle first layer with 1 tablespoon fruit mix, cut into small pieces, and 1 tablespoon broken nutmeats. Place 12 more balls over first layer; sprinkle with another tablespoon cut fruit and 1 tablespoon nut meats. Last, place remaining 12 balls. Pour any leftover butter or sugar over top. Cover with wax paper and a towel, and let cake stand in a warm place about 30 minutes, or until it rises to about ½ inch from top of pan.

Bake in a 350° F. oven about 35 minutes, or until top is brown. Remove from oven and let stand about 5 minutes; then place wax paper and a cake rack over top and turn cake out. *Immediately* tie a string around ring about 1 inch from bottom, to prevent balls from separating.

While cake is still hot, garnish top with about ¾ cup colorful fruit mix chopped medium-fine, or red and green candied cherries and yellow candied pineapple. Or cake may be drizzled with thin Coffee Cake Icing (page 510). When cake is cool, remove string carefully. Place cake on a round platter covered with a lace-paper doily, and serve. This makes a very colorful and delectable holiday coffee cake.

Filled Coffee Cake Squares

Serves 8 to 12

3 cups sifted all-purpose flour
¼ cup granulated sugar
½ teaspoon salt
½ cup firm butter or margarine
Grated rind of 1 small lemon or small orange
1 package dry yeast, combined with ¼ cup warm water (110° F. to 115° F.), stirred and allowed to stand about 5 minutes until dissolved
½ cup milk, first scalded, then allowed to cool to lukewarm
¼ cup egg yolks (3 large), beaten with a spoon

Combine flour, sugar, and salt, and sift together twice. Cut firm butter or margarine through dry ingredients until mixture looks like a coarse meal. Add grated rind.

Combine dissolved yeast with lukewarm milk and beaten egg yolks, and add all at once to dry ingredients. Stir with a spoon until well blended; turn out onto floured pastry cloth, and knead gently about 1 minute. Place in a greased bowl, brush top with melted butter, and let rise in room temperature until double in size. When doubled, cut dough into 2 pieces. Roll each to measure about 12 × 16 inches, and cut into halves. Fold dough over to facilitate handling. Pick up 1 piece of dough and transfer to a greased baking sheet. Spread it with about ½ cup any desired commercial cake filling or Pineapple Glaze Filling (page 514). Place second sheet of dough over filling. Pinch around ends to prevent filling from running out in baking, or press down with a fork. Do likewise with other half of dough; fill, etc. Let filled dough stand about 15 minutes in room temperature; then brush with leftover beaten egg white, and sprinkle each section with about 2 tablespoons chopped pecans. Bake in a 375° F. oven about 15 to 20 minutes, or until golden brown but not too dark. Remove from oven; let stand on cake rack until cold.

When cold, drizzle top with Quick Icing (below). Let icing set at least 30 minutes; then trim cake, and cut into 3-inch squares. These are delicious for snack parties, teas, or buffet parties.

Quick Icing for Filled Coffee Cake Squares

2 tablespoons orange or lemon juice (milk may be used instead)

About 1 cup sifted confectioners' sugar

Combine ingredients and beat until smooth, using enough sugar to form a thin icing. If milk is used instead of juice, add ½ teaspoon vanilla.

Pineapple Glaze Filling for Coffee Cake Squares

1 cup crushed pineapple with part of juice
1 tablespoon lemon or orange juice

1 tablespoon cornstarch, combined with ¼ cup granulated sugar

Combine all ingredients, and stir until well blended. Cook until thick and glazy, about 3 minutes after simmering begins.

Bundt Kuchen (Yeast-Raised Form Coffee Cake)

1 package dry yeast, combined with ¼ cup warm water (110° F. to 115° F.)
¾ cup lukewarm milk, first scalded, then cooled
1½ cups sifted all-purpose flour
½ cup butter or margarine
¾ cup granulated sugar, combined with ¼ teaspoon salt

2 large whole eggs
1 teaspoon lemon or orange extract
½ teaspoon vanilla
1¼ cups more flour
¾ cup grated pecans, combined with ¼ cup granulated sugar and ¼ teaspoon cinnamon

Prepare sponge in a 7-inch bowl with dry yeast combined with warm water. Let stand about 5 minutes; then add lukewarm milk and 1½ cups flour. Beat 2 or 3 minutes until smooth. Cover, and let stand in a warm place or in a bowl of lukewarm water until doubled, about 30 minutes.

About 10 minutes before sponge is ready, in a 8- or 9-inch bowl beat butter or margarine with electric mixer until creamy. Add sugar and salt, a little at a time, and beat well about 1 minute until light. Now add eggs, 1 at a time, and beat after each addition about ½ minute. Add extracts and beat until well blended. With a large wooden spoon add sponge, a little at a time, alternately with 1¼ cups flour, a little at a time, and beat after each addition until very smooth.

Pour about ⅓ of batter into an 8½ × 3¼-inch form pan that has been well greased with 1 tablespoon unsalted shortening and sprinkled with flour. Over batter in pan sprinkle grated pecan meats combined with sugar and cinnamon. Now pour rest of batter over filling, spread evenly, cover pan, and let cake rise until it is about ½ inch from top of pan. This will take anywhere from 1 to 2 hours, depending on temperature of room. Pan can be placed in a utensil of lukewarm water on a cold damp day.

Bake cake in a preheated 350° F. oven about 50 minutes, or until top is brown and cake feels firm to the touch. Remove from oven, let remain in pan about 15 minutes, then loosen around upper part and tube, and turn out onto a cake cooler. When cold, sprinkle with confectioners' sugar, or drizzle with Coffee Cake Icing (page 510).

Coffee Cake Orange Knots

Serves 8

Use 1 recipe Kuchen Dough (page 508), but reduce milk to ¼ cup, and add ¼ cup orange juice and 1 tablespoon grated orange rind.

After dough rises a second time, roll it to measure about 10 inches square. With a pastry wheel cut dough into strips ½ inch wide, and form knots. Let knots rise about 20 to 30 minutes; then bake them on a greased baking sheet about 15 minutes or until delicately brown but not too dark. Remove from oven, and while still hot, drizzle Orange Icing on top of each. These cakes are best served warm. If made in advance, do not ice until they are reheated.

Orange Icing for Coffee Cake Knots

1 teaspoon grated orange rind	About 2 cups, more or less, sifted con-
3 tablespoons orange juice	fectioners' sugar

Mix ingredients thoroughly, using enough sugar to make proper consistency for icing, and beat until smooth.

Flaky Thin Croissant Coffee Cakes

Prepare 1 recipe Flaky Croissant Luncheon or Dinner Rolls (page 500), but increase sugar to ⅓ cup, add ½ teaspoon lemon extract and 1 teaspoon vanilla. Cut dough in 4 uniform pieces. Roll each piece to measure about 12 × 12 inches. Spread center only with ¼ cup jam or preserve combined with 2 tablespoons more or less finely chopped nuts or cake crumbs. Fold over to enclose filling. Leave plain. Brush top with melted butter. Let stand until light, about 1 to 1½ hours. Then bake at 375° F. about 20 to 25 minutes, or until golden brown. Now shut off heat and let remain in oven for about 15 minutes to make crisp. Watch closely toward end to prevent burning. When cool, brush with corn syrup and drizzle with Coffee Cake Icing (page 510). Other fillings may be used in these cakes.

Brioche Streussel-Top Coffee Cake

Prepare beaten Quick French Brioche Dough (page 499). After it rises first time, beat it again thoroughly for about 1 minute, then pour and spread it with a fork into *two* 7 × 7 × 1¼-inch square foil pans, each well greased with 1 teaspoon unsalted shortening. Or may be baked in one large 9 × 9 × 2-inch square pan. We prefer the 2 smaller pans. Let stand in a warm room about 1 hour. Meanwhile prepare Streussel Topping given below. Keep it in a cool place.

Preheat oven at 375° F. at least 15 minutes in advance. When batter looks like it has doubled in size, *gently* brush top with yolk of egg combined with 1 tablespoon milk. Sprinkle top with ½ of Streussel Topping for 7-inch size (whole recipe for large), starting from side to center by spoonful. Bake 7-inch cakes about 20 minutes or until brown, about 25 to 30 minutes for the 9-inch size. Remove from oven, let stand about 5 minutes, loosen around sides with a dinner knife or spatula, place cake rack over top and turn over.

If to be served within a short time, drizzle top with Coffee Cake Icing (page 510). Or they may be stored in covered container and reheated at 350° F. for about 10 minutes, then iced. They are more delectable if reheated, but can be served cold.

Streussel Topping

3 tablespoons cold firm butter or margarine
¼ cup sifted all-purpose flour
¼ cup pecan meats, broken in medium pieces

¼ cup granulated sugar, combined with ¼ or more teaspoon of cinnamon

With pie blender (or fingers) cut butter through dry ingredients until mixture looks crumbly and moist. Keep in cool place until ready to be used. This will cover two 7-inch cakes or one 9 × 9.

Croissant Coffee Cake Rolls

Prepare recipe as for Coffee Cakes (page 515). For large rolls, cut dough in 2 pieces and roll each piece to measure about 10 × 22 inches. Brush with melted butter and sprinkle with ¼ cup very finely chopped nuts and a little cinnamon. Cut each into 6 wedges. Roll from large end to form croissants; place with open end down on ungreased baking sheet. Let stand about 1 to 1½ hours or until light. Bake at 375° F. for 20 to 25 minutes, or until golden brown. Shut off heat and let remain in oven about 15 minutes. When slightly cool, brush with corn syrup and drizzle with Coffee Cake Icing (page 510) and chopped nuts.

Note. These Coffee Cakes and Rolls are flakier baked in advance and reheated in a 350° F. oven for about 8 to 10 minutes. Then glaze and ice. Baked cakes and rolls can be frozen.

▶ DOUGHNUTS ◀

Basic Raised Dough for Doughnuts, Bismarcks, Etc.

Makes about 8 very large doughnuts, 12 medium bismarcks

½ cup scalded milk
¼ cup soft butter or margarine
¼ cup granulated sugar
½ teaspoon salt
1 large egg, beaten ½ minute with egg beater

½ teaspoon vanilla
1 package dry yeast, dissolved in ¼ cup warm water (about 110° to 115° F.)
About 3 cups sifted all-purpose flour

Pour scalded milk over butter and sugar. Add salt. When melted, add beaten egg and vanilla. When lukewarm, add dissolved yeast, and last sifted flour a little at a time to form a soft dough. When too stiff to mix with spoon, turn out onto floured pastry cloth and add only enough more flour to form soft dough that does not stick to hands. Knead for several minutes. Place in well-greased No. 5 or 6 bowl. Brush top of dough with melted fat, cover, and let rise in warm place until double. Turn out onto cloth and knead again 1 minute. Place in greased bowl, brush top with melted fat, and allow to rise again until double. After dough rises a second time, cut, or shape as desired.

Doughnuts

Pat and roll Basic Raised Dough (above) not more than ½ inch in thickness. Let stand about 2 minutes. Dip large cutter into flour each time and cut through dough. Place on very lightly floured wax paper or a towel. Cover with a towel and allow to rise until light (about ½ hour during cold weather, only about 15 to 20 minutes during very warm weather). Pick up with pancake turner and deep-fry at 360° F. until golden brown on one side, and then turn. Avoid turning more than once. Drain on cake rack or paper toweling. When cool, roll into granulated sugar, or sprinkle with confectioners' sugar or dip into Transparent Icing (page 519).

Note. Raised doughnuts that are a day old may be reheated on a cake rack with drip pan underneath at 325° F. for about 7 or 8 minutes. If they are more than a day old, it is best to wrap them in foil or paper bag and reheat for about 10 to 12 minutes. If unusually dry, drizzle them with a little warm water, then reheat.

Bismarcks

Pat and roll Basic Raised Dough (page 517) to ½ inch in thickness. Let stand about 2 minutes, then cut with large plain cutter dipped into flour. Let rise until light (about ½ hour during cold weather and 15 to 20 minutes during very warm weather); then deep-fry at 360° F., and proceed as with Doughnuts (above). When cold, pump a little jam or jelly into bismarcks with a No. 8 plain decorating tube and bag, or use special tube.

Dutch Apple Cake

Pat an roll ½ (or more) of Basic Raised Dough (page 517) about 10 inch square to fit a shallow 9-inch-square pan. Place in greased pan, pulling and stretching dough to fit and having it come up on all sides about 1 inch. Sprinkle dough with 3 tablespoons of dry bread crumbs and let stand about 15 minutes. Pare ¾ pound (2 large or 3 medium) uniform-sized Jonathan or winesap apples and cut into very thin slices. Lay them in parrallel rows on the crumbs and sprinkle top with about ⅓ cup sugar combined with ¼ teaspoon cinnamon and ⅛ teaspoon nutmeg. Combine 2 tablespoons melted butter or margarine, 1 egg yolk slightly beaten, and 2 tablespoons milk. Drizzle this over apples. Let stand about 15 minutes until light. Bake 45 to 60 minutes in 350° F. oven, or until crust is brown and apples are soft.

Fresh peaches, apricots, or plums may be used instead of apples. For fresh peaches, dip into boiling water for a minute or two and remove skins. Slice like apples and arrange in same way. For apricots and plums, do not peel and do not blanch, simply cut in halves, remove stones and arrange them with cut side up. Sprinkle with sugar, etc.

Knots

Leftover pieces of dough may be used for knots. Knead scraps a few seconds. Cover and let stand about 30 minutes. Cut into uniform-sized pieces and roll each piece of dough on unfloured pastry cloth until smooth into strands about 6 inches long and ¾ inch wide. Let strands stand about 5 minutes, make knots. Let rise until light (about 30 to 40 minutes) then deep-fry at 360° F., and proceed according to Doughnuts recipe (page 517).

Transparent Icing for Doughnuts, Bismarcks, Etc.

¼ cup boiling water, combined with
    2 teaspoons butter or margarine
2½ cups sifted confectioners' sugar (or

a little more depending on fine-
    ness of sugar)
1 tablespoon unbeaten egg white

In a 1-quart saucepan, combine boiling water combined with butter and the sifted confectioners' sugar, a little at a time. Stir until well blended. Add the tablespoon of unbeaten egg white, and with egg beater beat mixture only until smooth, but not foamy; ¼ teaspoon vanilla may be added.

This icing should be lukewarm, and can be kept over hot water during dipping process. Do not permit it to become too warm at any time. Dip upper part only of doughnuts into icing, and place them with icing side up on cake racks with pan underneath. Let stand at least 15 minutes before serving.

▶ PASTRIES ◀

Glacéed Pineapple-Orange Yeast Rolls

Makes about 16 medium rolls

1 package dry yeast, dissolved in ¼
    cup warm water (about 110 F.
    to 115° F.)
¼ cup butter, melted and lukewarm
¼ cup granulated sugar
1 large whole egg, well beaten
½ teaspoon salt
½ cup scalded milk, then cooled to
    lukewarm

2 tablespoons orange juice
About 3¼ cups sifted all-purpose flour,
    or enough to form a very soft
    dough
⅔ cup pineapple jam, mashed with a
    fork
About ¼ cup pecan meats

Combine all ingredients except jam and nuts in order given. Beat until smooth after each addition of flour. When too stiff to beat, turn out onto floured pastry cloth and knead gently for a minute or two, adding more flour to prevent clinging to hands. Place in greased bowl and let stand until about double in size. Turn out onto floured pastry cloth, knead again about ½ minute. Let rise second time, then roll to measure about 10 × 18 inches. Brush with melted butter, then spread dough as uniformly as possible with ⅔ cup pineapple jam. Sprinkle with about ¼ cup chopped pecan meats. Roll from large end into a long narrow roll. Cut roll in 12 uniform pieces. Place with open ends down into a 9 × 9-inch square pan that has been well greased on sides and bottom covered with 1 recipe of *cool* Caramel Glaze (below). Prepare glaze while dough is rising.

Caramel Glaze for Yeast Rolls

¼ cup butter or margarine
1 cup brown sugar, solidly packed

2 tablespoons water
1 teaspoon extract

Combine all ingredients in small saucepan and stir gently until well blended. Cook without stirring for 1 minute after it comes to the simmering point. Pour glaze into well-greased square pan and let cool about ½ hour before placing rolls over glaze. Let rolls stand in pan until they rise about 1 inch from top of pan. Then bake in a 375° F. oven about 40 minutes, or until very brown and firm to the touch. Remove from oven, place wax paper and cake rack over top and turn over. Pick up any glaze that remains in pan or drips onto paper, and pour over rolls. Let stand until cool before serving.

Sour-Cream Kippel Yeast Pastries

Makes 16 pastries

2 cups sifted all-purpose flour
1 teaspoon salt
¼ cup granulated sugar
¼ cup butter or margarine
1 egg yolk, slightly beaten with a fork
½ cup cool sour cream, combined with ¼ teaspoon baking soda
1 package dry yeast, combined with ¼ cup warm water (about 110° F. to 115° F.)

1 teaspoon vanilla
2 more tablespoons butter
About ⅓ cup thick jam, preserves, or jelly
1 egg white, beaten until it clings to bowl
1 tablespoon granulated sugar, combined with ¼ teaspoon cinnamon, to sprinkle on top
About ¼ cup slivered almonds

Combine and sift together flour, salt, and sugar. Cut ¼ cup butter into dry ingredients until mixture looks like a coarse meal. Add egg yolk, sour cream combined with baking soda, dissolved yeast, and vanilla. Beat until smooth. If dough appears too soft and sticky, add a little more flour. Turn it out onto a floured pastry cloth and knead gently about 1 minute, adding more flour if necessary, but keep dough as soft as possible. Place it in a greased bowl, cover, and let stand in refrigerator or a cold place (not over 50° F.) 3 to 4 hours, or until it doubles in size. Remove from bowl after it rises, and roll it to measure about 12 × 18 inches. Place on half of dough 2 tablespoons butter, broken up into small pieces, fold over to cover butter, and roll dough again a few inches larger. Continue to fold and roll a little, 2 more times. Now place it on wax paper on a flat surface, cover well with wax paper and a towel, and refrigerate about 30 minutes.

After 30 minutes (no longer unless refrigerator temperature is below 40° F.) remove it from refrigerator and cut into 2 pieces. Roll each piece to measure 8 × 16 inches. Cut into 2 uniform squares. Place 1 teaspoon jam, preserves, or jelly in center of each. Turn 2 of the points toward center to enclose filling, brushing with slightly beaten egg white to prevent opening, and pinch well. Place on a lightly greased baking sheet. Roll and fill second piece of dough in same way. Brush top of each well with stiffly beaten egg white, sprinkle with several slivers of almonds and a little sugar combined with cinnamon. Let stand on baking sheet in room temperature about 30 to 45 minutes or until light; then bake at 400° F. about 15 to 18 minutes, or until golden brown but not dark. When lukewarm, drizzle with Coffee Cake Icing (page 510).

Honey Glacéed Strawberry Yeast Rolls

Make about 16 medium rolls

Prepare Glacéed Pineapple-Orange Yeast dough (page 519). Let rise second time. Turn out onto floured pastry cloth, and cut in half. Roll each half of dough to measure about 6 × 18 inches. Brush with melted butter, then spread entire surface as evenly as possible with about 3 tablespoons mashed strawberry jam. Roll from large end to form a long narrow roll. Cut into 8 pieces and place with cut end down in small muffin pans that have been *well greased* and bottom covered with 2 teaspoons honey.

Let rise until light, about ½ hour, then bake in a 375° F. oven about 25 to 30 minutes for medium rolls. Or roll full recipe of dough to about 12 × 12 inches, spread with melted butter and about ⅓ cup strawberry jam. Roll and cut in 8 *large sections* and place in large muffin pans, greased, and bottom covered with 1 tablespoon honey. Let rise until light, about 40 minutes, then bake at 375° F. about 35 minutes, or until brown and firm to touch. When done, turn out onto wax paper at once. Let stand until cold before serving.

Basic Yeast Dough for Glazed Butterscotch Pecan Rolls, Butterhorns, Sweet Rolls

⅓ cup scalded milk
¼ cup very soft butter or margarine
2 tablespoons granulated sugar
About ½ teaspoon salt
1 large whole egg, beaten ½ minute with hand beater

1 package dry yeast, combined with ¼ cup warm water (about 110° to 115° F.); let stand about 5 minutes
About 2¼ cups sifted all-purpose flour
Melted butter

Pour scalded milk over soft butter or margarine, sugar, and salt. When melted, add well-beaten egg, and when lukewarm add dissolved yeast.

Add flour gradually and beat well. Turn out onto floured pastry cloth and knead gently several minutes, adding only enough flour to prevent dough from sticking, keeping it soft. Place in well-greased 6-inch bowl and brush top with melted butter. Cover bowl with wax paper and towel and let dough rise in a warm place (best temperature about 85° F.) until double in size—about 30 to 60 minutes, depending on temperature of room. When double in size, turn out onto pastry cloth and knead again about ½ minute. Let rise a second time, then roll, fill, etc.

Note. Pecan rolls may be reheated in a 350° F. oven for about 10 to 15 minutes just before serving. Brush with light or dark corn syrup if dull.

Syrup Glaze for Pecan Rolls

Over moderate heat stir and bring to a *full boil* ½ cup light brown sugar (packed), 3 tablespoons butter or margarine, and 3 tablespoons hot water. Remove from heat as soon as it comes to a boil in center. Do not cook further or glaze on rolls will become hard. Let syrup glaze cool about ½ hour until lukewarm before using, but do not allow to become cold. With spoon, *stir gently* each time when picking up glaze. This recipe makes about 10 level tablespoons of glaze, enough for 1 recipe rolls.

Cream Cheese-Kolachy Yeast Pastries

Serves 12

½ cup cream cheese	1 package dry yeast, combined with
2 tablespoons butter	¼ cup warm water (about
1 teaspoon salt	110° F.)
¼ cup granulated sugar	¼ cup cool milk
1 egg yolk	About 2 cups sifted all-purpose flour
Grated rind ½ lemon	2 more tablespoons butter

In a medium-size bowl combine cream cheese, 2 tablespoons butter, salt, sugar, and egg yolk. With mixer or spoon beat until smooth. Now add grated lemon rind, dissolved yeast, cool milk, and flour, a little at a time, forming a medium dough. Turn it out onto a floured cloth and knead gently about 1 minute, adding more flour if necessary to prevent sticking, but keep dough as soft as possible. Place it in a greased bowl, brush top with melted butter, and store in refrigerator until it doubles in size. This will take about 2 to 4 hours, depending on temperature of refrigerator. When dough has doubled in size (do not permit it to become overlight), roll it to measure about 12 × 18 inches, and on half of dough place 2 tablespoons butter broken up into small pieces. Fold over to enclose butter, and roll dough again to a few inches larger. Continue to fold and roll a little, 2 more times. This will give more layers to pastries. Now place dough on wax paper in flat pan, cover well with wax paper and a towel and keep in refrigerator about 30 minutes—not more than 30 minutes unless refrigerator temperature is below 40° F.

Round Kolachys. Cut full recipe of dough into halves after it has been refrigerated about 30 minutes. Roll each half to measure about 6 × 8 inches. With a 2½-inch round cutter, cut out rounds of dough. Reshape scraps gently, roll, and form more rounds. Allow dough rounds to stand on a very lightly greased baking sheet in room temperature (not over 70° F. if possible) about 20 minutes. Now with fingers form a wide indentation in each, and fill with about 1 teaspoon preserves, jam, prune paste, date paste, apricot paste, or heavy cheese mixture. Let stand about 45 to 60 more minutes in a cool room (not over 70° F.). Then bake in a preheated 375° F. oven about 15 to 20 minutes, or until golden brown but not dark. Remove, and sprinkle thickly with sifted confectioners' sugar or drizzle with Coffee Cake Icing (page 510).

Kolachy Pockets. Roll ½ recipe of dough into an 8 × 12-inch rectangle. Cut into 6 uniform 4-inch squares. Place about 1 teaspoon filling on center of each. Moisten inside of the 4 points of dough with a little beaten egg white; bring points together to enclose filling, and pinch well to prevent opening. Place pastries on a lightly greased baking sheet. Brush with slightly beaten egg white combined with 1 tablespoon water, and sprinkle with thin-slivered almonds. Let rise in cool room (not over 70° F.) about 45 to 60 minutes—longer if room is colder, less time if room is warmer. Pastries must feel light but not overlight. Bake in a preheated 375° F. oven about 20 to 25 minutes or until golden brown. When done, drizzle Coffee Cake Icing (page 510) over tops.

Individual Medium Pecan Rolls

Makes 16 medium rolls

Roll ½ recipe of the Basic Yeast Dough for Pecan Rolls (page 521) into a sheet that measures about 12 × 12 inches. Brush with melted butter; sprinkle with ¼ cup brown sugar, packed, 2 tablespoons chopped pecans, and a little cinnamon. Roll and cut into 8 uniform pieces. Cover sides and bottom of medium-sized muffin pans with soft butter or margarine and pad sides only with soft brown sugar. Pour ½ tablespoon Syrup Glaze (page 522) into each section. Over glaze arrange several small pecans, and over pecans, place rolls cut sides down, pressing gently. Brush top of rolls with melted butter. Let stand in warm room until they appear light, from 30 to 40 minutes, depending on temperature of room.

Bake in a 350° F. oven about 25 to 30 minutes. Remove from oven and at once turn out onto wax paper.

Pecan Roll Loaf

Make 1 loaf

Roll whole recipe of Basic Yeast Dough for Pecan Rolls (page 521) into a sheet that measures 14 × 16 inches. Brush with melted butter or margarine, sprinkle with ½ cup brown sugar, packed, ¼ cup medium chopped nuts, and a little cinnamon. Roll from small end, and cut into 8 uniform pieces. Brush sides and bottom of 9¾ × 5¾ × 2¾-inch pan well with soft butter, and pad sides only of pan ¾ way up with soft brown sugar. Pour about 10 tablespoons of Syrup Glaze (page 522) into pan, and cover glaze with pecans. Place rolls in pan with cut sides down, pressing down lightly. Brush top of rolls with melted butter. Cover and let rise in a warm room to about ½ inch from top of pan. Takes about 30 minutes, depending on temperature of room. Bake at 375° F. about 50 to 60 minutes, or until brown. Remove from oven and at once turn out onto rack covered with wax paper.

Pecan Roll Ring

Roll 1 recipe of Basic Yeast Dough for Pecan Rolls (page 521) into a sheet that measures 12 × 18 inches. Brush with melted butter and sprinkle with ½ cup of brown sugar, packed, ¼ cup finely chopped nuts, and a little cinnamon. Roll from small end and cut into 8 uniform pieces. Brush sides and bottom of 10 × 2-inch aluminum ring mold with very soft butter and pad sides only ¾ way up with brown sugar. Pour about 10 tablespoons of Syrup Glaze (page 522) into mold, cover with pecans, and place rolls over nutmeats pressing down gently. Brush tops of rolls with melted butter and let stand in warm room until they come to top of mold. Bake at 350° F. about 45 to 50 minutes or until brown. Remove from oven, place wax paper and a cake rack over rolls. Turn over at once.

If pecans cling to bottom of mold when turning rolls out, release them at once with a fork and place on rolls while hot.

Butterhorn Sweet Rolls

Makes about 16 rolls

Prepare Basic Yeast Dough for Pecan Rolls (page 521). For medium-size rolls, cut 1 recipe of dough into 2 pieces. Form each in round patty. (For very large rolls, roll full recipe into one 16-inch circle.) Roll pieces into 10-inch circles and let stand several minutes before cutting. Brush with melted butter. Cut in 8 wedges. Place a spoonful of any desired sweet filling used in coffee cakes on large end. Roll and form crescents. Place on silicone paper with open end down. Brush well with melted butter and let rise about 30 to 40 minutes. Bake at 425° F. about 15 to 20 minutes. When warm brush with corn syrup, drizzle with Coffee Cake Icing (page 510) and sprinkle top with chopped pecan meats. Drizzle a little more icing over nutmeats.

Basic Dough for Danish Pastries

Single recipe makes 12 very large individual pastries, or 18 medium

½ cup scalded milk
2 tablespoons soft butter
⅓ cup granulated sugar
½ teaspoon salt
2 large eggs, beaten with egg beater
    ½ minute
½ teaspoon vanilla
Rind of ½ lemon, or ½ teaspoon lemon extract
1 package dry yeast, combined with

¼ cup warm water (about 110° F. to 115° F.; for a faster rising dough, use 2 packages yeast dissolved in ½ cup warm water, and reduce milk to ¼ cup
About 3 cups sifted all-purpose flour
1 cup sifted cake flour
¾ cup cold butter (half margarine may be used); for extra rich flaky dough use 1 cup butter

Pour scalded milk over the 2 tablespoons butter, granulated sugar, and salt. Stir until dissolved. Now add the beaten eggs, vanilla, and lemon rind or extract. When lukewarm, add dissolved yeast. Sift flours, and add them to liquid, about 1 cupful at a time. When dough is medium consistency, beat it well until smooth. Continue to add rest of flour until it is difficult to beat it further. Turn out onto floured pastry cloth, and knead well for several minutes, adding only enough more flour to prevent stickiness, but keep dough as soft as possible. Place in well-greased 7-inch bowl. Brush top with melted butter, cover, and let rise until double in bulk. Takes about 1 hour. When double in bulk, turn out onto *very, very* lightly floured pastry cloth, and knead again about ½ minute. Cover and let rise a second time.

Meanwhile, wash the cold, firm butter until it is waxy for about 2 minutes. Squeeze out water. Divide it into 3 uniform parts, wrap in wax paper and refrigerate.

When dough has risen a second time, on floured pastry cloth roll it into a rectangle that measures about 8 × 14 inches, and distribute 1 of the pieces of butter, cut in small pieces, over ⅔ of the dough. Fold that portion of the dough having no butter on it toward you over the buttered part, and then fold the other ⅓ over the first 2, giving 3 thicknesses. Press edges together with rolling pin. Place on flat pan covered with wax paper and a towel or place into a large plastic bag. Refrigerate for about ½ hour.

After ½ hour, roll dough again to measure about 10 × 16 inches, distribute second piece of butter, fold same way. Wrap and refrigerate for ½ hour.

After ½ hour, roll dough again to measure about 12 × 18 inches. Distribute ⅓ (last) part of butter same way, fold over, etc. Dough must be refrigerated for at least 4 hours after all of butter has been rolled in. It may be refrigerated in *coldest part* for 12 hours (not longer than 24 hours if possible). Then cut, roll, fill, etc., as per directions given in each recipe. After pastries are filled and shaped, *they must stand* in room temperature about 1½ hours (sometimes longer during very cold weather) depending also on size of pastries, amount of yeast used, and temperature of room. Bake according to time given in recipes.

Important Facts Regarding Danish Pastries. During warm weather it is important to turn refrigerator to the coldest point, and to store dough in coldest part during entire procedure to prevent overfermentation. Do not keep dough longer than 24 hours in coldest part of refrigerator during warm weather. If it must be kept longer, it may be frozen for as long as 1 week. It is better to remove dough from freezer about 8 hours in advance and let it defrost in refrigerator until next day, then cut, roll, etc.

It is important to grease pans quite well for moist filled cakes, *or, better, to use silicone* paper without any greasing. This paper can be reversed and used a second time.

All cakes may be brushed with warm corn syrup before they are iced, to impart gloss, especially those that are not brushed with egg before baking.

It is better not to glaze and ice cakes until ready to be served. Pastries of this type are always more delectable and flakier *when reheated.* To do so reheat them at 350° F. on baking sheet for about 10 minutes, a little longer for large cakes, but watch closely to prevent burning.

Danish pastries will remain fresh for at least a week if wrapped well in plastic bag or heavy wax paper and refrigerated until ready to be reheated.

Danish Swirl

Makes 2 swirls

Roll ½ recipe of Basic Dough for Danish Pastries (page 525) into 8 × 16 rectangle. Brush with melted butter, sprinkle with ¼ cup finely chopped pecans and a little cinnamon to taste. Cut into 4 uniform strips. Roll and twist each strip. Place them in silicone-lined or well-greased 9-inch round cake pan (or 10-inch pie plate), starting in the center, forming a swirl. Leave a little space between strips. When entire pan is filled, adjust strips as uniformly as possible, by pressing down with fingers. Let cake rise about 1½ hours. Now brush entire surface with beaten whole egg (or egg white), sprinkle top with about 3 tablespoons coarsely broken pecan meats (do not chop, but break lengthwise with fingers). Bake at 375° F., about 25 to 30 minutes, or until golden brown. Remove from oven, let cool in pan on cake rack for 5 minutes. Loosen around sides, place rack over top, and turn out. Turn over again with right side up. May be brushed with corn syrup to add glaze. Drizzle with Coffee Cake Icing (page 510) before serving. Full recipe of Basic Dough for Danish Pastries will make 3 smaller swirls in 8-inch pans or pie plates.

Danish Pastry Luncheon or Dinner Rolls

Makes 24 large rolls

Prepare basic Danish Pastry Dough (page 525), reducing sugar to 2 table-spoons, and increasing salt to 2 teaspoons. Cut full recipe in 4 parts, then roll each piece into 8 × 12 rectangle. Cut same as for Danish Pastry Horns (page 528). Roll, etc. Bake about 15 to 20 minutes at 375° F.

Danish Pastry Pinwheels

Roll ⅓ of Basic Dough for Danish Pastries (page 525). Make 4 large or 8 medium to measure about 10 × 10 inch square. Cut into 4 large squares, or 8 medium. Cut through each point, leaving about 1 inch uncut in center. Wet center with water with tip of finger. Turn every other point toward center, pressing down well to prevent opening. After pastry is shaped, brush entire surface lightly with melted butter. Let stand on silicone-lined baking sheet about 1 hour. Bake at 375° F. about 15 to 20 minutes. When cool, brush with warm corn syrup, cover points with Coffee Cake Icing (page 510) and sprinkle with finely chopped nuts. Pour a little raspberry or strawberry jam into center and sprinkle with sifted confectioners' sugar just before serving.

Danish Pastry Snails

Roll ⅓ recipe of Basic Dough for Danish Pastries (page 525) into a rectangle about 8 × 12 inches. Brush with melted butter; sprinkle with about 1 tablespoon granulated sugar combined with ¼ teaspoon cinnamon, and 2 tablespoons very finely chopped nuts. Cut dough into 4 strips; roll both ends toward center, flatten each with hand. Brush with melted butter. Let stand about 1 to 1½ hours on silicone-lined pan. Bake at 375° F. about 15 to 20 minutes. Then glaze, ice, and sprinkle with nutmeats.

Danish Pastry Horns (or Crescents)

Pat and roll ⅓ recipe of Basic Dough for Danish Pastries (page 525) into a rectangle about 8 × 14 inches. Brush with melted butter. Cut into 4 wedges. Place a spoonful of the following cheese preparation (or any other preferred filling) on largest end: Combine ½ cup cream cheese with 1 egg yolk, ¼ teaspoon lemon extract, and ¼ teaspoon vanilla, 2 tablespoons granulated sugar, and a little milk if necessary, to form a thick consistency. Roll from large end, forming a crescent. Place on silicone-lined baking sheet with open ends down, brush with melted butter, and let rise in room temperature until very light for about 1½ hours. Bake at 375° F. 15 to 20 minutes until brown. With pancake turner remove from baking sheet and let cool on cake racks, then brush with corn syrup, icing, and sprinkle with nutmeats.

Danish Pastry Braid

For large braid, roll ½ recipe of Basic Dough for Danish Pastries (page 525) into a rectangle about 10 × 18 inches. Spread entire surface with ½ cup Almond Paste Filling (below) that is not too thin, or combine ½ cup commercial prepared almond filling with ¼ cup finely chopped nutmeats. Cut into 3 uniform strips. Roll each strip lengthwise to enclose filling, and twist slightly. Form braid pinching both ends well to prevent opening. Place on greased baking sheet or preferably covered with silicone paper. Cover with wax paper and towel and let rise in room temperature about 1½ hours. Bake at 375° F. about 25 to 30 minutes, or until golden brown. Remove from oven and when warm glaze, and drizzle with Coffee Cake Icing (page 510) if to be served within a short time. Best to prepare 3 medium-size braids from 1 recipe of dough. Roll each third to measure about 8 × 16 rectangle. Spread with ⅓ cup commercial almond filling combined with 3 tablespoons finely chopped nutmeats. Roll same as larger cake. Bake about 20 to 25 minutes at 375° F., or until golden brown. Ice, etc.

Almond Paste Filling

½ cup (¼ pound) commercial almond paste
½ cup granulated sugar (or brown sugar packed)
1 large whole egg, slightly beaten
1 cup soft cake crumbs, or cookie crumbs
1 teaspoon vanilla

1 tablespoon melted butter
About ½ cup fine-chopped pecan or walnut meats
About ¼ cup rich milk or cream, or enough to make spreading consistency
¼ teaspoon cinnamon (optional)

Cut almond paste in fine pieces; combine with the sugar. Slowly add beaten egg, and beat with electric mixer or spoon until smooth. Add cake crumbs, vanilla, butter, nutmeats, milk or cream, and cinnamon. Beat well until thoroughly blended.

Babas au Rhum

Makes 12 to 18 individual babas

4 large eggs
½ cup lukewarm melted butter or margarine
⅓ cup granulated sugar
¼ teaspoon salt

1 package dry yeast, combined with ¼ cup warm water (about 110° F.)
About 2½ cups sifted all-purpose flour

In a medium-size bowl, beat eggs about 1 minute with hand or electric beater. Add lukewarm melted butter or margarine, granulated sugar, salt, dissolved yeast, then the flour a little at a time. Beat until smooth for several minutes with electric beater, or 3 minutes with electric beater, or 5 minutes with a heavy spoon. Should be a stiff batter or until drops from spoon in very soft gobs. As soon as beating is completed, pour batter into well-greased individual plain or fancy tart molds. Any size small, medium, or large individual molds may be used. Fill molds about ½. Let stand in room temperature until dough rises almost to top of molds. Meanwhile, preheat oven to 375° F. Bake about 12 to 18 minutes, or until golden brown and firm to the touch, depending on size. When done, remove at once from molds and let stand until cold. Use at once or store in a covered container until needed. May be baked several days in advance.

To Serve. Prepare Hot Syrup (page 530). Drop Babas into simmering syrup and let remain in syrup for 5 or 6 minutes, turning them over several times, until they swell appreciably, to more than double original size. Remove them carefully from hot syrup, with a large *perforated spoon* or pancake turner, and let drain on cake coolers for at least 15 minutes. When cold, place them carefully in shallow petit fours white cups. Brush top of Babas with a little liqueur, then spread with a very little apricot or peach glaze that has been thinned out with corn syrup. (Apricot or peach jam may be put through a strainer for this purpose.) Garnish top of each Baba with a red well-drained maraschino cherry and green citron leaves. Green maraschino cherries may be cut to simulate leaves if preferred. Serve individually with Whipped Cream Brandy or Rum Sauce (page 372), or with brandy-flavored whipped cream.

Hot Syrup for Babas

1 pound granulated sugar (2¼ cups)
4 cups water
Juice of 1 large lemon, then cut up
skin in medium pieces and add to
other ingredients

¼ cup brandy, curaçao, or other
liqueur

Cook these ingredients in a 2-quart saucepan *only* until syrup is clear.
Then to hot syrup add about ¼ cup of brandy, curaçao or other liqueur.

▶ *Cakes and Tortes*

SPECIAL OCCASION CAKES

THERE ARE HUNDREDS OF CAKE RECIPES, BUT IF THEY ARE ANALYZED YOU will see that the cakes are closely related and come under one of two categories: the butter cake family and the sponge cake family. As you prepare the various cakes, it will be interesting to note that they branch out from a few basic recipes. Each recipe, however, is distinguished by certain characteristics. Full directions are given with each recipe in this section.

The terms "frosting" and "icing" are used interchangeably. Frostings may be cooked or uncooked. Ordinarily, sponge cakes are covered with richer icings than butter cakes because they do not contain any shortening. Slightly sweetened or unsweetened whipped cream that has been stabilized with a small amount of gelatin may be used to ice and fill some cakes.

Ingredients for butter, or shortening, cakes must be room temperature, about 70° F. during warm weather, 75° F. during cold weather. Remove ingredients from refrigerator several hours in advance during cold weather, only a short time during warm weather. Do not overheat cakes when you add the flour and liquid; it is important to lower speed at this point. Overbeating will make cakes heavy and streaky, especially during warm weather. Do not bake this type of cake in pans that are more than 2 inches deep unless indicated in recipes. Shallow pans will give a more desirable texture. Always test cakes for doneness by inserting a wood pin in or cake tester in center of cake before removing it from oven. If tester is dry, cake is done. If all shortening is used instead of butter or margarine, it is important to increase liquid by 1 tablespoon, and salt by ½ teaspoon.

▶ BUTTER CAKES ◀

What are butter cakes and how would you distinguish them from other cakes?

Cakes are divided into two general classifications. All cakes containing butter and other fats are classified as "butter cakes" and all those that do not contain butter are classified as "sponge cakes."

531

What are the important factors in successful cakemaking?
1. Standard level measurements.
2. Dependable balanced and tested recipe.
3. Good ingredients, such as top quality eggs, fine granulated sugar and cake flour.
4. Correct mixing technique, which becomes more or less automatic with practice and experience.
5. Correct temperature of ingredients; they should be at room temperature, cool, but not cold or warm.
6. Proper size and style of pan, correct baking temperature, and required length of time for baking.

Is it necessary to use all butter in cakes?
No. It is true that cakes made with all butter are very delectable in texture and flavor. However, half margarine and half butter may be used for excellent results. All margarine also produces good cakes. *Use the regular type margarine,* not the liquid or chiffon type if you prepare our recipes. If you prefer to use shortening instead of butter and margarine, it is important to increase milk by 1 tablespoon for each small recipe, and 2 tablespoons in larger recipes.

How can egg whites be whipped stiff, but not dry?
The whites are beaten to the point where they stand in glossy peaks, look "wet" and "shiny," and cling tightly to the beater when it is held straight up. This is the correct stage for all beaten whites, unless recipe states otherwise. If whipped to the dry stage whites become granular and will break up when folded into the main mixture. A soufflé would not rise properly and would be grainy in center if the whites were dry. This is one of the most important techniques to learn. Whites will not stand at all, once beaten, unless some sugar is added; when called for in recipe whites will remain firm much longer. (See page 564 for more detailed information.)

Why is cake flour used in cakemaking?
Cake flour is preferred in cakemaking because it has gone through a special milling process and contains less gluten than bread or all-purpose flour, thereby making cakes more velvety and tender. If using all-purpose flour use 2 tablespoons less for each cup of cake flour. The results are acceptable, but not as desirable.

Why do butter cakes sometimes shrink excessively?
If cakes are overbaked or if pans are well greased there will tend to be excessive shrinkage. Cakes tend to expand to a better volume if

sides of pans are not greased at all, but slight greasing is recommended if a smooth surface is desired on sides of cake when released from pan.

Should butter cakes be released from pans as soon as they are removed from oven?

No. It is best to allow cakes to remain in pans, on a cake cooler, for 10 to 15 minutes, thereby permitting cake cells to stiffen slightly before turning out. This will prevent breaking, and the cakes become sufficiently rigid to withstand the shock of handling.

How are cakes tested for doneness?

Cake is tested for doneness by inserting a toothpick or cake tester in center of the cake. If tester comes out clean without any of the batter adhering, the cake is done. Another indication that the cake is done is when it shrinks slightly from sides of pan and no dent is left when the center of the cake is touched *lightly* with finger. Tests should not be made, however, until cake has baked at least three-quarters of baking time suggested. It is important to watch cake the last quarter of baking time to prevent overbaking. Only approximate baking times are given in these recipes, because cakes are not always prepared under the most favorable conditions, such as temperature of ingredients when mixing cake, style and depth of pans used, quality of raw ingredients, correct oven temperature, etc.

What causes cakes to run over in baking?

1. Too much batter for the size of pan used; use less batter in pan.
2. Oven temperature is too low underneath cake; use higher temperature, or bake cake on lowest rack.
3. Too much baking powder. Be sure to loosen powder before measuring with standard measuring spoon, and level with edge of knife or spatula. Use type of baking powder designated in recipe.
4. Too much sugar. Our recipes have been tested many times, and if directions are followed, excellent results will be obtained.

Is it necessary to cut through butter-cake batters while in pan or to strike pan on table?

It is more important to do so in angel food and sponge cakes. For butter cakes, striking pan on table several times is sufficient.

What depth pan gives best results?

The depth of batter in pan influences texture of cake. If a fine velvety texture is desired, depth of pan should be at least 1⅓ inches, and sufficient batter should be used to permit cake to come to top of pan when it is done. A straighter-side pan will give cake a better texture than a pan with sloping sides. It is necessary to have pan filled a little more than half with batter for the majority of butter cakes, unless otherwise specified, as for Florentine Pastries.

If a recipe for a butter cake calls for 2-layer pans, can a 2-inch deep square pan be used successfully?

Yes. In this case, reduce baking temperature 25 degrees and bake 2-inch deep square cake for a longer time, testing last part of baking period.

What causes heavy cakes?

1. Oven temperature too low.
2. Oven temperature too high.
3. Overbeating of flour and milk.
4. Underbeating and overbeating of butter, sugar, and eggs. It is important to beat these ingredients with electric mixer or a heavy spoon until mixture is thick and fluffy and light in color, but not runny or oily. Fine granulated sugar (not the superfine) should be used. On a cool day the butter, sugar, and eggs should be beaten continuously 7 or 8 minutes before flour and liquid are added. *Reduce beating time on a warm day.*
5. Underbeating of flour and milk will also cause a heavy cake. Batter must be beaten only until smooth after each addition of flour and milk.

What causes hill in center of butter cake?

1. Too much flour.
2. Overbeating.
3. Too much batter in center of pan. Always spread batter to sides of pan, leaving a slight depression in center, unless otherwise specified.
4. Oven temperature too high.

When baking layer cakes, regardless of how evenly I distribute the dough in the two pans, invariably one side is higher than the other. What causes this?

This is caused by uneven heat distribution. Bake 1 layer at a time in center of rack for more perfect results.

What causes sugary crust?

1. Insufficient beating of butter, sugar, and eggs.
2. Use of very coarse granulated sugar; fine granulated sugar should be used (not the superfine).
3. Too much sugar.

Is it possible to overbeat butter, sugar, and eggs with the electric mixer for butter cakes?

Yes. There is an optimum amount of beating for these ingredients. It is learned principally from experience and close observation. Our timing is only a guide. A good rule, however, is to cream butter or shortening until it is soft enough to blend well with the sugar. Add sugar, about ¼ cupful at a time, and beat well after each addition, for about ½ minute. Then add eggs and beat each one in about 1 minute or until mixture is very *light but not runny.* Air incorporated during creaming process increases volume of cake and also given a finer texture and velvetiness to the finished cake. Fine granulated sugar should be used in cakemaking as it dissolves more quickly. Underbeating or overbeating these ingredients will produce an inferior cake.

What causes tunnels in cakes?

1. Overbeating when adding flour and liquid.
2. Too much baking powder; loosen baking powder, then measure.
3. Beating is best accomplished in a circular motion.

Is it necessary to preheat oven for cake baking?

Yes. After extensive tests made by leading universities' home economics departments, it was found that cakes baked in preheated ovens were superior in every way—and unless oven is preheated, baking time is difficult to gauge.

Can 3 layers of cake be baked in the oven at the same time?

Yes, provided there is sufficient space for 2 layers on the center rack and the third layer is not placed directly over the lower layers. The pans should not touch each other, nor should they touch the oven walls.

Can butter cakes be stored in refrigerator?

Yes, especially during warm weather and if cakes are to be held for more than 2 or 3 days. It is advisable, however, to remove butter cakes from refrigerator at least an hour before serving time, unless they are filled or spread with whipped cream. Extremely cold butter cakes have a firmer texture and are more desirable if kept in room temperature for an hour or longer before serving.

On what rack should cakes be baked?

Bake all cakes (unless otherwise specified in recipes) as near the center of oven as possible, and if baking 2 layers at one time, stagger layers in opposite corners, away from walls of oven, leaving space between each layer, so that the heat may circulate freely around the pans for uniform baking.

Three layers should be placed on two racks that are close together in the center of the oven and still allow for the lower cakes to rise without touching rack above. Two pans are placed on the lower rack and the third on upper rack, being sure not to place it directly over lower cake, but where there is most open space.

When 1 cake is baked, it should be placed on the center of the rack as close to the center of the oven as possible.

What causes a heavy, unbaked layer on bottom or center of cakes?
1. Must use a reliable balanced recipe.
2. Insufficient mixing; beat longer.
3. Too much liquid; reduce liquid.
4. Overbeating, especially on a warm day. Beat butter, sugar, and eggs until mixture has the consistency of a heavy whipped cream, and is not runny or oily.
5. Very soft flour; increase flour.
6. Warm ingredients; must be cool, but not cold.
7. Insufficient beating of yolks. Beat until very light.
8. Flours do vary from one season to another and if cakes are consistently soggy or form a heavy layer on bottom, decrease milk by 1 tablespoon for each cup in recipe, or increase flour by 2 tablespoons or a little more if necessary for each cup.
9. If batter for butter cakes appears too thin after it is completely beaten, it is better to add a little more flour provided batter was not overbeaten.

What causes a dry butter cake?
1. Too much flour.
2. Insufficient shortening.
3. Overbaking.
4. Not enough moisture.

What causes a heavy cake?
1. Overbeating of ingredients in first part, or when adding flour and milk.
2. On a warm day do not remove ingredients from refrigerator until 40 minutes before preparing butter cakes, and do not overbeat butter, sugar, and eggs. Mixture should appear like a heavy whipped cream and not runny or oily.
3. Insufficient beating or overbeating of butter, sugar, and eggs.

4. Too much shortening or flour.
5. Oven temperature too high.

What causes tops to split?
It is characteristic of some loaf and other cakes baked in deep pans to crack on top; this does not affect texture. Too much flour and too much heat will also cause some cakes to split on top.

What causes butter cake to fall?
1. Too much baking powder or other leavening.
2. Too much sugar.
3. Temperature too low.
4. Insufficient baking.
5. Leaving oven door open too long before cake has set.
6. Jarring oven door.
7. Ingredients too cold.

What causes cakes to stick to bottom of pan?
Butter cakes will stick if not enough unsalted fat has been used for greasing. Butter and margarine burn more rapidly and have a tendency to make cakes stick. It is better to use an unsalted soft (not melted) shortening, greasing pan well on bottom and very, very lightly on sides, then sprinkle surface with flour, and shake out loose flour.

Some recipes suggest not to grease sides of pans, but we have found that there is no difference in the volume of the cake if sides are greased very lightly. The cake is more easily released from pan with a dinner knife when sides have been lightly greased, and the surface is smoother to ice. Please use amount of shortening suggested in our recipes and proper size pans for best results.

Too strong bottom heat will also cause sticking. In this case bake cake on higher rack, or reduce temperature slightly.

What causes cakes to peak in center?
1. Too many eggs.
2. Not enough sugar.
3. Not enough baking powder.
4. Too much heat.
5. Too much flour.

What causes cakes to crumble or become too tender?
1. Too much sugar.
2. Not enough eggs.

3. Oven temperature too low.
4. Too much baking powder.

What causes excessive shrinkage of cake in oven or after removal from oven?

1. Too much milk.
2. Oven temperature is too high or too low.
3. Too much shortening.
4. Flour is too fresh.
5. Overbaking.
6. Overgreasing of baking pan.
7. Cake is placed in a draft or in a cold room to cool.

Why is part of the sugar in a butter cake sometimes added to the egg whites that are folded in last?

The addition of sugar stabilizes the whites and makes it easier to fold them into the batter. Folding should continue only until no bits of egg white appear in the batter.

Can brown sugar be substituted successfully in a butter cake calling for granulated sugar?

It is always better to use the type of sugar designated in the recipe, but if it must be substituted it is safer to do so by weight than by measure.

Mathon's Vanilla Cream Torte

From Mathon's Famous Seafood Restaurant, Waukegan, Illinois

Crust for 9 x 9 x 2-Inch Square Pan

2 cups graham cracker crumbs (finely crushed with rolling pin, then sifted)
¼ cup sifted granulated sugar
1 tablespoon all-purpose flour
¼ teaspoon cinnamon
½ cup butter or margarine, melted

Mix dry ingredients together well; add melted butter or margarine and with a large spoon blend well, then mix further with fingers until moist. Remove 1 cup to be used for top of torte. Pour rest of preparation into bottom of an ungreased 9 × 9 × 2-inch square pan. Press down with back of a large spoon and back of hand until uniform in thickness. Keep in refrigerator for at least 1 hour until firm to touch. Prepare filling just before it is to be poured into pan.

Filling for Vanilla Cream Torte

⅓ cup unsifted cornstarch
⅛ teaspoon salt
½ cup sifted granulated sugar
4 large egg yolks, combined with ¼
    cup cool milk
¾ cup instant dry milk, added about

1 tablespoon at a time to 3¾ cups
cool homogenized milk (stir until
smooth; bring milk to simmering
point)
About 2 teaspoons vanilla

Combine all ingredients except the milk and vanilla in a 3-quart heavy saucepan. Scald milk and at once add it slowly, about ¼ cup at a time, to the yolk mixture, stirring it quickly and continuously until all milk has been added. Now place pot over medium heat (not high) and cook for several minutes or bit longer, stirring continuously until custard begins to thicken and simmer (not boil). Now simmer (never boil) about 3 minutes, stirring quickly and continuously to prevent overcooking. Temperature of simmering custard should be about 185° F., never higher than 200° F. or it is likely to separate. Remove from heat and at once pour into a large bowl; add vanilla, stir, and quickly pour hot custard into cake pan lined with crumbs. Keep it on a cake rack while preparing Meringue Topping.

Meringue Topping for Vanilla Torte (and Other Tortes or Baked Desserts)

½ teaspoon cream of tartar
Pinch salt
½ teaspoon vanilla
4 very large egg whites, carefully sep-

arated, to measure ½ cup (room
temperature about 1 hour)
½ cup sifted granulated sugar

Add cream of tartar, salt, and vanilla to egg whites (in a 7- or 8-inch bowl). (Best temperature of egg whites 75° to 80° F.) Beat whites at high speed until medium and still slide out of bowl. Now add granulated sugar, about 1 tablespoon at a time, and beat after each addition until blended. After all the sugar has been added continue to beat about 1 more minute if using a powerful beater, a little longer if using a junior beater, or one that has less power, or beat until peaks or meringue are fairly stiff and ends slightly rounded, and meringue clings to beater. To stabilize meringue and prevent weeping, add preparation made with cornstarch given below, and continue to beat meringue low speed about ½ minute, *not longer. At once* spoon meringue onto hot filling, and with dinner knife or spatula spread it as evenly and flat as possible. Sprinkle top with reserved cup of graham cracker crumb mixture, and bake torte on lowest rack of a *preheated* 375° F. oven for about 15 minutes.

When done, remove from oven, and let torte cool on a cake rack in room temperature for several hours, then it must be refrigerated for at least 8 hours to prevent spreading. May be prepared day in advance, if kept in refrigerator.

Cornstarch Stabilizer for Meringue. In a very small saucepan combine 2 teaspoons cornstarch with 1 tablespoon cool water until smooth. Add ⅓ cup hot water, stir and cook over low heat until thick, then simmer only ½ minute. Use this lukewarm, as directed in meringue recipe.

To Serve Tortes. Loosen around sides of torte with a dinner knife. Cut into uniform squares or rectangles right in pan, same width as a pancake turner. With pancake turner release pieces carefully from pan, scraping bottom slightly to release crust. The first piece is likely to break slightly.

Chocolate Vanilla Cream Torte

To basic Vanilla Cream Torte, add 3 ounces of melted dark sweet chocolate (not baking chocolate) to the yolk mixture before adding scalded milk combined with the ¾ cup instant dry milk. Add vanilla. Increase sugar to ⅔ cup. If you prefer to use baking chocolate, increase sugar to ¾ cup. Proceed as per general directions (page 538).

Butterscotch Meringue Torte

Prepare filling by adding ¾ cup light brown sugar, solidly packed, to ¼ cup melted butter or margarine. Stir well, and add 4 yolks combined with ¼ cup milk and ⅓ cup cornstarch. Stir well until smooth. Now add 3¾ cups homogenized milk combined with ¼ cup instant dry milk, brought to the scalding point, *slowly* to the egg mixture, stirring continuously. Cook over medium heat until thick, then continue to cook slowly, at simmering point, about 3 minutes. Add 1 teaspoon or more vanilla, mix gently, and at once pour filling into pan lined with crumbs. Prepare meringue, and proceed as for Vanilla Cream Torte (page 538).

Lemon Meringue Torte

Use 1½ cups granulated sugar. Increase cornstarch to ⅔ cup. Combine ¼ cup cold water with the yolks from 4 large eggs. Use 3¼ cup boiling water instead of milk for a smoother custard, ½ cup, more or less, strained lemon juice, and 1 teaspoon lemon rind added to filling after it has simmered for several minutes. Stir well and continue to cook about 3 more minutes. Pour into pan lined with crumbs, etc. Prepare stabilized meringue, etc. (see page 538).

Note. These tortes are very delicate and delectable if directions are properly followed. Do not permit fillings to boil at any time, just simmer, below 200° F. Instant dry milk added to the fresh homogenized milk will stabilize the fresh milk and helps prevent a watery custard. It is important to refrigerate these tortes as soon as they are cool, for at least 8 hours. Best to prepare them a day in advance, if refrigerated.

If preferred, these tortes may be prepared without using the instant dry milk; and the cornstarch stabilizer may be omitted in the mixture, but do try the recipes as we suggest. You will be pleasantly amazed to see the difference in the finished product.

Lady Fingers Liqueur Torte

For No. 44 pan that measures 13 × 4½ × 2½ inches

4 packages commercial lady fingers
½ pound dark sweet chocolate (milk chocolate may be used); dipping chocolate excellent
1 cup butter, cold and firm (half margarine may be used)
2½ cups sifted confectioners' sugar
1 tablespoon vanilla
¾ cup egg yolks (about 8, best to measure), beaten at high speed for several minutes (in 7-inch bowl)
⅓ cup curaçao, combined with 1½ cups cool pineapple or orange juice (brandy, rum, or other liqueur may be used instead of curaçao)
1 cup of almonds, blanched in simmering water for several minutes, then slivered, and toasted on a baking sheet in 350° F. oven for about 10 minutes, turning them over every few minutes. Watch closely toward end. Commercially sliced almonds may be roasted and used. (Other nutmeats may be used instead)
About 2 cups of Chocolate Marshmallow Buttercream (page 610) for top decorations

Split 4 packages lady fingers.

Line pan with 2 thicknesses of heavy wax paper; bring paper up about an inch above rim, or use silicone paper. Now on bottom of pan, *over the wax paper*, place a stiff cardboard cut to fit pan, covered smoothly with foil. This will facilitate handling torte.

Cut chocolate up in small pieces and melt it over hot water. Stir, and when completely melted remove from hot water and let stand until *cool*, but not cold and not warm.

Prepare Filling. In an 8-inch bowl, beat the cold firm butter for several minutes until it looks like a heavy whipped cream. Add sugar, about ½ cup at a time, and beat after each addition until smooth, then beat about 2 more minutes after all sugar has been added. Add vanilla, and beaten yolks, a little at a time, beating only until well blended. Last, add cool chocolate, a little at a time, and beat only until no streaks appear.

In a shallow square or round pan or dish, combine the liqueur with fruit juice. Blend well. Dip split lady fingers into liquid, 1 at a time *quickly*. Don't let them soak or they will crumble. Lay fingers 3 or 4 in a row *lengthwise* over foil cardboard on bottom of pan, forming 5 to 6 rows.

Spread each of first 4 or 5 layers with ½ cup filling, and top layer with about 1 cup, reserving rest of filling for sides of torte. Refrigerate, or, better, place in freezer for about 1 hour, or until filling is very firm to touch and torte can be lifted out of pan without breaking.

To Decorate Torte. Lift it out of pan carefully with both hands and remove wax paper. Foil-covered cardboard will cling to bottom of cake, facilitating handling. Spread sides with remaining chocolate filling, and cover with 1 cup slivered toasted almonds, including about ½ inch of rim. Place torte on serving platter (preferably oblong or oval), and refrigerate.

Pipe 5 very large Chocolate Buttercream roses on nails with No. 124 rose tube. Insert them into a carton box with cover to hold them in place in freezer or coldest part of refrigerator until firm to touch. Best to freeze them for a short time. Meanwhile, with bag and No. 30 star tube, pipe 5 small mounds of Chocolate Buttercream on top of cake where roses will be placed. This will raise roses. When roses are firm to touch, release them carefully from nails with a small spatula or dinner knife, and place on top of each mound, holding a heavy toothpick in center of each to help place them in proper position. Now, with No. 70 leaf tube, pipe chocolate leaves on each side and ends of roses.

This torte is very beautiful and delicious decorated with chocolate roses and leaves. Instead of chocolate roses, it may be decorated with light buttercream or whipped cream scrolls or flowers. It is important to keep torte in coldest part of refrigerator until serving time. May be frozen if well wrapped.

Cinnamon Butter Cake

Serves 8

⅔ cup butter	1 teaspoon double-acting baking powder
1 cup granulated sugar	¼ teaspoon salt
2 large whole eggs, beaten with dover beater about ½ minute	4 teaspoons cinnamon
2 cups sifted cake flour	1 cup less 2 tablespoons buttermilk
1 teaspoon baking soda	

Have all ingredients at room temperature. Beat butter until creamy, add sugar, a little at a time, and beat about 1 minute. Add eggs, a little at a time, and beat about 3 minutes, or until light. Combine and sift dry ingredients several times and add to butter-and-egg mixture alternately with buttermilk. Beat only until batter is smooth. Pour into a shallow greased baking sheet that measures 11 × 15 inches. Bake about 15 minutes at 350° F., then 5 minutes at 400° F. Remove from oven; let cool in pan. When cold, spread with Butter Cinnamon icing. Let cake stand about 30 minutes before cutting into rectangles, squares, or as desired. Place whole pecan or walnut halves on each and press down lightly; or omit nuts and pipe icing rosette and leaves.

Butter Cinnamon

3 tablespoons soft butter	1 teaspoon vanilla
¼ cup cream or rich milk	2 cups, or more, sifted confectioners'
1½ teaspoons cinnamon	sugar

Beat butter; add cream or milk, cinnamon, and vanilla. Last, add sifted confectioners' sugar a little at a time, and beat until smooth. More or less sugar may be used to suit taste.

Tiny Cinnamon Cupcakes

Pour Cinnamon Butter Cake batter (page 542) into small cupcake pans (lined with paper cups) that measure about ¾ inch deep by 2 inches wide, having them a little more than half filled. Bake at 350° F. about 15 to 20 minutes, or until done. When cool, pipe a large round scroll of your favorite buttercream icing. Sprinkle center only with pistachio nuts.

Vienna Date Slices

Serves 8

¾ cup butter (half margarine may be used), cold and firm	¼ cup sifted confectioners' sugar, combined with 2 cups sifted all-purpose flour
½ cup cream cheese, cold and firm	2 teaspoons granulated sugar
1 egg yolk	

With electric mixer beat butter until creamy, add cheese and egg yolk, and beat until smooth. Add combined flour and sugar, and beat until smooth. Turn out onto a floured pastry cloth and knead gently about 1 minute. Form a flat 8-inch square. Wrap well in wax paper, and refrigerate until firm to the touch but not hard. (Dough may remain in refrigerator many hours, but it must stand in room temperature until it is slightly pliable.) When ready to use, cut dough into 2 pieces and roll each to measure about 8 × 12 inches. Spread ⅓ cup Filling for Vienna Date Slices (page 544) down center of dough. Turn dough over to enclose Filling. Do likewise with other piece of dough. Pick up carefully with both hands, and transfer to a very lightly greased baking sheet. Brush tops lightly with beaten egg white, and sprinkle each with 1 teaspoon granulated sugar. Bake at 400° F. about 25 to 30 minutes, or until golden brown. Let cool on baking sheet. Very delicious served warm or cold.

To serve, slice crosswise about ½ inch thick. Slices may be sprinkled with sifted confectioners' sugar.

Filling for Vienna Date Slices

Cook 1 package pitted dates (7½-ounce size) in 1 cup hot water in a covered saucepan about 10 minutes, or until very soft. Mash with a fork. Let cool. Add ¼ cup fine-chopped nuts. When cold, add about 3 tablespoons water to make paste of spreading consistency. This is enough filling for 2 recipes Vienna Dough.

Vienna Apricot Slices

Follow recipe for Vienna Date Slices (page 543), using Filling for Vienna Apricot Slices (below).

Filling for Vienna Apricot Slices

Cover ¼ pound dried apricots with ½ cup water, and cook in a covered saucepan about 15 minutes or until very soft. When done, mash with a fork. Let cool, and add ½ cup granulated sugar and 2 tablespoons chopped nuts. When cold, add 1 or 2 tablespoons water if necessary to make spreading consistency. This is enough filling for 1 recipe Vienna Dough.

Plain Layer Cake

For single layer 9 × 1½-inch round pan, or its equivalent

½ cup butter or margarine	with 2¼ teaspoons double-acting
1 cup granulated sugar	baking powder
2 medium eggs (to measure ⅓ cup)	⅔ cup milk
1¾ cups sifted cake flour, combined	½ teaspoon vanilla or other flavoring

Measure ingredients and let stand in room temperature about 2 hours during very cold weather, ½ hour during warm weather.

With electric mixer high speed (or heavy spoon) beat butter or margarine for about 1 or 2 minutes. Add sugar, a small amount at a time, and beat about 1 more minute. Add whole eggs, 1 at a time and beat until light, about 1 minute for each egg. And combine flour and baking powder, about ½ cup at a time, alternately with ¼ cup of milk, and beat after each addition at medium speed *only until smooth*. Overbeating cake when adding flour and milk will produce a heavy texture. Last, add vanilla and blend well.

Pour batter into a 9 × 1½-inch round layer cake pan (or equivalent square pan) having pan little more than half filled. (First grease well on bottom and lightly on sides with 1½ teaspoons soft unsalted shortening, and coat with flour, or grease lightly and line with wax paper. Shake out loose flour.) Spread batter in pan with back of spoon, making very *slight* depression in center of layer. Bake in preheated 350° F. oven 25 minutes, then increase temperature to 375° F. and bake about 10 more minutes, testing cake toward end to prevent overbaking. When done, remove from oven, let stand in pan on cake rack about 10 minutes, then loosen around sides and turn out onto cake cooler.

Buttermilk Layer Cake

½ cup butter or margarine
1 cup granulated sugar
2 medium eggs (⅓ cup)
1¾ cups sifted cake flour, combined

with ¾ teaspoon baking soda
and ¾ teaspoon cream of tartar
⅔ cup buttermilk
½ teaspoon vanilla or other flavoring

Prepare same as Plain Layer Cake (above).

Layers Baked in Various Size Pans

1 recipe batter makes one 9 × 1½-inch layer. Bake 25 minutes at 350° F., then about 10 minutes at 375° F.

1 recipe batter makes one 10 × 1⅓-inch layer. Bake 25 minutes at 350° F., then about 10 minutes at 375° F.

1½ recipes batter make two 9½ × 1-inch layers. Bake 20 minutes at 350° F., then about 10 minutes at 375° F.

1½ recipes batter make two 9 × 1¼-inch layers. Bake 25 minutes at 350° F., then about 10 minutes at 375° F.

1 double recipe batter makes one 12 × 1½-inch layer. Bake 45 minutes at 350° F., then about 10 minutes at 375° F.

1 recipe batter makes two 8 × 1-inch layers. Bake 20 minutes at 350° F., then about 10 minutes at 375° F.

Note. Bake cakes on center rack of oven. If baking 2 layers at one time, stagger layers in opposite corners, away from walls of oven, leaving space between layers. A third layer may be baked on upper rack at same time, being sure not to place it directly over lower layer, but where there is most open space. We like to use at least half butter for flavor and texture. If you use all hydrogenated shortening, add ½ teaspoon salt and 1 extra tablespoon liquid for each recipe. If you like a soft, moist texture prepare cake made with buttermilk. Refrigerate buttermilk cakes if they are to stand for more than 2 days during very warm weather. Remove from refrigerator about an hour before serving.

Florentine Pastry Squares

Pour batter for Individual Florentine Pastries (page 546), using only 2¼ cups of cake flour, in a 9 × 9 × 2-inch square pan, or preferably, in two

7 × 7 × 1¼-inch foil pans, first greased and floured with 1½ teaspoons unsalted shortening for large pans, and 1 teaspoon shortening for each 7-inch pan. Bake large cakes at 350° F. 35 minutes, then increase heat to 375° F. and bake about 10 more minutes. For 7-inch cakes, reduce baking time to 30 minutes at 350° F., then about 5 more minutes at 375° F., if necessary. When done, remove cakes from oven and let stand in room temperature about 10 minutes, then loosen around sides with a dinner knife, place cake rack over top, and gently turn them over. Let cool, then spread with Thin Orange Icing (page 547). Let stand until icing is slightly set. Then cut cake into uniform squares. With No. 27 star tube and Quick Buttercream Icing—No. 1 (page 614), pipe a rosette in center of each square. With No. 67 leaf tube, pipe green leaves.

Individual Florentine Pastries

Makes 24 individual cupcakes

¾ cup butter or margarine, medium consistency
1¼ cups sifted granulated sugar
2 very large whole eggs (to measure ½ cup); if short, add a little extra beaten egg or milk
1 teaspoon lemon or orange extract (or vanilla)
2½ cups sifted cake flour for individual cup cake pastries (use ¼ cup less flour if you bake this cake in square or round pans)

¼ teaspoon salt
1½ teaspoons double-acting baking powder and ½ teaspoon baking soda
½ cup commercial sour cream, combined with ½ cup homogenized milk, or omit sour cream and soda, and instead use ¾ cup homogenized milk, but increase double-acting baking powder to 2¼ teaspoons

With electric mixer or heavy spoon cream butter or margarine for about 1 or 2 minutes. Add sugar, a little at a time, and beat well after each addition until thoroughly blended, for about 1 more minute. Now beat eggs for ½ minute, and add them a little at a time to the shortening mixture, and continue to beat at high speed about 2 more minutes during cool weather, a little less time during very warm weather. Lower speed, and add flour that has been combined and sifted with baking powder, soda, and salt, about ½ cup at a time, alternately with ¼ cup of the liquid, beating after each addition *only* until smooth. For individual pastries pour batter into paper-lined large muffin molds, having them *not more* than half filled. Bake at 350° F. 25 to 30 minutes, or until brown, but not dry. Serve plain, or scoop out center and fill with various jams, jellies, cake fillings, or cream filling. Place tops on. Sprinkle with confectioners' sugar, and decorate with Quick Buttercream Icing—No. 1 (page 614) rosettes and leaves, using No. 27 star tube for rosettes, and No. 67 tube for leaves. Recipe may be cut in half.

Chocolate Florentine Pastries

Using basic recipe (page 546), reduce flour by ⅓ cupful and add ⅓ cup of unsifted cocoa to the flour and sift together several times. Add 1 teaspoon vanilla. Bake according to directions for Individual Florentine Pastries.

Thin Orange Icing for Florentine Pastries

About 1½ cups sifted confectioners' sugar, more or less, depending on consistency of icing desired

2 tablespoons orange juice, or 2 tablespoons water and 1 teaspoon orange extract

1 tablespoon melted butter or margarine

Add sifted sugar, little by little, to the orange juice and melted butter or margarine, and beat thoroughly until smooth. Spread on top of individual pastries; or spread on entire top of cakes baked in square pans.

Rainbow Butter Cake

For Turkhead pan that measures 8½ × 3¼, or little larger

¾ cup butter or margarine

1 cup and 2 tablespoons sifted granulated sugar

2 large whole eggs (½ cup)

1 teaspoon lemon

½ teaspoon vanilla extract

2¾ cups sifted cake flour

2¼ teaspoons double-acting baking powder

½ cup milk

Red, blue, and yellow food coloring

Have all ingredients room temperature about 1 or 2 hours during cold weather, not more than ½ hours during warm weather.

Cream butter or margarine about 1 minute in an 8½-inch bowl, add sugar a little at a time and beat about 1 more minute. Add eggs, 1 at a time, and beat about 1 minute at high speed for each egg if using a powerful mixer. Should look like a heavy whipped cream, not runny. Add extracts, then flour sifted with baking powder, about 1 cup flour at a time alternately with about 3 tablespoons of the milk, beating after each addition *only* until smooth.

To 1½ cups of the batter, add red coloring; to 1¼ cups add green coloring; and to 1¼ cups add yellow. Gently beat coloring into batters only until evenly blended. Grease form pan with 1 tablespoon and 1 teaspoon unsalted shortening and coat with flour. Shake out loose flour. First pour pink batter into pan carefully with a spoon and spread it gently; then with spoon pour in green batter; and last yellow batter. Spread very gently. Bake in preheated 325° F. oven 45 minutes; increase temperature to 375° F., and bake about 15 more minutes, or until done. Remove from oven and let cake remain in pan about 15 minutes, then loosen around edges of tube, and carefully turn it out onto cake cooler. When cool, ice, or simply sprinkle thickly with confectioners' sugar. Slice and arrange attractively on round platter to show rainbow.

Large Rainbow Butter Cake

For form pan or angel food pan that measures about 10 × 4 inches

1½ cups butter or margarine	5½ cups sifted cake flour
2¼ cups sifted granulated sugar	4½ teaspoons double-acting baking
4 large whole eggs (1 cup)	powder
1½ teaspoons lemon extract	1 cup and 2 tablespoons milk
1 teaspoon vanilla	

Follow general mixing directions (above). Divide batter, and to 3½ cups add red coloring; to 2¾ cups add green coloring; and to rest of batter add yellow coloring.

Grease pan with 1½ tablespoons shortening and coat with flour. Bake 1 hour at 325° F., then about 20 more minutes at 375° F., or until done. Remove from oven. Let stand on cake rack about 15 minutes, then carefully turn out onto rack.

For rainbow effect a tube pan must be used. Do not overbeat batter at any time.

Spiced Cake Squares

½ cup butter or margarine	About ¼ teaspoon ground cloves
1 cup soft light brown sugar, packed	¼ teaspoon cinnamon
2 large whole eggs (½ cup)	¼ teaspoon salt
1½ cups sifted cake flour	½ cup buttermilk, or ½ cup regular
½ teaspoon baking soda, and ¾ teaspoon double-acting baking powder	homogenized milk
	½ teaspoon vanilla (optional)

Have all ingredients room temperature about an hour, or remove chill from milk and eggs before using.

In an 8-inch bowl cream butter or margarine with electric mixer at high speed about 1 minute; add sugar a little at a time and beat about 1 more minute. Now add eggs, 1 at a time, and beat each in batter about 1 minute. After eggs are added, beat batter another minute or two if necessary to make batter light but not runny. Do not overbeat. Add sifted combined dry ingredients, about ½ cup at a time, alternately with about 2 tablespoons of milk, and beat after each addition only until smooth. Vanilla may be added if desired. Pour batter into two 7-inch square pans or foil pans (or a small 9 × 13 baking sheet for dainty small cakes.) Grease each pan well on bottom and lightly on sides with 1 teaspoon unsalted shortening, and coat pans with flour. Shake out loose flour. The 7-inch and the 9 × 13-inch baking sheet cake are baked at 350° F. for about 30 minutes, raising heat to 400° F. after 25 minutes if they appear moist on surface. Do not overbake. Test before removing from oven. When done, let stand about 10 minutes in pans, loosen around sides, and turn out onto cake coolers. When cool, mark each into 25 to 30 uniform small squares, oblongs, or diamonds if using them as tea cakes. Sprinkle tops with confectioners' sugar. With No. 27 star tube, pipe a tiny buttercream rosette and with No. 65 or 67 leaf tube pipe green on each leaves. Keep in covered container, until serving time, then cut through markings into small pastries. Arrange attractively on platter covered with doily. This cake is very delicious if spread with thin layer of Lemon Icing (page 619), or simply sprinkled well with confectioners' sugar.

Devil's Food Cake

For square pans

⅓ cup unsweetened unsifted cocoa, combined slowly with ⅓ cup cool water
⅔ cup butter or margarine
1½ cups sifted granulated sugar
2 large whole eggs (½ cup)
2 cups sifted cake flour, combined

with ½ teaspoon baking soda and 1¼ teaspoons double-acting baking powder
⅔ cup buttermilk (room temperature)
1 teaspoon vanilla
About ¼ teaspoon, or more, red food coloring (optional)

First, in a small bowl add water slowly to cocoa and stir until smooth. Let stand while preparing rest of cake. In an 8-inch bowl, beat butter or margarine about 1 minute, add sugar a little at a time, and beat about 1 more minute, until well blended. Add eggs, 1 at a time, and beat each about 1 minute or until batter is light, but not runny. On a warm day, do not overbeat. Add flour, combined and sifted with soda and baking powder, alternately with the buttermilk, about ½ cup flour at a time and ¼ cup buttermilk at a time. Beat after each addition at medium speed *only until smooth*. Overbeating will make cake heavy. Add vanilla, red coloring, and last the cocoa mixture, and beat *only* until blended. Pour batter into either one 9 × 9 × 2-inch square pan or two 7 × 7 × 1¼-inch square pans, greased and floured. (Use 1½ teaspoons unsalted shortening to grease large pan well on bottom and lightly on sides. Use 1 teaspoon shortening to grease each of the smaller pans. Then coat with flour and shake out loose flour.) Bake large cake at 350° F. 45 minutes; then raise temperature to 400° F. and bake about 10 more minutes. Bake smaller cake at 350° F. 30 minutes; then at 400° F. 10 more minutes. Remove from oven, let cakes remain in pans about 10 minutes, then loosen around sides and carefully turn out onto cake racks.

Round Devil's Food Cake

For two round 9 × 1½-inch layer-cake pans

½ cup unsweetened unsifted cocoa, combined slowly with ½ cup cool water (mix well until smooth)
1 cup butter or margarine
2¼ cups sifted granulated sugar
3 large whole eggs (¾ cup)

3 cups sifted cake flour, combined with ¾ teaspoon baking soda and 1¾ teaspoons double-acting baking powder
1 cup buttermilk (room temperature)
1½ teaspoons vanilla
About ½ teaspoon red food coloring (optional)

Grease each layer-cake pan well on bottom and lightly on sides with 1½ teaspoons unsalted shortening and coat with flour. Follow mixing directions above. Bake at 350° F. 30 minutes, then about 10 more minutes at 400° F.

This recipe can be baked in one 9 × 13 × 2-inch oblong pan, greased with 2 teaspoons shortening, and floured. Bake 45 minutes at 350° F., then 10 minutes at 400° F.

Note. During cold weather, remove ingredients from refrigerator about 1 hour before preparation of cake, and ½ hour during warm weather. Follow mixing directions as closely as possible. Overbeating or underbeating at any time will produce a heavy streaked cake. Chill may be removed from very cold eggs or buttermilk by placing them in a pan of warm water for a few minutes during very cold weather.

This cake is delectable if layers are split and filled with Quick French Buttercream Icing (page 613), or White Mountain Icing (page 612), or Stabilized Whipped Cream (page 615). Cakes filled with whipped cream must be refrigerated until shortly before serving.

Large Gold Cake

For 10 × 4-inch tube pan or 11¾ × 2¾-inch spring form pan or solid 12 × 3-inch pan

1¼ cups butter or margarine
2¼ cups sifted granulated sugar
1½ cups egg yolks, thoroughly beaten about 3 minutes with electric mixer

4 cups sifted cake flour
4 teaspoons double-acting baking powder
1 cup milk (room temperature)
2 teaspoons vanilla

Cream butter or margarine well with electric beater or wooden spoon for about 1 minute. Add sugar gradually and beat thoroughly 2 or 3 minutes. Add well-beaten egg yolks, a little at a time, and continue beating until batter is light and fluffy, about 3 minutes. Add combined flour and baking powder alternately with the milk, about 1 cup flour at a time, and beat only until light and smooth. Add flavoring.

Grease pan with 1 tablespoon or little more shortening, and coat with flour. Shake out loose flour. Bake about 1 hour in a 325° F. oven; then raise temperature to 375° F. and bake about 10 minutes longer. When done, remove from oven, let stand in pan about 15 minutes; loosen sides and around tube, and turn out onto cake cooler. When cold, sprinkle with confectioners' sugar, or frost as desired. This cake may also be baked in 3 round or square layers that measure about 9 × 1 ½ inches, at 350° F. about 40 minutes.

Small Gold Cake

For 8½ × 3¼-inch tube pan	*For 9 × 9 × 2-inch square pan, or two 7 × 7 × 1½-inch square pans*
½ cup butter or margarine	⅔ cup butter or margarine
1 cup sifted granulated sugar	1 cup and 2 tablespoons sifted granulated sugar
⅔ cup egg yolks, beaten with electric mixer about 2 minutes	¾ cup egg yolks, beaten with electric mixer about 2 minutes
2 cups sifted cake flour	2 cups sifted cake flour
2 teaspoons double-acting baking powder	2 teaspoons double-acting baking powder
½ cup milk	⅔ cup milk
1 teaspoon orange or other extract	1 teaspoon orange or other extract

Follow mixing directions for Large Gold Cake (above).

Grease form pan with 1 tablespoon or little more unsalted shortening, and coat with flour. Shake out loose flour. Bake form cake at 325° F. 45 minutes, then about 10 more minutes at 375° F. Remove from oven, and let stand in pan about 15 minutes, then loosen around edges and tube, and carefully turn out onto cake rack.

Grease 9 × 9 × 2-inch square pan with 1 ½ teaspoons unsalted shortening well on bottom and lightly on sides, and coat with all-purpose flour. Pour in full recipe of batter, and bake about 45 minutes at 325° F., then raise heat to 375° F. and bake about 10 minutes, or until done. Remove from oven, and let stand in pan on cake rack about 15 minutes, then loosen around sides, and turn out onto cake rack. *Or* pour batter into two 7 × 7 × 1 ½-inch square foil pans, well greased on bottom and lightly on sides with 1 teaspoon shortening, and coated with flour. Bake at 325° F. 35 minutes, then about 10 more minutes at 375° F. Let cool in pans on cake racks about 10 minutes; loosen around sides, and turn out onto cake racks.

Petit Fours (Lady Baltimore Cake)

For two 7 × 7 × 1-inch foil pans

⅔ cup butter or margarine
1 cup granulated sugar
2 cups sifted cake flour, combined with 1½ teaspoons double-acting baking powder
⅔ cup milk

1 teaspoon vanilla
½ cup egg whites, beaten until they cling to bowl, then add 2 tablespoons sugar and beat only until blended

Cream butter well, add sugar, little at a time, and beat for several minutes until light. Add sifted cake flour combined with baking powder, alternately with the milk, and beat until smooth. Add vanilla. Last, beat egg whites and pour into batter. Fold over and over until smooth. Bake in two 7 × 7 × 1-inch foil pans, each greased with 1 teaspoon shortening and sprinkled with flour, for about 40 minutes at 325° F., raising heat the last few minutes if necessary to 375° F. It is better to bake this cake a day in advance before cutting it into various sizes and shapes.

May be baked in small 9 × 13 baking sheet, which has been greased with 2 teaspoons shortening and floured, at 350° F. for about 30 minutes.

To Ice and Decorate. With a very sharp plan knife remove crusts from top and sides of cake, and shake off crumbs. Cut into desired sizes and shapes. Place on cake racks. With bag and plain opening on coupling, or No. 8 or 10 plain tubes, squeeze bulbs of Quick Buttercream Icing (page 621) in center of some if desired, or leave plain. Chill cakes for about 30 minutes or put in freezer for a few minutes, only until bulbs are firm (do not freeze), before covering with Quick Petit-Fours Fondant (page 620), then with a tablespoon or pot pour prepared fondant over each one, being careful to cover sides and corners. Pick up fondant that falls through rack and add a few drops of hot water if necessary, and pour again.

When icing on petit fours is set, release them from racks with a spatula, place on a flat surface and decorate.

Serve in white petit-four cups. Buttercream or Royal Icing (page 625) may be used to decorate these cakes. Cakes without buttercream bulbs are more delicious if split in halves and filled with a little jam or buttercream before covering with fondant.

Party-Style Fruit-Topped Petits Fours

Makes about 40

1 recipe of basic Petit Fours (Lady Baltimore Cake, above)
1½ recipes Quick Petit-Fours Fondant (page 620)

1 recipe Quick Buttercream Icing (page 621)
1 recipe Royal Icing (page 625)

Bake 1 recipe Petit Fours in a small baking sheet that measures about 9 × 13 inches (well greased with 2 teaspoons unsalted shortening, and floured) at 350° F. about 30 minutes, or until done. Pan will appear overfilled before baking, but it will not run over. When done, remove from oven. Let cake cool in pan about 10 minutes; then cut it into 3 crosswise sections while in pan. Carefully turn cake out onto a large rack or baking sheet, and let stand until cold. It is best to bake it a day in advance and refrigerate, to facilitate cutting.

Prepare Quick Buttercream Icing, and leave it white. Keep covered.

Prepare Royal Icing and color part green, for hulls and leaves of fruits. Keep covered.

Prepare 1½ recipes Quick Petit-Four Fondant, and keep covered over warm water.

Pear Petits Fours. Cut ⅓ of cake into ovals with a very small oval cutter (simply shape 1½-inch round cutter into oval). Remove crust from cakes.

Apple Petits Fours. Cut ⅓ of cake into rounds with a very small round 1¼-inch cutter. Remove crusts from cakes.

Strawberry Petits Fours. Cut ⅓ of cake into rectangles 1¾ inches long and 1 inch wide. Remove crusts from cakes.

Place cakes on racks with drip pan underneath. With No. 10 plain decorating tube (that fits coupling) pipe white buttercream pears on oval cakes, leaving ¼-inch space all around. With same tube pipe apples on round cake and strawberries on rectangles. Refrigerate cakes until fruits are firm to touch.

Remove ⅓ of fondant and put aside in a 1-quart suacepan, over warm water. To rest of fondant add a few drops yellow coloring and a little orange or lemon extract. Mix well, and with a large spoon pour fondant over Pear Petits Fours. Pick up any fondant that drops into drip pan and place back in pot. Now add a few drops green coloring, mix well, and pour over apples. To white fondant put aside, add red coloring and a little yellow for strawberries. Pour over cakes. Let cakes stand about 15 minutes.

Now with green Royal Icing (Buttercream Icing may be used instead) and No. 30 star tube, pipe green hulls on round ends of strawberries. Insert citron stems about ¾ inch long and 1⁄16 inch wide, tinted green. With a heavy pointed toothpick dipped into coloring, puncture strawberry part only. With No. 65 small leaf tube, pipe leaf on pear, and insert stem. With a heavy pointed toothpick dipped into dark melted chocolate (or a little cocoa and water made into a paste) puncture rounded part (or insert a tiny piece of currant or black raisin rolled in fingers into balls). Let fondant dry on Petits Fours at least 1 hour; then with a tiny painter's brush and very little red coloring (rub brush on white paper to remove excess coloring) tint round part of pear. Pipe green leaf on apple with No. 65 tube and insert citron stem. A little red coloring may be brushed on front part of apple.

Release cakes from racks very carefully with a flat dinner knife or spatula, and place them in a small petit-four cups. If not to be served within several hours, keep them in a tightly covered box in room temperature for 1 day. Store covered in refrigerator several days if necessary. They may be frozen.

Important Facts. Do not keep fondant over *very* hot water at any time, not over 150° F., and do not add more than about 1 teaspoon water if fondant thickens. It is best to reheat it over hot water (not hotter than 150° F.) when necessary, and do not overbeat. Let surface of Petits Fours dry well at least 1 hour before tinting.

Dorothy's Special Form Cake

For 8½ × 3¼-inch form pan

2 large whole eggs (scant ½ cup)
½ teaspoon lemon, ½ teaspoon almond, and ½ teaspoon vanilla extracts
½ cup butter or margarine
1 cup granulated sugar
2 cups sifted cake flour, combined with 1½ teaspoons double-acting

baking powder and ½ teaspoon baking soda
1 cup dairy sour cream (room temperature)
2 tablespoons granulated sugar, combined with ¼ teaspoon cinnamon
⅓ cup finely chopped pecan meats

In a 7-inch bowl combine the 2 large eggs and extracts. Beat with electric mixer at high speed about 3 minutes until thick.

In an 8- or 9-inch bowl, beat the butter until creamy, add the cup of sugar, a little at a time, and continue to beat for at least 1 minute at high speed.

Now add the beaten egg preparation to the sugar and butter, a little at a time, and beat at high speed for about 2 minutes. Combine the 2 cups sifted cake flour with the baking powder and soda, and sift together several times. Add flour to the egg and butter mixture, about ½ cup at a time, alternately with the cup of sour cream, about ¼ cup at a time, and beat after each addition until smooth.

Pour 2 cups of this preparation into form pan well greased with 4 teaspoons unsalted shortening, and floured. Now sprinkle 2 tablespoons of sugar combined with the cinnamon *over batter* in pan, and then the ⅓ cup of finely chopped pecans over sugar. Pour rest of batter into pan, and bake in preheated 350° F. oven 45 minutes, then raise temperature to 400° F. for 5 or 6 minutes if not done. Remove from oven, let remain in pan about 5 minutes, then loosen around upper edge and tube, place cake cooler over top and turn over carefully. Let stand until cool, then store. Sprinkle thickly with sifted confectioners' sugar or icing before serving.

Blitz Torte

For 9-inch pan

¾ cup granulated sugar
½ cup butter or margarine
6 egg yolks (½ cup)
½ teaspoon vanilla
½ cup half & half cream
1¾ cups sifted cake flour, combined with 3 teaspoons double-acting baking powder and ¼ teaspoon salt
½ cup sliced or slivered untoasted almonds

Cream butter, add sugar, a little at a time, then egg yolks, and continue to beat for about 5 minutes with electric mixer. Add vanilla, then sifted dry ingredients alternately with the cream, and beat after each addition only until smooth. Pour and spread batter into 2 round 9-inch well-greased and floured baking pans. Use 1¼ teaspoons unsalted shortening to grease bottom and sides of each pan. Pour and spread Meringue over the 2 unbaked layers. Sprinkle untoasted almonds on 1 layer (which will be used for the top).

Bake layers at 350° F. about 50 minutes, or until meringue is golden brown and crisp. When done, remove from oven and place on cake racks. Let stand about 15 minutes, then loosen around sides and turn cakes out onto racks carefully. When cold, place the layer without almonds on large serving platter with meringue side down (or up, as preferred). Spread with a thick layer of French Cream Filling (page 643), Bavarian Cream Filling (page 588), Chocolate Filling (page 691), ice cream, sliced strawberries, raspberry or strawberry jam, or buttercream icing. Place second layer over filling with meringue part up. Sprinkle with confectioners' sugar, cut and serve. Hot chocolate sauce, strawberry sauce, or any similar sauce may be served with this torte. It may also be decorated with large scrolls of whipped cream for special occasions.

Meringue for Blitz Torte

6 large egg whites (¾ cup)
¼ teaspoon salt
½ teaspoon cream of tartar
½ teaspoon vanilla
1½ cups granulated sugar

Beat whites, salt and cream of tartar about 3 minutes with electric mixer or 5 minutes with hand beater. Add the vanilla, then the sugar, about 1 tablespoon at a time, and continue to beat until well blended after each addition of sugar.

Dark Rich Fruit Cake

Makes 4-pound cake

2 pounds (4 cups solidly packed) fruit mix for a very rich fruit cake, or as little as 1½ pounds (3 cups) fruit mix may be used for a less rich cake, and do not decrease other ingredients

½ cup raisins or currants, simmered in small amount of water several minutes, drained (or omit and use ½ cup more fruit mix)

¼ cup light corn syrup poured over fruit mix (optional but makes cutting of cake easier); if fruit mix appears very dry, add ½ cup light corn syrup instead of ¼ cup

½ to ¾ cup brandy (light wine pineapple juice may be used instead)

½ cup butter or margarine, medium consistency

¼ cup granulated sugar

2 medium whole eggs

1½ cups sifted all-purpose flour, to which add ½ teaspoon baking soda, ¼ teaspoon salt, ¼ teaspoon allspice, ¼ teaspoon cinnamon, ¼ teaspoon ginger, ¼ teaspoon cloves and ¼ teaspoon nutmeg

1¼ cups very coarsely broken pecan meats or walnuts (less may be used)

Line bottom and sides of 9½ × 5½ × 2¾-inch oblong pan or 9 × 3-inch medium-round tube pan smoothly with 2 thicknesses of heavy wax paper. If using tube pan grease tube well and line rest of pan with paper.

Simmer raisins or currants, drain well, and combine them with the chopped fruit mix. Pour corn syrup and brandy over fruits and blend well. Cover tightly, if possible, and allow to stand for at least 2 hours or longer. This adds extra flavor as the brandy in the fruit gradually permeates through cake.

With spoon or electric beater, cream butter, add sugar, beat well, then add eggs, 1 at a time. Beat until light for about 2 minutes. Sift flour together with baking soda, salt, and spices. (For light-colored fruit cake, omit spices. Use blanched chopped almonds instead of pecans and white Sultana raisins instead of black. Add 1 teaspoon vanilla, orange or lemon extract to batter). Add ½ of dry ingredients to butter, sugar and egg mixture, a little at a time, beating until well blended. Now add fruit mix, about 1 cup at a time, alternately with the nutmeats. Last, add rest of dry ingredients. *Do not use electric beater when adding fruits to prevent crushing cherries.* Mix fruits in with heavy long spoon, and add remaining flour with spoon.

Drop batter into lined pan (hold paper in place with a little shortening if necessary). Press down batter as you drop it into pan, so that it will be solidly packed and evenly distributed. Bake in a 275° F. oven on a flat old baking sheet, and cover with well-greased aluminum foil, dome fashion. This will prevent drying out. It will take about 3½ hours or longer at 275° F. to bake, then if center of cake *is not firm*, remove foil, and continue to bake it about 15 minutes longer, raising temperature to 325° F. *Bake longer if using the larger amount of fruit mix.* Cakes are done when they feel firm to the touch. After cakes are removed from oven, let them stand on cake racks in pans until cool enough to handle, about 30 minutes, then loosen around edges, and turn out.

How to Glaze and Decorate Fruit Cakes. Brush cakes with warm light corn syrup. Let stand about 30 minutes, then decorate with glazed red cherries, blanched almonds, citron leaves, etc. Pour a little warm syrup over cherries and almonds. Let stand several hours until glaze is set. In storing fruit cakes after they are decorated make sure cover does not touch fruits.

Fruit cakes are very beautiful decorated with small marzipan fruits and Gum Drop Roses (page 628).

Fruit cakes should be baked at least 2 weeks before serving. They may be stored in a cool place or refrigerator for many months. It is better to have cake pans ⅞ filled before baking. Fruit cakes do not rise much in baking. Fruit cakes may be brushed *very* lightly with brandy every 2 or 3 weeks if to be kept for months. Store them in a tight container or wrap well in aluminum foil and keep in a *cool* place or refrigerator. May be frozen for 1 year.

Important. An extremely very sharp light-weight knife or one with a serrated-edge must be used in cutting fruit cake, and cake should be refrigerated for several hours or longer before slicing. Dip knife into hot water and cut cake with an easy sawing motion to avoid crumbling. Wipe knife with wet cloth often.

Note. This cake may be baked in various size pans. For large angel food pan that measures 10 × 4 inches, use double recipe of ingredients. Bake at 275° F. about 5 hours or longer, then remove foil, and bake until firm to the touch in center. May be baked in 1-pound coffee cans (lined with wax paper). One recipe will make 3 cakes. Bake at 275° F. about 2½ hours covered, then 15 minutes at 325° F., or until firm to touch in center. For bread pan 7½ × 3¾ × 2¼ inches, 1 recipe will make 2 cakes. Bake at 275° F. about 3 hours, then uncovered at 325° F. until firm to touch in center. For bread pan 5¾ × 3¼ × 2¼, 1 recipe will make about 5 cakes. Bake at 275° F. about 2 hours, then about 15 minutes uncovered at 325° F., or until firm to touch in center. Decorate as desired. Sometimes cakes take longer to bake. Must feel firm in center when done.

Fruit Cake Petit Fours

Cut dark or light fruit cake into squares or rectangles, about 1½ inches or larger. Place them on a cake rack and cover them with Quick Glossy

Chocolate Icing (page 619). Let icing on cakes set for ½ hour, then garnish center top of each with ¼ or ½ glazed cherry and 2 citron leaves, or with icing rosette and leaves; release from rack. Serve in petit-four cups. These chocolate Fruit Cake Petit Fours are not only beautiful but delicious, and unusual. This is an excellent way to use leftover fruit cake.

California Apricot Fruit Cake

⅔ cup butter or margarine

1 cup granulated sugar

3 medium whole eggs

½ teaspoon lemon and ½ teaspoon orange extract

2 cups sifted all-purpose flour, to which add ½ teaspoon baking soda, ½ teaspoon salt

2 cups fruit mix, solidly packed (1 pound)

1 cup white Sultana raisins simmered, covered, in about ½ cup hot water for 2 or 3 minutes, then drained thoroughly

1½ cups dried apricots, covered with 1 cup hot water, and steamed in covered saucepan, about 5 minutes, turning several times; drain thoroughly and cut into about ½-inch pieces (for less tart flavor use only 1 cup apricots but increase fruit mix by ½ cup)

1 cup coarsely broken pecan or walnut meats

⅓ cup apricot liquid

With electric mixer or heavy spoon, cream butter or margarine, add sugar, then eggs, 1 at a time, and beat each egg in about 1 minute. Add extracts. Mix well. Add ½ of sifted dry ingredients, a little at a time, and beat until smooth. Combine all fruits, nuts, and apricot liquid and add them, about a cup at a time, to the flour mixture, stirring in with a *heavy wooden spoon.* Electric mixer would crush fruits. Last, add rest of sifted dry ingredients and beat with spoon until smooth. Pour into an oblong pan that measures 13 × 2¾ × 4½, lined with 1 thickness of heavy wax paper. As you pour batter, press down well so that cake bakes uniformly. Bake covered with greased foil, on an old baking sheet in a 325° F. oven about 2½ to 3 hours, then raise temperature to 350° F. and bake about 15 more minutes, or until top is attractively brown and cake feels firm in center. Remove from oven, let stand on cake rack about 30 minutes. Now carefully loosen around sides, and turn over onto cake rack. Let stand until cold before storing in a tight container. *It is better not to keep this cake more than 2 or 3 weeks unless refrigerated or frozen.*

Miniature Fruit Cakes or Plum Puddings

May be baked in the miniature angel food pans that sell 6 to the set. Line with wax paper. Fill with Fruit Cake (above or page 556) or Plum Pudding (page 559) almost to top. Cover with greased foil, and bake on flat pan at 275° F. for about 1½ hours, then remove foil, increase temperature to 325° F. and bake about 15 more minutes, or until firm to the touch. Glaze and decorate.

Note. If top is not evenly browned when center feels firm to the touch, shut off heat, and place cake under broiler for a few minutes. Enough heat is retained in broiling unit to brown top attractively.

Flaming English Plum Pudding

For bowl 7 inches wide and 4 inches deep

⅓ cup milk
½ cup light molasses
¾ teaspoon baking soda
⅓ cup finely cut suet (fat from meat), or butter or margarine
¼ cup brown sugar, solidly packed
1 whole egg, beaten with a fork
2 cups sifted all-purpose flour
¼ teaspoon ground nutmeg
¼ teaspoon ginger
¼ teaspoon cloves
¼ teaspoon cinnamon

¼ teaspoon salt
¼ cup blanched almonds, chopped medium
½ cup black raisins, steamed several minutes, and thoroughly drained
¼ pound brown glazed figs, or extra fruit mix, cut in ¼-inch pieces
¼ pound pitted dates, cut in ¼-inch pieces
½ cup fruit mix, solidly packed
¼ cup brandy, wine, or fruit juices

In a large bowl, mix milk, molasses, and soda. Stir until thoroughly blended, for about ½ minute, then add the finely chopped suet, brown sugar, and beaten eggs. With heavy wooden spoon or electric mixer (low speed), beat until blended. Combine and sift together several times the flour, spices, and salt. Add sifted dry ingredients about a cup at a time to first mixture and beat unitl smooth after each addition. Last, with spoon, add nutmeats and cut-up fruits that have been moistened with the ¼ cup brandy, about a cup at a time, and beat until well blended.

Pour batter into a 7-inch heatproof bowl greased with 2 teaspoons unsalted shortening and sprinkled with flour. Batter should come up about ⅔ of way. Place on old baking sheet, cover bowl with greased foil. Bake pudding about 2½ hours at 300° F., or until firm to the touch in center. When done, remove from oven, and let stand about 5 minutes; loosen around sides, and turn over onto rack. When baked plum pudding is cold, store it in a tight container. May be baked several weeks in advance. Keep in cool place.

This plum pudding may be baked in various size deep pans. Adjust baking time accordingly. Empty coffee cans with covers may be used. Have them about ⅔ filled, put greased cover on, and bake about 2 hours at 300° F. If not done after 2 hours, raise temperature to 350° F. and finish baking a few minutes longer.

To Serve for Special Occasions. Bake in a deep bowl. If to be served warm, place pudding back in well-greased bowl in which it was originally baked about an hour before serving, cover it with greased foil, and place it on a rack in a deep pot, having water come up about halfway around bowl. Cover pot and allow water to boil vigorously for about 1 hour. Now remove it from water carefully, and turn pudding out onto serving platter. Arrange lemon or galax leaves on platter with various glazed candied fruits (or other fruits). Cut out a hole from top of pudding about 1 inch deep and 1 inch wide, with round cutter. Garnish around opening with a row or two of glazed cherries cut in halves and citron leaves, if desired. Fill opening with 2 or 3 small cubes of sugar that have been soaked in lemon or orange extract for at least 5 minutes; light and carry to table. Flame may be extinguished after a minute or two by holding cake server on top of pudding for a few seconds. Cut and serve with whipped cream flavored with a little brandy or rum, or as desired.

Poppy Seed Form Cake

Serves 8

½ cup butter
⅔ cup granulated sugar
1¾ cups sifted cake flour
2 teaspoons double-acting baking powder
⅔ cup cool milk, combined with ⅓

cup poppy seed (stir well and let stand about 1 hour)
½ teaspoon vanilla and ½ teaspoon lemon extract
½ cup egg whites
¼ cup more granulated sugar

In an 8-inch bowl cream butter well. Add sugar, a little at a time, and beat until light for about 2 minutes. Add sifted flour, combined with the baking powder, ½ cup at a time, alternately with about ¼ cup milk and poppy seed mixture, and beat until smooth after each addition. Add flavoring. With clean beaters, beat whites in a 7-inch bowl until they cling well to bottom and sides of bowl. Add the ¼ cup sugar, tablespoon at a time, and beat after each addition only until well blended. Pour beaten whites all at once into flour preparation, and with rubber scraper fold over and over *until no streaks* appear. Pour into an 8½ × 3¼-inch form cake pan that has been well greased with 1 tablespoon unsalted shortening, and sprinkle with flour.

Bake in a preheated 350° F. oven about 45 minutes, then increase temperature to 375° F. and bake about 10 more minutes, or until top is brown and cake is done when tested. Remove from oven, let remain in pan about 10 minutes, then loosen around upper edge and tube, and turn out onto cake cooler. When cool, sprinkle thickly with sifted confectioners' sugar, or drizzle with Cinnamon Butter Icing (page 616), or Lemon Icing (page 619).

Blueberry Cupcakes

Makes about 20 large or 40 small

½ cup butter or margarine
1¼ cups sifted granulated sugar
2 large eggs, beaten 1 minute
2 cups sifted cake flour
1½ teaspoons double-acting baking
    powder

¼ teaspoon salt
⅔ cup milk
½ teaspoon vanilla
½ cup fresh blueberries

With electric mixer or spoon, cream butter. Add sugar, a little at a time, and beat until thoroughly blended. Add beaten eggs, and continue to beat mixture about 2 minutes with electric beater or 3 minutes with spoon.

Add sifted flour combined with baking powder and salt alternately with milk, about ½ cup flour and ¼ cup liquid at a time. Add vanilla. Last, add blueberries and fold gently. Pour into large paper-lined muffin pans. They should be a little more than half filled. Bake at 350° F. about 30 minutes. Small muffin pans may be used instead of large ones, in which case bake at 350° F. about 25 minutes.

Do not overbake. Test toward end of baking with cake tester. When done, remove from oven and turn out onto a cake rack.

Grilled Pecan, Walnut, or Coconut Butter-Cake Squares

Serves 8

½ cup butter or margarine
1 cup granulated sugar
2 large whole eggs (room tempera-
    ture)
2 cups sifted cake flour
2¼ teaspoons double-acting baking
    powder

⅔ cup milk (room temperature)
1 teaspoon vanilla
2 tablespoons very soft butter or
    margarine
⅓ cup soft brown sugar
¾ cup fine-chopped nuts or coconut
3 tablespoons coffee cream

Cream ½ cup butter. Add granulated sugar, a little at a time, then eggs, 1 at a time, and beat until very light—about 2 minutes. Add flour combined with baking powder, alternately with milk, and beat only until smooth. Add flavoring. Pour into a square pan measuring 9 × 9 × 2 inches that has been well greased on bottom and very lightly on sides, and sprinkled with flour. Bake at 325° F. about 30 minutes; then raise heat to 375° F. and bake about 10 more minutes. Test cake before removing from oven.

When cake is done, let stand a few minutes, but while it is still warm, spread top with following mixture: Combine 2 tablespoons very soft butter or margarine with brown sugar. Cook over low heat until melted. Add chopped nuts or coconut, alternately with coffee cream, to make proper consistency to spread. Spread on cake and broil at 325° F., about 1 inch from heat, until bubbles form and top is brown. Watch closely to see that it does not burn. When cool, cut into squares in pan. If it is to be made in advance, let cool, cover with several thicknesses of wax paper, and store. Cut just before serving.

Mindy's Party-Size Banana Cake Squares

Serves 8 to 10

2 cups sifted cake flour
1⅓ cups sifted granulated sugar
2 teaspoons double-acting baking powder
½ teaspoon baking soda
½ teaspoon salt
1 cup mashed ripe bananas (2 very large), combined with ¼ cup commercial sour cream

½ cup soft butter or margarine
2 very large eggs or 3 medium
Another ¼ cup sour cream
1 teaspoon vanilla
½ cup medium chopped pecans or walnuts

Sift flour, sugar, baking powder, soda, and salt together 3 times. Pour into an 8- or 9-inch bowl. Add the cup mashed bananas combined with the ¼ cup sour cream, and the ½ cup butter or margarine. Beat at medium speed for about 2 minutes. Add the unbeaten eggs, the other ¼ cup sour cream, vanilla, and chopped nutmeats, and continue to beat for about 1 more minute.

Pour batter into 9 × 13 × 2-inch pan, well greased on bottom and lightly on sides with 2 teaspoons unsalted shortening, and floured or lined with silicone paper. Bake at 350° F. about 35 to 40 minutes. When done, remove from oven and let stand on cake rack about 15 minutes, then loosen around sides, place a long cake rack over top and turn over. Or cake may be left in pan, iced, and cut as needed.

Spread Cream Cheese Frosting (page 617) on entire surface of cake. Sprinkle with chopped nutmeats, or omit nutmeats, cut cake in squares and decorate top of each with buttercream (or cream cheese) rosette and leaves, made with No. 27 star tube, and 67 leaf tube.

Mindy's Party-Size Yummy Cake

Serves 8

¾ cup butter or margarine
1¼ cups sifted granulated sugar
3 medium eggs (to measure not more than ⅔ cup)
2¼ cups sifted all-purpose flour
1 teaspoon vanilla

2 teaspoons double-acting baking powder
½ teaspoon baking soda
½ teaspoon salt
1 cup commercial sour cream

Have all ingredients room temperature about 1 hour.

With electric mixer at high speed beat butter or margarine for about 1 minute after all sugar has been added. Add eggs, 1 at a time, and beat until light, about ½ minute for each egg. Sift dry ingredients together several times, then add them alternately with the sour cream, about ½ cup dry ingredients at a time, and ¼ cup cream at a time, at medium speed only until smooth. Add vanilla. Do not overbeat.

Pour 2½ cups of the batter into 13 × 9 × 2-inch pan, greased well on bottom and lightly on sides with 2 teaspoons unsalted shortening, and floured or lined with silicone paper.

Spread evenly, and sprinkle top of batter with ¾ cup of Sugar Cinnamon Topping. Pour rest of batter into pan, spreading gently, and cover with rest of cinnamon sugar preparation. Bake at 350° F. about 40 to 45 minutes. Remove from oven, let stand on cake rack for at least 15 minutes, then cover a long rack with wax paper, and turn cake over. It is better, however, to leave this cake right in pan, and cut it as needed. Lift out with cake server.

Sugar Cinnamon Topping and Filling for Yummy Cake

¼ cup granulated sugar
½ cup soft light brown sugar, packed
2 teaspoons, more or less, cinnamon

½ cup medium-chopped pecans or walnuts

In a small bowl combine these ingredients and mix them well. Use as directed in recipe.

▶ SPONGE CAKES ◀

Why is cake flour used in sponge cakes?
Because it gives a lighter and more tender cake.

Why is cream of tartar used in French pastry and angel food cakes?
Because it stablizes the egg whites, and also bleaches flour in angel food cake. If cream of tartar is omitted in these cakes, they shrink excessively after they are removed from oven.

Why are sponge cakes baked in ungreased pans?
So that they cling to bottom and sides of pan when inverted to cool. They should not be removed from the pan for at least an hour or until they are cool enough to retain their shape and volume. If removed while warm, the cakes will be heavy and soggy.

Why do sponge cakes fall out of pans while cooling?
1. Underbaking.
2. Greased pan.
3. Sometimes a new, very smooth pan will cause this. It is best to place empty new angel food pans made of tinware in a 350° F. oven for several hours. Aluminum pans do not require this treatment. Best to rub sides and bottom of all new Angel Food pans with steel wool.

Why do sponge cakes sometimes have a soggy bottom?
1. They may have been left in pan too long while cooling. They should be removed within 2 hours.
2. If cake is too close to table when inverted, this causes condensation of steam.
3. Insufficient beating of whites.
4. Flour is too soft.

Why is top of sponge cake sometimes too moist or sticky?
Insufficient baking. Raise temperature last part of baking period.

What causes a heavy, undersized sponge cake?
1. Too much mixing.
2. Too much heat.
3. Pan too large.
4. Removing cake from pan while still too warm; it should be quite cool.

What causes coarse-grained sponge cakes?
1. Insufficient mixing.
2. Oven temperature too low.
3. Very coarse sugar.

How can egg whites be whipped stiff, but not dry?
Do not store or beat egg whites in aluminum or copper bowls, as they affect the color of the beaten whites. It is best *not to use* plastic bowls as oftentimes (not always) they have a chemical that prevents volume development. Use crockery or stainless steel bowls.

For best results use the right size bowl indicated in recipes for that particular amount of whites. Eggs will beat up more quickly and give more volume when their temperature is about 75° F. Eggs separate more easily when they are quite cool, but not extremely cold or warm. Remove them from the refrigerator about 30 minutes in advance during cold weather; 15 minutes during warm weather. Separate carefully, cover bowl, and let whites remain in room temperature for about 1 hour or longer.

When whites are room temperature, beat them with electric mixer high speed until they just cling to bowl, testing often by tilting bowl, then beat a few seconds longer, ½ minute, depending on their use, or until they cling well to bottom and sides and *are stiff but not dry.* At this point the whites should cling tightly to beater when it is held upright unless otherwise specified in recipe. Further beating of whites will cause them to become granular, and they will disintegrate when combined with other ingredients. Beaten to the granular stage, cakes and soufflés would not rise properly, and the texture would be grainy and undesirable.

If you use this method of beating egg whites, we suggest adding sugar about ¼ cup at a time, and fold sugar into beaten whites gently but quickly with a long wooden spoon or a rubber spatula (plate scraper), *instead* of using electric mixer for this step. We also prefer to add rest of sugar combined with the flour with wooden spoon or rubber scraper. (See recipes for more details.) However, you may beat in sugar with the electric mixer in any of our recipes if you prefer, but it is riskier. Beat in sugar with electric mixer at high speed about ⅓ cup at a time until well blended. It is more difficult for the beginner and some experienced cake makers to judge when the sugar has been beaten in sufficiently when using this method. Folding the sugar with a long wooden spoon or rubber scraper into the beaten whites is an easier method, especially for the beginner.

What causes sugary or hard crust?
1. Too much top heat.
2. Overbaking
3. Very coarse sugar.
4. Insufficient blending of sugar with whites.
5. Too much sugar in recipe.

What causes tough sponge cakes?
1. Overbeating egg whites.
2. Overbaking.
3. Too much flour.

Why will egg whites oftentimes not beat up?
1. Because egg whites contain some yolk.
2. Because there is some grease in bowl or beaters.
3. Because eggs are of inferior quality. Use only top-grade eggs.

Is it necessary to use a flat wire beater to beat egg whites for sponge cakes?
No. Hand beater or electric beater gives excellent results.

Should egg yolks and dry ingredients be added with electric mixer?
It is best to fold in egg yolks and dry ingredients by hand with a long wooden spoon or rubber scraper. Mixing at this point must be gentle but quick.

Should sponge cakes be baked at a high temperature?
No. Best results are obtained when low or moderate temperatures are used, about 350° F., not over 375° F. Cakes containing a large proportion of eggs become tough when baked at too high temperatures.

Can sponge cake pans be used for butter cakes?
Yes, provided they are washed and scoured thoroughly after each use.

What causes sponge cakes to fall while baking?
1. Opening oven door too often, especially during first part of baking period.
2. Jarring of oven door.
3. Insufficient baking.
4. Ingredients may be too cold.

Can sponge cakes be refrigerated before and after icing?
Yes. When properly mixed and baked, they will remain moist for a week or longer if stored in a closed container in refrigerator.

Why are angel food cakes baked in tube pans?
Because this cake is very delicate and requires some support in center, especially when baked in a deep pan.

What happens if whites are overbeaten or underbeaten for angel food cake?
Underbeaten whites will cause cake to collapse or shrink excessively. Overbeaten whites will produce a dry tough cake.

What is meant by bleaching the flour in an angel food cake?
Cream of tartar is used to bleach flour. If omitted in angel food cake, finished cake would have a creamy or yellowish color instead of white.

Why must pan be inverted at once after baking sponge cakes?
To prevent cake from collapsing, because if cake is cooled in an upright position, or if it is removed while warm, the cell walls will not be sufficiently stiffened to maintain its volume and shape. As soon as angel food and sponge cakes are done, they must be turned upside down *at once.* So that they do not rest on upper crust, there must be an air space of at least 1½ to 2 inches between bottom of cake and

the top of table. If the pan is not equipped with a long tube in center or side supports, it can be suspended between 2 upturned round or square cake pans until cakes are cold, or pan with long tube may be placed over neck of a low, heavy, wide funnel. Sponge cakes baked in deep square pans can also be turned upside down so that edges rest on 2 other pans. Let hang until cold, then release cakes from pans with a plain dinner knife, holding knife close to sides of pan. Do likewise around tube.

Why is it not advisable to cool sponge cakes on cake cooler?
If sponge cake pan has a long tube, it may be inverted onto cake cooler; if not, it would stick to rack, making it difficult to release when cold, and would also be too close to table. It is always best to have cake raised about 1½ inches from table while cooling to permit circulation of air, thus preventing soggy cake and the possibility of its falling out of pan before it is sufficiently cool.

What causes heavy solid layer in sponge cakes?
1. Overmixing.
2. Underbeating egg whites or yolks.
3. Ingredients too warm, especially during hot weather.
4. Oven temperature too high or too low.

What causes angel food cakes not to rise?
1. Insufficient beating of egg whites. Beat until they cling to bowl, then about ½ more minute.
2. Overmixing when adding sugar and flour.
3. Omission of cream of tartar.

What causes large tunnels in sponge cakes?
1. It is necessary to cut through batter a few times and to strike pan against table before baking sponge cakes, and especially angel food cakes. All cakes that contain a large number of eggs are improved in texture if given this treatment.
2. Insufficient blending of sugar and flour with the egg whites.

Can wax paper be used on bottom of angel food pan?
It is not advisable to do so, unless specified in recipe, because it might cause cake to fall out of pan while cooling, and it also forms a depression on bottom of cake.

Is it best to combine all of the sugar for angel food and sponge cakes with the flour before adding to the beaten whites?

No. It is better to add part of sugar to the beaten whites and rest to the flour before the addition of any of the flour. This strengthens the egg whites and will produce a cake with more volume.

Why is part of the sugar combined with the flour in angel food and sponge cakes?

Sifting part of the sugar with the flour prevents formation of small balls —thus making it easier to incorporate the flour into the beaten whites. This method requires less mixing and results in a more tender cake with more volume.

Is it necessary to use top-quality fresh eggs for angel food and sponge cakes?

Yes, if a superior cake is desired. Eggs that are old will produce poorer cakes.

What causes a sponge roll to be heavy or soggy?

1. Insufficient baking.

2. Insufficient beating of egg whites and yolks.

3. If flour is too fresh and too soft. If batter appears thin, add 2 more tablespoons flour.

4. If you use our recipes, please allow cakes to cool for a short time, as per our directions, then trim, and roll loosely.

What causes a poor quality sponge cake?

The quality depends principally upon the freshness of the eggs and the extent of beating the egg yolks, also the whites or whole eggs, depending on recipe. Please follow directions.

French Pastry Cake

Serves 8

1 cup sifted cake flour	Pinch of salt
1 cup and 2 tablespoons sifted granulated sugar	1 teaspoon cream of tartar
	1 teaspoon vanilla
8 large eggs (1 cup whites and ¾ cup yolks)	

Combine flour with about ½ of the sugar and sift together several times. Separate eggs. In a small bowl, beat yolks for several minutes with egg or electric beater until very light. Wash beaters. Add pinch of salt to egg whites (that have been standing in room temperature about 1 hour in an 8- or 9-inch bowl), and at once with large egg beater, or better electric mixer, beat until foamy. Then sprinkle cream of tartar over entire surface and continue to beat until whites cling to bottom and sides of bowl. Beat for ½ more minute. With a large spoon, fold beaten egg yolks into whites a little at a time, then the flour combined with other ½ of sugar, about ¼ cup at a time, then the flour combined with other ½ of sugar, about ¼ cup at a time, and last vanilla (or any other flavoring). Pour into a round loose bottom ungreased deep pan, about 3½ × 9 inches. If using a solid pan without removable bottom, it is better to place a 3-inch-round (not larger) piece of wax paper on center bottom of pan, holding it in place with a little shortening. Cut through batter several times with a spatula or dinner knife to prevent deep tunnels.

Bake in a preheated 300° F. oven 45 minutes, then raise temperature to 325° F. and continue to bake about 15 more minutes, or until done. Test with a wood pin or cake tester in center of cake about 10 minutes before baking time is up. If it comes out dry, cake is done. Turn pan upside down on rack or 2 flat pans and let cake cool for about 2 hours, or until cold. It is better to remove cake from pan as soon as it is cold. Loosen sides and bottom with a spatula or dinner knife and turn out onto serving platter or cake rack.

French Pastry Cake

Serves 12 to 16

1½ cups sifted cake flour	¼ teaspoon salt
1¾ cups sifted granulated sugar	1½ teaspoons cream of tartar and 1½
12 large eggs (1½ cups whites and 1	teaspoons vanilla
cup yolks)	

Use deep angel food pan that measures about 4 × 10 inches, or loose bottom pan that measures about 12 × 3 inches. Follow procedure in recipe above, but increase baking time to 1 hour, then about 20 minutes at 325° F. Test last 10 minutes.

To Decorate Large Cakes With Basket of Roses. Use 1½ recipes Mrs. Miller's Quick French Buttercream Icing (page 613).

Add a little red coloring to 1 cup of white icing for roses; a little green coloring to ⅔ cup white icing for leaves, stems, and bulbs; a little yellow coloring to ⅔ cup white icing for basket. To rest of icing add 1 ounce or less of melted baking chocolate (or any coloring desired). Remove about 1 cup of this icing to be used for border. Spread the rest over the entire surface of cake as smoothly as possible.

For small cake with basket of roses it will take 1 recipe of Mrs. Miller's Quick French Buttercream Icing.

Any leftover icing may be wrapped in waxed paper and stored in refrigerator for about 1 week. Let stand in room temperature until medium consistency before using. Then stir gently and use. May be frozen for several months.

Tubes Used for Decorating Cake. Use No. 104 tube for large roses, carnations, etc. Use No. 67 tube for large leaves (No. 70 for extra large). Use No. 4 tube for stemming (No. 6 for thicker stemming) and bulbs underneath flowers. Use No. 27 for medium borders (No. 30 for larger borders) and basket work.

Angel Food Cake

Serves 12

1¾ cups egg whites	½ teaspoon salt
1¾ cups sifted granulated sugar	1½ teaspoons cream of tartar
1½ cups sifted cake flour	1½ teaspoons vanilla or other flavoring

Have eggs cool as they will separate more easily. Separate, cover, and allow whites to stand in a warm room for about 1 hour. Add ½ cup of the sugar to flour and sift together several times. Add salt to whites, and with electric mixer, beat until foamy. Add cream of tartar and continue to beat until whites cling to bottom and sides of bowl; then beat ½ more minute. With large wooden spoon, fold in rest of sugar, about ¼ a cupful at a time, blending gently. Now add flour that has been sifted with ½ cup of sugar, about ¼ cupful at a time, mixing only until smooth. Add flavoring and blend gently. Pour batter into an ungreased 10 × 4-inch tube pan. Cut through batter, especially on sides, a few times and gently strike pan on table. This will prevent large tunnels in cake. Bake cake in a preheated 350° F. oven for about 45 minutes, or until done. Be sure to test cake for doneness toward end of baking period before removing it from oven. When done, turn pan upside down and let stand until cake is cold, about 2 hours. Then with a dinner knife or spatula, loosen sides and go around tube. Loosen bottom of cake and turn out onto cake platter. Ice with Mrs. Miller's Quick French Buttercream Icing (page 613) or whipped cream, or serve as desired.

Springtime Violet Angel Food Cake

Make basic Angel Food Cake (above).

Prepare single recipe of Mrs. Miller's Quick French Buttercream Icing (page 613) or White Mountain Buttercream Icing (page 612). Add violet coloring to ⅓ cup of the icing for violet flowers; red coloring to ¼ cup of the icing for center of flowers; green coloring to 1 cup of the icing, to be used for leaves, stems, and part of combination border; yellow coloring to rest of icing, to be used for spreading on entire surface of cake, and for combination border on cake.

Single recipe makes about 4 cups of icing. Make about 30 violet flowers with 193 flower tube or No. 3 tin cookie tube and bag on wax paper. Place in freezer for at least 1 hour. Make borders with same No. 3 large cookie tube and bag, directly on cake. Make stems with No. 6 tube, directly on cake. Make centers with No. 6 tube, in center of each flower. Make violet leaves with No. 104 (or 67 or 70) tube, directly on cake.

Remove loose crumbs from cake and spread entire surface smoothly with pale yellow icing. Decorate around edge of opening in center of cake if desired, leave plain; or cover with round piece wax paper. Pipe leaves directly on cake, forming 4 bouquets. With small spatula or knife, lift violets from wax paper and place them at once onto leaves to prevent softening. It will take about 6 or 7 violets for each bouquet. Pipe 6 or 7 stems on right side of each bouquet. Pipe border of pale green and yellow icing on base of cake.

Two-Tone Angel Food Cake

Serves 12

Prepare 1 recipe white Angel Food Cake (page 570). After it is completely mixed, pour ½ the batter into another bowl. Add red coloring to suit taste; blend coloring well into batter with a mixing spoon. Pick up a heaping tablespoon of pink batter and drop into an ungreased angel food pan; then pick up white batter and continue to alternate until all of batter has been used up. Strike pan against table. Smooth top, and bake according to directions for Angel Food Cake. Any other color combination may be used.

When cake is cold, cover it with Strawberry or Raspberry Fluff Icing (page 619), and decorate with whole fresh berries when in season.

Chocolate Angel Food Cake

Serves 12

1 cup and 2 tablespoons sifted cake flour	1¾ cups egg whites, in 10- or 12-inch bowl
⅓ cup unsweetened cocoa	½ teaspoon salt
1¾ cups sifted granulated sugar	1½ teaspoons cream of tartar
	1 teaspoon vanilla or other extract

Sift flour, cocoa and ½ cup of the sugar together several times. Separate eggs, and let whites stand in room temperature about 1 hour. Preheat oven. Add salt to whites and with hand beater or electric mixer beat until foamy, add cream of tartar and continue to beat until they cling to bottom and sides of bowl. Now beat ½ more minute. Fold in sugar (less ½ cup added to flour), about ¼ cup at a time, vanilla, and last add dry ingredients sifted together in advance, about ¼ cup at a time, until no streaks appear. Do not overmix. Pour into ungreased 10 × 4-inch tube pan, and with a dinner knife or spatula cut through batter several times. Bake in 350° F. oven about 45 minutes. When done, remove from oven, turn upside down onto a cake rack and let stand only until cake is cold, about 2 hours. Loosen sides and around tube with a dinner knife, and turn out, then loosen around bottom of pan. These cakes may be left whole or cut into individual pastries, filled, and decorated.

Individual Chocolate French Pastries

Makes 24 very large pastries, or 36 medium

Prepare 1 recipe Chocolate Angel Food Cake (above). Cut cake cross-wise into 2 thick layers (or 3 flatter), then into individual portions. Spread with Mrs. Miller's Quick French Buttercream Icing (page 613); cover sides with finely chopped pecan meats, chocolate shots, toasted coconut, or as desired. Decorate top with buttercream flowers and other designs. Place in paper cups.

Chocolate Ice Cream Roll or Yellow Sponge Roll

Serves 8

7 large eggs, separated
¾ cup sifted cake flour, combined with ¼ cup unsweetened cocoa, if pre-paring chocolate roll (for yellow sponge roll, use 1 cup flour and omit cocoa)

Pinch of salt
¾ cup sugar
¾ teaspoon cream of tartar
1 teaspoon vanilla

First separate eggs, cover and let stand in room temperature about 1 hour. Grease a 12 × 18 pan with 1 tablespoon or little more unsalted shortening and sprinkle with cake flour. Shake off loose flour. Set oven at 400° F. Beat yolks for about 1 minute until light. Put aside. Sift the flour, cocoa, and ¼ cup of the sugar together several times in preparing chocolate roll. Pour egg whites into 10-inch bowl. Add pinch of salt and beat until foamy. Sprinkle cream of tartar over surface of whites, and continue to beat until they cling to bottom and sides of bowl. Now beat whites about ½ more minute. Fold in the beaten yolks, about ⅓ at a time, then fold in the re-maining ½ cup sugar, about 3 tablespoons at a time, and last fold in the flour, and cocoa mixture, about ¼ cup at a time. Fold in vanilla. Pour into greased and floured pan. Bake in preheated 400° F. oven 12 to 15 minutes, or until done. (If oven temperature is correct, it will take 15 minutes for chocolate roll, a little less time for yellow roll.) When done, remove from oven, loosen around sides with a dinner knife. Carefully turn it out onto large tea towel (or better onto long rack about 12 × 18 covered with towel). With a serrated-edge knife immediately cut away about ¼ inch of crisp edges all around. Now let cake stand uncovered (away from drafts) about 10 minutes (or until cool, but not cold, and not warm). Form short or long roll. If not to be filled soon, it is important to store it in a plastic bag, then unroll and fill.

If a short wide roll is desired, start from short end. When ready to be filled, unroll carefully, place on a sheet of wax paper, cover with 2 bricks of ice cream, *each brick cut into 6 uniform slices,* or stabilized whipped cream, marshmallow, French Cream Filling (page 669), etc., leaving about 1½ inches uncovered on small ends. Roll tightly.

For Ice Cream Roll, arrange on platter, pour chocolate sauce or whipped cream over top and serve from table; or it may be sliced and sauce served separately.

Note. This recipe may be cut in halves and baked in a 10 × 14-inch pan, greased with 3 teaspoons shortening and floured. Bake 10 or 12 minutes.

George Washington Roll

Serves 8

Prepare basic Chocolate or Yellow Sponge Roll (above). Roll from wide end, forming a long roll. Cut a stiff cardboard to measure about 3 inches wide and 16 inches long. Cover it with wax paper or foil, holding it down underneath with Scotch tape. When cake is cold, open and spread it with about 1¼ cups or little more of Mrs. Miller's Quick French Buttercream Icing (page 613). Or use 1 recipe of French Cream Filling (page 669), leaving about 2 inches all around uncovered with filling. Other fillings may be used.

To ½ cup icing add green coloring for stems and leaves. To 1 cup add red or yellow (or may be left white). Cut off about ¼ inch from ends of roll, and spread both ends with white icing and cover with chopped nuts. Now add 1 ounce (or little more) cool melted chocolate to rest of icing, blend well. Place roll on cardboard, spread entire surface with chocolate icing (or any color preferred). Mark with special marker or fork to simulate log. With green icing and No. 8 plain decorating tube, pipe a spray of stems; leaves with No. 67 or 70 tube. Pipe relief roses with white, pink, or yellow icing with No. 104 or No. 124 tube. George Washington Roll may be decorated with green citron leaves and glazed cherries instead of buttercream flowers.

Golden Sponge Upside-Down Cake

Serves 8

6 egg yolks
¾ cup granulated sugar
½ teaspoon vanilla
⅓ cup boiling water

1¼ cups sifted cake flour
1¼ teaspoons baking powder
¼ teaspoon salt

First prepare Topping (below). With electric beater, beat yolks about 2 minutes, or until thick and lemon-colored. Add sugar a little at a time, and continue beating until very light (about 1 minute). Add flavoring; then slowly add boiling water. Last, pour in sifted flour with baking powder and salt, all at once, and stir until smooth.

Pour cake batter over Topping, and bake in 350° F. oven about 35 to 40 minutes.

When done, allow to stand on cake cooler 5 minutes; then invert. Allow to cool and decorate with ½ pint whipped cream.

Topping for Sponge Upside-Down Cake

¼ cup butter
½ cup brown sugar

5 slices pineapple rings
5 red cherries

Melt butter and combine with brown sugar. Pour into bottom of an upside-down pan. Over it place pineapple rings with cherries in center of rings.

French Pastry Pecan Torte

For 3 × 9-inch pan or its equivalent

7 large or 8 medium eggs
Pinch of salt
1 teaspoon cream of tartar
1 cup and 2 tablespoons granulated sugar (add half of sugar to flour and sift together)
1 cup sifted cake flour
½ cup pecan meats, first measured, then put through food grater (should measure about ¾ cup after they are grated)
1 teaspoon vanilla

For 10 × 4-inch or 12 × 3-inch spring form pan

10 large or 12 medium eggs
¼ teaspoon salt
1½ teaspoons cream of tartar
1¾ cups sifted granulated sugar (add half of sugar to flour and sift together)
1¼ cups sifted cake flour
¾ cup pecan meats, first measured, then put through food grater (should measure about 1¼ cups after they are grated)
1½ teaspoons vanilla

Separate eggs. Beat yolks for several minutes with egg beater until very light. Wash beaters. Add salt to egg whites, and with electric beater, beat until foamy. Add cream of tartar and continue to beat until they cling to bowl, then beat ½ more minute. With a large spoon, fold beaten yolks into whites, a little at a time; fold in ½ of sugar, about ¼ cup at a time, then fold in the flour combined with rest of sugar, ¼ cup at a time. Last, add grated nuts and vanilla and blend gently until no streaks appear, but do not overwork. Pour into an ungreased pan that measures about 3 × 9 or its equivalent, or if preparing large recipe pour it into a 10 × 4 or about a 12 × 3 spring form pan. Bake small cake at 300° F. about 45 minutes, then raise temperature to 350° F. and bake about 15 more minutes, or until done when tested with a cake tester. If tester comes out dry, cake is done. Bake large cake at 300° F. about 1 hour, then about 15 more minutes at 350° F. When done, remove from oven, invert pan onto cake rack or 2 flat pans, and let stand until cold for at least 2 hours. When cold loosen around sides and bottom with a dinner knife or spatula and remove.

Heavenly Ice Cream Meringue Torte

Serves 8

French Pastry Pecan Torte (page 574)
Whip 2 to 4 cups 32% cream (depending on size of cake) until it clings to bowl

4 pints ice cream if using 1 layer of ice cream, or 8 pints ice cream if using 2 layers of ice cream
1 or 2 recipes Meringues for Ice Cream Torte (page 576)

Cut French Pastry Pecan Torte crosswise in 2 uniform layers, and place bottom layer in center of a 16-inch round platter or round cardboard. Cover layer of torte with a very thick layer of ice cream (about 1½ inches thick). Cover ice cream with second layer of torte. (To shape ice cream, line a 3 × 9 pan as smoothly as possible with wax paper, and pack bottom as solidly as possible with 4 pints ice cream. If 2 layers of ice cream are preferred, cover first layer while it is in pan with 2 round sheets of wax paper, having second sheet come up around sides as high as possible, to facilitate removal. Now pack in another 4 pints ice cream, smoothly as possible, and cover well. Slip into a plastic bag, and freeze until needed. This must be done at least 2 hours in advance, or can be stored in freezer for many days. To release ice cream from pan, go around sides with a dinner knife, lift out layer, peel off paper, and place ice cream on torte.) One layer (4 pints) is sufficient for 3 × 9 torte, but 2 layers (8 pints) may be used successfully. If ice cream appears soft, place entire filled torte into freezer for a short time, but do not let freezer too hard, or it will be difficult to cut. Remove from freezer and cut down into serving wedges, being careful to keep wedges as close together as possible. Put back into freezer while preparing stabilized whipped cream.

To Decorate. With bag and No. 3 star cookie tube, start at top of cut cake and pipe scrolls or straight designs of whipped cream to bottom of torte, spacing scrolls as uniformly as possible and leaving small open space between each to show torte. Pipe several rosettes on center top of torte, and garnish top of rosettes with a large meringue rose, surrounding rose with 7 or 8 green meringue scrolls. Place rest of roses alternately with green meringue scrolls around base of torte. Keep in freezer until ready to be served.

This torte may be completely filled and decorated with whipped cream several weeks in advance but omit meringues until shortly before serving. Let cream freeze hard on surface, then wrap it well. Remove from freezer about 1 hour before serving, *unwrapping at once.* Keep in refrigerator or may stand in room temperature for at least 30 to 45 minutes. Now place meringues on torte.

Note. For large 10 × 4 or about 12 × 3 pan, it is better to use 2 layers of ice cream (8 pints in all) if serving a large group; 1 quart whipping cream, using No. 7 star cookie tube to decorate, and 2 recipes of meringues.

To Serve. With cake server lift out 1 wedge at a time. If 2 layers of ice cream are used, simply serve only a wedge from top layer and 1 or 2 meringues. More meringues may be served separately. *If you are not equipped with a freezer (or large freezing section in refrigerator) this torte must be filled and served within a few minutes after it is completed.*

Meringues for Ice Cream Torte

Pinch of salt
½ teaspoon vanilla
½ cup fresh egg whites (in a No. 7 or 8 bowl), temperature of whites about 70° F., not warmer (Eggs must be as fresh as possible and of top quality for this purpose. Inferior, old eggs produce a softer meringue which cannot be used for fancy designs and roses. For best results eggs should be refrigerated until needed and not more than 2 or 3 days old after they are purchased.)
½ teaspoon cream of tartar
1 cup sifted granulated sugar
Red and green food coloring

Add salt and vanilla to egg whites, and with electric mixer beat until foamy. Add cream of tartar and beat about 3 minutes at high speed with electric beater, or until very stiff but not dry. Add the sugar, about a tablespoon at a time, and continue to beat only until sugar is well blended, about 1 minute. Divide meringue in 2 parts. To 1 add a little red coloring for the roses and to the other a little green coloring for the scrolls. Refrigerate green meringue until neded. Blend coloring into white meringue gently with a large spoon or mixer. As quickly as possible pipe roses onto ungreased rose nails with No. 124 rose tube. Insert them into a deep cardboard box (a candy box is excellent; or use an empty wax paper carton). Bake at 250° F. about 1½ to 2 hours, having door of oven slightly open to prevent discoloration. With No. 3 large star cookie tube and bag, pipe scrolls (about 3 inches long) onto a well-greased (use 1½ teaspoons unsalted shortening) 12 × 18 baking sheet. Bake at 250° F. about 1 to 1½ hours, keeping oven door slightly open. On a humid day leave meringues in oven with heat shut off to dry out well. Remove from oven, and when slightly cool, but not cold, release them with a small spatula from the nails and baking sheet. Keep well covered between wax paper until needed. If they soften during humid weather, reheat in a 250° F. oven for about 15 to 20 minutes. This recipe will make about 10 to 12 large roses, and 14 to 16 scrolls, enough to use for small or large ice cream torte. Double recipe may be used for large torte. Roses and scrolls can be baked in same oven at one time, leaving as much space between racks as possible. Move pans around if necessary.

Important. If meringues are prepared much in advance, they should be stored in boxes, separated with heavy wax paper, and refrigerated until ready to serve. Do not freeze. It is best not to prepare these meringues during very hot humid weather.

Viennese Whipped Cream Nut Torte

For 10 × 4-inch angel food tube pan, or its equivalent

For 9 × 3-inch angel food tube pan

13 large eggs (to measure 1⅔ cups of whites)
3½ cups sifted confectioners' sugar
3 cups of pecan meats, walnuts, filberts, or almonds, first measured, then very finely chopped or grated in mouli mill
½ cup light dry bread crumbs
1½ teaspoons vanilla
½ teaspoon salt
1 teaspoon cream of tartar

8 large eggs (to measure 1¼ cups whites)
2¼ cups sifted confectioners' sugar
2 cups pecans, walnuts, filberts, or almonds, first measured, then very finely chopped or grated in mouli mill
⅓ cup light dry bread crumbs
1 teaspoon vanilla
¼ teaspoon salt
⅔ teaspoon cream of tartar

Separate eggs very carefully. In a 10- or 12-inch bowl, with electric beater, beat yolks for about 2 minutes. Add sugar gradually and continue to beat for several more minutes. Add ¼ cup of the unbeaten egg whites, beat about 1 minute. Now add the chopped nuts that have been combined and mixed well with the bread crumbs to the yolk mixture, a little at a time, beating continuously until well blended. Add vanilla, then another ¼ cup of the unbeaten whites. Beat for several minutes.

In a separate 9- or 10-inch bowl pour rest of egg whites and salt. At once beat for a few seconds until foamy, then add the cream of tartar. Continue to beat until whites cling to bowl. *Beat ½ more minute.* Pour all the beaten egg whites at one time into first mixture and fold gently until thoroughly blended and no streaks appear, but do not overmix or under-mix. Pour into an ungreased loose-bottom 10 × 4 *tube pan*, cutting through batter a few times, and bake in 300° F. oven about 2 hours, testing cake the last 15 minutes. With cake tester or wood pin, test center of cake before removing from oven. When done, remove from oven, invert onto cake rack or 2 flat pans and allow to stand until absolutely cold for at least 5 hours. Then very carefully loosen around sides and tube with a dinner knife. Loosen bottom with dinner knife and lift out cake, place it on round card-board. Fill and decorate with whipped cream or any of the buttercream icings.

If cake breaks when removing from pan or runs over in baking, it was insufficiently mixed when adding beaten egg whites. It is better to allow this cake to stand 5 or 6 hours before removing from pan.

For small tube pan, 9 × 3 inches, follow procedure in recipe above, and bake about 1 hour and 30 minutes.

Very Important. If this type of cake is baked a day or two in advance, even if not iced, it must be kept in a very cold place or refrigerator, loosely wrapped in wax paper, to prevent rancidity in nutmeats. May be frozen for several months.

Chocolate-Filled Walnut Torte

Serves 12

Prepare 1 recipe Yellow Sponge Roll (page 572). Turn onto wax paper. Let stand until cold; then cut it into 4 uniform pieces.

Roast about ¾ cup walnut meats in a 300° F. oven about 10 minutes, turning them several times. Let stand until cold; then put through a nut chopper or grater.

Prepare 1 recipe Chocolate Filling for Walnut Torte.

Cut very stiff cardboard a little smaller than cake. Place cake on card-board.

Reserve 1 cup of filling for decorations on top of torte. Spread ⅓ cup on each layer. Spread rest of filling over entire sides and top of cake. Cover sides with chopped or grated walnuts. With No. 30 decorating tube (or No. 3 cookie tube) pipe attractive scrolls over entire top, and rosettes between scrolls. Keep in refrigerator until serving time.

Chocolate Filling for Walnut Torte

5 ounces baking chocolate, cut into small pieces	⅓ cup hot milk
½ cup butter or margarine	2 whole eggs
3½ cups sifted confectioners' sugar	2 teaspoons vanilla

Combine chocolate with butter or margarine and melt over hot water or very, very low heat. Add sifted confectioners' sugar alternately with hot milk, a little at a time. Add vanilla and eggs, 1 at a time, beating well after each addition. With electric mixer beat filling about 5 minutes after all ingredients have been added. Cover, and refrigerate about 1 hour or until very thick and cold. If too thin, add a little more sugar. If too thick, add a little more milk.

Dobos Torte

Serves 12

1¼ cups egg yolks, in a 10-inch bowl (room temperature at least 1 hour, covered, 75° F.)
2 cups sifted granulated sugar
1 cup very hot water (bring to boil, then keep covered until needed)
2½ cups sifted cake flour, combined with ½ teaspoon salt and 2¼ teaspoons double-acting baking powder
¾ cup pecans, first measured, then put through food grater

1½ teaspoons vanilla
5 cups Chocolate Buttercream Icing (page 610) to fill and spread on sides of cake
Another ¾ cup pecans, grated after measured, for sides and rim of cake
About ¾ cup pink or yellow buttercream for top decorations and ½ cup green for leaves

In a 10-inch bowl beat yolks at high speed for about 2 minutes until thick and lemon-colored. Add sugar, ¼ cup at a time, and continue to beat until very light, about 1 more minute after all sugar has been added. If using a small or old-type beater, beat a little longer. Lower speed and *slowly* add the very hot water, beating continuously. Now with a large spoon add flour combined with salt and baking powder all at once, and stir rapidly for about 2 minutes, or until batter is very smooth and thick. Last, fold in the grated pecans and vanilla, and blend well.

Pour batter into three 9 × 1½-inch round layer cake pans well greased on bottom and lightly on sides with 1½ teaspoons unsalted shortening for each pan, and coat with flour. Bake at 350° F. about 25 minutes, but watch closely after first 20 minutes. When done, remove from oven, let stand in pans about 5 minutes, then go down to bottom and around sides carefully with a dinner knife. Place rack on each and turn over. At once turn 1 of layers, having rounded side up. Let cool, then wrap and *refrigerate* for several hours or day in advance. This will facilitate splitting layers.

To Fill and Decorate. With a long serrated-edge knife, cut through center of each layer, making 6 layers in all. Place first layers on a round cardboard, about ½ inch smaller than cake. This will facilitate handling. Spread first layer with ½ cup Chocolate Buttercream Icing, then do likewise with 4 more layers. Now spread sides of layers with about 1 cup chocolate buttercream and cover with about 1 cup grated pecans.

To glaze sixth layer (for top of cake), place it on inverted side of a large baking sheet or round pan, with rounded side of cake up and wax paper underneath cake cut ½ inch smaller all around. Grease part of pan close to bottom of cake well with shortening to prevent caramel from sticking.

Prepare caramel glaze with ¾ cup sifted granulated sugar in an 8-inch skillet, *over medium heat.* As soon as sugar starts melting at bottom (takes several minutes but watch closely) *stir* until glaze is golden brown and clear and has no lumps, *but do not burn.* At once add 2 tablespoons soft butter or margarine, *lower heat* and continue to stir until butter is completely united with glaze.

At once pour glaze over top layer, and with back of large wooden spoon spread it as evenly as possible. Let stand for 2 or 3 minutes, then with long heavy oiled plain knife, make deep impressions of 12 (more or less) individual servings. *Go over impressions several times.* Let layer remain on pan until cold (or may be refrigerated for a few minutes). With dinner knife release any glaze that dropped onto pan. Slide pancake turner under cake with right hand and with left hand help pick up layer, and place it on top of other layers. Spread ½ cup of buttercream around outside of upper layer and cover with grated pecans.

Decorate each serving with a large buttercream rosette or full rose and green leaves. A chocolate border may be piped on base of cake with No. 30 star tube, or leave plain.

Continental Chocolate Mocha Torte

Serves 12 to 16

9 large eggs (to measure 2 cups), must be lukewarm (about 90° F.)
1½ teaspoons cream of tartar
1½ cups granulated sugar
1¼ cups sifted all-purpose flour (not cake flour)
8 ounces (½ pound) dark sweet chocolate, finely cut, combined with ½ cup warm strong brewed coffee, placed over *very* low heat only until melted and smooth, and starts to simmer, and stirred continuously to prevent scorching. Then add 2 teaspoons or less vanilla to chocolate and let stand until warm (not hot or cool)

In a large 10- or 12-inch bowl combine the warm eggs, cream of tartar, and granulated sugar. (If eggs are cool, place bowl with eggs in a utensil of hot water for a few minutes until they feel lukewarm to the touch. Warm eggs will make a higher and more delicate cake.) With electric mixer, at high speed, beat the eggs, cream of tartar, and granulated sugar about

10 minutes, a little longer if using a small or older-type beater. Now add flour, about ¼ cup at a time, *and with a large spoon* (not beater) fold and stir until smooth. Last, add the warm melted chocolate preparation, about 2 tablespoons at a time, and continue to fold and stir for 2 or 3 minutes until no streaks appear.

Pour batter into an ungreased large angel food pan that measures about 10 × 4 inches, and bake in a preheated 325° F. oven 1 hour, then raise heat to 375° F. and bake about 5 more minutes if necessary, or until done. Remove from oven and invert pan onto a cake rack covered with wax paper; let stand for several hours until cold. Top crust of this cake is likely to drop onto wax paper, which can be placed back onto cake after it is released from pan and turned out onto serving platter. To release cake from pan, when it is cold, go around sides and tube with a dinner knife and invert onto serving platter. Release bottom in same way.

To Ice and Decorate. Cut torte crosswise in 2 or 3 layers, spread with Continental Buttercream Custard and Icing (page 617), or whipped cream. Spread entire surface of cake with buttercream and cover sides with finely chopped or grated pecan meats, chocolate decorettes, or slivered toasted almonds. With bag and No. 3 large star cookie tube, pipe fancy scrolls of icing over entire top of cake. Milk chocolate curls may be made with a vegetable peeler and dropped directly on top of cake. (Milk chocolate must be room temperature several hours to curl well.)

Party-Style Glazed Strawberry Torte

Serves 8 to 12

French Pastry Cake (page 569) in heart or round 9 x 3 or 12 x 4-inch pan, increasing flour by ¼ cup for small cake, ⅓ cup for large cake; or use Gold Cake recipes (pages 550–551)
½ recipe Cream Filling (page 586) for small cake; full recipe for large cake
Prepare Glaze (page 582)
3 cups fresh strawberries for small cake; 4 cups for large cake, washed, drained, and dried thoroughly in a towel, then hulled
½ cup Quick Buttercream Icing—No. 1 (page 614), colored green
Thick piece of citron for stem, about 2 inches long and ¾ inch thick, or form stem with green gum drop (place citron stem in little green colored water for few minutes, then dry in a towel)

With a very sharp or serrated-edge knife (and scissors) cut around cake to simulate a large strawberry if using round pans. Scoop out about 1 inch of cake, leaving a 1½-inch wall all around to form rim. Now cut a stiff cardboard about ½ inch *smaller* than cake, and cover it smoothly with wax paper or foil, holding it in place with Scotch tape. Place cake over cardboard, then on a cake rack with drip pan underneath.

Fill opening of small torte with 1 or more cups Cream Filling (2 cups or more for large), spreading it smoothly and having it slightly higher in center. Place about ½ of strawberries on filling, leaving them whole if small, or cut in halves, reserving largest and most attractive ones for top. Now cut rest of berries in halves lengthwise and arrange them flat side down attractively, with pointed end of berries in same direction as point of cake, very close to each other, forming a mound in center, to simulate shape of strawberry as closely as possible. Pour cool glaze over entire surface of berries and rim of cake. With a spatula spread sides well with glaze. Refrigerate for about 20 minutes. With No. 7 large star cookie tube and green Quick Buttercream Icing, pipe a very large thick rosette on rounded end of torte, and insert a thick piece of citron for stem. Or use green gum drops for stems. Refrigerate.

To transfer torte to serving platter, loosen around bottom with a spatula or dinner knife; slip a pancake turner underneath with right hand, and place left hand underneath cardboard, and carefully transfer to a 14- or 16-inch round platter. Keep in a cold place or refrigerator until ready to serve. May be prepared a day in advance.

Glaze for Strawberry Torte

For 9 × 3 torte

3 tablespoons unsifted cornstarch
1 cup granulated sugar
⅛ teaspoon salt
¼ cup cool water
1 cup hot water
About ½ teaspoon red food coloring
2 tablespoons lemon juice

For 12 × 3 torte

⅓ cup unsifted cornstarch
1½ cups granulated sugar
¼ teaspoon salt
½ cup cool water, *and* 1½ cups hot water
About ¾ teaspoon red food coloring, and 3 tablespoons lemon juice

Combine cornstarch, sugar, salt, and cool water in a 2-quart saucepan; stir well until smooth. Add the hot water slowly and cook over moderate heat until thick, stirring continuously. Now lower heat and simmer about 5 minutes. Add coloring and lemon juice and cook about 1 minute. Place saucepan in ice water, stirring until glaze is smooth and cool; add little water if too thick.

Horn of Plenty Party Cake

Serves 12

In a 7-inch bowl prepare 1 small horn with 2 large eggs, ⅛ teaspoon cream of tartar, ¼ cup sugar, ½ teaspoon vanilla, ¼ cup cake flour, 1½ tablespoons cocoa. Mix this same as for large Sponge Roll (page 572), and bake in 9 × 9 square pan greased with 1½ teaspoons unsalted shortening and coated with flour. Bake about 10 to 12 minutes at 400° F. When done, loosen around sides, turn out onto square cake rack covered with towel. At once cut away crisp edges with a serrated-edge knife. Let cake stand about 10 minutes, then form a small horn of plnty, and keep it wrapped in towel until cool and ready to use.

Prepare Large Chocolate or Yellow Sponge Roll.

To Form Horn. When large roll is cool open and cut off 3 inches from long end, place small horn on top to form a foundation for large horn, and with hands carefully form a large horn of plenty, overlapping ends and holding in place with some Marshmallow Buttercream Icing (page 610) and wood pins wherever necessary, stuffing horn with cut-off pieces. At this point, it is better to wrap horn in wax paper firmly and refrigerate it for about ½ hour or longer. This will help to keep it in shape. Meanwhile cut a stiff cardboard same shape as horn but a little smaller all around. Cover it with foil or wax paper, holding in place underneath with tape if necessary.

Remove cake from refrigerator, place it on cardboard, then on a long cake rack. Spread entire surface and inside large open end of horn with about 2 cups of Chocolate Marshmallow Buttercream (page 610), then with a fork or special marker, mark lines on entire surface. Pick up horn with pancake turner or spatula and transfer to a large flat platter. With bag and No. 7 large cookie tube pipe a very thick fancy E scroll of Chocolate Marshmallow Buttercream on small end of horn, forming a curved tail. With same tube and Marshmallow Buttercream Icing form E border on rim of large open end. Refrigerate horn for about 15 minutes, but do not allow icing to become too firm before filling open end attractively with assorted fancy petit-four fruits and vegetables, small fancy cakes, fancy cookies, commercial ice cream molds, or as desired, holding them in place with a little icing. If horn has been iced and refrigerated long in advance (this can be done a day or two in advance, or it may be frozen), allow it to stand in room temperature for a short time so that fruits will cling to icing when filled. About 6 cups of buttercream are needed to decorate roll, or fill part of horn with Cream Filling (page 669), and use less buttercream.

Large Corn-on-the-Cob Pastry Cake

Prepare Chocolate Sponge Roll (page 572).

Prepare 1½ recipes Continental Buttercream Custard and Icing (page 617), or about 6 cups of any buttercream icing, if roll is to be filled with icing. It takes about 1½ to 2 cups of icing or *other filling* to spread inside of roll; about 1 cup to spread onto cake after it has been shaped, and about 3 cups for kernels on corn.

Prepare 1 recipe Gum Paste (page 584).

When sponge roll is cold, spread it with about 1½ cups (more or less) buttercream, cream filling, or fruit filling. Roll firm, and place it on a heavy cardboard (covered with wax paper or foil) cut about ½ inch smaller all around than roll. With a very sharp knife or scissors trim 1 end of cake into a *slight* point. Trim opposite end rounded. Place cake onto a long flat platter (at least 20 inches long) or 24-inch metal mat. Spread roll with about 1 cup of yellow buttercream icing. Then with No. 8 (or 10) plain tube and bag, pipe kernels on cake in uniform rows, starting from center top of large end, and then go from 1 side to the other straight down to tip. Make an opening on large rounded end of corn, and insert a thick gum paste stem (or one made with several green gum drops). Hold it in place with some crushed wax paper or foil until cake is cold. Refrigerate. Shortly before serving, place doilies around base of roll (or leave plain) and arrange corn husks on each side, starting with longest ones first. Place several various sizes on top.

To Make Corn Husks. Break off ⅓ cup of Gum Paste at a time, and on a very, very lightly floured (or rubbed with confectioners' sugar) pastry cloth, roll paste lengthwise to measure about 18 inches long and 3 inches wide. *At once* (before surface starts to dry) with a dinner knife cut to simulate husks of various sizes. *At once* mark top with dinner knife, forming fine lines. Place these husks on sides of a 2-pound long loaf rye bread (or anything else shaped about same as cake, being sure it has rounded ends). Place some on top of loaf also, inserting toothpicks to prevent sliding. Do not release from mold for at least 1 hour, then gently remove dry ones and place them on a flat sheet to dry out for a day or longer. (May be made weeks in advance and used as needed.) Scraps of gum paste may be kneaded in damp hand until united, then add little more sugar and work it well. Use about ¼ cup of scraps for stem. It is very important to keep any of the unused paste in a tightly closed plastic bag to prevent drying. Paste may stand several hours before rolling if necessary. Scrape cutting knife occasionally while forming husks, and release husks from pastry cloth with dinner knife if necessary. It is not necessary to keep rolling pin covered unless dough is a little too moist; in this case add more sugar to paste. This is one of the most beautiful pastries for special occasions. It may be surrounded with individual Petit-Four Fruits (page 591).

Gum Paste for Corn Husks, Leaves, and Other Decorations

2 level teaspoons plain gelatin, combined with 3 tablespoons cold water (stir gently; let stand several minutes until thick, then dissolve over simmering water)

¼ teaspoon green food coloring

1 teaspoon peppermint or lemon extract (optional)

About 4½ cups sifted confectioners' sugar (10X), or enough to prevent paste from sticking to hands

As soon as gelatin is dissolved and is quite hot, about 150° F., pour it into a No. 7 (medium size) bowl. Add coloring, extract, and the sifted confectioners' sugar, about a cup at a time, beating after each addition with a heavy wooden spoon. When paste is difficult to beat with spoon, turn it out onto a board, table top, or marble, and knead well until smooth and does not stick to hands, *adding more sugar if necessary*. As soon as paste is very firm and smooth, wrap it well in a plastic bag until ready to be rolled. Best to use it at once if possible as it rolls more easily. This is a basic gum paste and may be used for many decorations.

Cake Basket

Remove center of cake (see below for cakes that may be used), leaving about 2-inch rim for 9 × 3-inch cake; 2¼-inch rim for cake about 12 × 3 inches. Sprinkle top and sides with sifted confectioners' sugar, or lightly ice and cover with nutmeats or toasted coconut. Place on serving platter. If an angel food pan was used, fill bottom of opening with cake pieces. It is not necessary to cut down to bottom of cake unless a large amount of filling is preferred. Fill opening with our Cream Filling (page 586), Bavarian Cream Filling (page 588), or whipped cream, forming a slight mound in center of cake.

Color about ⅔ of Marshmallow Buttercream Icing (page 610) pink or yellow for rosettes or full roses; color rest of it green for leaves. With bag and No. 30 star tube, pipe large rosettes on entire surface of filling, scraping filling with tip of tube to prevent rosettes from sliding off. Use up all of rosette icing to give the basket a nice filled appearance. Then, with No. 67 leaf tube, pipe as many leaves as possible in between rosettes, as attractively as possible, reserving a little of the green for decorating handle. Roses may be made with No. 104 or 101 tube for this basket instead of rosettes.

Last, sprinkle handle with confectioners' sugar. Make 2 gashes on top inside of cake. Insert handle securely, going down about 2 inches to prevent it from tipping. With rest of green icing and leaf tube, pipe leaves around base of handle to help hold it in position, and to make it more attractive. Refrigerate cake or keep in a very cold place until ready to serve.

Note. Instead of buttercream decorations, this basket may be filled with fresh strawberries, washed and drained well, then dried in a towel, leaving hulls on; with fresh raspberries or blackberries, or sweet bing cherries. Or it may be filled with marzipan fruits. Meringue roses and leaves also make very attractive decorations and are edible.

Cakes That Can Be Used for Cake Basket

French Pastry Cake, baked in 9 × 3 solid pan, increasing flour by ¼ cup, or larger size, increasing flour by ½ cup, baked in a pan about 12 × 3-inch pan, are excellent for this dessert. Or you can use Angel Food Cakes or Sponge Cakes; also Gold Butter Cakes baked in deep pans. It is best to bake cake at least a day in advance, and to *refrigerate* it before you fill and decorate it.

Cookie Dough Handles for Cake Basket

Makes 2 handles

¼ cup shortening
⅓ cup granulated sugar
1 whole egg
½ teaspoon vanilla
½ teaspoon salt
1 tablespoon milk

About 1½ cups sifted all-purpose flour, or enough to form right consistency to handle dough (if too soft or too stiff, add more or less flour)

With electric mixer beat shortening, add sugar and beat well. Add whole egg and beat about 1 minute. Add vanilla and salt, then milk and flour alternately. Beat until smooth, adding last of flour with a spoon if dough is too heavy. Cut dough in 2 uniform pieces. Roll each one to form a long rope that measures about 18 inches long. Place them on large greased and floured baking sheet, forming a horseshoe, having open end 7 inches wide if to be used on cake baked in a 9 × 3 pan. For pan about 12 × 3 inches, form 10-inch ropes and 8-inch openings. With a fork mark handles gently. Bake in a 350° F. oven about 25 minutes, or until lightly colored, but not too dark. If handles appear soft, shut off heat and let remain in oven with door slightly open for about 30 minutes. Remove from oven and let cool on pan before using. Then carefully release with a wide spatula or pancake turner.

Cream Filling for Cake Basket

For 9 × 3-inch pan (use double recipe for 12 × 3-inch pan)

⅔ cup sugar
Pinch of salt
½ cup sifted all-purpose flour
2 tablespoons cornstarch

2 egg yolks, combined with ¼ cup cold milk, slightly beaten
2 cups warm milk
2 tablespoons butter
2 teaspoons vanilla

Combine dry ingredients and mix thoroughly. Add the egg yolk and cold milk, forming a paste. Pour in warm milk slowly and then cook until thick, stirring constantly. Cook several minutes after it thickens. Add butter, blend well. Let cool on cake rack, beating it occasionally to keep smooth. When cool add vanilla. Refrigerate for at least 2 hours before using.

Boston Cream Pie

Serves 8

Prepare ½ or ⅔ recipe of French Pastry Cake (page 568), increasing flour by ¼ cup, in a round loose-bottom pan that measures about 9 × 3 inches. This will give you a cake that is about 1½ inches high after it is baked. Any other sponge cake recipe may be used for this purpose. When cake is cool, release it from sides and bottom of pan. Wash bottom of pan.

To fill cake, split it in 2 layers. Place 1 layer on metal base of pan to facilitate handling and decorating. Pour 1 recipe of our Cream Filling (page 586) or preferably Bavarian Cream Filling (page 588) on top of first layer, spreading it carefully and uniformly, having it slightly rounded in center, and straight on sides. Now place other layer of cake over filling, and go around sides with a spatula to remove any loose filling or crumbs. If filling appears soft, refrigerate entire cake for an hour or longer. This will not be necessary if either filling was prepared a day in advance and refrigerated.

To Serve. Prepare 1 recipe Quick Glossy Icing (page 612). Remove cake from refrigerator and place it on a rack with a baking sheet underneath. Pick up icing and with a spatula cover sides of cake first. Now pour rest of icing all at once on top of cake and quickly spread it out as smoothly as possible. Pick up icing that drips into pan, and go around sides again. This cake may be refrigerated, then cut and serve as is; or for a special decoration, prepare a small recipe of Quick Glossy Icing with 3 tablespoons hot milk, 1 tablespoon soft butter, ½ teaspoon vanilla, about 2 cups of sifted confectioners' sugar, 1½ ounces melted chocolate. Beat well, and if too thin *after 20 minutes* add more sugar; if too thick or curdled, add a few drops hot milk or water. However, this *second icing must be thicker than the first.* Place icing in a bag with No. 8 plain tube (No. 10 may be used), and pipe a spiral on top of entire cake. With rest of icing pipe a border on base. One or more whipped cream or buttercream roses (white preferable) and green leaves may be placed in center of cake for very special occasions. Refrigerate cake for several hours before serving, but best not to ice too far in advance if a glossy icing is preferred. To serve, cut entire cake with a serrated-edge knife into serving portions, using a gentle sawy motion, keeping all portions together until serving time. This will give more attractive portions.

Bavarian Cream Filling

⅔ cup granulated sugar
¼ cup sifted all-purpose flour
2 tablespoons cornstarch
Pinch salt
2 egg yolks, combined with ¼ cup cold milk
2 cups warm milk

1 teaspoon vanilla
2 teaspoon plain gelatin, combined with ¼ cup cold water (let stand until thick)
1 cup whipping cream, beaten until it clings to bowl

Mix sugar, flour, cornstarch, and salt. Beat yolks slightly and combine with the ¼ cup cold milk. Add slowly to dry ingredients, forming a smooth paste. Add warm milk slowly and cook until thick and smooth, stirring constantly. Then simmer about 5 minutes. At once, while custard is very hot, add the thick gelatin and stir until completely melted. Pour into an 8-inch bowl and let stand until cool, stirring occasionally to prevent a crust from forming. When custard is *cool, but not cold,* add vanilla, and beat the cup of cream until it just clings to bowl. Fold cream into custard until it is evenly blended and no streaks appear. Cover and refrigerate for at least 4 hours or longer. Then pick it up with a large spoon, and place it on cake, spread gently. Place upper layer on and if filling appears soft, refrigerate cake for an hour or longer.

French Bouché Pastry Roses

Makes about 8 bouchés

2 eggs, very large
¼ teaspoon cream of tartar
Pinch salt

¼ teaspoon vanilla
3 tablespoons sifted granulated sugar
½ cup sifted cake flour

Separate eggs carefully, and allow whites to stand at room temperature in a 7-inch bowl about 1 hour. Add cream of tartar, salt, and vanilla, and at once beat at high speed until they form a soft meringue that barely slides out of bowl. Now add the sugar, about 1 teaspoon at a time, and beat after each addition for 2 or 3 seconds. Continue to beat until whites form stiff peaks, about 1 minute after all sugar has been added, but not dry. With a rubber scraper stir yolks well, and add them all at once to meringue, folding quickly but gently. Last, pour in all of flour at one time, and fold over and over only until ingredients appear moist but not smooth. Batter should appear coarse. *Immediately* place preparation in bag with No. 9 plain cookie tube, and press out thick 1½-inch mounds on medium-size baking sheet, that measures about 11 × 15 inches, covered with silicone paper, keeping mounds about 1 inch apart. Press down points. Sprinkle top with confectioners' sugar (with shaker) and bake at 400° F. about 7 minutes, or until lightly colored. (Do not prepare more than 1 recipe at a time for best results to prevent excessive spreading.) Remove from oven and let stand on rack until cool, then with spatula or dinner knife release cakes from paper.

To Fill and Decorate: When bouchés are cold, spread flat sides of cakes with thick layer of fluffy buttercream, Stabilized Whipped Cream (page 615), jams, fruit paste, or as desired. If using buttercream or Stabilized Whipped Cream, fill center, and spread top layer, coming down halfway. Now refrigerate or place in freezer for about ½ hour to set. This will facilitate handling.

Petals are piped onto cakes by picking up teaspoon of buttercream or Stabilized Whipped Cream, scraping it against edge of bowl each time (to remove surplus), then pressing spoon against bouchés, forming 2 rows of petals. Sprinkle top center of each pastry with a pinch of yellow or green sugar, or colored coconut.

Have buttercream medium consistency, not too soft, and not stiff. Stabilized Whipped Cream should be used at once or within 15 minutes for best results. Refrigerate pastries for several hours, or may be prepared day in advance even with Stabilized Whipped Cream if properly handled. Place on flat dish until firm.

Fourth of July Cake

Serves 8 to 12

1 recipe Yellow Sponge Roll (page 572)	About 2 cups Quick Buttercream Icing —No. 1 (page 614)
About 1 cup strawberry or raspberry jam or jelly	1 small package commercial red sugar (¼ cup)
	1 red-and-white candy stick

Prepare Yellow Sponge Roll. When done, let cool, and roll from small end, forming a thick roll. When cold, open and spread with raspberry or strawberry jam or jelly. Roll again and place on a large sheet of wax paper.

To Frost Roll. First spread ends of cake with white Quick Buttercream Icing; then frost entire surface as smoothly as possible, turning it over to frost underside. Place red sugar in a shaker with large openings. Sprinkle part of it on another sheet of wax paper. With a pancake turner lift off roll and place it over sugar, having open end down. Cover ends of roll with small round pieces of wax paper. Shake rest of red sugar gently over top and sides as uniformly as possible. Now lift up roll again and transfer to a long serving platter. Remove wax paper from ends. Insert a red-and-white candy stick into the center of one end for the fuse of a firecracker. Keep in a cold place or refrigerator until serving time. Cut crosswise into thick slices and serve.

Large Baked Alaska

Serves 12

Use either of cakes below, cut in 2 pieces, placed lengthwise on longer cardboard covered with foil. Follow directions for Baked Alaska (page 591). Use 4 pints ice cream. Increase egg whites for meringue to 1¼ cups, cream of tartar to ¾ teaspoon, salt to ¼ teaspoon, vanilla to 1½ teaspoons, sugar to 1¼ cups.

Butter Cake for Baked Alaska

⅓ cup butter or margarine
¾ cup granulated sugar
6 egg yolks, beaten about 2 or 3 minutes with egg beater
1¼ cups sifted cake flour, to which add

1½ teaspoons double-acting baking powder
¼ cup milk
½ teaspoon vanilla

Have all ingredients at room temperature for about 1 hour. Beat butter or margarine, add sugar, a little at a time, then the well-beaten yolks. Beat yolks, sugar, and butter several minutes. Add sifted cake flour and baking powder alternately with the milk, then add vanilla. Pour into well-greased and floured 9 × 9 × 2-inch square pan and bake about 30 minutes at 350° F.; then raise heat to 400° F. and bake about 10 more minutes. Remove from oven, let stand 10 minutes then loosen around sides and turn out onto rack.

Golden Sponge Cake for Baked Alaska

6 yolks
¾ cup granulated sugar
½ teaspoon vanilla
⅓ cup boiling water

1¼ cups sifted cake flour
¼ teaspoon salt
1 teaspoon double-acting baking powder

In a 7-inch bowl, with electric beater, beat yolks about 2 minutes, or until thick and lemon-colored. Add sugar, a little at a time, and continue beating until very light, about 1 more minute. Add flavoring, then slowly add boiling water. Last, pour in sifted flour with baking powder, all at once, and with electric mixer at medium speed beat until smooth.

Pour batter into a 9 × 9 × 2 inch-square pan that has been very lightly greased on bottom only with ¼ teaspoon unsalted shortening. Bake at 350° F. about 25 minutes, then raise heat to 400° F. and bake about 10 more minutes, or until done. Remove from oven, invert onto cake rack until lukewarm. To remove, loosen sides of cake and turn out.

Meringue for Baked Alaska

6 large egg whites (¾ cup)
½ teaspoon cream of tartar
⅛ teaspoon salt

¾ cup granulated sugar
1 teaspoon vanilla

In a No. 8 or 9-inch bowl, beat whites, cream of tartar and salt until they just cling to bowl, then add sugar, tablespoon at a time, and continue to beat at high speed about 1 minute with electric mixer, or until they cling to bowl, then beat ½ more minute. Add vanilla and beat until well blended. Leave white or add food coloring as suggested below, etc.

Baked Alaska

Serves 6

Either of the cakes on page 590 is suitable for Baked Alaska. When cake is baked, slice it crosswise and use ½ for a Baked Alaska that will serve 6 large portions.

About 15 minutes before serving prepare Baked Alaska as follows: Cut a cardboard same size exactly as cake, and cover cardboard with foil. Place cut and trimmed cake on foil-covered cardboard. Place it on a 17-inch stainless steel platter (or other heatproof platter). Place platter on a thick board (or on a large baking sheet).

Place 2 pints ice cream on cake, and keep in freezer until meringue is prepared.

Prepare meringue. Leave it white, or add a little green food coloring to about ⅔ of meringue, and red coloring to rest of it to make it pink. Spread green meringue over entire surface of cake and ice cream. Then, with No. 3 or No. 7 large cookie tube and bag, pipe fancy scrolls on top and sides of cake with the pink meringue. Sprinkle 1 tablespoon granulated sugar over entire surface and sides of cake. (This will prevent meringue from clinging to knife when cutting and serving.) Bake in a preheated 450° F. oven about 5 to 7 minutes, or until brown.

To Flame Alaska. Pour 1 tablespoon 80-proof brandy, curaçao, or rum over entire surface of cake. Light, slice, and serve at once. For large cake use about 2 tablespoons 80-proof liqueur.

Special Remarks. Have egg whites measured and ready in a No. 8 or 9-inch bowl for small cake (larger bowl for large recipe) at least an hour in advance, in room temperature. Have all necessary ingredients, beaters, etc., at hand before baking Alaska. It must not stand after it is baked. Be sure oven is preheated about 15 minutes in advance, set at 450° F. Have all individual serving plates and forks ready, also very sharp knife and cake server.

Petit-Four Fruits and Vegetables

Makes about 12 medium double cakes

¼ cup egg whites
¼ teaspoon cream of tartar
 Pinch salt
¼ teaspoon vanilla

3 tablespoons sifted granulated sugar
½ cup sifted cake flour
2 egg yolks

Separate eggs carefully, and allow whites to stand covered at room temperature in a 7-inch bowl about 1 hour; add cream of tartar, salt, and vanilla, and at once beat at high speed until they form a soft meringue that barely slides out of bowl. Now add the sugar, about 1 teaspoon at a time, and beat after each addition for 2 or 3 seconds. Continue to beat until whites are *stiff* peaks, about 1 minute after all sugar has been added, but not dry. With a large spoon stir yolks well, and add them at once to meringue, folding in quickly but gently. Last, pour in all of flour at one time, and fold over and over only until ingredients appear moist but not smooth. Batter should appear coarse. At once, place batter into pastry bag with No. 5 large plain cookie tube, or use plain opening of coupling, and form various fruits and vegetables as indicated below on inverted side of 12 × 18 baking sheet covered with silicone paper. Bake at 400° F. about 6 minutes, or until just done. Do not overbake, to prevent shriveling and toughening. Release cakes from paper with a dinner knife or spatula when cool. Store in closed container as soon as they are cool if not to be finished at once. These Petit-Four Fruits will remain fresh for several days if kept in a covered box in refrigerator or a cold place. Icing on cakes will shrivel slightly if kept in room temperature more than 1 day. May be frozen.

To Ice Petit-Fours. Place cakes on racks with drip pan underneath. Cover yellow cakes first by adding a drop or two of coloring to white Quick Petit-Four Fondant Icing (page 620). Then add a drop or two of red for carrots, and more red for strawberries and tomatoes. For apples, add green and a drop of yellow to white fondant. If it is necessary to use icing that drips into pan, release it with a rubber scraper, pour into pot and reheat it over hot water (not boiling) only until lukewarm. Too much heat makes fondant dull and sugary. Try to cover as many cakes as possible with first pouring. It is best to divide icing into 2 parts if the full assortment is made, using only about ⅓ of the icing for green and ⅔ for rest. Let cakes remain on racks until icing sets, then release them by sliding a dinner knife under each one; place them in petit-four cups, etc.

Strawberries. Form 2 medium pointed rounds for each strawberry. After they are baked and cooled, put together preferably with a light-yellow buttercream. Other fillings, such as custard, jams, or jellies may be used. Cover with red glossy Quick Petit-Four Fondant Icing, and at once sprinkle with red sugar. Insert imitation strawberry hull on large end.

Pears. Form 2 long pointed rounds for each pear. Bake, etc. Cover with yellow glossy Quick Petit-Four Fondant Icing, and at once before icing sets, sprinkle rounded part with commercial red granulated sugar. Insert a currant or small piece of raisin or a dot of melted chocolate on large end and imitation pear leaf on small end.

Bananas. Press out ½ of batter in one direction to simulate bananas, and rest of batter in opposite direction. Bake, etc. Put together with buttercream, etc. Cover with yellow glossy Quick Petit-Four Fondant Icing. Let icing set, then with a small stubby art brush and melted chocolate or cocoa, tint ends and top. Do same with little green coloring. Cocoa must be diluted in a very small amount of water to make a paste.

Apples. Press out 2 medium thick rounds for each apple. Press down points with damp finger. Bake and cool. Fill and place apples on cake rack, having them slightly tilted to show round part. Cover with light-green glossy Quick Petit-Four Fondant Icing. Use imitation apple leaf.

Tomatoes. Press out 2 large thick rounds for each. Press down points with damp finger. Bake, fill, and cover with red glossy Quick Petit-Four Fondant Icing, having them on rack with rounded side up. Before icing sets, make marks on tomatoes with back of knife. Use imitation strawberry leaf on top.

Carrots. Press out 2 long pointed strips of dough for each carrot. Bake and cool. Fill and cover with orange glossy Quick Petit-Four Fondant Icing. Before icing sets, mark across top to simulate carrot. Place imitation carrot leaf on large end.

Lady Fingers (Sponge Cake Type)

For 12 × 18-inch baking sheet

2 eggs, very large	½ teaspoon vanilla
¼ teaspoon cream of tartar	¼ cup sifted granulated sugar
Pinch of salt	½ cup sifted cake flour

Separate eggs and allow whites to stand in room temperature in a 7-inch bowl for about 1 hour. Add cream of tartar, salt, and vanilla, and at once beat at high speed until they form a soft meringue that barely slides out of bowl. Now add the sugar, about 1 teaspoon at a time, and beat after each addition until blended for 2 or 3 seconds. Continue to beat until whites form fairly stiff peaks and tip end only slightly rounded, but not dry. With rubber scraper stir yolks well, and add them all at once to meringue, folding in quickly and gently. Last, pour in all of flour at one time, and with rubber scraper fold over and over only until ingredients appear moist, but not smooth. Batter should appear coarse. Immediately place preparation into bag with plain opening of coupling (or use large No. 6 plain cookie tube in bag), and press out lady fingers on 12 × 18-inch baking sheet, covered with paper (silicone paper excellent), to measure 2½ to 3 inches long, keeping them about 1 inch apart. (One recipe will cover this size pan. Do not mix more than 1 recipe at a time for best results.) Sprinkle top of fingers lightly with sifted confectioners' sugar, and bake in a preheated 400° F. oven about 5 minutes, or only until *very, very* delicately colored (almost white), to prevent drying out. Remove from oven, let stand until cool, then carefully release them from paper with a spatula, or lift off with fingers. Spread flat sides lightly with jam, jelly, or sweet chocolate, and put 2 together. Sprinkle again with confectioners' sugar. Or use plain fingers to line pans for frozen desserts. Store in wax-paper-lined boxes, then in plastic bag to keep moist for 2 or 3 days. Sprinkle again with confectioners' sugar before serving. Single recipe will make about 15 pairs or 30 single fingers.

Lady Fingers Strawberry Bavarian Ice Box Mold

Serves 12

1 recipe Lady Fingers (page 593); 2 packages commercial lady fingers may be used instead
12-ounce package of sugared frozen strawberries or raspberries
¾ cup granulated sugar
½ cup egg whites
¼ teaspoon salt

2½ tablespoons plain gelatin, combined with ¾ cup cold water (let stand about 5 minutes, then dissolve over simmering water; let stand until lukewarm)
2 cups whipping cream, beaten to medium, still slides out of bowl
A little red coloring, if desired

Line 9 × 3-inch spring form pan with Lady Fingers, rounded side next to side of pan, holding them in position with a dab of butter, keeping fingers as close together as possible.

Combine berries, granulated sugar, egg whites, and salt in a 9- or 10-inch bowl. Beat at high speed with electric mixer about 10 minutes or longer, or until quite stiff. At once fold in dissolved lukewarm gelatin and blend thoroughly. Last, fold in the medium whipped cream. With a large spoon blend well until no streaks appear.

Carefully pour filling into pan lined with Lady Fingers. Garnish top with 8 fingers, having flat side down, arranging them to simulate a flower. When baking Lady Fingers, prepare a small round cake (about 1¼ inches in diameter) of the same dough. Place this in the center of mold. Refrigerate at least 8 hours.

To serve go around mold with a dinner knife, release clamp and remove sides of pan. Keep cake on bottom of pan for better support. Arrange on a round platter.

Mold is very attractive if top and sides are sprinkled with sifted confectioners' sugar before mold is placed on platter, and decorated with large scrolls of whipped Cream with No. 3 or 7 large star cookie tube.

▶ LARGE CAKES FOR SPECIAL OCCASIONS ◀

For these large recipes you will need an extra-large mixing bowl, about 13 × 5 inches (available in many department and hardware stores), and a standard-size electric mixer, not the junior size. You will need a large rack about 13 inches wide, either square or oblong, for the 15-inch wedding cakes and the large oblong cakes.

Grease sides and bottom of all pans lightly with unsalted shortening, unless otherwise specified, *and line bottom of all pans* with heavy wax paper or silicone paper, cut to fit smoothly. This prevents cakes from breaking when they are removed from pans. After they are removed from oven let cakes remain in pans on a cake rack *for at least 10 minutes for small cakes, 20 to 30 minutes for large cakes,* or as indicated in recipes, before turning them out onto rack.

Have all ingredients room temperature at least an hour in advance. Butter, margarine, or shortening should be of medium consistency. All butter, all margarine, or half of each can be used in these cakes. Remove chill from milk and eggs if necessary until just cool.

During warm weather it is best to use Quick Buttercream Icing (page 614), using half butter and half vegetable shortening, and water instead of milk, to prevent rancidity. During cold weather you can use other richer buttercream icings.

Cakes baked in aluminum pans require 25 degrees lower temperature than tinware pans. The 15 × 2½ inch, and smaller sizes, that come in a wedding cake set of 5, are available in many of the large hardware and department stores. The tinware 4-piece wedding cake pans are available in nearly all stores, and are very inexpensive. It is important to place empty new tinware pans in a 350° F. oven for about 3 hours for shallow pans and 5 hours for deep pans before using them, for proper heat penetration. This is done only once (when they are new). Aluminum pans do not require this treatment.

Any of the batters given for the various butter cakes in this section can stand in the refrigerator in the proper pans (or in a bowl), covered, for several hours or longer if you do not have oven space. You may have to increase baking time slightly. Remove batter from refrigerator about ½ hour for small cakes before baking, and 1 hour for large cakes, for batter stored in bowl, and let stand in room temperature.

Roses and other decorations can be made with Royal Icing (page 624) days in advance; let dry. They can be stored in boxes for many weeks or longer. Meringue powder for Royal Icing should be available from bakery shops if you buy it in small amounts. Be sure to state that it is for Royal Icing, then follow our mixing directions.

It is very important to support tier wedding cakes with heavy wood meat skewers cut same depth as cake, using 4 skewers for large layers, and 2 or 3 for smaller layers. Then place a stiff round cake cardboard between each layer. If using paper cardboard separators, line them with heavy wax paper, held in place with a little Scotch tape.

The professional plastic plate supports and plastic pegs are more sanitary and more secure than the homemade type. They are available from restaurant and bakery supply houses, and from many mail order houses, advertised in women's magazines. Directions come with these sets and are simple to follow.

It is not necessary to ice and decorate wedding and anniversary cakes in white icing. In recent years the pastel icings and decorations have become very popular and are attractive.

White Wedding Cake Made in 4-Tier Tinware Pans

For 12, 10, 8, and 6 × 2-inch pans

Large Recipe for Batter

2⅓ cups butter or margarine (half white shortening may be used), medium consistency

3 cups sifted granulated sugar

7 cups sifted cake flour, combined with 7 teaspoons double-acting baking powder and 1 teaspoon salt, and sifted together

2⅓ cups milk, cool, not cold

About 2 teaspoons vanilla

1¾ cups egg whites in 10-inch bowl (room temperature about 1 hour)

1 cup sifted granulated sugar

With electric mixer, beat butter for about 5 minutes, high speed, until creamy. Add sugar, about ½ cup at a time, and beat about ½ minute after each addition. Add flour combined with baking powder and salt, about 1 cup at a time, alternately with ⅓ cup of milk, and beat after each addition about 1 minute. Add flavoring. Now wash beaters thoroughly, and beat whites until they cling to bowl. Add the cup of sugar a little at a time, and beat after each addition until *well* blended, but not dry. Pour beaten whites, all at once, over batter, and with a long wooden spoon fold over and over until evenly blended and no streaks appear.

Pour full amount of batter into *one 12 × 2 pan*, *one 10 × 2 pan*, and *one 6 × 2 pan*, all greased well on bottom, and covered with heavy wax or silicone paper. Brush paper also with shortening. Grease sides of pans *as lightly as possible*, with shortening. Cover 2 small pans well with wax paper, or put into plastic bags, and refrigerate until first layer is done. This batter can remain in refrigerator for several hours. Place the largest pan (12 × 2) in center of a preheated 325° F. oven, and bake cake for about 1 hour, then increase temperature to 375° F. and bake about 10 more minutes, or until done when tested.

Meanwhile prepare the following batter to fit remaining 8 × 2 inch pan:

Small Recipe for Batter

⅔ cup butter or margarine (half white shortening may be used), medium consistency

1 cup sifted granulated sugar

2 cups sifted cake flour, combined with 1¾ teaspoons double-acting baking powder, and ¼ teaspoon salt, sifted together

⅔ cup milk, cool, not cold

1 teaspoon vanilla

½ cup egg whites in 7-inch bowl (room temperature about 1 hour)

2 tablespoons sifted granulated sugar

Follow same mixing directions as for large recipe. Pour into *one 8 × 2-inch* greased and papered pan. Cover well and refrigerate.

When first layer (12 × 2) is done, remove from oven, let stand on cake rack for about 20 minutes, then go around sides with a dinner knife, and turn out onto cake rack. Set oven again to 325° F. Now place remaining layers (the 10 inch, 8 inch, and 6 inch that were stored in refrigerator) into oven, leaving space between each layer, to allow heat to circulate properly. Bake 1 hour at 325° F., then 5 to 10 more minutes at 375° F. when properly tested. Remove from oven, and let stand on racks about 10 to 20 minutes, then release sides with a dinner knife, and turn over onto cake racks. Let cool, and store in plastic bags, on round cake cardboards, until ready to be iced and decorated.

Use Quick Buttercream Icing (page 614), Royal Icing (page 624), White Mountain Icing (page 611), or rich French-type Mrs. Miller's Buttercream Icing (page 613) to decorate. During warm weather, it is best not to use very rich buttercream icings.

Important. Have all ingredients room temperature (about 70° to 75° F.). If milk is cold remove chill over very low heat. Place container with egg whites in a pan of warm water if necessary for a few minutes. Have butter or margarine (and shortening) medium consistency. If all shortening is used, increase milk by ¼ cup for large recipe, 1 tablespoon for small recipe. If half shortening is used, increase large recipe by 2 tablespoons milk, and ½ tablespoon for small. This is an excellent white batter and can be refrigerated for several hours if you are equipped with only 1 oven. Be sure to keep it tightly covered for best results.

White Wedding Cake Made in 5-Tier Aluminum Pans

For 15, 12, 10, 7, and 4 × 2½-inch pans

Prepare 1 full large recipe for White Cake batter (page 596), and pour it into *one 15 × 2½-inch* aluminum pan, greased and lined with wax or silicone paper. Grease sides of pan *as lightly as possible with shortening*. Bake cake in 300° F. oven, 1 hour and 15 minutes, then increase temperature to

350° F. and bake about 15 more minutes, when tested. When done, remove from oven, let stand on cake rack about ½ hour, then loosen around sides with a dinner knife and turn out onto a very large rack (at least 13 inches in diameter). Baking rack from oven may be used for this purpose. When cold turn over onto a large 14-inch round cardboard or a pizza pan covered with silicone paper, or very flat platter.

Prepare 1 more full large recipe White Cake Batter (page 596) and pour it into *one 12 × 2½-inch* and *one 10 × 2½-inch* lined and greased pans. Cover the 10-inch layer well with wax paper or plastic bag *and refrigerate until ready to bake.* Place the 12-inch pan in preheated 300° F. oven and bake about 1 hour, then increase temperature to 350° F. and bake about 10 more minutes, when tested.

Now prepare small recipe for White Cake Batter (page 597), and pour it into *one 7 × 2½-inch* pan and *one 4 × 2½* pan, greased and covered with wax or silicone paper. Cover these pans well and refrigerate until ready to be baked.

When oven is clear, set it again to 300° F. and bake the 10-inch layer, 7-inch layer, and 4-inch layer (in center of oven) all at one time, leaving space between layers to allow the heat to circulate properly. Bake 1 hour at 300° F., then about 5 to 10 more minutes at 350° F. When done remove from oven, let stand on cake racks about 20 minutes, release sides with dinner knife, and turn out onto cake racks. Place them on round cake cardboards to prevent breaking and store in plastic bags until ready to decorate cake.

Use icings suggested on page 597 to decorate.

Whole Egg Cake Made in 5-Tier Aluminum Pans

For 15, 12, 10, 7, and 4 × 2½-inch pans

Large Recipe for Batter

2¼ cups butter or margarine	8 cups sifted cake flour, combined
4½ cups sifted granulated sugar	with 8 teaspoons double-acting
6 large whole eggs (to measure 1½	baking powder and ½ teaspoon
cups)	salt
2 teaspoons vanilla	2½ cups cool milk

With electric mixer, beat butter for about 5 minutes at high speed, until creamy. Add sugar, about ½ cup at a time, and beat about ½ minute after each addition. Add eggs, 2 at a time, and beat well for about 1 minute after each addition, then about 5 minutes after all eggs have been added. Add vanilla. Last, add flour sifted and combined with baking powder and salt, about 1 cup at a time, alternately with about ¼ cup of milk, and beat about ½ minute after each addition. Pour batter into *one 15 × 2½-inch* aluminum round pan, lightly greased on sides and bottom covered with silicone or wax paper. Bake at 300° F. about 1½ hours, then increase heat to 350° F. and bake about 15 more minutes, or until done, testing cake last few minutes. When done, remove from oven, let stand on rack about 20 to 30 minutes, then carefully release from sides, place large rack (at least 13 inches wide) over top and invert carefully. Remove paper and let cool.

Prepare another large recipe to pour into *one 12 × 2½-inch* aluminum pan and *one 10 × 2½-inch* aluminum pan, greased and covered with silicone or wax paper. Bake at 300° F. about 1 hour, then increase heat to 350° F. and bake about 10 more minutes, testing toward end. Prepare small recipe, below.

Small Recipe for Batter

½ cup and 1 tablespoon butter or margarine

1 cup and 2 tablespoons granulated sugar

2 large eggs (½ cup)

⅛ teaspoon salt

2 cups sifted cake flour, combined with 2 teaspoons double-acting baking powder

½ cup and 2 tablespoons milk

½ teaspoon vanilla

Following mixing directions as for large recipe. Pour batter into *one 7 × 2½-inch* and *one 4 × 2½-inch* aluminum pans, greased and covered with silicone or wax paper. Bake at 300° F. 45 minutes, then increase heat to 350° F. and bake about 10 more minutes. Test. Decorate with buttercream icing.

Whole Egg Cake Made in 4-Tier Tinware Pans

For 12, 10, 8 and 6 × 2-inch pans

Prepare large recipe for Whole Egg Cake (page 598). Pour into *one 12 × 2½-inch pan, one 10 × 2-inch pan,* and *one 6 × 2-inch pan,* greased and covered with silicone or wax paper. Bake at 325° F. about 1 hour, then increase heat to 375° F. and bake a few minutes longer if necessary, testing cake last few minutes. Refrigerate other 2 layers and bake at 325° F. about 45 minutes, then increase heat and bake a few minutes longer. Test.

Now prepare small recipe Whole Egg Cake (above) and pour into the 8 × 2-inch tinware pan. Bake about 45 minutes at 325° F., and then raise temperature to 350° F. and bake a few minutes longer. Test.

Whole Egg Butter Cake for Deep Pan

For 14 × 3½-inch pan

After many years of experimental work, we have developed a fool-proof Whole Egg Butter Cake recipe that can be baked in deep 3½-inch (or little deeper) pans. For other size pans, please follow directions for specific recipes.

3 cups butter or margarine (1½ pounds, room temperature)
5 cups sifted granulated sugar (2 pounds and 6 ounces)
2 cups whole eggs (8 to 10 whole eggs)
11 cups sifted cake flour

¼ cup double-acting baking powder
3½ cups homogenized milk (room temperature)
About 1½ tablespoons orange or lemon extract, or 1 scant tablespoon vanilla

Prepare 1 Large Recipe Whole Egg Cake (page 598). Line bottom of lightly greased 14 × 3½-inch pan with silicone or heavy wax paper as smoothly as possible. Grease top of paper lightly and grease sides of pans well. Pour in batter.

Bake these deep cakes at 300° F. about 2 hours, testing last 15 minutes, or according to schedule given for specific recipe. When done remove from oven, let stand on cake rack in pan about ½ hour; slice off round part if necessary. Then with a long dinner knife or spatula loosen around sides, place large wide rack on top of cake, hold *firmly* (close to table top) and turn over carefully. Let cake become cold before further handling or it is likely to break. Turn *over* onto another rack when cold.

Hyacinth Flower Pot Cake

Bake Large Gold Cake (page 550) in 16-inch oblong angel food aluminum pan, greased well on bottom and sides with 1 tablespoon unsalted shortening, then bottom lined with silicone or heavy wax paper, lightly greased. Bake cake 1 hour and about 20 minutes, at 300° F., testing last few minutes. Follow general mixing and cooling directions, etc. It is best to bake this cake at least 2 days in advance, and refrigerate it before decorating. Do not use other cakes, as they are likely to split.

To Decorate. Prepare Quick Buttercream Icing (page 614); add about 2 ounces melted baking chocolate. Spread entire surface and sides with chocolate icing, and, with No. 30 tube, pipe fancy scrolls as desired.

Several days in advance prepare Hyacinth Marshmallow Flowers with Royal Icing (page 628). Use as directed.

Sprinkle top of pot with green colored macaroon coconut or green sugar. Chill cake for several hours. Now place 5 flowers down center of pot, and arrange curved leaves in opposite directions in front of each flower, and 1 leaf on each end.

Note. Use flat oval or rectangular platter for this cake, covered with oblong or round doilies. Cake must be supported on a very stiff cardboard, cut a bit larger (¼ inch) all around base, and covered with smooth foil.

Large Diploma Cake

Prepare 2 Sponge Rolls (page 572) in 12 × 18 baking sheets, as per directions.

When rolled cakes are cool, open and place on wax paper, close to each other. Spread entire surface with buttercream. Lift up edge of paper and form one thick 18-inch long roll. Wrap firmly and refrigerate for at least 1 hour.

Meanwhile, cut a long stiff cardboard to measure a bit smaller (¼ inch) than cake. Cover with foil, flat as possible, holding it underneath with tape. Place cold roll on cardboard. Spread entire surface with pale yellow buttercream. With green icing and No. 5 plain large cookie tube, pipe bow in center. Now decorate with pale pink roses and green leaves, using No. 104 rose tube and No. 70 leaf tube, or as desired. Use long flat tray or 2 oblong 12 × 15-inch doilies.

If using buttercream rose decoration, please chill roses in refrigerator until *very very* firm, but do not freeze. To prevent them from sliding off roll, insert heavy toothpick through tiny open bud of rose, attaching it well to cake. Use No. 4 plain tube for writing name, best wishes, etc.

All-Occasion Oblong Party Cake

Makes about fifty 2-inch squares

Use an oblong baking pan that measures about 12 × 18 × 3 inches, or a roasting pan about 12 × 18 × 2½ inches deep. Prepare extra large Whole Egg Butter Cake recipe (page 598). Remove 3½ cups batter if using 12 × 18 × 2¼-inch aluminum pan. Pan should be a little more than half filled.

Grease bottom and sides of pan with unsalted shortening, and line with greased silicone or heavy wax paper. Bake cake at 300° F. for 1 hour and 30 minutes, testing cake last 15 minutes. May take a few minutes more or less, depending on type of pan used.

Do not have pan more than ⅔ filled with batter. If using a pan that measures about 11 × 17 at bottom, remove 3½ *cups of batter*, and put aside until large cake is baked. Then bake small cake in 9-inch square pan at 350° F. about 40 minutes.

Let large cake cool for about ½ hour in pan on cake rack before removing it from pan, then go around sides, place large rack over top of cake, holding firmly and turn over.

This cake may be iced and decorated in any way desired, for almost any occasion. Especially nice for large groups, as it is simple to cut into uniform squares. For Mother's Day decorations, use sprays of carnations. Or cake can be iced, cut into squares, left together, and top of each decorated with rosette and leaf.

Pineapple-Shaped Party Cake

For two 7-inch Pyrex bowls

1 cup butter (margarine or shortening)
1¾ cups sifted granulated sugar
4 large whole eggs (1 cup)
5 cups sifted cake flour, combined with 5 teaspoons double-acting baking powder

1 cup strained pineapple juice
¾ cup crushed pineapple, drained well, pressing out most of liquid
½ cup finely chopped pecan meats

First grease each bowl with 1½ teaspoons unsalted shortening and sprinkle well with all-purpose flour. Shake out loose flour. Light oven at 325° F.

Cream butter, add sugar, a little at a time, and beat well for about 1 minute. Add eggs, 1 at a time, and beat about 1 minute after addition of each egg. Now add flour sifted with baking powder, about 1 cup at a time, alternately with about 2 tablespoons pineapple juice. Beat only until smooth. Fold in the well-drained pineapple and finely chopped nuts. Stir and beat until well blended. Pour into greased and floured bowls and bake at 325° F. for 1 hour, then raise temperature to 375° F. and bake about 10 more minutes, or until firm to the touch. Remove from oven, let remain in bowls about 10 minutes, then go around top edge, place rack over each and invert carefully. Let cakes become cold. If you are equipped with only 1 bowl, half of batter can stand covered, refrigerated.

This cake can be baked in 2 medium-size bread pans, for same time.

To Fill and Decorate Cake. When cakes are cold, trim open ends if necessary to make them flat. Spread with pineapple filling and put the 2 cakes together to simulate body of pineapple. Insert a long wooden meat skewer through center top to help hold them together. Place cake on a rack. With paring knife make an opening on center top to measure about 1½ inches wide and 1 inch deep. Spread entire surface of cake and opening with about 1 cup of the chocolate icing. If icing on cake appears soft, place cake in refrigerator for a short time. Now place part of chocolate icing on one side of pastry bag and part of yellow streaked icing on opposite side, using No. 3 star cookie tube in bag. Starting at top of cake, pipe flat rosettes on entire surface. When finished, leave cake on rack, and place in refrigerator (or freezer if in hurry) until icing is firm to touch. When ready to arrange on serving platter, release bottom of cake from rack with a dinner knife, and with stiff pancake turner in right hand (or use 2 pancake turners if easier) lift up cake, supporting back part of cake gently with left hand. Transfer to serving platter. Wooden skewer may now be removed. Place a spray of green Royal Icing Pineapple Leaves in opening, or use top of a fresh pineapple.

To Form Pineapple Top. With bag and rest of green Royal Icing, on silicone paper held down with little shortening, form a thick foundation to measure 1½ inches wide and 2 inches high. Arrange the straight leaves in center, holding them in place with Royal Icing, and place leaves on each side, overlapping slightly where necessary, and hold down with more icing. Let dry in slightly warm oven, or room temperature for several hours or longer. Carefully turn it over to underside and let dry again, to prevent breaking when inserting into top of pineapple. It is best to prepare this several days in advance. When dry, with tiny brush tint leaves with a little green coloring, if desired. Insert spray into top opening of pineapple cake shortly before serving.

Pineapple Filling for Cake

½ cup well-drained crushed pineapple
⅓ cup pineapple juice
2 tablespoons granulated sugar

1 tablespoon cornstarch, combined with 2 tablespoons of water

Combine all ingredients and cook until thick, stirring continuously. Simmer about 5 minutes. Let become cold, then spread on flat sides of cakes and put together.

Chocolate Buttercream Icing for Pineapple Cake

½ cup cold firm butter or margarine
and ¾ cup white shortening
About 7½ cups sifted confectioners' sugar
3 or 4 tablespoons milk

2 teaspoons vanilla
1 ounce melted baking chocolate
¼ teaspoon red food coloring
½ teaspoon yellow food coloring

With electric mixer, beat butter and shortening about 5 minutes, or until it looks like a heavy whipped cream. Add confectioners' sugar, about 1 cup at a time, alternately with about ½ tablespoon of milk. Beat well after each addition. Add vanilla, then if icing appears heavy, continue to beat about 2 more minutes. If icing is too soft, add a little more sifted confectioners' sugar; if too heavy add a little milk. To ⅔ of this icing, add 1 once melted baking chocolate and ¼ teaspoon red coloring. Beat well. To rest of white icing add about ½ teaspoon yellow coloring, then fold in a few drops of red coloring mixing very slightly, to obtain marble effect.

Royal Icing Pineapple Leaves

¼ cup egg whites
Pinch of salt
¼ teaspoon cream of tartar

About 3¼ cups, or more, sifted confectioners' sugar

Combine egg whites, salt, cream of tartar, and 1½ cups of the sugar. Beat at high speed about 5 minutes. Add rest of sugar, ½ cup at a time, and continue to beat about ½ minute after each addition of sugar. Beat about 2 more minutes after all sugar has been added. If icing is too soft, add more sifted sugar; if too heavy, a few drops of water. Add green coloring and very little yellow. Flatten tip end of No. 7 large plain cookie tube slightly, and place tube in bag; half fill bag with green Royal Icing, and pipe 6 or 7 long curved leaves in one direction, and equal amount in opposite direction, on lightly greased baking sheet, or silicone paper held down smoothly with a little shortening. Now pipe about 7 long straight leaves to measure about 6 inches long; about 5 inches long for curved leaves. Cover rest of icing with a damp cloth or plastic bag until needed.

Place pan with leaves in a slightly warm oven (lighted at 300° F. and after about 3 minutes shut off heat). Let remain in oven for an hour or longer, then let remain in room temperature until cool. Turn them over, and if they are not very firm and dry, let stand in warm room for several hours, or, preferably, prepare a day in advance.

Party-Size Devil's Food Cake

For 11⅜ × 17¼ × 2¼-inch aluminum roasting pan

1½ cups unsweetened cocoa, loosened well with a spoon then measured, combined with 1½ cups cool water (not cold or warm)

2½ cups margarine or butter (1¼ pounds), medium consistency

4½ cups sifted granulated sugar

7 large whole eggs (to measure 1½ cups)

6 cups sifted cake flour, combined with 1½ teaspoons baking soda, *and* 4 teaspoons double-acting baking powder, 1 teaspoon salt

2 cups buttermilk, well shaken

1 tablespoon vanilla

About 1 tablespoon red food coloring (optional, but adds deep color)

First, in medium-size bowl slowly combine cocoa with cool water. Stir well until smooth and thick. If preparation appears too heavy to mix, add another tablespoon of water. Let stand while preparing rest of cake.

In a very large extra-size bowl, beat margarine or butter for about 5 minutes until creamy. Add sugar, about 1 cup at a time, and beat about 1 minute after each addition. Add eggs, 1 or 2 at a time, and beat until well blended, for about 1 or 2 minutes, after each addition, until batter looks creamy and light in texture. Add flour combined with baking soda, baking powder, and salt, about 1 cup at a time, and beat until smooth, then add about ½ cup buttermilk at a time and beat until well blended. Continue to add rest of flour and buttermilk, until smooth. Now add the vanilla, cocoa preparation slowly, and, last, the red food coloring, and beat only until evenly blended and no streaks appear. Pour into large roasting pan, sides greased and bottom lined with greased silicone paper or heavy wax paper. Spread and make slight depression in center. Bake at 300° F. about 1 hour and 20 minutes, or until done. Test last 15 minutes.

May be necessary to bake a little less or more time, depending on temperature of ingredients, accuracy of oven temperature, etc. If you use a pan smaller than 11⅜ × 17¼ × 2¼ inches, remove part of batter and bake separately. Pan should be little more than half filled before baking.

When done, remove from oven, place pan with cake in it on cake rack and let stand about ½ hour. To remove, loosen around sides with a dinner knife, place long wide rack over top and turn over carefully, holding ends of pan and rack firmly with both hands. Let cool and spread with Special Cream Cheese Chocolate Icing for Party-Size Cake (page 620).

Easter Egg Cake

Serves 12

½ cup butter or margarine
1 cup granulated sugar
⅓ cup egg yolks (5), beaten several minutes
2 cups sifted cake flour, or 1¾ cups all-purpose flour

2 teaspoons double-acting baking powder
⅔ cup milk
1 teaspoon flavoring

Note. This recipe requires an egg-shaped mold, which comes in 2 parts. Before using these very heavy novelty cake molds the first time, wash them thoroughly with soap and water, and dry well. Grease with unsalted shortening and place in a moderately hot oven (350° F. to 400° F.) for ½ hour. When cold, wash mold again in soap and water and use as suggested in each recipe. Have all ingredients at room temperature about 1 hour during cold weather.

Grease each side of mold with 1 teaspoon unsalted shortening and coat well with all-purpose flour. Light oven at 375° F. Cream butter well with electric mixer or spoon for several minutes. Add sugar a little at a time, and beat for several minutes. Add yolks and beat about 3 minutes. Add flour that has been sifted with the baking powder, about 1 cup at a time, alternately with ⅓ cup milk at a time, and beat after each addition only until batter is smooth. Add flavoring and blend well. Pour ½ of batter into each mold. Place molds on old baking sheet and bake at 375° F. about 40 minutes, or until firm to the touch. Remove from oven, and let stand in molds about 30 minutes, then gently turn cakes out onto rack. When cold, with a sharp knife trim flat sides and cast off a little from bottom, spread with a little icing (either Buttercream Icing, page 606, or White Mountain Icing, page 611), and put together to form an egg. Spread entire surface of cake with white icing. Sprinkle sides with macaroon coconut or leave plain. Place cake in center of a 14- or 16-inch round platter. With No. 4 or plain writing tube, pipe stems and bulbs of flowers with green icing, reserving some for the leaves. With No. 104 tube, pipe yellow and pink relief roses. With No. 67 tube and green icing pipe leaves. Other colors or decorations may be used. Place Individual Ice Cream Eggs around cake.

To Serve. With a very sharp or serrated-edge cake server or knife, first cut top layer crosswise. Then slice lower part. Serve with an Ice Cream Easter Egg (page 607), or as desired.

Buttercream Icing to Decorate Easter Egg Cake

⅓ cup butter or margarine, cold and firm
⅓ cup shortening, cold and firm
About 4 cups sifted confectioners' sugar
About ¼ cup cold milk
1 teaspoon vanilla

With electric mixer, at high speed, cream butter and shortening for several minutes until light and creamy. Add sifted confectioners' sugar, about ½ cup at a time, and beat well after each addition. Add vanilla. Last, add milk, about 1 tablespoon at a time until proper consistency is obtained. It may be necessary to add a little more or less milk, depending on temperature of ingredients and whether icing is to be used for spreading purposes or for flowers. Keep it heavier for flowers.

Divide and color the buttercream icing as follows:
Add a little green coloring to ½ cup icing for stems and leaves.
Add a little yellow coloring to ⅓ cup for yellow flowers.
Add a little red coloring to ⅓ cup for pink flowers.
Use rest of icing for spreading on entire surface of cake.

Individual Ice Cream Easter Eggs

To make 6 large or 8 small

2 pints ice cream (room temperature about 20 minutes)
4 cups macaroon coconut, divided and tinted pink, green, yellow, and white. (Add a few drops of coloring and equal amount of water to white coconut and work it with a fork until evenly colored, *then rub it well in palms of hands.*)

With an ice cream baller pick up ice cream and roll it into coconut. With hands shape gently to simulate an egg. Wrap each in wax paper and keep in freezer. These ice cream eggs may be prepared days in advance. In this case, wrap them well in wax paper, then place in a plastic bag, well sealed, and freeze.

Large Ice Cream Easter Egg

Remove ice cream from freezer about 20 minutes in advance. Line 2 egg molds that measure 7½ inches long and 2¾ inches deep with wax paper as smoothly as possible. Place 1 pint of vanilla ice cream in each, bringing it up on sides and bottom as uniformly as possible. Press down well. Fill center of each mold with 1 pint of lemon or orange ice, packing it down and having top as flat and smooth as possible. Put the 2 molds together and hold in place with heavy rubber bands or string, if necessary. Wrap well in several thicknesses of wax or freezer paper and freeze.

To Serve. Turn out onto a thin oval slice of cake or bread. Remove wax paper. Cake or bread will prevent mold from sliding on platter. Cover with white macaroon coconut and decorate with whipped cream or butter-cream icing, or, preferably, spread entire mold with whipped cream, and decorate top with a spray of flowers in the same pastel colors as cake. This can be done several hours in advance and kept uncovered in freezer until serving time, or wrap well after it is frozen and keep for a longer time. Remove from freezer about ½ hour before serving. It takes 1 pint whipping cream to cover and decorate mold.

Easter Lamb Cake

Serves 8 to 12

½ cup butter or margarine	2¼ teaspoons double-acting baking
1 cup granulated sugar	powder
2 large eggs	¾ cup milk
2½ cups sifted cake flour (or 2¼ cups all-purpose flour)	1 teaspoon vanilla or other flavoring

Note. This recipe requires a heavy lamb mold. Before using it the first time, wash it thoroughly with soap and water, and dry well. Grease with unsalted shortening and place in a moderately hot oven (350° to 400° F.) for 30 minutes. When cold, wash mold again in soap and water.

Have ingredients at room temperature at least 1 hour during cold weather.

With spoon or electric mixer cream butter or margarine well. Add sugar, a small amount at a time, and beat several minutes. Add eggs, 1 at a time, and beat each about 1 minute. Add flour (sifted with baking powder several times) alternately with milk combined with vanilla, and beat after each addition only until batter is smooth. Grease each side of lamb mold with 2 teaspoons unsalted shortening, and sprinkle with all-purpose flour. Shake out loose flour. Pour batter into the half containing the lamb's face. Insert a heavy toothpick in the nose for reinforcement, and a toothpick in each ear. Press toothpick down partly into batter. Cover with other half of mold, being sure the edges lock. Place mold on a small old baking sheet, and bake at 375° F. for 50 minutes. Remove from oven; let cool about 15 minutes before removing upper part. Let cake in lower part of mold cool further about 30 minutes; then gently turn it out onto a cake rack. Let it become cold before icing.

To Decorate. Prepare 1 recipe of Fluffy Icing (page 614). Spread it thickly onto cake. (It is best to have lamb lying on a piece of wax paper with a rack underneath.) Spread icing thickly on first side and sprinkle with macaroon coconut. Now place a sheet of wax paper on iced side and turn over gently onto another cake rack. Spread second side thickly with icing and sprinkle with macaroon coconut. Slice a thin layer from bottom of lamb and spread lightly with icing to make it flat and prevent toppling sideways. Stand it up on flat serving platter. Use currants or raisins for eyes and a piece of maraschino cherry for nose. Tie a colorful narrow ribbon around neck and make bow. Surround with green coconut or other garnish.

▶ *Icings and Frostings*

PROFESSIONAL CAKE DECORATING

▶ ICINGS AND FROSTINGS ◀

The terms icings and frostings are often used interchangeably.

Icing. Actually an icing is a thin liquid and confectioners' sugar preparation, used on yeast coffee cakes, cookies, and some pastries.

Frostings. These are usually a combination of butter or margarine and sifted confectioners' sugar, with a small amount of liquid and flavorings.

Cooked frostings. These are liquid and granulated sugar mixtures that are cooked like candy, requiring a candy thermometer for correct results.

Fluffy icings. A sugar-water and egg whites combination, usually beaten over boiling water to the proper consistency, as indicated in each recipe.

Royal icing. A combination of beaten egg whites and sifted confectioners' sugar, used principally for decorative purposes and for displays. Cakes are first covered with a soft icing, then decorated with flowers made with Royal Icing. These flowers can be made weeks or months in advance, allowed to dry completely, then stored in covered containers, and used as needed. Please see section on Professional Cake Decorating (page 623) for more details.

Note on the handling of egg whites. Egg whites used in any of these recipes, if suggested, or in cakes, must be carefully separated, as the least bit of yolk or fat will lessen the volume of the beaten whites, and often prevent whites from beating at all. Bowls and beaters must be free of grease and moisture. Do not use plastic bowls to store or beat whites, as the surface of nearly all plastic utensils have a chemical that deters proper volume. Do not use aluminum or copper, as they affect the color of beaten whites. Crockery or stainless steel bowls and utensils should be used for this purpose. (A stainless steel or enamel double boiler is indispensable in the preparation of fluffy icings beaten over boiling water, and for sauces.)

Marshmallow Buttercream Icing

½ cup cold, firm butter *and* ½ cup firm margarine

⅓ cup fresh egg whites (room temperature for at least 1 hour)

1½ cups granulated sugar

⅓ teaspoon cream of tartar

6 tablespoons cool water

1 teaspoon vanilla

Wash butter and margarine in ice water until pliable and waxy, for about 2 minutes. Squeeze out as much of water as possible and shake well. Now wrap in wax paper and store in coldest part of refrigerator until needed, but do not freeze.

Combine rest of ingredients in upper part of double boiler; mix well. Wipe sides with wet cloth to remove any sugar if necessary. If using an electric mixer, bring water to boil in lower part of boiler and remove from stove. Place upper part of boiler over water and *at once* beat ingredients for about 5 or 6 minutes (no longer) if using powerful beater, or until thick and icing forms deep swirls. If using an old mixer or small type, it may take a minute or two longer. If using hand beater, it is best to keep boiler over very low heat and beat for about 7 or 8 minutes. When done, remove icing to a bowl without scraping sides and bottom of double boiler. Measure 5 cups *or less* (not more). Cover with a damp cloth and let stand in room temperature or cool place *only* until icing is cool, but not cold, and not warm. Most desirable temperature is about 80° to 85° F.

When icing is cool, beat the cold, firm butter and margarine for about 3 to 5 minutes, or until it looks like whipped cream, but not runny. Now add the *cool* (not cold) marshmallow, a heaping spoonful at a time, and beat after each addition only until smooth.

Chocolate Marshmallow Buttercream. Add 1 or 2 ounces (not more than 2 ounces for full recipe) of cool melted baking chocolate, and blend well. Food coloring may be added to the basic icing.

Important Facts. If our directions are followed, excellent results are obtained.

If egg white preparation (called Marshmallow Icing or Seven-Minute Icing) feels sugary after it has been beaten, add 1 or 2 tablespoons hot water and continue to beat about 1 more minute. This condition is caused if water is not sufficiently hot; if top part of double boiler does not touch the very hot water; if icing is underbeaten; if it is overbeaten; if very coarse sugar is used; if sugar crystals are scraped from sides of double boiler. It is always best to wipe sides of boiler with a damp cloth before you start to beat icing. This Marshmallow Icing may be used as is or colored without combining with butter if preferred. Simple decorations can be made with it if you work at once as soon as icing is completed without letting it cool. If it is not to be combined with butter, spread it onto cake as soon as possible. If to be combined with butter, let stand only until cool, not cold.

All butter may be used in this buttercream icing, but half margarine or half firm white shortening gives a better *stand-up* quality for decorative purposes, especially during warm weather. Buttercream made with half white shortening takes on better color. Shortening does not require washing. Simply measure and refrigerate it until very cold and firm. It is not absolutely necessary to wash salted butter and margarine, but doing so produces a more delicate buttercream and the finished icing is less oily appearing. Unsalted butter does not require washing, but ¼ teaspoon salt must be added for flavor.

If finished buttercream appears coarse or too heavy to spread, place bowl in a pan of warm, *not hot,* water (about 120° F.) for several minutes, then stir and beat it vigorously for a few seconds. Remove as quickly as possible from warm water.

If finished buttercream is too soft to work with and form decorations it can be improved by beating an extra ½ cup cold, firm margarine or shortening (not butter) until like a heavy whipped cream (not too soft). Now add the soft buttercream, a heaping spoonful at a time to beaten margarine and beat after each addition only until smooth; or refrigerate soft buttercream for about ½ hour, scraping sides of bowl several times while in refrigerator. This condition is caused if marshmallow part is underbeaten; if it stands too long before combining with butter; if too much Marshmallow Icing is added. Best to measure not more than 5 cups after it is removed from double boiler, without scraping sides and bottom (⅓ cupful egg whites will not always give same amount of icing; less than 5 cupfuls Marshmallow Icing will give a heavier buttercream).

Leftover buttercream icing may be refrigerated for several days or weeks if tightly covered. Before using, let it remain in room temperature (at least an hour) until you can penetrate it easily with a spoon, then beat until smooth and use. It may be frozen for several months.

This information applies also to Mrs. Miller's Quick French Buttercream Icing, White Mountain Buttercream Icing, and similar icings.

Basic White Mountain Icing (Plain)

1½ cups sifted granulated sugar	½ cup fresh egg whites (room temperature about 1 hour in an 8-inch bowl)
½ teaspoon cream of tartar	
⅛ teaspoon salt	
½ cup hot water	½ teaspoon vanilla or other flavoring

In a 1-quart saucepan combine sugar, cream of tartar, salt, and hot water. Stir until smooth. Cook over moderate heat, stirring until comes to boiling point. Now continue to cook *without stirring further* until syrup reaches

244° or 246° F. This takes about 10 minutes over moderate heat after boiling starts, but best to use thermometer. *Wash sides* of pan with brush dipped into hot water during cooking process. When syrup reaches 244° or 246° F. *shut off* heat and leave saucepan on burner if using gas stove. Remove if using electric range. At once start beating egg whites until very stiff, about 1 minute after they cling to bowl. Now pour hot syrup slowly and continuously into center of beaten whites and continue to beat at high speed until icing is lukewarm and stiff, for about 5 more minutes. Add vanilla and blend well. As soon as icing is completed, spread it onto cake and decorate. If it stands more than a few minutes, it will soften slightly making it more difficult to form flowers and other designs but can be used for spreading and simple decorations. A few drops of food coloring may be added to icing and mixed thoroughly. This is an excellent icing for spreading and decorative purposes if properly made and will hold up well on cakes for a day or two without graining and retain decorations. One recipe will cover 2 or 3 layers, depending on size and decorations.

White Mountain Buttercream Icing

Prepare 1 recipe of Basic White Mountain Icing; cover and let stand until it is cool, but not cold. Best temperature about 80° to 85° F., just tepid. Meanwhile, in ice water wash 1 cup (or little more) medium firm butter for several minutes or until it feels waxy and smooth. *Half margarine or hydrogenated shortening may be used. Do not use all margarine or all shortening.* Wrap washed butter and shortening in wax paper and keep in coldest part of refrigerator until very firm.

Measure out 4 cups of basic icing. In an 8-inch bowl beat the butter at high speed for several minutes until it looks like a heavy whipped cream, not runny. At this stage, add the icing, a large spoonful at a time, and beat after each addition only until smooth. This is a delectable French-type buttercream icing and holds up better during warm weather than other buttercreams of this type. It may be colored, or 2 ounces (not more) of lukewarm melted baking chocolate may be added to full recipe.

During very warm weather it is best to use half shortening and half butter in this icing for better standup quality.

Quick Glossy Icing

¼ cup hot milk
2 tablespoons soft butter
1 teaspoon vanilla

About 4 cups sifted confectioners' sugar
3 ounces melted baking chocolate

Combine ingredients in the order given, *adding chocolate last,* and beat with spoon until smooth. Let stand about 20 minutes. If icing becomes too thick or dull before spreading onto cake, add a little hot milk or water. If it is too thin add more sifted confectioners' sugar.

Mrs. Miller's Quick French Buttercream Icing

⅔ cup homogenized milk

¾ cup cold, firm butter *and* ¾ cup cold firm margarine (All butter may be used, but icing holds up better if half margarine or shortening is used. Icing made with half white shortening colors better. At least half butter should be used for flavor. Do not use all margarine or all shortening.)

About ⅛ teaspoon salt (or omit) if using salted butter and margarine; if using part unsalted shortening, increase salt to about ½ teaspoon

1½ cups superfine granulated sugar, or 1¼ cups regular granulated sugar (superfine sugar gives better results)

2 teaspoons, or less, vanilla

2 ounces of cool melted baking chocolate (not more) for whole recipe; use less chocolate if part of icing is used for colored flowers, etc.

Scald milk and let stand until lukewarm, about 90° F. While milk is cooling, with electric mixer at high speed, beat the cold firm butter and margarine (broken up in small pieces) for 3 or 4 minutes, or until it looks like a heavy whipped cream, but not too soft or runny. Add salt, then sugar, about ¼ cup at a time, and beat after each addition for about ½ minute. Beat 1 or 2 more minutes after all sugar has been added. Combine vanilla with the tepid milk, then add about 2 tablespoons milk at a time to butter preparation, beating after each addition only until well blended. Beat about 2 more minutes after all milk has been added. Separate icing and add coloring; or add cool (not cold, or warm) melted baking chocolate. Beat *only* until well blended. Do not use more than 2 ounces chocolate for full recipe. One ounce is usually sufficient if part of icing is used for colored decorations. More chocolate will curdle icing.

This is a delectable buttercream icing for spreading and decorative purposes. Full recipe makes about 4 cups. If icing becomes too soft to work with at any time, especially during warm weather, in a separate medium-size bowl, beat ½ cup of cold firm regular (not liquid type) margarine (no butter) until like a heavy whipped cream, then add the very soft buttercream icing to the margarine, heaping spoonful at a time, and beat after each addition only until well blended. Cakes covered with this buttercream must be kept in refrigerator, or very cold place, until shortly before serving. Do not keep for longer than 1 week refrigerated. Can be frozen for several months.

Fluffy Icing

¼ cup egg whites
1 cup granulated sugar
¼ cup water
¼ teaspoon cream of tartar

½ teaspoon flavoring
⅛ teaspoon salt
Coloring if desired

Combine all ingredients in upper part of a double boiler. Mix well. If using electric beater, bring water in lower part of boiler to a good boil and remove from heat. Place upper part (containing ingredients) over lower part, and at once beat 5 or 6 minutes, or until icing is thick and forms deep swirls if using powerful beater. Beat longer with junior mixer. If beating with hand beater, keep complete boiler over very low heat and beat 7 or 8 minutes. When done, add coloring if desired, or leave white.

Quick Buttercream Icing—No. 1

¼ cup butter or margarine, *and* ¼
cup shortening, cold and firm
2½ cups sifted confectioners' sugar

½ teaspoon vanilla
About 2 tablespoons cold milk or
water, if needed

With electric mixer, beat butter or margarine and shortening for several minutes only until creamy but not runny. Add sifted confectioners' sugar, about ½ cup at a time, and beat well after each addition. Add vanilla. Now add 2 tablespoons of cold milk or water, a little at a time. It may be necessary to add a little more or less milk or water, depending on temperature of ingredients and whether icing is to be used for spreading purposes or for flowers. Use less liquid for flowers.

For Chocolate Icing, add 1 ounce or less of melted baking or semisweet chocolate.

Quick Buttercream Icing—No. 2

1 cup butter or margarine, *and* 1 cup
white shortening, cold and firm
2 pounds sifted 10X confectioners'
sugar

About ⅓ cup of lukewarm water
1½ teaspoons, more or less, vanilla, or
other flavoring

With electric mixer, high speed, beat butter or margarine and shortening about 5 minutes until it looks like whipped cream. Add about ½ the sifted confectioners' sugar, cup at a time, and beat after each addition for at least ½ minute. Add vanilla. Now start adding a little of the lukewarm water (not warm or cold) alternately with rest of sugar, beating well. This icing makes excellent roses and other designs and it is best to test consistency before adding all of liquid. It may be necessary to add little extra water for spreading purposes.

This is an excellent inexpensive icing for cakes decorated during warm weather (or at any other time). Add flavoring and coloring, and beat well.

Stabilized Whipped Cream

1 teaspoon plain gelatin, combined with 2 tablespoons cold water

1 cup 32% whipping cream (at least 24 hours old and very cold), at least 40° F. or put in freezing compartment for about 15 minutes

¼ cup confectioners' sugar (if desired)

Coloring (if desired)

¼ teaspoon vanilla (if desired)

First measure and assemble all ingredients. Combine gelatin and cold water, stir; let stand until thick, then place over simmering water, being sure that gelatin is completely dissolved. While gelatin is cooling, beat the cream until it is of medium consistency. At this point pour the dissolved warm gelatin into the center of the cream *all at once,* and continue to beat. If sugar, vanilla, or coloring are to be added, they must be added before cream is fully beaten. Beat only until cream *clings well to bowl.* Overbeating will cause it to curdle. If this cream is to be used for spreading or decorative purposes, use it at once, then refrigerate decorated cake. If to be used as a filler or topping, cream may stand in refrigerator for hours covered.

Important Facts. Successful whipping of cream depends on four important factors—properly chilled whipping cream between 35° and 40° F.; chilled narrow bowl of proper size; chilled whipper; aging of cream. Cream that is at least 24 hours old is best as it increases in viscosity and whips up more quickly. It is best to place cream in the freezing compartment or coldest part of refrigerator for about 15 to 30 minutes, or until it is slightly icy on the sides of bowl, or at least extremely cold, about 35° to 40° F. Then whip it as quickly as possible. Use a small narrow bowl for small amounts of cream to be whipped so that beaters are submerged in the cream as far as possible. Always cover leftover whipped cream or cream whipped in advance tightly, and refrigerate it until needed. If *unstabilized* cream that has been whipped in advance and stored in refrigerator softens, it may be rewhipped for a few seconds until it clings to bowl. Never rewhip stabilized whipped cream.

If cream turns buttery or curdles during beating process it was too warm when beaten or it was overbeaten. Keep cream as cold as possible until ready to be beaten. During warm weather, place bowl containing cream in a large pan or bowl of *ice and water and beat.*

Hungarian Buttercream Icing and Filling

1½ cups butter (best to use half white shortening), cold and firm
5 large egg yolks (to measure slightly more than ⅓ cup)

1½ cups sifted granulated sugar, combined with ½ cup hot water
1 teaspoon, or more, vanilla
Add ¼ teaspoon salt, if using half white shortening

In an 8-inch bowl, with electric mixer at high speed, beat butter and shortening for several minutes until it looks like a whipped cream, but not runny. Cover with plate and let stand in a cool room (or refrigerator) while preparing rest of recipe.

In 7-inch bowl, beat, at high speed, yolks of eggs for about 2 minutes. Cover with a plate and let stand in room temperature.

In a 1-quart saucepan (not larger) combine the granulated sugar and ½ cup of hot water. Blend thoroughly and wash sides of pan. Cook over moderate heat, stirring continuously until boiling begins. Now continue to cook without stirring to 240° F. Wash sides of pan with brush dipped into hot water when necessary. Do not stir and do not jar pot after boiling begins, to prevent graining. As soon as syrup reaches 240° F., remove gently from heat, and at once pour it slowly into beaten yolks, in a steady stream, beating continuously from the start, for about 5 minutes. Cover this preparation with a thick wet towel (wrung out well) and let stand until temperature drops to about 80° F., stirring it very gently from sides of bowl with a rubber scraper several times. Do not allow to become cold, just tepid. May be forced in a pan of ice water. When beaten yolks are ready, pour them, heaping spoonful at a time, into the cool butter preparation, and beat after each addition only until smooth. Add vanilla. May be colored.

For Chocolate and Mocha Buttercream. For chocolate flavor, add 2 ounces (or less, not more) of cool melted baking chocolate, and blend well. For mocha flavor, add 1 teaspoon or more instant coffee dissolved in ¼ teaspoon hot water, and blend thoroughly. Keep this icing tightly covered in room temperature if to be used within an hour or two. It may be refrigerated for several days, but must stand in room temperature about 2 hours. When it feels medium, stir well, and use. Cakes decorated or filled with this buttercream must be refrigerated if to stand for more than several hours.

Cinnamon Butter Icing

Combine 2 tablespoons soft butter with 2 tablespoons hot milk or cream, then add about 1½ cups or more sifted confectioners' sugar combined with ¼ teaspoon or more cinnamon, and ½ teaspoon vanilla. Beat until smooth. Drizzle over cake.

Continental Buttercream Custard and Icing

Makes about 4 cups

1 cup sifted granulated sugar
⅔ cup sifted all-purpose flour
¼ teaspoon salt, if using part shortening
2 egg yolks, combined with ½ cup cool milk

1½ cups hot milk (during very hot weather, it is better to use 1⅓ cups hot water instead of milk)
1 cup cold, firm salted butter, cut into small pieces (half margarine or shortening may be used)
2 teaspoons vanilla

In a 2-quart saucepan combine sugar, flour, and salt, if using part shortening. Add yolks combined with cool milk, forming a smooth mixture. Now add the hot milk slowly and cook until thick, stirring continuously over low heat. Let simmer about 5 minutes and continue to stir. Remove from heat and let cool on cake rack or force in pan of ice water, beating custard vigorously to keep it smooth and prevent crust from forming. When custard is just cool (about 85° F.), but not cold or warm, in an 8-inch bowl, beat cold, firm butter until it looks like a whipped cream, for about 5 minutes.

Add cool custard, large spoonful at a time to the beaten butter, and with electric mixer beat after each addition *only* until smooth. Last, add vanilla. May be colored; or for chocolate, add only 1 square (1½ tablespoons melted) cool melted baking chocolate. More chocolate makes icing softer and might curdle.

Note. It is better to spread this type of icing on cake, or to make roses (or other decorations) as soon as icing is completed, without refrigerating it first. If it has been refrigerated or kept in a cold place and then beaten, it is likely to curdle. However, cakes may be filled and decorated, then refrigerated for several days, or frozen for several months, *or icing can be* refrigerated about 45 minutes and stirred gently from sides, to keep uniform consistency for roses. Use at once.

Cream Cheese Frosting

3-ounce package cream cheese, or ½ cup (room temperature about ½ hour
¼ cup butter (room temperature about ½ hour)

3 cups sifted confectioners' sugar, or little more if needed
1 tablespoon cream or milk
1 teaspoon vanilla

In 7-inch bowl, combine cream cheese and butter. Beat for several minutes until creamy, but not runny nor too warm. Add the confectioners' sugar, about ½ cup at a time, alternately with the milk or cream. Add vanilla.

Beat until well blended. If icing is too soft, add a little more sifted confectioners' sugar.

Quick Coffee Cake Icing for Danish Pastries or Doughnuts

Combine 3 tablespoons hot milk with 1 teaspoon vanilla and about 3 cups sifted confectioners' sugar. Beat until smooth. This is enough icing for full recipe of pastries.

Transparent Icing for Italian Cakes

About 3 cups, or less, sifted confectioners' sugar
¼ cup boiling water

½ teaspoon, or more, lemon extract
Finely chopped or grated pistachio nuts

Add sifted confectioners' sugar to the ¼ cup boiling water and beat until smooth; add ½ teaspoon lemon extract. This is a thin icing. More sugar may be added for a thicker icing. Dip rounded part of cakes into icing and let drain on cake racks. Sprinkle center with pinch of pistachio nuts at once before icing sets. Cakes may be sprinkled thickly with confectioners' sugar instead of iced.

Special Glossy Chocolate Coating

For cookies and small cakes

½ pound dipping chocolate (or other sweet chocolate), cut in small pieces

¼ cup shortening (do not use butter or margarine)

Place chocolate and shortening in upper part of double boiler over cold water, and bring water to a boil. Shut off heat, and at once beat chocolate and shortening until completely melted and quite hot, but not over 150° F. if possible. Remove from hot water and pour coating into a small shallow heatproof Pyrex dish. Let stand until temperature drops to 110° to 125° F. For a thin coating, have temperature about 125° F.; for thicker coating about 110° F. If temperature of coating drops below 100° F. it will be less glossy. If coating cools during dipping process, place heatproof dish in a pan of hot water and stir until warm.

Butter or margarine cannot be used successfully in this coating because of the moisture content unless they are melted and only top part is used, and measured after it is removed. Sediment or moisture will cause curdling and dullness.

Any leftover coating may be left right in glass dish, covered tightly and stored in refrigerator or a cold place for several weeks. It may be placed in a pan of simmering water and stirred gently until of proper temperature.

Dark or light dipping chocolate, or combination of both will give best results. However, other semisweet or sweet chocolate may be used, but coating will be less glossy.

Quick Glossy Chocolate Icing

1½ tablespoons hot milk, combined with 1 tablespoon soft butter or margarine
About 1 cup sifted confectioners' sugar

½ teaspoon vanilla
1 ounce melted baking chocolate (or dark sweet chocolate)

In a 5- or 6-inch bowl combine hot milk and soft butter. Add sifted confectioners' sugar and vanilla. Beat until smooth. Last, add melted chocolate and mix thoroughly. Let icing stand about 30 minutes, covered, then if it appears too thick or dull before spreading on cake, add a few drops of milk or water. If too thin, add more sifted confectioners' sugar. It is best not to ice cakes made with this icing more than several hours before serving if a very moist, glossy icing is preferred. Prepare double recipe to ice top and sides of 1 large square cake or 2 small square cakes. Prepare triple recipe to ice top and sides of 2 large layers.

Lemon Icing

For tops of two 7 × 7-inch cakes, or one 9 × 13-inch cake

Combine ¼ cup melted butter with 1½ tablespoons of lemon juice, 1 tablespoon cream, and enough confectioners' sugar (about 2½ to 3 cups), to make proper consistency for spreading.

Fresh Strawberry or Raspberry Fluff Icing

1 cup fresh strawberries, washed, drained thoroughly and then hulled, or 1 cup raspberries, washed gently, and drained well
1¼ cups sifted granulated sugar

1 egg white (carefully separated from yolk; do not use yolk)
⅛ teaspoon salt
Few drops of red food coloring

Place all ingredients in an 8- or 9-inch bowl, and with electric mixer beat at high speed until light and quite stiff—for about 10 minutes, more or less, or until it clings to bowl. This icing will hold up for several hours in refrigerator.

Strawberry or Raspberry Fluff Icing Made with Quick Frozen Berries

1 package frozen berries (10- or 12-
   ounce size)
½ cup sugar

1 egg white
⅛ teaspoon salt
Few drops of red food coloring

Prepare same as for fresh berries (page 619). Icing made with frozen berries is softer and best results are obtained if prepared shortly before using. If it softens appreciably before it is used, it may be beaten again for several minutes.

Strawberry or Raspberry Fluff Freeze

Prepare basic Fluff Icing (page 619). Then fold in 1 cup of whipping cream that has been beaten to medium consistency, not too stiff. Turn temperature control of your refrigerator to coldest point. Pour fluff into refrigerator trays and freeze for 5 or 6 hours, or until firm to the touch. Or store in freezer, well wrapped.

To Serve Fluff Freeze. Spoon into sherbet glasses and garnish top with a thick scroll of whipped cream, using No. 3 or No. 7 cookie star tube and bag. Sprinkle finely chopped pistachio or green colored nutmeats on center top for additional color.

Special Cream Cheese Chocolate Icing for Party-Size Cake

½ pound cream cheese (1 cup)
About 1 pound sifted confectioners'
   sugar

¼ cup half & half cream
1 teaspoon vanilla
2 ounces baking chocolate

With electric mixer beat cheese until creamy. Add 3 cups of the sifted confectioners' sugar, about 1 cup at a time, and beat well. Now add 2 tablespoons of cream, little at a time, until well blended. Add rest of sugar and beat well. Add 2 ounces cool melted baking chocolate.

Beat until well blended and thick. Now add rest of cream, about 2 tablespoons, and the vanilla, and beat until smooth and of spreading consistency. Little more or less cream may be used, depending on consistency of icing desired.

Quick Petit-Fours Fondant Icing

¾ cup hot water
1½ cups sifted granulated sugar
1 teaspoon corn syrup, or ⅛ teaspoon
   cream of tartar

About 6 to 7 cups sifted confectioners' sugar, depending on fineness of sugar

In a 2-quart saucepan combine water, granulated sugar, and corn syrup. Stir until completely mixed. Wash sides of pan with wet brush as necessary. Bring to a full boil to 220° F. over medium heat, and at once remove from heat. Place on cake rack and let stand about 10 minutes, or until temperature drops to about 170° F. (It is best to use a thermometer for this icing.) Now add 6 cups sifted confectioners' sugar, 1 cup at a time, and beat until very smooth. Let icing stand until it feels lukewarm, about 90° F. to 95° F. When lukewarm, dip finger into icing, let drip for a few seconds and if icing is transparent, add more sugar to form proper pouring consistency that is not transparent. A teaspoon hot water may be added if fondant is too thick. Add extract.

Quick Buttercream Icing for Bulbs on Petit Fours

Excellent for general purposes and decorating

¼ cup butter and ¼ cup shortening, cold and firm

About 3 cups sifted confectioners' sugar

About 2 tablespoons cool milk or water, if needed

1 teaspoon vanilla

With electric mixer at high speed beat cold, firm butter and shortening until light. Add sifted confectioners' sugar, about ½ cup at a time and beat well after each addition. Add vanilla, and last the liquid, about 1 table-spoonful at a time, until proper consistency is obtained. It is important to beat icing quite well before adding liquid. It may be necessary to add a little more or less milk depending on temperature of ingredients and whether icing is to be used only for spreading purposes or for flowers. Keep icing heavier for borders and flowers on other cakes.

Chocolate Whipped Cream

⅓ cup sifted confectioners' sugar

1 cup whipping cream (24 to 48 hours old and very cold, about 35° to 40° F.)

2½ tablespoons sifted cocoa

1 teaspoon vanilla

Sift cocoa and confectioners' sugar until they are well blended. Add vanilla and whipping cream slowly and blend well. Beat with electric or hand beater until mixture clings well to bowl.

Chocolate Syrup Whipped Cream

1 cup whipping cream (best 1 or 2 days old, and extremely cold)

⅓ cup commercial chocolate syrup

Beat cream in a small No. 7 bowl at high speed until it just clings to bowl. Then lower speed and add chocolate syrup in a steady stream, slowly, and continue to beat only until well blended, about half a minute. *Do not overbeat,* thus preventing curdling.

Chocolate Syrup Whipped Cream is delicious as a filling for cakes, and it may be used as an icing. Use No. 3 cookie tube and bag to make beautiful scrolls and other designs.

Lemon Cream Cheese Icing

3-ounce package cream cheese	1 tablespoon milk or cream
About 2 cups sifted confectioners' sugar	⅛ teaspoon salt
	½ teaspoon lemon extract

Beat cheese until creamy, about 1 minute. Add sugar a little at a time, alternately with milk, and beat until smooth after each addition. Add salt and lemon extract, and beat until well blended. A drop or two of yellow food coloring may be added. A little more milk or sugar may be added, depending upon consistency desired.

Chocolate Cream Cheese Icing

3-ounce package cream cheese	⅛ teaspoons salt
About 2½ cups sifted confectioners' sugar	1 teaspoon vanilla
2 tablespoons milk or cream	1 ounce unsweetened chocolate, melted and cooled

Beat cheese until creamy, about 1 minute. Add sugar a little at a time, alternately with milk, and beat until smooth after each addition. Add salt and vanilla; blend well. Last, add cool melted chocolate and beat about 1 minute until smooth. A little more or less sugar may be used, depending on consistency desired. This is a delectable icing for brownies.

Maple Butterscotch Frosting

2 cups brown sugar, packed	¼ cup butter or margarine
1 cup granulated sugar	2 tablespoons corn syrup
¾ cup milk	⅛ teaspoon salt

Combine all ingredients in a 2-quart saucepan, blend well, and cook slowly until simmering begins, stirring continuously; then let boil about 1 minute, without stirring. Remove from heat; let stand on a cake cooler until warm (not hot and not cool). Then with a large wooden spoon beat preparation several minutes until it begins to lose its high gloss and stickiness. Let stand until cool. Now if icing is too thick, add about 1 tablespoon cream or milk, a little at a time, to make proper consistency for spreading. This frosting has a nice soft gloss if it is used the day it is made. Recipe makes enough for 2 medium-size layers.

Maple Marshmallow Icing

1½ cups brown sugar, packed	¼ teaspoon salt
¼ cup water	1 teaspoon maple flavoring
2 large egg whites	½ teaspoon vanilla
1 teaspoon corn syrup	

Combine all ingredients in upper part of a double boiler, place over lower part, and follow directions for Marshmallow Buttercream Icing (page 610), omitting butter. Recipe makes enough icing for 2 medium-size layers.

▶ PROFESSIONAL CAKE DECORATING ◀

Most of the decorating described in this section is done with Royal Icing, and in order to turn out satisfactory work the icing must be of the proper consistency. Royal Icing is made with fresh egg whites and sifted confectioners' sugar, or meringue powder (which is made from dried egg whites) and sifted confectioners' sugar. It can be purchased from bakers' supply houses or from some bakeries. Royal Icing is used primarily for decorative work. Cakes may be iced with Buttercream or White Mountain Icing, and decorated with Royal Icing flowers and lattice work.

Royal Icing flattens out after it stands for a while. For flowers, do not prepare more than can be used within an hour. For stemming, borders, and other flat work, it can be used within several hours *if icing is beaten each time before filling bag.*

Do not add more sugar than suggested amount, if possible. If it is difficult to press icing through the tube at any time, remove tube from coupling and wash it thoroughly in hot water, making certain that there are no particles of hard icing in tube. Then if it is still difficult to press out, add a little more egg white or a few drops of water, *very little* at a time. If it is too soft and designs or flowers do not stand up, add a little more sifted confectioners' sugar and beat thoroughly with electric mixer or spoon.

Royal Icing flowers may be made weeks or months in advance, allowed to dry thoroughly, then stored in a covered container for future use. Nails or molds on which flowers or other decorations are made must be lightly greased with *unsalted* shortening. To hasten drying, light oven at 300° F. for 5 minutes; *then shut off.* Place flowers (placed on a stand or heavy carton) in oven and let remain as long as possible. Flat flowers dry within an hour or two. Thick flowers take many hours, and it is advisable to let them stand a day if possible. Always test by removing 1 carefully and observing bottom. If it is still soft, do not remove the rest.

Buttercream roses and whipped-cream roses are piped onto ungreased nails and then stored in refrigerator until firm enough to remove with a paring knife. Do not remove flowers from refrigerator until rest of cake is completed, or they will soften.

Numbers of Tubes and Their Uses

Star tubes Nos. 24, 27, 29, 39, 30 (and all other star tubes) make:

> E border
> Single rosette border
> Double rosette border
> Scallops
> Basket
> Candleholders

Leaf tubes Nos. 65, 67, and 70 make leaves.

Nos. 4, 6, and 8 (also No. 2) make stems and imitation leaves.

Nos. 101, 104, and 124 make roses. (Use No. 104 for a medium-size rose.) These tubes also make relief roses and carnations.

Bulbs on relief roses are made with Nos. 4, 6, and 8 tubes.

Bulbs on carnations are made with Nos. 4, 6, and 8 tubes.

Writing is done with a No. 2 tube.

Bell flowers on small pastries, mints, etc., are made with No. 2 and No. 4 tubes. Tiny flat flowers are made with the same tubes.

Tiny flowers on sugar cubes are made with a No. 24 tube, with No. 2 tube for center. (Royal Icing must be used.)

Quick Practice Icing

Beat ½ pound cold firm vegetable shortening until light (about 5 minutes). Then gradually add about 1½ cups sifted cake flour, or 2 cups sifted confectioners' sugar, and continue to beat until thoroughly blended and fluffy. Color as desired and keep in a cool place. It may be used many times for practice work. If too soft, add a little more flour or sugar. *This icing is for practice only,* and is not edible.

Royal Icing

Use 8-inch bowl

1 pound sifted 10X confectioners' sugar

¼ cup meringue powder, combined with ⅔ cup cool water (stir well, and let stand about 15 minutes)

Add ½ of sugar to the meringue powder preparation and beat about 5 minutes. Now add rest of sugar, about ½ cup at a time, and beat after each addition about 1 minute.

This makes an excellent light icing for flowers, borders, etc. For a heavier icing, cover icing with a damp towel, let stand about 1 hour, then add another 1½ cups or less of 10X sifted confectioners' sugar, ½ cup at a time, and beat about 1 minute after each addition. This heavier icing may be preferred for flowers and other decorations made long in advance. Use as soon as possible after it is made for best results, and beat it each time before filling bag. If icing stands more than ½ hour, it is best to beat with mixer.

Royal Icing Made with Fresh Egg Whites

Use 7-inch bowl

¼ cup fresh egg whites
Pinch of salt
¼ teaspoon cream of tartar

About 3¼ cups, or more, sifted 10X confectioners' sugar

This type of icing is used for lattice work, long lilies of the valley and other long decorative leaves that must be much less fragile.

Combine egg whites, salt, cream of tartar, and 1½ cups of sugar. Beat at high speed about 5 minutes. Now add rest of sugar, ½ cup at a time, and continue to beat about ½ minute after each addition. Beat about 2 more minutes after all sugar has been added. Another ¼ cup or little more sugar may be added if icing appears soft. Best to have it stiff as possible for this type of work. If too stiff at any time, add a few drops of water or a little egg white, and beat well. *Use this icing as soon as possible after it is made,* and beat well each time before filling bag.

Special Decorations

Before baking large fancy cakes, it is wise to plan decorations, so that sufficient flowers and other ornaments may be made several days in advance. Decorations made with Royal Icing can be stored in covered boxes for several months or longer, provided decorations are thoroughly dry.

If it is difficult to remove ornaments made with Royal Icing from greased pans after they are thoroughly dry, place pans in a 200° F. oven 2 or 3 minutes; then remove carefully.

Cakes that are to be covered with light icings should first be spread smoothly with a thin coating of the icing and if using Royal or White Mountain Icing allow to stand in room temperature for several hours.

If using buttercream, store in refrigerator. Then spread again, as smoothly as possible, with a thicker layer of icing.

Dahlias, Single, Double, and Triple. Use No. 104 tube on a No. 7 nail, or on a nail with slight depression. This flower can be made only with Royal Icing. Pipe center with No. 4 tube.

Pompoms. Use No. 4 tube on No. 3 or No. 6 nail. Sprinkle top with colored corn meal or farina. Make only with Royal Icing.

Poinsettias. Make directly on cake with any decorative icing, such as Royal, Buttercream, White Mountain, etc. Use No. 67, No. 70, or No. 71 tube for petals, No. 4 for yellow centers. Add red coloring to basic icing for petals; add yellow for centers.

Birds. Use No. 2, No. 4, or No. 6 tube directly on cake with Buttercream, White Mountain, or Royal Icing. If using Royal Icing, they may be made on a lightly greased pan, allowed to dry, then carefully removed and transferred to cake. Use No. 2 tube to pipe eyes in a contrasting color.

Swans' Necks for Cream Puffs. Use No. 6 plain decorating tube for small and No. 10 for large. (No. 27 or No. 30 may also be used.)

Stork. Use No. 4, No. 6, No. 8, or No. 10 plain decorating tube for neck and outline of body. Use No. 2 or No. 4 tube for legs and feet. Fill in body with plain large tube or No. 30 star tube. Pipe storks directly on cake with Buttercream, White Mountain, or Royal Icings.

Bell Flowers. Use No. 2, No. 4, No. 6 tube for stems, centers and bells. Flowers are very attractive made with green stems, blue bells, and yellow center. Any icing may be used.

Tiny Flat Flowers for Place Cards and Mints. Use No. 1, 59°, 13, 101, 65, 2, 4 or 6 tube for entire flower. Make with any icing.

Pears and Strawberries. Use plain opening of coupling. Use citron for stems, small currants for rounded part of pear. Sprinkle round part with red sugar. Pipe leaf on pear with No. 4 tube. Use large star tube for hull on strawberry.

Chrysanthemum Flowers. Prepare Royal Icing (page 624) using only 1 pound of sifted confectioners' sugar. Icing for this flower should not be too stiff. Beat icing each time you fill bag, and keep it covered with a damp cloth (not too wet). Place 2-inch squares wax paper on lightly greased flat No. 7 flower nail. With bag and plain opening of coupling, half filled with colored icing, pipe a 1 inch thick and 1 inch wide mound of icing on top center of wax paper, having it slightly higher in center. With No. 80 decorating tube, start at top and pipe pointed ½-inch petals, keeping rounded side of tube on outside. As flower is completed, gently release wax paper and flower from nail, and place it on inverted side of a baking sheet.

To dry out flowers, light oven at 300° F. for about 3 minutes. *Shut off heat.* Place pan with flowers in warm oven and let remain for several hours or longer, to dry out well. Best to make them day or longer in advance. May be kept for several months.

Lattice Handles for Wedding Cakes, etc. Prepare Royal Icing Made with Fresh Egg Whites (page 625). Use as soon as it is made for best results. Beat each time you half fill bag. Cut rectangles of wax paper that measure about 2¼ inches wide and 3½ inches long. Grease underside of papers lightly and place them with greased side down on standard large rolling pin (supporting pin) with crushed paper toweling or dish towel on baking sheet. With bag and No. 24 star tube, pipe an outline in one direction, then in opposite direction, forming lattice. To reinforce lattice, pipe tiny rosette or E border around edge with No. 24 star tube.

To dry out lattice handles, light oven for about 3 minutes at 300° F. *Shut off heat.* Place baking sheet with rolling pin into oven and let remain for several hours. Then let stand in warm, dry room for at least 24 hours to dry out thoroughly. Test by lifting 1 off. If seems to stick, place pan in a warm oven for a few seconds (not minutes), which will facilitate removal. Place lattice on a flat pan until needed. May be made long in advance, but be sure to dry them out thoroughly before storing.

Easter Lilies. Prepare Royal Icing Made with Fresh Egg Whites (page 625). Use icing at once, and beat it each time you half fill bag. Grease inside and rim of No. 12 lily nail fairly well with unsalted shortening. With bag and No. 71 special lily tube, pipe 6 petals, making lily slightly thick in bottom center where 6 to 7 yellow stamens are placed in as far as possible. This flower will take at least 24 hours to dry according to general directions given above for lattice work. Test dryness of flowers by pulling 1 stamen. If stamen comes away from center, flower is not ready to be released from nail. Let stand several hours longer.

Lilies of the Valley Leaves for Wedding Cakes. Prepare Royal Icing Made with Fresh Egg Whites (page 625). Color about ⅔ of it green, leave rest white. Beat icing well each time you half fill bag, and keep covered with damp cloth. Use as soon as made for best results. Line a flat lightly greased baking sheet with silicone paper (or heavy wax paper). With bag, green icing, and No. 70 large leaf tube, pipe straight long leaves to measure about 2½ inches. Now with white icing and No. 4 plain tube, pipe white dots on leaves. Place pan in oven, heated about 3 minutes at 300° F. *Shut off heat.* Let remain for at least 8 hours, or until very dry. Use as suggested. Can be made long in advance. For narrower leaves use No. 67 tube.

Full Roses. Prepare Royal Icing Made with Fresh Egg Whites (page 625). Use No. 104 tube for medium roses; 124 tube for large. Pipe them on lightly greased No. 7 flower nail, keeping wide end of tube down. If you are not equipped with a large number of nails, place 2-inch squares wax paper on lightly greased nail, and as soon as rose is completed, release from nail, and place on inverted side of a flat baking sheet.

Carnations. Use No. 104 tube for medium carnations, keeping large end down. Carnation petals are made with tube directly onto top of cake with buttercream or other decorating icing. Make thick bulb with green icing and No. 8 or 10 plain decorating tube; stems with No. 6 or 8 plain decoratting tubes, imitation long narrow leaves with No. 8 or plain decorating tubes.

Marshmallow Flowers. Cut each large fresh marshmallow into 5 sections, leaving ½ inch uncut in center. Flatten each section with fingers, and with scissors trim corners to simulate petals. Roll a small piece of the discarded marshmallow into a tiny ball and dip it into diluted yellow coloring for center. Place tiny round ball in center, pressing it down lightly. With tip of a toothpick or wooden skewer dipped into diluted red coloring, make some lines in center of flower. *For leaves*, cut additional marshmallows into halves and then into slices. With fingers shape them to simulate leaves. Spread leaves out on wax paper and let dry at least 1 hour; then with a tiny brush tint top with diluted green coloring. Let dry again a short time. These flowers are very attractive to decorate tops of large or individual cakes. They may also be used to garnish dessert molds and mousses.

Gum Drop Roses. Purchase large *fresh* gum drops. Steam gum drops in top part of double boiler 10 minutes *if dry*. For large roses, use them whole, for small roses, cut in desired size. Place gum drops on a thick layer of granulated sugar, and with rolling pin roll them to desired thickness, *adding granulated sugar as needed to prevent sticking*. For small roses, cut through with a 2-inch cutter, forming rounds. Use 3-inch cutter for large roses. *Roll rounds again* to make them little thinner. Now cut each round in halves. Let stand uncovered on wax paper in room temperature for a few minutes (or if very moist for several hours). Form center of rose with 1 of halves, then place 5 to 7 more halves around center forming rose, pinching bottom well to form a base. If base is too thick, cut off a little. Place a narrow strip of aluminum foil around base if necessary to support petals until they are dry, or place each rose in several thicknesses of medium-size glassine paper candy cups.

Make rose buds with scraps of petals and leaves.

Use green gum drops to make gum drop leaves. Roll same as for petals but a little thicker. Cut each in 2 pieces. With scissors trim to simulate leaves. With dinner knife mark veins. Make 4 leaves for each rose. For thick leaves roll whole gum drops into an oval and shape. Green food coloring may be added to yellow or white gum drops if necessary, and kneaded well in hands and on board to make green, adding little granulated sugar as needed.

Hyacinth Marshmallow Flowers. Several days in advance prepare Hyacinth Flowers with Royal Icing (page 624). Insert heavy green tinted long wooden skewers (5¼ inches long) through 2½ large marshmallows. With deep pink royal icing and No. 24 star tube pipe tiny rosettes on entire surface. Insert flowers into a solid loaf of bread or egg box, until you are ready to use them. To tint meat skewers, paint lower half with slightly diluted green coloring. Let dry well on cake rack before using.

To make hyacinth leaves, with tip of plain No. 9 cookie tube, flattened slightly, prepare leaves with tough Royal Icing Made with Fresh Egg Whites (page 625), on lightly greased smooth pan or *silicone paper*. Make about ten 5-inch-long curved leaves in one direction and 10 in opposite direction. Let dry well.

► *Desserts*

CHEESE CAKES, STRUDELS, PUFF PASTRY, AND TARTS

THE TYPE OF DESSERT SERVED DEPENDS SOMEWHAT UPON THE NATURE OF the meal. However, a good rule to follow is to serve the rich, heavy desserts with a light luncheon or dinner, or just the reverse. Dessert molds that are attractively decorated or garnished enhance the buffet table for special occasions. They are very practical because they may be prepared in advance, and will serve many people.

Hollywood Two-Tone Cheese Cake

Serves 8 to 12

1¼ cups graham cracker or zwieback crumbs or very light dry bread crumbs, and ¼ teaspoon cinnamon (crush until very fine with rolling pin or put through food mill; sift and measure)

¼ cup granulated sugar
⅓ cup warm melted butter or margarine

Combine all ingredients and mix thoroughly using fingers or fork until well blended and moist. Grease ¾ way on sides and entire bottom of 9-inch loose bottom round pan (without tube) with 2 teaspoons unsalted shortening. Cover sides of pan with about 1 cup of crumb mixture, having it come up to about 1 inch from top of pan, and press down with back of spoon. Pour rest of crumb mixture into bottom of pan, and with a large spoon press down until smooth and compact. Keep in refrigerator or freezer while preparing Filling.

Pour First Part of Filling into pan, spread until smooth and uniform. Bake in preheated oven, 375° F. 25 minutes. Remove from oven, place on cake rack and let stand in room temperature about 15 minutes. Raise temperature of oven to 475° F. About a minute or two before time is up, prepare Second Part of Filling.

With a large spoon, pour Second Part of Filling over cool baked First Part of Filling, *starting from side to center*. Spread evenly, as gently as possible. Bake in 475° F. oven about 10 minutes. Remove from oven and let stand in room temperature on cake rack for 5 or 6 hours, or until absolutely cold before removing cake from pan. When cold, go around sides of cake with a spatula or dinner knife, and remove cake carefully.

To Serve. *Do not cut until following day.* Cover cake with wax paper and store in coldest part of refrigerator for at least 8 hours or longer. When ready to serve, cut into wedges and with a spatula or server release carefully from bottom of pan. For special occasions, top of each may be decorated with pink cream cheese rosette and green leaves. This cake may be refrigerated for several days after it is cut and stored on wax paper in a covered box.

Special Remarks. Remove all ingredients for this cake from refrigerator 2 hours before preparation. Entire top of cake may be covered with extra crumb mixture before baking, but cake is more attractive and unusual with plain top. Before releasing cake from pan, loosen crumbs on sides of pan, allowing them to drop on edge of cake. This forms a rim, imparting a more finished appearance.

First Part of Filling

1 pound cream cheese (room tempera- 3 medium eggs or 2 very large (½
 ture 2 hours)   cup)
½ cup granulated sugar   ¾ teaspoon vanilla

Combine all ingredients one at a time, and with electric mixer or heavy wooden spoon beat until smooth, about 2 or 3 minutes.

Eggs in First Part of Filling may be separated. Beat yolks with other ingredients. Then beat whites until they cling to bowl and fold into cheese mixture until well blended and no streaks appear. This method will give a slightly higher cake with a lighter texture. This cake is about 1½ inches high when ready to be served.

Second Part of Filling

1 pint commercial sour cream (do not ¼ cup granulated sugar
 use home-type sour cream)   1 teaspoon vanilla

With a spoon mix these ingredients only until well blended.

Small Cream Cheese Cake

Serves 8

Whites from 3 large eggs   ½ cup granulated sugar
3 tablespoons granulated sugar   ½ teaspoon vanilla and ¼ teaspoon
1 pound cream cheese   lemon extract
Yolks from 3 large eggs

Follow directions for large cake (below). Reduce crumbs to 1⅓ cups, sugar to ¼ cup, cinnamon scant ½ teaspoon, melted butter or margarine ⅓ cup. Line sides of 3 × 9-inch round pan with 1 cup of crumb mixture, about halfway; 1 cup for top. Pour rest on bottom.

Prepare filling same as for large cake, reducing baking time to about 50 minutes, or until cake rises in center, and cracks slightly.

Cream Cheese Cake

Serves 8 to 12

2 cups golden dry bread crumbs (or graham crackers or other cookie crumbs, using only ¼ cup of sugar)

½ cup granulated sugar, combined with about ½ teaspoon cinnamon
½ cup warm melted butter or margarine

Blend dry ingredients thoroughly, add warm melted butter or margarine, and with a fork and hands, stir until moist and evenly blended. Grease bottom and ⅔ of sides of a 9 × 3-inch loose-bottom pan with 3 teaspoons soft unsalted shortening. Cover ⅔ of sides with 1½ cups of the crumb mixture, pressing down with a tablespoon. Put aside 1 cup of crumb mixture for top. Pour rest of crumb mixture into bottom of pan, and with hand and spoon, press down to uniform thickness. Now place pan into refrigerator (or freezer) and let stand for *at least ½ hour*, or until firm to touch.

Pour filling into crust-lined pan. Sprinkle remaining cup of crumbs over top uniformly. Place 4 thicknesses of lightweight aluminum foil or double thickness freezer foil on outside of pan, holding it in place with paper clips or pins, having foil come up only as high as pan. (The aluminum foil will help prevent excessive baking on outside of cake. Aluminum foil may be used over again several times.) Bake cake at 375° F. for about 1 hour and 10 minutes, or until it comes up in center and cracks slightly. Remove from oven at once and let stand in room temperature on a cake rack *away from drafts until cold.* (This will take several hours.) Then release cake gently from sides with a dinner knife. Best to keep it on bottom of pan in refrigerator for several more hours. Cut into serving pieces and decorate top of each with a scroll of whipped cream (or icing) if desired, or leave plain.

Filling for Cream Cheese Cake

Whites from 6 large eggs
⅓ cup granulated sugar
2 pounds (4 cups) cream cheese
Yolks from 6 large eggs

1 cup granulated sugar
1 teaspoon vanilla and ½ teaspoon lemon extract

Remove ingredients from refrigerator at least 2 hours before mixing. Light oven and set at 375° F.

Place egg whites in an 8-inch bowl and beat them until they cling to bottom and sides. Now add the ⅓ cup of sugar and continue to beat about ½ more minute, at high speed. Refrigerate beaten whites while mixing other ingredients. In a 10-inch bowl combine the cheese, yolks, the 1 cup granulated sugar, and extracts. With electric mixer beat until smooth for about 2 or 3 minutes. If mixing with a spoon or junior beater, add 1 ingredient at a time and *beat until smooth* for several minutes. Pour beaten whites all at once into cheese mixture, and with a long spoon blend until no streaks appear.

Sour Cream Cheese Cake

Serves 8 to 12

2½ cups graham cracker crumbs (or zwieback crumbs)	¼ cup granulated sugar, combined with ¼ teaspoon cinnamon
	½ cup melted butter or margarine

Combine ingredients and with a fork blend until moist. Reserve 1 cup for top. With a spoon press remaining crumbs on sides and bottom of greased 9-inch spring form pan, all the way to top. Refrigerate for at least 30 minutes or until crumbs are firm.

Pour Filling into crumb-lined pan, sprinkle reserved cup of crumbs over the top evenly. Place aluminum foil (several thicknesses lightweight, or 2 thicknesses heavyweight) around sides of pan, holding it in place where the ends meet with a clip or pin.

Bake at 350° F. about 1 hour to 1 hour and 15 minutes, or until cake rises in center even with sides. Shut off heat, and allow cake to remain in oven with door partly open for about 1 hour. Remove from oven and let cool on cake rack for several hours. When cool, release from sides of pan, and refrigerate cake (leaving bottom of pan under cake until serving time). Cake may be baked several days in advance if wrapped and refrigerated. It may be cut into serving wedges after it is cold, and stored in a wax-paper-lined box for several days in refrigerator, or it may be removed from pan and frozen for several weeks.

Filling for Sour Cream Cheese Cake

4 egg whites, beaten until they cling to bowl, then add ¼ cup sugar (sugar added to whites is in addition to the ¾ cup)	1 pint dairy sour cream
	¼ cup cornstarch, sifted with ¾ cup granulated sugar
1 pound cream cheese, medium consistency (not too cold or too firm)	4 egg yolks
	½ teaspoon vanilla and ½ teaspoon lemon extract

It is important to have all ingredients room temperature about 2 hours.

First, beat egg whites, add sugar, and beat 1 more minute. Refrigerate. With electric mixer beat cheese until creamy; add sour cream, a little at a time, the cornstarch combined with the sugar, yolks, and flavoring, and continue to beat only until smooth. Last, remove beaten whites from refrigerator, pour them into custard, and with mixer beat slowly only until evenly blended.

New-York-Type Cream Cheese Cake

Serves 12

1 cup sifted all-purpose flour
½ teaspoon baking powder
¼ cup granulated sugar
½ teaspoon vanilla or lemon extract
⅓ cup butter or shortening

1 very small egg, beaten with a fork, and a little milk if dough appears too dry after egg has been added (should be the consistency of a medium cookie dough that can be rolled easily)

Sift dry ingredients together several times. Add vanilla or lemon extract and the butter. Cut through ingredients, using pastry blender, until they look like fine meal. Add beaten egg, and a little milk only if necessary. Blend with a knife or fork until dough leaves sides of bowl. Turn out onto a pastry cloth and knead gently a few seconds. Cut dough into 2 parts. Wrap 1 part in wax paper and refrigerate. Shape first piece of dough into a flat round and place it on bottom of an ungreased loose-bottom spring form pan that measures about 9 × 3 inches. Roll dough to fit pan. Trim off edges evenly. Place sides of pan on and bake at 325° F. about 20 to 25 minutes or until crust is delicately brown and firm to the touch. Remove from oven and let cool.

Remove other half of dough from refrigerator and cut it into 6 uniform pieces. With covered rolling pin, roll each piece about 3 inches wide and 5 inches long. Place pieces of dough on sides of ungreased cool pan, 1 piece at a time, and press well with floured fingers. (Cutting dough in small pieces facilitates handling—thus preventing breaking of longer pieces of rich dough.) Pour Filling into pan and bake at 325° F. about 1 hour, or until cake rises in center even with sides and takes on a very delicate color. Then bake about 10 minutes more or until surface cracks. Shut off heat. Let cake remain in oven for at least 1 hour, keeping oven door partly open. Let cake cool on a rack away from drafts. Be sure to let it stand until it is cold before releasing from pan and serving. It is best to refrigerate it for several hours before cutting.

It may be sprinkled thickly on top and sides with sifted confectioners' sugar before cutting, or cover top with one of the berry or fruit glazes (below and page 636). This cake will rise high and settle to original size after it is cold.

Filling for New-York-Type Cheese Cake

1 pound cream cheese (best to purchase half-pound packages)
⅓ cup sifted all-purpose flour
3 tablespoons cornstarch
¼ teaspoon salt
1 teaspoon vanilla
Rind of small lemon and small orange (or 1 teaspoon lemon flavoring)

⅓ cup egg yolks
1 cup cream
2 tablespoons butter
¾ cup egg whites
1¼ cups granulated sugar, combined with ⅓ cup hot water and cooked to 248° F.

In a large 10-inch bowl place 1 pound of cream cheese. Add the flour, cornstarch, salt, vanilla, rinds, and egg yolks, a little at a time, beating with electric mixer until smooth and well blended. Then add hot cream (about 150° F.) and butter slowly, beating only until smooth. Let this mixture stand while preparing cooked meringue.

Pour the unbeaten egg whites in an 8- or 9-inch bowl. In a very small saucepan (not more than 1-quart size) cook the granulated sugar and water until it reaches 248° F. This takes about 6 or 7 minutes. For best results a thermometer must be used. Wash sides of pan with brush dipped into hot water while syrup is cooking and do not stir after syrup begins to boil. As soon as it reaches 248° F., *shut off heat* and let saucepan remain on burner. Start to beat egg whites *immediately* until they cling to bowl, then beat ½ more minute. Now slowly, in a steady stream, add hot syrup, beating all the time with electric mixer. After all syrup has been added, continue to beat whites at high speed about 2 more minutes. Pour this meringue into cheese mixture and with electric beater, *at low speed*, beat only until smooth and no streaks appear. Pour into crust-lined pan and bake according to directions above.

Strawberry Glaze for Top of Cheese Cake

Made with 12-ounce package sweetened frozen strawberries

3 tablespoons cornstarch
¼ cup granulated sugar (or less, or may be omitted)
1 cup strawberry juice (measure juice

and add enough water if necessary to make 1 cup)
Strawberries, defrosted and drained for about 30 minutes

Combine the cornstarch and sugar. Slowly add the cup of juice. Mix well and cook over moderate heat until thick, then simmer about 5 minutes. If glaze is too thick, add a little water. Add red coloring. Let glaze cool for about 10 minutes, stirring it gently several times, then combine it with the drained strawberries. Let cool another few minutes, then carefully pour on top of cake with a spoon, being careful not to drip glaze on sides of cake. Refrigerate until cake is ready to be served, or for at least 2 hours.

Cherry Glaze for Top of Cheese Cake

Made with 10- or 12-ounce package sweetened frozen cherries

Use 3 tablespoons cornstarch and ½ cup or less granulated sugar. One tablespoon lemon juice may be added to cooked glaze. Prepare same as Strawberry Glaze.

Raspberry Glaze for Top of Cheese Cake

Made with 10- or 12-ounce package sweetened frozen raspberries

Prepare same as Cherry Glaze.

Fresh Strawberry Glaze for Top of Cheese Cake

Made with 1 pint fresh strawberries

Wash, drain, and dry berries on towel. Remove hulls. Cut berries in halves. Place them on top of cheese cake with rounded sides up. Prepare glaze with 1 cup water added slowly to 3 tablespoons cornstarch, ¾ cup granulated sugar, and ¼ cup fine-cut berries. Let simmer about 5 minutes after it thickens. Add red coloring. Let glaze stand until cool (but not cold), then pour carefully with a spoon over berries, etc.

Bavarian Cream Cheese Cake Dessert

For 9 × 3½-inch loose-bottom pan

¾ pound commercial vanilla or chocolate cookies, crushed with rolling pin until fine, then sifted, to make about 3 cups (cream-filled chocolate cookies may be used)

¼ cup granulated sugar
½ cup butter or margarine, first measured, then melted, warm

Combine crumbs and sugar and blend well. Add warm melted butter or margarine, and with a fork stir until moist, then rub in palms of hands. Remove 1 cup and put aside for top of dessert. Grease bottom and sides of pan to top with 2 teaspoons soft shortening. Cover sides of pan with about 1 cup of crumb mixture, pressing down with back of soup spoon, or fingers. Pour rest of crumb mixture into bottom of pan, and with fingers or back of spoon press down to uniform thickness. *Now* place pan in refrigerator or freezer while preparing Filling.

When Filling is ready pour into pan lined with crumbs. Spread top evenly and sprinkle with reserved cup of crumbs. Refrigerate for at least 24 hours, but do not freeze. Keep cold as possible.

To Serve. Let stand in room temperature about 15 minutes. Now go around sides several times with a long heavy dinner knife to release from sides of pan. Lift out, leaving dessert on bottom part of pan. With plain sharp knife cut into wedges, releasing crust from bottom with knife. Serve cold.

Important. For an extra-rich cheese cake, increase cream cheese to 2 pounds and gelatin to 5 teaspoons combined with ½ cup cold water. Leave rest of recipe as is. Can be frozen for 1 month.

Filling for Bavarian Cream Cheese Cake Dessert

1 pound cream cheese (2 half-pound packages)

1 tablespoon and 1 teaspoon plain gelatin, combined with ⅓ cup cold water

¼ cup sifted all-purpose flour

¼ cup granulated sugar

½ cup cool milk, combined with about ⅓ cup egg yolks

1¼ cups warm milk

1½ teaspoons vanilla

½ teaspoon lemon extract

¼ teaspoon salt

1½ cups sifted granulated sugar

½ cup hot water

⅔ cup egg whites (5 large eggs), carefully separated, in an 8- or 9-inch bowl

Place cream cheese in a 10- or 12-inch bowl, and let stand room temperature about 1 hour, until medium consistency, but not too soft.

Soak plain gelatin in cold water. Stir and let stand until thick. Put aside. In a 2-quart saucepan add flour, granulated sugar, and mix well. Add cool milk combined with yolks a little at a time, stirring after each addition, until smooth. Now add warm milk, a little at a time, and blend well. Cook over medium heat until thick, stirring continuously, to prevent lumping. Let simmer, for about 5 minutes. If custard appears slightly lumpy, beat with fluffy beater for about 1 minute until smooth. Shut off heat, *and at once* add the thick soaked gelatin preparation, and stir until completely melted. Cover and let stand in room temperature until needed.

With electric mixer, beat cream cheese for about 1 minute. Add hot custard, a little at a time, and continue to beat, medium speed, until smooth. Add vanilla, lemon extract, and salt, and blend well. Keep in room temperature while preparing cooked meringue.

At once in a 1-quart saucepan, combine the 1½ cups sugar with the ½ cup water. Stir well. Place over medium heat, and continue to stir only until boiling begins. *Do not stir further.* Wash crystals from sides of pan from time to time with brush dipped into hot water. Cook syrup to 244° F., shut off heat, but keep pot on burner if using gas stove. If using electric, remove from burner, and place on cool part of stove. *At once* start to beat egg whites until they cling to bowl, *then beat about 1 more minute.* Add hot syrup in a slow steady stream in center of beaten whites, beating at high speed, and about 2 more minutes after all syrup has been added.

Pour meringue, about ¼ at a time into the custard preparation, *and with rubber scraper* fold over and over until evenly blended and no streaks appear.

Magic Cheese Torte

Serves 8

2¼ cups chocolate cookie crumbs (or graham cracker crumbs)	⅓ cup warm melted butter or margarine
⅓ cup granulated sugar	

Combine all ingredients and blend well until moist. Reserve 1 cup for top. With a spoon, press remaining crumbs evenly on sides and bottom of greased spring-form pan, about 9 × 3 inches. Refrigerate for at least 30 minutes. Prepare Filling.

Pour Filling into crumb crust and sprinkle the cup crumbs evenly over top. Refrigerate torte for at least 6 hours before serving. Do not bake.

To Serve. Loosen around sides with a dinner knife. Cut into serving wedges and serve extremely cold. Top of wedges may be decorated with a scroll of whipped cream, or entire top of torte may be decorated with 1 cup heavy cream beaten until stiff. This is a very delectable creamy dessert for special occasions.

Filling for Magic Cheese Torte

1⅓ cups sweetened condensed milk (1 tall can)	½ teaspoon vanilla
1 pound cream cheese, medium consistency	6 tablespoons lemon juice
½ teaspoon lemon extract	½ cup heavy cream, beaten until it just clings to bowl

Add milk, a little at a time to cheese, and beat with electric mixer until smooth. Add extracts and lemon juice, a little at a time, and blend well. Last, pour whipped cream into cheese mixture, and with electric mixer at very low speed beat only until evenly blended and no streaks appear.

Angel Lemon Custard Torte

Serves 12

1 recipe of small Angel Food Cake (page 570)	1 tablespoon unflavored gelatin, combined with ¼ cup cold water
6 whole eggs	¾ cup lemon juice
1¼ cups sifted granulated sugar	Rind of 1 lemon

First, bake small Angel Food Cake. When cake is cold, remove from pan, wash pan, dry and oil lightly the sides, bottom, and tube. With hands break up ¾ of the Angel Food Cake into 2- to 3-inch pieces and put in pan.

Separate eggs and put whites in a No. 8 bowl. Combine unflavored gelatin and water and set aside.

In a 1-quart saucepan, blend the egg yolks, ¾ cup granulated sugar, lemon juice, and lemon rind. Cook over low heat until it coats wooden spoon. (This takes about 7 to 8 minutes.) Do not allow to boil as it will curdle; stir constantly. Shut off heat, add congealed gelatin at once, and mix with spoon until gelatin is completely melted. Pour in a 9-inch bowl.

Beat egg whites with hand or electric beater until stiff, then add ½ cup granulated sugar, a little at a time, and continue to beat until sugar is well blended, about 1 minute. Pour beaten egg whites all at once into cooked lemon custard, and fold with wooden spoon until no trace of egg whites appears. Pour over broken pieces of Angel Food Cake, using a knife or spatula so that lemon custard is well distributed throughout the pieces of Angel Food Cake. Refrigerate for 8 hours or longer.

Pineapple-Cheese Glaze Torte

Serves 8

⅔ cup cold butter or margarine	½ teaspoon baking powder
⅔ cup sifted confectioners' sugar	1 small egg, slightly beaten
2 cups sifted all-purpose flour	About 1 tablespoon milk
¾ teaspoon salt	

Combine dry ingredients and sift several times. Cut in shortening with pie blender until it looks like fine meal. Add *only* enough combined beaten egg and milk to form a *medium dough* that leaves sides of bowl. Turn out onto lightly floured pastry cloth and knead gently for a few seconds. Use ⅔ of dough for bottom and side crusts and the rest for lattice strips and rim. Roll larger piece of dough to fit a 10-inch layer-cake pan that has been greased with 1 teaspoon unsalted shortening. Sprinkle 2 tablespoons dry bread crumbs on dough and press dough gently. Spread with Filling (page 640) and then pour cool Glaze (page 640) over Filling.

Roll rest of dough like a thin pie crust, and with pastry wheel cut it into ½-inch strips. Place strips on top of pineapple Filling to form lattice. Brush around edges with egg yolk combined with 1 tablespoon milk, pressing dough slightly to form a depression for rim. With scraps of dough, make a long narrow rim for crust, and press down lightly. Brush entire top with milk. Bake at 400° F. for about 1 hour. When done, remove from oven and place on cake rack to cool. Keep in very cold place or refrigerator until ready to be served. This torte is served very cold. May be baked a day or two in advance.

Individual servings may be topped with whipped cream.

Filling for Pineapple-Cheese Glaze Torte

1 pound creamed cottage cheese
2 whole eggs, or 3 egg yolks, slightly
    beaten
½ cup granulated sugar

2 tablespoons sifted flour
1 teaspoon vanilla
A little lemon rind or ½ teaspoon
    lemon extract

If cheese is very moist, drain thoroughly, pressing out surplus moisture. Combine beaten eggs and cheese, add remaining ingredients, and beat until thoroughly blended. Spread evenly over dough.

Glaze for Pineapple-Cheese Glaze Torte

No. 2½ can crushed pineapple (or
    less)
2 tablespoons corn starch

½ cup granulated sugar
¾ cup pineapple juice

Drain pineapple thoroughly. Combine 2 tablespoons of crushed pineapple juice with 2 tablespoons of cornstarch and blend well. Add cornstarch mixture to pineapple juice and ½ cup granulated sugar. Mix well and cook over moderate heat, stirring constantly, until thick and glazy, about 5 minutes. Pour glaze over well-drained pineapple, mix, and let stand until cool. When pineapple glaze is cool, pour it with a teaspoon very carefully over the cheese filling.

Angel Orange Custard Torte

Serves 12

1 recipe of small Angel Food Cake
    (page 570), baked in a 9 × 3-
    inch tube pan
1¼ cups sifted granulated sugar
1 tablespoon unflavored gelatin, com-
    bined with ¼ cup cold water

¾ cup orange juice
Rind of one orange
½ teaspoon orange food coloring
    added to custard

Prepare like Angel Lemon Custard Torte (page 638).

Chocolate Mint Refrigerator Torte

Serves 8 to 12

Prepare 1 recipe Small Gold Cake (page 551). Pour 2 cups of the batter into a greased and floured 9 × 3-inch loose-bottom round pan. Pour rest of batter into a greased and floured 9-inch square pan. Bake cakes at 350° F. about 25 to 30 minutes, or until firm to the touch, raising temperature to 400° F. for a few minutes if necessary. Remove cakes from oven, let remain in pans about 5 minutes, then turn them out onto cake coolers until cold.

Wash the 9 × 3 loose-bottom round pan and dry it well. Place the round cake back into pan. Cut part of square cake into 16 uniform strips to measure 1 inch wide and ½ inch thick and 2 inches long. Place these strips around sides of pan, holding in place with dab of butter if necessary, leaving about ½-inch space between each one. Now cut 8 strips to measure ¾ inch wide, ½ inch thick, and about 3½ inches long for top of cake; also cut out a small round with open end of No. 7 cookie tube or small cutter for center of cake. Cover and put aside until needed. Prepare Filling (below).

Pour Filling into round pan lined with cake as soon as it is ready. Garnish top with the 8 strips of cake and round one for center. Refrigerate torte for at least 8 hours or longer before serving. May be made a day in advance.

To Serve Torte. Loosen around sides carefully with a dinner knife or spatula. Release cake, leaving it on bottom part of pan to prevent breaking. Sprinkle cake with sifted confectioners' sugar on sides and top, cut and serve as is, *or for special occasions* whip another cup of cream until stiff. With No. 3 or No. 7 star cookie tube, pipe large scrolls of whipped cream between strips of cake and in center, also on sides where strips of cake join filling. Instead of scrolls, pink or yellow relief roses may be piped with No. 104 or No. 127 rose tube, and leaves with No. 70 tube. Place cake in center of large round platter with doily and surround, if desired, with fancy cookies or small cakes.

Note. For vanilla torte, omit peppermint extract and increase vanilla to 1 tablespoon. Any other cake that cuts well, or lady fingers, may be used instead of Gold Cake.

Chocolate Mint Filling for Refrigerator Torte

¾ pound (1 cup melted) dark sweet chocolate cut in small pieces
½ cup hot water
½ cup granulated sugar
1 tablespoon peppermint extract

1 teaspoon vanilla
2 cups (1 pint) whipping cream, beaten until medium thick (should slide slightly out of bowl but be neither runny nor stiff)

Melt chocolate over simmering water, then add the hot water and granulated sugar. Cook together over simmering water about 7 minutes (in upper part of double boiler), stirring continuously until it thickens slightly. Remove from hot water and let stand about 10 minutes on cake cooler, or until it is just warm, not too warm and not cool, stirring it often during the cooling process. When warm, add the peppermint extract and vanilla, and mix well. Beat cream until it is medium thick. Pour chocolate preparation into cream *all at once* and with a large spoon mix gently until well blended and no streaks appear. Pour at once into round pan lined with cake.

French Fruit Flans

Serves 16 to 20

¼ cup unbeaten egg whites
½ pound commercial almond paste, cut up in small pieces, in 8-inch bowl
¾ cup soft butter or margarine

⅓ cup sifted granulated sugar
1 teaspoon vanilla
½ teaspoon salt
About 2 cups sifted all-purpose flour

Add egg whites, a little at a time, to the broken-up pieces of almond paste, and with electric mixer beat until smooth. Add the soft butter or margarine, about ¼ cup at a time, and beat until well blended, for about 2 minutes. Add the granulated sugar, a little at a time, then the vanilla and salt. Last, add the flour, about ½ cup at a time, and beat after each addition only until smooth. If dough feels very soft and sticky add little more flour.

Place 11- or 12-inch loose-bottom cheesecake round pan over a wide sheet of silicone paper, and with pencil make outline. Cut paper to fit pan, leaving a 2-inch wide strip on each side, to help release shell from pan after it has been baked and is cold. Grease pan lightly on bottom and sides so that paper adheres smoothly. Now spread dough as smoothly as possible over paper, having it come up on sides about ⅓ inch thick and 1 inch high (not thin, to prevent burning). Do this with fingers, and if necessary dampen hands lightly, or place sheet of wax paper over dough and press down to uniform thickness.

Bake in a preheated 350° F. oven about 35 minutes, or until golden brown, but not too dark. When done, remove from oven, and let remain in pan on a cake rack until cold. To remove flan from pan, carefully lift it out by holding protruding strips of paper firmly in fingers, and place shell on a flat stiff round cardboard, about same size, leaving the silicone paper underneath, cutting off the 2 strips. If using a loose-bottom pan, leave shell on metal bottom. Flan will have to have firm support underneath to prevent it from crumbling when cutting into serving pieces. It will be easier and safer to handle this dessert if you place the empty shell into a 12-inch round flat platter (a 12-inch pizza pan is excellent), leaving cardboard underneath for extra protection.

To Fill Flan. Prepare 1 recipe French Cream Filling (page 643), and let it cool to lukewarm, stirring it often while cooling. Spread ½ of filling over bottom of flan shell. Place 1 package of lady fingers (split) on top of filling, and drizzle them with 2 or 3 tablespoons of curaçao, brandy, or other liqueur. Pour and gently spread rest of cream filling over lady fingers. If filling is stiff, add a little milk to make it proper consistency for spreading, but it must not be runny. Now down center of flan arrange a row of overlapping bananas, sliced crosswise about ⅓ inch thick, and at once brush bananas with lemon or pineapple juice to prevent darkening. On each side of banana slices, place a row of fresh strawberries (washed and well drained on a towel), or red raspberries. If strawberries are large, cut them in halves. On sides of berries, place rows of fresh (or canned) pineapple wedges cut into about 1½-inch pieces. (Pineapple may be colored green by placing it in water to which a little green food coloring has been added for a few minutes. Then run cold water over it to remove surplus color. Drain well and dry on towel.) On outside of pineapple rows, place more sliced bananas, fresh blueberries, or dark grapes. See Suggested Fruits.

To Glaze Top of Flan. Prepare 1 recipe of Flan Glaze (page 644). With a spoon carefully pour glaze over fruit, filling in empty spots.

With a spatula spread a little glaze around edge of pastry. Let cool about 15 minutes, then cover edge with 1 cup sliced toasted almonds. To toast, spread 1 cup sliced almonds on baking sheet, and place in a 350° F. oven for about 10 to 12 minutes, or until golden color, stirring them several times after the first 5 minutes, to keep them uniform in color. Let almonds cool, then use as directed. Flan must be refrigerated or kept in a very cold place until serving time. To serve, with a very sharp knife, cut into serving pieces. Lift out with pie server. If using pizza pan, a border of whipped cream or cream cheese or buttercream icing may be piped on rim of pan with No. 3 star cookie tube.

Suggested Fresh Fruits

2 very large or 3 medium bananas, cut about ⅓ inch thick

1 pint strictly fresh strawberries, washed, drained thoroughly in a towel, and if large cut in halves

1 small fresh pineapple, cut in about 1½-inch wedges, and ⅓ inch thickness, tinted light green. Add green food coloring to enough cool water to submerge pineapple wedges, and allow pineapple to remain in colored water about 10 minutes, then pour into strainer, and run cold water over pineapple. Remove surplus moisture from pineapple in paper towels.

1 pint fresh cherries or large black or red grapes, or fresh blueberries

Any other fresh or canned fruit combinations may be used in these tortes.

French Cream Filling for Flan

½ cup granulated sugar
¼ cup sifted all-purpose flour
2 tablespoons cornstarch
Pinch of salt

2 egg yolks, combined with ¼ cup cold milk
2 cups warm milk
1 tablespoon butter
1 teaspoon vanilla

In a 2-quart saucepan combine sugar, flour, cornstarch, and salt. Add the combined egg yolks and ¼ cup cold milk slowly, and stir until smooth.

Now add warm milk, a little at a time, and cook over medium heat until thick and smooth, stirring continuously. After it thickens, lower heat and let simmer gently about 5 minutes, stirring it occasionally. When done, add tablespoon of butter and a drop or 2 of yellow food coloring, if necessary, and blend well. Let hot filling cool on cake rack in room temperature for about 30 minutes, beating it several times to prevent crust from forming. When lukewarm add vanilla, and if filling appears too stiff, add a little milk or cream to make it proper consistency. Use filling while lukewarm.

Glaze for French Fruit Flans

¼ cup cornstarch, combined with ½ cup cool water
1 cup granulated sugar

1¾ cups hot water
A drop or 2 of yellow food coloring
2 teaspoons lemon juice

In a 2-quart saucepan pour the cornstarch, add cool water, a little at a time, stirring until smooth. Add granulated sugar alternately with the hot water, stirring after each addition. Cook over medium heat until thick, stirring continuously. Let simmer for about 5 minutes. Remove from heat, add drop or 2 of yellow coloring (not more), then the lemon juice, and let glaze stand until lukewarm. Glaze must be stirred (do not beat) often while it is cooling to keep it at uniform consistency. If it appears too thick when ready to use, add a little water as needed. Best to use it on fruits when lukewarm.

Crêpes Suzette

Serves 6

½ cup whole eggs, beaten with egg beater about ½ minute
1 cup sifted all-purpose flour
1 cup milk (room temperature)
2 tablespoons melted butter or margarine

1 teaspoon brandy or triple sec or other liqueur (optional)
A little lemon rind, or ¼ teaspoon lemon extract

Beat eggs, add flour, a little at a time, alternately with the milk and melted butter or margarine, the liqueur, the rind of lemon, and salt. Beat with egg beater only until smooth. Cover, and let stand about 15 minutes or longer.

For a 7-inch skillet, pour about ⅔ of *a quarter cup measurement*. Brush skillet well with a little melted shortening for first pancake only, then occasionally if they stick. The butter added to the batter makes it unnecessary to grease skillet. After pouring batter into skillet, let cook for a *few seconds*, lift from heat and tilt pan back and forth while batter is still thin so that pancakes will be uniform in thickness. Cook until brown on first side over moderate heat; turn and cook second side until golden color. Roll each one, or pile flat on platter. After preparing first pancake, more milk or flour may be added to *regulate* thickness. It is better to cool skillet slightly before pouring batter for each crêpe but do not have skillet cold. This gives a thinner pancake. Pancakes may be prepared several hours in advance. Makes about 18 very thin pancakes if using 7-inch skillet. Smaller skillets may be used. In this case, use less batter (about 2 level tablespoons).

To Serve. When ready to be used, melt part of L'Aiglon Butter in a chafing dish. A skillet may be used instead. In this case, keep skillet over very low heat. Add *rolled* or flat crêpes to the melted L'Aiglon Butter, 1 at a time, turning often, then roll each if necessary. In preparing a large number of these crêpes at one time, they may be piled on top of one another. *Drain off all excess butter that remains in chafing dish after crêpes are heated through.* Now pour at least ¼ cup or more warm 80 proof liqueur over crêpes; cover dish for several minutes, then remove cover, light, and bring flaming to table. *Or* prepare before guests in dining room. Be sure to continue turning crêpes in liqueur until flame burns out, and serve as soon as possible as a dessert or light luncheon dish. Melt any left-over L'Aiglon Butter and serve it hot in a separate dish. Other liqueurs may be used, or several may be combined. If flame continues to burn too long, it may be extinguished by covering chafing dish for a few seconds.

For breakfast or luncheon dishes, these pancakes may be spread with jellies, jams, softened cream cheese, commercial sour cream, cottage cheese, etc., then rolled, sprinkled with sifted confectioners' sugar, or syrup. For luncheon or supper dishes fill with creamed seafood or poultry preparations.

L'Aiglon Butter for Crêpes Suzette

½ cup cold, firm butter
1 cup sifted confectioners' sugar
Rind of 1 small orange and 1 very
    small lemon

½ cup warm orange juice
⅓ cup warm triple sec or any other
    liqueur at least 80 proof

With electric beater beat the butter until light and creamy. Add sugar, rinds, and warm juice, *a little at a time*, and continue to beat until thoroughly blended. If butter separates, place bowl in a pan of hot water for a few minutes and beat well until smooth.

Classic Puff Paste Dough

1 pound salted butter (do not use
    substitutes)
4½ cups sifted all-purpose flour
1 teaspoon cream of tartar

1 teaspoon salt
Yolks of 2 eggs, slightly beaten and
    combined with 1¼ cups cold
    water

Let butter stand in room temperature until it is medium consistency, but not soft. Then wash it in ice water, working it with hands until pliable and waxy. Press out water, divide into 4 equal portions, and place each piece between sheets of wax paper. With rolling pin flatten each piece to measure about 8 × 8 inches round. Store butter in freezing compartment or coldest part of refrigerator until it is hard.

Meanwhile sift flour, cream of tartar, and salt together, several times; add dry ingredients to yolks and water, a little at a time. Mix as well as possible with a spoon. Turn out onto lightly floured pastry cloth and knead dough well for about 5 minutes, or until smooth. If dough is sticky, add a little more flour, keeping it of *medium consistency* (not too soft and not too firm). It may be necessary to use more or less flour. After dough has been kneaded and does not stick to hands, cover it with a bowl and let stand in a cool room for about 30 minutes during warm weather, and 1 hour during cold weather, or until ripe enough to roll easily. After dough has ripened, place it on a *lightly floured pastry cloth*, and with *ball-bearing rolling pin*, roll into a rectangle about 12 × 24 inches, keeping corners as square as possible, pulling into shape with fingers if necessary. Lay 1 portion of the hard butter, broken up in small pieces, over ⅔ of the dough, then fold the bare part of dough over ½ of the butter, then the butter part over top of the dough. This forms 3 layers of dough with 2 layers of butter in between. With rolling pin press down ends of dough to enclose butter. Place dough on wax paper in a flat pan, cover well with wax paper and towel or plastic bag. Let rest in refrigerator or cold place (temperature about 40° F.) about 30 minutes. *This makes 1 rolling.*

Puff paste made with all butter is rolled and folded 6 times in all if using our recipes and methods. After each rolling, mark number of rollings on edge of dough with a skewer or keep record on a piece of paper. (Recipe may be cut in half. In this case, divide butter into 3 uniform portions. Roll dough each time to 8 × 16 inches. And give it 6 rollings in all.)

After 30 minutes, roll dough again to 12 × 24 inches, and enclose second portion of butter same way. Cover, etc., and let stand in refrigerator 30 minutes. *This makes 2 rollings.*

After 30 minutes, roll again to 12 × 24, and enclose third portion of butter, etc. *This makes 3 rollings.*

After 30 minutes, roll again to 12 × 24, and enclose fourth portion of butter, etc. *This makes 4 rollings.*

After 30 minutes, roll again to 12 × 24. Fold into 3 layers as above *without butter* inasmuch as all 4 pieces of butter have ben rolled into dough already. Refrigerate for 30 minutes. *This makes 5 rollings.*

After 30 minutes, roll again to 12 × 24. Fold into 3 layers as above *without butter* inasmuch as all 4 pieces of butter already have been rolled into dough. *This makes 6 rollings.* After the sixth rolling, dough should rest in refrigerator well wrapped about 3 hours or longer before baking. (It may be refrigerated for 2 days. In this case wrap it very well in plastic bag to prevent drying out. Or it may be *frozen* for 1 week if properly wrapped. Frozen dough must be removed from freezer at least 8 hours in advance and refrigerated until pliable enough for rolling.)

Before using dough that has been refrigerated, it is better to allow it to stand in room temperature for about 30 minutes before rolling and cutting, to prevent excessive shrinkage. Do not store dough in coldest part of refrigerator. Most desirable temperature is about 40° F. during the rolling and storing process.

Very Important. Before basic finished dough is cut into 4 uniform pieces, rolled and shaped, *about ⅓ of the ends must be cut away with a long plain sharp knife.* This will help to keep the pastries symmetrical during the baking process.

It is very important to allow rolled dough to stand on pastry cloth about 3 minutes before cutting it into the various shapes and to turn them over, especially for the patty shells. This will prevent excessive shrinkage and finished pastries will be more symmetrical. Use very sharp, plain knife or plain pastry wheel to cut dough, and turn pastries over after cutting whenever possible. This helps to puff the layers upward.

After individual pastries are rolled and cut out, they must stand on baking sheet well covered in coldest part of refrigerator (about 40° F.) until very cold and firm to the touch, about 30 minutes, but do not freeze. Then bake them in 400° F. oven 15 or 20 minutes; reduce heat as suggested for the various pastries, *slip another baking sheet underneath,* to prevent excessive browning at the bottom, and finish baking. Puff pastries should be watched very closely toward end of baking period and should not be baked too dark in color. If possible, allow finished pastries to remain in oven with heat shut off and door partly open after baking time is up.

It is usually best to use medium-size baking sheets instead of large to prevent overbrowning of pastries around edges of pans.

Unfilled puff pastries may be baked in advance and stored, well wrapped, in refrigerator or a cold place for about 2 weeks. They may be frozen for several months. If necessary they may be reheated in a very slow oven, about 300° F. for about 10 minutes, to recrisp them.

Cream Slices

Makes 12 large individual servings or 16 medium

With plain sharp knife cut away about ⅓ inch from ends of dough, then cut 1 recipe Classic Puff Paste Dough into 4 equal parts. Roll each piece 10 × 14 inches, keeping corners as square as possible and gently pulling corners with fingers if necessary. Place on silicone paper on flat baking sheet; *puncture well with a fork.* Let rest in refrigerator 30 minutes, then cut crosswise through center of dough, turn over, and bake it 15 minutes at 400° F. Then reduce heat to 250° F., slip another pan underneath, and bake about 20 more minutes, watching closely toward end. Shut off heat when nicely colored and let dry out in oven with door slightly open. Two recipes of French Cream Filling fill entire recipe. Takes 1 recipe for Icing for tops.

To Fill Slices. Use 1 cup of French Cream Filling (page 669) for each ¼ recipe of pastry. When pastry is cold, trim edges with a serrated knife, press layers down gently, spread filling on pastry and cover with another sheet of pastry, having flat side up. Now drizzle top with thin Icing, or simply sprinkle with sifted confectioners' sugar. It is best to fill this pastry at least 2 hours in advance, refrigerate, then cut into individual servings with a serrated-edge knife. Can stand about 4 hours after they are filled and before serving. Top of individual slices may be decorated with a scroll of whipped cream.

Note. If more than 1 layer of French Cream Filling is preferred in slices, roll each ¼ recipe of dough thinner, about 12 × 18. Proceed same as above. Use 3 sheets of baked pastry with 2 layers of filling between slices, having flat side of pastry on top.

Icing for Puff Pastries

About 3 cups sifted confectioners' sugar

¼ cup milk
1 teaspoon vanilla

Add sugar to the hot milk and vanilla and beat well until smooth.

Strawberry Almond Pancakes

Serves 6 to 8

4 small packages (3 ounces each) cream cheese
¼ cup sugar
1½ tablespoons grated lemon peel
3 tablespoons lemon juice
16 French pancakes (Crêpes Suzette, page 644)

2 cups sliced and sugared strawberries
1 tablespoon lemon juice
¼ cup slivered almonds
¼ teaspoon almond extract

Beat softened cream cheese with sugar, lemon peel, and lemon juice until light and fluffy. Put 2 tablespoons of filling on each pancake, and roll. Place, open end down, in a shallow baking dish. Chill until serving time, then heat in a hot oven (400° F.) just until pancakes are hot.

Combine strawberries, lemon juice, almonds, and almond extract. Heat or not as desired. (Contrast of hot pancake and cold strawberries is very pleasant.) Spoon over filled pancakes and serve at once.

Cream Rolls

With plain sharp knife cut away about ⅓ inch from ends of dough, then cut 1 recipe Classic Puff Paste Dough (page 645) into 4 equal parts. Roll each piece into a rectangle measuring about 8 × 20 inches. Let stand several minutes, then cut into 4 uniform strips. Roll each strip over a very well-greased (use shortening) cream roll form, starting from one end, leaving about ¼ inch of form uncovered and having edges of dough overlap about ⅓ inch. Wet edge of dough with beaten egg white as you roll, being careful not to drop any egg white on form to prevent sticking. Place on silicone paper on baking sheet, let rest in refrigerator 30 minutes, being sure to have open end down. Bake in 400° F. oven about 20 minutes, then reduce heat to 250° F. and bake about 20 more minutes. If they are nicely colored, release them from forms and place them on baking sheet into oven to dry out at 250° F., or if well colored, shut off heat and let dry out, with oven door partially open.

These rolls are delicious filled with sweetened whipped cream, White Mountain Icing (page 612), marshmallow cream, cream filling, chocolate or lemon filling, etc. Sprinkle tops with sifted confectioners' sugar before serving.

Apple or Other Fruit Turnovers

Makes 32 medium-size or 16 very large

With plain sharp knife cut away about ⅓ inch from ends of dough, then cut 1 recipe Classic Puff Paste Dough (page 645) into 4 equal parts. Roll each into a strip about 9 × 17 inches. Cut into 8 medium uniform squares or 4 very large, and turn upside down. Brush edges with well-beaten egg white. Place a spoonful of cooked fruit on each square. (Thick creamed chicken or other thick fillings may be used.) Fold over to form a triangle. Press edges together well and place on silicone paper on baking sheet. With a fork puncture top twice. Chill for 30 minutes. Bake at 400° F. about 20 minutes, then reduce heat to 250° F. and bake about 20 more minutes, or until done. When cool, drizzle top with icing.

Apple Filling for Turnovers

In a covered saucepan cook until tender, for about 10 minutes, 1 pound of Jonathan or winesap apples that have been pared, cored, and sliced thin, with 2 tablespoons water and ¼ cup granulated sugar. When done, add 2 tablespoons butter, a little cinnamon and nutmeg, and a few pieces of chopped pecan meats and about 2 tablespoons raisins. Let filling stand until cold before using. This recipe makes enough for about 12 medium-size turnovers. Raisins and nutmeats may be omitted.

Patty Shells

Makes 12 large shells

With plain sharp knife cut away about ⅓ inch from ends of dough, then cut 1 recipe Classic Puff Paste Dough (page 645) into 4 equal parts. Roll each to measure 8¼ × 12¼ inches. Let stand several minutes, then with a 4-inch cutter, cut out 6 rounds. (*An open 2½ can* may be used to cut patty shells if a 4-inch cutter is not available.) From 3 of the rounds cut out centers with a 2-inch cutter. Turn all rounds and rings over and place them on silicone paper on baking sheet. Puncture entire surface of solid rounds and rings with a fork and brush them with beaten egg white. Place rings over solid rounds, and brush rings carefully with egg white. Chill 30 minutes or longer, then bake at 400° F. 20 minutes; reduce heat to 250° F. and bake about 20 more minutes, or until golden brown. Shut off heat and allow them to remain in oven to dry out if necessary, leaving oven door partially open. These shells may be made smaller for hors d'oeuvres and fruit tarts. For higher patties, divide dough into 3 uniform parts instead of 4, and roll same size. Will make only 9 if cut this way. Leftover scraps may be used for cheese sticks or turnovers.

Cheese Sticks

Makes about 60 sticks

With sharp knife cut away about ⅓ inch from ends of dough, then cut 1 recipe Classic Puff Paste Dough (page 645) into 4 equal parts. Roll each to measure 6 × 20 inches. Puncture well with a fork and brush with well-beaten egg white. Sprinkle each with 2 tablespoons grated parmesan cheese, ¼ teaspoon salt, and a little paprika. Press cheese into dough gently with uncovered rolling pin. With pastry wheel cut into 16 uniform short strips about 1¼ inches wide and 6 inches long. Twist, place on silicone paper on baking sheet. Let stand in refrigerator about 30 minutes, then bake at 400° F. about 10 minutes, or until puffed and very lightly colored. Reduce heat to 250° F. and continue to bake about 10 more minutes, watching closely toward end that they do not burn. Leave in oven with heat shut off and door partially open to dry out.

Puff Paste Palm Leaves

Makes about 75

With plain sharp knife cut away ⅓ inch from ends of dough, then cut 1 recipe Classic Puff Paste Dough (page 645) into 4 uniform pieces. Roll each to measure 8 × 18 inches. Sprinkle lightly *with part of ⅓ cup granulated sugar;* pat and roll a little, fold in half crosswise, sprinkle again with part of sugar. Continue to roll a little and sprinkle with rest of ⅓ cup of sugar and fold over, until dough measures about 12 inches long and 3 inches wide, about ½ inch thick. Then with a very sharp plain knife, cut in ½-inch-wide slices. Pick up with a spatula and place on silicone paper with cut side down on a 12 × 18-inch baking sheet, *leaving about 2-inch spaces between each.* Refrigerate for 30 minutes, then bake in a 400° F. oven about 10 minutes on first side, or until *delicately* brown underneath, but not dark. After 10 minutes, turn them over with a spatula and bake for *about* 10 more minutes or longer. Watch closely that they do not burn. Remove those that are sufficiently brown before time is up. Takes 1⅓ cups granulated sugar to roll in for the entire recipe cut in 4 pieces. These pastries are delicious served at afternoon teas, with ice cream, sherbets, etc. They may be rolled into granulated sugar just before serving, if desired.

Quick Puff Paste Apple Strudel

Makes 4 strudels

Roll ¼ recipe of New Easy Quick Puff Paste (page 654) to measure 8 inches wide and 14 inches long. Spread Apple Filling (page 652) down center lengthwise of pastry. Sprinkle top of apples with a little cinnamon and nutmeg if desired. Bring sides of pastry up to top of apples, but do not overlap. Press down small ends. Transfer (with both hands) to medium-size baking sheet, ungreased, or *preferably covered with silicone paper.* Bake in preheated 400° F. oven about 20 minutes, or until golden color; reduce heat to 350° F. Brush entire top surface and sides of pastry with well-beaten egg white combined with ¼ teaspoon salt or lemon juice, if desired, but not necessary. Continue to bake at lower temperature about 25 more minutes, or until underside is brown and crisp. Let remain in oven with heat shut off if necessary, or bake a few minutes longer. When done, lift off of pan with 2 pancake turners to prevent breaking; when lukewarm or cool, drizzle top with Quick Coffee Cake Icing (page 618), or simply sprinkle with sifted confectioners' sugar. To serve, cut crosswise in 2-inch pieces. May be frozen for several weeks after they are baked.

Apple Filling

3 medium sweet apples (Jonathan, winesap or delicious best), peeled and sliced thin (about 12 ounces); other fruits may be used

2 tablespoons granulated sugar
2 tablespoons raisins or currants, and 2 tablespoons broken pecan meats (optional)

In a small skillet combine thinly sliced apples and sugar, blend well, and cook over medium heat about 3 minutes, until slightly softened, but still firm. Let cool. Fold in raisins and pecan meats, if desired, or may be omitted.

Russian Blintzes

Makes 12 to 16

2 large whole eggs
½ cup sifted all-purpose flour
½ cup cool milk

½ teaspoon salt
2 tablespoons lukewarm melted butter or margarine

Beat eggs with dover beater about ½ minute. Add all other ingredients and continue to beat *only* until smooth. Cover and let stand at least 15 minutes or longer.

Brush a hot 6- or 7-inch skillet with melted butter or margarine for first blintze only. Pour 1½ to 2 tablespoons of batter, depending on size of skillet and thickness of pancake desired, then tilt pan back and forth until batter is evenly distributed. Cook over *moderate* flame about a minute or two until underside is brown. *Do not cook second side.* Turn out onto a flat cookie sheet covered with wax paper, having brown side up. Blintzes may be piled on top of one another after they are cooked on 1 side. *Stir batter each time it is picked up for frying.*

If blintzes are to be prepared in advance and reheated, it is better to cook them lightly first time. They may be prepared a day in advance and stored, covered, in refrigerator.

To Fill Blintzes. Place 1 tablespoon or more of filling lengthwise in center of each. Flatten a little, fold over, and tuck in edges. When all have been filled, sauté in hot butter, over moderate flame, with *flap side down* first, until golden brown, watching closely, for they brown very quickly. Turn over and fry second side. Pour any remaining butter in skillet over blintzes. They are now ready to be served with commercial sour cream, syrup, or simply sprinkled with additional hot butter and confectioners' sugar. This is for the fruit and cheese blintzes.

Blintzes in Casserole

Prepare and sauté blintzes. Place attractively in baking casserole. Brush with melted butter and reheat at 300° F. for about 15 minutes just before serving. Do not overbake; cook only until heated through.

Frozen Blintzes

Prepare, let cool completely, wrap for freezing. To defrost allow to stand in room temperature for at least 4 hours. Reheat in small amount of butter on both sides over moderate flame and serve.

Cottage Cheese Filling for Blintzes

Fills 12 to 16 blintzes

About ¼ cup cream, more or less, depending on dryness of cheese
1½ cups dry cottage cheese, or cream cheese
¾ teaspoon salt

About ⅓ cup granulated sugar (more or less, to suit taste)
A little grated lemon or orange rind (optional)
About ¼ teaspoon cinnamon combined with sugar (optional)

Add cream to cheese, a little at a time, and beat until smooth. Add all other ingredients and blend well. Two tablespoons raisins or currants may be added to this filling.

Apple Filling for Blintzes

Fills 12 to 16 blintzes

1½ pounds Jonathan or winesap apples (4 very large or 6 medium), peeled and sliced thin
¼ cup butter

⅓ cup granulated sugar (more or less, to suit taste)
¼ teaspoon cinnamon and ⅓ teaspoon nutmeg
¼ teaspoon salt

Sauté sliced apples in the ¼ cup butter for about 5 minutes, turning often. Add sugar and other ingredients and continue to cook for about 5 more minutes. Two tablespoons raisins or currants may be folded into cooked apples. Let mixture cool before using.

Strawberry Filling for Blintzes

Fills 12 to 16 blintzes

1 pint fresh strawberries, washed, drained on towel for at least an hour, then hulled

⅓ cup zweiback or cookie crumbs
⅓ cup granulated sugar

Cut small berries in halves, large ones in 4 pieces lengthwise. Combine with the crumbs and sugar just before they are to be placed in blintzes.

Raspberry and Blueberry Filling for Blintzes

Fills 12 to 16 blintzes

1 pint fresh raspberries or blueberries, washed, drained on towel for at least an hour

¼ cup zweiback or cookie crumbs
¼ cup granulated sugar

Leave berries whole. Combine with crumbs and sugar, and so forth.

Fresh Peach Filling for Blintzes

1½ pounds fresh peaches. Place in colander and dip into boiling water for about 1 minute. Remove skin, and brush at once with lemon or other citrus juice. Slice thin, and brush again with citrus juice (to prevent discoloration)

¼ cup butter
¼ cup granulated sugar (more or less, to suit taste)
¼ teaspoon salt
¼ teaspoon cinnamon and ⅛ teaspoon nutmeg

Proceed as for apple filling for blintzes.

New Easy Quick Puff Paste

4 cups sifted unbleached all-purpose flour (or more if needed)
3 teaspoons, or less, salt

2 cups *soft* swiftning, divided in 4 half cups (spreading consistency)
1¼ cups warm water, combined with 2 slightly beaten egg yolks

Sift flour and salt together into an 8-inch bowl. Add ½ cup of the soft shortening, and with pie blender cut through until it looks like a very fine meal. Add the warm water and yolks, all at once, and with a large wooden spoon blend well, until difficult to mix further. Turn dough out onto floured pastry cloth and knead gently several minutes until smooth. If dough is sticky and clings to hands during kneading process, *add a little more flour*, keeping it medium consistency. Now place smooth dough into well-greased 8-inch bowl, cover tightly in plastic bag, and place in freezer about 15 minutes, or in coldest part of refrigerator for 30 minutes.

After 15 minutes in freezer (or 30 if in refrigerator) roll dough to measure about 12 × 24 inches, and with rubber scraper spread ½ cup of the soft shortening over entire surface. Fold in thirds, place on flat baking sheet covered with wax paper, wrap well, and place in freezer 15 minutes (or coldest part of refrigerator 30 minutes). Repeat rollings and spreading of shortening in 15- (or 30-)minute intervals until all shortening has been used. *After last rolling*, pastry must be kept in freezer at least 30 minutes, not more than 40 minutes, if to be used at once, or in refrigerator 1½ hours, or as long as 2 days (not longer), well wrapped. May be frozen for 2 weeks. If pastry feels very stiff when ready to use, let stand in room temperature, covered, a few minutes, but not until it gets soft. Cut off rolled ends from dough.

Note. Use this New Quick Puff Paste as indicated in various recipes. It may also be used in recipes calling for Classic Puff Paste made with all butter.

Dough for Strudels

Small Recipe for 1 Very Large or 2 Medium Strudels

To be stretched on table that measures about 16 × 20 inches

2 medium eggs (⅓ cup)
½ teaspoon salt
⅓ cup lukewarm water
About 2¼ cups sifted all-purpose flour
1 tablespoon (or little more) salad oil
   to brush onto rolled dough

About ½ cup hot melted butter or margarine for each large strudel; ¼ cup for medium size
About ½ cup light dry bread crumbs for each large strudel; ¼ cup for medium size

Large Recipe for 2 Very Large or 4 Medium Strudels

To be stretched on table that measures about 30 × 30 inches

3 very large eggs (¾ cup)
¾ teaspoon salt
¾ cup lukewarm water
About 4½ cups sifted all-purpose flour
2 tablespoons (or little more) salad oil to brush onto rolled dough

About ½ cup warm melted butter or margarine for each large strudel; ¼ cup for each medium
About ½ cup light dry bread crumbs for each large strudel; ¼ cup for each medium

In an 8- or 9-inch bowl, with a spoon or fluffy beater, beat eggs a few seconds. Add salt, lukewarm water, then the flour, about 1 cup at a time, and beat well after each addition. When dough appears thick, beat it until smooth, then continue to add as much of the flour as possible, until dough leaves sides of bowl. It does not always take the full amount of flour and sometimes more, depending on quality of flour, size of eggs, etc. When dough is too stiff to mix with spoon, turn it out onto a floured board, and with floured hands knead it for about 1 minute, adding only enough more flour to prevent stickiness. Now pick up dough and strike it against board, and knead and strike for about 5 minutes, or until dough feels very smooth. If dough sticks to hand or board during the kneading and striking process, add little more flour, but only enough to prevent sticking to board. Use 1 teaspoon oil on board toward end of striking. Keep dough as soft as possible, even if it sticks a little, just so it can be handled.

After dough has been sufficiently kneaded and beaten, place it on a lightly oiled board or flat surface; brush top of dough with salad oil. Cover with a warm bowl, and let stand in warm room for about 1 hour, or longer during cold weather, but not more than 1½ hours. While dough is ripening, prepare filling, and cover bridge table with a large smooth cloth (bed sheet excellent). Sprinkle and rub entire surface of cloth with about ¼ cup sifted all-purpose flour to prevent dough from sticking.

When dough is ripe, with rolling pin roll it as *thin and as large as possible* over floured cloth. Large recipe should measure *at least* 24 × 24 inches; small recipe about 16 × 16 inches. *Brush entire surface with the salad oil.* Pull cloth so that dough hangs slightly on one end of table, and with floured hands stretch dough carefully, bringing it down on sides as quickly as possible, moving cloth whenever necessary to facilitate stretching. When dough has been stretched quite large, with scissors cut away heavy edges, and continue to stretch it further, working slowly and gently. Again cut away heavy edges. Dough should be as thin and transparent as tissue paper after it is completely stretched. Allow fully stretched dough to dry a little for about 10 to 15 minutes before filling and rolling, but it must not become brittle.

Because dough is quite large after it has been stretched completely, it is better to cut away the hanging parts and transfer them to another table with a cloth. At this point, again stretch part of dough remaining on top of table if it appears thick and moist. It is rather difficult to reach center of dough in the beginning and this is an excellent time to stretch it thinner in that area.

Start working by first cutting pieces of hanging stretched dough to measure about 18 inches long if using a 12 × 18 baking sheet. Cut smaller for smaller baking sheets. *Place very moist sheets down first.* Drizzle pieces of dough with part of ½ cup of hot melted butter or margarine and sprinkle each sheet with part of the ½ cup dry crumbs. Pile sheets on top of one another. Place filling on one end of dough, or as per directions given with each filling; fold end of dough nearest you over filling, helping to hold it in position with hands when starting, then lift cloth and roll. When completely rolled, pick up strudel with 2 pancake turners or both hands, and place it on a lightly greased 12 × 18-inch baking sheet or, best, covered with silicone paper. Two strudels can be baked at one time on a 12 × 18 sheet. Drizzle and brush top gently with hot melted butter or margarine, and bake at 375° F. about 30 to 40 minutes (temperature and time vary somewhat with the different fillings). Watch closely toward end to prevent burning.

Apple Strudel

Serves 8

About 2½ pounds (5 cups) peeled, thinly sliced apples (Jonathan or winesap)

½ cup granulated sugar

⅓ cup raisins or currants, simmered several minutes, then dried in a towel

⅓ cup coarsely broken pecan meats

½ teaspoon cinnamon and ¼ teaspoon nutmeg

⅓ cup light dry bread crumbs sprinkled over apples (this is plus crumbs sprinkled on dough)

About 2 tablespoons melted butter may be drizzled over apples

Combine ingredients and blend well for filling when ready to be used, not in advance. Place filling on end of dough that is about 18 inches wide for 12 × 18-inch pan. Bake at 375° F. about 30 to 40 minutes. Serve warm.

Cream Cheese Strudel

Makes 1 strudel

1 egg yolk
1 pound cream cheese (room temperature)
⅔ cup granulated sugar

½ teaspoon vanilla and ½ teaspoon lemon extract
¼ cup raisins or currants, simmered several minutes, then dried on towel (optional)

Add yolks to cheese that is medium consistency, not too soft, blend well; add sugar and beat until smooth. Add extracts and raisins and mix gently. Place on one end of dough that is about 14 inches wide, and roll. Drizzle with butter, etc., and bake at 375° F., about 35 to 40 minutes, until brown. Serve lukewarm, not cold, nor too hot. More filling may be used for a thicker strudel.

Cherry Strudel

Serves 8

1 large can sour water-packed cherries, or 1 pound fresh, sour pitted cherries
¼ cup dry bread crumbs

½ cup granulated sugar
¼ cup coarsely broken pecan meats
¼ cup raisins or currants, simmered a few minutes and dried in a towel

If using canned cherries, drain them very thoroughly for several hours, and dry them in a towel. If using fresh cherries, steam them in about ¼ cup water about 15 minutes, or until tender. Remove pits. Combine all ingredients just before using, and place on end of dough cut about 14 inches wide. For a thicker strudel, more filling may be used. Bake in a 375° F. oven about 35 to 40 minutes. Serve warm.

Fresh Strawberry Strudel

Serves 8

1 quart of fresh strawberries
¾ cup granulated sugar

½ cup light dry bread crumbs

Wash berries, drain well, and hull. Dry them in a towel. Just before using, sprinkle berries with the granulated sugar and crumbs and with hands mix gently. Place them on end of cut dough, about 14 inches wide, then roll, etc. More filling may be used for a thicker strudel. Bake at 400° F. about 30 to 35 minutes, or until delicately brown. Serve lukewarm or cold.

Pecan Strudel

Cut stretched dough into several pieces about 14 inches wide. Brush or drizzle each with melted butter and sprinkle each layer with 2 tablespoons of granulated sugar (instead of crumbs). Now drizzle entire top layer with warm melted butter and cover entire surface with about 1½ cups very finely chopped (not grated) pecan meats. Roll and transfer to lightly greased baking sheet. After it has been placed on baking sheet and before baking, brush a dinner knife with butter, and cut strudel crosswise into about ¾-inch slices, being careful not to move slices out of position. Drizzle a little warm melted butter into slits. Bake at 375° F. about 30 minutes. When cold cut through sections again, and separate slices, sprinkle with sifted confectioners' sugar, and serve cold.

Baklava

Serves 12

1 small recipe Strudel Dough (page 655), stretched as thin as possible
¾ cup hot melted butter
About 3 cups, more or less, of finely chopped, not grated, pecan or walnut meats

Syrup made with 1 cup granulated sugar and ⅔ cup water, simmered about 5 minutes after it begins to boil (add 1 teaspoon vanilla to syrup); or use 1 cup hot honey

Brush a 9 × 9 × 2-inch square pan with melted butter and line with silicone paper. Place 4 layers of dry Strudel Dough on bottom, drizzling or brushing each layer with hot melted butter. Cover with about 1 cup of chopped nuts, then with 2 layers of the thin dough; brush with hot melted butter, and continue to place the dough and nutmeats alternately in pan, leaving 3 layers of dough for the top of Baklava. Place the last 3 layers on top, brushing or drizzling each with hot melted butter. Brush a dinner knife with butter and cut Baklava lengthwise, then crosswise, making 16 individual pieces. Pour rest of hot melted butter into knife slits, between squares. Bake about 40 minutes at 300° F. Pour the hot syrup or honey over entire surface and continue to bake about 20 more minutes, or until pastry absorbs the syrup and is golden brown.

When done, remove from oven, place it on cake rack and let cool. When cool, cut through sections again, and lift out 1 section at a time. Sprinkle with confectioners' sugar. May be prepared several days or longer in advance. Cover and store in a cool place.

Note. Room in which strudels are stretched should be warm and free from drafts. Majority of strudels are best served warm (but not hot), or they may be baked in advance and reheated for about 15 minutes in a

325° F. oven. In reheating strudels, it is best to cut them into serving pieces, keeping them close together on baking sheet, then reheat, and serve warm. Sprinkle dessert strudels with sifted confectioners' sugar just before serving.

All strudels except the strawberry freeze well. Cream cheese strudel can be frozen for about 1 week.

All margarine may be used instead of butter. We like to use at least half butter for extra flavor.

Gus's Creamy Rice Pudding

Serves 6 to 8

1 quart, less ¼ cup, cool homogenized milk
½ cup granulated sugar
¼ teaspoon salt
½ cup uncooked rice (do not wash)

2 egg yolks (or 1 whole egg), combined with ¼ cup cool milk, stirred well
½ to 1 teaspoon vanilla
A little cinnamon for top (optional)

Combine milk, sugar, salt, and uncooked rice. Stir well and bring to a boil. Now cover pot, lower heat and let simmer (not boil) gently for 1 hour, *stirring several times.* After 1 hour, remove from stove. Add about ½ cup of hot pudding, a little at a time, to the beaten yolks and cool milk. Then pour the yolk mixture into pot of rice, and stir continuously for about 1 minute. Add vanilla, stirring well. Pour at once into medium-size bowl (about 7-inch size) and let remain on cake rack until cool enough to serve, or it may be refrigerated after it is cool and served cold.

Top may be sprinkled lightly with cinnamon. Very delicious, quickly prepared.

Raisins (¼ cup), simmered about 2 minutes, and dried in a towel, may be folded into pudding before serving.

Baked Rice Pudding

¾ cup uncooked rice, cooked gently in 2 cups hot water about 25 to 30 minutes or until done
½ cup granulated sugar, more or less
2 large whole eggs, slightly beaten

About ½ teaspoon salt
2 cups scalded milk
¼ cup raisins, simmered about 5 minutes (optional)

In a 1½-quart greased baking dish combine cooked rice and all other ingredients in the order given, stirring in each one with a large spoon until well blended. Bake uncovered in a preheated 350° F. oven about 1 hour to 1 hour and 15 minutes, or until blade of knife comes out clean when tested in center of pudding. If top is not brown when pudding is done, place it under broiler a few minutes, but watch closely.

Serve warm or cold with milk or cream.

Sautéed Glazed Apple Slices

4 large Jonathan or winesap apples, cored but unpeeled (remove about ¼ inch from each end and cut each apple in 2 pieces crosswise, making thick slices)

About ¼ cup hot butter or margarine
½ cup brown sugar
About 2 tablespoons hot water

In a large skillet sauté apple slices in butter or margarine until golden brown on each side. Sprinkle with brown sugar and 1 tablespoon water. Continue to cook and turn apple slices several minutes until they take on a nice glaze. Now cover apples and steam gently 2 or 3 minutes. Add second tablespoon water if necessary, to prevent scorching. Apples should be crisply tender, not too soft.

Peach Flambeau

Soak 8 pieces of loaf sugar (or ¼ cup granulated sugar) in ¼ cup orange juice and ¼ cup lemon juice for about 15 minutes. Pour entire mixture into a chafing dish, and heat until sugar is completely melted. Place 12 plain, brandied, or pickled peaches in chafing dish. Baste with the juices and cook for about 5 minutes. *Drain off any liquid that remains in chafing dish,* pour about ⅓ cup 80-proof brandy over peaches, cover for a few minutes, and light. Keep turning and basting peaches until flame burns out. Flame may be extinguished by covering dish for a moment or two. Pour the leftover liquor in chafing dish over fruits before serving. These desserts are very festive and attractive if prepared in dining room in presence of guests. Serve with ice cream or Whipped Cream Brandy Sauce (page 372).

Cherry Ice Cream Flambeau

Prepare as above, using Bing cherries. Pour them over ball of ice cream and top with whipped cream or Whipped Cream Brandy Sauce (page 372).

Peach and Cherry Flambeau

Prepare as above, using canned Bing cherries and peaches. Arrange peach in a sherbet glass, round side up. Pour cherries over peaches and on sides. Top with whipped cream or Whipped Cream Brandy Sauce (page 372).

Pear and Apricot Flambeau

Prepare as page 660, using pears and apricots.

Peachy Crisp Dessert

Serves 8

No. 2½ can sliced freestone peaches, thoroughly drained
2 tablespoons granulated sugar, combined with 2 tablespoons flour and ¼ teaspoon cinnamon

⅓ cup brown sugar
¼ cup melted butter or margarine
3 cups whole corn flakes (do not crush)
1 whole red maraschino cherry

Arrange well-drained sliced peaches (except 7 slices) in greased 9-inch round glass pie plate or 10 × 6 × 2-inch oblong dish. Sprinkle top with granulated sugar, flour, and cinnamon (that have been sifted together several times).

Sprinkle brown sugar and melted butter or margarine over corn flakes, and blend gently with 2 forks. Pour corn flakes over peaches. Sprinkle very lightly with cinnamon. Bake at 375° F. about 20 minutes, or until corn flakes appear glossy and crunchy.

Remove from oven, garnish top with the 7 slices of peaches, to simulate a flower. Place whole red cherry in center. To serve, pick up with a large serving spoon, and serve plain or with whipped cream on top.

Peachy Crisp Dessert Made with Fresh Peaches

Plunge 2 pounds of fresh peaches into boiling water for 1 minute, cool slightly, peel, and slice. Use instead of canned peaches as above. Pour 2 tablespoons of lemon juice over sliced fresh peaches to prevent discoloration as soon as they are sliced.

Crunchy Lemon or Orange Dessert

Serves 6

⅓ cup butter or margarine
¾ cup brown sugar, packed
1½ tablespoons flour

3 tablespoons water
3¾ cups corn flakes (do not crush)
Lemon or orange sherbet (or ices)

Melt butter or margarine, add sugar and flour, and stir well. Add water, and cook, stirring gently over low heat. Cook 5 minutes at simmering point after simmering begins, and stir gently. At once pour syrup over corn flakes and with 2 forks blend well. Pack into lightly buttered individual Mary Ann ring molds, and refrigerate for several hours or longer.

To serve, go around upper edge with paring knife, and turn out onto dessert plate. Fill center with a ball of lemon or orange sherbet or ice (other fillings may be used). Garnish top with well drained red maraschino cherry and green citron leaves, or serve plain. Serve at once.

Crunchy Dessert Ring

Serves 8

⅔ cup butter or margarine
1½ cups brown sugar, packed
3 tablespoons flour
⅓ cup water
6 cups corn flakes (do not crush) in large bowl

1 quart, more or less, fresh strawberries, raspberries, or sliced peaches
1 cup or more heavy cream, beaten until stiff

Melt butter or margarine, add sugar and flour, and stir well. Add water, and cook, stirring gently over low heat. Cook 7 or 8 minutes at simmering point after simmering begins, and stir gently. At once pour hot syrup over corn flakes and with 2 forks blend well. Pack into lightly buttered standard-size ring mold (about 7-cup capacity). Press down gently with large spoon. Refrigerate for several hours or longer.

To serve, loosen ring around upper edge and tube. Gently turn it onto large round serving platter (14- or 16-inch size). Fill center with stiffly whipped unsweetened cream, and surround with 1 quart or more fresh strawberries, raspberries, or sliced peaches. Cut through ring, pick up with a large serving spoon, and serve at once. Keep this dessert in refrigerator until ready to be served.

Individual Party Basket Desserts

Serves 8

¼ cup butter or shortening
⅓ cup soft brown sugar
½ teaspoon vanilla
¼ cup finely grated nuts (put through mouli mill)

1 cup sifted all-purpose flour
1 tablespoon milk, or enough to form a stiff dough

Cream butter, add sugar, and beat well. Add vanilla and nuts. Last, add flour alternately with the milk, forming a stiff dough. Knead gently for a few seconds. Form a 12-inch rope. Cut off ⅓ of dough and put it aside for handles of baskets. Cut remaining dough into uniform pieces. Roll each piece into a 4-inch round. Place over outside of lightly greased tartlet molds that measure 3 inches across the top. Puncture with a fork. Place them on a baking sheet, and bake in a 350° F. oven about 20 minutes or until delicately brown and firm to the touch. Remove from oven, let stand about 5 minutes, then gently release tarts from molds. Let them become cold.

To make handles, cut ⅓ of dough into 8 uniform pieces. Roll each into a narrow 6-inch rope. Lay them on a lightly greased baking sheet and bend to simulate handles with a 2½-inch base. Bake about 10 to 12 minutes in a 350° F. oven or until done, but watch closely toward end to prevent overbaking.

To Fill Baskets. Fill ⅔ of basket with ice cream, sherbet, custard, or any desired filling. Pipe a large scroll of whipped cream or icing on top of filling. Insert handles. With No. 24 star tube, pipe several pink quick buttercream rosettes on handle, and with No. 65 leaf tube, pipe several green leaves.

Note. These baskets may be made and filled in advance with ice cream or sherbet and decorated with scroll of whipped cream or buttercream icing, and frozen. In this case, do not insert handles until shortly before serving, when cream or icing is partially defrosted. Remove baskets from freezer about 30 minutes before serving, and keep them in refrigerator or a cold place. Cream fillings do not freeze well.

Muerbe Teig Dough for Tarts

⅓ cup sifted confectioners' sugar, or 2 tablespoons granulated sugar

1 cup sifted all-purpose flour, combined with ¼ teaspoon salt *and* ¼ teaspoon baking powder

⅓ cup firm butter, margarine, or shortening

About 2 tablespoons milk or cold water

Combine measured dry ingredients and sift together. Cut shortening into dry ingredients with a pie blender until it looks like fine meal. Add about 2 tablespoons milk or water to form a medium dough, blending ingredients well with a fork until mixture leaves sides of bowl. Dough must not be sticky nor too dry. Knead gently on lightly floured pastry cloth a few seconds. Wrap and chill if necessary, or use at once.

Cut dough into 6 uniform pieces for very large tart molds that measure about 3½ inches across top; 8 pieces for large boat molds and medium-size round molds about 2¾ inches wide; cut into 16 uniform pieces for very small boat molds.

Roll dough in rounds about 4½ inches for 3½ inch size. Roll dough in rounds about 3½ inches for 2¾ inch size. Roll dough in ovals about 3 × 5 for large boat molds. Roll dough in ovals about 2 × 4 for smallest boat molds.

Place rounds or ovals on outside of *very lightly greased* molds. Puncture tops and sides gently with toothpick, here and there. Place on a baking sheet and bake at 350° F. about 20 to 35 minutes, depending on size and thickness of dough used, but watch closely toward end and remove those that are brown on outer edge of baking sheet. Let cool slightly, then gently release from molds.

When shells are cold, fill and glaze them according to directions given in each recipe. If filled tarts are to stand more than an hour after they are filled and glazed, refrigerate on cake rack placed on baking sheet to keep crisp. It is best to serve these tarts within several hours after they are completed, to prevent breakage. Shells and filling may be prepared a day or two in advance, but do not fill too far in advance.

Cream Filling for Tarts

For 8 tarts

¼ cup sifted all-purpose flour
1 tablespoon cornstarch
¼ cup granulated sugar
Pinch of salt

1 egg yolk, combined with ¼ cup cold milk
1¼ cups warm milk
1 teaspoon butter
1 teaspoon vanilla

Combine measured dry ingredients and mix well. Add the yolk and cold milk, little at a time, stirring until smooth. Pour warm milk over egg mixture and then cook gently until thick, stirring continuously until simmering begins. Let simmer about 5 minutes after it thickens. Add butter, and when cool add vanilla. Beat several times during the cooling process to prevent a crust from forming. Cover and refrigerate for at least 2 hours before using. If filling is too thick when cold, add a little cool milk or water and beat well. In preparing a double recipe, use ¼ cup less of the warm milk.

Fruit Syrup Glaze for Tarts

When using canned fruits

1½ tablespoons cornstarch, combined with ¼ cup cool water
¼ cup granulated sugar

⅔ cup strained sweet fruit syrup (from any canned fruit)

Combine ingredients in the order given. Mix well. Cook over moderate heat until comes to the boiling point, stirring continuously. Simmer about 5 or 6 minutes. This is a basic glaze, and food coloring may be added. Let glaze stand until *lukewarm* before pouring it over fruits, stirring it gently several times in the beginning. If too thick add a little water. This will cover at least 8 tarts. Use ¼ cup less liquid for double recipe.

When using fresh fruits

1½ tablespoons cornstarch, combined   ½ cup hot water (or unsweetened
    with ¼ cup cool water   strained pineapple juice)
½ cup granulated sugar

Combine ingredients in the order given, mix well, and follow general cooking directions as for Fruit Syrup Glaze. This will cover at least 8 tarts. Use ¼ cup less liquid for double recipe.

    How to Glaze Tarts. Place filled tarts on cake coolers, having drip pan underneath. With a spoon pour lukewarm glaze over fruit very carefully to prevent spilling on outside of shell. If glaze is too thick, reheat it slightly or add a few drops of water. Any glaze that drips into pan may be picked up with a spoon, reheated if necessary and used. Allow glaze on tarts to set in a cool place for about 15 minutes before covering edges with plain finely chopped nuts, slivered lightly toasted almonds, or green pistachio nuts. Place tarts in paper cups before serving. It is best not to fill and glaze these tarts until several hours before serving to prevent breaking. Shells and cream filling may be prepared a day in advance.

Pear Tarts

Pour Cream Filling (page 664) into large or medium round tart shells; have them about ¾ filled. Arrange a well-drained pear over filling, rounded side up. With a small artist's brush, tint round side of pear with red coloring, and spread from center out with brush or blend with tip of finger. With a spoon pour lukewarm uncolored glaze over pear. Cover edges of tarts with finely chopped nuts. Insert an artificial pear leaf on small end, or use strip of citron.

Peach and Apricot Tarts

Pour Cream Filling (page 664) into round tart shells, having them about ¾ filled. Arrange a well-drained firm peach or apricot half over filling, round side up. (Cling peach halves are firmer and more attractive than the Freestone for this purpose.) With a small artist's brush, tint round side of fruit with red coloring, and spread from center out with brush, or, better, blend with tip of finger. With a spoon pour over fruit *lukewarm* glaze to which a drop or two of yellow coloring has been added. Cover edges of tarts with finely chopped nuts. Insert green leaf or strip of citron.

Pineapple Tarts

Pour Cream Filling (page 664) into round tart shells, having them about ¾ filled. Arrange a well-drained *small* pineapple ring over filling. Place a little more filling in opening of pineapple, then a whole drained maraschino cherry or fresh strawberry in center. With a spoon pour over fruit lukewarm glaze to which a drop or two of yellow coloring has been added. Now insert a green citron leaf on each side of cherry. Cover edges of tarts with finely chopped or lightly toasted slivered almonds.

Royal Anne Light Sweet Cherry Tarts

Pour Cream Filling (page 664) into tart shells, having them ¾ filled. Arrange 8 or 9 canned pitted cherries over filling, as close together as possible. It is better to have Cream Filling higher in center for cherry tarts. Add a drop of red and a drop of yellow coloring to basic fruit glaze. When lukewarm, pour it over cherries. Cover edge of tarts with chopped or slivered almonds. One No. 2½ can is sufficient for 8 tarts.

Black Bing Dark Sweet Cherry Tarts

Follow general directions for Light Cherry Tarts, but add a little red coloring to glaze.

Banana Tarts

Pour Cream Filling (page 664) into boat (or round) shells, having them about ¾ filled. Arrange thinly sliced bananas over filling. At once pour lukewarm pale yellow glaze over bananas to prevent discoloration. Cover edges with chopped nuts.

Fresh Strawberry or Raspberry Tarts

Pour Cream Filling (page 664) into tart shells, having them about ¾ filled. Place ½ strawberries over filling, forming a slight dome. If using raspberries, do not cut. Add red coloring to glaze. When lukewarm, pour it over fruit. Cover edges with green or plain chopped nuts.

Glazed Open-Face Berry or Fruit Pies

Pour 1 recipe of Cream Filling (page 664) into a 9-inch baked pie shell (page 734). Arrange well-drained berries or fruits over filling, as attractively as possible. Pour 1 recipe of glaze over fruits. Decorate edge of pie with large scrolls of whipped cream with a No. 3 or No. 7 cookie tube and bag. (Takes 1 cup whipping cream.) These pies are very beautiful and delicious for company meals.

Chou Paste

For cream puffs and éclairs

1 cup hot water, combined with ½ teaspoon salt
6 tablespoons butter or margarine
1 cup sifted all-purpose flour

1 scant cup whole eggs (4 very large eggs or 5 medium; best to measure)

Place salt, water, butter or margarine in a 2-quart saucepan and bring to a full boil. As soon as mixture comes to a boil, add the sifted flour all at once, lower heat and with wooden spoon stir vigorously for 2 or 3 minutes until mixture leaves sides of pan and is very smooth. Remove from stove, transfer to 8-inch bowl, let cool slightly for several minutes, then add eggs, 2 at a time, beating with electric mixer until smooth. After all eggs have been added, beat entire mixture for 3 minutes. If recipe is doubled or tripled, beat 4 or 5 minutes after all eggs have been added. If paste feels warm, chill it for a few minutes until cool but not cold. It may be necessary to use fewer eggs when preparing more than 2 recipes at one time. Paste may be prepared day in advance and refrigerated covered, but must be warmed up at room temperature before using.

To Shape Cream Puffs and Éclairs. Place spoonfuls of paste in desired size rounds on lightly greased baking sheet, heaping them higher in center, leaving about 2-inch space between each one. For more uniform results, it is better to use bag and large No. 9 plain tin cookie tube to form the various size cream puffs.

To shape éclairs it is important to use tube, forming 6-inch oblongs, leaving 2-inch space between each. If paste appears too soft and does not hold its shape, it may be placed over very hot simmering water (not boiling) for several minutes, stirring continuously until it stiffens. This condition is caused by undercooking preparation, underbeating, or too much egg. Single recipe will make:

About 30 small puffs
    Bake 15 minutes at 400° F. then about 20 minutes at 325° F.
About 18 medium puffs
    Bake 15 minutes at 400° F. then about 30 minutes at 325° F.
About 8 large puffs
    Bake 15 minutes at 400° F. then about 40 minutes at 325° F.
About 8 large éclairs
    Bake 15 minutes at 400° F. then about 50 minutes at 325° F.

When puffs are done, they may be left in oven to dry out further, with heat shut off and door partially open. If they are not crisp when removed from oven, they may be baked for a few more minutes at 325° F. Puffs and éclairs may be baked several days in advance and stored in covered container, then if they are soft, reheat them in a 400° F. oven for about 10 minutes, let cool, then fill.

Cream puffs may be filled with chicken or other salads; thick creamed dishes, etc., for main luncheon and supper dishes. For cocktail and snack parties, fill small puffs with seafood or chicken salad.

To Fill Ice Cream Puffs and Éclairs. Small puffs may be filled with French Cream Filling (page 669), using bag and No. 8 or 10 decorating tube (or special tube). For large puffs or éclairs, cut them open on 1 side only and fill with spoon or slice off top. With spoon cover top of large puffs and éclairs with Icing, and let stand on cake cooler with drip pan underneath for a short time. Small puffs may be iced by dipping upper part into Icing and turning over quickly, shaking puffs for a few seconds. If Icing is transparent on puffs, add more sugar to Icing in bowl. If it is not smooth, add a few drops of milk or water.

Cream Puff Swans

Bodies of swans are formed and baked same as for Cream Puffs. Heads and necks are made with No. 8 plain decorating tube for medium, and No. 10 tube for large. Pipe paste onto *lightly* greased baking sheet forming the letter "S," then pipe head and beak. Bake about 10 minutes for medium, 15 minutes for large, at 400° F. Watch closely the last minute or two to prevent burning. If soft, shut off heat, leave oven door open, and let dry out for a few minutes.

To Form Swans. Slice off top part of Cream Puff, fill lower part with French Cream Filling (page 669) and with No. 3 cookie tube pipe a thick collar of whipped cream on top. Shortly before serving, insert neck, and make wings with top of puff that was sliced off, cutting it in 2 parts. Use a small piece of another puff for tail end. With No. 4 tube and dark pink or green Icing, pipe eyes on sides of head. Sprinkle entire top of swan with sifted confectioners' sugar. Keep refrigerated until ready to serve.

Icing for Cream Puffs and Éclairs

¼ cup soft butter or margarine	About 4 cups sifted confectioners'
⅓ cup hot milk	sugar
1 teaspoon vanilla	2 ounces melted baking chocolate

Combine butter or margarine with hot milk and vanilla. Stir until butter is melted. Add confectioners' sugar little at a time and beat until smooth.

Last, add the melted baking chocolate (or add food coloring if preferred). Let chocolate icing stand at least 20 minutes before using.

If it is too thick, add a little more milk or water; if too thin, add more sifted confectioners' sugar.

French Cream Filling (Top of the Stove Custard)

Makes about 2 cups

½ cup granulated sugar
¼ cup sifted all-purpose flour *and* 2 tablespoons cornstarch
⅛ teaspoon salt
1 or 2 egg yolks
¼ cup cool milk

2 cups warm milk
1 tablespoon butter
1 teaspoon vanilla
1 or 2 ounces baking chocolate (optional)

Mix sugar, flour, cornstarch, and salt. Beat yolk slightly and combine with the ¼ cup cool milk. Add slowly to dry ingredients, stirring until smooth. Add warm milk, little at a time, stirring until well blended. Cook over moderate heat until thick, stirring continuously. Now lower heat and simmer about 5 minutes. Remove from heat and add butter. Stir well. If chocolate filling is preferred, add 1 or 2 ounces of baking chocolate, cut up in small pieces, and beat until well blended. Beat filling several times during cooling process to keep it uniform in consistency and prevent crust from forming. When cool, add vanilla, and if custard appears too thick, add a little cool milk or, cream and blend well. Must be refrigerated for several hours before using.

Velvety Chocolate Sauce

For ice-cream desserts, éclairs, etc.

2 ounces baking chocolate, cut into small pieces
1 cup hot homogenized milk (about 130° F.)

2 cups sifted confectioners' sugar
1 tablespoon butter
1 or 2 teaspoons vanilla

In a 1-quart saucepan melt chocolate over hot water. Add about ¼ cup of the hot milk, then all of the sugar, a little at a time, then rest of milk, a little at a time, beating after each addition until smooth. Cook over medium heat (stirring continuously until sauce is removed from stove) until thick, then lower heat and simmer about 5 minutes. It is important to stir this sauce for entire cooking time to prevent scorching. Remove from heat, add the butter and stir well. Add vanilla after it has cooled a little. It may be served warm or cold. If sauce is too thick, a tablespoon or two of hot water may be added to make right consistency. It may be prepared days in advance if refrigerated in a tightly covered container. Reheat over hot water just before serving.

Cream Puff Log

Serves 8

Prepare 1 full recipe Chou Paste (page 667), *using only ¾ cup whole eggs.* Chill, then with a large spoon place paste lengthwise in center of a well-greased 12 × 18-inch baking sheet, forming a solid long roll that is about 2½ inches wide and 1¼ inches thick, and 14 inches long. With a wet spatula smooth log. Bake at 450° F. 20 minutes, then reduce heat to 325° F. and continue to bake (without opening oven door until last few minutes) about 60 more minutes. After this, puncture log with sharp point of knife or skewer and let remain in oven with heat shut off and door slightly open for about 30 more minutes. Remove from oven and allow to become cold before cutting and filling.

To Fill. With a serrated-edge knife cut upper part of log lengthwise very carefully. Place bottom of log on a stiff cardboard covered with foil. Pour a full recipe or less of plain Cream Filling (page 664) or Bavarian Cream Filling (page 588) into log carefully. Place upper part of log on filling. Refrigerate until ready to be served. Sprinkle with sifted confectioners' sugar. Now place log on oblong or oval serving platter; cut into serving portions. Keep portions together and decorate top with a scroll of whipped cream using No. 3 cookie star tube, and garnish each scroll with red cherries, or strawberries and citron leaves.

Banana Cream Puff Log

Serves 8

Pour and spread half recipe of Cream Filling (page 664) in log (see above), then arrange sliced bananas on filling (2 large bananas). Cover bananas with rest of filling and a layer of whipped cream if desired. Decorate, etc.

Strawberry or Raspberry Cream Puff Log

Serves 8

Follow directions for Banana Log, using 1 pint of strawberries or raspberries instead of bananas.

La Neige Dessert (Soft French Custard)

¾ cup egg yolks (little more or less)
Pinch of salt
½ cup granulated sugar
¼ cup cornstarch, combined with ¼ cup milk

3¾ cups hot milk
About 1 teaspoon vanilla and 1 teaspoon crunch flavoring

Stir yolks well with spoon and strain into a 2-quart saucepan. Add the salt, sugar, a little at a time, and the cornstarch combined with milk. Very slowly add the hot milk, and cook over moderate heat until it begins to thicken, *stirring continuously.* Now lower heat and let simmer (not boil) for about 3 minutes. At once pour into a bowl and with egg beater beat for about ½ minute. Let stand in room temperature until cool, *stirring gently several times* (do not beat), add flavoring, *stir gently,* and refrigerate for at least 8 hours, but do not freeze.

Shortly before serving cut through French Meringues with a teaspoon, and arrange them on top of La Neige Dessert, in sherbet glasses, to simulate a flower. Garnish center of flower with a well-drained red maraschino cherry or a fresh strawberry, or simply place a whole meringue on each dessert.

French Meringues

½ cup fresh egg whites
Pinch of salt
¼ teaspoon cream of tartar

½ cup sifted granulated sugar
½ teaspoon vanilla

In a 7-inch bowl combine the egg whites, salt, and cream of tartar. Beat until eggs whites cling to bowl; add the granulated sugar, a little at a time, and beat about 1 more minute or until stiff, *but not dry.* Add vanilla and any desired food coloring, or leave white. With a large spoon pick up beaten whites and lower them into hot water (not boiling). Cover pan. Let cook for about 1 minute. When meringues have doubled in size, remove them with a perforated ladle. Do not keep pan over heat while cooking. Let meringues drain in colander for at least 15 minutes, then place them in a bowl, cover and let stand in refrigerator until ready to be served. Better not to prepare these meringues more than an hour or two before serving.

Meringues for Ice Cream Desserts, Etc.

½ cup *cool* fresh egg whites (not warmer than 70° F.)
Pinch salt

½ teaspoon cream of tartar
1 cup granulated sugar, sifted
½ teaspoon vanilla

Pour cool egg whites into an 8- or 9-inch bowl. Add salt and cream of tartar. At once beat at high speed with electric mixer about 3 minutes, or 5 minutes with hand beater. *Now* add the sugar, about 1 tablespoon at a time, and beat only until blended. Add vanilla. (It will take about 1 to 1½ minutes to beat in sugar.) Overbeating will break down meringue and designs will not retain their shapes. It is very important to use eggs that are top quality and as fresh as possible. Old eggs or those of inferior quality are watery and will not produce a stiff meringue. For double recipe beat 1 or 2 more minutes. A double recipe may be prepared at one time if you are equipped with 2 ovens. Meringues may be placed on all 3 racks in oven at the same time provided they are shifted around during baking process to prevent overbrowning. Bake at 250° F., referring to time given in each recipe.

It is best to leave oven door slightly open (about 1 inch) from the start or after meringues have partially baked to prevent overbrowning, and to keep heat as low as possible if they are baking too rapidly. When baking time is up let meringues remain in oven with heat shut off for a short time. This will insure crisp, tender meringues. Underbaking will make them tough and chewy. If they are browning too rapidly on bottom, place pan on another pan of same size. If tops of meringues are browning too rapidly, place them on lower rack.

It is important to form the various meringues on baking sheets or on rose nails as soon as possible and to refrigerate rest of meringue to prevent softening. If the last part of meringue appears spongy, stir it gently, and place it into bag and pipe designs as soon as possible. Refrigerated meringue retains its puffiness for about 30 minutes if top-quality fresh eggs are used. After meringues have been formed they may be kept in refrigerator for about 1 hour if oven space is not available.

Large 12 × 18-inch baking sheets are greased with 1½ teaspoons unsalted shortening; smaller baking sheets with 1 teaspoon. Grease rose nails as lightly as possible, or they may be used ungreased. A dab of shortening will be sufficient to grease a dozen rose nails. Too much grease will cause roses to slide off nails during baking.

Meringues may be made days or weeks in advance provided they are kept in a closed container, with wax paper in between each layer and refrigerated, or kept in a cold room. If they become soft and sticky during humid weather, they may be reheated at 250° F. for about 15 minutes. Then let cool and use as desired. *Best not to prepare meringues during very warm humid weather.* Do not freeze.

Roses. Use No. 104 tube and bag for medium and large roses; No. 124 or 127 tube for extra-large. Pipe them onto *very* lightly greased (or ungreased) rose nails. Place them on a wooden stand if available. An empty egg carton, covered candy box, or wax paper carton is excellent for this purpose, or lift roses off nail and place on lightly greased pan and bake. The No. 124 or 127 larger rose tubes do not fit into coupling, so simply use bag with tube without coupling. Bake roses at 250° F. for about 1½ hours, following general directions given above. When cool release from nails.

Leaves. Add green coloring to basic meringue. Use No. 67 tube and bag for medium; No. 70 best for large leaves. Bake about 45 minutes, following general directions.

Meringue Cookies. Use No. 3 large cookie tube and bag. Form various shapes. Decorate with red glazed (or very well-drained and dried on a towel) maraschino cherries, green citron leaves, chopped nuts, colored sugar, or as desired. Bake about 1 hour, etc.

Ice Cream Shells. With plain opening of coupling and bag (or No. 3 or 7 cookie star tube), pipe rings on well-greased baking sheets. Fill in center of ring, and go over edge several times. Bake about 1½ hours, etc. Very flat meringue discs may be made for ice cream desserts, topped with a rose and with leaves inserted on sides of rose. Bake discs about 1 hour. Follow general directions.

Birds. Use plain opening of coupling for large birds, or decorating tubes with large plain opening for small birds. Pipe them onto greased baking sheets, etc. Bake about 1 hour.

Swans. Use plain opening of coupling and make shells as given above. Make wings, 1 for right side and 1 for left side, and tails. Pipe swans' necks and heads, all with the same opening of coupling. Bake shells about 1½ hours; necks, wings and tails about 1 hour.

Fill ⅔ of shell with ice cream or fruit and then pipe a thick scroll of heavy or stabilized whipped cream over ice cream. Make a gash in whipped cream or ice cream to insert necks, wings and tails. Do not fill until just before serving. With pointed end of wooden skewer dipped into red coloring, paint eyes on swans. One recipe meringue will make 4 to 5 complete swans, depending on size.

Individual Ice Cream Easter Eggs

Makes 6 large or 8 small

2 pints ice cream (room temperature about 20 minutes)
4 cups macaroon coconut, divided and tinted pink, green, yellow, and white (add a few drops of color- ing and equal amount of water to white coconut and work it with a fork until evenly colored, *then rub it well in palms of hands*)

With an ice cream baller pick up ice cream and roll it into coconut. With hands shape gently to simulate an egg. Wrap each in wax paper and keep in freezer. These ice cream eggs may be prepared days in advance. In this case, wrap them well in wax paper, then place in a plastic bag, well sealed, and freeze.

Large Ice Cream Easter Egg

Remove ice cream from freezer about 20 minutes in advance. Line 2 egg molds that measure 7½ inches long and 2¾ inches deep with wax paper as smoothly as possible. Place 1 pint of vanilla ice cream in each, bringing it up on sides and bottom as uniformly as possible. Press down well. Fill center of each mold with 1 pint of lemon or orange ice, packing it down and having top as flat and smooth as possible. Put the 2 molds together and hold in place with heavy rubber bands or string, if necessary. Wrap well in several thicknesses of wax or freezer paper and freeze.

To Serve. Turn out onto a thin oval *slice of cake*. Remove wax paper. Cake will prevent mold from sliding on platter. Cover with white macaroon coconut and decorate with whipped cream or buttercream icing, or preferably, spread entire mold with whipped cream, and decorate top with a spray of flowers in pastel colors same as for cake. This can be done several hours in advance and kept uncovered in freezer until serving time, or wrap well after it is frozen and keep for a longer time. Remove from freezer about ½ hour before serving. Takes 1 pint whipping cream to cover and decorate mold.

Ice Cream Petits Fours and Molds

Remove brick ice cream from freezer and store in refrigerator about 20 to 30 minutes, or until slightly soft. Cut each brick lengthwise into 2 thick slices.

For Petits Fours. With a very sharp plain or serrated-edge knife cut ice cream into rectangles, triangles, or squares. Cut rounds with 2-inch cutter; hearts with medium or large cutter. Place them at once on flat pan covered with wax paper *with another pan filled with ice underneath to prevent ice cream from melting at bottom.* Immediately put pan in freezer until ice cream is very stiff.

Shortly before decorating petits fours, whip 1 cup of cream in a No. 7 bowl until cream barely clings to bottom and sides. Now divide in half. Add green to 1 portion and red to other (or leave white). Beat only until well blended and cream just clings to bowl.

With bag and No. 27 star tube pipe entire surface of ice cream with green, pink, yellow, or white whipped cream, forming E design. Put back into freezer at once if they appear soft. Then with No. 27 tube pipe a large rosette in center of each, and with No. 67 tube pipe leaves. Or pipe relief roses or full roses with No. 104 tube. Place back in freezer until very firm to touch. Then release them from wax paper with a spatula if necessary, or lift up with fingers and place each in a petit-four cup.

Slip entire pan or box into a large plastic bag if not to be served within a few hours. May be kept for several months if properly wrapped.

For Ice Cream Molds. Use irregular pieces of ice cream left over from rounds and hearts or cut up brick and let stand in bowl a few minutes until soft enough to pack into heart and other style molds. With small spatula pack ice cream down into mold, forming a slight mound in center. Put in freezer until very, very firm. To release from molds, dip them into warm water (about 125° F.), not too hot, for about 15 seconds, remove, wipe ouside of molds, and shake ice cream out onto hand or pan covered with wax paper. Now put into freezer again until surface of molds is firm. Then proceed to decorate same as for petits fours.

One pint brick ice cream will make about 12 medium-size petits fours or molds. One cup cream will cover and decorate 12 to 16, depending on size. *These ice cream molds and petits fours must be kept at zero or lower to prevent softening.*

Ice Cream Sherbet Torte

Serves 8 to 12

½ pound chocolate cookies, graham crackers, vanilla wafers, or zwieback

½ cup sifted confectioners' sugar

½ cup melted butter or margarine

3 pints chocolate ice cream (or other flavor)

2 pints lime sherbet (or other flavor)

With rolling pin crush cookies into very fine crumbs (should measure 2½ cups). Combine with the confectioners' sugar and melted butter or margarine, and with a fork or by hand blend well. Pour 1¼ cups onto bottom of ungreased 9 × 3-inch loose-bottom round pan, and with back of large spoon press down crumbs until uniform and compact. Place in refrigerator for at least 30 minutes.

Allow 3 pints of chocolate ice cream (any other ice cream may be used) to stand in room temperature or refrigerator until of medium consistency, not too stiff and not soft. Pour and pack ice cream over crust evenly with back of spoon. Place in freezer and let stand until firm to touch.

Allow 2 pints of lime (or any other kind) sherbet to stand in refrigerator or room temperature until medium consistency. Pour and spread this evenly over chocolate ice cream.

Sprinkle about 1 cup of the crumb mixture over top of sherbet carefully and evenly. Place back in freezer for several hours, or until firm to touch.

When torte is firm, go around sides with a spatula or dinner knife and release from sides of pan, but leave it on metal bottom. Place rest of crumb mixture around sides as evenly as possible. If torte is to be served within a short time, top may be decorated with large scrolls of whipped cream, with No. 3 cookie tube, or fancy flower decoration. Let it remain uncovered in freezer until ready to be served, but not more than 2 hours. If to be kept longer, it is best to wrap it in wax paper, then in freezer paper. Torte may be prepared weeks in advance, left plain or decorated, if properly wrapped. Remove from freezer and either keep in room temperature about 1 hour before it is to be served, or store in refrigerator about 2 hours before it is needed. Arrange fancy small cakes or cookies around torte.

Party-Size Ice Cream Bombe

Makes 24 good-size portions

4 pints butter pecan or vanilla ice cream
3 pints chocolate ice cream
2 pints orange ice or sherbet
Thin slice sponge cake

1 cup whipping cream, or 3 cups whipping cream and 3 teaspoons gelatin
Green and red food coloring

Leave ice cream and sherbet in room temperature about 30 minutes to soften slightly.

Line bowl with wax paper as smoothly as possible. Spread the 4 pints of butter pecan or vanilla ice cream on bottom and sides of 8-inch Pyrex bowl, pressing down well to make uniform thickness. Place bowl in freezer for a few minutes if ice cream appears soft. Then spread the 3 pints of chocolate ice cream over the first. Chill again if necessary. Last, place the 2 pints of orange ice or sherbet in center, and press down well. Cover top with several thicknesses of waxed paper and wrap bowl in foil or freezer paper. Let remain in freezer for at least 8 hours. May be prepared several weeks in advance if properly wrapped.

To Serve. Remove paper and place a thin layer of sponge cake on flat side of bombe. With a dinner knife, loosen sides and turn bombe out onto a large round platter. Remove all paper from sides and top of ice cream. Dip a spatula or dinner knife into water and go over entire surface to make it as smooth as possible.

To Decorate Bombe. Whip 1 cup of cream until medium consistency, then add a little green coloring to ⅓, and red coloring to ⅔. Continue to beat only until cream clings to bowl. Pipe a spray of relief roses on rounded part with stems and leaves. Surround bombe with fancy small cakes or cookies.

For a Very Fancy Decoration on Bombe. Whip 2 cups of cream until medium thick, then add 2 teaspoons gelatin combined with 4 tablespoons cold water; let stand until thick, then dissolve over simmering water, and let stand until warm. Continue to beat cream after gelatin has been added only until it clings to bowl. With No. 3 cookie tube, pipe cream onto bombe, starting from the top, to form a swirl. Then whip 1 more cup of cream, stabilize it with 1 teaspoon gelatin combined with 2 tablespoons cold water, until thick, then dissolve over simmering water, and let cool. Add red coloring to ⅔ of the partially beaten cream, and green coloring to ⅓ of the partially beaten cream. Continue to beat only until it clings to bowl. Make roses with pink cream using No. 104 or No. 127 tube, and transfer them to top of mold. Pipe green leaves with green whipped cream and No. 70 leaf tube, all around and between roses.

To serve 12, recipe may be cut in half, using 7-inch bowl.

Rhubarb Sauce

Hothouse rhubarb that is obtainable in February and March is light pink and not very tart. Home-grown or garden-type, available in early spring, has dark reddish to green stalks and is very tart. Always select rhubarb with red color, as it has better flavor and is less tart. Wash, dry well, and store in hydrator until ready to be used.

Wash rhubarb and do not dry. Remove leaves and trim ends. *Do not peel.* Cut into about 1-inch pieces. Cook in tightly covered saucepan (without adding water) for about 7 or 8 minutes over moderate heat, turning several times. For each pound of uncooked rhubarb, add about ½ cup granulated sugar after rhubarb is partially tender. Continue to cook 2 or 3 minutes longer. A cup of strawberries that have been washed, drained thoroughly, then hulled, may be added to rhubarb when adding sugar. In this case, use ¾ cup of sugar.

Honey Crispettes

Serves 4 to 6

2 whole large eggs
2 tablespoons water
About 1½ cups sifted all-purpose flour (more or less, to form medium dough)

½ teaspoon baking powder
1 cup honey, combined with ⅓ cup water

Beat eggs until frothy for a few seconds, add the water, then the flour sifted with baking powder, a little at a time, to form a medium dough. Knead dough gently for a minute or two until smooth. Cover with a bowl and let ripen for about 20 minutes. Cut in 2 pieces, roll each piece into a very thin sheet. Cut into strips and knot; or cut in triangular shapes, oblongs, squares, etc., and make a gash in center of each. Deep-fry at 375° F. until delicately brown on one side, then turn over and brown second side. Watch closely, as they brown rapidly. Drain on cake coolers or paper towels until cool.

To Make Glaze. In a small saucepan combine the cup of honey and ⅓ cup water, blend well, and bring to a boil. Lower crispettes into foamy honey glaze and lift out with a pair of tongs or long metal skewer. Drain on cake cooler with a baking sheet underneath. A frying basket can be used to glaze these crispettes if large quantities are being prepared. Simply place several of them in the basket at one time, lower into the foamy honey glaze for 2 or 3 seconds, and lift out. Keep honey over low heat while working, and be sure it is simmering gently or foamy before dipping crispettes. Let them stand until cold before serving. Best served within 2 days after they are glazed.

Sugared Crispettes. Simply cover crispettes thickly with sifted confectioners' sugar. Shake off loose sugar and serve with tea, coffee, desserts, or as desired.

Rhubarb and Strawberry Sherbet

Proceed as for Rhubarb Sauce (page 677). When rhubarb and strawberries are tender, *fold in an extra cup (or more) of strawberries*, but do not cook further. Pour into bowl, let stand until cool, then store in refrigerator until very cold. Pour into sherbet glasses and decorate top with a scroll of whipped cream or with any soft icing, using bag and No. 3 star cookie tube. Very delicious and attractive. Increase sugar to 1 cup if preparing this combination.

Apple Dumplings

Serves 8

6 medium-size apples, peeled and cored

Pie-crust Dough (page 732) made with 2 cups flour, using only ½ cup shortening, or Baking Powder Biscuit Dough (page 476) made with 2 cups all-purpose flour

6 tablespoons brown sugar, solidly packed (granulated sugar may be used instead)

6 tablespoons butter or margarine, medium consistency

Cinnamon and nutmeg

Prepare dough; chill if necessary. Roll dough to measure 14 × 21 inches. Cut it into 6 uniform squares. Place a peeled and cored apple on each. Fill each opening of apple with 1 tablespoon butter, 1 tablespoon sugar, and a little cinnamon and nutmeg. Enclose the apple completely in the dough, bringing the 4 corners of the dough to the top, pinching well, and using a little milk or water if necessary to seal. Place each one carefully in a baking dish that measures about 12 × 8 × 2 inches, leaving a space on each side and between each apple. Brush tops with milk, and prick in several places. Bake in 425° F. oven for about 20 minutes.

Pour Plain Syrup over tops, reduce heat to 350° F., and continue baking for about 40 more minutes, or until crust is brown and apples are tender. Test toward end of baking. Serve apple dumplings with cream, Lemon Sauce, or as desired.

Plain Syrup for Apple Dumplings

1½ cups water
½ cup sugar
1 tablespoon butter

⅛ teaspoon nutmeg
⅛ teaspoon cinnamon

Combine all ingredients and bring to a boil. Simmer about 1 minute.

Lemon Sauce for Apple Dumplings

1 cup sugar
2 cups cool water added slowly to 1 tablespoon cornstarch (more cornstarch can be used)
⅛ teaspoon salt

¼ teaspoon nutmeg
¼ teaspoon cinnamon
1 large lemon, with the rind, cut into small pieces
1 tablespoon butter

Cook all ingredients together until boiling point; lower heat and simmer about 5 minutes. For a thicker sauce increase cornstarch to 2 tablespoons. Strain before serving.

Baked Apples

Serves 4

4 Rome Beauty apples
4 tablespoons brown sugar
4 teaspoons butter

1 cup hot water
Pinch of cinnamon
Pinch of nutmeg

Wash and core apples. Pare upper part of each apple.

Place apples in a baking dish. Fill center of each apple with 1 tablespoon brown sugar and 1 teaspoon soft butter. Sprinkle each apple with cinnamon and nutmeg. Add cup of hot water in baking dish. Cover and bake at 400° F. for about 40 to 45 minutes, or until apples are tender. At the end of 20 minutes, remove cover and baste apples. Cover again and finish baking.

Baked apples may be served hot or cold, with or without cream.

Butterscotch Custard in Casserole

Serves 6 to 8

¾ cup dark or light brown sugar, solidly packed
6 large eggs
1 teaspoon vanilla

¼ teaspoon salt
1 quart cream-line milk (if using homogenized milk, cook custard about 1½ hours)

Press brown sugar on bottom of 10 × 6½ × 2-inch oblong glass heatproof casserole as uniformly as possible. In a medium-size bowl beat the 6 eggs for about ½ minute with electric or hand beater. Add the vanilla, salt, and, very slowly, 1 quart *scalded* milk. Pour this mixture slowly over brown sugar in casserole. Place casserole in a large utensil with hot water coming up at least halfway, and bake at 300° F. for about 1 hour, more or less, or until knife comes out clean when tested in center of baked custard. Cook longer if using homogenized milk. If top of custard is not brown when set, place it under broiler for a minute or two and watch closely to see that it does not burn. Let cool in room temperature on cake rack, then refrigerate until ready to be served. For special occasions decorate top of custard with 1 cup whipping cream beaten until stiff, using No. 3 star cookie tube.

The brown sugar in this dessert separates from the custard, forming a delicious syrup on the bottom, which is picked up with a spoon and served over each portion of custard.

Date, Nut, and Raisin Rice Custard

Serves 6 to 8

2 whole eggs	¼ teaspoon salt
2 cups hot milk	2 cups cooked rice
1 tablespoon butter	¼ cup dates, chopped
3 tablespoons sugar	¼ cup pecans, chopped
1 teaspoon vanilla	¼ cup raisins
⅛ teaspoon nutmeg	

Beat eggs, add milk, butter, sugar, vanilla, nutmeg, salt, cooked rice, dates, pecans, and raisins. Blend well.

Pour into large baking dish (1½-quart) and bake at 350° F. for about 1 hour, or until blade of knife inserted in center of custard comes out clean. Be sure to set baking dish into another pan of hot water.

For individual cups bake about 45 minutes. Very delicious served hot with the Lemon Sauce below.

Lemon Sauce for Custard

½ cup granulated sugar	1½ tablespoons lemon juice
1 tablespoon cornstarch	⅛ teaspoon nutmeg
1 cup boiling water	Dash of salt
2 tablespoons butter	

Mix sugar and cornstarch, and add boiling water gradually. Cook for 5 minutes, stirring constantly. Add butter, lemon juice, nutmeg, and salt. Serve while hot.

Chocolate Mousse in Sherbet Glasses

Serves 4

¼ pound dark sweet chocolate (⅓ cup after melted)
2 tablespoons hot water
2 egg yolks slightly beaten

1 teaspoon vanilla
2 egg whites beaten until they cling to bowl
1 tablespoon granulated sugar

In a very small saucepan cook chocolate (cut in small pieces) and hot water, *over very low heat*, until smooth. Add the hot chocolate mixture, a spoonful at a time, to the slightly beaten egg yolks, and beat until smooth. Add vanilla. Beat whites until they cling to bowl; add the 1 tablespoon granulated sugar and beat until well blended. Pour whites into chocolate mixture and stir until no streaks appear. Pour into sherbet glasses about ⅔ full. Refrigerate at least 6 hours. Before serving, pipe a large scroll of whipped cream on top of each and sprinkle with slivered pistachio nuts, or garnish with a well drained maraschino cherry and green citron leaves. Serve with cookies or small cakes.

▶ *Cookies*

BARS AND SLICES,
PLAIN AND FANCY

THE SMART HOMEMAKER ALWAYS HAS A JAR OF COOKIES ON HAND TO BE served with tea, coffee, or ice cream when the unexpected guest drops in, or to her family when she has been too occupied to prepare another dessert.

Cookies are easily prepared and have the advantage of keeping for a longer time than cakes. This chapter contains some recipes for very fancy cookies suitable for serving on special occasions or for using as gifts.

Important. From the standpoint of flavor it is better to use at least half butter in cookies. However, all margarine will give good results. Butter or margarine should be of medium consistency, and the other ingredients room temperature. Beat butter or margarine, sugar, and eggs until very light, for several minutes, before you add the dry ingredients and the liquid. Then beat only until smooth after each addition. Cookies keep well for several weeks if properly wrapped and refrigerated, or they may be frozen for several months. Separate layers with sheets of wax paper.

Decorations for Cookies

Green Stems and Leaves

In many of our recipes for fancy top layered gelatin molds and fancy cookies, petit fours, etc., we suggest citron leaves, stems, etc. The most useful item for this work is candied citron peel, an ingredient used in holiday fruit cakes. It is available in many fancy grocery stores, sold by the piece or halved. Citron is a fruit peel (from the orange family) that is grown for the peel alone and which, after some special treatment, is candied. It is light to dark green with some yellow tint.

For Stems. With a very sharp knife slice citron lengthwise about ⅛ inch thick, then into about 1-inch narrow strips, about ⅛ inch wide.

For Leaves. With a very sharp knife slice same thickness, then trim to uniform width about ¼ to ⅓ inch wide. Now cut strips into diamond shapes. This is a quick and excellent way to make leaves.

For other decorations, scraps and trimmings may be cut into small pieces. For additional color, it is important to soak these decorations in some green colored water (add few drops green coloring to warm water) for about 10 minutes, not longer. Then drain them well, rinse under clear cool water, and dry them thoroughly on paper towels. May be used at once, or let dry completely, and store in a cool dry place for several weeks or longer, in a covered container, use as indicated in recipe.

Green candied pineapple may also be cut up and used in same way. Green maraschino or candied cherries are sometimes used.

Green Nuts for Decorative Purposes

When a recipe calls for pistachio nuts, you can use pecan meats, prepared as follows: Put pecan halves through a medium nut chopper, or crushed with rolling pin. Add a few drops of green food coloring combined with few drops water, working coloring into nutmeats with a fork, then blend them further in palms of hands. Spread nuts on a cookie sheet and allow to dry in room temperature for an hour or longer. When dry, it is important to put the colored nutmeats through a food mill or grater. Use as indicated in recipes.

Butter Cookies (Muerbes)

Makes about 50 to 60 cookies

1 cup (½ pound) butter or margarine, medium consistency
⅔ cup granulated sugar
Yolks of 2 eggs

1 teaspoon lemon, orange, or vanilla extract
About 2¼ cups sifted all-purpose flour

Cream butter or margarine well for about 1 minute. Gradually add sifted sugar and egg yolks, 1 at a time, and beat about 1 or 2 minutes. Add extract and last sifted flour, a little at a time, using only enough to form a dough that will go through a plastic bag and No. 3 cookie star tube. Beat well. *Be sure to test dough after adding 2¼ cups of sifted flour. If too soft, add a little more flour.* Place into bag and squeeze at once into desired shapes on lightly greased baking sheets. Decorate with glazed red cherries, citron, nuts, etc., or with green and red maraschino cherries. This dough may also be put through a cookie press using a little less flour. Bake in a 350° F. oven about 20 minutes, or until golden brown. Place on upper rack last 5 minutes of baking.

If any cookie mixtures are too stiff to go through bag and tube at any time, add a little milk or water, a teaspoonful at a time, until they are of proper consistency. Have bag less than half filled and do not allow dough to stand more than necessary after it is mixed.

How to Make Fancy Muerbes

1. Press dough into a closed ring, overlapping a little. Decorate each cookie with half or quarter glazed cherry and 2 citron leaves.
2. Press dough into the letter "C." Decorate ends with small pieces of citron and red cherries. Sprinkle center of cookies with pinch finely chopped nuts and bake. After they are baked, 2 may be put together with a little melted sweet chocolate.
3. Press dough into rosettes having ends tapered. After they are baked, put 2 together with melted sweet chocolate. Dip small end into melted sweet chocolate and cover with chocolate shots, green or plain chopped nuts. Serve in bonbon cups.
4. Add little melted baking chocolate to basic mixture. With chocolate mixture press out rosettes, having points tapered. Press out same size rosette with yellow mixture. Decorate small end with half glazed cherry and 1 citron leaf.
5. Add red or green food coloring to basic dough and form into different shapes *with bag or cookie press*. Very attractive for teas, parties, etc.
6. Add little extra flour to basic mixture. Roll and cut different shapes. Pipe contrasting color cookie mixture on top with No. 3 cookie star tube.

Quick Dainty Butter Cookies

½ cup butter (half margarine may be used)
¾ cup sifted confectioners' sugar
1 tablespoon milk
½ teaspoon vanilla
About 1½ cups sifted all-purpose flour

Beat butter until creamy. Add sugar a little at a time, and beat about 2 minutes. Add milk and vanilla alternately with sifted flour, and beat after each addition until smooth. Turn dough out onto a pastry cloth and knead gently about ½ minute. If dough is too soft, add a little more flour, or chill it 1 hour or longer to facilitate handling.

Roll dough on a floured pastry cloth about ¼ inch thick (not too thin), and with a small (not more than 2-inch size) round crinkle cutter (other styles may be used) cut through dough. Pick up cookies with spatula and place on lightly greased baking sheets. Reknead scraps gently, roll, and cut out. Bake in a preheated 350° F. oven about 15 to 20 minutes. Do not let them get too dark. When cold, roll cookies in confectioners' sugar. If preferred, top of cookies may be brushed with egg yolk combined with 1 tablespoon milk, then sprinkled with chopped nutmeats, colored sugar, or decorettes before they are baked.

Christmas Cookie Canes

Prepare basic dough for Yuletide Cookies (below). Divide it in 2 parts (if making all canes). Add red coloring to 1 part. Leave rest white.

Dough must not be too dry for canes and it is best to test it before adding more than 2½ cups of flour. Dough must form strips without cracking and without sticking to hands. If too soft, canes will spread; if dough is too dry, it will crack in the handling. If too dry at any time during the shaping process, a few drops of water may be added. If too soft, add very little more flour. To shape medium-size canes, pick up 1 level measuring teaspoon of each color, and roll into pencil-like strips 5 inches long. Lay contrasting strips next to each other and twist the 2 together. Now gently roll combined strips on pastry cloth. With both hands pick them up carefully and transfer to well-greased baking sheet, and bend to simulate canes, leaving at least 1 inch space between each. Bake at 300° F., about 20 minutes, then shut off heat; leave oven door partially open and allow canes to dry out for about 15 minutes. It is important to use low baking temperature for these cookies to prevent discoloration. Look at them after first 15 minutes and if they appear to bake too rapidly, reduce heat to lowest point, or shut off entirely, and let dry out in oven. When done, release them from pan at once with pancake turner to prevent sticking and breaking. Let cool on racks or any flat surface. When cold, they may be tied with colorful narrow ribbon. Make lovely holiday gift for children, and tree decorations.

Yuletide Cookies

Makes about 50

¾ cup white shortening	About 2½ to 3 cups sifted all-purpose
1 cup granulated sugar	flour, or enough to form a me-
1 egg yolk	dium dough that does not stick
½ teaspoon salt	to hands
1½ teaspoons lemon or orange extract	¼ cup milk

With electric mixer or spoon, beat shortening, add sugar, little at a time, and beat well about 1 minute. Add yolk and salt, and beat for about 2 minutes. Add extract, then flour alternately with the milk, and beat after each addition until dough is smooth.

Christmas Cookie Wreaths

Prepare basic dough for Yuletide Cookies (above), leaving it white or adding green coloring. On a floured pastry cloth, roll dough a little less than ¼ inch thick, but not too thin. With a scalloped 2½-inch round cutter, cut through dough. With a small 1-inch plain round cutter (or open end of No. 7 star cookie tube) cut out centers, forming rings. Reknead centers and shape. Bake cookies on a well-greased baking sheet at 300° F. about 15 to 20 minutes; then shut off heat, leave oven door partially open, and let dry about 15 minutes. With pancake turner release cookies from baking sheet as soon as they are removed from oven, and place on cake coolers. When cold, decorate tops with 3 green leaves (No. 65 tube), and at once place 1 red cinnamon candy on each leaf, pressing down gently.

Double Christmas Cookie Wreaths

Proceed as for single wreaths (above), but from half of rings cut out ¼-inch pieces. When cookies are cold, slip the 2 rings together, concealing open end under solid surface, and hold together with a dab of icing. Decorate with 3 groups of leaves and cinnamon candies, as suggested for single wreath.

Christmas Cookie Leaves or Trees

Prepare basic dough for Yuletide Cookies (page 685), and add green coloring. On a floured pastry cloth, roll dough a little less than ¼ inch thick. With leaf or tree cutter, cut out cookies. Pick up with spatula and place on a well-greased baking sheet. Bake at 300° F. about 15 to 20 minutes; then shut off heat, leave door partially open, and let dry about 15 minutes. Release from pan as soon as they are removed from oven, and let cool on cake racks. When cold, cover entire surface lightly with a very thin Royal Icing (page 624), and at once sprinkle with colored sprinkles.

Christmas Bells

Prepare basic dough for Yuletide Cookies (page 685). Add red coloring to half, and green to other half. On a floured pastry cloth, roll dough a little less than ¼ inch thick. With bell cutter, cut out cookies. With a thick wooden skewer make a hole on upper part of each bell. Bake on a well-greased baking sheet at 300° F. about 15 to 20 minutes; then shut off heat, leave door partially open, and let dry out about 15 minutes. Release from pan as soon as they are done. When cold, place 1 red and 1 green bell together, and tie with red or green string, or very narrow ribbon. Pipe a rosette on lower part of each with No. 27 star tube, and green leaves with No. 65 tube.

Holiday Turkey Cookies

Prepare basic dough for Yuletide Cookies (page 685). Divide into 3 parts. Leave 1 part white; add red coloring to 1 and green to the other. Now combine half of white with whole part of red, and other half of white with whole part of green. Work together with hands to simulate marble, but do not work it too thoroughly. White should be conspicuous. Roll red-and-white dough on a floured pastry cloth a little less than ¼ inch thick, and with a 1½-inch round cutter, cut out cookies. Roll green-and-white dough same thickness, and with a 2-inch *turkey cutter,* cut out cookies. Bake on a well-greased baking sheet at 300° F. about 15 to 20 minutes; then shut off heat, leave door open, and leave in oven to dry out about 15 more minutes. Release from pan as soon as they are done, and let cool on cake racks. When cold, pipe a tiny rosette (with No. 24 star tube) of yellow icing on side of turkey's head, and at once place a red cinnamon candy over icing to simulate eye. Put aside, and with same tube and green icing pipe a long thick strip of icing on each round cookie. Gently stand turkey upright in center of icing, and do not disturb for at least 15 minutes. Serve around a mold, or as desired.

Note. This is an excellent recipe for use with any Christmas cookie cutter, such as Santa Claus, reindeer, rabbit, angel child, etc. Some of cookies may be brushed with egg yolk combined with 1 tablespoon milk, then sprinkled with green and red sugar, colored decorettes, or chopped nutmeats. Red cinnamon candies may be used for eyes and buttons. It is better to roll dough about ¼ inch thick if using very large cutters and to lift cookies up from pastry cloth with a wide pancake turner to prevent breaking. Bake thicker cookies about 5 minutes longer.

Butterscotch Filled Wafers

Makes about 40

½ cup butter or margarine
⅓ cup soft brown sugar, solidly packed
1 large whole egg
¼ teaspoon maple flavoring and ¼ teaspoon vanilla flavoring

About 1¾ cups sifted all-purpose flour, combined with ¼ teaspoon baking soda and sifted together several times (keep dough soft)

With electric mixer or spoon beat butter or margarine, add sugar, a little at a time, then egg, and beat about 2 minutes. Add flavorings and last sifted flour and baking soda, beating only until smooth. Knead very gently a few seconds. If dough is very soft, add a little more flour, wrap in wax paper and keep in refrigerator for about ½ hour, or until firm enough to roll. Use at once if it can be handled. Roll small amount at a time on lightly floured pastry cloth, to about ⅛ inch thickness. Cut out with 1½-inch round cutter, pick up with spatula and place on lightly greased pan or silicone paper.

Brush half of wafers with slightly beaten egg white combined with

¼ teaspoon lemon juice or ⅛ teaspoon salt and sprinkle with shredded blanched almonds. Bake at 350° F. about 8 to 10 minutes in center of oven, or until delicately brown, watching closely toward end as they burn easily. Remove with spatula onto cake cooler or flat surface. When cold spread flat side of plain rounds with Roasted Nut Filling and place together with rest of rounds. Sprinkle very lightly with confectioners' sugar.

Roasted Nut Filling

1 cup of pecans	2 tablespoons butter
½ cup light brown sugar, solidly packed	1 egg yolk
2 tablespoons hot water	½ teaspoon vanilla

Spread pecans on a baking sheet and roast in a 300° F. oven for about 10 minutes, turning several times to prevent burning. *Then* put through a fine nut chopper or grater.

In a 1-quart saucepan, combine brown sugar, hot water, butter, and egg yolk. Cook over very low heat about 5 minutes after mixture begins to simmer, stirring *very gently*. Let stand until lukewarm; then add vanilla and grated pecans, to form a medium-thick paste of spreading consistency. If too thick, add a few drops of hot water. If too thin, add more grated pecans. This is a very delicious nut filling for cookies, tartlets, and coffee cakes. May be stored in refrigerator in a closed container for several months.

Almond or Pecan Chocolate Turtles

Makes about 40

Large blanched *untoasted* almonds, or medium or large pecan halves (do not use small)	Slightly beaten egg white (whole egg or yolk), combined with ¼ teaspoon lemon juice about ½ hour before using
Prepare basic dough for Butterscotch Filled Wafers (page 687)	

Place 3 almonds or pecans together on *ungreased (or better on silicone paper)* baking sheet. Form balls of dough with 1 level measuring teaspoon or little more. Dip ½ of ball into beaten egg white and place it on top of nutmeats, flattening slightly with fingers, pushing nutmeats together with left hand; or dip small end of nutmeats into whites and insert them on bottom part of dough rounds. Bake on *upper rack* of oven, at 350° F. about 12 to 15 minutes, watching very closely toward end to prevent nutmeats from burning. Upper part of cookies may appear slightly soft, but will become crisp when cold. Remove with spatula onto cake cooler and let stand until cold. Pour Chocolate Icing for Cookies and small

Cakes over entire surface of cookies and nutmeats. Let drain well. Pick up icing that drips off, add a few drops of hot water and re-use. Do not remove cookies for at least 30 minutes. When set, release with spatula or dinner knife.

Chocolate Icing for Cookies and Small Cakes

Covers about 12 to 15 cookies

1 tablespoon melted butter or margarine
2 tablespoons hot milk
½ teaspoon vanilla
About 1 cup sifted confectioners' sugar

1 ounce finely cut baking chocolate or dark sweet chocolate (melt chocolate over hot water, watching closely, stir, and remove as soon as melted)

Combine butter or margarine, hot milk, vanilla and sifted confectioners' sugar. Beat until smooth. *Last,* add melted chocolate and beat until thoroughly blended. Let stand until cool, covered, for at least 15 minutes. Now if icing appears too thin, add more sifted confectioners' sugar. If too thick add a few drops of hot water. With a spoon or small saucepan pour icing over cookies. Pick up icing that falls onto pan, add several drops of hot water if it is too thick, and re-use. Do not remove cookies from rack for at least 30 minutes, then release with spatula or dinner knife.

Butterscotch Pyramids

Makes about 30

1 recipe basic dough Butterscotch Filled Wafers (page 687)
1 recipe Roasted Nut Filling (page 688)

Glazed red cherries and citron leaves, or decorating icing
Confectioners' sugar

Roll dough about ⅛ inch in thickness. With a 2-inch, 1½-inch, and 1-inch cutter (may be made smaller), cut out an even number of rounds. With spatula transfer to lightly greased baking sheet, and bake at 350° F. about 8 to 10 minutes, watching very closely toward end. When done, remove with spatula to flat surface. When cold, spread with Roasted Nut Filling or cool melted sweet chocolate, starting with flat side of smallest round, and put together to simulate a pyramid. Sprinkle thickly with sifted confectioners' sugar. Place a dab of butterscotch filling underneath a ¼ of a red glazed cherry and garnish top of pyramid. Place tiny green citron leaves on each side of cherry. Or omit cherry and citron, and with No. 24 tube pipe icing rosette, scraping surface slightly with tip of tube, and with No. 65 pipe green leaves.

Chocolate Brownies

Makes about 30 squares

There are many versions of brownies. True brownies should be moist and of a chewy consistency. The important thing is not to overbeat the ingredients and not to overbake them. They keep well in refrigerator several weeks, if tightly covered.

½ cup butter or margarine
2 squares (2 ounces) unsweetened chocolate
2 eggs
1 cup granulated sugar
¾ cup sifted all-purpose flour, combined with ¼ teaspoon baking powder

⅛ teaspoon salt
½ cup, or more, broken pecan or walnut meats
1½ teaspoons vanilla
1 tablespoon corn syrup (optional)

Over very low heat melt butter or margarine and chocolate, stirring to prevent scorching. Let cool. In a medium-size bowl beat eggs with egg beater a few seconds (not too long). Add sugar a little at a time, and beat with spoon until smooth. Add flour combined with baking powder, and with spoon beat until well blended. Add cool chocolate preparation and mix well. Last, add salt, broken nutmeats, vanilla, and corn syrup. (Corn syrup may be omitted, but it gives brownies a nice chewy consistency.) Beat preparation only until well blended, and pour into an 8 × 8 × 2-inch pan) that has been greased with 2 teaspoons unsalted shortening and coated with flour. Bake in a preheated 350° F. oven about 35 minutes. When done, remove from oven and let stand in pan about 5 minutes; then carefully turn it out onto a cake cooler.

When cool, cover with Chocolate Cream Cheese Icing (page 622) or your favorite icing. Cut into squares and serve.

Continental Glossy Chocolate Cakes

Makes about 30

1 recipe basic dough Butterscotch Filled Wafers (page 687)
1 recipe Chocolate Icing for Cookies and Small Cakes (page 689)

Finely chopped or grated pistachio nuts

Roll basic dough for Butterscotch Filled Wafers about ¼ inch in thickness (thicker than for wafers). Cut out with 1½-inch cutter. Bake about 12 to 15 minutes at 350° F., watching closely that they do not burn. When done, transfer to flat surface. When cold, spread flat side of half with

Special Chocolate Filling for Cookies and Small Cakes. Put together with rest of rounds. Arrange on cake racks, leaving space between them, and cover with Chocolate Icing for Cookies and Small Cakes. Pick up icing that drips onto pan, add few drops of hot water, and re-use. Sprinkle center *only* of each cake with a pinch of finely chopped or grated pistachio nuts. Do not remove from rack for at least 30 minutes or longer.

Cakes filled with this chocolate custard should be kept in a cold place for not more than 2 days. If to be kept longer, use Roasted Nut Filling (page 688).

Special Chocolate Filling for Cookies and Small Cakes

2 ounces finely chopped unsweetened baking chocolate	1 tablespoon hot water
15-ounce can sweetened condensed milk	1 teaspoon vanilla

In upper part of double boiler melt the 2 ounces of chopped chocolate. Add 1 can of condensed milk and cook over boiling water for 6 or 7 minutes or longer, until it thickens, stirring constantly. Then remove from heat; add 1 tablespoon hot water and blend well. When lukewarm, add 1 teaspoon vanilla. Let stand until cold. If too thick a little more hot water may be added. Store in refrigerator.

This is an excellent filling for cookies and small cakes and holds up better than the standard chocolate fillings. It may also be used in pastry bag with large star tube for decorating and filling tartlets, etc., *but omit the tablespoon hot water.* Store cookies filled with this icing in refrigerator or cold place not more than 2 or 3 days.

Chocolate Log Cookies

Makes about 60 cookies

⅓ cup hot water added slowly to ⅓ cup unsweetened cocoa, or 2 ounces melted baking chocolate	Yolks of 2 eggs
	1 teaspoon vanilla
	¼ teaspoon baking soda
1 cup (½ pound) butter	About 3 cups sifted all-purpose flour
¾ cup granulated sugar	

In a 5-inch bowl add hot water slowly to cocoa (unless using chocolate) mix well and let cool. Cream butter thoroughly about 1 minute; add sugar gradually and beat well. Add egg yolks, 1 at a time, and continue beating until light, about 2 minutes. Add vanilla and cool cocoa mixture (or chocolate). Add combined baking soda and flour, a little at a time, to form dough that will go through plastic bag and No. 7 cookie star tube.

After adding about 2½ cups sifted flour, test dough in bag, and if it is too soft, add more flour gradually. As much as 3¼ cups of flour may be used. Always have bag *less than half filled*. Dough must be pressed out at once onto inverted side of slightly greased pans or it will toughen and be difficult to press out through bag. If dough is too stiff to squeeze through bag, add about a teaspoon or two of water or milk. Leave about 1½ inch space between each cookie and bake in a 350° F. oven 20 to 30 minutes, or until firm to the touch. Place on upper rack of oven last 5 minutes. When done, remove or loosen at once from pans, and place on cake racks. When cold, brush top only with warm corn syrup to impart glaze during cool dry weather. Let stand on cake coolers until glaze sets, then cover both ends of cookies with Chocolate Frosting and finely chopped green or plain nutmeats.

Chocolate Frosting for Log Cookies

Add 3 tablespoons hot water to 3 tablespoons unsweetened cocoa. Mix until smooth; add 2 tablespoons of very soft butter, 1 tablespoon milk, ½ teaspoon vanilla. Stir until smooth. Add sifted confectioners' sugar (about 2½ to 3 cups) gradually to form a medium-soft frosting that will not run.

Chocolate Mellow Bars

Serves 8

⅓ cup butter or margarine
⅓ cup sugar
2 eggs, separated
1 cup sifted flour, combined with ½ teaspoon baking powder
¼ teaspoon salt
½ teaspoon vanilla
1 ounce unsweetened chocolate, melted
½ cup chopped nutmeats
1 cup brown sugar, well packed

Cream butter or margarine and add sugar. Add egg yolks and beat 2 minutes. Add flour combined with baking powder and salt. Mix well; then add vanilla, chocolate and nuts. Spread dough ¼-inch deep in a greased 9 × 9 × 2-inch pan. Beat egg whites until stiff; then add brown sugar and blend well. Pour meringue over dough and bake about 30 minutes in a preheated 350° F. oven. When cool, cut into squares.

Walnut or Pecan Butter Crescents

Makes about 50 to 60 cookies

1 cup (½ pound) butter, medium consistency
1 cup sifted confectioners' sugar (do not use granulated)
About 2¼ cups sifted all-purpose flour (as much as 2¾ cups flour may be used)
½ pound pecans or walnuts (2 cups), chopped medium (not grated)

In an 8-inch bowl, cream butter about 1 minute; add sifted confectioners' sugar, a little at a time, then vanilla, and beat about 1 minute. Add sifted flour alternately with the chopped nutmeats, beating well after each addition. Mold at once with fingers into desired shapes, such as crescents, rounds, and ovals. Bake on very lightly greased inverted side of pan, about 20 to 25 minutes in a 350° F. oven until golden brown. Bake on upper rack last 5 minutes. When cold, dip into confectioners' sugar.

Chocolate-Chip Chewies

Serves 12

1 cup butter or margarine	½ teaspoon salt
½ cup granulated sugar	½ teaspoon baking soda
1 cup brown sugar	1 teaspoon baking powder
2 egg yolks	¾ cup chocolate chips
1 tablespoon cold water	2 egg whites
1 teaspoon vanilla	¾ cup chopped pecans
2 cups sifted flour	

Cream butter or margarine well with electric beater, add granulated sugar and ½ cup of the brown sugar, and beat until well blended. Add egg yolks, water, and vanilla, and beat 3 minutes at high speed. Add combined dry ingredients and beat until completely blended. Place preparation on a 10 × 15-inch cookie sheet that has been lightly greased with 1 teaspoon unsalted shortening. With damp hand, flatten uniformly on cookie sheet. Sprinkle chocolate chips on top. Beat egg whites until stiff. Then add remaining ½ cup brown sugar and beat about 1 minute. Spread this meringue evenly over entire top of batter. Last, sprinkle chopped pecans over meringue. Bake at 375° F. 35 to 40 minutes, or until top is brown. Cut into squares while still warm.

Vienna Pineapple Fingers

Makes about 24

¼ pound (½ cup) butter, medium consistency	¼ pound (½ cup) cream cheese, medium consistency
	1¼ cups sifted all-purpose flour

With electric mixer or spoon, beat butter and cheese only until smooth. Add flour and beat until well blended. Knead gently a few seconds on floured pastry cloth. Shape into a flat square that measures about 8 inches. Wrap in wax paper and store in refrigerator (on flat dish or pan) for at least 4 hours, or until firm. If dough is very stiff when ready to be rolled, let stand in room temperature about 10 minutes.

Cut dough into 4 uniform pieces. Roll each piece to measure *about* 9 × 9 *inch square*. With pastry wheel, trim off uneven edges. Cut each sheet into 6 uniform pieces. Place 1 scant teaspoon pineapple jam in center of each, spreading *lengthwise about 1 inch*. Fold over lengthwise to enclose filling, using spatula or knife. Then turn up edges about ½ inch and press down with spatula or knife. Brush each pastry lightly with melted butter and sprinkle with a scant ¼ teaspoon of Cinnamon-Sugar (prepared by combining ½ teaspoon cinnamon with 4 tablespoons granulated sugar and sifted together until well blended). Now with spatula pick up and place onto ungreased baking sheet or silicone paper. If pastries appear soft (or during warm weather) it is best to chill them for 15 minutes before baking. Then bake at 325° F. about 30 to 35 minutes, or until delicately brown and crisp. Watch closely that they do not burn. Lift out of pan carefully and let cool on racks. When cold, store in closed container. May be prepared several days in advance and are more delicious if reheated for about 5 minutes at 300° F. Serve lukewarm, but not hot.

Vienna Anchovy Fingers

Prepare dough for Vienna Pineapple Fingers and roll as above. Spread center of each with about 1 inch anchovy paste from tube. Fold over, etc. Sprinkle top with paprika. Bake, etc. Serve as hors d'oeuvres or with soups or salads.

Vienna Parmesan Fingers

Prepare dough for Vienna Pineapple Fingers and roll as above. Sprinkle center thickly with parmesan cheese. Fold, and transfer to baking sheet. Sprinkle top well with parmesan cheese and little paprika. Serve slightly warm with soups and salads.

Vienna Cream-Cheese Cookies

Cream together ½ pound cream cheese and ½ pound butter. Add gradually about 2½ cups sifted all-purpose flour, forming a smooth dough. Knead gently several minutes. Wrap in wax paper and keep in refrigerator overnight. Roll about ⅓ inch thick. Cut into desired shapes, make slight depression in center, and squeeze a dab of jam in center of each. Or cut into squares, wet edges with a little beaten egg, place a little jam on each, and turn them over, pinching ends well together so that they do not open in baking. Bake at 400° F. about 20 minutes depending on thickness and size. When they are cold, sprinkle with confectioners' sugar.

Horn of Plenty Cookies

Makes about 30

½ cup butter
¼ cup sifted granulated sugar
¼ cup sifted confectioners' sugar
1 egg yolk
1 teaspoon vanilla

1½ cups sifted all-purpose flour, combined with 1 tablespoon cocoa and sifted together until well blended
1 tablespoon milk

Cream butter, add sugars, little at a time, egg yolk and vanilla, and beat for about 1 minute at high speed with electric mixer. Add flour combined with cocoa, about ½ cup at a time, and a little of the milk at a time. Beat only until well blended. Now if dough feels sticky or very soft, add a little more flour (about ¼ cup) forming a medium dough that is not dry or too soft. Turn out onto lightly floured pastry cloth and knead gently a few seconds.

To Shape Horns of Plenty. Use slightly rounded measuring teaspoon dough for each. Shape to simulate thick small horns. With fingers curve horns gracefully and place them on 12 × 18 baking sheets greased with 1½ teaspoons shortening (1 teaspoon for smaller baking sheet). With back of dinner knife make marks on top of horns, and with finger form a slight wide opening on large end. When all horns are shaped, brush them with egg white that was combined with ⅛ teaspoon salt. (Beat white and salt a few seconds with fork and let it stand at least 15 minutes before using. Salt will thin out white of egg, making it easier for spreading.) Now fill in open end of horns with small pieces of candied green and yellow pineapple, red cherries, and broken pieces of pecan meats. Brush entire surface of filling with egg white. Bake at 300° F. about 25 to 30 minutes, then shut off heat and let dry in oven with door open for about 15 minutes, or longer.

Basket Cookies

Makes about 25

Prepare 1 recipe Horn of Plenty Cookies dough (above). Make handles with ½ measuring teaspoon basic dough, forming 4-inch ropes. Place them on greased baking sheet at least 1 inch apart forming horseshoe shapes, having open end of handles 1 inch wide. Now on floured pastry cloth with covered rolling pin, roll part of basic dough (not all at one time) about ⅛ inch in thickness (not too thin). With pastry wheel or knife cut dough in 1½-inch squares. With dinner knife mark top of each to simulate weave of basket. Brush handles very carefully with egg white. With spatula pick up basket part and place it over lower part of handle, pressing down gently.

With fingers taper lower part of basket slightly. Brush with egg white. May be filled same as Horns. They are also very attractive if tiny pink, yellow, and white rosettes are piped near open end of basket with No. 24 rosette tube, after they are baked and cold. Use tiny 65 leaf tube and green icing for leaves. Royal Icing (page 624) is best for this purpose. (Quick Butter-cream Icing, page 614, may be used). Bake baskets about 20 to 25 minutes at 300° F., then shut off heat and let dry out for about 15 more minutes with door open. Carefully release them from baking sheets when cool.

Pineapple-Shaped Cookies

Makes about 25

Prepare dough for Horn of Plenty Cookies (page 695), omitting the tablespoon cocoa. To ¼ of the recipe add a drop or 2 of green food coloring for leaves of pineapple. To rest of dough add a little yellow and red coloring (also about ½ teaspoon cocoa, optional). Blend well. Form leaves of pineapple with ½ measuring teaspoon of green dough. Shape it to simulate a small fan, and place on greased baking sheet. After all of leaves are formed, mark through them with dinner knife. Brush tops well with egg white combined with ⅛ teaspoon salt. With a very *slightly rounded* measuring teaspoon of orange dough form bodies of pineapple in long narrow ovals (as they will spread some in baking). Attach bodies to green part, overlapping well, and press down to prevent coming apart after they are baked. Pinch lower part of green attached to orange paste to make it very narrow. Brush entire surface with egg white. (Pineapples may be shaped with brown basic dough, then pipe 3 leaves on upper part with green Royal Icing using No. 65 leaf tube). Bake at 300° F. about 20 to 30 minutes, then shut off heat and let dry out in oven for about 15 minutes, but do not allow to discolor appreciably. Remove from oven and when luke-warm, release carefully with spatula or dinner knife and let cool on racks or flat surface.

Hazelnut Macaroons

Makes about 50

1 pound grated hazelnuts (filberts), put through a food grater (4 cups solidly packed after they are grated)	¼ teaspoon salt
	1 teaspoon vanilla or other flavoring
	1¾ cups egg whites
2½ cups granulated sugar	Another ¼ cup egg whites or extra grated nuts, only if necessary
2 cups sifted confectioners' sugar	

In a 4-quart saucepan combine all ingredients, and with a large wooden spoon stir well until moist. Cook over low heat, stirring very gently, continuously, for about 10 minutes, or until preparation is quite hot, but not over 175° F. Thermometer may be used for stirring after the first 5 minutes and temperature watched closely. When it reaches anywhere from 170° to 175° F., remove from heat, and pour into a bowl. Let stand in room temperature until cool, *stirring it gently several times, but not too often.*

When preparation is cool, place a small amount into a bag with plain opening of coupling and press out several rounds on a baking sheet covered with silicone paper. If your oven has strong bottom heat, it is better to use a double thickness of paper or double baking sheet to prevent overbrowning on bottom. With damp (not wet) tip of finger press down points of macaroons. If macaroon mixture appears too heavy, it is important to make test and add more whites. If it spreads out appreciably and does not form a point, add a little more grated nuts. After baking the sample of macaroons, let cool about 15 minutes, then release them from paper with a spatula or dinner knife. Now observe texture. If macaroons are hollow, add a little more grated nuts to rest of basic preparation; if too solid, add a little more egg whites. These macaroons are baked about 15 to 20 minutes in a preheated 350° F. oven, or until lightly colored and just firm to the touch but not too dry.

Note. As soon as macaroons are cold, they should be placed in boxes or other containers, tightly covered and overwrapped to prevent drying out. Then they may be stored for about 1 week in a cold place or refrigerator. May be frozen for 1 month. They may be left plain or filled with buttercream or jam after they are baked then put together. Follow specific directions given with each macaroon recipe.

Hazelnut Filled Macaroons

Spread flat sides of macaroons (or with finger make depression on flat sides) with Buttercream Icing (page 614) or jam. Put 2 together. Dip 1 end into lukewarm (about 110° F.) Special Glossy Chocolate Coating (page 698). Let dry for about 30 minutes, then serve, or store filled macaroons in covered box for several days—or longer, if refrigerated. They will become more tender but still crisp.

Hazelnut Logs

With bag and plain opening of coupling press out 3-inch ropes of Macaroon dough on silicone paper, leaving about an inch space between each one. Bake about 15 to 20 minutes as per general directions. When cold, dip part of 1 end into Special Glossy Chocolate Coating (page 698), or leave plain.

Jumbo Hazelnut Crescents

Pick up 1 slightly rounded tablespoon of basic macaroon dough, and roll it gently into coarsely chopped or sliced hazelnuts. Form a 4-inch rope and then shape into crescent. Place on silicone paper and bake 20 to 25 minutes, or until just firm to the touch. When cold, dip about 1 inch of both ends into Special Glossy Chocolate Coating (below), or leave plain.

Hazelnut Mushrooms

Prepare various size round macaroons with part of basic preparation. Bake according to general directions. To rest of preparation *add enough more grated or chopped nuts to form a stiff mixture* that will hold its shape. With hands form various size cones to simulate stems of mushrooms, kind of long, and wide at bottom. Place them upright on silicone paper, and bake about 20 to 25 minutes, or until firm to the touch. When cold, dip flat ends about ⅛ inch up into Special Glossy Chocolate Coating (below). Make depression on flat side of round macaroons, and dip part way into chocolate coating. Place round macaroons on top of stems and let stand for about 30 minutes to dry in a cool room. Or omit glossy coating, and spread and fill underpart of cap with Buttercream Icing (page 614)) or jam, and put together in same way. May be sprinkled lightly with cocoa.

Special Glossy Chocolate Coating for Cookies and Small Cakes

½ pound dipping chocolate (or other sweet chocolate), cut in small pieces

¼ cup shortening (do not use butter or margarine)

Place chocolate and shortening in upper part of double boiler over cool water, and bring water to a boil. Shut off heat, and at once beat chocolate and shortening until completely melted and quite hot, but not over 150° F. if possible. Remove from hot water and pour coating into a small shallow heatproof dish. Let stand until temperature drops to 110° to 125° F. For a thin coating, have temperature about 125° F.; for thicker coating about 110° F. If temperature of coating drops below 100° F. it will be less glossy. If coating cools during dipping process, place heatproof dish in a pan of hot water and stir until warm.

Macaroon cookies are best dipped at about 110° F. After cookies or cakes are dipped or covered with this special coating, shake off surplus coating, and scrape cookies gently against edge of dish. Place them on wax paper and let remain in a cool room (below 70° F. if possible) for at least 30 minutes before serving. If cookies or cakes are to be stored after they are iced, allow them to remain in a cool room at least 1 hour, then place them in single layers in flat boxes. Cover tightly, and store in a cool place or refrigerator. It is best not to place more than 1 layer in each box. If they have been refrigerated, remove and let stand in room temperature covered for at least an hour before serving. This will help to retain gloss.

Butter or margarine cannot be used successfully in this coating because of the moisture content unless they are melted and only top part is used and measured after it is removed. Sediment or moisture will cause curdling and dullness.

Any leftover coating may be left right in glass dish, covered tightly and stored in refrigerator or a cold place for several weeks. Then it may be placed in a pan of simmering water and stirred gently until of proper temperature.

Oriental Almond Cookies

Makes about 40

1 cup shortening (half butter may be used)

½ cup granulated sugar *and* ½ cup brown sugar, solidly packed

1 large whole egg, slightly beaten and combined with 2 table-spoons water

1½ teaspoons almond extract and ½ teaspoon vanilla

2½ cups sifted all-purpose flour, combined with 1 teaspoon baking soda and ½ teaspoon salt, sifted together several times

About 1 cup blanched almonds, left whole or split in 2 lengthwise (to blanch almonds drop into boiling water and simmer 2 minutes; let cool slightly, then with fingers remove skins)

1 egg yolk, combined with 1 teaspoon water and slightly beaten

With electric mixer or heavy spoon beat shortening for several minutes. Add sugars, little at a time, and continue to beat until well blended. Now add the whole egg combined with the 2 tablespoons water and beat 3 or 4 minutes, or until mixture appears light. Add extracts, and last dry ingredients, about ½ cup at a time, and beat after each addition only until smooth. This is a soft dough, but if too soft, add ¼ cup more flour. Chill for at least 1 hour.

In palm of hands form *very smooth* balls with 1 level tablespoon of dough; flatten them slightly, place on lightly greased baking sheet, about 1½ inches apart. Brush tops with beaten yolk mixture and place a whole or split almond in center of each, pressing down gently. For plain cookies, omit almonds. Bake cookies at 325° F., about 25 to 30 minutes, or until golden brown, watching closely last few minutes to prevent burning. Remove those that are done if necessary, and continue to bake rest. Release cookies from baking sheet with a spatula or dinner knife while still warm, and place them on cake coolers or any flat surface. When cold, store in a covered container until ready to be served. Delicious served with oriental food.

Lady Windermere's Fan Cookies

Makes about 40

¾ cup butter or margarine, medium consistency
½ cup soft brown sugar, solidly packed
2 cups sifted all-purpose flour
2 tablespoons cool milk

1 egg yolk, slightly beaten and combined with 1 tablespoon water
Dark or light sweet melted chocolate
Pistachio nuts, finely chopped or put through nut grater

Cream butter or margarine well, add sugar and beat about 1 or 2 minutes. Add flour and the 2 tablespoons milk, little at a time, and beat only until smooth. Knead dough gently a few seconds. If too soft add little more flour. May be chilled. Roll on lightly floured pastry cloth about ¼ inch thick, and cut out with a 3-inch round fluted cutter. Cut each round into 4 wedges, and crease with dull edge of knife to represent folds of fan. Transfer with spatula to lightly greased baking sheet or silicone paper. With a tiny camel's hair paint brush, brush each with egg yolk combined with water. Bake at 325° F. about 15 to 20 minutes, or until very lightly colored, but not dark. Remove with spatula. When cold, dip small ends into cool melted sweet chocolate, draining well, then into chopped pistachio nuts. Place on wax paper in a cool place until chocolate sets.

Valentine Tartlets

Makes about 24

Prepare Lady Windemere's Fan dough. Roll about ¼ inch (or thicker). With a 2-inch cutter, cut out rounds. From half, cut out centers with a tiny heart cutter (other style cutters may be used). Transfer to very lightly greased baking sheet or silicone paper. Brush cut-out rounds very lightly with slightly beaten egg white or yolk combined with water, using tiny camel's hair paint brush. Sprinkle each with a little pistachio nuts. Bake 15 to 20 minutes at 325° F., watching closely that they do not become too dark. Bake solid rounds little longer. When done, remove with spatula and let cool. When cold, pour a small mound of red Apricot Glaze in center only of solid rounds. Sprinkle cut-out rounds with very little confectioner's sugar and place over solid rounds. May be prepared several days in advance and stored in covered containers to prevent drying out of jam.

Apricot Glaze or Filling for Cookies, Tartlets, Etc.

½ cup sieved apricot or peach jam or preserves, measured after it has been put through sieve

1 tablespoon cornstarch, combined with ⅓ cup cool water, mixed until smooth

Combine ingredients and cook over moderate heat, stirring continuously until smooth and thick, about 5 minutes after it begins to simmer. Let cool. If too thick when cool, add a few drops of water. *For red glaze,* add a little red food coloring and blend thoroughly.

Raspberry Hearts

Bake tiny hearts cut out from Valentine Tartlets. Brush lightly with beaten egg and sprinkle center of each with a pinch of pistachio nuts. Bake 10 to 12 minutes at 325° F., watching closely that they do not burn. When cold, put 2 together with smooth red jam or melted chocolate. Sprinkle lightly with confectioners' sugar.

Basic Short Pecan Dough

Makes about 24

½ cup butter or margarine
⅓ cup brown sugar, solidly packed
2 yolks of eggs
½ teaspoon vanilla

½ cup grated pecans, solidly packed
About 1¼ to 1½ cups sifted all-purpose flour, to form a medium dough, not too soft, and not dry

Beat butter or margarine about ½ minute; add sugar, and beat another ½ minute, then add yolks and beat another ½ minute. Now add vanilla, and grated nuts alternately with the flour, small amount at a time, and beat only until smooth. Do not overbeat at any time. Turn dough out onto a lightly floured cloth and knead gently a few seconds. Chill dough if necessary for a few minutes, or use at once.

Sonia's Thimble Cookies

Makes about 25 to 30

½ cup butter, medium consistency
¼ cup soft brown sugar
1 egg yolk
1 cup sifted all-purpose flour
1 egg white, slightly beaten, com-

bined with ¼ teaspoon lemon juice ½ hour before using (for dipping)
About ½ cup finely chopped nuts
Jelly or smooth jam

Cream butter, add sugar and beat well, then add yolk and beat about 1 minute. Blend in flour until dough is smooth. Chill in refrigerator for about 1 hour if dough is too soft to handle. Form balls with ½ tablespoon dough. Dip ½ of each ball into beaten egg white, then into finely chopped nutmeats. Place with nut side up on greased baking sheet or, better, on silicone paper and with thimble make a depression in center of each. Bake at 300° F. in center rack about 10 minutes. Remove from oven and with thimble press centers down again. Continue to bake in center of oven for about 15 more minutes at 300° F. If not brown, raise heat to 350° F. and bake on upper rack about 5 more minutes. Watch closely. When cookies are cold, with tip of teaspoon or pastry bag and No. 10 tube, fill centers with smooth jam or jelly. May be sprinkled very lightly with sifted confectioners' sugar.

Continental Cherry Surprise Macaroons

Roll Basic Short Pecan Dough (page 701) about ¼ inch in thickness. With a round scalloped 2-inch cutter, cut dough. Place on each a half red or green maraschino cherry, flat side down, that has been well drained and dried on a towel. Now with bag and plain opening of coupling pipe a thick bulb of Hazelnut Macaroon preparation (page 696) over cherry to cover it completely. Bake on ungreased baking sheet about 15 to 20 minutes at 350° F., but watch closely last few minutes to prevent over-browning. Very delicious and unusual.

Continental Raspberry Macaroon Rings

Follow directions for Cherry Surprise Macaroons, omitting cherry. With bag and No. 10 plain decorating tube, pipe a ring of Hazelnut Macaroon preparation (page 696) on top edge of each basic cookie, leaving ⅛ inch space. Bake about 15 to 20 minutes at 350° F. When cool, fill opening with raspberry jam or any other filling.

Hazelnut Rosette Cookies

Makes about 40

1 cup butter (half margarine may be used)
¾ cup sifted granulated sugar
1 egg yolk
¼ teaspoon salt (if using unsalted shortening)

½ teaspoon vanilla or other extract (optional)
About 2¼ cups sifted all-purpose flour
½ cup hazelnuts (filberts), first measured, then put through a food grater

In an 8-inch bowl beat butter until creamy. Add sugar, a little at a time, and beat well. Now add egg yolk, salt, and extract, and beat about 2 minutes. Last, add flour, about ½ cup at a time, with grated nutmeats, a little at a time. Before adding last of flour, test dough by placing it in bag with

No. 7 large star cookie tube. Have bag a little less than half filled. Squeeze out large rosettes, and if dough is soft, add rest of flour. If dough becomes too difficult to squeeze out toward end, add a few drops water and mix well. Bake on ungreased baking sheets at 350° F. about 15 to 20 minutes, or until delicately colored but not too dark. Remove from oven, and let remain on baking sheets until lukewarm; then carefully release them with a spatula. Store in a covered container when cold. Cookies may be left plain and sprinkled with confectioners' sugar before serving, or tops may be garnished with strips of green citron and pieces of red cherry before they are baked. May be shaped into balls in palms of hand.

Grandma's Old-Fashioned Cookies

Makes about 60 to 70

About 1 cup egg yolks (bit more or less), beaten with electric mixer about 3 minutes
1¼ cups butter or margarine, medium consistency
1¼ cups sifted granulated sugar
1¼ teaspoons vanilla or lemon extract

About 4½ cups sifted all-purpose flour, or enough to form a medium dough, that does not stick to hands or pastry cloth
2 teaspoons double-acting baking powder

Beat yolks in a medium-size bowl and put aside. Now with electric mixer beat butter or margarine about 1 minute; add sugar a little at a time and continue to beat until smooth, about 1 more minute. Add beaten yolks, a little at a time, and beat about 2 minutes after all yolks have been added. Add extract. Now sift flour and baking powder together 2 or 3 times, and add it, about ½ cup at a time, to the yolk mixture, beating after each addition until smooth. When dough becomes too stiff to beat with mixer, turn it out onto a floured pastry cloth, and knead gently about 1 minute, adding more flour if necessary to prevent stickiness. Test a small amount of dough by forming a roll on floured pastry cloth. If it does not stick and holds its shape enough flour has been added. Add little more flour if needed.

To shape cookies, use ½ tablespoon of dough for each, and with hand roll gently on lightly floured pastry cloth, forming 5-inch narrow ovals. Shape ovals into the letters 6, 8, and 9, or as desired. Place on lightly greased baking sheet. May be brushed with yolk combined with 1 tablespoon milk, and tops sprinkled with shredded almonds. Bake at 350° F. about 20 minutes, or until delicately colored, not too brown. When cool, cookies may be rolled in sifted confectioners' sugar. Do not sugar them until you are ready to serve. May be stored in a closed container for several weeks. May be frozen for several months.

Recipe may be cut in half.

Pinwheel Cookies

Makes about 40

¾ cup soft butter (or half butter and
    half margarine)
½ cup sifted granulated sugar
½ cup sifted confectioners' sugar

1 whole egg
1 teaspoon vanilla
About 2½ cups sifted all-purpose flour

Cream butter thoroughly; add sugars, a little at a time, then egg. Beat well until very light. Add vanilla. Last, add flour, a small amount at a time. Dough should not be sticky or heavy. Divide dough into 3 portions. Add yellow coloring to one part, green to one and red to third part. Work colorings into doughs with a fork until thoroughly blended, and if necessary, knead dough gently a few seconds until there are no streaks.

Use ¼ cup of each dough. With a covered rolling pin, roll each portion on a sheet of heavy wax paper to measure about 4 inches wide and 10 inches long. Put the 3 doughs together, pat gently with hand, and press around ends with fingertips. Cut off uneven parts, and roll from long end. Wrap tightly in wax paper, and keep in refrigerator until firm. It may be kept in freezing compartment, in which case it will be ready to slice in about 30 minutes.

When roll is firm, cut crosswise into ¼-inch slices. Place on a lightly greased baking sheet about 1 inch apart. Bake at 325° F. about 15 minutes; then shut off heat and allow cookies to remain in oven, with door slightly open, about 10 more minutes. Watch closely toward end, as they lose their attractive colors if overbaked.

Quick Checkerboard

Using dough for Pinwheel Cookies, form 4 uniform narrow rolls. Put together. Wrap in wax paper and keep in refrigerator until firm. Proceed as for Pinwheel Cookies.

Marble Cookies

Work leftover pieces of dough from Pinwheel Cookies until smooth, and roll on wax paper. Wrap tightly and chill. Bake according to directions above.

Solid Centers

Using dough for Pinwheel Cookies, roll ¼ cup dough 4 inches wide and 10 inches long. With ½ cup of contrasting dough form a roll that measures about 1 inch wide and 10 inches long. Place on first dough and enclose roll. Wrap tightly in wax paper and keep in refrigerator until firm. Proceed as above.

Louise's Cinnamon Snaps

Makes about 30 cookies

½ cup butter or margarine	1½ cups sifted all-purpose flour
½ cup granulated sugar	1 teaspoon baking soda
1 whole egg	1 teaspoon cinnamon
1 tablespoon molasses	¼ teaspoon salt

Cream butter or margarine, add sugar and egg, and beat several minutes until light. Add molasses and blend well. Combine all dry ingredients and sift twice; add to butter mixture, a little at a time, and beat until smooth. Pick up level ½ tablespoon at a time. Drop into granulated sugar, and form balls. Place on well greased inverted side of a baking sheet, at least 2½ inches apart, to prevent running together. Bake at 350° F. about 25 minutes, or until brown but not burned. These cookies require close watching toward end. Remove cookies on outer edges if they are done, and continue to bake the rest. Shut off heat and allow cookies to remain in oven with door slightly open. This will make cookies crisp. When done, remove at once with a spatula to prevent sticking to pan. Let cool before storing.

If cookies are not crisp throughout when they are cold, they were insufficiently baked.

Rye Flour Dainty Wafer Cookies

Makes about 24

¾ cup butter	bined and sifted with 1 cup sifted
½ cup granulated sugar, combined	rye flour
with ¼ teaspoon cinnamon	½ teaspoon baking powder
1 cup sifted all-purpose flour, com-	

Cream butter, add sugar and cinnamon, and beat well. Add flours combined with baking powder, forming a medium dough. If dough appears too moist, add a little more flour; if it appears too dry as flour is being added, do not use all the flour. Chill dough, wrapped in wax paper, about 30 minutes. Roll about ⅛ inch thick. With a 2-inch cutter, cut out rounds. From one end cut a hole toward top with a very small cutter (end of a decorating tube may be used). Pierce with a fork on opposite end 3 or 4 times. Pick up with a spatula and transfer to a lightly greased baking sheet. Bake at 325° F. about 10 minutes, or until delicately brown. Watch closely toward end, as these wafers burn easily. Remove with a spatula to prevent breaking. When they are cold, sprinkle with confectioners' sugar. This is a very delicate and delicious wafer.

Snowball Butter Cookies

Makes 50 to 60

1 cup (½ pound) butter	½ teaspoon liquid food coloring (yellow, red, or green)
¼ cup sifted confectioners' sugar	
1 teaspoon vanilla	3¼ cups sifted all-purpose flour

Let butter stand in room temperature 30 minutes. Cream butter with electric beater until creamy, add sugar, and beat well. Add vanilla and food coloring; blend well. Add flour about ½ cup at a time and beat until smooth. Shape into balls, using about 1 tablespoon dough for each snowball. Place on inverted side of a lightly greased 12 × 18-inch baking sheet, leaving about 1½-inch spaces between them.

Bake in a 350° F. preheated oven about 30 minutes. When done and still hot, roll in confectioners' sugar. Keep in an airtight cookie jar or other container until cold. Re-roll in confectioners' sugar before serving.

Banana Oatmeal Cookies

Makes about 36 to 40 cookies

1½ cups sifted all-purpose flour	¾ cup cold shortening
1 cup granulated sugar	1 whole egg, well beaten
½ teaspoon baking soda	1 cup mashed ripe bananas
1 teaspoon salt	1¾ cups rolled quick oats
¼ teaspoon nutmeg	½ cup chopped nuts
¾ teaspoon cinnamon	

Sift together flour, sugar, soda, salt, nutmeg, and cinnamon into a mixing bowl. Cut in cold shortening until mixture looks like fine meal. Add well-beaten egg, bananas, rolled oats, and nuts. Beat until thoroughly blended. Drop by teaspoonfuls, about 1½ inches apart, onto a very lightly greased cookie sheet. Bake at 400° F. in a preheated oven about 12 to 15 minutes, or until done. Remove from cookie sheet immediately.

Brown Sugar Cookies

Makes about 40

1 cup butter or margarine	½ teaspoon vanilla
½ cup brown sugar, solidly packed	2⅓ cups sifted all-purpose flour, combined with ½ teaspoon baking soda
1 egg yolk	
½ cup finely chopped nuts (optional)	

Cream butter or margarine well, add sugar a little at a time, then the egg yolk. Beat until light. Add the nuts and mix thoroughly. Add vanilla and, last, the flour and baking soda, little at a time. Beat only until smooth. Place dough in a bag with plain opening of coupling, having bag less than half filled. Press 1-inch balls onto *lightly* greased pan, spacing balls about 1 inch apart. Bake at 350° F. for about 15 to 20 minutes, or until *delicately* brown. Watch toward end of baking, as they burn very quickly. When done, remove from oven and let stand until cool.

For special occasions these cookies are more attractive if topped with half pecan or walnut meat and if the top of each is brushed with slightly beaten egg white after nut is on. Bake as above. When they are cold they may be sprinkled with sifted confectioners' sugar.

Pecan-Date Cookies

Makes about 30

¾ cup butter or margarine	About 2 cups sifted all-purpose flour
⅔ cup sifted confectioners' sugar	½ cup fine-chopped dates
1½ teaspoons vanilla	½ cup fine-chopped pecan meats
2 tablespoons milk or cream	Additional sifted confectioners' sugar

With electric mixer beat butter or margarine about 3 minutes until light. Add sugar and continue to beat until smooth. Add vanilla and milk or cream, and blend well. Now add about ½ of flour, little at a time, then chopped dates and nuts. Add rest of flour, forming a firm dough that does not stick to hand. Pick up 1 level tablespoon at a time and form smooth balls. Place on a very lightly greased baking sheet, *about 2 inches apart*, and bake at 300° F. about 25 to 30 minutes, or until lightly colored but not brown. Let cool. Just before serving, roll in sifted confectioners' sugar, and arrange attractively on serving platter, piling them up high.

Apricot or Peach Meringue Sticks

Makes about 24

⅔ cup butter	(put through a food mill or
½ cup granulated sugar	strainer if lumpy)
1 large whole egg	2 egg whites
½ teaspoon vanilla	½ cup granulated sugar
About 2 cups sifted flour, combined	1 tablespoon flour
with ¼ teaspoon baking soda	1 cup nuts, chopped medium-fine
⅔ cup smooth apricot or peach jam	

Cream butter, add sugar, and beat about 1 minute. Add egg and beat another minute. Add vanilla, then flour a little at a time, and continue to beat only until smooth. Dough should be soft but not sticky. If sticky, add a very little more flour. Spread dough in a lightly greased 10 × 14-inch baking sheet. Flatten by placing wax paper over dough and pressing another baking sheet over it or press down with palms of hands. Remove upper sheet and paper, and spread jam over entire surface of dough as evenly as possible. Bake at 400° F. about 15 minutes.

About 5 minutes before baking time is up, beat egg whites until they cling to bowl; then add ½ cup granulated sugar, a little at a time, and 1 tablespoon flour. Beat until well blended, about 1 minute. Fold nuts into meringue. After dough has baked 15 minutes, remove from oven and quickly spread meringue over entire surface. Continue to bake another 15 minutes at 400° F., or until meringue is brown. Remove, and when mixture is cool, cut into sticks about 1 inch wide and 3 inches long. Red raspberry or blackberry jam may be used instead of apricot or peach.

Czechoslovakian Pastry Boats

Makes about 35

1 cup sifted all-purpose flour	½ cup soft butter or margarine
⅛ teaspoon, or more, cinnamon	½ teaspoon lemon extract
1 cup sifted confectioners' sugar	About 2 or 3 teaspoons cool water (if
¼ teaspoon salt	needed)
½ cup pecan meats, first measured, then put through fine nut grater (not chopped)	

Combine first 4 dry ingredients, and sift them into an 8-inch bowl. Add grated nutmeats, and with hands blend well. Now add the soft butter or margarine and extract, and with fingers mix ingredients until moist. If preparation appears dry, add 2 or 3 teaspoons of water, little at a time, until pastry holds its shape when pressed in hand.

Spread ⅔ (or little more) level standard measuring tablespoon of pastry smoothly into inside of lightly greased boat molds that measure about 3½ inches long, making a slight cavity. Bake in a preheated 325° F. oven about 20 to 25 minutes, or until golden brown, but not too dark. Remove those that are done before time is up, if necessary, to prevent overbaking. Let boats cool on molds about 15 minutes, then release them carefully, inserting point of paring knife in one end if necessary.

To Decorate Boats. These pastries are very rich and delectable and do not require fillings. Simply sprinkle them lightly (with shaker) with sifted confectioners' sugar, *then* with blue or green Buttercream Icing (page 614) and No. 30 star tube pipe a long oval scroll in each pastry. Insert a sail made of sugar wafer in center, and with No. 24 or 27 star tube pipe a pink rosette on each side of sail, and blue or green leaves with No.

65 or 67 tube. Arrange on flat platter with doily, alone, or with other small cakes or cookies.

Assorted Small Czechoslovakian Pastry Forms

Reduce amount of sugar in above recipe to ¾ cup. Mix as per general directions. Spread inside of lightly greased continental small molds with basic pastry preparation, making a slight depression. Bake in a 325° F. oven about 20 minutes.

To Decorate. Place on platter with open end down; sprinkle with confectioners' sugar (with shaker). For chicks, bunnies, etc., make eyes with No. 24 star tube, and pipe tiny leaves on each side of rosette. Rest of forms may be decorated in same way, or as desired.

Note. A small amount of fruit paste, jam, or sweet chocolate may be spread in cavities of these pastries, and 2 of same size and shape put together. May be made several weeks in advance if refrigerated, or kept in cold place, or may be frozen.

Party-Style Leaf Cookies

Makes about 60 cookies

⅓ cup butter (best to use half white shortening)	1 teaspoon lemon extract or other flavoring
¾ cup sifted confectioners' sugar	1¼ cups sifted all-purpose flour
2 tablespoons granulated sugar	About ⅓ cup milk
1 whole egg	

Cream butter, add sugars little at a time, then egg, and beat about 2 minutes. Add flavoring. Then add flour, a little at a time, alternately with milk, and beat after each addition *only* until smooth. Add a little green coloring if desired. Grease inverted side of a medium-size baking sheet with 1 teaspoon unsalted shortening. Lay leaf stencil on baking sheet and spread dough over it with a spatula. Remove excess dough, and lift spatula upward off pan. Repeat until entire pan is covered. Sprinkle with red, green, and yellow sugar, or leave plain if it is to be coated with chocolate. Bake in a 300° F. oven about 12 to 15 minutes, or until edges are lightly browned, but watch closely the last minute or two to prevent overbrowning. Remove from oven, lift off with a pancake turner, and let cool on cake racks or any other flat surface.

To Coat with Chocolate. Cut as fine as possible about ¼ pound (4 squares) semisweet dark chocolate. Place it over warm water, about 120° F., and let stand until chocolate begins to melt. Remove from warm water before chocolate is fully melted, and stir well until smooth. Temperature of melted chocolate must not exceed 92° F., to maintain glossiness on cookies. Let melted chocolate stand a few minutes until cool; then with an artist's brush paint green leaves attractively. *Keep melted chocolate over lukewarm water while coating cookies.* Let coated cookies remain in a cool room, not over 70° F., a few minutes, or refrigerate 5 minutes.

These dainty cookies are very delicious and attractive for special occasions. Store them in a box, with wax paper between layers. Keep in refrigerator during humid weather. They may be recrisped in a 300° F. oven about 4 or 5 minutes. Let cool. Those coated with chocolate cannot be put back into oven.

Peanut Butter Cookies

Makes about 30

½ cup butter or margarine
½ cup granulated sugar
¼ cup brown sugar, solidly packed
½ cup moist best-quality peanut butter
1 whole egg
½ teaspoon vanilla

1½ cups sifted all-purpose flour, combined with ½ teaspoon baking soda
⅛ teaspoon salt
Whole large roasted peanuts (optional)

Cream butter, add sugars, a little at a time, then peanut butter. Beat until thoroughly blended. Add egg, and beat until light. Add vanilla. Last, add combined flour, baking soda, and salt, a small amount at a time. Beat after each addition only until smooth. Measure about 1 teaspoon dough for each cookie, and shape with hands into small balls. Place about 1 inch apart on a very lightly greased baking sheet. Mark with a fork *or brush with beaten egg and place a whole peanut on each.* Bake about 15 to 20 minutes at 350° F., or until they are delicately brown. Watch closely last few minutes, as they burn very easily. These cookies may be sprinkled with sifted confectioners' sugar.

Coconut Macaroon Cookies—No. 1

Makes about 30 macaroons

¾ cup granulated sugar
3 tablespoons white corn syrup
¾ cup egg whites

2¼ cupfuls macaroon coconut
¼ cup sifted all-purpose flour

Combine above ingredients in a 2-quart saucepan and beat until moist. Keep over moderate heat until very hot, about 150° F., stirring continuously. Remove from heat, add ¾ teaspoon vanilla and ¼ teaspoon salt. Let mixture stand in refrigerator for at least 4 hours then pick up about

1 tablespoonful at a time and shape to simulate strawberries, pears, or other cookies, dampening hands occasionally. If preparation is too soft, add little more coconut.

Coconut Macaroon Strawberries

Add a little red coloring to ⅔ cup cold dough Coconut Macaroon Cookies No. 1 (above)

Add green coloring to rest of dough Citron strips cut at least 1 inch long for stems, then colored green

Form uniform-size balls with about 1 scant tablespoon red coconut macaroon mixture, then shape them to simulate strawberries. With ½ teaspoon of the green preparation form tiny balls, then flatten, and place them on thick round part of strawberries for hulls. Insert strips of citron for stems. Bake on a 12 × 18 baking sheet greased with 1 tablespoon unsalted shortening and coated with flour, or, better, covered with silicone paper, in a 350° F. oven about 15 minutes, but do not allow cookies to discolor. Remove from oven and with spatula release cookies from hot pan at once to prevent sticking. Let cool on wax paper, or on cake coolers.

Coconut Macaroon Cookies—No. 2

Makes about 25 macaroons

⅔ cup egg whites
1 cup sifted granulated sugar
2½ cups dry commercial macaroon coconut
1 tablespoon cornstarch

⅛ teaspoon salt
1 teaspoon vanilla
2 tablespoons white corn syrup, then add 1 more tablespoon *if too dry*

In a 2-quart saucepan combine all ingredients and mix thoroughly until very moist. Place over moderate heat and allow mixture to become hot (about 150° F.), stirring it continuously, about 5 minutes. Remove from heat, let cool for about ½ hour. Place mixture into a pastry bag with large No. 7 star cookie tube. Press out thick rosettes that measure about 1½ inches wide and 1¼ inches high, on a 12 × 18 baking sheet that has been greased with 1 tablespoon shortening and sprinkled with flour, shaking off excess flour, or better on silicone paper. Decorate top of each with ¼ or ½ glacéed red cherry and two green citron leaves, *or leave plain.* Bake in a 350° F. oven about 18 to 20 minutes or until golden brown. When done, remove from oven, and at once release macaroons from baking sheet with a pancake turner or a wide spatula. Place them on wax paper or cake racks until cold. To impart glaze tops may be brushed with warm corn syrup several hours before serving during dry weather.

Coconut Macaroon Pears

Add little yellow coloring to ¾ cup cold dough Coconut Macaroon Cookies No. 1 (page 710)
Add several drops of green to rest of preparation

Citron strips cut 1 inch long for stems, then colored green
Small currants, or raisins cut in small pieces and rolled to simulate balls
Commercial red sugar

Form uniform-size balls with about 1 scant tablespoon yellow coconut mixture, then shape to simulate pears. Form tiny ovals with ¼ teaspoon green, then flatten to simulate leaves, and place on small end of pears. Insert citron strips for stems. Place small currant on rounded end, and sprinkle a little red sugar on each. Bake on 12 × 18 baking sheet greased with 1 tablespoon unsalted shortening and coated with flour, or cover with silicone paper, in a 350° F. oven for about 15 minutes, but do not allow cookies to discolor. Remove from oven, and with spatula release cookies from hot pan at once to prevent sticking. Let cool on wax paper, or cake coolers.

Macaroon Swans

Makes about 50

1 pound commercial almond paste
½ to ⅔ cup unbeaten egg whites
⅔ cup sifted granulated sugar

⅔ cup sifted confectioners' sugar
½ teaspoon extract

Cut almond paste in small pieces. Add only ½ cup of the unbeaten egg whites to start with, little at a time, and with electric mixer beat until smooth. Add sugars, little at a time, then extract, and a drop or 2 of yellow food coloring. Beat well for a few seconds. If preparation appears the least bit lumpy, put it through a food mill or strainer. Now test preparation by pressing out 2 or 3 rounds onto baking sheet. It contains enough egg whites if a point is raised and does not flatten out. If a very thick long point is raised, add little more egg whites, but seldom more than ⅔ cup for entire recipe provided almond paste is not too dry. If almond paste can has been opened, store paste in wax paper, then in small plastic bag, and refrigerate. Remove from refrigerator several hours in advance, and if it appears too dry and firm, brush it well with warm water, place in upper part of double boiler, cover, and allow water underneath to boil vigorously for about 10 to 15 minutes, or until paste has softened. Now combine it at once with other ingredients.

To Shape Swans. Cover baking sheet with silicone paper (or grease medium-size baking sheet with 1 teaspoon unsalted shortening and coat with flour; shake off loose flour). Place a pointed piece of blanched almond on pan. With left hand hold almond in place, then with pastry bag and No. 10 plain decorating tube, press out head on almond, and continue to press graceful long neck, increasing pressure to form body, and decreasing pressure toward end to form pointed tail end. Make eyes with very tiny pieces of currants or raisins, rolled in fingers to form balls. *Or eyes may be made with tip of toothpick dipped into dark melted baking chocolate (or cocoa and bit of water)* after swans are baked and lukewarm. Insert a whole split blanched almond into thick part of body with rounded end of almond down. Bake in 300° F. oven about 25 to 30 minutes, or until delicately colored but not too brown. Now shut off heat, and let dry for about 15 minutes in oven with door partly open. Remove from oven, let stand on pans about 10 minutes, or until lukewarm, then release them carefully with a spatula or dinner knife to prevent breaking. With tiny artist's brush tint beak, wing, and top of head lightly with red coloring.

Blanched Almonds for Swans

Drop almonds with skins on into hot water and let simmer about 5 minutes. Drain and pour cold water over almonds. Between thumb and forefinger remove skins. While almonds are still very moist, split them lengthwise in 2 halves, inserting point of paring knife through rounded end. With knife cut some of these split almonds in narrow point pieces for beaks. Each split almond will make 2 or 3 beaks, cut lengthwise. Use whole split almond for wings, as suggested above.

Macaroon Grapes

Makes about 40

To ½ cup recipe for Macaroon Swans add little green food coloring. With rest of dough form foundations with No. 10 plain tube. With same tube and basic preparation pipe grapes on foundation. With same No. 10 tube and green preparation pipe stem about 1 inch long, and with green paste and No. 70 leaf tube, pipe a large wide leaf on rounded part of grapes. Before using left tube, open tip end well with dinner knife. Bake in a 300° F. oven on silicone paper about 25 to 30 minutes, then shut off heat and let dry in oven with door open for about 15 minutes. When cool, release from pans with spatula, etc.

Basic Almond Paste Macaroon Cookies

Makes about 50 to 60

1 pound commercial almond paste	¾ cup sifted confectioners' sugar
½ to ⅔ cup unbeaten egg whites	1 teaspoon vanilla
¾ cup granulated sugar	Food coloring as suggested in recipes

Cut almond paste in small pieces. Add only ½ cup of the unbeaten whites to start with, little at a time, and beat with electric mixer (or may be mixed with hand) until smooth. Add sugars, little at a time, then vanilla and food coloring. Beat well for about ½ minute. If mixture appears the least bit lumpy, it is important to put it through a food mill or strainer. Test mixture by pressing out 2 or 3 rounds onto baking sheet. It contains enough egg whites if a small point is raised and does not flatten out. If a very thick long point is raised, add rest of egg whites. If rounds flatten out after they are pressed onto baking sheet too much egg was used. In this case cookies will spread out appreciably and lose their identity after they are baked. It is therefore very important to add egg whites little at a time and make suggested test; ½ cup egg white is usually sufficient.

Macaroon cookies are commonly baked on silicone paper. After they have been baked and are cool, release them from papr with a dinner knife or spatula. Instead of using paper, a 12 × 18-inch baking sheet may be greased with 1½ teaspoons of soft unsalted shortening and sprinkled with flour. Shake off loose flour. In this case, remove cookies from pan with spatula while they are still warm, but not at once, to prevent sticking. If macaroons brown too rapidly on underside because of strong bottom heat, bake them on a double thickness of paper or double baking sheet. It is better to shut off heat as soon as these cookies are delicately colored and feel dry to the touch, in about 25 minutes, then let remain in oven with door slightly open for about 10 minutes. Almond paste macaroons may be kept at least 1 week provided they are stored in a tight container after they are cold. They freeze very well for several months if properly wrapped.

Glaze for Almond Paste Cookies

Use *lukewarm* light corn syrup. Commercial glazes that dry quickly may be purchased from bakers' supply houses. Home-type glaze makes cookies attractive but it is best not to use it on a humid day as it remains sticky. If these cookies are to be packed for gifts or if they are to be kept covered it is better to omit glaze. For home use, brush top part only very lightly with syrup and keep cookies on racks until glaze is set. It may take several hours depending on humidity in room. These cookies, however, are very beautiful and attractive without glaze.

Almond Paste Pears

Remove ½ cup of the preparation from 1 full recipe Basic Almond Paste mixture. Add a few drops of green food coloring to be used for leaves on pears. Add a drop or 2 of yellow coloring to rest of mixture. With bag and plain opening of coupling (or a very large plain tube) press out 1½-inch bodies of pears. Then with No. 8 or 10 plain decorating tube, pipe green leaf on pointed end of pear, and insert a small strip of citron for stem cut about ¾ inch long. On large end place a very small currant or piece of raisin or dot of melted chocolate. With tip of damp forefinger dipped into commercial red sugar, gently tint round part of pears. Bake at 300° F. about 25 minutes, or until delicately colored, but not brown. Watch closely the last few minutes to prevent discoloration. Let remain in oven with heat shut off and oven door slightly open for a few minutes if necessary. When done, remove from oven, etc.

Almond Paste Strawberries

Paste for strawberries must be a little heavier because of the added red coloring. Remove ½ cup of preparation from 1 full recipe of Basic Almond Paste mixture. Add a few drops of green coloring to be used for hulls on strawberries. Add red food coloring to rest, and with a bag and plain opening of coupling (or very large plain tube) press out 1½-inch strawberries. With a No. 3 star cookie tube and bag pipe hulls on large end. Then use ¾-inch strips of citron for stems. Bake at 300° F. about 25 minutes, but watch closely toward end to prevent discoloration. Let remain in oven with heat shut off and door partially open for a few minutes if necessary.

Almond Paste Drops

With plain opening of coupling press out 1, 2, 3 or 4 rounds of Basic Almond Paste mixture. Decorate tops with halves of glazed cherries, green citron leaves, split blanched almonds, etc. Bake at 300° F. about 25 to 30 minutes.

Almond Paste Crescents

Drop small portions of Basic Almond Paste mixture into coarsely chopped nuts and form crescents. Make them small as they increase in size in baking. Bake about 25 to 30 minutes in 300° F. oven.

Chocolate Macaroons

Add 1½ ounces of melted baking chocolate to ¾ recipe Basic Almond Paste mixture, and a few drops of green or red coloring to ¼ of the recipe. Blend well. Follow general mixing and baking directions.

Chocolate Macaroon Swirls

With plain opening of coupling press out 1 inch rounds of chocolate maca-roon mixture (page 715). With plain No. 6 or 8 tube and green or red mixture, pipe a swirl on top of each.

Chocolate Macaroons with Rosette Tops

Press out 1-inch rounds of chocolate macaroon mixture, then with No. 3 star cookie tube, pipe small green or red rosette on top of each.

Chocolate Macaroon Cigarettes

With plain opening of coupling, press out 3-inch strips of chocolate maca-roon mixture. With plain No. 6 or 8 decorating tube, pipe green or red scroll design on top.

Chocolate Macaroon Logs

With No. 3 cookie tube, pipe 3-inch logs with chocolate macaroon mixture. After they are baked and cold, brush ends only with corn syrup or chocolate icing and cover with chopped green nuts.

Chocolate Macaroon Rosettes

With No. 3 or No. 7 star cookie tube, press out rosettes with chocolate macaroon mixture. Garnish top of each with ¼ or ½ glacéed cherry and citron leaves.

Continental Leaf Cookies

Make about 3 dozen cookies

½ pound commercial almond paste
2 egg whites, unbeaten (¼ cup)
3 tablespoons water

¾ cup sifted confectioners' sugar
1 teaspoon vanilla

Cut almond paste into small pieces. Add egg whites little at a time. With hand or electric mixer, blend carefully to make a smooth mixture. Then with wooden spoon or electric mixer, mix in water, confectioners' sugar, and vanilla. If lumpy, it must be put through food mill or strainer. If too thick, add *very little* more water, 1 teaspoon at a time.

Grease inverted side of baking sheets (12 × 18 inches) with 2 teaspoons of shortening. Sprinkle with all-purpose flour; shake well to remove loose flour. Lay leaf stencil on baking sheet and spread dough over it with a spatula. Remove excess dough and lift stencil straight up. Repeat until entire pan is covered. Sprinkle with colored sugar, being careful not to drop sugar on pan to prevent cookies from sticking. Bake in a 300° F. oven about 10 to 12 minutes, or until delicately brown. Watch closely to prevent burning. *As soon as they are done, remove from baking sheet with a wide pancake turner or they will stick and break.* When cookies are cold, place in airtight box with wax paper in between layers. This will keep them crisp.

Karydato (Walnut or Pecan Grecian Pastries)

Makes about 36

3 large egg whites	¾ cup farina
½ cup butter or margarine	1½ cups medium-chopped walnuts or
⅔ cup granulated sugar, combined with 1 teaspoon cinnamon	pecans
3 egg yolks	2 tablespoons brandy or fruit juice

In a 6- or 7-inch bowl beat whites until they barely cling to bowl. Let stand room temperature while preparing rest of pastry. In 8-inch bowl beat butter or margarine until creamy, add sugar combined with the cinnamon, little at a time, and beat about 1 minute. Add yolks and beat about 2 more minutes. Now add the farina alternately with the chopped nutmeats and brandy, and beat until smooth. Last, pour all of beaten whites into bowl; stir and blend until no streaks appear.

Pour into greased 9-inch square pan, bottom covered with very well-greased silicone or heavy wax paper, sprinkled with flour. (This is important to release pastry without breaking.) Spread evenly and bake at 375° F., about 30 minutes, or until slightly firm in center of pastry. Remove from oven and let stand about 5 minutes. Now go around sides all the way down with a dinner knife. Place square cake rack over top of pan and turn over carefully. Peel off paper, then turn pastry carefully with right side up.

Combine 3 tablespoons granulated sugar with 3 tablespoons brandy or fruit juice. Keep over low heat only until comes to a boil, stirring gently. With brush spread this syrup over entire surface of pastry. Let stand until cold before cutting into small rectangles, squares, or diamonds. Sprinkle with sifted confectioners' sugar, and with No. 27 star tube and 65 leaf tube decorate with small icing rosette and leaves. This pastry may be prepared without addition of syrup.

May be kept at least 2 weeks, well wrapped and refrigerated, or stored in a cold place. May be served as a dessert, cut in about 2½-inch squares, topped with whipped cream.

Revani (Grecian Walnut Brandy Cakes)

Makes about 36

4 egg yolks
⅔ cup sifted granulated sugar
2 tablespoons brandy (light sweet wine or fruit juice may be used)
1⅓ cups walnuts or pecans, chopped medium

⅛ teaspoon cinnamon and ⅛ teaspoon cloves added to ⅓ cup cracker meal
¼ cup melted butter
4 egg whites

In a 7-inch bowl, beat egg yolks with electric mixer for about 1 minute. Transfer to 8-inch bowl, add sugar little at a time, and continue to beat. Add the brandy, chopped nuts, cinnamon and cloves combined with cracker meal, and the melted butter, beating after each addition until well blended. Last, beat egg whites until they cling to bowl; add all at once to other ingredients, and fold in until no streaks appear. Pour into a 9 × 9-inch square pan that has been well greased with *2 teaspoons unsalted shortening* and sprinkled well with all-purpose flour, shaking out loose flour. A smaller pan may be used if a thicker pastry is preferred. Bake in a 375° F. oven for about 35 minutes, or until firm to touch. When done, remove from oven and let stand in pan about 5 minutes, then loosen around sides, and carefully turn over onto cake rack. For additional moisture and flavor, pastry may be brushed with 2 tablespoons of brandy, wine, or fruit juice when cool. When cold, transfer to a board, cut into diamonds, squares, or rectangles. Sprinkle with sifted confectioners' sugar, leave plain, or decorate center of each with a buttercream rosette and leaves. Use No. 24 or 27 tube for rosettes and No. 65 or 67 leaf tube for leaves.

These pastries keep well for at least a week if stored in tightly covered container and kept in a cool place. May be frozen.

Marzipan Slices

Makes about 32 slices

½ cup butter or margarine, medium consistency
⅓ cup sifted granulated sugar
½ teaspoon vanilla
Yolk of 1 large egg, combined with ⅓ cup cool milk, beaten few seconds

About 2 cups sifted all-purpose flour, combined and sifted with ½ teaspoon baking soda
½ cup red raspberry jam (not more), beaten with a fork until creamy

With electric mixer or heavy spoon, beat butter or margarine about 1 minute. Add sugar, little at a time, and beat until well blended. Add vanilla, then yolk of egg combined with the milk alternately with sifted flour and soda, forming a very soft dough. Spread with floured hand into a 10 × 14-inch baking sheet, first greased then covered with greased silicone or heavy wax paper. Bring dough up to top on all sides of pan. Place wax paper and another pan on top of spread dough. Press down to flatten surface of dough, and to make it uniform in thickness. Remove paper from top of dough, and *refrigerate* pan until filling is ready. (This is very important.) Measure the ½ cup of raspberry jam, and beat it with a fork until creamy. Put aside until needed. Prepare Almond Paste Filling for slices.

Remove pan from refrigerator, and spread the ½ cup of beaten raspberry jam on top of dough evenly and gently. With a spoon pour the green Almond Paste Filling over the jam gently, and with a fork or spoon (or rubber scraper) spread it very carefully so as not to mix it with jam. Bake in a 350° F. preheated oven for 35 to 40 minutes, or until top is delicately brown and just firm to the touch, but not too solid. After the first 20 minutes look at pastry and if filling has puffed, puncture it gently with a fork. When done, remove from oven, place it on a cake rack to become cold. When cold, spread entire surface carefully and smoothly with the Glossy Chocolate Icing. Allow to stand for several hours before cutting, then with a sharp knife cut *right in pan* into rectangle slices, squares, or diamonds. Lift each out with a small spatula or dinner knife. Tops may be decorated with tiny buttercream rosettes and leaves, or with whole pecan or walnut halves. If nutmeats are used, they must be placed on icing before icing is fully set. Keep in covered container until serving time.

Almond Paste Filling for Marzipan Slices

1 unbeaten egg white *and* 3 large whole eggs
½ pound commercial almond paste, cut into small pieces
½ cup sifted granulated sugar
1 teaspoon vanilla
3 tablespoons soft butter or margarine
A few drops green food coloring

Add unbeaten egg white and the 3 whole eggs, 1 at a time, to the almond paste, and with electric mixer beat until well blended. Add sugar, little at a time, vanilla and soft butter or margarine, and beat until smooth. Now add a few drops of green food coloring and blend well. If preparation appears lumpy, it is better to put it through a food mill or strainer.

Glossy Chocolate Icing for Marzipan Slices

3 tablespoons hot milk
1 teaspoon vanilla
1 tablespoon soft butter
About 2 cups sifted confectioners' sugar
2 ounces of melted baking chocolate

Combine all ingredients in the order given, adding chocolate last to prevent curdling, and beat until smooth. Cover bowl, and let icing stand at least 30 minutes. If icing appears too thin, add more sifted confectioners' sugar. If it is too thick and dull, add a little warm milk or water, to make proper consistency.

Dream Meltaway Slices

Makes 32 slices

⅓ cup very soft butter (margarine may be used)
½ cup sifted confectioners' sugar
Yolk of 1 large egg
½ teaspoon vanilla
About 1½ cups sifted all-purpose flour
½ teaspoon baking soda

2 tablespoons milk
2 whole eggs
1 cup brown sugar, packed solid
1 teaspoon vanilla
½ cup fine-chopped nuts
½ cup coconut (or omit coconut and use ½ cup more nuts)

Cream butter thoroughly. Add sugar, a little at a time, and beat until smooth. Add egg yolk, then vanilla and, last, sifted flour and baking soda, alternately with milk, forming a very soft dough. With wet hand spread *thickly* on bottom and *thinly* on sides of a greased 9 × 9-inch square pan. Then pour and spread with a fork the following filling:

With a spoon beat 2 whole eggs; add brown sugar, vanilla, nuts, and coconut. Mix very thoroughly. *(Instead of coconut an extra ½ cup nuts may be used.)*

Bake at 400° F. about 20 minutes; then reduce heat to 300° F. and bake about 15 more minutes, or until firm to the touch.

When mixture is done, loosen sides and turn onto a cake cooler. When it is cold, cut, with crust side up, into 4 uniform strips and each strip into 8 slices. Sprinkle lightly with confectioners' sugar or decorate with tiny colored rosettes and green leaves made with Quick Butter Icing (below), using No. 24 star tube for rosettes and No. 65 for leaves.

Quick Butter Icing

Cream ¼ cup butter; add 1 tablespoon cream, ½ teaspoon vanilla, and enough sifted confectioners' sugar (about 1¼ cups) to form proper consistency for spreading. Beat about 5 minutes. For flowers and leaves, add a little more confectioners' sugar.

Frangipan Tartlets

Prepare 1 recipe dough for English Cherry Tartlets (page 721). Spread into medium molds according to directions. Pour Frangipan Filling into each pastry-lined mold, having filling come up almost to top. Cover tops well with shredded untoasted almonds and sprinkle with sifted confectioners' sugar. Bake at 350° F. about 20 minutes (or less, depending on size) in center of oven, then increase temperature to 400° F. and bake about 7 or 8 minutes on upper rack, or until delicately brown, but not dark. Remove from oven and turn over onto wax paper, or lift out of molds carefully and let cool on racks. Store in covered container until ready to be served. Best served same day.

Frangipan Filling for Tartlets

½ cups commercial firm almond paste (¼ pound), combined with 2 tablespoons hot water
2 large whole eggs, slightly beaten with fork

¼ cup granulated sugar
1 tablespoon melted butter
½ teaspoon vanilla
Green or red coloring

Moisten almond paste with the 2 tablespoons hot water and work it with hands or electric mixer until smooth. Add slightly beaten eggs, alternately with sugar, and beat with spoon or electric mixer. Last, add melted butter, vanilla, and several drops of green or red coloring. Beat until thoroughly blended.

English Cherry Tartlets

Makes sixteen 2¾ × 1-inch tartlets

¼ cup butter, medium consistency
¼ cup granulated sugar
1 large whole egg
½ teaspoon vanilla
1 cup sifted all-purpose flour, com-

bined with ¼ teaspoon baking soda
About ¼ cup more flour, if dough is too soft
Thick cherry preserves or jam

Beat butter until creamy, add sugar, little at a time, then egg, and beat well about 2 minutes. Add vanilla and, last, flour, combined and sifted with baking soda. Beat only until smooth when adding flour. Grease very small cupcake molds (¾ inch deep and 2 inches wide at top) lightly with unsalted shortening. Place 1 *scant* tablespoon of dough in each and with *damp finger* spread dough evenly on bottom and sides. Store in refrigerator while preparing Filling for English Cherry Tartlets (page 722).

When filling is ready, remove dough-filled molds from refrigerator.

Place about ½ teaspoon cherry preserves or jam on bottom of each unbaked tartlet. Pour filling into each mold, having it come up almost to top. Bake at 350° F. in center of oven 20 minutes, then place on upper rack and bake about 10 more minutes—raising temperature to 400° F. Bake until tops are golden brown. When done remove from oven, and turn over gently onto wax paper. Let stand until cold. When ready to serve, sprinkle well with sifted confectioners' sugar, and place about 1 level teaspoon cherry preserve or jam on top center of each. Other preserves or jams may be used instead of cherry. Best served same day.

Note. These tartlets may be made in molds of other sizes. Small tartlet molds that come 30 to the set, or similar ones that measure 1¾ inches wide across top opening and ¾ inch deep are available. Use about ½ tablespoon dough in each. Fill these, after they are baked and cold, with a little jam and a rosette of buttercream or chocolate filling. For medium-size fancy tart molds that measure about 2¾ inches wide across top opening, and 1 inch deep, use about 1 tablespoon of dough in each.

Filling for English Cherry Tartlets

⅔ cup cream cheese
¼ cup granulated sugar
1 tablespoon soft butter

1 whole egg
¼ teaspoon lemon or orange extract

Beat cream cheese, granulated sugar, soft butter, whole egg, and extract *only* until smooth.

Chewy Apricot Pecan Bars

Makes about 50

⅔ cup shortening, medium consistency
2½ cups brown sugar, packed
3 large eggs
1 teaspoon vanilla
1 teaspoon baking powder, combined with 2 cups sifted all-purpose flour

½ teaspoon salt
¾ cup dried apricots, cut into pieces the size of large raisins
¾ cup chopped walnut meats or pecans

Cream shortening, add sugar, a little at a time, and beat well. Add eggs, 1 at a time, and beat until well blended. Beat about 2 or 3 minutes after all eggs have been added or until mixture looks like a heavy whipped cream. Add vanilla, flour combined with baking powder, and salt. Beat until smooth. Fold in the chopped (uncooked) apricots and chopped nuts. Pour into a 10 × 14-inch baking sheet that has been well greased with 2 teaspoons unsalted shortening and sprinkled with flour. With a fork spread batter as evenly as possible. Bake in a 400° F. oven about 20 minutes, or until it rises in center and is brown. Do not bake further if a moist chewy bar is desired. Remove from oven; let stand on a cake rack until lukewarm without removing from baking sheet. Cut into bars about 1 inch wide and 2½ inches long. When cool, and just before serving, roll well in sifted confectioners' sugar. Shake off loose sugar and arrange bars attractively on a serving platter. Store these bars in a tightly covered container.

Date Bars

Makes about 40

¼ pound butter or margarine
¼ cup brown sugar
2 egg yolks

1 cup all-purpose flour
¼ teaspoon salt
½ teaspoon baking powder

With beater cream butter or margarine well, add brown sugar, and beat until well blended. Add egg yolks, and beat about 5 minutes until light. Last, add flour to which salt and baking powder have been added, a small amount at a time, and beat only until blended. Place preparation in a greased and floured 9 × 9 × 2-inch pan, and with a damp hand, press down uniformly. Dough is heavy and must be pressed down by hand. Bake in a 350° F. oven about 15 minutes or until it is a very light golden brown.

About 5 minutes before cookie dough is done, prepare Topping for Date Bars. Spread Topping over cookie dough evenly; then place back in 350° F. oven and bake an additional 20 minutes, or until Topping is golden brown in color. When cool, leave in pan and cut into bars of desired size.

Topping for Date Bars

2 egg whites
¾ cup brown sugar
2 tablespoons all-purpose flour

7½-ounce package pitted dates, cut into small pieces
1 cup chopped pecans

Beat egg whites until stiff. Add brown sugar and beat until well blended. Add flour to cut-up dates. (This helps to separate the pieces.) Last, add dates and pecans, and blend well.

Crunchy Cocoa-Filbert Bars

Serves 6 to 8

⅔ cup butter or margarine
1 cup brown sugar, packed
1 egg yolk
1 teaspoon vanilla
1¼ cups sifted all-purpose flour, combined with 2 tablespoons cocoa, ½ teaspoon baking soda, ½ teaspoon cinnamon

⅔ cup filberts, crushed with rolling pin until medium-fine
1 egg white, beaten until frothy
1 additional cup crushed filberts for topping

With electric mixer or a spoon, beat butter or margarine, add sugar, and beat well. Add egg yolk and continue to beat about 2 minutes, or until fluffy. Add vanilla and sifted dry ingredients alternately with ⅔ cup crushed filberts. Place dough in a greased 11 × 15-inch baking sheet (using 2 teaspoons unsalted shortening for greasing), spread and pat dough with hand until it is smooth and uniform in thickness. Dampen hand occasionally if dough sticks. Brush entire surface thickly with beaten egg white, and sprinkle with 1 cup crushed filberts, pressing down gently with hand to prevent filberts from rolling off when cutting. Bake at 350° F. about 25 minutes, or until firm to the touch and brown. Shut off heat, and let remain in oven with door partially open about 10 minutes to insure crispness throughout, but watch closely that they do not burn. Remove from oven, let stand about 7 or 8 minutes, and while in pan cut into uniform medium-size bars. Keep on a cake rack until cold.

When cold, sprinkle entire surface with confectioners' sugar. These bars are especially attractive if drizzled with Cocoa Icing before they are separated. When icing is set, pick up bars with a spatula and arrange attractively on a serving platter.

Cocoa Icing

Combine 3 tablespoons cocoa, ¾ cup sifted confectioners' sugar, ½ teaspoon vanilla, and about 1½ tablespoons hot milk. Beat until smooth.

Crunchy Peanut Bars

Serves 6 to 8

⅔ cup butter or margarine
1 cup brown sugar, packed
1 egg yolk
1 teaspoon vanilla
1½ cups sifted all-purpose flour, combined with ½ teaspoon baking soda, ½ teaspoon cinnamon

⅔ cup salted peanuts put through a nut chopper
1 egg white, beaten until frothy
1 additional cup chopped peanuts for topping

With electric mixer or a spoon, beat butter or margarine, add sugar, and beat well. Add egg yolk and continue to beat about 2 minutes, or until fluffy. Add vanilla and sifted dry ingredients alternately with ⅔ cup chopped peanuts. Place dough in a greased 11 × 15-inch baking sheet (using 2 teaspoons unsalted shortening for greasing); spread and pat dough with hand until it is smooth and uniform in thickness. Dampen hand occasionally if dough sticks. Brush entire surface thickly with beaten egg white, and sprinkle with 1 cup chopped peanuts, pressing down gently with hand to prevent peanuts from rolling off when cutting. Bake at 350° F. about 25 to 30 minutes, or until firm to the touch and brown. Shut off heat, and let remain in oven with oven door partially open about 15 minutes to insure crispness throughout.

Remove from oven, let stand about 7 or 8 minutes; then while still warm in pan cut into uniform medium-size bars. Keep on a cake rack until cold; then pick up carefully with a spatula and store in a covered container. If bars are not crisp throughout when cold, place them back in a 300° F. oven 7 or 8 minutes; then shut off heat and leave in oven with door partially open a short time. These bars are very attractive if sprinkled with sifted confectioners' sugar just before serving.

Crunchy Chips

Makes about 40 cookies

¾ cup butter or margarine
¾ cup soft brown sugar
1 whole egg
2½ cups sifted all-purpose flour, combined with ¼ teaspoon salt and 1 teaspoon baking powder

¼ cup milk
½ cup chopped nuts
1 cup semisweet chocolate chips or drops
1 teaspoon vanilla

Cream butter or margarine with sugar a few minutes. Add egg, beat an additional minute, then add flour combined with salt and baking powder, alternately with milk. Beat until smooth. Add nuts, chocolate chips, vanilla and blend well. Drop on a greased baking sheet and flatten with floured fork to give an attractive top appearance. Bake in a preheated 375° F. oven about 20 to 25 minutes, or until golden brown.

Gingerbread-Man Cookies

Makes about 18 cookies

½ cup shortening
½ cup granulated sugar
½ cup unsulphured molasses
1 egg
2½ cups sifted all-purpose flour
½ teaspoon salt

½ teaspoon baking soda
1 teaspoon baking powder
½ teaspoon ginger
½ teaspoon cloves
1 teaspoon cinnamon
½ teaspoon nutmeg

Cream together shortening, sugar, and molasses until creamy. Add egg and beat well about 2 minutes. Sift together all dry ingredients. Add to batter about 1 cup at a time and mix thoroughly. Chill in refrigerator about 1½ to 2 hours.

Roll out on a lightly floured pastry cloth about ¼ inch thick. Using a large gingerbread-man cookie cutter, measuring about 6 inches, cut cookies and place on inverted side of a 12 × 18-inch greased baking sheet. Press in pieces of raisins or currants for eyes, mouth, nose, and buttons. Bake in a preheated 350° F. oven about 10 to 12 minutes. Gingerbread-man cookies are very attractive if frosted with Transparent Icing (page 618). If cookies are to be frosted, use raisins just before frosting sets on cookies.

Lady Finger Butter Cookies

1 cup butter or margarine, cold and firm

½ cup granulated sugar

1 teaspoon vanilla

2 cups sifted all-purpose flour (¼ cup more flour may be used for a less rich cookie)

Cream butter or margarine thoroughly with electric mixer about 5 minutes. Add sugar a little at a time, and continue to beat until well blended. Add vanilla and, last, flour, a little at a time, and beat after each addition only until smooth.

To shape, place dough in a pastry bag with plain opening of coupling and press out fingers that measure about 4 inches long and ¾ inch wide on a very lightly greased baking sheet. Bake at 350° F. about 15 to 20 minutes, or until very lightly colored. Remove from oven. When cookies are cold, sprinkle thickly with sifted confectioners' sugar, or place 2 together with a little melted sweet chocolate. Both ends of cookies may be dipped into cool melted chocolate. Let stand on wax paper in a cool place, not over 70° F., until chocolate is set. Arrange attractively on a serving platter.

Strudlicky

Makes about 24

½ cup butter, medium consistency

3 large egg yolks (¼ cup)

¼ teaspoon lemon rind, or ½ teaspoon lemon extract

About 1 cup sifted cake flour, more or less

Beat butter, add yolks, and beat about 2 minutes. Add lemon rind, then flour, a little at a time, forming a smooth medium dough that is not too soft and not so dry that it crumbles in rolling. Form balls with 1 level tablespoon dough. Roll on a well-floured pastry cloth, and with well-floured rolling pin roll to measure about 3½ inches. Place 1 teaspoon Meringue Filling on each. Fold over to form pillows, and go around edges with a pastry wheel to seal. Pick up with a spatula and transfer to an *ungreased* baking sheet. Bake about 15 to 18 minutes at 350° F., or until *lightly* colored. Remove, and when they are cold, cover well with sifted confectioners' sugar. Bake 12 to 15 minutes at 350° F.

Meringue Filling for Strudlicky

1 egg white

2 tablespoons granulated sugar

½ teaspoon vanilla

¼ cup nuts, chopped medium-fine

In a small bowl beat egg white until it clings to bowl. Add vanilla and granulated sugar, and beat about 2 minutes, or until mixture is very stiff. Fold in chopped nuts and use as soon as possible to fill Strudlicky.

Toffee Squares

Makes about 40 large squares, or 80 medium

1 cup butter or margarine
1 cup granulated sugar
1 egg yolk
1 teaspoon vanilla
2 cups sifted all-purpose flour, com-

bined with ½ teaspoon baking soda and 1 teaspoon cinnamon
1 egg white, beaten until foamy
1 cup pecan meats, chopped medium

Cream butter, add sugar, egg yolk, and vanilla. Beat well for several minutes with electric mixer or spoon. Add flour combined with baking soda and cinnamon, little at a time, and beat until smooth. Place dough in a greased baking sheet that measures about 11 × 16 inches, and flatten with damp hand to prevent sticking, then cover entire surface with wax paper and another pan. Press down until flat. Remove paper and upper pan. Brush top of dough well with beaten egg white. Sprinkle chopped pecans over egg white and with hand press nuts down gently. Bake at 350° F. about 35 to 40 minutes. Remove from oven, and at once *while still hot and in baking sheet* cut into squares, or as desired.

Finnish Pecan or Walnut Dreams

Makes about 50

½ pound cold firm butter (half margarine may be used)
¼ cup granulated sugar
½ teaspoon vanilla

2 cups sifted all-purpose flour
½ cup *finely* chopped nuts (or put through nut grater)

With electric mixer, beat cold firm butter *until very light*, about 5 minutes. Add sugar, little at a time, and continue to beat for about 2 or 3 minutes. Add flavoring, then flour, little at a time, and beat only until smooth. Last, add finely chopped nuts and mix well. Press through plastic bag and plain opening of coupling into large rounds on ungreased baking sheet, leaving about 1 inch space between each cookie. Chill in refrigerator until firm to the touch, about 20 minutes. Then bake at 350° F. about 20 to 30 minutes, or *until delicately colored*, but not brown. When done, remove from oven, let stand until cold, then cover thickly with sifted confectioners' sugar. If to be stored do not cover with sugar until ready to be served or packed as gifts. If dough is too stiff to go through pastry bag, it may be shaped into balls with hands.

Fancy Fruitlet Cookies

Makes about 30

⅔ cup soft butter or margarine
½ cup less 1 tablespoon (7 tablespoons) sifted granulated sugar
½ teaspoon lemon, banana, or strawberry extract

1½ cups sifted all-purpose flour (or little more)
Food colorings
Citron stems, cut about ¾ inch long (or use long stems from cloves)
A little commercial red sugar

With electric mixer or spoon beat butter or margarine ½ minute; add sugar, little at a time, and beat for about 1 minute after all sugar has been added. Now add extract and the flour, about ¼ cup at a time, and beat only until smooth. Divide dough into colors desired, and shape as per directions.

Bake all cookies on ungreased baking sheet in a 300° F. oven about 35 minutes or a little longer (only 25 minutes for bananas), but watch closely toward end of baking to prevent discoloration. Cookies may be left in oven, *with heat shut off, and oven door slightly open,* for a few minutes to dry out if necessary.

Apples. Add a little green coloring to dough, and blend in with a heavy fork or spoon until no streaks appear. Add a little more flour if soft. Use 1 rounded standard measuring teaspoonful, and in palms of hands shape into smooth ball. Insert stem. Bake according to directions. When cold, cookies may be lightly tinted, up and down direction, with a little red coloring, but not necessary.

Pears. Add a little yellow coloring to dough, blend well, etc. Use 1 rounded standard measuring teaspoonful, and in palms of hands form smooth balls, then cone shape, bending small end sightly. Place on baking sheet. Insert stems. With ⅛ teaspoon green dough form tiny flat ovals to simulate leaves, and place firmly near stem on pears. Sprinkle rounded part with pinch of commercial red sugar, and with toothpick or tip of wooden skewer dipped into cool melted dark chocolate (or little cocoa and water paste) puncture bottom of pear. Bake as per general directions.

Bananas. Add a little yellow coloring to dough and a little more flour. With a slight bit more than 1 level standard measuring teaspoonful of dough form 2½-inch ovals. Place on baking sheet, curving them slightly. Dip toothpick into cool melted chocolate or cocoa preparation, scraping surplus against edge of dish, and tint top and ends of bananas. Do likewise with toothpick dipped into green coloring. Bake as per general directions for about 25 minutes.

Strawberries. Add a little red coloring, not too much as cookies will darken after baking. Add a little more flour if soft. Use 1 rounded teaspoonful and shape into smooth balls, cone shape. Dip entire *top only* of berries onto a thick layer of red commercial sugar. Place on baking sheet with sugar side up. With scant ¼ teaspoonful green dough form flat circles to simulate hulls, and place them on top (not on end) of rounded part, pressing down gently. Now insert stem, and bake as per general directions.

Note. To make citron stems, cut dry citron into slices about ⅟₁₆ inch thick, then into strips not less than ¾ inch long. Drop stems into small amount of water combined with green coloring for a few minutes (not more than 10 minutes); drain well on paper toweling. Spread out on flat pan and let dry well, uncovered in room temperature for a day or two in advance. Dry stems can be kept for many months in a covered container and used as needed. Stems must be inserted halfway into cookie to prevent them from dropping out.

Rich Flaky Butter Horn Pastries

Makes about 36

1 cup salted butter, cold and firm (half margarine may be used)
2 cups sifted all-purpose flour
1 egg yolk, slightly beaten and combined with ¾ cup commercial sour cream
About ⅔ cup any preferred filling

With pie blender, cut cold firm butter into flour until it looks like coarse meal (same as for pie dough). Now add yolk combined with sour cream, and with a dinner knife or fork stir until dough leaves sides of bowl. Turn out onto lightly floured pastry cloth, and knead very gently for a few seconds. Divide dough into 3 equal portions and form a flat circle with each. Wrap well in wax paper and refrigerate for at least 8 hours. May be kept for several days if wrapped in wax paper or in plastic bag.

To Bake. Roll each piece to measure 12 inches round, not smaller, and not more than 13 inches. With pastry wheel (or knife) cut each circle into 12 uniform wedges. Place ½ teaspoon of heavy filling on large end of each, and roll to form crescents; or roll each piece 10 × 10 inches square and cut into 16 uniform squares. Put ½ teaspoon filling on each. Brush edges with beaten whites and fold over into triangle. Place them on ungreased baking sheet with open end down for crescents and bake at 350° F. about 20 to 25 minutes, or until lightly colored, but not too brown. When cool, but not cold, sprinkle thickly with sifted confectioners' sugar, and serve.

These pastries are best served slightly warm, but not hot, nor cold. They may be baked several days in advance and reheated on a baking sheet in a 350° F. oven for about 7 minutes before serving. Sprinkle thickly with confectioners' sugar just before serving.

For Cocktail Flaky Horns. Use a stiff seafood, chicken, meat or mushroom preparation. If made in advance, they must be refrigerated, then reheated at 350° F. for about 10 minutes just before serving. See hors d'oeuvres section for various fillings.

Jam or Preserve Fillings for Flaky Horns

Use ½ cup any preferred jam or preserve; put through a food mill if necessary, or crush with a fork. Then add about ¼ cup or more finely chopped or grated pecans to form a *stiff* consistency.

▶ *Pies*

Pɪᴇ ʜᴀꜱ ʙᴇᴇɴ ᴄᴀʟʟᴇᴅ Aᴍᴇʀɪᴄᴀ'ꜱ ᴍᴏꜱᴛ ꜰᴀᴍᴏᴜꜱ ᴅᴇꜱꜱᴇʀᴛ, ᴀɴᴅ ɪɴ ɴᴏ ᴏᴛʜᴇʀ part of the world can one find pies as delectable and interesting in variety. Pies are usually served with a light meal because they are rich in protein and because of their satiety value. When properly prepared, they will not upset the digestion of any normal person.

Because raw products oftentimes vary in quality, pie crust made from any good standard recipe is not always uniform. It is therefore advisable to select top brands of flour and shortening. After some experience you will learn whether it is necessary to increase or decrease shortening. Bakers usually test a new batch of flour or shortening and guide themselves accordingly. Detailed mixing instructions are given with each recipe in this section.

Fats. Our recipes have been developed with unbleached all-purpose flour and the newer type hydrogenated lard and shortenings. These fats have better keeping qualities, have more body, do not impart objectionable fatty flavors to the crust, and are much easier to manipulate, especially for the beginner, than the *old-type soft lards.* For extra flavor, we like to use half butter. Hydrogenated fats can remain in room temperature for many months without becoming rancid. They may be measured at room temperature, then must be refrigerated until cold and firm, but not too hard, if using our recipes and methods. If you prefer to use the old-fashioned lard, reduce amount slightly.

Liquids. Ice water is commonly used in pie pastry, but we prefer very cold milk because it browns the crust better and is more nutritious. We cannot give the exact amount of liquid to use, for the amount varies slightly depending on the temperature of the ingredients, the fineness of division of the ingredients, quality of flour, and other factors. It is very important to have all ingredients cold and to work as quickly as possible. If ingredients are warm or too finely divided, less liquid will be required, thus producing a crumbly overrich crust that is difficult to handle. More liquid than the maximum amount suggested in our recipes will make crust less tender. During warm weather we suggest chilling the fat-flour mixture in refrigerator for at least an hour before adding the cold liquid, then return

731

it to the refrigerator for a short time if it feels too soft to handle before rolling.

Pie Plates. Our recipes have been developed to fit deep standard-size heatproof glass pie plates and aluminum pie plates with a satiny finish.

Basic Pie Dough for Open-Face Pie

For 10-inch pie plate

1¼ cups sifted all-purpose flour
¾ teaspoon baking powder
1 teaspoon salt, if using unsalted shortening; ¾ teaspoon salt, if using half butter

½ cup and 2 tablespoons cold firm shortening (half butter may be used for extra flavor)
About 3 or 4 tablespoons cold milk or water

Sift flour, baking powder, and salt into a 7- or 8-inch bowl. With pie blender cut cold, firm (not hard) shortening into dry ingredients until it looks like very coarse meal, not too fine. Some of the shortening should be the size of small peas. Now add the cold milk or water, *very little at a time*, over different parts of mixture, tossing quickly with a fork or dinner knife until all particles cling together when pressure is used. It is best not to use less than 3 tablespoons of liquid and not more than 4 if possible. Too little liquid makes dough break when rolling; too much liquid toughens pastry. When pastry appears moist, but not wet, turn it out onto a lightly floured pastry cloth, and knead it very gently for a few seconds (not minutes). Pie dough should be handled as little and as lightly as possible, but it is important to mix the ingredients sufficiently and to knead dough for a few seconds to facilitate rolling and prevent it from splitting and cracking around the edges when rolled. The little extra shortening called for in pie dough recipes will compensate for a little extra handling. Let pastry stand in cool room or refrigerator about 15 minutes, wrapped, before rolling.

Form a thick round patty with full recipe of dough. If it feels soft, wrap in wax paper and *refrigerate* for about ½ hour, but do not allow dough to become too firm. If it is refrigerated for a longer time and pastry feels too firm, let stand covered in room temperature about ½ hour. Pastry will roll more easily and prevent cracking around edges if it is not too firm. If ends of rolled dough crack, pinch them together and continue to roll to proper size.

Roll full recipe of dough on lightly floured pastry cloth, from center out in all directions, forming a 14-inch circle. Before dough is fully rolled, with a long spatula loosen it from cloth several times, and gently move it around, rubbing a little more flour onto cloth if necessary to prevent sticking, turning pastry over once or twice before it is completely rolled. Now fold the circle of pastry through center, then into quarters; lift it up carefully with both hands and place it into ungreased 10-inch pie plate so that fold is across the center of the dish. Unfold dough without stretching and allow it to fall loosely into angles of pan. With hands pat out air to make pastry fit snugly. Form a rim with the extra hanging dough so that the folded edge is about ¼ inch beyond edge of plate rim. Let stand in refrigerator about 15 minutes before baking.

The pie dough must be held down to prevent it from buckling and rising. Two methods are commonly used. A heavy plate a little smaller may be greased on the outside and set into the pastry-lined plate. A heavy plate is required to keep the crust in place. Bake in preheated 400° F. oven 15 minutes, then lower temperature to 300° F. and finish baking crust for about 10 more minutes, watching it closely the last few minutes to prevent overbrowning. Crust may be left in oven to dry out with heat shut off and oven door partially open for a few minutes.

The second method is to prick the pastry with a sharp-tined fork closely all over the bottom sides and rim to allow trapped air to escape. Do not puncture crust at any time for custard pies. Look at crust after first 5 minutes of baking, and if any bubbles appear, puncture. Bake about 15 to 20 minutes at 400° F., or until golden brown and crisp. This method will take less time to bake. For custard pie, the first method is preferred as it makes a more perfect smooth shell. *Do not puncture for custard pie.*

Individual Pie Shells

3½ inches across top

Divide full recipe of Basic Pie Dough into 8 uniform pieces. Shape each gently into balls, and roll into 4½-inch circles. Place on inverted side of pie plates, pressing down gently. Puncture top and sides with a fork. To facilitate handling, place them on a baking sheet, and bake at 400° F. about 15 minutes, or until golden brown and crisp. Remove those that are done before time is up if necessary. They may be left in oven with heat shut off for a short time to dry out.

Dough for 8-Inch Pie Plate

1 cup sifted all-purpose flour	6 or 7 tablespoons shortening
1 scant ½ teaspoon baking powder	About 3 tablespoons cold milk or
½ tablespoon salt	water

Follow general mixing directions for Basic Pie Dough for Open-Face Pie. Form a thick round patty, and roll from center out to measure 12-inch circle. Fit into pie plate, chill, and bake at 400° F. about 15 to 18 minutes, or until golden color. Let dry few minutes with heat shut off.

Dough for 9-Inch Pie Plate

1⅛ cups sifted all-purpose flour
½ teaspoon baking powder
¾ teaspoon salt

7 tablespoons shortening
About 3 to 4 tablespoons cold milk
or water

Follow general mixing directions for Basic Pie Dough for Open-Face Pie (page 732). Form a thick round patty, and roll from center out to measure 13-inch circle. Fit into pie plate, chill, and bake at 400° F. about 15 to 18 minutes, or until golden brown. Let dry out few minutes with heat shut off.

Butterscotch Pie

For 8-inch pie shell (page 733)
Use 1½ recipes for 9-inch pie shell (above)
Use double recipe for 10-inch pie shell (page 732)

¼ cup unsifted cornstarch (loosen with spoon)
⅔ cup, or less, light brown sugar, packed (old-fashioned type)

2 or 3 yolks, combined with ¼ cup cool milk, mix well
⅛ teaspoon salt
2 cups warm milk
½ teaspoon vanilla

In 2-quart saucepan combine cornstarch and brown sugar. Mix well. Add warm yolks combined with cool milk (little at a time; mix until smooth) and the salt. Now pour warm milk slowly into preparation, stirring continuously, and cook over medium heat until thick, stirring all the time to prevent scorching and lumping. Then lower heat and simmer about 5 minutes. Add ½ teaspoon vanilla just before pouring into crust. If filling is to stand after it is cooked, stir gently several times, to prevent crust from forming. Keep covered if to be used hot until you pour it into crust, or refrigerate uncovered if to be used cold.

Chocolate-Vanilla Cream Pie

For 8-inch pie shell (page 733)
Use 1½ recipes for 9-inch pie shell (above)
Use double recipe for 10-inch pie shell (page 732)

¼ cup unsifted cornstarch (loosen with spoon)
¾ cup sifted granulated sugar
Yolks of 2 or 3 eggs, combined with ¼ cup cool milk, mix well
⅛ teaspoon salt
2 cups hot milk

2 ounces unmelted dark sweet chocolate, cut into small pieces (3 tablespoons melted), or 1½ ounces unmelted dark baking chocolate, cut into small pieces
About 1 teaspoon vanilla

In 2-quart saucepan combine the cornstarch and granulated sugar. Blend well. Add yolks of eggs combined with the cool milk, little at a time, and mix thoroughly. Add salt and hot milk slowly. Cook over medium heat until thick, stirring continuously, and simmer about 5 minutes. Add unmelted broken-up chocolate and stir well until completely melted and well blended, *off heat*. Add vanilla. If filling must stand, stir several times, to prevent crust from forming.

Old-Fashioned Lemon Pie

For 8-inch pie shell (page 733)
Use 1½ recipes for 9-inch pie shell (page 734)
Use double recipe for 10-inch pie shell (page 732)

⅓ cup unsifted cornstarch (loosen with spoon)
1 cup sifted granulated sugar
⅛ teaspoon salt
2 or 3 yolks, combined with ¼ cup cool water

1⅓ cups very hot water, added slowly
Rind of lemon (optional)
⅓ cup, or less, lemon juice
1 tablespoon butter or margarine

In a 2-quart saucepan, combine all ingredients *except* lemon juice and butter. Stir until smooth, and cook over medium heat until thick, stirring continuously. After it thickens, add the lemon juice, little at a time; blend and continue to simmer about 5 minutes. If too thick add little water. Shut off heat, add butter. Stir several *times*, then keep tightly covered only until you prepare Meringue Topping (page 736). Bake as per directions given in Meringue Topping recipe.

Lemon Chiffon Pie

For 8-inch pie shell (page 733)
Use 1½ recipes for 9-inch pie shell (page 734)
Use double recipe for 10-inch pie shell (page 732)

2½ tablespoons unsifted cornstarch
½ cup sifted granulated sugar
⅛ teaspoon salt
Yolk of 1 large egg, combined with 2 tablespoons water
⅔ cups hot water

⅓ cup, or less, lemon juice
1 tablespoon butter or margarine
2 teaspoons plain gelatin, combined with ¼ cup cold water
1 large egg white (scant ¼ cup)
2 tablespoons granulated sugar

In a 1-quart saucepan combine the cornstarch, ½ cup granulated sugar, salt, and the yolk combined with 2 tablespoons water, little at a time. Add ⅔ cup hot water slowly, stirring all the time. Cook over medium heat until thick, stirring continuously. If very thick add little more water. After it thickens, add lemon juice slowly, and continue to cook about 5 more minutes. Remove from heat, and add the softened gelatin and tablespoon butter or margarine; stir until completely melted. Stir several times, cover tightly. *In a 7-inch (narrow bottom) bowl*, with egg beater, beat the 1 egg white until it clings to bowl. Add the 2 tablespoons sugar, little at a time, and beat until well blended. *At once* pour hot filling, heaping tablespoon at a time, to the beaten meringue, and fold in quickly until evenly blended and no streaks appear. *At once* (do not let remain in bowl) pour filling into baked crust. Cover with Meringue Topping (below) and bake as per directions.

Note. Instead of Meringue Topping, these pies are delicious covered with a thick layer of whipped cream. Use about 1 cup unwhipped cream for 8- or 9-inch pies. For 10-inch pies, use 1½ cups unwhipped cream, beaten until clings to bowl. Not necessary to add sugar.

Meringue Topping

For 8-inch pie
Use 1½ recipes for 9-inch pie
Use double recipe for 10-inch pie

3 large egg whites (½ scant cup)
2 teaspoons cornstarch
2 tablespoons cool water
⅓ cup hot water

¼ teaspoon cream of tartar, or 1 teaspoon lemon juice
6 tablespoons granulated sugar
½ teaspoon vanilla for Butterscotch and Chocolate pie

Separate eggs very carefully; place whites in a 7-inch bowl, cover and let stand room temperature at least 1 hour. Most desirable temperature of whites about 75° to 80° F.

Prepare filling for pie; stir it twice after removed from heat; cover until meringue is ready.

Prepare stabilizer for meringue with 2 teaspoons cornstarch combined with 2 tablespoons cool water. Stir until smooth, add ⅓ cup hot water (use very smallest saucepan) and cook until thick, stirring continuously, then simmer *only* ½ *minute*. Let stand in pan of cold water until just warm, while preparing Meringue Topping. Stir 2 or 3 times.

Pour hot filling into cool baked pie shell. *At once* start to prepare Meringue Topping. Add the cream of tartar or 1 teaspoon lemon juice to unbeaten egg whites, and beat at high speed to medium soft consistency. Add sugar, about a teaspoon at a time, and beat after each addition until blended.

Beat about 2 more minutes after all of sugar has been added, or until *peaks are fairly stiff and tip end slightly rounded. At this point* pour the warm stabilizer *all at once* into meringue, scraping it from saucepan with rubber spatula, *and continue* to beat meringue at low speed, about ½ minute, or until evenly blended.

At once, with a tablespoon cover about ⅓ inch of rim of crust with meringue. This will prevent meringue from sliding off when cutting. Heap rest of meringue onto pie filling, large spoonful at a time, *pressing down gently,* to prevent open spaces in finished meringue. Now with rubber spatula spread meringue as smoothly as possible, on sides and top, keeping it very slightly rounded in center. *Place pie on center rack of 375° F. pre-*heated oven, and bake about 18 to 20 minutes for small pies, or until meringue is medium golden color, not too dark, and not too light. Remove from oven, and let stand on cake rack in room temperature to cool for about 2 hours, then it may be refrigerated for at least 2 more hours before cutting; or may be stored in refrigerator for 2 days if properly prepared, as per directions. This meringue does not have tendency to stick to knife when cutting, unless it is overbaked. If necessary wipe knife each time with a wet cloth as you cut it into individual servings. *For large pies bake meringue about 5 minutes longer.* Meringue may be prepared without addition of cornstarch stabilizer, but not as desirable.

Custard Pie

A less rich crust will give better results when preparing Custard Pie. Use all shortening, reducing amount to ½ cup for 10-inch size; 7 tablespoons for 9-inch. An inner plate must be used in preparing pie shell, *and crust must not be punctured at any time.* Follow general mixing and baking directions on page 732. Partially prebake crust at 400° F. with a smaller greased inner plate for about 18 minutes, or until it is nicely colored and you can remove inner plate with tip of a dinner knife without sticking to crust. Bake longer if inner plate cannot be removed easily.

About 10 minutes before pie shell is ready, prepare filling, let stand a few minutes if necessary. Then remove inner plate, reduce temperature to 300° F. Leave plate with crust in center of rack. With small saucepan pour carefully into partially baked crust, *reducing temperature to 300° F.* Be careful not to spill filling on crust. Wipe bottom of saucepan with paper toweling each time before pouring. Sprinkle top lightly with grated nutmeg, very delicious, but not necessary, *and bake at the reduced 300° F. temperature* about 40 to 50 minutes for 9-inch size; 55 to 60 minutes for 10-inch *or until* custard does not cling to blade of paring knife inserted halfway between edge of plate and center of custard (or off center). Filling will continue to cook as it cools.

Let cool on cake rack at least an hour, then may be refrigerated for several hours or longer. If our directions are followed this custard will not become watery even a day or two later. Do not overbake, and temperatures of oven must be accurate. Best to test temperatures of your oven with a good portable thermometer before baking custards. The instant dry milk helps to stabilize the homogenized milk. Homogenized milk without the addition of the dry milk may be used, but results are not as desirable.

Custard Pie Filling

For 9-inch pie shell

1 scant cup whole eggs (4 very large)
½ cup sifted granulated sugar
⅛ teaspoon salt
½ teaspoon vanilla
⅔ cup instant dry milk, added about

a tablespoon at a time to to 2⅔ cups cold homogenized milk, stir well, then scald milk (bubbles form around edges) over medium heat; stir

For 10-inch pie shell

5 very large eggs (1¼ cups)
⅔ cup sifted granulated sugar
⅓ teaspoon salt
¾ teaspoon vanilla
¾ cup instant dry milk, added about

a tablespoon at a time to 3¼ cups cold homogenized milk, stir well, then scald milk (bubbles form around edges) over medium heat; stir

In an 8- or 9-inch bowl, with fluffy or egg beater, beat eggs for a few seconds, add sugar, little at a time, and beat until well blended. Add salt, vanilla, and a little yellow food coloring if needed. *Now slowly* add the scalded milk (about a tablespoon at a time to prevent cooking of eggs) and mix well.

Southern Pecan Pie

For 9-inch pie shell (page 734)

1⅓ cups sifted all-purpose flour
7 tablespoons shortening
¼ teaspoon baking powder

½ teaspoon salt
About 3 tablespoons cold milk or water

For 10-inch pie shell (page 732)

1¼ cups sifted all-purpose flour
½ cup shortening
⅓ teaspoon baking powder

⅔ teaspoon salt
About 4 tablespoons cold milk or water

A less rich crust will give better results when preparing Southern Pecan Pie Fillings. Prepare single pie crust dough, following directions for Basic Pie Dough for Open-Face Pie (page 732). Be sure there are no tears or holes in pastry. Patch with scraps of leftover pastry if necessary. *Partially* prebake crust about 18 minutes at 400° F., or until it is very lightly colored.

Remove upper plate. Lower oven temperature to 325° F. Prepare and pour Southern Pecan Pie Filling into crust and bake at 325° F. about 1 hour and 15 minutes, or until filling rises in center even with sides, but do not overbake. Watch closely the last 15 minutes as oftentimes filling will be done within 1 hour. When done, remove from oven and let cool on a cake rack before cutting. Refrigerate if pie is to be kept more than 2 hours after it is cool. Decorate with whipped cream if desired.

Southern Pecan Pie Filling

For partially baked 9-inch pie shell

2 cups white corn syrup	2 tablespoons melted butter
¼ cup sifted all-purpose flour	1½ teaspoons vanilla
¼ cup light brown sugar, solidly packed	¾ cup small pecan meats, or broken pieces (optional)
4 very large eggs (1 cup)	

For partially baked 10-inch pie shell

2½ cups white corn syrup	2½ tablespoons melted butter
⅓ cup sifted all-purpose flour	2 teaspoons vanilla
⅓ cup light brown sugar, solidly packed	1 cup small pecan meats, or broken pieces (optional)
5 very large eggs (1¼ cups)	

With electric mixer add corn syrup a little at a time to flour and brown sugar, and blend until smooth. Beat eggs a few seconds with electric mixer. Add eggs, melted butter, and vanilla slowly to syrup mixture. Now add pecan meats, and with a spoon beat about 1 minute until smooth.

Pecan meats may be omitted; this pie is delicious without them. Decorated with whipped cream.

Rum or Brandy Pie

For 10-inch pie shell (page 732)

Pour Filling into cool baked pie shell, and let stand in refrigerator at least 3 hours. Then cover entire top with a thin layer of sponge cake or French Pastry Cake (page 568) that has been baked in a 9- or 10-inch round pan. (Half recipe of French Pastry or any sponge cake may be baked in a 9- or 10-inch wax-paper lined pan.) When done, let stand until cold, then remove, and cut cake into 4 uniform wedges. Cut each wedge in about ⅓ inch thickness crosswise, and place on pie. (One cake is sufficient for 2 pies.) After cake is placed on pie filling, it may be brushed lightly with about ¼ cup brandy, rum, cordial, or liqueur, then decorated with Topping (page 740).

Spread Topping, reserving 1½ cups for border, on top and sides of cake as smoothly as possible. With No. 3 star cookie tube, pipe an attractive border on rim and edge. Sprinkle top with shaved curled milk chocolate. Store in refrigerator until ready to be served. May be prepared and decorated several hours in advance. *This pie should be absolutely cold and set before cutting.* It is therefore better to prepare it at least 4 hours before serving.

Other cordials or liqueurs such as cointreau, triple sec, orano, curaçao, etc., may be used in this pie instead of brandy or rum.

Filling for Rum or Brandy Pie

1¼ cups whipping cream, beaten until just clings to bowl
5 egg yolks
¾ cup granulated sugar
¼ cup rum, brandy, or other liqueur

2 teaspoons plain gelatin, combined with ¼ cup cold water (stir, and let stand until thick, about 5 minutes, then dissolve over simmering water)

First whip cream and refrigerate until needed. With electric mixer, in 8-inch bowl beat yolks about 2 minutes; add sugar, little at a time, and continue to beat about 2 more minutes, or until very light. Add the ¼ cup rum or other liqueur and mix well. Add the dissolved lukewarm gelatin slowly and beat until well blended. Last, fold in whipped cream until no streaks appear.

Topping for Rum or Brandy Pie

1 teaspoon plain gelatin, combined with 2 tablespoons cold water
1¾ cups whipping cream
¼ cup sifted confectioners' sugar

1 teaspoon brandy or crunch flavoring
¼ teaspoon vanilla

Let combined plain gelatin and cold water stand until thick, about 5 minutes, then dissolve over simmering water. Remove from water, and while cooling, beat whipping cream until of medium consistency. At this point, add the *warm* gelatin all at once, and beat only until blended. *Before it is stiff,* add sifted confectioners' sugar, and flavoring. Continue to beat *only* until cream is stiff, but not curdly. Remove 1½ cups of the whipped cream for border. Keep in refrigerator.

Banana Cream Pie

For 10-inch pie shell (page 732)

Prepare French Cream Filling (below). When it is cold, pour it into a 10-inch baked pie shell. Slice 3 to 4 bananas about ¼-inch thick, and distribute evenly on top of cream filling. Beat 1 pint whipping cream until stiff, adding ¼ cup confectioners' sugar. Spread ⅔ of whipped cream on top of bananas. Place rest of whipped cream in bag with No. 3 or No. 7 star tin cookie tube, and decorate as desired.

Banana Cream Pie can be decorated with whipped cream and placed in the refrigerator for several hours in advance.

French Cream Filling

¾ cup granulated sugar
3 tablespoons cornstarch
⅓ cup sifted all-purpose flour
Pinch of salt
2 egg yolks

¾ cup cold milk
3 cups warm milk
1½ tablespoons butter
1½ teaspoons vanilla

Mix sugar, cornstarch, flour, and salt. Beat egg yolks slightly and combine with ¾ cup cold milk. Add to dry ingredients, forming a smooth paste. Add warm milk slowly and cook until thick and smooth, stirring constantly. Cook about 5 minutes after it thickens. Add butter, and when mixture is cool, add vanilla. A little yellow coloring may be added.

Let filling stand in room temperature until cool, beating it several times. If filling appears too stiff when it is cool, add enough more cold milk or cream to make it of proper consistency. Beat thoroughly with a spoon or until smooth. When cool, cover and keep in refrigerator at least 2 hours before using.

Lime Chiffon Pie

For 10-inch pie shell (page 732)

1½ cups granulated sugar
½ cup lime juice and rind of 3 limes
Yolks of 5 large eggs
2 teaspoons plain unflavored gelatin, combined with 2 tablespoons

cold water and allowed to stand until thick
½ teaspoon green coloring
Whites of 5 large eggs (⅔ cup)

Combine ¾ cup of the sugar with lime rind, lime juice, and slightly beaten egg yolks; cook over very low heat until sugar is completely dissolved and lime custard coats spoon. Do not allow it to boil—just simmer. Stir continuously while cooking. Add thick gelatin mixture to very hot lime custard and keep over low heat, stirring constantly, only until completely melted. Remove from heat and pour into a 9-inch bowl. Add green coloring, and blend well.

Beat egg whites until they just cling to bowl. Add remainder of sugar (¾ cup) and beat only until blended; overbeating of whites will give a dry, undesirable filling. Pour egg whites all at once into hot custard and fold over and over until well blended. Pour into a cold baked 10-inch pie shell. Let stand until cold. Decorate with whipped cream rosettes, using No. 3 star cookie tube.

Orange Cream Pie

For 10-inch pie shell (page 732)

¾ cup granulated sugar
⅓ cup flour
¼ cup cornstarch
¼ teaspoon salt
2 egg yolks
¾ cup cold milk

3 cups warm milk
1½ tablespoons butter
1½ teaspoons vanilla
¼ teaspoon orange coloring
1 teaspoon orange extract

Mix sugar, flour, cornstarch, and salt. Beat egg yolks slightly and combine with ¾ cup cold milk. Add to dry ingredients, forming a smooth paste. Add warm milk slowly and cook until thick and smooth, stirring constantly. Cook about 5 minutes after it thickens. Add butter and when mixture is cool, add vanilla, orange coloring, and orange extract. Allow to stand in refrigerator 2 hours or longer. When filling is cool, place in baked pie shell and arrange sections of oranges over complete top of cream filling. Decorate with 1 cup whipping cream that has been beaten until stiff. This pie may be prepared several hours in advance.

Pumpkin Chiffon Pie

For 10-inch pie shell (page 732)

½ cup granulated sugar, or ¾ cup
   brown sugar, solidly packed
¼ cup cornstarch
¼ teaspoon salt
Slightly beaten yolks of 2 large eggs
¼ cup cold milk
1¾ cups cooked or canned pumpkin
About 1 teaspoon pumpkin pie spices
   (for dark filling), or ½ teaspoon
   ginger (for yellow filling)

2 tablespoons boiling water
1 cup hot milk
2 tablespoons soft butter
1 tablespoon plain gelatin, combined with 4 tablespoons cold water
Whites of 3 large eggs
¼ cup granulated sugar

Combine sugar, cornstarch, and salt. Add egg yolks, slightly beaten and combined with ¼ cup milk, forming a smooth paste. Add pumpkin and mix well. Then add spices that have been combined with boiling water to form a paste. Mix until smooth. Add hot milk slowly. Cook until mixture comes to a boil; then continue to cook slowly about 5 minutes, stirring constantly. Add butter and *thick* gelatin preparation and blend thoroughly. While pumpkin mixture is cooling slightly, at once beat egg whites until they cling to bowl. Add ¼ cup granulated sugar, and continue to beat only until blended. Add hot pumpkin, a heaping spoonful at a time, to egg whites, and fold in quickly, until evenly blended. Pour into a baked pie shell.

Place pie on a cake cooler and allow to stand *until cold;* finally, decorate with whipped cream, using No. 3 cookie tube. Keep in refrigerator. May be prepared several hours in advance.

Yuletide Eggnog Pie

For 10-inch pie shell (page 732)

¼ cup granulated sugar

⅛ teaspoon salt

2 egg yolks, slightly beaten

1½ cups warm eggnog (commercial type)

2 teaspoons plain gelatin, combined with ¼ cup cold water; stir and let stand until thick

2 tablespoons pecan meats, broken in large pieces

1 teaspoon vanilla or brandy flavoring

2 large egg whites, beaten until they just cling to bowl, then add 2 tablespoons granulated sugar and beat only until blended; refrigerate

¾ cup whipping cream, beaten until it just clings to bowl; refrigerate

2 tablespoons red maraschino cherries, well drained and dried on a towel, sliced in rings

2 tablespoons green maraschino cherries, well drained and dried on a towel, sliced in rings

Combine ingredients same as for Yuletide Eggnog Mold (page 447). Pour into cold baked pie shell, spread smoothly and refrigerate for at least 4 hours. Shortly before serving, whip 1 cup of cream until stiff and with bag and No. 3 cookie tube, pipe a collar around inside edge of pie to simulate a Christmas wreath. Cut 6 or 8 well-drained (and dried in a towel) red maraschino cherries, or glazed, in halves or leave whole. Place them on border about an inch apart, and garnish each cherry with 2 green citron leaves (or green maraschino cherries may be cut lengthwise into 6 sections and used for leaves). Cherries and leaves may be omitted and shredded sweet corn chocolate may be sprinkled over top.

Yuletide Eggnog Custard Cup Desserts

Will make 8

Prepare 1 recipe Yuletide Eggnog Pie filling (above). Pour into 8 oiled custard cups or small molds. Refrigerate for at least 4 hours. To serve, loosen around edges and turn out onto individual dessert plates. Garnish top with a large rosette of whipped cream and green leaves. Or place ½ maraschino cherry on top of whipped cream rosette and place 2 citron or green cherry leaves on each. Serve small fancy cakes or cookies with this dessert.

Individual Yuletide Eggnog Pies or Tarts

Will make 8 individual pies

Proceed same as for Yuletide Eggnog Pie. Pour into 8 cold baked individual pie shells (page 733). Refrigerate for at least 4 hours. Decorate each with whipped cream, cherries, and leaves, or as desired.

Apple Custard Meringue Pie

For 9-inch unbaked pie shell (page 734)

2 tablespoons dry bread crumbs	¼ to ⅓ cup brown sugar, packed
1 pound apples (Jonathan or winesap preferable), peeled and sliced thin	A little cinnamon and nutmeg
	1 tablespoon butter, broken up into small pieces

Sprinkle bottom of unbaked pie shell with 2 tablespoons dry bread crumbs. Arrange apples in pie shell. Sprinkle sugar, cinnamon, and nutmeg over apples. Add butter. Bake at 450° F. 15 minutes; then reduce heat to 350° F. and cover pie with double thickness of aluminum foil to prevent drying out. Bake about 30 minutes at 350° F. Meanwhile prepare Custard Filling. When pie crust and apples are done, remove from oven; pour hot filling over top. Keep on a cake cooler. Raise temperature to 400° F. while preparing Meringue Topping (below).

As soon as meringue is ready, at once spread over filling, being sure to cover part of rim of shell with meringue. Sprinkle top of meringue with 1 teaspoon granulated sugar. Place back into oven and bake at 400° F. about 15 to 18 minutes, or until golden brown. Remove, and let cool on a cake rack. Then refrigerate or keep in a cold place several hours before cutting. This is a most unusual and delectable pie.

Custard Filling for Apple Pie

¼ cup granulated sugar	1 cup warm milk
¼ cup sifted all-purpose flour	1 tablespoon butter
⅛ teaspoon salt	1 teaspoon vanilla
3 egg yolks, combined with ½ cup cool milk	

Combine granulated sugar, flour, salt, egg yolks and ½ cup cool milk. Stir until smooth. Add warm milk. Cook until thick over medium heat; then cook very slowly about 5 minutes. When done, add butter and vanilla.

Meringue Topping for Apple Custard Pie

⅛ teaspoon salt	3 large egg whites
¼ teaspoon cream of tartar	½ cup brown sugar
½ teaspoon vanilla	

Add salt, cream of tartar, and vanilla to egg whites in a No. 7 bowl, and beat until they form a very soft meringue that still slides out of bowl. Add sugar a little at a time, and continue to beat at high speed about 1 more minute after all sugar has been added until meringue forms stiff peaks.

Fresh Strawberry Glazed Pie

For 10-inch pie shell (page 732)

1 recipe French Cream Filling (page 741)

At least 1 pint strictly fresh strawberries—or better, 1 quart (wash berries, drain well, dry on a towel, remove hulls, and cut into halves if large)

Glaze for Strawberry Pie

½ pint whipping cream

Pour French Cream Filling into baked pie shell. Spread evenly. Place strawberry halves over filling, cut side down. Pour cool glaze evenly over berries. Place pie in refrigerator at least 1 hour before decorating with whipped cream. Beat cream until it is stiff. With a No. 3 cookie tube and bag, pipe a double border around edge of pie.

Glaze for Strawberry Pie

Combine 1 cup water with 2½ tablespoons cornstarch and 1 cup granulated sugar (or less). Cook in a small saucepan until mixture is thick, stirring constantly. Lower heat and simmer about 5 minutes. When clear, add 2 tablespoons lemon juice and a little red food coloring. Stir until thoroughly blended. Let glaze stand until cool, stirring it several times. If it appears too thick, add 1 or 2 tablespoons of water to make it of proper consistency, but not thin. Test by pouring a teaspoonful on berries.

Fresh Peach Glazed Pie

Follow directions for Fresh Strawberry Glazed Pie.

Use 4 to 6 peaches. Dip into boiling water about 1 minute. Remove skins. Brush peaches at once with lemon juice to prevent discoloration. Brush again with lemon juice after they are cut. Arrange attractively on French Cream Filling. Prepare glaze and add few drops of yellow coloring. Decorate with whipped cream.

Fresh Blueberry Glazed Pie

Proceed as with Fresh Strawberry Glazed Pie (substituting fresh blueberries for the strawberries), but add ½ cup blueberries to glaze ingredients and cook together. Strain glaze if lumpy. It is best to use 1 quart blueberries in this pie.

Fresh Raspberry Glazed Pie

Follow directions for Fresh Strawberry Glazed Pie, substituting fresh raspberries for the strawberries.

Fresh Blackberry Glazed Pie

Prepare like Fresh Blueberry Glazed Pie, substituting fresh blackberries for the blueberries. Add a little red coloring to glaze.

Frozen Cherry Glazed Pie

Use 11-ounce package frozen cherries. Defrost. Drain juice, and add enough water to make 1 cup. Combine juice with ½ cup granulated sugar and about 2½ tablespoons cornstarch. Cook until thick and clear, about 5 minutes after it simmers. Add 2 tablespoons lemon juice and some red coloring. Proceed as with Fresh Strawberry Glazed Pie.

Frozen Strawberry or Raspberry Glazed Pie

Proceed as with Frozen Cherry Glazed Pie. Use 11-ounce package of berries and only ¼ cup sugar for strawberries and ½ cup sugar for raspberries.

California Fruit Pie

For 10-inch pie shell (page 732)

1 recipe French Cream Filling (page 741)	Canned peaches, pears, apricots, sliced pineapple, Bing cherries
1 recipe Glaze (below)	Fresh strawberries, grapes, bananas

Prepare French Cream Filling and glaze. While glaze is cooling, place cream filling in baked pie shell. Tint round part of pears and peaches with red food coloring. Arrange fruits attractively on top of cream filling. Pour lukewarm glaze, with a teaspoon, over fruits and cream filling. Cover edge of pie with sliced toasted almonds, or a border of whipped cream. Place in refrigerator several hours before serving.

Glaze for California Fruit Pie

½ cup strained pineapple, peach, pear, or apricot syrup	1 tablespoon cornstarch, combined with 2 tablespoons cold water
¼ cup sifted granulated sugar	

Cook fruit syrup, sugar, cornstarch, and water until mixture is thick and clear, stirring constantly to prevent lumping. Takes 5 to 6 minutes. Let stand until lukewarm, stirring it several times before pouring it over fruit.

Pineapple Cream Pie

For 10-inch pie shell (page 732)

1 cup granulated sugar
½ cup pineapple juice
Yolks of 4 large eggs
2 teaspoons plain gelatin, combined with 2 tablespoons cold water and allowed to stand until thick

No. 2 can crushed pineapple, strained (1¼ cups)
Whites of 4 large eggs
1 cup whipping cream

Combine ½ cup sugar with pineapple juice and slightly beaten egg yolks. Cook over very low heat until sugar is completely dissolved and custard coats spoon. Do not allow it to boil; just simmer for 2 or 3 minutes. Stir continuously while cooking. Add thick gelatin mixture to very hot custard, stirring constantly until completely melted. Remove from heat and pour into a No. 9 bowl. Add strained crushed pineapple to hot custard mixture and blend well.

Beat egg whites until they just cling to bowl.

Add *other* ½ cup of sugar to whites and beat only until blended. Pour egg whites all at once into hot custard and fold over and over until well blended. Pour into cold baked pie shell.

When pie is cool, place it in refrigerator for several hours. Then beat whipping cream until it clings to bowl. Decorate pie.

Fresh Blueberry Glazed Cheese Pie Torte

For 10-inch pie shell (page 732)

2 slightly beaten egg yolks
¼ teaspoon salt
¾ cup granulated sugar
⅓ cup lemon juice
1 tablespoon plain gelatin, combined with ½ cup cold water, allowed to stand until thick

½ pound cream cheese, beaten with spoon until smooth
2 egg whites
¼ cup sugar
1 pint less ⅓ cup fresh blueberries, washed and dried in a towel

Combine egg yolks, salt, ¾ cup sugar, and lemon juice. Blend well and cook in a heavy saucepan (or in top part of double boiler) until custard coats spoon, then simmer 2 minutes. Add thick gelatin mixture and stir until completely dissolved. Let custard stand until it is cool (but not cold), stirring it several times while it is cooling. When custard is cool, but not cold and set, add it a little at a time to beaten cream cheese, and blend well. Now beat egg whites until they cling to bowl, add ¼ cup sugar, and beat about 1 more minute. Fold egg whites into custard and blend thoroughly. Pour custard into cool baked pie shell and let stand in refrigerator at least 2 hours until cold and firm. Meanwhile prepare Blueberry Glaze.

When custard is cold and set, pour uncooked blueberries over it and spread as evenly as possible. Now pour lukewarm glaze over berries carefully with a spoon. Cover edges of pie with slivered toasted almonds, or decorate with a large scroll of whipped cream. Or pie may be cut into serving pieces, and topped with a spoon of whipped cream. Refrigerate at least 4 hours before serving. It may also be served without decoration.

Blueberry Glaze

¼ cup cornstarch
1¼ cups cool water
1¼ cups granulated sugar

⅓ cup fresh blueberries, washed and dried in a towel
¼ teaspoon salt
1 tablespoon lemon juice

Combine cornstarch with cool water; add granulated sugar, ⅓ cup berries, and salt. Mix well and cook until thick and smooth, stirring constantly, crushing berries on side of pan to extract color and juice. Simmer about 5 minutes after glaze thickens. Add lemon juice. Let glaze stand until lukewarm.

Fresh Blueberry Glazed Cheese Tartlets

Proceed as for Fresh Blueberry Glazed Cheese Pie Torte, but pour into individual pie shells (page 733).

Streussel-Top Fresh Peach Cream Pie

For 9-inch unbaked pie shell (page 734)

2½ cups fresh peaches, measured after they are peeled and brushed with lemon juice
1 cup commercial sour cream
2 tablespoons all-purpose flour

¾ cup granulated sugar
1 teaspoon vanilla
¼ teaspoon salt
1 whole egg, slightly beaten with fork

Slice peeled peaches medium-thick, about ½ inch, and brush with a little lemon juice. Combine all ingredients except peaches. Mix until smooth. Add peaches to filling and blend gently. Pour into unbaked pie crust, and bake at 400° F. about 25 minutes. Then sprinkle top with Streussel Topping and continue to bake about 10 more minutes or until Streussel is melted.

Streussel Topping for Peach Pie

3 tablespoons firm butter
3 tablespoons sifted all-purpose flour

3 tablespoons nuts, chopped medium-fine

Combine all ingredients. With a pastry blender cut through until it looks like coarse meal.

Fresh Peach Cream Pie

For 10-inch pie shell (page 732)

1 recipe French Cream Filling (page 741)
2 pounds large fresh peaches

1 cup whipping cream
Several well-drained red maraschino cherries

Prepare French Cream Filling and refrigerate several hours until cold and stiff.

Plunge peaches into boiling water 1 minute, then into cold water. Peel and cut into medium-thick slices. At once brush them with lemon or pineapple juice to prevent discoloration.

Beat cream until it clings to bowl. (Stabilize cream with gelatin during warm weather.)

Pour filling into baked pie shell, and spread evenly. Place all except 9 peach slices over filling. Spread peaches with whipped cream, as smoothly as possible. Form 3 flowers with 3 slices of peaches and a maraschino cherry on top of whipped cream. Refrigerate until serving time.

Canned peaches can be used instead of fresh during the winter months.

Fresh Peach Meringue Pie

For 10-inch unbaked pie shell (page 732)

2 pounds fresh ripe peaches
2 tablespoons lemon juice
3 tablespoons dry bread crumbs
½ cup brown sugar, packed, combined with 2 tablespoons minute tapioca
1½ teaspoons granulated sugar

Plunge peaches into boiling water about 1 minute. Peel, and slice medium-thick. Add lemon juice and mix gently.

Sprinkle bottom of unbaked crust with bread crumbs. Place sliced peaches in crust. Sprinkle combined brown sugar and tapioca over peaches. Bake at 425° F. about 35 minutes, *covering top and sides* of pie with aluminum foil after 20 minutes. Meanwhile prepare Butterscotch Cream Filling (page 750).

When pie is done, remove from oven. Pour hot filling over peaches. Keep on a cake cooler. At once prepare Brown-Sugar Meringue and spread over top, being sure to cover about ⅓ of rim of crust. This will prevent meringue from sliding off when cutting. Sprinkle top of meringue with 1½ teaspoons granulated sugar. Place back into oven and bake at 400° F. about 15 to 18 minutes, or until meringue is brown. Remove, and let cool on cake rack. Let stand until cold.

Butterscotch Cream Filling for Fresh Peach Pie

½ cup brown sugar, packed	1½ cups warm milk
¼ teaspoon salt	1 tablespoons butter
¼ cup sifted all-purpose flour	1 teaspoon vanilla
3 egg yolks, combined with ½ cup cool milk	

Combine sugar, salt, and flour. Add egg yolks combined with milk, a little at a time, forming a smooth mixture. Add warm milk. Cook until thick, stirring constantly. Simmer (do not boil) about 3 or 4 minutes; then add butter. Remove from stove. Let stand a few minutes; then add vanilla and mix well. Let stand until ready to be poured over peaches. Filling should be quite warm when poured over peaches.

Brown-Sugar Meringue for Fresh Peach Pie

⅛ teaspoon salt	½ cup brown sugar, packed
3 large egg whites	½ teaspoon vanilla

Add salt to egg whites in a 7- or 8-inch bowl. Beat them until they barely cling to bowl. Add sugar, about 1 tablespoon at a time, and beat until well blended; then add vanilla and continue to beat about 1 more minute, or until stiff.

Streussel-Top Apple Pie

For 10-inch unbaked pie shell (page 732)

Apple Filling

3 pounds Jonathan or winesap apples	¾ teaspoon cinnamon
½ cup hot water	¼ teaspoon nutmeg
1 cup granulated sugar	¼ cup brown sugar
3 tablespoons bread crumbs	

Peel and core apples, and slice into 16 sections. Combine apples, water, and granulated sugar in a large skillet. Cover and cook slowly until tender, turning often. (This takes 10 minutes.) Do not cook too soft. Allow to cool. Then pour into an unbaked pie crust that has been sprinkled with the 3 tablespoons bread crumbs. Sprinkle apples with the cinnamon, nutmeg, and brown sugar. Bake in a 425° F. oven 25 minutes. Then place Streussel Topping over apples and continue to bake for 15 to 20 minutes longer. If Streussel is not brown, place under broiler a few minutes.

Streussel Topping for Apple Pie

6 tablespoons cold firm butter   ½ cup coarsely broken pecans
¾ cup sifted all-purpose flour   ½ cup granulated sugar

Blend all ingredients with pie blender until crumbly. Keep in refrigerator
until ready to be used.

Basic Pie Dough for 2-Crust Pie

For 10-inch pie plate

2¼ cups sifted all-purpose flour
¾ teaspoon baking powder
1½ teaspoons salt if using unsalted
    shortening; only 1 teaspoon if
    using half salted butter
1 cup cold, firm shortening (half

butter may be used for extra
flavor; if using old-fashioned
lard, use 2 or 3 tablespoons less)
About 5 or 6 tablespoons cold milk
or water

Sift dry ingredients together and pour into an 8-inch bowl. With pie blender
cut cold, firm shortening into dry ingredients until it looks like very coarse
meal, not too fine. Some of the shortening should be the size of small peas.
Now add the cold milk or water, very little at a time, over different parts
of mixture, tossing quickly with a heavy fork or dinner knife, until all
particles cling together when pressure is used. It is best not to add less than
5 tablespoons of liquid and not more than 6 if possible. Too little liquid makes
dough break easily when rolled; too much liquid toughens pastry. When
dough appears moist, but not wet, turn it out onto a lightly floured pastry
cloth, and knead it a few seconds (not minutes). Pie dough should be
handled as little, and as lightly, as possible, but it is important to mix the
ingredients sufficiently and to knead it a few seconds to facilitate rolling
and prevent it from splitting and cracking around edges. The little extra
shortening called for in pie dough recipes will compensate for a little
extra handling. Best to refrigerate dough for at least 15 minutes before
rolling.

   Now divide the dough into 2 pieces, and form round thick patties. On a
warm day or if pastry feels soft, it is better to wrap it well in wax paper and
to refrigerate it for about an hour, more or less, but do not allow it to
become too firm. If pastry feels very firm when ready to be rolled, let
stand in room temperature for a few minutes. This will prevent edges
from cracking and facilitate rolling. If edges crack, pinch them together
gently. Roll dough for lower crust on lightly floured pastry cloth with
covered rolling pin from center out in all directions, forming a 12½-inch
circle for a deep 10-inch pie plate. Before dough is fully rolled, with a long
spatula loosen it from cloth several times and move it around carefully,

rubbing a little more flour onto cloth if necessary to prevent sticking, turning dough over once or twice before it is fully rolled. Now fold the circle of pastry through center, then into quarters. Lift it carefully with both hands and place into ungreased pie plate so that fold is across center of dish. Unfold dough without stretching and allow it to fall loosely into angle of plate. With hands gently pat out air to make pastry fit snugly. Cut away any uneven hanging dough from rim.

For fruit fillings sprinkle 3 tablespoons dry bread crumbs as evenly as possible over bottom of dough, pressing down gently with back of hand or back of large spoon. Pour filling into crust, following directions given for various filling. Brush rim with milk or water. *Now* roll dough for upper crust to measure about 13½-inch circle, using same procedure as for lower crust. Puncture it well with a fork to allow steam to escape, cut away uneven edges, fold pastry through center, then into quarters. With both hands carefully place it on filling so that fold is across center of plate. Unfold pastry without stretching and bring it down, forming a rim, tucking overhanging dough under lower crust so that it is about ¼ inch beyond edge of the plate. Go around rim with a fork dipped into flour occasionally, or pinch with fingers. Brush top of pie with milk, excluding rim.

Bake in a preheated 400° F. oven 25 minutes. Remove from oven only long enough to place a strip of foil (cut 2½ inches wide and 36 inches long) around rim of pie, holding it firmly in place with a pin or paper clip; return pie to oven at once, and continue to bake about 15 to 20 more minutes. (The strip of foil will prevent overbrowning of rim.) If top of pie is not brown after 45 minutes, place pie in broiler close to burner *with heat shut off*, until brown, for about 2 minutes, but watch closely.

For lattice top, roll upper crust into a 12-inch circle, and with pastry wheel cut into about 16 strips that measure ¾ inch wide. Carefully place strips on filling starting with short strips, attaching them to wet rim, pressing down firmly. Form rim with scraps if desired. Now gently brush top of strips with milk. Bake as directed.

Dough for 2-Crust 8-Inch Pie Plate

1⅔ cups sifted all-purpose flour	¾ cup cold firm shortening
½ teaspoon baking powder	About ¼ cup cold milk or water
1 teaspoon salt	

Mix as per general directions for Basic Pie Dough for 2-Crust Pie. Divide in 2 pieces. Roll piece for bottom crust to measure 10 inch round. Roll piece for upper crust to measure 11 inches.

Large Apple Pie

For 10-inch 2-crust pie shell (page 751)

3 pounds Jonathan or winesap apples
2 tablespoons lemon juice
1 cup granulated sugar, combined
    with 2 tablespoons cornstarch

⅔ cup hot water
3 tablespoons dry bread crumbs
Little cinnamon and nutmeg

Peel and core apples. Cut each apple into 8 or 16 uniform sections. Combine lemon juice, sugar, cornstarch, and hot water in a large deep skillet or 4-quart saucepan. Add apples and mix well. Cover and cook slowly until crisply tender, but not too soft, about 7 to 10 minutes, depending on size and quality of apples. When done, pour into a bowl and let stand until cold. This may be done hours or a day in advance.

Roll dough for lower crust as per general directions for 2-Crust 10-inch Pie. Sprinkle top of dough with the 3 tablespoons dry crumbs. Pour cold apple filling over crumbs. Sprinkle top of apple with a little cinnamon and nutmeg. Roll dough for upper crust, and proceed as per general directions for 2-crust pie.

Small Apple Pie

For 8-inch 2-crust pie shell (page 752)

1½ pounds Jonathan or winesap apples
1 tablespoon lemon juice
½ cup granulated sugar, combined
    with 1 tablespoon cornstarch

⅓ cup hot water
1½ tablespoons dry crumbs
Little cinnamon and nutmeg

Follow general cooking directions given for larger recipe (above). Bake 8-inch pie about 35 to 40 minutes. It is important to place strip of foil around rim after first 20 minutes to prevent overbrowning, and return pie to oven for about 15 to 20 more minutes.

Louise's Apple Squares

For 9 × 13-inch baking sheet

Prepare crust with 3 cups sifted all-purpose flour, 1½ teaspoons salt, 1 teaspoon baking powder, 1¼ cups cold firm shortening, and about ½ cup cold milk or water.

Mix same as for Basic Pie Dough for 2-Crust Pie (page 751). Divide in 2 pieces; roll 1 piece for lower crust to measure about 12 × 16 inches (not larger). Sprinkle with about ¼ cup dry bread crumbs. Peel and slice thin 3 pounds (or little less) Jonathan or winesap apples, and arrange them as evenly as possible on top of crumbs. Sprinkle top of apples with about ½ cup or little more granulated sugar, and a little nutmeg and cinnamon.

Brush edge of lower crust lightly with milk or water. Now on floured pastry cloth, roll second piece of dough for upper crust to measure about 12 × 16 inches; puncture it well with a fork, fold in half, then in quarters.

With both hands carefully pick up pastry, and place it over apples. Unfold pastry without stretching, and cover filling, forming a small rim, cutting away uneven edges. Press down with fingers to seal. Brush top with milk. Bake in a preheated 425° F. oven 30 minutes, then lower temperature to 325° F. and bake about 35 to 40 more minutes, or until upper crust is very brown, but not burned. It may be necessary to puncture top crust during the baking process, and to press it down with hand gently to prevent hollow space between filling and upper crust. When done, sprinkle thickly with sifted confectioners' sugar, or better drizzle with icing made with 1¼ cups sifted confectioners' sugar, 2 tablespoons hot milk or water, and ½ teaspoon vanilla, beaten until smooth.

To Serve. Cut into squares right in pan and lift out with server.

Note. An aluminum pan would be excellent for this pastry. If using tinware, it must be burned out in a 350° F. oven for at least 5 or 6 hours to conduct heat and prevent a light lower crust. Use a dark tinware pan if available.

Canned Blueberry Pie

For 10-inch 2-crust pie shell (page 751)

2 cups blueberry syrup (drained from berries)
About ¾ cup granulated sugar
½ teaspoon salt

¼ cup cornstarch, combined with ¼ cup blueberry syrup or water
1 tablespoon lemon juice
2 No. 2 cans best-quality blueberries, well drained

Follow general directions given for Canned Cherry Pie filling (page 755).

Fresh Blueberry Pie

For 10-inch 2-crust pie shell (page 751)

4 cups fresh blue berries (1 quart)
1 cup granulated sugar
½ teaspoon salt

¼ cup cornstarch, combined with ¼ cup cold water
¾ cup hot water
1 tablespoon lemon juice

Wash and pick over blueberries; drain well. Combine sugar, salt, ½ cup of the blueberries, diluted cornstarch, and the ¾ cup hot water. Cook over low heat until thick, then simmer for about 5 minutes, crushing berries with back of spoon or fork. Now add the 1 tablespoon lemon juice and mix well. Pour glaze over rest of blueberries and let stand until cold. If filling appears too thick when it is cold, add a little water. Follow general baking directions given for Canned Cherry Pie filling (below).

Canned Cherry Pie

For 10-inch 2-crust pie shell (page 751)

1¼ cups cherry liquid (drained from cherries)
1¼ cups sifted granulated sugar
½ teaspoon salt
¼ cup cornstarch, combined with ¼ cup cherry liquid or water

1 tablespoon lemon juice
Red food coloring
3¾ cups water-packed red sour cherries (2 No. 2 cans or 2½ No. 303 cans)

Combine the 1¼ cups cherry liquid, granulated sugar, salt, cornstarch mixture, and lemon juice in a small quart saucepan. Mix well and cook until thick, stirring continuously until smooth. Lower heat and simmer about 5 minutes. Add some red food coloring, and pour glaze over the well-drained cherries, and let stand until preparation is cold. If filling appears too thick when it is cold, a little water or cherry liquid may be added. Use half recipe of filling for 2-Crust 8-inch Pie Shell.

Fresh Peach Pie

For unbaked 10-inch 2-crust pie shell (page 751)

2 pounds of fresh peaches
1 cup sifted granulated sugar
¾ cup water

3 tablespoons cornstarch, diluted with ¼ cup water
⅛ teaspoon salt
3 tablespoons bread crumbs

Place peaches in a colander and dip into boiling water about 1 minute. Remove skins, slice about ½ inch thick, and brush with lemon juice.

Prepare glaze with the sugar, water, and cornstarch diluted with water. Mix well and cook until thick and clear, stirring constantly. Always cook glaze several minutes after it comes to the boiling point. Add salt. Pour hot glaze over sliced peaches; mix gently and allow to become cold. Then pour them into unbaked pie crust that has been sprinkled with bread crumbs. Bake as per general directions for 2-Crust pie.

Fresh Strawberry or Raspberry Pie

For unbaked 10-inch 2-crust pie shell (page 751)

Use 4 cups strawberries. Wash, drain thoroughly, dry on towel, and *then* hull.

Prepare glaze with 1¼ cups granulated sugar, 1 cup water, and 3 or 4 tablespoons of cornstarch diluted in ¼ cup cold water. Mix well and cook until thick and clear, stirring constantly. Always cook glaze several minutes after it comes to the boiling point. Add some red food coloring after it is done, and ⅛ teaspoon salt. Pour hot glaze over whole berries; mix gently and allow to become cold. Then pour them into unbaked pie crust that has been sprinkled with 3 tablespoons of bread crumbs. Wet rim of lower crust and place on upper crust that has been pricked with fork, turning ends under so as to form a seam. Be very careful not to tear crusts, or filling will run out in baking. Follow general baking directions for 2-crust pie. Place on a cake cooler. *Do not cut until cold.* Use ½ recipe for 8-inch pie.

If pie is to stand more than 7 or 8 hours, it is better to use only 3 tablespoons cornstarch; otherwise filling is quite thick.

Rhubarb Pie

For unbaked 10-inch 2-crust pie shell (page 751)

5 cups unpeeled diced rhubarb (2 pounds)
1¾ cups, more or less, granulated sugar
½ teaspoon salt
¼ cup all-purpose flour

3 whole eggs
2 tablespoons dry bread crumbs
2 tablespoons soft butter
Yolk of egg, beaten and combined with 1 tablespoon milk

To prepare rhubarb for pie, remove ends, wash thoroughly, and dry on a towel. Cut into uniform lengthwise strips, then crosswise into pieces 1 inch long and ¼ inch wide.

Mix sugar, salt, and flour, and add to diced rhubarb. Beat eggs lightly with a fork and stir into mixture. Fill unbaked pie shell that has been sprinkled with dry bread crumbs, and dot butter over the top of the rhubarb filling; then top with lattice strips of dough. *Use ⅔ of pie dough for bottom crust and rest for lattice.* Brush rim of lower crust with milk before placing lattice strips on it. Brush lattice strips with egg yolk combined with milk.

Bake at 450° F. for 20 minutes, then reduce heat to 350° F. and bake about 30 minutes longer.

Mince Pie

For unbaked 10-inch 2-crust pie shell (page 751)

Prepare 1 recipe of Basic Pie Dough for 2-Crust Pie. Pour Filling for Mincemeat Pie into unbaked pie crust that has been sprinkled with the 3 tablespoons dry bread crumbs. Roll dough for upper crust and place it over mincemeat. Follow general directions for 2-crust filled pies.

For smaller 8-inch pie, use ½ recipe filling.

Filling for Mincemeat Pie

1 tablespoon brandy   4 cups commercial mincemeat

Blend brandy thoroughly with the mincemeat.

Strawberry-Rhubarb Pie

For unbaked 10-inch 2-crust pie shell (page 751)

Proceed as for Rhubarb Pie (page 756). Instead of 5 cups rhubarb, use 3 cups rhubarb and 2 cups cleaned, hulled whole strawberries. A very delicious combination.

▶ Italian Dishes

STANDARDIZED RECIPES OF FOREIGN DISHES ARE A THING OF THE PAST. EACH chef now adds his individual touches.

The repertory of Italian dishes is so vast that it has been a gigantic task to pick out those we are including in this section.

We have, therefore, chosen some of the leading dishes that are served in the finest hotels and restaurants everywhere, and that will appeal to the discriminating person with a fine sense of appreciation.

We are listing the most common products used in Italian cooking. These are available not only in all Italian grocery stores, but in a majority of supermarts, and other stores.

Mozzarella. A mild domestic cheese made from part whole milk and part skim cow's milk. It is used principally on Italian pizza, lasagna casseroles, special Italian fried and toasted sandwiches and appetizers, and many other dishes. It is also an excellent table cheese and is usually included on an hors d'oeuvre platter.

Scamorza–Mozzarella. We have been told by the largest manufacturer of these cheeses that they are identical. The only difference is that the mozzarella comes in ½ pound pear-shape whole pieces; the scamorza comes in 1 pound size. They can be kept refrigerated for many weeks, and also freeze well.

Parmesan and Romano. These are not the same. They are usually grated and sprinkled on pastas and numerous other Italian preparations. The parmesan is milder and preferred by some people. A majority of Italians prefer the romano, which has a much stronger flavor. It is always better to purchase these cheeses by the piece and to grate them at home, as needed, for best flavor. However, a majority of Americans buy them grated and use them in small amounts.

Ricotta. A soft creamy cheese, similar in appearance to cream cottage cheese, but should never be used interchangeably as some recipes suggest. Ricotta is made from fresh whole milk, and can be held under refrigeration for several days, but does not freeze well. Can be eaten plain, as an appetizer, but it is principally used in lasagna casseroles and ravioli dishes. Also excellent in cannoli pastries, and as a filler combined with whipped cream in fancy layered sponge cakes. It also makes delectable dessert tortes, etc.

758

Italian-style Canned Tomatoes. Usually peeled whole plum tomatoes. American-style peeled tomatoes may be used instead.

Italian-style Tomato Paste. This is a thick paste, and excellent in Italian sauces and other dishes. Use as directed in recipes. Available in all Italian stores and supermarts, in 6- and 12-ounce cans.

Oregano. The most popular herb used in Italian cookery. There is now a powdered type, but we like the oregano dry leaves, that you first measure then crush between your fingers. *Use only ¼ the amount of powdered if you do not have the leaves.* Do the same with basil leaves and similar herbs.

Garlic. Fresh garlic is preferred in Italian cooking, but you can use ¼ teaspoon garlic salt or ⅛ teaspoon garlic powder in place of 1 small clove garlic. It is best to put fresh garlic through a garlic press, or chop very, very fine. The best way to store fresh garlic is in a small uncovered jar, or with a punctured cover. Do not refrigerate and do not keep tightly covered, as it will mold more easily.

Parsley. Fresh parsley is always preferred to the dry. In an emergency you can use a little dry parsley.

Mushrooms. Sautéed fresh mushrooms are delicious added to Italian sauces and other preparations. Or you can use dry mushrooms, soaked for a short time, then used as directed on label or in recipe.

Olive Oil. Used in Italian cookery. You may prefer the more bland salad oils. Lard is also commonly used in Italian cooking.

Flour. Use unbleached all-purpose flour in ravioli paste, noodles, manicotti, and other pasta dishes, also in yeast breads.

Italian Sausage. Comes hot and mild. It is mainly made with all pork shoulder, seasoned with finochio (fennel seed), salt, and Italian-style crushed red pepper. It has become so popular in recent years that it is available in all Italian stores and supermarts. Look for a good brand, or you can make your own from our excellent recipe. It is served as a main dish, baked or broiled, in sauces for Italian pasta dishes, in appetizers, and principally on Italian pizza and in the Italian appetizer calzoni.

Spaghetti, Macaroni, Mostaccioli, Lasagna, and Other Commercial Pastas. Available in all stores. Look for the brands that are made with enriched No. 1 semolina, wheat germ added. Do not overcook pasta in Italian dishes. Most Italians prefer it al dente—cooked to medium or firm, not soft.

Dry Wines in Cooking. Any good grade of dry white or red wine may be used. It enhances many of the dishes.

How to Cook Spaghetti, Macaroni, etc.

For 1 pound of pasta, add 2 tablespoons salt to about 4 quarts of water and bring to a good rolling boil. Now add the spaghetti or macaroni slowly so that boiling is not disturbed. Do not break long pasta, but simply hold it upright for a minute or two until it begins to soften, pushing it gently into the boiling water.

Cook thin spaghetti 8 to 10 minutes; if thick, about 12 to 15 minutes. Very thick macaroni may take as long as 25 minutes, depending on personal taste. The Italians however prefer their pasta cooked al dente, on the firm side. We suggest that you cook these products by taste-testing until desired tenderness is obtained. A tablespoon of shortening may be added to the water to prevent the pasta from clinging together. Adjust heat to prevent boiling over, and keep water at a brisk boil. Do not cover pot. Stir once in a while. When done, pour into a colander and drain thoroughly. If to be served at once, arrange it on a large platter (or individual plates), and *at once* pour a little sauce over it, and blend with 2 forks. (This will prevent pasta from sticking together if you are delayed a few minutes.) Then pour more simmering sauce over top and sprinkle with grated Italian cheese. Arrange meat balls or other meat around edge of platter, and garnish ends with parsley bouquets. Serve at once.

How to Cook Ravioli, Tortellini, Manicotti, etc.

Follow general cooking directions for spaghetti and macaroni. You will notice, however, that this type of pasta will float to the top within a few minutes. To preclude stirring during the boiling process (anywhere from 5 to 20 minutes) we suggest that you place a double thickness of a wet dish towel on inside top of pot, directly over the pasta, covering entire surface. The wet towel will prevent boiling over, and keep items wet and tender. When done, pour gently into a colander, or pick up with a perforated ladle or large spoon, draining them thoroughly. Follow detailed directions given with each recipe.

Note. See section on Home Freezing for instructions on freezing Italian dishes.

▶ APPETIZERS ◀

Please see Hors d'Oeuvres section for additional Italian appetizers.

Italian Antipasto Platter

Form a mound in center of a large round platter with 1 pound well-drained fresh ricotta cheese that has been seasoned with 2 tablespoons fine-chopped fresh green onion and stems, 1 tablespoon grated Italian cheese, ½ teaspoon salt, ⅛ teaspoon white pepper, and ¼ teaspoon dried oregano or basil leaves. Instead of ricotta cheese, center of platter may be mounded with well-drained giardiniera (mixed pickled vegetables in wine vinegar) that may be purchased in jars, or with crab meat, tuna fish, etc.

Surround ricotta or giardiniera with thin-sliced capocollo, prosciutto, Italian salami, Italian vinegar peppers, black ripe olives, artichoke hearts, Italian provolone or mozzarella cheese, Italian fresh finochio, sliced tomatoes drizzled with Italian salad dressing, anchovies, etc.

These food items are also very attractive served in a 2-tier platter. Italian Antipasto can be served as the first course of dinner, or as a light luncheon or supper with Garlic-flavored Bread (page 814).

Pizza Neapolitan Appetizer

Makes two 12-inch pizza shells

This delectable snack (also served as a main luncheon and supper dish, and at cocktail parties) originated in Naples, Italy, but has become a national eating habit in the United States. Many versions have been developed in recent years, but we are giving you the authentic recipe in this section. You may modify it if you wish.

The original topping was made with fresh uncooked tomatoes and other ingredients. The fresh tomatoes were simply sliced and placed on top of pizza dough without precooking (as sometimes is suggested in recipes). However, none of the authoritative Italian cookbooks recommend precooking tomatoes; the majority of them suggest using canned, peeled tomatoes, as we do in our recipe. If you prefer to precook fresh tomatoes for about 15 minutes, slowly, you may do so. There will be some evaporation in doing so, therefore, please measure tomatoes after they are cooked for best results.

We like to use a top brand of Italian or regular canned peeled tomatoes (a 14- to 16-ounce can), and without draining, crush tomatoes with hands into small pieces, then add 1 can of Italian-style tomato paste (6 ounce size) to 2 cups of crushed tomatoes. Stir until well blended with seasonings suggested in recipe. This amount of filling is sufficient for two 12-inch round pizzas, using 1 cup and 2 tablespoons (a bit more or less) for each pizza.

Pizza Dough Neopolitan

1 cup lukewarm milk or water
¼ cup melted shortening
1 teaspoon salt
1 teaspoon sugar
1 package dry yeast, combined with ¼ cup warm water (about 110° to 115° F.) until dissolved

About 3½ cups sifted all-purpose flour, or enough to form a medium dough that does not stick to hands during kneading process

In an 8- or 9-inch bowl combine lukewarm milk or water, melted shortening, salt, and sugar. Blend well, add the dissolved yeast, then the flour, about 1 cup at a time, and beat after each addition with a long heavy wooden spoon until smooth. When too stiff to beat, turn dough out onto floured pastry cloth, add more flour if very sticky, and knead dough for several minutes, adding more flour to prevent stickiness, forming a dough that is not too soft and not too stiff. Cut dough into 2 even parts; knead each into a ball for a few seconds, place on a floured flat pan, brush top lightly with melted fat or oil, cover with wax paper and towel and let stand in room temperature about 20 minutes, or about double in bulk, but not overlight.

When dough has doubled in size, roll each piece about 1 inch larger than a well-greased aluminum 12-inch round pizza pan (use 2 teaspoons shortening to grease each pan). Oblong pan that measures about 9½ × 13½ inches, forming an oblong, may be used. Place dough into greased pan having it come up on sides, at least ½ inch, forming a rim. Let dough stand in pan about 20 minutes. Meantime, preheat oven to 400° F. Now puncture pizza shell on entire surface with a fork, and bake in center of 400° F. oven about 10 to 12 minutes, or until *very, very* lightly colored (almost white) and partially set. Look at pizza after it has baked about 5 minutes, and if it has puffed up in any area, *puncture it well* with a fork and press down gently with back of fork or hand, to keep flat. This is very important. Continue to bake for about 5 or 6 more minutes. (Refrigerate second unbaked pizza shell if you have only 1 oven.) Remove baked shell from oven, and carefully slide onto cake racks to become cold. Shell may now be filled, or stored in refrigerator and filled and baked a day or two later.

These shells may also be prepared several weeks in advance if properly wrapped and frozen. Separate shells with 2 thicknesses of wax paper, and stack them on top of each other. Place on a solid surface to freeze. Wrap properly. Allow to defrost as needed, fill, bake, etc.

Note. This revolutionary method of preparing pizza saves last-minute preparation of yeast dough. Shells are simply filled and baked, without waiting. The bottom crust is always more crisp and tender because of the double baking. The filling is also more desirable as it does not dry out when it is baked on the pizza for the 25 to 30 minutes that is required with the conventional method.

If you prefer to use the conventional method, simply allow rolled dough to stand in pizza pans about 20 minutes, then fill them with tomatoes, etc., and bake at once for about 25 minutes at 400° F. on center rack of preheated oven, or until underside of pizza is brown and crisp. If you prefer this method, we suggest that you reheat pizza for only 5 or 6 minutes in 350° F. oven after it has baked the first time and cooled slightly, even if made hours or a day in advance. Pizza is always served reheated to be delectable, to melt cheese, and crisp crust.

Pizzas that have been filled and completely baked may be refrigerated for 2 or 3 days if properly wrapped in wax paper, or may be frozen. To reheat, place cold pizza in preheated 350° F. oven center rack for about 7 or 8 minutes if not frozen, about 9 or 10 minutes if frozen. In reheating pizza place directly on rack in center of oven, not on a baking sheet. This will insure a more crisp, tender undercrust.

Filling for Pizza Neopolitan

14- to 16-ounce can of Italian or American peeled tomatoes (about 2 cups)
6-ounce can Italian-style tomato paste
¼ cup salad oil

¼ teaspoon baking soda
1 teaspoon salt
¼ teaspoon pepper
¼ teaspoon garlic powder

Crush tomatoes with hands into fine pieces. Add tomato paste and all other ingredients, and stir well for about 1 minute until thoroughly blended. This makes enough filling for 2 pizzas. Stir well again and measure 1 cup and 2 tablespoons or bit more for each. At once spread evenly over the partially baked shell (or unbaked one, as you prefer). Sprinkle with one of the toppings given below.

Note. Many different toppings may be used on Pizza. Sautéed green pepper strips; sautéed fresh mushroom; sautéed onions; and other vegetables or seafoods may be used.

Mozzarella or Scamorza Cheese Topping

For one 12-inch pizza

¾ teaspoon coarse oregano, crushed in fingers
About 2 tablespoons grated Italian cheese

About 1 cup (¼ pound) shredded (or cut thin narrow strips) mozzarella or scamorza cheese

Sprinkle oregano, then cheeses over entire surface.

Sausage-Mozzarella or Scamorza Cheese Topping

For one 12-inch pizza

Sauté ⅓ to ½ pound ground pork in ½ tablespoon fat for 7 or 8 minutes, then season with ¼ teaspoon salt, ½ teaspoon finochio seed (fennel), and ⅛ teaspoon black pepper. Blend ingredients well in skillet for about 1 minute, separating pieces of meat as you sauté them. Prepared Italian sausage (available in nearly all Italian grocery stores and majority of supermarts) may be used instead. Simply remove meat from casing and sauté in same way, but omit seasonings suggested. Sprinkle entire surface of pizza with ¾ crushed coarse oregano, about 2 tablespoons grated Italian cheese, and 1 cup shredded mozzarella. Meat may be placed under or on top of the shredded mozzarella or scamorza. We prefer to cover meat with the shredded cheese, then bake pizza.

Important. Best not to freeze sausage-topped pizza for more than 2 weeks, or to refrigerate for not more than 2 days, to prevent spoilage and change in flavor. Other pizza may be frozen for several months if properly wrapped. Can be reheated frozen, at 350° F. for about 9 or 10 minutes.

Anchovy-Mozzarella Topping

For one 12-inch pizza

Reduce salt in filling to ¼ teaspoon for each pizza. Sprinkle top with about 1½ tablespoons canned anchovies, broken in very fine pieces, before covering with the mozzarella cheese and other ingredients given in Mozzarella or Scamorza Cheese Topping.

To Bake Pizza in Prebaked Shells. Pizzas that are prepared with partially prebaked shells are first placed on a cake rack (or a flat cookie sheet) and filled. Then slide them carefully directly onto center rack of preheated 400° F. oven (not in pizza pan) and bake them for about 18 to 20 minutes, or until the underside is golden brown and crisp, but not burned. With a fork lift up 1 side of pizza while in oven to observe color underneath. If light, bake it a few minutes longer. Good pizza should always be crisp and tender when done. This baking style does not require reheating if you serve it as soon as done and is quite hot. Slide pizza out of oven with a fork onto a cake rack or flat pan. Let stand 2 or 3 minutes if too hot too handle. Cut with pizza wheel or very sharp knife.

To Bake Pizza in Unbaked Shells. This style must be baked right *in the pizza pan*, at 400° F. center rack, for about 25 minutes, or until underside is golden brown. Test the same way. It is always best to bake this style in advance and reheat it at 350° F. for about 7 or 8 minutes just before serving. Follow serving instructions for prebaked pizza (above).

Calzoni Squares

Serves 6 to 8

2¼ cups sifted all-purpose flour	¾ cup butter or margarine, firm
1½ teaspoons double-acting baking powder	1 very large egg, well beaten with fork and combined with ¼ cup milk
¾ teaspoon salt	

Sift dry ingredients together in 8-inch bowl. Add butter or margarine, and with pie blender cut through until it looks like fine meal. Add beaten egg and milk all at once, and with large spoon blend thoroughly until leaves sides of bowl. If mixture appears dry, add little more milk. If too soft, add very little more flour. Turn out onto floured pastry cloth and knead gently about 1 minute, or until smooth, adding more flour if sticky. Cut dough in 2 pieces, using about ⅔ for bottom crust, ⅓ for top. If dough feels soft, best to wrap it in wax paper and chill for about ½ hour or longer.

To Fill Calzoni. Roll ⅔ recipe of pastry dough to measure about 11 × 16 inches for bottom crust. Place it in 9 × 13 × 1-inch *dark well-greased baking sheet* (1 teaspoon shortening to grease pan), bringing it up on all sides of pan. Pour filling into pan, and spread as evenly as possible. Now on floured pastry cloth roll other piece of dough to measure about 10 × 15 inches, puncture it well with a fork, fold in half, pick up carefully with both hands, and place it on top of filling. Go around edges with a fork to seal well, cutting off any surplus dough. Brush entire top with milk.

Bake in preheated 375° F. oven about 30 minutes, or until dark golden color. Remove from oven, place on cake rack and let become lukewarm before cutting. This pastry is best served lukewarm or cold, but not hot. It may be prepared in advance, and stored in refrigerator until shortly before serving, then reheat at 350° F. for about 10 minutes until lukewarm.

Ricotta and Sausage Filling for Calzoni

2 large whole eggs, well beaten with fork

1 pound fresh Italian ricotta (do not drain)

¼ to ½ cup milk, depending on moisture in ricotta

1 pound fresh Italian sausage, cut in 3-inch pieces, sautéed in small amount fat until well browned, turning several times. Then add ¼ cup water, cover skillet and steam for about 10 minutes. Let cool, then slice ¼ inch thick, and cut in 2 or 3 pieces to facilitate cutting squares. (Instead of fresh Italian sausage, ½ pound of top-quality dry commercial peperoni sausage may be used. Simply slice peperoni same as for fresh, and combine with other ingredients.)

¼ cup grated Italian cheese

⅛ teaspoon black pepper

About ¾ teaspoon salt (½ teaspoon if using commercial peperoni sausage)

2 tablespoons fresh chopped parsley, or ½ teaspoon dry parsley, or crushed oregano

In a 10-inch bowl add the beaten eggs to the ricotta, and stir until well blended. Add milk, and beat well. Add all other ingredients in the order given, and stir until evenly mixed.

14-Inch Pizza

Use ⅔ recipe of basic pizza dough rolled about 15 inch round. Follow other detailed directions given for 12-inch size (page 761). For a very thick peasant-style pizza you can use full recipe of dough.

Use 1½ recipes of filling for ⅔ recipe of dough. Use double recipe filling for full recipe thick dough. Follow general directions, but increase baking time about 5 to 10 minutes, or until undercrust is brown. Bake in aluminum pan.

▶ SAUCES ◀

Basic Italian Tomato Sauce

Makes five 8-ounce cups

¼ cup finely chopped onion
1 clove garlic, chopped, or put through garlic press
¼ cup celery, finely chopped
2 tablespoons, or more, oil, shortening, or butter
No. 2½ can Italian- or American-style tomatoes
2 cans Italian-style tomato paste (6 ounce size)
About 1½ teaspoons salt
1 dry bay leaf, crumbled fine
1 teaspoon sugar

¼ teaspoon nutmeg
½ teaspoon coarse oregano or ¼ teaspoon powdered
⅛ teaspoon pepper
¼ cup chopped fresh parsley
¼ cup grated Italian cheese
Italian Meat Balls (page 795)
1 cup fresh mushrooms, sliced and sautéed in 1 tablespoon butter (optional)
¼ cup dry wine (optional)
About ½ teaspoon baking soda (optional)

Sauté onion, garlic, and celery slowly in the 2 tablespoons or more hot oil or shortening for about 5 minutes. Press tomatoes through a food strainer, or simply crush them with hands until medium pieces. Add tomatoes and tomato paste to the sautéed vegetables and all other ingredients except baking soda, mushrooms, and meat balls. Simmer in a covered saucepan for about 1 hour if using baking soda. Cook at least 4 hours if soda is omitted. Stir sauce often as it scorches very easily, and keep heat low. Add browned meat balls and simmer about 30 minutes, covered. Sautéed fresh mushrooms may be added the last 15 minutes. Wine may now be added if desired, and continue to simmer about 15 minutes.

Baking soda should be added the last 10 minutes. (It helps to neutralize acidity in tomatoes, making sauce more palatable.) Add soda, little at a time, and cook sauce several minutes. Taste and add rest of soda, not to exceed ½ teaspoon.

If sauce appears too thick at any time, a little water or dry wine may be added. If too thin, cook it uncovered for about 15 minutes.

This is enough sauce for 6 very large portions, 8 medium, and 12 small servings.

May be prepared several days in advance if refrigerated. May be frozen for several months.

Tomato Sauce

In 2 tablespoons shortening sauté 1 tablespoon of finely chopped onion or 1 small clove of garlic. Add 1-ounce can of Italian-style tomato paste and 1 can of water. A teaspoon of instant bouillon or cube may be added. Season with about ¼ teaspoon salt, 2 tablespoons of grated Italian cheese, pinch of baking soda, a little nutmeg, all-spice, and pepper. Cook slowly in covered saucepan about 15 minutes. Add a little more water toward end of cooking if it becomes too thick. Should be the consistency of a medium custard. This amount of sauce will be sufficient for about 12 cutlets. Extra sauce may be prepared and served separately. Simmer 15 minutes.

Quick Tomato Sauce

¼ cup fine-chopped opion	1 teaspoon sugar
1 small clove garlic, chopped fine	¼ teaspoon nutmeg
¼ cup fine-chopped celery	½ teaspoon oregano leaves
2 tablespoons butter	¼ teaspoon pepper
2 (6-ounce) cans Italian-style tomato paste	¼ cup chopped parsley
1 cup water	¼ teaspoon baking soda
1¼ teaspoons salt	¼ cup parmesan cheese

Fry onion, garlic, and celery slowly in butter about 5 minutes. Add tomato paste and water, and mix well. Add all other ingredients, and cook sauce about 15 minutes in a covered saucepan.

Italian Meat Sauce

Prepare recipe for Italian Meat Balls (page 795), but instead of forming balls fry meat loosely, separating it with a fork as it is browning. Season meat with various ingredients, omitting bread crumbs, egg and milk, then add it to sauce the last 15 minutes. Meat may be increased to 1 pound.

Sauce Bolognese

Makes 5 cups of sauce; serves 8 to 10

This very rich dark sauce is served principally in Bologna, in the better restaurants and homes, in the northern part of Italy. There are many versions, depending on personal taste and the locality. Some recipes suggest adding rich cream to the completely cooked sauce just before serving, and others use only a small amount of tomatoes or tomato paste to add color. We hope that you will enjoy our version of this interesting sauce.

½ pound of raw whole chicken livers, well drained and dried in a towel, sautéed in 2 or 3 tablespoons hot butter or oil for 7 or 8 minutes, then chopped fine

½ pound of ground beef or pork, sautéed in 2 tablespoons butter or oil for 7 or 8 minutes, separating meat with a fork as you sauté it

½ cup finely chopped carrots

¼ cup finely chopped onion

½ pound fresh mushrooms, washed, dried well, chopped medium

⅓ cup finely chopped celery

¼ cup more butter or oil

1 clove garlic, put through garlic press

½ teaspoon marjoram, crushed in fingers

1 crushed bay leaf

About 1 teaspoon salt

⅛ teaspoon nutmeg

2 teaspoons sugar

¼ teaspoon black pepper

No. 2½ can Italian or American tomatoes, crushed with hands in small pieces

6-ounce can Italian-style tomato paste

1 cup or more vegetable or meat stock, or add instant bouillon to water

½ cup, more or less, dry red or light wine (optional)

½ teaspoon baking soda (optional, but improves taste of sauce)

Cook chicken livers and meat as directed above. Put aside. Sauté vegetables in the ¼ cup butter or oil for about 10 minutes. Pour meat and cooked vegetables into a 3- or 4-quart saucepan. *Add seasonings and all other ingredients listed,* and simmer for about 1 hour if baking soda is used; about 2 hours if soda is omitted. Stir sauce often, and cook it over very low heat, *covered,* and simmer; do not boil, or it is likely to scorch. When sauce is done, taste and add more seasoning if necessary. If it is too thick, add more wine or stock, to make proper consistency.

Some chefs like to add 2 or 3 tablespoons of flour blended well with same amount of very soft butter to the hot sauce, and immediately stir until simmering begins. Let simmer about 5 minutes.

Nina Miroballi's Italian Mushroom Sauce

Serves 6 to 8 or more

1 pound fresh mushrooms

¼ cup hot oil or butter

1 medium size onion, chopped fine

1 clove garlic, or ½ teaspoon garlic powder

1 medium green pepper, cut into ½-inch strips

1 cup celery, chopped fine

½ cup parsley, chopped fine

1 teaspoon crushed oregano

About 2 teaspoons salt

¼ cup grated Italian cheese

¼ teaspoon black pepper

No. 2½ can Italian plum tomatoes, crushed with hands into small pieces

About ¼ teaspoon baking soda

Wash mushrooms in lukewarm water. Dry them thoroughly on a towel. If small leave whole; if medium slice thick. Sauté mushrooms in the ¼ cup hot oil or butter, and cook gently about 5 minutes. Add all other ingredients except baking soda, and simmer about 1 hour, stirring frequently. If sauce appears too thin, cook it uncovered a few minutes longer. If too thick, add little water or stock, or tomato juice. Add baking soda the last 10 minutes and simmer gently. Taste and season further if necessary. Serve on macaroni products or on vegetables.

Pesto à la Genovese

Makes about 1½ cups

Pesto à la Genovese is a delectable and famous Italian sauce, served principally in the northern part of Italy on homemade fettuccini (noodles) and other pasta. It can be served on any commercial pasta, but the taste and texture of the homemade is superior. This rich, unusual sauce is also served on poached and broiled fish, on baked potatoes, and some vegetables.

To prepare the fettucini (noodles) or other pasta, cook them until crisply tender (al dente) for about 7 or 8 minutes, more or less, depending on the thickness. Drain well, and to each portion of pasta, add a tablespoon of butter and a tablespoon of consommé (or you can use the cooking water from the pasta). With 2 forks quickly blend noodles well with the butter and liquid. Now cover top of each portion with about 2 tablespoons of pesto; *carry to the table at once,* and again blend noodles as you serve them.

To use pesto on poached and broiled fish, baked potatoes, and vegetables, cook foods as per directions in recipes, arrange them on an attractive platter. At once, while foods are hot, cover top of each portion with 1 or 2 tablespoon of pesto, and serve immediately.

The special ingredients listed below are available in a majority of Italian grocery stores and in some supermarts. Parsley can be substituted for fresh basil leaves, but the taste is different and not as delectable.

1½ cups fresh basil leaves
⅓ cup fresh parsley (Italian parsley preferable)
⅓ cup fresh marjoram, or frozen or fresh spinach
¾ cup pine nuts (omit, if not available, but they add a distinctive flavor)
4 large cloves of fresh garlic, put through garlic press

1 cup grated Italian cheese (parmesan or romano)
About ⅔ cup olive oil (any domestic salad oil may be used); instead of using all oil, half soft butter may be used
About ½ teaspoon salt
¼ teaspoon black pepper

Wash fresh basil leaves, parsley, and marjoram. Dry them thoroughly in a towel. Cut into small pieces. Place vegetables and all other ingredients into a blender, at high speed, covered, for about 1 minute, or until pesto is smooth. If you do not have a blender, place all ingredients *except oil* (or half butter) in a mortar with a pestle, and mash well, then add oil and the soft butter, little at a time, and blend well, until it looks like a smooth thick sauce or paste. If too thick, add a little more oil. Taste and add more salt if needed.

Anchovy Pesto

1 tablespoon anchovy paste
½ cup grated parmesan or romano cheese
1 cup butter, medium consistency (salted butter preferable)
½ teaspoon oregano leaves, crushed in fingers

2 large cloves of garlic, put through garlic press
¼ cup fresh basil or parsley, chopped as fine as possible, or ½ teaspoon dry basil

Combine all ingredients in a medium-size bowl, and with a large heavy wooden spoon (or preferably electric mixer) beat only until well blended.

Salt is omitted in this preparation because of the anchovy paste and salted butter. Taste and season if necessary.

Use as indicated in recipe for Pesto à la Genovese. This sauce is especially delicious served on very thin commercial spaghetti, cooked al dente, blended well just before serving. It is also delectable on broiled French or Italian bread. Serve hot.

Note. If pesto is made in advance or is left over, it may be placed in a container with a very thin film of oil brushed on the surface, covered well, and refrigerated for at least a week. Let become soft in room temperature about 1 hour before using.

▶ PASTA ◀

Tortellini (Pasta Rings)

This popular dish, served principally in the northern part of Italy, can be made in tiny rings and served in chicken soup; or made larger and served like ravioli. They may be covered with Sauce Bolognese (page 767); Sauce for Cannelloni French-Style (page 776); or your favorite tomato sauce. They are also very delicious rolled in warm melted butter after they are well drained and very hot, then sprinkled with freshly grated Italian cheese, as an accompaniment to meat or poultry dishes, or as an entrée.

To Make Tortellini. Prepare Homemade Egg Noodles (page 778). Prepare Chicken Filling for Cannelloni (page 776) or Ricotta Filling for Ravioli (page 773).

After noodle dough stands until it is soft, roll it as per directions. Dough must be rolled paper-thin for small tortellini or they will be bulky. Cut in 2-inch rounds, place about ½ teaspoon filling on each; wet edges with finger dipped into beaten egg white. Fold each round, forming half circle. Pinch around ends to seal well. To form the authentic tortellini, pull points very gently, dampen edges lightly with egg white, and wrap each around your forefinger like a ring, pinching ends well to prevent opening. This may take a little practice, but is very simple after you make the first few. However, may be simply sealed without forming ring.

There is a waste of dough in forming rounds. A simpler method is to cut the thin rolled dough into 2-inch squares, place the ½ teaspoon filling on each, wet edges and seal. Place the filled and formed tortellini on a lightly floured tea towel before cooking, and cover with another towel until you are ready to cook them. Best not to let them stand more than an hour in room temperature, to prevent filling from souring. They may be cooked a day in advance about 15 minutes, then reheated for several minutes in simmering water, and served with sauce, or as desired.

To Cook Tortellini. Lower gently into a large pot of boiling salted water, adding a tablespoon of shortening to water. As soon as they float to the top, cover them with a wet tea towel, inside top of pot. This will keep them moist and it will not be necessary to stir them, until tender, for about 15 minutes. When done, pour a little cold water into pot to check steam, drain tottellini in a colander, and serve as desired. If not to be served at once, drain them well, pour melted butter over them, to prevent clinging together. Or you may blanch them with cold water, drained well, and stored on wax paper, separating them with more wax paper. Cover well and refrigerate, or may be frozen for several weeks. Reheat in simmering water for several minutes. Test 1 before serving.

Ravioli

Makes about 24 medium-sized

1½ teaspoons shortening, melted	About 2½ cups sifted all-purpose
½ teaspoon salt	flour or enough to form firm
Yolk of 1 egg, slightly beaten	dough that does not adhere to
¾ cup lukewarm water	hands

Melt shortening and combine with salt, beaten egg yolk, and lukewarm water. Beat in about 2½ cups sifted flour, a little at a time, to form firm dough that does not stick to hands during kneading process. Turn out onto well-floured pastry cloth and knead a few minutes until smooth. Cover with warm bowl and allow to stand in room temperature about 60 minutes. (This ripens dough, making it easier to roll.) Roll into a rectangle about 18 × 22 inches. Brush upper half of dough with well-beaten egg white combined with ¼ teaspoon salt. Arrange 1 rounded teaspoon of filling over dough, leaving at least 1 inch space between each section, and cover with lower half of dough. Press dough, starting in center and around each section to press out air; puncture if necessary to release air. Cut into squares with ravioli wheel, and with fingers *pinch around ends if open.* Keep on lightly floured towel, and turn over occasionally. Let stand about 1 hour before boiling.

When ready to be cooked, lower gently into about 3 quarts rapidly boiling water to which 1 tablespoon salt and 1 tablespoon shortening have been added. Cover ravioli with wet tea towel inside top of pot and boil *gently* about 20 minutes, more or less, depending on size and thickness of dough, but do not cook so long that they break. (Wet towel will keep ravioli moist and stirring will not be necessary during boiling process.) When done, pour a little cold water into utensil to cool water *slightly,* remove with perforated ladle, and drain thoroughly. Arrange on large or individual plates, sprinkle with grated Italian cheese and cover with Basic Italian Tomato Sauce (page 766).

These ravioli may be prepared a day in advance. In this case cook them only 15 minutes, blanch them thoroughly with cold water after they are cooked, place in single layers on a flat baking sheet or platter, covered with wax paper, and wax paper in between each layer. Recook them in simmering salted water for about 5 minutes just before serving.

Meat and Spinach Filling for Ravioli

¾ pound fresh ground beef, veal, lamb, or pork, or leftover roasted meat, chicken, etc.

2 tablespoons oil, butter, or shortening

½ cup cooked spinach, chopped very fine

About ¼ cup chopped parsley

1¼ teaspoons salt

2 tablespoons dry bread crumbs

⅛ teaspoon nutmeg

¼ teaspoon pepper

1 small clove garlic, put through garlic press, finely chopped, or 1 small onion, finely chopped

2 tablespoons grated Italian cheese

1 large egg

If using fresh ground meat, sauté it slowly in 2 tablespoons fat for about 10 minutes separating it with a fork. If using cooked meat, chop fine and sauté only a few minutes. Add finely chopped spinach and other ingredients, except egg, to the meat. Cook together over low heat for several minutes until thoroughly blended. Add egg and beat quickly. Turn off heat. When cool, it may be put through a fine food chopper, *or use as is.* If it is too dry, add more egg to bind mixture; if too soft, add another 2 or more tablespoons bread crumbs.

Ricotta Filling for Ravioli

1 pound fresh ricotta, drained well
1 egg yolk
¼ cup chopped parsley
1 teaspoon sugar

1 teaspoon salt
⅛ teaspoon pepper
2 tablespoons grated Italian cheese

Drain the ricotta. Add the egg yolk, parsley, sugar, salt, pepper, and grated cheese. Beat until well blended, and consistency of a heavy custard. Do not have filling too soft.

Baked Stuffed Lasagna

Serves 6 to 8

1¼ recipes Basic Italian Tomato Sauce
    (page 766)
1¼ recipes Meat Balls (page 795)
1 pound lasagna macaroni

6 tablespoons grated Italian cheese
½ pound, or less, mozzarella or sca-
    morza cheese, sliced very thin

Prepare Basic Italian Tomato Sauce and Meat Balls.

Drop lasagna macaroni into 4 quarts rapidly boiling salted water (1½ tablespoons salt) and cook gently about 25 to 30 minutes, or until crisply tender. Add 1 tablespoon of shortening to water to prevent lasagna from sticking together. When done, pour little cold water into utensil and drain lasagna well in a colander.

Prepare Ricotta Filling for Lasagna (page 774).

Grease a heatproof glass baking dish that measures 12 × 8 × 2 inches (or use 17-inch stainless steel platter) with 2 teaspoons unsalted shortening. Pour ½ cup of the tomato sauce into dish and spread as evenly as possible. Over sauce arrange 3 layers of cooked lasagna macaroni, ½ cup additional sauce. Sprinkle with 2 tablespoons Italian cheese, ½ of thinly sliced mozzarella cheese, a few meat balls, cut into small pieces, and ½ of the Ricotta Filling, spreading as evenly as possible. Cover with 2 or more layers of the cooked lasagna. Pour another ½ cup sauce over lasagna, sprinkle with another 2 tablespoons Italian cheese, rest of sliced mozzarella cheese, a few meat balls, cut into small pieces, and rest of Ricotta Filling, spreading as evenly as possible. Finish with 3 or more layers of cooked lasagna macaroni. Sprinkle with 2 tablespoons of Italian cheese, and cover entire surface with about 1¼ cups of tomato sauce. Spread as evenly as possible.

Bake in a 350° F. oven about 1 hour if ingredients are warm, or about

1¼ hours if ingredients have been standing and are cool. If sauce boils over toward end, lower heat to 300° F. and place a baking sheet or piece of foil directly below casserole, not on floor of oven.

To Serve. To prevent spreading when serving, Baked Stuffed Lasagna must stand in room temperature about *30 minutes* (not more than 45) after it is baked. This dish will remain quite hot for at least 45 minutes. If top appears dry, pour a little sauce over entire surface just before cutting into 8 or more uniform portions. Lift each portion out with flexible pancake server.

Lasagna may be baked a day or several hours in advance if refrigerated, then reheated in a 350° F. oven for about 30 to 45 minutes if it is quite cool. If slightly warm, reheat for about 20 to 30 minutes, or when meat thermometer inserted in center of lasagna registers about 150° F.

Small leftover portions may be reheated in a deep skillet or saucepan in a small amount of hot water to produce steam. Cover pan and steam gently about 10 minutes or until heated through. Pour sauce over each portion just before serving.

Ricotta Filling for Lasagna

Combine 1½ pounds fresh ricotta cheese with 2 slightly beaten eggs, ¼ cup grated Italian cheese, ¼ cup fresh parsley, cut fine, 1½ teaspoons salt, ¼ teaspoon black pepper. Beat together until thoroughly blended. Should be the consistency of a soft custard.

Cannelloni Italian-Style (Manicotti)

Makes 24; serves 8 to 12

¼ cup lukewarm water
2 egg yolks
1 large whole egg
½ teaspoon salt

About 2¼ cups sifted all-purpose flour, or enough to form a medium dough that does not stick to hands when kneading

Combine water, yolks, whole egg, and salt in a medium-size bowl. Stir well and add flour, little at a time, and beat until smooth after most of flour has been added. When too stiff to beat with spoon, turn dough out onto a floured pastry cloth, and knead several minutes, adding more flour if sticky, forming a medium dough that does not cling to hands and is smooth. Cover dough with a warm bowl and let stand about ½ hour to ripen before rolling.

When dough is ripe, cut it into 6 uniform pieces. Roll each piece to measure 8 inches square. Cut each square into 4 uniform pieces, making a total of twenty-four 2-inch pieces. (They will increase in size after they are cooked in water.)

In a 4-quart saucepan ¾ filled with water, add about 1 tablespoon salt and 2 tablespoons shortening. Bring water to a good full boil. Drop pieces of dough into boiling water, 1 at a time, at about 5-second intervals, stirring gently with a long spoon with left hand. Now cover top of water in pot with a wet kitchen towel. Towel will keep noodle squares moist and stirring will not be necessary as they cook gently for about 6 or 7 minutes—until crisply tender. (They will become more tender after they are filled and baked.) When done, pour a little cold water into pot, and carefully drain noodle squares in a colander. After they drain well, place them on towels to remove any surplus moisture, or they will be difficult to fill and roll.

To Fill. Spread ¼ cup of Ricotta Filling on each piece of cooked noodle dough, leaving about ½ inch space without filling on each end. Roll firmly like a jelly roll, and place in well-buttered 17-inch stainless steel platter (or other heatproof platter about same size) *keeping open ends down,* leaving about ½ inch space between each roll, as they will increase in size during the baking process. Prepare 1¼ recipes of Basic Italian Tomato Sauce (page 766). Spread sauce on first layer. Sprinkle with about 2 tablespoons grated Italian cheese. Place rest of rolls on top and sides of lower layer, and spread with more sauce, reserving part of sauce to serve separately. Sprinkle with 2 tablespoons cheese. Cover baking dish with a well-greased piece of foil, dome-fashion, and bake in preheated 400° F. oven about 30 minutes. If sauce begins to run out of dish, lower heat to 300° F. and finish baking. Remove from oven, and *let rest* about 10 minutes before serving. Pick each up carefully with a large oval serving spoon or pancake turner. Serve rest of sauce and more grated cheese separately.

Note. These cannelloni may be prepared a day in advance, and stored on large platter or baking sheet on wax paper. Brush them with melted butter or margarine, but do not spread with sauce until you are ready to bake them. Separate layers with heavy wax paper, and cover with wax paper, and refrigerate. Then bake as suggested, but increase baking time by 10 minutes. May be frozen; best without sauce.

Ricotta Filling for Cannelloni (Manicotti)

3 pounds (6 cups) fresh Italian ricotta, drained if very wet
3 large whole eggs, slightly beaten with a fork
About 1½ teaspoons salt
1¼ teaspoons sugar
¾ teaspoon black or white pepper
⅓ cup finely chopped fresh parsley, or 1 tablespoon dry
⅓ cup grated Italian cheese

Beat ricotta with a large spoon or electric mixer. Add eggs, 1 at a time, and blend well after each addition until smooth. Add all other ingredients, 1 at a time, and beat until well mixed.

Cannelloni French-Style

Makes 24

Prepare 1 recipe of noodle dough for Cannelloni Italian-style (page 774).

To Fill Cannelloni. Place 1 rounded tablespoonful cool Chicken Filling for Cannelloni French-Style on 1 end of each square of noodle dough, bringing it close to ends. Form an oval and roll firmly. Arrange on well-buttered 17-inch steel platter (or other flat baking dish) leaving about ½ inch space between each roll, *with open ends down*. Spread first layer with a little of the Sauce for Cannelloni French-Style and sprinkle with ¼ cup grated parmesan cheese. Place rest of cannelloni over first row, between openings and in any open spaces. Sprinkle with another ¼ cup grated cheese, and cover with rest of sauce. Sprinkle entire surface with paprika, and bake at 350° F. about 40 minutes if ingredients are room temperature. If casserole was put together early and refrigerated, bake about 50 minutes. Place under broiler to brown if necessary before serving.

Garnish ends of platter with vegetable flowers and parsley, and serve hot, with a salad and dessert. No side dishes necessary as this is a complete and very satisfying meal.

Chicken Filling for Cannelloni French-Style

1 pound, net weight, cooked chicken meat, chopped medium with cleaver or heavy knife (2 pounds uncooked chicken breast or legs and thighs, simmered in 2 cups *unseasoned* water for about 30 minutes, or until tender, will give 1 pound net reserve stock from the cooked chicken, to be used for sauce)

5 slices bacon, cut into very small pieces and pan-fried until medium (drain well), or ½ cup cooked ham, chopped fine
About ½ teaspoon salt
¼ teaspoon pepper
1½ cups of Sauce for Cannelloni French-Style

Mix all ingredients well and let cool.

Sauce for Cannelloni French-Style

¾ cup butter or margarine
1 cup very finely chopped green onion and stems, mixed
1 small clove garlic, put through garlic press
3-ounce can mushrooms, chopped fine

¾ cup sifted all-purpose flour
1½ cups reserved chicken stock, combined with 2 cups of milk and liquid from mushrooms
¾ teaspoon oregano
About 2 teaspoons salt
2 tablespoons dry sherry wine

Melt butter or margarine, add finely chopped onion, garlic, and mushrooms, and sauté for several minutes. Add flour and blend as smooth as possible. Add warm stock combined with milk and mushroom liquid, and seasonings. Cook until thick, then let simmer about 5 minutes. Add wine, and cook another minute. Taste sauce, and season further if necessary. This sauce should be of medium consistency. If too thick, add little more liquid. Add 1½ cups of this sauce to the cooked chopped chicken and other ingredients in Chicken Filling for Cannelloni French-Style, and mix well. Let filling cool. Put rest of sauce aside to be used later.

Gnocchi Romano

Makes 24 to 30; serves 4 to 6

½ cup hot water
¼ cup butter or margarine
½ teaspoon salt
½ cup sifted all-purpose flour
2 large whole eggs (½ cup or bit less)
1 cup mashed Idaho potatoes (add no milk, no butter, no salt), or instant Idaho potatoes (reduce water by 2 tablespoons; add no milk)
Another ½ cup sifted all-purpose flour
¼ cup grated Italian cheese

In a 2-quart saucepan combine hot water, butter or margarine, and salt. Bring to a boil, lower heat to medium, and add the ½ cup flour all at once. Stir vigorously for about 2 minutes until smooth and mixture leaves sides of pan. Remove from heat, pour into 7- or 8-inch bowl, and at once add eggs, 1 at a time, and beat after each addition until very smooth. Electric mixer or heavy wooden spoon may be used. Now add the mashed potatoes and mix thoroughly with heavy spoon until smooth. Turn out onto floured pastry cloth, and add the other ½ cup of flour alternately with the grated Italian cheese, little at a time, kneading gently until smooth. If preparation feels *too* soft, add a little more flour, not more than ¼ cup. Keep dough *soft*, but it must hold its shape when rolled and cut.

Divide dough into 2 uniform pieces. On lightly floured pastry cloth roll each piece with hands into a 22-inch rope. Cut on bias in about 2½-inch pieces, measured from point to point. Pick gnocchi up with small spatula and place on a plate, then lower them carefully into rapidly boiling salted water. A 10-inch deep skillet ¾ filled with boiling water, seasoned with 2 teaspoons salt, will hold half of gnocchi (about 12 to 15). When gnocchi float to top, in about 3 or 4 minutes, *let boil gently about 1 minute* (not more than 2 minutes necessary). Stir gnocchi *gently* with long spoon until they are done. Remove with slotted spoon, drain well, and place into skillet with melted butter or margarine over very low heat. Serve at once sprinkled with grated Italian cheese or Basic Italian Tomato Sauce (page 766). Keep gnocchi hot, covered, over *very, very* low heat for a few minutes while second batch is cooking.

If preferred, drained cooked gnocchi may be poured into an ovenproof flat casserole. Pour Basic Italian Tomato Sauce over top, and sprinkle with cheese. Bake about 15 minutes before serving if ingredients are warm; about 25 to 30 minutes if ingredients are cool.

Gnocchi may be cooked hours or day in advance. Drain in colander, pour cold water over them gently, to prevent sticking when storing, well covered, in refrigerator. To reheat, cover them with warm water, and gently bring to a boil. Let simmer about 2 or 3 minutes, drain well, and serve as desired.

Frozen Gnocchi. Prepare and cook gnocchi as per general directions. Drain and separate with wax paper; wrap for freezing about 2 weeks in advance. To serve frozen gnocchi, lower them into warm water, lightly salted, and bring to a gentle boil. As soon as they float to the top of water, in about 5 minutes, let boil gently about 2 minutes for small amount, about 3 minutes for large amount. Drain thoroughly and serve rolled in soft butter, and sprinkle with grated Italian cheese. Or arrange well-drained cooked gnocchi on an attractive oval platter, pour Basic Italian Tomato Sauce over top, and sprinkle with Italian cheese.

Homemade Egg Noodles

3 large whole eggs
2 teaspoons salad oil

⅔ teaspoon salt
About 2 cups sifted all-purpose flour

Pour eggs into a medium-size bowl and beat them with a wire whisk or egg beater for about ½ minute. Add the oil and salt and blend well. Now with a large heavy wooden spoon add flour, about ½ cup at a time, and beat after each addition for a few seconds. When dough becomes too stiff to beat in bowl, turn it out onto a well-floured pastry cloth, and knead it for several minutes until dough is quite firm and smooth, but not dry. Add more flour if necessary to prevent a sticky dough. Cover with a bowl and let stand in a warm room for about 30 minutes or longer to ripen.

When dough is ripe, cut it in 2 pieces, and roll each piece on floured pastry cloth to measure about 18 inches round, or thinner, depending on what it is to be used for. For *tortellini*, dough must be rolled as thin as possible, then cut into small rounds or squares, about 1½ to 2 inches. For *fettuccine*, allow rolled dough to stand in room temperature about 30 minutes, turning it over several times. After 30 minutes touch dough. It must not be the least bit sticky and not so dry that it is brittle. Fold it over, or form a roll. Place it on a board, and with a very sharp knife cut dough into desired width. Separate, and spread noodles on a flat surface. They may be cooked at once, or allowed to dry thoroughly, then stored for future use.

Gnocchi Verdi (Green Gnocchi)

Serves 4

2 tablespoons butter or margarine

10-ounce package uncooked frozen spinach, defrosted, surplus moisture pressed out through a strainer, chopped very fine (unless already chopped)

½ cup Italian ricotta, well drained

¼ cup sifted all-purpose flour

2 large eggs, beaten only until yolks and whites are well mixed

¼ cup grated Italian cheese

½ teaspoon salt

¼ teaspoon black pepper

⅛ teaspoon nutmeg

Boiling water in a 3- or 4-quart pot, combined with 1 teaspoon salt

About ¼ cup melted butter in medium-size skillet, and more grated Italian cheese

Melt butter or margarine in good-size skillet, add well-drained chopped spinach and cook over medium heat until moisture has evaporated and spinach begins to cling to bottom of pan. (This will take several minutes.) Now add the drained ricotta, and continue to cook for 3 or 4 minutes, stirring until well blended. Pour this preparation into a large bowl, add the flour, mix well, then add beaten eggs, grated Italian cheese, salt, pepper, and nutmeg. Beat preparation with a heavy spoon for about 2 minutes. Cover and refrigerate for at least 1 hour. May stand in refrigerator for at least 12 hours.

To cook, shape balls in palms of damp hands with about 1 rounded tablespoon of the preparation, dampening hands occasionally with a wet cloth. Place smooth-shaped gnocchi on wax paper until they are all ready. Now lower them into rapidly boiling salted water, and cook *gently at simmer point (do not boil)* about 5 minutes, or until gnocchi appear a little larger and slightly firm to the touch. Stir them gently during the cooking process, and do not cook too many at one time. Pick up cooked gnocchi with a perforated spoon, let drain well, and place them in a skillet with melted butter or margarine. Keep covered over *very* low heat (just to keep warm) or in a 250° F. oven until all have been cooked.

Sprinkle them with grated Italian cheese and serve in an attractive dish as an accompaniment with meat or poultry. They are also delicious rolled into Basic Italian Tomato Sauce (page 766), and sprinkled with grated cheese.

▶ MAIN DISHES ◀

Breast of Chicken Alfredo

Prepare 1 pound chicken breasts, each breast cut in 2 pieces. With cleaver flatten breast slightly. Pour Marinade Alfredo over chicken breasts, cover and refrigerate for at least 2 hours, turning breasts over several times.

(It is better not to bone and skin breasts when using this method. They will be more moist and more tender.)

To Bake. Sift together ½ cup all-purpose flour with 1½ teaspoons paprika, ½ teaspoon salt, ¼ teaspoon pepper, 1 tablespoon Italian cheese. Remove breasts from marinade, hold in fingers and let drain a few seconds. Now cover them completely with flour preparation, shaking off loose flour. Sauté gently in about ¼ inch of half butter and half oil or shortening about 5 minutes on each side until breasts are light golden color. They will darken further in the oven. Place them on a rack or trivet with drip pan underneath, and bake in a 350° F. preheated oven about 35 minutes for medium breast, 40 minutes for large, or until rib bones can easily be removed from meat. Pour ½ cup hot water into drip pan after a few minutes, then more liquid if necessary. Brush about 1 tablespoon melted butter over each breast the last 10 minutes. Serve in a bed of Noodles Alfredo (page 781), or as desired.

Marinade Alfredo

2 tablespoons salad oil	1 tablespoon grated Italian cheese
1 tablespoon lemon juice	¼ teaspoon coarse oregano, crushed
1 sliver fresh garlic, or ⅛ teaspoon garlic salt	½ teaspoon salt
	¼ teaspoon black pepper

Combine all ingredients in medium bowl, and with egg or wire beater, beat about 1 minute.

Note. Place poultry to be marinated into an enamel, glass, or stainless steel utensil, and not in other utensils made of metal, as very often the acid in the marinade will act upon the metal chemically and develop an unpleasant taste in the meat or poultry, and other foods. Let food soak in the marinade for time suggested in recipe, turning it over, and basting it often with a large spoon with marinade in pan. Keep in refrigerator, but let stand in room temperature for about 1 hour before cooking, either in or out of marinade.

Sautéed Breast of Chicken or Turkey Alfredo

It is important to bone chicken breasts for this purpose. Skin may be left on or removed. If using turkey breasts slice about ½ inch thick. Marinate same as for Breast of Chicken Alfredo. Drain, and cover with seasoned flour. Sauté breast in about ⅓ inch of hot butter and half oil or unsalted shortening, about 7 or 8 minutes on each side, over medium heat. When good golden color on underside, turn over carefully and sauté second side about 7 or 8 minutes. Because breast of chicken or turkey is a very tender meat, it will be cooked through according to these directions provided meat is boned and cut not more than ½ inch thick. Test by cutting through thick piece with side of dinner fork. If not tender, *cover skillet, lower heat* and simmer several minutes. Do not add any water if possible. Serve with Noodles Alfredo (below).

Note. To suit those who prefer only white meat of turkey, Premium Deep-Basted Breast of Young Turkey is available. They are vacuum sealed and frozen while still fresher than fresh. Weights range from 3½ to 7 pounds. Have breast slightly frozen as it will slice more smoothly and easily.

Noodles Alfredo

Prepare your own Homemade Noodles (page 778), or use top-quality (1 pound) wide egg noodles. Cook them in salted boiling water gently about 10 minutes, or until crisply tender. When done, drain well, pour into a large heated attractive serving bowl or chafing dish. *At once* add ½ cup soft unmelted butter and ½ cup freshly grated Italian cheese for each pound of noodles, and with 2 forks blend well. About ¼ cup or little more of *warm* rich cream may be blended into noodles just before you are ready to serve them. It is better not to heat butter and to have cream just warm for better flavor.

Seasoned noodles may be poured onto an oval serving platter, forming a nest. Arrange baked or sautéed breasts of chicken or turkey down center. Sautéed fluted mushrooms may be placed on top of each breast. Sauce Poulet (page 332) may be served separately, but it is not necessary with these moist delicious noodles.

Chicken Cacciatore (Hunter-Style)

Serves 4

2 tablespoons butter and 2 tablespoons oil, or other shortening
3-pound drawn frying chicken, cut in serving pieces
1 clove garlic, cut fine, or put through garlic press
½ teaspoon oregano or thyme, crushed in fingers
¼ teaspoon black pepper

About 1½ teaspoons salt
⅓ cup flour
½ cup, or more, dry white wine, combined with 1 cup canned or fresh tomatoes, cut into medium pieces
½ pound fresh mushrooms, sliced thick and sautéed in 2 tablespoons butter

Heat butter and oil. Brown chicken slowly on all sides, over medium heat, until very brown. Sprinkle with remaining ingredients except mushrooms. Cover skillet or saucepan, and simmer about 40 minutes, adding more wine or tomatoes if chicken appears dry. Turn chicken several times during cooking process. When it is tender, add fresh sautéed mushrooms. Cook uncovered about 5 minutes. Add little gravy coloring if needed.

Arrange cooked chicken attractively on serving platter, and pour remaining sauce and mushrooms over top. May be served in bed of Risotto Milanese (page 805) or noodles, etc.

Chicken Legs and Thighs Alfredo

Prepare same as Breast of Chicken Alfredo (page 779), but increase cooking time about 15 minutes, depending on size. If the leg and thigh are left in 1 piece, it may take an extra 10 minutes to become tender. Test before removing from oven. If you can penetrate thickest part of leg with a two-tined fork or point of paring knife easily and there is no pink color visible, meat is done.

Chicken Tetrazzini

Serves 6

3-pound drawn frying chicken	About ½ pound or more fresh mushrooms, sautéed in 2 tablespoons butter
2 cups hot water	
Salt as suggested	
½ pound broad egg noodles or spaghetti	A little pepper
	Several slivers garlic
2 tablespoons melted butter	Additional salt, pepper, and cheese
2 tablespoons grated Italian cheese	

Steam chicken in the 2 cups hot water and 2 teaspoons salt, about 40 to 60 minutes, or until tender. Let stand until cool enough to handle. *Strain stock for sauce.* Remove meat from bones, and cut chicken into pieces about 3 inches long.

Cook noodles in gently boiling unsalted water about 10 minutes, or until crisply tender, but not too soft. Then pour a *little* cold water into utensil and drain noodles thoroughly. Pour noodles into bowl and at once season with 1 teaspoon salt, 2 tablespoons melted butter, cheese, and 1 cup of Sauce for Chicken Tetrazzini (page 783).

Sauté mushrooms in the 2 tablespoons butter for 5 minutes. Season with ½ teaspoon salt, pepper, and slivers of garlic, and continue to cook several minutes.

Pour and spread noodle mixture into a flat, buttered baking dish that measures about 10 × 1⅓ inches (round or oblong casserole may be used). A 17-inch stainless steel platter is excellent. Place the sautéed mushrooms over noodles, pour a little of the sauce over mushrooms, then cover with the cut chicken. Season with about ½ teaspoon salt and a little pepper. Pour rest of sauce (that has cooled for about 15 minutes) over chicken and sprinkle top with about ¼ cup grated Italian cheese and drizzle with 2 tablespoons melted butter. Bake at 350° F. about 30 minutes, then broil about 5 minutes, or until golden brown. Serve hot.

Sauce for Chicken Tetrazzini

¾ cup sifted all-purpose flour
½ cup melted butter
1 cup warm milk or cream
2 cups warm chicken stock

1½ teaspoons salt
2 tablespoons dry sauterne or sherry wine

Blend flour into melted butter, gradually add milk or cream *and* chicken stock stirring constantly. Cook until thick and smooth, then simmer 5 minutes, adding salt and wine toward end. Let cool about 15 minutes before pouring over top of chicken. If too thick, add 1 or 2 tablespoons of milk.

Chicken Dinner Vesuvio

Serves 4

3-pound frying chicken, cut up
½ cup sifted all-purpose flour, combined with 2 teaspoons paprika, ½ teaspoon crushed oregano leaves, ½ teaspoon garlic salt, 1 teaspoon salt, 1 tablespoon Italian cheese

¼ cup hot oil, combined with ¼ cup butter
About ¼ cup stock or water
¼ cup dry wine (optional)

Wash chicken under cold running water, drain it thoroughly, but have it slightly damp so that coating will cling better. Roll each piece into the flour sifted with seasonings, pressing coating on with both hands. Sauté chicken in the hot oil combined with butter over medium heat until brown on both sides, but not too dark, as it will darken more in the oven. Place it on an attractive heatproof serving platter. Add about ¼ cup of stock or water to drippings in skillet and pour over the chicken. Place Browned Potatoes around and in between open spaces in platter. Bake in a preheated 350° F. oven about 1 hour, or until tender, removing the breast after 40 minutes. Baste chicken with drippings in pan or additional butter the last 10 minutes. If drippings appear scant, add about ¼ cup more stock or dry wine.

To Serve. About 5 minutes before removing chicken from oven, place cooked peas or string beans in small heaps in open spaces between chicken and potatoes, and continue to bake a few minutes longer. If breast was removed before other pieces of chicken were done, remember to place it back into the oven just before you add the vegetable.

Browned Potatoes for Chicken Vesuvio

About 2 pounds red boiling potatoes, peeled, and cut into quarters, washed and dried thoroughly
About ¼ cup or more hot oil or unsalted shortening

½ teaspoon salt
¼ teaspoon pepper
2 tablespoons Italian cheese

Brown potatoes well in the hot oil. Remove from fat, season with the salt, pepper, and Italian cheese.

Peas or String Beans for Chicken Vesuvio

¼ cup sliced or chopped onion
¼ cup hot oil or shortening
1 package defrosted frozen peas or string beans

1 teaspoon salt
¼ teaspoon pepper
1 tablespoon parmesan cheese
¼ teaspoon crushed oregano

Sauté onion in the ¼ cup hot oil for several minutes. Add defrosted vegetable and seasonings. Cover and cook gently only until tender—about 7 or 8 minutes for beans; 3 minutes for peas.

Chicken Milano

3-pound frying chicken, cut into serving pieces
¼ cup oil and ¼ cup butter, heated
1 large clove garlic, minced
1 large onion, chopped fine
½ cup celery, chopped fine
1 green pepper, chopped fine
½ cup dry sauterne wine

6-ounce can tomato paste
½ cup stock or water
1 teaspoon crushed oregano
¼ teaspoon baking soda
About 1½ teaspoon salt
½ teaspoon pepper
¼ cup grated Italian cheese

Wash chicken pieces and dry them thoroughly. Brown them in the hot oil combined with butter, then add garlic, onion, celery, and green pepper, and continue to cook for about 5 more minutes, but do not scorch. Combine sauterne wine, tomato paste, stock or water, and all of seasonings; blend well and pour over the sautéed chicken. Cover pan and simmer gently about 50 minutes, removing breast after 35 to 40 minutes. When chicken is tender, remaining sauce may be thickened with ½ tablespoon corn starch dissolved in 2 tablespoons water. Continue to cook until thick, then simmer about 3 minutes. Serve chicken on a bed of flat egg or green noodles, mixed vegetables, or Risotto Milanese (page 805).

Chicken Stew Italian-Style

5-pound stewing chicken, cut into serving pieces
½ cup hot oil or shortening
1 large onion, sliced thin
1 clove garlic, chopped fine
About 2 teaspoons salt
½ teaspoon pepper
½ teaspoon crushed oregano

About ½ teaspoon dry celery or parsley
3 cups tomatoes, broken in small pieces
¼ cup dry wine
2 tablespoons flour, combined with ¼ cup cool water
1 pound noodles or other fancy pasta
¼ cup or more grated Italian cheese

Brown chicken well in the hot oil or shortening. Add all other ingredients except the noodles and grated Italian cheese. Let chicken simmer, covered, over very low heat for 2½ to 3 hours, depending on tenderness. Add little more wine or stock toward end if necessary.

About 15 minutes before chicken is tender, cook noodles in boiling salted water until crisply tender (al dente), drain well, and add to tomato drippings in pan (first remove chicken and place it in center of a hot serving platter). Blend noodles well with the sauce, adding the grated Italian cheese. Arrange noodles around chicken. Very delicious served with a salad bowl.

Osso Buco (Shin Bones of Veal)

Serves 4 to 8

There are several versions of this famous Italian dish that is served principally in the northern part of Italy.

4 shins of veal (have butcher saw into about 4-inch pieces, not less than 3 inches)
¼ cup butter and ¼ cup oil, melted and hot
Salt
Pepper
Crushed oregano leaves
Flour
2 cups of peeled fresh or canned undrained tomatoes, broken up into medium-size pieces
½ cup of stock or water
3 cups carrots, cut in 3-inch-thick wedges
3 cups pascal celery, cut in 3-inch-thick wedges

3 cups medium-size onions, cut lengthwise into ¾-inch-wide slices
1 large, or more, clove of fresh garlic, cut fine, or put through garlic press
½ cup mixed butter and oil, melted and hot
About 1½ teaspoons, or bit more, salt
¼ teaspoon black pepper
1 teaspoon, or less, crushed oregano leaves
¼ cup fresh parsley, cut medium fine, or 1 tablespoon dry (optional)
2 medium bay leaves, crumbled into fine pieces

Wash shins under cool running water. Dry them well in a towel. Trim if necessary. Brush each generously with part of ¼ cup melted butter and ¼ cup oil, and sprinkle with salt, pepper, and crushed oregano leaves. Roll meat in flour, covering it well and completely with the flour. Brown the shins in rest of the hot butter and oil slowly on all sides until they are very brown. (This will take about 20 minutes. Don't rush it.) Now place shins in a Dutch oven upright to prevent marrow from falling out. Pour remaining drippings over meat. Cover top of shins with tomatoes and stock or water. Cover pot and bring to boiling point on top of stove. Meanwhile, preheat oven to 350° F. Place covered pot into preheated oven and bake shins for about 1½ hours, or until meat is almost tender.

Meanwhile, peel and cut vegetables. Sauté vegetables in the ½ cup hot butter and oil over medium heat, turning them over frequently, for about 15 minutes, but do not allow to brown. Mix remaining seasonings together and sprinkle them over vegetables, blending them well the last 5 minutes.

Remove pot from oven (after 1½ hours) and pour off all liquid into a 2-quart saucepan. Thicken liquid with ⅓ cup sifted flour combined slowly with ½ cup cool water, stirring to keep it smooth. Let simmer about 5 minute after it thickens. Pour sauce, sautéed vegetables, *and about 1 cup light dry wine* over shins, and sprinkle top with rind of 1 small lemon. Cover pot and return to oven, and continue to bake at 350° F. for about 20 more minutes, or until meat is *very tender* when tested with a 2-tined fork. If not done, continue to bake about 15 minutes and make test. Do not overcook as vegetables will lose their attractiveness and flavor. For extra color and taste 1 package of frozen green peas may be added the last 7 or 8 minutes. Or omit peas, and add 1 cup fresh celery leaves, cut into about ¾-inch pieces.

When meat is tender, taste sauce and add a little more salt if needed. Place shins in center of a large platter, allowing 1 for each person if they are small (a large shin will serve 2 nicely). Surround meat with the colorful, delectable vegetables, and pour small amount of peas and carrots over each shin. Or shins may be served on a bed of Risotto Milanese (page 805) or any type of fancy-cut, well-seasoned, and buttered pasta, cooked al dente, or egg noodles. There will be enough rich sauce to serve with each shin.

Note. Beef shins may be used instead of veal shins.

Parmesan Veal Cutlets

Veal steak about ½ inch thick
Salt and pepper
Pinch of oregano
Light dry bread crumbs (not white)

Well-beaten egg to which add 1 tablespoon water
Swiss cheese

Cut veal into desired pieces and pound with meat tenderer. Sprinkle with salt and pepper and pinch of oregano. Cover with bread crumbs, dip into diluted egg, then cover with crumbs again, pressing down crumbs. Let meat stand on wax paper for about 20 minutes, turning it over several times while standing. Fry slowly in about ¼ inch unsalted shortening or oil until golden brown on 1 side, then fry second side. Place on a trivet, add ½ cup hot water to drippings. Cover and cook *slowly* about 30 minutes or until tender, adding more water if drippings appear dry. Pour a spoonful of Tomato Sauce (page 767) on each cutlet and place a slice of Swiss cheese over sauce, sprinkle with paprika and cover saucepan again. Continue to cook slowly about 10 minutes more, or meat may be placed in a greased baking sheet or heatproof platter after the first steaming. Then pour sauce and place cheese over sauce. Bake uncovered in a 400° F. oven about 10 minutes for a drier crust.

Veal Chops Cacciatore

Serves 4 to 6

2 pounds veal chops, sliced about ¾ inch thick

2 tablespoons shortening and 2 tablespoons butter

1 small clove garlic

About 1½ teaspoons salt

¼ teaspoon pepper

¼ teaspoon oregano leaves

¼ cup light dry wine

¾ cup tomatoes (fresh or canned)

2 tablespoons grated parmesan cheese

2 tablespoons flour

¼ cup mushroom liquor or tomato juice

1 large fresh green pepper, cut into 1 x 2-inch pieces and sautéed in 1 tablespoon oil until delicately brown and almost tender, about 5 minutes

1 small can button mushrooms, drained (save liquor)

Brown veal chops in shortening and butter. Sprinkle with seasonings, turning chops over to season other side. Add wine, tomatoes, and cheese. Cover skillet tightly and simmer about 30 to 40 minutes, or until meat is tender. Combine flour with mushroom liquor or tomato juice and stir until smooth. Add to meat. Add sautéed green pepper and drained mushrooms. Cover skillet, and simmer about 7 or 8 minutes. When done, arrange chops on an oval or oblong platter. Pour sauce over meat, and serve with spaghetti, macaroni, noodles, rice, or potatoes.

Plain Breaded Veal Cutlets

Proceed same as for Parmesan Veal Cutlets (page 786), but omit sauce and cheese on top of cutlets. Plain breaded veal cutlets may be served with any type of gravy or tomato sauce.

Note. If a crisp crust is preferred on veal cutlets, cover them with egg and crumbs, as per general directions. Let stand, etc. Do not have them sliced more than ½ inch in thickness, better ¼ inch, to insure thorough cooking. Deep-fry cutlets at 325° F. in oil or shortening for about 7 or 8 minutes, until golden brown and crisp. Or they may be baked on a rack with drip pan underneath at 350° F. for about 20 to 30 minutes after they have been browned in hot fat in a skillet on top of stove. Pour about 1 cup of hot water in drip pan to prevent smoking. When meat is tender, pour sauce on top and place sliced cheese over sauce, and continue to bake until cheese is fully melted—for about 7 or 8 minutes.

If Premium quality veal is used and it is sliced less than ½ inch thick, it may be covered with egg and crumbs, etc., then fried slowly in ¼ inch of oil or shortening about 7 or 8 minutes on each side without braising.

Veal Scaloppine à la Genovese

Serves 4

1 small clove garlic
2 tablespoons butter, oil, or shortening
1 pound thinly sliced veal steak, cut in 3-inch squares
1 teaspoon salt
A little pepper
Pinch of sage and nutmeg
2 tablespoons all-purpose flour
1 teaspoon capers (optional)

1 small onion, sliced very thin
½ cup sauterne or other dry white wine, combined with ⅓ cup tomato paste purée
¼ pound fresh mushrooms, sliced medium and sautéed in 1 tablespoon butter
1 tablespoon stuffed green olives, sliced in rings (optional)

Sauté garlic in the butter for about 5 minutes. Remove garlic and discard it. In same butter, brown meat lightly on both sides, over moderate heat. When meat is brown, sprinkle it with the salt, pepper, sage, nutmeg, flour, capers, onion, and the wine and tomato paste. Cover, and simmer about 15 to 20 minutes, turning meat several times. If liquid in skillet appears scant during cooking process, add a little more wine or tomato juice. When meat is tender, add the sautéed mushrooms and the tablespoon olive rings. Cook together uncovered about 7 or 8 minutes.

When ready to serve, arrange meat attractively on bed of mixed vegetables, noodles, or as desired. May be sprinkled with a small amount of finely chopped fresh parsley or fresh green onions.

Evelyn Russo's Neapolitan-Style Leg of Veal

Have butcher prepare leg of veal for roasting. Rub meat with cut clove of garlic. Cut remaining garlic in small pieces and insert into meat, making openings with paring knife. Sprinkle entire surface with about 2 teaspoons (or less) oregano, 2 teaspoons salt, ½ teaspoon black pepper, a little very finely minced parsley (about 1 teaspoon), and about 2 tablespoons grated Italian cheese. Drizzle about ¼ cup melted butter or oil over meat, and then 1 cup of tomatoes and juice, first crushed with hands or put through food mill.

Roast meat on a trivet at 300° F., about 35 minutes per pound if bone is left in, or about 45 minutes per pound if bone has been removed. Best to use meat thermometer. While meat is roasting, baste it often with drippings in pan, and add a little hot stock or dry light wine to drippings *whenever necessary to prevent scorching.* Drizzle veal with another ¼ cup melted butter or oil after first 2 hours. For large leg of veal weighing more than 6 or 7 pounds, pour another ½ cup tomatoes when meat is half done. Tomatoes scorch very easily, even at low temperatures. *Keep adding hot water or stock to drippings as often as is necessary.* The water and drippings will make a delicious gravy after meat is done. Measure drippings and add more water if necessary. Thicken with 2 tablespoons cornstarch diluted in 2 tablespoons cool water *for each cup of gravy.* Season further if necessary, and simmer about 7 or 8 minutes. Sautéed mushrooms may be added to gravy if desired. *Turn meat over when half done.* Sliced and serve as suggested for Leg of Lamb (page 790).

Peppered Steak with Sautéed Mushrooms Italian-Style

Serves 4 to 6

¼ cup oil	1 pound beef tenderloin, cut in about
1½ pounds fresh green peppers (4	2-inch squares and ¼ inch thick
large)	(veal or pork tenderloin may be
Fresh garlic	used)
Salt and pepper	¼ cup flour
About 1½ teaspoons oregano	¼ cup sherry or sauterne
½ cup butter or oil	½ cup crushed tomatoes
½ pound firm fresh mushrooms; if	2 medium firm red tomatoes, or 6
small leave whole, if large cut	bell tomatoes
in thick slices	

In the ¼ cup oil sauté the green peppers, cut into about 1½-inch squares, and several slivers of garlic for about 5 minutes, turning them often to prevent browning. Season with 1 teaspoon salt, ¼ teaspoon pepper, and ½ teaspoon oregano. Cover and steam about 5 minutes, turning them several times. Do not cook any longer than necessary. Peppers should be crisply tender and still green. Put aside.

In about ¼ cup butter or oil (butter preferable) sauté several slivers of garlic and the mushrooms. Cook only about 3 minutes, turning them often. Should be very crisply tender and light in color. Season with ½ teaspoon salt, ⅛ teaspoon pepper, and ½ teaspoon oregano. Pour mushrooms into peppers.

In ¼ cup butter sauté several slivers garlic for about 1 minute, add meat and cook about 2 or 3 minutes on each side over moderate high heat, or until brown. Season with about 1¼ teaspoons salt, ½ teaspoon oregano, ¼ teaspoon pepper, ¼ cup flour, ¼ cup sherry or sauterne wine and ½ cup tomatoes crushed into medium pieces. Cover skillet and steam about 5 minutes (longer for veal and pork) until tender, turning several times.

Cut up 2 red firm tomatoes in large pieces, about 1½ inches. Combine them with the sautéed peppers and mushrooms. Just before serving, cook all vegetables together over moderate heat, about 5 minutes, turning several times, *only until heated through.* Do not overcook at this point in order to preserve color and flavor. *Drain well.*

To Serve. Mound *drained* vegetables on an oblong or oval platter. Arrange meat over vegetables and pour sauce over all. Or meat may be combined with drained vegetables and then mounded on serving platter. Serve at once as a main dish, or as an accompaniment to Spaghetti (page 759), Lasagna (page 773), Ravioli (page 771), etc.

Flank Steak Bracciole Italian-Style

Serves 4

1 flank steak, or 1 pound round steak	1 tablespoon parmesan cheese
1 teaspoon salt	2 tablespoons chopped parsley
½ teaspoon pepper	2 strips bacon or salt pork
1 clove chopped garlic	

Have butcher cut flank steak into 2 lengthwise pieces and remove skin; put in rest of ingredients, roll meat, and hold in place with wood pins. Sauté until golden brown on all sides in ½ cup very hot shortening. Add meat to Basic Italian Tomato Sauce (page 766) and cook about 2 hours, depending on tenderness of meat. Test for doneness. Flank steak is slightly stringy but has much flavor.

Continental-Style Leg of Lamb

Prepare 1 leg of lamb, boned for oven. Let stand at room temperature at least 1 hour in advance. (Allow about 45 minutes per pound for roasting of meat if it has been boned. If bones have not been removed, allow about 30 minutes per pound.) Make several incisions in meat, and insert small slivers of garlic. Rub entire surface of lamb with cut clove of garlic. Sprinkle well with salt and pepper, about ½ teaspoon thyme, ½ teaspoon rosemary. Combine 2 tablespoons of tomato paste with ¼ cup sauterne wine, 1 cup of stock or water. Place meat on a trivet in a shallow roasting pan, with fat side up, having meat thermometer in thickest part. Pour liquids over meat and roast at 325° F. until done. Baste about every 15 minutes with drippings in pan, adding more stock or water as needed to prevent scorching. It may be necessary to *add another cup of liquid (stock or water)* during the roasting process. The tomato paste causes drying of the drippings but adds color and flavor. The leftover drippings and liquid when meat is done make a very tasty and attractive gravy.

Important. When meat has been roasting about half of time, turn it over on opposite side, and continue to roast and baste for the balance of cooking time. This will flavor and brown meat more evenly and prevents charring. A meat baster is very convenient in basting this meat.

When lamb is done, remove and place it on a warm platter. Prepare gravy by removing most of fat from drippings and add enough more stock or water to drippings in roasting pan to make amount of gravy desired. For each cup, add 2 tablespoons cornstarch (or 3 tablespoons flour), combined with 2 or 3 tablespoons water to make smooth paste. Combine with drippings and cook, stirring continuously, until thick, then simmer about 5 minutes. Taste and season further if necessary. Two tablespoons dry sherry or sauterne wine may be added to gravy.

To Serve. Slice lamb lengthwise into thin slices. (This is the continental way of carving lamb and it is desirable because top-quality lamb is very tender and can be sliced with the grain, which is an exception to the rule.) Place sliced lamb on a thick bed of well-seasoned and buttered peas, or Vegetable Casserole Continental (page 809), Rice Pilaf (page 312), or buttered noodles. Pour sauce over entire surface of meat, or part of sauce can first be poured over vegetables, rice, or noodles. Garnish top of meat with very large sautéed mushrooms, with rounded part up. Place vegetable flowers and parsley bouquet on each end for special occasions. This is a very delectable way to prepare lamb and is enjoyed even by people who do not like lamb roasted in the standard way.

Lamb Casserole Neapolitan

Serves 6

½ cup sliced onion
¼ cup hot butter and ¼ cup shortening
¼ pound fresh mushrooms, sliced
2 cups thick tomatoes and juice, combined with ¼ teaspoon baking soda
About 2 teaspoons salt
½ teaspoon dried basil or mint, crushed in fingers

½ teaspoon coarse-ground black pepper
½ pound cooked narrow yellow noodles or fine spaghetti
About 2 cups leftover roasted lamb (or other leftover meat), cut into 1-inch pieces
About ½ cup grated Italian cheese for top

Sauté onion in butter several minutes. Add mushrooms, and cook 3 or 4 more minutes. Add tomatoes and all seasonings, and simmer, covered, about 10 minutes. Now add cooked noodles and meat; blend well. Pour into a casserole that measures about 12 × 8 × 2 inches. Sprinkle top with grated cheese and bake at 400° F. about 20 to 25 minutes. This is an excellent 1-dish meal, served with a salad and dessert.

Stuffed Green Peppers with Rice and Meat

Serves 6

6 large green peppers	¼ teaspoon garlic salt
5 tablespoons oil	3 cups cooked rice (1 cup uncooked)
1 pound ground beef	6-ounce can tomato paste, combined
1½ teaspoons salt	with 2 cans cold water
¼ teaspoon pepper	½ cup fresh pulled bread crumbs
½ teaspoon oregano	

Wash peppers; remove cores, centers and seeds. Sauté peppers in 2 tablespoons oil on all sides. Fry ground beef in other 3 tablespoons oil; season with salt, pepper, oregano, and garlic salt. Add cooked rice and ⅓ cup diluted tomato paste.

Stuff peppers with rice and meat mixture. Place stuffed peppers in a large pie plate or casserole. Put pulled bread crumbs on top of each pepper, and drizzle top with melted butter. Pour rest of diluted tomato paste in pie plate or casserole, and bake in preheated 350° F. oven about 30 minutes, or until peppers are soft.

Sicilian-Style Spaghetti and Meat Casserole

Serves 8

2 tablespoons shortening	2 cans (6-ounce size) Italian tomato
1 small onion, chopped fine	paste, combined with about 2
1 clove garlic, chopped fine	cups stock or water
1 pound ground beef (or half pork)	¼ teaspoon baking soda
1½ tablespoons salt	1 pound spaghetti, cooked in 3
½ teaspoon pepper	quarts salted water (with 1 ta-
¼ cup minced parsley	blespoon salt) until tender,
About ¾ cup grated Italian cheese	about 15 minutes, drained well
½ teaspoon oregano	1 cup walnuts, toasted in a 300° F.
1 large can tomatoes (No. 3 size),	oven about 10 minutes, then put
crushed with hands or put	through a nut chopper
through a food mill	

In a large 3- or 4-quart saucepan heat shortening. Add chopped onions and garlic, and cook about 5 minutes. Add ground meat, and continue to cook about 7 or 8 minutes until brown. Add salt, pepper, parsley, ¼ cup cheese, oregano, tomatoes, and tomato paste with stock or water. Mix well. Cover, and simmer about 1 hour. Add baking soda last 10 minutes.

Spread bottom of a large casserole that measures about 12 × 8 × 2 inches with part of meat sauce, then with a layer of well-drained cooked spaghetti, another layer of sauce, a layer of toasted walnuts, and about 2 tablespoons cheese. Continue to place spaghetti and other ingredients in layers until casserole is filled. Top it with sauce, making 3 layers in all. Bake at 350° F. uncovered about 35 minutes if ingredients are warm, or 45 minutes if casserole was prepared in advance. Sprinkle top with parsley just before serving. Serve extra leftover meat sauce separately.

Neapolitan Spaghetti Casserole

Serves 6

¾ pound spaghetti, macaroni, or any specialty pasta
½ pound bacon, cut fine
1 pound ground beef
½ pound sliced mushrooms
½ cup chopped onions
½ cup green pepper, cut fine
2 tablespoons butter or margarine
1½ teaspoons salt

⅛ teaspoon pepper
½ teaspoon oregano
1 medium clove garlic, chopped fine
¼ cup parsley
6-ounce can tomato paste, combined with 1½ cups water and ¼ teaspoon baking soda
¾ cup parmesan cheese

Cook pasta about 15 minutes, or until tender; rinse with cold water; drain. In a saucepan fry bacon until medium-crisp, add ground beef, and cook about 7 minutes until done, mixing as it cooks. In another saucepan sauté mushrooms, onions, and green pepper about 5 minutes in butter. Add all vegetables, seasonings, and ½ of tomato mixture to meat. Cover pan, and cook about 6 or 7 minutes.

Place ½ of cooked pasta in a well-buttered casserole. Sprinkle with ½ the parmesan cheese. Over this place meat and vegetable mixture. Now cover with remaining pasta, then cheese, and last, the other ½ of tomato mixture. Cover casserole with foil to prevent top from drying out, and bake 30 minutes at 375° F.

Polpettine alla Toscana (Tuscany-Style Meat Balls)

Serves 8

1 pound ground veal
1 pound ground cooked ham
1 onion, chopped medium-fine and sautéed in 2 tablespoons butter
¼ teaspoon pepper

¼ cup fine-chopped celery, sautéed with onion
1 teaspoon salt
1 large or 2 small eggs, slightly beaten

Combine ingredients and mix thoroughly. Shape medium-size balls, using a rounded tablespoonful of meat for each. Sauté slowly in a small amount of oil or butter until brown. May be served plain, or simmer in Sauce Toscana.

Sauce Toscana

½ cup chopped fresh green onion
¼ cup fine-chopped carrots
¼ cup fine-chopped celery leaves
¼ cup oil or butter
2 tablespoons flour
1½ cups vegetable or meat stock (or

water combined with instant bouillon)
2 tablespoons tomato paste
About 1 teaspoon salt
¼ teaspoon pepper
¼ teaspoon thyme leaves

Sauté onion, carrots, and celery leaves in oil or butter about 5 minutes. Sprinkle flour over cooked vegetables; then add stock combined with tomato paste and seasonings. Add meat balls, cover pan, and simmer about 30 minutes.

Polpettine are delicious served with Italian risotto, polenta, or in a bed of green buttered noodles.

Neapolitan Meat Casserole

Serves 8

½ cup fine-chopped onion
1 large clove garlic, chopped fine
¼ cup celery, chopped fine
2 tablespoons oil
2 cans (6-ounce size) Italian-style tomato paste
1 cup water
2½ teaspoons salt
1 teaspoon granulated sugar
1 teaspoon oregano
¼ teaspoon pepper
½ cup parsley, chopped

¼ cup parmesan cheese
¼ teaspoon baking soda
1 pound ground lean beef
¼ cup butter
½ teaspoon salt
¼ cup oil
6 large green peppers (each pepper cut into 6 pieces)
½ teaspoon salt
About 2 cups pulled bread crumbs
1½ cups shredded mozzarella cheese

Sauté onion, garlic, and celery in 2 tablespoons oil about 3 minutes. Add tomato paste and water, and blend well. Add next 7 ingredients. Cover pan, and allow sauce to simmer about 10 minutes. While sauce is cooking, fry ground beef in ¼ cup butter about 7 minutes; add ½ teaspoon of salt.

In another skillet heat ¼ cup oil, and fry green peppers about 5 minutes; season with ½ teaspoon salt. Cover skillet, and steam peppers about 5 minutes more, or until crisply tender.

Place ground beef in bottom of a 12 × 8 × 2-inch casserole; pour tomato sauce over meat. Over sauce arrange sautéed green peppers uniformly.

Cover peppers with bread crumbs, and last, sprinkle mozzarella cheese over top of casserole. Bake uncovered at 350° F. about 30 minutes, or until brown. If not brown after 30 minutes, place under broiler a minute or two.

Italian Meat Balls

Serves 4

½ pound ground beef, pork, veal or lamb (best to use half beef and half pork)
1 tablespoon chopped fresh parsley, *or* ¼ teaspoon coarse oregano (or more)
2 tablespoons grated Italian cheese

About ½ teaspoon salt
¼ teaspoon black pepper
¼ teaspoon garlic powder, or 1 clove garlic, chopped fine
1 large whole egg, beaten with fork
¼ cup cool milk or water
¼ cup dry bread crumbs

In medium-size bowl, combine ingredients in the order given, and with a large fork or spoon beat in each ingredient. Now let preparation stand at least 20 minutes. Form 12 medium-size smooth balls, and fry slowly in about 2 tablespoons very hot shortening or oil until golden brown. Do not turn balls until they are brown on underside, and do not crowd pan.

Add balls and drippings to Basic Italian Tomato Sauce (page 766) after it has simmered about 1 hour if using baking soda, 4 hours if soda is omitted. Add several tablespoons water to drippings in skillet, scrape well with wooden spoon and add to sauce. Simmer balls slowly in sauce about 30 minutes, but watch carefully toward end that they do not overcook and fall apart.

Note. Instead of cooking in sauce, meat balls may be served plain.

Helen Camp's Pork Tenderloin Spiedini, Italian-Style

Serves 8

¼ cup finely chopped onion
½ cup, or little more, hot melted butter or margarine
About 1¼ cups dry bread crumbs
About ⅓ cup grated Italian cheese
½ teaspoon crushed oregano or basil leaves
1 large thick pork tenderloin, weighing at least 1 pound, after trimmed, cut in 1-inch-thick slices, then flattened with a heavy

cleaver to about ¼ inch thickness
About ¼ cup more melted butter or margarine to brush onto meat
About ¾ teaspoon salt
About ¼ teaspoon black pepper
1 egg, beaten and seasoned with ¼ teaspoon salt and ⅛ teaspoon pepper or margarine
Onion, sliced into ¼-inch-thick pieces
Bay leaves

Sauté the finely chopped onion in the ½ cup melted butter or margarine for about 2 minutes without browning. Shut off heat. Add the dry crumbs, and stir well until moist and well blended. Add the grated Italian cheese and the crushed oregano, and blend thoroughly. Now brush each slice of meat well with the melted butter or margarine, and sprinkle each piece with a bit of salt and pepper. Place a rounded tablespoon of crumb mixture on each, spreading it lightly. Roll to enclose filling. Hold together with heavy toothpick.

After all rolls are shaped, dip each one into beaten egg. Drain well and cover meat with remaining crumb preparation. Place on wax paper and let stand about 20 minutes, turning them over twice.

To cook, place breaded Spiedini in a well-greased 10-inch heatproof pie plate or other heatproof dish, separating each roll with a slice of onion cut about ¼ inch thick, and with whole or pieces of bay leaves. Bake in a preheated 400° F. oven, about 30 to 35 minutes, on the center rack. Brush or drizzle a little melted butter or margarine on top of each roll the last 5 minutes, to help keep them moist and delicious. Serve Creamed Fresh Mushrooms separately, or as desired.

To Freeze Spiedini. Place Spiedini a ½ inch apart on a flat paper-lined pan. Wrap well. Can be frozen for about 2 months. To bake frozen Spiedini, arrange them on baking dish same as unfrozen. Not necessary to defrost them first, but increase baking time about 5 minutes.

Creamed Fresh Mushrooms for Spiedini

¼ cup finely chopped green onion, mixed with ¼ cup green stems
½ pound fresh mushrooms, washed and dried well, then cut in thick slices
¼ cup hot butter or margarine
2 teaspoons cornstarch, combined with ⅔ cup milk

¼ teaspoon salt, little more if needed
¼ teaspoon dry oregano or basil leaves
⅛ teaspoon pepper
1 tablespoon dry wine
2 tablespoons green onion stems, ½ inch long (optional)
Pimiento strips (optional)

Sauté chopped onion and mushrooms in the hot butter or margarine for about 5 minutes. Add dissolved cornstarch and milk and cook until thick, stirring constantly. Simmer about 3 minutes. Add seasonings and wine and cook 2 more minutes. Two extra tablespoons green onion stems, ½ inch long, and pimiento strips may be added for more color.

Italian-Style Braised Pork Loins

Serves 6

Use pork loins weighing at least 2 pounds. Rub meat well with salt and pepper, and brown it well on all sides in a small amount of butter with a cut clove of garlic. Add 1 can Italian-style tomato paste combined with ½ cup stock or water. Season with about 1 teaspoon salt, ½ teaspoon pepper, ½ teaspoon oregano, 2 tablespoons Italian cheese, and 1 tablespoon parsley. Cover and simmer about 2 hours, or until tender, testing meat so as not to overcook. It should be tender when tested with a fork. When done, let rest in sauce for at least 15 minutes before slicing attractively. Serve with vegetables or any macaroni dish.

Broiled Halibut Steak with Pizzaiola Sauce

Serves 4

2 tablespoons oil	½ teaspoon crumbled oregano leaves
2½ cups (No. 2 can) tomatoes	1 teaspoon dried parsley flakes
2 tablespoons tomato paste	¼ teaspoon ground black pepper
1 teaspoon salt	¼ teaspoon garlic powder
¼ teaspoon baking soda	2 (1-inch) halibut steaks

Heat oil in a 2-quart saucepan. Add remaining ingredients except halibut, and cook uncovered 20 to 30 minutes over low heat until sauce is of medium thickness.

Broil halibut steaks at 450° F. 2 inches from heat about 15 minutes. Do not turn over. Pour sauce over broiled halibut steaks in a bed of cooked rice.

Italy, a fisherman's paradise, is known for its delicious seafood. Pizzaiola Sauce, made with a tomato base and deftly seasoned with oregano and parsley, adds a fragrant flavor and aroma to fish, shrimp, or lobster.

Italian Scamorza Omelet

Serves 2 or 3

3 tablespoons butter and shortening	⅛ teaspoon oregano or thyme
4 eggs	⅛ teaspoon white pepper
2 tablespoons rich milk or cream	1 tablespoon fine-chopped parsley
1 tablespoon grated parmesan cheese	½ cup coarsely shredded scamorza or
½ teaspoon salt	mozzarella cheese

In a 7- or 8-inch shallow skillet melt butter and shortening over low heat until they sizzle, but do not allow to become brown. With dover beater, beat eggs, cream, parmesan cheese, salt, oregano, pepper, and parsley about ½ minute. Pour into hot butter. Have heat low. Cook eggs slowly until bottom of omelet is congealed. Then lift up sides with spatula, to allow uncooked eggs to run underneath and cook. Continue to cook until omelet is done. If top of omelet appears too moist, it may be cooked covered a few seconds. Pour shredded scamorza or mozzarella cheese over ½ of omelet. Fold over, and turn out onto serving platter. Serve with thick slices of tomato on lettuce, brushed with Italian Salad Dressing (page 368) and sprinkle with a little oregano, sautéed Broccoli Parmesan (page 800), and buttered Garlic-flavored Italian Bread (page 814).

Mozzarella in Carozza (Italian Fried Sandwich)

Remove crust from white sliced bread if desired, or leave on for a more substantial sandwich. Brush lightly with butter. Fill with thin-sliced mozzarella or scamorza cheese. Make sandwich; cut into 2 rectangular pieces. Dip each piece into well-beaten egg combined with 2 tablespoons milk, about ½ teaspoon salt, and a little pepper. Pick up with tongs or fingers and pan-fry in about ¼ inch very hot butter or other fat until brown on each side. Serve at once as a light luncheon or snack with sliced tomatoes. Sandwiches are very attractive if arranged on an oblong or oval platter, overlapping each other slightly. Surround with sliced tomatoes or serve a quick mushroom sauce separately.

▶ SAUSAGES ◀

Italian Pork Sausages

Remove surplus fat from fresh pork shoulder and cut meat into *very* small pieces, or put through a coarse meat grinder. Weigh chopped meat, and for each pound of meat, season with about

1 teaspoon salt	½ to 1 teaspoon Italian-style crushed
1¼ teaspoon finochio (fennel seed)	dry red pepper (optional)

Spread meat on a large flat dish or pan, combine seasonings and sprinkle over entire surface of meat, little at a time, mixing in with hands as seasonings are added. Cover well with waxed paper, and keep in refrigerator for several hours or until ready to be used, not later than 8 hours.

Meanwhile soak pork casings in lukewarm water for about 15 minutes, then rinse them thoroughly until all salt has been removed and casings feel soft. Place casing on narrow end of Italian sausage funnel (available in many hardware stores). Put a small amount of meat through funnel into casing; then push rest of casing onto tube of funnel. Fill, and prick sausage with a pointed metal skewer or cake tester. Form about 5-inch sausages, and twist casing. Do not pack meat into casings too firmly or too loosely.

Store finished sausage in refrigerator for about 24 hours to develop flavor before cooking. It is best to freeze sausage (for not more than 3 weeks) if not to be cooked within 3 days. Allow it to defrost on shelf of refrigerator for several hours before cooking, or it may be cooked frozen, increasing cooking time for about 7 or 8 minutes.

To Roast Italian Sausage. Place sausage on rack with drip pan underneath, leaving a small space between each piece. If links are long, best to cut them into 3- or 4-inch sizes. Roast in 400° F. preheated oven 20 minutes, turning them over after first 10 minutes, if you are preparing only 1 or 2 pounds. For larger amounts, increase time to 15 minutes on each side. Now remove from oven and place under broiler (at same temperature) until brown, about 5 minutes on each side. This is an excellent way to prepare large amounts of sausage, as it requires less attention.

To Pan-fry and Braise Italian Sausage. Brush skillet well with melted shortening. When hot, add sausage pieces and cook over *medium* heat until brown on each side. When sausage is nice and brown, add about ¼ or more hot water, cover skillet tightly, and simmer (over very low heat or simmer burner) for about 20 minutes, depending on thickness of sausage. Turn occasionally, and add more hot water if it evaporates, enough to produce steam when cover is lifted off. When done, remove cover and continue to cook sausage for several minutes until it takes on an attractive color and most of moisture has evaporated. One pound of sausage will serve 2 or 3 with other foods.

Italian sausage is very delicious added to spaghetti sauce, and also served on or with Italian pizza along with fried peppers, etc.

Note. Fresh Italian sausage is available in Italian grocery stores and in a majority of supermarts.

Italian Sausage and Maccaroni Casserole

Serves 4

1 pound Italian or other fresh sausage	¼ cup sifted all-purpose flour
½ pound macaroni	1¼ cups warm milk
¼ cup butter or shortening	1 teaspoon salt

Pan-fry sausage as per general directions (page 798). When done, let cool a few minutes, then cut sausage into about ½-inch slices crosswise.

Cook macaroni in boiling salted water about 25 to 30 minutes, or until tender, but not too soft. In a separate saucepan melt the ¼ cup butter, blend in flour, and then add milk gradually, stirring constantly. Or bring milk to scalding point, and add it all at once to flour mixture, and at once stir and cook until thick and smooth. Add ¼ cup of the cheese, holding aside other ¼ cup. Add salt, and blend well, and cook until cheese has melted.

Combine ⅔ of the sauce with well-drained cooked macaroni in a large bowl or saucepan. Now pour and spread ½ of macaroni in well-buttered casserole. Place cooked sausage over macaroni, then cover sausage with rest of macaroni, and sprinkle top with the remaining ¼ cup of cheese. Bake 30 uncovered minutes at 425° F., or until top is brown.

Italian Sausages with Green Peppers

Serves 4 to 6

2 pounds Italian sausages	½ teaspoon oregano leaves, crushed
1 pound fresh green peppers	½ teaspoon salt

Cut sausages into about 3- to 4-inch pieces. Remove stems and seeds from green peppers. Slice lengthwise about 2 inches wide.

Place sausage pieces in a greased skillet, and fry over medium heat on all sides about 5 minutes. Then add green peppers, oregano, and salt, and fry over low heat about 5 more minutes. Cover saucepan, and simmer slowly about 15 minutes, or until sausage is tender.

▶ VEGETABLE DISHES ◀

Baked Broccoli à la Parmesan

Serves 6

1 bunch broccoli, or 2 packages frozen broccoli	1 cup broccoli liquid, water, or meat stock
¼ cup shortening	¼ cup sifted flour
1 large clove garlic, cut up	1 teaspoon salt
¼ pound fresh mushrooms	¼ teaspoon nutmeg
6-ounce can Italian-style tomato paste	A little pepper
	¼ cup grated parmesan cheese

Cook broccoli (see page 280), adding 1 teaspoon salt. (Or cook frozen broccoli according to instructions on package.) Slice quite thin, and arrange in buttered pie dish that measures about 10 × 1½ inches.

In a saucepan melt shortening, add garlic, and cook several minutes. Add mushrooms that have been washed and dried thoroughly, then sliced. Let cook about 5 minutes, turning often. Add tomato paste and broccoli liquid (or water or meat stock) combined with flour. Season with salt, nutmeg, pepper; add cheese. Cook all together in a covered saucepan about 15 minutes.

Pour sauce over broccoli in baking dish and sprinkle with more parmesan cheese. Bake at 350° F. about 30 minutes.

Sautéed Broccoli Parmesan

Cook broccoli as per general directions (page 280). Drain well. Just before serving, sauté broccoli about 5 minutes in melted butter to which a sliver of fresh garlic has been added. Sprinkle well with grated parmesan cheese, and serve with omelet.

Baked Stuffed Eggplant Slices

Serves 4 to 6

The old theory that the juice in eggplant is poisonous has been disproved by the best authorities. The same notion was current at one time about tomatoes. It is not necessary to press eggplant under a weight, as this renders eggplant tasteless and dry. Select firm, glossy eggplants that are not too large. Keep in a cool dry place if not cut. Unused parts should not be pared and must be wrapped in wax paper and kept in hydrator. Skin on eggplant becomes soft after it is cooked. It may or may not be removed. *Eggplant is more palatable when pared.* Because of its bland flavor, vegetables such as onions, tomatoes, etc., enhance eggplant.

1 medium-size eggplant	1 teaspoon salt
1 or 2 well-beaten eggs	½ teaspoon black pepper
¼ cup hot oil	¼ cup minced parsley
1 medium-size onion, sliced thin	2 tablespoons grated parmesan cheese
¼ cup shortening	½ cup dry bread crumbs
1 pound ground beef, veal, pork, lamb, or leftover meat	Additional grated parmesan cheese for top

Cut eggplant lengthwise into 2 pieces. Pare (skin may be left on), and cut into slices about ¼ inch thick. Dip slices into beaten egg, and sauté in the hot oil until brown on each side. Sauté onion in shortening about 5 minutes; add ground meat, and cook about 10 minutes longer, or until nicely browned. Add salt, pepper, minced parsley, ¼ cup sauce (below), cheese, and then bread crumbs. Mix well.

Arrange sliced sautéed eggplant in a flat baking dish that measures about 10 × 1⅓ inches. Sprinkle slices very lightly with a little salt and pepper; cover with meat mixture and a little of the sauce. Continue until all eggplant, meat, and most of sauce have been used, reserving part of sauce for top. Sprinkle top with 3 or 4 tablespoons cheese. Bake at 350° F. in a covered dish (another plate of same size may be used as a cover, or use greased foil) about 1 hour, or until tender, removing cover last 15 minutes. Test by cutting through with a fork and tasting.

Sauce for Baked Stuffed Eggplant Slices

1 small onion, cut fine	1 teaspoon salt
2 tablespoons shortening	1 tablespoon grated parmesan cheese
6-ounce can Italian-style tomato paste, combined with 2 cans water	¼ teaspoon pepper

Sauté onion in shortening; add combined tomato paste and water. Cook all together slowly in a covered saucepan about 10 minutes; then season with salt, cheese, and pepper.

Note. Quarter pound or more mozzarella cheese sliced very thin may be placed on each layer as you are putting casserole together.

Louise's Italian Eggplant Casserole

Serves about 8

2 large eggplants, peeled
3 eggs, beaten with a fork
¼ cup oil
6 hard-coked eggs, sliced
¼ cup chopped parsley

Salt and pepper
1 pound scamorza or mozzarella cheese, sliced thin
¾ cup parmesan cheese

Wash and dry eggplants; slice into ¼-inch slices. Dip each slice into beaten egg and then fry (preferably in oil) until golden brown on both sides. Moisten bottom of the casserole with a little Quick Tomato Sauce (page 767). Place a layer of eggplant slices in 2-quart casserole. Salt and pepper slices lightly. Sprinkle *part* of the hard-cooked eggs, parsley, scamorza cheese, and parmesan cheese over eggplant. Top with *part* of sauce. Now start another layer the same way, using eggplant, salt and pepper, eggs, parsley, cheeses, and sauce until all ingredients have been used. Bake at 375° F. about 45 minutes.

This makes an excellent and tasty main dish for meatless days.

Italian-Style Potato Salad Platter—No. 1

Serves 6 to 8

2 pounds red boiling potatoes, cooked gently until tender, but not too soft (new potatoes best)
4 plum tomatoes, or 2 medium-size firm tomatoes, cut into ½-inch chunks
¼ cup fresh green onion, cut into ½-inch pieces
¼ cup onion stems, cut into ½-inch pieces
½ cup fresh green pepper, cut into narrow ½-inch strips

½ cup Italian fresh finochio, *or* Pascal celery, cut crosswise about ⅓ inch wide
About 2 teaspoons salt
¼ teaspoon coarse-ground black pepper
1 tablespoon fresh basil, cut into small pieces, *or* ½ teaspoon dried basil, crumbled
About ¼ cup salad oil, combined with 2 tablespoons wine vinegar, well blended

Peel and cut potatoes into medium-thick slices, and combine with all other ingredients. Mix gently, and mound in center of a large round platter. Surround salad with sliced capoccolo, Italian salami, provolone cheese, tiny vinegar peppers, etc.

Italian-Style Potato Salad Platter—No. 2

Serves 6 to 8

2 pounds red boiling potatoes, cooked gently until tender but not too soft (new potatoes best)

½ pound Italian salami, cut into long narrow strips about 3 inches long and ¼ inch wide

¼ cup fresh green onion, cut into ½-inch pieces

¼ cup onion stems, cut into ½-inch strips

½ cup Pascal celery, cut crosswise about ⅓ inch wide

About 1½ teaspoons salt

¼ teaspoon coarse-ground black pepper

½ teaspoon dried basil, crumbled

1 teaspoon finochio (fennel seed)

About ¼ cup salad oil, combined with 2 tablespoons wine vinegar, well blended

Peel and cut cold cooked potatoes into medium-thick slices, and combine them with all other ingredients. Mix gently, and mound in center of a large round platter. Surround salad with slices of tomatoes and cucumbers, brushed well with Italian or French dressing, and topped with curled anchovies.

Note. These potato salad platters make an excellent light luncheon or supper dish with buttered Garlic-flavored Italian Bread (page 814).

Italian Potato Omelet

Serves 3 to 4

3 medium-size potatoes, boiled with skins on, then peeled, and sliced medium-thick

1 small onion, sliced thin or chopped

About ¼ cup shortening (or part butter)

About ½ teaspoon salt

⅛ teaspoon black pepper

¼ teaspoon oregano leaves, crumbled

3 eggs, well beaten with a fork and combined with ½ teaspoon or less salt and ⅛ teaspoon pepper

Combine cut potatoes, onion, and seasonings, and drop into hot fat in an 8-inch skillet. Sauté potatoes about 5 minutes; turn over and sauté another 5 minutes. Now beat eggs with a fork, add salt and pepper, and pour over entire surface of potatoes. Continue to cook until eggs are set on underside; then with a pancake turner, turn potatoes over and cook a few minutes longer, but do not let them become too dry. This is very delicious as a main family luncheon or supper dish, or may be served with meat, fish, or poultry.

Neapolitan Fresh Green Bean Salad

Serves 3

1 package frozen beans, cooked until crisply tender, and well drained, or canned beans
1 teaspoon salt
½ teaspoon black pepper
⅛ teaspoon Italian red pepper

½ teaspoon oregano leaves, crushed
2 tablespoons salad oil
¼ cup wine vinegar
1 small clove garlic, slivered
8 pitted black ripe olives, crushed with bottom of a glass

Blend all ingredients thoroughly. Cover, and refrigerate at least 1 hour. To serve, pour into center of a round platter, forming a mound. Surround it with leafy lettuce or endive, and arrange wedges of tomatoes around base of salad, over lettuce. Brush tomatoes with some of dressing in salad. This is a very delicious and substantial salad.

Italian-Style Roasted Fresh Green or Red Peppers

Serves 3 to 4

1 pound large thick fresh green or red peppers
1 small clove garlic, crushed or chopped fine
About ½ teaspoon salt

1/16 teaspoon cayenne or Italian red pepper (optional)
About ¼ teaspoon, or less, crushed oregano leaves
About 1 tablespoon, or less, salad oil

Preheat oven to 550° F. Place peppers directly on center rack of oven, and roast about 10 minutes for thin-skinned peppers, 15 minutes for thick-skinned, or until they start to brown and blister. Now turn them over and around every few minutes (additional 5 to 10 minutes) until most of the skin is brown. Remove from oven and let cool. Peel all loose and burned skin. Break into long strips about ¾ inch wide, discarding seeds and core.

Place in a bowl and add all other ingredients. Blend thoroughly with a heavy spoon or fork, and refrigerate for several hours to develop more flavor.

These peppers are usually served cold, but may be served slightly warm if desired. They make excellent meatless sandwiches, and are also very delicious served with roasted Italian sausage, fried chicken, and other sautéed or roasted meats. They keep well for about 1 week in refrigerator, or may be frozen for about 1 month.

Italian-Style Broiled Peppers

Some cooks like to broil fresh peppers. Set temperature to 500° F., place peppers on a baking sheet, about 2 inches from heat source. Broil on each side about 10 to 12 minutes, depending on thickness, but watch closely not to burn or overcook them. Prepare as above.

Note. Thick peppers are preferred for these methods of cooking.

Green or Red Peppers Stuffed Italian Style

Serves 6

10 slices white bread from which crust has been removed (several days old)
¼ cup cider vinegar, combined with ¼ cup cool water
2 tablespoons oil
1 large clove or 2 small cloves garlic, chopped fine

About ½ teaspoon salt
¼ teaspoon black pepper
1 tablespoon oregano or thyme
¼ cup chopped parsley
2-ounce can anchovies, cut in small pieces
2 tablespoons grated parmesan cheese
6 medium-size sweet peppers

Cut bread in ½-inch cubes or break with fingers. Pour vinegar and water over bread, a small amount at a time; add oil and all other ingredients (except peppers), mixing together lightly. Wash peppers, dry thoroughly. With a paring knife or teaspoon, remove cores, seeds, and inner white membranes. Sprinkle insides with salt. Fry on all sides in small amount of oil until brown, turning carefully so that they do not break. Skin may be peeled off. Have heat medium high. Remove carefully, and let stand until cool enough to handle. Stuff with bread-crumb mixture. Place on a baking sheet, sprinkle with salt; cover and bake at 350° F. about 1 hour if peppers are thick, less if peppers are thin-skinned or peeled. After 1 hour, remove cover, and bake 15 more minutes. Test, and if not tender, bake few minutes longer.

Risotto Milanese

Serves 8 to 12

½ cup butter or margarine
1 small clove garlic, chopped fine, or ¼ cup chopped onion
½ cup finely chopped fresh mushrooms
1 pound rice
About 3 cups chicken stock (or other stock) or instant bouillon, com-

bined with ⅛ teaspoon saffron
½ cup solid tomatoes, cut in small pieces, or crush with hand
About 1 tablespoon salt (less if stock is salted)
About ¼ cup grated parmesan cheese

Melt butter or margarine, but do not brown. When quite hot, add the garlic or onion, mushrooms, and rice. Cook over moderate heat about 10 minutes, turning often. Then add all other ingredients. Blend well, cover saucepan and bring to boiling point. Lower heat and simmer until rice is tender, for about 30 minutes. *Stir very gently once or twice toward end.* If rice appears dry and hard when time is up, add a little more stock or water and continue to cook, covered, a few minutes longer. When done, it may be kept tightly covered for about 20 minutes (off the stove) before serving. Serve with meat, poultry, or seafood.

Stuffed Zucchini, Italian-Style

Serves 4

2 zucchini (½ pound each)	½ teaspoon salt
1 small onion, sliced thin	A little pepper
2 tablespoons shortening	2 tablespoons parsley, chopped fine
½ cup peeled fresh tomatoes or canned tomatoes	⅓ cup bread crumbs
	Melted butter or margarine
2 tablespoons parmesan cheese	

Wash zucchini; drop whole into enough boiling unsalted water to cover. Cook *gently* about 10 to 15 minutes in covered saucepan until crisply tender, *not too soft.* Drain; let stand until cool enough to handle. Cut into halves lengthwise; remove pulp carefully with a teaspoon, and mash or cut up.

In a saucepan sauté onion in shortening. Cook until lightly brown; add mashed or cut-up scooped center of zucchini, fresh or canned tomatoes, cheese, salt, pepper, chopped parsley, and bread crumbs. Cook all together about 7 or 8 minutes. Brush entire surface of zucchini shells with melted butter or margarine, sprinkle with salt, and stuff with this mixture. Drizzle top with melted butter. Place on a flat baking dish, and bake about 30 minutes at 350° F. Broil several minutes before serving.

Zucchini may be stuffed with leftover or freshly chopped cooked meats and served as a main dish.

Zucchini and Veal Chops in Casserole

Serves 6

2 pounds medium-size zucchini (not too large)	sliced ½ inch thick, sautéed in 4 tablespoons fat
About ½ cup shortening	1½ teaspoons salt
1 pound onions	½ teaspoon papper
1 teaspoon salt	About 4 tablespoons hot water
½ teaspoon pepper	2 tablespoons flour
½ teaspoon oregano leaves	¼ cup grated Italian cheese
½ teaspoon dried basil leaves, crushed in fingers	About 1½ cups or more fresh or canned tomatoes, cut into large pieces
2 pounds veal chops with kidney,	Salt and pepper

Wash zucchini; cut off both ends. Do not peel. Cut lengthwise in halves, then crosswise into 2-inch chunks. Sauté zucchini in part of shortening until lightly browned on white parts. Cut onions into large chunks, and sauté them in part of shortening until lightly colored. Combine onions with zucchini, and season them with the 1 teaspoon salt, ½ teaspoon pepper, ½ teaspoon oregano, and ½ teaspoon basil. Cover, and steam for 5 minutes.

Sauté veal chops in 4 tablespoons (or more if necessary) hot fat until nicely browned on 1 side; turn over and brown other side. Season with 1½ teaspoons salt and ½ teaspoon pepper. Add about 4 tablespoons water, cover skillet tightly, and steam meat about 35 to 45 minutes, or only until tender. Good-quality veal will be tender in 35 minutes.

Place cooked meat in bottom of a 12 × 8 × 2-inch oblong heatproof casserole. Sprinkle meat with 2 tablespoons flour. Pour cooked zucchini and onions over meat. Sprinkle with about ¼ cup grated Italian cheese. Pour tomatoes over top, leaving large spaces uncovered with tomatoes to show green of zucchini. Season top of tomatoes very lightly with ½ teaspoon salt and a little pepper. Bake at 375° F. about 20 minutes just before serving; about 30 minutes if casserole was prepared long in advance and ingredients are cold.

Ham and Zucchini in Casserole

Serves 4 to 6

1 very large onion, sliced thin	¼ teaspoon dried basil
¼ cup shortening	¼ teaspoon thyme leaves
1½ pounds small zucchini, washed but not peeled	½ pound ham, cut into long, very narrow strips (2 inches long)
1½ cups canned tomatoes, drained	2 tablespoons flour, combined with drained-off tomato juice
1½ teaspoons salt	
¼ teaspoon pepper	4 tablespoons parmesan cheese

Sauté onion in ¼ cup very hot fat about 5 minutes. Add zucchini that have been sliced about ¼ inch in thickness, then tomatoes, salt, pepper, basil, and thyme. Cover, and simmer about 10 minutes, or until zucchini slices are crisply tender but not too soft. Pour off surplus tomato liquid from zucchini. Pour zucchini into greased casserole that measures about 10½ × 6½ × 2 inches. Place cut ham over zucchini. Leftover cooked ham is excellent for this purpose. Prepare a sauce with 1 cup drained tomato juice (add water to make up difference if necessary) and the 2 tablespoons flour. Cook until thick; then simmer about 5 minutes. Pour sauce over ham as uniformly as possible. Sprinkle top with grated parmesan or other cheese. Bake at 400° F. about 15 minutes if ingredients are warm, about 20 to 25 minutes if casserole was prepared in advance. When done, and just before serving, sprinkle well with minced parsley. This makes an excellent luncheon or supper dish. Serve with mashed or boiled potatoes.

Zucchini Stew, Italian-Style

Serves 4 to 8

¼ cup butter or margarine
1 pound ground beef
2 teaspoons salt
¼ teaspoon pepper
½ teaspoon oregano leaves
½ cup sliced onions

1 cup green peppers, cut into ½ inch squares
2 pound medium-size zucchini (4-ounce size)
2 cups canned tomatoes
1 tablespoon cornstarch, combined with 2 tablespoons water

Melt butter or margarine, and when hot fry ground meat until done, about 7 or 8 minutes. Season with salt, pepper, and oregano. Add sliced onions and green peppers. Also add zucchini (unpeeled) that have been sliced ½ inch thick. Last, add tomatoes and blend well. Cover saucepan, and simmer gently about 20 minutes, or until squash is tender when tested with a fork.

When cooked, add cornstarch and water, and simmer uncovered about 5 minutes, stirring occasionally.

Zucchini Omelet in Casserole

Serves 6 to 8

1 large clove garlic, chopped fine
2 pounds very small (4-ounce size) zucchini, washed, with ends removed but not peeled, then cut into thin ½-inch slices
¼ cup buttter and ¼ cup oil

½ teaspoon dried basil, crushed in fingers
About 2 teaspoons salt
¼ teaspoon black pepper
¼ cup grated Italian cheese
4 large whole eggs
Paprika

In a large skillet or saucepan sauté garlic and zucchini in hot fat 7 or 8 minutes, turning often. Add all seasonings, and continue to cook several more minutes, or until zucchini is crisply tender but not too soft. This may be done several hours in advance. Then about 30 minutes before serving, beat eggs slightly and combine them with vegetable mixture. Pour into a well-buttered 9-inch glass pie plate or oblong casserole that measures about 10 × 6 × 2 inches. Bake in 400° F. oven about 25 to 30 minutes, or until eggs are set in center of casserole. Remove from oven, sprinkle top with paprika, and cut into wedges if baked in pie plate; cut into squares if baked in oblong casserole. Very delicious served hot with meat, poultry, or fish.

Fresh Vegetable Minestrone Soup

½ cup melted butter or margarine
½ cup chopped onions
1 clove garlic, put through garlic press or chopped fine
1 medium fresh green pepper, cut into ½-inch strips, ¼ inch wide
1 cup pascal celery cut crosswise into ⅓-inch-thick crescents
¼ cup fresh carrots, sliced ¼ inch thick crosswise
1 cup fresh green beans, cut into ½-inch pieces
¼ cup fresh parsley, chopped medium fine
1½ cups fresh or canned tomatoes, crushed or cut in about 1-inch pieces

8 cups boiling stock, or use instant boullion dissolved in hot water
¼ cup grated Italian cheese
1 bay leaf
½ teaspoon marjoram or oregano leaves, crushed in fingers
½ teaspoon black pepper
About 1 tablespoon salt, more if needed
1 cup or more cubed unpeeled zucchini squash, or fresh spinach
1 cup or more cubed potatoes, ½ inch size
1 cup or more partially cooked macaroni, cut into 1-inch pieces

In the ½ cup hot butter or margarine sauté onions, garlic, green pepper, and celery, for about 5 minutes. Add all other ingredients, except the cubed zucchini, cubed potatoes, and partially cooked macaroni. Cover pot and simmer ingredients for about 1 hour. Now add the zucchini, potatoes, and macaroni and continue to cook about 20 minutes longer. Minestrone must be thick. Cook uncovered toward end if necessary, or add little more stock or water if too thick. Taste and add more seasoning if necessary. Serve additional Italian grated cheese separately.

Note. There are many versions of this soup and it varies from region to region in Italy, and often from cook to cook. It makes a delicious and satisfying family meal served with broiled garlic bread for luncheon or supper dish. Some cooked ham cubes may be added the last few minutes for a more substantial soup.

Vegetable Casserole Continental

4 packages frozen mixed vegetables
1½ teaspoons salt
¼ teaspoon pepper

½ teaspoon oregano
About ½ teaspoon garlic salt
¼ cup melted butter

Cook frozen vegetables in 1½ cups boiling water about 5 minutes, drain thoroughly and reserve vegetable liquid for sauce. Season vegetables with rest of ingredients, mix well, and pour them into a greased 17-inch steel baking platter (or any style casserole preferred). Prepare Sauce Continental (page 810) and spread it over vegetables.

Bake at 400° F. about 15 minutes if vegetables are warm; 20 minutes if casserole was put together in advance. When done, sprinkle entire surface with very finely chopped parsley or fresh green onion stems, and garnish center with whole or thickly sliced sautéed mushrooms.

If this casserole is to be used as a bed for Continental-Style Sliced Lamb or Neapolitan-Style Veal, omit mushrooms from top. One-half cup sautéed sliced mushrooms may be added to the vegetables with other ingredients.

Sauce Continental for Vegetable Casserole

½ cup finely chopped onion
¼ cup butter or margarine
¼ cup sifted all-purpose flour
1½ cups reserved vegetable liquid, combined with 1 can Italian-style tomato paste or tomato sauce

¼ cup grated Italian cheese
¼ teaspoon oregano
¼ teaspoon pepper
1 teaspoon salt
¼ teaspoon baking soda
2 tablespoons dry wine

In a 2-quart saucepan sauté the chopped onion in the ¼ cup fat for about 5 minutes. Add flour and stir well, forming a smooth paste. Add lukewarm vegetable liquid combined with the tomato paste slowly, then all other ingredients listed. Stir well and simmer about 10 minutes. Let sauce cool for about 20 minutes, stirring it occasionally, then pour it over the cooked vegetables and spread out smoothly.

Evelyn Russo's Italian Lentil Minestrone

½ pound (about 1 cup) lentils, washed in cool water several times, removing any foreign matter and imperfect black lentils
5 cups of meat or vegetable stock, or 5 cups water combined with 2 teaspoons instant bouillon (any flavor)
About 1 teaspoon salt
⅛ teaspoon black pepper
¼ teaspoon oregano leaves, crushed in fingers, or ⅛ teaspoon powdered oregano
¼ teaspoon garlic
¼ cup canned or fresh tomatoes, peeled and cut into very small pieces, or 2 tablespoons tomato paste, or 3 tablespoons tomato purée
About 1 pound, or less, fresh Italian

pork sausage, cut into 2-inch pieces and sautéed in ¼ cup of oil or other fat until brown, but not too dry
1 cup, or more, fresh carrots, cut in 2-inch-thick wedges, then simmered until crisply tender, about 10 minutes (drain well, and season with about ⅛ teaspoon salt and 1 tablespoon butter)
1 package frozen whole spinach, first cooked about 3 minutes after it is thawed and begins to simmer, seasoned with ½ teaspoon salt (drain spinach well, cut it into large pieces with scissors, season it with ⅛ teaspoon garlic salt or bit less powder and 1 tablespoon butter or margarine; blend well)

Combine lentils with the 5 cups of liquid. Add salt, black pepper, oregano, garlic powder and tomatoes, and cook gently (simmer) about 40 minutes in a covered pot. Now add sautéed sausage and drippings in skillet and continue to cook about 35 more minutes. Do not add carrots and spinach until you are ready to serve. Taste and season further if necessary. Last, add the carrots and blend well. Just before serving minestrone fold the hot cooked spinach into entire preparation, blending it gently for a few seconds to keep spinach slightly separated, in mounds, from the lentils.

If minestrone appears too thin after adding sautéed sausage, continue to cook uncovered. If it appears too thick, add little more liquid. This preparation is best served medium consistency.

Minestrone may be prepared without adding carrots and spinach. If it becomes very thick after refrigerated, add a little water or stock, stir well, and reheat over very low heat.

Serve grated Italian cheese separately, also garlic broiled bread, and an Italian salad bowl.

Pasta and Fagioli (Pasta with Navy Beans)

½ pound dried navy beans, soaked in cold water for about 12 hours
5 cups cold water
2 teaspoons salt
¼ teaspoon pepper
½ teaspoon oregano
1 bay leaf
½ teaspoon garlic salt

¼ cup fresh parsley, or ½ tablespoon dry
⅓ cup oil
½ cup onions, chopped fine
½ cup celery and leaves, chopped fine
2 cups (No. 2 can) tomatoes, cut into medium pieces
¼ pound uncooked elbow macaroni, or other cut pasta

Drain soaked beans, and pour them into a 3-quart saucepan. Add the 5 cups cold water, salt, pepper, oregano, bay leaf, garlic salt, and parsley. Cover pot and bring to a boil. Lower heat and cook gently about 1 hour. Test beans to see if they crush easily between fingers. Cook until tender if necessary.

In a separate saucepan heat oil, add the chopped onion and celery, and sauté for about 5 minutes. Add tomatoes to cooked onion and celery and cook 5 minutes longer. Now pour tomato preparation into bean pot, blend well, and cook uncovered about 20 minutes. Last, add the pasta, stir well and continue to cook until pasta is tender, but not too soft, about 15 more minutes. Taste and add more seasoning if needed. Serve grated Italian cheese separately. If preparation is too thick, add little more stock or water. If too thin, cook uncovered a few minutes longer before you add the pasta.

This is a very popular family-style thick soup and is often served as a luncheon or supper dish with Italian or French bread.

Suppli di Ricotta e Spinaci (Ricotta Spinach Croquettes)

1 pound fresh ricotta, well drained, pressing out surplus water through strainer

10- or 12-ounce package chopped spinach, cooked about 5 minutes, then drained thoroughly (chop spinach if necessary)

1 large egg, beaten with a fork a few seconds

About 1 teaspoon salt

¼ teaspoon pepper

½ teaspoon oregano leaves, crushed in fingers, or ¼ teaspoon powdered oregano

¼ teaspoon garlic salt or powder

¼ cup grated Italian cheese

To prepare, combine all ingredients in the order listed in a large bowl, and beat well for about 2 minutes. Cover and refrigerate for about an hour, or may be refrigerated for as long as 12 hours. Pick up 1 rounded tablespoon of the filling at a time, and shape it into thick 2½-inch smooth rounds, for plain suppli. For cheese-filled suppli, place ¾-inch square cube of mozzarella or gruyère cheese in center of each, and cover completely with preparation. Now flatten top of each slightly.

Dip suppli into well-beaten egg combined with 1 tablespoon water, let drain well, spreading out fingers, then cover with light dry unseasoned bread crumbs. May be dipped a second time into egg and crumbs, but not necessary. Place crumbed suppli on wax paper and let stand in room temperature 10 to 15 minutes, turning them over after 5 minutes. Sauté in about ¼ inch of hot oil or unsalted shortening. (Temperature of fat should be about 300° F. Temperature can be ascertained by tilting skillet and inserting deep-fat thermometer.) Cook over medium low heat (not high) about 3 minutes on each side, or until they are good golden color and crisp. Turn over gently and brown second side.

Serve hot with meat or poultry, or serve as a light family luncheon or supper dish covered with tomato meat sauce. Suppli may be kept warm in a 250° oven for about ½ hour. Leftovers may be reheated in a small amount of hot fat, in covered skillet, about 2 minutes on each side. Very delicious even reheated.

Spinach and Steamed Potatoes, Italian-Style

Cook 2 pounds fresh spinach until just tender in ¼ cup hot water (or cook 2 packages frozen spinach, according to directions on package).

Sauté 1 clove garlic in 2 tablespoons olive or vegetable oil until garlic is light brown. Add this to cooked spinach and pot liquor. Add 4 medium-size steamed potatoes from which skins have been removed, about 1 teaspoon salt, and ⅛ teaspoon cayenne pepper. Cook all together about 7 or 8 minutes, turning often. Serve hot. Instead of potatoes, about 1 cup cooked navy beans or lima beans may be combined with spinach.

Potato Croquettes, Italian-Style

Peel and wash 1 pound Idaho potatoes and cut in uniform large pieces (about 2 inches). Cook 20 to 30 minutes or until soft (do not overcook) in about 1 inch boiling unsalted water, in covered saucepan. Drain well, dry out over low heat. *Mash at once* while very hot and to 2 cups (little more or less) add 1 *very small* beaten egg (only enough to hold ingredients together), 1 teaspoon salt, ⅛ teaspoon pepper, 1 tablespoon (more or less) fresh parsley chopped fine, 1 tablespoon Italian grated cheese, ¼ teaspoon onion or garlic salt. Mix well, and let cool. Then divide into 8 uniform portions (about ¼ cup each) and form oval croquettes. Roll in fine dry light bread crumbs, then into beaten egg combined with 1 tablespoon water, then into crumbs again. Let stand on wax paper at room temperature about 20 minutes, turning over several times. Shake off loose crumbs and deep-fry at 375° F. for several minutes until golden brown and crisp. May be kept warm in a very, very low oven on cake rack for about 15 minutes, or croquettes may be fried to a lighter color in advance and refried at 350° F. for several minutes just before serving; or may be completely fried and reheated on cake rack with drip pan underneath in 350° F. oven for about 12 to 15 minutes (not longer or they are likely to crack). May be pan-fried in about ¼ inch of hot unsalted shortening or cooking oil several minutes on each side, instead of frying in deep fat.

Fresh Vegetable Salad Bowl

1 large head of iceberg lettuce, cut or broken into medium-size pieces (other lettuce may be used instead)

Tomatoes, cut into 1-inch pieces

Cucumber, peeled and sliced thin (optional)

About ½ cup radishes, sliced thin crosswise

About ½ cup fresh green onions, cut into 1-inch pieces

About ½ cup watercress or red cabbage (optional)

Have these ingredients cold, crisp and thoroughly drained and dried on towels. Pour salad dressing over them to moisten. Mix well and serve. This salad is very attractive if served in a salad bowl that has been lined with fresh romaine lettuce or other greens. On top of vegetables arrange 6 or 7 slices of tomatoes that have been cut crosswise; over tomatoes arrange 6 or 7 *thin rings* of green pepper cut crosswise. Pour more dressing over tomatoes and peppers. Sprinkle top with medium chopped green onion or parsley. *Any fresh salad vegetable may be used in this salad bowl.*

▶ BREAD ◀

Garlic-Flavored Italian or French Bread

Serves 6 to 8

¼ teaspoon salt
1 or 2 large cloves fresh garlic, cut very fine or better put through garlic press

½ cup soft butter or margarine
A long loaf of Italian or French bread (about 1 pound size)

Add salt and garlic to butter or margarine and blend well. Slice bread diagonally to within ½ inch of crust. Spread garlic-butter between slices and over top. Place loaf on a baking sheet in a 400° F. oven for about 15 minutes. Or wrap in aluminum foil and bake for about 25 minutes. Serve as soon as possible. Bread will be more crisp if top part of foil is left open.

Anchovy-Garlic Italian or French Bread

Add about 1 teaspoon (more or less) anchovy paste to soft butter in basic recipe above.

Parmesan Tomato Garlic French Bread

Serves 6 to 8

1 long loaf French bread (about 14 inches long)
⅓ cup cold, firm butter, beaten about 5 minutes with electric mixer, combined *with* 1 very large or 2 medium cloves garlic, put through garlic press
6 tablespoons grated parmesan or romano cheese

Another ¼ cup grated parmesan cheese
About 1 teaspoon crushed oregano, or ½ teaspoon powdered oregano
2 or 3 medium-size fresh tomatoes, sliced into thin rounds, then in halves
A little salt

Cut French bread lengthwise in halves. Spread each half with ½ of beaten butter combined with garlic. Sprinkle 3 tablespoons parmesan or romano cheese on each half, and about ¼ teaspoon crushed oregano. Now with a sharp serrated knife cut bread into diamond shape. Place a thin ½ slice of tomato on each piece of bread. Sprinkle tomatoes with a little parmesan cheese, pinch of oregano, and a bit of salt. Bake in preheated 350° F. oven about 12 to 15 minutes. Serve as soon as possible.

Very unusual and delectable bread. May be put together several hours in advance. Keep in cool place. Bake just before serving.

▶ DESSERTS ◀

Savory Tea Biscuits, Continental-Style

Serves 6 to 8

Prepare basic Tea Biscuits (page 476). Cut dough using 2-inch or smaller cutter. Roll dough ½ inch thick. Let cool after they are baked. Split in halves and cover lower half with 1 teaspoon Continental Filling. Place top on, and spread top with about ¼ teaspoon filling. Reheat at 400° F. about 7 or 8 minutes just before serving. These biscuits may be filled hours in advance and stored in a covered container in refrigerator or a cold place until ready to be reheated.

These biscuits are delectable served with seafood or poultry salads, soups, chafing dish preparations, or as snacks. Also very delicious if made smaller for hot hors d'oeuvres.

Continental Filling for Tea Biscuits

For about sixteen 2-inch biscuits

½ cup soft butter or margarine
¼ cup, or more, grated Italian cheese
1 medium or large clove of garlic, put through garlic press, or chopped very fine

¾ teaspoon coarse oregano, crushed between fingers, or ¼ teaspoon powdered
⅛ teaspoon black pepper

Combine all ingredients and beat until well blended. May be made several days in advance if stored in a covered container in refrigerator. Let stand in room temperature until soft before using.

Italian Ricotta Cake Torte

Serves 12 to 16

9 × 3-inch Sponge (page 572), Angel Food (page 570), or small French Pastry (page 568) Cake
1 recipe Ricotta Filling for Torte (page 816)

2 cups or less whipping cream, beaten until it clings to bowl
Milk or dark sweet chocolate

Split a 9 × 3-inch round Sponge Cake (or small Angel Food or French Pastry Cake). Cover lower part with Ricotta Filling. Place upper layer on top of filling. Now whip 2 cups or less of cream until it clings to bowl. (Cream for spreading may be stabilized with 1 teaspoon gelatin combined with 2 tablespoons cold water.) Let stand until thick, then dissolve over simmering water. Add dissolved gelatin to medium whipped cream all at once and continue to beat *only* until cream clings well to bowl. At once spread this cream over entire top and sides of torte. Then garnish top with shaved milk chocolate curls. Best to allow chocolate to stand in a warm room for several hours before curling it with a vegetable peeler.

For fancy designs, pipe part of cream onto torte with decorating bag and No. 3 star cookie tube. Refrigerate for at least 1 hour before cutting and serving.

Ricotta Filling for Cake Torte

½ cup whipping cream beaten until it clings to bowl
1 pound fresh ricotta, well drained
1 cup sifted confectioners' sugar
1 teaspoon plain gelatin, combined with 2 tablespoons cold water until thick, then dissolved over simmering water
1 teaspoon vanilla

Whip the ½ cup cream and refrigerate. With mixer beat drained ricotta for about 1 or 2 minutes, add sifted confectioners' sugar and beat only until well blended. Dissolve gelatin and fold it into the ricotta mixture. Add vanilla. *At once* fold whipped cream into ricotta until evenly blended. Refrigerate filling for at least 3 hours before spreading onto cake (1½ recipes of filling may be used in a 9 × 3-inch cake).

Ricotta Pie Torte

For 10-inch deep glass pie plate

Crust for Ricotta Pie Torte

1½ cups sifted all-purpose flour, combined with ¼ teaspoon baking powder and 2 tablespoons granulated sugar
½ cup cold firm butter or margarine
1 large egg, beaten about ½ minute with egg beater
About 1 or 2 tablespoons milk or water, if needed
¾ teaspoon shortening

Sift dry ingredients together into a medium-size bowl. Add butter or margarine, and with pie blender cut through until mixture looks like a coarse meal. Add well-beaten egg, a little at a time, and with a large heavy fork or dinner knife blend until pastry leaves sides of bowl, adding a little milk or water if ingredients appear dry. Turn out onto floured pastry cloth and knead gently about ½ minute. Form a flat round, wrap in wax paper, and chill for about 30 minutes, but do not allow to become too firm.

When ready to be baked, turn dough out onto lightly floured pastry cloth, and with covered rolling pin roll from center out in all directions, forming a 13½-inch round, releasing it from bottom several times with a spatula as you roll. Fold in halves, then in quarters, pick up with both hands and carefully place it into lightly greased 10-inch pie plate. Form rim with hanging dough. Now grease outside of a 9-inch glass plate with ¾ teaspoon unsalted shortening, and place it inside of large plate lined with pastry. This inner glass plate will keep crust smooth and prevent pastry from buckling. Prebake crust at 350° F. about 20 minutes, or until very lightly colored and partially set. Remove from oven, and carefully lift out inner plate. Now, to prevent rim of pastry from burning, place a piece of foil cut about 36 inches long and 2½ inches wide, lightly greased, around rim of plate, holding it in place with a pin or clip. Pour filling into crust, and continue to bake at 350° F. about 40 more minutes or until set. When done, remove torte from oven, and let cool on cake rack. Refrigerate.

To Serve. Spread top with lightly sweetened whipped cream, and make fancy scrolls with No. 3 star cookie tube. Cut in wedges. It will take about 1½ cups whipping cream, beaten till clings to bowl, for fancy decorations. Top of torte may also be garnished with a few chocolate curls.

Filling for Ricotta Pie Torte

1½ pounds moist Italian ricotta cheese that comes in small packages or in bulk (Do not drain. If ricotta appears unusually heavy or dry, add ¼ cup milk or cream. Ricotta can be purchased in nearly all Italian grocery stores; also in majority of chains.)
⅔ cup sifted granulated sugar
4 large whole eggs (1 cupful)

1 teaspoon vanilla
¼ cup or less well drained (dried on towel) maraschino or glazed red cherries, sliced in thin rings.
¼ cup pecan or walnut meats, broken with fingers in coarse ¼-inch pieces
2 tablespoons or little more candied orange or lemon peel cut into ½-inch pieces (optional)

Have all ingredients at room temperature for several hours. Pour ricotta into 8- or 9-inch bowl. Beat with electric mixer for about 2 minutes. Add sugar, little at a time, then eggs, 1 at a time, beating each one in for about ½ minute. Add vanilla, and last fold in the sliced cherries, broken nutmeats, and candied peel. Mix thoroughly and pour into partially baked crust as per directions above. These ingredients must not be too cold. If ingredients are cool increase baking time about 5 minutes.

Whipped Cream Ricotta Pie

For 9-inch pie plate

1⅓ cups fine chocolate crumbs (commercial chocolate cream-filled cookies are excellent if crushed with rolling pin until very, very fine, then blended well), or graham cracker crumbs

2 tablespoons granulated sugar
⅓ cup warm butter or margarine, melted

Combine all ingredients in a medium bowl and stir until evenly blended, rubbing in palms of hands if necessary. Pour into pie plate and with back of large spoon press crumbs into uniform thickness on bottom and sides of plate. Place in refrigerator or freezer until crust is very firm to the touch.

As soon as filling is prepared, pour into cold pie shell and spread evenly. Sprinkle top with about ¾ cup of dry chocolate crumbs (not combined with butter and sugar). Refrigerate for at least 6 hours before serving.

To Serve. Place dish in a shallow pan with warm water for about 2 minutes. Lift out, wipe dish well. Now loosen around edge, cut into wedges, and lift out with pie server. Crumb crusts are very difficult to release from dish, so follow instructions carefully. If you prepare similar desserts in pans with loose bottom (cheese cake pan), simply cover bottom and sides of pan with a very hot damp turkish towel for 2 or 3 minutes. Cut, and serve.

Filling for Whipped Cream Ricotta Pie

1 pound fresh ricotta cheese
1 teaspoon, or little more, vanilla
1½ cups, or less, sifted confectioners' sugar
1 cup, or less, whipping cream, beaten until just clings to bowl, not too stiff and not dry

2 teaspoons plain gelatin, combined with ¼ cup cold water (stir gently and let stand until thick, then dissolve over simmering water)

With electric mixer beat ricotta for about 2 minutes, add vanilla and the sifted confectioners' sugar, about ¼ cup at a time, and continue to beat after each addition until smooth. Whip the cream and refrigerate until needed. Now dissolve thickened gelatin in pan of simmering water. Add dissolved warm gelatin slowly to the ricotta mixture, and blend well. *At once* pour in beaten cream, and with rubber scraper or long spoon fold in until evenly blended and no streaks appear. Immediately pour filling into cold pie shell, and spread evenly.

Italian Cannoli Pastries

Serves 12

1 cup sifted all-purpose flour
¼ teaspoon salt
3 tablespoons sifted confectioners' sugar

1 tablespoon butter or shortening
1 small egg, slightly beaten and combined with 1 tablespoon light wine or water

Sift dry ingredients together several times. Cut in butter with pie blender until it looks like very fine meal. Add only enough beaten egg and liquid to form a medium dough, not too firm and not too soft. Turn out onto lightly floured cloth and knead a few seconds. Cover dough with warm bowl and let stand in room temperature about 30 minutes or little

longer. Divide dough into 12 uniform round pieces. Roll pieces in thin
5½-inch rounds to fit cannoli forms. Place *loosely* on lightly greased
forms, wetting 1 inch of lap with cool water and sealing well to prevent
opening. (Have about 1-inch lap.) Let stand 10 minutes, then deep-fry
at 375° F. until golden brown and crisp. Keep cannoli submerged in fat
during frying process to brown evenly, holding them down with frying
basket or a heavy metal trivet, or a long spoon. When done, remove
carefully with tongs or 2 forks. Place on cake rack. When cool enough to
handle, remove from forms. When shells are cold, fill with Ricotta Filling,
whipped cream, chocolate, lemon, plain custard filling, or ice cream.
Sprinkle edges with green nuts if desired, and top with sifted confectioners'
sugar.

Cannoli shells may be prepared several days in advance. Store in wax
paper, in a paper bag in cool, dry place.

Ricotta Filling for Cannoli

1 pound fresh Italian ricotta, well drained
About ¾ cup sifted confectioners' sugar
Enough cream to form proper consistency, about 2 tablespoons, *only if ricotta is very dry*
About 2 tablespoons ¼-inch pieces sweet chocolate
1, or more, teaspoons vanilla
1 tablespoon chopped citron or candied orange peel, cut into ¼-inch pieces
1 tablespoon chopped glazed cherries, cut into ¼-inch pieces
1 tablespoon coarsely broken pecan or walnut meats

With electric mixer or spoon, beat ricotta for a few seconds, then add
sifted confectioners' sugar, little at a time, and continue to beat until
very light, about 2 minutes. Add only enough cream to make proper
consistency, the vanilla, and other ingredients. Mix thoroughly and keep
in coldest part of refrigerator until ready to be used, for *at least 2 hours*.
Ricotta, sugar, and cream may be beaten a day in advance and kept very
cold. *Shortly before serving, add other ingredients.* This is enough filling
for 8 to 10 cannoli shells, depending on size. Do not fill cannoli more
than 1 hour before serving.

Zuppa Inglese

Serves 12 to 16

French Pastry Cake (page 568), or any other sponge or angel food cake
½ cup brandy or other liquor
1 cup candied fruit mix (used in fruit cakes), soaked in ¼ cup brandy or other liquor
1 recipe French Cream Filling (page 741)
½ cup egg whites, room temperature
¼ teaspoon salt
½ teaspoon vanilla
½ cup sifted granulated sugar
2 more tablespoons granulated sugar

Split cake crosswise in 2 sections. Place lower half on a heatproof platter. Brush it with ¼ cup of the liquor, then cover it with soaked fruit mix. Spread the French Cream Filling over fruit. Place upper half of cake over filling. Brush cake with other ¼ cup liquor.

Now in 7-inch bowl combine egg whites and salt. Beat until mixture clings to bowl. Add the ½ cup sugar, about 2 tablespoons at a time, and beat until well blended, and meringue clings to bowl when turned upside down. Beat in vanilla. At once pile meringue on top of cake, having it slightly rounded in center. Sprinkle top of meringue with the 2 tablespoons sugar. Bake in a preheated 400° F. oven 7 or 8 minutes, or until lightly colored. Remove from oven, let cool, then refrigerate for at least 4 hours before serving.

This is a very rich delicious dessert, and should be served in small wedges.

Note. Instead of meringue, dessert may be covered with whipped cream without placing in oven.

Biscotti Croccanti (Italian Toasted Almond Slices)

Serves 12

¼ cup soft butter or margarine	1 tablespoon double-acting baking powder
¾ cup granulated sugar	
4 medium-size eggs	¾ cup whole raw almonds with skins on
¼ teaspoon salt	
1 teaspoon vanilla	About 1 teaspoon anise seed (optional)
3½ cups sifted cake flour, or more if necessary	

With electric mixer or spoon, beat butter or margarine, add sugar a little at a time, then eggs 1 at a time, beating in each egg about 1 minute. Add salt, vanilla, and about ½ of flour that has been combined with baking powder, and beat with a spoon *only until smooth.* Add ½ of almonds and beat until blended. Then add rest of flour and almonds. Beat until well blended. Dough should be as light as possible if a light texture is desired.

Divide dough into 4 uniform portions. Form each portion into a roll on a well-floured pastry cloth. Pick up carefully and place on a well-greased and floured baking sheet that measures about 12 × 18 inches. *With hands pull roll to fit width of sheet,* keeping it as uniform and smooth as possible. Do likewise with other 3 portions of dough, keeping them about 3 inches apart. Brush tops of rolls with milk, and bake at 400° F. about 20 to 25 minutes, or until golden brown and firm to the touch. Do not overbake.

Remove from oven; let stand covered with a towel for several hours. Then place rolls on a cutting board and with a very sharp plain knife cut into ½-inch slices. Place on an ungreased baking sheet with cut sides down, and toast at 400° F. about 15 to 20 minutes, turning them over and around until delicately brown and crisp. Watch closely toward end to prevent burning. Let cool, and store in a closed container. They may be rolled in sifted confectioners' sugar before serving.

Important. It is best to use an electric mixer for the beating of the butter, sugar, and eggs. Beat flour and almonds with spoon only until well blended. As little flour as possible should be used, to keep these slices light in texture.

Italian Fennel Cakes

Serves 8 to 12

¼ cup butter or margarine
⅔ cup granulated sugar
3 large whole eggs (¾ cup)
1 tablespoon, or less, Italian finochio (fennel seed)
1 teaspoon lemon flavoring

½ teaspoon vanilla flavoring
About 2¼ cups sifted all-purpose flour, combined and sifted with 2½ teaspoons double-acting baking powder

Cream butter or margarine, add sugar, little at a time, and beat well for 1 minute. Add 1 whole egg at a time and beat each 1 minute at high speed (little longer by hand). Add fennel seed, lemon and vanilla flavorings, and, last, the sifted flour and baking powder (all at once) and mix *with spoon* only until smooth, forming a medium dough, not too soft. Place dough into pastry bag and with large plain cookie tube or opening of coupling press out small rounds (about 1 inch) onto greased baking sheet. If dough is too stiff to go through bag, add a little water. Bake at 375° F. in center of oven about 15 minutes, then place on upper rack and bake about 7 or 8 minutes, or until delicately brown, but not too dry; bake longer for very crisp cakes. When cold, dip rounded part into Transparent Icing and sprinkle center top with a pinch of finely chopped or grated green nuts, or leave plain.

Dough may be chilled and shaped in hands forming balls instead of using pastry bag. Cakes may be sprinkled thickly with confectioners' sugar instead of iced.

Transparent Icing for Fennel Cakes

About 3 cups, or less, sifted confectioners' sugar
¼ cup boiling water

1 teaspoon lemon extract
Finely chopped or grated pistachio nuts

Add sifted confectioners' sugar to the ¼ cup boiling water and beat until smooth; add 1 teaspoon lemon extract. (This is a thin icing. More sugar may be added for a thicker icing.) Dip rounded part of cakes into icing and let drain on cake racks. Sprinkle center with pinch of pistachio nuts at once before icing sets.

▶ *Oriental Cookery*

IF WE WERE ASKED FOR ONE OF THE HIGHLIGHTS IN OUR MANY ADVENTURES in cooking, we should probably say mastering the art of Oriental cookery. Our experience, like that of most people, with this particular type of food was limited to restaurant eating until we had the opportunity of delving into the intricacies of cooking it. The chef with whom we worked (see below) had his own way of measuring, temperature usage, and timing. We finally interpreted these into everyday cooking terms. Now any housewife can easily follow and have success with our recipes in Oriental cookery.

This was made possible for us by the courtesy and helpful assistance of the management of the famous Shangri-La Restaurant, 222 North State Street, Chicago. Time after time we were graciously received and admitted to the kitchens of this popular eating place to watch and question their noted chef, Jimmie Chang, on recipes you will see here. We were also allowed to try the recipes in the restaurant kitchen under the guidance of the chef and later in our school under the supervision of the restaurant's genial host, Jimmie Moy. All of which makes us deeply grateful to Shangri-La for this delightful excursion into the realm of Oriental cookery.

Most of us are interested in serving balanced meals. In Oriental cookery this is surprisingly easy to do. This very old, very delicious method of cookery might have stepped right out of one of today's books on nutrition. It follows closely balanced, nutritious food requirements. For a tantalizingly different taste you have only to try Oriental sauces. They give the final, inspired touch which always makes a dish superb eating. We hope you will find these recipes as exciting as we did when working on them at Shangri-La.

Most of the food items used in these dishes may be purchased in American grocery stores. The rest of them are available in the Oriental stores. Whenever chicken stock is suggested in these recipes, chicken instant bouillon or cubes may be added to hot water and used in its place.

Peanut oil is ordinarily used. However, other oils, except olive oil, may be used.

▶ APPETIZERS ◀

Noodle Dough

For 18 large egg rolls or 32 individual ones

1 very large egg (¼ cup), beaten with a fork
⅔ cup lukewarm water
2 teaspoons salt

About 2½ cups sifted all-purpose flour, or enough to form dough that does not stick to hand, but keep it as soft as possible

Combine all ingredients except flour. Add flour, little at a time, and beat until dough leaves sides of bowl. Turn out onto floured pastry cloth and knead until smooth, adding more flour to prevent dough from sticking to hands, but keep it soft as possible. Cut dough into 2 pieces after it has been kneaded and shape each into square piece. Cover with bowls and let ripen for about 10 minutes during warm weather, about 20 minutes during cold weather. Then roll each piece to measure about 20 inches square. Trim off uneven ends, and cut each sheet into sixteen uniform 4½-inch squares or nine 6-inch squares. After squares are cut, let them stand on wax paper on cookie sheets for about 15 minutes, turning them over several times to dry out slightly, *but not become brittle. Watch this closely.* (See directions for making Cantonese Egg Rolls, page 824).

Note. This noodle dough makes excellent tender fried Won Tons, served instead of rolls or bread with Cantonese food.

Chinese Fried Noodle Nests

1 pound moist Chinese noodles will make about 10 to 12 nests

Purchase moist Chinese noodles in Oriental bakeries or grocery stores. There are two kinds, thin and thick. Either may be used. To form individual nests, use a No. 2½ can from which the top and bottom have been removed with a can opener that leaves smooth edges. Make sure can is clean and dry. Place it in a deep saucepan (2- or 3-quart size) half filled with cooking oil. Pick up ⅓ cup moist noodles that have been in room temperature about 1 hour, and lower gently into hot fat between 385° F. and 400° F. Fry until puffed and lightly browned; then turn over and brown upper part. Lift out with a long skewer or fork, and drain on cake rack.

When ready to serve, fill nests with Chicken à la King (page 222), other creamed dishes, or Chop Suey (page 850), and arrange on plate with 2 small peach or apricot halves or pineapple fingers decorated with cream cheese or whipped cream and a glazed or maraschino cherry and 2 citron leaves.

Fried Crisp Noodles—No. 1

Roll dough same as for egg rolls; let stand for about 30 minutes, turning it over several times, then fold dough over and over, and cut it as thin as possible with very sharp knife. Fry noodles at 375° F. to 400° F. until golden brown and crisp for several minutes, turning them over once.

Fried Crisp Noodles—No. 2

Purchase moist Chinese noodles, as suggested for Noodle Nests. Drop by handful into deep hot fat, between 385° F. and 400° F. and fry until golden color and crisp, on the underside, then turn over and fry until lightly browned. This will take only 2 or 3 minutes. Watch closely not to overbrown. Serve with many Oriental dishes.

These noodles may be fried several days in advance and kept well wrapped in wax paper in a cool dry place. If they do not appear crisp when ready to be served, they may be reheated in a 350° F. oven on a baking sheet for about 5 minutes.

Cantonese Egg Rolls Appetizers

Prepare 1 recipe Noodle Dough (page 823). Or purchase noodle dough squares that measure about 7 inches if making large rolls, or 4-inch squares for individual size, from Oriental noodle factories or stores. (These factories supply the leading Chinese restaurants.) They are more economical and satisfactory than homemade noodle dough. There are about eighteen 7-inch squares to the pound. Keep them in their original wrapper, covered with a very damp towel, until ready to be used (to prevent drying out), and store in refrigerator. It is best to use them within 3 days after they are purchased.

Cut off about 1½ inches from all corners of large noodle square, about 1 inch from individual. Measure ¼ cup Filling for Egg Rolls solidly packed and form a 5-inch roll; about 1 tablespoon for individual. Place filling on wide end of dough nearest you. Brush edges of dough with well-beaten egg combined with ¼ teaspoon salt and roll up, turning edges in while rolling. Keep rolls on wax paper until all have been completed. As soon as rolls are completed, heat oil to 360° to 375° F. Dip rolls into Cantonese Fritter Batter, then lower into hot fat carefully and dry until *very lightly colored* and set for about 2 minutes. Lift out and drain on cake coolers. If to be kept more than an hour before serving, cover and store in refrigerator. About 30 minutes before serving, remove from refrigerator, let stand in room temperature. When ready to be served, lower gently into hot oil 360° to 375° F. and fry until golden brown and crisp, about 5 minutes. Remove from fat, cut each roll crosswise into 3 or 4 pieces and serve at once. Serve individual rolls whole.

Cantonese Fritter Batter

1 medium egg	¼ cup sifted all-purpose flour
2 tablespoons chicken stock or milk	½ teaspoon salt

Combine all ingredients in a small bowl and, with egg beater, beat until smooth. Cover and let stand about 10 minutes, or longer. If batter is too thin, add a little more flour; if too thick add more liquid. Best to have a thin batter.

Filling for Egg Rolls

For 8 large egg rolls

1 cup cooked shrimp
1 cup cooked pork, veal, or ham, finely chopped with knife
1 cup celery, chopped very fine
½ cup canned Chinese water chestnuts, chopped (not too fine)
½ cup fresh green onion and stems, chopped very fine, or 2 tablespoon chopped dry onion

1¼ teaspoons salt (less if using ham or seasoned meat)
1 teaspoon sugar
⅛ teaspoon black pepper
3 tablespoons, or little more, melted butter
2 tablespoons, or little more, peanut butter

Chop all ingredients except shrimp with heavy knife or cleaver. Do not grind.

To prepare shrimp, cook ½ pound in gently boiling water for about 5 minutes if large, about 3 minutes if medium. Then shell, remove vein, and chop into very small pieces. This will give about 1 cup chopped shrimp (1 cup canned shrimp may be used; reduced salt to 1 teaspoon). Combine all ingredients in a bowl, and with hands work well until thoroughly blended. If mixture appears too dry, add a little more peanut butter. Mixture should appear moist and hold its shape when pressed in hand but not wet or too dry. Cover and store in refrigerator until ready to be used. May be prepared a day in advance but *must be refrigerated.*

Boiled Won Tons (Chinese Ravioli)

Prepare like Cantonese Filled Won Tons. Instead of dropping into deep fat, cook in boiling water about 15 minutes. Serve with Won Ton Gravy.

Won Ton Gravy

In 2 tablespoons peanut oil, sauté ½ cup fine-chopped green onion and ½ cup fine-chopped mushrooms about 5 minutes. Then add 1 cup chicken stock combined with 1 tablespoon cornstarch, 1 teaspoon soy sauce, ¼ teaspoon Chinese molasses, and ½ teaspoon salt. Cover, and simmer about 5 minutes, or until thick and transparent. Pour this sauce over Cantonese Fried or Boiled Won Tons, and sprinkle top with fine-chopped fresh green onion.

Cantonese Filled Won Ton Appetizers (Fried)

Makes about 40; serves 12

1 recipe Noodle Dough (page 823), or ½ pound of commercial Chinese noodle dough	1 whole egg, combined with ¼ teaspoon salt, beaten 15 minutes in advance

Cut moist noodle dough in about 2½-inch squares. Place 1 slightly rounded teaspoon of Won Ton Meat Filling on each, spreading it flat. Brush edges of squares with beaten egg, fold over, forming triangles. Press edges well together. Puncture top 2 times with toothpick.

Deep-fry Won Tons in peanut oil as soon as possible after they are filled, at 350° F., until golden brown and crisp on 1 side, then with fork turn over and fry second side. Lift out with perforated spoon, and drain on cake racks. May be kept hot in a low oven (about 250° F.) for about 15 minutes, or they may be deep-fried hours in advance, refrigerated then reheated on cake racks with drip pan underneath in a 350° F. oven for about 8 to 10 minutes. Do not refry.

Won Ton Meat Filling

½ pound (1 cup packed) very finely ground lean raw pork, chicken, or beef (cooked meat may be used)	1 teaspoon cornstarch
	1 tablespoon finely chopped fresh green onion and stems
⅛ teaspoon pepper	About 1 teaspoon salt
2 tablespoons finely chopped water chestnuts	2 teaspoons soy sauce

Combine all ingredients and blend well.

Cantonese Fried Shrimp

Serves 6 as appetizer

1 pound raw shrimp	1 tablespoon cornstarch
1 very large egg or 2 small (⅓ cup)	About ¾ cup sifted flour, combined with ¾ teaspoon baking powder
½ cup chicken stock, milk or water (more or less, depending on flour)	¼ teaspoon garlic salt
2 teaspoons salt	

Shell shrimp and remove vein if necessary. Split lengthwise. If shrimp are very large, flatten with cleaver and cut in 2 pieces to insure thorough cooking. If small or medium, may be left in 1 piece. Wash under cold running water and drain very thoroughly for about 15 minutes, then on paper towel.

Combine all ingredients (except shrimp) in a bowl, and with egg beater beat until smooth. Cover and let stand at least 15 minutes. Drop well-drained *raw, split* shrimp into batter. Pick up 1 at a time, drain a little, and drop into deep hot oil, about 350° F. Do not fry too many in first frying at one time to prevent clinging together. Fry until *very light brown* if to be prepared in advance and refried. If to be served at once, fry until *golden* brown and crisp, about 5 minutes. Best to fry second time. Drain on cake cooler and serve as soon as possible. If after frying 1 or 2 shrimp the coating appears too thin, add a little more flour. If it appears too thick, add a little more liquid.

These shrimp may be fried first time several hours or a day in advance, stored in refrigerator after they are cool, then refried for several minutes before serving, or until crisp and golden brown. *Watch second frying as they darken quickly.* Keep temperature about 350° F.

Serve with Cantonese Sweet-Sour Sauce (page 834) or Hot Sauce (page 835).

Won Tons with Chicken

Serves 2 generously

¼ cup hot oil, to which add ½ teaspoon salt

½ cup raw chicken, cut into flat strips about ½ inch wide, 1 inch long

2 tablespoons chicken stock

¼ cup pineapple, cut into 2-inch chunks

¼ cup fresh green pepper, cut into 2-inch squares

¼ cup fresh red firm tomatoes, cut into 2-inch pieces

¼ cup pineapple juice

2 tablespoons cider vinegar

¼ cup brown sugar

2 teaspoons cornstarch

½ teaspoon salt

In hot oil sauté raw chicken strips about 1 minute on each side. Then add stock, cover pan, and steam chicken gently about 10 minutes. After 5 minutes, pour off liquid from chicken. Combine chicken with pineapple, green pepper, and tomato.

In a separate saucepan, cook together pineapple juice, cider vinegar, brown sugar, cornstarch, and salt. After it comes to boil, lower heat, and simmer about 5 minutes. Combine this sauce with chicken and vegetables.

To serve, arrange about 8 to 10 fried Won Tons on serving platter, and spread cooked chicken with vegetables and sauce over them. Sprinkle top with cut fresh green onions and serve at once with Cantonese-Style Fried Rice (page 852).

Oriental Shrimp Appetizer

Serves 6 to 8

½ pound cooked whole large shrimp (1 pound before cooking), 25 to 30 shrimp

1 large can Chinese water chest- nuts (net weight of chestnuts 4 ounces), each cut in 2 slices (if some of the chestnuts are small, leave whole)

To cook shrimp, drop into boiling unsalted water and let simmer about 5 minutes as soon as they come to boiling point. Remove shells and vein, if necessary. If using top-quality cooked canned shrimp, omit salt in marinade. If shrimp are very large and thick, it is better to split in halves lengthwise.

Pour Oriental Marinade over the cooked whole shrimp and sliced water chestnuts. Mix well and let marinate for at least 2 hours, turning them over occasionally. When ready to be prepared, drain well. Wrap a thin whole or ½ slice of bacon around a whole shrimp and slice of water chestnut firmly, and secure with plain heavy toothpick. This may be done hours or a day in advance if refrigerated in a covered container.

To Serve. Place appetizers on cake racks with drip pan underneath (pour 1 cup hot water in pan to prevent smoking) and oven-bake at 425° F. about 8 minutes on first side, then turn over and bake about 7 more minutes on second side. Remove from oven, and replace toothpicks with frilled ones if desired. Serve hot. These appetizers may be *completely cooked* hours in advance and stored in refrigerator, covered, as soon as they are cold, then reheated in oven at 400° F. on racks for about 7 or 8 minutes. May be frozen for 1 week. Reheat for about 10 minutes if frozen.

Oriental Marinade

3 tablespoons soy sauce, combined with ½ cup chicken or meat stock (or water)

1 teaspoon Chinese molasses

¼ teaspoon, or less, salt (omit if using canned shrimp)

¼ teaspoon garlic or onion salt

¼ teaspoon black pepper

Stir ingredients well for about ½ minute.

Note. Place meat to be marinated into an enamel, glass, or stainless steel utensil, *and not in other utensils made of metal* as very often the acid in the marinade will act upon the metal chemically and develop an unpleasant taste in the food. Let food soak in the marinade for time suggested in recipe, turning it over and basting it often with a large spoon with marinade in pan. Keep in refrigerator, but let stand in room temperature for about 1 hour before cooking, either in or out of marinade.

Oriental Chicken Liver Appetizer

Makes about 20; serves 6

½ pound chicken livers, each cut in 2 or 3 pieces, depending on size
5-ounce can Chinese water chestnuts, each sliced lengthwise in 2 pieces
¼ pound bacon, each slice cut in 2 pieces crosswise (not lengthwise)

Place a piece of chicken liver and a thick slice of chestnut on one end of bacon, roll tightly, and insert a heavy toothpick through bacon, chestnut, and liver to hold together as securely as possible. Place appetizers into bowl of Marinade for Oriental Chicken Livers, cover and refrigerate for several hours or longer. *Omit salt* if marinated for longer han 2 hours.

To Serve. Place 1 cup hot water in a drip pan. Arrange marinated appetizers on a cake rack, leaving about an inch space between each one, and bake in a preheated 450° F. oven 10 minutes; turn over and bake another 8 to 10 minutes. Plain toothpicks may be removed and replaced with frilled picks.

Serve appetizers on a heated platter. Will remain hot for about 15 minutes. They may remain in oven with heat shut off and door slightly open for a short time if necessary before serving.

These appetizers may be completely prepared and baked for a little shorter time, several hours or a day in advance, if refrigerated, then reheated on cake racks in a 400° F. oven for about 6 or 7 minutes just before serving.

Marinade for Oriental Chicken Livers

2 tablespoons soy sauce, combined with ¼ cup water or stock
¼ teaspoon salt
¼ teaspoon garlic salt
¼ teaspoon black pepper

Combine all ingredients and stir until well blended.

Yuon Stuffed Mushrooms (Appetizer)

Serves 6 to 8

Purchase 1 pound large firm white mushrooms. Wash in cool water, and drain in a colander at least 15 minutes. Remove stems carefully. Sprinkle inside of mushroom caps with salt, and stuff with Cantonese Meat Filling, having meat high and rounded.

In a medium-size skillet (with cover), pour 2 tablespoons peanut oil,

¼ cup chicken stock, ¼ teaspoon salt. Place filled mushrooms in skillet. Cover, and steam *gently* over medium heat about 15 minutes for small mushrooms, 20 minutes for medium-size, and 25 minutes for large. Keep heat only high enough to produce steam. If moisture evaporates toward end, add another ¼ cup stock. When mushrooms are done, there should be at least ¼ cup drippings in skillet. Pour drippings over mushrooms before serving.

Yuon Stuffed Mushrooms may also be served as an accompaniment or main dish. In this case, prepare gravy with ½ cup stock combined with 1 tablespoon cornstarch, 1 teaspoon soy sauce. Add to drippings, and cook together until thick and clear. Pour over mushrooms and sprinkle top with fine-chopped green onion. The mushroom stems may be sliced thin, sautéed, and added to gravy.

Cantonese Meat Filling

½ pound fine-ground lean pork	1 teaspoon cornstarch
½ teaspoon salt	1 tablespoon chopped fresh green
⅛ teaspoon pepper	onions and stems, or ½ table-
1 tablespoon fine-chopped water chest-	spoon chopped onion
nuts	1 teaspoon soy sauce

Combine all ingredients, blend thoroughly with hands, and stuff.

Cantonese Squab (Appetizer)

Serves 4

Have 2 squabs or Cornish hens drawn and split into halves. Steam in about 1 inch of stock prepared as follows: to each cup of chicken stock add ½ teaspoon Chinese molasses, ½ teaspoon salt, ½ teaspoon sugar, ⅛ teaspoon Oriental dark seasoning powder.

Place birds on a rack and pour stock over them. Cover pan, and steam about 30 minutes, turning several times. Do not overcook. Drain well, then dry on towel. Cut into medium-size pieces. A few minutes before serving, drop cut-up squab into deep hot peanut oil, 375° F., and cook until brown and crisp. Season with salt and pepper before serving. Serve with any sauce.

Sautéed Shrimp, Garlic Sauce (Appetizer)

Serves 6

Remove shells and veins from 1 pound fresh shrimp. Wash thoroughly under cold running water and drain well. Split shrimp lengthwise in 2 pieces. Sauté them several minutes in ¼ cup peanut oil to which ½ teaspoon salt has been added, turning often. Add 1 teaspoon Black Bean-Garlic Sauce (page 835) and ¼ cup chicken stock. Cover, and cook over moderate heat about 5 more minutes. Last, thicken with 1 tablespoon cornstarch diluted in 2 tablespoons stock, and add ¼ teaspoon Chinese molasses, about ½ teaspoon salt, ⅛ teaspoon pepper. Cover, and cook over moderate heat only until thick and glazy, about 5 minutes, turning several times. Mound on dish and sprinkle top with fine-cut fresh green onions and stems.

Chicken Livers en Brochette (Appetizer)

Serves 6

Wash ½ pound livers. Drain well, then cook about 5 minutes in a little water to which ¼ teaspoon Chinese molasses, ¼ teaspoon salt, and ½ teaspoon sugar have been added. Let remain in liquid until cool; then drain very well. Cut peeled water chestnuts into pieces about ½ inch wide and 1 inch long. After they are cut, chestnuts may be steamed in a small amount of water several minutes, but they are tastier if used raw. Cut chicken livers about 1 inch long and ½ inch wide. Place each piece of liver on a slice of bacon, roll a little, then enclose water chestnut; continue to roll and hold together with toothpick. Place on a platter on rack over hot water. Water should reach rack but not platter. Cover pan, and steam about 15 minutes. A few minutes before serving, drop into deep hot fat, about 375° F., and cook about 2 or 3 minutes. Serve as soon as possible.

Oriental Barbecued Beef or Pork Tenderloin Appetizers on Bamboo Sticks

Makes about 15 to 20 appetizers; serves 6 to 8

6 inch very thin bamboo sticks
1 pound of beef or pork tenderloin, sliced about ¼ inch thick, 1¼ inch squares (not larger) (top-quality aged sirloin tip or top of round may be used; sprinkle with meat tenderizer about 10 minutes after they are removed from marinade and before they are sautéed)
Small can mushrooms
Cocktail onions
Pineapple cubes or water chestnut cubes

Insert pointed end of bamboo sticks through 1 piece of meat, then through a very small canned mushroom cap, small cocktail onion, cube of pineapple or water chestnut, then another piece of meat. Place appetizers in a medium-size flat container, and cover with marinade. Refrigerate for at least 8 hours, turning them over several times.

To Cook. Drain well, and sauté over *medium* heat on well-oiled flat side of griddle pan, or heavy large skillet, about 1 minute on each side. It may be necessary to lower or increase heat from time to time, also to add a little more oil or a little water on griddle during cooking process. Do not overcook. May be kept hot on heatproof dish or other flat pan in very low oven (250° F.) for about ½ hour. Or appetizers may be grilled hours or a day in advance, cooled, then refrigerated. Shortly before serving remove from refrigerator and brush them with leftover marinade, reheat on griddle or in skillet about ½ minute on each side, *or large amount may be reheated in a 350° F. oven for about 10 minutes just before serving.*

To Serve. Arrange appetizers on a 12- or 14-inch round platter, with bowl of Hot Sauce (page 835) in center, or serve without sauce.

Marinade for Oriental Appetizers on Bamboo Sticks

2 tablespoons granulated sugar
2 tablespoons catsup
¼ cup soy sauce
½ teaspoon Chinese molasses
¼ teaspoon salt

¼ teaspoon pepper
¼ teaspoon garlic or onion salt
1 cup chicken or meat stock (add bouillon cube to 1 cup hot water)

Combine all ingredients and blend thoroughly. Pour over appetizers.

Oriental Barbecued Shrimp Appetizers on Bamboo Sticks

Serves 8 to 12

Cook 2 pounds *medium-size* (not large) raw shrimp in simmering water about 3 to 5 minutes. When cool, drain well, and place on bamboo sticks same as meat appetizers (above). Very delicious.

Hot Oriental Delight Appetizers

Makes about 45

1 can Chinese water chestnuts (6½ or 8 ounce size), chopped medium, not too fine
3-ounce can chopped mushrooms, chopped fine
4½-ounce can shrimp, or 1 cup freshly cooked, chopped medium, not too fine
½ teaspoon salt if using freshly cooked shrimp and unsalted cooked pork

(omit salt if using canned shrimp and ham)
2 teaspoons soy sauce
¼ teaspoon pepper
¼ cup fresh green onion and stems mixed, chopped fine
¾ pound of ham or cooked pork (1½ cups packed), chopped fine
5 whole eggs
4 cups light bread crumbs

Prepare White Sauce with 3 tablespoons melted butter or margarine. Add ¼ cup sifted all-purpose flour; stir until smooth, then add ½ cup lukewarm milk. Cook, stirring continuously until thick and smooth. Simmer 2 or 3 minutes. Add a little more milk if sauce is too thick to blend well.

Add all ingredients (except eggs and bread crumbs) to White Sauce and stir well until evenly blended. Cover, and refrigerate for 2 hours or longer, or until firm enough to handle and shape. Can be prepared day in advance.

To shape, pick up 1 level tablespoon of preparation, and with hands shape into very smooth balls, dampening hands *slightly* if sticky. Cover balls with light bread crumbs, then dip into well-beaten whole eggs; let drain (add no water to eggs). Roll again in crumbs, then in egg, and the third time in crumbs. (This is important to prevent bursting and to produce a crisp crust.) Place on wax paper and let stand about 20 minutes, turning them over several times. Lower gently into deep hot fat, about 375° F., until lightly colored, for about 2 minutes, then refry a second time just before serving, at 375° F. for about 2 minutes. It is best to fry these appetizers a second time for crisp crust even if they are to be served within a short time. They may be fried once a day in advance, and then refried shortly before serving. Store them in covered container in refrigerator. Or they may be frozen for several weeks. Let stand covered in room temperature for about 2 hours after removing from freezer, or defrost for longer time in refrigerator.

Important. If using French-fry basket, place 8 to 10 appetizers in basket at one time, and lower into fat. They will brown evenly if placed in fat at one time. In reheating the second time twice as many may be placed in basket at one time, at 375° F. Do not allow fat to cool, but increase heat as necessary.

Serve in chafing dish, or on a large platter around a bowl of Hot Sauce (page 835). Frilled toothpick on top center of each adds color, and makes appetizer easy to pick up.

Cantonese Barbecue Ribs and Pork Appetizer

2 pounds ribs, pork tenderloin, or pork loin
¼ cup granulated sugar
2 tablespoons catsup
2 tablespoons soy sauce
½ teaspoon Chinese molasses
2 teaspoons salt
¼ teaspoon black pepper
¼ cup chicken stock

For marinade, combine all ingredients (except meat) and mix well. Pour over meat on both sides. Cover with wax paper, and let stand in refrigerator 7 or 8 hours or longer, turning occasionally and brushing several times with sauce that settles in dish while standing.

About 2 hours before serving, remove meat from refrigerator, place it on a rack with drip pan underneath, adding about 1 cup cold water in drip pan to prevent smoking.

Ribs. Roast ribs at 350° F. about 1½ hours, turning them over after 45 minutes, and baste them occasionally with leftover marinade. After 1½ hours, test ribs, and if not done, roast a little longer. Very thick back ribs may take 25 or 30 minutes longer. It is better to have them a little overcooked than undercooked. Before serving, cut with a very sharp knife into single ribs and serve with sauce. If meat is browning too rapidly, cover loosely with aluminum foil or lower temperature to 325° F. Ribs are done when you can pull them apart easily.

Pork Tenderloin. Follow above directions. Roast about 2 hours if tenderloins are large and thick, turning over after 1 hour. Chinese cooks use the center and leanest part of a pork loin for this purpose.

Pork Loin. Prepare same as tenderloin, but cook for longer time, allowing about 40 minutes per pound for 3- or 4-pound pieces. Use meat thermometer and cook to 170° F. Oriental cooks trim the pork loin, removing most of visible fat. It is more moist and tender than the pork tenderloin.

▶ SAUCES ◀

Sweet-Sour Sauce—No. 1

Serves 12

¼ pound dry apricots, combined with 1 cup water and cooked until very soft, or use canned apricots

¼ teaspoon salt

½ cup, more or less, granulated sugar

About ½ cup, more or less, cider or white vinegar

Cook apricots in water in covered saucepan very slowly about 30 minutes, or until very soft and most of water has been absorbed by apricots. When soft, put apricots through food mill.

Combine all ingredients and with egg beater, beat until smooth and thoroughly blended. Taste and season further if necessary. Serve with Cantonese appetizers. May be made days in advance and stored in covered jar in refrigerator.

Sweet-Sour Sauce—No. 2

Serves 8

¼ cup vinegar

½ cup pineapple juice

⅓ cup brown sugar, solidly packed

1½ tablespoons cornstarch, combined with 2 tablespoons water

About 1 teaspoon salt

Combine all ingredients in saucepan and bring to boiling point, stirring constantly. Let simmer about 5 minutes. Let cool. May be made in advance. If sauce is too thick, thin out with pineapple juice or vinegar. Serve with Cantonese appetizers and Him Soon York (page 838).

Hot Sauce

Serves 12

½ cup cool water
About 1½ tablespoons dry mustard, more or less, to suit taste

About ¾ cup catsup
About 1 teaspoon salt

Combine all ingredients and, with egg beater or large spoon, beat until smooth and thoroughly blended. Serve with Cantonese appetizers. May be made days in advance and stored in covered jar in refrigerator.

Mustard Sauce

Serves 12

To each cup mayonnaise, add about 1 teaspoon dry mustard, 1 teaspoon sugar, 3 tablespoons prepared mustard, or enough to suit taste. Add a little lemon juice if too thick. Serve with Cantonese appetizers.

Black Bean-Garlic Sauce

¼ cup Chinese black beans, washed thoroughly under running water and drained
2 large cloves garlic, peeled and chopped very fine
1 teaspoon fresh ginger, chopped very fine (optional)

½ teaspoon salt
¼ teaspoon black pepper
1 tablespoon soy sauce
1 tablespoon peanut oil

Wash beans thoroughly under running water, drain well, and chop fine. Combine the chopped black beans, chopped garlic, and chopped ginger. Place in bowl, add rest of ingredients, blend well. Keep tightly covered in refrigerator until ready to be used. May be kept for several days or longer. Serve with lobster and other seafood.

▶ MAIN DISHES ◀

Lobster Almond Din

Makes 2 large or 3 medium servings

½ cup fresh green pepper, cut into 1-inch squares and boiled 1 minute

½ cup cooked pascal celery, cut crosswise into ½-inch pieces, cooked 5 minutes

½ pound cooked lobster meat (1 pound raw)

½ cup Chinese pea pods, cut diagonally in 2 pieces, or leave whole

½ cup Chinese water chestnuts, sliced medium, lengthwise

½ pound fresh mushrooms, sliced, sautéed for 2 or 3 minutes

¼ cup hot oil

1½ teaspoons, more or less, salt

¼ teaspoon black pepper

¼ teaspoon garlic salt

¾ cup cool chicken stock, combined with 1½ tablespoons cornstarch

3 tablespoons pimiento, cut into 1-inch squares

About 15 to 20 blanched, whole, or better *split*, toasted salted almonds

First cook celery in small amount of hot water in covered pan for about 5 minutes. Cook green pepper about 1 minute. Drop cooked lobster, pea pods, chestnuts, green pepper, mushrooms, and celery into hot oil, and cook over moderate heat about 5 minutes, turning often. Add seasonings, blend well, and cook about 2 more minutes. Now add the chicken stock and cornstarch. Cover and cook over moderate heat until thick and simmer 5 minutes, turning occasionally while it thickens. Fold in pimiento squares. If it appears too thick, add a little more stock. Heap on serving dish and sprinkle top with the toasted salted almonds. Serve at once with Cantonese-Style Fried Rice (page 852).

Instead of fresh lobster meat, canned lobster, frozen lobster meat, or small lobster tails that have been boiled about 5 minutes then shelled and cut, may be used. Some fish stores sell fresh lobster meat by the pound. It is more economical and practical to buy this way than to cook live lobsters.

Chicken Almond Din

Serves 3 or 4

Follow directions for Lobster Almond Din, but instead of lobster, use ¾ pound (1½ cups) raw chicken cut into very flat pieces, about 1 inch wide and 2 inches long. Drop raw chicken into hot oil and cook for several minutes, turning as it fries. Then cover, and steam about 5 minutes over moderate heat. Add other ingredients, and proceed as for Lobster Almond Din.

Serve with Cantonese-Style Fried Rice (page 852).

Beef Mandarin-Style

Serves 4 to 6

½ pound (1½ cups cut) Chinese bok toy, sliced into flat pieces about 3 inches long, ½ inch wide, or ½ pound fresh Chinese pea pods, left whole, or cut in 2 pieces, lengthwise
1 cup fresh celery, cut crosswise ½ inch wide, then cooked in small amount of water, covered tightly, for about 5 minutes (blanch at once with ice water)
¾ cup, more or less, Chinese water chestnuts, sliced medium thick
½ pound fresh mushrooms, sliced medium thick and sautéed about 2 minutes

½ cup hot oil
1 pound beef (or pork) tenderloin, sliced ¼ inch thick and into 2-inch squares (aged top of round or sirloin may be used)
1 teaspoon salt
¼ teaspoon pepper
¼ teaspoon garlic powder
1 teaspoon Chinese molasses
1 tablespoon soy sauce
1½ tablespoons cornstarch, combined with about ¾ cup chicken stock
⅓ cup pimiento, cut into 1-inch squares

Sauté the first 7 ingredients in ¼ cup hot oil for 5 minutes. In other ¼ cup of hot oil sauté meat 2 minutes on each side. Add salt, pepper, and garlic powder to sautéed meat. Cook molasses, soy sauce, and cornstarch combined with chicken stock in covered saucepan until thick, stirring several times. Then let simmer uncovered about 5 minutes. Fold in pimiento squares.

To Serve. Drain hot cooked vegetable thoroughly. Mound them on a warm oval platter, and arrange beef with molasses sauce over vegetables as smoothly as possible. Sprinkle entire top with finely chopped green onions and stems. Or, if preferred, blend vegetables with meat, then mound on platter. Serve Cantonese-Style Fried Rice (page 852) separately.

Sautéed Shrimp—Sweet and Sour

Instead of pork in Him Soon York recipe, use ½ pound fresh shrimp, shelled, veins removed, then split into halves lengthwise. If shrimp are very large, flatten with heavy knife or cleaver, and cut into *strips* for this purpose. Dip into Cantonese Fritter Batter (page 825), and fry in deep fat at 350° F. until brown—about 5 minutes. Then proceed according to directions in Him Soon York recipe.

Him Soon York (Sweet-Sour Pork)

Makes 2 large or 3 medium servings

½ pound (1 cup solidly packed) pork tenderloin, or very lean pork, cut very thin, about ¼ inch wide, 2 inches long
1 recipe Cantonese Fritter Batter (page 825)
Hot oil for deep-frying meat
1 recipe Sweet-Sour Sauce—No. 2 (page 834)
¼ cup oil

1 cup (1 large) fresh green pepper, parboiled about 1 minute (instead of green pepper, 1 cup pea pods may be added last)
1 cup canned or fresh pineapple, cut into 1½-inch pieces
1 cup very firm red tomatoes, cut into 1½-inch pieces (⅓ cup pimiento cut into 1-inch squares may be used instead of tomatoes)

Dip meat into Cantonese Fritter Batter; pick up 1 piece at a time, lower into hot oil (350° F.) and fry a few pieces at a time until golden brown (not too dark, as meat will darken more after it is combined with other ingredients, and cooked again). Takes about 5 minutes to fry; watch closely.

Make Sweet-Sour Sauce—No. 2. Put aside. In a large skillet, pour the ¼ cup oil. When hot, add the fresh green pepper that has been parboiled for 1 minute only and cut in 1½-inch squares. Add the cooked pork strips and pineapple and cook together for 2 or 3 minutes, mixing very gently as it cooks. Now add the Sweet-Sour Sauce—No. 2, blend gently, cover pan and cook over moderate heat until thick and transparent, about 5 minutes. Last, fold in the tomatoes and cook all together about 2 minutes, being careful not to crush tomatoes. When done, mound attractively on dish and serve with Cantonese-Style Fried Rice (page 852).

Chicken Chow Mein

Makes 2 large servings or 3 medium

¼ cup oil
1 cup uncooked chicken, cut in 3-inch very flat narrow strips, about ¼ inch wide (it will take 1 pound of breasts of chicken to give about 1 cup)
½ cup pascal celery, cut in very narrow flat 3-inch strips
½ cup Chinese bok toy, cut in very narrow 3-inch strips
½ cup Chinese pea pods, cut diagonally in 2 pieces, or leave whole

¼ cup Chinese water chestnuts, cut in thin slices
¼ pound sliced fresh mushrooms, sautéed 2 minutes
1 cup fresh or canned bean sprouts, well drained
2 teaspoons salt
½ teaspoon garlic salt
2 tablespoons cornstarch, combined with 1 cup chicken stock
¼ cup pimiento strips, cut about 1 inch long (optional)

In a large skillet heat the ¼ cup of oil. Add chicken strips and sauté for several minutes over moderate heat, turning continuously to prevent browning. Add all of vegetables and seasonings, except pimiento, blend well, cover skillet and cook about 7 or 8 minutes over low heat. Now add the cornstarch combined with 1 cup chicken stock, and continue to cook until thick, then for 3 or 4 minutes, turning gently. Fold in pimiento strips for additional color. If too thick, add a little more chicken stock or water.

To Serve. Place these cooked ingredients over a bed of Fried Crisp Noodles (page 824). Garnish top with ½ cup blanched, slivered, toasted salted almonds and 1 cup chopped fresh green onion and stems. Serve at once.

Shrimp Chow Mein

Serves 3 to 4

Use 1 pound or less of raw shrimp. Remove shells, if necessary, split shrimp in halves lengthwise and then cut into long narrow pieces. Wash thoroughly and dry well. Then follow same procedure as for Chicken Chow Mein.

Bali Bali Cantonese Boned Chicken Dinner

Serves 4

4 tender chicken legs including thighs, weighing about ½ pound each	2 tablespoons soy sauce
	1 teaspoon salt
2 cups chicken stock (add instant bouillon to hot water)	¼ teaspoon pepper
	1 teaspoon sugar
1 teaspoon Chinese molasses	

Place chicken legs on a low trivet, add all other ingredients, and cook gently in a covered saucepan (or deep skillet) until tender, about 35 to 40 minutes. Do not overcook. Turn legs over after first 20 minutes. When done, remove from heat and let meat stand in liquid until lukewarm. Now with hands carefully release bone from leg, by twisting bone end back and forth (if necessary make slight slit on underside of leg, not on top), and pull bone out from tip end. Do likewise with thigh bone, keeping meat and skin as intact as possible. About 15 minutes before serving, roll meat in well-seasoned flour (to ¾ cup flour, add 1 teaspoon paprika, ¼ teaspoon salt, ⅛ teaspoon white pepper). Shake off loose flour. Now sauté chicken, placing it down in ¼ inch hot fat with thick part first until golden brown over medium heat. Turn over and sauté second side.

Arrange attractively on bed of Cantonese Vegetables (page 851). Rice may also be served separately. May be served without boning.

Cantonese Chicken Slices

Serves 2

¼ cup hot peanut oil
½ cup raw chicken, cut about 2 inches long, 1 inch wide, ¼ inch thick
½ cup pea pods, cut diagonally or leave whole
½ cup fresh mushrooms, sliced thick
¼ cup Chinese water chestnuts, peeled and sliced thin
About 1 teaspoon salt
A little pepper
½ cup chicken stock
1 tablespoon cornstarch
¼ teaspoon garlic salt
Green onions

In hot peanut oil, sauté chicken about 3 minutes stirring it, but do not allow to brown. Add pea pods, mushrooms, and chestnuts, and cook uncovered about 7 or 8 minutes, turning often. Season with salt and pepper. Last, thicken with chicken stock combined with cornstarch and seasonings. Cook covered over low heat until thick and glazy. Let simmer about 3 minutes. If too thick, add more stock. Pile high on serving dish and sprinkle top with fresh green onions cut into 1-inch pieces. Serve with Cantonese-Style Fried Rice (page 852).

Fresh Lobster Cantonese-Style

Serves 2 to 3

¼ cup ground lean raw pork
¼ cup hot oil
½ pound cooked lobster meat
1 teaspoon Black Bean-Garlic Sauce (page 835)
About ¾ teaspoon salt
¼ teaspoon black pepper
½ cup chicken stock
1 large whole egg
1 tablespoon cornstarch, combined with ½ cup cool chicken stock and ½ teaspoon Chinese molasses (a little more stock may be added if necessary after lobster is cooked)

Sauté ground pork in hot oil about 5 minutes, turning it continuously to prevent browning. Add cooked lobster meat that has been cut in very large pieces, about 1 × 2 inches. Season with Black Bean-Garlic Sauce, salt, and pepper. Cook all together 2 or 3 minutes, turning often. Add chicken stock, then slightly beaten egg, and mix gently. Cover pan, and cook over moderate heat 2 or 3 minutes (until egg sets), turning gently toward end. Last, add cornstarch mixture. Cover, and simmer over moderate heat 5 minutes until thick, turning several times. Serve with Fried Rice (page 852).

Instead of fresh lobster meat, canned or frozen lobster meat, or small lobster tails that have been boiled about 5 minutes, then shelled and cut, may be used.

Pressed Duck Cantonese

Serves 6

Prepare 1 large fully drawn Premium duckling, defrosted, and washed under cold running water (do not remove any of the skin), then placed on a trivet in 4 cups boiling water, 2 tablespoons soy sauce, ¼ cup sliced onion, ¼ cup celery and leaves, 1 small bay leaf, 1 teaspoon salt. Cook gently about 1½ hours, or until you can loosen leg from body. When done, remove duck from liquid and let stand until cool enough to handle, *but still warm.*

Now carefully remove all of skin with fingers and a small knife, keeping pieces as large and as intact as possible. Release meat from bones, and with scissors cut into medium-size pieces, about 2 inches long, ¼ inch thick, or smaller.

On a large board or inverted side of very large baking sheet, place six 5-inch squares of silicone paper (or heavy wax paper). Divide duck skin into 6 portions, and place it on papers, forming 3-inch rounds. Sprinkle top of skin with little salt and pepper, and a scant teaspoon of flour on each.

Place cut-up duck meat in a bowl, and season it with 1 teaspoon salt, ½ teaspoon poultry seasoning, ⅛ teaspoon pepper, 1 teaspoon granulated sugar, 1 tablespoon cornstarch, and, last, add 1 tablespoon soy sauce. Mix all ingredients well. Divide meat evenly into 6 portions, and pile it on top of skin, pressing it down firmly with hand, to make it compact and of uniform thickness. Brush top of each with well-beaten egg, and sprinkle each with about ¾ teaspoon flour. Cover meat with individual square pieces of wax paper and put in freezer for about 40 minutes, *or until very firm.* Otherwise remove from freezer and keep covered in coldest part of refrigerator (not in freezer after they are firm). If they soften in room temperature, they are likely to fall apart. In this case put back into freezer only until firm before you fry them.

About 15 minutes before you are ready to fry them, prepare batter with 2 medium eggs, ¼ cup stock or milk, ½ cup sifted all-purpose flour, 1 teaspoon salt. Beat until smooth, cover and let stand. Prepare Duck Sauce.

To Fry. Gently release patties from paper, and brush both sides lightly with batter. Place on pancake turner, and at once lower gently into hot oil, about 400° F., and cook 5 or 6 minutes, or until brown and crisp. They may be fried in advance to lighter color and refried at 350° F. for 2 or 3 minutes just before serving. The second frying will give a more crisp coating.

To Serve. Pack Plain Cooked Rice or preferably Cantonese-Style Fried Rice (page 852) in a 7-inch lightly oiled bowl. Turn out onto 14- or 16-inch platter. Surround with duck patties. Brush patties with Duck Sauce and sprinkle top of each with slivered sautéed almonds and finely chopped green onion. Serve rest of sauce separately.

Duck Sauce

Pour stock from simmered duck into a large Pyrex cup. Let stand a few minutes, and remove most of fat that settles at the top. For each cup of stock, use about 1½ tablespoons (or little more) cornstarch diluted in 2 tablespoons cold water, ¼ teaspoon salt, ⅛ teaspoon Chinese molasses, 1 teaspoon soy sauce. Cook until thick, and simmer about 5 minutes. Taste and season further if necessary. Prepare at least ¼ cup sauce for each serving.

Egg Foo Yong (Omelets)

Makes about 10 to 12 patties; serves 4 to 6

1½ cups Chinese bean sprouts (1 can)	¼ cup very narrow celery strips, about 2 inches long and ⅛ inch thick (optional)
1½ cups cooked ham or meat, sliced thin and cut into long narrow 2-inch strips, or crab meat, shrimp, etc.	
	About 1 teaspoon salt (only ¼ teaspoon salt if using ham or salted meat)
¾ cup onions, sliced thin lengthwise	
8 eggs	¼ teaspoon pepper

Drain bean sprouts thoroughly, pressing out water. Mix well with meat and onions. Beat eggs *slightly* with fork and add salt and pepper. Pour eggs over other ingredients and mix very lightly with 2 forks. At once pour ¼ cup of mixture for each omelet into a frying pan containing ⅛ inch of very hot oil or other fat. Cook over moderate heat until well set and brown on 1 side (about 3 or 4 minutes on each side). Turn over carefully with pancake turner and brown other side. Avoid turning more than once. Pour Quick Gravy over Egg Foo Yong while hot, or serve separately. Serve attractively around molded plain or Chinese Fried Rice (page 852). Sprinkle top of rice with paprika.

Quick Gravy for Egg Foo Yong

Combine 3 cups boiling water with 4 teaspoons instant beef bouillon. Stir until dissolved. Let stand until lukewarm. In another saucepan, melt ¼ cup of butter or margarine, add ¼ cup of cornstarch and blend well; then add lukewarm bouillon stock very slowly, stirring constantly. Cook until thick and let simmer about 5 minutes. About 1 tablespoon soy sauce and 1 teaspoon Chinese molasses may be added.

Roasted Cornish Hens Oriental

Serves 6

3 tablespoons wine vinegar	1 small clove garlic, sliced or chopped
1½ teaspoons paprika	
¾ teaspoon savory or rosemary herb	⅓ cup soy sauce
2 teaspoons salt	1 teaspoon Chinese molasses
½ teaspoon black pepper	½ cup salad oil
1 teaspoon sugar	3 Cornish hens, defrosted and cut in halves

Mix all ingredients except Cornish hens until well blended, and at once pour over split hens in a deep utensil. Let marinate for at least 8 hours, turning hens over and around a few times.

About 1½ hours before serving, arrange hens *on rack* with flesh side down, in a large shallow roasting pan, or broiler pan excellent. Pour about 2 cups hot water in bottom of pan to prevent smoking, and roast at 375° F., 30 minutes, then turn hens over and continue to roast about 30 to 40 minutes, depending on size of birds. It is important to brush birds often with leftover marinade after the first 15 minutes. Test 1 of the hens for doneness by loosening leg from body. If it is resistant, continue to cook longer. When done, brush with glossy gravy made with drippings in pan and any remaining marinade.

To Prepare Gravy. Add water or chicken stock to drippings in pan (or use water and instant bouillon). For each cup of gravy add 1½ tablespoons starch diluted in 2 tablespoons water. Taste and season further with little salt, pepper, and soy sauce, if desired. Cook until thick and glazy, about 5 minutes after simmering begins. Sliced sautéed mushrooms may be added to sauce. Brush birds with glaze before serving. Serve on a bed of Cantonese-Style Fried Rice (page 852), Cantonese Vegetables (page 851), or both. Garnish ends of platter with vegetable flowers and parsley bouquet. Sprinkle top with finely chopped green onion and stems if desired.

Rice may be molded in a 7-inch bowl and surrounded with glazed hens. Paper frills may be placed on leg ends.

Top-of-the-Stove Braised Cornish Hens

Marinate according to general directions for Cornish Hens Oriental (above). Drain well and brown birds in a small amount of butter. Place with meat side up, add ¼ cup water or stock, cover skillet, and steam about 25 minutes if small, 30 minutes if large birds. Cook uncovered last 5 minutes.

Braised Duck Cantonese

Serves 4 to 6

1 duck weighing about 5 or 6 pounds
3 cups hot water
Duck giblets
2 teaspoons salt
1 medium sliced onion
3 cups very hot water
1 tablespoon soy sauce
½ cup flour

Oil or butter
¼ cup cornstarch, combined with ¼ cup cool water
1 tablespoon more soy sauce
1 teaspoon Chinese molasses
½ teaspoon salt
¼ teaspoon pepper

Remove neck skin and any surplus fat from duck; wash it under cool running water, and place it with breast side up on a trivet in a large saucepan or Dutch oven. Add 3 cups very hot water, giblets, 2 teaspoons salt, sliced onion, and 1 tablespoon soy sauce. Cover tightly and simmer duck for about 1 hour, or until tender, when legs leave body without effort.

When duck is tender, remove from pot and let stand in room temperature until cool enough to handle. Then with poultry shears or heavy knife cut into serving pieces. Sprinkle each piece well with flour, shaking off loose flour. Sauté in very hot oil or butter until golden brown and crisp on each side.

Now prepare gravy with ¼ cup cornstarch combined with ¼ cup cool water, 1 tablespoon soy sauce, 1 teaspoon Chinese molasses, ½ teaspoon salt, ¼ teaspoon pepper, and 2 cups of strained duck stock. Cook until thick and glazy, then simmer about 5 minutes. Taste and season more if necessary with a little soy sauce, molasses, etc. Cooked giblets may be cut up and added to sauce.

To Serve. Pack Cantonese-Style Fried Rice (page 852) in a 7-inch greased bowl. Unmold onto a 16- or 17-inch round platter and surround rice with sautéed duck. Brush pieces with little of the glazy sauce, and sprinkle top with a bit of finely chopped green onion, if desired. Serve separately.

Dowel Sea Piquat (Sparerib Dish)

Serves 1 generously

Cut 1 pound raw spareribs into single ribs, then crosswise into 1½-inch pieces. Have butcher do this for you, as it requires a cleaver. Sauté in a small amount oil until brown on both sides. Cover, and steam about 60 minutes, or until done, adding about 2 tablespoons stock or water. When almost done, season with salt, pepper, and 1 teaspoon Black Bean-Garlic Sauce (page 835). Last, thicken with 1 teaspoon cornstarch in ¼ cup stock and ¼ teaspoon Chinese molasses. Cook until thick and glazy in a covered saucepan over low heat. Mound on a serving dish and garnish top with fresh green onion cut fine.

Gay Long Beef with Broccoli

Serves 2

2 cups broccoli (stem ends only), peeled and sliced in long flat pieces about ¼ inch thick, 3 inches long, 1 inch wide
Chicken stock or water
Salt
½ pound beef (or pork) tenderloin, sliced ½ inch thick and cut into 2-inch squares

3 tablespoons hot oil
1 tablespoon cornstarch
¼ teaspoon pepper
¼ teaspoon garlic salt
½ teaspoon Chinese molasses
½ teaspoon soy sauce

Steam broccoli in a small amount of chicken stock or water until tender but not soft—about 7 or 8 minutes. Season it with about ½ teaspoon salt when done. *Reserve the liquid.*

To oil, add ½ teaspoon salt. Sauté meat about 2 minutes on each side over moderately high heat. Combine well-drained broccoli with meat. Last, add ¾ cup stock reserved from broccoli, combined with cornstarch, seasonings, Chinese molasses, and soy sauce. Cover, and cook over low heat until thick and transparent—about 7 or 8 minutes—turning several times. Serve with Cantonese-Style Fried Rice (page 852). (Use flower end of broccoli in other dishes.)

Beef Tenderloin with Pea Pods

Serves 2 generously

½ pound beef (or pork) tenderloin, sliced about ¼ inch thick and 2 inches square
¼ cup hot oil, to which add ½ teaspoon salt
¼ pound Chinese fresh pea pods (1 cup), cut into 2 pieces diagonally, or leave whole
½ cup canned button mushrooms (one 3- or 4-ounce can), cut into 2 pieces (if large)

1 small can Chinese water chestnuts, sliced medium thick
1 tablespoon cornstarch
¾ cup chicken stock
¼ teaspoon Chinese molasses
1 teaspoon soy sauce
1 teaspoon salt
¼ teaspoon black pepper
About 2 tablespoons pimiento, cut into 1-inch squares (optional)

Sauté meat in hot oil about 2 minutes on each side until lightly brown but not dry. Add vegetables, and continue to cook about 5 minutes over moderate heat, turning often. Last, add cornstarch combined with chicken stock and seasonings. Cover, and cook over low heat until mixture is thick and glazy (about 5 minutes), turning gently several times. Serve with Cantonese-Style Fried Rice (page 852).

Beef Tenderloin with Fresh Bean Sprouts

Serves 2 to 3

½ pound beef (or pork) tenderloin, cut ¼ inch thick into 2-inch squares

⅓ cup very hot oil, to which add ½ teaspoon salt

½ pound fresh Chinese bean sprouts, or 1 can, well drained

½ cup fresh green onions and stems, cut into 1-inch pieces

1 tablespoon cornstarch
½ cup chicken stock
¼ teaspoon Chinese molasses
1 teaspoon soy sauce
½ teaspoon salt
¼ teaspoon black pepper

In hot oil sauté meat until lightly brown but not dry—about 2 minutes on each side. Add bean sprouts and onions, and continue to cook about 5 minutes over medium heat, turning often. Last, add cornstarch combined with stock and seasonings. Cover, and cook over low heat until thick and glazy—about 5 minutes. Mound on a dish and serve with Cantonese-Style Fried Rice (page 852).

Beef Tenderloin with String Beans

Serves 2 to 3

2 cups string beans
About 10 ounces beef tenderloin or other tender beef sliced thin, cut into 1 x 2-inch pieces

¼ cup oil, to which ½ teaspoon salt and several slivers garlic have been added

1 tablespoon cornstarch, diluted in ½ cup string-bean stock or chicken stock
½ teaspoon salt
⅛ teaspoon black pepper
½ teaspoon Chinese molasses

Use long Chinese string beans if they are available. They are about 2 feet long and are prepared as are other string beans. If they are not available, 1 package frozen string beans may be used.

Cut beans into 2-inch pieces and steam in a small amount of water or chicken stock in a covered saucepan about 7 or 8 minutes, or until crisply tender. As soon as done, drain and pour cold water over them to set color.

Sauté meat in seasoned oil about 6 or 7 minutes, turning often. Do not allow it to dry out. Add string beans and continue to sauté several minutes, turning often. Add cornstarch diluted with stock and seasonings. Cover, and cook about 5 minutes over moderate heat until thick and glazy, turning several times. Mound attractively on a dish and serve with Cantonese-Style Fried Rice (page 852).

Javanese-Style Shrimp

Serves 2 or 3

1 pound fresh shrimp
Hot peanut oil
½ cup fresh lean ground pork
About 1 teaspoon Black Bean-Garlic Sauce (page 835)
¼ cup chicken stock
2 whole eggs, slightly beaten with a fork

2 tablespoons fresh green onions and tops
1 tablespoon cornstarch, combined with ½ cup cool chicken stock
1 teaspoon Chinese molasses
1½ teaspoons salt
¼ teaspoon black pepper
⅓ cup hot peanut oil

Shell shrimp if necessary, remove vein, split lengthwise if they are large. In hot peanut oil, sauté raw shrimps and ground pork about 5 minutes, turning often to prevent browning. Add Black Bean-Garlic Sauce and chicken stock. Cover, and steam over moderate heat about 7 minutes. Remove cover, add slightly beaten eggs. Stir quickly, add green onions, and, last, cornstarch combined with chicken stock to which molasses and seasonings have been added. Mix well, cover pan, and cook over moderate heat until thick and transparent—about 7 minutes. Serve with Cantonese-Style Fried Rice (page 852).

Chinese Pea Pods with Cabbage

Serves 6 to 8

4 tablespoons peanut oil
½ cup thin-sliced onion
4 cups shredded cabbage (1 small head)

1 pound Chinese pea pods
1½ teaspoons salt
¼ teaspoon pepper

Heat oil; add onion and shredded cabbage. Cover, and cook over low heat until crisply tender, about 8 minutes.

Remove tips and strings from Chinese pea pods; then cut them into halves or leave whole. Add peas and seasonings to cooked cabbage. Cover, and steam about 5 minutes.

Serve with meat, poultry, or fish.

Chinese Pineapple Lamb

Serves 6

1½ pounds boneless lamb	Salt and pepper
2 tablespoons oil	1 cup beef stock or bouillon
¼ cup chopped onion	1 can bean sprouts
1 cup sliced celery	No. 2 can pineapple chunks, drained
1 can (or 4 ounces) mushrooms and	1 tablespoon cornstarch
liquor	3 tablespoons soy sauce

Cut lamb into thin slices about 2 inches square. Brown in hot oil; add onion and celery, and brown lightly. Add mushrooms and liquor, seasonings, and bouillon. Cover, and simmer 1 hour. Add bean sprouts and pineapple. Blend cornstarch and soy sauce, and stir into hot mixture. Cook until thickened and glazy and simmer about 3 minutes, stirring carefully. Serve over hot chow-mein noodles or steamed rice.

Shrimp and Green Pepper Oriental

Serves 4

¼ cup hot cooking oil	¼ teaspoon black pepper (more or less to suit taste)
1 pound fresh green peppers (about 6 medium-size or 4 large)	⅓ teaspoon dried rosemary (more or less to suit taste)
1 clove garlic, cut fine	1½ tablespoons cornstarch, combined with ¾ cup stock and about ½ teaspoon commercial gravy coloring or Chinese molasses
1 pound uncooked deveined and shelled shrimp	
About 1¼ teaspoon salt	

Cut peppers lengthwise into 1½-inch strips. Discard core and seeds. Sauté over medium heat in hot oil with garlic about 5 minutes or until lightly brown but not soft. Now add shrimp and seasonings, blending ingredients well. Cover skillet, and cook about 5 minutes, turning ingredients twice during cooking process. Remove cover, and add cornstarch combined with stock (water combined with a teaspoon instant bouillon may be used) and gravy coloring. Continue to cook uncovered several minutes or until glazy and thick.

To Serve. Cook ½ pound Chinese Rice (page 853). Arrange rice in an oval or round platter, and make a deep opening in center of rice. Pour shrimp and peppers with sauce in opening and serve at once.

Japanese Sukiyaki Dinner

Serves 4

¼ cup hot peanut oil

¾ pound beef tenderloin or rib eye steak, sliced thin about ⅛ inch into 2-inch squares (top-quality aged sirloin tip or top round, or pork tenderloin, may be used)

Granulated sugar, salt, and little pepper as needed

1 pound, or less, fresh spinach leaves (remove all stems), dried on a towel, or 10- or 12-ounce package frozen (instead of spinach, romaine lettuce may be used; use leaves and stems); cut spinach in 2-inch pieces

2 or 3 cups stock (use liquid from any vegetables, or add bouillon cube to water)

1½ cups carrot wedges, cut about 2 inches long, ⅓ inch wide, first simmered in ½ cup water about 5 minutes in covered saucepan (reserve liquid)

4 large dry Oriental mushrooms (or more), first soaked about 1 hour in very hot water, then remove stem from center and cut mushrooms in ½-inch-wide pieces, about 1½ inches long

1 cup red or white onions, cut lengthwise about ⅛ inch thick and 2 inches long

1 small can (about 6 ounce size) sliced or whole bamboo shoots (not diced), cut lengthwise if whole, about 2 inches long and ⅓ inch wide

1½ cups fresh green onion and stems, cut lengthwise about 2 inches, including onion part (if onion part is large, cut lengthwise in half)

2 cups, or more, canned bean thread noodles, washed thoroughly under cold water, drained well. (Sauté ¼ cup finely chopped onion in ¼ cup oil for several minutes, add noodles, and season with about 1¼ teaspoons salt, ⅛ teaspoon pepper, and cook together several minutes. Put aside until needed. Cut noodles with scissors before pouring into skillet.)

8 square pieces of fresh or canned tofu (soy bean curd), cut ¾ inches thick and wide (optional)

In a 12-inch heavy skillet (electric skillet may be used) heat oil. Add meat in single layer, and at once sprinkle top with 1 teaspoon granulated sugar, ½ teaspoon salt, ⅛ teaspoon pepper. Cook about 1 minute on each side, turning over. Push meat aside in skillet.

Add well-drained spinach, or preferably romaine lettuce. Cut up leaves about 2 inches, cut stem end of Romaine smaller. Cook only about 1 minute, season with ¾ teaspoon salt, ⅛ teaspoon pepper. Do not cook more than a minute or two. It will cook further as other ingredients are added. Push aside.

Now start adding about ¼ cup stock at a time, and more as needed. Add precooked carrots, and sauté about 1 minute. Season with 1 teaspoon sugar, ¼ teaspoon salt, and push aside.

Add presoaked and cut-up mushrooms and sauté about 1 minute. Season with ¼ teaspoon salt, ⅛ teaspoon pepper. Push aside.

Add more liquid as required, to cause steaming. Add red or white sliced onions and sauté about 1 minute. Season with ½ teaspoon sugar, ¼ teaspoon salt, ⅛ teaspoon pepper. Push aside.

Add bamboo shoots, cook about 2 minutes. Season with ¼ teaspoon salt, ⅛ teaspoon pepper, and push aside. Add little stock.

Add fresh green onion and stems. Season with ¼ teaspoon salt, cook about 1 minute. Push aside.

Add precooked and seasoned noodles, and simmer about 3 minutes, turning them well.

Last, add tofu squares, season with ¼ teaspoon sugar, and gently cook them for about 1 minute. (Fresh tofu preferred.)

Serve right from skillet, or arrange on a large heated platter in separate groups. May be served from a large flat chafing dish as soon as done, or from electric skillet.

Chop Suey

Serves 6

About 2 tablespoons oil, butter, or shortening
1½ pounds veal, pork, or beef, cut in 1¼-inch cubes (pork shoulder excellent)
About 1½ teaspoons salt
About ¼ teaspoon black pepper
1½ cups hot water
2 cups celery, cut ½ inch wide, 1 inch long
½ teaspoon salt
2 cups onions, sliced ½ inch wide, 1 inch long

1 small can pimiento, cut ½ inch wide and 1 inch long (optional)
1 small can mushrooms, or ¼ pound fresh mushrooms sautéed in butter for several minutes (optional)
¼ cup cornstarch, combined with ¼ cup cold water
About ½ tablespoon Chinese molasses and 2 tablespoons soy sauce (more may be used)

Over moderate heat, heat oil or other fat in large frying pan. When very hot, add meat and brown it well. Do not fry too much meat at one time. Season meat with about 1½ teaspoons salt and a little black pepper. Use a deep narrow skillet or covered saucepan. Add 1½ cups of hot water and cook very slowly at simmering point until tender, 40 to 60 minutes if using veal, or pork; about 1½ hours for beef, depending on quality of meat and kind of utensil used, or until fork-tender. Do not uncover often. If meat appears dry, add a little more water. Keep heat very low. Stir occasionally.

Melt 1 tablespoon of butter in medium saucepan; add cut celery and about 1 cup of water cover tightly and cook about 5 minutes until *crisply* tender, but not soft. Add onions, cook about 5 minutes. Add 1 teaspoon salt and mix well.

When meat and vegetables are tender, combine them and add the green onion tops, pimiento, and mushrooms. Add cornstarch combined with water, Chinese molasses and soy sauce. Cook until thick and glazy, about 5 minutes, then let simmer about 5 more minutes.

Meat may be decreased in this recipe; in that case increase amount of vegetables. For Vegetable Chop Suey, omit meat and increase mushrooms to 1 pound. If Chop Suey appears too thick or dry after it is done, a little water may be added. Taste and season further if necessary.

Cantonese Vegetables

Serves 4

1 cup Chinese fresh pea pods, cut diagonally in 2 pieces or leave whole	¼ cup pimiento, cut in ½-inch squares, or ½ cup crisply cooked carrot slices
1 cup fresh thick-sliced mushrooms, or one (3-ounce) can sliced	¼ cup oil
2 cups bok toy (Chinese greens), cut in 2-inch pieces, 1 inch wide, ¼ inch thick	1 tablespoon soy sauce
	1 teaspoon sugar
	½ teaspoon salt
1 large can (about 6 ounces) Chinese water chestnuts, sliced medium thick	½ cup chicken stock
	1½ tablespoons cornstarch
	2 tablespoons water

Over moderate heat, sauté vegetables in the ¼ cup hot oil for about 7 or 8 minutes, turning them over several times. Season with soy sauce, sugar, salt. Last, add chicken stock combined with cornstarch, dissolved in 2 tablespoons water. Cook until thick, then simmer about 5 minutes. Taste and season further if necessary. Extra sauce may be prepared if serving rice also with this dish.

▶ RICE ◀

Plain-Cooked Rice

Serves 3 to 4

The Oriental people wash rice several times in cold water (but not necessary), drain it well, and cook 1 cup rice with 1½ cups boiling water or chicken stock. Cover saucepan and bring to a quick boil. Then lower heat and cook very slowly about 25 to 30 minutes, or until rice is done but not soft. If rice is too firm when cooking time is up, pour about ¼ cup more water over top and continue to cook a few minutes longer. This will give about 3 cups of plain rice. If preferred rice may be cooked according to directions given on package. If using converted rice, please follow directions given on package.

Cantonese-Style Fried Rice

Serves 3 to 4

Heat ¼ cup oil in a large skillet. When very hot, add 1 slightly beaten egg and cook 2 or 3 minutes, breaking egg into small pieces with a fork as it cooks. Add ¼ cup ground cooked meat or seafood (meat or seafood may be omitted if rice is served as an accompaniment to a substantial Oriental dish). Then add 3 cups plain-cooked rice, about 1 teaspoon salt, ¼ teaspoon pepper, ¼ cup finely chopped green onion, and about 2 or 3 tablespoons soy sauce.

Blend ingredients well and cook over moderate heat for about 7 or 8 minutes. This rice may be prepared in advance if refrigerated and reheated in upper part of double boiler over vigorously boiling water for about 10 minutes just before serving. Mold in custard cups or bowl.

Chinese Fried Rice

Serves 4 to 6

½ cup oil

3 eggs, slightly beaten

1½ cups baked or boiled ham, roasted meat, bacon, shrimp, crab meat, or lobster, cut in ¼-inch small pieces

4½ cups cooked rice (12 ounces before cooking)

½ cup onion, sliced thin lengthwise

About 1½ teaspoons salt (only 1 teaspoon if using salted meat)

A little pepper

1 can Chinese bean sprouts, thoroughly drained

1 tablespoon soy sauce

⅓ cup fresh green onion tops, cut ½ inch long (optional)

2 tablespoons pimiento, cut into ½-inch squares (optional)

In a large skillet, heat ½ cup oil. Add slightly beaten eggs and cook for a few seconds, but do not allow eggs to become *too* firm. Break up with a fork during cooking process. Add the meat, rice, onion, salt and pepper, and, last, the bean sprouts and soy sauce. Mix well with 2 forks. Cook together *only* until hot, about 10 minutes, covering pan for a few minutes. If it appears too dry, 2 tablespoons or more of fat may be added. One-third cup of fresh green onion tops and 2 tablespoons of pimiento squares may be added for additional color. Brush a 7-inch bowl with shortening, pack rice into mold, turn over onto platter and surround with Egg Foo Yong (page 842), or as desired.

Chinese Rice—No. 1

Serves 6

1 pound best quality rice
3¼ cups hot water

1 teaspoon salt (optional)

Combine rice with about 3¼ cups of hot water. Add salt. Cover saucepan tightly and bring to a quick boil. Lower heat and simmer slowly about 25 to 30 minutes, or until well puffed and dry. Keep heat very low and stir gently 2 or 3 times. If rice appears too firm toward end of cooking, sprinkle it with a little more hot water and continue to cook a few minutes longer. When rice is done, shut off heat and allow it to remain covered about 20 minutes. This will fluff up and loosen rice from bottom and sides of pan. May be cooked in double boiler about 1 hour, or until tender.

Chinese Rice—No. 2

The majority of rice growers today recommend cooking rice without washing in cold water as Oriental cooks do. In a 2-quart saucepan combine 1 cup rice with 2 cups cold water and about 1 teaspoon salt. Cover and bring to a good boil for about 1 minute. Lower heat and simmer about 14 minutes, or until rice is done. For more details follow directions given on package. If using precooked or other types of rice, follow directions on package. We prefer our Method No. 1.

▶ DESSERTS ◀

Dessert Rice Mold Imperial

Cook 1 cup standard-type rice in 3 cups simmering water and ½ teaspoon salt, in tightly covered saucepan, until very soft, about 25 to 30 minutes, over very low heat. Drain well, and measure 3½ cups cooked.

In a large bowl (about 10-inch size) combine cooked rice and hot Cream Filling. Blend thoroughly. Let stand until lukewarm. May be forced over cold water. Meanwhile, beat 1 cup of whipping cream until barely clings to bowl. Fold it into the lukewarm rice preparation, mixing gently and well blended. Add ½ cup of candied fruit (cut into ¼-inch pieces) that has been marinated in 2 tablespoons of brandy or pineapple juice, without draining. Fruit may be omitted. Add 1 teaspoon vanilla or other flavoring. Pour into a 7-cup very lightly oiled tower mold. Refrigerate for at least 24 hours.

To Serve. Loosen around upper edge of mold with dinner knife, rub top of mold and a platter with cold water. Place 12- or 14-inch platter over top of mold and invert. Top of mold may be decorated with a large cream cheese or buttercream (or whipped cream) rose or rosettes, and green leaves. Or garnish with a group of fresh strawberries held in place with toothpicks, and green citron leaves. Surround base with fresh strawberries, kumquats, or clusters of Frosted Grapes (page 435), and green leaves, or as desired.

Serve plain whipped cream, or Whipped Cream Brandy and Rum Sauce (page 372) or crushed sweetened strawberries separately, or *serve plain.*

For large party-size mold, double above recipe and pour into tyrolean mold that measures 7¼ inches tall and 9 inches wide at open end.

Cream Filling

1 cup granulated sugar
¼ cup sifted all-purpose flour
2 tablespoons cornstarch
⅛ teaspoon salt

2 egg yolks, combined with ¼ cup cool milk
2 cups warm milk
1½ tablespoons plain gelatin, combined with ½ cup cold water (stir and let stand until thick)

In a 2-quart saucepan combine sugar, flour, cornstarch, and salt. Add yolks combined with cool milk, a little at a time, and stir until smooth. Add warm milk slowly, and cook until thick and smooth, stirring continuously. Let simmer about 5 minutes. Now at once shut off heat, and immediately add the thickened gelatin preparation. Stir until dissolved.

Oriental Almond Cookies

1 cup shortening (half butter gives better flavor)
½ cup granulated sugar and ½ cup brown sugar, solidly packed
1 large whole egg, slightly beaten and combined with 2 tablespoons water
1½ teaspoons almond extract
½ teaspoon vanilla
2½ cups sifted all-purpose flour, combined with 1 teaspoon baking

soda and ½ teaspoon salt, sifted together several times
About 1 cupful blanched almonds; they may be left whole or split in 2 lengthwise (to blanch almonds drop into boiling water and simmer 2 minutes, let cool slightly, then with fingers remove skins)
1 egg yolk, combined with 1 tablespoon water and slightly beaten

With electric mixer or heavy spoon beat shortening for several minutes. Add sugars, little at a time, and continue to beat until well blended. Now add the whole egg combined with the 2 tablespoons water, and beat 3 or 4 minutes, or until mixture appears light. Add extracts, and last dry ingredients, about half cup at a time, and beat after each addition only until smooth. This is a soft dough. Chill for at least 1 hour.

In palm of hands form *very smooth* balls with 1 level tablespoon dough; flatten them slightly, place on lightly greased baking sheet, about 1½ inches apart. Brush tops with beaten yolk mixture and place a whole or split almond in center of each, pressing down gently. For plain cookies, omit almonds. Bake cookies at 325° F. about 25 to 30 minutes, or until golden brown, watching closely last few minutes to prevent burning. Remove those that are done if necessary, and continue to bake rest.

Release cookies from baking sheet with a spatula or dinner knife while still warm, and place them on cake coolers or any flat surface. When cold, store in a covered container until ready to be served.

► *Smörgåsbord,*

OR AMERICAN-STYLE BUFFET

A BUFFET SPREAD OFFERS AN EXTREMELY CONVENIENT WAY TO ENTERTAIN a number of persons. The guests are not seated, but partake of refreshments standing. The food is placed upon an attractively laid table, usually all at the same time, although it may be served in two or three courses. Plates, silver, and napkins are on the table to make the service prompt and easy. Small tables should be placed about in conspicuous places in order that one may have an opportunity to dispose of a cup or a glass; otherwise guests will use the buffet table and spoil its beauty. This method of serving is particularly adapted to special occasions, such as wedding breakfasts, luncheons for twelve or more, evening entertaining, Sunday-night suppers, card parties, and wedding-anniversary parties.

► HOW TO SERVE SMÖRGÅSBORD ◄

The arrangement and service of a buffet luncheon and an evening spread are practically the same. The buffet luncheon often presents heavier and more varied courses than would ordinarily be served at night, and in the evening the table is lighted with candles. If candles are used, candelabra are better than candlesticks for two reasons: first, they give better light; second, they contribute height, which is important because a buffet table is always more heavily laden than the ordinary table and therefore looks best when lights are dominatingly high.

The buffet table is preferable for many reasons: it needs less space, can be made to look more attractive, and calls for fewer dishes and less service.

The luncheon cloth is the preferred table covering. Although a damask cloth may be used, a lace or embroidered one is better.

There are no special directions for setting a buffet table. After laying the linen, place the center decoration. Flowers may be taller than for dinner, though not heavy or massive. An artistic grouping of fruit or vegetable-carved flowers may take the place of fresh flowers. *Objects of utility are of first importance;* and unless there is ample space for both, objects that are solely for ornament are omitted. Flowers in the center of the table are lovely, but if the table is crowded, they had better be omitted.

The arrangement of the dishes depends largely upon the menu and the number of guests. It is better to replenish dishes and supplies from a serving table or the pantry than to have the table appear crowded.

The important dishes of food are placed down the length of the table as close to the centerpiece as possible, with appropriate serving silver grouped about them. Place the plates in piles, never too high; from 8 to 12 are sufficient in one stack, and should be replaced as used. Place 1 piece of serving silver on each side of the platter or dish and parallel to it. Place rows of silver forks near serving dishes in some conventional pattern. The person who is serving places 1 fork upon each plate before passing it, or guests may help themselves. Napkins are laid near the corners of the table. Napkins of luncheon size may be folded square; if large, they are folded in triangles. They are placed on the table overlapping one another. The object is to separate them so that 2 will not be taken up together.

The buffet menu must be chosen with care so that the food may be easily handled. Ordinarily knives and small dishes are not used, unless there are sufficient tables and chairs to accommodate all guests.

As a rule, beverages are served from a side table, but a colorful punch may be used in center of the buffet table.

Rolls are usually served with hot courses. Dainty sandwiches, from which crusts have been removed, are served with cold courses.

▶ *Teas*

AND COFFEE-MAKING

Afternoon tea is a pleasant method of entertaining friends. There are three general types of tea: the formal tea, the informal tea, and high tea. The accompaniments for an informal tea are simple—a hot bread, thin bread-and-butter sandwiches, and cookies. The formal tea is more elaborate and is served to a larger group. A beverage or two, dainty sandwiches, small cakes and cookies, and dainty candies are the usual accompaniments.

The two most common types of tea—informal and formal—are most popular. The musicale, tea dance, and garden party are merely elaborations of informal and formal teas.

▶ HOW TO SERVE TEA ◀

For a Small Informal Tea, when you have a maid, no table is set. The maid brings to the drawing room, living room, or porch the tray with the tea service, which she places on a small table previously made ready to receive it. The hostess either makes the tea and pours it or has it made and brought in for her to pour. If the tea is made by the hostess, the maid must see that the equipment for making and serving is complete. Sandwiches and small cakes and cookies are brought in on a tea wagon, or they may be placed on the table. The tea service should be arranged to simplify the pouring—the teapot at the right hand, cream, sugar, and lemon in front, and cups and saucers at the left. Small tea plates may be provided for the sandwiches and cakes, with a folded napkin on each plate. With plates, omit saucers for cups, as it would be very awkward and inconvenient to carry both.

In a house without a maid, the hostess would, of course, set the tray with everything except the boiling water before her guests arrive, leaving the water kettle on the range in the kitchen.

When slices (or sections) of lemon are served, a lemon fork or pick should accompany the serving dish. If you like, stud the lemon slices with cloves.

For the More Formal Type of Tea and When Serving Large Groups, the dining-room table is used. Spread it with the finest linen, and place the tea service at one end of the table and the coffee service at the other end, or pour both coffee and tea from each end. Both beverages are generally offered when large groups gather.

A centerpiece of cut flowers and dishes of dainty mints or candies make the center of the table look attractive. The sandwiches, small cakes, and cookies are placed on the table symmetrically. Two friends of the hostess usually pour at either end of the table so that the hostess is free to greet her guests.

Stacks of small tea or salad plates, napkins, and spoons (and sometimes salad forks) are arranged at each end of the table. Cups are placed at the left of the person pouring. Place a dinner napkin near the tray, for the pourer to use to protect her gown.

When serving large groups, it is better to prepare the tea in the kitchen and have it brought to the dining room in a silver pitcher and poured into the teapot as needed. Water must be kept boiling in the kitchen kettle so that it may be ready when needed.

In the late afternoon, lighted candles are used, as they always add balance and beauty to a table. The most popular hours for large teas are 4 to 6 or 5 to 7. On a bright day, shades should be drawn.

A **High Tea** is a company supper served buffet style: All the food and dishes are on the table. This type of service is very popular on a late Sunday afternoon and evening from 5 to 8. For this, plan a more hearty menu if men are among the guests. Friends of the hostess or members of the family may help serve the refreshments, and a maid should be in attendance to remove cups and plates and bring fresh ones, as well as to replenish all dishes of food. When serving large groups, place sugar, cream, and lemon slices conveniently so that guests may serve themselves.

Best Method of Making Tea

Tea may be put into a tea ball or a muslin bag and taken out when sufficiently steeped. These containers should not be more than half full, to allow the tea leaves room to swell and to give off their full amount of flavor. The quantity of dry tea to be used in proportion to water is not fixed; it depends on the grade of tea and the strength desired. An old rule reads, "A teaspoon of tea to a cup." This is an excellent rule to use when trying a new tea, but most people will find that it is not necessary to use so much tea. The housewife must experiment with her particular kind, and suit it to the tastes of her family or guests.

The method of making tea is not so variable. Experts insist that there is only one way. Freshly boiling water is necessary; otherwise the tea is flat and insipid. Pour the boiling water on the required amount of leaves in a teapot. If an infusion with a maximum of aroma of tannin or astringent flavor is desired, allow it to brew for 3 minutes; then remove the tea container or pour off the liquid into another warm pot and serve at once. More "body" is given by longer brewing, which extracts more tannin. Five minutes should be sufficient time.

Iced Tea

Make tea in usual way. The clearest iced tea is made by pouring the hot liquid over cracked ice rather than by cooling it slowly and chilling in the refrigerator. If it is to be poured over cracked ice it must, of course, be made doubly strong, as the ice dilutes it.

Russian Tea

24 cups of boiling water
 4 sticks of cinnamon
 1 teaspoon heads from whole cloves
    (remove heads and discard stems;
    the essence is in the heads)

Juice of 6 oranges
Juice of 3 lemons
2 cups granulated sugar
Rum or preserved ginger

Steep 5 heaping teaspoons of tea, preferably Orange Pekoe or Gunpowder, in 2 cups of boiling water for 5 minutes. *Do not use aluminum or metal utensils, as it will cloud the tea.*

Add cinnamon and cloves to 24 cups boiling water and boil for 5 minutes; then add orange juice and lemon juice, also sugar and strained tea. Bring mixture to boiling point. Serve with flask of rum or with preserved ginger, as desired.

▶ GENERAL DIRECTIONS FOR COFFEE-MAKING ◀

For best results buy top-quality coffee. Use 1½ to 2 level tablespoons (1 rounded tablespoon) of coffee for 1 standard measuring cup of water, more or less. Find out with a little experiment the exact amount needed to insure the flavor you prefer. Experiment also with various types of coffee makers and with varying amounts of time for brewing.

The coffee maker must be sparkling clean, and it is therefore important to scrub it well after each use to remove the oils that cling to the sides of the coffee maker. Be careful not to submerge the base of your automatic coffee maker in water. Use only fresh cold water in preparing coffee. Water from the hot tap does not produce fresh-tasting coffee.

It is always best not to buy coffee in large quantities—not more than 1 week's supply. The fresher the coffee, the better. In 1950 The National

Coffee Association recommended keeping the coffee in the original container in the bottom of the refrigerator, because removing coffee from its original container permits air to pass through the coffee, thus drying out some of the oils that give coffee its flavor. Keeping the can of coffee covered and in the refrigerator keeps these flavor oils intact.

Automatic Coffee Makers

Automatic coffee makers are foolproof if you follow the rules above and the directions given by the manufacturers. Be sure to use the right grind.

Glass-Maker Method

Use very fine grind

Measure coffee and water. Bring water to a boil. Insert the upper bowl. As water rises to the upper bowl, reduce heat and stir coffee and water a few seconds. Allow coffee to remain in upper bowl and to gurgle at least 2 minutes—a little longer for a stronger brew. Remove from heat. When coffee has siphoned in lower bowl, remove upper bowl and serve as soon as possible, or keep at an even temperature over very low heat.

Percolator Method

Use regular grind

Measure water and pour it into percolator. Bring water to the boiling point before inserting basket containing measured coffee. Then reduce heat and allow coffee to percolate slowly about 8 to 10 minutes, more or less, to suit taste. If you want to keep coffee hot, remove the basket, and place percolator over very low heat.

Drip Method

Use fine grind

Measure coffee and place it in upper section. Measure water and bring to the boiling point. At once pour fresh boiling water over coffee in upper container, and let drip through the coffee. If coffee appears weak, it may be poured again over grounds immediately. For best results, do not prepare a few cups of coffee in a large maker of this type. Follow directions given by manufacturers.

▸ *Party-Style Punches*

Party-Style Fruit Punch

Makes about 50 to 60 punch cupfuls

2 cans concentrated frozen orange juice (6-ounce can)
2 cans concentrated frozen lemonade (6-ounce can)
1 large can crushed pineapple with juice
2 packages frozen strawberries or raspberries (10- or 12-ounce size)

3 fresh limes (or lemons) cut in halves lengthwise, then cut in thin slices
2 large bottles gingerale or 8 bottles 7 UP (more gingerale or 7 UP may be used)
About 36, or more, ice cubes to start with (add more as needed)

Shortly before serving combine all ingredients in a large 6- or 7-quart punch bowl. Stir well. For an alcoholic punch, add a bottle of brandy or other liqueur. Garnish edge of platter underneath bowl with fresh galax or lemons, fresh kumquats, etc. Or garnish entirely with large clusters of season, such as cherries, strawberries, lady apples, tiny pears, small limes or lemons, fresh kumquats, etc. Or garnish entirely with large clusters of black, red, and green grapes, alternating the colors.

This punch may be made in smaller amounts and served at any time in attractive tall glasses instead of punch cups. Garnish top with sprig of fresh mint.

For a more tart punch, add 1 more can concentrated frozen lemonade or lemon juice. For a sweeter punch add some sugar first dissolved in boiling water and cooled.

Elinor's Eggnog Punch

Makes 5 pints

6 eggs
1¼ cups granulated sugar
1 pint coffee cream

1 pint milk
1 pint, more or less, bourbon
1 jigger, more or less, rum

Separate eggs. Beat whites until they cling to bowl. Add ½ cup sugar to whites and beat until blended. Beat yolks several minutes with electric mixer. Add rest of sugar (¾ cup) to yolks and continue to beat about 2 more minutes. Add egg-white mixture to yolks, a little at a time, and blend well. Add cream and milk, a little at a time, and stir until smooth. Last, add the bourbon and rum. Top may be sprinkled with nutmeg.

For a nonalcoholic punch, use commercial eggnog. French Boiled Meringues (pages 671–672) are very attractive and delicious served on top of this punch. A little bourbon or rum may be added to commercial eggnog.

Yuletide Punch Bowl

1 pound cranberries, cooked in covered saucepan with 4 cups water until skins pop, for about 10 minutes; put through sieve or food mill and discard skin

Add 2 cups sugar to cranberries and cook about 1 minute to dissolve sugar, let stand until cold

1 package frozen strawberries
½ cup lemon juice
4 quarts gingerale or water
Ice cubes, or crushed ice
2 small fresh limes or lemons, sliced thin

Combine all ingredients in punch bowl. Add ice cubes or crushed ice a few minutes before serving. Float lime slices on top.

Christmastide Fruit Punch

Makes about 4 quarts

2 cups (1 pint) cranberry juice cocktail (can be purchased in bottles)
2 cups (No. 2 size can) pineapple juice (sweetened or unsweetened)
6-ounce can frozen lemonade
6-ounce can frozen orange juice

10-ounce package frozen raspberries or strawberries
1 large attractive fresh lime, cut in halves lengthwise, then in thin slices
1 quart gingerale
About 30 ice cubes

Combine all ingredients except gingerale and ice cubes in a punch bowl or other container and refrigerate until serving time. Last add the gingerale and ice cubes. Stir well until ice cubes are half melted and serve as a punch or fruit juice cocktail. This is a very delicious and colorful nonalcoholic fruit punch and may be served during the holidays for cocktail, snack, and buffet parties.

Champagne Hors D'Oeuvres Punch

Serves about 50 people

2 fifths champagne
2 fifths sauterne wine
2 fifths sparkling water

4 jiggers curaçao
4 jiggers brandy
4 jiggers grenadine or sugar

Champagne, wine, and sparkling water should be refrigerated for several hours before preparing punch. Place a block of ice or about 50 ice cubes in punch bowl. Add brandy, curaçao, and grenadine. Mix well; then add the champagne, pouring it slowly, and, last, the sparkling water. Stir gently until very cold. Garnish large platter underneath bowl with Christmas holly or other similar decorations during the holiday season. Recipe may be cut in half. We also recommend serving a nonalcoholic fruit juice punch at large parties (see below).

Eastertide Fruit Punch

Makes about 30 punch cupfuls

1 stick cinnamon, combined with 2 cups water, 2 cups granulated sugar (more sugar may be used) and ¼ teaspoon whole cloves; cook together about 5 minutes after simmering begins; strain and cool

1 pint bottled grape juice, or 1 can frozen combined with 1½ cups water

2 cans frozen lemon juice, combined with 4 cups water

1 quart gingerale

Just before serving combine all ingredients in a punch bowl. Add ice cubes. Garnish top with thinly sliced lemon wedges and a few sprigs of fresh mint leaves. Garnish platter with lemon or galax leaves and clusters of various grapes available, or with colorful small fresh fruits, or leave plain.

Fresh Blueberry Punch

Serves 12

1 cup fresh blueberries
2 cups water
1 can frozen lemonade

2 cups ginger ale
1 pint orange ice milk
About 15 or 20 ice cubes

Cook blueberries in water very slowly 7 or 8 minutes. Then put through a strainer and press out as much of pulp as possible. Cool.

Combine all ingredients and blend well. Serve in a punch bowl, or in tall attractive glasses. Garnish edge of each glass with fresh mint or lemon leaves and a red cherry on stem.

Lime Punch

Serves 12

1 can frozen lime juice
1 can frozen lemonade
4 cans water

2 cups lime ice milk
2 cups ginger ale
About 15 ice cubes

Combine all ingredients, and beat well. Add ice cubes just before serving. Serve in a punch bowl, or in tall attractive glasses. Garnish edge of each glass with fresh mint or lemon leaves and a red cherry on stem.

Party-Style Tea Punch

Serves 24

1 cup sugar	2 cups pineapple juice
2 cups water	1 quart gingerale or 7 UP
2 cups strong tea	Thin lemon slices
1 can frozen lemon juice or lemonade	Few sprigs mint
1 can frozen orange juice	¼ cup sliced maraschinos

Cook sugar and water only until clear. Let cool. Just before serving, combine all ingredients in the order given, except the sugar and water syrup. Now add syrup to suit taste, and about 24 ice cubes. Serve in center of table in an attractive punch bowl. Garnish platter underneath with lemon leaves and fresh flowers or fruits in season if desired.

► *An Introduction to Wines*

WE ARE GIVING YOU IN THIS CHAPTER SOME IMPORTANT BUT LIMITED FACTS regarding wine in cooking. For an invaluable common-sense practical guide for anyone who wants to know things about wines that are rudimentary to the connoisseur; who wants to familiarize himself with the different classes and types of wines and their characteristics; wants to know how to select wines and what the labels on wine bottles mean; what wines go best with certain foods and dishes; wants to know how to serve wines; the proper temperatures at which various wines are at their best and the glassware in which they should be served; wants to know how best to use wines to enhance the deliciousness of dishes and other information, we heartily recommend *The American Guide to Wines* by Ruth Ellen Church, Food and Wine Editor of the Chicago *Tribune*, and author of several other outstanding cookbooks. In addition to all this important material regarding wines, she has included 100 delectable and practical gourmet dishes in her *American Guide to Wines*. This book is now available in paperback nationally, and in our opinion it is the best book of its kind for the homemaker and gourmet cook as well.

Wine has been associated with food through the ages. For generations, it has been the "secret" ingredient of famous chefs. In continental cuisine it is indispensable, and it has been said that wine, both as a flavoring in food and as a beverage to accompany it, enhances the flavor of more different foods than any other seasoning except salt.

For smart, gracious, traditional—yet moderate, simple, and inexpensive— entertaining, wine has no equal, for there is a wine to suit every guest and every occasion. Contrary to general opinion, the serving of wine is easier and simpler than that of almost any other beverage. It is served chilled or unchilled, depending on the wine, the weather, or the consumer's preference, but the effort is confined to pouring from bottle to glass.

When one is just learning to enjoy wine, it is well to know that there are only 5 kinds of wine. They are: appetizer wines, so-called because they are best for before-meal serving; red table wines, served at room temperature with the main course; white table wines, also served with the main course, but well chilled for fullest taste appeal; dessert wines, served with dessert or with evening refreshments; and sparkling wines, excellent at any time, but especially nice when you've something to celebrate.

The appetizer wines to remember are sherry and vermouth, served in 2- to 3-ounce glasses before dinner, with or without hors d'oeuvres. The best-known red table wines are claret and burgundy. All red table wines are made dry (not sweet) to go with the main-course foods. They are at their best when served in 5- to 8-ounce glasses, and at room temperature, with steaks, roasts, or the humble but good stews and spaghetti dishes. Most popular members of the white table-wine family are sauterne and rhine wines. These white table wines, whether dry or semisweet, are all very delicate in flavor and are at their best when served well chilled in 5- to 8-ounce glasses with chicken or fish, with luncheons, and with sandwiches at the bridge table.

Port, muscatel, and tokay are the best known dessert wines. Because of their natural sweetness, these wines are served at dessert time, with or without coffee, or with refreshments, and in the evening. These rich heavy-bodied wines are served either at room temperature or slightly chilled, according to preference, and in 2- to 3-ounce glasses. Champagne and sparkling burgundy are the most popular of the sparkling wines for parties and festive occasions, and are always served very cold and in portions of approximately 4 to 6 ounces.

▶ WINE BUYING AND STORING ◀

There are wide variances in price in the same-size bottle and in the same type of wine. That is because some wines cost more to produce, age, bottle, and sell than others. Wines fall into three grades of quality, generally referred to as "standard," "choice," and "premium."

It is wise to buy table wines in the size of container that can be emptied a few days after opening. Table wines are perishable, just as milk is, and once open to contact with air, they should be used within a week—sooner if the weather is warm. When table wine is bought by the gallon for economy's sake, it should be decanted into smaller bottles and recorked. Appetizer and dessert wines will keep almost indefinitely after the bottle is opened.

Unopened bottles of wine are best placed in a cool spot that won't get too warm, won't freeze, and where the temperature is as even as possible. In wineries, the ideal temperature has been found to be between 50° to 60° F.; in homes, the wine cellar temperature should stay under 80° F. Corked bottles of table wines and sparkling wines should be placed on their sides for storage so that the corks are kept moist and air is sealed out. Dessert wines and bottles with screw tops may stand upright.

▶ THE SERVING OF WINE ◀

There is no set ritual for wine service at a home dinner. The bottle may be placed on the table and passed around, the guests helping themselves. The host or hostess may pour, and in this case it is customary for the host to pour a bit of wine into his own glass first. A slow turn of the bottle before raising it from the glass helps prevent dripping. It is customary to fill the glasses only about two-thirds full so that the drinker may savor the delightful bouquet of the wine.

When only 1 wine is served, the wine glass is placed at the right of the water goblet. When 2 wines are served, the wine glasses may be arranged in a straight line at the right of the goblet or to form a triangle with the water goblet. As soon as the course is served, the appropriate wine is poured. Then, if a second wine is to be served, the first glass is removed, whether empty or not, with the china and silver of the course it accompanies.

At elaborate dinners where several wines are served, no more than 2 wine glasses should be on the table at one time. Additional glasses are brought at the proper time.

When a different wine is served with each course, they are usually matched like this: sherry or champagne with hors d'oeuvres; sherry with soup; dry white table wine with fish or shellfish; a second table wine with the entrée, red or white according to the kind of food; a third table wine or sparkling wine with *pièce de résistance;* a sixth wine (any dessert wine) with dessert; a seventh wine, like port or burgundy, with cheese.

▶ WINE IN COOKING ◀

Wine is an indispensable part of good cooking, and few professional chefs would think of cooking without it. The same factors that make wines harmonize with foods on the table—their ability to balance the sweetness, acidity, saltiness, and bitterness of foods and to supply aroma, acidity, and smoothness for foods that lack those qualities—account for its use in cooking. It is not distinguishably the flavor of wine that is imparted. In fact, a dish cooked with wine does not taste like wine, and the alcoholic content of wine, just like that of vanilla, is lost when subjected to heat.

While almost any wine can be used with almost any food, there are natural taste harmonies between certain wines and certain foods, and a knowledge of these is part of the knack of cooking.

Dry sherry is perhaps the most versatile wine in cooking, blending harmoniously with a great variety of foods. The great advantage over other cooking wines is that it can be kept for several months on the pantry shelf even after the bottle has been opened. Other dry wines should be used within a week after they are opened.

Fish and seafood of all kinds are natural flavor-mates with sherry. Sometimes the seafood is marinated in sherry for a short time so that the flavor of the wine permeates the food. Sometimes, instead, a dash of sherry is added shortly before the dish is removed from the heat.

A number of outstanding chicken dishes are made with sherry. So are numerous sauces for ham and other meats, as well as sauces for puddings. Fruits for appetizer and dessert use and many luscious "made" desserts combine exceptionally well with sherry.

Next to sherry in popularity for cookery are the white table wines. Their light flavors go especially well with fish, chicken, and veal. Cheese dishes and seafood curries are improved when rhine wine or sauterne replaces part of the liquid called for in the recipe.

Red table wines, as might be expected, go particularly well in dishes made with red meats. Red wines also can often be interchanged with white wine if their color does not interfere.

Pot roasts, stews, and low-cost variety meats like kidneys, liver, and heart are greatly helped by the use of red table wine in their preparation. Marinating these less expensive cuts of meat in red or white table wine improves their flavor and texture. And the wine marinade makes a most delicious gravy.

Dessert wines such as sweet sherry, port, and muscatel are most appropriately used to add flavor to dessert and sweet sauces. Mixed diced fruit are particularly good when soaked in port. And a little muscatel added to the mincemeat does wonders for mince pie.

▶ *Vegetable Carving*
AND BUTTER MOLDING

▶ VEGETABLE CARVING ◀

American Beauty Roses

Select nice round white turnips, potatoes, or beets. Peel and trim as round and smooth as possible. With a sharp paring knife, starting at bottom, make impression of petals and cut through very carefully. When bottom row of petals has been cut, remove part of turnip before starting next row. Continue in this manner until the entire rose is formed. Do not make more than 4 or 5 rows. These roses may be carved several days in advance and kept in a plastic bag in refrigerator. A day or so before using, place roses in tinted water, and allow to remain in water until desired color is obtained. Roses may be kept for several weeks if turnips are very fresh and firm.

Pond Lily

Select nice firm turnips that measure about 3 inches wide and 2 inches high (or higher). Pare and scrape as smooth as possible. With point of a knife, mark a circular line around the top of turnip $\frac{1}{3}$ of the way down. Turn turnip upside down and mark petals. Remove the triangular pieces of turnip between petals. Insert tip of knife between each petal and the main portion of the turnip, and press petals outward from the turnip very carefully so that they do not break. Smooth off body of turnip before starting the next row.

For the second row of petals, mark a second circular line about $\frac{1}{4}$ inch above where first line was made. This marks the tip of the second row of petals. Cut second row of petals as before. Remove triangular pieces and loosen petals.

For third row, working toward top of turnip, cut this row same as second, removing triangular pieces between petals. But this time, instead of smoothing out the surface as in the 2 previous rows, scoop out the center of the turnip in a cone-shaped piece.

Place the turnip upside down in cold water, and keep in refrigerator 1 hour or longer.

For yellow lily, add a few drops of yellow coloring to the soaking water. For a pink lotus, add a little red coloring to water.

Green Pads for Lily

From small end of a large green pepper, remove about 1 inch. Cut about 6 petals, and remove triangular pieces. Use a small sharp paring knife. Do not cut too close to bottom or petals will break. If pepper is very thick, remove part of pulp from leaves very carefully; also remove seeds and trim center, forming a flat surface. When ready to use lily, remove it from water and place it in center of green-pepper base. Hold in place with toothpicks if necessary. Fill center of lily with grated carrot.

Daffodil or Jonquil

Cut medium-thick slices of round white turnips. Peel, and cut each slice into 6 petals, leaving a small space uncut in center. Trim each petal slightly rounded. After having cut as many flowers as desired, form oval-shaped centers from thick leftover pieces of turnips. Trim and shape like a cone; scoop out center from large end of cone, and scallop edges. Place a toothpick through petal base of turnip; place cone-shaped part of turnip on top center and tint in yellow-colored water until desired color is obtained.

Cosmos

Cut thin slices of round white turnip. Remove skin, and cut into 6 sections, leaving a small space uncut in center. Trim each petal slightly round; then with a pastry wheel or fork, mark edge of petals. Dip into water colored pink, yellow, orchid, or blue. Drain well, and sprinkle center of cosmos with poppy seed. Place in center of each flower a small round grapefruit skin, lemon skin, or carrot, cut with small end of an olive pitter or knife. Use wood pin to hold together.

Daisies

Cut slices of round white turnip. Trim if necessary, or cut uniformly with a round cutter. Cut into 16 sections, leaving a small space uncut in center. Cut around each section to simulate petals. Place a thick round piece of carrot in center of each, and hold together with a toothpick. Keep in cold water if daisies are to be used within a few hours. They may be kept in a plastic bag in refrigerator several days.

Zinnias

Cut same as daisies, using 3 rounds of different sizes. Tint pastel shades; hold together with toothpicks. Place a tiny yellow carrot center on each. Sprinkle center with poppy seed or coarse-ground pepper.

Tulips

Select medium-size oval potatoes or turnips (turnips preferable). Peel, leaving a smooth surface, and cut 4 petals. With a potato baller or other gadget, scoop out center very carefully. Tint, and place several green toothpicks in center of each, with currants or raisins on points of toothpicks. These tulips are very attractive when arranged in an oblong container as a centerpiece for table or platter.

Scalloped Oranges, Grapefruit, Lemons, Melons, Tomatoes, Hard-Cooked Eggs

With point of a sharp knife, cut through center of fruit, etc. Pull apart and use as desired.

Plum Tomato Tulips

Select firm, attractive plum tomatoes. Wash and dry them well. With a very sharp or serrated-edge paring knife, cut 3 *rounded* petals on small end of tomato, leaving about ¼ inch space at the top, and come down about halfway. With knife carefully remove center of tomato, leaving a thick base. With a heavy wooden skewer make a good opening on large end of tomato if to be used as a tulip. *Before filling tomatoes,* if to be used as an hors d'oeuvre in compartment dish, *slice off a little from bottom* to prevent it from toppling over.

With bag and large plain cookie tube or plain opening of coupling, fill center of tomatoes with Deviled Egg Preparation (page 48) or any smooth meat or seafood mixture. Place a small round slice of ripe olive on top center of each. Insert a firm long green onion stem in opening on bottom of each and arrange attractively on top of a large hand-molded salad, or on meat and other platters.

Colonial Doll Centerpiece

For sandwich platter, cold meats, etc.

Place a bunch of curly endive, leaf lettuce, escarole, or sweet peas in opening of a china doll head. Place it over a cone-shaped holder made of heavy paper or styrofoam. Tie a ribbon around bosom; decorate skirt with small carved flowers, parsley, grated carrots, or as desired.

Daisy Centerpiece

For hors d'oeuvres platter

Select firm white round turnips or potatoes at least 3 inches in diameter to make large flowers. With a sharp knife, slice about ⅛ inch thick. Cut through with a daisy cutter. For center, use a thick round slice of carrot. Hold together with heavy toothpicks. Place on ½ of an orange, apple, grapefruit, or potato. Fill in open spaces with parsley or green leaves. These flowers may also be used to garnish cold-meat platters, finger sandwiches, and tea sandwiches. *If using potatoes, dip flowers into lemon juice to prevent darkening.* Use smaller vegetables if a small cutter is used.

Fresh Pineapple Centerpiece

For hors d'oeuvres platters, etc.

With a long sharp knife cut off about ⅓ of the pineapple crosswise, including green top. Place it with flat side down in center of a large platter of hors d'oeuvres, canapés, fruit salads, etc. Insert vegetable-carved flowers (held together with toothpicks) between green leaves. Very attractive and unusual.

Pickle Fans

Slice small pickles into 5 or 6 sections, to about ¼ inch from bottom. Spread sections. Thin radish slices cut into halves may be placed between them. Use as garnish for potato salad, etc.

▶ BUTTER MOLDING ◀

Butter Paddling of Lilies

Place paddles in boiling water for 1 minute *only when new.* Then soak them in ice water for about 1 hour or less before using. Wash butter in ice water, squeezing it with hands until waxy and free of lumps, dipping hands into warm water occasionally. With corrugated side of paddles, form balls of uniform size, then with plain side flatten balls into thin patties. Dip paddles into ice water often to prevent butter from sticking. Mold each patty to simulate a lily, curving 1 side. Make centers with small pieces of butter on corrugated side of paddles. Decorate each lily with parsley or green butter leaf. It is better not to have butter too hard or too soft when molding to prevent it from sticking to paddles.

Butter Paddling of Grapes

Shape a foundation of washed butter. Make about 20 to 30 medium-sized balls. Keep in ice water. Arrange on foundation of washed butter; then add green coloring to more soft, washed butter and work it with a fork. With hand, continue to work butter until thoroughly blended. Allow green butter to stand in ice water until firm. Make stem; then make leaves by shaping ovals of butter and flattening them. With knife, mark lines on leaves to simulate veins. Arrange on grapes. If butter adheres to paddles, wash paddles in warm water and soak again in ice water for a few minutes.

For large bunch of grapes, use 1 pound butter. Remove ¼ cup to be colored green for leaves and stem. Use ½ cup for foundation. Make balls with the rest of grapes.

Butter Paddling of Roses

With corrugated side of paddles, form balls of uniform size, then with plain sides, flatten them into thin patties. *Cut patties in halves.* Dip paddles into ice water often to prevent sticking. Mold half patty to simulate a rose center. Then arrange about 7 or 8 half patties around center to form a rose. Place on platter and garnish with parsley or green butter leaves. These roses may be made in various sizes.

Pickling and Preserving

▶ PICKLING ◀

Home-Style Bread-and-Butter Pickles

4 pounds gherkin pickles
1¾ cups granulated sugar
1¼ cups cider vinegar
¾ cup water

1 clove garlic
½ teaspoon salt
1 tablespoon pickling spices

Wash gherkin pickles; dry. Cut into ½-inch slices. Place sugar, water, and cider vinegar in a saucepan and bring to the boiling point. Fill two 1-quart sterilized jars or one 2-quart sterilized jar with sliced pickles; add clove of garlic cut into 3 or 4 pieces, and ½ teaspoon salt and spices to each jar. Pour boiling vinegar syrup slowly over pickles, filling jar to within 1 inch of top. Adjust cover and seal at once.

This recipe does not require processing.

Barbecue Pickles

⅔ cup cider vinegar
⅔ cup hot water
1¼ pounds brown sugar (2½ cups solidly packed)
2 teaspoons whole allspice
2 teaspoons whole black pepper

2 tablespoons salad oil
1 large clove garlic, sliced thin
10 large firm dill pickles, or 2-quart jar of dill pickles, sliced about ⅓ inch thick

Combine vinegar, hot water, brown sugar, and spices. Cook slowly, uncovered, about 20 minutes after it comes to the simmering point. Pour oil and garlic over sliced pickles and mix well. When vinegar mixture is ready, pour it over pickles while hot, and mix well. When mixture is cold, place in a tightly covered jar and let stand 3 or 4 days before serving. Pickles will keep well several weeks or longer in refrigerator or other cold place. After pickles have been eaten, liquid may be used as a salad dressing. Freshly cooked or canned beets may be prepared in same way.

Pickled Sliced Carrots

4 bunches carrots
About 2½ cups cider vinegar
½ cup granulated sugar

1 large clove garlic
1 teaspoon salt
1 small hot red pepper, sliced

Wash and peel carrots. Steam in a small amount of hot water until crisply tender—about 10 minutes. Drain and slice. Bring cider vinegar and sugar to the boiling point. Fill sterilized jars with sliced carrots; add garlic, salt, and red pepper. Pour boiling vinegar syrup over sliced carrots slowly to within 1 inch of top of jar. Adjust cover and seal tight.

This recipe does not require processing.

Pickled Beets

4 pounds fresh beets
1¾ cups granulated sugar
1 tablespoon pickling spices
1¼ cups cider vinegar

¾ cup water
1 clove garlic
A few thin slices onion

Wash beets, leaving 1 or 2 inches of stem on. Steam in a small amount of hot water until crisply tender—about 30 to 45 minutes. Do not overcook. Drain, and rinse with cold water. Remove skins, and slice. Place sugar, water, vinegar, and pickling spices in a saucepan and bring to the boiling point. Place sliced beets in a sterilized 2-quart jar or in two 1-quart jars; add clove of garlic, cut into 3 or 4 pices, and onion slices. Pour hot vinegar syrup slowly over beets, filling jar to within 1 inch of top. Seal tight.

This recipe does not require processing.

Assorted Pickled Vegetables

All the following vegetables may be used for a colorful and flavorful assortment of pickled vegetables: *carrots, green peppers, red peppers, eggplant, cucumbers, cauliflower, celery, green beans, and green tomatoes.*

To fill a 2-quart jar of Assorted Pickled Vegetables, use about 3 cups cider vinegar and 4 tablespoons granulated sugar.

Steam separately until crisply tender, in a small amount of hot water, cauliflower, carrots, eggplant, and green beans. Do not overcook.

Slice green peppers, celery, cucumbers, and red peppers into long strips. Just before you are ready to use them, pour boiling water over them and let stand a few minutes. Do not cook or blanch green tomatoes—just cut in quarters.

After vegetables are cooked or blanched, and then sliced, place them attractively in a sterilized 2-quart jar. A clove of garlic, a small hot red pepper sliced, and a little fresh dill will give additional flavor. Pack vegetables firmly and then pour hot vinegar syrup over them slowy. Adjust cover and seal tight.

This recipe does not require processing.

Pickled Green Tomatoes

Cut green tomatoes into quarters and prepare the same way as Assorted Pickled Vegetables above.

Pickled Green Peppers

Wash green peppers and dry them. Remove seeds, and slice lengthwise. Prepare in the same way as Assorted Pickled Vegetables above.

▶ PRESERVING ◀

Note. If commercial pectins are used in preserves, jams, and jellies, please follow directions given by manufacturers and their recipes.

Strawberry Preserves

8 cups strawberries (2 quarts)	½ teaspoon red food coloring
4 cups granulated sugar (2 pounds)	

Select firm, well ripened strawberries. Wash and drain carefully, dry them on a towel, and remove hulls. Measure, and place in a 6-quart kettle. Add sugar. Place kettle over low heat and heat slowly to a full rolling boil; then boil rapidly about 15 minutes, or until thermometer registers 220° F. to 222° F. Stir occasionally, being sure not to crush strawberries. Remove from stove, skim with a ladle, add red coloring, and mix gently. If using Mason jars, pour at once while hot into sterilized jars and seal at once. If using jelly glasses, pour into sterilized jelly glasses. Melted paraffin can be poured over preserves at once, or after preserves have cooled. When paraffin has set, cover jelly glasses with lids, or with double thickness of wax paper, tied securely.

Apricot Preserves

Makes 5 half-pint jelly glasses

3 pounds apricots	4½ cups granulated sugar
1 cup water	½ cup unstrained fresh lemon juice

Wash apricots. With a paring knife, cut apricots into small pieces or in halves, removing stones. Skins may be left on if desired. Bring water and sugar to the boiling point. Add lemon juice, then apricots. Cook apricots in syrup over medium heat about 40 minutes until clear—or until thermometer registers 220° or 222° F. Pack in sterilized jars, filling to within ½ inch of tops. If using Mason jars, seal at once. If using jelly glasses, allow to cool; then pour melted paraffin over jelly. When paraffin is set, seal.

Red Raspberry Jam

Makes 3 to 4 half-pint jelly glasses

1 quart raspberries	4½ cups granulated sugar
¼ cup water	

Wash and drain raspberries. Crush with pie blender or potato masher. Add ¼ cup water to each quart (4 cups) berries. Cook until soft—about 5 minutes. Add sugar, bring to boiling point, place thermometer in saucepan and cook to 220° to 222° F., stirring occasionally. Pour while hot into sterilized jars. Seal.

Blackberry, dewberry, loganberry, and youngberry jams are made in the same way.

Peach Jam

Makes about 4 half-pint jelly glasses

About 2½ pounds peaches	3 cups granulated sugar
½ cup water	

Wash, peel, pit, and crush peaches, and measure 4 cups. Place in a large kettle with water. Boil 10 minutes. Add sugar, and over medium heat boil until thick—about 20 minutes, or until thermometer registers 220° to 222° F., stirring occasionally. Pour while hot into sterilized jars. Seal.

Currant Jelly

2 quarts currants	3 cups granulated sugar
1 cup water	

Wash and pick over currants, but do not remove stems. Mash in bottom of a preserving kettle. Add water, cover, and simmer 15 minutes. Put into a jelly bag and drain off juice. Measure 4 cups juice into kettle. Bring to the boiling point and boil 5 minutes. Add sugar, again bring to a boil, and boil 5 to 8 minutes, or until thermometer registers 220° F. Pour into sterilized jelly glasses, and cover with melted paraffin. When paraffin is set, place covers on jelly glasses.

Continue cooking 4 cups juice at a time, as above, until all juice is cooked.

Grape Jelly

Wash and pick over grapes and remove stems before putting into a preserving kettle. Mash, heat to the boiling point, cover, and simmer 30 minutes. Strain through a heavy jelly bag. Do not squeeze bag. Measure 4 cups juice into large preserving kettle and let boil 5 minutes. Add 3 cups sugar, bring again to the boiling point, and boil about 3 minutes, or until jelly sheets from spoon and thermometer registers 220° F. to 222° F. Skim, and pour into sterilized jelly glasses, and cover with melted paraffin. When paraffin is set, place covers on jelly glasses.

Continue cooking 4 cups juice with 3 cups sugar until all juice is cooked.

► *Home Freezing*

TODAY MORE HOMES ARE EQUIPPED WITH A FREEZER THAN EVER BEFORE. Freezing in the home, when properly done, is one of the simplest and least time-consuming methods of preserving many foods. More of the original flavor, color, texture, and nutritive value is usually retained during freezing than when these foods are preserved in any other way. It is important, however, to select for freezing foods of the highest quality, and to follow directions for freezing carefully.

This chapter is not intended to cover every phase of home freezing, but to serve as a supplement to the booklet you obtain from your freezer manufacturer, which covers the technical operation and maintenance of the unit and provides other valuable information.

We are not including freezing of fresh fruits and vegetables inasmuch as few homemakers are interested in this phase of freezing. You will find detailed directions in your freezer instruction booklet covering this subject. In the majority of cases it is more economical to purchase these items commercially frozen.

General Rules for Successful Freezing

1. Select top-quality foods, and freeze them as soon as possible after they are packaged.

2. Follow instructions given in the booklet furnished by the manufacturer of your freezer as to the technical operation and maintenance of the unit.

3. Freeze all food at zero or lower.

4. Do not store foods in the freezer section of a conventional refrigerator for more than a week or two, *unless* it is a combination refrigerator-freezer, having two separate doors, that operates on two different thermostats, and the freezing compartment maintains zero temperature, or lower. It is advisable to keep a refrigerator-freezer thermometer in either type, to make sure of correct storage temperatures.

5. Put no more unfrozen food in a home freezer than will freeze within 24 hours. Usually this will be about 3 pounds of food to each cubic foot of its capacity. Overloading slows down the rate of freezing, and foods that

freeze too slowly may lose quality or spoil. For quickest freezing, place packages against freezing plates or coils, and leave a little space between packages so air can circulate freely. After freezing, packages may be stored close together.

6. Liquid or semiliquid foods expand when frozen. Allow at least ½-inch head space in small containers and 1 inch in larger ones.

7. Use only *moisture-vapor-proof* packaging for best results, and follow directions given by the manufacturer for sealing, etc.

8. Label and date all packages clearly. Use older packages first.

9. Do not refreeze foods that have been completely thawed out (except cakes and other baked foods, such as coffee cakes, breads, and rolls). If meats are still partially frozen, they can be refrozen, but should be used as soon as possible. Completely thawed meats should be cooked at once, then may be refrozen if you cannot eat it within a day or two. We do not like to refreeze poultry even if it is not competely thawed out. It is best to cook it, then freeze. Completely defrosted fish and creamed preparations should be discarded. If they are still partially frozen, cook them at once, and serve as soon as possible.

10. Pack foods tight to cut down on the amount of air in the package, and when food is packed in a freezer bag, press air out of the unfilled part of the bag. Press firmly to prevent air from getting back in. Seal immediately, following directions given by the manufacturer.

11. *Whenever possible,* defrost all foods, wrapped, on a refrigerator shelf.

12. For best results, do not store foods longer than the suggested maximum time.

Wrapping Foods Correctly for Freezing

Package or wrapping material for freezing must be *moisture-vapor-proof* and of the right size and shape. Freezer packaging is available in many types—flat or shaped, rigid or collapsible, and made of paper, plastic, metal, glass, or foil. All include complete instructions for proper use and are either self-sealing or have directions for sealing. The best wrapping material will not give adequate protection to the food if the package is not carefully wrapped. The two most common methods of wrapping are:

Drugstore Wrap. Tear off a sheet of freezer wrapping material about 1½ times as long as would be required to go once around the food being wrapped. Place food in the center of the paper. Bring opposite sides of the paper together evenly over food. Fold down in a series of folds until the paper is tight against the food. Make pointed-end folds, pressing paper close to the end surfaces of the food to avoid air pockets. Turn end folds under package and seal with freezer tape. Label package and freeze.

Butcher Wrap. Tear off a sheet of freezer wrapping material about 2 times as long as would be required to go once around the food being wrapped. Place the food across the corner. Bring corner over the food and roll toward the opposite corner. Midway of roll, tuck the two side corners into the center of the package, pulling tight and excluding air by pressing toward the open ends. Continue rolling until the package is compact and all the sheet is used. Seal well with freezer tape. Label package and freeze.

Freezer Wrapping Material

Rigid Containers, such as cartons or jars, are excellent for storing liquids and foods packed in liquid. Because liquid expands when frozen, allow 1-inch heat space in large containers, and ½-inch in small, and place a piece of cellophane or foil, cut to the shape of the container, over the food. Most rigid containers have tight-fitting lids, so that no other sealing is necessary after the lid is closed down.

Plastic Films come in two handy forms: *sheets* in dispenser rolls with a cutting edge, which can be used for wrapping meat, poultry, cheese, butter, baked goods, etc.; and *bags*, one of the most popular freezing wrappings, which are adaptable to many foods since they come in various sizes and are easily sealed by twisting the open end tightly, bending double and then securing it with a rubber band or any closure available. These bags are very convenient for cookies, nuts, rolls, and many other items that are likely to be needed a few at a time. They are also excellent for chickens and turkeys.

Coated Laminated Paper is excellent for meats, poultry, cheeses, etc. Place food on the coated side for wrapping, and be sure to follow directions given by the manufacturer.

Aluminum Foil. Use only freezer-weight foil. Household foil does not give adequate protection for long storage. Foil is easily molded and one of the best protective wrappings. It is usable in the oven, so that many foods can be taken directly from freezer to oven without unwrapping. It is also reusable if handled carefully and is excellent for wrapping irregularly shaped foods. Foil needs no sealing. Always place food on the shiny side of foil when wrapping.

Recommended Storage Periods of Various Foods in Your Freezer
at Zero or Lower

Most books on home freezing recommend longer storage periods for many foods than those specified below. However, from our many years of actual experience in this work, we have found that while foods stored for very long periods are acceptable, they lose more flavor, color, and texture.

Uncooked Meats, Poultry, and Fish

Beef	8 months	Seasoned sausage	1 month
Lamb, mutton, fresh		Bacon, sliced	1 month
pork, veal	6 months	Hams and bacon slabs	2 months
Chicken and turkey	4 months	Variety meats	2 months
Lean fish and game	4 months	Shellfish and fatty fish	2 months
Ground meat and			
unseasoned sausage	2 months		

Dairy Products

Eggs	3 months	Heavy (32 to 40%) Cream	2 months
Butter	6 months	Ice Cream	2 months
Milk	1 month	Cheese	3 months

Prepared Foods

Stews	3 months	Chili con carne	6 months
Spaghetti sauce and		Casseroles	3 months
meat balls	3 months	Macaroni and cheese	2 months
Chop suey	3 months	Chicken and meat pies	3 months
Chicken à la King and		Meat loaves, seasoned	1 month
similar dishes	2 months	Soups	3 months
Baked beans	6 months		

Potatoes—Cooked

French-fried	2 months	Stuffed baked	3 months
Hash browned or		Candied sweet	3 months
fried slices	2 months		

Cooked Meats, Poultry, and Seafood

Breaded or batter-		Lobster or crab meat	1 month
fried chicken	2 months	Cooked fish, any kind	1 month
Sliced turkey or chicken	1 month	Croquettes	1 month
Sliced roast	1 month	Uncoated fried meats	
Cooked shrimp, plain		or poultry	1 week
or breaded	1 month	Leftover cooked foods	2 weeks

Canapés, Hors d'Oeuvres, and Sandwiches

Open-face canapés		Pastry filled hors	
and hors d'oeuvres	2 weeks	d'oeuvres	2 months
		Sandwiches	2 weeks

Baked Goods

Pies unbaked, berry, apple, mince	2 months	Doughnuts, any kind	1 month
		Coffee cakes, baked	3 months
Pies baked, berry, apple, mince	4 months	Quick breads	3 months
		Yeast bread, baked	6 months
Chiffon and whipped-cream pies	1 month	Yeast rolls, baked	3 months
		Fruit cakes and plum puddings	12 months
Baked pie shells	3 months		
Unbaked pie shells	2 months	Cheese cakes and pies	1 month
Cakes, baked	4 months	Whipped-cream or ice-cream tortes	2 months
Cookies, baked	6 months		

Fruits and Vegetables

Blanched vegetables	6 months	Fruit juices and purées	6 months
Prepared fruits	6 months		

Miscellaneous

Nutmeats	6 months	Candied fruit mix	6 months
Candies	6 months	Coffee in original cans	6 months
Dipped chocolates	6 months	Commercial pre-cooked foods	1 month
Bread crumbs	3 months		
Crackers, any kind	3 months	French garlic bread, sliced and buttered	1 month
Raisins or other dried fruits	6 months		

▶ MEATS AND POULTRY ◀

Fresh Meat

Meat is the most costly food in a freezer and therefore requires careful attention in buying, wrapping, freezing, thawing, and cooking. It is usually advisable to have meat boned, not only because it saves space but also because bones are likely to punch holes in the wrappings. If bones are left in, whether in steaks or roasts, cover the sharp edges first with an extra layer of wrapping material, or some suet. This will prevent puncturing the outer wrapping. Package meat in amounts convenient for a single meal, and wrap flat rather than rolled, to reduce thawing time.

To prevent extensive loss of fluid and flavor, meat should be cooked before it is fully defrosted, or very soon after, especially if it has cut surfaces. Defrosted meat is cooked in the same way as unfrozen meat, but if it is cooked before being defrosted, the temperature and time of cooking need to be changed. The cooking temperature must be reduced at least 25 degrees and the cooking time increased about 15 to 25 minutes per pound for roasts that are solidly frozen, less time for those partially frozen.

It is always best to defrost meat in its original wrappings, and in the refrigerator. Allow at least 5 hours per pound for large pieces, less for thinner cuts. Then meat may be left in room temperature for a short time to defrost further if necessary, but it is safer to start cooking meat before it is entirely defrosted. Meats will take half as long to defrost in room temperature, and only about 1 hour per pound in front of an electric fan or in a very, very slow oven (about 200° F.). In order to make sure frozen meat is cooked to the desired degree of doneness—rare, medium, or well done—it is very important to use a meat thermometer. The thermometer is inserted into the meat when it has cooked for at least 2 hours, or when you can penetrate the thickest muscle with a heavy metal skewer. If the meat is cooking too slowly or too rapidly toward the end, the heat may be increased or decreased. Be sure to add some water or stock to the drippings in the roasting pan if they appear to be scorching.

Steaks, Chops, Ground Meat, Variety Meats, Stew Meat. In stacking steaks, chops, and hamburgers, it is very important to place 2 pieces of wax paper between layers, for easy separation without complete thawing when ready to cook. They freeze and defrost more quickly if stored in small packages, and also retain more freshness. Whenever possible, do not salt ground meat of any kind before it is frozen. If it is salted, it will not keep as long as unsalted meat. It is always best to defrost hamburgers and thin cuts of steaks and chops before cooking. Thick steaks may be broiled frozen, but cooking time must be increased and they must be broiled at much lower temperatures to insure proper cooking in center. Check a thick steak for doneness by making a small cut close to the bone before removing it from the broiler, and observe the color. If chops, cutlets, and other similar cuts are to be breaded (coated with egg and crumbs), they must first be thawed completely, or else coatings will not cling to meat.

It is always best to defrost hamburgers and thin steaks completely provided you cook them as soon as they are defrosted, or very soon after. If they stand around more than a short time, the flavor is not as desirable. However, they may be cooked slightly frozen. *In an emergency* they can be cooked in the completely frozen state provided you lower the temperature and increase cooking time. Test interior of meat by making a gash in center and observe color.

Cured Meats

Processors do not generally recommend freezing bacon, luncheon meats, frankfurters, dry and semidry sausage, but they can be frozen for about 1 month in an emergency. The Brown 'N Serve cooked pork sausages freeze well for several months. Hams may be frozen for 1 or 2 months, but special care must be taken to double-wrap the meat, so that the odor of the smoke and seasonings will not penetrate other foods. Smoked meats lose flavor after a short time, and those with fat start to become rancid after 2 or 3 weeks. We do not recommend freezing sliced luncheon meats. The majority of these meats can be refrigerated for 2 or 3 weeks if you follow directions on label.

Poultry

Most of the poultry today sold in supermarkets and other retail stores is eviscerated ready to cook or to freeze. This type of poultry is always more desirable because it is dressed and drawn by experts and is of top quality. It is available whole or cut up into pieces.

Broilers. Split the bird in 2 along the backbone, or ask your marketman to do this for you. Separate the halves with 2 layers of wax paper to prevent them from freezing together. Wrap the giblets, except the livers, separately and place them beside the bird. Livers may not be stored longer than 2 months. Wrap the birds in any moisture-vapor-proof freezer paper or foil, following general directions for wrapping. Or, if you prefer, place them in plastic freezer bags, squeezing out all the air possible, and twist top of the bag tightly, bending double, and fastening well with a rubber band. Label and date package, and freeze at once.

Fryers and Other Cut-up Poultry. Cut bird into serving pieces unless you have purchased it this way. Wrap each piece in wax paper, and pack according to general directions. Individual pieces frozen in this way may be removed as needed, and the remainder left in the freezer. A complete bird may be packed in each wrapper, or you may prefer to pack breasts together, thighs together, etc., depending on how you wish to use the bird.

Whole Roasting Birds and Turkeys. Purchase eviscerated whole birds. Tie the wings and legs close to the body to facilitate wrapping and to save space. Pad any protruding bony parts with small wads of wax paper to prevent puncturing the outside wrapper. Wrap in freezer paper, foil, or a plastic bag, according to general directions.

Stuffing Poultry Before Freezing. It is not safe to freeze home-stuffed poultry, either before or after roasting, in the home freezer. Commercially frozen stuffed birds are prepared by experts under carefully controlled conditions, and are frozen at a very, very low temperature, which cannot be done in the home freezer successfully. If you purchase commercially frozen stuffed turkeys, be sure to follow directions on the label for storage and cooking.

If you wish to stuff a frozen bird for roasting, it must be thawed completely to insure thorough cooking. Unstuffed poultry may be cooked in the frozen state, but cooking time must be half again as long as for defrosted poultry, and temperature must be reduced at least 25 degrees. If cut-up poultry is to be breaded, it must be completely defrosted to prevent the coating from dropping off in cooking. It is always best to cook poultry as soon as possible after it is defrosted, to preserve flavor and moisture. Follow directions on label for defrosting of frozen turkey.

▶ FISH AND SHELLFISH ◀

Fish

To preserve the flavor and freshness of fish, it should be frozen the day it is caught or purchased. If this is not convenient, it should be kept extremely cold until ready to be frozen. Clean and wash fish, unless this has already been done. Leave whole, or cut it as desired. Separate cut pieces with 2 thicknesses of wax paper; wrap whole fish individually in wax paper. Then overwrap in aluminum foil or any other moisture-vapor-proof paper. Aluminum foil is excellent inasmuch as the fish may be baked or broiled in the same foil.

It is not necessary to defrost fish before cooking unless the pieces need to be separated, or unless it is to be breaded or dipped into a batter for deep frying. Cooking time of frozen fish must be increased and temperature decreased to prevent scorching and insure thorough cooking. To test fish for doneness, cut through it with a fork. If it flakes, do not cook it further. If you prefer to defrost fish, it is always best to do so slowly in its freezer wrapping in the refrigerator, for about 8 to 12 hours. In an emergency it can be defrosted more quickly in room temperature or in front of a fan. The important thing, however, is to cook the fish as soon as possible after it has defrosted, to prevent loss of moisture and flavor. Fish can be stored up to 6 months, but a shorter storage of about 3 months is preferable. Never refreeze defrosted raw fish.

Raw Shrimp, Oysters, Lobster Tails, Crab Meat

Uncooked shellfish spoils more easily than other foods. It should be overwrapped and frozen as soon as possible, and stored not more than 2 months. Never refreeze defrosted raw shellfish. If it has defrosted, cook it before wrapping and freezing, and store it *not more than 2 weeks.*

Cooked Shrimp, Lobster, Crab Meat

Frozen shrimp or lobster tails may be cooked without defrosting. Increase cooking time slightly for partially defrosted seafood, but do not overcook. Cook according to general directions, but for a little less time, if they are to be frozen after they are cooked and reheated before serving. These foods have a tendency to toughen if stored more than several weeks. *Maximum storage time should be 1 month.* Remember that slow defrosting in the refrigerator will always give better results.

▶ DAIRY PRODUCTS ◀

Eggs

Whole Eggs must be shelled before they are frozen, to prevent cracking; then they may be frozen with or without separating. Break eggs, and stir them just enough to blend yolks with whites, but do not beat in any air. To each pint (2 cups) add 1 teaspoon of salt or 1 tablespoon of sugar. Mix well. Pour into rigid containers, leaving 1 inch head space for expansion. Frozen eggs must be completely thawed before using. Three and one-half tablespoons are equivalent to 1 large egg. Eggs may be stored up to 3 months.

Egg Whites. Egg whites need no special treatment. Simply separate them from yolks very carefully, and store enough in 1 container for an angel-food cake, a meringue, or any other specific recipe. Do not add any salt or sugar, and do not beat. Pour into rigid containers, leaving 1 inch head space for expansion. Defrost completely before using; then cover, and leave in room temperature about 1 hour. The most desirable temperature of egg whites for angel-food cakes is about 75 ° to 80° F., for baked meringues about 70° F. Two tablespoons egg whites equal 1 large egg white. They may be stored up to 3 months.

Egg Yolks. Measure the required amount for a gold cake or any other recipe. To each cup of yolks add 1 tablespoon of sugar (if they are to be used for a cake). Stir well. Or you can use ½ teaspoon of salt to each cup of yolks if they are to be used for general cooking purposes. Pour into rigid containers, leaving 1 inch head space for expansion. Defrost completely before using. When following cake recipes in this book, it is suggested that 1 tablespoon of warm water should be added to each cup of defrosted yolks before beating them. No reduction of sugar or liquid needs to be made. One and one-half tablespoons of defrosted yolks equal 1 large egg yolk. They may be stored up to 3 months.

Whipping Cream

Frozen whipping cream takes longer to beat, and the volume is a little less. It is good in cooked desserts that call for heating the cream first, and it is excellent for recipes in candy-making that calls for heated cream, like caramels and similar candies. Defrosted cream is not very desirable in coffee as freezing causes fat to separate and the oil rises.

Whipped cream freezes very well on cakes and other desserts. Or it may be whipped, sweetened to taste, then formed into large rosettes with No. 7 decorating tube and bag, or into mounds, on a flat pan covered with wax paper. Freeze them uncovered for several hours until firm to the touch; then slip them, on the pan, into a freezer bag, seal and freeze. They may be stored for 2 months. To serve, place a frozen rosette or round on top of each dessert, allowing about 15 minutes for them to defrost.

Milk

Pasteurized homogenized milk freezes fairly well for about 1 month. It is best to purchase it in cartons if it is to be frozen. Otherwise pour it into rigid freezer containers, leaving 2 inch head space. Shake it well before pouring.

Butter

Butter freezes very well up to 6 months. It is always best to overwrap it to preserve flavor.

Ice Cream

Ice cream freezes very well for about 2 months in the original cartons, but should be overwrapped to be kept creamy.

Cheese

Most cheeses keep well in the refrigerator for several weeks. It should be noted that with the exception of a few smooth-bodied cheeses such as bleu, camembert, and limburger, freezing will affect the body and texture of most cheeses. However, they will still be suitable for cooking uses even though they may appear crumbly or mealy. Storage life is about 3 months.

For best results, cheese should be tightly wrapped in foil or plastic bags. If the original wrapper has a full unbroken seal, the products may be frozen without additional wrapping. Cheese such as cheddar or Swiss which has been cut into small cubes for freezing should not be stored for longer than 3 weeks. Cheese such as cheddar, Swiss, pasteurized processed American cheese (slices and/or loaf), processed cheese spread (loaf), and cream cheese may be stored in the freezer for up to 3 months if well wrapped.

Cream cheese which has been frozen should be used only for cooking;

during freezing this cheese tends to become crumbly and thus it will not have the usual smooth-spreading consistency in uncooked dishes. Top-quality cream cheese can be refrigerated for a month or longer.

▶ HOW TO FREEZE YOUR OWN PREPARED FOODS ◀

The home freezer is a great convenience in relieving the hostess of much of the stress and strain involved in preparing for a large party. You can cook your own favorite foods well in advance and freeze them—and feel relaxed on the day of the party. The freezer is particularly gratifying for storing foods you have prepared for holiday meals, since it enables you to spend with your family and friends many of the hours you would other-wise spend in the kitchen.

What Not to Freeze

There are few foods that cannot be frozen. They include gelatin molds, puddings, custards (either baked or boiled), mayonnaise and other similar dressings, hard-cooked egg white (unless chopped very fine in small amounts in hors d'oeuvres), green salads and other vegetables, fresh un-cooked fruits, creamed cottage cheese (unless combined with cream in cheese dips, etc., or used in small decorations on canapés and other hors d'oeuvres). Research may provide directions later for preparing good frozen products from some of these foods.

Commercially prepared puddings, custard desserts, salad molds, cream pies, etc., are made with special commercial thickening agents, which do not separate on freezing, but they are not available in retail stores at the present time. Some freezer books suggest freezing these foods in the home, but in our opinion the results are not satisfactory. We find that they break down and become watery, and lose much flavor as well as their attractive appearance. You can plan to prepare these foods a day or two in advance and simply refrigerate them until serving time.

Creamed Dishes, Stews, Chop Suey, Various Sauces, and Similar Preparations

If foods prepared for the freezer are to be heated before serving, it is advisable to undercook them slightly—especially rice and macaroni prod-ucts, and potatoes and vegetables in stews and casseroles. Prepare recipes as usual, seasoning them lightly (more seasoning may be added at serving time) and reducing the amount of fat if possible. Cool the pan of food at once uncovered, in ice water or very cold water, or set it in a very cold place. Quick cooling of the food after it is cooked helps to keep its natural flavor, color, and texture. It also prevents the growth of bacteria that may cause spoilage. Place the cooled food at once into moisture-vapor-proof containers, in meal-size amounts, packing the food tight to reduce the amount of air in the package. In quart containers the food may be stored in 2 or 3 layers, separated by double thicknesses of water-resistant material such as cellophane. This will facilitate separating the frozen blocks of food and shorten the reheating time. Since liquid expands as it freezes, allow 1-inch head space when packing liquid and semiliquid foods in large containers, about ½ inch in small ones. To assure a good closure, keep the sealing edges free from moisture or food. When packaging foods with freezer material that comes in sheets, wrap them as tight as possible, seal properly, and freeze at zero or below as soon as they are packed.

To Reheat. These foods can be reheated either in the oven or on top of the range. Reheating in a double boiler or saucepan is faster, but food reheated in the oven requires less attention and the texture is usually better. When using a double boiler, start with warm, not hot, water in the lower pan. Reheating over direct heat requires constant attention, and the food must be stirred often and gently. Allow at least 30 minutes, and serve as soon as possible. Generally it is better to reheat frozen cooked main dishes without thawing. However, in order to transfer the food to a cooking utensil, it will be necessary to place the frozen package in warm water for a few minutes to loosen it. Only ovenproof containers can safely be taken from the freezer and put directly into a hot oven for reheating. If you prefer to thaw food completely before reheating, it is best to place it in the refrigerator if thawing will take more than 4 hours in room temperature. This will prevent growth of bacteria that may cause spoilage.

To heat prepared frozen foods in the oven, use a cover on the container until thawing is completed. The cover may be removed to permit browning, if you wish, but thawing will be much quicker in a covered dish. If the container used for heating does not have a lid, cover it with well-greased kitchen-weight foil, shiny side down.

Casseroles. Many dishes, such as individual or large casseroles, may be frozen in the containers in which they were baked, and will be ready for reheating at serving time. Gravies and sauces in casseroles and similar dishes should contain as little fat as possible, to avoid separation. Commercially packed prepared foods containing sauces and gravies are made with special thickening agents that do not separate on freezing, but these products are not available in retail stores at the present time. Large casseroles will take about 1½ hours to reheat in the frozen stage, and the oven temperature must not exceed 325° F., to prevent overbrowning before the interior is hot. If casseroles are allowed to defrost in the refrigerator overnight, heating time is reduced to about 1 hour. A meat thermometer may be placed in the center of the casserole the last few minutes of baking. It is ready to serve when the temperature reaches about 150° F., never over 180° F. Do not overheat.

If you are not equipped with several or more casseroles and other covered dishes, *and also wish to save space in the freezer,* we suggest that you line flat casseroles with wet parchment paper or heavy foil, extending it above rim. Fill them with the food, freeze until hard. Now lift out food, wrap for freezing, and return to freezer.

To reheat above preparations, place the frozen food back into original container, then into oven set at 325° F. Any food reheated in the oven must reach an internal temperature of at least 150° F., to be safe and heated through. Temperature can go as high as 180° F. This is ascertained by placing a meat thermometer into center of food when it is soft enough, moving thermometer up and down slowly until a stationary point is reached, and the juices simmer for about 10 to 15 minutes around the edges.

Today authorities warn that food must not be allowed to cool at room temperature, and suggest that before freezing food should be chilled at once in ice water or in refrigerator. An easy rule to remember is to keep hot foods hot (at least 140° F.) and cold foods cold (below 45° F.) at any time, not only for freezing. Food kept for more than 3 or 4 hours between 60° and 120° F. may not be safe to eat. Salmonella, a tiny, infectious bacteria that contaminates food, thrives at room temperature. It is destroyed at a temperature of 40° F. or below, and 140° F. or above. Salmonella is a year-round danger, and it becomes more common during the summer months when picnickers eat foods that have been improperly stored. It thrives in usual picnic foods such as potato salads, milk, and milk products, poultry, and fish. If you cannot maintain these foods at the proper temperatures, don't take them along unless they are going to be cooked at the picnic site. Convenience foods can also become contaminated if not prepared according to directions, and temperature of the hot preparation is below 150° F. before it is served. Best to test interior temperature with a meat thermometer.

French-Fried Potatoes

Prepare according to general directions. Let them become cold; then wrap for freezing. To serve, spread them out on a baking sheet and place in a preheated 425° F. oven for about 15 minutes, watching closely, turning them over the last few minutes.

Hash Browned or Fried Brown Potato Slices

Prepare according to general directions. Wrap and freeze. To serve, heat same as French-fried potatoes, or sauté them in a very well-greased covered skillet about 6 or 7 minutes on each side, turning them over with a pancake turner.

Stuffed Baked Potatoes

Prepare according to general directions. Wrap and freeze. To serve, bake them without defrosting in a preheated 350° F. oven about 30 to 45 minutes, or until heated through and browned.

Boiled Potatoes

Boiled potatoes do not freeze well. If they must be used in stews and casseroles, be sure to undercook them. Or omit them, and add freshly cooked potatoes to the stew after it has been completely reheated.

Cooked Spaghetti, Noodles, Macaroni, and Rice

Freezing of these foods is not recommended unless they are used in casseroles or combination dishes. It takes longer to defrost them than to cook them, and they are never as desirable. They become mushy unless they are *undercooked* before freezing.

Italian Ravioli, Manicotti, and Stuffed Cannelloni

These foods may be frozen for several weeks. Some commercial brands are frozen with the sauce in some localities, but we find them more desirable if they are frozen without sauce. The sauce may be prepared in advance and frozen separately, *then it is reheated before you add it to the various frozen pasta items.* This not only shortens the reheating time, but prevents the ricotta-filled items from becoming watery and curdling from overcooking if the sauce is frozen in the same container with the product.

Ravioli may be frozen uncooked, or partially boiled. Cooked ravioli will require only a few minutes to become tender. Uncooked (raw) ravioli will need about 20 minutes of gentle boiling, if you use our basic recipes and directions.

Pasta squares for cannelloni and manicotti are best when partially cooked, then filled, and frozen, preferably without sauce. To recook place in a heatproof casserole or other flat baking dish, leaving ½ inch space between each. Now cover with heated Italian sauce (or sauce indicated in recipe), cover casserole with well-greased foil or cover of casserole. Bake in preheated 400° F. oven about 30 minutes, remove cover and bake about 10 more minutes, or until center of food is very hot and reaches temperature of at least 150° F. when tested with a meat thermometer (to be safe for eating). Do not allow temperature to go over 180° F. to prevent overcooking.

Stuffed Lasagna

Ricotta stuffed lasagna may be frozen for not more than 2 weeks, the shorter the freezing period, the better. Place casserole frozen into a preheated 375° F. oven for about 1 hour and 20 minutes. Best to test with a meat thermometer. Interior temperature should be at least 150° F. and not more than 180° F. When time is up, spread extra sauce over entire top, shut off heat, and leave in oven, with door open for about 15 minutes. Then serve as per directions.

Soups

All kinds of homemade soups freeze well. To save space in the freezer, prepare them in concentrated form, adding more liquid as needed when they are defrosted for serving. Broth soups are easily defrosted over direct low heat. Cream soups are best reheated in a double boiler to prevent scorching, unless you stir them continuously over very low heat. Remember to leave 1 inch head space in each container when freezing.

Coated Fried Chicken, Meats, and Croquettes

Cut-up coated (with egg and crumbs or thick 'batter) fried chicken, cutlets, and croquettes freeze very well for about 2 months. The coating protects these foods against drying out. Prepare, cool, and wrap them well for freezing. To reheat, place chicken or cutlets without thawing on a baking sheet or heatproof dish in a 400° F. oven for about 40 to 60 minutes, depending on the thickness and size of the pieces. Turn them over after the first 20 minutes, and move them around from time to time until they are heated through and crisp. For an unusual dry coating, lower heat to 300° F. and continue to bake them a little longer. Croquettes are better if thawed on a refrigerator shelf for about 8 hours, then reheated on a baking sheet in a 350° F. oven about 15 to 20 minutes. Test after 15 minutes, as they are likely to burst if overheated. If they are heated through before you are ready to serve them, simply shut off the heat, and leave the oven door partly open.

To Refry. If you prefer to reheat these foods by refrying them in deep fat (instead of reheating in oven for a much longer time), *it is important that you allow foods to defrost in refrigerator (not room temperature)* about 8 hours or longer in advance, and to keep them refrigerated until a few minutes before you are ready to serve them. To reheat, lower them gently into deep hot fat, about 350° F., a few pieces at a time, until they are deep golden color and crisp. Takes about 5 minutes for large pieces, 3 minutes for smaller items. They are more crisp and delectable reheated this way.

Cooked Meat

It is best not to freeze leftover cooked meats unless they are packed in sauces and gravies. Leftover meats may be frozen for a very short time, not more than 1 week, as they have a tendency to become rancid, dry, and tough.

Large Pieces of Leftover Roasts, Ham, Poultry. Do not allow leftover foods to remain in room temperature more than a few minutes after the meal is over. Refrigerate them as soon as possible to prevent contamination, then wrap them for freezing in amounts that you will serve in 1 meal. Serve them cold, or reheat only until heated through, and serve at once. It is best to serve them within 1 or 2 weeks. Breaded foods may be frozen for about 2 months.

Chicken and Meat Pies

Chicken and meat pies keep very well in the freezer for 3 months. Prepare, let cool, and store in the plates they are baked in, if possible. Follow general wrapping and freezing directions. To serve, place pies unthawed in a 400° F. oven about 45 minutes for individual sizes, 1 hour or longer for larger sizes. Meat thermometer inserted in center should register about 150° F.

Bread Crumbs for Coating Meats, Poultry, Fish, etc.

Bread crumbs will become rancid after a few days if left in room temperature, in about 2 weeks if refrigerated. However, large amounts may be prepared at one time when convenient, and frozen for several months in plastic bags. Then you can remove whatever amount is needed for one meal, and leave the rest in the freezer. Buttered crumbs may also be frozen.

Hors d'Oeuvres, Canapés, and Sandwiches

These foods freeze well for about 2 weeks, if properly made and wrapped. Do not use crackers, large amounts of mayonnaise or other salad dressings, fresh crisp vegetables, jellies, or hard-cooked egg whites. *Very small amounts* of mayonnaise or salad dressings may be combined with chicken, meat, or seafood fillings to give moisture and flavor. Almost any other type of filling and bread may be used. Spread the bread with softened butter or margarine (not mayonnaise or salad dressing) to prevent fillings from soaking bread. Cut sandwiches into halves, or as desired, and wrap individually in freezer cellophane or heavy wax paper. Then pack a number of them in freezer bags or airtight boxes. Mark, and freeze. Open-face canapés and hors d'oeuvres can be frozen in single layers in flat boxes or baking sheets. If baking sheets are used for storage, allow hors d'oeuvres to freeze uncovered; then slip the pan into a large freezer bag. Seal, etc. To defrost, allow about 2 hours in room temperature, about 4 hours in the refrigerator. Pastry hors d'oeuvres with various fillings, which are served hot, can be frozen unbaked. Place them in a 400° F. oven about 15 minutes just before serving. If they are filled and baked before freezing, reheat them without defrosting in a 400° F. oven for 7 or 8 minutes.

Yeast Breads and Coffee Cakes

Practically every kind of *baked* yeast bread, rolls, and coffee cake freezes well. Freezing *unbaked* yeast doughs is not recommended (except for Danish pastry yeast dough and similar rich doughs, that can be frozen for about 1 week), inasmuch as the storage life is very short and uncertain, and handling very complicated. Loaves of bread and large coffee cakes should be completely baked. Small yeast rolls, however, may be prepared, shaped, and allowed to rise for half the usual time, baked in a preheated 300° F. oven for about 25 minutes, or until they are slightly colored, and cooled well, before they are wrapped for freezing. To serve these rolls, place them on a baking sheet in a cold oven set at 400° F. and bake until they are brown and crisp on the outside, about 15 minutes. Serve them at once. Fully baked rolls may be reheated in the same way for about 10 minutes. Whole loaves of bread and coffee cakes will be defrosted in a 300° F. oven in about 30 minutes, or in room temperature in about 2 hours. Defrosted coffee cakes may be reheated in a 400° F. oven for about 10 to 15 minutes, depending on size.

Quick Breads

Quick breads made with baking powder, such as Banana Nut Bread, Date and Nut Bread, etc., also freeze well. It is advisable to slice these breads after they are baked and cooled well before freezing. Then wrap them carefully, and freeze. They have a tendency to tear if sliced after they are frozen. They will defrost in room temperature in about 1 hour. Frozen baked muffins, corn bread, baking powder biscuits, and similar breads are acceptable, but not as good as fresh. They do not keep as well as frozen baked yeast breads. Do not store them for more than 1 month. To serve, allow them to defrost, in their wrappings, in room temperature for about 1 hour. Then reheat them in a 425° F. oven for about 6 or 7 minutes. Or reheat them from the frozen state at 375° F. for about 15 minutes.

Frozen Cakes

Baked cakes freeze very well and have a long storage life of 4 to 6 months if properly wrapped. Freezing *cake batters* is not recommended inasmuch as there is no advantage in doing so, and also because the volume of the cake will be smaller and it is likely to sink in the center. Before freezing, cakes may be frosted with buttercream icings and other uncooked icings, or with whipped cream. Icings containing large amounts of egg whites and syrups do not freeze well. Filled cakes have a tendency to become soggy after they are frozen, except those filled with buttercream icing or whipped cream. Do not use cream fillings in cakes to be frozen. It is better to fill them after they are defrosted. A decorated cake must be placed on a cardboard and frozen uncovered for several hours, then covered with wax paper, and overwrapped with freezer paper or slid into a large plastic bag. If possible, store decorated cakes in deep boxes so that they can remain covered during the thawing process. Any paper or covering that clings to a decorated cake must be removed as soon as it is placed in room temperature or in the refrigerator, to protect the decorations. Otherwise, always defrost undecorated cakes unwrapped, either in the refrigerator about 8 hours or in room temperature about 4 hours. For the best possible texture, it is important to thaw butter cakes completely and to let them remain in room temperature at least 1 hour before serving.

Fruit Cakes, Plum Puddings

These items freeze very well for 6 months or longer. To defrost, let them stand in room temperature unwrapped for at least 12 hours. Fruit cakes cut better if they are cold. Use a very sharp knife, and wipe it with a wet cloth after cutting each slice.

Cheese Tortes, Cheese Cakes, and Whipped Cream Tortes

Most cheese cakes freeze well for about 1 month. They must be baked before freezing. Let them become very cold; then cut them into serving portions, release them from the pans with a pie server, and place them on a flat surface covered with freezer paper. Any type of torte or dessert containing whipped cream or ice cream freezes well for about 2 months. They can be placed in the freezer uncovered for several hours until firm to the touch, then wrapped for freezing. It is best to defrost decorated tortes unwrapped in the refrigerator if they have been stored in deep boxes, allowing several hours.

Pies (Fruit, Berry, and Mince)

The most desirable pies for freezing are fruit, berry, and mince pies. They may be frozen either baked or unbaked. Fruit and berry pies have a better flavor and the crust is flakier if they are frozen *unbaked,* and since it takes almost as long to thaw *baked* frozen pies as it does to cook *unbaked* ones, there is no time advantage in baking them before freezing. However, this is a matter of preference, and it might be well for you to try both methods. To prevent peaches, apricots, and apples in pies from turning dark, it is important to pour about 2 tablespoons of lemon juice over the fruit as soon as it is sliced and before combining it with other ingredients. It is also advisable to increase the thickening agent in berry and fruit pies by 1 tablespoon. Prepare them according to directions, but if you are freezing 2-crust pies before baking, do not cut vents in the upper crust. Cut the vents after the frozen pie has baked 15 minutes.

Wrapping Pies for Freezing. If you intend to freeze pies in the plates in which they are prepared, we recommend using the dull aluminum pie plates (not the aluminum foil). They are easy to handle, do not break, and brown undercrust beautifully. It is a good investment to spend several dollars for these permanent aluminum pie plates if you like to freeze a few pies at one time. If you prefer to bake pies before freezing, allow them to become cold on a cake rack, then place another plate (this can be foil or paper plate) over each one to prevent crushing, and slip them into plastic bags, and seal tightly. If you are freezing unbaked pies, wrap them in the same way.

To Bake Pies. Bake uncooked pies (without defrosting) in a preheated 425° F. oven on *lowest rack* about 45 to 50 minutes for small pies, 1 hour or longer for large thick pies. Then if they are not brown, lower temperature to 350° F. and continue to bake until brown, about 15 more minutes, but watch closely the last few minutes.

To Thaw a Cooked Pie. Place pie in a 400° F. oven about 40 minutes, or let it stand room temperature about 8 hours, and reheat at 400° F. about 10 minutes, *on lowest rack.*

Pies Baked in Aluminum Foil Plates. If you prefer to use foil plates (instead of aluminum or glass plates) proceed as above, but grease bottom and sides of plates with soft butter or margarine before you place in the crust and the filling. This will help to brown undercrust. You can do this with any pie plate if the undercrust does not usually brown well. Pies prepared in foil plates should be baked on lowest rack at 425° F. on an old dark baking sheet (or aluminum pan) to brown underside and make it crisp.

Other Pies

Chiffon pies, pies containing whipped cream, and pecan, pumpkin, and cheese pies freeze well for a short period—not more than 1 month for best results. These pies must be baked before freezing and do not need to be thawed in the oven. Simply let them stand in the refrigerator unwrapped for about 8 hours, or until defrosted. Cream and custard pies do not freeze well. The commercially sold frozen cream pies are made with special thickening agents (not available to the homemaker at the present time) that do not cause curdling. Meringue toppings on pies should be avoided because they toughen during freezing.

Pie Shells or Sheets

Baked pie shells freeze very well, but to prevent breaking, it is important to stack them carefully with 2 sheets of wax paper between them, and to store them in a box. Wrap them for freezing according to directions above. It is better not to freeze thick pieces of pie dough, as they would take a long time to defrost and consequently become warm. Instead, it is advisable to roll circles of dough to the proper size for your pie plates, and to store them on flat round pizza pans of stiff round cardboard (a little larger than the dough) covered with wax paper. Separate them with 2 layers of paper before wrapping. Pastry circles must be completely defrosted but still cold before placing them in pie plates.

Doughnuts, Cream Puffs, Éclairs, Meringues

All doughnuts freeze very well for about 1 month. Pack them as soon as possible after they have cooled. To serve, simply let them defrost, covered, in room temperature for several hours. Serve without reheating. Cream puffs and éclairs may be filled with whipped cream or ice cream, but not cream filling, before freezing. Let them defrost uncovered in the refrigerator about 30 minutes before serving.

Cookies

Cookies freeze very well whether baked or unbaked. There is no advantage to freezing them unbaked. Frozen baked cookies will thaw in about 2 hours, unwrapped, in room temperature. Unbaked frozen cookies may be placed directly in the oven without defrosting, allowing several minutes more baking time. If baked cookies are packed for freezing, be sure to place wax paper between layers. If they are to be used for gifts, pack them attractively, overwrap, and freeze.

Chocolate-Dipped Candies, Nuts, Raisins, etc.

Chocolate-dipped candies and the majority of other candies freeze very well for at least 6 months. Defrost them in a cool room, not over 70° F., or in the refrigerator for at least 8 hours. They should be kept *wrapped,* to prevent discoloration, before being defrosted. Then they may be kept for 2 weeks in the refrigerator. Nuts, raisins, and dried fruits freeze very well.

▶ *Menus*

1. Hollywood Salad Appetizer
   Breast of Chicken Imperial
   Turkish Pilaf (Rice with Mushrooms, etc.)
   Asparagus with Hollandaise Sauce
   Fresh Sautéed Mushrooms
   French Pastry Cake
   Coffee

2. Clear Bouillon with Petites Quenelles
   Broiled Porterhouse or Sirloin Steak, or Planked Beef Tenderloins
   French-fried Potatoes
   Vegetables Mornay in Casserole
   Fresh Vegetable Salad Bowl
   Viennese Nut Torte
   Coffee

3. Quick Vegetable Meat Ball Soup
   Barbecued Spareribs with Bread Dressing, or Barbecued Chicken
   Barbecue Sauce
   Cole Slaw with Cooked Salad Dressing
   Baked Potatoes
   Homemade White Bread
   Rainbow Butter Cake with Strawberry or Raspberry Fluff Icing
   Coffee

4. French Onion Soup
   Roasted Duckling with Moist Dressing and Orange Sauce
   Sweet Potato Delights
   Mushrooms and Spinach Baked in Casserole
   Strawberry Glazed Tarts or Strawberry Shortcake
   Coffee

5. Cream of Potato and Green Onion Soup

Baked Stuffed Whitefish
French-fried Onion Rings
Asparagus Salad
Whole Wheat Bread
Cherry Pie
Coffee

6. Gumbo Chicken Soup
   Sautéed Breasts of Chicken (or any other chicken dish)
   Grilled Pineapple and Tomato Slices
   Baked Potatoes
   Yeast Rolls
   Meringues with Ice Cream
   Coffee

7. Cream of Mushroom Soup
   Beef Bordelaise with Gravy
   Potato Croquettes
   Brussels Sprouts, Sautéed
   Fresh Vegetable Salad Bowl
   Lemon Chiffon Pie
   Coffee

8. Oysters à la Rockefeller Appetizer
   Baked Chicken Monte Carlo
   Fresh Lima Beans and Corn, Baked in Casserole
   Pear Salad
   Rum Pie
   Coffee

9. Bird of Paradise Fruit-Salad Appetizer
   Roasted Stuffed Cornish Hens with Special Tetrazzini Gravy
   Asparagus in Casserole
   Crêpes Suzette with l'Aiglon Butter
   Coffee

10. Big Apple Cocktail
    Roast Stuffed Turkey or Chicken
    Sweet Potatoes in Orange Cups
    Cranberry Mold
    Butterhorns
    Pecan Pie or Flaming Plum Pudding
    Coffee

11. Hot Mushroom Meringue Appetizers
    Baked Ham with Special Raisin Sauce
    Glazed Sweet Potatoes
    Strawberry-Rhubarb Mold
    Clover Leaf Rolls
    Butter Easter Lilies
    Apple Squares
    Coffee

▶ LUNCHEON OR SUPPER MENUS ◀

1. Shrimp Salad Mold
   Horseradish Sauce
   Celery and Olives
   Hot Parker House Rolls or Finger Sandwiches
   Muerbes and Chocolate Log Cookies
   Coffee or Tea

2. Shrimp de Jonghe
   Brioche Luncheon Rolls
   Fresh Vegetable Salad Bowl
   Brioche Streussel-Top Coffee Cake
   Coffee or Tea

3. Chop Suey or Egg Foo Yong
   Chinese Rice
   Butterhorns
   Glazed Pecan Rolls
   Coffee or Tea

4. Chicken à la King
   Baking Powder Biscuits
   Apple Pie
   Coffee or Tea

5. Chicken Croquettes with Sauce
   Duchesse Potatoes
   Julienne Glazed Carrots
   Fresh or Frozen Peas
   Cream Puffs or Éclairs
   Coffee or Tea

6. Vegetable Daisy Meat Platter
   Fresh Vegetable Salad Bowl
   Homemade White Bread
   Coffee or Tea

7. Corned Beef with Boiled Cabbage, Potatoes, and Carrots
   Bohemian Rye Bread
   Fresh Peach Pie or Blueberry Pie
   Coffee or Tea

8. Shrimp Creole with Rice
   Hot Rolls
   Angel Food Cake with La Neige Dessert
   Coffee or Tea

9. Hostess French-fried Shrimp
   Special Hostess Sauce
   Pineapple Cream Cheese Mold
   Fruit Salad Dressing
   Coffee or Tea

10. Stuffed Zucchini
    Fluffy Mashed Potatoes in Casserole
    Braided Yeast Rolls
    Italian Fennel Cakes
    Coffee or Tea

11. Mushrooms and Spinach Baked in Casserole
    Knotted Yeast Rolls
    Buttercream-Filled Coffee-Cake Loaf
    Coffee or Tea

12. Fricassee of Chicken
    Fluffy Dumplings
    Steamed Frozen Corn
    Devil's Food Cake Squares
    Coffee or Tea

13. Eggplant, Vegetable, and Meat Stew
    Cucumbers in Sour Cream
    Bohemian Rye Bread
    Toffee Squares
    Coffee or Tea

14. Baked Stuffed Summer Squash
    Fluffy Mashed Potatoes
    Parker House Yeast Rolls
    Danish Pastries
    Coffee or Tea

15. Spinach, Broccoli, or Asparagus Baked Mold
    Pork Sausage Links
    Cheese Sauce
    Twin Yeast Rolls
    Chocolate Log Cookies
    Coffee or Tea

16. Pineapple Bird Salad or Cantaloupe Bird Salad
    Finger Sandwiches
    Ice Cream Chocolate Roll or George Washington Roll
    Coffee or Tea

17. Happy Jack Salad
    French Dressing
    Assorted Finger Sandwiches
    Raised Doughnuts, Bismarcks, or Crullers
    Coffee or Tea

▶ ITALIAN SUPPERS OR DINNERS ◀

1. Breast of Chicken or Turkey Alfredo
   Noodles Alfredo
   Sauce Poulet
   Party-Style Citrus Fruit Mold
   Ricotta Torte
   Coffee

2. Continental-Style Roast Leg of Veal or Lamb
   Vegetable Casserole Continental
   Risotto Milanese
   Cucumber Salad Mold
   Zuppa Inglese
   Coffee

3. Spaghetti or Ravioli with Meat Balls
   Pan-fried Eggplant Slices

Fresh Vegetable Salad Bowl
Garlic-Flavored Italian Bread
Spumoni Ice Cream and Italian Fennel Cakes

4. Italian-Style Braised Pork Loins
Potatoes Vesuvio in Casserole
Green or Red Peppers Stuffed Italian-Style
Fresh Vegetable Salad Bowl
Florentine Pastry Squares

5. Lasagna in Casserole
Peppered Steak
Baked Broccoli à la Parmesan
Italian Fresh Finochio and relishes
Cannoli Pastries
Coffee

6. Pizza, with various toppings
Italian Broiled or Roasted Sausage
Italian Toasted Almond Slices
Chianti Wine
Coffee

7. Chicken Cacciatore or Veal Scallopini
Zucchini and Tomatoes au Gratin
Fresh Vegetable Salad Bowl
Individual Florentine Pastries
Coffee

8. Osso Buco with various vegetables
Caesar Salad Bowl
Italian Broiled Tomato Garlic Bread
Zuppa Inglese

9. Cannelloni (Manicotti) Italian-Style
Veal Steak Parmesan
Zucchini Stew
Piquant Salad Bowl
Whipped Cream Ricotta Pie Torte

10. Tortellini Bolognese with Sauce Bolognese
Chicken Milano
Sautéed Broccoli Parmesan

Anchovy Salad Bowl
Italian Fennel Cakes

11. Chicken Vesuvio with Potatoes and Vegetables Vesuvio
Summer Salad Bowl
Italian Garlic Bread
Marzipan Slices

▶ ORIENTAL BUFFET DINNERS AND SUPPERS ◀

1. Beef Mandarin-Style with assorted vegetables
Cantonese-Style Fried Rice
Won Tons with Chicken
Hot Rolls
Vienna Pineapple Flaky Pastries
Fruit Punch
Tea

2. Lobster Almond Din
Cantonese-Style Fried Rice
Beef Tenderloin with Fresh Bean Sprouts or Pea Pods
Fresh Fruit Platter: pineapple, strawberries, etc.
Hot Rolls
Oriental Cookies and Tea

3. Chicken or Shrimp Chow Mein with Fried Noodles
Cantonese Sautéed Vegetables
Braised Duck Cantonese
Cantonese-Style Fried Rice
Hot Rolls
Strawberry Rhubarb Mold
Tea

4. Him Soon York (Sweet-Sour Pork)
Cantonese-Style Fried Rice
Lobster Cantonese Style
Hot Rolls
Pineapple-Shaped Fruit Salad Mold
Tea

5. Cantonese Pressed Duck
Sautéed Chinese Vegetables

Cantonese-Style Fried Rice
Cantonese Chicken Slices
Hot Rolls
Pineapple Salad Mold and Muerbe Cookies
Tea

6. Bali Bali Chicken
   Vegetables for Bali Bali Chicken
   Boiled Won Tons
   Dowel Sea Piquat
   Hot Rolls
   Fresh Fruit Platter in Season
   Tea

▶ COCKTAIL PARTIES ◀

For large groups—more than 12

1. Seafood Horn-of-Plenty (filled with marinated whole glazed shrimp)
   Hot Mushroom Filling in Chafing Dish, surrounded with crackers, etc.
   Stuffed Olive Pinwheels
   Coronation Appetizers
   Individual Strawberry Appetizers (made with various fillings)
   Punch

2. Pineapple Hors d'Oeuvres Centerpiece (made with chicken livers, etc.)
   Shrimp Louisiana in Chafing Dish
   Hot Ham Bouches
   Caviar-Egg Appetizer
   Hotel Rainbow Canapés
   Punch

3. Chaud-Froid Salmon or Seafood Salad Mold
   Fluffy Cheese Dip
   Russian Blintzes (filled with seafood)
   Lobster Thermidor Dip in Chafing Dish
   Bonbons Elites
   Punch

4. Colonial Doll Hors d'Oeuvres Centerpiece, surrounded with Cold Meat
   Sweet Pea Appetizers
   Stuffed Olive Pinwheels
   Swan Shrimp Appetizer

Crab Meat Dip, surrounded with melba toast, etc.
Punch

5. Chaud-Froid Curved Fish Mold (seafood of any kind)
Hot Chicken Dip in Chafing Dish
Hot Asparagus Roquefort Rolls
Cheese Meat Swirls
Kippered Herring, molded
Punch

▶ COCKTAIL PARTIES ◀

For small groups

1. Cheese Apple Centerpiece
Ham and Cheese Soufflé Hors d'Oeuvres
Hot Mushroom Meringues
Sunbonnets
Gherkin Fan Appetizer

2. Large Strawberry Cheese or Seafood Centerpiece
Deviled-Egg Bird Appetizers
Shrimp in Cocktail Sauce Hors d'Oeuvres
Crab Meat au Diable in Patty Shells
Gruyère-Caviar Hors d'Oeuvres

3. Crab Meat au Diable in Chafing Dish
Bacon-Egg Canapés
Mushroom Crescents or Diamonds
Cheese-Meat Swirls
A Man's Favorite Appetizer

▶ ORIENTAL HORS D'OEUVRES COCKTAIL PARTIES ◀

1. Cantonese Barbecue Ribs
Cantonese Roasted Pork Slices
Yuon Stuffed Mushrooms
Oriental Chicken Liver Appetizer
Honolulu Fresh Strawberry Pineapple Appetizers
Oriental Shrimp Appetizer

2. Cantonese Egg Roll

Oriental Bacon Shrimp Appetizer
Sautéed Shrimp in Garlic Sauce
Chicken Liver en Brochette
Cantonese Squab or Cornish Hen Appetizer

3. Lobster Oriental in Chafing Dish
Pancho Almond French-fried Shrimp with Pancho Sauce
Stuffed Lobster and Shrimp Appetizers
Fresh Pineapple-Shrimp Appetizers
Fresh Shrimp or Lobster Melon Appetizer

Dipping Sauces for Oriental Appetizers

Sweet-Sour Sauce—No. 1
Sweet-Sour Sauce—No. 2
Hot Sauce
Mustard Sauce
Special Dressing for Seafood-Fruit Appetizers

▶ ITALIAN COCKTAIL PARTIES ◀

1. Italian Pizza, with various toppings, cut into small squares
Italian Tomato-Tuna Appetizers
Anchovy Dip
Italian Salami Hors d'Oeuvres Puffs
Wine

2. Ricotta-Sausage Filled Squares (Calzoni)
Italian Salami-Anchovy Appetizer
Italian Cornucopias
Plum-Tomato Tulip Spray Hors d'Oeuvres
Wine

3. Italian Antipasto Platter
Assorted Plum-Tomato Hors d'Oeuvres
Italian Salami Hors d'Oeuvres Puffs
Parmesan Garlic Dip
Wine

4. Tomato Dip
Scrambled Egg and Salami Appetizers
Italian Prosciutto and Melon Appetizers

Italian Meat Ball Appetizers in Chaflng Dish or served on toothpicks
Wine

▶ PARTY-STYLE BUFFET SUPPERS (COLD) ◀

For large groups

1. Chaud-Froid Chicken Salad Mold, garnished with fresh tomato
   slices, etc.
   Party-Style Potato Salad Mold (with embedded Cream Cheese Roses)
   surrounded with Baked Sliced Ham
   Party-Style Vegetable Salad Mold
   Ice Cream Fruit Salad Mold
   Fruit Salad Dressing
   Hollywood Two-Tone Cheese Cake
   Small Fancy Cookies and Cakes
   Hot Rolls or Finger Sandwiches
   Coffee
   Punch

2. Lobster Salad Imperial, molded
   Horseradish Sauce
   Hyacinth Party Chicken Salad Mold
   Cucumber Salad Mold, surrounded with sliced corned beef
   Pineapple Salad Mold, with delectable Fruit Salad Dressing
   Chocolate Almond Pastry Torte
   Hazelnut Macaroons
   Hot Rolls or Finger Sandwiches
   Coffee
   Punch

3. Crab Meat Salad Ravigote, molded and garnished
   Assorted Relishes
   Turkey Salad Superb, molded and garnished
   Tomato Aspic Salad Mold, surrounded with cold sliced meat and
   cheeses
   Cartwheel Grapejuice Salad Mousse, with various fruits
   Dobos Torte
   Pineapple-shaped Party Cake, surrounded with dainty cookies and
   small cakes
   Hot Rolls or Finger Sandwiches
   Coffee
   Punch

4. Shrimp Salad Louisiana, molded and garnished
   Chaud-Froid Hand-Molded Ham Salad, garnished
   Horseradish Sauce
   Party-Style Citrus Fruit Mold, garnished and surrounded with cold
   meats
   Colonial Doll Dessert Mold with Fruit Salad Dressing
   Assorted Fancy Cookies and Small Cakes
   Hot Rolls or Finger Sandwiches
   Coffee
   Punch

▶ HOLIDAY BUFFET SUPPERS OR DINNERS (HOT) ◀

1. Roast Turkey with Dressing, Gravy
   Sweet Potato Fluff in Casserole with Special Orange Sauce
   Mixed Vegetables Mornay in Casserole
   Cranberry Mold, with glazed fruits
   Fruit Salad Dressing
   Yuletide Party-Style Torte Pie
   Assorted Yuletide Cookies
   Hot Rolls
   Coffee
   Punch

2. Baked Ham, glazed and garnished
   Sweet Potato Meringue in Casserole
   Yuletide Star Cranberry-Raspberry Salad Mold
   Asparagus with Hollandaise Sauce
   Fruit Cake Petits Fours
   Apple Strudel or Apple Slices
   Hot Rolls
   Coffee
   Punch

3. Roast Stuffed Ducklings, glazed and garnished
   Sweet Potato Delights on pineapple rings
   Casserole of Spinach
   Butterfly Fruit Salad Mold
   Fruit Salad Dressing
   Southern Pecan Pie, decorated with whipped cream
   Marzipan Slices
   Hot Rolls

Coffee
Punch

4. Stuffed Roasted or Broiled Cornish Hens with Wild Rice and special
     Tetrazzini Gravy
   Glazed Sweet Potatoes in Casserole—Flamed
   Buttered Peas and Carrots
   Grape Mold, garnished with fruits
   Lady Finger Raspberry or Strawberry Ice Box Torte, surrounded with
     Fancy Coconut Pear and Strawberry Cookies
   Hot Rolls
   Coffee
   Punch

▶ HOLIDAY OPEN HOUSE BUFFET SUPPER (COLD) ◀

For large group

Turkey Salad Superb, surrounded with relishes
Holly Wreath Seafood Buffet Mold
Poinsettia Buffet Log
Boneless Glazed and Decorated Ham
Assorted Fancy Petits Fours
Flaming English Plum Pudding
Dainty Finger Sandwiches
Holiday Candies and Bonbons
Coffee

▶ FORMAL OR HIGH TEA ◀

For large groups, weddings, anniversaries, etc.

1. Bar-le-duc French Cream Cheese Mold, with melba toast and dainty
     crackers
   Fancy Sandwich Loaf, with various fillings, decorated
   Crescent Tea Sandwiches
   Basket Tea Sandwiches
   Continental Leaf Cookies
   Karydato Grecian Pastries
   Tiny Filled Cream Puffs
   Bonbons
   Salted Nut Meats

Tea and Coffee
Punch

2. Hyacinth Salad Mold, with dainty finger sandwiches
   Cloverleaf Tea Sandwiches
   Hotel Rainbow Canapés
   Sunbonnets with various toppings
   Petit Fours, small
   Coconut Macaroons
   English Tartlets
   Tea and Coffee
   Punch

3. Confetti Party Mousse, with dainty triangle sandwiches
   Chicken-Almond Salad open-face canapés
   Twin Meat Swirls
   Coronation Appetizers
   Watercress Filling on small Bread Crescents, decorated
   Anchovy Walnut Spread on small Diamond-shaped Breads, decorated
   Frangipan Tartlets
   Fancy Muerbe Cookies
   Toffee Square Cookies
   Tea and Coffee
   Punch

▶ INFORMAL AFTERNOON TEA ◀

For small intimate groups

Any of the Open-Face Canapés in Hors d'Oeuvres section
Dainty Finger Sandwiches, with various fillings
Small Glazed Pecan Rolls
Spiced Cake Squares
Banana Bread, sliced thin
Date and Nut Bread, sliced thin
Tea and Coffee

▶ GOURMET BUFFET DINNERS OR SUPPERS (HOT) ◀

For 12 or more

1. Lobster Thermidor in Chafing Dish or Casserole
   Baked Chicken Monte Carlo in Casserole
   Sauce Parisienne

Asparagus with Hollandise Sauce
Flaky Croissant Dinner Rolls
Caesar Salad Bowl
Flaming French Crêpes Suzette
Coffee
Champagne Punch

2. Breast of Chicken Kiev
Whole Fillet Beef Wellington in Puff Paste
Special Mushroom Gravy
Mushroom, Green Bean, and Carrot Medley Glacé
Bahama Salad Bowl with special dressing
Baba Rum Cakes around Molded Ice Cream Bombe
Hot Brioche Dinner Rolls
Coffee
Wines

3. Cold or Hot Chateaubriand Dinner with various vegetables and topped
with Carved Sautéed Mushrooms
Shrimp de Jonghe in Casserole
Potatoes Delmonico in Casserole
Kentucky Limestone Salad Bowl with special dressing
Danish Pastry Dinner Rolls
Heavenly Ice Cream-filled Pastry Meringue Torte
Coffee
Wines

▶ SUMMERTIME BUFFET SALAD BAR (COLD) ◀

For large groups

Carved Watermelon Centerpiece, filled with melon balls, or used as a
punch bowl and surrounded with Fresh Peach Baskets, glazed
Fresh Pineapple Birds of Paradise, filled with Fruit Salad Dressing or
cut-up fresh pineapple and fresh strawberries
Shrimp Arnaud, molded and garnished, surrounded with relishes
Crab Meat Salad Ravigote, molded and surrounded with fresh tomato
slices
Chicken Salad Superb on a bed of Molded Salad Greens
Quick Flaky Cheese Sticks, melba toast, Dainty Finger Sandwiches
Fresh Blueberry Party-Style Mold
Assorted Fancy Small Cakes and Cookies
Fresh Fruit Punch
Iced Coffee or Tea

Almond
Blanched, for swans, 713
Chocolate turtles, 688–89
Continental leaf cookies,
716–17
Cookies, Lady Winder-
mere's fan, 700
Cookies, Oriental, 699
Din, chicken, 836–37
Din, lobster, 836
Filling, frangipan, for
tartlets, 721
Paste crescents, 715
Paste drops, 715
Paste filling for marzipan
slices, 719
Paste macaroon cookies,
713–14
Paste pears, 714–15
Paste strawberries, 715
and shrimp appetizers,
Pancho, 9–10
Strawberry pancakes, 648–49
Toasted, slices, Italian,
820–21
Anchovy
Appetizers, Switzerland, 77
and salami appetizer,
Italian, 71
Vienna fingers, 694
APPETIZERS, 1–87
bread cases, 4–5
bread foundations, 2–3
bread foundations, sautéed,
3
centerpiece, bleu cheese
mold, 57
centerpiece, cheese "apple,"
50–51
centerpiece, cheese "pear,"
51–52
centerpiece, cheese "pumpkin," Epicurean, 55–56
centerpiece, cheese "strawberry," 51
centerpiece, chicken liver
paté, 56–57
centerpiece, Colonial doll,
62
centerpiece, "daisy," 4

centerpiece, glazed shrimp,
58
centerpiece, lobster, 52
centerpiece, "pineapple," 50
freezing and storing, 1–2
glaze for, 3
pastry dough, basic, 4
patty shells, 4–5
APPETIZERS, COLD, 46–87
Anchovy, Switzerland, 77
Anchovy-salami, Italian, 71
Antipasto platter, Italian,
760–61
Bacon-egg, 66
Bon bon elites, 70
Calzoni squares, 764–65
Caviar-egg, 67
Caviar "grape," 68
Caviar and Gruyère, 66
Cheese-meat swirls, 69–70
Chicken, sesame breast of,
71
Cornucopias, Italian, 68
Coronation, 67
Crab meat salad ravigote,
61–62
Crab meat in tomato cups,
64
Egg-bacon, 66
Egg birds, deviled, 47–48
Egg-caviar, 67
Egg, crab apple, 48–49
Egg roses, 49
Eggs, colored Easter, 48
Eggs, deviled, fancy stuffed,
48
Eggs, hard-cooked, 46–47
Eggs, tulip, 47
Gherkin fan, 69
Gruyère and caviar, 66
Herring, kippered, snack
mold, 64
Honolulu pineapple-straw-
berry bird, 73
Horn of plenty, seafood
cocktail, 53–55
Hotel Rainbow canapés, 70
Italian antipasto platter,
760–61
Italian cornucopias, 68

Italian prosciutto and
melon, 77–78
Italian salami-anchovy, 71
Italian tomato-tuna fish, 75
Lobster salad Imperial, 59–
61
Meat-cheese swirls, 69–70
Meat, cold "sweet pea," 74
Melon and prosciutto,
Italian, 77–78
Olive pinwheels, stuffed,
68–69
Olive, surprise, 68
Peanut butter party sand-
wiches, 65
Pickle, dill, stuffed, 76–77
Pineapple-shrimp, 75
Pineapple-strawberry bird,
Honolulu, 73
Prosciutto and melon,
Italian, 77–78
Sailboat, 70
Salami-anchovy, Italian, 71
Salmon, 63
Sandwich loaf, 52–53
Sandwiches, basket tea, 65
Sandwiches, clover leaf
party, 65
Sandwiches, crescent party,
66
Sandwiches, dainty finger,
64
Sandwiches, dainty triangle,
65
Sandwiches, peanut butter
party, 65
Sandwiches, tulip party,
65–66
Sardine crescents, 77
Sardines on toast, 74–75
Seafood basket, 73–74
Seafood cocktail horn of
plenty, 53–55
Seafood platter, 62–63
Sesame breast of chicken,
71
Shrimp in cocktail sauce,
67
Shrimp-pineapple, 75
Shrimp, glazed, farci, 76

Shrimp salad Louisiana, 58–59
Shrimp, swan, 71
Sunbonnet canapés, 69
Strawberry, 72–73
Strawberry-pineapple bird, Honolulu, 73
Tomato aspic, 60–61
Tomato, plum, tulip spray, 50
Tomato tulip, 49
Tomato-tuna fish, Italian, 75
APPETIZERS, HOT, 5–46
Almond-shrimp, Pancho, 9–10
Bacon-frankfurter, 38
Bacon-sausage, 38–39
Bacon-tamale, 38
Beef tenderloin, Oriental barbecued, on bamboo sticks, 831–32
Blintzes, chicken, 26
Blintzes, crab meat, 26
Blintzes, lobster, 26
Blintzes, shrimp, 26
Calzoni squares, 34–35
Cantonese barbecued ribs and pork, 13, 833–34
Cantonese cocktail strudels, 31–32
Cantonese egg rolls, 824–25
Cantonese filled won ton, 826
Cantonese fried shrimp, 826–27
Cantonese squab, 830
Cervelat filling, 43
Cheese, cream, rolled, toasted, 40–41
Cheese and ham soufflé, 21
Cheese, Italian, 37
Cheese roll-ups, toasted, 40
Cheese soufflé, 20
Cheese sticks, quick flaky, 19–20
Cheese, Swiss, and sardine, grilled, 40
Chicken blintzes, 26
Chicken liver filling, 43
Chicken liver, Oriental, 16, 829
Chicken livers en brochette, 831
Chicken, won tons with, 827–28
Chili tacos, cocktail, 26–27
Crab meat au diable, 24
Crab meat blintzes, 26
Crab meat filling, 42
Crab meat, flaky, 28–29
Crab meat soufflé, 22–23
Crab meat thermidor in pastry shells, 42–43

Croquettes, cocktail, 33–34
Dolmas, Turkish, 24–28
Egg Rolls, Cantonese, 824–25
Egg, scrambled, and salami filling, 43
Frankfurter-bacon, 38
Frankfurter filling, 43
Ham, baked hot molded glazed, 29–31
Ham bouches, 7
Ham and cheese soufflé, 21
Ham filling, 43
Ham rolls, toasted, 39–40
Hamburger, petit, 44
Hamburgers, cocktail, stuffed, 45
Italian cheese, 37
Italian meatball, 38
Italian-style sautéed shrimp, 36–37
Lobster blintzes, 26
Lobster filling, 42
Lobster à la Newburg, 41–42
Lobster tails, stuffed, gourmet, 9
Man's favorite, a, 43–44
Meat ball, Italian, 38
Meat balls, Swedish, 44–45
Meat cocktail strudel, 31–32
Mozzarella, 35–36
Mushroom bouches, 8
Mushroom meringues, 7
Mushroom pastry crescents or diamonds, 5–6
Mushroom soufflé, 21–22
Mushroom surprises, 6
Mushrooms in chafing dish, 7–8
Mushrooms, Yuon stuffed, 829–30
Noodle dough, 823
Noodle nests, Chinese fried, 823–24
Noodles, fried crisp, 824
Oriental, on bamboo sticks, 14–15
Oriental barbecued beef tenderloin, on bamboo sticks, 831–32
Oriental barbecued pork tenderloin, on bamboo sticks, 831–32
Oriental barbecued shrimp, on bamboo sticks, 832
Oriental chicken liver, 16, 829
Oriental delight, 16, 832–34
Oriental pagoda, 41
Oriental shrimp, 15, 828–29

Oysters, french-fried, remoulade, 46
Oysters Rockefeller, 24–25
Pancake-sausage, miniature, 38
Pastry squares, 32–33
Pizza, 14-inch, 765–66
Pizza, Neopolitan, 761–62
Pork and ribs, Cantonese barbecued, 13, 833–34
Pork tenderloin, Oriental barbecued, on bamboo sticks, 831–32
Roll-ups, brown 'n serve, 40
Roquefort puffs, 39
Salami, Italian, puffs, 37
Salami and scrambled egg filling, 43
Sardine and swiss cheese, grilled, 40
Sausage-bacon, 38–39
Sausage-pancake, miniature, 38
Seafood gourmet, in patty shells, 18–19
Seafood melty, 23–24
Shrimp-almond, Pancho, 9–10
Shrimp blintzes, 26
Shrimp, Cantonese fried, 12, 826–27
Shrimp de Jonghe, 34
Shrimp filling, 42
Shrimp, French-fried, remoulade, 45–46
Shrimp, French-fried, stuffed, 8
Shrimp Louisiana (in chafing dish), 10–11
Shrimp, Oriental, 15, 828–29
Shrimp, Oriental barbecued, on bamboo sticks, 832
Shrimp, Pancho, luncheon-style, 10
Shrimp, sautéed, garlic sauce, 830–31
Shrimp, sautéed, Italian style, 36–37
Sombreros, 25–26
Strudels, Cantonese cocktail, 31–32
Strudels, meat cocktail, 31–32
Swedish meat balls, 44–45
Tacos, cocktail chili, 26–27
Tamale-bacon, 38
Won ton, Cantonese filled, 826
Won tons, 13–14
Won tons, boiled, 825–26
Won tons with chicken, 827–28

Apple
Baked, 699
Big, fruit cocktail, 346
Blintzes, 653
Dumplings, 678–79
Petit fours, 553
Pie, custard meringue, 744–45
Pie, large, 753
Pie, small, 753
Pie, Streussel-top, 750–51
Slices, sautéed glazed, 660
Squares, Louise's, 753–54
Strudel, quick puff paste, 651–52
Turnovers, 649–50
Apricot
Bars, chewy pecan, 722
California fruit cake, 558
Canned, pie, California fruit, 746–47
and pear flambeau, 661
and pear gelatin mold, party-style, 425–26
and pineapple salad, 364
Sticks, meringue, 707–708
Tarts, 665
Vienna slices, 544
Arroz con Pollo, 225–27
Artichoke(s)
Bottoms, stuffed, 273
Buttered, 272
With cheese sauce, 273
Stuffed, 340
Stuffed, de luxe, 273-74
Asparagus, 274
in casserole, 409
and cheese casserole, puffy, 409
Deviled eggs in casserole, 413
Luncheon rolls in casserole, 410
and ham, creamed, noodle casserole, 404
Majestic in casserole, 410
Mold, 314–16
Mornay, broiled, 281
and mushroom omelet, Swiss, 261
and olive salad mold, 356
Omelet in casserole, 261–62
Salad, 362–63
and scrambled eggs soufflé, 268
Vegetables vinaigrette, 318–19
Avocado
Bird salad, 360–61
Cup, crab meat, salmon or tuna salad in, 358
Babas au Rhum, 529
Bacon
cooking, 195

and corn casserole, 413
drippings, 195
and fried eggs, 259
Bagels, 502–503
Baked Alaska, 590–91
Baklava, 658–59
Banana(s)
Cake squares, Mindy's party-size, 562
California fruit pie, 746–47
Cream pie, 740–41
Cream puff log, 670
French fruit flans, 642–43
Nut bread, 488
Oatmeal cookies, 706
Petit-four fruits and vegetables, 591–93
and pineapple salad, 363
Tarts, 666
Bar-Le-Duc French cream cheese mold, 450–51
Batter
Cantonese fritter, 11, 825
Crispy-crust, 214
Crispy-crust, for French-fried Cornish hens, 294
Crispy-crust, for shrimp and fish, 245
for French-fried fish, shrimp and onion rings, standard, 244–45
for French-fried onion rings, 294
for Pancho almond-shrimp appetizer, 10
for white wedding cake, 596–97
for whole egg cake, 598–99
Bean(s)
Baked, home-style, 275
Dilled, Louisiana, 276
Dilled, Louisiana, in casserole, 276
Green, fresh, 277
Green, fresh, salad, 360
Green, fresh, salad Neopolitan, 804
Green, with new boiled potatoes and onions, 277–78
Green, salad, German hot sweet-sour, 362
Kidney, red, salad, 359
Lima, fresh, 274
Lima, fresh, and corn baked in casserole, 275
Lima, and sausage casserole, 410
Lima, and spinach Continental, 278
Mushroom and carrot medley glace, 278–79
Navy, pasta with (Pasta and Fagioli), 811

with sautéed toasted almonds, 277
Sprouts, fresh, beef tenderloin with, 846–47
String, beef tenderloin with, 846–47
String, for chicken Vesuvio, 784
String, fresh green, 277
String, marinated, 279
String, medley, 279
Wax, fresh, 277
Wax, with new boiled potatoes and onions, 277–78
BEEF
general information, 117–31
cooking, 120–31
Corned, Premium, 118–19
Pro'Ten roasts, 117
special cuts, 119–20, 141
timetable for broiling, 131
timetable for roasting, 128
Balls, porcupine, in casserole, 396
Barbecued boneless rolled, 192
Barbecued hamburgers, 193
Barbecued short ribs, 192
Barbecued spareribs, 191-92
Barbecued steaks and chops, 193
Beefburger, green pepper, jumbo stuffed baked and broiled, 122
Beefburger, mushroom and green pepper, jumbo stuffed, 122
Beefburgers, green pepper, 149–50
Beefburgers, green pepper and mushrooms, 148–49
Beefburgers, mushroom, 148
Beefburgers, onion, 149
Bordelaise, 144
Calf's liver, baked whole, 194
Casserole à la duchesse, 394–95
Chateaubriand, 137–39
Cheeseburger, baked and broiled, jumbo, 147–48
Cheeseburger dinner or luncheon, broiled, 150
Cheeseburger pie, 152
Chicken-fried, 195
Chili con carne, 155
Corned, 139–40
Cornish pasties, 151

Creole round steak roll, 152
Fillet of, Wellington, 134–37
Frankfurter quails, 193
Frankfurters à la duchesse, 194
Gay Long, with broccoli, 845
Ground
  Cornish pasties, 151
  hamburgers, barbecued, 193
  hamburgers, deviled, 151
  hamburgers with smothered onions, 144–45
  meat balls, Italian, 795
  meat balls, Swedish, 44–45
  meat casserole, Neopolitan, 794–95
  meat loaf de luxe, 142–43
  meat and spaghetti casserole, Sicilian-style, 792–93
  meat patties, puffy, 153
  meat and rice, stuffed green peppers with, 792
  Pastitso in casserole, 397–98
  Polpettini alla Toscana, 793–94
  stuffed cabbage leaves, 142–43
Hamburger hors d'oeuvres, petit, 44
Hamburgers, barbecued, 193
Hamburgers, cocktail stuffed, 45
Hamburgers, deviled, 151
Hamburgers with smothered onions, 144–45
Italian meat balls, 795
Japanese Sukiyaki Dinner, 849–50
Liver, calf's, baked whole, 194
Mandarin-style, 837
Meat balls, Italian, 795
Meat balls, Swedish, 44–45
Meat casserole, Neopolitan, 794–95
Meat loaf de luxe, 142–43
Meat patties, puffy, 153
Meat and rice, stuffed green peppers with, 792
Meat and spaghetti casserole, Sicilian-style, 792–93
Oxtails, potted, 156
Pastitso in casserole, 397–98
Patties, puffy, 153

Polpettini alla Toscana, 793–94
Pot roast, 141–42
Roast, hash in casserole, baked, 395–96
Rolled, barbecued boneless, 192
Sauerbraten (American-style), 155–56
Short ribs, barbecued, 192
Spareribs, barbecued, 191–92
Steak, chicken-fried, 154
Steak, flank, Braccioli, Italian-style, 789
Steak, peppered, with sautéed mushrooms, Italian-style, 789–90
Steak, round, roll, Creole, 152
Steak, Swiss, 154
Steaks, barbecued, 193
Steaks, pan-broiled, 132–33
Steaks, Salisbury, broiled or sautéed, 145–46
Stew and biscuits in casserole, 393–94
Stew gourmet, 140–41
Stroganoff in chafing dish, 395
Stuffed cabbage leaves, 142–43
Sukiyaki Dinner, Japanese, 849–50
Swedish meat balls, 44–45
Tenderloin appetizer, Oriental barbecued, on bamboo sticks, 831–32
Tenderloin with fresh bean sprouts, 846
Tenderloin with pea pods, 845–46
Tenderloin with string beans, 846–47
Tenderloin, whole roasted, 133–34
Tongue-chicken mold, 470
Wellington, fillet of, 134–37
Beet greens, 262
Beets, 279–80
  Carmelized glazed, 279
  Pickled, 876
  Supreme, quick, 280
Biscuits
  Baking powder, 764–77
  Savory pinwheel, 389
  Savory tea, Continental-style, 477–78
  Shortcake, for berries and other fruits, 478
Bismarcks, 518
blackberry, fresh, glazed pie, 746

Blintzes, 26, 652–54
Blueberry
  Blintzes, 653
  Canned, Pie, 755
  Cupcakes, 561
  Fresh, glazed cheese pie torte, 747–48
  Fresh, glazed cheese tartlets, 748
  Fresh, glazed pie, 745
  Fresh, party-style mold, 429–30
  Fresh, pie, 755–56
  Glaze, 748
  Pancakes, 480–81
Bouches, hot, 7–8
Bouillon, Court, 239
  for poached fish, 249
Bread crumbs *see* Meat and Poultry Coatings
BREADS, QUICK, 475–91
  Biscuits, baking powder, 476–77
  Biscuits, savory tea, Continental-style, 477
  Biscuits, shortcake, 478
  Bread, banana nut, 488
  Bread, corn, 489
  Bread, corn, sticks, 489
  Bread, date and nut, 488–89
  Bread, date and nut, pineapple, 490
  Coffee cake, Danish cinnamon, 491
  Coffee Cake, Madelaine's, 491
  Gingerbread, 490
  Popovers, 485
  see also Doughnuts, non-yeast; Pancakes; Waffles
BREADS, YEAST, 492–531
  freezing, 494
  ingredients, 492–94
  Babas au Rhum, 529
  Bagels, 502–503
  Bagels, poppy seed or caraway, 503
  Bohemian rye, 505
  Braided rolls, 497
  Brioche, kneaded, luncheon or dinner rolls, 499–50
  Brioche rolls, quick French, 499
  Brioche Streussel-top coffee cake, 516
  Brioches, French, 498–99
  Bundt Kuchen, 514–15
  Butterhorn dinner or luncheon rolls, 497–98
  Cinnamon-raisin, 506–507
  Cloverleaf rolls, 496–97
  Coffee cake braid, 509–10

Coffee cake, brioche Streussel-top, 516
Coffee cake, Bundt Kuchen,
514-15
Coffee cake, cinnamon ball,
511-12
Coffee cake, croissant, flaky
thin, 515-16
Coffee cake, croissant rolls,
516-17
Coffee cake dough, Kuchen,
508
Coffee cake doughs, refrigerated, 509
Coffee cake loaf, butter-
cream filled, 511
Coffee cake orange knots,
515
Coffee cake, pecan, filled,
509-10
Coffee cake rolls, butter-
cream yeast, individual,
512
Coffee cake rolls, croissant,
516-17
Coffee cake squares, filled,
513-14
Coffee cake, Swedish tea
ring, 510
Coffee cake, walnut, filled,
509-10
Coffee cake, wreath, Yule-
tide, 512-13
Corn-meal yeast pan, 498
Cream cheese-Kolachy
yeast pastries, 522-23
Croissant, flaky, luncheon
or dinner rolls, 500-501
Danish pastries, basic
dough for, 525-26
Danish pastry braid, 528
Danish pastry crescents, 528
Danish pastry horns, 528
Danish pastry luncheon or
dinner rolls, 527
Danish pastry pinwheels,
527
Danish pastry snails, 527
Danish swirl, 526-27
Dough, basic yeast, for
glazed butterscotch
pecan rolls, butter-
horns, sweet rolls, 521-
22
English muffins, 501-502
French (home-style), 505-
506
French, anchovy-garlic, 814
French, garlic flavored, 814
French, parmesan tomato
garlic, 814
Honey glacéed strawberry
yeast rolls, 521
Hot cross buns, 503-504

Italian, anchovy-garlic, 814
Italian, garlic flavored, 814
Knotted rolls, 497
Old-fashioned rolls, 497
Parker house rolls, 496
Pecan roll loaf, 524
Pecan roll ring, 524
Pecan rolls, individual
medium, 523
Pineapple-orange yeast
rolls, glacéed, 519-20
Raisin-cinnamon, 506-507
Rolls, basic recipe for yeast
raised, 495-96
Sour cream kippel yeast pas-
tries, 520-21
Twin rolls, 496-97
White, plain, 504
Whole wheat, 507
see also Doughnuts, yeast;
French toast; pastries
Broccoli
Baked, à la Parmesan, 800
Gay Long beef with, 845
and ham roll-ups in casse-
role, 401-402
Mold, 314-16
Mornay, broiled, 281
Parmesan, sautéed, 800-801
Brownies, chocolate, 690
Brussels sprouts, 281-82
breaded and deep-fried, 282
sautéed, 282
Butter
for browning, 323
cinnamon, 543
clarified, 328-29
kneaded, 323
L'Aiglon, for Crepes Su-
zette, 479, 645
Maitre d'hotel, 329-30
Whipped, 79
see also Sauces: butter
Butter molding
paddling of grapes, 874
paddling of lilies, 873
paddling of roses, 874
Butters and Spreads, 78-82
see also Butter; Mayon-
naise; Salad Dressings
Cabbage, 314
Chinese, 314
Chinese pea pods with,
847-48
Green, 282
and onions sautéed, 188,
282-83
Red, 283
Sautéed, 188
Cake decorating, professional,
623-29
CAKE(S), BUTTER, 531-63
general information, 531-
38

Almond slices, toasted, Ital-
ian, 820-21
Apricot, California, fruit,
558
Apricot slices, Vienna, 544
Banana, squares, Mindy's
party-size, 562
Biscotti Croccanti, 820-21
Blueberry cupcakes, 561
Brownies, chocolate, 690
Chocolate, Continental
glossy, 690-91
Cinnamon, 542-43
Cinnamon cupcakes, tiny,
543
Coconut, 561-62
Coffee see BREADS,
QUICK: Coffee cakes;
BREADS, YEAST:
Coffee cake
Cupcakes, blueberry, 561
Cupcakes, cinnamon, tiny,
543
Date slices, Vienna, 543-44
Devil's food, 549
Devil's food, party-size,
604-605
Devil's food, round, 550
Fennel, Italian, 821
Florentine pastries, choco-
late, 547
Forentine pastry squares,
545-46
Florentine pastry squares,
individual, 546
Form, Dorothy's special, 554
Form, poppy seed, 560
Fruit, California Apricot,
558
Fruit, dark rich, 556-57
Fruit, miniature, 558-59
Fruit, petit fours, 558-59
Gold, large, 550-51
Gold, small, 551
Italian Fennel, 821
Lady Baltimore, 552
Layer, buttermilk, 545
Layer, plain, 544-45
Pecan squares, grilled, 561
Petit fours, 552
Petit fours, fruit topped,
party-style, 552-54
Pudding, plum, 558-59
Pudding, plum, flaming
English, 559-60
Rainbow, 547-48
Rainbow, large, 548
Spiced squares, 548-49
Squares, Banana, Mindy's
party-size, 562
Squares, coffee cake, filled,
513-14
Squares, Florentine pastry,
545-46

Squares, Florentine pastry, individual, 546
Squares, pecan, grilled, 561
Squares, spiced, 548–49
Vienna apricot slices, 544
Vienna date slices, 543–44
Walnut, 561–62
Yummy, Mindy's party-size, 562–63
Zuppa Inglese, 819–20
CAKE(S), SPONGE (FRENCH PASTRY, ANGEL FOOD), 563–94
general information, 563–68
Angel food, 570
Angel food, chocolate, 571–72
Angel food, springtime violet, 570–71
Angel food, two-tone, 571
Baked Alaska, 591
Baked Alaska, large, 590–91
Basket, 585–87
Bavarian ice box mold, lady finger strawberry, 594
Corn-on-the-cob pastry, large, 583–85
Diploma, large, 601
Fourth of July, 589
French bouché pastry roses, 588–89
French pastries, chocolate, individual, 572
French pastry, large, 568–70
Horn of plenty party, 582–83
Ice cream roll, chocolate, 572–73
Lady fingers, 593–94
Lady fingers, strawberry Bavarian ice box mold, 594
Petit-four fruits and vegetables, 591–93
Roll, chocolate ice cream, 572–73
Roll, George Washington, 572–73
Roll, yellow, 573
Strawberry Bavarian ice box mold, lady fingers, 594
Upside-down, golden, 574
Cakes, Cheese see Cheese cake
Cakes, Coffee see BREADS, QUICK: Coffee cake; BREADS, YEAST: Coffee cake
CAKES, SHAPED AND SPECIAL OCCASION
Basket, 585–87

Corn-on-the-cob pastry, large, 583–85
Devil's food, party-size, 604–605
Diploma, large, 601
Easter egg, 605–606
Easter egg, ice cream, large, 607
Easter eggs, ice cream, individual, 606
Easter lamb, 607–608
French bouché pastry roses, 588–89
French pastry, 569–70
Horn of plenty party, 582–83
Hyacinth flower pot, 600
Lady fingers, 593–94
Lady fingers strawberry Bavarian ice box mold, 594
Large, 594–95
Oblong party, all-occasion, 601–602
Petits fours (Lady Baltimore Cake), 552
Pineapple-shaped, party, 602–604
Wedding, white, made in 4-tier tinwear pans, 596–97
Wedding, white, made in 5-tier aluminum pans, 597-98
Whole egg, made in 4-tier tinware pans, 599
Whole egg, made in 5-tier aluminum pans, 598–99
Calzoni squares, 34–35, 764–65
Cantaloupe
Melon birds, 364
Melon boats, 367–68
Salad basket, 345
Carrot(s), 283
Bean, mushroom and, medley glacé, 278–79
Carmelized glazed, 284
and creamed peas à la duchesse, 405
Deviled eggs in casserole, 413
Julienne glazed, 284–85
mold, baked, 283
Vegetables vinaigrette, 318–19
Whole glazed, 284
Whole toasted, 283–84
CASSEROLES, 374–417
freezing, 2, 376–77, 890–92
Asparagus, 409
Asparagus and cheese, puffy, 408

Asparagus and ham, creamed, noodle, 404
Asparagus luncheon rolls, 411
Asparagus majestic, 410
Asparagus omelet, 261–62
Asparagus and tuna, 385
Bacon and corn, 413
Bean, lima, and sausage, 410
Beans, dilled, Louisiana, 276
Beans, lima, fresh, and corn, baked, 275
Beef, à la duchesse, 394–95
Beef stew and biscuits, 393
Blintzes, 652
Broccoli and ham roll-ups, 401–402
Butterscotch custard, 679–80
Carrots and creamed peas, à la duchesse, 405
Cheese and asparagus, puffy, 409
Chicken, breast of, Epicurean, 392–93
Chicken creole, 391
Chicken custard, 388
Chicken Monte Carlo, baked, 387–88
Chicken-mushroom Mornay, 388–89
Chicken timbales in green pea, 390
Corn and bacon, 413
Corn and fresh lima beans, baked, 275
Egg and potato scallop, 411
Eggplant Grand'mère, 412
Eggplant, Louise's Italian, 802
Eggs, deviled, 413
Eggs, deviled, and shrimp, Mornay, 380
Eggs and spinach Florentine baked, 264
Haddock, broiled fillet of, Piquant, 386
Haddock, fillet of, Mornay, 384–85
Halibut, broiled, and cheese, 386–87
Ham and asparagus noodle, creamed, 404
Ham and duchesse sweet potatoes, 402–403
Ham and green noodle, 401
Ham luncheonettes, party-style, 400–401
Ham and spinach roll-ups, 182–83
Ham and zucchini, 807–808
Lamb chops, baked shoulder, and potatoes, 190
Lamb, Neopolitan, 791–92

Lobster Oriental, 377–78
Lobster thermidor, 253–54
Macaroni, baked, 417
Macaroni, baked elbow, and pork sausages, 400
Macaroni and pork, Louisiana, 399
Macaroni-salmon, 383
Macaroni sizzling squares, baked, 403–404
Meat, Neopolitan, 794–95
Meat and spaghetti, Sicilian-style, 792–93
Noodle, creamed ham and asparagus, 404
Noodle, green, and ham, 401
Noodle, green, soufflé, 415–16
Noodle, green, and tuna, 385–86
Noodles Romanoff, 416
Pastitso, 397–98
Perch, broiled fillets of, Piquant, 386
Pork chops and potatoes, baked, 190
Pork, curried, 398
Pork and macaroni, Louisiana, 399
Pork sausages and baked elbow macaroni, 400
Pork shoulder and mushroom, 399–400
Pork tenderloin and mushroom, 400
Potato and egg scallop, 411
Potato, new, 308
Potatoes Delmonico, 305
Potatoes Vesuvio, 304
Quick, 417
Salmon, 383–84
Salmon-macaroni, 383
Sausage and lima bean, 409–10
Savoy, 396–97
Shrimp and deviled eggs Mornay, 380
Shrimp jambalaya, 381
Shrimp and rice, Creole, in individual, 382–83
Shrimp supreme, 381–82
Spaghetti and meat, Sicilian-style, 792–93
Spaghetti, Neopolitan, 793
Spinach, 407
Spinach and egg, curried, 407
Spinach and eggs Florentine, baked, 264
Spinach and ham roll-ups, 182–83
Spinach timbales and ham, 180–81

Sweet potato fluff, 414–15
Sweet potatoes meringue, 309–10
Tuna and asparagus, 385–86
Tuna-green noodle, 385–86
Tuna-mushroom, 384
Turkey and dressing, 392
Turkey, breast of, Epicurean, 392–93
Turkey timbales in green pea, 390
Veal, baked, 174
Veal chops and potatoes, baked, 190
Veal chops and zucchini, 806–807
Vegetable and mushroom medley, 406
Vegetable, Continental, 809–10
Vegetables, mixed, Mornay, 408
Zucchini and ham, 807–808
Zucchini omelet, 808
Zucchini stew, company-style, 319
Zucchini and veal chops, 806–807
Cauliflower, 285
Centerpiece on vegetable platter, 285–86
Sautéed, 286
Scalloped, 285
Caviar
and egg canapés, 67
"grape" hors d'oeuvres, 68
and Gruyère hors d'oeuvres, 66
Celery, 286
creamed, 286
CHAFING DISHES
preparing, 375–76
Beef Stroganoff in, 395
Chicken-mushroom Mornay in, 388–89
Crab meat au diable, 378
Crab meat Creole, 378–79, 381
Crab meat and rice, creamed, 379
Lobster Creole, 381
Lobster Oriental, 377–78
Shrimp Louisiana, 379
CHEESE
American, cocktail strudel, 32
Appetizers, Italian, 37
and asparagus casserole, puffy, 409
and crab meat ring mold, 552
Cream, appetizer, 2
Cream, mold, Bar-Le-Duc French, 450–51

Cream, mold, pineapple, 448–49
Cream, rolled, toasted, 40–41
Fruits, stuffed glazed, 441–42
Gruyère, and ham Quiche Lorraine, 94
and halibut casserole, baked, 386–87
Ham and mushroom French toast sandwiches, 265–66
and ham souffle hors d'oeuvres, 21
Italian, appetizers, 37
Mozzarella in Carozza, 798
Mozzarella hors d'oeuvres, 35
Ricotta-sausage calzoni, 35
Ricotta spinach croquettes, 812
Roll-ups, toasted, 40
Roquefort puffs, 39
Scamorza omelet, Italian, 797–98
Souffle hors d'oeuvres, hot, 20
Sticks, 650
Sticks, quick flaky, 19–20
Swiss, French toast sandwiches, 266
Swiss, and sardine appetizers, grilled, 40
see also Cheese Cake; Fondues; Pizza; Rarebits
Cheese Cake
Cream, 632–33
Cream, Cookies, Vienna, 694
Cream, dessert, Bavarian, 636–38
Cream, New-York-type, 634–36
Cream, small, 631–32
Cream, strudel, 657
Hollywood two-tone, 630–31
Parmesan, Vienna fingers, 694
Pie torte, fresh blueberry glazed, 747–48
and pineapple glaze torte, 639–40
Sour cream, 633–34
Tartlets, fresh blueberry glazed, 748
Torte, magic, 638
Cherry
Bing, canned, pie, California fruit, 746–47
Black bing dark sweet, tarts, 666
Canned, pie, 755

Frozen, pie, glazed, 746
Flambeau, ice cream, 660
Light sweet, tarts, Royal
    Anne, 666
Macaroons, Continental sur-
    prise, 702
and peach flambeau, 660
Strudel, 647
Tartlets, English, 721–22
CHICKEN
general information, 196–
    202, 206–207
timetable for roasting, 208
trussing, 207
types, 196-97
Almond Din, 836–37
Arroz con Pollo, 225–27
Barbecued, 221–22
Blintzes, 26
Breast of, Alfredo, 779-80
Breast of, Alfredo, sautéed,
    780–81
Breast of, Epicurean, in cas-
    serole, 392–93
Breast of, Romanoff, 217–18
Breast of, sesame, cold hors
    d'oeuvres, 71–72
Breasts, 200–202
Breasts for fancy dishes,
    209–10
Breasts Imperial, 220–21
Breasts, sautéed (braised),
Broiled, 217
Buffet log, molded poinset-
    tia, 457–58
Butter-crisp baked, 216
Cacciatori, 781–82
Chaud-froid mold, 461–62
Cooked, souffle, 268
Cornish hens, broiled, 232–
    33
Cornish hens, crispy-crust
    French-fried, 233–34
Cornish hens, gourmet style,
    229–31
Cornish hens, Oriental, 233
Cornish hens, Oriental,
    roasted, 843
Cornish hens, top-of-the-
    stove, braised, 845–46
Creole in casserole, 391
Croquettes, 223–24
Custard casserole, 388
Deep-fat fried, breaded, 214
Deep-fat fried, crunchy-
    crust, 215–16
Deep-fried, 213–14
Dinner, Bali Bali, Canton-
    ese, boned, 839–40
Dinner Vesuvio, 783–84
French-fried, crispy-crust
    (in deep fat), 213–14
Fricasee, 227–28
Kiev, 218–19

A la King, 222–23
Legs and thighs Alfredo,
    782
Liver
    appetizer, a man's favor-
        ite, 43–44
    appetizer, Oriental, 16,
        829
    en brochette, filling, 43
    mushroom pate, 137
    pate hors d'oeuvres cen-
        terpiece, 56–57
Milano, 784
Monte Carlo in casserole,
    baked, 387–88
and mushroom Mornay in
    casserole, 388–89
Oven-fried, breaded, braised,
    215
Pan-fried, breaded, braised,
    215
Pan-fried in the rough, 211
Pie, 228–29
in the pot with vegetables,
    220
Regal in casserole, 391–92
and rice curry, company-
    style, 224–25
Salad mold, 467–68
Saad superb, molded, 354
Slices, Cantonese, 840
Squab appetizer, Cantanese,
    830
Stew, Italian-style, 785
Tetrazzini, 782–83
Timbales in green pea cas-
    serole, 391
and tongue mold, 470
Vesuvio, 783–84
Whole roasted, 207–208
Whole simmered, 211–12
Won tons with, 827–28
see also POULTRY
Chili
con carne, 115
Tacos, cocktail, 26–27
Chives, 286
Chocolate
Almond turtles, 688–89
Brownies, 690
Cake, angel food, 571–72
Cakes, Continental glossy,
    690–91
Chip chewies, 693
Chips, crunchy, 725
Cookies, log, 691–92
Crunchy chips, 725
Filled walnut torte, 578–79
Filling, special, for cookies
    and small cakes, 691
Florentine pastries, 547
Fondue, Swiss milk, 92
French pastries, individual,
    572

Ice cream roll, 572–73
Macaroon cigarettes, 716
Macaroon logs, 716
Macaroon rosettes, 716
Macaroon swirls, 716
Macaroons, 715
Macaroons with rosette
    tips, 716
Mellow bars, 692
Mint refrigerator torte,
    640–41
Mocha torte, Continental,
    580–81
Mousse in sherbet glasses,
    681
Pecan turtles, 688–89
Sauce, velvety, 669
Swiss milk, fondue, 92
and vanilla cream pie, 734
and vanilla cream torte,
    540
Chowders *see* SOUPS AND
    CHOWDERS
Coffee, 860–61
Coffee cake *see* BREADS,
    QUICK: Coffee cake;
    BREADS, YEAST: Cof-
    fee cake
COOKIES, 682–730
Almond chocolate turtles,
    688–89
Almond, Oriental, 699–700,
    854–55
Almond paste crescents, 715
Almond paste drops, 715
Almond paste pears, 714–15
Almond paste strawberries,
    715
Anchovy fingers, Vienna,
    694
Apricot pecan bars, chewy,
    722
Apricot meringue sticks,
    707–708
Banana oatmeal, 706
Bars, chewy apricot pecan,
    722
Bars, crunchy cocoa-filbert,
    723–24
Bars, crunchy peanut, 724–
    25
Bars, date, 723
Basket, 695–96
Brown sugar, 706–707
Brownies, chocolate, 690
Butter, 683–84
Butter crescents, pecan,
    692–93
Butter crescents, walnut,
    692–93
Butter, lady finger, 726
Butter, quick dainty, 684
Butterhorn pastries, rich
    flaky, 729–30

Butterscotch filled wafers, 687–88
Butterscotch pyramids, 689
Canes, Christmas cooky, 684
Checkerboard, quick, 704
Cherry surprise macaroons, Continental, 702
Chocolate cakes, Continental glossy, 690–91
Chocolate chip chewies, 693
Chocolate logs, 691–92
Chocolate mellow bars, 692
Christmas bells, 686
Christmas leaves, 686
Christmas trees, 686
Cinnamon snaps, Louise's, 705
Coconut macaroon, 710–11
Cream cheese, Vienna, 694
Crunchy chips, 725
Crunchy cocoa-filbert bars, 723–24
Czechoslovakian pastry boats, 708–709
Czechoslovakian pastry forms, small assorted, 709
Date bars, 723
Date-pecan, 707
Dream meltaway slices, 720
Finnish pecan or walnut dreams, 727
Fruitlet, fancy, 728–29
Gingerbread-man, 725
Hazlenut crescents, jumbo, 698
Hazlenut filled macaroons, 697
Hazlenut logs, 697
Hazlenut macaroons, 696–97
Hazlenut mushrooms, 698
Hazlenut rosette, 702–703
Holiday turkey, 686–87
Horn of plenty, 695
Lady finger butter, 726
Lady Windermere's fan, 700
Leaf, Continental, 716–17
Leaf, party-style, 709–10
Macaroon, basic almond paste, 713–14
Macaroon, chocolate, cigarettes, 716
Macaroon, chocolate, logs, 716
Macaroon, chocolate, rosettes, 716
Macaroon, coconut, 710–11
Macaroon grapes, 713
Macaroon pears, 712
Macaroon rings, Continental raspberry, 702
Macaroon strawberries, coconut, 711

Macaroon swans, 712–13
Macaroon swirls, chocolate, 716
Macaroons, chocolate, with rosette tips, 716
Macaroons, Continental cherry surprise, 702
Macaroons, hazlenut, 696–97
Macaroons, hazlenut filled, 697
Marble, 704
Marzipan slices, 718–20
Muerbes, 683–84
Oatmeal banana, 706
Old-fashioned, Grandma's, 703
Oriental almond, 699–700
Parmesan fingers, Vienna, 694
Peach meringue sticks, 707–708
Peanut bars, crunchy, 724–25
Peanut butter, 710
Pecan bars, chewy apricot, 722
Pecan butter crescents, 692–93
Pecan chocolate turtles, 688–89
Pecan-date, 707
Pecan dough, basic short, 701
Pineapple fingers, Vienna, 693–94
Pineapple-shaped, 696
Raspberry hearts, 701
Raspberry macaroon rings, Continental, 702
Revani, 718
Rye flour dainty wafer, 705–706
Solid centers, 704–705
Strudlicky, 726–27
Tartlets, English Cherry, 721–22
Tartlets, Frangipan, 720–21
Tea biscuits, savory, Continental-style, 815
Thimble, Sonia's, 701–702
Toffee squares, 727
Valentine tartlets, 700–701
Vienna anchovy fingers, 694
Vienna cream cheese, 694
Vienna parmesan fingers, 694
Vienna pineapple fingers, 693–94
Walnut butter crescents, 692–93
Walnut dreams, Finnish, 727
Wreaths, Christmas, 685–86

Wreaths, double Christmas, 686
Yuletide, 685
Corn
  and bacon casserole, 413–14
  creamed fresh, off cob, 287
  on cob, 287
  and eggs, scrambled, 264–65
  Fritters, 287
  Frozen, steamed, 288
  Griddle cakes, 482-83
  and ham fritters, 288
  and lima beans, baked in casserole, 275
  Oysters, 483
  Soufflé, 268–69
  Steamed, 287
Cornish hens see CHICKEN: Cornish hens
Crab meat
  Appetizers, flaky, 28-29
  au diable, 24, 378
  Blintzes, 26
  Chaud-froid seafood mold, 458–61
  and cheese ring mold, 452
  Creole, 378–79
  Filling appetizer, 29
  Pilaf, 250
  Quiche Lorraine, 95
  and rice, creamed (in chafing dish), 379
  Salad in avocado cup, 359
  Salad ravigote, 61–62
  Salad ravigote, molded, 351–52
  Salad à la Reefer, molded, 352–53
  Seafood basket hors d'oeuvres, 73–74
  Souffle, 22–23, 269
Cranberry
  and calavo salad with turkey slices, 367
  Fluff mold, 433
  Gelatin mold, 431–32
  Molds, individual, 431
  and raspberry mold, yuletide star, 434
Cream
  Filling, butterscotch, for fresh peach pie, 750
  Filling, French, 669
  Filling for tarts, 664
  Pie, banana, 740–41
  Pie, Boston, 587–88
  Pie, chocolate-vanilla, 734–35
  Pie, fresh peach, 755
  Pie, orange, 742
  Pie, pineapple, 747
  Puff log, 670
  Puff log, banana, 670

Puff log, raspberry, 670
Puff log, strawberry, 670
Puff swans, 668
Torte, Mathon's vanilla, 538
Whipped, torte, Viennese
  nut, 577–78
CREOLE DISHES
Chicken, in casserole, 391
Crab meat (in chafing
  dish), 381
Halibut steak, 247
Lobster, 381
Okra stew, 294
Sauce, 335
Shrimp, in chafing dish, 380
Shrimp and rice in indi-
  vidual casseroles, 382–
  83
Veal cutlets, 164
Crepes Suzette, 478–79, 644–
  45
Croquettes
Chicken, 223–24
Cocktail, 33–34
Potato, Italian-style, 483
Ricotta spinach, 812
Croutons, 346
Cucumber(s), 288
Salad mold, 471
in sour cream, 289
CURRY DISHES
Chicken and rice, company-
  style, 224–25
Lamb stew, 159
Pork casserole, 398
Rice for French fried Corn-
  ish hens, 234
Spinach and egg casserole,
  405–406
Custard
Butterscotch, in casserole,
  679–80
Chicken, in casserole, 391
Continental buttercream,
  617
Eggnog, cup desserts, Yule-
  tide, 743
La Neige dessert, 670–71
Rice, date, nut and raisin,
  680
Soft French, 670–71
Top of the stove, 669
Dandelion greens, 314
Danish pastry *see* BREADS,
  YEAST: Danish pastry
Date
Bars, 723
and nut bread, 488–89
and nut bread, pineapple,
  490
Nut and raisin rice custard,
  680
and pecan cookies, 707
Slices, Vienna, 543–44

DESSERT(S), 630–81
Cherry ice cream flambeau,
  660
Crunchy lemon, 661
Crunchy orange, 661
Crepes Suzette, 644–45
La Neige, 670–71
Peach and apricot flambeau,
  661
Peach and cherry flambeau,
  660
Peach flambeau, 660
Peachy crisp, made with
  fresh peaches, 661
Ring, Crunchy, 662
Sautéed glazed apple slices,
  660
Strawberry almond pan-
  cakes, 648–49
Strawberry almond pan-
  cakes, 648–49
Swiss milk chocolate fon-
  due, 92
Yuletide eggnog custard
  cup, 743
see also BREADS, CAKES,
  PIES, Puddings, etc.
Dips, 84–87 *see also* Butters
  and Spreads; Dips, hot
Dips, hot, 95–97
Dolmas, Turkish, 27–28
DOUGH
Biscuit, baking powder, 393
Chou paste, 667
Coffee cake Kuchen, 508
Cookie, handles for cake
  basket, 586–87
for croissant rolls, flaky,
  500
for Danish pastries, basic,
  525-26
for doughnuts, basic raised,
  517
for hot hors d'oeuvres,
  basic pastry, 4–5
Kuchen, 508
Pecan, basic short, 701
Pie, for open-face pie,
  basic, 732–33
Pie, for 8-inch pie plate, 733
Pie, for 9-inch pie plate, 734
Pie, for 2-crust pie, basic,
  751–52
Pie, for 2-crust 8-inch pie
  plate, 752
Pie shells, individual, 733
Pizza, Neopolitan, 761–63
Puff paste, classic, 645–47
Puff paste, new easy quick,
  654
Short pecan, basic, 701
for tarts, Muerbe Teig,
Yeast, basic, for glazed
  butterscotch pecan rolls,

butterhorns, sweet rolls,
  521–22
Doughnuts, non-yeast
Buttermilk balls or puffs,
  487–88
Buttermilk fried, 486–87
French, 485–86
Smetana puffs, 487
Doughnuts, yeast
Basic dough for, 517
Bismarcks, 518
Dutch apple cake, 518
Knots, 518–19
DRESSINGS *see* STUFF-
  INGS AND DRESS-
  INGS
DRESSINGS, SALAD *see*
  SALAD DRESSINGS
Duck
Cantonese braised, 844
Cantonese pressed, 841–42
Roast, gourmet style, 231–
  32
see also POULTRY
Dumplings
Apple, 678–79
Fluffy baking powder, 227–
  28
Eggnog
Custard cup desserts, Yule-
  tide, 743
Mold, Yuletide, 447–48
Eggplant
Balkan lamb with, 159
Casserole, Louise's Italian,
  802
Grand'mère, 412
Halves, stuffed, 289
Slices, pan-fried, 289–90
Vegetables and meat stew,
  290
EGG(S), 256–69
cooking hints, 256–57
determining quality, 257
sizes and colors, 257–58
and asparagus, in casserole,
  261–62
and bacon canapes, 66
Benedict, 264
Birds, deviled, 47–48
and caviar canapés, 67
Coddled, 346
Colored Easter, 48
Coronation appetizers, 67
Crab apple appetizers, 48–
  49
Deviled, 413
Deviled fancy stuffed, 48
Deviled, and shrimp Mor-
  nay in casserole, 380–
  81
Foo Yong, 842
Fried (or sautéed), 258–59
Fried, and bacon, 259

Fried, basic, 260
and green peppers, 298
Hard-cooked, 46–47
Nests à la Rosinia, fluffy, 263–64
Omelets, 260–63
Fluffy, 262–63
luncheon, or supper, 260–61
potato, Italian, 803–804
Scamorza, Italian, 797–98
Swiss mushroom asparagus, 261
Zucchini, in casserole, 808
Poached, 258
and potato scallop in casserole, 411
Roses, 49
Salad mold, 468
Scrambled, 259–60
Scrambled, and asparagus, 265
Scrambled, and corn, 264–65
Spinach, curried, casserole, 405–406
and spinach Florentine baked in casserole, 264
Supreme, 263
and tomatoes, peppers pan-fried with, 298
Tulip, 47
see also French toast; SOUFFLE DISHES
Endive, 290, 314
Boiled, Italian-style, 290–91
with spareribs, Italian-style, 291
Escarole, 291, 314
Fennel cakes, Italian, 821
FILLINGS FOR DESSERTS, PASTRIES, PIES, ETC.
Almond paste, 528
Almond paste, for marzipan, 701
Apple, for blintzes, 653
Apple, for German pancakes, 480
Apple pie, 750
Apple, for strudel, 652
Apple, for turnover, 649–50
Apricot, for cookies, tartlets, etc., 701
Blueberry, for blintzes, 653
Blueberry, uncooked, for German pancakes, 480
Boston cream, 588
Brandy pie, 740
Buttercream, Hungarian, 616

Buttercream for yeast rolls, 512
Butterscotch cream, for fresh peach pie, 750
for cheese cake, 631
for cheese cake, Bavarian cream dessert, 637–38
for cheese cake, cream, 632–33
for cheese cake, New-York-type, 635
for cheese cake, sour cream, 633–34
for cheese-pineapple glaze torte, 640
for cheese torte, magic, 638
Chocolate mint, for refrigerator torte, 641
Chocolate, for walnut torte, 578–79
Continental, for savory tea biscuits, 477
Continental, for tea biscuits, 815
Cottage cheese, for blintzes, 653
Cream, Boston, 587–88
Cream, French, 669, 741
Cream, French, for flan, 643–44
Cream for rice mold, 854
Cream, for tarts, 664
for cream torte, vanilla, 539
Frangipan, for tartlets, 721
French cream, 669, 741
French cream, for flan, 643–44
Jam, for flaky horns, 730
Meringue for Strudlicky, 726–27
for mincemeat pie, 750
Nut, roasted, 688
Peach, fresh, for blintzes, 654
Peach, fresh, for German pancakes, 480
Pineapple, for cake, 603
for pineapple-cheese glaze torte, 640
Pineapple, for coffee cake braid, 509
Pineapple glaze, for coffee cake squares, 514
Preserve, for flaky horns, 730
Raspberry, for blintzes, 653
Raspberry, uncooked for German pancakes, 480
Ricotta, for cake torte, 816
Ricotta, for cannoli, 819
for ricotta pie torte, 817
for Ricotta whipped cream pie, 818
for rum pie, 740

Southern pecan pie, 740
Strawberry, for blintzes, 653
Strawberry, uncooked, for German pancakes, 480
Sugar cinnamon, for yummy cake, 563
Tartlets, English cherry, 722
for tarts, cream, 664
for Valentine salad mold, 456–57
for Vienna apricot slices, 544
for Vienna date slices, 544
FILLINGS FOR MEAT, POULTRY, SEAFOOD, VEGETABLES, ETC.
Cervelat, 43
Chicken, for Cannelloni, French-style, 776
Chicken liver, 43
for chicken pie, 228–29
Crab meat, 29, 42
for egg rolls, 825
Egg, scrambled, and salami, 43
for eggplant Grand'mère, 413
Frankfurter, hot, 43
Green pepper, 146
Green pepper beefburger, 150
Green pepper and mushroom, 148
Ham, 43
Lobster, 42
Lobster tail, 42
Meat, Cantonese, 830
Meat, for pastry squares, 33
Meat and spinach, for ravioli, 773
Meat strudel, 31–32
Meat, for tamales, 411–12
Mozzarella, hors d'-oeuvres, 36
Mushroom, 148
Mushroom and green pepper, 147
Onion, 149
for pineapple mold, 428–29
for pineapple-raspberry mold, 437
for pizza Neopolitan, 763
for potatoes Vesuvio, 304
for raspberry-pineapple, mold, 437
Ricotta, for cannelloni (manicotti), 775
Ricotta, for lasagna, 774
Ricotta, for ravioli, 773
Ricotta-sausage for calzoni, 35, 765
Roquefort, 177

Salami and scrambled egg, 43
Seafood gourmet, special, 19
for Shamrock mold, 422–23
Shrimp, 8, 42
Spinach and meat, for ravioli, 722–73
Strudel, Cantonese, 31
Wonton meat, 14, 830
FISH
breaded, deep-fried, 244–45
fillets, marinade for, 236–37
pan-fried, 345–46
poached, 248–49
soufflé, 269
steaks, baked with bread stuffing, 243
see also Haddock, Halibut, Perch, Pompano, Salmon, Sardine, Trout, Tuna, White-fish
Fondues
preparing, 88–90
American cheese, 91
Beef, bourguignon, 91–92
Cheddar cheese, 91
Swiss cheese, classic, 90–91
Swiss milk chocolate, 92
additional recipes, 92
Frankfurter(s)
Baked macaroni sizzling squares, 403–404
à la duchesse, 194
Quails, 193
Rarebit, 99
Freezing, home
general rules, 880–84
recommended storage periods, 882–84
wrapping for, 881–82
Dairy products, 888–90
Fish and shellfish, 887–88
Meat, cured, 885–86
Meat, fresh, 884–85
Prepared foods, 890–900
breads, cakes, pies, etc., 896–900
hors d'oeuvres, 895–96
pasta dishes, 893–94
potato dishes, 892–93
soups, 894
stews, casseroles, etc., 890–92
French toast
California, 266
Grilled, 265
Sandwiches, ham, cheese, and mushroom, 265–66
Sandwiches, Swiss cheese, 266
Fritters
Batter for Cantonese, 11
Corn, 287–88

Corn and ham, 288
Frog's legs provincial, sautéed, 248
Frying, deep-fat, 8–9, 123–24, 184, 301–302
Garlic, 291
Garnish for special occasions, 434, 438
Gelatin see MOLDS
Gherkin fan appetizers, 69
GLAZE FOR DESSERTS, PIES, ETC.
for almond paste cookies, 714
Apricot, for cookies, tartlets, etc., 701
Blueberry, 748
for California fruit pie, 746–47
Caramel, for yeast rolls, 520
Cherry, for top of cheese cake, 636
Fruit syrup, for tarts, 664
for pineapple-cheese glaze torte, 640
Raspberry, for top of cheese cake, 636
Strawberry, fresh, for top of cheese cake, 635–36
for strawberry pie, 745
Strawberry, for top of cheese cake, 636
for strawberry torte, 582
Syrup, for pecan rolls, 522
Water, for tarts, 665
GLAZE FOR MEAT, SEAFOOD, MOLDS, ETC.
for chateaubriand, mushrooms, and top of stuffed artichokes, 340
for chateaubriands, 139
Clear, 55, 239
Clear aspic, 460–61
Clear, for molds, etc., 464
French dressing, 58
for fruit mold, 431–32
Gravy for mock chicken legs, 167
Gravy for turkey, 206
for ham, 178
for orange daisies, decorating hams, 179–80
Orange, special, for sweet potato fluff, 332, 414–15
Oriental, 41
for shrimp farci, 76
Tomato, for lobster mold, 465
for Vegetables, 279
Grape
Frosted, 435–36
Juice salad mousse, cartwheel, 443–44

and pear salad, 365
Purple, mold, 434–36
GRAVY
browned flour for, 322
butter for margarine for browning, 323
preparing, 321–24
au jus, 325–26
Brown, 325
Brown, thick, for beef stew in casserole, 394
Brown, thick, à la duchesse, 394–95
Brown, thickened, 326
for chicken legs, 332
Chicken pan, 331
Chicken pan, quick, 209
Chicken, quick, 209
from chicken stock, 331
for duckling, roast, 231
for Egg Foo Yong, quick, 842–43
Glaze, for chicken legs, 332
Glaze, for roasted turkey, 330–31
Glaze, for turkey, 206
for mock chicken legs, 167
Mushroom, 326
Mushroom, for French-fried Cornish hens, 234–35
for pot roast of beef, 142, 326–27
for Shish Kabob, 162
Tettrazini, special, for Cornish hens, 231
Thick brown, for beef stew in casserole, 394
Thick brown, à la duchesse, 394–95
Thickened, 321–22
Thickened brown, 326
Thickened, for roasted meats, 129
Tomato, for tamales, 412
Won ton, 826
Haddock
Broiled, 243–44
Broiled fillets, 246
Broiled fillets, Piquant, 386
Fillet of, Mornay in casserole, 384–85
Halibut
Baked, and cheese casserole, 386–87
Broiled, 243–44
Steak, broiled, with Pizzaiola sauce, 797
Steak à la Creole, 247
Steaks, broiled with soufflé topping, 246–47
Steaks, with tomato-cheese sauce, 240
HAM
fully cooked, 178

scoring and glazing, 178
uncooked, 178
uncooked, cooking schedule
  for, 179
and asparagus, creamed,
  noodle casserole, 404
Asparagus luncheon rolls in
  casserole, 411
Baked hot molded glazed,
  appetizer, 29–31
Bouches, hot, 7
and broccoli roll-ups in
  casserole, 401–402
Buffet log, molded poinsettia, 457–58
Cheese-meat swirls, 69
Cheese and mushroom
  French toast sand-
  wiches, 265–66
Cold sliced baked, calavo-
  strawberry salad with,
  367
and corn fritters, 288
Cutlets Madrid, 179
and green noodle casserole,
  401
and Gruyère cheese Quiche
  Lorraine, 94
Italian prosciutto and melon appetizer, 77–88
Loaf, glazed, 181–82
Mold, chaud-froid, 461–62
Rolls, toasted, 39-40
Salad mold, chaud-froid,
  466–67
Salad platter, party-style,
  362
and spinach roll-ups in casserole, 182–83
and spinach timbales cas-
  serole, 180–81
and sweet potatoes duchesse
  in casserole, 402–403
and zucchini in casserole,
  807–808
Herring, kippered, snack
  mold, 64
Honey dew melon
birds, 364
boats, 367–68
salad basket, 345
Ice cream
Bombs, party-size, 676–77
Cakes
  Easter egg, large, 607,
    674
  Easter eggs, individual,
    606, 673
  meringue torte, heavenly,
    575–76
  roll, chocolate, 572–73
  sherbet torte, 675–76
Flambeau, cherry, 660
Molds, Baba crown, 449

Molds, fruit salad, 444–45
Petit fours and molds,
  674–75
ICINGS AND FROSTINGS,
  608–23
definitions, 608
Butter, cinnamon, 616
Butter, quick, 720
Buttercream, chocolate
  marshmallow, 610
Buttercream, chocolate, for
  pineapple cake, 603
Buttercream, Continental,
  617
Buttercream, to decorate
  Easter egg cake, 606
Buttercream, French, Mrs.
  Miller's quick, 613
Buttercream, Hungarian,
  616
Buttercream, marshmallow,
  610–11
Buttercream, quick, 614–15
Buttercream, quick for bulbs
  on petits-four, 621
Buttercream, white moun-
  tain, 612
Butterscotch, maple, 622–23
Chocolate buttercream for
  pineapple cake, 603
Chocolate coating, quick
  glossy, 619
Chocolate coating, special
  glossy, 618–19
Chocolate coating, special
  glossy, for cookies and
  small cakes, 698–99
Chocolate, for cookies and
  small cakes, 689
Chocolate cream cheese, 622
Chocolate, cream cheese,
  special, for party-size
  cakes, 620
Chocolate, glossy for marzi-
  pan slices, 719–20
Chocolate, for log cookies,
  692
Chocolate marshmallow but-
  tercream, 610
Chocolate syrup whipped
  cream, 621–22
Chocolate whipped cream,
  621
Cinnamon butter, 616
Cocoa, 724
Coffee cake, 510
Coffee cake, quick, for Dan-
  ish pastries or dough-
  nuts, 618
for coffee cake squares,
  filled, quick, 514
Cream cheese, 617–18
Cream cheese, chocolate, 622
Cream cheese, chocolate,

special, for party-size
  cakes, 620
Cream cheese, lemon, 622
for cream puffs, 668
for eclairs, 668
Fluffy, 614
Glossy chocolate coating,
  quick, 619
Glossy chocolate coating,
  special, for cookies and
  small cakes, 698–99
Glossy, chocolate, for mar-
  zipan slices, 719–20
Glossy, quick, 612–13
Lemon, 619
Lemon cream cheese, 622
Maple butterscotch, 622–23
Maple marshmallow, 623
Marshmallow buttercream,
  610–11
Marshmallow buttercream,
  chocolate, 610
Marshmallow maple, 623
Orange, for coffee cake
  knots, 515
Petit fours fondant, quick,
  620–21
Pineapple leaves royal,
  603–604
Raspberry, fresh, fluff, 619
Raspberry fluff freeze, 620
Raspberry fluff made with
  quick frozen berries,
  620
Royal, made with fresh egg
  whites, 625
Strawberry fluff freeze, 620
Strawberry fluff made with
  quick frozen berries,
  620
Strawberry, fresh, fluff, 619
Transparent, for doughnuts,
  bismarcks, etc., 519
Transparent, for Fennel
  cakes, 821
White mountain, basic
  (plain), 611–12
see also CAKE DECORAT-
  ING, PROFESSIONAL
ITALIAN DISHES, 758–821
pasta, how to cook, 759–60
typical ingredients, 758–59
Almond, toasted, slices,
  820–21
Anchovy pesto, 770
Anchovy-salami appetizer,
  71
Antipasto platter, 160–61
Beans, green, fresh, salad,
  Neopolitan, 804
Biscotti Croccanti, 820-21
Biscuits, savory tea, Conti-
  nental-style, 815
Bolognese sauce, 767-68

Bread, anchovy-garlic, 814
Bread, garlic-flavored, 814
Bread, parmesan tomato garlic, 814
Broccoli à la parmesan, baked, 800
Broccoli parmesan, sautéed, 800-801
Calzoni squares, 34-35, 764-65
Cannelloni, 774-75
Cannelloni, French-style, 776
Cannoli pastries, 818-19
Cheese appetizers, 37
Chicken, breast of, Alfredo, 779-80
Chicken, breast, sautéed, 780-81
Chicken cacciatori, 781-82
Chicken dinner Vesuvio, 783-84
Chicken legs and thighs Alfredo, 782
Chicken tetrazzini, 782-83
Cornucopias, 68
Croquettes, potato, 483, 813
Eggplant casserole, Louise's 802
Eggplant slices, baked, stuffed, 801-802
Endive, boiled, 290-91
Endive with spareribs, 291
Fennel cakes, 821
Gnocchi Romano, 777-78
Gnocchi Verdi, 779
Halibut steak, broiled with Pizzaiola sauce, 797
Ham and zucchini stew, 808
Lamb casserole Neopolitan, 791-92
Lamb, leg of, Continental-style, 790-91
Lasagna, baked stuffed, 773-74
Macaroni and sausage casserole, 799-800
Manicotti, 774-75
Meat balls, 795
Meat ball appetizer, 38
Meat balls, Tuscany-style, 793-94
Meat casserole, Neopolitan, 794-95
Meat and rice, stuffed green peppers with, 792
Minestrone, Evelyn Russo's lentil, 810-11
Minestrone, fresh vegetable, 809
Mozzarella hors d'oeuvres, 35-36
Mushrooms, Nina Miroballi's, 768-69

Noodles Alfredo, 781
Noodles, egg, homemade, 778
Omelet, potato, 262, 803-804
Omelet, scamorza, 797-98
Omelet, zucchini, 808
Pasta and Fagioli (pasta with navy beans), 811
Peppers, broiled, 804-805
Peppers, green or red, fresh, roasted, 804
Peppers, greed or red, stuffed, 805
Peppers, green, with sausages, 800
Pesto à la Genovese, 769-70
Pizza, 14-inch, 765-766
Polpettine alla Toscana, 793-94
Pork loins, braised, 796-97
Pork sausages, 798-99
Pork tenderloin Spiedini, Helen Camp's, 795-96
Potato croquettes, 483, 813
Potato omelet, 803-804
Potato salad platter, 802-803
Prosciutto and melon, 77-78
Ravioli, 771-73
Rice and meat, stuffed green peppers with, 792
Ricotta cake torte, 815-16
Ricotta pie torte, 816-17
Ricotta pie, whipped cream, 817-18
Risotto Milanese, 805-806
Salad bowl, fresh vegetable, 813
Salami-anchovy appetizer, 71
Salami hors d'oeuvres puffs, 37
Sausage with green peppers, 800
Sausage and macaroni casserole, 799-800
Sausages, pork, 798-99
Scamorza omelet, 797-98
Shrimp, sautéed, 36-37
Spaghetti and meat casserole Sicilian-style, 792-93
Spaghetti casserole, Neopolitan, 793
Spareribs, endives with, 291
Spinach and steamed potatoes, 812-13
Steak, peppered, with sautéed mushrooms, 789-90
Suppli di Ricotte e Spinaci

(Ricotta Spinach Croquettes), 812
Tomato sauce, 727
Tomato sauce, basic, 766-67
Tomato sauce, quick, 767
Tomato-tuna fish appetizer, 75
Tomatoes, fresh grilled parmesan, au gratin, 318
Tortellini (pasta rings), 770-71
Turkey, breast of, Alfredo, sautéed, 780-81
Vegetable casserole Continental, 809-10
Veal chops cacciatori, 787
Veal cutlets, plain breaded, 787-88
Veal, leg of, Evelyn Russo's Neopolitan-style, 788-89
Veal scallopini à la Genovese, 788
Whipped cream ricotta pie, 817-18
Zucchini and ham in casserole, 807-808
Zucchini omelet, 808
Zucchini stew, 808
Zucchini, stuffed, 806
Zucchini and veal chops in casserole, 806-807
Zuppa Inglese, 819-20
Jam
peach, 878
red raspberry, 878
Javanese-style shrimp, 847
Jelly
currant, 878-79
grape, 879
Karydato, 717
LAMB
Premium, 118
timetable for broiling chops, 131
timetable for roasting, 128
Barbecued, 192
Breast of, barbecued, 161
Casserole Neopolitan, 791-92
Chinese pineapple, 848
Chops
baked, and potatoes in casserole, 190
braised shoulder, 153
grilled, 157
maintenon, 160-61
oven-broiled, 156-57
pan-broiled, 157
savory, and fresh green peppers, 158-59
Curry stew, 159
with eggplant, Balkan, 159

Leg of, Continental-style, 790–91
Meat loaf de luxe, 142–43
Meat balls gourmet, 151
Mock chicken legs, 166–67
Pastitso in casserole, 397–98
Riblets, braised barbecued, 160
Shanks, braised, 158
Shashlik, 162
Shashlik en brochette, 163
Shish Kabob, 161–62
Stew, curry, 159
Stew, spring, 157
Stuffed cabbage leaves, 143–44
La Neige Dessert (Soft French), 670–71
Lasagna, baked stuffed, 773–74
Lemon
Custard torte, angel, 638–39
Dessert, crunchy, 661–62
Pie, chiffon, 735–36
Pie, old-fashioned, 735
Torte, meringue, 540–41
Lettuce, 291
Romaine, 314
Lime chiffon pie, 741–42
Liver
Calf's, baked whole, 194
Chicken-fried, 195
Lobster
Almond Din, 836
Blintzes, 26
Broiled, 250–51
Broiled live, 251–52
Fresh, Cantonese-style, 840–41
hors d'oeuvres centerpiece, 52
and melon appetizer, 75–76
à la Newburg, 41–42
Quiche Lorraine, 95
Salad Imperial, 59–61
Salad Imperial, molded, 354–55
Salad mold, chaud-froid, 464–65
Souffle, 269
Tails, 252
Tails, boiled, 252
Tails, broiled precooked, 252
Tails, broiled without pre-cooking, 253
Tails thermidor, 252
Thermidor in casserole or chafing dish, 253–54
Macaroni
Baked in casserole, 417
Baked elbow, and pork sausages, casserole, 400

Baked sizzling squares, 403–404
for green pepper veal stew, 176
and Italian sausage, casserole, 799–800
and pork casserole, Louisiana, 398
and salmon casserole, 383
Manicotti, 774–75
Margarine
for browning, 323
Kneaded, 323
Whipped, 53, 79
see also Butter
MARINADE(S)
Alfredo, 780
for breast of chicken (or turkey) Romanoff, 218
Burgundy, 163
Lobster tail, 9
Meat, 120, 162
Meat, for beef, veal or lamb, 339–40
Oriental, 15, 41, 828–29
for Oriental appetizers on bamboo sticks, 832
for Oriental chicken liver, 829
for poultry and meat, 20
for seafood and fish fillets, 236–37, 334
for vegetables, 473
Marzipan slices, 718–19
Mayonnaise
Chaud-froid, 54, 463–64
Dressing, 370–71
Dressing, Tarragon, 63
Gelatin, 82
Stabilized, 61–62
Stabilized for crab meat ravigote, 352
Whipped cream, 344
MEASURING, xi–xii
MEAT
aging and storing, 116–17
grades and quantities, 114–16
methods of cooking, 114, 120–31
Premium, 117–18
timetables, 128, 131
see also BEEF; LAMB; PORK; VEAL; etc.
Meat and Poultry coatings
Bread crumbs, 125–27
browned, 126
commercial, 125–26
red-colored, 72–73
Corn flake coating, 126
Cracker crumbs, 126
Crumb, for breast of chick-en (or turkey) Roman-off, 218

Other commercial coatings, 126
Seasoned flour for coating, 126–27
Seasoned flour for coating chicken, 216
Melon
Medley salad mold, 438–39
and prosciutto, Italian, 77–78
see also Cantaloupe; Honey dew melon; Watermelon
MENUS, 901–15
Meringue
for Baked Alaska, 590–91
for Blitz torte
Brown-sugar, for fresh peach pie, 750
Brown-sugar, special Filling for Strudlicky, 726–27
French, 671
for ice cream desserts, etc., 671–73
for ice cream torte, 576
Topping (for pies), 736–37
Mince pie, 756–57
Mint, chocolate, refrigerator torte, 640–41
MOLD, 418–74
preparing, 418–22
Almond cream, Bavarian, 452–53
Apricot-pear gelatin, party-style, 425–26
Asparagus, 314–16
Baba crown ice cream, 449
Bar-Le-Duc French cream cheese, 450–51
Bavarian almond cream, 452–53
Blueberry, fresh, party-style, 429–30
Broccoli, 314–16
Chaud-froid chicken or meat, 461–62
Chaud-froid fish or seafood, 458–61
Chaud-froid ham salad, 466–67
Chaud-froid lobster salad, 464–65
Chaud-froid salmon or sea-food, 462–64
Cheese and crab meat ring, 452
Cheese and potato, baked, 302–303
Chicken salad, 467–68
Chicken-tongue, 470
Christmas tree, 434
Citrus fruit salad, party-style, 432–33

Crab meat and cheese ring, 452
Confetti party mousse, 440–41
Cranberry fluff, 433
Cranberry, gelatin, 431–32
Cranberry, individual, 431
Cranberry-raspberry, yuletide star, 434
Cream cheese, Bar-Le-Duc French, 450–51
Cream cheese, pineapple, 448–49
Cucumber salad, 471
Egg salad, 468
Eggnog, yuletide, 447–48
Fish or seafood, chaud-froid, 458–61
Fruit gelatin ring, Della Robbia, large party-size, 427–28
Fruit gelatin ring, standard-size Della Robbia, 426–27
Fruit, pineapple-shaped, 428–29
Fruit salad, butterfly, party-style, 436–37
Fruit salad doll, Colonial, 423–24
Fruit salad, ice cream, 444–45
Grape juice salad mousse, cartwheel, 443–44
Grape, purple, 434–36
Ham salad, chaud froid, 466–67
Hyacinth party-style, 453–55
Ice cream fruit salad, 444–45
Lime horseradish, 469
Meat or chicken, chaud-froid, 461–62
Melon medley salad, 438–39
Multifruit salad, 439
Pineapple cream cheese, 448–49
Pineapple-raspberry, 437–38
Pineapple-shaped fruit, 428–29
Poinsettia buffet log, 457–58
Potato, baked, and cheese, 302–303
Potato, baked, ring, 303–304
Potato salad, party-style, 472–73
Raspberry-cranberry, yuletide stars, 434
Raspberry-pineapple, 437–38
Rhubarb-strawberry, 439–40

Rhubarb-strawberry egg, 440
Rice dessert, Imperial, 451–52
Sabayon salad mousse, 445–46
Salmon salad, chaud-froid, 462–64
Seafood buffet, holly wreath, 455–56
Seafood or fish, chaud-froid, 458–61
Seafood salad, chaud-froid, 462–64
Shamrock, party-style, 422–23
Spinach, 314–16
Tulip, party-style, 442–43
Valentine salad, 456–57
Vegetable salad, garden, 469–70
Vegetables, marinated, individual, 465–66
Mousse, chocolate, in sherbet glasses, 681
Muerbes, 683
Fancy, 684
Muffins, English, 501–502
Mushroom(s), 292
Asparagus omelet, Swiss, 261
Bouches, 8
Broiled, 292
in chafing dish, hot, 7–8
and chicken liver paté, 137
Chicken
and chicken Mornay in casserole, 388–89
Dip, hot, 96
Fresh, creamed, for Spiedini, 796
Fresh, sautéed, 292
Ham and cheese, French toast sandwiches, 265–66
Marinated, 252
Meringues, hot, 7
Pastry crescents or diamonds, 5–6
and pork shoulder in casserole, 399–400
and pork tenderloin in casserole, 399–400
Quiche Lorraine, 94
Sautéed carved, for beef tenderloin, 134
Soufflé appetizer, 21–22
and spinach baked in casserole, 292–93
Stuffed, baked in cream, 293
Surprises, 6
Turkish pilaf, 312
and vegetable medley in casserole, 404–405

Yuon stuffed, appetizer, 829–30
Noodle(s)
Alfredo, 781
creamed ham and asparagus, casserole, 404
Dough, 823
Egg, homemade, 778
Fried crisp, 824
Green, and ham casserole, 401
Green, souffle in casserole, 415–16
Nests, Chinese fried, 823–24
Romanoff, 416
Okra, 293–94
Stew, Creole-style, 294
Omelets see EGG(S): Omelets
Onion(s), 294
and cabbage, sauteed, 188, 282–83
Glazed, 295
and new boiled potatoes with green or wax beans, 277–78
Rings, french-fried, 294
Rings, french-fried, batter for, 294
Sautéed, 294
Smothered, 145
ORIENTAL COOKERY, 822–55
Almond cookie, Oriental, 854–55
Almonds and rice, fried, 313
Barbecued beef tenderloin appetizer on bamboo sticks, 831–32
Barbecued pork tenderloin, on bamboo sticks, 831–32
Barbecued ribs and pork, appetizer, Cantonese, 833–34
Barbecued ribs and pork, Cantonese, 13
Barbecued shrimp on bamboo sticks, 832
Beef with broccoli, Gay Long, 845
Beef Mandarin-style, 837
Beef tenderloin appetizer, barbecued, on bamboo sticks, 831
Beef tenderloin with fresh bean sprouts, 846–47
Beef tenderloin with pea pods, 845–46
Beef tenderloin with string beans, 846–47
Black bean barbecue sauce, 835

Cabbage, sauteed, with sweet-sour spareribs, 187–88
Chicken Almond Din, 836–37
Chicken chow mein, 838–39
Chicken dinner, Bali Bali Cantonese, boned, 839–40
Chicken liver appetizer, Oriental, 16, 829
Chicken livers en brochette appetizer, 831
Chicken slices, Cantonese, 840
Chicken, won tons with, 827–28
Chop suey, 850–51
Chow mein, chicken, 838–39
Chow mein, shrimp, 839
Cornish hens, braised, top-of-the-stove, 843–44
Cornish hens, Oriental, 233
Cornish hens, Oriental, roasted, 843
Dessert rice mold, Imperial, 853–54
Dowel Sea Piquet, 844–45
Duck, braised, Cantonese, 844
Duck, pressed, Cantonese, 841–42
Egg rolls appetizer, Cantonese, 11–12, 824–25
Gay Long beef with broccoli, 845
Him Soon York, 838
Hot sauce, 835
Japanese Sukiyaki dinner, 849–50
Lobster Almond Din, 836
Lobster, fresh, Cantonese-style, 840–41
Lobster Oriental, 377–78
Mushrooms, Yuon stuffed, appetizer, 829–30
Mustard sauce, 835
Noodle dough, 823
Noodle nests, Chinese fried, 823–24
Noodles, crisp fried, 824
Oriental appetizer on bamboo sticks, 14–15
Oriental delight appetizer, hot, 16–17, 832–33
Pea pods with cabbage, Chinese, 847–48
Peppers, green, and strimp, Oriental, 848
Pork, sweet-sour, 838
Pork tenderloin appetizer, barbecued, on bamboo sticks, 831–32

Rice and almonds, fried, 313
Rice, Chinese, 853
Rice, fried, Cantonese-style, 852
Rice, fried, Chinese, 852–53
Rice mold Imperial, dessert, 853–54
Rice, plain-cooked, 851
Sauces, 17–18, 834–35
Shrimp appetizer, barbecued, on bamboo sticks, 832
Shrimp appetizer, Oriental. 828–29
Shrimp chow mein, 839
Shrimp, fried, Cantonese, 12, 826–27
Shrimp and green peppers, Oriental, 848
Shrimp, Javanese-style, 847
Shrimp, Oriental, 15
Shrimp, sautéed, garlic sauce appetizer, 830–31
Shrimp, sautéed—sweet and sour, 837
Spareribs, sweet-sour, with cabbage, sautéed, 187–88
Squab appetizer, Cantonese, 830
Sukiyaki Dinner, Papanese, 849–50
Sweet-sour sauce, 834–35
Sweet-sour spareribs with sauteed cabbage, 187–88
Vegetables, Cantonese, 851
Won ton appetizer, filled, Cantonese, 826
Won tons, 13–14
Won tons, boiled, 825–26
Won tons with chicken, 827–28
Yuon stuffed mushrooms appetizer, 829–30

Oyster(s)
Remoulade, french-fried, 46
à la Rockefeller, 249–50
Rockefeller appetizers, 24–25
Stew, 105
Oxtails, potted, 156
Pancakes
Corn oysters, 483
Crepes Suzette, 478–79
German, 479–80
Griddle cakes, 480
blueberry, 480–81
corn, 482–83
Hush puppies, 484–85
Potato croquettes, Italian-style, 483

Potato, fresh, 306, 484
Potato, Swiss-style, in skillet, 305–306
Southern rice, 480
Strawberry almond, 648–49
Parsley, 295
Parsnips, 295–96
baked, 296
pan-fried, 296
PASTA
how to cook, 759–60
Cannelloni, French-style, 776
Cannelloni, Italian-style, 774–75
Casserole Savoy, 396–97
Gnocchi Romano, 777–78
Gnocchi Verdi, 779
Lasagna, baked stuffed, 773–74
Macaroni, baked, in casserole, 417
Macaroni, baked elbow, and pork sausages, casseroles, 400
Macaroni, baked, sizzling squares, 403–404
Macaroni, for green pepper veal stew, 176
Macaroni and Italian sausage, casserole, 799–800
Macaroni and pork casserole, Louisiana, 398
Macaroni and salmon casserole, 383
Manicotti, 774–75
Noodle, creamed ham and asparagus, casserole, 404
Noodle dough, 823
Noodle, green, souffle in casserole, 415–16
Noodle nests, Chinese fried, 823–24
Noodles Alfredo, 781
Noodles, egg, homemade, 778
Noodles, fried crisp, 824
Noodles, green, and ham casserole, 401
Pastitso in casserole, 397–98
Quick casserole, 417
Spaghetti casserole, Neopolitan, 793
Spaghetti and meat casserole, 792–93
Tortellini (pasta rings), 770–71
Won ton appetizer, fried, filled, Cantonese, 826
Won tons, 13–14
Won tons, boiled, 825–26

Won tons with chicken, 827–28
Pastitso in casserole, 397–98
PASTRIES
Apple dumplings, 678–79
Apple turnovers, 649–50
Baklava, 658–59
Banana cream puff log, 670
Cannoli, Italian, 818–19
Cheese sticks, 19–20
Cream cheese-Kolachy yeast, 522–23
Cream puff, dough for, 667–68
Cream puff log, 670
Cream puff log, banana, 670
Cream puff log, raspberry, 670
Cream puff log, strawberry, 670
Cream puff swans, 668–69
Cream slices, 647–48
Danish, Babas au Rhum, 528–29
Danish, basic dough for, 525–26
Danish, braid, 529–30
Danish, horns, 528
Danish, luncheon or dinner rolls, 527
Danish, pinwheels, 527
Danish, snails, 527
Danish swirl, 526–27
Dough, basic yeast, for glazed butterscotch pecan rolls, butterhorns, sweet rolls, 521–22
Dough, classic puff paste, 645–47
Dough, for large pastries, 151
Flan, French fruit, 624–44
Fruit turnover, 649–50
Honey crispettes, 677–78
Patty shells, 650
Pecan roll loaf, 524
Pecan roll ring, 524–25
Pecan rolls, medium, individual, 523
Pineapple-orange, glacéed, yeast rolls, 519–20
Puff paste, new easy quick, 136–37, 654
Puff paste palm leaves, 651
Popovers, 485
Raspberry cream puff log, 670
Strawberry cream puff log, 670
Strawberry, honey glacéed, yeast rolls, 54
Sour cream Kippel yeast, 520–21
Strudel, apple, 656–57

Strudel, apple, quick puff paste, 651–52
Strudel, cherry, 657
Strudel, cream cheese, 657
Strudel, dough, 655–56
Strudel, pecan, 658
Strudel, strawberry, fresh, 657
Turnover, apple, 648–50
Turnover, fruit, 649–50
see also BREAD;
CAKE(S); COOKIES; DESSERTS; PIE(S)
Pea(s)
and carrots, creamed, à la duchesse, 405
for Chicken Vesuvio, 784
Creamed, for turkey timbales, 390
Green, paprika, 297
Pods, beef tenderloin with, 845–46
Pods with cabbage, Chinese, 847–48
and salmon salad, 361
Sautéed in onion butter, 297
Soufflé, 268
Peach
and apricot tarts, 665
Canned, pie, California, fruit, 746–47
and cherry flambeau, 660
Crisp dessert, 661
Crisp dessert made with fresh peaches, 661
Dessert ring, crunchy, 662
Flambeau, 660
Fresh, filling for blintzes, 654
Fresh, pie, 755
Fresh, pie, cream, 748
Fresh, pie, glazed, 745
Fresh, pie, meringue, 749–50
Meringue sticks 707–708
Pear
Almond paste, 714–15
and apricot flambeau, 661
and apricot gelatin mold, party-style, 425–26
Calavo-cranberry salad with turkey slices, 367
Calavo-strawberry salad with cold sliced baked ham, 367
Canned, pie, California fruit, 746–47
and grape salad, 365
hors d'oeuvres centerpiece, 51–52
Macaroon, coconut, 712
Mint, salad with cold sliced lamb, 367

Petit-four fruits and vegetables, 591–93
Petits four, 553
Salad, standing, 364–65
Tarts, 665
Pecan
Baklava, 658–59
Bars, chewy apricot, 722
Butter crescents, 692–93
Butter-cake squares, grilled, 561
Chocolate turtles, 688–89
Czechoslovakian pastry boats, 708
Czechoslovakian pastry forms, assorted small, 710
Date cookies, 707
Dough, basic short, 701
Filling, roasted nut, 688
Pie, Southern, 738–39
Strudel, 658
Topping for date bars, 723
Topping, Streussel, for apple pie, 751
Torte, French pastry, 574–75
Pepper(s)
Green, 158, 297
Green, broiled, Italian-style, 804–805
Green, and eggs, 297
Green, fresh, roasted, Italian-style, 804
Green, Italian sausages with, 800
Green, pan-fried, 297
Green, pan-fried with tomatoes and eggs, 298
Green, sautéed for veal stew, 176
Green, stuffed, Italian-style, 805
Green, stuffed with rice and meat, 792
Green, succotash-stuffed baked, 298–99
Green, for veal chops provincial, 174
Red, 297
Red, broiled, Italian-style, 804–805
Red, fresh, roasted, Italian-style, 804
Red, pan-fried, 297
Red, pan-fried with tomatoes and eggs, 298
Red, stuffed, Italian-style, 805
Perch
Baked stuffed fillet, 243
Broiled fillets Piquant, 386
Fillet of, Mornay in casserole, 384–85

Pickles and Pickling
Barbecue ribs, 875
Beets, 876
Gherkin fan appetizers, 69
Green peppers, 877
Green tomatoes, 877
Home style bread-and-butter pickles, 875
Sliced carrots, 876
Vegetables, assorted, 876–77

PIE(S), 731–57
dough
for open face pie, basic, 732–33
for 8-inch pie plate, 733
for 9-inch pie plate, 734
for 2-crust pie, basic, 751–52
for 2-crust 8-inch pie plate, 752
ingredients, 731–32
shells, individual, 733
Apple custard meringue, 744–48
Apple, large, 753
Apple, small, 753
Apple squares, Louise's, 753–54
Apple, Streussel-top, 750–51
Banana cream, 740–41
Berry, glazed open face, 666
Blackberry, fresh, glazed, 746
Blueberry, canned, 754
Blueberry, fresh, 754–55
Blueberry, fresh, glazed, 745
Blueberry, fresh, glazed cheese pie torte, 747–48
Boston cream, 587–88
Brandy, 739–40
Butterscotch, 734
California fruit, 746–47
Cherry, canned, 755
Cherry, frozen, glazed, 746
Chocolate-vanilla cream, 734–35
Cream, banana, 740–41
Cream, Boston, 587–88
Cream, chocolate-vanilla, 734–35
Cream, orange, 742
Cream, peach, fresh, 749
Cream, peach, fresh, Streussel-top, 748–49
Cream, pineapple, 747
Cream, whipped, ricotta, 817–18
Custard, 737–38
Eggnog, individual, 744
Eggnog, Yuletide, 743

Fruit, California, 746–47
Fruit, glazed open-face, 666
Lemon chiffon, 735–36
Lemon, old-fashioned, 735
Lime chiffon, 741–42
Meringue topping, 736–37
Mince, 756–57
Orange cream, 742
Peach, fresh, 755
Peach, fresh, cream, 749
Peach, fresh, cream, Streussel-top, 748–49
Peach, fresh, glazed, 745
Peach, fresh, meringue, 749–50
Pecan, Southern, 738–39
Pineapple cream, 747
Pumpkin chiffon, 742–43
Raspberry, fresh, 755–56
Raspberry, fresh, glazed, 746
Raspberry, frozen, glazed, 746
Rhubarb, 756
Rhubarb-strawberry, 757
Ricotta, whipped cream, 817–18
Rum, 739–40
Southern pecan, 738–39
Strawberry, fresh, 755–56
Strawberry, fresh, glazed, 745
Strawberry, frozen, glazed, 746
Strawberry-rhubarb, 757
Whipped cream ricotta, 817–18

Pineapple
and apricot salad, 364
and banana salad, 363
Canned sliced, California fruit pie, 746–47
Centerpiece, bird of paradise, 343–44
Centerpiece, hors d'oeuvres, 50
and cheese glaze torte, 639–40
Cream cheese molds, 448–49
Cream pie, 747
Cocktail, birds of paradise, individual, 344
Date and nut bread, 488–89
Fingers, Vienna, 693–94
Lamb, Chinese, 848
and raspberry mold, 437
Salad Tahiti, birds of paradise, individual, 344
and shrimp appetizer, 75
Strawberry bird appetizer, Honolulu, 73
Tarts, 665–66
Pizza
14-inch, 765–66

Neopolitan, appetizer, 761–64
Plum
Pudding, 558–59
Pudding, flaming English, 559–60
Polpettini alla Toscana, 793–94
Pompano en Papillote, 24–42
Popovers, 485
Poppy seed form cake, 560
PORK
grades, 114–15
Tend'r Lean, 117–18
timetable for roasting, 128
Casserole Savoy, 396–97
Chops, baked crisp crust, 185
Chops, deep-fat fried, 184
Chops, pan braised breaded, 183–84
Chops, plain braised, 184
Chops, plain broiled, 183
Chops, plain fried, 184
Chops and potatoes, baked, in casserole, 190
Chops, stuffed broiled, 183
Dowel Sea Piquat, 844–45
Hocks with boiled vegetables or sauerkraut, 188–89
Loin, baked, Continental-style, 187
Loins, barbecued, 192
Loins, Italian-style braised, 796–97
and macaroni casserole, Louisiana, 399
Meat balls, Italian, 795
Meat dinner, vegetable daisy, 186
Meat loaf de luxe, 142–43
Meat patties, Continental, 176–77
Meat and spaghetti casserole, Sicilian-style, 792–93
Mock chicken legs, 166–67
Pastitso in casserole, 397–98
and ribs appetizer, Cantonese barbecued, 833–34
Roast, and sauerkraut, 190–91
Sausage and lima bean casserole, 410
Sausages and elbow macaroni, baked, casserole, 400
Sausages with green pepper, Italian, 799–800
Sausages, Italian, 798–99
Sausages and macaroni casserole, Italian, 799–800

Shoulder and mushroom casserole, 399–400
Spareribs, barbecued, 191–92
Spareribs, sweet-sour, with sauteed cabbage, 187–88
Stroganoff in chafing dish, 395
Stuffed cabbage leaves, 143–44
Sweet-sour, 838
Tenderloin appetizer, Oriental barbecued, or bamboo sticks, 831–32
Tenderloin patties, deep-fat fried, 184
Tenderloin, barbecued baked, 189
Tenderloin and mushroom casserole, 399–400
Tenderloin patties, baked crisp crust, 185
Tenderloin patties, Creole-style, 189–90
Tenderloin Spiedini, Helen Camp's Italian-style, 795–96
Potato(es), 299
Baked, 299–300
Baked, fancy-cut buttered, 307
Boiled, 299
Browned, for chicken Vesuvio, 784
and cheese mold, baked, 302–303
Croquettes, Italian-style, 483, 813
Delmonico in casserole, 305, 415
Duchess, 301
and egg scallop in casserole, 411
French-fried, 301–302
Lyonnaise, 302
Mashed, fluffy, 307
New boiled, and onions, green or wax beans with, 277–78
New sautéed whole, 305
Omelet, Italian, 262
Pancake, Swiss-style, in skillet, 305–306
Pancakes, fresh, 306, 484
Ring mold, baked, 303–304
Salad with bleu cheese and sour cream, 356–57
Salad, German hot, 357
Salad mold, party-style, 472–73
Salad, molded, 355
Salad platter, Italian-style, 802–803

Scalloped cream, 306–307
Slices, pan-fried brown in omelet pan, 300–301
Slices, pan-fried brown, in skillet, 301
Steamed, and spinach, Italian-style, 812–13
Sweet see Sweet potato(es)
Vesuvio in casserole, 304
POULTRY
cooking in water, 123
deep-fat frying, 123–24
freezing, 197–98
marinades, 202
toughness, 197
types, 196–97
see also CHICKEN; DUCK; TURKEY
Poultry Coatings see Meat and Poultry coatings
Preserves
Apricot, 877–78
Strawberry, 877
Pudding
Plum, 558–59
Plum, flaming English, 559–60
Rice, baked, 659–60
Rice, Gus's, 659
see also Custard
Pumpkin, 311
Baked, 311
Chiffon pie, 742–43
Punch
Blueberry, fresh, 864
Bowl, Yuletide, 863
Champagne hors d'oeuvres, 863–64
Christmastide fruit, 863
Eastertide fruit, 864
Elinor's eggnog, 862–63
Fruit, 862
Lime, 864–65
Tea, 865
Quiche Lorraine
Basic, 93–94
Crab meat, 95
Ham and Gruyère cheese, 94
Italian-style, 35–36
Lobster, 95
Mushroom, 94
Shrimp, 95
Radish tops, 314
Rarebits
Frankfurter, 99
Ham, 99
Open-face sandwiches, 100
Sardine, 97
Shrimp and cheese, 98
Spanish Welsh, 98
Tomato, on toast with anchovies, 97–98

Welsh, 99–100
Raspberry
Blintzes, 653
and cranberry mold, Yuletide star, 434
Cream puff log, 670
Dessert ring, crunchy, 662
Flans, French fruit, 642
Fresh, pie, 755–56
Fresh, pie, glazed, 746
Frozen, pie, glazed, 746
Hearts, 701
and pineapple mold, 437–38
Salad, tropical, 365
Ravioli, 771–73
Revani (Grecian Walnut Brandy Cakes), 718
Rhubarb
Pie, 756
Sauce, 677
and strawberry egg mold, 440
and strawberry mold, 439–40
and strawberry pie, 757
and strawberry sherbet, 678
Rice
Arroz con Pollo, 225–27
and almonds, fried, 313
and chicken, curry, company-style, 224–25
Chinese, 312–13, 853
and crab meat, creamed (in chafing dish), 379
Curried, for French-fried Cornish hens, 234
for curry of veal, 175
Custard, date, nut and raisin, 680
Dessert mold Imperial, 451–52, 853–54
Fried, Cantonese-style, 852
Fried, Chinese, 852–53
and meat, with stuffed green pepper, 792
Plain-cooked, 851–52
Pancakes, Southern, 480
and shrimp Creole, in individual casseroles, 382–83
Spanish-style chicken with, 219–20
Turkish pilaf, 312
Wild, Gourmet, Alice Pope Gierum's, 311
Wild, mold, 311–12
Rolls see BREADS
Romaine, 314, 360
Rutabagas, 319
SALAD DRESSINGS
Bahama, 373
Brandy sauce, whipped cream, 372
Cooked, for cole slaw, 371

French, Continental-style, 368
French, modified, 369
French, Piquant, 373
Fruit, 371
Gourmet Goddess, 370
Horseradish whipped cream sauce, 372
Italian, Continental-style, 368
Italian, modified, 369
Kentucky limestone, 373
Mayonnaise *see* Mayonnaise
Piquant French, 373
Roman, 369–70
Roquefort, 370
Roquefort, Pope's cream, 372–73
Rum sauce, whipped cream, 372
Russian, for Romaine Lettuce, 360
Sauce Louisiana, 374
Special, for seafood fruit appetizer, 75–76
Sour cream, zesty, 369, 474
Superb, 368
Tart, 76
Vinaigrette tarragon, 63
Whipped cream, horseradish sauce, 372
Whipped cream brandy sauce, 372
Whipped cream rum sauce, 372
Zesty sour cream, 369, 474
Salad greens, 313–14
SALADS, SALAD BOWLS, AND SALAD MOLDS, 342–74
Anchovy, 347
Apple, big, fruit cocktail, 346
Apricot-pineapple, 364
Asparagus, 362–63
Athenian, 360
Avocado bird, 360–61
Avocado and shrimp with Russian dressing, 351
Bahama, 347
Banana-pineapple, 363
Bean, green, 360, 362
Bean, red kidney, 359
Beans, green, Neopolitan fresh, 804
Caesar, 345–46
Calavo-cranberry, with turkey slices, 367
Calavo-strawberry, with cold sliced baked ham, 367
Cantaloupe, 345
Cantaloupe melon birds, 364
Chicken, superb, molded, 354

Citrus fruit, party-style, 432–33
Cole slaw, 348
Cole slaw, molded, 348
Crab meat in avocado cup, 358
Crab meat, ravigote, molded, 348
Crab meat, à la Reefer, molded, 352
Florida, 365
Fruit, Colonial doll, 423–24
Fruit, fresh, 364
Fruit salad, butterfly, party-style, 436–37
German, hot, sweet-sour, 362
Grape-pear, 365
Ham, party-style, 362
Happy Jack, 366
Hollywood, 365–66
Honey dew, 345
Honey dew melon birds, 364
Kentucky limestone, 249–50
Lettuce, molded, 348
Lobster, Imperial, molded, 354–55
Melon boats, 367–68
Mold, asparagus-olive, 356
Mold, chaud-froid ham, 466–67
Mold, chaud-froid lobster, 464–65
Mold, chaud-froid salmon or seafood, quick, 462–64
Mold, Colonial doll,
Mold, egg, 468
Mold, ice cream fruit, 444–45
Mold, multifruit, 439
Mold, potato, party-style, 472-73
Mold, Sabayon mousse, 445–47
Mold, Valentine, 456–57
Mold, vegetable, buffet party, 473–74
Molds, petit gourmet relish, 357–58
Molds, vegetable, marinated, individual, 358
Pear mint, with cold sliced lamb, 367
Pear, standing, 364–65
Pineapple-banana, 363
Pineapple birds of paradise, centerpiece, 343–44
Pineapple birds of paradise, Tahiti, individual, 344
Piquant, 348–49

Potato, with bleu cheese and sour cream, 356–57
Potato, German, hot, 357
Potato, Italian-style, 802–803
Potato, molded, 355
Raspberry, tropical, 365
Romaine lettuce with Russian salad dressing, 360
Salmon, crunchy, 361–62
Salmon-pea, 361
Saratoga, 347
Seafood cocktail, gourmet, 359
Shrimp, Louisiana, molded, 350–51
Shrimp, molded, 349–50
Shrimp, in tomato poinsettia, 357
Summer, 348
Tomato basket, 363
Tomato rose, 363
Tuna, in avocado cup, 358
Turkey, superb, molded, 354
Vegetable, fresh, 346–47, 813
Waldorf, 363–64
Watermelon, 344–45
see also MOLDS
Salami, Italian
and anchovy appetizers, 71
hors d'oeuvres puffs, 37
Salmon
Casserole, 383–84
for hors d'oeuvres, 63
and macaroni casserole, 383
and pea salad, 361
Salad in avocado cup, 358
Salad, crunchy, 361–62
Salad mold, chaud-froid, quick, 462–64
Whole poached, gourmet-style, 238–39
Salt, in meat cookery, 120–21
Saltimbocca, 165–66
Sardine
Crescents, 77
Rarebit, 97
on toast, 74–75
SAUCES FOR DESSERTS
Brandy, whipped cream, 446–47
Chocolate, velvety, 669
Custard, 453
Lemon, for apple dumplings, 679
Lemon, for custard, 680
Rhubarb, 677
Rum, whipped cream, 446–47
Whipped cream brandy, 446–47

Whipped cream rum, 446–47
see also TOPPINGS FOR DESSERTS, ETC.
SAUCES FOR MEATS, POULTRY, SEAFOOD
preparing, 321–24, 327
Amandine, 329
Anchovy pesto, 770
Arnaud, 255, 335–36
Barbecue, 193, 222
Bearnaise, 341–42
Bechamel, 327
Black bean-garlic, 835
Bolognese, 767–68
Brandy, whipped cream, 339, 372
Butter, brown or black, 329
Butter, green, for oysters, 250
Butter, hot, 328–29
for Cannelloni, French-style, 776–77
Chaud-froid, 460
Cheese, for baked vegetable mold, 330, 405–406
Cheese, for fillet of perch, 243
Cheese, for macaroni squares, 403–404
Cheese-olive, 410
Cheese, for spinach timbales and ham casserole, 181
Cheese, thick, for ham and broccoli roll-ups, 402
Cheese, thick, for ham and spinach roll-ups, 182
Cheese-tomato, for halibut steak, 240
for chicken fricassee, 227
for chicken tetrazzini, 330, 783
Continental, for vegetable casserole, 810
Cranberry, old-fashioned whole, 333–34
Cream, for scalloped potatoes, 307
Creole, 335
Creole, for baked stuffed whitefish, 238
Curry, for pork casserole, 398
Curry, special, for chicken and rice curry, 225
Curry, for spinach and egg casserole, 405–406
Duck, 842
for eggplant slices, baked stuffed, 801–802
Fish, 249
French dressing, Reefer, 353

French dressing, special, for Cornish hens, 229–30, 333
Gingersnap raisin, special, 182, 337
Gourmet, 153, 342
Gourmet dressing, for salmon and seafood dishes, 333, 342
Hollandaise, 340–41
Horseradish whipped cream 372
Hostess, special, 150, 334
Hot, 18, 337–38, 835
Hot, served with Shashlik, 162
Lemon, 28
Lemon-Mayonnaise, 241
Lemon, for Turkish Dolmas, 338
Louisiana, 59, 374
Madrid, for ham cutlets, 179
Madrid, for veal chops, 172
Maintenon, 171
Mayonnaise-horseradish, whipped cream, 374
Medley, 405
Meat, Italian, 767
Mornay, for broccoli or asparagus, 281
Mornay, for mixed vegetables, 407–408
Mushroom, Nina Miroballi's Italian, 768–69
Mushroom, thick, 146
Mushroom, thick, special, for Salisbury steaks, 338
Mustard, 18, 338
Newburg, 41–42
Pancho dipping, 10, 338
Parisienne, 330, 387–88
Pesto à la Genovese, 769–70
Piquant, for broiled fillets of haddock or perch, 386
Pizzaiola, 797
for Pompano en Papillote, 242
for potato-cheese mold, 303
for potato ring mold, 304
Poulet, for chicken Alfredo, 332
Ravigote, 61–62
Reefer French dressing, 353
Reefer tartar, 353
Regal, 391–92
Remoulade, 46
Rum, whipped cream, 339, 372
Seafood tartar, 60, 336
Shrimp, 240–41
Smetana, for veal balls, 170

Sour cream, zesty, 474
Sweet-sour, 17–18, 337, 834–35
Tarragon Dressing, Vinaigrette, 336
Tarragon mayonnaise dressing, 335
Tartar, 334, 336
Tartar, seafood, 336
Tartar, Reefer, 353
Tomato, 727
Tomato-cheese, for halibut steak, 240
Tomato, Italian, basic, 766–67
Tomato juice, for Creole shrimp and rice, 383
Tomato, quick, 767
Tomato, quick, for parmesan veal cutlets, 334–35
Tomato, for veal patties farci, 173
Toscana, 794
Veloute, 327
Vinaigrette tarragon dressing, 336
Whipped cream brandy, 339, 372
Whipped cream, horseradish, 372
Whipped cream mayonnaise-horseradish, 374
Whipped cream rum, 339, 372
White, 17
White, medium, 224, 328
White, thick, 142, 223–24 328
White, thin, 327–28
Zesty sour cream, 474
see also TOPPINGS FOR SPECIALTY DISHES
Sauerbraten (American-style), 155–56
Sausage *see* PORK
Scallops
breaded deep-fried, 244-45
Louisiana, 249
SEAFOOD   (SHELLFISH)
see Crab meat; Lobster; Oysters; Scallops; Shrimp
Shashlik, 162
en brochette, 163
Sherbet
Lemon crisp dessert, 661
Orange crisp dessert, 661
Rhubarb and strawberry, 678
Torte, ice cream, 675–76
Shish kebab, lamb, 161
Shrimp
and almond appetizers, Pancho, 9–10

Appetizer, Oriental, 828–29
Arnaud, 255
and avocado salad with Russian dressing, 351
Blintzes, 26
Breaded deep-fried, 244–45
and cheese rarebit, 98
Chow mein, 839
Colonial doll mold, 350
Creole, in chafing dish, 380
Creole, and rice, in individual casseroles, 382–83
de Jonghe, 34, 254–55
and deviled eggs Mornay in casserole, 380–81
Egg roll, Cantonese, 11–12
Fried, appetizers, Cantonese, 826–27
Fried, Cantonese, 12
Glazed, 55
and green peppers, Oriental, 848
Hot snack, 96
Jambalaya, 382
Javanese-style, 847
Louisiana, in chafing dish, 10–11, 379
Oriental, 15
Oriental barbecued, on bamboo sticks, 832
Pancho, luncheon style, 10
Pilaf, 250
Quiche Lorraine, 95
Remoulade, French-fried, 45–46
Salad Louisiana, molded, 350–51
Salad molded, 349–50
Salad in tomato poinsettia, 351
Sautéed, garlic sauce, 830–31
Sautéed, Italian-style, 36–37
Sautéed, sweet and sour, 837
Seafood cocktail horn of plenty, 53–55
Seafood gourmet appetizer in patty shells, 18–19
Seafood melty appetizers, 23–24
Souffle, 269
Stuffed french-fried, gourmet, 8–9
Supreme, in casserole, 381–82
Smorgasbord, 856–57
SOUFFLE DISHES
Asparagus, 268
Broccoli, 268
Cheese, 267–68
Cheese, hot, hors d'oeuvres, 20
Chicken, cooked, 269

Corn, 268–69
Crab meat, hot, 22–23
Fish, 269
Green noodle, casserole, 415–16
Ham and cheese hors d'oeuvres, 21
Meat, cooked, 269
Mushroom, appetizer, 21–22
Pea, 268
Shellfish, 269
Spinach, 268
Vegetables, mixed, 268
Soup stocks, 101
Brown meat, 101–102
Chicken, 226
Clarified (clear), 103
Fish (fumet), 102–103
Meat essence, 103
Meat glaze, 103
White meat, 102
White poultry, 102
SOUPS AND CHOWDERS
Beef barley vegetable, 106
Bouillon with petite quenelles, clear, 106
Chicken gumbo, 104
Chowder, clam, 111–12
Chowder, corn, 112
Chowder, corn tomato, 111
Chowder, scallop, 113
Chowder, vegetable clam, 112
Cream of asparagus, 110
Cream of cauliflower, 109
Cream of celery, 109
Cream of chicken, 110
Cream of corn, 111
Cream of mushroom, 108
Cream of pea, 108–109
Cream of potato and green onion, 110
Cream of spinach, 109
Cream of tomato, 108
Cream of two colors, 111
Cream soups, preparation, 107–108
Hearty ham and bean, 107
Lentil wiener, 106–107
Minestrone, fresh vegetable, 809
Minestrone, Evelyn Russo's lentil, 810–11
Onion, French, 103–104
Onion, quick. 104
Oyster stew, 105
Scotch broth, 106
Vichyssoise, 105–106
Spinach, 314
Casserole, 407
and egg, curried, casserole, 407
and eggs Florentine, baked, 264

and ham roll-ups, 182–83
Mold, 314–16
Pie, 314
Supreme, 316
Timbales and ham, 180–81
Squash
Acorn, baked, 317
Hubbard, 316
Summer, baked stuffed, 316–17
Strawberry
Almond pancakes, 648–49
Almond paste, 715
Appetizer, 72–73
Blintzes, 653
and calavo with cold sliced baked ham, 367
Coconut Macaroon, 711
Cream puff log, 670
Dessert ring, crunchy, 662
Flans, French fruit, 642–43
Fresh, pie, 755–56
Fresh, pie, California fruit, 746–47
Fresh, pie, glazed, 745
Fresh, strudel, 657
Frozen, pie, glazed, 746
Fresh, tarts, 666
Lady fingers, Bavarian ice box mold, 594
Petit-four fruits and vegetables, 591–93
Petits fours, 553
and pineapple bird appetizer, Honolulu, 73
and rhubarb egg mold, 440
and rhubarb mold, 439–40
and rhubarb pie, 757
and rhubarb sherbet, 678
Torte, glazed, party-style, 581–82
Strudel
American cheese cocktail, 32
Apple, quick puff paste, 651–52
Apple, 656–57
Baklava, 658–59
Cantonese cocktail, 31
Cherry, 657
Cream cheese, 657
Dough, 655–56
Meat cocktail, 31–32
Pecan, 658
Strawberry, fresh, 657
Strudlicky, 726–27
STUFFINGS AND DRESSINGS
Bread, for barbecued ribs, 191–92
Bread, for chicken, 208
Bread, for Cornish hens, 230
Bread, for duckling, 232
Bread, for turkey, 203–204

Bread, for whitefish, baked stuffed, 237–38
for pork chops, 183
Rice, wild, for Cornish hens, 230
for turkey casserole, 392
for veal birds, 169
for veal chops Madrid, 171–72
for veal patties farci, 172–73
Succotash, 298–99
Sukiyaki dinner, Japanese, 849–50
Sweet potato(es)
carmelized glazed, 310
Delight for casserole, 403
Delights, 309
Delights, petit, 30–31
Fluff in casserole, 414–15
Meringue in casserole, 309–10
in orange cups, 310–11
Oven-glazed, 308–309
Pan-glazed, 308
Syrup
hot, for Babas, 530
for pancakes, waffles, etc., 482
Plain, for apple dumplings, 679
Tacos, cocktail chili, 26–27
Tamales, Mexican, 404
Tarts and Tartlets
dough for, 663–65
Apricot and peach, 665
Banana, 666
Cherry, black bing dark sweet, 666
Cherry. Royal Anne light sweet, 666
Eggnog, individual yuletide, 744
Peach and apricot, 665
Pear, 665
Pineapple, 665–66
Raspberry, fresh, 666
Strawberry fresh, 666
Tartlet, blueberry, fresh, glazed cheese, 748
Tartlet, English cherry, 721–22
Tartlet, Frangipan, 720–21
Tartlet, Valentine, 700–701
Tea, 858–60
Iced, 860
Russian, 860
Timbales
Chicken, in green pea casserole, 390
Spinach, and ham casserole, 180–81
Turkey, in green pea casserole, 390

Timetables
for broiling meats, 131
for roasting chicken, 208
for roasting meats, 128–29
for roasting turkey, 205
Tomato(es)
Aspic, 60–61
Aspic mold, 471
Basket salad, 363
Cups, crab meat in, 64
and eggs, peppers pan-fried with, 298
Fresh grilled parmesan, au gratin, 318
Fresh, poinsettia, 458
Plum tulip hors d'oeuvres spray, 50
Rarebit on toast with anchovies, 97
Slices, stuffed glazed, 318
Stewed, 317
Tulip, hors d'oeuvres, 49
TOPPINGS FOR DESSERTS, PIES, ETC.
for brandy pie, 740
for Danish cinnamon coffee cake, 491
for date bars, 723
Meringue, for tortes, 539
for rum pie, 740
for sponge upside-down cake, 574
Streussel, 516
Streussel, for apple pie, 750
Streussel, for peach pie, 749
Sugar cinnamon for yummy cake, 563
see also ICINGS AND FROSTINGS; SAUCES FOR DESSERTS, ETC.
TOPPINGS FOR SPECIALTY DISHES, MOLDS, PIZZA, ETC.
Anchovy-mozzarella, 764
Anchovy, savory, 83
Braunschweiger, 169
Custard, for Pastitso, 398
for hyacinth party-size mold, 454
Mozzarella cheese, 763
Pizza, 763–64
for potato salad mold, party-style, 473
for raspberry-pineapple mold, 437
Rockefeller, 25
Roquefort, 177
Sausage-mozzarella cheese, 763–64
Sausage-scamorza cheese, 763–64

Scamorza cheese, 763
Special, for broiled fish, 246
for Valentine salad mold, 456
see also GRAVY; SAUCES FOR MEATS, ETC.
Tortellini, 770–71
TORTES
Blitz, 555
Blueberry, fresh, glazed cheese pie, 747–48
Butterscotch meringue, 540
Cheese, magic, 638
Chocolate filled walnut, 578–79
Chocolate mint refrigerator, 640–41
Chocolate mocha, Continental, 580–81
Dobos, 579–80
Chocolate-vanilla cream, 540
French pastry pecan, 574–75
Ice cream meringue, heavenly, 575–77
Ice cream sherbet, 675–76
Lady fingers liqueur, 541–42
Lemon custard, angel, 638
Lemon meringue, 540–41
Nut, Viennese whipped cream, 577–78
Orange custard, angel, 640
Pecan, French pastry, 574–75
Pineapple-cheese glaze, 639–40
Strawberry, glazed, party-style, 581–82
Vanilla cream, Mathon's, 538–40
Walnut, chocolate filled, 578–79
Whipped cream nut, Viennese, 577–78
see also CAKES
Tortilla bases, 25–26
Trout, lake, baked, with shrimp sauce, 240–41
Tuna
and asparagus casserole, 385
and green noodle casserole, 385–86
and mushroom casserole, 384
Salad in avocado cup, 358
TURKEY
general information, 197, 202–206
timetable for roasting, 205
Breast of, Epicurean, in casserole, 392–93
Breast of, Romanoff, 217–18

Breast of young, deep basted, 206
Breasts, 200–202
Breasts of, Alfredo, sauteed, 780–81
and dressing in casserole, 392
Fruit salad, 366–67
Neck and giblets, 203
Roast, butter-basted, 206
Roasting, 203–206
Salad superb, molded, 354
Slices, Calavo-cranberry salad with, 267
see also POULTRY
VEAL
Premium, 118
timetable for roasting, 128
Baked, in casserole, 174
Balls Smetana, 170
Barbecued, 192
Birds Bordelaise, 167–68
Birds Smetana, 168–69
Chops, baked, and potatoes in casserole, 190
Chops cacciatori, 787
Chops Madrid, 171–72
Chops Maintenon, 170–71
Chops, pan-braised breaded, 183–84
Chops, plain braised, 184
Chops, plain broiled, 183
Chops Provincial, 173–74
Chops à la Sauterne braised, 174
Chops, stuffed broiled, 183
Collops Braunschweiger, 169
Curry with rice, 174–75
Cutlets à la Creole, 164

Cutlets, Parmesan, 786–87
Cutlets plain breaded, 175–76, 787–88
Deep-fat fried, 184
Leg of, Evelyn Russo's Neopolitan-style, 788–89
Maréchal, 164
Meat balls gourmet, 151
Meat patties, Continental, 176–77
Mock chicken legs, 166
Osso Buco, 785–86
Paprika, Hungarian, 163
Pastitso in casserole, 397–98
Patties farci, 172
Scaloppini à la Genovese, 788
Stew, green pepper, 176
Stew Tarragon, 173
Vegetable carving, 870–73
VEGETABLE(S), 270–320
general information, 270–72
Cantonese, 851
Casserole Continental, 809–10
Fresh, minestrone soup, 809
Fresh, salad bowl, 813
Garden, salad mold, 469–70
Medley and mushroom, in casserole, 406
Mixed, Mornay casserole, 408
Mixed, Soufflé, 268
Molds, marinated, individual, 465–66
Quick casserole, 417

Salad mold, buffet party, 473–74
Vinaigrette, 318–19
Waffles, 475
Pecan, 476
Walnut
Baklava, 658–59
Butter-cake squares, grilled, 561
Butter crescents, 692–93
Finnish dreams, 727
Karydato, 717
Revani, 718
Torte, Chocolate-filled, 578–79
Watercress, 314
Watermelon salad basket, 345
Whitefish
Broiled, 243–44
Fillets Hollandaise, 241
Fillets en Papillote, 242–43
Whole baked stuffed, à la Creole, 237–38
Wines
buying and storing, 867–68
in cooking, 868–69
kinds, 866–67
serving, 868
Yeast, 492–93
Zucchini
Halves, broiled, 320
and ham, in casserole, 807–808
Omelet in casserole, 308
Stew, 319–20
Stew in casserole, company-style, 319
Stew, Italian-style, 808
Stuffed, Italian-style, 806
and veal chops in casserole, 806–807